T0189290

Communications in Computer and Information Science   **955**

Commenced Publication in 2007
Founding and Former Series Editors:
Phoebe Chen, Alfredo Cuzzocrea, Xiaoyong Du, Orhun Kara, Ting Liu,
Dominik Ślęzak, and Xiaokang Yang

More information about this series at http://www.springer.com/series/7899

Ashish Kumar Luhach · Dharm Singh
Pao-Ann Hsiung · Kamarul Bin Ghazali Hawari
Pawan Lingras · Pradeep Kumar Singh (Eds.)

Advanced Informatics for Computing Research

Second International Conference, ICAICR 2018
Shimla, India, July 14–15, 2018
Revised Selected Papers, Part I

 Springer

Editors
Ashish Kumar Luhach
Department of Computer Science
and Engineering
Maharshi Dayanand University
Rohtak, Haryana, India

Dharm Singh
Namibia University of Science
and Technology
Windhoek, Namibia

Pao-Ann Hsiung
National Chung Cheng University
Minxiong Township, Chiayi County
Taiwan

Kamarul Bin Ghazali Hawari
Electrical and Electronics Engineering
Universiti Malaysia Pahang
Pekan, Pahang, Malaysia

Pawan Lingras
Saint Mary's University
Halifax, NS, Canada

Pradeep Kumar Singh
Department of Computer Science
and Engineering
Jaypee University of Information
Technology
Kandaghat, India

ISSN 1865-0929   ISSN 1865-0937 (electronic)
Communications in Computer and Information Science
ISBN 978-981-13-3139-8   ISBN 978-981-13-3140-4 (eBook)
https://doi.org/10.1007/978-981-13-3140-4

Library of Congress Control Number: 2018960620

This Springer imprint is published by the registered company Springer Nature Singapore Pte Ltd.
The registered company address is: 152 Beach Road, #21-01/04 Gateway East, Singapore 189721, Singapore

Preface

The Second International Conference on Advanced Informatics for Computing Research (ICAICR 2018) targeted state-of-the-art as well as emerging topics pertaining to advanced informatics for computing research and its implementation for engineering applications. The objective of this international conference is to provide opportunities for the researchers, academics, industry professionals, and students to interact and exchange ideas, experience, and expertise in the current trends and strategies in information and communication technologies. Moreover, participants were informed about current and emerging technological developments in the field of advanced informatics and its applications, which were thoroughly explored and discussed.

ICAICR 2018 was held during July 14–15 in Shimla, India, in association with Namibia University of Science and Technology and technically sponsored by the CSI Chandigarh Chapter and Southern Federal University, Russia.

We are very thankful to our valuable authors for their contribution and our Technical Program Committee for their immense support and motivation for making the first edition of ICAICR 2018 a success. We are also grateful to our keynote speakers for sharing their precious work and enlightening the delegates of the conference. We express our sincere gratitude to our publication partner, Springer, for believing in us.

July 2018

Ashish Kumar Luhach
Dharm Singh
Pao-Ann Hsiung
Kamarul Bin Ghazali Hawari
Pawan Lingras
Pradeep Kumar Singh

Organization

Conference General Chair

Pao-ann Hsiung   National Chung Cheng University, Taiwan

Conference Chairs

Kamarul Bin Ghazali Hawari   Universiti Malaysia Pahang, Malaysia
Dharm Singh   Namibia University of Science and Technology,
                                    Namibia

Conference Co-chairs

Pljonkin Anton   Southern Federal University, Russia
Ashish kr. Luhach   Maharishi Dayanand University, Rohtak, India
   (Professional Member
   of CSI)
Pardeep Kumar Singh   Jaypee University of Information Technology, Solan,
   (Professional Member   India
   of CSI)

Technical Program Committee

Chairs

Pawan Lingras   Saint Mary's University, Canada
Pelin Angin   Purdue University, USA

Co-chairs

Vivek Kumar Sehgal   Jaypee University of Information Technology, India
Ritesh Chugh   CQ University, Australia
Ioan-Cosmin Mihai   A.I. Cuza Police Academy, Romania
Abhijit Sen   Kwantlen Polytechnic University, Canada

Members

K. T. Arasu   Wright State University Dayton, Ohio, USA
Mohammad Ayoub Khan   Taibah University, Kingdom of Saudi Arabia
Rumyantsev Konstantin   Southern Federal University, Russia
Wen-Juan Hou   National Taiwan Normal University, Taiwan
Syed Akhat Hossain   Daffodil University, Dhaka, Bangladesh
Zoran Bojkovic   University of Belgrade, Serbia
Sophia Rahaman   Manipal University, Dubai

Thippeswamy Mn	University of KwaZulu-Natal, South Africa
Lavneet Singh	University of Canberra, Australia
Pao-ann Hsiung	National Chung Cheng University, Taiwan
Wei Wang	Xi'an Jiaotong-Liverpool University, China
Mohd. Helmey Abd Wahab	Universiti Tun Hussein Onn, Malaysia
Andrew Ware	University of South Wales, UK
Shireen Panchoo	University of Technology, Mauritius
Sumathy Ayyausamy	Manipal University, Dubai
Kamarul Bin Ghazali Hawari	Universiti Malaysia Pahang, Malaysia
Dharm Singh	Namibia University of Science and Technology, Namibia
Adel Elmaghraby	University of Louisville, USA
Almir Pereira Guimaraes	Federal University of Alagoas, Brazil
Fabrice Labeau	McGill University, Canada
Abbas Karimi	IAU, Arak, Iran
Kaiyu Wan	Xi'an Jiaotong-Liverpool University, China
Pao-Ann Hsiung	National Chung Cheng University, Taiwan
Paul Macharia	Data Manager, Kenya
Yong Zhao	University of Electronic Science and Technology of China, China
Upasana G. Singh	University of KwaZulu-Natal, South Africa
Basheer Al-Duwairi	Jordan University of Science and Technology, Jordan
M. Najam-ul-Islam	Bahria University, Pakistan
Ritesh Chugh	CQ University Sydney, Australia
Yao-Hua Ho	National Taiwan Normal University, Taiwan
Pawan Lingras	Saint Mary's University, Canada
Poonam Dhaka	University of Namibia, Namibia
Amirrudin Kamsin	University of Malaya, Malaysia
Ashish kr. Luhach	Maharishi Dayanand University, Rohtak, India
Pelin Angin	Purdue University, USA
Indra Seher	CQ University Sydney, Australia
Adel Elmaghraby	University of Louisville, USA
Sung-Bae Cho	Yonsei University, Seoul, Korea
Dong Fang	Southeast University, China
Huy Quan Vu	Victoria University, Australia
Basheer Al-Duwairi	JUST, Jordan
Sugam Sharma	Iowa State University, USA
Yong Wang	University of Electronic Science and Technology of China, China
T. G. K. Vasista	King Saud University, Saudi Arabia
Nalin Asanka Gamagedara Arachchilage	University of New South Wales, Australia
Durgesh Samadhiya	National Applied Research Laboratories, Taiwan
Akhtar Kalam	Victoria University, Australia
Ajith Abraham (Director)	MIR Labs, USA
Runyao Duan	Tsinghua University, China

Miroslav Škoric	IPEE Section, Austria
Al-Sakib Khan Pathan	IPTC, Malaysia
Amina Jackel	Windsor University, Canada
Pei Feng	Southeast University, China
Ioan-Cosmin Mihai	A.I. Cuza Police Academy, Romania
Abhijit Sen	Kumamoto Polytechnic, Japan
R. B. Mishra	Indian Institute of Technology (BHU), India
Bhaskar Biswas	Indian Institute of Technology, IIT (BHU), India

Contents – Part I

Contents – Part II

Information Systems

Networks

Security and Privacy

Computing Methodologies

Integrating Ontology Learning and R for Providing Services Efficiently in Cities

Anjali Hora[(⊠)] and Sarika Jain

National Institute of Technology, Kurukshetra, Haryana, India
horaanjali@gmail.com, jasarika@nitkkr.ac.in

Abstract. With the advancement in Artificial Intelligence, Intelligent systems are being implemented that are able to perform cognitive functions like human beings but due to the complexity in this domain and lack of measure of semantics in program, it is difficult to analyze that how these functions are performed, what functions are to be considered, to what degree they are to be considered. As ontology has been proven the excellent mean of providing semanticity, definitions that are machine understandable are created through ontology. The purpose of creating knowledge representation through ontology that is to analyze the data related to urban services. In this way, intelligent systems will use the definitions created through ontology for doing analysis. This is to be done to provide services in cities in a better way. This paper deals with the learning of base ontology in specific domain from a relational database by making use of plug-in available in Protégé. By populating the ontology through learning, functions available in R will be used to remove the redundant/implied ontological terms. This will evaluate/curate the ontology.

Keywords: MySQL · R language · Ontology learning · Semantic web
Protégé

1 Introduction

Serving the cities and community in a better way is the urgent need of government. In collaboration with University of Toronto and IIT Bombay, definitions that are machine understandable and helps to build intelligent systems for doing analysis are created using ontology. A 'virtual tower of Babel' currently exists in terms of how data related to urban services are available. Babel here refers to "confusion". Providing services require a good strategy that fulfills the requirement of the people of the city. Knowledge based system [10] will help to better analyze and optimize how the public is served. The task will be to create a relation schema through mysql and convert it into ontology by learning it so that it can give us some meaningful result.

The concept of ontology learning came into the picture when there is an urgent need to convert the source information into ontology so that query searching becomes meaningful and more accurate. Data is available in the form of ontology with repeated/implied/unintelligible ontological terms.

In this paper our main focus is to provide learning mechanism to ontology from other information sources. It is always necessary to convert the whole information

© Springer Nature Singapore Pte Ltd. 2019
A. K. Luhach et al. (Eds.): ICAICR 2018, CCIS 955, pp. 3–12, 2019.
https://doi.org/10.1007/978-981-13-3140-4_1

source (be it a database or web or set of documents) automatically into a Knowledge-based application that provides meaning to that source of information so that analyzing that data becomes easy. Data is available in the form of documents, on the web and on relational databases. Relational databases as information source are based on records (in the form of rows and columns). It is purely based on query searching using database languages like MySQL, SQL, dBase, MS Access, FoxPro, oracle etc. But lack of providing meaning to data is the major drawback of relational databases. Data is so huge that companies use data warehouses that support management's decision making process as well. But this way of decision making process has drawbacks like extra reporting work, maintenance, security, processing speed, ad hoc query searching etc. Web as source of information is another way for fetching data but attempts at gaining intellectual control over data like text, image, and sound proves to be daunting. Document as source of information lacks complete knowledge of data.

Out of so many source of information, Relational databases are one of them. Relational database management system like mysql, oracle, Microsoft sql server etc. have the ability to connect with open source text mining tools (R, Java, Perl, LingPipe), file interfaces (XML, CSV), ODBC, JDBC, DBI, Text vendor supplied connector. We will make use of this ability of RDBMS by connecting it with plug-in called data master [5] in protégé. Our approach is to populate the base Ontology using the plug-in called datamaster available in protégé, IDE which is GUI based and easy to implement so that we can analyze the data as it provides meaning to the data. The data becomes more understandable when we will remove repeated/implied ontological terms using package ontologyX [8] available in R language.

2 Literature Study

The framework in the approach described by Mayank Singh et al. [1] is similar to BD2OWL but has additional features that identified problems and deficiencies. By converting the whole relational database in 3NF [2] and then defining certain rules for learning, classes, properties, hierarchy, cardinality, instances and implementing these rules in OWL language. Word Net and ontology learning layer cake [3] for converting the text document into the ontology is used in other approaches. Ontology learning through the web by making use of architecture called OntoLearn [4]. OntoLearn's architecture supports a three-phase process of terminology extraction and filtering, semantic interpretation, and domain-concept-forest generation. Methods are available for improving the quality of terms and definitions by identifying circular and unin-telligible terms/definitions in ontologies and taxonomies on the basis of intelligibility index and circularity index [11]. Domain experts are testing the score in these indexes to determine the quality of terms. Plug-ins like data master available in Protégé is used to convert Relational schema into ontology. Note that in above approaches, Usage of R language has not taken place for improving the ontology.

Other approaches use different relational databases [9] like oracle 11 g [12] for the purpose of ontology learning whereas our approach uses mysql connector that is JDBC driver connector/j for connectivity of database with protégé. A file with .owl extension will automatically be generated when conversion of a database into ontology using datamaster plug-in will take place. Term ids will be generated in .obo file when .owl file is converted into .obo file in ROBOT. Data is present in meaningless way on web and processing of that data is required. OWL [13] provides machine interpretability of Web content than that supported by XML, RDF, and RDF Schema (RDF-S) by providing additional vocabulary along with a formal semantics. OWL is rich with vocabulary for describing properties and classes. In this way, Query searching by humans becomes more efficient.

ROBOT [7] tool provides us with command line interface for the conversion of OWL code into OBO format. This is done as the package Ontology index [6] used in our approach works under OBO format only. get_ontology and minimal_set function in an Ontology Index package are used for reading the ontology and removing the repeated/implied ontological terms respectively. The data imported in R language can be used with different packages available in R language.

3 Proposed Approach to Implementation

Following table depicts the schema for providing services to cities.

The relational schema given in Table 1 above contains four tables. First Table that is E_detail contains information about the employee working under different services. Second Table that is E_service consist of information regarding the services. Third Table that is Equipment_detail consists of information regarding the machinery corresponding to different services. Fourth Table that is Equipment_services consist of information regarding the quantity and cost corresponding to different services.

Table 1. Relational schema

Relation	Foreign key	Primary key
E_detail(E_id int, salary int, address varchar(20))	E_id in E_detail references to E_id in E_service	E_id
E_service(E_name varchar(20), services varchar(20), E_id int)	Services, E_id in E_service references to Services, E_id in Equipment_detail	Services, E_id
Equipment_detail(Equipment varchar (20), quantity int, purchasing_area varchar(20))	Equipment in Equipment_detail references to Equipment in Equipment_services.	Equipment
Equipment_services(Equipment varchar(20), cost int, Quantity int, services varchar(20))	None	None

In First Table, E_id in E_detail references to E_id in E_service. In Second Table, Services, E_id in E_service references to Services, E_id in Equipment_detail. In Third Table, Equipment in Equipment_detail references to Equipment in Equipment_services. In Fourth Table, there is no foreign key. Creation of database in cloud using

Amazon Web Services will take place as it offers broad set of global compute, Storage, database, Analytics, Application and deployment services that help organizations move faster, lower IT costs and scale applications.

3.1 Ontology Learning

Protégé, an open source ontology editor comes with plug-in like data master [5], onto base that helps to convert the relational database into ontology. We can also populate the base ontology already present in the protégé or create a whole new ontology.

In order to access a database using a specific JDBC driver, put the JAR file containing the JDBC driver in your class path. A convenient way is to put the JAR file containing the JDBC driver (for example mysql-connector-java-5.1.6-bin.jar for MySQL)in the[PRO-TEGE_INSTALLATION_DIR]/plugins/edu.stanford.smi.protegex.datamaster directory and restart Protégé. Learning of ontology will take place in protégé and corresponding OWL file will be saved. Out of so many source of information, Relational databases are one of them. Relational database management system like mysql, oracle, Microsoft sql server etc. have the ability to connect with open source text mining tools (R, Java, Perl, Ling Pipe), file interfaces (XML, CSV), ODBC, JDBC, DBI, Text vendor supplied connector. We will make use of this ability of RDBMS by connecting it with plug-in called data master in protégé.

For activating the data master panel, click on Project- > Configure. Click on data master tab check box. Then, click OK.

Figure 1 shows the plug-in activation tab in protégé. Figure 2 shows the panel when the connection is built. For connection, Jdbc driver: com.mysql.jdbc. Driver, Jdbc URL: It is the complete path in mysql where the database are present (here, mysql://localhost:3306/database where database is the name of schema we created), User login: It will take the username that we created at the time of installation,

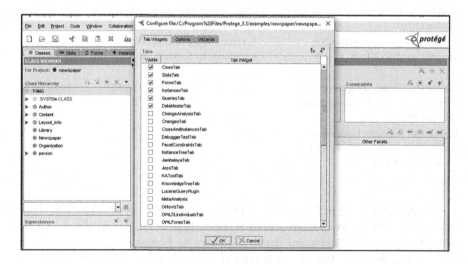

Fig. 1. Plug-in activation tab

Password: It will take the password that we created at the time of installation of mysql. Figure 3 Shows the data master panel where tables E_detail and E_services are imported into the ontology.

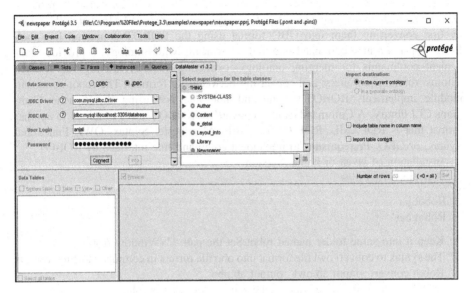

Fig. 2. Data master panel after connection builds

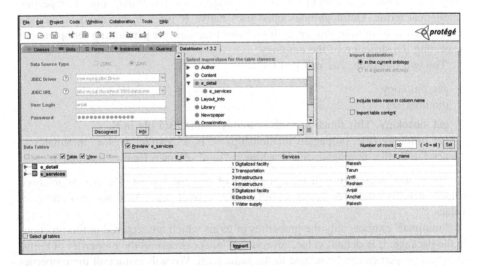

Fig. 3. Data master panel while importing the table into ontology

3.2   Command Used for Format Conversion

Our ontology may contain similar terms. Removal of repeated ontological terms through one of the packages called "OntologyIndex" [6] in R will take place through our approach. OWL file gets saved corresponding to ontology learnt in protégé. Ontology which are available in a Web Ontology Language (OWL) format will be used by first converting them into OBO format using the ROBOT command line tool. ROBOT [7] is a new command-line tool for working with ontology. It provides convenient commands for merging ontology, extracting subsets, filtering for selected axioms, running reasoners, and converting between file formats. The robot-command module implements ROBOT's command line interface using the Apache Commons CLI library. A Command called "convert" in ROBOT saves ontology to another format that is RDFXML, RDF OWL, Turtle, Manchester Syntax, OWL Functional Syntax, or OBO. Prerequisites to implement command line interface by ROBOT.

Installation of java8 or higher version

Download two files

Robot.jar
Robot.bat

Keep it into same folder named robot.Set the path C:/Windows/robot
The syntax to convert owl file format into obo file format in command line interface is
Robot convert –input ab.owl –output ab.obo
It will create a file say ab.obo in the same folder that is robot.

3.3   Usage of R

A package named OntologyIndex in R language is used for removing the repeating ontological terms. Ontologyindex class uses native R types to represent ontological terms and sets of ontological terms. It includes functions for performing set operations respecting the structure of the ontology.

The two functions that will be used are:

get_ontology
minimal_set

get_ontology. This function reads ontology from OBO file in R.
get_ontology (file, propagate_relationships = "is_a", extract_tags = "minimal")
get_OBO (file, propagate_relationships = "is_a", extract_tags = "minimal")

Here "file" argument will fetch the path of obo file format. "Propagate_relationships" includes character vector of relations. "extract_tags" that has two character values.

"minimal" extracts only the properties of terms which are required to run functions in the package. It is default value. "everything" that extracts all the properties of terms. Different properties can be related to the same term. We will extract all the properties get_ontology will create the index of properties with corresponding terms where terms can be repeated. The snippet to read a file using get_ontology by converting it from owl file format to obo file format.

Read the ab.obo file in r language

```
>Install.packages("ontologyIndex")
>library(ontologyIndex)
>basedir <- "C:/Windows/robot"
> infile <- file.path(basedir,'ab.obo')
>get_ontology(infile,extract_tags = "minimal")
>outfile<-get_ontology(infile,extract_tags = "minimal")
>outfile
```

minimal_set. minimal_set function maps a set of ontological terms onto a non-redundant set.

minimal_set removes redundant/implied terms from a set of terms.

minimal_set (ontology, terms)

Here "ontology" argument fetches ontology_index object. "terms" will fetch us character vector of ontological terms. In this way, we will get the non-repeated terms. Unintelligible/flawed terms can also be removed.

Term Ids for each term in standardized ontology is in the form of GO:0007411, say for gene ontology. There is no mechanism for generating term ids for ontology created through protégé. Also, functions like minimal_set requires term ids in specific format.

```
> minimal_set(go, c("GO:0007411","GO:0007415"))
```

will remove the terms if same or if having flaw.

Remove the repeated ontological terms from our ontology

```
>minimal_set(outfile,c("doc_id_INSTANCE","user_id_INSTA
NCE","user_id_INSTANCE"))
```

This will remove the repeated terms but as the terms are not provided with defined ids, it will take any string as terms for the ontology. The ontology must be standardized and has defined term ids. This limitation can be solved by patenting the ontology.

Following figures corresponding to the relational schema gives us the idea about how the changes will take place in ontology in graphical form. The diagrams below show that how our base ontology will look like after applying functions from R language.

In this way, Ontology maintenance will take place in a very simple way without manually managing the complete Ontology.

Figure 4 corresponds to the ontology that requires curation. Figure 5 shows the ontology when curation has been done after applying functions available in R packages. Repeated ontological terms like Bending machine that corresponds to Infrastructure, Water supply, Electricity will be removed using the function minimal_set and will point to all three terms only once. We are able to minimize the cost of tools used for each service by pointing them only once with all services that requires them. Thus, we are able to minimize the total amount that will spend on tools while providing services in cities. However, this will increase the completion time that will act as the limitation for this paper.

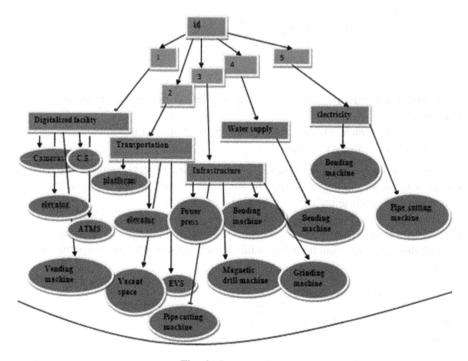

Fig. 4. Base ontology

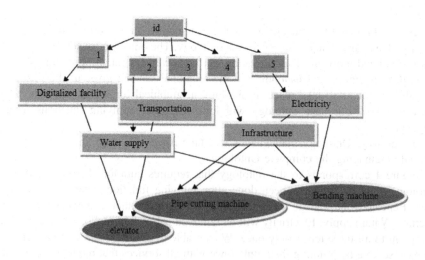

Fig. 5. Ontology after applying functions in ontology index package in R

4 Future Scopes

While merging different Ontology's of same domain, it is possible that same terms can occur more than once in Ontology that leads to repeated terms. This approach of removing the redundant/implied terms in ontology using R will help us to ignore the extraneous data. Ontology learning on the other hand will help Companies to automatically convert the different sources of information into Ontology. This will provide meaning to that data and will also help them to find the insights of that data.

Also, it will decrease the load of creating ontology's manually.

5 Conclusion

Data in huge amount is present that needs to be analyzed and then decisions need to be taken on the basis of an analyzation. The purpose of this paper is to analyze data through ontology and make use of that analyzation in taking decisions. Also, an approach for ontology management is also provided with this paper using packages available in R. With learning mechanism, we are able to generate our ontology automatically. With Ontologyindex package, we are able to maintain our ontology by removing flawed terms. As the packages available for ontology management in R can only be used with some standardized ontologies under Open Biomedical Ontology Foundry, Future work will be to make our own packages in R language that supports any domain specific Ontology.

References

1. Jain, V., Singh, M.: A framework to convert relational database to ontology for knowledge database in semantic web. Int. J. Sci. Technol. Res. 2(10), 9–12 (2013)
2. Li, M., Xiao-Yong, D., Shan W.: Learning ontology from relational database. In: Proceedings of 2005 International Conference on Machine Learning and Cybernetics, vol. 6. IEEE (2005)
3. Buitelaar, P., Cimiano, P., Magnini, B.: Ontology learning from text: an overview. Ontol. Learn. Text: Methods Eval. Appl. 123, 3–12 (2005)
4. Missikoff, M., Navigli, R., Velardi, P.: Integrated approach to web ontology learning and engineering. Computer 35(11), 60–63 (2002)
5. Nyulas, C., O'Connor, M., Tu, S.: Datamaster–a plug-in for importing schemas and data from relational databases into protege. In: 10th International Protégé Conference, pp. 15–18 (2007)
6. OntologyIndex. https://cran.r-project.org/web/packages/ontologyIndex/index.html
7. Overton, J.A., Dietze, H., Essaid, S., Osumi-Sutherland, D., Mungall, C.J.: ROBOT: a command-line tool for ontology development. In: Proceedings of the International Conference on Biomedical Ontology (ICBO), pp. 131–132. CEUR Workshop Proceedings (CEUR-WS. org), Lisbon (2015)
8. Lee, J.J.Y., et al.: Text-based phenotypic profiles incorporating biochemical phenotypes of inborn errors of metabolism improve phenomics-based diagnosis. J. Inherit. Metab. Dis., 1–8 (2018)

9. Bakuya, T., Masato, M.: Relational database management system. U.S. Patent No. 5,680,614. 21 October 1997

10. Wang, X., Chan, C.W., Hamilton, H.J.: Design of knowledge-based systems with the ontology-domain-system approach. In: Proceedings of the 14th International Conference on Software Engineering and Knowledge Engineering. ACM (2002)

11. Köhler, J., et al.: Quality control for terms and definitions in ontologies and taxonomies. BMC Bioinform. **7**(1), 212 (2006)

12. Mogotlane, K.D., Fonou-Dombeu, J.V.: Automatic Conversion of Relational Databases into Ontologies: A Comparative Analysis of Protégé Plug-ins Performances. arXiv preprint arXiv:1611.02816 (2016)

13. McGuinness, D.L., Van Harmelen, F.: OWL web ontology language overview. W3C Recomm. **10**(10), 2004 (2004)

Overlapped Sunflower Weighted Crop Yield Estimation Based on Edge Detection

Hemant Rathore[1([⊠])], Vijay Kumar Sharma[1], Shubhra Chaturvedi[2],
and Kapil Dev Sharma[1]

[1] Department of Computer Science and Engineering, Rajasthan Institute
of Engineering and Technology, Jaipur, Rajasthan, India
rathorehemant0@gmail.com
[2] Department of Botany, Government College Malpura, Tonk, Rajasthan, India

Abstract. Today agriculture field's demands to develop such an intelligent system those provide accurate and timely information for an estimation of crop productivity. This paper designed an automated decision support system to estimate sunflower crop productivity information with interface between camera and computer software. The earlier steps of system generate overlapped flower yield information and latter steps count the seed from the flower head. Some beautiful flowers in the nature have Fibonacci relationship in their seeds pattern, i.e. sunflower, pineapple etc. The implementation parts based on two color model RGB and HSV. HSV provide better results for overlapped flower. The technique use image segmentation, morphological operation for overlapped flower count and edge detection for seed count.

Keywords: Edge detection · Morphological operation · Segmentation
Filters

1 Introduction

Study of flowers is done in Floriculture [1]. The study of modern flower crops comes under the floriculture which is sub-branch of horticulture [1]. Yield estimation is the main part of the agriculture's accuracy. The precision agriculture has main application of the yield estimation. Precision agriculture is the early estimation of the crop for preplanning and decision of every stage of crop. The entire problem in every stage of flowers can be solved by precision agriculture using computer & machine vision based decision with full automation. This paper presented the sunflower yield calculation of crop from flowers shape analysis [2]. The man made estimation system gives better results even if there is variation in fields or weather conditions [3–7]. For developing a new computing algorithm basic yield estimation model is inferred in Fig. 1 below.

Object detection, shape detection and texture detection are the three main parts of counting algorithm [8–11]. It is easy to estimate the object from binary image in matlab. Hence, firstly it is important to use segmentation technique for extracting flower form the background and convert in to binary image [12]. In the fifteenth century scientist Leonardo discovered Fibonacci series [13]. The sun magic flower known as sunflower. It has clockwise and anticlockwise spires. These spires have

© Springer Nature Singapore Pte Ltd. 2019
A. K. Luhach et al. (Eds.): ICAICR 2018, CCIS 955, pp. 13–22, 2019.
https://doi.org/10.1007/978-981-13-3140-4_2

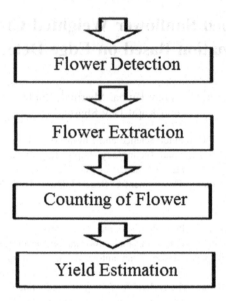

Fig. 1. Basic model for yield estimation

number relationship (i.e. 34 anticlockwise and 55 clockwise or 55 anticlockwise and 89 clockwise). For any size of sunflower they come with Fibonacci number, even if head size of sunflower very. It is very complex to count number of seeds from a sunflower because many seeds presented in both spires and they intersect. In Fig. 2 show the algorithm steps of sunflower yield estimation.

2   Development Algorithm

The Development steps of proposed algorithm are divided into two parts, first for flower count and second for seed count:

The flower count step includes 6 steps, in which input is taken as RGB image and output is generated in the form of flower count. In next seed count steps includes the cropping the sunflower head followed by seed count operation.

2.1   For Flower Count

Step 1: First of all Capture RGB images from the field of the sunflower
The first step of yield estimation of sunflower is capturing the image of sunflowers from the sunflower field. The sunflower image is captured by the high-quality camera which is stationary. The image captured by camera is the RGB image. The RGB image has the basic color of any object like Red, Green, and Blue. Future this RGB image to pass to next step which remove the noise from the RGB image.

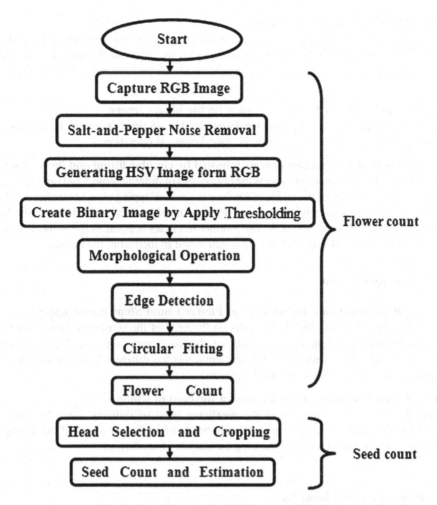

Fig. 2. Development algorithm's process flowchart

Step 2: Remove the noise from the captured image
Salt and pepper noise is common in captured image by camera. So remove the Salt and pepper noise by the Median filter. The output pixels of the image are determined by calculating the median of the neighborhood pixels and replace the pixel by the calculated median pixel. In this filter, the median value is placed on image pixel value.

Step 3: Convert the RGB capture image to HSV image
Different flowers have the different color. The color extraction has a range of hues value because the flowers contain shades of color. After the color transformation, the hue range is calculated. The HSV color model used for flower extraction. The transformation of RGB image gives better segmentation. The segmentation of the flowers is better using HSV color model then compared to RGB color model.

Step 4: Generate the binary image

After detection of flowers, they are extracted from the background using Otsu thresholding technique segmentation process. After the segmented image is called the binary image in which flower region is white and the background is black and vice versa. It is easy to count objects from the binary image.

Step 5: Apply Morphological operation on the binary image

The image is reconstructed using the finite number of time operation i.e. Dilation, Erosion, Opening, and Closing after the morphological operation.

Step 6: Apply edge detection process followed by circular fitting and flower count

The basic process of detection detects the boundaries of different object and outline of an object and background of the image and indicates the overlapping object boundaries. The image segmentation using the canny edge. Find the number of circles and their radius by using the imfindcircles commands. The number of circles is equal to the number of the flower head and the size of each flower is calculated in inch from the radius.

2.2   For Seeds Count

Step 1: Head selection after all steps of Flower Count Steps then cropping

After the circular fitting, the circle marks on the head of the sunflower then count the sunflower head and find an estimation of the sunflower cropping. Heads of the sunflowers are not the same size. Different sunflower has different head size then select the different sunflower head for next step seed count.

Step 2: Seed Counting and estimation of the crop of sunflower

After the head count, then select the sunflower head of different size. After head selection, the seeds are count form different heads of sunflower and find the average weight of the seeds which give the crop estimation of sunflower.

3   Experimental Results

During the image capturing process there is some chance to add the noise due to any regions like environment condition etc. Hence here is need to remove such kind of noise [14–16]. RGB to HSV conversion is necessary because the flower area can be detected on the basis of hue value [17, 18]. It is easy to extract the different regions by using segmentation technique [19]. The circular fitting or curve fitting tool box used to count the number of flower [20–22]. It provides the facility to create, modify and access the fitting objects [20–22]. The methods command of MATLAB results the curve fitting objects.

For example,

f = fittype ('a * x^2 + b * exp (n * x)'); methods (f)

The number of objects or circles gives the result Flower yield calculation.

Figure 3 infers the results obtained after execution of flower count steps. From the results it is clear that accuracy of flower count is near about 92%.

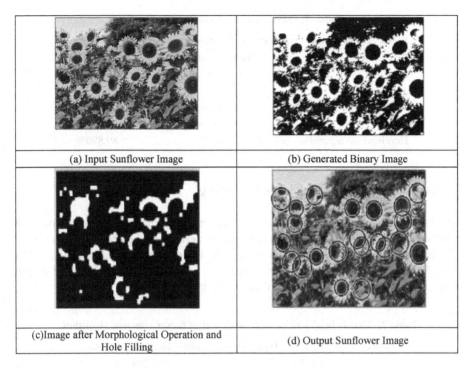

| (a) Input Sunflower Image | (b) Generated Binary Image |
| (c)Image after Morphological Operation and Hole Filling | (d) Output Sunflower Image |

Fig. 3. Obtained result of proposed technique

4 Accuracy of Flower Count Steps

The number of flower count is equal to the result of the length function of MATLAB. For example:

length (centers);

The accuracy of proposed flower count steps can be computed by comparing it with the manual count.

$$\text{Accuracy} = (\text{AFC} / \text{MC}) * 100 \qquad (1)$$

Here,

AFC = Algorithmic flower count
MC = Manual count

In Table 1 shows the Summary for the accuracy of different kinds of flowers.

From above table it can be concluded that the flower count steps of proposed algorithm provides the 89.896% or 90% accuracy. For sunflower it results accuracy approximately 92%. Input and output image from figure no 2 it is clear that head count is 22 out of 24, here the accuracy is 91.67%.

Table 1. Development algorithm accuracy

S. No.	No of image processed	Type of flowers	Accuracy
1	18	Yellow gerbera	92.31%
2	22	White marigold	87.53%
3	8	Water lily	82.48%
4	18	Yellow marigold	95.50%
5	15	Common yellow sunflower	91.66%
Development algorithms over all accuracy			89.896%

5 Head Size Based on Circular Fitting

Figure 2 shows overlapped flower count or flower head count. Sunflower is found in many verities but yellow sunflower is common. In agriculture the head size is normally measured in inch. It very from 4 inch to 12 inch. The maximum head size exists up to 27 inch. Table 2 shows the radius of sunflowers reflected as result, from the output image in Fig. 2 and its equivalent full head size in inch.

Table 2. Details head size of each sunflower of flower counting algorithm.

Flower count	Radius	Head size = 2*radius	Head size in inch
1	13.615	27.23	10.7205
2	13.2777	26.5554	10.4549
3	15.1792	30.3584	11.9521
4	14.6327	29.2654	11.5218
5	11.4672	22.9344	9.0293
6	13.9376	27.8752	10.9745
7	13.5606	27.1212	10.6776
8	10.0707	20.1414	7.92969
9	12.1582	24.3164	9.57339
10	11.1913	22.3826	8.81205
11	8.5658	17.1316	6.74473
12	8.1214	16.2428	6.39481
13	15.224	30.448	11.9874
14	15.9961	31.9922	12.5954
15	13.0219	26.0438	10.2535
16	13.6835	27.367	10.7744
17	12.4706	24.9412	9.81938
18	14.5105	29.021	11.4256
19	14.5679	29.1358	11.4708
20	12.2001	24.4002	9.60638
21	12.0045	24.009	9.45237
22	15.5084	31.0168	12.2113

1 inch = 2.54 cm or 1 cm = (1/2.54 = 0.393701) inch

In this paper we categorize three kinds of sunflower heads; these are Large, Medium and Small [23].

So close picture of such kind of head is taken and count the seed of individual head using edge detection.

Apply the following Mathematical formula to seed estimation:

$$SE = FC((SH_L + SH_M + SH_S)/3)$$ (2)

Here,

SE: Total seed count
FC: flower count
SH_L: Number of seed in large head (greater than 10").
SH_M: Number of seed in medium head (7" >= and <=10").
SH_S: Number of seed in small head (less than 7").

Here we can categorize the head in more, according to size which give more accurate yield results.

Following Fig. 4 infer the edge detection.

Table 3 shows the Results of average weight yield. From the Pearson Education, "Data analysis on the Web" the average weight of a seed is 142 mg [24].

So yield estimated weight can be derived from it.

$$Yield\,weight = SE * seed\,average\,Weight$$ (3)

6 Accuracy of Crop Estimation

The accuracy of crop estimation of sunflower can be computed by comparing with the manual count average weight

$$Accuracy = (ACW / MCW) * 100$$ (4)

Here,

ACW = Algorithmic Count Weight
MCW = Manual Count Weight

In the Table 4, the input image has 24 head and output image has 22 head, then the weight accuracy of 22 head out of 24 is 92.28%.

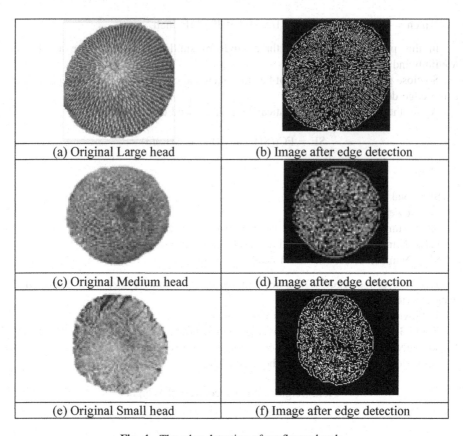

Fig. 4. The edge detection of sunflower heads

Table 3. Shows the results of average weight yield

No. of flower	SH$_L$	SH$_M$	SH$_S$	SE	Total yield weight
22	1224	997	799	22147	3.145 kg
25	1182	951	862	24958	3.544 kg
30	1190	961	878	30290	4.301 kg
18	1235	1020	828	18498	2.627 kg
23	1169	905	858	22479	3.192 kg

Table 4. Shows the results of crop estimation of sunflower

Manual flower count	Algorithmic flower count	Weight of sunflowers by manual	Weight of sunflowers by proposed technique	Accuracy
24	22	3.408 kg	3.145 kg	92.28%
27	25	3.834 kg	3.544 kg	92.44%
33	30	4.686 kg	4.301 kg	91.78%
20	18	2.840 kg	2.627 kg	92.50%
25	23	3.550 kg	3.192 kg	89.91%

7 Conclusion

This paper presents the sunflower crop yield estimation technology with the help of the application of image processing. To comparing our results on the basis of seed weight [24]. Our results meet the accurate crop productivity. it can be concluded that the technique provides the accurate estimation of sunflower weighted crop. The proposed technique is used for precise agriculture. In future scope, we will focus on other types of crop.

References

1. Chadha, K.L.: Horticulture: new avenues for growth. The Hindu Survey of Indian Agriculture, 155–160 (1999)
2. Wang, Q., Nuske, S., Bergerman, M., Singh, S.: Automated crop yield estimation for apple orchards. In: 13th International Symposium on Experimental Robotics (ISER 2012), pp. 1–15 (2012)
3. Stajnko, D., Rakun, J., Blanke, M.: Modelling apple fruit yield using image analysis for fruit colour, shape and texture. Europ. J. Hortic. Sci. **74**, 260–267 (2009)
4. Bairwa, N., Agrawal, N., Gupta, S.: Development of counting algorithm for overlapped agricultural products. In proceeding of National Conference on Recent Advances in Wireless Communication and Artificial Intelligence (RAWCAI-2014) (2014)
5. Zhou, R., Damerow, L., Sun, Y., Blanke, M.: Using colour features of cv. 'Gala' apple fruits in an orchard in image processing to predict yield. Precis. Agric. **13**, 568–580 (2012)
6. Stajnko, D., Rozmana, Č., Pavloviča, M., Beber, M., Zadravec, P.: Modeling of 'Gala' apple fruits diameter for improving the accuracy of early yield prediction. Sci. Hortic. **160**, 306–312 (2013)
7. Kelman, E., Linker, R.: Vision-based localisation of mature apples in trees images using convexity. Biosyst. Eng. **118**, 174–185 (2014)
8. Bairwa, N., Agrawal, K.N.: Counting algorithm for flowers using image processing. Int. J. Eng. Res. Technol. (IJERT) **3**, 775–779 (2014)
9. Gil, J., Kimmel, R.: Efficient dilation, erosion, opening and closing algorithms. In: Goutsias, V.J., Vincent, L., Bloomberg, D. (eds.) Mathematical Morphology and its Applications to Image and Signal Processing, Palo-Alto, USA, June 2000, pp. 301–310. Kluwer Academic Publishers (2000)
10. Haralick, R.M., Shanmugam, K., Dinstein, I.: Textural Features for image classification. IEEE Trans. Syst. Man Cybernatics **3**(6), 610–621 (1973)
11. Guru, D.S., Sharath, Y.H., Manjunath, S.: Texture features and KNN in classification of flower images. IJCA (2010). Special Issue on Recent Trends in Image Processing and Pattern Recognition RTIPPR
12. Patel, H.N., Patel, A.D.: Automatic segmentation and yield measurement of fruit using shape analysis. Int. J. Comput. Appl. **45**(7) (2012). (0975 – 8887)
13. Aggelopoulou, A.D., Bochtis, D., Fountas, S., Swain, K.C., Gemtos, T.A., Nanos, G.D.: Yield prediction in apple orchards based on image processing. Precis. Agric. **12**, 448–456 (2011)
14. Sharma, V.K., Srivastava, D.K., Mathur, P.: Efficient image steganography using graph signal processing. IET Image Process. **12**(6), 1065–1071 (2018)

15. Kaur, S., Kaur, S.: Performance evaluation of different filters in image denoising for different noise. Int. J. Innov. Res. Sci. Eng. Technol. **5**(7) (2016). ISSN (Online) 2319-8753, ISSN (Print) 2347-6710
16. Singh, P., Shree, R.: A comparative study to noise models and image restoration techniques. Int. J. Comput. Appl. **149**(1) (2016). (0975 – 8887)
17. Saravanan, G., Yamuna, G., Nandhini, S.: Real time implementation of RGB to HSV/HSI/HSL and its reverse color space models. In: International Conference on Communication and Signal Processing, India, 6–8 April 2016 (2016)
18. Nnolim, U.A.: Design and implementation of novel, fast, pipelined HSI2RGB and log-hybrid RGB2HSI color converter architectures for image enhancement. Microprocess. Microsyst. **39**(4–5), 223–236 (2015)
19. Nilsback, M.E., Zisserman, A.: Delving into the whorl of flower segmentation. In the Proceedings of British Machine Vision Conference, vol. 1, pp. 27–30 (2004)
20. Islam, S., Ahmed, M.: A study on edge detection techniques for natural image segmentation. Int. J. Innov. Technol. Explor. Eng. (IJITEE) **2**(3) (2013). ISSN 2278-3075
21. Wang, H.: Robust statistics for computer vision: model fitting, image segmentation and visual motion analysis, Ph.D thesis, Monash University, Australia (2004)
22. Yuen, H.K., Princen, J., Illingworth, J., Kittler, J.: A comparative study of hough transform methods for circle finding. Image Vis. Comput. **8**, 71–77 (1990)
23. Ahmad, S.: Environmental effects on seed characteristics of sunflower. J. Agron. Crop Sci. **187**(3), 213–216 (2001)
24. StatCrunch: Data Analysis on Web. College of Western Idaho, Pearson Education 2017–2018

Integration of RESTful Services in Agro Advisory System

Mahesh Titiya[1](✉) and Vipul Shah[2]

[1] Government Engineering College, Rajkot 360005, India
mdtitiya@gmail.com
[2] Dharmsinh Desai University, Nadiad 360005, India
vashahin2010@gmail.com

Abstract. There is a large amount of data related to agricultural practices being collected via different sources but it is not being u sed for maximum benefit for the farmers due to lack of mediums for the information to flow and other factors like language differences, lack of technology to access that information etc. Information Communication Technology (ICT) can helps to bridge that gap by creating systems that are easier to access and are able to answer the basic questions for the farmers which helps the farmers to increase the production of the crop. Such a system should make use of all the data sources available and provide processed information that makes sense to the user. We have developed ontology based Agro-Advisory System to fulfill these requirements. It is acknowledged based system. The knowledge base is maintained in the form of ontology. Ontology contains cotton crop knowledge. Ontology is integrated with RESTful web services to develop our system. Farmers can ask their queries related to cotton crop cultivation by Android mobile and get recommendations on their mobile which improves cotton crop productivity. The system is also able to send notification and alert to farmers if any adverse change in weather condition.

Keywords: RESTful services · Ontology
Semantic web · Recommended system · RESTful architecture

1 Introduction

In the domain of agriculture the farmers have mainly questions regarding which crop is to cultivate, the weather conditions, process to cultivate crop, and information regarding the disease and pest affecting the crop. It is not feasible for the expert to present physically every time to answer the queries of farmers. Due to which the farmers may not able to clearly understand the answer of expert for specific query asked by farmers. So there is communication gap between the farmers and expert. It is desirable to capture agriculture expert's knowledge in a system that understands farmer's queries appropriately and gives the recommendations for it. We have developed ontology based Agro-Advisory System to

© Springer Nature Singapore Pte Ltd. 2019
A. K. Luhach et al. (Eds.): ICAICR 2018, CCIS 955, pp. 23–34, 2019.
https://doi.org/10.1007/978-981-13-3140-4_3

fulfill these requirements. Ontology is integrated with RESTful web services to develop our system.

RESTful services work seamlessly over the internet. They can be written in java languages and combined with various other technologies to build complex systems. The basic characteristics of web services are composition in which atomic services can be combined to form a new service that can answer queries without having to create them separately.

We have integrated such RESTful services with a variety of data sources. We are using Structured Query Language (SQL), Resource Description Framework (RDF) and Geographical data which are stored separately. We have written web services to retrieve the information, process them if necessary and display them on a mobile device or on a web browser in either plain text, tabular or map format.

2   KisanMitra: Ontology Based Agro Advisory System

We have build up system named KisanMitra which uses data sources such as knowledge base in the form of Ontology and Geographical data Sources. These data sources are integrated using RESTful services. KisanMitra gives answers to queries of farmers on their mobile regarding pest and disease prevention techniques to be used based on the query asked by frames, the information regarding weather condition, and soil. Our system is very much user friendly to farmers which requires very less training to use it.

3   Analysis and Design of System

We propose to create a mobile phone based and automated Agro advisory system for the cotton farmers in Gujarat state. To achieve this we will be using various concepts in ICT that will help us to create a feasible and useful solution. Figure 1 is proposed architecture of the system.

3.1   Components of System

The SQL database:- This database contains information which does not changes regularly. The database contains information regarding farm survey number, soil of farm, NPK ratio of farm, latitude and longitude of farm etc. The information will be entered by farmers during registration. The SQL database also contains weather information which is updated regularly by admin. The SQL Queries are run to fetch data from SQL database and stored on PostGreSql server database which is on cloud. The information stored on PostGreSql database available to user using available RESTful services.

The RDF knowledge base:- This is main components of system which contains knowledge base for the Cotton Crop. It contains information regarding Climatic

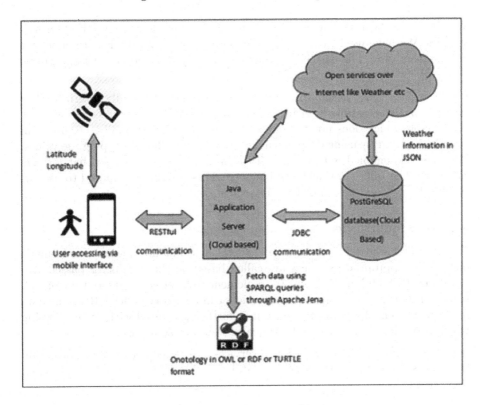

Fig. 1. KisanMitra system architecture

Condition, Disease and Pest affecting cotton crop, Irrigation techniques, Irrigation for cotton crop at regular interval, Pesticide and Insecticide to be used for Cotton crop etc. We are using SPARQL Queries and reasoners on the RDF knowledge base to generate the result for users queries. We have used Apache Jena [10] framework to retrieve the data from ontology through query and communicate the results of query using RESTful web services.

Geographic database:- It contains information regarding the farm location, farm latitude and longitude. The Geographical information stores in the POSTGIS database which is an extension of PostGreSql. This data helps to show the current location of farmer's farm on the Google Earth or Google Map. We have also added more information like farmers name shown with farm location, number of pest or disease on a farm. It will help farmers to better understand current and deduce patterns if any without analyzing a lot of tabular and plain text data.

RESTful Services:- This component drives whole system. The relevant data based on farmers queries are fetched from SQL database and RDF knowledge base and displayed to users on their mobile using RESTful services. The web services are using REST based architecture which is more suited to the world-wide web considering the similarities in the basic operations between the two.

We have used Java language and JAX-RS API for implementing RESTful web services. We have used Eclipse as an Integrated Development Environment for development of it. The RESTful services are deployed on cloud so that it can be accessible by user from their mobiles.

User Interface (UI):- KisanMitra system is having user friendly interface. The system can be accessible by using UI of our system. The user interface is made very simple which does not take lot of input from user manually. i.e. user can submit the input by using drop down menus instead of the user typing the values. We have also enabled our system with local language support so that farmers can enter their query in their local language. Less training is required to use our system due to good design of User Interface.

3.2   RESTful Services

The RESTful web services are used to fetch relevant information for farmer's query. The appropriate services are called based on the parameter passed. We have used RESTful architecture to implement web services. The output of web services is in the JSON format. The services can be invoked once URL is fixed on deployment. The JSON format output is further processed with JSON Parsing which is displayed on the mobile device or web browser of user.

SQL based web services:- These web services can be used to fetch information from the Structured Query Language databases. The Fig. 2 shows the SQL based web services.

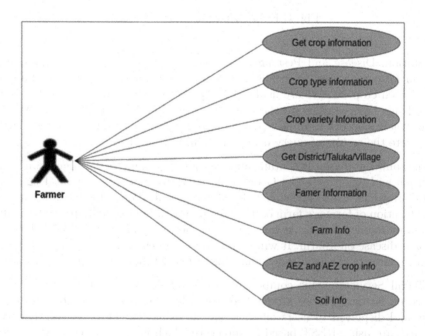

Fig. 2. SQL based web services

Location Based Service:- This service display the current location of the farm on Google Map based on the parameter passed as farm survey number or current location. The Latitude and Longitude is provided to display current location information of farm. The service can be accessed using URl would be: URL/services/AEZLocationInfo_Service/latitude. Figure 3 shows the flow of it.

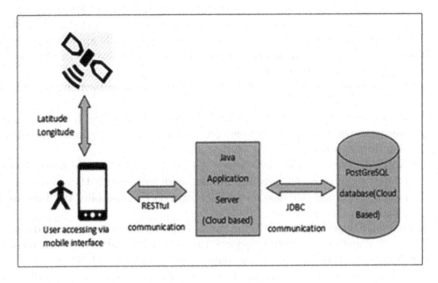

Fig. 3. Location based service

Weather Service:- This service gives information about the current climatic condition of the specific location. The location information is provided with Latitude and Longitude of specific location. This service does not require any human intervention. It is autonomous service. Figure 4 shows the flow of it.

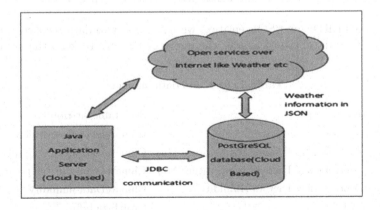

Fig. 4. Weather based service

4 Developing Mobile Interface and Web Service Integration

1. Mobile interface is developed for accessing the web services which displays the recommendation of query of farmers on their mobile. We have used mobile phones as a medium of interaction between the farmers and knowledge base which is in the form of ontology. As the Android operating system is widely used in most of mobiles. We have decided to created mobile application which runs on it. We have used Android studio version 1.4 to develop it. Our application has 3 major components:
   (a) Information centre: It provides all the information like farmer info, village info, weather info etc.
   (b) Recommendation centre: provides recommendations for farmer's query like pest preventions techniques for pest and cure for disease based on symptoms and observations on cotton plant.
   (c) Notifications and map data where the user can see all the notifications related to adverse change in climatic conditions which they received in mobile. A farmer can also see view of farm on their mobile. We have used google api services for it.
2. Adding RDF based data (OWL format) and preparing web services to query that data using Apache Jena Services that use RDF data to return recommendations to the user based on parameters provided. These services use the POST operation to transmit the SPARQL query so cannot be directly accessed via a web browser. Below are the services developed.
   (a) Disease cure by Observations appear on plant.
   (b) Pest and its prevention techniques by Observations.
   (c) Disease and its cure by symptoms.
   (d) Disease Observations, Pest Observations, Disease Symptoms and Disease Symptoms by part.
3. Android mobile interface is created which retrieve RDF data using sparql queries. We have made recommendation centre through which user can select the query.
4. Mapping of RDF and SQL entities, we have used two data resources, ontology and sql database to answer the query of farmer. To keep the system in

Table 1. RDF and data mapping

OWL/RDF concept	SQL table/attribute
Climate-Clouds	ClimateData-Description
Climate-Metrological Factors-Temperature-Max	ClimateData-max_tempreature
Climate-Metrological Factors-Temperature-Min	ClimateData-min_tempreature
Climate-Metrological Factors-Humidity	ClimateData-humidity
Crop-CropType	CropTypeInfo
Climate-Clouds	CropVarietyInfo
Soil	Soil

synchronization, we have performed a data mapping between the SQL and RDF data which is shown in Table 1.

5. Figures 5 and 6 showing the service composition designed for the current system: Here two services one to parse and other to query the RDF ontology is used to obtain the final result. This composition is used for all the services in the Recommendation centre of our application.

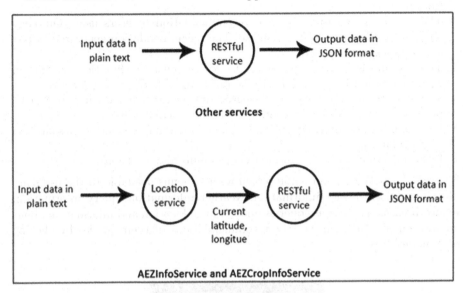

Fig. 5. SQL database service

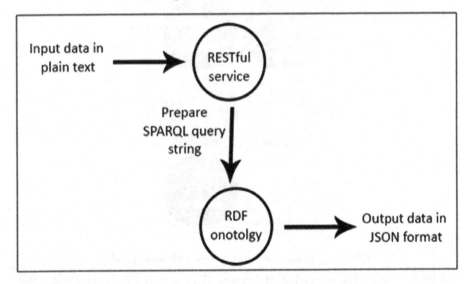

Fig. 6. RDF database service

5   Results

We have built the system which has the following functionalities.

1. Access of variety of information related to Cotton Crop such as Climatic condition, Soil for Cotton Crop, Varieties of Cotton Crop, Pest and Disease affecting cotton crop etc. on user mobile which need to have internet connection.
2. The system is generating proper recommendation to users using Ontology Knowledge Base and SQL Database. The recommendation generated in fast and easy way to farmers.
3. The system also helps the farmers to get the current climatic condition of current location by passing Latitude and Longitude of current location.
4. The pest attacks report can be presented on a map on live data and authorized personnel can judge if intervention is needed to control it.
5. Farm and farmer information can be viewed on a map for better presentation of information.
6. Data collection can be performed via formhub to collect data.

Figure 7 shows the system home screen with a menus available to the users are my information, farmer information, weather information, query information, report disease, pest/disease queries, map of farm location and information about application. Farmers can get the recommendations of their queries by clicking on "queries" icon.

Fig. 7. Snapshots of home screen with user detail

Figure 8 shows the query list of farmers. This screen will be available after clicking on a select box of queries. It includes all the queries that generally asked by the farmers. A farmer can select the query from this list.

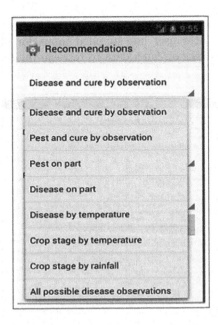

Fig. 8. Snapshots of query list

Figure 9 shows the screen available to farmers after clicking disease and cure by observation submenu. Observation and affected part of the cotton plant are given as an Inputs for the query.

Fig. 9. Recommendations centre

Figure 10 shows the result of query asked by farmers. This screen will be available to the used after user has supplied input for observation and part affected and then use clicks on fetch data to retrieve the result of query.

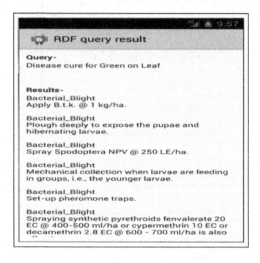

Fig. 10. Recommendations of query

6   Conclusion

Agro-Advisory systems like eSagu, aAQUA, mKrishi, are in use to help farmers by improving their farming practices. This thesis presents a new Agro-Advisory system named as "KisanMitra" which is an Android based and uses new semantic web technologies like ontology, SPARQL query language and reasoning capabilities. The system can generate automatic recommendations based on farmers queries regarding crop and their farming so agro experts are not needed at the other end. The user/farmers will be able to access a variety of data like soil types, cotton crop varieties, farmer information, pest/disease affecting cotton crop, insecticide, pesticide, fungicide which needs to be used to prevent disease/pest. The farmers will get recommendation or relevant information on their mobile phones without being concerned about the source of data. The system can generate alert and notification and sends to farmers if there is adverse change in climate condition so that farmers can take precautionary steps before heavy damage occurs. To access our system the mobile device only needs to communicate with the web services through internet. The interface for the mobile phone system is very user friendly which does not require much training. Our Kisan-Mitra system is pioneer and pilot work to develop agro advisory system using ontology. This system will be also a model for building agro advisory system for other crop which leads to increase in the yield or production of crop.

7   Future Scope

Our system can be more useful to farmers if we could include current climate condition data and weather prediction techniques. Weather predictions can be made more accurate depending on previous data. We are currently limited by data space which we have on cloud, upon more space we can add more data which helps us to determine weather patterns accurately. Recommendations can be made better using better reasoning and inference logic in our ontology. More farms may be mapped in our system that will help to increase the reach and benefit more users. Other elements like water sources/warehouses may also be mapped to provide more information like nearest water body or nearest warehouse.

References

1. Hendler, J., Berners-Lee, T., Lassila, O.: The Semantic Web. Scientific American, New York City (2001)
2. XML: Extensible markup language. http://www.w3.org/XML/
3. Rdf: Resource description framework. http://www.w3.org/RDF/
4. Stephan, G., Pascal, H., Andreas, A.: Knowledge Representation and Ontologies. In: Studer, R., Grimm, S., Abecker, A. (eds.) Semantic Web Services, pp. 51–105. Springer, Heidelberg (2007). https://doi.org/10.1007/3-540-70894-4_3
5. Owl: Web ontology language. http://www.w3.org/2001/sw/wiki/OWL
6. Noy, N.F., McGuinness, D.L.: Ontology development 101: a guide to creating your first ontology. Stanford Knowledge Systems Laboratory, 25 2001
7. Laliwala, Z., Sorathia, V., Chaudhary, S.: Semantic and rule based event-driven services-oriented agricultural recommendation system. In: 26th IEEE International Conference on Distributed Computing Systems Workshops (ICDCSW06), pp. 24–30, July 2006
8. Noy, N.F.: Tools for mapping and merging ontologies. In: Staab, S., Studer, R. (eds.) Handbook on Ontologies. International Handbooks on Information Systems, pp. 365–384. Springer, Heidelberg (2004). https://doi.org/10.1007/978-3-540-24750-0_18
9. Koutu, G.K., Shastry, P.P., Mishra, D.K., Mandloi, K.C.: Handbook of Cotton, 1st edn. Studium Press (India) Pvt. Ltd., Delhi (2012)
10. Bhalotia, G., Hulgeri, A., Nakhe, C., Chakrabarti, S., Sudarshan, S.: Keyword searching and browsing in databases using BANKS. In: Proceedings - International Conference on Data Engineering, pp. 431–440 (2002)
11. S. Exchange and R. Development, eSagu : An IT- based personalized agroadvisory system for augmenting livelihoods of farmers, December 2006
12. Ramamritham, K., Bahuman, A., Duttagupta, S.: aAqua: a database-backended multilingual, multimedia community forum. In: Proceedings of the 2006 ACM SIG-MOD International Conference on Management of Data, Ser. SIGMOD 06, pp. 784–786 (2006)
13. Shinde, S., Piplani, D., Srinivasan, K., Singh, D., Sharma, R., Mohnaty, P.: mKR-ISHI: simplification of IVR based services for rural community. In: Proceedings of the India HCI 2014 Conference on Human Computer Interaction, Ser. IndiaHCI 14, pp. 154–159 (2014)

14. G.K. Centre: AGRISNET - Information Network for Farmers, no. 3, March 2011
15. Roy, M., Ghosh, C.K.: The benefits of the e-learning agricultural project Kissanker-ala to digital immigrants and digital natives. Turk. Online J. Distance Educ. **14**(2), 150–164 (2013)
16. Agropedia: A free and open source java framework for building semantic web and linked data applications. http://agropedia.iitk.ac.in
17. M. sabesh cicr: approved package of practices for cotton. http://www.cicr.org.in/pop/gj.pdf
18. Mehta, S.C., Agrawal, R., Kumar, A.: Forewarning crop pests and diseases: IASRI methodologies, pp. 67–77, Iasri (2005)
19. Sparql protocol and query language for rdf. http://www.w3.org/TR/rdf-sparql-query
20. Le, S.: Semantic web holds promises for ocean observing needs, in Oceans (2008)
21. Horridge, M., Knublauch, H., Rector, A., Stevens, R., Wroe, C.: A practical guide to building OWL ontologies using the Protg-OWL Plugin and CO-ODE Tools, pp. 0–117, vol. 27. The University Of Manchester (2004)
22. Pappu, N., Sarkar, R., Prabhakar, T.V.: Agropedia: humanization of agricultural knowledge. IEEE Internet Comput. **14**(5), 57–59 (2010)
23. Bichindaritz, I.: Mmoire: a framework for semantic interoperability of casebased reasoning systems in biology and medicine. Artif. Intell. Med. **36**(2), 177–192 (2006)
24. Sini, M., Yadav, V., Prabhakar, T.V., Singh, J., Awasthi, V.: Knowledge models in agropedia indica (2008)
25. Rajasurya, S., Muralidharan, T., Devi, S., Swamynathan, S.: Semantic information retrieval using ontology in university domain. CoRR, vol.abs/1207.5745 (2012)

Neural Network Models for Prediction of Evaporation Based on Weather Variables

Rakhee[1(✉)], Archana Singh[1], and Amrender Kumar[2]

[1] CSE, Amity University, Noida, India
rakheesharma234@gmail.com
[2] Agricultural Knowledge Management Unit, ICAR-IARI, Delhi, India

Abstract. Artificial Neural networks (ANNs) is a computation method that can be utilized for predictions. In this study prediction of evaporation using ANN's multilayer perceptron (MLP) is attempted considering different weather variables *viz*. Relative Humidity Morning & Evening, Bright Sunshine Hours, Rainfall, Maximum & Minimum temperature, Mean Temperature and Mean Relative Humidity. The analysis is done over different parts of India *viz*. Raipur, Pantnagar, Karnal, Hyderabad and Samastipur. Weather of four lag weeks from week of forecast is considered for the model development. The lag periods were also utilized to develop weather indices. Subsequent two years were not included while developing the model for predicting evaporation for different locations. The performance of the developed models was evaluated based on Root Mean Square Error (RMSE).

Keywords: Artificial Neural Networks · Prediction models · Weather indices Backpropagation algorithm · Mean absolute percentage error

1 Introduction

In agricultural field, a weather based model can be an effective tool to predict the future scenario for the crops. Weather is an important factor that influence the crop yield and pest infestation in the field, thus prediction of evaporation is important to monitor the crop water requirement and management of available resources. Most of the researchers have established linear relationship between the input variables and the output variable, but due to high complex data in agriculture and non-linear nature of weather data, the research focus has shifted toward development of non-linear model for prediction. For the development of non-linear model Artificial Neural Network (ANN) has evolved out in better way than any other technique. Its application become largely focus on solving complex problems with great ease. Different problem domains *viz*. medical, stocks, finance, engineering, security, character recognition, agriculture etc. have utilized ANN technique to solve their problem domains. The advance characteristic features of ANN includes mapping capabilities that is they can easily map input patterns to their associated outputs. They can predict new outcomes from the past data. The artificial neural network can also form full patterns from the noisy or incomplete data.

Time-series analysis was used for predicting relative humidity and forecasting of temperature [1]. MLP network is formed using three layers with 6 neurons in hidden

© Springer Nature Singapore Pte Ltd. 2019
A. K. Luhach et al. (Eds.): ICAICR 2018, CCIS 955, pp. 35–43, 2019.
https://doi.org/10.1007/978-981-13-3140-4_4

layer and sigmoid activation function to forecast temperature [2]. another researcher [3] have predicted temperature forming ANN using three layer MLP network, in this training is done through back propagation and relative humidity, atmospheric temperature, atmospheric pressure, wind velocity and wind direction are considered as independent variable. Researchers [4, 5] have also applied neural network technique for plant disease forecasting. Most of them have worked on the comparison of ANN and traditional statistical methods and found that ANN work better than these traditional methods. Some researchers have forecasted [6] wheat productivity of Junagadh (Gujarat) using data on weather conditions to develop ANN model and found that the results based on ANN are better than those from multiple linear regression model (MLR). [7] Developed neural network model for forecasting crop yield (rice, wheat, sugarcane for central plain zone, eastern plain zone,) and important diseases of mustard crop in different locations using weather variables. Multilayer perceptron (MLP), a neural network architecture was found to be better than weather indices model on basis of MAPE.

It is recommended from the study that one hidden layer is first choice for any feed forward network formation but if one hidden layer with large number of neurons could not perform well then second layer with few processing neurons could be attempted. In this study, prediction of evaporation is done using ANN technique. MLP algorithms namely backpropagation and conjugate gradient descent is applied using one hidden layer consisting of seven neurons. In the network formation, hyperbolic activation function is used. The input layer consist of independent variables (various combination of weather variables) and output layer consist of evaporation as output variable.

2   Data

Different locations of India were considered for the model development. In this study, weekly meteorological data for different locations *viz.* Raipur (21.25° N, 81.62° E): 1985–2012; Karnal (29.68° N, 76.99° E): 1973–2005; Pantnagar (29.02° N, 79.49° E): 1970–2008; Hyderabad (17.38° N, 78.48° E): 2006–2012; Samastipur (25.86° N, 85.78° E): 1984–2010. Weather variables *viz.* maximum & minimum temperature (maxt & mint), relative humidity in the morning & in the evening (rhi & rhii), rainfall (rf), bright sunshine hours (bsh), evaporation (evap), mean temperature (meant), mean relative humidity (meanrh) were used. Various combinations of independent variables were considered i.e. (i) maxt (ii) meanrh (iii) meant and meanrh (iv) meant, meanrh and bsh (v) meant, meanrh, bsh and rf (vi) meant, meanrh, bsh and rf.

3   Methodology

3.1   Generation of Weather Indices

In this methodology two indices were developed for each weather variables *viz.* (i) The first indices consist of total accumulation of weather variable, this represents the total accumulation of weather (ii) second indices consist of weighted value of weather variables, weight being as correlation coefficients between variable to forecast and weather variables in respective weeks, this indicates the distribution of weather with special reference to its importance in different week in respect to week of forecast. On the same pattern the combined effect of weather variable (taken two weather variable at a time) were also attempted. The form of the model was [8–11].

$$Y = a_0 + \sum_{i=1}^{p} \sum_{j=0}^{1} a_{ij} Z_{ij} + \sum_{i \neq i'}^{p} \sum_{j=0}^{1} b_{ii'j} Z_{ii'j} + \varepsilon \tag{1}$$

$$Z_{ij} = \sum_{w=n_1}^{n_2} r_{iw}^{j} X_{iw} \tag{2}$$

$$Z_{ii'j} = \sum_{w=n_1}^{n_2} r_{ii'w}^{j} X_{iw} X_{i'w} \tag{3}$$

where

Y   Forecast variable
X_{iw} i^{th} weather variable in wth week
r_{iw} correlation coefficient between Y and i^{th} weather variable in wth week
$r_{ii'w}$ correlation coefficient between Y and product of X_i and $X_{i'}$ in wth week
p   number of weather variables
n_1 initial week for which weather data was included in the model
n_2 final week for which weather data was included in the model
E   error term

    In this study results based on the interaction of weather variables were not found to be satisfactory thus have considered only single weather variables as independent variable.

3.2   Model Based on Artificial Neural Networks

Artificial Neural Network consists of processing units which communicate to one another by sending signals over a large weighted connection. The network is adapted based on the architecture of human brains which consists of neurons to receive and transmit the signals to another neuron and thus eventually forming a network. Similarly, ANN consist of processing units and connections i.e. artificial neurons and weights between them respectively. The artificial neuron transports the signals to another neurons and so on to form the network. The values stored in the weights simulate the information so that network learn, memorize and then form relationships to form a stronger network. ANNs can learn and generalize from experience. Neural network consists of neurons, connections between them i.e. weights and three layers namely input layer, hidden layer(s) and output layer. The network is trained using the data with known output, the procedure is termed as supervised learning. After training, the network model formed is used to predict the output of new input data. In the present study, two algorithms is used to train the neural network namely back propagation and conjugate gradient descent respectively. Evaporation considered to be output unit and weather variables were the input units. One hidden layers having seven neurons were used in the network. Activation function is needed in hidden units to introduce non-linearity into the model. Choice of activation function depends on heuristic rules for example if learning involves deviation from average, use hyperbolic tangent and logistics activation function is used for classification problems [12]. The hyperbolic tangent function is presented mathematically as

$$f(x) = [e^x - e^{-x}]/[e^x + e^{-x}] \tag{4}$$

In this study hyperbolic function (tanh) is used as activation function with one hidden layer having seven neurons for training neural network to predict evaporation for different places in India.

4 Learning Algorithm Used

4.1 Backpropagation

Backpropagation is a common method to train a neural network. The algorithm calculates the weights which is used in the network formation. It calculates the gradient to adjust the weights of the neuron which is a fundamental unit of the ANN. Here in this algorithm, error function is to be minimized with respect to weights and the bias. If the study consider linear activation function then the activation of the output unit is calculated as linear function of input units, weights and the bias respectively. Multilayer perceptron (MLP) is learned by back propagation method, it is a supervised procedure in which neural network is created based on data having known outputs. Figure 1 represents the flow chart of Backpropagation algorithm working method to minimize the errors. The model for the neural network first calculate the error and if its minimized then this model is ready for prediction, otherwise the model will first update the parameters (weights) and train the network again with the updated weights and then calculate the error to see whether it is minimized or not. Once the model with minimized error is ready, the prediction can be performed. The training to model is given by some learning algorithms, These algorithms were mainly classified into three broad categories namely Supervised learning, Unsupervised learning and reinforced learning. In Multilayer Perceptron supervised learning algorithm is used to train the network. The neural network is created arranging the neurons in successive layers. The information flows form input neurons to output neurons via hidden layers. In this study one hidden layer having seven neurons were considered to develop the model.

4.2 Conjugate Gradient Descent

Conjugate gradient descent (CGD) is the most popular iterative method for solving linear equations. The basic back propagation algorithm adjust the weights in negative

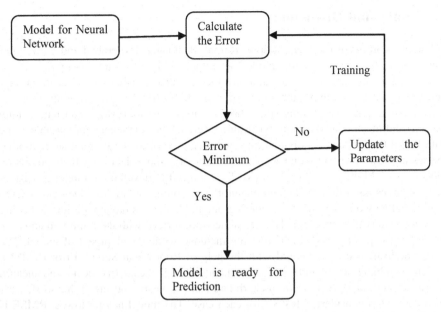

Fig. 1. Flow chart followed by backpropagation algorithm to minimize the error while training the model

direction of the gradient, in this direction performance function is decreasing. If performance function is decreasing more rapidly in negative gradient direction it doesn't mean convergence attains at faster rate. In CGD, the search is performed along conjugate directions, it attains faster convergence. In CGD algorithm firstly, vector sequence of iterates were generated, the residuals corresponding to these iterates were also generated along with the directions used to update these residuals and iterates. The algorithm now selects the direction vectors as a conjugate of its successive gradients obtained as the process progresses. These directions are determined sequentially at each step of iterations.

5 Evaluation Criteria Used

Root Mean Square Error (RMSE) is used to evaluate the performance of the prediction models. Mathematically represented as follows

$$RMSE = \sqrt{\frac{1}{m} \sum_{i=1}^{m} (o - p)^2} \tag{5}$$

6 Results and Discussion

Different locations of India *viz.* Raipur, Karnal, Pantnagar, Hyderabad and Samastipur were considered for prediction model development. In this study evaporation was considered as dependent variable and all other weather variables *viz.* maximum temperature (maxt), minimum temperature (mint), rainfall (rf), relative humidity morning (rhi), relative humidity evening (rhii), bright sunshine hours (bsh), mean temperature (meant) and mean relative humidity(meanrh) were taken as independent variables. The data for all the locations is divided into two sets; one forms the training set and other the testing test. Two subsequent year were out of sample data on which prediction model is run. Multilayer perceptron (MLP) is utilized to develop the model consisting of two phases algorithm of Backpropagation and Conjugate Gradient Descent (CGD). The neural network is formed considering one hidden layers having 7 neurons having hyperbolic activation function. The neural network formed with the training data is run for two subsequent years which were not included while development of model. The model performance is monitored with the help of Root Mean Square Error (RMSE), various combinations of independent variables like (i) meant (ii) meant and meanrh (iii) maxt and maxrh (iv) meant, meanrh and bsh (v) meant, meanrh, bsh and rf; were tried and tested considering RMSE for each case. The model having lowest RMSE is the best to predict the evaporation. Table 1 represents the RMSE for different locations considering various combinations of independent variables.

Table 1. RMSE for different location with various combinations of weather variables

S. No.	Locations	MeanTemp	MeanTemp and MeanRh	MaxTemp and MaxRh	MeanTemp, MeanRh and Bsh	MeanTemp, MeanRh, Bsh and Rf
1.	Raipur	1.55	0.98	1.04	1.10	1.14
2.	Karnal	1.88	1.04	1.15	1.20	1.10
3.	Pantnagar	1.49	1.47	1.71	2.01	3.12
4.	Hyderabad	2.21	0.95	2.73	2.46	2.54
5.	Samastipur	1.32	1.01	1.33	2.35	1.05

Table 1 shows that the combination of mean temperature (average value of maxt and mint) and mean relative humidity (average value of rhi and rhii) have least RMSE for all the considered locations. The model developed using mean temperature and mean relative humidity as independent variables provides close approximation of predicted values with the observed one for all the locations. Figure 2 Shows the graphs of observed and predicted values for these locations. The graphs were shown only for the combination of MeanTemp and MeanRh to predict the evaporation as it has least value of Root Mean Square Error and thus provides better accuracy with the developed model.

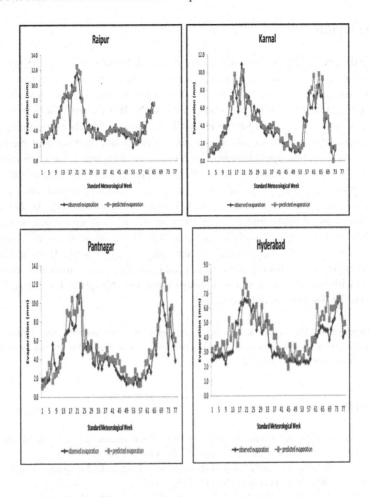

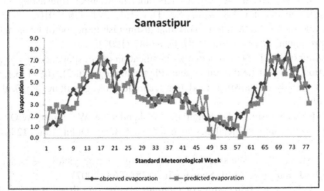

Fig. 2. Graphs representing observed and predicted values of evaporation for various locations using mean temperature and mean relative humidity as independent variables

7 Conclusion

In this study prediction of evaporation for different locations (Raipur, Karnal, Pant-nagar, Hyderabad and Samastipur) using various combinations of weather variables *viz.* (i) meant (ii) meant and meanrh (iii) maxt and maxrh (iv) meant, meanrh and bsh (v) meant, meanrh, bsh and rf, was done using ANN. Weather of four weeks lag from week of forecast is considered for the model development. Weather based indices were also developed and considered as independent variables but the results of prediction in such case is not in close approximation with observed ones hence the error rate is very high, thus, four-week lag data of all-weather variables were considered as independent variables against evaporation as dependent variable. Predictive model was run on two subsequent years which were not considered in model development. Artificial neural network was formed using multilayer perceptron having two algorithms namely back propagation and conjugate gradient descent. Various combinations of independent variables were tried, and their evaluation were tested using RMSE. Lowest RMSE for all the locations were found with meant and meanrh. This indicates that model developed with meant and meanrh as independent variable gives better prediction of evaporation for the considered locations.

Acknowledgments. The work would not have been possible without the data. we thank Agricultural Knowledge Management Unit, ICAR-IARI, New Delhi for providing us with the data from various locations of India.

References

1. Mathur, S., Kumar, A., Chandra, M.: A feature based neural network model for weather forecasting. World Acad. Sci. Eng. Technol. **34**, 66–73 (2007)
2. Hayati, M., Mohebi, Z.: Application of artificial neural networks for temperature forecasting. World Acad. Sci. Eng. Technol. **28**, 275–279 (2007)
3. Santhosh Baboo, S., Kadar Shereef, I.: An efficient weather forecasting system using artificial neural network. Int. J. Environ. Sci. Dev. **1**(4), 321–326 (2010)
4. Dewolf, E.D., Francl, L.J.: Neural network that distinguish in period of wheat tan spot in an outdoor environment. Phytopathology **87**(1), 83–87 (1997)
5. Dewolf, E.D., Francl, L.J.: Neural network classification of tan spot and stagonespore blotch infection period in wheat field environment. Phytopathology **20**(2), 108–113 (2000)
6. Madhav, K.V.: Study of statistical modeling techniques in agriculture. Ph.D. thesis, IARI, New Delhi (2003)
7. Kumar, M., Raghuwanshi, N.S., Singh, R., Wallender, W.W., Pruitt, W.O.: Estimating Evapotranspiration using artificial neural network. J. Irrig. Drain. Eng. **128**(4), 224–233 (2002)
8. Agrawal, R., Mehta, S.C.: Weather based forecasting of crop yields, pests and diseases - IASRI models. J. Ind. Soc. Agril. Statist. **61**(2), 255–263 (2007)
9. Chattopadhyay, C., et al.: Forecasting of *Lipaphis erysimi* on oilseed Brassicas in India - a case study. Crop. Prot. **24**, 1042–1053 (2005)

10. Chattopadhyay, C., et al.: Epidemiology and forecasting of *Alternaria* blight of oilseed *Brassica* in India - a case study. Zeitschrift für Pflanzenkrankheiten und Pflanzenschutz **112**, 351–365 (2005)
11. Desai, A.G., et al.: *Brassica juncea* powdery mildew epidemiology and weather-based forecasting models for India - a case study. J. Plant Dis. Prot. **111**(5), 429–438 (2004)
12. Klimasauskas, C.: Applying neural networks. Part 3: Training a neural network (1991)

Energy Management System for Analysis and Reporting in the Advanced Metering

Abhishek Singh[1]([✉]), Pratibha Pandey[1], and Balgovind Gupta[2]

[1] Department of Computer Science and Engineering,
Institute of Engineering and Technology, Dr. A.P.J. Abdul Kalam University,
Lucknow, India
singhabhishek.0815@gmail.com, ppratibha14@gmail.com
[2] Landis+Gyr, Noida, Uttar Pradesh, India
balgovindgupta@gmail.com

Abstract. A smart meter is a device which is used to collect the consumption demand data from home appliances. Energy Management System for analysis and reporting is data communication based software that received encrypted data from electronic energy meter reading Instrument and electronic energy meter. It displays data in user readable format after some required conversion. This paper presented an overview of Advance metering infrastructure and Energy management system. Later, described the security and functionality of the Energy management system. After that it shows the different report obtained by the Energy managements system which includes six months of Billing History, Tamper details, Load Survey up to sixty days and more according to user requirement using Crystal report. Load survey data are represented in tabular and graphical format. User can view all, daily, monthly and many more presentation format.

Keywords: Smart grid · Security · Advanced Meter Reading (AMR)
Head End System (HES) · Energy Management System (EMS)
Advanced Metering Infrastructure (AMI)

1 Introduction

Smart meter is an advanced energy meter that measures the energy consumption of a consumer and display on demand data that provides added information to the utility company compared to a regular energy meter [1]. The user is able to see the daily weekly and monthly consumption by means of display installed at home [14]. It is possible to manage the power consumption for energy optimization purposes, both in terms of costs for the customer and energy saving in this way [2]. Here, Fig. 1 represents the advanced metering infrastructure (AMI) extending Advance meter reading (AMR) mechanism by enabling duplex communication between the meters that permits instructions to be sent from utility datacenter to other meters for various purpose that includes Billing information, pricing information, time of delay, load forecasting,

A. K. Luhach et al. (Eds.): ICAICR 2018, CCIS 955, pp. 44–53, 2019.
https://doi.org/10.1007/978-981-13-3140-4_5

Demand side Management/Demand-Response actions, or remote service disconnects, load forecasting and outage management [10].

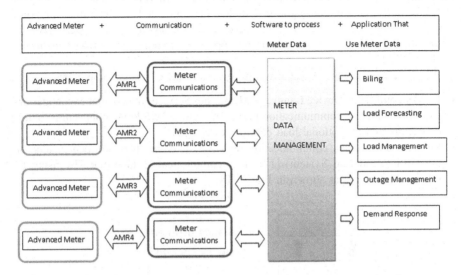

Fig. 1. Advanced metering infrastructure block diagram (conventional)

In order to analyze and view the data of energy electric meter, author has proposed Energy management system for reporting and analysis of that data. Energy management system is capable of presenting different category of data like Power factors, Tariff energy, Voltage Phase data etc. To view and analyze the electric meter data for single meter or group of meters, for reading the data collected now or past, the energy management system has well featured Graphical user interface (GUI). It also has Data analysis and presentation tool that presents various set of data such as Tamper record, billing records, cumulative energies, History Data, Maximum demand and Instantaneous value. Data is collected from the energy meter using International Electro-Technical Commission (IEC) protocol (62056-46) [4]. Data presented in the form of reports like general report, Instant report, and main energy Consumption reports etc. This Energy Management system is also used for generation of bill by the third party on the basis of billing section parameters which includes Cumulative energy, Load factors, voltage imbalance etc.

2 An Overview of Advanced Metering Infrastructure (AMI) and Energy Management System for Analysis (EMS)

Advanced metering infrastructure consist of advanced meters or smart meters that monitor the various factors like power usage, communicate and control to optimize the energy usage, implement data management systems to store and process metering and control data [3]. The major functionality of Advanced metering infrastructure (AMI) include Energy Audits and Accounting, Demand Response or Demand Side Management, Quick communication of abnormality alarms, prepaid and postpaid model for Green energy into a grid for efficient billing cycle [9]. Meter must support a common communication protocol that connects with head end system (HES) [16]. To get this functionality a robust system and duplex communication between devices is required [13, 15].

The Extended advanced metering Infrastructure have 3 basic components:

- DLMS compliant (Device Language Messaging Service) meters that exchanges and uses data with fast communication port (Minimum of 9.6 kbps) connect/disconnect contactors and an optional load control switch [17].
- Modems and duplex communication network for connection between meters and the HES (Head End System) [12]. This communication take place by using the standard Interfaces as shown in Fig. 2 [18].

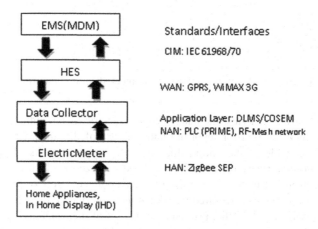

Fig. 2. Advanced metering infrastructure system interface

- Head End System (HES) and Meter Data Management (MDM) scheduling, Software Data collecting, setting threshold values and meter configuration are the key functions performed by head end system. Head end interface system is directly connected to various types of meters via collector or directly with meters attached modem [5, 6].

Energy Management system for analysis and reporting is meter data management (MDM) software. The Energy Management System supports set of data from smart meter and digital meter of various types with minor changes, so that data is uploaded in proper format and path of energy Management System without any manual intervention once the menu is selected. It supports local readout directly from meter through optical interface.

3   Energy Management System Security and Architecture

3.1   Energy Management System for Analysis and Reporting Security

Energy management system for analysis and reporting first received encrypted data from electronic energy meter. The transfer of data must be fraud proof and highly reliable [11]. The EMS (Energy Management System) software shall have a data analysis module, which shall import the data collected from these meters. The entire data stored in the EMS shall be encrypted [8] on the basis of various encryption technique. The Energy Management System that secures the system throughout all the operation is the unique feature of proposed Energy Management System [19]. The security of the system will be maintained on the basis of password and registration key check during the application startup. The system's security is maintained by registration key and password while starting application, generated files will be in encrypted and retained in non-readable format.

3.2   Energy Management System for Analysis and Reporting Architecture

Modified architecture of Energy Management system (EMS) fetch the data from an electric energy meter, after that Energy Management System for analysis and reporting generate raw data, when there is communication with meter. SLG (Encrypted, Protected Data/log File) file is generated and it contains all the details of electric meter raw data. This raw data is uploaded into database and from database user collect the information of meter (Fig. 3).

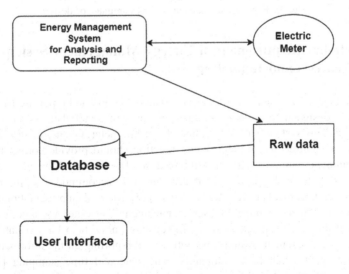

Fig. 3. Energy management system for analysis and reporting architecture

The programming architecture of Energy management system for analysis and reporting will follow 3-layered architecture application layer, presentation layer, business layer and data layer.

- In application layer where forms is design using the controls like textbox, labels, command buttons etc. and the presentation layer is controlled by resource file manager. All the label captions are displayed according to the values in the resource file.
- In business layer is the class where the functions which get the validate various data from the application layer and passes through the data access layer. All validations are kept in this layer. Validation is performed according to the rules defined in external validation file.
- In Data layer the class which gets the data from the business layer and sends it to the database or vice-versa. This layer only interacts with the database. We write the database queries or use stored procedures to access the data from the database or to perform any operation to the database (Fig. 4).

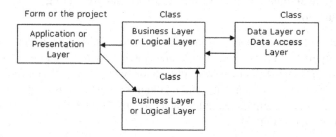

Fig. 4. Energy management system summary of design

4 Functional Requirement of Energy Management System for Analysis and Reporting

Energy Management System is software for data collection and reporting from energy meters. It is designed to collect, organize and present meter data for effective data management. This system is used to collect data from meter. Quality of service such as correctness, response time, reliability etc. function should provide correct result and response time of communication should be low. The Energy Management System development platform should be such that it can easily accommodate in future various meters types and protocols of IEC based meters [22]. Meter data presentation in tabular and graphical formats. Multilevel user management Scheduler for automatic meter reading Consumer & meter data storage Exhaustive online help Easy installation [7].

In Energy management system for analysis and reporting all the information about abnormality events shall be accompanied with date and time stamping [19]. This information is displayed in the sequence in which it happened. The screen visible to user on error will include Exception Number, Exception Summary and the error log will contain Exception Details (exception stack trace) Date-time stamp and all errors will be logged so no unhandled exceptions thrown by the system [20] (Table 1).

Table 1. Energy management system for analysis and reporting function

Functional requirement	Main functions
License and user management	License key to take care of the security of the application and consumer data management
EMS definition	EMS definition on the basis of active meters consumers etc.
Data acquisition and configurations	Retrieve meter data and settings by direct communication from Meter and set COM port setting and serial port communication
Authenticated billing code (ABC) and temper detection	ABC used to transfer bills, other meter information and used to detect tempers
Reports	EMS facilitates user to view and print the selected type of data report

4.1 User Group

Energy Management System user group is divided into user management, change password, application login details and logoff. User management interface is used to add, view and edit user's detail. Change Password is used to change the password of the EMS (Energy Management system). Application login details help in adding more security to the system and through which users identify the user login time and its identity.

4.2 Energy Management System Definition

Energy Management System definition through we identified Area definition, Group definition, Active meter, Inactive meters and free consumers.

4.3 Configurations

Users can set COM port (communication port) setting and Serial Port communication setting like Baud rate, Bit Rate, Parity, and Stop Bit according to need.

4.4 Authenticated Billing Code

It is a unique and innovative feature to transfer meter status and other billing data to utility in secure or encrypted form.

4.5 Tamper Detection

Separate Records are kept for tampers in meter. Multiple folders are designated to collect record data from folders, these folders are called as compartment. Sometimes some changes are made in energy meters such that it registered less energy than actually consumed. The Energy Management system is designed to detect all the tempers, its type and instantaneous parameters when temper event has occurred.

5 Advantages of Energy Management System for Analysis and Reporting

5.1 Reliability

All errors are logged in Proposed Energy Management System. There would be no unhandled exceptions thrown by the system. Proper messages will be shown to the user if any error occurs and the application should never exit or crash in any case.

5.2 Security

Inputs are validated and critical log activity is maintained. The log will have the information of user who involve in the operation, operation detail, date-time stamp.

5.3 Maintainability

Energy Management system (EMS) supports the future changes which includes bug fixing new application addition and addition of any other requirement which is needed at later stage.

5.4 Data Rate

Data rate is related to related with how fast the data is communicated between Energy management system and Head End System (HES) [21]. Proposed Energy Management system provide Minimum data rate 10 kbps.

6 Report and Results

EMS (Energy Management system) for analysis and reporting helps user to view, analyze and print the different report of data which include detailed report, meter wise report, date wise report and group wise report. The data is stored in tabular form of corresponding databases which can be identified by meter number. Data parsing modules and meter data collection carries meter data. Reports is divided into three Sections.

1. *General Section*
   Which includes meter data analysis report, instant report, general report and transaction log. For example, Meter data analysis report further includes general details and instantaneous details etc (Fig. 5).

Meter Data Analysis Report

Meter ID	: 0000081	Location	: ---
Consumer ID	: ---	Region	: ---
Consumer Name	: ---	Division	: ---
Installation Date	: ---	Circle	: ---
Meter Voltage Rating	: ---	Contract Demand(kW)	: ---
Meter Current Rating	: ---	Active Meter	: No

General Details

Description	Value
Meter ID	0000081
Meter DateTime	14/02/2013 12:33
Reading DateTime	14/02/2013 12:31:47
PC Dump DateTime	14/02/2013 13:40:57
Firmware Version	10.19X
Manufacturing Date & Time	00/00/0000 00:00
Meter Rating	00V, 00-00 A
Accuracy Class	1
Meter Constant (Impulse/kWh)	3200

Instantaneous Details

Description	Value
Voltage (V)	244.91
Phase Current (A)	00.00
Neutral Current (A)	00.00
Phase Power (kW)	00.00
Neutral Power (kW)	00.00
Power Factor	+0.00
Present Month Average PF	0.13

Fig. 5. General section meter data analysis report

2. **Billing Section** of reports is on the basis of Main energy, Main energy consumption, Maximum demand, Billing load factor, Billing Average PF details (Fig. 6).

Billing Average PF Details	
History	Average Power Factor
01	0.80
02	0.75
03	0.74
04	0.74
05	0.78
06	0.00
07	0.00
08	0.00
09	0.00
10	0.00
11	0.00
12	0.00

Billing Load Factor	
History	Billing Load Factor
01	00.81
02	00.70
03	00.81
04	00.63
05	00.80
06	00.00
07	00.00
08	00.00
09	00.00
10	00.00
11	00.00
12	00.00

Fig. 6. Billing section meter data analysis report

3. **Other section** of reports contains tamper event history details, load survey, daily survey. Other section is useful for detecting at what time which type of tamper is occur (Fig. 7).

Tamper Event History Details

History	Tamper Occurrence	Tamper Restoration
Tamper Events : Earth Tamper		
01	13-03-13 15:15	00-00-00 00:00
02	13-03-13 14:55	13-03-13 15:12
03	13-03-13 14:51	13-03-13 14:52
04	13-03-13 14:45	13-03-13 14:48
05	13-03-13 14:40	13-03-13 14:42
06	13-03-13 14:29	13-03-13 14:37
07	13-03-13 14:15	13-03-13 14:26
08	13-03-13 13:45	13-03-13 13:59
09	13-03-13 13:36	13-03-13 13:42
10	13-03-13 13:12	13-03-13 13:33
11	13-03-13 13:03	13-03-13 13:09
12	13-03-13 12:17	13-03-13 13:00
13	13-03-13 12:11	13-03-13 12:14
14	13-03-13 12:05	13-03-13 12:08
15	13-03-13 11:54	13-03-13 12:02
16	13-03-13 11:48	13-03-13 11:53
17	13-03-13 11:41	13-03-13 11:45
18	13-03-13 11:21	13-03-13 11:38
19	13-03-13 11:15	13-03-13 11:17
20	13-03-13 11:10	13-03-13 11:12
21	13-03-13 10:50	13-03-13 11:07
22	13-03-13 10:45	13-03-13 10:47
23	13-03-13 10:40	13-03-13 10:42
24	13-03-13 10:36	13-03-13 10:37
25	13-03-13 10:25	13-03-13 10:33
Tamper Events : Reverse Tamper		
01	14-11-12 17:34	14-11-12 17:47
02	07-11-12 15:17	07-11-12 15:52

Fig. 7. Other section meter data analysis report

7 Conclusion

Energy Management System for analysis and reporting software is windows based user friendly system software. The Energy Management System can easily accommodate with various meters types in future. It supports local data readout directly from meter. The Data transfer shall be highly reliable and fraud proof. Energy management system software shall provide all details adequate for analysis and abnormal event data. The software shall have the facility to convert all the consolidated information data of all parameters into ASCII format. The information about meter reading date, billing readings, energy and its maximum demand is be presented in such a way that a user should easily understand.

References

1. Depuru, S.S.S.R., Wang, L., Devabhaktuni, V., Gudi, N.: Smart meters for power grid – challenges, issues, advantages and status. In: Power Systems Conference and Exposition (PSCE), pp. 1–7. IEEE, March 2011
2. Garrab, A.: A new AMR approach for energy saving in smart grids using smart meter and partial power line communication. In: REVET Conference, pp. 263–269. IEEE, March 2012
3. Selvam, C.: Advanced metering infrastructure for smart grid application. In: Recent Trends in Information Technology (ICRTIT) 2012, pp. 145–150. IEEE, April 2012
4. IEC (62056-46): Electricity metering – data exchange for meter reading, tariff and load control – part 46: data link layer using HDLC protocol. http://www.iec.ch/smartgrid/standards
5. King, C.: Integrating advanced metering data into enterprise. In: Power System Conference and Exposition PSCE 2009, p. 1. IEEE/PES, March 2009

6. Lee, J.: Customer energy management platform in the smart metering. In: 14th Asia-Pacific Network Operation and Management Symposium 2012, pp. 1–4. IEEE, September 2012
7. Xiao-min, B.: Functional analysis of advanced metering infrastructure in the smart grid. In: Power System Technology (POWERCON) Conference, pp. 1–4. IEEE, October 2010
8. Thomas, M.S., Ali, I.: A secure way of exchanging the secret keys in advanced metering infrastructure. In: Power System Technology (POWERCON), pp. 1–7. IEEE, October-November 2012
9. Son, Y.S.: Home energy management system based on power line communication. In: Consumer Electronics (ICCE) 2010 Digest of Technical Papers, pp. 1380–1386. IEEE, January 2010
10. Park, J., Lin, Y., Moon, S.-J., Kim, H.-J.: A scalable load-balancing scheme for advanced metering infrastructure network. In: Proceedings of the 2012 ACM Research in Applied Computation Symposium, pp. 383–388. ACM, October 2012
11. Ye, F., Qian, Y., Hu, R.Q.: A security protocol for advanced metering infrastructure in smart grid. In: 2014 IEEE Global Communications Conference, pp. 649–654 (2014)
12. Elafoudi, G., Stankovic, L., Stankovic, V.: Power disaggregation of domestic smart meter readings using dynamic time warping. In: 2014 6th International Symposium on Communications Control and Signal Processing (ISCCSP), pp. 36–39 (2014)
13. Ghasempour, A.: Optimizing the Advanced Metering Infrastructure Architecture in Smart Grid (2016)
14. Stoilov, D., Atanasov, V., Jordanov, F., Angelov, I.: Losses in electricity distribution networks, Technical University of Sofia (2016)
15. Shahinzadeh, H., Hasanalizadeh-Khosroshahi, A.: Implementation of smart metering systems: challenges and solutions. Indones. J. Electr. Eng. 12(7), 5104–5109 (2014)
16. Ghasempour, J.A.: Optimizing the advanced metering infrastructure architecture in smart grid (2016)
17. Yang, J., Huang, G., Wei, C.: Privacy-aware electricity scheduling for home energy management system. Peer-To-Peer Netw. Appl. (2/2018) (2016). ISSN 1936-6442
18. Kumar, S., Lim, H., Kim, H.: Energy optimal scheduling of multi-channel wireless sensor networks for wireless metering. In: Electronics Information and Communications (ICEIC) 2016 International Conference (2016)
19. Ohsaki, H., Nakamoto, Y., Yokoi, N., Moribe, H.: Performance comparison of IP and CCN as a communication infrastructure for smart grid. In: Proceedings - International Computer Software and Applications Conference, vol. 3, pp. 523–528 (2015)
20. Khan, M.F., et al.: Communication technologies for smart metering infrastructure. In: Electrical Electronics and Computer Science (SCEECS) IEEE Students' Conference (2014)
21. Brettschneider, D., et al.: On homomorphic encryption for privacy-preserving distributed load adaption in smart grids. In: Communications (ICC) IEEE International Conference (2016)
22. Kumar, V., Hussain, M.: Secure communication for advance metering infrastructure in smart grid. In: 11th IEEE India Conference on Emerging Trends and Innovation in Technology, INDICON (2015)

Human Action Recognition in Video

Dushyant Kumar Singh[✉]

Department of CSE, MNNIT, Allahabad, India
dushyant@mnnit.ac.in

Abstract. In the world of automation every event needs some kind of auto response. Automatic responses can only be made when events are perceived automatically. With camera as a source of visual sensing, some intelligent system fitted with camera can make automatic visual perception possible for any event. Recognizing human activities for some automated response can be one challenge under this problem domain. In this paper, motion feature of a moving object is used for recognizing human action/activity. Histogram of Oriented Gradient (HOG) features with Support Vector Machine (SVM) classifier is used for classifying the human actions into 5 basic categories i.e. bending, boxing, handclapping, jogging and jumping. Pre-Processing involves Lucas-Kanade Algorithm to extract the human silhouette and Skeletonization operation to generate human skeletons. Skeletons are secondary features which are made input to SVM for activity classification. Experiments are conducted on KTH database and Weizmann database for accuracy calculation.

Keywords: Human action recognition · Optical flow
Lukas-Kanade · Skeletonization · HoG · SVM

1   Introduction

Over the years, technology has got advanced and people have started using visual images and videos to convey as much information as possible. Videos have become an inseparable part of our life. Every computer, laptop, tablet and even mobile phones can record, store and share videos. To recognize the activity of human in real life is the main purpose of human action recognition. Human activity is the complex and highly diverse task, so recognizing accurate activity is challenging. Its use in proactive computing is interested and attracted a lot of people in research in different application areas [1]. A reliable system capable of recognizing human actions in a video sequence has a wide range of application such as surveillance, healthcare, human computer interactions and entertainment [2].

Generally, human action recognition involve two important blocks. The first block is human silhouette extraction from the video. The tracking of the object is based on optical flows among video frames. The second important block is feature extraction and classification of human action from the extracted feature.

© Springer Nature Singapore Pte Ltd. 2019
A. K. Luhach et al. (Eds.): ICAICR 2018, CCIS 955, pp. 54–66, 2019.
https://doi.org/10.1007/978-981-13-3140-4_6

There are different types of methods for extracting human silhouette such as Background subtraction Technique [3,4], RGB-H-CbCr Skin Colour model [5], Voila jones Algorithm [6] and Optical Flow Technique [7]. Since, motion is one of the prominent feature of any moving object, so our approach uses Optical Flow Technique to extract the human silhouette from the video.

The preprocessing involves extracting human silhouette and the skeleton. There are different techniques to extract features such as histogram of oriented gradients (HOG) [8], motion information histogram (MIH) [9], bag of features (BOF) and many more. Artificial neural network (ANN) is an influential tool of information processing [10]. Our proposed work uses Support Vector Machine (SVM) [11] for action classification from the feature vector. The concluding point is to obtain successful results and the methods to improve the human action recognition system.

The remaining paper is organized as follows: Sect. 2 discussed the optical flow technique to extract human silhouette. In Sect. 3, the activity classification algorithm is proposed which involve HOG feature extraction on skeleton and classification using SVM. The experimentation details of the proposed algorithm are discussed in Sect. 4. In Sects. 5 and 6, described the results and the conclusion followed by future work respectively.

2   Optical Flow Technique

Optical flow is the method to calculate the motion of objects, edges and surfaces between two frames in a video. It is the relative motion between the scene and an observer(may be a human or a camera). Motion field is the 2-D projection of a 3-D motion onto the image plane. Optical flow is the apparent motion of the brightness pattern in an image sequence. The optical flow method calculates the motion in terms of velocity vector at every pixel positions of a frame at any time instance t. This motion is exactly the relative displacement of a pixels in two adjacent frames.

Optical Flow algorithms works upon two assumptions for calculating velocity of moving pixel. These are Brightness Constancy and Temporal Persistence. Brightness constancy means that intensity of any pixel (x, y) remain same during displacement/motion. This can be modeled by the given Eq. 1.

$$I(x, y, z) = I(x + \delta x, y + \delta y, t + \delta t) \tag{1}$$

Partial differering w.r.t. time, we get

$$I_x u + I_y v + I_t = 0 \tag{2}$$

$$V.I = I_t \tag{3}$$

This equation is defined as Optical Flow Constraint Equation or Gradient Constraint Equation. In Eq. 3,

$$V = (u, v) \qquad \text{Velocity vectors}$$
$$I = (Ix, Iy) \quad \text{Partial derivatives of intensity}$$

There are 2 unknown components of V (u & v) in a single linear equation i.e. Gradient constraint equation. This constraint of solving one equation for two unknowns is resolved by third assumption and that is Spatial Coherence. And the method for velocity vector calculation using this assumption is proposed by Lucas-Kanade Algorithm.

2.1   Lucas-Kanade Algorithm

The Lucas-Kanade algorithms is used to calculate optical flow. [12] In this method, a widely used two frame differential method for calculating components of V. It assumes that the flow is constant in a local neighbourhood around the central pixel under consideration at any given time. In simpler terms the motion vector in any given region do not change but merely shift from one position to another.

The flow field is estimated using some additional constraint. This method is assumed that the flow V is constant in a small window of pixels of size mXm. A differential equation is written for each pixel i.e. 1....n. Here n is square of 'm'. n equations with m >1, which is centered at pixel (x, y) can be found as:

$$I_{x(q1)}V_x + I_{y(q1)}V_y = I_{t(q1)} \tag{4}$$

$$I_{x(q2)}V_x + I_{y(q2)}V_y = I_{t(q2)} \tag{5}$$

$$\begin{matrix} . & . & . \\ . & . & . \end{matrix}$$

$$I_{x(qn)}V_x + I_{y(qn)}V_y = I_{t(qn)} \tag{6}$$

where q1, q2, ...qn are the pixels inside the window, and Ix(qi), Iy(qi), It(qi) are the partial derivatives of the image I with respect to position x, y and time t, evaluated at the point qi and at current time t.

These equations can be written in matrix form as A.V $=$ B where, A $=$ Spatial matrix V $=$ Velocity matrix B $=$ Temporal matrix.

The Lucas-Kanade Algorithm solves the determined system of equations by the Least Squares Principle [5]

$$A.V = B \tag{7}$$

Multiplying both sides with A Transpose

$$A^T A.V = A^T B \tag{8}$$

Therefore,

$$V = (A^T A)^{-1} A^T b \tag{9}$$

Sobel Operator is a differential operator of convolution technique, that technique is frequently used for spatial derivatives computing [13]. The gradient of the image intensity is computed using this method. It is used a small window (3X3 kernels) to convolve the whole image, because of the small window it takes very less time. This technique is also identified edges of an image. The temporal derivative (It) is calculated by subtracting the second frame from the first frame.

3 Feature Extraction and Classification

In pattern recognition, feature plays an important role. Feature represents the coded information that is intended to facilitate learning and generalization for better human interpretations. Sometimes input data contained redundant images, and it also takes the large time to process and produce a set of features. These features are transformed into a reduce set of features is called Feature Vector. One of the methods used for feature extraction is Motion Information Histogram (MIH) [9]. MIH separates the objects from background and then uses histogram of the extracted objects to classify actions. Motion information histogram is calculated using the following equation:

$$MIH = (FB \oplus FC) - FB \tag{10}$$

where, FB indicates the previous frame, FC is current frame and the operator is exclusive OR. The movement of the extracted object from the input frame helps to calculate the MIH by using the motion information of the object.

Similarly, a change in movement and motion of the extracted objects accompanies a change in centre points of the extracted objects. For a particular action performed by the object the centre points traces a unique path of motion for us to classify these accordingly. And this is second method of feature extraction.

The third method is Skeletonization [14] with the HOG feature extraction [8]. The general shape is represented by skeleton extraction. To preserve the object properties such as topological and hierarchical properties, we used Skeletonization algorithm. The other existing algorithms are required high memory and also these are computationally intensive. The aim of Skeletonization is to extract a region-based shape feature representing the general form of an object.

Histogram of Oriented Gradient or HOG descriptors are the most common features that are used in image processing for object detection kind of tasks. This technique evaluates the gradients for their orientation in some smaller-smaller subsamples of an image. In HOG descriptors, the shape and appearance of localized object within an image can be described using gradient intensity distribution.

4 Proposed System

The entire processing for action/activity classification under this system is a 6 step procedure.

A. Pre Processing
B. Lucas-Kanade Algorithm
C. Thresholding
D. Skeletonization
E. HOG feature extraction
F. Recognition with SVM.

The flow diagram of the proposed human action recognition system is shown in Fig. 1. In this approach, data set containing activities such as bending, boxing, handclapping, jogging and jumping is divided into 2 parts i.e. training set and test set. The proposed system is also divided into two parts i.e. Object detection and activity classification parts. Object recognition is done by Lucas-Kanade Algorithm and the classification done using HOG feature extraction with SVM classifier.

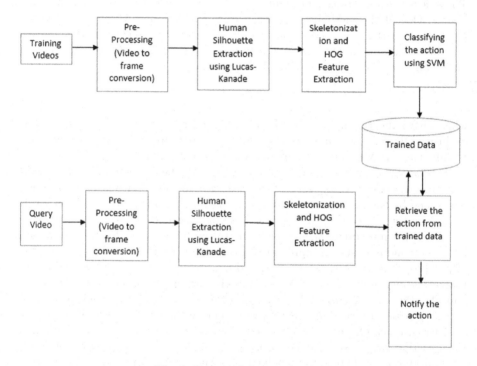

Fig. 1. Proposed system design

4.1   Pre-processing

Lucas-Kanade Algorithm requires two consecutive frames of the video. Frames are extracted from video and sampled. Sampling is done to select the prominent/key frames to be processed. This in turn reduces the total number of frames to be processed and helps in faster and real-time processing. Filtering is also applied on the sampled frames to reduce the noise occurring due to environment affects. Filtered sampled frames are then made input to the Object/Human detection algorithm.

4.2 Lucas-Kanade Algorithm

The Lucas-Kanade Method utilize optical flow estimation of the moving points as analyzed in two consecutive frames. The flow is estimated by solving the Optical Flow equation assuming that the flow in the local neighbourhood is constant. The flow is estimated using Least Square Principle. Following are the results when Lucas-Kanade Algorithm is applied on the image input containing moving object. Figure 2 shows the direction of velocity vectors that we get on applying the algorithm on two adjacent frames with moving object. Figure 3 shows the mapping of these velocity vectors (u, v) on the (x, y) plane.

Fig. 2. Velocity vectors over the image with their directions

4.3 Thresholding

Current intermediate output is the velocity vector plot of the frames obtained by the Lucas-Kanade Algorithm. Next task is to extract the moving human in the foreground from the rest of the background. As can be seen from the output obtained by applying the algorithm on the frames, the velocity vectors are dense near the movement in the image.

The value of the velocity vectors near the human being have high values. These velocity values are stored in a matrix. Median of these velocity values in the matrix is calculated, which is a value that clearly differentiate the motion of human and the static background. Median value is then used as a threshold for detecting the human being in the frames.

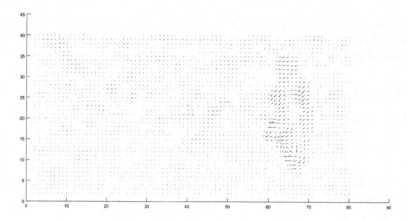

Fig. 3. Velocity (u, v) plotted on (x, y) plane

Figure 4 shows the output in which any values above the threshold are made white (value 1) and all the values below this threshold or the background pixels are made black (value 0). This way we extract the human, which is shown over a black background in white pixels.

Fig. 4. Detected moving human being

4.4 Skeletonization

Skeletonization is the process of thinning the object blob. This is helpful in finding different body parts and analysing their movements. This is an important step in processing phase. Skeletonization is a crucial process for many applications such as OCR, pattern recognition, etc. Skeletonization is a process for reducing foreground regions in a binary image to a skeletal residuum which retains the extent and connectivity of the original region while reducing the foreground pixels atmost. The flow chart for the method to obtain the skeleton is shown in Fig. 5.

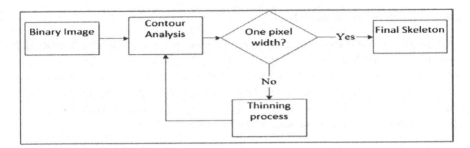

Fig. 5. Steps for Skeletonization

The skeleton is formed by repeatedly applying the thinning process on the input image frame, until a single pixel width object is obtained. Skeleton result is shown in the Fig. 6.

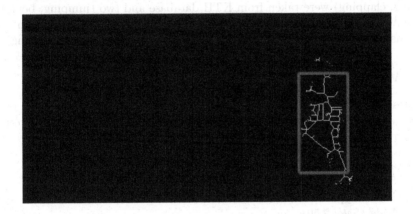

Fig. 6. Steps for Skeletonization

4.5 HOG Feature Extraction

To detect the object in image processing and computer vision, here we used the Histogram of Oriented Gradient (HOG) feature descriptors. In this method, we count the occurrences of gradient orientation in a local area of an image. In HOG descriptors, the distribution of intensity gradients or edge directions is used to describe the local object appearance and shape within an image. These descriptors are implemented to divide an image into the small connected region, and these small regions are called cells. Every cell is compiled a histogram of gradient directions or edge orientations a histogram of gradient directions or edge orientations.

4.6   Classification Using SVM

After getting the dataset of feature vector for every action, we train our model according to the classifier i.e. Support Vector Machine (SVM). The very first step is to convert the spreadsheet to a valid classifier input type i.e. a table. The feature vector table is imported to the Classification Learner App. The data is imported after selecting the Cross Validation Field. Finally we train our model with the help of Median Gaussian SVM Classifier.

5   Result and Analysis

Data required for experimentation is collected from KTH [15] and WEIZMANN [16] database for training and testing. The KTH is a well-recognized publicly available dataset for single human action recognition. The dataset has 5 actions (boxing, jogging, clapping hands, jumping and bending), three of which (boxing, jogging, clapping) were taken from KTH database and two (jumping, bending) from WEIZMANN database. A total of 318 videos have been used from both databases, 206 of which are used for training and the remaining for testing.

5.1   Visual Analysis

Figures 7 and 8 well presents the video results for indentifying actions. Input video can be browsed and played and then the algorithm recognizes the respective actions in that video frame.

- Data Set 1
    Specification -
    Video Type: RGB, Black and White
    Video Size: 2.50 s
    Frame Rate: 30 fps
    Others: Homogeneous Outdoor Background, Static Camera.
- Data Set 2
    Specification -
    Video Type: RGB, Black and White
    Video Size: 2.50 s
    Frame Rate: 30 fps
    Others: Homogeneous Outdoor Background, Static Camera.

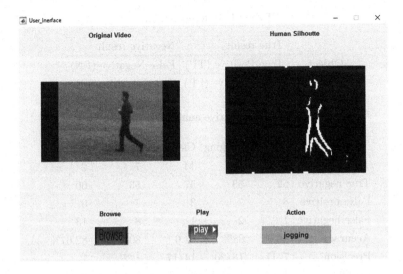

Fig. 7. Visual analysis of jogging action

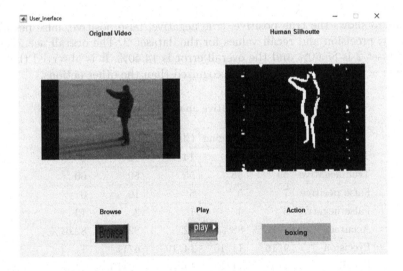

Fig. 8. Visual analysis of boxing action

5.2 Quantitative Analysis

Table 1 is reference table for the performance evaluation parameters.

Table 2 shows the true positive, true negative, false positive, false negative, accuracy, precision and recall values for the dataset 1. The overall accuracy of the dataset 1 is 86.65% and the overall error is 13.35%. It is observed that the clapping action is more accurately recognized than the other actions.

Table 1. Reference table

	True result	Negative result
Object	True Positive (TP)	False Negative (FN)
No object	False Positive (FP)	True Negative (TN)

Table 2. Quantitative analysis of dataset 1

	Boxing	Jogging	Clapping	Jumping	Bending
True positive	14	13	14	7	2
True negative	52	53	57	53	60
False positive	8	7	3	7	0
False negative	1	2	1	8	13
Accuracy	88%	88%	94.6	80%	82.67%
Precision	7/11	13/20	14/17	1/2	1
Recall	14/15	13/15	14/15	7/15	2/15

Table 3 shows the true positive, true negative, false positive, false negative, accuracy, precision and recall values for the dataset 2. The overall accuracy of the dataset 2 is 85.60% and the overall error is 14.40%. It is observed that the clapping action is more accurately recognized than the other actions.

Table 3. Quantitative analysis of dataset 2

	Boxing	Jogging	Clapping	Jumping	Bending
True positive	9	11	14	12	2
True negative	53	55	55	50	60
False positive	7	5	5	10	0
False negative	6	4	1	3	13
Accuracy	82.67%	88%	92	82.67%	82.67%
Precision	9/16	11/16	14/19	6/11	1
Recall	3/5	11/15	14/15	12/15	2/15

Figure 9 shows the comparison of different values of Dataset 1 and Dataset 2. It clearly shows that the prediction of Boxing, Hand-clapping is better for dataset 1 while for dataset 2 jumping is better. Jogging and Bending have the same accuracy for both the datasets. The Overall Accuracy of the model for dataset 1 is better than that for dataset 2, which is 86.65% and 85.60% respectively.

The results are also analyzed by a confusion matrix for action classification on TPR and FNR parameters. Figure 10 shows the confusion matrix for every action as made under the median Gaussian classifier. It presents the percentage of correctness of each action.

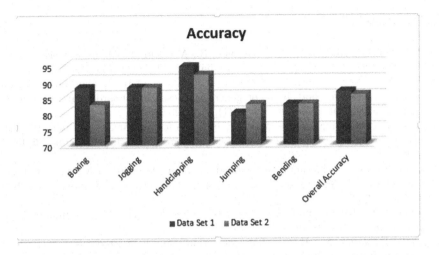

Fig. 9. Accuracy graph of action recognition on two dataset.

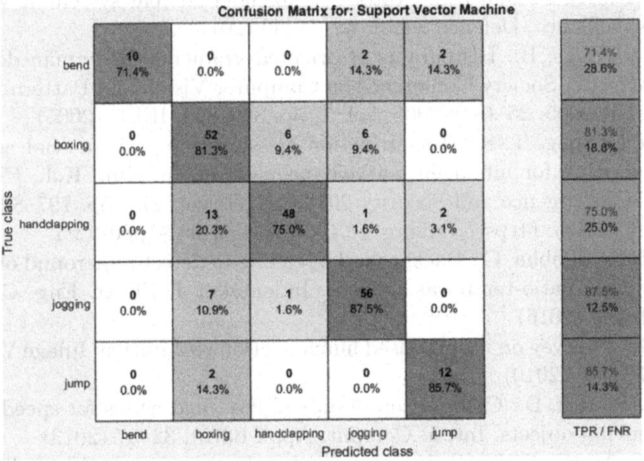

Fig. 10. Confusion matrix for SVM classifier

6   Conclusion

The paper presented a new method using Lucas-Kanade algorithm and Skeletonization with HOG features for action recognition. Final classification of the human actions in the test dataset is done by using the SVM Classifier. The accuracy of the system designed come out to be 80.9%. The result provides suitable evidence that this method can be used in real life applications such as surveillance, healthcare industry and home assistance programs.

References

1. Abu-Ain, W., Abdullah, S.N., Bataineh, B., Abu-Ain, T., Omar, K.: Skeletonization algorithm for binary images. Procedia Technol. **1**(11), 704–709 (2013)
2. Jati, A.N., Novamizanti, L., Prasetyo, M.B., Putra, A.R.: Evaluation of moving object detection methods based on general purpose single board computer. Indonesian J. Electr. Eng. Comput. Sci. **14**(1), 123–129 (2015)
3. Goswami, P.P., Singh, D.K.: A hybrid approach for real-time object detection and tracking to cover background turbulence problem. Indian J. Sci. Technol. **9**(45), 7 (2016)
4. Basavaraj, G.M., Kusagur, A.: Crowd anomaly detection using motion based spatio-temporal feature analysis. Indonesian J. Electr. Eng. Comput. Sci. **7**(3), 737–747 (2017)
5. Singh, D.K., Kushwaha, D.S.: ILUT based skin colour modelling for human detection. Indian J. Sci. Technol. **9**(32) (2016)
6. Viola, P., Jones, M.: Rapid object detection using a boosted cascade of simple features. In: Proceedings of the 2001 IEEE Computer Society Conference on Computer Vision and Pattern Recognition, CVPR 2001, vol. 1, p. I. IEEE (2001)
7. Singh, D.K., Kushwaha, D.S.: Automatic intruder combat system: a way to smart border surveillance. Defence Sci. J. **67**(1), 50 (2017)
8. Dalal, N., Triggs, B.: Histograms of oriented gradients for human detection. In: IEEE Computer Society Conference on Computer Vision and Pattern Recognition 2005, CVPR 2005, 25 June 2005, vol. 1, pp. 886–893. IEEE (2005)
9. Kwak, N.J., Song, T.-S.: Human action classification and unusual action recognition algorithm for intelligent surveillance system. In: Kim, K.J., Chung, K.-Y. (eds.) IT Convergence and Security 2012. LNEE, vol. 215, pp. 797–804. Springer, Dordrecht (2013). https://doi.org/10.1007/978-94-007-5860-5_95
10. Kumar, N.S., Shobha, G.: Background modeling to detect foreground objects based on ANN and spatio-temporal analysis. Indonesian J. Electr. Eng. Comput. Sci. **2**(1), 151–160 (2016)
11. Poppe, R.: A survey on vision-based human action recognition. Image Vis. Comput. **28**(6), 976–990 (2010)
12. Patel, E., Shukla, D.: Comparison of optical flow algorithms for speed determination of moving objects. Int. J. Comput. Appl. **63**(5), 32–37 (2013)
13. Aslani, S., Mahdavi-Nasab, H.: Optical flow based moving object detection and tracking for traffic surveillance. World Acad. Sci., Eng. Technol., Int. J. Electr., Comput., Energ., Electron. Commun. Eng. **7**(9), 1252–1256 (2013)
14. Tschirren, J., Palágyi, K., Reinhardt, J.M., Hoffman, E.A., Sonka, M.: Segmentation, skeletonization, and branchpoint matching — a fully automated quantitative evaluation of human intrathoracic airway trees. In: Dohi, T., Kikinis, R. (eds.) MICCAI 2002. LNCS, vol. 2489, pp. 12–19. Springer, Heidelberg (2002). https://doi.org/10.1007/3-540-45787-9_2
15. Schuldt, C., Laptev, I., Caputo, B.: Recognizing human actions: a local SVM approach. In: Proceedings of the 17th International Conference on Pattern Recognition, 2004, ICPR 2004, 23 August 2004, vol. 3, pp. 32–36. IEEE (2004)
16. Blank, M., Gorelick, L., Shechtman, E., Irani, M., Basri, R.: Actions as space-time shapes. In: 2005 Tenth IEEE International Conference on Computer Vision, ICCV 2005, 17 October 2005, vol. 2, pp. 1395–1402. IEEE (2005)

Defuzzified Strategy of Interval Valued Triskaidecagonal Fuzzy Number Assigning in the Failure of Marine Main Engine

A. Rajkumar[(⊠)] and D. Helen

Department of Mathematics, Hindustan Institute of Technology and Science, Chennai 603103, India
arajkumar@hindustanuniv.ac.in, helen.br@outlook.com

Abstract. This paper illustrates the various representation of interval-valued Triskaidecagonal fuzzy number. In order to attain the failure mode in Marine Main Engine, the Fault analysis method has been used. The whole concept of application on interval valued Triskaidecagonal fuzzy number approaches the cause and effect of failure modes to make convenient with deffuzied methods.

Keywords: Fuzzy number · Triskaidecagonal · Interval-valued fuzzy number
Signed distance · Fault tree method · Triskaidecagonal fuzzy number

1 Introduction

This article has been indicated as a case study of fault tree analysis (FTA) method in marine engineering application. The two stroke engine is mainly used for the force of the ship in reliability testing facility. Due to the uncontrollable working conditions or weather conditions, it is difficult to get the failure value of the undesired event of FTA. In [6], Cai et al. Proposed system failure by use of fuzzy methodology. Fault tree analysis is used to get more reliable and reasonable results based on influencing factors of experts. Fault tree is built based on a top event with cause and effect presents the intermediate event with shows graphically as a rectangle. The subsequent intermediate events correlates lead to the top event. In [7], Singer approached FTA concept in reliability analysis. The main engine's fault tree are faults of the multi cylinder, failure to the turbocharger and common components. Fuzzy set theory is applied in Fault tree method. In 1965, L.A Zadeh proposed degree of membership for fuzzy sets is a real numbers between [0, 1]. Determining the degree of membership in practical application is very difficult. Since approximate reasoning, many scholars have used the concept of interval valued fuzzy numbers and gave the expression of interval valued fuzzy numbers.

The fault tree of cylinder unit includes cylinder cover piston liner group failure, piston rod and combustion and start air components failure. The fault of piston cylinder is the main faults is the groups includes failures of cylinder head, piston, piston rings, liner and jacket. In [4], Rafat presented a Marine main engine's fault tree to find the minimal cut set of first order. The faults of piston crank group are illustrated among the specific components are the piston rod, the stuffing box, crosshead bearings, a connecting rod and crankpin bearings. The starting and combustion process are highlighted

© Springer Nature Singapore Pte Ltd. 2019
A. K. Luhach et al. (Eds.): ICAICR 2018, CCIS 955, pp. 67–79, 2019.
https://doi.org/10.1007/978-981-13-3140-4_7

includes faults to the exhaust valve, the air starting value, fuel injectors with high pressure pipes and fuel pump. The turbocharger is classified in to fault of turbine functioning components, compressor and common elements. The fault of crank system contains the damage to main bearings, thrust bearing and the shaft. The fault sub tree analyzed main engine is the tree of camshaft.

2 Preliminaries

2.1 Definition

An interval valued fuzzy set $\tilde{R}$ on R is given by $\tilde{R} = \left\{ (x, [\mu_{\tilde{R}^L}(x), \mu_{\tilde{R}^U}(x)]) \right\}$ $\forall x \varepsilon R$ Where $0 \leq \mu_{\tilde{R}^L}(x) \leq \mu_{\tilde{R}^U}(x) \leq 1$ and $\mu_{\tilde{R}^L}(x), \mu_{\tilde{R}^U}(x)\varepsilon[0, 1]$ denoted by $\mu_{\tilde{R}}(x) = [\mu_{\tilde{R}^L}(x), \mu_{\tilde{R}^U}(x)]$, $x \varepsilon R$ or $\tilde{R} = [\tilde{R}_L, \tilde{R}_U]$

2.2 Definition

An interval valued Triskaidecagonal fuzzy number ϖ on R is given $\varpi = \left\{ (x, [\mu_{\varpi^L}(x), \mu_{\varpi^U}(x)]) \right\} \forall x \varepsilon R$ Where $0 \leq \mu_{\varpi^L}(x) \leq \mu_{\varpi^U}(x) \leq 1$ and $\mu_{\varpi^L}(x), \mu_{\varpi^U}(x)\varepsilon[0, 1]$ as $\mu_{\tilde{A}}(x) = [\mu_{\varpi^L}(x), \mu_{\varpi^U}(x)]$, $x \varepsilon R$ or $\varpi = [\varpi_L, \varpi_U]$

Assume $\varpi^L = (\ell_1, \ell_2, \ell_3, \ell_4, \ell_5, \ell_6, \ell_7, \ell_8, \ell_9, \ell_{10}, \ell_{11}, \ell_{12}, \ell_{13}; \delta)$ and $\varpi^U = (\varsigma_1, \varsigma_2, \varsigma_3, \varsigma_4, \varsigma_5, \varsigma_6, \varsigma_7, \varsigma_8, \varsigma_9, \varsigma_{10}, \varsigma_{11}, \varsigma_{12}, \varsigma_{13}; \gamma)$ where $0 < \delta \leq \gamma \leq 1$

$$\varsigma_1 < \ell_1 < \varsigma_2 < \ell_2 < \varsigma_3 < \ell_3 < \varsigma_4 < \ell_4 < \varsigma_5 < \ell_5 < \varsigma_6 < \ell_6 < \varsigma_7 < \ell_7 < \varsigma_8 < \ell_8 < \varsigma_9 < \ell_9 < \varsigma_9 < \ell_{10} < \varsigma_{10} < \ell_{11} < \varsigma_{11} < \ell_{12} < \varsigma_{12} < \ell_{13} < \varsigma_{13}$$

$\ell_1, \ell_2, \ldots, \ell_{13}, \varsigma_1, \varsigma_2 \ldots \varsigma_{13} \varepsilon R$. The membership function of ϖ_L, ϖ_U is defined as follows

$$\mu_{\varpi_{TD}}L(x) = \begin{cases} \delta\left(\frac{1}{6}\frac{x-\ell_1}{\ell_2-\ell_1}\right) & \ell_1 \leq x \leq \ell_2 \\ \delta\left(\frac{1}{6} + \frac{1}{6}\frac{x2-\ell_2}{\ell_3-\ell_2}\right) & \ell_2 \leq x \leq \ell_3 \\ \delta\left(\frac{2}{6} + \frac{1}{6}\frac{x-\ell_3}{\ell_4-\ell_3}\right) & \ell_3 \leq x \leq \ell_4 \\ \delta\left(\frac{3}{6} + \frac{1}{6}\frac{x-\ell_4}{\ell_5-\ell_4}\right) & \ell_4 \leq x \leq \ell_5 \\ \delta\left(\frac{4}{6} + \frac{1}{6}\frac{x-\ell_5}{\ell_6-\ell_5}\right) & \ell_5 \leq x \leq \ell_6 \\ \delta\left(\frac{5}{6} + \frac{1}{6}\frac{x-\ell_6}{\ell_7-\ell_6}\right) & \ell_6 \leq x \leq \ell_7 \\ \delta\left(1 - \frac{1}{6}\frac{x-\ell_7}{\ell_8-\ell_7}\right) & \ell_7 \leq x \leq \ell_8 \\ \delta\left(\frac{5}{6} - \frac{1}{6}\frac{x-\ell_8}{\ell_9-\ell_8}\right) & \ell_8 \leq x \leq \ell_9 \\ \delta\left(\frac{4}{6} - \frac{1}{6}\frac{x-\ell_9}{\ell_{10}-\ell_9}\right) & \ell_9 \leq x \leq \ell_{10} \\ \delta\left(\frac{3}{6} - \frac{1}{6}\frac{x-\ell_{10}}{\ell_{11}-\ell_{10}}\right) & \ell_{10} \leq x \leq \ell_{11} \\ \delta\left(\frac{2}{6} - \frac{1}{6}\frac{x-\ell_{11}}{\ell_{12}-\ell_{11}}\right) & \ell_{11} \leq x \leq \ell_{12} \\ \delta\left(\frac{1}{6}\frac{\ell_{13}-x}{\ell_{13}-\ell_{12}}\right) & \ell_{12} \leq x \leq \ell_{13} \\ 0 & x > \ell_{13} \end{cases}$$

$$\mu_{\overline{\varpi_{TD}}}U(x) = \begin{cases} \gamma\left(\frac{1}{6}\frac{x-\varsigma_1}{\varsigma_2-\varsigma_1}\right) & \varsigma_1 \leq x \leq \varsigma_2 \\ \gamma\left(\frac{1}{6}+\frac{1}{6}\frac{x2-\varsigma_2}{\varsigma_3-\varsigma_2}\right) & \varsigma_2 \leq x \leq \varsigma_3 \\ \gamma\left(\frac{2}{6}+\frac{1}{6}\frac{x-\varsigma_3}{\varsigma_4-\varsigma_3}\right) & \varsigma_3 \leq x \leq \varsigma_4 \\ \gamma\left(\frac{3}{6}+\frac{1}{6}\frac{x-\varsigma_4}{\varsigma_5-\varsigma_4}\right) & \varsigma_4 \leq x \leq \varsigma_5 \\ \gamma\left(\frac{4}{6}+\frac{1}{6}\frac{x-\varsigma_5}{\varsigma_6-\varsigma_5}\right) & \varsigma_5 \leq x \leq \varsigma_6 \\ \gamma\left(\frac{5}{6}+\frac{1}{6}\frac{x-\varsigma_6}{\varsigma_7-\varsigma_6}\right) & \varsigma_6 \leq x \leq \varsigma_7 \\ \gamma\left(1-\frac{1}{6}\frac{x-\varsigma_7}{\varsigma_8-\varsigma_7}\right) & \varsigma_7 \leq x \leq \varsigma_8 \\ \gamma\left(\frac{5}{6}-\frac{1}{6}\frac{x-\varsigma_8}{\varsigma_9-\varsigma_8}\right) & \varsigma_8 \leq x \leq \varsigma_9 \\ \gamma\left(\frac{4}{6}-\frac{1}{6}\frac{x-\varsigma_9}{\varsigma_{10}-\varsigma_9}\right) & \varsigma_9 \leq x \leq \varsigma_{10} \\ \gamma\left(\frac{3}{6}-\frac{1}{6}\frac{x-\varsigma_{10}}{\varsigma_{11}-\varsigma_{10}}\right) & \varsigma_{10} \leq x \leq \varsigma_{11} \\ \gamma\left(\frac{2}{6}-\frac{1}{6}\frac{x-\varsigma_{11}}{\varsigma_{12}-\varsigma_{11}}\right) & \varsigma_{11} \leq x \leq \varsigma_{12} \\ \gamma\left(\frac{1}{6}\frac{\varsigma_{13}-x}{\varsigma_{13}-\varsigma_{12}}\right) & \varsigma_{12} \leq x \leq \varsigma_{13} \\ 0 & x > \varsigma_{13} \end{cases}$$

Then

$$\varpi = [\varpi^L, \varpi^U] = \left[\left[\begin{array}{c}(\ell_1, \ell_2, \ell_3, \ell_4, \ell_5, \ell_6, \ell_7, \ell_8, \ell_9, \ell_{10}, \ell_{11}, \ell_{12}, \ell_{13}; \delta), \\ (\varsigma_1, \varsigma_2, \varsigma_3, \varsigma_4, \varsigma_5, \varsigma_6, \varsigma_7, \varsigma_8, \varsigma_9, \varsigma_{10}, \varsigma_{11}, \varsigma_{12}, \varsigma_{13}; \gamma)\end{array}\right]\right]$$

is called the level (δ, γ) Interval valued Triskaidecagonal fuzzy number (Fig. 1).

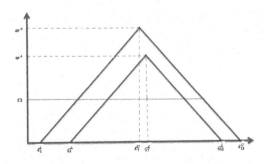

Fig. 1. Interval valued Triskaidecagonal fuzzy number

3 Application of Marine Main Engine Failure Using Interval Valued Triskaidecagonal Fuzzy Number

ч 1-Indicates the system failure to start of Main Engine.

ч 2-Indicates the failure to start of Engine due to cylinder unit 1 Failure

ч3-Indicates the failure to start of Engine due to cylinder unit 2 Failure. (Table 1)

Table 1. Components of marine main engine

Name of the components			
ч 77- Fuel cams	ч16- Bed Plate	ч 30-Crankshaft components	ч 54-Exhaust valve Cam
ч38- Stuffing box	ч40-Piston rod-connecting rod	ч5- Auxiliary blowers	ч 46-Shaft Failure
ч32- Cylinder cover	ч44- Air Starting valve	ч22- Camshaft	ч23-Cylinder cover-piston-liner group failure
ч39- Crosshead Bearing	ч56- Fuel injection	ч18- Scavenge air receiver	ч53- Bearings
ч17- Chain Drive	ч62-Radial Bearing	ч58- High pressure pipe	ч 49-Main Bearings
ч42- Exhaust Valve	ч51- Thurst Bearing	ч36-Cylinder Jacket	ч 14-Crankshaft
ч33- Piston &Piston rings	ч35- Liner	ч 60-Fuel Pump	ч21- Air Cooler

Parallel System: The fuzzy reliability R ps of the parallel system shown below can be evaluated by using the expression as follows:

$$\tilde{R}_{ps}^{i} = 1 \ominus \prod_{j=1}^{n} (1 \ominus \tilde{R}_{j}^{i}) = 1 \ominus [(1 \ominus (r_{11}, r_{12}, r_{13} ; r'_{11}, r_{12}, r'_{13})) \square \quad \ldots\ldots\ldots$$

$$\square \quad (1 \ominus (r_{n1}, r_{n2}, r_{n3} ; r'_{n1}, r_{n2}, r'_{n3}))]$$

Step-1:

$ų_7 = 1\Theta (1 \Theta ų_{23}) (1 \Theta ų_{24}) (1 \Theta ų_{25})$
$ų_8 = 1\Theta (1 \Theta ų_{26})$
$ų_{26} = 1\Theta (1 \Theta ų_{32}) (1 \Theta ų_{33}) (1 \Theta ų_{34}) (1 \Theta ų_{35}) (1 \Theta ų_{36})$
$ų_9 = 1\Theta (1 \Theta ų_{27})$
$ų_{27} = 1\Theta (1 \Theta ų_{37}) (1 \Theta ų_{38}) (1 \Theta ų_{39}) (1 \Theta ų_{40})(1 \Theta ų_{41})$

$ų_{10} = 1\Theta (1 \Theta ų_{28})$
$ų_{28} = 1\Theta (1 \Theta ų_{42}) (1 \Theta ų_{43}) (1 \Theta ų_{44})$
$ų_{43} = 1\Theta (1 \Theta ų_{56}) (1 \Theta ų_{57}) (1 \Theta ų_{58}) (1 \Theta ų_{59}) (1 \Theta ų_{60})$
$ų_{11} = 1\Theta (1 \Theta ų_{29})$
$ų_{29} = 1\Theta (1 \Theta ų_{45}) (1 \Theta ų_{46}) (1 \Theta ų_{47}) (1 \Theta ų_{48})$
$ų_{45} = 1\Theta (1 \Theta ų_{61}) (1 \Theta ų_{62}) (1 \Theta ų_{63}) (1 \Theta ų_{64})$
$ų_{48} = 1\Theta (1 \Theta ų_{65}) (1 \Theta ų_{68}) (1 \Theta ų_{69}) (1 \Theta ų_{70})$

$ų_{12} = 1\Theta (1 \Theta ų_{30})$
$ų_{30} = 1\Theta (1 \Theta ų_{49}) (1 \Theta ų_{50}) (1 \Theta ų_{51})$
$ų_{49} = 1\Theta(1 \Theta ų_{71})(1 \Theta ų_{72})(1 \Theta ų_{73})(1 \Theta ų_{74})(1 \Theta ų_{75})(1 \Theta ų_{76})$
$ų_{13} = 1\Theta (1 \Theta ų_{31})$
$ų_{31} = 1\Theta (1 \Theta ų_{52}) (1 \Theta ų_{53}) (1 \Theta ų_{54})(1 \Theta ų_{55})$
$ų_{52} = 1\Theta(1 \Theta ų_{77})(1 \Theta ų_{78})(1 \Theta ų_{79})(1 \Theta ų_{80})(1 \Theta ų_{81})(1 \Theta ų_{82})(1 \Theta ų_{83})$
$ų_{53} = 1\Theta(1 \Theta ų_{84})(1 \Theta ų_{85})(1 \Theta ų_{86})(1 \Theta ų_{87})(1 \Theta ų_{88})(1 \Theta ų_{89})$
$ų_{54} = 1\Theta(1 \Theta ų_{90})(1 \Theta ų_{91})(1 \Theta ų_{92})(1 \Theta ų_{93})(1 \Theta ų_{94})(1 \Theta ų_{95})(1 \Theta ų_{96})$

Step-2:

$ų_2 = 1\Theta(1 \Theta ų_7)(1 \Theta ų_8)(1 \Theta ų_9)(1 \Theta ų_{10})(1 \Theta ų_{11})(1 \Theta ų_{12})(1 \Theta ų_{13})$
$ų_6 = 1\Theta(1 \Theta ų_{14})(1 \Theta ų_{15})(1 \Theta ų_{16})(1 \Theta ų_{17})(1 \Theta ų_{18})(1 \Theta ų_{19})(1 \Theta ų_{20})(1 \Theta ų_{21})(1 \Theta ų_{22})$

Step-3:

$ų_1 = 1\Theta (1 \Theta ų_2) (1 \Theta ų_3) (1 \Theta ų_4) (1 \Theta ų_5) (1 \Theta ų_6)$

Similarly linguistic values can frame out for all the components. (Table 2)

Table 2. Linguistic values of marine main engine failure using Fault tree analysis method with Interval valued Triskaidecagonal fuzzy number

Component	Lower bound	Upper bound
$u3$	$(0.003,0.005,0.007,....0.025,0.027;\delta)$	$(0.001,0.004,0.006,...0.024,0.026;\gamma)$
$u4$	$(0.005,0.009,0.014,.....0.034,0.035;\delta)$	$(0.003,0.005,0.007,...0.034,0.036;\gamma)$
$u5$	$(0.007,0.008,0.009,....0.028,0.030;\delta)$	$(0.006,0.008,0.010,...0.035,0.037;\gamma)$
$u14$	$(0.010,0.012,0.014,....0.032,0.034;\delta)$	$(0.009,0.011,0.014,....0.035,0.037;\gamma)$
$u15$	$(0.012,0.014,0.016,....0.038,0.039;\delta)$	$(0.011,0.013,0.015,....0.040,0.042;\gamma)$
$u16$	$(0.015,0.017,0.018,....0.040,0.042;\delta)$	$(0.013,0.015,0.016,....0.042,0.044;\gamma)$
$u17$	$(0.017,0.019,0.021,....0.042,0.044;\delta)$	$(0.016,0.018,0.020,....0.043,0.045;\gamma)$
$u18$	$(0.024,0.026,0.028,....0.046,0.048;\delta)$	$(0.020,0.022,0.024,....0.047,0.049;\gamma)$
$u19$	$(0.028,0.030,0.032,....0.050,0.052;\delta)$	$(0.024,0.027,0.030,....0.052,0.054;\gamma)$
$u20$	$(0.030,0.032,0.034,....0.052,0.054;\delta)$	$(0.026,0.028,0.032,....0.055,0.059;\gamma)$
$u21$	$(0.036,0.038,0.040,....0.058,0.060;\delta)$	$(0.032,0.035,0.038,....0.061,0.063;\gamma)$
$u22$	$(0.038,0.040,0.042,....0.060,0.062;\delta)$	$(0.034,0.036,0.038,....0.064,0.066;\gamma)$
$u23$	$(0.041,0.043,0.045,....0.065,0.067;\delta)$	$(0.039,0.042,0.044,....0.067,0.069;\gamma)$
$u24$	$(0.053,0.055,0.057,....0.075,0.077;\delta)$	$(0.045,0.047,0.049,....0.078,0.080;\gamma)$
$u25$	$(0.057,0.059,0.061,....0.079,0.081;\delta)$	$(0.050,0.052,0.054,....0.083,0.085;\gamma)$
$u32$	$(0.059,0.063,0.067,....0.085,0.087;\delta)$	$(0.055,0.057,0.059,....0.088,0.090;\gamma)$
$u33$	$(0.061,0.062,0.063,....0.072,0.073;\delta)$	$(0.059,0.060,0.061,....0.079,0.080;\gamma)$
$u34$	$(0.063,0.065,0.067,....0.085,0.087;\delta)$	$(0.060,0.062,0.064,....0.088,0.089;\gamma)$
$u35$	$(0.066,0.068,0.070,....0.088,0.090;\delta)$	$(0.063,0.065,0.067,....0.089,0.091;\gamma)$
$u36$	$(0.069,0.070,0.072,....0.090,0.092;\delta)$	$(0.065,0.067,0.069,...0.091,0.093;\gamma)$
$u37$	$(0.071,0.073,0.075,....0.093,0.095;\delta)$	$(0.069,0.072,0.074,...0.095,0.097;\gamma)$
$u38$	$(0.072,0.073,0.074,....0.083,0.084;\delta)$	$(0.070,0.071,0.072,...0.086,0.087;\gamma)$
$u39$	$(0.074,0.076,0.077,....0.091,0.092;\delta)$	$(0.071,0.073,0.075,...0.092,0.093;\gamma)$
$u40$	$(0.077,0.078,0.079,....0.094,0.095;\delta)$	$(0.073,0.075,0.077,...0.094,0.096;\gamma)$
$u41$	$(0.080,0.081,0.082,....0.091,0.092;\delta)$	$(0.077,0.079,0.081,...0.096,0.098;\gamma)$
$u42$	$(0.084,0.086,0.087,....0.096,0.097;\delta)$	$(0.080,0.082,0.083,...0.098,0.099;\gamma)$
$u44$	$(0.086,0.087,0.088,....0.098,0.099;\delta)$	$(0.083,0.085,0.086,...0.099,0.101;\gamma)$
$u46$	$(0.090,0.091,0.092,....0.102,0.103;\delta)$	$(0.087,0.089,0.091,...0.106,0.107;\gamma)$
$u47$	$(0.093,0.095,0.097,....0.113,0.115;\delta)$	$(0.090,0.092,0.094,...0.117,0.119;\gamma)$
$u50$	$(0.103,0.105,0.107,....0.125,0.127;\delta)$	$(0.096,0.099,0.103,...0.127,0.129;\gamma)$
$u51$	$(0.107,0.109,0.121,....0.139,0.141;\delta)$	$(0.102,0.104,0.106,...0.143,0.145;\gamma)$
$u55$	$(0.120,0.122,0.124,....0.142,0.144;\delta)$	$(0.118,0.122,0.123,...0.144,0.146;\gamma)$
$u56$	$(0.125,0.126,0.128,....0.146,0.148;\delta)$	$(0.120,0.122,0.125,...0.150,0.152;\gamma)$
$u57$	$(0.130,0.132,0.134,....0.152,0.154;\delta)$	$(0.127,0.130,0.133,...0.157,0.159;\gamma)$
$u58$	$(0.133,0.135,0.137,....0.158,0.160;\delta)$	$(0.130,0.133,0.135,...0.159,0.162;\gamma)$
$u59$	$(0.137,0.139,0.141,....0.163,0.166;\delta)$	$(0.135,0.137,0.140,...0.166,0.169;\gamma)$
$u60$	$(0.140,0.142,0.144,....0.168,0.170;\delta)$	$(0.136,0.138,0.141,...0.172,0.174;\gamma)$

Step-1:

μ_7=(0.143593,0.148993,0.154369,0.159724,0.165055,0.171238,0.177392,0.182648,0.187882,0.193094,0.198283,0.20345,0.208595;0.128133,0.134501,0.139938,0.148961,0.157924,0.164157,0.177392,0.187019,0.192235,0.198297,0.205175,0.211173,0.216284)

μ_8=(0.280068,0.287716,0.296063,0.302837,0.310303,0.316969,0.323584,0.330148,0.33594,0.342409,0.348828,0.355198,0.361518;0.267681,0.27467,0.281607,0.290763,0.302838,0.31327,0.323584,0.33375,0.340945,0.350209,0.358668,0.365646,0.37119)

μ_9=(0.322102,0.327213,0.331569,0.336623,0.340932,0.345931,0.352316,0.358654,0.362849,0.367718,0.372558,0.377366,0.381465;0.311776,0.31916,0.325755,0.331575,0.337351,0.343797,0.352316,0.36075,0.367017,0.37255,0.37873,0.384855,0.390265)

μ_{10}=(0.589893,0.595466,0.600996,0.606461,0.610955,0.61944,0.625547,0.631598,0.637995,0.643452,0.648844,0.65375,0.659007;0.578592,0.586177,0.593697,0.601534,0.608816,0.615482,0.625547,0.634556,0.642123,0.648797,0.655766,0.661803,0.667722)

μ_{11}=(0.793355,0.798159,0.803099,0.808164,0.812886,0.817942,0.823087,0.827913,0.832403,0.836404,0.840088,0.844484,0.848024;0.784462,0.79142,0.799392,0.805934,0.811852,0.818423,0.823087,0.830636,0.836356,0.841789,0.846876,0.85018,0.853602)

μ_{12}=(0.794586,0.798558,0.805166,0.809671,0.813856,0.817732,0.822443,0.825941,0.829379,0.832759,0.83608,0.838925,0.842139;0.786281,0.791674,0.798197,0.803791,0.810137,0.814946,0.822443,0.828087,0.832336,0.83627,0.840152,0.844329,0.847847)

μ_{13}=(0.997980.998099,0.99823,0.998352,0.99847,0.998587,0.998722,0.998814,0.998896,0.998982,0.999054,0.999121,0.999176;0.997741,0.99795,0.998159,0.998325,0.998476,0.998614,0.998722,0.998863,0.998954,0.999041,0.999115,0.999181,0.999244)

Step-2:

μ_2=(0.999985,0.999987,0.999989,0.999991,0.999992,0.999993,0.999995,0.999995,0.999996,0.999997,0.999997,0.999998,0.999998;0.999981,0.999984,0.999987,0.99999,0.999992,0.999993,0.999995,0.999996,0.999997,0.999997,0.999998,0.999998,0.999998)

μ_6=(0.191794,0.20657,0.220311,0.23306,0.251,0.250303,0.28357,0.296844,0.311321,0.3241350.336737,0.348452,0.359984;0.169938,0.18592,0.204085,0.223502,0.241709,0.258729,0.28357,0.304869,0.318502,0.335373,0.349842,0.36269,0.375977)

Step-3:

ʯ1=(0.9999883,0.99999,0.999992,0.999993,0.999994,0.999995,0.999996,0.999997,0
.999997,0.999998,0.999998,0.999999,0.999999;0.999984,0.999987,0.99999,0.99999
2,0.999994,0.999995,0.999996,0.999997,0.999998,0.999998,0.999999,0.999999,0.99
9999)

Case:1 If $0 \le \Omega < \delta$, then

$$\varpi_l^L(\alpha) = \frac{6\Omega}{\delta}(\ell_2 - \ell_1) + \ell_1$$

$$\varpi_r^L(\alpha) = \frac{6\Omega}{\delta}(\ell_{13} - \ell_{12}) + \ell_{13}$$

$$\varpi_l^U(\alpha) = \frac{6\Omega}{\gamma}(\varsigma_2 - \varsigma_1) + \varsigma_1$$

$$\varpi_r^U(\alpha) = \frac{6\Omega}{\gamma}(\varsigma_{13} - \varsigma_{12}) + \varsigma_{13}$$

Where $\left\{\varpi_l^L(\Omega), \varpi_l^U(\Omega)\right\}, \left\{\varpi_r^L(\Omega), \varpi_r^U(\Omega)\right\}$ are the $\Omega-$ cuts of left and right side of level (δ, γ) Interval valued Triskaidecagonal fuzzy number.

Case:2
If $\delta \le \Omega \le \gamma$, then

$$\varpi_l^U(\Omega) = 6\alpha(\varsigma_7 - \varsigma_6) - 5\varsigma_7 + 6\varsigma_6$$

$$\varpi_r^U(\Omega) = 6\alpha(\varsigma_9 - \varsigma_8) - 4\varsigma_8 + 5\varsigma_9$$

Definition: Signed distance
$\kappa_0(h, 0), h\varepsilon R$ is define as $\kappa_0(h, 0) = h$ and is called the signed distance from k to 0. κ_0 meant is When (i) h > 0, $\kappa_0(h, 0) = h > 0$ (i.e.) h is the right and distance from 0 is h. (ii) h < 0, $\kappa_0(h, 0) = h < 0$ (i.e.) h is the left and distance from 0 is -h.
When $0 < \delta < \gamma$, we obtain the signed distance of from 0

$$\varpi = \begin{bmatrix} (\ell_1, \ell_2, \ell_3, \ell_4, \ell_5, \ell_6, \ell_7, \ell_8, \ell_9, \ell_{10}, \ell_{11}, \ell_{12}, \ell_{13}; \delta), \\ (\varsigma_1, \varsigma_2, \varsigma_3, \varsigma_4, \varsigma_5, \varsigma_6, \varsigma_7, \varsigma_8, \varsigma_9, \varsigma_{10}, \varsigma_{11}, \varsigma_{12}, \varsigma_{13}; \gamma) \end{bmatrix}$$

Case: 1 $0 \le \Omega \le \delta$

$$\kappa_0(\varpi_l^U(\Omega), 0) = \varpi_l^U(\Omega), \kappa_0(\varpi_l^L(\Omega), 0) = \varpi_l^L(\Omega),$$

$$\kappa_0(\varpi_r^L(\Omega), 0) = \varpi_r^L(\Omega), \kappa_0(\varpi_r^U(\Omega), 0) = \varpi_r^U(\Omega)$$

The signed distance of the interval $[\varpi^L(\Omega), \varpi^U(\Omega)]$ from 0 is given by

$$\kappa_0\left[(\varpi_l^L(\Omega), \varpi_l^U(\Omega)), 0\right] = \frac{1}{2}\left[\kappa_0(\varpi_l^U(\Omega), 0) + \kappa_0(\varpi_l^L(\Omega), 0)\right] = \frac{1}{2}\left[\varpi_l^U(\Omega) + \varpi_l^L(\Omega)\right]$$

$$= \frac{1}{2}\left[\ell_1 + \varsigma_1 + \frac{6\Omega}{\gamma}(\varsigma_2 - \varsigma_1) + \frac{6\Omega}{\delta}(\ell_2 - \ell_1)\right]$$

(1)

$$\kappa_0\left[(\varpi_r^L(\Omega), \varpi_r^U(\Omega)), 0\right] = \frac{1}{2}\left[\kappa_0(\varpi_r^U(\Omega), 0) + \kappa_0(\varpi_r^L(\Omega), 0)\right] = \frac{1}{2}\left[\varpi_r^U(\Omega) + \varpi_r^L(\Omega)\right]$$

$$= \frac{1}{2}\left[\ell_{13} + \varsigma_{13} + \frac{7\Omega}{\gamma}(\varsigma_{13} - \varsigma_{12}) + \frac{7\Omega}{\delta}(\ell_{13} - \ell_{12})\right]$$

(2)

The signed distance of $\left[\varpi_l^L(\Omega), \varpi_l^U(\Omega)\right] \cup \left[\varpi_r^L(\Omega), \varpi_r^U(\Omega)\right]$ from 0 is given by

$$\kappa_0\left(\left[\varpi_l^L(\Omega), \varpi_l^U(\Omega)\right] \cup \left[\varpi_r^L(\Omega), \varpi_r^U(\Omega)\right], 0\right) = \frac{1}{2}\left[\kappa_0((\varpi_l^L(\Omega), \varpi_l^U(\Omega)), 0) + \kappa_0((\varpi_r^L(\Omega), \varpi_r^U(\Omega)), 0)\right]$$

$$= \frac{1}{4}\left[\ell_1 + \varsigma_1 + \frac{6\Omega}{\gamma}(\varsigma_2 - \varsigma_1) + \frac{6\Omega}{\delta}(\ell_2 - \ell_1) + \ell_{13} + \varsigma_{13} + \frac{6\Omega}{\gamma}(\varsigma_{13} - \varsigma_{12}) + \frac{6\Omega}{\delta}(\ell_{13} - \ell_{12})\right]$$

$$= \frac{1}{4}\left[\ell_1 + \varsigma_1 + \ell_{13} + \varsigma_{13} + \frac{6\Omega}{\gamma}(\varsigma_2 - \varsigma_1 + \varsigma_{13} - \varsigma_{12}) + \frac{6\Omega}{\delta}(\ell_2 - \ell_1 + \ell_{13} - \ell_{12})\right]$$

(3)

The function in Eq. 3 is continuous on $0 \leq \Omega \leq \delta$ with respect to Ω, we can find the average value by integration

$$\frac{1}{\delta}\int_0^\lambda \kappa_0\left(\left[\varpi_l^L(\Omega), \varpi_l^U(\Omega)\right] \cup \left[\varpi_r^L(\Omega), \varpi_r^U(\Omega)\right], 0\right) d\alpha$$

$$= \frac{1}{8}\left(-4\ell_1 + 2\varsigma_1 + 8\ell_{13} + 2\varsigma_{13} + 6\ell_2 - 6\ell_{12} + \frac{6\delta}{\gamma}(\varsigma_2 - \varsigma_1 + \varsigma_{13} - \varsigma_{12})\right)$$

$$\kappa_0(\dot{P}_1, 0) = 0.999996205$$

Case: 2 $\delta \leq \Omega \leq \gamma$ The signed distance of $\left[\varpi_l^U(\alpha), \varpi_r^U(\alpha)\right]$ from 0 is given

$$d_0\left[(\varpi_l^U(\Omega), \varpi_l^U(\Omega)), 0\right] = \frac{1}{2}\left[d_0(\varpi_l^U(\Omega), 0) + d_0(\varpi_l^U(\Omega), 0)\right] = \frac{1}{2}\left[\varpi_l^U(\Omega) + \varpi_l^U(\Omega)\right]$$

$$= \frac{1}{2}\left[6\Omega(\varsigma_7 - \varsigma_6) - 5\varsigma_7 + 6\varsigma_6 + 6\Omega(\varsigma_8 - \varsigma_7) + 5\varsigma_9 - 4\varsigma_8\right]$$

$$= \frac{1}{2}\left[6\Omega(\varsigma_7 - \varsigma_6 + \varsigma_8 - \varsigma_7) - 5\varsigma_7 + 6\varsigma_6 + 5\varsigma_9 - 4\varsigma_8\right]$$

This function is also continuous function and the average value is calculated by integration.

$$\frac{1}{\gamma - \delta} \int_\lambda^\rho (\kappa_0(\varpi_l^U(\Omega), \varpi_r^U(\Omega)), 0) d\Omega$$

$$= \frac{1}{\gamma - \delta} \frac{1}{4} \begin{bmatrix} 6\gamma^2(\varsigma_7 - \varsigma_6 + \varsigma_9 - \varsigma_8) + (-10\varsigma_7 + 12\varsigma_6 + 10\varsigma_9 - 8\varsigma_8)\gamma \\ -6\delta^2(\varsigma_7 - \varsigma_6 + \varsigma_9 - \varsigma_8) + (-10\varsigma_7 + 12\varsigma_6 + 14\varsigma_9 - 14\varsigma_8)\delta \end{bmatrix}$$

$$\kappa_0(\dot{P}_1, 0) = 0.99999837594$$

Centroid Distance for lower bound:

$$\frac{\delta}{12}[-\ell_1 + 2\ell_7 - 2\ell_{12} + \ell_{13}] + \frac{\delta}{6}[-\ell_3 - \ell_2 - \ell_4 - \ell_5 - \ell_6 + 5\ell_7 + \ell_9 \\ - 5\ell_8 + \ell_{10} + \ell_{11} + 2\ell_{12}] + \delta[\ell_8 - \ell_7]$$

$$\int \mu_A(x)dx = 0.00000112602 \qquad (i)$$

$$\frac{\delta}{12}[-\ell_3^2 - \ell_2^2 - \ell_4^2 - \ell_5^2 - \ell_6^2 - \ell_7^2 + \ell_8^2 + \ell_9^2 + \ell_{10}^2 + \ell_{11}^2 + 2\ell_{12}^2] + \frac{\delta}{36}[\frac{2\ell_2^3 - 3\ell_1\ell_2^2 + \ell_1^3}{\ell_2 - \ell_1} + \frac{2\ell_3^3 - 3\ell_2\ell_3^2 + \ell_2^3}{\ell_3 - \ell_2} + \frac{2\ell_4^3 - 3\ell_3\ell_4^2 + \ell_3^3}{\ell_4 - \ell_3}$$
$$+ \frac{2\ell_5^3 - 3\ell_4\ell_5^2 + \ell_4^3}{\ell_5 - \ell_4} + \frac{2\ell_6^3 - 3\ell_5\ell_6^2 + \ell_5^3}{\ell_6 - \ell_5} + \frac{2\ell_7^3 - 3\ell_6\ell_7^2 + \ell_6^3}{\ell_7 - \ell_6} - \frac{2\ell_8^3 - 3\ell_7\ell_8^2 + \ell_7^3}{\ell_8 - \ell_7} - \frac{2\ell_9^3 - 3\ell_8\ell_9^2 + \ell_8^3}{\ell_9 - \ell_8} - \frac{2\ell_{10}^3 - 3\ell_9\ell_{10}^2 + \ell_9^3}{\ell_{10} - \ell_9}$$
$$- \frac{2\ell_{11}^3 - 3\ell_{10}\ell_{11}^2 + \ell_{10}^3}{\ell_{11} - \ell_{10}} - \frac{2\ell_{12}^3 - 3\ell_{11}\ell_{12}^2 + \ell_{11}^3}{\ell_{12} - \ell_{11}} + \frac{2\ell_{12}^3 - 3\ell_{13}\ell_{12}^2 + \ell_{13}^3}{\ell_{13} - \ell_{12}}]$$

$$\int X\mu_A(x)dx = 0.00000182933 \qquad (II)$$

Centroid distance for lower bound = 1.62459814

Centroid distance for upper bound:

$$\frac{\gamma}{12}[-\varsigma_1 + 2\varsigma_7 - 2\varsigma_{12} + \varsigma_{13}] + \frac{\gamma}{6}[-\varsigma_3 - \varsigma_2 - \varsigma_4 - \varsigma_5 - \varsigma_6 + 5\varsigma_7 + \varsigma_9 \\ - 5\varsigma_8 + \varsigma_{10} + \varsigma_{11} + 2\varsigma_{12}] + \gamma[\varsigma_8 - \varsigma_7]$$

$$\int \mu_A(x)dx = 0.0000027 \qquad (i)$$

$$\frac{\gamma}{12}[-\varsigma_3^2 - \varsigma_2^2 - \varsigma_4^2 - \varsigma_5^2 - \varsigma_6^2 - \varsigma_7^2 + \varsigma_8^2 + \varsigma_9^2 + \varsigma_{10}^2 + \varsigma_{11}^2 + 2\varsigma_{12}^2] + \frac{\gamma}{36}[\frac{2\varsigma_2^3 - 3\varsigma_1\varsigma_2^2 + \varsigma_1^3}{\varsigma_2 - \varsigma_1} + \frac{2\varsigma_3^3 - 3\varsigma_2\varsigma_3^2 + \varsigma_2^3}{\varsigma_3 - \varsigma_2} + \frac{2\varsigma_4^3 - 3\varsigma_3\varsigma_4^2 + \varsigma_3^3}{\varsigma_4 - \varsigma_3}$$
$$+ \frac{2\varsigma_5^3 - 3\varsigma_4\varsigma_5^2 + \varsigma_4^3}{\varsigma_5 - \varsigma_4} + \frac{2\varsigma_6^3 - 3\varsigma_5\varsigma_6^2 + \varsigma_5^3}{\varsigma_6 - \varsigma_5} + \frac{2\varsigma_7^3 - 3\varsigma_6\varsigma_7^2 + \varsigma_6^3}{\varsigma_7 - \varsigma_6} - \frac{2\varsigma_8^3 - 3\varsigma_7\varsigma_8^2 + \varsigma_7^3}{\varsigma_8 - \varsigma_7} - \frac{2\varsigma_9^3 - 3\varsigma_8\varsigma_9^2 + \varsigma_8^3}{\varsigma_9 - \varsigma_8} - \frac{2\varsigma_{10}^3 - 3\varsigma_9\varsigma_{10}^2 + \varsigma_9^3}{\varsigma_{10} - \varsigma_9}$$
$$- \frac{2\varsigma_{11}^3 - 3\varsigma_{10}\varsigma_{11}^2 + \varsigma_{10}^3}{\varsigma_{11} - \varsigma_{10}} - \frac{2\varsigma_{12}^3 - 3\varsigma_{11}\varsigma_{12}^2 + \varsigma_{11}^3}{\varsigma_{12} - \varsigma_{11}} + \frac{2\varsigma_{12}^3 - 3\varsigma_{13}\varsigma_{12}^2 + \varsigma_{13}^3}{\varsigma_{13} - \varsigma_{12}}]$$

$$\int X\mu_A(x)dx = 0.00000258 \qquad (II)$$

Centroid distance for upper bound = 0.955555556

Euclidean distance: $\sqrt{\sum_{i=1}^{n}|x_i - y_i|^2}$, $ED = \sqrt{(x_1 - y_1)^2 + (x_2 - y_2)^2 + (x_3 - y_3)^2 + (x_4 - y_4)^2 + \ldots\ldots(x_{13} - y_{13})^2}$

$ED = \sqrt{0.00000000032}$, where n = 13

Failure Modes & Effects Analysis of Marine Main engine:

- Tabulation of components, consequences and safeguards are they associated with failure modes.
- Identification/assessment of risk is derived from looking at each component in the case of multi-unit cylinder)
- FTA- approach is commonly referred (Table 3).

Table 3. Failure mode and Effect analysis

Identification	Failure of marine main engine		
Description	A distance approach of Triskaidecagonal interval valued fuzzy number analyzed with fault detection of marine main engine		
Acceptance level of failure modes	[0.999983, 0.999999]		
Risk priority level of failure	0.999996		
Distance method	**SD**	**CD**	**ED**
	Case-1: 0.999996202 **Case:2** 0.99999837594	**LB:**1.62459814 **UB:** 0.955555556	$\sqrt{0.00000000032}$
Effects	Ship accident		
Safeguards	Prevent the malfunctions of common components and main cylinder		

4 Conclusion

Thus Having the importance of distance for Interval valued Triskaidecagonal fuzzy number; a effective distance formula is presented for its computation. The performance of the Fault tree of marine main engine is analyzing using distance formula have compared with Centroid distance, Euclidean distance, and Signed distance to appeared as a appropriate condition for Interval valued Triskaidecagonal fuzzy number and conveniently distance methods presented in the approach of FTA in Marine Ship to find the effect and causes of failure modes. Further research is needed to propose distance formula for Interval valued Triskaidecagonal fuzzy number to find out more accuracy.

References

1. Rajkumar, A., Helen, D.: New arithmetic operations of triskaidecagonal fuzzy number using alpha cut. In: Pant, M., Ray, K., Sharma, T.K., Rawat, S., Bandyopadhyay, A. (eds.) Soft Computing: Theories and Applications. AISC, vol. 583, pp. 125–135. Springer, Singapore (2018). https://doi.org/10.1007/978-981-10-5687-1_12
2. Rajkumar, A., Helen, D.: New arithmetic operations in inverse of triskaidecagonal fuzzy number using alpha cut. In: Pant, M., Ray, K., Sharma, T.K., Rawat, S., Bandyopadhyay, A. (eds.) Soft Computing: Theories and Applications. AISC, vol. 583, pp. 115–123. Springer, Singapore (2018). https://doi.org/10.1007/978-981-10-5687-1_11
3. Rajkumar, A., Helen, D.: Tree trigger success of door bell using fuzzy number. Int. J. Pure Appl. Math. 114(5), 71–77 (2017). ISSN: 1311-8080 (printed version); ISSN: 1314-3395 (online version)
4. Devadoss, A.V., Praveena, N.J.P.: Analysis of system failure of single cylinder vertical diesel engine using fuzzy fault tree through interval valued hexadecagonal fuzzy numbers. Int. J. Pure Appl. Math. 117(14), 253–259 (2017)
5. Laskowski, R.: Fault tree analysis as a tool for modeling the marine main engine reliability structure. Int. J. Pure Appl. Math. 41(113), 71–77 (2015). ISSN 1733-8670
6. Cai, K.Y., Wen, C.Y., Zhang, M.L.: Fuzzy states as a basis for a theory of fuzzy reliability. Microelectr. Reliab. 33(15), 2253–2263 (1993)
7. Singer, D.: A fuzzy set approach to fault tree and reliability analysis. Fuzzy Sets Syst. 34(2), 145–155 (1990)
8. Praveena, N.J.P.: Application of interval valued hexadecagonal fuzzy numbers in project network, 14(117), 253–259 (2017). ISSN 1311-8080

Application of Triskaidecagonal Fuzzy Number in Home Appliances Using Sequencing Problem

A. Rajkumar[✉] and D. Helen

Department of Mathematics, Hindustan Institute of Technology and Science,
Chennai 603103, India
arajkumar@hindustanuniv.ac.in, helen.br@outlook.com

Abstract. The new method of Triskaidecagonal fuzzy number are being proposed in this paper. A generalized Triskiadecagonal fuzzy number is solved in order to obtain the accurate solution for the numerical problem using the technique of Sequencial approach. Thus a generalized Triskiadecagonal fuzzy number is solved concerning the real life situation by comparing the Triangular, Trapezoidal and Dodecagonal fuzzy number using the technique of Sequencial approach. It is concluded by analysis that the application of Triskaidecagonal fuzzy number performs more potency in the human activities.

Keywords: Sequencing · Triskaidecagonal fuzzy number · Lexical values

1 Introduction

Fuzzy numbers are frequently used as universal approximates. It is also seen while dealing with the home appliances with known order. The scheduling procedures available today are not only quite realistic, but also possess a fast solution generating capability. Sequencing refers to the order, in which it represents an order or a list or an order. It finds widespread applications, both in manufacturing and service industries. Govindarajan [8] proposed a new method to solve sequencing problem with generalized fuzzy numbers by a ranking function for obtaining the solution. Laxminarayan Sahoo [9] proposed a new method for job sequencing problem using Trapezoidal Fuzzy numbers. The concept of Triskaidecagonal fuzzy number is used in the home appliances to enhance in proving the accurate result. Thus it has been examined with alpha cut as a very effective approximately. Then the defined problem has been converted into crisp job sequencing using Yager's ranking index method [9]. Thus the defuzzification method involves in Triangular,Trapezoidal and Dodecagonal Fuzzy number in order to compare the optimal solution with Triskaidecagonal fuzzy number. The idle time of the machine and the optimal solution for the job is also obtained. The results found here is precise and accurate while comparing with other existing Fuzzy numbers. The produced result is analyzed and steps had been taken to calculate time units to implement the success by using the Fuzzy numbers.

© Springer Nature Singapore Pte Ltd. 2019
A. K. Luhach et al. (Eds.): ICAICR 2018, CCIS 955, pp. 80–87, 2019.
https://doi.org/10.1007/978-981-13-3140-4_8

2   Preliminaries

Triskaidecagonal Fuzzy Number (TDFN): A fuzzy number $m_{\overline{TD}}$ is a dodecagonal fuzzy number denoted by $m_{\overline{TD}} = (a_1, a_2, a_3, a_4, a_5, a_6, a_7, a_8, a_9, a_{10}, a_{11}, a_{12}, a_{13})$ (Fig. 1 and Tables 1, 2, 3).
where are real numbers and its membership function

$$\mu_{\overline{TD}}(x) = \begin{cases} \frac{1}{6}\left(\frac{x-a1}{a2-a1}\right) & a_1 \leq x \leq a_2 \\ \frac{1}{6} + \frac{1}{6}\left(\frac{x2-a2}{a3-a2}\right) & a_2 \leq x \leq a_3 \\ \frac{2}{6} + \frac{1}{6}\left(\frac{x-a3}{a4-a3}\right) & a_3 \leq x \leq a_4 \\ \frac{3}{6} + \frac{1}{6}\left(\frac{x-a4}{a5-a4}\right) & a_4 \leq x \leq a_5 \\ \frac{4}{6} + \frac{1}{6}\left(\frac{x-a5}{a6-a5}\right) & a_5 \leq x \leq a_6 \\ \frac{5}{6} + \frac{1}{6}\left(\frac{x-a6}{a7-a6}\right) & a_6 \leq x \leq a_7 \\ 1 - \frac{1}{6}\left(\frac{x-a7}{a8-a7}\right) & a_7 \leq x \leq a_8 \\ \frac{5}{6} - \frac{1}{6}\left(\frac{x-a8}{a9-a8}\right) & a_8 \leq x \leq a_9 \\ \frac{4}{6} - \frac{1}{6}\left(\frac{x-a9}{a10-a9}\right) & a_9 \leq x \leq a_{10} \\ \frac{3}{6} - \frac{1}{6}\left(\frac{x-a10}{a11-a10}\right) & a_{10} \leq x \leq a_{11} \\ \frac{2}{6} - \frac{1}{6}\left(\frac{x-a11}{a12-a11}\right) & a_{11} \leq x \leq a_{12} \\ \frac{1}{6}\left(\frac{a13-x}{a13-a12}\right) & a_{12} \leq x \leq a_{13} \\ 0 & x > a_{13} \end{cases} \qquad (1)$$

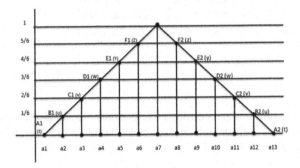

Fig. 1. Triskaidecagonal fuzzy number

Table 1. Triangular and trapezoidal fuzzy lexical scale

Lexical terms	Lexical view point (Triangular)	Lexical view point (Trapezoidal)
Very Low-VL	(0.5, 1.0, 1.5)	(0.05, 0.45, 0.85, 1.25)
Low-L	(1.5, 2.0, 2.5)	(0.5, 1.0, 1.5, 2.0)
Medium-M	(2.5, 3.0, 3.5)	(2.0, 2.5, 3.0, 3.5)
High-H	(3.5, 4.0, 4.5)	(3.0, 3.5, 4.0, 4.5)

Table 2. Dodecagonal and triskaidecagonal fuzzy linguistic scale

Lexical terms	Lexical view point (Dodecagonal)	Lexical view point (Triskaidecagonal)
Very Low	(0.13, 0.14, 0.15, 0.16, 0.17, 0.18, 0.19, 0.20, 0.21, 0.22, 0.23, 0.24)	(0.04, 0.05, 0.06, 0.07, 0.08, 0.09, 0.10, 0.11, 0.12, 0.13, 0.14, 0.15, 0.16)
Low	(0.17, 0.18, 0.19, 0.20, 0.21, 0.22, 0.23, 0.24, 0.25, 0.26, 0.27, 0.28)	(0.10, 0.11, 0.12, 0.13, 0.14, 0.15, 0.16, 0.17, 0.18, 0.19, 0.20, 0.21, 0.22)
Medium	(0.22, 0.23, 0.24, 0.25, 0.26, 0.27, 0.28, 0.29, 0.30, 0.31, 0.32, 0.33)	(0.12, 0.13, 0.14, 0.15, 0.16, 0.17, 0.18, 0.19, 0.20, 0.21, 0.22, 0.23, 0.24)
High	(0.36, 0.39, 0.42, 0.45, 0.48, 0.51, 0.54, 0.57, 0.60, 0.63, 0.66, 0.69)	(0.20, 0.21, 0.22, 0.23.0.24, 0.25, 0.26, 0.27, 0.28, 0.29, 0.30, 0.31, 0.32)

Table 3. Membership functions of using Alpha cut

Membership functions of using Alpha cut	
$x = \alpha (a_2 - a_1) + a_1, x = -\alpha (a_3 - a_2) + a_3$	–Triangular
$x = \alpha (a_2 - a_1) + a1, x = -\alpha (a_4 - a_3) + a_4$	–Trapezoidal
$\begin{cases} [5\alpha(a_2 - a_1) + a_1, 5\alpha(a_{11} - a_{12}) + a_{12}] \\ [5\alpha(a_3 - a_2) + 2a_2 - a_3, 5\alpha(a_{10} - a_{11}) + 2a_{11} - a_{10}] \\ [5\alpha(a_4 - a_3) + 3a_3 - 2a_4, 5\alpha(a_9 - a_{10}) + 3a_{10} - 2a_9] \\ [5\alpha(a_5 - a_4) + 4a_4 - 3a_5, 5\alpha(a_8 - a_9) + 4a_9 - 3a_8] \\ [5\alpha(a_6 - a_5) + 5a_5 - 4, 5\alpha(a_7 - a_8) + 5a_8 - 4a_7] \end{cases}$	–Dodecagonal
$\begin{cases} [6\alpha(a_2 - a_1) + a_1, -6\alpha(a_{13} - a_{12}) + a_{13}] \\ [6\alpha(a_3 - a_2) + 2a_2 - a_3, -6\alpha(a_{12} - a_{11}) + a_{11} - 2a_{12}] \\ [6\alpha(a_4 - a_3) - 2a_4 + 3a_3, -6\alpha(a_{11} - a_{10}) + 3a_{11} - 2a_{10}] \\ [6\alpha(a_5 - a_4) - 3a_5 + 4a_4, -6\alpha(a_{10} - a_9) + 4a_{10} - 3a_9] \\ [6\alpha(a_6 - a_5) - 4a_6 + 5a_5, -6\alpha(a_9 - a_8) + 5a_9 - 4a_8] \\ \quad [6\alpha(a_7 - a_6) - 5a_7 + 6a_6, -6\alpha(a_8 - a_7) + a_8] \end{cases}$	–Triskaidecagonal

3 Problem

If different types of furniture pass through five prefinishing stages in the same order, the processing time varies considerably at each stage based on the size and complexity of each type of furniture (Table 4).

Table 4. Scale variable of expert

Type	Stage1	Stage2	Stage3	Stage4	Stage5
Chair	M	M	M	M	M
Desk	M	VL	L	M	H
Lamp	H	M	M	L	M
EndTable	H	VL	M	L	M
CoffeeTable	M	M	VL	M	M

Figuring an optimal sequency for processing the five types of furniture through the five stages to minimize the total elapsed time and total idle time at stages 1, 2, 3, 4 & 5?

Definition: Yager's ranking index is defined by $y(A) = \int_0^1 0.5(A_\alpha^L + A_\alpha^U)$ where (A_α^L, A_α^U) is the α - level cut of the fuzzy number A. When putting membership function is equal to a.

Applying Yager's methods, to find (0.5, 1.0, 1.5)

$$\text{When} \qquad y(A) = \int_0^1 0.5(2) = 1$$

Similarly for other linguistic values, we obtain

$$y(A) = \int_0^1 0.5(4) = 2, y(A) = \int_0^1 0.5(6) = 3, y(A) = \int_0^1 0.5(8) = 4$$

$$VL - [1], L - [2], M - [3], H - [4]$$

When for Trapezoidal,

$$y(A) = \int_0^1 0.5(1.3) = 0.65, y(A) = \int_0^1 0.5(2.5) = 1.25, y(A) = \int_0^1 0.5(5.5) = 2.75,$$

$$y(A) = \int_0^1 0.5(7.5) = 3.75$$

$$VL - [0.65], L - [1.25], M - [2.75], H - [3.75]$$

When for Dodecagonal,

$$y(A) = \int_0^1 0.5(2.75) = 1.375, y(A) = \int_0^1 0.5(2.25) = 1.125,$$

$$y(A) = \int_0^1 0.5(1.85) = 0.925, y(A) = \int_0^1 0.5(5.25) = 2.625$$

$$VL - [0.925], L - [1.125], M - [1.375], H - [2.625]$$

When for Triangular

$$y(A) = \int_0^1 0.5(1.2) = 0.6, y(A) = \int_0^1 0.5(1.92) = 0.96, y(A) = \int_0^1 0.5(2.16) = 1.08,$$

$$y(A) = \int_0^1 0.5(3.12) = 1.56$$

$$VL - [0.6], L - [0.96], M - [1.08], H - [1.56]$$

4 Algorithm for Sequencing Problem

Let us consider 'm' machine as $A_1, A_2, \ldots, A_m$. Any Problem can be considered into two complicated machines. Thus $A_{i1}, A_{i2}, A_{i3} \ldots A_{im}$ can be dealt with times on machines $A_1, A_2, \ldots, A_m$ respectively.

Then if $\min_i A_{i1} \geq \max_i A_{ij}, j = 2, 3.., m - 1$ (or)

$$\min_i A_{im} \geq \max_i A_{ij}, j = 2, 3.., m - 1$$

Introduce two imaginary machines G and H such that

$$G = M_{i1} + M_{i2} + M_{i3} + M_{i4}, \quad H = M_{i2} + M_{i3} + M_{i4} + M_{i5}$$

If the least possible value in G process = ith job first. Similarly the least possible value in H process = jth job last.

If there is a tie. ie., $M_{i1} = M_{j2}$ steps of action is being taken the ith job first and jth job in the last. Blot out the jobs has already been refered and done until all the jobs have been mandated. After breakthrough the optimum sequence could be found consequently (Tables 5, 6, 7 and 8).

1. Total Passing time is the period between the first job and the last job by calculating the total elapsed time with initial time zero. Time out of machine A is the time in the next machine. Summation will be in the order of optimum sequence.
2. Idle time in machine A = The total elapsed achieved time – Completed optimum sequence on machine A.

Table 5. Total elapsed time of triangular fuzzy number

Stages	Chair		Desk		Lamp		EndTable		CoffeeTable	
	In	Out	In	Out	In	Out	In	Out	In	Out
2	0	3	3	4	4	6	6	9	9	13
4	3	7	7	8	8	11	11	13	13	16
5	7	10	10	13	13	14	14	17	17	20
1	10	13	13	16	16	19	19	22	22	25
3	13	17	17	20	20	23	23	25	25	28

The Total Passing duration is = 28 time units

Idle time of Stage 1 = Total Passing time – Time finish up by Stage 1
$$= 28 - 17 = 11 \text{ time units}$$

Idle time of Stage 2 = Total Passing time – Time finish up by Stage 2
$$= 28 - 11 = 17 \text{ time units}$$

Idle time of Stage 3 = Total Passing time − Time finish up by Stage 3
$$= 28 - 12 = 16 \text{ time units}$$

Idle time of Stage 4 = Total Passing time − Time finish up by Stage 4
$$= 28 - 13 = 15 \text{ time units}$$

Idle time of Stage 5 = Total Passing time − Time finish up by Stage 5
$$= 28 - 16 = 12 \text{ time units}$$

Table 6. Total elapsed time of trapezoidal fuzzy number

Stages	Chair		Desk		Lamp		End Table		Coffee Table	
	In	Out	In	Out	In	Out	In	Out	In	Out
2	0	2.75	2.75	3.4	3.4	4.65	4.65	7.4	7.4	11.15
4	2.75	6.5	6.5	7.15	7.15	9.9	9.9	11.15	11.15	13.9
5	6.5	9.25	9.25	12	12	12.65	12.65	15.4	15.4	18.15
1	9.25	12	12	14.75	14.75	17.5	17.5	20.25	20.25	23
3	12	15.75	15.75	18.5	18.5	21.25	21.25	22.5	23	25.75

The Total Elapsed duration is = 25.75 time units

Idle time of Stage 1 = Total Passing time − Time finish up by Stage 1
$$= 25.75 - 15.75 = 10 \text{ time units}$$

Idle time of Stage 2 = Total Passing time − Time finish up by Stage 2
$$= 25.75 - 9.55 = 16.2 \text{ time units}$$

Idle time of Stage 3 = Total Passing time − Time finish up by Stage 3
$$= 25.75 - 10.15 = 15.6 \text{ time units}$$

Idle time of Stage 4 = Total Passing time − Time finish up by Stage 4
$$= 25.75 - 10.75 = 15 \text{ time units}$$

Idle time of Stage 5 = Total Passing time − Time finish up by Stage 5
$$= 25.75 - 14.71 = 11.04 \text{ time units}$$

Table 7. Total elapsed time of dodecagonal fuzzy number

Stages	Chair		Desk		Lamp		EndTable		CoffeeTable	
	In	Out	In	Out	In	Out	In	Out	In	Out
2	0	1.375	1.375	2.3	2.3	3.425	3.425	4.8	4.8	7.425
5	1.375	2.75	2.75	4.125	4.125	5.05	5.05	6.425	7.425	8.8
1	2.75	4.125	4.125	5.5	5.5	6.875	6.875	8.25	8.8	10.175
4	4.125	6.75	6.75	7.675	7.675	9.05	9.05	10.175	10.175	11.55
3	6.75	9.375	9.375	10.75	10.75	12.125	12.125	13.25	13.25	14.625

The Total Elapsed duration is $= 14.625$ time units

Idle time of Stage 1 = Total Passing time − Time finish up by Stage 1
$$= 14.625 - 9.375 = 5.25 \text{ time units}$$

Idle time of Stage 2 = Total Passing time − Time finish up by Stage 2
$$= 14.625 - 5.975 = 8.65 \text{ time units}$$

Idle time of Stage 3 = Total Passing time − Time finish up by Stage 3
$$= 14.625 - 6.175 = 8.45 \text{ time units}$$

Idle time of Stage 4 = Total Passing time − Time finish up by Stage 4
$$= 14.625 - 6.375 = 8.25 \text{ time units}$$

Idle time of Stage 5 = Total Passing time − Time finish up by Stage 5
$$= 14.625 - 8.125 = 6.5 \text{ time units}$$

Table 8. Total elapsed time of triskaidecagonal fuzzy number

Stages	Chair		Desk		Lamp		EndTable		CoffeeTable	
	In	Out	In	Out	In	Out	In	Out	In	Out
2	0	1.08	1.08	1.68	1.68	2.76	2.76	3.36	3.36	4.44
5	1.08	2.16	2.16	3.72	3.72	4.8	4.8	5.88	5.88	6.96
4	2.16	3.24	3.24	4.32	4.32	5.28	5.28	6.24	6.24	7.32
1	3.24	4.32	4.32	5.4	5.4	6.96	6.96	8.52	8.52	9.6
3	4.32	5.4	5.4	6.36	6.36	7.44	7.44	8.52	9.6	10.2

The Total Elapsed duration is $= 10.2$ time units

Idle time of Stage 1 = Total Passing time − Time finish up by Stage 1
$$= 10.2 - 6.36 = 3.84 \text{ time units}$$

Idle time of Stage 2 = Total Passing time − Time finish up by Stage 2
$$= 10.2 - 4.44 = 5.76 \text{ time units}$$

Idle time of Stage 3 = Total Passing time − Time finish up by Stage 3
$$= 10.2 - 4.8 = 5.4 \text{ time units}$$

Idle time of Stage 4 = Total Passing time − Time finish up by Stage 4
$$= 10.2 - 5.16 = 5.04 \text{ time units}$$

Idle time of Stage 5 = Total Passing time − Time finish up by Stage 5
$$= 10.2 - 5.88 = 4.32 \text{ time units}$$

5 Conclusion

Comparing the result of Dodecagonal, Trapezoidal and Triangular with Triskaidecagonal fuzzy number, which makes easy to understand and helps to formulate uncertainty in actual environment. Here increasing the fuzzy number always reduces the total elapsed time and the idle time of entire function. In such a way Sequencing approach serves an application for the decision makers in real life situation using fuzzy numbers.

References

1. Rajkumar, A., Helen, D.: New arithmetic operations of triskaidecagonal fuzzy number using alpha cut. In: Pant, M., Ray, K., Sharma, T.K., Rawat, S., Bandyopadhyay, A. (eds.) Soft Computing: Theories and Applications. AISC, vol. 583, pp. 125–135. Springer, Singapore (2018). https://doi.org/10.1007/978-981-10-5687-1_12
2. Rajkumar, A., Helen, D.: New arithmetic operations in inverse of triskaidecagonal fuzzy number using alpha cut. In: Pant, M., Ray, K., Sharma, Tarun K., Rawat, S., Bandyopadhyay, A. (eds.) Soft Computing: Theories and Applications. AISC, vol. 583, pp. 115–123. Springer, Singapore (2018). https://doi.org/10.1007/978-981-10-5687-1_11
3. Selvam, P., Rajkumar, A., SudhaEaswari, J.: Dodecagonal fuzzy number [DDFN]. Int. J. Control Theory Appl. 9(28), 447–461 (2016)
4. Banerjee, S.: Arithmetic operations on generalized trapezoidal fuzzy number and its applications. An Off. J. Turk. Fuzzy Syst. Assoc. 3(1), 16–44 (2012)
5. Zimmermann, H.J.: Fuzzy Set Theory and its Application, 4th edn. Springer, Heidelberg (2011)
6. Zadeh, L.A.: The concept of a Linguistic variable and its Application to approximate reasoning (Part II). Inf. Sci. 8, 301–357 (1975)
7. Dubois, D., Prade, H.: Operations on fuzzy numbers. Int. J. Syst. Sci. 9(6), 613–626 (1978)
8. Govindarajan, R., Kripa, K.: Fuzzy sequencing problem using generalized triangular fuzzy numbers. Int. J. Eng. Res. Appl. 6(6, Part-1), 61–64 (2016)
9. Sahoo, L.: Solving job sequencing problems with fuzzy processing times, vol. 3, no. 4 (2017)

Kernel Functions of SVM: A Comparison and Optimal Solution

Subham Panja[(⊠)], Akshay Chatterjee, and Ghazaala Yasmin

St. Thomas' College of Engineering and Technology, Kolkata 700 023, India
subhampanja13@gmail.com,
akshay.chatterjee2015vit@gmail.com,
me.ghazaalayasmin@gmail.com

Abstract. Classification with better accuracy for all type of data set for a single classifiers is still a challenge in the domain of Machine learning. Improving the efficiency of classifiers is still a challenge for researchers. This notion has motivated to give comparative solution for the classifiers with the proposition of optimal solution. The classification algorithm can be applied for many application to improve its accuracy such as Gender and age classification, face etc. This is just to relinquish a boost to the svm algorithm researches in the various classification fields through the different kernel functions. The proposed methodology has propounded an optimal solution on the usage of kernel functions. There have been many researches on the kernel function comparisons. Here, a better and accurate solution has been applied on dataset for male female and transgender which is new gender has been classified and has been expectant to come up with a better accuracy.

Keywords: Support vector machine · Kernel function · Classification

1 Introduction

Since 90's image reorganisation and classification studies are raising hand in every inch of momentary researches in the field of soft computing. In 1990, scientists came with new solutions like SVM and CNN. We are working on SVM kernel functions. While classifying some object researchers are using the SVM with different kernel functions [1–4, 7]. In feature classification or texture classification we are using different kernel functions for classification [13]. This research have been clearly done before [10] but no final and accurate solution has been given for a particular application. So we are going to give a basic map for what case we can use what type of kernel functions for the accuracy to be better and the time to be lesser. It will give a better practice in mobile computing. Recognising digits by Neural Network has been a long trend [14]. Support vector machine is just an assistant to it. Support vector machine is the supervised model to analyze data by a series of the classification and regression algorithms.

© Springer Nature Singapore Pte Ltd. 2019
A. K. Luhach et al. (Eds.): ICAICR 2018, CCIS 955, pp. 88–97, 2019.
https://doi.org/10.1007/978-981-13-3140-4_9

1.1 Literature Review

Lots of research papers are written on SVM for recognizing and classification with the help of the kernel functions and their comparison. Many papers have discussed on the evolution of kernel functions [2, 3]. Some have used for image classifications [7]. Some have discussed about the kernel usage [1, 4, 5, 12]. Comparison has also been done among all these kernel functions [8–11]. Some paper help to find the best choice among SVM kernels namely linear, polynomial and RBF kernels then we find to make a comparison between SVM with the absolute choice of kernel. Some study has been made out on the use of evolution and approaches in similar with SVMs. Some paper presents an a element called K tree, that is the method of Programming using genetics to find a kernel for a particular data domain. KTree is advanced and elongated version of the Genetic Kernel SVM. Some paper bring a method for support vector machine classification with help of indefinite kernels. Instead of initially minimizing non convex error function, the method finds the support vectors and a proxy kernel matrix used in solving the error. Some help the problem of adding multiple feature channels for the purpose of best image classification. The Support vector machine classifiers have been tested on several binary datasets. Many types of kernel function namely: linear, radial basis function, polynomial Kernel and sigmoid kernel are used to perform task and all four give other results. Linear kernel gives the absolute performance a framework is developed based on Support Vector Machines (SVM) for classification using polarimetric features found from multi-temporal Synthetic Aperture Radar (SAR) imageries. The present study is an experimental comparison of these machines with a advanced approach.

2 Support Vector Machine

As we discussed earlier this is a supervised model that helps in classifying and analyzing. Given a set of different data as an input it will just find out what are the various types are there and classify them in non probabilistic and binary form. It Is a path from the artificial neural network which was unable to give the same accuracy to the functions what svm performs. It follows different algorithms like support vector classification, support vector clustering, etc. Classification algorithm is solved using some functions of kernel like: Linear, Polynomial and Radial Basis function.

3 Classification

Support Vector Machine (SVM) is basically a classifying method that does the classification tasks by making hyper planes in many dimensional space that separates different class into different sectors. SVM finds both regression and classification tasks. For that variables a new variable is made instead of 0 and 1. It is then dependent on three different types of variables (A, B, C) of new kind: A:{1, 0, 0}, B:{0, 1, 0}, C:{0, 0, 1}.

Now it is of two types:

- Type 1 Classification SVM (known as C-SVM classification)
- Type 2 Classification SVM (known as nu-SVM classification).

Type 1 Classification SVM (C-SVM): This function deals with the error correcting function.

$$\frac{1}{2}w^Tw + C\sum_{i=1}^{N}\xi_i \qquad (1)$$

Where the constraints are:

$$y_i\left(w^T\phi(x_i) + b\right) \geq 1 - \xi_i \text{ and } \xi_i \geq 0, i = 1, \ldots, N \qquad (1.1)$$

where C is the holding constant, w is the coefficient of vector, b is a constant, and ξ_i represents parameters for handling data (inputs) that is hard to separate. The index i labels the N training cases. The kernel ϕ is used to transform data from the input (independent) to the feature space. C is our error determining factor. If it is large then i = error is there. To avoid over fitting, we should carefully choose the factor c.

Type 2 Classification SVM (NU-SVM): It reduces the error function.

$$\frac{1}{2}w^Tw - v\rho + \frac{1}{N}\sum_{i=1}^{N}\xi_i \qquad (2)$$

subject to the constraints:

$$y_i\left(w^T\phi(x_i) + b\right) \geq \rho - \xi_i, \xi_i \geq 0, i = 1, \ldots, N \text{ and } \rho \geq 0 \qquad (2.1)$$

REGRESSION: Here we have to estimate the dependency of functional variable x on the another one y. As usual our function here will be based on the single function f(x) plus some noise. Regression is of two types:

- Regression Type 1 (also known as epsilon-SVM regression)
- Regression Type 2 (also known as nu-SVM regression).

Regression SVM Type 1 (also known as epsilon-SVM regression):
For this one the error function is going to be:

$$\frac{1}{2}w^Tw + C\sum_{i=1}^{N}\xi_i + C\sum_{i=1}^{N}\xi_i^{\bullet} \qquad (3)$$

Where the constraints are going to be:

$$\begin{aligned}
w^T\phi(x_i) + b - y_i &\leq \varepsilon + \xi_i^{\bullet} \\
y_i - w^T\phi(x_i) - b_i &\leq \varepsilon + \xi_i \\
\xi_i, \xi_i^{\bullet} &\geq 0, i = 1, \ldots, N
\end{aligned} \qquad (3.1)$$

Regression SVM Type 2 (also known as nu-SVM regression):
Here our error function will be:

$$\frac{1}{2}w^T w - C\left(v\varepsilon + \frac{1}{N}\sum_{i=1}^{N}\left(\xi_i + \xi_i^{\bullet}\right)\right) \tag{4}$$

Constraints:

$$\begin{aligned}
(w^T\phi(x_i) + b) - y_i &\leq \varepsilon + \xi_i \\
y_i - (w^T\phi(x_i) + b_i) &\leq \varepsilon + \xi_i^{\bullet} \\
\xi_i, \xi_i^{\bullet} &\geq 0, i = 1, \ldots, N, \varepsilon \geq 0
\end{aligned} \tag{4.1}$$

KERNEL FUNCTIONS: Support vector machines are using the four types of kernel functions:

Start with the Linear function followed by Polynomial function Radial Basis Function and Sigmoid function A basic overview of all the functions is the:

$$K(X_i, X_j) = \begin{cases}
X_i \bullet X_j & \text{Linear} \\
(\gamma X_i \bullet X_j + C)^d & \text{Polynomial} \\
\exp\left(-\gamma|X_i - X_j|^2\right) & \text{RBF} \\
\tanh(\gamma X_i \bullet X_j + C) & \text{Sigmoid}
\end{cases} \tag{5}$$

Where:

$$k(X_i, X_j) = \phi(X_i) \bullet \phi(X_j)$$

i.e., the kernel function is the fot product of the input dataset mapped into high dimensional transformational plane by transformation ϕ.

Gamma is the adjustable parameter of certain kernel functions.

4   Kernel Functions

Support vector machines are using the four types of kernel functions: Linear, Polynomial, Radial Basis function and Sigmoid functions. The kernel function is the dot product of the input dataset mapped into high dimensional transformational plane by transformation ϕ. Gamma is the adjustable parameter of certain kernel functions.

5   Experimental Results

For a polynomial of nth degree we are to find for what values of n our novelty of classification will go higher with a suitable time (Fig. 1).

For a three degree polynomial. we are taking 10 inputs datasets here and expects a time taken to be around 0 secs.

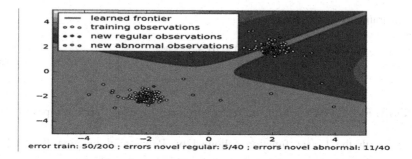

We are taking 40 inputs datasets here and expects a time taken to be around 0 seconds.

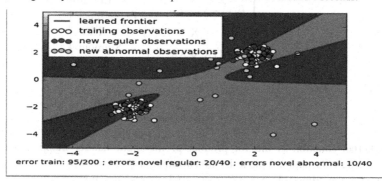

Now we are trying for a fifty degree polynomial: We are taking 10 inputs datasets here and expects a time taken to be around 0 seconds.

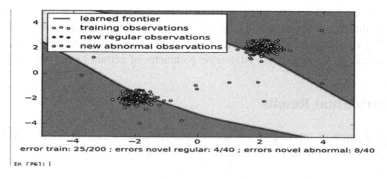

Fig. 1. Various kernel polynomial functions in a comparison form showing their experimental results along with time taken.

We are taking 20 inputs datasets here and expects a time taken to be around 0 seconds.

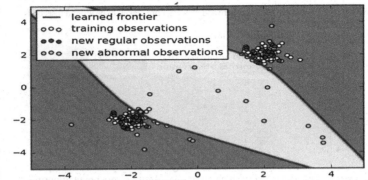

error train: 10/200 ; errors novel regular: 3/40 ; errors novel abnormal: 6/40

Overall results for input dataset size 10:

Degree	Error%	Time	Error Novel Regular	Error abnormal irregular
3	28	0	5	11
5	12.5	0	4	8
10	50.5	0	21	3

Overall results for input dataset size 20:

Degree	Error%	Time	Error Novel Regular	Error abnormal irregular
3	47	0	20	7
5	5	0	5	5
10	20.5	0	5	4

Overall results for input dataset size 40:

Degree	Error%	Time	Error Novel Regular	Error abnormal irregular
3	47.5	0	20	10
5	76	0	23	3
10	34	0	13	3

Fig. 1. (*continued*)

Comparison among Radial basis function with different input dataset size (Fig. 2):

We are taking 10 inputs datasets here and expects a time taken to be around 0 seconds.

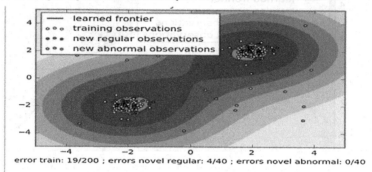

error train: 19/200 ; errors novel regular: 4/40 ; errors novel abnormal: 0/40

We are taking 20 inputs datasets here and expects a time taken to be around 0 seconds.

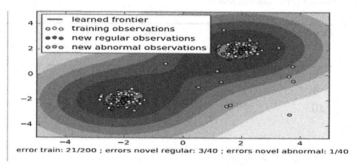

error train: 21/200 ; errors novel regular: 3/40 ; errors novel abnormal: 1/40

We are taking 40 inputs datasets here and expects a time taken to be around 0 seconds.

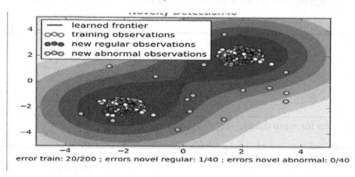

error train: 20/200 ; errors novel regular: 1/40 ; errors novel abnormal: 0/40

Degree	Error%	Time	Error Novel Regular	Error abnormal irregular
10	9.5	1	4	0
20	10.5	1	3	1
40	10	1	1	0

Fig. 2. Showing the time taken and error percentage by RBF at different dataset size

6   Experimental Interface

For a polynomial function in svm classification, higher the number of datasets or inputs and lower the degree, better the accuracy and lesser the time taken. For a radial basis function in svm classification, time taken will be greater than expectation but accuracy will be far better than polynomial function with the least degree at any cost and at any input dataset size. For a radial basis function in svm classification, lower the number of datasets or inputs, better the accuracy (Fig. 3).

Function	Error%	Time	Error Novel Regular	Error abnormal irregular
Radial basis function	9.5	1	4	0
Polynomial degree 3	47.5	0	20	10

Fig. 3. Comparing best levels of poly 3 kernel function and radial basis kernel function

The result below is retrieved from the language classification dataset. Here we get maximum precision in Linear Kernel function in and recall is also maximum there. So here we get best results in Linear Kernel function. True positives (TP) values that are positive that were correctly named by the classifier. True negatives (TN) signifies which are negative that were correctly recognized by the classifier. False positives (FP) are the negative tuples that were incorrectly authenticated as positive False negatives (FN) are the positive tuples that were mislabelled as negative (e.g., tuples of class buys computer = yes for which the classifier predicted buys computer = no) (Fig. 4).

Kernel Function	True Positive	True Negative	Precision	Recall
Linear	76	24	76	72.5
Polynomial	23	77	23	19
Radial Basis Function	80	20	80	76.5

Fig. 4. Comparing kernel functions on the basis language classifier dataset

Precision can be defined as follows:

$$\frac{TP}{TP + FP}$$

Recall is defined as:

$$\frac{TP}{TP + FN}$$

7 Conclusion

Finally in this paper we achieved a summary how the kernel functions come to play in various fields. This comparison will let the next generation writers to make a basic comparison how the kernel functions vary according to their methods. According to our experiment we found the rbf as the most active. Somewhere we got that a polynomial kernel function with lesser degree is giving a better accuracy. This will help a lot in mobile computing where time is a major fact. Many people have given the papers on these kinds of comparison of the kernel functions [8–11]. We are giving an optimal picture of how this kernel functions can be implemented in case of a polynomial or rbf method argument. But for general view we are concluding that if it's a polynomial function, lesser the degree, more the input dataset in number, less the time be taken and more accuracy will be reached but the reverse will play the role in RBF (not the condition given as degree of polynomial).

Acknowledgement. This chapter does not contain any studies with human participants or animals performed by any of the authors.

References

1. Hofmann, M.: Support vector machines—Kernels and the kernel trick. Notes, 26 2006
2. Howley, T., Madden, M.G.: The genetic evolution of kernels for support vector machine classifiers. In: 15th Irish Conference on Artificial Intelligence (2004)
3. Liu, L., Bo, S., Xing, W.: Research on Kernel Function of Support Vector Machine
4. Lin, H.-T., Lin, C.-J.: A study on sigmoid kernels for SVM and the training of non-PSD kernels by SMO-type methods. Submitt. Neural Comput. 3, 1–32 (2003)
5. Luss, R., d'Aspremont, A.: Support vector machine classification with indefinite kernels. In: Advances in Neural Information Processing Systems (2008)
6. Yekkehkhany, B., et al.: A comparison study of different kernel functions for SVM-based classification of multi-temporal polarimetry SAR data. Int. Arch. Photogramm. Remote. Sens. Spat. Inf. Sci. 40(2), 281 (2014)
7. Scholkopf, B., et al.: Comparing support vector machines with Gaussian kernels to radial basis function classifiers. IEEE Trans. Signal Process. 45(11), 2758–2765 (1997)
8. Hsu, C.-W., Lin, C.-J.: A comparison of methods for multiclass support vector machines. IEEE Trans. Neural Netw. 13(2), 415–425 (2002)

9. Camastra, F.: A SVM-based cursive character recognizer. Pattern Recogn. **40**(12), 3721–3727 (2007)
10. Platt, J.: Probabilistic outputs for support vector machines and comparisons to regularized likelihood methods. Adv. Large Margin Classif. **10**(3), 61–74 (1999)
11. Bruzzone, L., Prieto, D.F.: A technique for the selection of kernel-function parameters in RBF neural networks for classification of remote-sensing images. IEEE Trans. Geosci. Remote Sens. **37**(2), 1179–1184 (1999)
12. Cherkassky, V., Ma, Y.: Practical selection of SVM parameters and noise estimation for SVM regression. Neural Netw. **17**(1), 113–126 (2004)
13. Baudat, G., Anouar, F.: Kernel-based methods and function approximation. In: 2001 Proceedings of the International Joint Conference on Neural Networks. IJCNN 2001, vol. 2. IEEE (2001)

Big Data Analytics in *Ralstonia solanacearum* Genomics

Shivani Chandra[1(✉)], Alka Grover[1], Piyush Garg[1],
and Shalini Jauhari[2]

[1] Amity Institute of Biotechnology, Amity University Uttar Pradesh, Noida
201301, India
{schandra4,agrover}@amity.edu,
piyushgarg555@gmail.com
[2] School of Life Sciences, Starex University, Gurugram, India
shalinijauharijain@gmail.com

Abstract. *Ralstonia solanacearum* is a phyto pathogen that causes bacterial wilt disease. The pathogen is widely spread throughout the globe infecting over 200 species in about 50 plant families. It is a soil borne phyto-pathogen. This species complex consists of thousands of different strains of bacterial pathogens with a very vast range of plant hosts from banana, potato, brinjal to tomato, tobacco and olives. The strains with genetic variations have been divided into four phylotypes: phylotype I, phylotype II A and II B, phylotype III, and phylotype IV. The pathogen is extremely difficult to combat as there is no effective control method. Rapid progress in high throughput whole genome sequencing technology has contributed towards generating enormous amount of Big data. Genomics revolution has provided whole genome sequence data of several strains of *Ralstonia* and techniques from Big data analytics, contributed to remarkable progress in the field of *Ralstonia* genomics. Big data analytics is widely used in different research fields due to its efficiency and effectiveness. This paper discusses the outcomes and advantages of Big data analytics in the field of *Ralstonia* genomics.

Keywords: *Ralstonia solanacearum* · Genomics · Big data analytics

1 Introduction

The soil bacterium *Ralstonia solanacearum*, causes bacterial wilt disease to almost all the plants of family solonacae. The disease results in major economical losses in both monocot and dicot plants. Over 200 plant species ranging from shrubs, trees and annual plants are infected by this pathogen. The bacterium was previously known as *Pseudomonas solanacearum* [1]. GMI1000 strain was the first *Ralstonia solanacearum*, genome sequenced in 2001 [2]. The completion of whole genome sequence of strain GMI1000, has been a major achievement. Availability of many other complete genome sequences of this bacterium has contributed to the growth of genomic data that facilitate the researchers to study signature sequences of different strains of this bacterium. Big data in the field of genomics is represented in volume, velocity and variety [3].

© Springer Nature Singapore Pte Ltd. 2019
A. K. Luhach et al. (Eds.): ICAICR 2018, CCIS 955, pp. 98–107, 2019.
https://doi.org/10.1007/978-981-13-3140-4_10

A few years have been spent to understand the data, categorize, and sort the data. By the year 2017 a total of 19 complete genome sequences are available in the databanks (Fig. 1). Many other genomes are being sequenced. The Big data available for the *Ralstonia solanacearum* have been categorized in different forms like number of chromosomes and plasmids, number of genes, number of expressed genes, proteins etc.

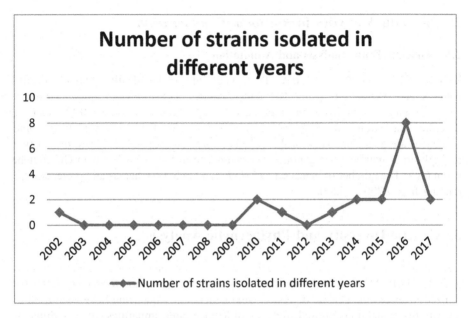

Fig. 1. *Ralstonia solanacearum* genome sequencing

1.1 Big Data on Cloud

Big data is a term that describes large amounts of data. This data is available in structured or unstructured form. A structured data is the form of data sets in which the structure is defined. It contains a schema and is organized with parameters that make it readable and easy to analyze, whereas unstructured data is the raw data which does not consist of defined schema [4]. It is very difficult to retrieve useful information from unstructured data. Volume, variety and velocity are the primary characteristics of Big data. The volume of data is the quantity of the data generated, produced or stored. The variety of data is the nature and different types of data generated, produced or stored. E. g. text, ids, images, videos, logs etc. The velocity of data is the speed at which data is generated, stored and processed [5]. In the terms of genomic data, the complete genome sequence provides the volumes. RNA sequencing, resequencing of genomic data and transcriptomics provide the variety of data and the increase in number of whole genome sequencing gives the volume. However, the challenge is to process, analyze, manage, and store the Big data [6]. Cloud computing provides services that can be utilized to analyze genomic data. It provides the programming platforms, software and infrastructure which not only analyze the data but also manages genomics data [7]. Most of the software used for analytics is an open source. One of the examples of such frame work is Hadoop. It has been used to provide infrastructure for the processing of genomic data [8]. Hadoop is the core platform of Big data. It helps to sort data in such a way that it is useful for analysis [9]. Hadoop has the capability to withstand faults in data and also scale up the data from one server to many servers [10].

2 Big Data Analytics in *Ralstonia solanacearum*

2.1 Genome Data Analysis and Annotation

Various large scale data sets have been analyzed for the identification of specific patterns and correlations using Big data analytics. For *Ralstonia solanacearum* a variety of data sets are available. First genome sequenced was GMI1000 [2]. Table 1 describes the strains of *Ralstonia solanacearum*. So far, 19 complete genome sequences are available. Most of the genomes carry one chromosome and one or two megaplasmids with average genome size ranging from 5.4 to 5.8 Mb with GC content about 66%. The number of genes ranged from 4700 to 5900 whereas and proteins were ranging from 4700 to 5200.

3 Genetic Diversity and Phylogenetic Analysis

Genetic diversity of *Ralstonia* has been assessed using many molecular markers such as PCR-RFLP, AFLP, 16S rRNA sequencing analysis. Also, bioinformatics tools were utilized to access the genetic diversity. Next generation sequencing have been used to identify functional domains and study the differences and similarities between different strains. Pathogen associated molecular patterns were also generated using bioinformatics tools and variations were studied amongst different strains and host.

Phylogenetic analysis of *Ralstonia sp.* have demonstrated that the species complex contains four phylotypes. These phylotypes correspond to geographic origin. The phylotype I strains originated in Asia, phylotype II strains came from North America and South America, phylotype III strains originated in Africa, and phylotype IV strains are from the Indonesian archipelago. Software such as Maximum Unique Matches index (MUMi) were used to calculate genomc distances and a new phylogenetic tree has been generated for *Ralstonia solanacearum* species complex.

3.1 Comparative Genomics

Since *Ralstonia solanacearum* has got unusual wide host range, researchers have also used comparative genomics to study the differences in genomes of different strains. Comparison of the genomes was done at whole genome sequence level to compare amongst different strains of same phylotypes or different strains from different phylotypes. The Big data obtained from lining up the sequences of different genomes have also been utilized to identify signature sequences which are specific to either candidate disease resistance genes, virulence genes or host specificity.

Table 1. Genome sequence of *Ralstonia solanacearum* strains (https://www.ncbi.nlm.nih.gov/genome/genomes/490).

S.No.	*Ralstonia solanacearum* Strain	Size (MB)	GC%	Replicons	Genes	Protein	Reference
1	GM11000	5.81092	66.96	Chromosome:NC_003295 PlasmidpGMI1lOOOmp: NC_003 296.1	5208	4984	Salanoubat et al. [2]
2	P082	5.43026	66.64	Chromosome:NC_017574.1 Plasmid megaplasmid: NC_017575.1	4867	4638	Xu et al. [26]
3	PSI07	5.60562	66.29	Chromosome:NC_014311 Plasmid mpPSI07:NC_014310.1	4972	4749	Remenant et al. [17]
4	UY031	5.41168	66.57	Chromosome:NZ_CP012687.1 Plasmid unnamed:NZ_CPO 12688.1	4797	4548	Guariachi-Sousa et al. [27]
5	KACC10722	5.46326	66.43	Chromosome:NZ_CP0l4702.1 Plasmid unnamed: NZ_CP014703.1	4897	4704	Song et al. (2016)
6	UW163	5.59624	66.57	Chromosome:NZ_CP012939.1 Plasmid pUW163a: N_CP012940.1 Plasmid pUW163a:N_CPO12941.1 Plasmid pUW163b: N_CP012942.1	5012	4759	Ailloud et al. [13]
7	IBSBF1503	5.53025	66.66	Chromosome:NZ_CP01294.3 Plasmid unnamed: NZ_CP012944.1	4903	4659	Ailloud et al. [13]
8	YC40-M	5.75213	66.70	Chromosome:NZ_CP015850.1 Plasmid unnamed:NZ CP015851.1	5142	4892	Li et al. (2016)
9	KACC10709	5.60824	66.04	Chromosome:NZ_CP016904.1 Plasmid unnamed: NZ_CP016905.1	5011	4725	Kim et al. (2016)
10	0E1-1	5.76297	66.87	Chromosome:NZ_CP009764.1 Plasmid unnamed: NZ_CP009763.1	5095	4870	Ohnishi et al. (2015)
11	FJAT-1458	6.0599	66.77	Chromosome:NZ_CP016554.1 Plasmid unnamed:016555.1	5442	5166	Chen et al. (2016)
12	EP1	6.04297	66.70	Chromosome:NZ_CP015115.1 Plasmid unnamed: NZ_CP015116.1	5400	5144	Li et al. (2016)
13	FJAT-91	5.87409	66.87	Chromosome:NZ_CP016612.1 Plasmid unnamed: NZ_CP016613.1	5227	4955	Chen et al. (2016)
14	SEPPX05	5.99693	66.87	Chromosome:NZ_CP021448.1 Plasmid unnamed: NZ_CP021449.1	5503	5163	Hua et al. (2017)
15	CQPS-1	5.89344	66.84	Chromosome:NZ_CP016914.1 Plasmid NZ_CP016915.1	5243	4808	Liu et al. [28]

(*continued*)

Table 1. (*continued*)

S.No.	Ralstonia solanacearum Strain	Size (MB)	GC%	Replicons	Genes	Protein	Reference
16	FQY_4	5.80525	66.79	Chromosome:NC_020799.1 Plasmidmegaplasmid: NC_021745.1	5192	4972	Cao et al. [29]
17	CMR15	5.59037	66.80	Chromosome:NC_017559.1 Plasmid CMR15_mp: NC_017589.1 Plasmid pRSC35: NC_017558.1	5041	4814	Remenant et al. [17]
18	RS-10-244	5.68831	66.85	Chromosome:NZ_CM002755.1 plasmid unnamed1 NZ_CM002756.1	5119	4731	Ramesh et al. [12]
19	RS-09-161	5.75792	66.69	Chromosome:NZ_CM002757.1 Plasmid unnamed1 NZ_CM002758.1	5143	4812	Ramesh et al. [12]

3.2   Identification of Specific Genes

With the availability of Big data on genome sequences of various strains of *Ralstonia solanacearum*, scientists have deciphered the host pathogen relationship. Comparative genomics approach and phylogenetic analyses have identified genes that are specific to virulence, host specificity and disease resistance. Sequence knowledge of these genes has enabled researchers to isolate and validate genes that play important roles. Also, the precise location of the genes has been successfully utilized to clone the genes, and study the host pathogen relationship. Researchers are using the Big data to design primers and amplify genes of interest from a variety of strains. The similarities and difference in the strains are elucidating genes that are specific for a given strain or climate. For example, candidate genes for host specificity; T3E were identified in different but closely related *Ralstonia* ecotypes [13]. Comparative genome analysis of gene expression data of *Ralstonia solanacearum* have revealed that one gene *hrpB* controls multiple virulence pathways by acting as regulatory switch [14]. Furthermore, pan genomic microarray approach was acquired by researchers to analyze the genomes of bacteria. This approach was useful to understand the evolution of this genome with the knowledge of genes gained and lost during the course of evolution [15]. Comparative genomics was also used to analyze three different genomes of *Ralstonia solanacearum*: GMI1000, Po82, and CMR15. The study revealed that the genomes were similar at nucleotide level however the arrangement of the genes was different in each strain [16].

4 Results and Discussion

Whole genome sequence and annotation of *Ralstonia solanacearum* are available from different parts of the world including America, Africa, Caribben [11]. Recently, isolates from India have also been sequenced [12]. The Big data available at NCBI website with reference to genes and proteins of this pathogen is summarized in Table 2.

Table 2. Big data available at NCBI website.

Genes		
EST	68,113	Expressed sequence tag sequences
Gene	87,473	Collected information about gene loci
GEODataSets	240	Functional genomics studies
GEO Profiles	157	Gene expression and molecular abundance profiles
HomoloGene	1	Homologous gene sets for selected organisms
PopSet	610	Sequence sets from phylogenetic and population studies
UniGene	8	Clusters of expressed transcripts
Proteins		
Conserved domains	89	Conserved protein domains
Protein		Protein sequences
Protein clusters	7,900	Sequence similarity-based protein clusters
Structure	201	Experimentally-determined biomolecular structures

Big data analytics of all these genomes revealed that all the strains of *Ralstonia solanacearum* consists of a few common genes designated as core genome. The other genes are unique to specific strains and are designated as dispensable genome. This part of the genome carries genes present in most of the strains but not in all strains (Fig. 2).

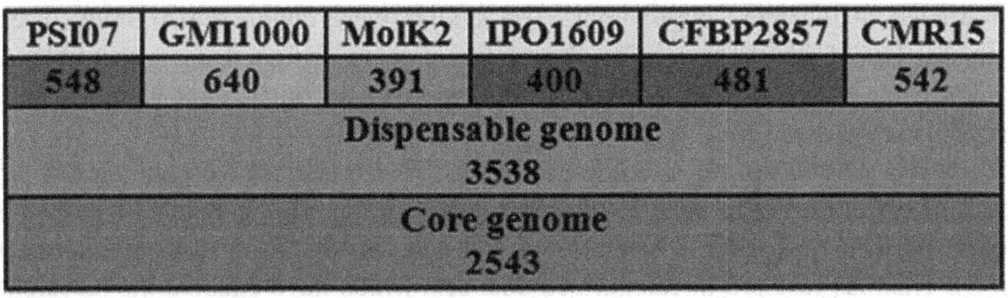

PSI07	GMI1000	MolK2	IPO1609	CFBP2857	CMR15
548	640	391	400	481	542
Dispensable genome 3538					
Core genome 2543					

Fig. 2. Genome arrangement of *Ralstonia solanacearum* strains.

Comparison of genome sequences clearly indicated that the species complex have a common pathology. The genes that are unique to strains are host specific and are present only that specific strain. These unique genes are involved either in determining the virulence or host specificity or adaptation of the hosts. It also explains the evolutionary divergence of the strains. These unique genes are determined by using algorithm that sorts homolog predictions. These genes are considered to be involved in adaptation in different environments or unique hosts. This implies that the genes involved are related but have been evolved to specific mechanisms [13, 17, 18]. Transcriptome analysis, RNA sequencing, genome resequencing and differential Gene expression of a few strains of *Ralstonia Solanacearum* have also been conducted to study the pathogen. The study suggested that the phylogenetically close pathogens were significantly different. Gene expression was more strain specific than host specific especially with respect to virulence related genes [13]. Transcriptome analysis of GMI1000 strains was conducted to investigate the role of specific genes that governs pathogenicity i.e. HrpB genes, by using constructs of microarray. The microarray results showed that 50 *hrpB* genes were down-regulated whereas 143 *hrpB* genes were up-regulated. These results enhance the understanding of the mechanism by which specific strains are working [19]. In another research it was reported that each strain of *Ralstonia* has a unique effector repertoire. This repertoire encodes for both strain-specific effector variants and these variations are shared among the strains [19]. As mentioned above, most of the *Ralstonia* genomes contain one chromosome and a few megaplasmids. Megaplasmids were also studied separately to understand their role. The analysis of the genes present in the plasmids inferred that most of these genes produce phytohormones. Also, a number of genes that were involved in pathogenicity and host specificity were located on these plasmids. These plasmids also contain genes that provide resistance to bactericides such as UV irradiation, antibiotics, and copper. This suggests that the plasmids of this pathogen also carry genes that are important for the survival of the pathogen [20]. The avirulence (avr) and virulence (vir) genes are involved in pathogenicity and host specificity respectively [21, 22].

It was further confirmed by genome wide analysis of gene expression data that hrp gene is involved in controlling multiple virulence pathways by acting as regulatory switch [14]. Genetic diversity of different strains has been assessed and the pathogen has been divided into four phylotypes.

Further, based on genome analyses of different strains the *Ralstonia solanacearum* species complex was categorized into three species [23, 24]. Genetic diversity has also been studied in localized populations. The studies were conducted to study disease resistance. Based on these studies the cultivars were assigned as susceptible and resistant to the disease. Also, markers were developed in other plant varieties on the basis of these studies [23–25].

Ralstonia solanacearum is complex species. Researchers have generated a large amount of data in order to analyze this pathogen. The big data generated by scientists all over the world has been sorted, stored and analyzed by using hadoop framework (Fig. 3). This has resulted in categorized data sets which have enabled the researchers to pin point their research. The import and export facility has expedited the analysis of big data available. Thus big data analytic techniques have played a major role in *Ralstonia* genomics.

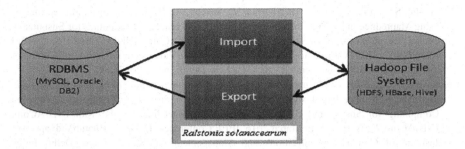

Fig. 3. Hadoop framework for *Ralstonia solanacearum* big data

5   Conclusion

Advances in sequencing techniques have generated unprecedented amount of data. This Big data available for *Ralstonia solanacearum* have proven to be useful in deciphering the species complex at different levels. The genome, proteome and transcriptome analyses have enabled the scientists to elucidate methods to combat this pathogen. Big data analytics has provided new tools such as Hadoop in sorting the data and unearth the hidden information in desired format. This suggests that cloud based computational biology and Big data analytics has a great potential in revolutionalizing *Ralstonia solanacearum* genomics.

References

1. Boucher, C., Genin, S.: The Ralstonia solanacearum-plant interaction. In: Talbot, N.J. (ed.) Annual Plant Reviews, Plant Pathogen Interactions. Wiley (2009)
2. Salanoubat, M., et al.: Genome sequence of the plant pathogen Ralstonia solanacearum. Nature **415**(6871), 497–502 (2002)
3. Chand, M., Shakya, C., Saggu, G.S., Saha, D., Shreshtha, I.K., Saxena, A.: Analysis of big data using apache spark. In: 2017 4th International Conference on Computing for Sustainable Global Development, Proceedings of the 11th INDIACom, INDIACom-2016, 1st–3rd March 2017, IEEE Conference ID 40353. BharatiVidyapeeth's Institute of Computer Applications and Management (BVICAM), New Delhi, India (2017)
4. Saxena, A., Kaushik, N., Kaushik, N.: Implementing and analyzing big data techniques with spring framework in Java & J2EE. In: Second International Conference on Information and Communication Technology for Competitive Strategies (ICTCS). ACM Digital Library (2016)
5. Yesugade, K., Bangre, V., Sinha, S., Kak, S., Saxena, A.: Analyzing human behaviour using data analytics in booking a type hotel. In: 2017 4th International Conference on Computing for Sustainable Global Development, Proceedings of the 11th INDIACom, INDIACom-2016, 1st–3rd March 2017, IEEE Conference ID 40353. BharatiVidyapeeth's Institute of Computer Applications and Management (BVICAM), New Delhi, India (2017)

6. Sendre, S., Singh, S., Anand, L., Sharma, V., Saxena, A.: Decimation of duplicated images using Mapreduce in bigdata. In: 4th International Conference on Computing for Sustainable Global Development, Proceedings of the 11th INDIACom, INDIACom-2016, 1st–3rd March 2017, IEEE Conference ID 40353 2017. BharatiVidyapeeth's Institute of Computer Applications and Management (BVICAM), New Delhi, India (2017)
7. Saxena, A., Kaushik, N., Kaushik, N., Dwivedi, A.: Implementation of cloud computing and big data with Java based web application. In: 2016 3rd International Conference on Computing for Sustainable Global Development, Proceedings of the 10th INDIACom, INDIACom-2016, 16th–18th March 2016, IEEE Conference ID 37465. BharatiVidyapeeth's Institute of Computer Applications and Management (BVICAM), New Delhi, India, pp. 3043–3047 (2016)
8. Chhawchharia, A., Saxena, A.: Execution of big data using map reduce tecnhique and HQL. In: 2017 4th International Conference on Computing for Sustainable Global Development, Proceedings of the 11th INDIACom, INDIACom-2016, 1st–3rd March 2017, IEEE Conference ID 40353. BharatiVidyapeeth's Institute of Computer Applications and Management (BVICAM), New Delhi, India (2017)
9. Jain, S., Saxena, A.: Integration of spring in Hadoop for data processing. In: 2017 4th International Conference on Computing for Sustainable Global Development, Proceedings of the 11th INDIACom, INDIACom-2016, 1st–3rd March 2017, IEEE Conference ID 40353. BharatiVidyapeeth's Institute of Computer Applications and Management (BVICAM), New Delhi, India (2017)
10. Jain, S., Saxena, A.: analysis of hadoop and mapreduce tectonics through hive big data. Int. J. Control. Theory Appl. **9**(14), 3811–3911 (2016)
11. Peeters, N., Carrère, S., Anisimova, M., Plener, L., Cazalé, A.C., Genin, S.: Repertoire, unified nomenclature and evolution of the type III effector gene set in the Ralstonia solanacearum species complex. BMC Genom. **14**, 859 (2013)
12. Ramesh, R., et al.: Genome sequencing of Ralstonia solanacearum Biovar 3, Phylotype I, Strains Rs-09-161 and Rs-10-244 Isolated from eggplant and Chili in India. Genome Announc **2**(3), e00323–14 (2014)
13. Ailloud, F., Lowe, T.M., Robene, I., Cruveiller, S., Allen, C., Prior, P.: In planta comparative transcriptomics of host-adapted strains of Ralstonia solanacearum. PeerJ **4**, e1549 (2016)
14. Occhialini, A., Cunnac, S., Reymond, N., Genin, S., Boucher, C.: Genome-wide analysis of gene expression in Ralstonia solanacearum reveals that the hrpB gene acts as a regulatory switch controlling multiple virulence pathways. MPMI **18**(9), 938–949 (2005)
15. Lefeuvre, P., Cellier, G., Remenant, B., Chiroleu, F., Prior, P.: Constraints on genome dynamics revealed from gene distribution among the *Ralstonia solanacearum* species. PlosOne (2013). https://doi.org/10.1371/journal.pone.0063155
16. Chandra, S., Grover, A.: Analysis of Ralstonia solanacearum genomes: GMI1000, Po82, and CMR15 using comparative genomics approach. In: 2017 - 4th International Conference on Computing for Sustainable Global Development, Proceedings of the 11th INDIACom, INDIACom-2017, 01st–03rd March 2017, IEEE Conference ID 40353. Bharati Vidyapeeth's Institute of Computer Applications and Management (BVICAM), New Delhi, India (2017)
17. Remenant, B., et al.: Genomes of three tomato pathogens within the Ralstonia solanacearum species complex reveal significant evolutionary divergence. BMC Genom. **11**, 379 (2010)
18. Guidot, A., Prior, P., Schoenfeld, J., Carrere, S., Genin, S., Boucher, C.: Genomic structure and phylogeny of the plant pathogen Ralstonia solanacearum inferred from gene distribution analysis. J. Bacteriol. **189**(2), 377–387 (2007)
19. Sun, Y., et al.: Genome sequencing and analysis of Ralstonia solanacearum phylotype I strains FJAT-91, FJAT-452 and FJAT-462 isolated from tomato, eggplant, and chili pepper in China. Stand. Genomic Sci. **12**, 29 (2017)

20. Vivian, A., Murillo, J., Jackson, R.W.: The roles of plasmids in phytopathogenic bacteria: mobile arsenals? Microbiology **147**, 763–780 (2001)
21. Vivian, A., Gibbon, M.J.: Avirulence genes in plant pathogenic bacteria: signals or weapons? Microbiology **143**, 693–704 (1997)
22. Vivian, A., Arnold, D.L.: Bacterial effector genes and their role in host-pathogen interactions. J. Plant Pathol **82**, 163–178 (2000)
23. Grover, A., et al.: Genotypic diversity in a localized population of Ralstonia solanacearum as revealed by random amplified polymorphic DNA markers. J. Appl. Microbiol. **101**(4), 789–806 (2006)
24. Dutta, P., Rahman, B.: Varietal screening of tomato against bacterial wilt disease under subtropical humid climate of Tripura. Int. J. Farm Sci. **2**(2), 40–43 (2012)
25. Reddy, A.C., Vekant, S., Singh, T.H., Awath, C., Reddy, K.M., Reddy, D.C.L.: Isolation, characterization and evolution of NBS-LRR encoding disease-resistance gene analogs in eggplant against bacterial wilt. Eur. J. Plant Pathol. **143**(3), 417–426 (2015)
26. Xu, J., et al.: The complete genome sequence of plant pathogen Ralstonia solanacearum strain Po82. J. Bacteriol., JB-05384 (2011)
27. Guarischi-Sousa, R., et al.: Complete genome sequence of the potato pathogen Ralstonia solanacearum UY031. Stand. Genomic Sci. **11**(1), 7 (2016)
28. Liu, Y., et al.: Genome sequencing of Ralstonia solanacearum CQPS-1, a phylotype I strain collected from a highland area with continuous cropping of tobacco. Front. Microbiol. **8**, 974 (2017)
29. Cao, Y., et al.: Genome sequencing of Ralstonia solanacearum FQY_4, isolated from a bacterial wilt nursery used for breeding crop resistance. Genome Announc. **1**(3), e00125-13 (2013)

A Comparative Fuzzy Cluster Analysis of the Binder's Performance Grades Using Fuzzy Equivalence Relation via Different Distance Measures

Rajesh Kumar Chandrawat, Rakesh Kumar[✉], Varinda Makkar,
Manisha Yadav, and Pratibha Kumari

Lovely Professional University, Punjab, India
{Rajesh.16786,rakesh.19437}@lpu.co.in

Abstract. The aim of this paper is to classify the performance grades of binders for NCHRP 90-07 using fuzzy equivalence clustering via Minkowski, Mahalanobis, Cosine, Chebychev and Correlation distance function. The performances of binders were graded in terms of high specific and equal stiffness temperature at three different parameters. The five distance functions namely Minskowski ($w = 2$), Mahalonobis, Cosine, Chebychev and Correlation are successfully applied in the clustering methodology to achieve a better separation analysis. The clusters are discovered by all five distances and distinguished for suitable value of membership grade. We also include a theoretical comparison between the clustering performances by these distances. The Mahalonobis distance function trialed first time in the equivalence fuzzy clustering methodology and accomplished the desirable objectives. The core effectuations of Mahalonobis and Chebychev distance over other four distances on the clustering performance of binders are investigated.

Keywords: Fuzzy equivalence class clustering
Binders high specific temperature · Distance function

1 Introduction

Clustering is a data analysis method which is used regularly in the strategy formulation, study of market and business system planning. Partition of commodities is a conventional issue in the inventory control and management. In most industries, there are different types of materials and components of machine or other apparatus to be managed for achieving desired goal. In order to enrich the efficiency of material management, an expert idea is to sort different materials into groups. However, different enterprises have different requirements in this area. Hence, the precision-based cluster analysis may not be practical. Furthermore, a clustering method based on fuzzy equivalence relation can comfortably tackle the separation analysis under fuzzy environment. The conventional clustering is aimed to assign each data point to only one cluster. But the fuzzy clustering assigns different degree of satisfaction to each level where the membership of a level is shared among various clusters. In this paper we are

A. K. Luhach et al. (Eds.): ICAICR 2018, CCIS 955, pp. 108–118, 2019.
https://doi.org/10.1007/978-981-13-3140-4_11

proposing the fuzzy equivalence class clustering using Minkowski, Mahalanobis, Cosine, Chebychev and Correlation distance function on the performance grading of different binders used in Turner–Fairbank Highway Research Center Polymer Research Program [19]. It was observed by Shenoy in his research that the super pave specification parameter $|G*|/\left(\frac{1}{Sin\delta}\right)$ is not tolerable in classification polymer modified binders for high temperature performance grading of paving asphalts. It was a matter of concern to subtilize this parameter to gain more consciousness in the pavement performance and also detect other latent parameters that may better relate the rutting resistance. The refined super pave specification parameter, namely, $|G*|/\left(1 - \frac{1}{tan\delta.Sin\delta}\right)$ has the highest merit for possible use. It is a viable alternative for getting the high temperature specification, such that it becomes more sensitive to field performance. Owing to the variations in the phase angle δ, the parameter $|G*|/(1 - \left(\frac{1}{tan\delta.sin\delta}\right)$ can easily attain its efficiency as compared to the original super pave specification parameter. Another alternative would be to first define an equal stiffness temperature $(T_e °C)$, when the complex shear modulus ($|G*|$) takes a specific value of 50 kPa. This takes care of the rheological contribution coming from one portion of the term $|G*|/\left[1 - \frac{1}{(tan\delta.Sin\delta)}\right]$. The result in terms of high specification temperature $\left(T_{TH}^\circ C\right)$ being defined as $(T_e °C)/\left[1 - \frac{1}{(tan\delta.Sin\delta)}\right]$ and it is more meaningful to achieve eminent high specification temperature. To get the better discrimination between the performances of bindersat different membership grades with specification parameter $|G*|/\left(\frac{1}{.sin\delta}\right)$, $|G*|/(1 - \left(\frac{1}{tan\delta.sin\delta}\right)$ and $\left(T_e^\circ C\right)/\left[1 - \frac{1}{(tan\delta.Sin\delta)}\right]$, the fuzzy equivalence class clustering is proposed. Cluster analysis is one of the leading approaches to acknowledge the patterns. In order to get better classification of objects, the idea of fuzzy clustering was represented by many researchers. In this direction, they made significant contributions in the development of making a decision in existence of fuzziness, incomplete information. The first fuzzy clustering approach was initiated by Bellman et al. [1] and Ruspini [2] then Dunn [3] explained the Well-Separated Clusters and Optimal Fuzzy Partitions. Tamura et al. [4] figure out an n-step procedure using max-min fuzzy compositions (max-min similarity relation) and achieved a multi-level hierarchical clustering. Now fuzzy clustering has been extensively examined and practiced in multifarious areas by Bezdek et al. [5], Bezdek [6], Aldenderfer et al. [7], Trauwaert et al. [8], and Yang et al. [9–11]. Groenen [12] used Minskowski distance function to get fuzzy cluster analysis. Yang et al. [13] concentrated on Cluster analysis based on fuzzy relations and a clustering algorithm is created for the max-t similarity relation matrix. Then three critical max-t (max-min, max-prod and max-Δ) compositions are compared. Liang et al. [14] determined the best number of cluster using a cluster validity index by taking suitable λ cut value. At first, the trapezoidal fuzzy numbers is defined based on subject's attributes rating. The distance between two trapezoidal fuzzy numbers is computed subsequently to obtain the compatibility relation then the categorization of objects was done by fuzzy equivalence relation. Then Recently, Gustafson et al. [15], Fu et al. [17] and Kumam et al. [18] concentrated on fuzzy clustering analysis based on equivalence class and illustrated the desirable cluster. Bataineh et al. [16] compared the performances of fuzzy C-mean clustering algorithm and subtractive clustering algorithm according to their capabilities. The aim of this paper is to classify the binder's performances using fuzzy equivalence clustering via Minkowski Cosine, Chebychev, Correlation and a new (Mahalanobis) distance function. The reliability and adequacy of the Mahalonobis distance on the clustering performance of Binders is examined over Minkowski and other distance functions.

2 Clustering Analysis Method

2.1 Mathematical Preliminaries

In this paper, some primal attributes of fuzzy cluster analysis are reviewed. First, we recapitulate the basics of fuzzy sets and fuzzy relations.

Definition 1. Let X be an universal space then a fuzzy set on X, is defined by $\tilde{A} = \{(x, \mu_{\tilde{A}}(x)) | x \in X$ and $\mu_{\tilde{A}}(x) \rightarrow [0, 1]\}$ where $\mu_{\tilde{A}}(x)$ is the membership function or grade defined in X which gets values in the range [0, 1].

Definition 2. Let $\tilde{A}$ and $\tilde{B}$ are two fuzzy sets, defined on universal spaces X and Y then a fuzzy relation on $(X \times Y)$, is defined by $\tilde{R} = \{[(x, y), \mu_{\tilde{R}}(x, y)] | (x, y) \in X \times Y\}$ where

$$\mu_{\tilde{R}}(x, y) \leq \min\{\mu_{\tilde{A}}(x), \ \mu_{\tilde{B}}(x)\}$$

Definition 3. Let $\tilde{R}_1$ on $(X \times Y)$ and $\tilde{R}_2$ on $(Y \times Z)$ be two fuzzy relations then the max-min composition $\tilde{R}_1 \circ \tilde{R}_2$ is defined by $\tilde{R}_1 \circ \tilde{R}_2 = \left\{ \left[(x, z), \max_{y \in Y} \{ \min\{ \mu_{\tilde{R}}(x, y), \right. \right.$ $\mu_{\tilde{R}}(y, z)\}\}] | x \in X, y \in Y, z \in Z\}$.

Definition 4. Let $\tilde{R}$ be a fuzzy relations on $(X \times X)$ then

(1) $\tilde{R}$ is called reflexive if $\mu_{\tilde{R}}(x, x) = 1, \forall x \in X$
(2) $\tilde{R}$ is called ε-reflexive if $\mu_{\tilde{R}}(x, x) \geq \varepsilon, \forall x \in X$
(3) $\tilde{R}$ is called weakly reflexive if $\mu_{\tilde{R}}(x, y) \leq \mu_{\tilde{R}}(x, x)$ and $\mu_{\tilde{R}}(y, x) \leq \mu_{\tilde{R}}(x, x) \forall x \in X$.

Definition 5. A fuzzy relation $\tilde{R}$ is called symmetric if $\mu_{\tilde{R}}(x, y) = \mu_{\tilde{R}}(y, x) \forall x, y \in X$.

Definition 6. A fuzzy relation $\tilde{R}$ is called transitive if $\mu_{\tilde{R}}(x, z) \geq \max_{y \in Y} \{ \min\{ \mu_{\tilde{R}}(x, y), \mu_{\tilde{R}}(y, z)\}\}; \forall x, y, z \in X$.

Definition 7. A fuzzy relation $\tilde{R}$ on X is said to be compatible on X if it is reflexive and symmetric.

Definition 8. A fuzzy relation $\tilde{R}$ on X is said to be transitive on X if it is reflexive, symmetric and transitive.

2.2 The Construction of a Fuzzy Compatible and Equivalence Relation

To obtain the Fuzzy cluster analysis through equivalence class, the distances between the crisp data sets is required here we are proposing the Mahalonobis, Chebychev, Minkowski, Cosine and Correlation metric distance respectively on crisp data. Let X be an universal space and X_{ik} and $X_{jk} \in X$ then the Minkowski metric distance on crisp data is defined as

$$D_{w(i,j)_k} = \left[\sum_{k=1}^{n} |X_{ik} - X_{jk}|^w\right]^{\frac{1}{w}} \tag{1}$$

The Minkowski's measure holds for $w \in [1, \infty)$. For the special case of $w = 1$, it becomes Hamming distance, and when $w = 2$, it is Euclidean distance.

The Mahalonobis distance is defined as

$$M_{d(i,j)_k} = \left\{\left[(X_i - X_j)^T V^{-1} (X_i - X_j)\right]\right\}^{1/2} \tag{2}$$

where V is the sample covariance matrix. If the covariance matrix V is the identity matrix, then the $M_{d(i,j)}$ reduce to the Euclidean distance. If V is diagonal, then the determined distance measure is called a normalized Euclidean distance defined as $M_{d(i,j)_k} = \sqrt{\frac{\sum_{k=1}^{n} |X_{ik} - X_{jk}|^2}{V}}$.

The Cosine distance is defined as

$$D_{cos(i,j)_k} = 1 - \frac{\sum_{k=1}^{n} X_{ik}.X_{jk}}{\sqrt{\sum_{k=1}^{n} (X_{ik})^2}.\sqrt{\sum_{k=1}^{n} (X_{jk})^2}} \tag{3}$$

The Correlation distance is defined as

$$D_{corr(i,j)_k} = 1 - \frac{\sum_{k=1}^{n} (X_{ik} - \overline{X_{ik}}).(X_{jk} - \overline{X_{jk}})}{\sqrt{\sum_{k=1}^{n} (X_{ik} - \overline{X_{ik}})^2}.\sqrt{\sum_{k=1}^{n} (X_{jk} - \overline{X_{jk}}))^2}} \tag{4}$$

Where $\overline{X_{ik}} = \frac{1}{n}\sum_{k=1}^{n} X_{ik}$ and $\overline{X_{jk}} = \frac{1}{n}\sum_{k=1}^{n} X_{jk}$.

And the Chebychev distance is defined as

$$D_{max(i,j)} = \max_k |X_{ik} - X_{jk}| \tag{5}$$

According to the distances, the fuzzy compatible relation matrix is yielded. For Minkowski class $(w = 2)$ the relation matrix is

$$\tilde{R}(X_i, X_j) = 1 - \delta\left[\sum_{k=1}^{n} |X_{ik} - X_{jk}|^2\right]^{\frac{1}{2}}$$

$$\text{Where } \delta = \left\{max\left[\sum_{k=1}^{n} |X_{ik} - X_{jk}|^2\right]^{\frac{1}{2}}.\right\}^{-1} \tag{6}$$

And the Fuzzy compatible relation matrix for Mahalonobis distance is generated by

$$\tilde{R}(X_i, X_j) = 1 - \lambda \left\{ \sqrt{[(X_i - X_j)^T S^{-1}(X_i - X_j)]} \right\}.$$

$$\text{Where } \lambda = \left\{ max \sqrt{[(X_i - X_j)^T S^{-1}(X_i - X_j)]} \right\}^{-1} \tag{7}$$

The Fuzzy compatible relation matrix for Cosine distance is

$$\tilde{R}(X_i, X_j) = 1 - \gamma \left\{ 1 - \frac{\sum_{k=1}^{n} X_{ik} . X_{jk}}{\sqrt{\sum_{k=1}^{n} (X_{ik})^2} . \sqrt{\sum_{k=1}^{n} (X_{jk})^2}} \right\}$$

$$\text{Where } \gamma = \left\{ max \left\{ 1 - \frac{\sum_{k=1}^{n} X_{ik} . X_{jk}}{\sqrt{\sum_{k=1}^{n} (X_{ik})^2} . \sqrt{\sum_{k=1}^{n} (X_{jk})^2}} \right\} \right\}^{-1} \tag{8}$$

The Fuzzy compatible relation matrix for Correlation distance is

$$\tilde{R}(X_i, X_j) = 1 - \rho \left\{ 1 - \frac{\sum_{k=1}^{n} (X_{ik} - \overline{X_{ik}}) . (X_{jk} - \overline{X_{jk}})}{\sqrt{\sum_{k=1}^{n} (X_{ik} - \overline{X_{ik}})^2} . \sqrt{\sum_{k=1}^{n} (X_{jk} - \overline{X_{jk}}))^2}} \right\}$$

$$\text{Where } \rho = \left\{ max \left\{ 1 - \frac{\sum_{k=1}^{n} (X_{ik} - \overline{X_{ik}}) . (X_{jk} - \overline{X_{jk}})}{\sqrt{\sum_{k=1}^{n} (X_{ik} - \overline{X_{ik}})^2} . \sqrt{\sum_{k=1}^{n} (X_{jk} - \overline{X_{jk}}))^2}} \right\} \right\}^{-1} \tag{9}$$

The Fuzzy compatible relation matrix for Chebychev distance is

$$\tilde{R}(X_i, X_j) = 1 - \sigma \{ max_k |X_{ik} - X_{jk}| \} \text{ Where } \sigma = \{ max \{ max_k |X_{ik} - X_{jk}| \} \}^{-1} \tag{10}$$

After the fuzzy compatible relation matrix, the Fuzzy transitive closures were constructed for each matrix. If $\tilde{R} \circ \tilde{R} \subseteq \tilde{R}$ then $\tilde{R} \circ \tilde{R} = \tilde{R}_T^2$ is said to be transitive closure of $\tilde{R}$ for $k = 1$. If $\tilde{R} \circ \tilde{R} \not\subseteq \tilde{R}$ then construct $\tilde{R}^2 \circ \tilde{R}^2$. If $\tilde{R}^2 \circ \tilde{R}^2 \subseteq \tilde{R}^2$ then $\tilde{R}_T^4$ is said to be transitive closure of $\tilde{R}^2$ for $k = 2$. If there are n-elements in the universal space then the fuzzy transitive closure is achieved until $2^k \geq n - 1$.

The α-cut relation can be obtained from a transitive fuzzy relation by taking the pairs which have membership degrees no less than α.

$$\tilde{R}_\alpha = \{ [(x, y), \mu_{\tilde{R}}(x, y) \geq \alpha] | (x, y) \, \epsilon \, X \times Y \}. \tag{11}$$

3   Experimental Data

The experimental data used was taken from the research [19] under NCHRP (National Co-operative Highway Research Program) and TFHRC (Turner–Fairbank Highway Research Center).

4   Result

Using descried methodology, the performance grades of binders were targeted for Mahalonobis metric, Minkowski (w = 2) metric, Chebychev matric, Cosine matric and Correlation metric distances. The fuzzy compatible relation matrices and transitive closure are derived for each distance (Figs. 1, 2, 3, 4 and 5).

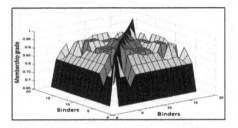

Fig. 1. Graphical representation of results achieved by Minskowski distance.

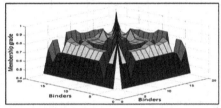

Fig. 2. Graphical representation of results achieved by Mahalonobis distance.

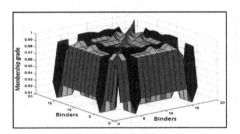

Fig. 3. Graphical representation of results achieved by Cosine distance.

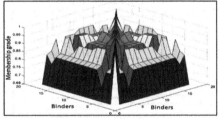

Fig. 4. Graphical representation of results achieved by Chebychev distance.

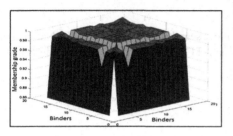

Fig. 5. Graphical representation of results achieved by Correlation distance.

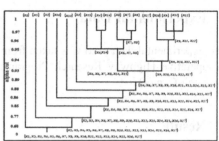

Fig. 6. Clustering tree by Minkowski distance

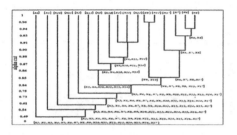

Fig. 7. Clustering tree by Mahalonobis distance.

Fig. 8. Clustering tree by Correlation distance.

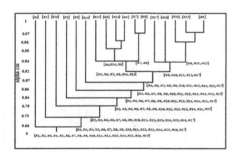

Fig. 9. Clustering tree by Chebychev distance.

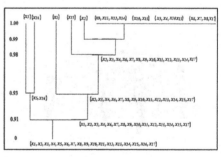

Fig. 10. Clustering tree by Cosine distance.

5   Analysis

All the binders are separated according to their performances at different level of α by using Minkowski, Mahalonobis, Cosine, Correlation and Chebychev distance differently. It is observed by Fig. 6 that Binder x_1 = flux (B6224) is detached first at

$\alpha = 0.68$, then Polymer-modified binder x_5 = Elvaloy No. 1 (B6228) is separated at $\alpha = 0.77$ and after that x_2 = unmodified base (B6225) separated at $\alpha = 0.85$. Similarly $x_{16}, x_{13}\ldots, x_{12}$ are clustered successively at different high degree of α. The desired clusters are also identified from clustering tree for suitable value of α for example if $\alpha = 0.90$, then the clusters are: $\{\{x_1\}, \{x_5\}, \{x_2\}, \{x_{16}\}, \{x_{13}\}, \{x_3\}, \{x_4, x_6, x_7, x_8, x_{14}, x_{15}\}, \{x_9, x_{10}, x_{11}, x_{12}, x_{17}\}\}$.

The total number of clusters can be obtained from clustering tree by Minkowski metric distance for different alpha and they are described as: If $\alpha \in [00.68]$ then N(c) = 1, If $\alpha \in (0.680.77]$ then N(c) = 2. Similarly if $\alpha \in (0.770.85]$, N(c) = 3. If $\alpha \in (0.850.86]$, N(c) = 4.

If $\alpha \in (0.860.88]$, N(c) = 5. If $\alpha \in (0.880.89]$ N(c) = 6. If $\alpha \in (0.890.93]$, N(c) = 7.

If $\alpha \in (0.930.94]$, N(c) = 8. If $\alpha \in (0.940.95]$, N(c) = 9. If $\alpha \in (0.950.96]$, N(c) = 11.

If $\alpha \in (0.960.97]$, N(c) = 13. If $\alpha \in (0.971]$ N(c) = 17.

According to the Clustering tree by Mahalonobis metric distances, it is observed by Fig. 7 that the binder x_1 = flux (B6224) is detached first at $\alpha = 0.49$, then Polymer-modified binder x_5 = Elvaloy No. 1 (B6228) is separated at $\alpha = 0.54$. After that x_{16} = B6252 is separated at $\alpha = 0.64$. similarly $x_{15}, x_2\ldots, x_8$ are clustered successively at different high degree of α. The desired clusters are also identified for suitable value of α. If the $\alpha = 0.90$, then the binders are separated differently as compared to Minkowski and other distances and the clusters are: $\{\{x_1\}, \{x_5\}, \{x_{16}\}, \{x_{15}\}, \{x_2\}, \{x_{13}\}, \{x_3\}, \{x_{10}\}\{x_4, x_{11}, x_{14}\}, \{x_9, x_{12}\}, \{x_6, x_7, x_8\}\}$.

The total number of clusters can be obtained from clustering tree by Mahalonobis metric distance or different alpha and they are described as: If $\alpha \in [00.49]$ then N(c) = 1. If $\alpha \in (0.490.54]$ then N(c) = 2. Similarly If $\alpha \in (0.540.61]$, N(c) = 3. If $\alpha \in (0.610.73]$, N(c) = 4.

If $\alpha \in (0.730.75]$, N(c) = 5. If $\alpha \in (0.750.84]$, N(c) = 6. If $\alpha \in (0.840.85]$, N(c) = 7. If $\alpha \in (0.850.86]$, N(c) = 8. If $\alpha \in (0.860.87]$, N(c) = 9. If $\alpha \in (0.870.88]$, N(c) = 10. If $\alpha \in (0.880.90]$, N(c) = 11. If $\alpha \in (0.900.91]$, N(c) = 12. If $\alpha \in (0.910.93]$, N(c) = 14. If $\alpha \in (0.930.94]$, N(c) = 15. If $\alpha \in (0.940.96]$, N(c) = 16. If $\alpha \in (0.961]$, N(c) = 17.

According to the Clustering tree by Correlation distances it is observed by Fig. 8 that Binder x_1 = flux (B6224) is detached first at $\alpha = 0.87$, then Polymer-modified binder x_5 = Elvaloy No. 1 (B6228) is separated at $\alpha = 0.96$. Similarly remaining binders are clustered into two groups after $\alpha = 0.99$. The desired clusters are also identified from clustering tree for suitable value of α for example if $\alpha = 0.90$, then the clusters are: $\{\{x_1\}, \{x_2, x_3, x_4, x_5, x_6, x_7, x_8, x_9, x_{10}, x_{11}, x_{12}, x_{13}, x_{14}, x_{15}, x_{16}, x_{17}\}\}$.

The total number of clusters can be obtained from clustering tree by Correlation distance for different alpha and they are described as: If $\alpha \in [00.87]$ then N(c) = 1, If $\alpha \in (0.870.96]$ then N(c) = 2. Similarly if $\alpha \in (0.960.99]$, N(c) = 3. If $\alpha \in (0.99 \ 1]$, N(c) = 4.

According to the Clustering tree by Chebychev distances. It is observed by Fig. 9 that Binder x_1 = flux (B6224) is detached first at $\alpha = 0.66$, then Polymer-modified binder x_5 = Elvaloy No. 1 (B6228) is separated at $\alpha = 0.73$ and after that x_{16} = polymer-modified Ethylene–Styrene–Inter polymer No. 2 (B6252) is separated at $\alpha = 0.79$ Similarly $x_2, x_3 \ldots, x_9$ are clustered successively at different high degree of α. The binders are separated differently as compared to the Mahalonobis Cosine and Correlation distances but the separation is quite similar to the Minskowski metric distance. The desired clusters are also identified from clustering tree for suitable value of α for example if $\alpha = 0.90$, then the clusters are:$\{\{x_1\}, \{x_5\}, \{x_{16}\}, \{x_2\}, \{x_3\}, \{x_{13}\}, \{x_4, x_6, x_7, x_8, x_9, x_{10}, x_{11}, x_{12}, x_{14}, x_{15}, x_{17}\}\}$.

The total number of clusters can be obtained from clustering tree by Chebychev distance for different alpha and they are described as: If $\alpha \in [00.66]$ then N(c) = 1, If $\alpha \in (0.660.73]$ then N(c) = 2. Similarly if $\alpha \in (0.73\ 0.79]$, N(c) = 3. If $\alpha \in (0.79\ 0.84]$, N(c) = 4.

If $\alpha \in (0.84\ 0.86]$ N(c) = 5. If $\alpha \in (0.86\ 0.87]$ N(c) = 6. If $\alpha \in (0.87\ 0.92]$, N(c) = 7.

If $\alpha \in (0.92\ 0.94]$, N(c) = 8. If $\alpha \in (0.94\ 0.95]$, N(c) = 12. If $\alpha \in (0.95\ 0.96]$, N(c) = 13.

If $\alpha \in (0.96\ 0.97]$, N(c) = 15. If $\alpha \in (0.97\ 1]$ N(c) = 17.

According to the Clustering tree by Cosine distances it is observed by Fig. 10 that no binder is separated till $\alpha = 0.91$ and after $\alpha = 0.91$ two binders x_5 = Elvaloy No.1 (B6228) and x_{16} = polymer-modified Ethylene–Styrene–Inter polymer No. 2 (B6252) are detached together as a one cluster. After the $\alpha = 0.93$ binder x_5, x_{16} and binder x_1 = flux (B6224) are detached separately. Similarly remaining binders are clustered successively at different high degree of α. The desired clusters are also identified from clustering tree for suitable value of α.

The total number of clusters can be obtained from clustering tree for different alpha and they are described as: If $\alpha \in [00.91]$ then N(c) = 1, If $\alpha \in (0.91\ 0.93]$ then N(c) = 2. Similarly if $\alpha \in (0.93\ 0.98]$, N(c) = 4. If $\alpha \in (0.980.99]$, N(c) = 5. If $\alpha \in (0.99\ 1)$, N(c) = 6. If $\alpha = 1$ N(c) = 9.

The following graph shows the number of clusters achieved by Mahalonobis, Chebychev, Minskowski ($w = 2$), Cosine, and Correlation distance with respect to different membership grade. The all distances illustrate the same number of cluster (N(c) = 1) till membership grade $\alpha = 0.49$. After the $\alpha = 0.49$, there exits significant difference in the number of cluster by all five distance functions. The Mahalonobis distance quantize more number of cluster than other four distances function for each $\alpha \in (0.49\ 0.97]$. The clustering performance achieved by Chebychev distance function is quite better than Minskowski ($w = 2$) distance and substantially finer than Cosine and Correlation distance function. The Mahalonobis, Chebychev, and Minskowski ($w = 2$) demonstrate the same number of cluster (N(c) = 17) for each $\alpha \in (0.97\ 1]$. Overall the Mahalonobis distance shows the viable feasibility as compared to Chebychev, Minskowski ($w = 2$), Cosine, and Correlation distance function in terms of desired number of clusters (Fig. 11).

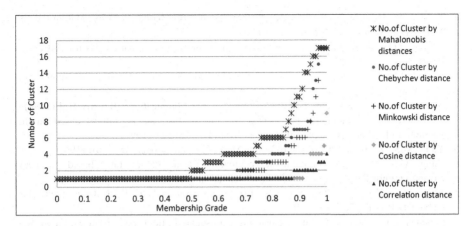

Fig. 11. The comparison of clustering by Mahalonobis, Chebychev, Minkowski, Cosine and Correlation distances.

6   Conclusion

In this paper a Comparative fuzzy equivalence class clustering of binders based on their performance, is proposed. The performances of binders were graded in terms of high specific temperature at three different parameters. Five distance functions namely Minskowski (w = 2), Mahalonobis, Cosine, Chebychev and Correlation are applied in the separation methodology and it is a first attempt where the Mahalonobis distance function is used for equivalence fuzzy clustering. The fuzzy compatible relation matrices and transitive closures are derived for each distance function. Then the separate cluster analysis is done for Minskowski, Malonobis, Cosine, Chebychev and Correlation distance function and the desired clusters are identified for suitable value of membership grade. It was observed that the overall clustering performance of binders by Mahalonobis distance function is better than the performance by Minskowski and other distance function. The overall Performance achieved by Chebychev distance function is quite better than Minskowski $(w = 2)$ distance and substantially finer than Cosine and Correlation distance function. Mahalonobis distance function produce more number of cluster at most of the α-level. The separation stages by Mahalonobis distance are also extensively better than other distance. So the fuzzy cluster analysis by Mahalonobis distance function can provide effective grip in the separation analysis and strategy formulation.

References

1. Bellman, R., Kalaba, R., Zadeh, L.A.: Abstraction and pattern classification. J. Math. Anal. Appl. **2**, 581–585 (1966)
2. Ruspini, E.H.: A new approach to clustering. Inform. Control **15**, 22–32 (1969)
3. Dunn, J.C.: Well-separated clusters and the optimal fuzzy partition. J. Cybern. **4**, 95–104 (1974)

4. Tamura, S., Higuchi, S., Tanaka, K.: Pattern classification based on fuzzy relations. IEEE Trans. Syst. Man Cybern. **1**, 61–66 (1978)
5. Bezdek, J.C., Harris, J.D.: Fuzzy partitions and relations: an axiomatic basis for clustering. Fuzzy Sets Syst. **1**, 111–127 (1978)
6. Bezdek, J.C.: Pattern Recognition with Fuzzy Objective Function Algorithms. Plenum Press, New York (1981)
7. Aldenderfer, M., Blashfield, R.: Cluster Analysis. Sage Publications, Beverly Hill (1984)
8. Trauwaert, E., Kaufman, L., Rousseeuw, P.: Fuzzy clustering algorithms based on the maximum likelihood principle. Fuzzy Sets Syst. **42**, 213–227 (1991)
9. Yang, M.S.: A survey of fuzzy clustering. Math. Comput. Model. **18**, 1–16 (1993)
10. Yang, M.S., Su, C.F.: On parameter estimation for normal mixtures based on fuzzy clustering algorithms. Fuzzy Sets Syst. **68**, 13–28 (1994)
11. Yang, M.S., Ko, C.H.: On cluster-wise fuzzy regression analysis. IEEE Trans. Syst. Man Cybernet.–Part B **27**, 1–13 (1997)
12. Groenen, P.J.F., Jajuga, K.: Fuzzy clustering with squared Minkowski distances. Fuzzy Sets Syst. **120**(2), 227–237 (2001)
13. Yang, M.-S., Shih, H.-M.: Cluster analysis based on fuzzy relations. Fuzzy Sets Syst. **120**, 197–212 (2001)
14. Liang, G.-S., Chou, T.-Y., Han, T.-C.: Cluster analysis based on fuzzy equivalence relation. Eur. J. Oper. Res. **166**, 160–171 (2005)
15. Gustafson, N., Pera, M.S., Ng, Y.-K.: Generating fuzzy equivalence classes on RSS news articles for retrieving correlated information. In: Gervasi, O., Murgante, B., Laganà, A., Taniar, D., Mun, Y., Gavrilova, Marina L. (eds.) ICCSA 2008. LNCS, vol. 5073, pp. 232–247. Springer, Heidelberg (2008). https://doi.org/10.1007/978-3-540-69848-7_20
16. Bataineh, K.M., Naji, M., Saqer, M.: A comparison study between various fuzzy clustering algorithms. Jordan J. Mech. Ind. Eng. (JJMIE) **5**(4), 335–343 (2011). ISSN 1995-6665
17. Fu, P., Gu, X., Wang, Q.: Fuzzy clustering analysis of goods classification based on equivalence relation in inventory management. Int. J. Adv. Comput. Technol. (IJACT) **5** (2013)
18. Kumam, W., Pongpullponsak, A.: Fuzzy logic and fuzzy clustering for medical service value model. In: International Multi Conference of Engineers and Computer Scientists, IMECS 2013, Hong Kong, 13–15 March 2013, vol. II (2013)
19. Shenoy, A.: The high temperature performance grading of asphalts through a specification criterion that could capture field performance. J. Transp. Eng. **130**(1), 132–137 (2004)

Enhancing the Efficiency of Decision Tree C4.5 Using Average Hybrid Entropy

Poonam Rani, Kamaldeep Kaur[(✉)], and Ranjit Kaur

Lovely Professional University, Phagwara, Punjab, India
ranipoonam405@gmail.com, Kaurdeep230@gmail.com,
reetbansal09@gmail.com

Abstract. Getting the efficient and effective decision tree is important, because of its numerous applications in mining and machine learning. Different modifications have been done on the splitting criteria in the decision tree. Different entropy concepts are introduced by different scholars. Shannon's entropy, Renyi's entropy, and Tsalli's entropy are those entropies which can affect the overall efficiency of decision tree C4.5. This research implemented new average hybrid entropy that has combined statistical properties of Reyni's and Tsalli's entropy, Average Hybrid entropy is the average between the maxima of Reyni's and Tsalli's entropy. The overall idea is, applying Average Hybrid entropy on the basis of instances and integrates those instances after pruning. This makes the pruning process easy and gives better results. Research is done on three standard datasets Credit-g, Diabetes, and Glass dataset taken from UCI repository; it is proved that the average hybrid entropy is having the more efficient results.

Keywords: Shannon's entropy · Reyni's entropy · Tsalli's entropy
Data mining · Machine learning · C4.5 · Decision tree · J48 classifier

1 Introduction

A decision tree is the supervised learning algorithm. Although it is one of the earlier algorithms introduced in machine learning and in data mining process, still it is an important and in-demand area of research. The reason behind it is that it provides better results and it is flexible in nature. It is also easy to understand. Information gain and entropy are the two main execution parts concerned with C4.5 decision tree algorithm. The overall thought is to identify the unspecified or hidden instances using the known rules of formation for the instances. The key plan is to split the tree for getting the resultant leaves which will act like our instances.

In a decision tree, the key inspiration is to quantify the homogeneity for the given dataset. Here to find the information gain of instances through which one can split the dataset accordingly. The algorithm starts in a way by splitting the nodes on the basis of their information gain and the node with highest information gain is selected as parent node or root node of the tree. And the base of calculating the info gain is entropy calculation. Information gain is mainly recorded between entropy before and after the split. Further, the maximum gain point becomes the split value and recursively this

© Springer Nature Singapore Pte Ltd. 2019
A. K. Luhach et al. (Eds.): ICAICR 2018, CCIS 955, pp. 119–134, 2019.
https://doi.org/10.1007/978-981-13-3140-4_12

function will go on till the minimum leaf child occur or the maximum gain point arises. By the end, we can get the highest purity homogeneity, group.

There are different entropies already introduced like Shannon's entropy, Renyi's entropy, and Tsalli's entropy in decision tree [1]. Shannon's entropy is the earlier one and also useful for the research purpose as well. In [2] the researchers have used Shannon's entropy to know the influence of the landslide causing, they also mentioned the vulnerability. This is default entropy as well. But according to [3] refinement is required in Shannon's entropy for getting the better results. But if do the comparative study on the basis of split criteria [4, 5] Reyni's entropy and Tsalli's entropy gives better efficiency results. But the overall thing is choosing the best approach for the maximum efficiency. For this evaluation, can combine the best statistical properties of the Reyni's and Tsalli's we can generate the average hybrid entropy [6]. This average hybrid entropy contains one more divergence variable named Dp which provides more accurate results [7–11].

Zhong [12] have published a paper on the analysis of cases based on the decision tree. The authors have been proposed an improved version of the decision tree classifier on the bases of Taylor method and entropy. The entropy is working as the backbone of the decision tree. So, they have picked this entropy concept and enhance the performance of the ID3 decision tree. Gajowniczek et al. [1] published a paper on Comparison of a decision tree with Reyni and Tsalli's entropy applied for imbalanced churn dataset. In this paper, they modified the decision tree C4.5. They have experimented the α parameter. By changing the α parameter in the algorithm and apply it on the given dataset they analysis the efficiency difference. At the end they have shown the better results of using the Reyni and Tsalli's entropy as compared to the standard Shannon's entropy. Wang et al. [5] presents a paper on unifying the split criteria of decision trees using Tsalli's entropy. They have used the Tsalli's entropy in splitting criteria of the decision tree and introduced new algorithm. They also elaborate the concept of the variable α. Results are clearly shown that the newly proposed algorithm is giving better results as compared to the standard entropy that is Shannon's entropy Mehmet et al. [6] On Statistical Properties of Jizba-Arimitsu Hybrid Entropy. In this paper, the scholar has provided the statistical properties of the Hybrid entropy. They have actually combined the properties of Renyi's and Tsalli's entropy. In this entropy important factor is $\frac{q+1}{2}$, which defines that yes this is average hybrid entropy. This is called average because this provides average between Renyi's and Tsalli's entropy. They have concluded that this entropy can be defined and used in mathematics, physical and statistical application. This will provide the connection bond because of fisher metric and will give the more precise evaluation of the model parameter [9].

Further Paper is divided into section organization which contains rest of the detail about this implementation; Sect. 2 contains the materials and methods Sect. 3 presents the improved decision tree. Section 4 describes the algorithm for the average hybrid entropy. Section 5 presents the experiments and a result Sect. 6 provides the conclusion part.

2   Materials and Methods

2.1   Data Sets

To evaluate and identify the implementation progress results, three datasets are used namely Credit-g, Diabetes and Glass datasets. These datasets are extracted from the UCI repository. UCI is the machine learning repository. All the datasets available in the UCI repository are standard datasets. All three datasets are experimented using the four different entropies. And these data sets are evaluated and compared on various parameters such as accuracy, true positive rate, false positive rate, precision and recall and ROC for all entropies.

2.2   Entropy

It is known as the sum of the probability of each class label times the log probability of that respective label [13]. In decision tree, we need to calculate entropy two times. Firstly we have to calculate it for the individual attribute, and then calculate it for the combined attributes.

2.3   Gain Ratio

In decision tree learning, information gain ratio is a ratio of information gain to the intrinsic information. It is used to reduce a bias towards multi-valued attributes by taking the number and size of branches into account when choosing an attribute.

2.4   Shannon's Entropy

A simple formula to calculate Shannon's entropy is given below-

$$\mathbf{E}(S) = \sum_{i=1}^{c} -\mathbf{pi} \log_2 \mathbf{pi} \tag{1}$$

Here s describes the support whether the set will further classify as yes class or no class. $\sum_{i=1}^{c} -pi \log_2 pi$ will provide the summation of all the values of the set. Further logarithm base 2 will be implemented and minus the one set's value from another [14].

To calculate the gain ratio the formula is-

$$\text{Gain}(T, X) = \text{Entropy}(T) - \text{Entropy}(T, X) \tag{2}$$

The main fundamental of the decision tree is to identify the attribute having the highest information gain, which will further act as the root node. This is intuition gets from the homogeny of dataset and identifies the best class label at the end. Here T, X are two different attributes from which the attribute having highest value will be considered as root attribute [14].

These two are Shannon-Boltzmann-Gibbs entropy based formulas. But as we see from [15] there are other methods to use these entropies in an efficient manner.

2.5 Renyi's Entropy

The formula to calculate Renyi's entropy-

$$H\alpha(X) = \frac{1}{1-\alpha} \log\left(\sum_{i=1}^{n} p_i^\alpha\right) \tag{3}$$

Here the variable X is a generates the all possible outcomes 1, 2, ..., n. Further corresponding probability pi will be calculated for each i = 1, ..., n. logarithm base 2 will be called for all the calculation. If the probabilities are for all i = 1, ..., n, then all the Renyi's entropies of the distribution are equivalent [16].

2.6 Tsalli's Entropy

Formula to calculate Tsalli's entropy-

$$S_q(p_i) = \frac{k}{q-1} \cdot \left(1 - \sum_{i=1}^{} p_i^q\right) \tag{4}$$

This is same as the Renyi's entropy but here the factor q is introduced. Here q is the real number. This is a helpful factor to calculate the entropy in a different manner [15].

2.7 Average Hybrid Entropy

Entropy is a concept used for the different domains. This is the concept of physics uses for the thermodynamics, statistics and for informational concepts. In decision tree classification entropy leads to finding the best class label. In [6] Jizba and Arimitsu introduced new hybrid entropy. This entropy contains the statistical properties of Reyni's and Tsalli's entropy. Mainly the continuous divergence and continuous average entropy are working differently for measuring from the Reyni's and Tsalli's entropy. In [5] it is clearly mentioned all different entropies and statistical properties of the average hybrid entropy as well. Recently various scholars introducing the hybrid entropy concept, but there are some properties missing as well. In [6] all properties are clearly defined for the hybrid entropy. The average entropy is also known as average hybrid entropy because it is an average between Reyni's and Tsali's entropy [7]. The average hybrid entropy is defined as:

$$A_q(p) = D\frac{q+1}{2}(p). \tag{5}$$

Now, discussion of the different interesting properties has to encounter. First of all, this is clearly described for the parameter q > 0, which is properly matched with Renyi's and Tsalli's entropy. One more thing is that in this entropy fisher metric is used which is also similar to the Reyni's and Tsallis entropy. If the value of q becomes 1 then it will similar to the Shannon entropy. For Reyni's entropy q is defined as $q \leq 1$, similarly in the average hybrid entropy q work for $q \leq 1$.

In actual scenario the important factor is q + 1/2. This provides average between the Reyni's and Tsalli's entropy [8]. We can examine from here

$$x\frac{q+1}{2}y = x+y+\left(1-\frac{q+1}{2}\right)xy = x+y+\frac{1-q}{2}xy = 2\left(\frac{x}{2}q\frac{y}{2}\right). \tag{6}$$

Here the order of q is non- extensive. According to Kolmogov-Nagumo function the average hybrid entropy defined as [9].

$$ln\frac{q+1}{2}(x) = \frac{x\,1-(q+1)/2-1}{1-\frac{q+1}{2}} = 2\frac{x(1-q/2-1)}{1-q} = 2\,lnq(\sqrt{x}) \tag{7}$$

In deformed logarithm, average hybrid entropy can also be defined [10].

$$\begin{aligned}\ln qn \ge \ln q + 12n \ge \ln n \text{ for } q \le 1,\\ \ln qn \le \ln q + 12n \le \ln n \text{ for } q \ge 1\end{aligned} \tag{8}$$

After defining these forms it is clear that average hybrid entropy lies between maxima of Tsalli's and Reyni's entropy.

3 Improved Decision Tree

There are different classification algorithms but decision tree provides more accurate results and fewer complexes as well. Hereby combing the Reyni's and Tsalli's entropy, we generated the Average Hybrid Entropy [7]. This is defined as:

$$A_q(p) = D\frac{q+1}{2}(p) \tag{9}$$

Here D is same as α defined in Renyi's and Tsalli's entropy. Here the parameter α is used to adjust the measure depending on the shape of probability distributions [1]. Q is also the same variable as defined by the sales entropy [5]. The actual change is going to be done using the equation $\frac{q+1}{2}$. This defines the Average maxima between Renyi's entropy and Tsalli's entropy.

Pruning is a very important step in decision tree distribution. This helps the decision tree to reduce the overfitting and increase the efficiency. This reduces the complexity of the decision tree and provides the ability to classify instances [17].

Data mining is interdisciplinary field, where the statistical and algorithmic combination can be useful to get the effective outcomes. Entropy is the concept of physics and Average Hybrid Entropy is derived from the statistical properties of the Renyi's and Tsalli's entropy. The modification has been done on the entropy formula. Fisher matrix and Cramer Rao bond depicts that the maxima (calculated in Average Hybrid Entropy) will definitely affect the final calculated results [9, 10], because Cramer Rao bond works on removing the biasness of the decision tree classifier algorithm. Fisher matrix is again directly linked with the respective outcomes. This is totally depends on the maximum likelihood estimates, calculated by the fisher matrix. This estimation will be reducing the error rate using the Average Hybrid Entropy. By choosing the combined statistical properties new entropy concept has been introduced and further implementation describes that all the factors mentioned here are perfectly satisfied and affect the overall results. Further the flow chart for the Average Hybrid Entropy classifier algorithm is describe, the process of the implementation is inspiration for getting the appropriate results for the research purpose.

Figure 1 describes the flow chart for the Average Hybrid Entropy decision tree algorithm.

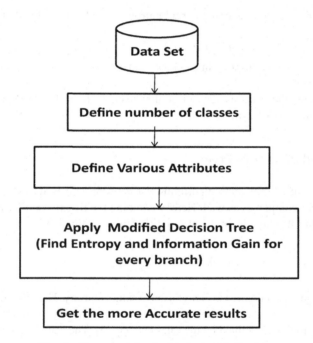

Fig. 1. Flow chart for the implemented algorithm

For implemented improved decision tree the concept of Average Hybrid Entropy is used. In Weka, the C4.5 algorithm is available in J48 classifier Tree. This paper describes the algorithm along with implementation. For achieving the increased efficiency, implemented work used pruning, inside pruning there are instances, these instances also affect the efficiency. So, until decision tree reaches to its leaf node iteration should be there to obtain the average hybrid methodology formula and calculate the overall efficiency.

4 Algorithm for Average Hybrid Entropy

To implement the algorithm Weka tool has been used and for the coding purpose Net Beans IDE platform also involved here. In Weka algorithm, the C4.5 source code is available as J48 classification algorithm. For checking the results datasets also used from the Weka. Overall results clearly specify that the proposed work having best accuracy results. In this paper compare the Average Hybrid Entropy with the Shannon's, Renyi's and Tsalli's entropy as well. By using these practical tools finally get the best accuracy with fewer complexities.

```
// Pruning distribution for decision tree ( training instances, data, leaf_node, instances,
//son_nodes, local_instances, local_split_model)
training instances =data;
if(!leaf_node)
        // call local instances and split data
     for (each instance<son_node.lenght)
        // call distribution for local instances
Else
             // check whether there are more instances at the  leaf
             // call hybrid entropy prune the decision tree

        if ( instances empty)
                  //stop pruning the further instances
        end if
end
else
end if
```

5 Experimental Results

This research implemented the average hybrid entropy in the decision tree and modified the decision tree for obtaining the information gain of nodes, After implementing the Average Hybrid Entropy results are clearly showing that newly implemented hybrid entropy is having more accurate results as comparing the Shannon's, Reyni's and Tsalli's entropy. For achieving the output graph three datasets are used, named as Credit-g, Diabetes and Glass dataset. Respective results for each dataset are 72.60%, 75%, 68.22% these are the providing better accuracy results. There are some factors on which these entropies have to be compared that are TP Rate (true positive rate), FP Rate (false positive rate), Precision and ROC Area. 10 fold cross validation is also used for evaluation of the accuracy factor. Graph depicts that Average Hybrid entropy contains better results. The reason is maxima factor of Renyi's and Tsalli's entropy.

Accuracy is overall efficient output results which provide more purity in the dataset results. This will further help in better data mining process. TP is true positive rate; the instances which are actually positive and accurate for the final results. FP is the false positive rate; the instances which are incorrect and involved to produce the final results. Precision is another factor involved in the final accuracy results. It is something which gives the exactness of the accuracy. The area under ROC curve (AUC) defines the overall accuracy.

Further the table values and their respective line graphs representing the accuracy results and showing that the implemented decision tree having average hybrid entropy gives the better accuracy results.

Table 1. Values for the respective entropy for credit-g data set

Credit-g dataset evaluation					
C4.5	Accuracy	TP rate	FP rate	Precision	ROC area
Shannon's entropy	70.50%	0.705	0.475	0.687	0.639
Reyni's entropy	71.40%	0.714	0.45	0.7	0.662
Tsallis entropy	71%	0.71	0.46	0.695	0.637
Average hybrid entropy	72.60%	0.726	0.453	0.709	0.673

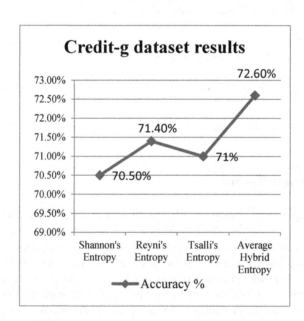

Fig. 2. Line graph representation for credit dataset

Table 1 clearly depicts the overall evolution of decision tree after applying the 4 different entropies on the Credit-g dataset. The affecting factors are overall Accuracy (how many correctly classified instances after the execution), TP rate (True Positive rate depicts the instances that are labeled in the correct class.), FP rate (label classes which are not involved in the correct instances but it should be), Precision (all the relevant instances) and ROC. ROC is also known as AUR which means the area under ROC curve. This value is directly proportional to the accuracy factor. The respective values are given in Table 1, which clearly presents that Average Hybrid Entropy gives the best results as a statically values that are; Accuracy is 72.60%, TP rate is 0.726, FP rate is 0.453, precision values is 0.709 and ROC Area value is 0.673. Here Fig. 2 presents the graph view for the Credit-g dataset. This clearly shows the differences in the graphical view. 72.60% is the highest accuracy value after applying the Average hybrid Entropy.

Table 2. Values for the respective entropy for Diabetes dataset

Diabetes dataset evaluation					
C4.5	Accuracy	TP rate	FP rate	Precision	ROC area
Shannon's entropy	73.83%	0.738	0.327	0.735	0.751
Renyi's entropy	74.35%	0.743	0.321	0.74	0.758
Tsalli's entropy	74.48%	0.745	0.331	0.74	0.74
Average hybrid entropy	**75%**	**0.75**	**0.323**	**0.745**	**0.754**

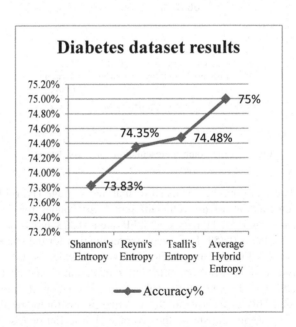

Fig. 3. Line graph representation for Diabetes dataset

In Table 2 all the factors which are involved in the overall results and evaluation purpose have encountered and their respective values are mentioned as well. This table draws all factor values for the different entropies implemented on the Diabetes dataset.

Table 3. Values for the respective entropy for glass data set

Glass dataset evaluation					
C4.5	Accuracy	TP rate	FP rate	Precision	ROC area
Shannon's entropy	66.82%	0.668	0.13	0.67	0.807
Reyni's entropy	67.76%	0.678	0.125	0.677	0.824
Tsallis entropy	67.76%	0.678	0.125	0.678	0.823
Average hybrid entropy	**68.22%**	**0.682**	**0.124**	**0.682**	**0.834**

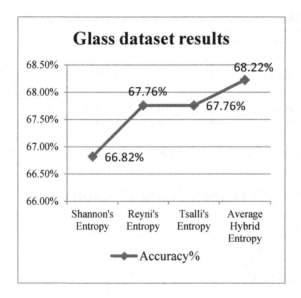

Fig. 4. Line graph representation for glass dataset

After every single evaluation, the results show that the Average Hybrid Entropy gives the best results on this dataset as well. Different factor values for Average Hybrid Entropy are; Accuracy is 75%, TP rate is 0.75, FP rate is 0.323, precision value is 0.745 and AUC or ROC value is 0.754. Line graph representation for the Diabetes dataset is given in Fig. 3. In this Fig, accuracy factor is involved which is 75% is the highest value for the Average Hybrid Entropy after implementation on the Diabetes dataset.

Similarly, Table 3 is showing all the values after evaluation of different entropies on the Glass dataset. This table shows all the affecting factors for the results same as the previous datasets. Consequently shows the Average Hybrid Entropy is giving the best results that are; Accuracy is 68.22%, TP rate is 0.682, FP rate is 0.124, the Precision value is 0.682 and ROC value is 0.834. Figure 4 is drawn after evaluating the factor accuracy. This Line graph representation showing the clear enhancements of the results. 68.22% is the highest accuracy factor measured by involving Average Hybrid Entropy on the Glass dataset.

Table 4. Results of the implemented work on the basis TP rate, FP rate, precision, ROC area factors

C4.5	Dataset	Accuracy	TP Rate	FP Rate	Precision	ROC Area
Shannon's Entropy		70.50%	0.705	0.475	0.687	0.639
Renyi's Entropy		71.40%	0.714	0.45	0.7	0.662
Tsalli's Entropy	Credit-g	71%	0.71	0.46	0.695	0.637
Average Hybrid Entropy		**72.60%**	**0.726**	**0.453**	**0.709**	**0.673**
Shannon's Entropy		73.83%	0.738	0.327	0.735	0.751
Renyi's Entropy		74.35%	0.743	0.321	0.74	0.758
Tsalli's Entropy	Diabetes	74.48%	0.745	0.331	0.74	0.74
Average Hybrid Entropy		**75%**	**0.75**	**0.323**	**0.745**	**0.754**
Shannon's Entropy		66.82%	0.668	0.13	0.67	0.807
Renyi's Entropy		67.76%	0.678	0.125	0.677	0.824
Tsalli's Entropy	Glass	67.76%	0.678	0.125	0.678	0.823
Average Hybrid Entropy		**68.22%**	**0.682**	**0.124**	**0.682**	**0.834**

Further Table 4 is showing the overall comparisons of the decision tree after implementing Shannon's entropy, Renyi's entropy, Tsalli's entropy and Average Hybrid Entropy. There are three datasets availed from the UCI repository. UCI repository provides the standard datasets for the research scholars for doing the different analysis. Three datasets are involved for the analysis for the complete results and evaluations. These datasets are Credit-g dataset, Diabetes dataset, and Glass dataset. After all the implementation based on the main factors (Accuracy, TP rate, FP rate, Precision, and ROC) consequently the Average Hybrid Entropy is giving the best results for all the datasets. On the bases of accuracy factor the Credit-g dataset shows 72.60% accuracy, Diabetes dataset presents 75% accuracy and on the Glass dataset, the Average Hybris Entropy gives the 68.22% accuracy. These are showing that this is one of the entropy which can affect the overall decision tree efficiency.

Here Fig. 5 shows the bar graph representation for the comparison of all the datasets on the different mentioned entropies. This is showing the enhancement of the decision tree algorithm's efficiency is achieved by implementing the Average Hybrid Entropy. Accuracy % factor is used for showing the graph results. Three datasets are involved in the for the evaluation purpose their respective results for the different entropies are shown in Fig. 5. To see the progress of the Diabetes dataset the highest accuracy value is 75% that is using the Average Hybrid Entropy. For the second dataset named Credit-g, the highest accuracy has been achieved using the Average Hybrid Entropy that is 72.60%, last but not least for the third dataset Glass the accuracy value is 68.2%. Here we can clearly see the enhancement of efficieny in decision tree algorithm using Average Hybrid Entropy. For the overall evaluation this is clearly showing that the Average Hybrid Entropy imprving more than 2% as compared to the standard entropy for the same dataset.

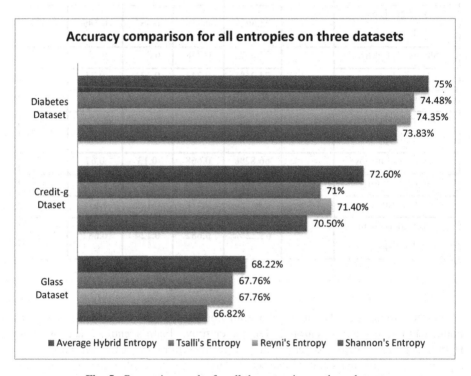

Fig. 5. Respective results for all the entropies on three dataset

The area under ROC curve (AUC) defines the overall accuracy. An area under 0.5 is counted as worthless. The higher area under ROC defines the excellent accuracy results. Here different ROC is shown for separate entropies for the **glass dataset**. The ROC value defines the overall difference. ROC is directly responsible for the final accuracy results. From the following Figs we can easily define what Shannon's entropy is having ROC area **0.807**, similarly Renyi's entropy having ROC area value **0.824**, further Tsalli's entropy having the ROC curve area value **0.823** and finally for the average hybrid entropy the ROC area value is 0.834 Which is the highest value and having excellent ROC area. The ROC area, when it comes near more to the value 1 then we can say that this is excellent value for the accuracy. Here the blue color defines the more excellence part. More the ROC or AUC area involved in the results the more accurate and precise results that would be. Following Figs are showing the ROC details for different entropies after implementation on the Glass dataset (Figs. 6, 7, 8 and 9).

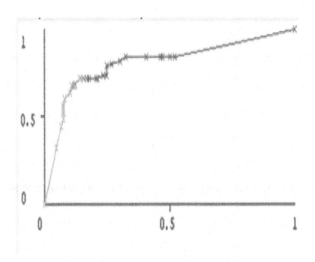

Fig. 6. ROC curve of Shannon's entropy having for glass dataset having ROC area 0.807

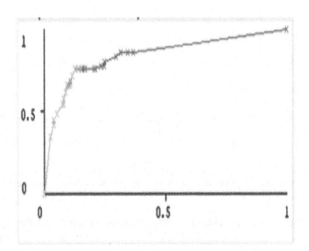

Fig. 7. ROC curve of Renyi's entropy having for glass dataset having ROC area 0.824

TP and TN here are the same because both are the sum of all true classified examples, regardless their classes. False positives, which are items incorrectly labeled as belonging to the class. False negatives items are which were not labeled as belonging to the positive class but should have been. Precision is another factor involved in the

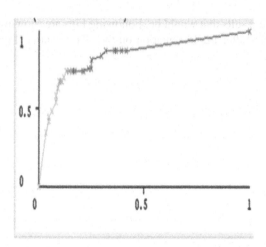

Fig. 8. ROC curve of Tsalli's entropy having for glass dataset having ROC area 0.823

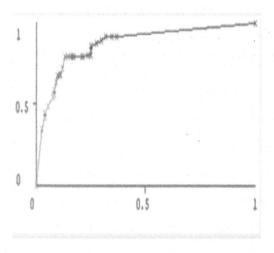

Fig. 9. ROC curve of average hybrid entropy having for glass dataset having ROC area 0.834

final accuracy results. It is something which gives the exactness of the accuracy. Here different formulas for the calculation of all these important factors are given:

Sensitivity = TP / TP + FN   **False-Positive Rate** = FP / FP + TN

Specificity = TN / TN + FP   **True-Negative Rate** = TN / TN + FP

Precision = TP / TP + FP   **False-Negative Rate** = FN / FN + TP

True-Positive Rate = TP / TP + FN   **Accuracy**= (TP+TN)/ (TP+TN+FP+FN)

Table 5. Analysis of average hybrid entropy on three datasets

Analysis for the average hybrid entropy			
Accuracy parameters	Datasets		
	Credit-g dataset	Diabetes dataset	Glass dataset
True positive	0.75	0.75	0.682
False positive	0.453	0.323	0.124
Accuracy	72.60%	75%	68.22%
Precision	0.709	0.745	0.682

In the Table 5 here mentioned about the analysis results for Average Hybrid Entropy after performing on different datasets. All these factors calculated according to the class type. Here mentioned table represents the weighted average values for all the datasets.

6 Conclusions

In the era of machine learning and data mining, there is need of more effective and accurate decision tree algorithm, that's why enhancement of research on this topic is preferable. Decision tree uses the concept of split criteria and pruning the instances on the basis of information gain and entropy. The C4.5 algorithm is available as a source code in Weka software. To increase the efficiency there are different entropy introduced. Shannon's entropy is the standard one. Reyni's entropy and Tsalli's entropy are redefined through statistical properties. Average Hybrid Entropy is a collective form of Reyni's and Tsalli's entropy. By using the pruning properties of instances this paper implemented this Average Hybrid entropy. Consequently, it gives the better results from the previous one. It provides the more precise bond with the nodes has to be pruned in the decision tree. Different datasets from UCI repository have been picked for evaluating the results that are Credit-g, Glass and Diabetes datasets. Overall it is clear that 72.60% accuracy gives for the Credit-g, 75% and 68.22% accuracy provides for the Diabetes and Glass datasets respectively. Overall evaluation is showing that Average Hybrid Entropy enhanced the more than 2%accuracy as compared to the standard entropy. In future, more elaboration has to be performed on the basis of statistical properties of the different entropies and should be tested against the continuous as well as discrete values as a future work.

References

1. Gajowniczek, K., Ząbkowski, T., Orłowski, A.: Comparison of decision trees with Rényi and Tsallis entropy applied for imbalanced churn dataset. In: Computer Science and Information Systems, pp. 39–44 (2015)
2. Sharma, L.P., Patel, N., Ghose, M.K., Debnath, P.: Influence of Shannon's entropy on landslide-causing parameters for vulnerability study and zonation—a case study in Sikkim. India. Arab. J. Geosci **5**, 421–431 (2012)

3. Truffet, L.: Shannon Entropy Reinterpreted (2017)
4. Lima, C.F.L., De Assis, F.M., De Souza, C.P.: Decision tree based on Shannon, Rényi and Tsallis entropies for intrusion tolerant systems. In: 5th International Conference Internet Monitoring and Protection, ICIMP 2010, pp. 117–122 (2010)
5. Wang, Y., Song, C., Xia, S.-T.: Unifying Decision Trees Split Criteria Using Tsallis Entropy (2015)
6. Dogra, A.K.: A review paper on data mining techniques and algorithms. Int. Res. J. Eng. Technol. **4**, 1976–1979 (2015)
7. Ilić, V.M., Stanković, M.S.: Comments on " On q-non-extensive statistics with non-Tsallisian entropy". Phys. A Stat. Mech. Appl. **466**, 160–165 (2017)
8. Contreras-Reyes, J.E., Arellano-Valle, R.B.: Kullback-Leibler divergence measure for multivariate skew-normal distributions. Entropy **14**, 1606–1626 (2012)
9. Bercher, J.F.: Some properties of generalized Fisher information in the context of nonextensive thermostatistics. Phys. A Stat. Mech. Appl **392**, 3140–3154 (2013)
10. Bercher, J.-F.: On generalized Cramér-Rao inequalities, generalized Fisher information, and characterizations of generalized q-Gaussian distributions. J. Phys. A: Math. Theor. **45**, 255303 (2012)
11. Teimouri, M., Nadarajah, S., Hsing Shih, S.: EM algorithms for beta kernel distributions. J. Stat. Comput. Simul. **84**, 451–467 (2014)
12. Zhong, Y.: The analysis of cases based on decision tree. In: 2016 7th IEEE International Conference on Software Engineering and Service Science, pp. 142–147 (2016)
13. tackOverflow. https://stackoverflow.com/questions/1859554/what-is-entropy-and-information-gain
14. An Introduction to Data Science. http://saedsayad.com/decision_tree.htm
15. Wikipedia. https://en.wikipedia.org/wiki/Tsallis_entropy
16. Wikipedia. https://en.wikipedia.org/wiki/Rényi_entropy
17. Wikipedia. https://en.wikipedia.org/wiki/Pruning_%28decision_trees%29

Stock Market Price Prediction Using SAP Predictive Service

Sanjana Devi and Virrat Devaser[✉]

Department of Computer Science and Engineering,
Lovely Professional University, Phagwara, Punjab, India
sanjanasanjull1995@gmail.com, virrat.14591@lpu.co.in

Abstract. Stock market price prediction is one of the most active areas of research among analysts from last few decades. Stock market price prediction is nothing but a process of trying to find the stock cost price for next trading day or next few days. A good prediction strategy may help to yield more profit. Different techniques and instruments are utilized to forecast the stock market price like artificial neural system, fuzzy logic, machine learning, Support Vector Machine, ARIMA model, R programming. Different algorithms are utilized to execute all these methods more precisely like Naïve Bayes, K-means, genetic Algorithms and Data mining algorithms and so on. The main intention is to increase the accuracy of forecast the stock market. Here, we are going to create a model with the help of Amazon web services, SAP Cloud Appliance Library. The Model is integrated with cloud to manage the dataset easily. SAP predictive services help to predict the future outcome in better way. Beauty of this model is it can handle large amount of data very easily. Like if user have historical data in the form of big data, it can not only easily managed in cloud environment but analyzing those data in very short time span is also possible with the help of SAP, because SAP is in-memory database.

Keywords: Data forecasting · Stock market price prediction
Cloud appliance library · Amazon web services · SAP predictive services

1 Introduction

Data Forecasting is the hot topic in the area of research that can be either in the stock or medical field or similar areas. Forecasting is nothing but the process of predicting the future value by analyzing the present and past data. The forecast is only an estimation of some factor an incentive at some predefined future day and age. Data forecasting can be done in various different areas like weather forecasting, in the medical field, to predict that whether a particular patient can have specified disease or not, in schools/colleges to predict the student performances etc. Using historical data to predict the future trends is nothing but data forecasting. Business person, companies use forecasting to allocate their budget and plan their future projects to maximize their profit, to analyze their performance and risks what they can face in future. Forecasting can be used to predict GDP (Gross Domestic Product), unemployment changes, or how it changes in a year. A statistician uses forecasting in every possible situation wherever

© Springer Nature Singapore Pte Ltd. 2019
A. K. Luhach et al. (Eds.): ICAICR 2018, CCIS 955, pp. 135–148, 2019.
https://doi.org/10.1007/978-981-13-3140-4_13

it requires forecasting for ensuring profits for future. Forecasting is not a simple procedure and it consists of numbers of steps. Various steps are explained as follows:

- First, we have to analyze the situation and identifying the variables on the basis of the situation that we want to predict.
- After analyzing the situation we have to select a dataset, and according to our requirement clean the dataset.
- Then that dataset is analyzed to predict the future value.
- At last, verification is done to compare the predicted value with the actual results to validate the procedure in the more accurate way.

Data forecasting has applications in the various fields like weather forecasting, Supply Chain Management and so on. One of the biggest applications of Data Forecasting is Stock Market Price Prediction.

Stock market in some cases is known as equity market or share market is only a collection of merchants and purchasers of shares or stocks which represents to organizations or market claims including securities enrolled on the stock trade. Stock price prediction is the process of predicting the future outcome by analyzing the past historical data by using some algorithms with the help of some tools. A Successful prediction of future value is one which provides more accuracy as compared to the other techniques and help to yield maximum profit. There are various factors which affect the stock market like political events, new product launching in market. Political events like new policies of RBI (Reserve Bank of India), WTO (World Trade Organization) etc. affect the stock market [1]. Although, there are number of methods to predict the future outcome but the main concern these days is to increase the accuracy in such a way that it will help to predict the future value close enough to the actual value. According to a theory named as Random Walked Theory [2], it states that stock market follows random trend in spite of following some logical trend so we can't predict it. In past, according to the number of researchers, stock market cannot be predicted because it is based on non-linear and random phenomenon. But on the contrary researchers always took this as a challenge used various latest tools to understand and overcome this kind of chaotic behavior. However, Stock price prediction can be done using number of techniques like using fuzzy logic we can provide a probabilistic results of upcoming outcomes, using some artificial intelligence techniques like artificial neural network where we can train the neural network for analyzing the data, using SVM (Support Vector Machine), DS Theory, kNN Theory, using some programming languages also like R programming etc.

The various methods used for stock price prediction can broadly classify into three categories:

- **Technical analysis (charts based):** In this, it is assumed that future price can be predicted by analyzing the trends that are followed by the past stock price.
- **Data Mining Technologies:** various data mining techniques are used in this like artificial neural network, SVM and various genetic algorithms etc.
- **Fundamental Analysis Techniques:** Fundamental analyses follow the concept that for every company's growth, monetary funds are the basic requirement. If company works well, it well get more benefits or rewards in terms of monetary resources

results more growth or rise in stock price. Some of the famous fundamental analysis techniques are P/E (price-earning) ratio analysis etc.

Dealing with Mispricing: The main concern is to increase accuracy in predicted stock price so that mispricing is reduced. Mispricing is nothing but difference between actual price and predicted price. This digression between the predicted price and actual price can be considered as the threshold. Traditionally threshold could be considered as the function of cost. But now threshold may be considered as changed with various factors. There are certain factors that can affect the value of threshold like volatility, liquidity, short-sales. By managing these factors or even one of them led to manage threshold value [3].

So, for reducing the threshold value i.e. mispricing between predicted value and actual value, we will create a model, which will use cloud for storage purpose and SAP Predictive services for predicting better results. In this model we will identify the factors which will affect the results more generously. These identified factors will provided more weightage as compare to another, and there may be some factors which doesn't affect the results. We can simple ignore those factors by excluding them on the analysis time. Although they are present in dataset, but excluding them at the analysis time leads to reduce complexity.

In this paper we are going to explain how we will implement the model. In second section we discuss some previously used techniques along with the merits and demerits of each. In third section, we will discuss our technique to enhance this prediction more accurately. In the next section we will discuss experimental results. At last we are going to conclude it along with its future scope.

2 Literature Survey

In Random Walked Theory in 1973, Burton Malkiel states that Stock market do not follow any logical trend so it cannot be predicted. These non- linear and random methods followed by the stock tend to made it unpredictable. This theory fits perfectly in some cases because all techniques used for prediction didn't provide much accuracy [2, 4].

According to Heimstra [5] the stock market follows some trends but we don't know the exact pattern. Some random and vague information is present only. To analyze the incomplete and vague information, fuzzy logic is the good option. A fuzzy model created which will compare the market valuations to investment conditions. If there is no fixed historical values exist for this comparison so fuzzy logic is the good option. The investment condition can be determined using factors like inflation, business cycle etc. It provides acceptable results but it can be enhanced by further tuning [6].

Fundamental analysis approach can also be followed some real-world data analysis. There are some factors that affect changes in stock price either in government or other exchange companies. It also depends on the belief of people which can be analyzed in the form of sentiments that are expressed in social media sites and news articles etc. so sometimes sentimental analysis can be used with other techniques like a neural network to predict the stock market price.

According to another strategy neural network can be used to predict the closing price of stock by analyzing the behavior of stock. A three step process including collecting sample data, preprocessing and predicting future close price, is followed using Artificial neural network [7]. In another research a multi-agent architecture framework is designed to find the correlation between the factors that affect the stock and the market trends which will help to predict stock value [8–10].

Both neural network and fuzzy logic have their own merits and demerits. By combining their merits Hybrid neuro fuzzy system came to existence. First, fuzzy logic is implemented, on the basis of results, a decision tree was designed. It will help to decide which factors (open price, close price, trade ratio) from the complete sample affect the results. On the basis of these results artificial neural network was applied. A Neuro-fuzzy system basically is a model where artificial neural network and fuzzy logic is implemented. Fuzzy logic is used to implement IF-THEN rules and on the basis of these IF-THEN rules implementation analysis done and interconnection are done using the neural network where there is an input layer, output layer and a number of hidden layers are also present [11].

Support Vector Machine is the supervised learning based method to be used with the existing scenario to get more accurate and comfortable results. The complete methodology followed for the SVM is divided into two parts:

- In the first part, SVM filter is used which will help in feature selection by using correlation technique.
- In the second part, a model named quasi linear function is used to process that selection function for predicting the future stock in more accurate way.

This system not only helps to predict the stock price but also helps to control the overfitting problem in the stock market prediction. This system has various advantages like best feature subset is selected the subset which contains only those features which are highly related to the output function so that it helps to increase the accuracy. As we eliminate the least significant features which help to get most significant data and to remove the noisy data easily. Ranking helped to easily pick up the best features [12, 13].

Machine Learning technique is also used to predict next day's cost price. For this we have to train the system using past historic data. On the basis of that training, it will help to predict the stock price for the next trading day. The main aim is to train the model so that it will provide most accurate results. We not only want to predict the movement of stock price but also try to check the ratio of movement with the fixed amount of time. For example 10% rise in stock price. A methodology named Equity stock price movement is tried to predict the same. Equity price movement is nothing but movement in stock price in a normal working environment. This methodology is considered as a classification techniques where if there is movement in stock market price which is 10% or higher then it will be considered as good else it will be categorized in the bad category.

Similarly, if there are a large number of stocks are there, there may be some stocks that are not more useful. So we can categorize the stock again in two categories one is good and other is bad. Some basic parameters or useful indicators are selected. These indicators can be selected on the basis of feature selection procedure. That useful or best-suited features are considered as the base features and on the basis of the feature subset, various stocks are categorized. We have to categorize in the good or bad category. If stock contains all essential features or does not contain any leas significant feature we can accept that stock and put it in the category of good stock. There may be some stock that doesn't even contain single useful indicator we simply discard that stocks without even categorizing them [14].

As per Ryota [15], time series model was created which will help to extract the interrelationships between the different stock values, predicted stock values. This will help to understand the trends which were followed by stock price. It calculated variation pattern which helps to analyze the changes in stock.

The naïve method also known as Naïve Bayes method can also be used to predict the future stock price. Here the author proposed a model which mainly includes two operations one is automation and another is a prediction. Using Automation, one can fix the prices for the shares and according to it; shares can be automatically bought or sold. In the prediction it can be of two types, one is a dummy and another is in real time. In dummy prediction, we can predict the value of future stock where in case of real we can find the value of current stock price [16].

According to another strategy stock price prediction can be done also using the technical and fundamental analysis where one can perform technical analysis on the historical data by using some artificial intelligence technique. For performing fundamental analysis, social media data is used with the help of sentimental analysis. Sentimental analysis with technical analysis provide more efficient and accurate results [17, 18].

R programming can also be used to predict the future outcome. It will not only help to analyze the prediction value but also very efficient to give accurate results. R studio help to run the code in effective way and it is also available on cloud based environment which will help to run web based program in R programming language [19].

As these days due to large number of transactions and money being put in stock markets, it leads to large and complex historic data. This data may leads to some problem in analyzing and storing this large amount of data in the specified format. This problem can be resolved with cloud platform. So In the present work we are going to devise a model which will integrate cloud services along with SAP predictive services to predict the future value for the stock.

3   Present Work

We are going to implement a model for stock market prediction using SAP HANA predictive services and cloud computing. This predictive service we can access using SAP HANA on demand interface. We can elaborate this process by using the SAP HANA studio where we can access data and analysis and prediction based on historical data can be done on the basis of the predictive services.

SAP HANA is basically is a column oriented, in memory relational database management system which is managed and developed by the SAP SE (System, Application & products in data processing) where SE stands for Software Enterprise. HANA is basically stands for high-performance analytic appliance, is an application based on in-memory database where data resides in memory i.e. in RAM instead of hard disk drive. That's why this may have fastest data accessing and processing capabilities.

We can use this as on premise or in cloud environment. Cloud based tool can have some services that we are not able to use in studio. For Stock price prediction we are going to use predictive analysis service which provides functionality for predicting stock market price by processing the historical data. Historical data that we are going to analyze will be taken from National Stock Exchange. We can analyze the data by using the workbench or can be using the SAP HANA. If we are going to use HANA studio, we have to first load the data into the SAP HANA studio and then we have to connect SAP HANA with the predictive service workbench where we can analyze the data. These services are basically of two types:

SAP Predictive Services: The SAP Cloud Platform Predictive service provides two types of services, which are accessible on the cloud as one single application. Every one of them offers distinctive functionalities and afterward tends to various types of users:

- **Business Services:** These Services are basically designed for business analyst. These services are very easy to use. These services are specifically designed to provide only predictive analysis. Each service is designed in such a way that it can easily answer any business query.
- **Predictive Analytics Integrator Services:** Here, non-predictive applications, which are generally cloud based, integrated to use predictive models. Basically this kind of services is designed for the people who have knowledge about machine learning or good data analyst. This will enable effective use of predictive models along with real life scenario.

Every service set is a gathering of Restful web administrations which are prepared to be coordinated in the cloud application or expansion we are creating. As an engineer, we can profit by the component rich and simple to-utilize advancement condition that the SAP Cloud Platform offers. The other significant advantage of these administrations is that we can utilize the REST APIs with any programming dialect that helps the HTTPS convention. We can either use java or HTML5.

The main concern here is how to use cloud platform for SAP predictive services. Basically if we want to use cloud platform services for any tool or techniques we can access it either using Amazon Web Services or using Microsoft Azure. We were working with AWS (Amazon web services). So in this model we combined three things i.e. Amazon web services, Sap predictive Service and Cloud Appliance Library.

3.1 Motivation for This Model

Since, for the stock price prediction our main concern is to predict the future value for stock in more accurate manner. As we all know volume of data is increasing every hour. So here, our main concern is to manage such a large amount of data and to analyze it in efficient way so that it helps to predict the results more accurate because the large amount of data leads to more accurate prediction. For example: if we have to analyze large amount of data like in TBs, etc. it is quite difficult to manage this much amount of data with any tools that are currently being used by analysts.

To solve this problem, we have come with an idea of creating this model which will integrate three things i.e. cloud environment (Cloud Appliance Library), SAP, AWS

(Amazon Web Services). When we talk about cloud, we can access cloud services using Amazon Web Services. Managing such large amount of data can easily be done using cloud and this data can be analyzed to predict the results using SAP services. If we talk about SAP predictive services, due to some reasons we are using these services described as follow:

- For predicting close price, a large amount of historical data is required that can managed only by cloud services.
- The SAP provides services which were implemented on cloud platform.
- SAP is an in-memory relational database, which means it will able to analyze the large amount of data in very little time span.

3.2 Methodology Implemented

This Process includes different steps which will help us to understand complete methodology easily. The complete flow of the process is described as following (Fig. 1):

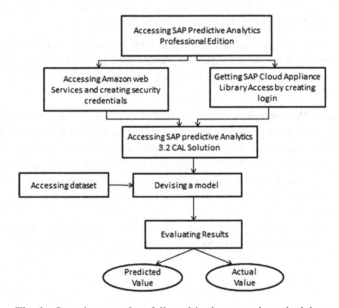

Fig. 1. Stepwise procedure followed in the research methodology

The list of steps followed in the complete process was described as following:

(1) The very first thing is we have to access the SAP Predictive Services by creating its login.
(2) When we login successfully, we have to access cloud service provider i.e. Amazon Web services, SAP Cloud Appliance Library. This will enable us to Access SAP Predictive Services CAL Solution.

(3) After this, we have created an instance of SAP Predictive Analytics by using CAL solution for it.
(4) When we successfully created an instance and connected to the Remote desktop, we have to devise a model which will enable us to predict the future stock price by analyzing the historical data.
(5) Once model builds successfully we can analyze the result by comparing the predicted value with actual value for measuring the model's accuracy.

We have to access the SAP Predictive Analytics Services Professional Edition. We can access these services by creating a trial account. Once we created login, for implementing this API, there are three requirements that must be fulfilled:

a. There must be access to cloud services. Cloud services can be accessed either through Amazon Web Services or using Microsoft Azure. We are using Amazon Web Services for accessing cloud services.
b. There must be access to SAP Cloud services. For this, we have to create a login for accessing SAP services.
c. These two services must be integrated into cloud appliance library, so we can manage our dataset stored on cloud platform using SAP services by accessing SAP predictive Analytics Cloud Appliance Library Solution.

The important thing is we are accessing SAP Predictive Analytics-Professional Edition. As this is a professional Edition basically used by professional for getting an industrial solution. This is a paid service of SAP. For accessing this we have to access AWS and SAP Cloud Appliance Library.

Step 1: Amazon Web Services: Amazon Web Services is just a service provided by Amazon which will provide cloud computing solutions to the industry, customers and individuals. It provides a solution to various services along with virtual environment having functionality similar to the real environment. Different services Elastic Compute Cloud (EC2) service is used for whatever computation we have done on a cloud platform. EBS (Elastic Block Storage) service is used for storing dataset for which we want to compute results.

After following steps they mentioned, once we have created an account successfully on AWS. After that, we have to create security credentials (Fig. 2).

Fig. 2. Creation of security credentials in AWS

Once we have created access key successfully, a file named with rootkey.csv downloaded. This file includes access key id and access secret key. Once we have created this access key, it will become active after 12 h. So, we can use these access key for creating an instance of the required services after 12 h only.

Step 2: The next step is to get the SAP Cloud Appliance Library Account: For this, we have first click on the link mentioned in email.

When we clicked on this link, a list of service is there which contain all the services that were provided by the SAP. The very first thing is to create a login account for SAP CAL. Click on the login option in the top right corner. A signup page will open, if you have SAP account, you can simply upgrade that account to SAP CAL account by accepting terms and conditions and by filling some basic details. Once we have created the account successfully, now we can access whatever service we require (Fig. 3).

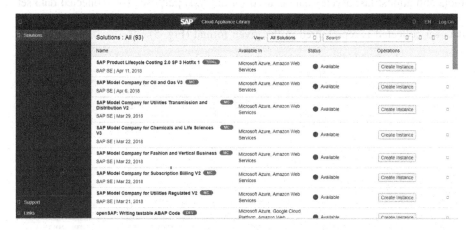

Fig. 3. SAP CAL solution list

Step 3: After accessing the Amazon Web Services and Cloud Appliance Library the next step is to access the SAP predictive Analytics CAL solution. We have to create an instance to access this service. When we clicked on the solutions tab here, it will provide an option to create an instance. After clicking on the create instance tab, we have to specify some details. One important thing is we have to specify access key and a secret key which we have created in amazon web services account. Once we specify those credentials, it will test the connection. If all the details were correct it will allow the instance for being created (Fig. 4).

As shown in figure once instance created successfully, we can connect to remote desktop by clicking on connect option. After this we are able to access the remote desktop and it enables us to create a model, deploy a model and use a model according to our requirement. We can manage and analyze the dataset by using this model for predicting the better future results.

Fig. 4. Successful instance creation

When we were successfully able to access the SAP Predictive Analytics solution through remote desktop, the second step is to collect the dataset and preprocess it according to requirement.

Historical data used for this work is collected from National Stock Exchange of India and almost last 5 years data is used for analysis purpose. This collected data set may contain some error or missing values. So we have preprocessed the data first. The data set collected is represented in the given format (Fig. 5).

	A	B	C	D	E	F	G	H	I	J	K	L	M	N	O	P
1	Symbol	Date	Expiry	Open	High	Low	Close	change in	LTP	No.ofcont	Turnoveri	OpenInt	Changein(	Percentag	UnderlyingValue	
2	NIFTY	1/1/2016	3/31/2016	7985	8050	7974.2	8036.7	0.011846	8039.95	1404	8442.67	39900	39900	100.00%	7963.2	
3	NIFTY	1/4/2016	3/31/2016	7995	8005.25	7853	7864.1	-0.02195	7865	1877	11135.59	87750	47850	54.53%	7791.3	
4	NIFTY	1/5/2016	3/31/2016	7892.95	7894.7	7841	7864.95	0.000108	7855.6	1815	10712.62	154125	66375	43.07%	7784.65	
5	NIFTY	1/6/2016	3/31/2016	7836.65	7882	7790.25	7812.15	-0.00676	7810.25	1936	11385.69	190725	36600	19.19%	7741	
6	NIFTY	1/7/2016	3/31/2016	7740.35	7758.7	7632.3	7643	-0.02213	7633.4	2845	16381.01	249750	59025	23.63%	7568.3	
7	NIFTY	1/8/2016	3/31/2016	7670	7696.75	7651.1	7659.3	0.002128	7664.5	1923	11064.57	260175	10425	4.01%	7601.35	
8	NIFTY	1/11/2016	3/31/2016	7587.65	7668.5	7560.05	7639.7	-0.00257	7645	2182	12455.29	277875	17700	6.37%	7563.85	
9	NIFTY	1/12/2016	3/31/2016	7636.4	7638.3	7555	7584.05	-0.00734	7580.6	1197	6812.02	303075	25200	8.31%	7510.3	
10	NIFTY	1/13/2016	3/31/2016	7628	7653.65	7481.05	7626.5	0.005566	7621.3	2335	13259.41	323625	20550	6.35%	7562.4	
11	NIFTY	1/14/2016	3/31/2016	7550	7662	7504.4	7587.65	-0.00512	7584.85	2390	13580.6	356250	32625	9.16%	7536.8	
12	NIFTY	1/15/2016	3/31/2016	7577.05	7606.15	7482.3	7494.55	-0.01242	7491	1532	8663.61	368025	11775	3.20%	7437.8	
13	NIFTY	1/18/2016	3/31/2016	7494.1	7522.2	7402	7416.5	-0.01052	7410	2401	13430.57	390000	21975	5.63%	7351	
14	NIFTY	1/19/2016	3/31/2016	7439.45	7518.55	7421.7	7483.5	0.008953	7480	2723	15271.98	410475	20475	4.99%	7435.1	
15	NIFTY	1/20/2016	3/31/2016	7404	7404.2	7275.05	7344.45	-0.01893	7354	5261	28927.47	507000	96525	19.04%	7309.3	
16	NIFTY	1/21/2016	3/31/2016	7408	7430	7285	7319.75	-0.00337	7327	4430	24393.94	613650	106650	17.38%	7276.8	
17	NIFTY	1/22/2016	3/31/2016	7379.6	7464	7359.5	7455.45	0.018201	7463	3485	19417.08	646950	33300	5.15%	7422.45	
18	NIFTY	1/25/2016	3/31/2016	7479	7505.15	7437.3	7458.65	0.000429	7456.45	4011	22467.52	748200	101250	13.53%	7436.15	
19	NIFTY	1/27/2016	3/31/2016	7456.45	7491	7437	7455.75	-0.00039	7453.7	3278	18342.11	820950	72750	8.86%	7437.75	
20	NIFTY	1/28/2016	3/31/2016	7449.45	7492.85	7447.9	7463.4	0.001025	7467.4	4768	26699.55	913050	92100	10.09%	7424.65	
21	NIFTY	1/29/2016	3/31/2016	7444.45	7592.2	7444.45	7581.75	0.01561	7580	5789	32690.72	985200	72150	7.32%	7563.55	

Fig. 5. Historical data

Preprocessing of Historical Data: We were focusing on predicting next day's close price. For this we have to check number of attributes which may affect the next day's close price. There are number of attributes which may affect the close price but our main concern is to select the variable which highly affect the price like open price, min max, trading quantity etc. we mainly focus on the two parameters i.e. change in Open Interest and change in Close price.

- Change in OI (open Interest) referred as Total percentage of change in open interest of today with respect to previous day where Open interest is number of open (delivered or not closed) shares that exist on one day.
- Change in close price percentage is the percentage of total change in close price of trading day with respect to close price of previous day.

After processing the dataset completely, we can analyze this dataset by using the model which we created on remote desktop with the help of predictive analytics services. We can store this dataset directly on remote desktop also using cloud services and we can access this dataset through SAP HANA schema also. We can easily access the dataset and analyze it for predicting the future value (Fig. 6).

Symbol	Date	Close	change in price %	ChangeinOl
NIFTY	2016/01/01	8036.7	0.011845658	39900
NIFTY	2016/01/04	7864.1	-0.021948	47850
NIFTY	2016/01/05	7864.95	0.000108	66375
NIFTY	2016/01/06	7812.15	-0.006759	36600
NIFTY	2016/01/07	7643	-0.022131	59025
NIFTY	2016/01/08	7659.3	0.002128	10425
NIFTY	2016/01/11	7639.7	-0.002566	17700
NIFTY	2016/01/12	7584.05	-0.007338	25200
NIFTY	2016/01/13	7626.5	0.005566	20550
NIFTY	2016/01/14	7587.65	-0.00512	32625
NIFTY	2016/01/15	7494.55	-0.012422	11775
NIFTY	2016/01/18	7416.5	-0.010524	21975
NIFTY	2016/01/19	7483.5	0.008953	20475

Fig. 6. Processed dataset view

4 Experimental Results and Discussion

SAP Predictive services provide efficient results. It will allow us to create model according to our requirement which will not only provide effecting results but display results in highly efficient way.

Since we all know that in stock market prediction, our main concern is to increase the accuracy. It became very difficult when it comes to the dealing with a large amount of data i.e. big data. So, SAP predictive services along with cloud appliance library solution fit best for solving this price prediction problem.

Here, we want to predict the close price for the next day. When we select target variable which we want to predict, automatically an identical column will be created with the name kts_1 which will provide predicted value for the complete period from starting date to till the date we want to forecast (Fig. 7).

This graph will provide comparison between actual close price and kts_1 which is predicted close price. As this is predictive model, we are predicting future close price. Only one column value will be created and predicted by default. It also provides some outlier value which lies in this graph.

An excel report will be generated automatically which include the actual and predicted value of close price (Fig. 8).

So, in this way this model provides more accuracy in case of future prediction. We are not only able to predict the value of next day but we can compare the predicted value with the actual value to get how much accuracy our model will provide.

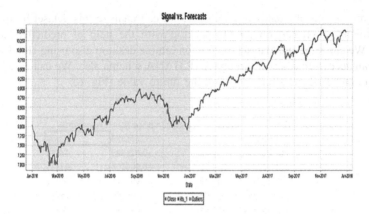

Fig. 7. Comparison between close price (actual value) and kts_1 (predicted value)

Signal vs. Forecasts

	Close	kts_1
'2016-01-0'	8036.7	
'2016-01-0'	7864.1	
'2016-01-0'	7864.95	7865.42
'2016-01-0'	7812.15	7808.19
'2016-01-0'	7643	7667.08
'2016-01-0'	7659.3	7660.7
'2016-01-1'	7639.7	7637.48
'2016-01-1'	7584.05	7578.73
'2016-01-1'	7626.5	7629.6
'2016-01-1'	7587.65	7581.67
'2016-01-1'	7494.55	7471.92
'2016-01-1'	7416.5	7413.7
'2016-01-1'	7483.5	7488.98
'2016-01-2'	7344.45	7338.43

Fig. 8. An excel generated automatically containing predicted price and actual price

4.1   Comparison with Existing Techniques

Although there were a number of techniques to predict stock price, we prefer to use SAP Predictive services. Because of some following reasons

- The main concern is to predict the future stock price by analyzing a large amount of data. So here, we have to implement prediction process along with managing a large and complex dataset. SAP Predictive Services provides integration with cloud environment with the help of Amazon Web Services.
- This module provides a user-friendly graphical user interface which can also be implemented using R programming. To reduce the complexity we have implemented this model using graphical user interface.
- Till now, no any existing technique is used with the cloud platform for predicting stock market price.

SAP provides better results as compared to the previous techniques. This not only helps to increase the performance of the model but also enable us to get more accuracy as compared to the previous techniques (Fig. 9).

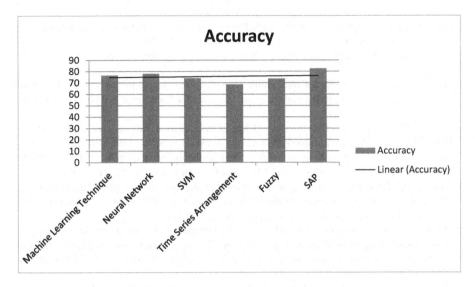

Fig. 9. The comparison with existing techniques

As shown in this graph, SAP Predictive services increase accuracy as compared to the other techniques. In this techniques complexity of the model reduced because in this model complete dataset is managed and analyzed in the cloud platform.

5   Conclusion and Future Scope

In this paper, we devised a model which will help us to predict stock market close price in very easy and efficient way. Data can easily be managed by using cloud services. These services we can easily accessed using AWS. Data analyzed using SAP services. Large amount of data can easily access and managed using this model. If dataset containing any error or missing values, this can be automatically analyzed using this model. No need to traverse complete dataset. This model increases efficiency along with accuracy in prediction.

Further this model can be improved using some regression techniques, where results can be improved by changed the value of different factors which were effect the stock price. We can classify the weather the future stock of a company will arise or not. We can check for fraud detection also. We can implement techniques like neural network.

References

1. Chen, D., Bin, F., Chen, C.: The Impacts of Political Events on Foreign Institutional Investors and Stock Returns : Emerging Market Evidence from Taiwan, vol. 10, no. 2 (2005)
2. Van Horne, J.C., Parker, G.G.C.: Theory : An Empirical Test. (1967)
3. Shankar, R.L.: Mispricing in single stock futures: empirical examination of Indian markets Mispricing in single stock futures: empirical examination of Indian markets, pp. 1–36 (2015)
4. Dupernex, S.: Why might share prices follow a random walk? Stud. Econ. Rev. **21**, 167–179 (2007)
5. Hiemstra, Y.: A stock market forecasting support system based on fuzzy logic. In: 1994 Proceedings of the Twenty-Seventh Hawaii International Conference on System Sciences, vol. 3, pp. 281–287 (1994)
6. Setnes, M., Van Drempt, J.H.: Fuzzy modeling in stock-market analysis, pp. 250–258 (1999)
7. Andrade de Oliveira, F., Enrique Zarate, L., de Azevedo Reis, M., Neri Nobre, C.: The use of artificial neural networks in the analysis and prediction of stock prices. In: 2011 IEEE International Conference on Systems, Man, and Cybernetics, pp. 2151–2155 (2011)
8. Iuhasz, G., Tirea, M., Negru, V.: Neural network predictions of stock price fluctuations. In: Proceedings-14th International Symposium on Symbolic and Numeric Algorithms for Scientific Computing, SYNASC 2012, pp. 505–512 (2012)
9. Olatunji, S.O., Al-Ahmadi, M.S., Elshafee, M., Fallatah, Y A.: Saudi Arabia stock prices forecasting using artificial neural networks. In: Fourth International Conference on the Applications of Digital Information and Web Technologies (ICADIWT 2011), pp. 81–86 (2011)
10. Sood, P.K., Devaser, V.: Stock price prediction for a sectorial leader in NSE using neural network. Int. J. Appl. Eng. Res. **10**(55), 2067–2074 (2015)
11. Nair, B.B., Dharini, N.M., Mohandas, V.P.: A stock market trend prediction system using a hybrid decision tree-neuro-fuzzy system. In: Proceedings- 2nd International Conference on Advances in Recent Technologies in Communication and Computing ARTCom 2010, pp. 381–385 (2010)
12. Lin, Y., Guo, H., Hu, J.: An SVM-based approach for stock market trend prediction. In: Proceedings of the International Joint Conference on Neural Networks (2013)
13. Basu, A., Watters, C., Shepherd, M.: Support vector machines for text categorization, pp. 1–7 (2002)
14. Milosevic, N.: Equity forecast: predicting long term stock price movement using machine learning. J. Econ. Libr. **3**(2), 8 (2016)
15. Ryota, K., Tomoharu, N.: Stock market prediction based on interrelated time series data. In: 2012 IEEE Symposium on Computers & Informatics, Isc. 2012, pp. 17–21 (2012)
16. Shubhrata, M.D., Kaveri, D., Pranit, T., Bhavana, S.: Stock Market Prediction and Analysis Using Naïve Bayes. Int. J. Recent Innov. Trends Comput. Commun. **4**(11), 121–124 (2016)
17. Attigeri, G.V., Manohara Pai, M.M., Pai, R.M., Nayak, A.: Stock market prediction: a big data approach. In: 35th IEEE Region 10 Conference TENCON 2015, January, 2016
18. Thomas, M.M.: A review paper on BIG Data. Int. Res. J. Eng. Technol. **4**(4), 2395–56 (2015)
19. Kelley, K., Lai, K., Wu, P.-J.: Using R for data analysis: a best practice for research. In: Best Practices Quantitative Methods, pp. 535–572 (2008)

RNN-LSTM Based Indoor Scene Classification with HoG Features

Ambica Verma[✉], Shilpa Sharma, and Priyanka Gupta

School of Computer Science and Engineering, Lovely Professional University,
Phagwara, Jalandhar, India
er.ambica@gmail.com, shilpa13891@gmail.com,
priyankaquick@gmail.com

Abstract. The machine learning and artificial intelligence models have evolved with unenvisaged swiftness over the past decade. The machine learning and artificial intelligence models work on the basis of the mathematical models, which are capable of processing the financial, image, video, audio, audio-visual and several other forms of data. In this paper, the work has been carried upon the bulk image data representing the variety of indoor scenes. The goal is to detect the type of indoor scene, which can be utilized by variety of artificial intelligent application for various purposes. The indoor scene recognition has been performed over the computer vision & pattern recognition (CVPR), 2009 dataset, which is consisted of 15620 images. The deep learning mechanism known as recurrent neural network (RNN) has been incorporated for the classification of the indoor scene data over the histogram of oriented gradient (HoG) based features. Specifically, the forget gates based recurrent mode called Long short-term memory (LSTM) has been incorporated for the classification of the indoor scene data. The performance of the proposed model has been analyzed over the CVPR09 dataset using 50 and 100 randomly drawn test cases. The proposed model has been found 92% accurate in comparison with SVM (88%), KNN (80%) and Naïve Bayes (86%). The F1-measure based performance assessment also proves the robustness of LSTM based model with 96% accuracy over 92% of Naïve Bayes, 93% of SVM and 88% of KNN.

Keywords: Deep learning · Recurrent neural network
Long-short term memory · LSTM · Indoor scene recognition · CVPR'09

1 Introduction

Scene classification is aimed at labeling an image into semantic categories (room, office, mountain etc). It is an important task to classify, organize and understand thousands of images in stable and efficient processing. From the perspective of the scene recognition application, these models are found useful and productive in various scenarios in the computing world. As accurate classification of an image, as better as it helps in better organization and browsing of the image data. Scene classification is highly valuable in remote navigation also (Fig. 1).

The above figure describes the RNN neural networks for the supervised applications. Indoor scenes are cluttered with many objects. The indoor scene images may contain repeated objects among the imagery of different areas at home, office or

© Springer Nature Singapore Pte Ltd. 2019
A. K. Luhach et al. (Eds.): ICAICR 2018, CCIS 955, pp. 149–159, 2019.
https://doi.org/10.1007/978-981-13-3140-4_14

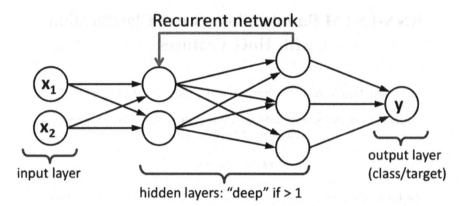

Fig. 1. A typical architecture of scene recognition models using the supervised recurrent neural network (RNN) algorithms

shopping areas. The existence of the objects, different combinations, etc is very important for the recognition of the scene, which may play the important role for the category evaluation in the classification algorithms. The classification algorithms such as support vector machine (SVM), neural network (NN), k-nearest neighbor (kNN), etc are used to determine the classes of the target or testing data by analyzing it in reference with the training data. As its mentioned previously that the indoor scene data is higly cluttered, which according to this study, must be decluttered in order to remove the objects or regions with low significance and by keeping the higher significance objects. The decluttering or selection of the high significance features can be performed by using the texture, pattern, color or other kinds of features descriptors, which involves scale invariant feature transformation (SIFT), fast retina key points (FREAK), speeded up robust features (SURF), etc. For the successful implementation of the indoor scene recognition application, a perfect combination of the classification algorithm and image feature descriptor is required. For this combination, this paper uses the RNN-LSTM based classification model with histogram of oriented gradients (HoG) based features.

2   Related Work

Espinace et al. [1] has worked on the scene detection in natural imagery for the robotic objects. The robots are entirely dependent upon the computer vision based models to identify and recognize the objects in the visual objects. In this paper, the focus is kept on the detection and localization of the multiple objects in the common categories such as furniture, doors, etc in order to facilitate the robots to move around the given premises. Giannoulis et al. [2] has worked towards removing the complexity for event detection and scene classification by incorporating the multi-layered object detection methods. Antanas et al. [3] has developed the kernel program to classify the natural scene images with application of multiple object relations. This scheme works by evaluating the combinations of various objects in the target scene in order to identify the scene. Gupta et al. [4] has worked upon the RGB image database, where the perception based scene recognition techniques are applied over the given image set. This technique emphasizes the use of grouping of the objects in the specific combination in the bottom-up approach coupled with semantic behavior in order to recognize the type of scene in the target image.

Juneja et al. [5] has developed the scene recognition approach to determine the type of scene on by analyzing the distinctive but partial regions in the given image. Monadjemi et al. [6] experimented upon the high definition images to determine the kind of target scene. This model uses the texture based features to determine the type of the scene on a whole, which means the focus lies upon the complete image matrix, rather than individual objects. Duda et al. [7] worked towards the robotic vision (eventually computer vision) to help the robots to understand the type of scene in order to execute the location specific program to achieve a task. Fitzpatrick et al. [8] developed the category oriented scene classification model. This model uses the supervised knowledge based model to determine the various sets of objects in order to determine the scene. Quattoni et al. [9] has analyzed the causes of failed detection of the scenes. This study remarked the detection of the target objects by using the different exemplars within the set of objects in each class. Li et al. [10] has worked upon the low-level feature based scene type detection. This model is empowered by the object filtering method, which recognizes several kinds of objects in the certain combination in order to correctly recognize the scene.

3 Methods and Materials

The scene recognition model is prepared to facilitate the robots to identify their surroundings. The idea behind this project is to implement the scene or surrounding specific program selection in the robots in to complete the tasks. For example, a robot may need to clean the bedroom floor and not the lobby between 12PM to 4PM. Hence, the robot must be aware of its surroundings, and should not clean the lobby, if the time is between 12PM and 4PM, but it can clean the bedroom in the meanwhile. This model utilizes the combination of histogram of oriented gradients (HoG) and Recurrent neural networks to classify the scenes in the target image. The HoG feature descriptor is a color based feature descriptor, which describes the features of target image in block-wise pattern. The image is divided into smaller blocks, and HoG of each block is computed. The HoG matrix represents a reduced size matrix than the original images in the binarized paradigm. This matrix is further converted to the vector in order to prepare the feature matrix for multiple images altogether. HoG features obtained from all of the images in the training and testing datasets are analyzed using the HoG feature descriptor, and the final feature matrices are prepared for both training and testing data. The recurrent neural network (RNN) is utilized to classify the pattern (from images). A RNN classifier can be classified as sub-class of ANN (artificial neural network), which has the ability to create the unit-oriented connections between the neurons in order to realize the directed cycle. This behavior is known as the exhibit dynamic temporal behavior. RNNs utilize the internal memory for the processing of subjective sequences from the input data. This ability empowers RNNs to handle the unsegmented and non-connected component structures with higher accuracy than any other form of ANNs. A typical LSTM (Long short-term memory) based ANN is considered as the deep learning alternative with ability to utilize the vanishing gradients to resolve the pattern recognition problem. LSTM model is complimented by the RNNs, which can be explained as "forget" gates.

These forget gates are used to process the information under the backward propagation paradigm. The algorithm of the proposed model is described below:

Algorithm 1: Indoor Scene Recognition with Recurrent Neural Networks

---

1. Input testing image matrix
2. Divide the image matrix to smaller blocks of MxN size, for example 2x2, 3x3 or 4x4
3. Create an empty matrix of zeros equal to the size of input image → hogM
4. Run the iteration for each of the block
   - i.   Acquire the pixels in the current block
   - ii.   Compute the mean of pixels in the current block
   - iii. Covert the pixels with value higher than or equal to the new value of 1
   - iv.   Covert the pixels with value lower than to the new value of 0
   - v.   Update the pixels accordingly in *hogM* matrix
   - vi.   If it's the last iteration
        a. Exit the loop
   - vii. Otherwise
        a. Go to 4(a)
5. Transform *hogM* matrix to *hogV* vector
6. Acquire the training image database
7. Create a empty training matrix (2-D) → *trainMat*
   - i.   Row size equals to the number of images
   - ii.   Column size equals to the total number of pixels
8. Run the iteration of each of training image to extract the HoG features
   - i.   Create an empty image matrix for *trM* to handle the features of current image in training database
   - ii.   Run the following on the current training image
        a. Acquire the pixels in the current block
        b. Compute the mean of pixels in the current block
        c. Covert the pixels with value higher than or equal to the new value of 1
        d. Covert the pixels with value lower than to the new value of 0
        e. Update the pixels accordingly in *trM* matrix
        f. If it's the last iteration
            i. Exit the loop
        g. Otherwise
            i. Go to 4(a)

   - iii. Cover the *trM* matrix to *trV* vector
   - iv.   Update the corresponding feature row in *trainMat* for current image with *trV* vector
   - v.   If it's the last image

```
        a.  Exit the loop
   vi.  Otherwise
        a.        Goto 8(b)(i)
```

9. Create the RNN-LSTM object from the corresponding
   library
10. Set the input parameters for RNN-LSTM to perform
    the classification of the given data
11. Train the RNN-LSTM classifier with the training
    matrix *trainMat*
12. Test the RNN-LSTM classifier with *hogV* feature
13. Analyze the output matrix returned by RNN-LSTM
14. Return the classification result

4 Results and Discussion

The results of the proposed model have been analyzed using the various performance
indicators as well as the statistical type 1 and type 2 errors. The statistical type 1 and 2
errors include the true positive (TP), false positive (FP), false negative (FN) and true
negative (TN) cases, which indicates all four aspects of the results to represent the false
or correct acceptance and reject of the test cases. Two experiments are performed over
the proposed model for the purpose of cross-validation with 50 and 100 test cases
(image samples), which are drawn randomly by using the random permutation series
generation for the selection of the testing candidates.

The above figure shows the results observed from the proposed model in the form
of type 1 and 2 errors for the scenario with 50 test cases, which are also presented in the
following Table 1. According the data analysis of 50 test cases, the RNN-LSTM model
for 50 cases has been recorded with 44 TPs, 2 TNs, 3 FPs and 1 FN, whereas the SVM,
KNN and Naïve Bayes are recorded with 41, 38 and 39 TPs, 3, 2 and 4 TNs, 2, 2 and 3
FPs and 4, 8 and 4 FNs respectively.

Table 1. Performance analysis of multiple classification models over 50 test cases

Parameter	SVM	KNN	Naïve bayes	RNN-LSTM
TP	41	38	39	44
TN	3	2	4	2
FP	2	2	3	3
FN	4	8	4	1
TOTAL	50	50	50	50
Accuracy	0.88	0.80	0.86	0.92
Precision	0.95	0.95	0.93	0.94
Recall	0.91	0.83	0.91	0.98
F1-measure	0.93	0.88	0.92	0.96

The RNN-LSTM model is discovered with 92% accuracy, 94% precision, 98% recall and 96% of F1-measure, which is greatest among the four classification models. The second best classification model (SVM) has been recorded with 88% accuracy, 95% precision, 91% recall and 93% F1-measure, where the proposed RNN-LSTM model outperformed the SVM with nearly 1-7% on different performance indicators, which is also evident from the following figure (Fig. 2).

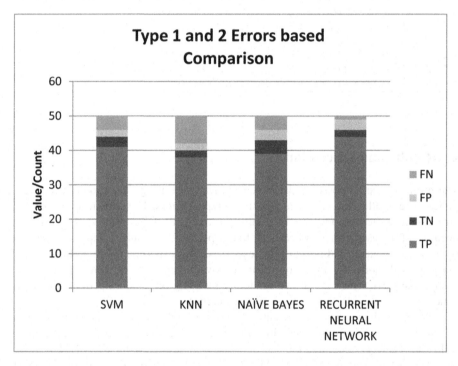

Fig. 2. Comparison of the different classification models based upon statistical type 1 and type 2 errors for 50 samples

The above figure displays the results obtained for the different classification models used for scene recognition with 100 test cases. In second experiment with 100 test cases, the RNN-LSTM model has been recorded with 88 TPs, 6 TNs, 2 FPs and 4 FN, whereas the SVM, KNN and Naïve Bayes are recorded with 81, 77 and 80 TPs, 5, 4 and 6 TNs, 3, 5 and 7 FPs and 11, 14 and 7 FNs respectively.

According to Table 2, which is observed for 100 test cases, the RNN-LSTM model is discovered with 94% accuracy, 98% precision, 96% recall and 97% of F1-measure, which is highest from all four classification models. The nearest classification model (SVM) has been recorded with 86% accuracy, 96% precision, 88% recall and 92% F1-measure, where the proposed RNN-LSTM model outperformed the SVM with nearly 2-8% on different performance indicators (Fig. 3).

Table 2. Performance analysis of multiple classification models over 100 test cases

Parameter	SVM	KNN	Naïve bayes	RNN-LSTM
TP	81	77	80	88
TN	5	4	6	6
FP	3	5	7	2
FN	11	14	7	4
Total	100	100	100	100
Accuracy	0.86	0.81	0.86	0.94
Precision	0.96	0.94	0.92	0.98
Recall	0.88	0.85	0.92	0.96
F1-Measure	0.92	0.89	0.92	0.97

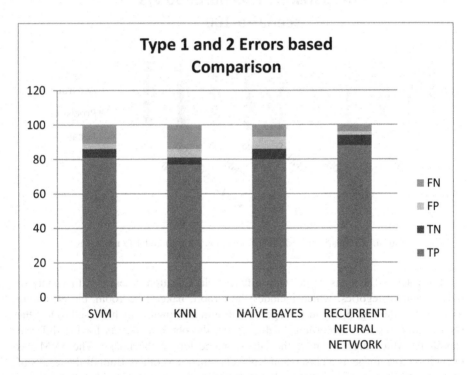

Fig. 3. Comparison of the different classification models based upon statistical type 1 and type 2 errors for 100 samples

The Fig. 4 shows the results obtained for the scenarios designed with different scenarios including 50 and 100 test cases. The results of both scenarios are compared on the basis of accuracy, precision, recall and f1-measure parameters. These scenarios are compared to know the performance loss due to the higher number of test cases in scenario with 100 test cases against the scenario with 50 cases. The SVM is observed with performance loss with rise in the number of test cases, which decreased by 2% from 88% to 86%, where the Naïve Bayes classification model remains constant in both of the test cases with accuracy of 86%. The KNN and RNN are observed with the higher overall accuracy with the rise in the samples, where KNN is increased by 1% and RNN is reportedly increased by 2%. Hence, the RNN is proved to be more efficient than all other supervised models for the data classification with higher number of samples.

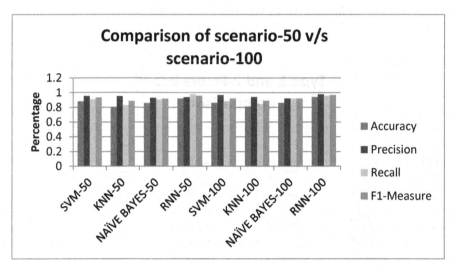

Fig. 4. Comparison of different scenarios with 50 and 100 test cases

The category analysis model with different classification is tested with variety of indoor scene categories, which includes the airport, bakery, bedroom, closet, dining room etc. In the Fig. 5, the test image of bedroom is shown, which is used to test the classification models. According to this figure, the obtained results for the different classifiers, which are shown as the labels on the top of the image. The SVM has recognized this image as a closet, and KNN classified it as office. Both of the results of these classifiers are unacceptable, hence considered wrong and added to the false negative cases. On the contrary, the Naïve Bayes and RNN recognized with its true category, i.e. bedroom, which is considered a correct result and added to the true positive cases.

Original:bedroom | SVM:closet | KNN:office | Naive Bayes:bedroom | RNN:bedroom

Fig. 5. The results obtained from the proposed model after classification with proposed model in comparison with other models

5 Conclusion

The proposed model has been designed around the application of RNN, specifically long-short term memory (LSTM) based RNN to determine the indoor scenes by matching the testing image with the large pre-classified database of indoor scenes. Total 67 types of indoor scenes are present in the CVPR 2009 dataset, out of which all of the indoor scenes are incorporated for the testing and training purposes in the proposed model. The proposed model has been tested with 50 and 100 test cases, which are drawn randomly from the dataset of above 15000 indoor scene images. The performance analysis includes the statistical assessment, where proposed model has been recorded with the best results with highest true positive cases (44 and 88) and true negative cases (2 and 6) in comparison to the other algorithms, which creates the leading performance engine for indoor scene classification. The proposed model has been found highly accurate with nearly 92% and 94% of accuracy in the case of 50 and 100 test cases respectively. Also, the F1-measure of 96% and 97% is found to be highest among all of the classification algorithms for 50 and 100 test cases respectively. In the case of 100 test cases, the proposed RNN-LSTM model has been recorded with 92% accuracy and 96% of F1-measure against the SVM (88% and 93%), KNN (80% and 88%) and Naïve Bayes (86% and 92%).

References

1. Espinace, P., Kollar, T., Roy, N., Soto, A.: Indoor scene recognition by a mobile robot through adaptive object detection. Robot. Auton.Syst. **61**(9), 932–947 (2013)
2. Giannoulis, D., Stowell, D., Benetos, E., Rossignol, M., Lagrange, M., Plumbley, M.D.: A database and challenge for acoustic scene classification and event detection. In: 2013 Proceedings of the 21st European Signal Processing Conference (EUSIPCO), pp. 1–5. IEEE (2013)
3. Antanas, L., Hoffmann, M.E., Frasconi, P., Tuytelaars, T., De Raedt, L.: A relational kernel-based approach to scene classification. In: 2013 IEEE Workshop on Applications of Computer Vision (WACV), pp. 133–139. IEEE (2013)
4. Gupta, S., Arbelaez, P., Malik, J.: Perceptual organization and recognition of indoor scenes from RGB-D images. In: 2013 IEEE Conference on Computer Vision and Pattern Recognition (CVPR), pp. 564–571. IEEE (2013)
5. Juneja, M., Andrea, V., Jawahar, C.V., Zisserman, A.: Blocks that shout: distinctive parts for scene classification. In: 2013 IEEE Conference on Computer Vision and Pattern Recognition (CVPR), pp. 923–930. IEEE (2013)
6. Monadjemi, A., Thomas, B.T., Mirmehdi, M.: Experiments on high resolution images towards outdoor scene classification. Technical report, University of Bristol, Department of Computer Science (2002)
7. Duda, R.O., Hart, P.E., Stork, D.G.: Pattern Classification. John Wiley and Sons, Hoboken (1999)
8. Fitzpatrick, P.: Indoor/outdoor scene classification project. Pattern Recognition and Analysis
9. Quattoni, A., Torralba, A.: Recognizing indoor scenes. In: 2009 IEEE Conference on Computer Vision and Pattern Recognition CVPR 2009, pp. 413–420. IEEE (2009)
10. Li, L.-J., Su, H., Lim, Y., Fei-Fei, L.: Objects as attributes for scene classification. In: Kutulakos, K.N. (ed.) ECCV 2010. LNCS, vol. 6553, pp. 57–69. Springer, Heidelberg (2012). https://doi.org/10.1007/978-3-642-35749-7_5
11. Antanas, L., Hoffmann, M., Frasconi, P., Tuytelaars, T., De Raedt, L.: A relational kernel-based approach to scene classification. In: 2013 IEEE Workshop on Applications of Computer Vision (WACV), pp. 133–139. IEEE (2013)
12. Mesnil, G., Rifai, S., Bordes, A., Glorot, X., Bengio, Y., Vincent, P.: Unsupervised and transfer learning under uncertainty-from object detections to scene categorization. In: ICPRAM, pp. 345–354 (2013)
13. Zhang, L., Zhen, X., Shao, L.: Learning object-to-class kernels for scene classification. IEEE Trans. Image Process. **23**(8), 3241–3253 (2014)
14. Li, L.-J., Su, H., Fei-Fei, L., Xing, X.P.: Object bank: a high-level image representation for scene classification and semantic feature sparsification. In: Advances in Neural Information Processing Systems, pp. 1378–1386 (2010)
15. Alberti, M., Folkesson, J., Jensfelt, P.: Relational approaches for joint object classification and scene similarity measurement in indoor environments. In: AAAI 2014 Spring Symposia: Qualitative Representations for Robots (2014)
16. Russakovsky, O., Lin, Y., Yu, K., Fei-Fei, L.: Object-centric spatial pooling for image classification. In: Fitzgibbon, A., Lazebnik, S., Perona, P., Sato, Y., Schmid, C. (eds.) ECCV 2012. LNCS, pp. 1–15. Springer, Heidelberg (2012). https://doi.org/10.1007/978-3-642-33709-3_1
17. Espinace, P., Kollar, T., Roy, N., Soto, A.: Indoor scene recognition by a mobile robot through adaptive object detection. Robot. Auton. Syst. **61**(9), 932–947 (2013)

18. Fredembach, C., Schroder, M., Susstrunk, S.: Eigenregions for image classification. IEEE Trans. Pattern Anal. Mach. Intell. **26**(12), 1645–1649 (2004)
19. Mojsilovic, A., Gomes, J., Rogowitz, B.E.: ISEE: perceptual features for image library navigation. In: SPIE Human Vision and Electronic Imaging (2002)
20. Kollar, T., Roy, N.: Utilizing object–object and object–scene context when planning to find things. In: International Conference on Robotics and Automation (2009)
21. Dollar, P., Tu, Z., Perona, P., Belongie, S.: Integral channel features. In: British Machine Vision Conference (2009)
22. Vasudevan, S., Siegwart, R.: Bayesian space conceptualization and place classification for semantic maps in mobile robotics. Robot. Auton. Syst. **56**, 522–537 (2008)
23. Espinace, P., Kollar, T., Soto, A., Roy, N.: Indoor scene recognition through object detection. In: IEEE International Conference on Robotics and Automation (2010)

A Roadmap to Deep Learning: A State-of-the-Art Step Towards Machine Learning

Dweepna Garg[1(✉)], Parth Goel[1], Gokulnath Kandaswamy[2], Amit Ganatra[1], and Ketan Kotecha[3]

[1] Devang Patel Institute of Advance Technology and Research, Charotar
University of Science and Technology, Changa, Anand, Gujarat, India
dweeps1989@gmail.com, er.parthgoel@gmail.com,
amitganatra.ce@charusat.ac.in
[2] Lovely Faculty of Technology and Sciences, Lovely Professional University,
Phagwara, Punjab, India
kgnathit@gmail.com
[3] Faculty of Engineering, Symbiosis International University, Pune, India
drketankotecha@gmail.com

Abstract. Deep learning is a new era of machine learning and belonging to the area of artificial intelligence. It has tried to mimic the working of the way the human brain does. The models of deep learning have the capability to deal with high dimensional data and perform the complicated tasks in an accurate manner with the use of graphical processing unit (GPU). Significant performance is observed to analyze images, videos, text and speech. This paper deals with the detailed comparison of various deep learning models and the area in which these various deep learning models can be applied. We also present the comparison of various deep networks of classification. The paper also describes deep learning libraries along with the platform and interface in which they can be used. The accuracy is evaluated with respect to various machine learning and deep learning models on the MNIST dataset. The evaluation shows classification on deep learning model is far better than a machine learning model.

Keywords: Deep learning · Deep learning models · Deep learning libraries
MNIST dataset

1 Introduction

Deep Learning handles too much complicated information and simplifies the entire tasks. Geoff Hinton, Yann Lecun, Andrew Ng, Andrej Karpathy and Yoshua Bengio are the most popular researchers of Deep learning [1]. Google and its self-driving cars, Apple, NVIDIA and its GPU, Toyota are the various companies dealing with deep learning. The main motive of deep learning is to make the machine intelligent in the way the human brain works. The various deep architectures and learning models help in learning the features of numerous images and other objects. Neural networks are used to make the smart computers that can understand the complex patterns. The complex patterns are broken down in simpler patterns with the help of the deep

© Springer Nature Singapore Pte Ltd. 2019
A. K. Luhach et al. (Eds.): ICAICR 2018, CCIS 955, pp. 160–170, 2019.
https://doi.org/10.1007/978-981-13-3140-4_15

networks. The accuracy of these networks has found to yield good results. Deep networks were inspired by our human brains. The training time and the accuracy are the two parameters which get affected due to vanishing gradient problem [2]. The term gradient refers to the rate with which the cost changes with respect to bias or weight. The network gets trained quickly if the gradient is large else the net gets trained slowly. The process used for training a neural net is called *back-propagation*. It is so called because it calculates the gradient from right to left. Back-prop takes a lot of time in training the network on Central Processing Unit (CPU) compared to Graphical Processing Unit (GPU). GPU is specially designed for the calculation of huge matrix.

2 Neural Network

The concept of deep learning mainly focuses on neural networks. Neural Network improves the accuracy of perceptron and follows the same process that human brain works [3]. It was observed that the accuracy of prediction could be improved by using a layered stack of perceptrons. It is resulted in multi-layer perceptron (MLP). The neural network consists of various nodes interconnected to one another via the edges. These interconnected nodes are known as neurons. A set of input is received, complex calculations are performed and the output of the same is used to solve a problem. The neural network consists of mainly input layer, the hidden layer and the output layer (Fig. 1).

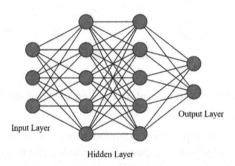

Fig. 1. Architecture of neural network

A set of input is passed from the input layer to the first hidden layer and it is passed to the next layer and then to the next until the output layer is reached. In the output layer, the classification results are determined by the scores at each node. Forward propagation is the concept wherein the series of events starts from the input and then every activation is sent to the next layer and then the next, all the way to the output layer. The reverse of the above operation is referred to as back-propagation. In forward prop: each node has the same classifier; if one repeats an input, then the same output is obtained. The node of the hidden layers receives the same input but does not fire out the same value as each set of input is modified by unique weights and biases. Each edge is assigned a unique weight and each node with a unique bias. The net is trained by comparing the output from the forward propagation with the correct output that is known and the cost is calculated by considering the difference between the two. The network is trained in order to make the cost as small as possible. Once the network is trained well, then the neural network has the ability to make accurate predictions each time. Neural networks are used for various classification tasks where an object can fall into one of the categories.

3   Restricted Boltzmann Machine (RBM)

Geoff Hinton's approach leads to the creation of RBM [4]. He is often referred to as the father of deep learning. Restricted Boltzmann machine is two layers shallow network which translates the input into a set of numbers that encodes the input. It automatically finds the patterns in the data by reconstructing the input. This model was built to overcome the vanishing gradient problem. There are mainly two passes in RBM namely the forward and the backward pass (Fig. 2).

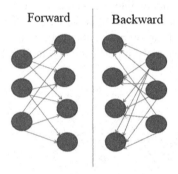

Fig. 2.   Backward and forward pass of Restricted Boltzman machine

In the forward pass, the input node is combined with an individual weight and one overall bias. The result of this is then passed to the hidden layer which may or may not activate. The backward pass combines each activation with the individual weight and overall bias. The result of this is then passed to the visible layer for reconstruction. In order to determine the quality of the result, the reconstruction is compared against the original input by the visible layer. RBM uses a measure called KL Divergence for the visible layer [5]. The steps from forward pass to visible layer are repeated with varying weights and biases until the input and re-construction are as close as possible. As the data required for RBM need not be labeled, so it can be used as an unsupervised model for solving the real-time applications related to photos, videos, voices and sensors. RBM actually makes the decisions about the important features and the way they can be combined to form the patterns. RBM is a family of feature extraction of deep nets.

4   Deep Belief Network

Geoff Hinton proposed Deep belief network which is regarded as one of the alternatives to backpropagation. The network structure of DBN resembles the multi-layer perceptron but with respect to training, they are entirely different. A stack of RBMs can be viewed as a deep belief network [6]. The training of DBN starts with reconstructing the input to an accurate extent by the first RBM. The hidden layer of the first RBM is called the visible layer for the next and the next RBM is trained using the outputs from the first RBM. This process continues until every layer of the network is trained (Fig. 3).

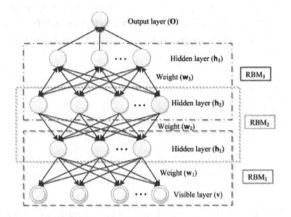

Fig. 3. Diagrammatic representation of deep belief network [7]

The entire input is learned by each RBM layer. On the other hand, the entire input is fine-tuned in succession by the deep belief network in order to improve the model. The reason behind the good performance of DBN is due to the stack of RBMs which outperforms a single unit. The models of RBM have an ability to detect inherent patterns in the data. Small changes in the weights and biases can alter the net's perception of the patterns and a little improvement in the total accuracy. DBN only needs a small labelled dataset, which is important for real-world applications. With the help of GPUs, the training process gets complete in a reasonable amount of time and hence it can be stated that DBN is a solution to the vanishing gradient problem.

5   Convolutional Nets

The concept of Convolutional neural networks (CNN) [8] was given by Yann Lecun. Facebook is using CNN for its facial recognition software. Early in the year 2015, an object recognition challenge was carried out wherein a machine was able to beat a human. This challenge made the AI popular. ImageNet [9] dataset became popular because it has 1000 different categories of images and researcher set it as a benchmark to evaluate their algorithm for classification. Starting with the convolutional layer of

CNN, each node in the convolutional layer is calculated with its weight and common bias of the layer. RELU (rectified linear unit) is the activation function which is generally used in CNN. The problem of vanishing gradient comes into the picture as the CNNs are trained using backpropagation. Mainly, intermediate layer uses RELU activation because it works on the same kind of patterns so, the difference in the gradient is very small. Dimensionality reduction is carried out using the pooling layer. The sequential combination of the multiple convolutional layers and the RELU layers builds up the complex patterns. These layers are unable to understand the meaning of the pattern. So in order to classify the data samples, network ends with the fully connected layer. On the other hand, the neurons in the convolutional layer, perform this convolution operation. The neurons are connected to every other neuron in the adjacent layers. Same weight and the bias parameters are shared among the neurons of the given filter because of that filter looks for the same pattern in different sections of the image (Fig. 4).

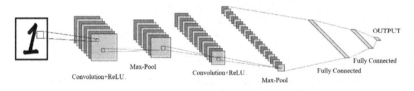

Fig. 4. Architecture of convolutional neural network

With the introduction of the pooling layer, only the relevant patterns are identified by convolution and RELU. GPU's are used to train the CNNs. The only drawback of CNN is that it requires a huge amount of categorized data for training, which is a very difficult task to collect for a real-world application. Table 1 shows comparison among Convolution Neural Networks on ImageNet Dataset for image classification of 1000 categories. They are trained using Gradient Descent with backpropagation. ReLU and dropout are used as an activation function and regularization respectively.

Table 1. Comparison of Convolution Neural Networks

Network name	Error rate		GPU used	No. of days for training	No. of layers
	Top-1 (%)	Top-5 (%)			
AlexNet [10]	37.5	17.0	2 GTX 580 3 GB	6	8
ZF Net [11]	36	14.8	GTX 580	12	7
VGG Net [12]	24.8	7.5	4 Nvidia Titan black	2 to 3 weeks	19
GoogLe Net [13]	–	6.7	CPU based	–	22
Microsoft ResNet [14]	–	3.57	8 GPU	–	152

6   Recurrent Neural Nets

Recurrent Neural Networks (RNN) has gained popularity due to the work of Juergen Schmidhuber, Sepp Hochreiter, and Alex Graves. RNN is the best to use when the data changes with time. The built-in feedback loop of the RNN acts as a forecasting engine and the output of a layer is added to the subsequent input layer and fed back into the same layer (Fig. 5).

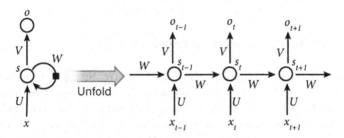

Fig. 5. Architecture of recurrent neural network [15]

In RNN, a sequence of values is received as an input, and sequence of values are produced as an output [16]. With an ability of RNN to work with sequences, it is used in various applications like document classification, forecasting the demand in supply chain planning, image captioning and classifying the video's frame by frame. Typically, an RNN is an extremely difficult network to train. The problem of vanishing gradient persists as these nets use backpropagation. Gating technique is used to address the problem of vanishing gradient and it helps the network to decide when to ignore the current input, and when to remember it for future time stamps. The most popular techniques are GRU and LSTM [17]. Other techniques include gradient clipping, steeper gates, and better optimizers. GPUs are used to train a recurrent networks.

7   Autoencoders

The autoencoders are two layered model. They are very shallow, i.e. it comprises of an input layer, hidden layer and output layer [18]. RBM is a popular example of autoencoder. The autoencoders mainly work with two steps- encoding and decoding. In this, the weights encode the features in the hidden layers and the same weights then decode the image in the output layer. The feature extractor of autoencoder first encodes and then reconstructs to the best of its accuracy deciding which data feature is most important (Fig. 6).

Autoencoders are trained with backpropagation using the metric called loss. A Loss is the information lost when the network tries to reconstruct the input. Small loss values would reconstruct the image very similar to the original. Deep autoencoders are used for dimensionality reduction and they perform better than their predecessor principal component analysis (PCA).

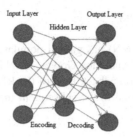

Fig. 6. Architecture of autoencoders

8 Recursive Neural Tensor Network (RNTN)

Richard Socher gave the concept of RNTNs. Recursive Neural Tensor Networks or RNTNs are best when it is used to discover the hierarchical structure of data [19]. The basic components of RNTN are parent group (referred to as the root) and the child groups (referred to as the leaves). The root is connected to both leaves, but the leaves are not connected to each other. The leaf groups receive the input, and the root uses a classifier to fire out a class and a score. Each group is simply a collection of neurons. The number of neurons decides the complexity of the input data. The features are the word vectors which serve as the basis of sequential classification. These are grouped into subphrases, which are then combined into a sentence that can be classified by sentiment and other metrics. Table 2 shows a comparison of deep learning models with them applications and complexity.

Table 2. Highlights of deep learning models

Deep learning model	Best fit for	Model complexity	Application	Pioneered author
CNN	Supervised learning	High (Layers of CNN are repeated several times followed by a few fully connected layers)	Image classification, object recognition	YannLecun, Geoff Hinton
RNN	Supervised learning	High (Higher than CNNs due to management of current layer and output of previous layer)	Image captioning, speech recognition, classification of video frame by frame, text processing, time series analysis	Juergen Schmidhuber, SeppHochreiter and Alex Graves
Auto encoder	Unsupervised learning	Low (2 layer)	Labelling of dataset, important features selection	Geoff Hinton
RBM	Unsupervised learning	Low (2 layer)	Labelling of dataset, important features selection, feature extractor	Geoff Hinton

(continued)

Table 2. (*continued*)

Deep learning model	Best fit for	Model complexity	Application	Pioneered author
DBN	Supervised learning	High (Stack of RBMs)	Image recognition	Geoff Hinton
RNTN	Supervised learning	High (hierarchical structure)	To analyze data that have a hierarchical structure, i.e. Sentiment analysis and natural language Processing	Richard Socher

9   Comparison of Deep Learning Library

Basically, all deep learning libraries are open sources and supporting all types of deep learning architectures. They are able to analyze untrusted data like text, speech and images. Each library supports CUDA and capable to run networks on NVIDIA GPUs. Table 3 shows comparison of Deep Learning Libraries. TensorFlow [20] becomes very popular because of its huge resources which are made by Google and widely used in many projects. It has network visualization facility through tensorboard. It helps us to debug the deep network.

Table 3. Comparison of deep learning library

Software	Creator	Platform	Written in	Interface
TensorFlow	Google Brainteam	Linux, Mac OS, Windows	C ++, Python	Python, (C/C ++ public API only for executing graphs)
Keras [21]	François Chollet	Linux, Mac OS, Windows	Python	Python
Deeplearning4j [22]	Adam Gibson	Linux, Mac OS, Windows, Android (Cross-platform)	C, C ++	Java, Scala
Caffe [23]	Yangqing Jia	Linux, Mac OS, Windows	C++	Python, Matlab
Theano [24]	University de Montréal	Cross-platform	Python	Python
Torch [25]	Ronan Collobert, Kavukcuoglu, Clement	Linux, Mac OS, Windows, Android, iOS	C, Lua	Lua,C, utility library for C ++/OpenCL
Microsoft Cognitive Toolkit-CNTK [26]	Microsoft Research	Windows, Linux	C++	Python, C++, Command line, BrainScript (. NET on roadmap)

10 MNIST Dataset

The MNIST [27] dataset consist handwritten digits in range of 0 to 9. It is a subset of NIST [28] which is one of the largest set available of handwritten digits. The number of images of training data is 55,000 along with 10,000 images of test data and 5,000 images of validation data in MNIST dataset. Size of each digit image is 28 × 28. There are mainly 2 parts of the MNIST data point namely an image of a handwritten digit indicated as "x" and another is the corresponding label for each image indicated as "y". These labels are used for recognition of digit while training and testing. The images along with the corresponding labels are contained in both the training set and the test set. The image of MNIST dataset has a range between zero and nine of hand-written digit. So the total number of possibilities is only ten of an image.

11 Experimental Setup

The experiment is performed on Core i5 processor, 8 GB RAM, Ubuntu Operating System. The following figures show the accuracy with different architectures of machine learning and deep learning models using different activation function on MNIST dataset. Each experiment runs with 5000 iterations. Batch size and learning rate are 64 and 0.0001 respectively. The graphs below depict the accuracy of each model. The *y-axis* in the graph indicates the accuracy and *x-axis* indicates the number of iterations. It is seen that the convolutional neural network is able to classify the images in a more accurate manner as compared to the other machine learning models (Figs. 7, 8, 9 and 10).

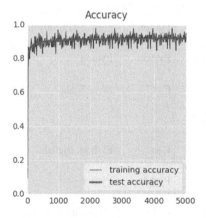

Fig. 7. Neural network with 1 layer Accuracy = 92.20%

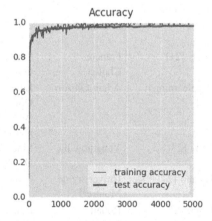

Fig. 8. Neural network with 5 layers using ReLU Accuracy = 98.24%

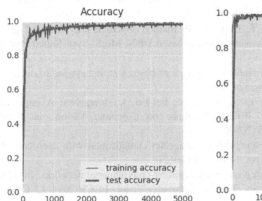

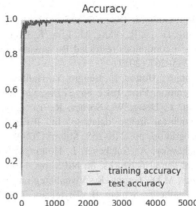

Fig. 9. Convolutional Neural Network (CNN) with Dropout = 0.70 Accuracy = 98.52%

Fig. 10. Convolutional Neural Network (CNN) with Batch Normalization Accuracy = 9.45%

12 Conclusion

In this paper, a roadmap to the deep learning is presented. It summarizes the structure and the application areas to which the deep learning models can be the best applied. The future of deep learning lies in the field of computer vision where ConvNets and RNNs can be combined and use for video analytics and reinforcement learning. The challenging issue is to choose an appropriate dataset along with the deciding factor that whether to use the off-the-shelf representations or to fine-tune the parameters. The paper also concludes that when the different models are implemented on MNIST dataset, for deep learning models, the accuracy is comparatively higher than the other machine learning models. Hence, deep learning is considered to be the state-of-art step towards machine learning.

References

1. Deep Learning Research Groups. http://deeplearning.net/deep-learning-research-groups-and-labs/
2. Pascanu, R., Mikolov, T., Bengio, Y.: On the difficulty of training recurrent neural networks. In: 30th International Conference on Machine Learning, pp. 1310– 1318. JMLR.org, Atlanta, GA, USA (2013)
3. Abraham, A.: Artificial neural networks. In: Sydenham, Peter H., Thorn, Richard (eds.) Handbook of Measuring System Design, pp. 901–908. Wiley, London (2005)
4. Sutskever, I., Hinton, G., Taylor, G.: The recurrent temporal restricted Boltzmann machine. In: NIPS'2008, Curran Associates, Inc., pp. 1601–1608 (2009)
5. Fischer, A: Training Restricted Boltzmann Machines. KI-Künstliche Intelligenz. **29**, 441– 444 (2015)

6. Hinton, G.E., Simon, O., Yee-Whye, T.: A fast learning algorithm for deep belief nets. Neural Comput. **18**, 1527–1554 (2006)
7. Huang, H., Li, R., Yang, M., Lim, T., Ding, W.: Evaluation of vehicle interior sound quality using a continuous restricted Boltzmann machine-based DBN. Mech. Syst. Signal Process. **84**, 245–267 (2017)
8. Lecun, Y., Bottou, L., Bengio, Y., Haffner, P.: Gradient-based learning applied to document recognition. Proc. IEEE **86**, 2278–2324 (1998)
9. Deng, J., Dong, W., Socher, R., Li, L.-J., Li, K., Fei-Fei, L.: ImageNet: A large-scale hierarchical image database. In: IEEE Conference on Computer Vision and Pattern Recognition, pp. 248–255. Miami (2009)
10. Krizhevsky, A., Sutskever, I., Hinton, G., E.: ImageNet classification with deep convolutional neural networks. In: NIPS, pp. 110–1114 (2012)
11. Zeiler, M.D., Fergus, R.: Visualizing and understanding convolutional networks. In: Fleet, D., Pajdla, T., Schiele, B., Tuytelaars, T. (eds.) Computer Vision–ECCV 2014. LNCS, vol. 8689. Springer, Cham (2014)
12. Simonyan, K., Zisserman, A.: Very deep convolutional networks for large-scale image recognition. In: International Conference on Learning Representations (2015)
13. Szegedy, C., Liu, W., Jia, Y., Sermanet, P., Reed, S., Anguelov, D., et al.: Going deeper with convolutions. In: IEEE Conference on Computer Vision and Pattern Recognition, pp. 1–9. Boston (2015)
14. He, K., Zhang, X., Ren, S., Sun, J.: Deep residual learning for image recognition. In: IEEE Conference on Computer Vision and Pattern Recognition, pp. 770–778. Las Vegas, NV (2016)
15. LeCun, Y., Bengio, Y., Hinton, G.E.: Deep learning. Nature **521**, 436–444 (2015)
16. Graves, A.: Generating Sequences With Recurrent Neural Networks, CoRR. (2013)
17. Hochreiter, S., Schmidhuber, J.: Long short-term memory. Neural Comput. **9**, 1735–1780 (1997)
18. Hinton, G.E., Zemel, R.S.: Autoencoders, minimum description length, and Helmholtz free energy. Adv. Neural. Inf. Process. Syst. **6**, 3–10 (1994)
19. Socher, R., Perelygin, A., Wu, J., Chuang, J., D. Manning, C., Ng, A., et al.: Recursive deep models for semantic compositionality over a sentiment Treebank. In: Conference on Empirical Methods in Natural Language Processing (2013)
20. Abadi, M., Barham, P., Chen, J., Chen, Z., Davis, A., Dean, J., et al.: Tensorflow: A system for large-scale machine learning. In: 12th USENIX Conference on Operating Systems Design and Implementation. pp. 265–283, USENIX Association, Savannah, GA, USA (2016)
21. Keras: The Python Deep Learning library. https://keras.io/
22. Deeplearning4j: Open-source, Distributed Deep Learning for the JVM. https://deeplearning4j.org/index.html
23. Caffe| Deep Learning Framework. http://caffe.berkeleyvision.org
24. Bergstra, J., Bastien, F., Breuleux, O., Lamblin, P., Pascanu, R., Delalleau, O., et al.: Theano: deep learning on gpus with python. In: Neural Information Processing Systems. Big Learn workshop (2011)
25. Collobert, R., Kavukcuoglu, K., Farabet, C.: Torch7: a matlab-like environment for machine learning. In: Neural Information Processing Systems. Big Learn workshop (2011)
26. Agarwal, A., Akchurin, E., Basoglu, C., Chen, G., Cyphers, S., Droppo, J., et al.: An Introduction to Computational Networks and the Computational Network Toolkit. Microsoft Technical Report MSR-TR-2014-112 (2014)
27. The MNIST database of handwritten digits. http://yann.lecun.com/exdb/mnist
28. NIST Handprinted Forms and Characters Database. https://www.nist.gov/srd/nist-special-database-19

Morphology Analysis and Time Interval Measurements Using Mallat Tree Decomposition for CVD Detection

Navdeep Prashar[1](✉), Meenakshi Sood[2], and Shruti Jain[2]

[1] Department of Electronics and Communication Engineering,
Bahra University, Solan, India
nav.prashar@gmail.com
[2] Jaypee University of Information Technology, Solan, India
{meenakshi.sood, shruti.jain}@juit.ac.in

Abstract. Electrocardiogram signal is used to identify the heart related abnormalities as cardiovascular disease. Automatic detection and analysis of abnormalities of long duration of ECG signals is tedious and quite subjective as it is difficult to decipher the minute morphological variations. In this paper, Morphology Analysis and Time Interval Measurements using Mallat Tree Decomposition (MTD) are done to obtain the signal in the desired form for calculation of heart rate. ECG signals are analyzed with various mother wavelets using MTD, and analyzed on the basis of performance matrices. It was found for this research work bior 3.9 wavelet is well suited for the processing of ECG signal. Heart rate using Peak Detection Algorithm (PDA) is calculated after pre-processing technique and bior 3.9 wavelet. The experiments were carried out on MATLAB R2016a environment.

Keywords: Cardiovascular disease · Mallat Tree Decomposition
Heart rate · Time interval measurement · Morphology analysis

1 Introduction

Cardiovascular disease (CVD) is a major disorder that results in to hypertension and myocardial infarction. Approximately 30% of worldwide deaths are due to CVD disease [1, 2]. Early detection of CVD disease is an important step to prevent these deaths. Therefore, a regular analysis of ECG signal is required for early detection [3, 4]. An ECG signal consists of five waves namely *P*, *Q*, *R*, *S*, and *T* which performs four main events: the *R-R* interval, the *P-Q* interval, the *QRS* complex, and the *S-T* interval [5]. These events contain their own peaks to analyze the morphology, amplitude and time duration for CVD detection [6–8]. All the important features such as duration and amplitude on this recording must lies within normal range. P wave is the upright positive deflection with respect to baseline in the waveform. The duration and amplitude of this wave should be less than or equal to 0.11 s and 0.25 mV respectively. *P-Q* is measured from the beginning of *P* wave to the start of the *QRS* complex. *QRS*

A. K. Luhach et al. (Eds.): ICAICR 2018, CCIS 955, pp. 171–181, 2019.
https://doi.org/10.1007/978-981-13-3140-4_16

complex being the most prominent feature of entire waveform have the duration and amplitude range lies in between 60–100 ms and 2.5–3.0 mV respectively. Resting state of ventricles signified by T wave in which repolarization process takes place. The S-T segment requires approximately 320 to 350 ms. Repolarization period of ventricles is from 100–250 ms having amplitude in between 0.1–0.5 mV [9]. Machine Learning based ECG analysis is required for an accurate detection of peaks which is a very tedious task as this signal is affected by Baseline Wander noise, Power line interference noise, Burst noise and Electromyography noise [10–12]. False detection of R-wave leads to undesired results which further resulted in to poor signal-to-noise ratio (SNR) [13]. Many researchers have done research on heart rate calculation, feature extraction [14–20], ECG compression, R-R interval analysis, and P, S, & T wave detection which are mainly categorized in to three categories: Time Detection Technique, Transform Domain Detection Techniques, & Morphologic Filtering Techniques and Template Matching Methods [21].

Wavelet transform has become an important computational tool for performing Signal Processing. It overcomes the shortcomings of time window size which does not vary with frequency. Authors in [22] uses wavelet transform which is applied to extract the coefficients and they uses autoregressive modelling for calculating temporal structure of an ECG signal [22]. A new technique is presented by authors in [23] in which feature sets has been obtained using mathematical morphology. A novel ECG obfuscation method has been formulated which uses cross correlation based template matching approach to distinguish all ECG features [24]. Another method of feature extraction based on Discrete Wavelet Transform (DWT) has been designed to solve the problem of non-stationary ECG signals by providing stable features [25]. A modified technique based on the combined wavelet transform is presented in which two wavelets a Quadratic Spline Wavelet (QSWT) for QRS detection and the Daubechies six coefficient (db6) wavelet for P and T detection have been used [26]. Authors in [27] uses technique based on cepstrum coefficient method for feature extraction and artificial neural network (ANN) models for the classification and has developed a model which gives the accuracy of 97.5% to diagnose cardiac disease [27]. An integrated feature extraction approach has been proposed using Principal Component Analysis and DWT that shows the wavelet features are more significant than time domain feature for better discrimination [28]. An author in [29] proposes an automatic ECG feature extraction system based on DWT for various feature extraction.

In this research paper, distinct families of discrete wavelets have been applied for multilevel decomposition of MIT-BIH Arrhythmia v5 ECG input signal to extract the R-R interval, P-Q interval, QRS complex, and S-T interval along with Heart Rate calculation. This paper is further organized as follows: Sect. 2 introduces signal decomposition using Mallat Tree Decomposition (MTD). Section 3 describes the methodology which is followed by results and discussions and concluded in the last.

2 Signal Decomposition Using Mallat Tree Decomposition Algorithm

DWT derived from sub-band coding result in less computation time and reduced number of required resources. In DWT time scale representation of signal is obtained using digital filtering technique. The signal is passed through filters having different cut-off frequency at different scales. The DWT function is given by

$$W_\psi(j, k) = \frac{1}{\sqrt{m}} \sum x(n) \, \psi_{j,k}(n) \tag{1}$$

where $x(n)$ = input signal, $1/\sqrt{m}$ is a normalizing term, m is the number of samples in the sequence and n is integer = 0, 1, 2 ... m–1.

The DWT is defined by MTD algorithm in which output is computed by successive low pass and high pass filtering of discrete signal as shown in Fig. 1.

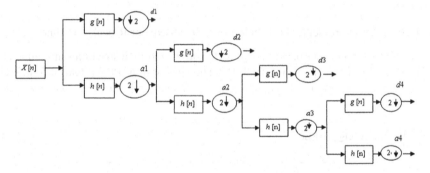

Fig. 1. Multilevel decomposition at level4

In Fig. 1, $x[n]$ is the input signal which is decomposed into two: high pass filter $g[n]$ and low pass filter $h[n]$. Each stage comprises of two digital filters and two down samplers (by 2) to produce further varying frequency digital signals. The down sampled output of first high pass filter $g[n]$ and low pass filter $h[n]$ give detail coefficient $d1$ and approximation coefficient $a1$ respectively. The approximation coefficient $a1$ is further decomposed and this process continues till the set level of decomposition. In this research paper, 4 level of decomposition is used which provide $d1$, $d2$, $d3$, $d4$ as detailed coefficients and $a4$ as an approximation coefficient. Different families of DWT such as Daubechies, Biorthogonal, Reverse Orthogonal, Symlets and Coiflets have been used for signal decomposition.

3 Methodology

Input signal of ECG with 100 record databases from MIT-BIH Arrhythmia v5 is taken from Physio Bank ATM. This input ECG signal has length of 1460 samples which is sampled at rate of 360 Hz. The following steps are followed for Peak Detection (morphology analysis) and computation of different intervals (time interval measurement).

Step 1: MIT-BIH Arrhythmia database ECG signal 100 m.mat is loaded.

Step 2: Pre-processing: Input ECG signal is fed to digital FIR High pass filter using Blackman windowing technique to remove Base Line Wander noise with cut-off frequency 0.5 Hz. The order of filter is taken $N = 10$ by defining the window length i.e. $N + 1 = 11$ [11].

Step 3: Compute Heart Beat rate of pre-processed signal: Output of FIR High pass filter is used to compute the Heart rate of an ECG signal is defined by Eq. 2.

$$Heart\,Rate \;=\; \frac{Sample\,Rate \,\times\, 60}{R_2 \,-\, R_1} \tag{2}$$

where R_2 and R_1 represents the location of two subsequent R peaks on time scale.

Step 4: Different ECG peaks (*P, Q, R, S,* and *T*) and their location (amplitude and time) has been detected using Peak Detection Algorithm (PDA). Out of 5 different waves/peaks, *R* peak has the maximum amplitude of an ECG signal in every cycle.

Peak Detection Algorithm

Input – Pre-processed signal (*Y*)

Output – Peak Detection

---

1. Define Sample Rate
2. Detection of *R* peak: The point with maximum amplitude gives the *R* peak location.

If *R* peak is located for each cycle (R_{peak}) , then different other peaks are detected by the following methods :

3. Detection of *P* peak : *P* peak location detection is given as

$$a = \left[R_{peak} - \left(\frac{Sample\,Rate \times 25}{Beat} \right) \right] : \left[R_{peak} - \left(\frac{Sample\,Rate \times 5}{Beat} \right) \right]$$

P peak amplitude= max(*Y*(*a*));

4. Detection of Q peak: Q peak location detection is given as

$$b = \left[R_{peak} - \left(\frac{Sample\ Rate \times 10}{Beat} \right) \right] : \left[R_{peak} - \left(\frac{Sample\ Rate \times 1}{Beat} \right) \right]$$

Q peak amplitude $= \min(Y(b))$;

5. Detection of Speak : S peak location detection is expressed as

$$c = \left[R_{peak} + \left(\frac{Sample\ Rate \times 1}{Beat} \right) \right] : \left[R_{peak} + \left(\frac{Sample\ Rate \times 5}{Beat} \right) \right]$$

Speak amplitude $= \min(Y(c))$;

6. Detection of T peak : T peak location detection is represented as

$$d = \left[R_{peak} + \left(\frac{Sample\ Rate \times 10}{Beat} \right) \right] : \left[R_{peak} + \left(\frac{Sample\ Rate \times 30}{Beat} \right) \right]$$

T peak amplitude $= \max(Y(d))$;

    End

Step 5: Detection of Time Interval Measurements: After detecting different ECG peaks, different intervals are calculated. R-R interval is calculated by Eq. 3

$$R\text{ - }R\text{ interval} = (R_2 - R_1)/\text{sample rate} \tag{3}$$

where R_2 and R_1 are the locations of two subsequent R peaks.
P-Q interval is given by Eq. 4

$$P\text{ - }Q\text{ interval} = (Q_{peak} - P_{peak})/\text{sample rate} \tag{4}$$

where Q_{peak} and P_{peak} are the location of Q and P peak in that particular cycle.
QRS complex is calculated by Eq. 5

$$QRS\text{ complex} = (S_{peak} - Q_{peak})/\text{sample rate} \tag{5}$$

where S_{peak} and Q_{peak} are the location of S and Q peak in that particular cycle.
S-T interval is given by Eq. 6

$$S\text{ - }T \text{ interval} = \left(T_{\text{peak}} - S_{\text{peak}}\right)/\text{sample rate} \tag{6}$$

where T_{peak} and S_{peak} are the location of T and S peak in that particular cycle.

Step 6: Decomposition level is set at level 4 to maintain the balance to remove noise without removing important features. Different wavelet families are used: Daubechies, Biorthogonal, Reverse Orthogonal, Coiflets and Symlets.

Step 7: In this step, performance metrics of different wavelet families has been examined using different parameters to find out which wavelet transform is better for ECG signal computation.

1. Signal-to-noise ratio (SNR) is calculated as root mean square amplitude of signal and noise.

$$\text{SNR} = 10 \log_{10} \left(E_{\text{signal}}/E_{\text{noise}}\right)^2 \tag{7}$$

2. Mean Square Error (MSE) signifies the difference between Original signal and cleaned signal without noise.

$$MSE = 1/N \sum_{n=1}^{N} [x(n) - y(n)]^2 \tag{8}$$

3. Percent root mean square difference (PRD) is used to measure the distortion and is defined by Eq. (9)

$$PRD = \sqrt{\frac{\sum_{n=1}^{N} [x(n) - y(n)]^2}{\sum_{n=1}^{N} [x^2(n)]}} \tag{9}$$

In Eqs. 8 and 9, $x(n)$ is noisy input signal and $y(n)$ represents filtered signal.

Step 8: On the basis of performance parameters best wavelet method is analysed which is used for the further experiments. Wavelet coefficients using MTD are extracted and smoothing of coefficients has been done using Global Thresholding followed by denoising.

Step 9: After getting the wavelet coefficients using MTD, different peaks of an output signal has been detected using Peak Detection Algorithm as explained in step 4 which are compared with the peaks obtained after pre-processing techniques.

Step 10: Different time intervals of wavelet coefficients obtained using MTD has been calculated by equations used in Step 5 and compared the results obtained after pre-processed signals.

4   Results and Discussions

In this section, output of an ECG signal has been observed at different stages. In first stage, output has been obtained after removing baseline wander noise. In second stage, output of an ECG signal has been obtained after performing multilevel decomposition using MTD. The best wavelet on the basis of performance parameters such as SNR, MSE and PRD has been selected which is followed by extracting coefficients. Lastly peaks of ECG signal are detected and different time measurement intervals are calculated which are compared with the values obtained after pre-processing.

4.1   Removal of Baseline Wander Noise by Pre-processing Technique and Detection of Various Peaks

To remove low frequency Baseline wander noise, FIR filter has been designed using Blackman window technique explained by Prashar *et al.* [11]. Order of filter is $N = 10$ and window length is $N + 1$. Peaks of the filtered output ECG signal have been detected using Peak Detection Algorithm shown in Fig. 2.

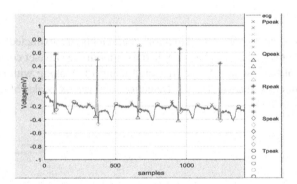

Fig. 2. Time domain analysis of Output ECG signal after filtered by Blackman window with Peak Detection.

4.2   Performing Multilevel Decomposition Using Mallat Tree

The output of High pass FIR filter is fed to the different wavelet families. Different families of wavelet used in this paper are Daubechies- db4, db5, db6, db7, db8, Biorthogonal-bior3.5, bior3.7, bior3.9, Reverse Orthogonal – rbio4.4, rbio5.5, rbio6, Coiflets-coif4, coif5 and Symlets –sym4, sym5, sym6, sym9. Table 1 shows the performance metrics of different wavelets families in terms of SNR, MSE and PRD. Result shows that bior3.9 wavelet is well suited for ECG signal processing as it has high SNR and low value of MSE and PRD among all the wavelet families.

Table 1. SNR comparison of window based FIR filters

Wavelet families	Type	SNR	MSE	PRD
Daubechies	**db4**	25.0144	2.0134e−04	0.0561
	db5	24.6097	2.2101e−04	0.0588
	db6	24.3737	2.3335e−04	0.0604
	db7	24.5116	2.2606e−04	0.0595
	db8	24.0698	2.5027e−04	0.0626
Biorthogonal	**bior3.5**	26.3158	1.4921e−04	0.0483
	bior3.7	26.4652	1.4416e−04	0.0475
	bior3.9	26.5396	1.4172e−04	0.0471
Reverse orthogonal	**rbio4.4**	24.4049	2.3168e−04	0.0602
	rbio5.5	24.9515	2.0428e−04	0.0565
	rbio6.8	25.1085	1.9703e−04	0.0555
Coiflets	**coif 4**	25.1166	1.9666e−04	0.0555
	coif5	24.8627	2.0850e−04	0.0571
Symlets	**sym4**	24.8996	2.0674e−04	0.0569
	sym5	24.6218	2.2039e−04	0.0587
	sym6	25.2806	1.8937e−04	0.0552
	sym9	24.8941	2.0700e−04	0.0569

Detailed coefficients and approximation coefficients are extracted from the ECG signal. Global Thresholding has been applied to smooth the wavelet coefficient. Lastly, different peaks of denoised signal are detected using PDA along with computation of different time interval measurements. Detection of various peaks of denoised ECG signal is shown in Fig. 3.

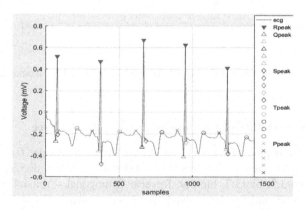

Fig. 3. Detection of peaks of denoised signal using PDA

Table 2 shows the computation of Heart Rate after pre- processing of an ECG signal and after processing by bior3.9 wavelet.

Table 2. Heart Rate computation

Heart Rate per minute	Heart Rate computation after High pass FIR filter	Heart Rate computation after processing by bior3.9 wavelet
	74.8882	74.8256

Table 3 shows the various peak errors such as P peak error, Q peak error, R peak error, S peak error and T peak error. Peak error is computed by equation

Table 3. Different peak error computation

Peak type	Peak error (%)
R peak error	0.2000
P peak error	2.000
Q peak error	0.4000
S peak error	2.4000
T peak error	2.4000

Table 4. Calculation of different peak intervals

S. No.	Types of intervals	Indications	Normal values of intervals (sec)	Output after high pass FIR filter (sec)	Output after processing by bior3.9 wavelet (sec)
1	R-R interval	Useful to calculate Heart Rate	0.6–1.2	0.8014	0.8021
2	P-Q interval	P-Q interval specifies the certain medical conditions. P-Q interval over 0.2 s indicates first degree of Heart blockage. Prolongation also indicates Hypokalemia, acute rheumatic fever	0.12–0.2	0.1378	0.1333
3	QRS complex	It indicates the depolarization of the right and left ventricle of human heart. Useful in diagnosing Cardiac arrhythmia, myocardial infraction	0.06–0.1	0.0461	0.0517
4	S-T interval	Variations in ST interval indicate the disease like transmural myocardial infarction	0.32–0.35	0.3451	0.3479

$$Peak\,Error = abs\left(x_p - x'_p\right) \qquad (10)$$

where x_p is output from high pass filter and x'_p is identified after MTD.

Table 4 shows the time level measurement of different peak intervals i.e. *R-R* interval, *P-Q* interval, *QRS* complex and *S-T* interval in every cycle of an ECG signal at two levels: (a) Output of ECG signal after High pass FIR filter using Blackman window and (b) Output of ECG signal after processing through bior3.9 wavelet.

5 Conclusion

The manual detection method is not suitable for a long-term monitoring system, and whenever an ECG is acquired from a patient body, a lot of noises accumulate with it, so proper detection is not feasible. Machine Learning based ECG analysis is required for an accurate detection of peaks which is a very tedious task as this signal is affected by various noise. In this paper, Morphology Analysis and Time Interval Measurements using Mallat Tree Decomposition (MTD) are done to obtain the signal in the desired form for calculation of heart rate. ECG signals are analyzed with various mother wavelets using MTD, and analyzed on the basis of performance matrices.

References

1. Alwan, A.: Global Status Report on No Communicable Diseases 2010, pp. 9–31. World Health Organization, Geneva (2011)
2. Palanivel, S., Sukanesh, R.: Experimental studies on intelligent, wearable and automated wireless mobile tele-alert system for continuous cardiac surveillance. J. Appl. Res. Technol. **11**, 133–143 (2013)
3. Dilaveris, P.E., et al.: Simple electrocardiographic markers for the prediction of paroxysmal idiopathic atrial fibrillation. Am. Heart J. **135**, 733–738 (1998)
4. Elgendi, M., Eskofier, B., Dokos, S., Abbott, D.: Revisiting QRS detection methodologies for portable, wearable, battery-operated, and wireless ECG systems. PLoS ONE **9**, e84018 (2014)
5. Hasan, M.A., Mamun, M.D.: Hardware approach of R-peak detection for the measurement of fetal and maternal heart rates. J. Appl. Res. Technol. **10**, 835–844 (2012)
6. Bashour, C., et al.: Characterization of premature atrial contraction activity prior to the onset of postoperative atrial fibrillation in cardiac surgery patients. Chest **126**, 831S–832S (2004)
7. Tran, T., McNames, J., Aboy, M., Goldstein, B.: Prediction of paroxysmal atrial fibrillation by analysis of atrial premature complexes. IEEE Trans. Biomed. Eng. **51**, 561–569 (2004)
8. Tsipouras, M.G., Fotiadis, D.I., Sideris, D.: Arrhythmia classification using the R-R- interval duration signal. IEEE Comput. Cardiol. **2002**, 485–488 (2002)
9. Surawicz, B., Childers, R., Deal, B.J., Gettes, L.S.: AHA/ACCF/HRS recommendations for the standardization and interpretation of the electrocardiogram. J. Am. Coll. Cardiol. **53**, 976–981 (2009)
10. Benitez, D., Gaydecki, P.A., Zaidi, A., Fitzpatrick, A.P.: The use of the Hilbert transform in ECG signal analysis. Comput. Biol. Med. **31**, 399–406 (2001)

11. Prashar, N., Dogra, J., Sood, M., Jain, S.: Removal of electromyography noise from ECG for high performance biomedical systems. Netw. Biol. **8**(1), 12–24 (2018)
12. Prashar, N., Jain, S., Sood, M., Dogra, J.: Review of biomedical system for high performance applications. In: 4th IEEE International Conference on signal processing and control (ISPCC 2017). 21–23 September, Jaypee University of Information technology, Waknaghat, Solan, H.P, India, pp. 300–304 (2017)
13. Köhler, B.-U., Hennig, C., Orglmeister, R.: QRS detection using zero crossing counts. Prog. Biomed. Res. **8**, 138–145 (2003)
14. Dogra, J., Sood, M., Jain, S., Prashar, N.: Segmentation of magnetic resonance images of brain using thresholding techniques. In: 4th IEEE International Conference on signal processing and control (ISPCC 2017), Jaypee University of Information technology, Waknaghat, Solan, H.P, India, pp. 311–315 (2017)
15. Sharma, S., Jain, S., Bhusri, S.: Two class classification of breast lesions using statistical and transform domain features. J. Glob. Pharma Technol. (JGPT) **9**(7), 18–24 (2017)
16. Rana, S., Jain, S., Virmani, J.: Classification of focal kidney lesions using wavelet-based texture descriptors. Int. J. Pharma Bio Sci. **7**(3), 646–652 (2016)
17. Bhusri, S., Jain, S., Virmani, J.: Classification of breast lesions using the difference of statistical features. Res. J. Pharm. Biol. Chem. Sci. (RJPBCS) **7**(4), 1365–1372 (2016)
18. Rana, S., Jain, S., Virmani, J.: SVM-based characterization of focal kidney lesions from B-mode ultrasound images. Res. J. Pharm. Biol. Chem. Sci. (RJPBCS) **7**(4), 837–846 (2016)
19. Bhusri, S., Jain, S., Virmani, J.: Breast lesions classification using the amalagation of morphological and texture features. Int. J. Pharm. Bio Sci. (IJPBS) **7**(2), 617–624 (2016)
20. Jain, S.: Classification of protein kinase B using discrete wavelet transform. Int. J. Inf. Technol. **10**(2), 211–216 (2018)
21. Burte, R., Ghongade, R.: Advances in QRS detection: modified Wavelet energy gradient method. Int. J. Emerg. Trends Sign. Proc. **1**, 23–29 (2012)
22. Zhao, Q., Zhan, L.: ECG feature extraction and classification using wavelet transform and support vector machines. In: International Conference on Neural Networks and Brain, ICNN&B 2005, vol. 2, pp. 1089–1092 (2005)
23. Tadejko, P., Rakowski, W.: Mathematical morphology based ECG feature extraction for the purpose of heartbeat classification. In: 6th International Conference on Computer Information Systems and Industrial Management Applications, CISIM 2007, pp. 322–327 (2007)
24. Sufi, F., Mahmoud, S., Khalil, I.: A new ECG obfuscation method: a joint feature extraction and corruption approach. In: 2008 International Conference on Information Technology and Applications in Biomedicine, ITAB 2008, pp. 334–337 (2008)
25. Tamil, E.M., Kamarudin, N.H., RosliSalleh, M., Idris, Y.I., Noor, N.M., Tamil, A.M.: Heartbeat Electrocardiogram (ECG) Signal Feature Extraction Using Discrete Wavelet Transforms (DWT)
26. SaxenaS, C., Kumar, V., Hamde, S.T.: Feature extraction from ECG signals using wavelet transforms for disease diagnostics. Int. J. Syst. Sci. **33**(13), 1073–1085 (2002)
27. Jen, K.K., Hwang, Y.R.: ECG feature extraction and classification using cepstrum and neural networks. J. Med. Biological Eng. **28**(1), 31 (2008)
28. Martis, R.J., Chakraborty, C., Ray, A.K.: An integrated ECG feature extraction scheme using PCA and wavelet transform. In: Annual IEEE India Conference (2009)
29. Srisawat, W.: Implementation of real time feature extraction of ECG using discrete wavelet transform. In: 10th International Conference on Electrical Engineering/Electronics, Computer, Telecommunications and Information Technology (ECTI-CON) (2013). 10.1109/ECTICon.2013.6559628

Automated Optical Disc Segmentation and Blood Vessel Extraction for Fundus Images Using Ophthalmic Image Processing

Charu Bhardwaj[(✉)], Shruti Jain, and Meenakshi Sood

Department of Electronics and Communication Engineering, Jaypee University
of Information Technology, Waknaghat, Solan, India
cbcharubhardwaj215@gmail.com,
{shruti.jain,meenakshi.sood}@juit.ac.in

Abstract. Diabetic Retinopathy that is characterised by the progressive deterioration in retinal blood vessels is considered the root cause of severe vision loss in diabetic patients. This situation can be reduced upto much extent by regular screening and diagnosis. Precise automatic segmentation of optical disc and automated blood vessel extraction results in effective diagnosis of diabetic retinopathy reducing the chances of vision loss. A considerable progress has been made by various researchers towards automating the ophthalmic image processing via computer aided screening but maintaining the image quality as that of the original fundus image is still a challenge. In this paper, authors have evaluated Optical Disc Segmentation methods based on thresholding, region growing algorithm and mathematical morphology for effective removal of optical disc to facilitate blood vessel extraction. A new blood vessel extraction technique using Mathematical Morphology and Fuzzy Algorithm is proposed for precise blood vessel extraction. Two open access standard fundus image databases, DRIVE and STARE were exploited for performance evaluation of the proposed approach. This approach is effective in identifying optical disc to extract the blood vessels near the optical disc area which plays an important role in early diagnosis of diabetic retinopathy.

Keywords: Diabetic retinopathy · Ophthalmic image processing
Computer aided screening · Optical disc segmentation · Blood vessel extraction

1 Introduction

Diabetic Retinopathy (DR) is characterised by long term accumulated damage to the retina occurring due to diabetes mellitus which are marked by the appearance of different lesions like microaneurysms, exudates, haemorrhages, neovascularisation, etc. DR is considered as the major cause of vision loss in most of the diabetic patients and it occurs due to the change in retinal blood vessels which may swell and leak out fluid into the retinal area. These blood vessels may close off completely arresting the oxygen supply to the retina. The other major cause of DR is blood vessel overgrowth leading to bifurcated blood vessel pattern. The newly grown blood vessels are weak and fragile and may leak out blood and fluid into the retinal areas [1]. Broad classification of DR

© Springer Nature Singapore Pte Ltd. 2019
A. K. Luhach et al. (Eds.): ICAICR 2018, CCIS 955, pp. 182–194, 2019.
https://doi.org/10.1007/978-981-13-3140-4_17

falls into two categories Non-Proliferative Diabetic Retinopathy (NPDR) and Proliferative Diabetic Retinopathy (PDR) [2]. The two main structures used for fundus image analysis are optical disc and blood vessels. Optical disc (OD) is the brightest part and it usually appears bright yellowish circular or oval shaped region appearing in the fundus photography. Blood vessels originate from the centre of the optical disc and they are responsible for supplying nutrition to the eye [3]. Segmentation and removal of OD is essential step in image processing for automated detection of DR lesions as inaccurate removal of OD may hamper the detection of bright lesions like EXs leading to misclassification. Since blood vessels appear as dark elongated structures in fundus photography, imprecise detection of blood vessels may impede the detection of dark lesions like MAs and HEMs [4].

Various researchers have contributed to the remarkable improvement in the screening and diagnosis methods by automated optical disc segmentation and blood vessel extraction. In [5], a novel approach based on histogram matching for optical disc segmentation was proposed. In this method, some of the fundus images from the dataset were used to create the template and then the average of histograms for each color component was calculated to localize the centre of the optical disc. Correlation between each of the R, G, B components of the original image and template is also computed and the point which has the maximum correlation value is selected as the centre of optic disc. Authors in [6] proposed an Automated Diabetic Retinopathy Detection System to process the fundus images so that they have similar quality as that of angiogram to obtain better clarity of lesions. Segmentation of optical disc is done employing speed up robust features and blood vessel extraction is done using morphological image processing operations. Authors in [7] employed clustering approach with a novel correction procedure and vessel transform for automatic optical disc detection. To detect the boundaries of the optical disc, the proposed algorithm is integrated with scale space analysis. The work presented in [8] employed High Resolution Fundus image database (HRF database) and for the enhancement of optical disc, histogram equalization function is applied on green channel of fundus image. For OD segmentation speed up robust features function is exploited and the evaluation of results is done using Receiver Operating Characteristics curve (ROC curve). The method proposed in [9] is a modification of vessel transform by using vessel vector-based phase portrait analysis (VVPPA) and a hybrid between VVPPA and a clustering method used in vessel transform. Exceptional performance was achieved in [10] for blood vessels and optic disc segmentation in retinal images by employing the extraction of the retina vascular tree using graph cut technique. Markov random field (MRF) image reconstruction method is utilised for optic disc segmentation by removing vessels from optical disc region. In [11] extraction of retinal vascular tree is done using graph cut method and this blood vessel information is utilized to identify the approximate position of optical disc which is further fed to ANN classifier. Authors in [12] used various image processing techniques like adaptive histogram equalization and image filtering. Optical disc and the blood vessels are detected and removed using morphological operations and employing Otsu thresholding algorithm for better results. Study implemented in [13] utilises adaptive histogram equalization based preprocessing technique and robust distance transform is used for blood vessel segmentation. After reviewing all these articles it was revealed that inadequate illumination of fundus images and their poor quality leads to inability to analyse them after applying image processing techniques. Therefore, image pre-processing methods plays a major role to improve contrast and illumination for further image analysis steps for OD segmentation, OD removal and extraction of blood vessels. The color and intensity properties of MAs are similar to those of blood vessels due to which most of the methods listed in the literature misses the MAs adjacent to blood vessels and some MAs that are too small or blurred to be seen with the naked eyes. Thus the authors in this research work came up with a solution for optical disc segmentation and blood vessel extraction to facilitate the ophthalmologists for effective diagnosis of eye related diseases using fundus image analysis. In this paper, authors have implemented and critically analysed different OD segmentation methods and proposed a Mathematical Morphology based Fuzzy Algorithm for efficient extraction of blood vessels. Fundus images are obtained from standard publically available DRIVE and STARE databases. The RGB images are converted to green channel as only this channel has maximum intensity out of all the R, G and B channels. Further, histogram equalization is performed to enhance image quality followed by optical disc segmentation of equalized image and blood vessel extraction is done using the proposed approach. Various performance metrics were evaluated to validate the proposed method. Rest of this article is organized as: Sect. 2 comprises of Materials and methods presenting the proposed algorithms for optical disc segmentation. Experimental results comparing different OD detection methods are discussed in Sect. 3 followed by conclusion and future work in Sect. 4.

2   Materials and Methods

2.1   Fundus Image Databases

This research work utilizes two of the publically available standard databases for fundus image analysis. Some of the fundus image databases referred in the literature are as follows; DRIVE [14], STARE [15], DIARETDB0 [16], DIARETDB1 [17], MESSIDOR [18]. The detailed explanation of different databases is given Table 1. These databases are beneficial for image testing, blood vessels extraction, segmentation [19], feature extraction [20] and classification [21] for DR screening and detection.

Out of all the databases discussed in the table above, DRIVE and STARE databases are commonly used databases for fundus image analysis. To generalize our research work, the proposed algorithm was implemented on images obtained from DRIVE and STARE databases and experiments are performed on these databases.

2.2   Different OD Segmentation Techniques

Thresholding: Thresholding is the most common segmentation method and it is used in many of the applications due to its simplicity of implementation and computation speed. Thresholding is used in such applications where the image can be divided into two groups; the main object and the background depending upon the pixel intensity values. Let us consider an image $f(x, y)$, which is composed of a light object on a dark

Table 1. Description of publically available databases for fundus images

Sr. no.	Fundus image database	Field of view (FOV)	Image resolution	Database description
1.	DRIVE [14]	45°	768 × 584	20 color testing images and 20 color training images with extracted blood vessels.
2.	STARE [15]	35°	605 × 700	400 images with masked and extracted blood vessels.
3.	DIARETDB0 [16]	50° FOV with varying imaging settings	1500 × 1152, 1936 × 1296	130 color fundus images of which 20 are normal and 110 contain signs of the diabetic retinopathy.
4.	DIARETDB1 [17]	50° FOV with varying imaging settings	1500 × 1152, 1936 × 1296	89 color images out of which 84 images contains the sign of non-proliferative DR and remaining 5 are normal fundus images containing no sign of DR.
5.	MESSIDOR [18]	45° FOV	1440 × 960, 2240 × 1488, 2304 × 1536	1200 colored fundus images, out of which 800 images are acquired with pupil dilation and 400 without dilation.

background such that all of the image pixels are distributed into two dominant modes of the dynamic range of pixels. Then select a threshold value based on the intensity variation of foreground and background objects to exactly separate these two modes and extract the object from the background [22, 23]. The algorithm used for thresholding is explained in the following section.

Algorithm 1

Input: Image f (x,y)
Output: Segmented image after extracting the optical disc

BEGIN
Step 1: Take the input image and convert the RGB image into gray scale image.
Step 2: As OD is the brightest part in the fundus image, select a threshold value to extract the brightest object from the image and rest is considered as the background.
Step 3: At any point (x,y) in the image at which $f(x,y) > T$ is considered an object point and otherwise the point is considered as background.
Step 4: The optical disc segmented part $g(x,y)$ is given by

$$g(x,y) = \begin{cases} 255 \ (White) & if \ f(x,y) > T \\ 0 \ (Black) & if \ f(x,y) \le T \end{cases}$$

Step 5: Fundus image after extracting the optical disc is obtained by subtracting the segmented part from the original gray scale image.
END

Region Growing: This procedure groups pixels or small sub-regions into larger regions based on some predefined criteria for growth. It involves the selection of initial seed point and then growing the regions by appending those neighbouring pixels to the seed point having similar properties to those of the seed point. The properties upon which the similarity is calculated may be a specific range of intensity or color. The region growing in this technique depends upon the homogeneous neighbouring pixels around the seed. The selection of similarity criteria depends upon the image type of the data available and also on the problem under consideration.

Algorithm 2

Input: Original Image f (x,y)

Output: Segmented image after extracting the optical disc

BEGIN

Step 1: input image and convert the RGB image into grayscale image.
Step 2: Calculate the centre of the optical disc and take that point as the initial seed point S (x,y) array containing 1's at the location of the seed point and 0's elsewhere.
Step 3: All the connecting pixels in the neighbourhood of S (x,y) fulfilling the similarity criteria are eroded to one pixel and labelled as 1 and all other pixels in S are labelled as 0.
Step 4: Set a threshold value as the absolute difference between the seed and the pixels at (x,y). This threshold is considered as the stopping criteria that give the difference in the intensity values differentiating a darker and a brighter region.
END

Mathematical Morphology (MM): Morphology is an image processing tool that is particularly suitable for extracting and analyzing region shapes like boundaries, skeletons, etc. in images. For morphological operations, a structuring element is used that is a small subset or a sub image used to investigate the image under study to determine the properties of interest. Green channel image is complemented followed by adaptive histogram equalization to apply morphological operations. Morphological opening function is used and the morphologically opened image is subtracted from the histogram equalized image to obtain optical disc segmented image.

2.3 Proposed Methodology

This research work anticipates the importance of OD segmentation and blood vessel extraction in the diagnosis and computer aided screening of fundus images. The fundus images obtained from the databases lack clarity due to poor contrast as they are under illuminated and these images also have larger dimensions which increase the system complexity. These artefacts are removed from the image by using image pre-processing techniques.

Figure 1. gives the block diagram of proposed approach for this research work. Fundus images are collected from fundus image databases [14, 15] and are pre-processed utilizing steps like intensity conversion, image denoising and image contrast enhancement. The various Optical disc segmentation algorithms were implemented on fundus images taken from DRIVE and STARE databases. The centroid of the image is determined followed by detection of optical disc boundaries using morphological operations for optical disc segmentation and removal. After critical analysis of all these OD segmentation techniques, authors proposed a Mathematical Morphology based Fuzzy Algorithm approach for optical disc removal. Various performance metrics are evaluated to validate the proposed method. The algorithm for the proposed approach is depicted in the flowchart shown in Fig. 2.

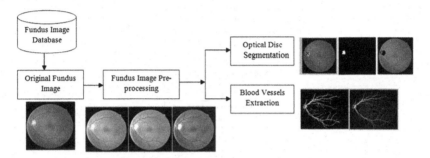

Fig. 1. Block diagram for the proposed approach

2.4   Performance Evaluation Metrics

For this research work various performance metrics are also incorporates to validate the result of the proposed approach and it was found that fuzzy approach when combined with MM approach gives better results in terms of Structural Similarity Index (SSIM), Root Mean Square Error (RMSE), Peak Signal to Noise Ratio (PSNR) and run time elapsed when the extracted blood vessels are compared with the ground truth images.

3   Results and Discussion

3.1   Experiment 1

DRIVE database [14] is considered for this experiment to investigate and analyze the effectiveness of all the algorithms explained in the Sect. 2.2. All the experiments are performed using MATLAB2013 software and a tabular comparison is also presented to investigate parameters of ground truth blood vessel images and extracted blood vessels for better quality assessment. In this experiment the OD segmentation using thresholding function is investigated and is shown in Fig. 3. The figure depicts the original image, grayscale converted image, segmented part of optical disc along with the output fundus image after removing the OD. The drawback of this approach lies in setting a new threshold value every time for a new fundus image to be processed. A constant threshold value does not work for this segmentation approach as the intensity of OD is not same for all the fundus images.

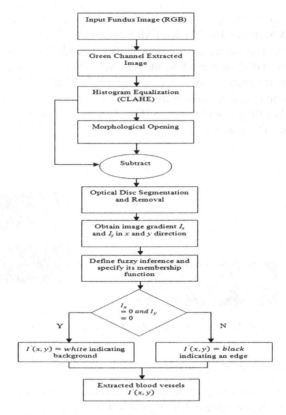

Fig. 2. Flowchart of proposed approach for OD segmentation and blood vessel extraction

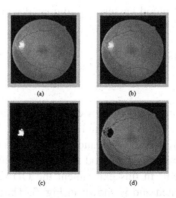

Fig. 3. Optical disc segmentation using thresholding function (a) Input fundus image from DRIVE database, (b) grayscale converted image, (c) segmented part using thresholding and (d) output fundus image after OD segmentation

Region growing process is initiated through a seed point. Selection of seed point is the important criteria for region growing process and is an open challenge. Centre of optical disc is obtained and this point is considered as the seed point for region growing process. After selecting an initial seed point, regions are grown by appending to each seed those neighboring pixels those having the properties similar to the seed point. The absolute intensity difference between the seed point and pixel at point (x, y) to stop growing the region is set as stopping criterion. Figure 4. depicts the results obtained by OD Removal using Region Growing algorithm. Segmentation is done using Region growing process and the segmented part is shown along with the output fundus image.

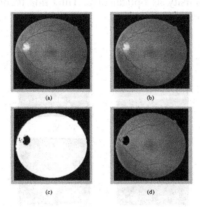

Fig. 4. optical disc removal using region growing approach (a) Input fundus image from DRIVE database, (b) grayscale converted image, (c) segmentation using region growing process and (d) output fundus image after OD segmentation using region growing

The results of Optical Disc elimination done using the MM approach are given in Fig. 5. Figure consists of the original fundus image depicted in Fig. 5(a), green channel is extracted as it is the maximum intensity channel and shown in Fig. 5(b). Segmented part of OD is shown in Fig. 5(c) and the output fundus image after OD segmentation is shown in Fig. 5(d).

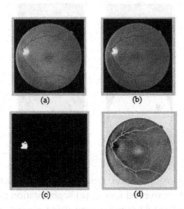

Fig. 5. Optical disc elimination using mathematical morphology approach

3.2 Experiment 2

Structured Analysis of Retina (STARE) consists of 20 fundus images captured by
TopCon TRV-50 fundus camera with 35 degrees of FOV. Each image is digitized to
605 × 700 pixels with 24 bits per pixel resolution. Ground truth vessel segmentation
was created for all the twenty images which are labelled manually by the professional
expert [15]. Thresholding method for OD segmentation was investigated and it is
shown in Fig. 6. Figure 6 depicts the original image, grayscale image, segmented part
along with the output fundus image after removing the optical disc. It can be seen that
for STARE database thresholding function segments all other parts also in the fundus
image having similar intensity as optical disc. Thus this technique does not perform
better for STARE database.

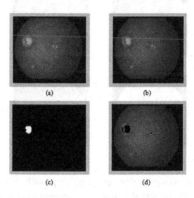

Fig. 6. Optical disc segmentation using thresholding function (a) Input fundus image from
STARE database, (b) grayscale converted image, (c) segmented part using thresholding and
(d) output fundus image after OD segmentation

Figure 7. gives the output of Region based Growing Segmentation method. It is the
visualization of original image along with the output image of optical disc after
applying Region Growing Algorithm.

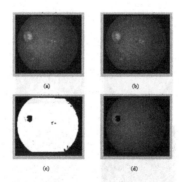

Fig. 7. Optical disc removal using region growing approach (a) Input fundus image from
STARE database, (b) grayscale converted image, (c) segmentation using region growing process
and (d) output fundus image after OD segmentation using region growing

Optical disc elimination done using MM approach is shown in Fig. 8. It consists of the original fundus image and green channel extracted image in Fig. 8(a) and (b). Segmented part is shown in Fig. 8(c) and the output fundus image after OD segmentation is shown in Fig. 8(d). It is clear from the visualization of results obtained from evaluating both DRIVE and STARE databases that MM yields better quality blood vessels after OD removal as compared to the other mentioned two techniques; Thresholding and Region Growing.

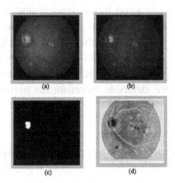

Fig. 8. Optical disc elimination and blood vessel extraction using MM approach

3.3   Extraction of Blood Vessels

After evaluating the optical disc segmentation results using all the approaches, it was revealed that MM approach gives the best results. Fuzzy algorithm is applied on output blood vessels obtained using MM algorithm. The results after applying fuzzy approach are shown in Fig. 9.

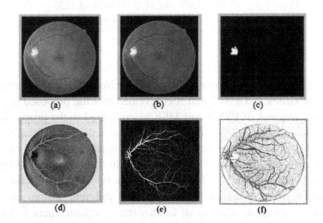

Fig. 9. Blood vessel extraction using proposed approach for DRIVE database image (a) Input fundus image from DRIVE database, (b) green channel converted image, (c) segmented region, (d) CLAHE converted image, (e) blood vessels after OD segmentation and (f) output of blood vessel extraction after applying fuzzy approach

It is seen that proposed approach yields better results for optical disc elimination and also blood vessels are better extracted using this method. Performance assessment of the proposed approach for optical disc elimination and blood vessel extraction is done in Table 2. Area in pixels for the extracted optical disc was calculated. The ground truth of blood vessels were available in the DRIVE database, thus on comparing the extracted blood vessels with the ground truth blood vessels labeled by hand, metrics like RMSE, PSNR, SSIM and run time elapsed are calculated. The range of SSIM is in between 0 to 1 and it is a similarity based parameter providing the statistical similarity information about extracted blood vessels and ground truth blood vessels. RMSE and PSNR are pixel intensity based parameters and they are also exploited in this research work to analyze the image quality of extracted blood vessels. Performance assessment of all the images taken from DRIVE database is done but the results for 10 images are reported in this paper. The ground truth images for original hand labeled images are missing for STARE database therefore the performance evaluation is done only for DRIVE database.

Table 2. Performance assessment parameters of proposed technique for blood vessel extraction using DRIVE database

Sample image	OD Area (pixels)	RMSE	PSNR	SSIM	Runtime elapsed (seconds)
Image_1	2213	0.9619	48.4681	0.8809	2.8248
Image_2	2024	0.9538	48.5420	0.8840	3.0535
Image_3	2036	0.9665	48.4266	0.8790	3.2653
Image_4	2044	0.9403	48.6656	0.8882	2.8248
Image_5	3116	0.9508	48.5690	0.8845	3.1663
Image_6	3694	0.9573	48.5098	0.8822	3.2183
Image_7	4426	0.9549	48.5314	0.8837	2.9538
Image_8	2516	0.9499	48.5772	0.8851	3.1135
Image_9	1935	0.9570	48.5123	0.8826	3.1138
Image_10	2009	0.9600	48.4856	0.8817	3.2743

Blood vessel extraction algorithms discussed in this paper are also compared with the existing approaches in Table 3 and it is revealed that the proposed approach gives the better results in terms of PSNR and MSE as compared to the proposed techniques discussed in [24] and [25]. PSNR should be high for better image quality, and PSNR computed in [24] gives the highest value approximately equal to 8 dB for method employing adaptive median filter. The proposed technique employed in this work has PSNR value of 48 dB which is much higher than reported in [24]. Another comparison is made with the work done in [25] comparing different histogram equalization approaches for comparative analysis of fundus image enhancement techniques. This comparison also reveals that our approach gives the better contrast enhancement as it employs CLAHE approach for histogram equalization which gives highest PSNR value out of all other HE approaches.

Table 3. Tabular comparison of existing techniques with proposed techniques

Sr. No.	Employed techniques	MSE	PSNR
1.	Adaptive median filter (30)	10305.77	8.00
2.	CLAHE (31)	129.49	27.01
3.	Proposed approach	0.96	48.53

4 Conclusion

In this research work, segmentation techniques are exploited for optical disc segmentation. A novel approach is proposed using mathematical morphology for optical disc removal and improving the blood vessel extraction by applying fuzzy algorithm. The experimentation was performed on all the images obtained from both the datasets but due to space constraints results form single image from each of the database are visualised. The proposed approach was concluded the most effective approach for identifying the optical disc to extract the blood vessels near the optical disc area for early diagnosis of diabetic retinopathy. For critical analysis, RMSE, PSNR, SSIM and run time elapsed were calculated, comparing the ground truth blood vessel images obtained from DRIVE database and extracted blood vessels using proposed technique. The future work in this field comprises further image analysis for feature extraction and classification to detect the lesions like MAs, HEMs, EXs, etc. to facilitate ophthalmic services for early detection of DR.

References

1. Eye smart eye health information from the American academy of ophthalmology. The Eye MD Association
2. Amin, J., Sharif, M., Yasmin, M.: A Review on Recent developments for detection of Diabetic Retinopathy. Hindawi Publishing Corporation Scientifica. (2016)
3. Ortega, M., Penedo, M.G., Rouco, J., et al.: Retinal Verification using a feature points based biometric pattern. EURASIP J. Adv. Signal Process. 2 (2009)
4. Kar, S.S., Maity, S.P.: Automatic detection of retinal lesions for screening of diabetic retinopathy. IEEE Trans. Biomed. Eng. 65(3), 608–618 (2016)
5. Dehghani, A., Moghaddam, H.A., Moin, M.S.: Optical disc localization in retinal images using histogram matching. EURASIP J. Image Video Process. 2012, 19 (2012)
6. Patwari, M., Manza R., et al.: Automated localization of optical disc, detection of microaneursyms and extraction of blood vessels to bypass angiography. In: Advanced in Intelligent Systems and Computing (2015)
7. Muangnak, N., Aimmanee, P., et al.: Vessel transform for automatic disc detection in retinal images. IET J. Inst. Eng. Technol. 9, 743–750 (2015)
8. Rathod D., Monza R., et al.: Localization of Optical Disc using HRF database (2015)
9. Muangnak, N., Aimmanee, P., Makhanov, s: Automatic optic disc detection in retinal images using hybrid vessel phase portrait analysis. Int. Fed. Med. Biol. Eng. 56, 583–598 (2017)
10. Gonzalez, A.S., Kaba, D., Li, Y., Liu, X.: Segmentation of the blood vessels and optic disc in retinal images. IEEE J. Biomed. Health Inform. 18(6), 1874–1886 (2014)

11. Jestin, V.K.: Extraction of blood vessels and optic disc segmentation for retinal disease classification. In: Recent Advances in Computer Science, pp. 440–444 (2015)
12. Phyo, O., Khaing, A.S.: Automatic detection of optical disc and blood vessels from retinal images using image processing techniques. Int. J. Res. Eng. Technol. 3(3), 300–307 (2014)
13. Prakash, R.S., Aditya, R., Sameer, Y., Parameswari, S., Kumar, G.S.: Retinal blood vessel extraction and optical disc removal. Int. J. Res. Eng. Technol. 4(04), 80–83 (2015)
14. Staal, J.J., Abramoff, M.D., Niemeijer, M., Viergever, M.A., Ginneken, B.V.: Ridge based vessel segmentation in color images of the retina. IEEE Trans. Med. Imaging 23, 501–509 (2004)
15. Hoover, A., Kouznetsova, V., Goldbaum, M.: Locating blood vessels in retinal images by piecewise threshold probing of a matched filter response. IEEE Trans. Med. Imaging 19(3), 203–210 (2000)
16. Kauppi, T., et al.: DIARETDB0: evaluation database and methodology for diabetic retinopathy algorithms. In: Machine Vision and Pattern Recognition Research Group, vol. 73, pp. 1–17. Lappeenranta University of Technology, Finland (2007)
17. Kauppi, T., Kalesnykiene, V., Kamarainen, J., et al.: The DIARETDB1 diabetic retinopathy database and evaluation protocol. In: Proceedings of the British Machine Vision Conference (BMVC 2007) Warwick, UK, pp. 1–10 (2007)
18. MESSIDOR: Methods for Evaluating Segmentation and Indexing technique Dedicated to Retinal Ophthalmology (2004). http://messidor.crihan.fr/index-en.php
19. Dogra, J., Sood, M., Jain, S., Prashar, N.: Segmentation of magnetic resonance images of brain using thresholding techniques. In: Proceedings of the IEEE International Conference on Signal Processing and Control (ISPCC 2017), pp. 311–315 (2017)
20. Bhusri, S., Jain, S., Virmani, J.: Breast lesions classification using the amalagation of morphological and texture features. Int. J. Pharma Bio Sci. 7(2), 617–624 (2016)
21. Sharma, S., Jain, S., Bhusri, S.: Two class classification of breast lesions using statistical and transform domain features. J. Glob. Pharma Technol. 9(7), 18–24 (2017)
22. Gonzalez, R.C., Woods, R.E.: Digital Image processing, 2nd edn. Prentice-Hall, Englewood Cliffs (2002)
23. Rajaiah, R.P., Britto, R.J.: Optic disc boundary detection and cup segmentation for prediction of glaucoma. J. Glob. Pharma Technol. 3(10), 2665–2672 (2014)
24. Swathi, C., Anoop, B.K., et al.: Comparison of different image pre-processing methods used for retinal fundus images. In: IEEE Conference on Emerging Devices and Smart Systems (ICEDSS 2017), pp. 175–179 (2017)
25. Yadav, S.K., Kumar, S., Kumar, B., Gupta, R.: Comparative analysis of fundus image enhancement in detection of diabetic retinopathy. In: IEEE Region 10 Humanitarian Technology Conference (R10-HTC), pp. 1–5 (2016)

Implementation and Performance Assessment of Gradient Edge Detection Predictor for Reversible Compression of Biomedical Images

Urvashi$^{(\boxtimes)}$, Emjee Puthooran, and Meenakshi Sood

Department of Electronics and Communication Engineering,
Jaypee University of Information Technology, Waknaghat, HP, India
survashi2793@gmail.com,
{emjee.puthooran,meenakshi.sood}@juit.ac.in

Abstract. Technological advancement of medical imaging techniques are progressing constantly, dealing with images of increasing resolutions. In hospitals, medical imaging techniques like X-rays, magnetic resonance imaging and computed tomography etc. are of high resolution consuming large storage space. Such high resolution of medical images transmitted over the network utilizes large bandwidth that often results in degradation of image quality. So, compression of images is only a solution for efficient archival and communication of medical images. Predictive based coding technique is explored in this paper for medical image compression as it performs well for lossless compression. This paper presents a comparative investigation on 2D predictor's coding efficiency and complexity on CT images. It was observed that among 2D predictors Gradient Edge Detection (GED) predictor gave better results than Median Edge Detector (MED) and DPCM. GED predictor at proper threshold value achieved approximately same results in terms of various performance metrics as Gradient Adaptive Predictor (GAP) though it is less complex.

Keywords: Compression · Predictors · Coding efficiency · Complexity

1 Introduction

Digital image processing has a great demand for transmission and storage of data efficiently with the rapid advancement in information and communication technology. In biomedical area, technology of medical images are progressing dramatically and dealing with images of increasing resolutions. Healthcare departments deal with abundant amount of medical images and terabytes of digital data is generated by hospital per year [1, 2]. Currently various medical imaging techniques are in use like magnetic resonance (MR), X-rays and computerized tomography (CT) that produce enormous amount of data as these techniques normally contains set of 2D frames that represent cross sectional part of human body. This growing amount of medical data makes a demand for effectual techniques of compression that are used for proper storage and communication [3]. Efficient compression techniques are required to deal

© Springer Nature Singapore Pte Ltd. 2019
A. K. Luhach et al. (Eds.): ICAICR 2018, CCIS 955, pp. 195–205, 2019.
https://doi.org/10.1007/978-981-13-3140-4_18

with the rapid expansion of medical data, to save time and to shrink storage space. Additionally, telemedicine is an application that requires progressive lossy to lossless compression. Since compressed image file sizes require less time for transmission so it is valuable for telemedicine application [4]. Medical image compression has been proved as a very important aspect to get a successful real time application of telemedicine along with an efficient storage and transmission. Compression technique removes the irrelevant and redundant bits from the image and accelerates the transmission speed. Compression results in lesser number of bits to represent the information. An efficient compression technique can reduce file size and transmission time, i.e. improving effectiveness of the image transmission system. Generally used image compression techniques are discussed.

Lossy compression technique does not provide exact replica of original image but it results in higher compression ratio. Lossy technique system is not acceptable in medical field because any loss of information result in false and it may create issue. So it is not preferred technique for compression of medical images [5, 6]. Lossless compression of image is an appropriate technique in medical field as it results exact replica of original image [7]. Diagnosis of image cannot afford any deficiency in diagnostically important regions of interest (ROIs). Thus it is necessary to have an approach that brings a high compression rate maintaining good quality of medical images. There are many compression techniques available in literature like transformation coding, entropy encoding and dictionary encoding.

As it is essential that compression and reconstruction of signal should be efficient without any loss of medical information as little loss of data especially in medical field is unbearable because it may lead to diagnose mistakenly [8].

Related Work

It is seen in literature that predictive coding performs well for lossless compression technique and efficiency of compression system depends upon the choice of predictors. Choice of is necessary for predictor for efficient prediction results in reduction of redundancy from the image that further contributes for better compression ratio. Many researchers have reported applying predictive coding technique on medical images for lossless compression.

In [9], author reviewed various image compression techniques based on medical image compression. In the rising field of telemedicine and teleradiology, comparative analysis of compression techniques and their applications has been carried out. In [10] predictive coding with a simple context-based entropy coder is offered and different predictor efficiency were analyzed with higher bit depth, achieving approximately same bit rate as standard predictor algorithm. [11] In this paper, author examined various compression techniques and it was explored that although medical image compression is an emerging need, but it encounters higher dimensionality of challenges and complicatedness for catering the increasing demands of the medical science. Authors in [12] proposed threshold controlled gradient edge detection which combines MED predictor and GAP. It is seen that GED predictor can achieve comparable bit rates as more complicated GAP predictors. In [13], author has used differential pulse code modulation for image compression lossless and near-lossless compression method and due to its high compression ratio and simplicity; it is an efficient technique for lossless compression. Enhanced DPCM transformation is used in this method which has a good energy compaction and Huffman encoding was used for image coding. In [14], proposed prediction based algorithms on the detection of edges and assessment of local gradients. MED and GAP were analyzed and comparative analysis of these predictors were also done in terms of entropy. Authors in [15] adopted a compression method that is based on a combination between predictive coding and bit plane slicing for compression of medical and natural image samples. High system performance is achieved by this lossless compression technique with high compression ratio. The main objectives through this research paper are to find the more efficient prediction algorithm by comparing different 2D predictors for image prediction. Another objective of this paper is to analyze the effectiveness of varying resolution values on entropy of prediction error image. The rest of this paper is organized as follows. In Sect. 2, details of prediction based compression is presented. In Sect. 3 results and discussion are shown. Conclusion of paper is drawn in Sect. 4.

2 Materials and Methods

2.1 Data Set

Different medical images of CT-scan are collected from CIPR [16] and OSRX [17] for validation, testing and examine coding efficiency of different predictors on patient's medical images. Details of CT medical test samples are shown in Table 1. These datasets are commonly used datasets having CT images of varying resolutions. In this research work, CT images are taken to test the algorithms and there is no effect in the performance of algorithms with varying image modality, resolution and number of images.

Table 1. Dataset details of CT medical test images

TAG	Sequence name	Modality	Image size
CIPR-CT-01	CT_Aperts	CT	256×256
CIPR-CT-02	CT_carotid	CT	256×256
CIPR-CT-03	CT_skull	CT	256×256
CIPR-CT-04	CT_wrist	CT	256×256
OSRX_CT_01	BREBIX	CT	512×512
OSRX_CT_01	MAGIX	CT	512×512
OSRX_CT_02	CEREBRIX	CT	336×336

2.2 Predictive Based Lossless Image Compression

Additional amount of bits and information that do not provide any relevant information is called redundancy [18]. Neighboring pixels in an image are related to each other and correlation between these pixels results in interpixel redundancy. Neighboring pixels are used to calculate the value of current pixel and difference between adjacent pixels can be used to represent an image to reduce the interpixel redundancy. Basic Scheme of predictive coding technique is shown in Fig. 1.

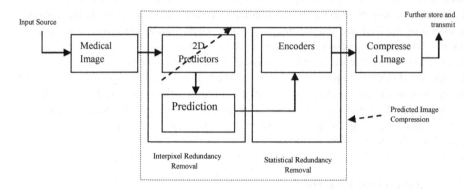

Fig. 1. Scheme of predictive coding technique

In predictive coding technique, interpixel redundancy is removed by 2D predictors and statistical redundancy is removed by encoders like Huffman and Arithmetic coding.

2.3   2D Predictors Used in Predictive Based Coding Techniques

Most important part of lossless predictive coding technique is prediction as it exploits interpixel redundancy from the image. 2D predictors can also be used for removing redundancy from volumetric images when operated slice by slice. 3D volumetric medical data is splitting into 2D image slices and separately enhance and predicted by the 2D predictor algorithms. Basic arrangement of pixels in causal template is denoted as follows:

$$
\left.
\begin{aligned}
&X_{i,j} = X\,[i, j],\ X_N = X\,[i, j-1],\ X_W = X\,[i-1, j], \\
&X_{NW} = X\,[i-1, j-1],\ X_{NE} = X\,[i+1, j-1], \\
&X_{NN} = X\,[i, j-2],\ X_{WW} = X\,[i-2, j],\ X_{NNE} = X\,[i+1, j-2].
\end{aligned}
\right\} \quad (1)
$$

Where $X_{i,j}$ is current pixel and X_N (North pixel), X_W (West pixel), X_{NW} (North–West pixel), X_{NE} (North-East pixel), X_{NN} (North-North pixel), X_{WW} (West–West pixel) X_{NNE} (North-North-East pixel) are neighbour pixels in causal template. The various 2D predictors taken into consideration in the work are Median Edge Predictor (MED), Gradient Adjusted Predictor (GAP), Differential Pulse Code Modulation (DPCM) and Gradient Edge Predictor (GED).

Median Edge Detection Predictors (MED): The value of current pixel $X_{i,j}$ is predicted by Median edge detector that selects the median value among neighboring pixels X_N, X_W and $X_W + X_N - X_{NW}$ (pixels are shown in Eq. 1). It is uses three causal pixels which are used to select one of the three sub-predictors depending upon whether it is horizontal edge or vertical edge [19].

Gradient Adjusted Predictors: GAP is based on the gradient estimation which is done around the current pixel. It can adapt itself to the intensity gradients of immediate neighbors of predicted pixel. For gradient estimation six causal pixels are used and predicted value is determined on some threshold. Threshold use in this predictor is fixed and typical values of threshold are 8, 32 and 80 [12].

Differential Pulse Code Modulation (DPCM): Differential encoding compression method predicts the current signal value based on the past encoded signal values. Error signal is obtained by taking difference of original value and predicted value and then encoded. It gives good compression ratio for images with high correlation between neighbouring pixels [20]. Error signal having peaked histogram is containing small error value.

Gradient Edge Detection: MED and GAP predictors have their own merits and demerits and GED predictor takes the advantage of both predictors. It is finest combination of simplicity and efficiency. It uses local gradient estimation on proper threshold value (T) as that of GAP and chooses between three sub predictors, defined as in MED predictor [4]. Threshold values used in standard GAP predictor are fixed but in GED predictor value of threshold is user defined. On proper threshold value GED provides efficient results as that of GAP. Like MED, it is also simple to implement. Algorithm of GED is as follows:

$$
\left.
\begin{aligned}
&\text{Av} = |\text{NW} - \text{W}| + |\text{NN} - \text{N}| \\
&\text{Ah} = |\text{WW} - \text{W}| + |\text{NW} - \text{N}| \\
&\text{if Av} - \text{Ah} > \text{T}, \text{Px} = \text{W} \\
&\text{else if Av} - \text{Ah} < -\text{T}, \text{ Px} = \text{N} \\
&\text{else Px} = \text{N} + \text{W} - \text{NW} \\
\\
&\text{where, T} = \text{Threshold} \\
&\text{Av, Ah} = \text{vertical and horizontal gradients} \\
&\text{Px} = \text{Predicted pixel}
\end{aligned}
\right\}
\tag{2}
$$

2.4 Performance Metrics

Different predictors for medical images are examined with various evaluation metrics as entropy, Peak Signal-to-Noise Ratio, Structural Similarity Index (SSIM). Entropy is final step in predictive coding technique that removes the statistical redundancy from the image [21, 22]. Entropy of an image is calculated as:

$$
H(X) = -\sum_{x} p(x) \log p(x)
\tag{3}
$$

Where, $p(x)$ is probability of a symbol x.

Quality of an image is express in terms of PSNR and its typical value is 30 db for 8 bit depth. It depends upon Mean Square Error (MSE), lower the value of square error higher will be PSNR and better quality of an image is obtained [23]. PSNR is calculated by

$$
\begin{aligned}
\text{PSNR} &= \frac{10\log_{10}(255)^2}{\text{MSE}} \\
\text{MSE} &= \frac{1}{\text{MN}} \sum \sum \frac{\text{error}^2}{\text{rows} \times \text{columns}} \\
\text{RMSE} &= \sqrt{\text{MSE}}
\end{aligned}
\tag{4}
$$

SSIM is the combination of luminance, contrast and structure and based on mean and variance. Value of SSIM is lies between 0 and 1 and predicted image is more similar to original image if SSIM approaches to 1 [8].

$$
\text{SSIM}(x, y) = \frac{\left(2\mu_x\mu_y + c_1\right)\left(2\sigma_{xy} + c_2\right)}{\left(\mu_x^2 + \mu_y^2 + c_1\right)\left(\sigma_x^2 + \sigma_y^2 + c_2\right)}
\tag{5}
$$

3   Results and Discussion

Results of several 2D predictors of predictive coding technique for the various CT-scan databases are presented, implemented in MATLAB 2013.

Medical images of Computed Tomography (CT) are compressed using 2D predictors MED, DPCM, GAP and GED are obtained and shown in Figs. 2, 3. It is found that interpixel redundancy is better removed by GAP than the MED and DPCM predictor as GAP provides less entropy and RMSE of prediction error image. Results of GED predictor are approximately same as that of GAP predictor. Original image and residual image obtained from MED, GAP, DPCM and GED predictors are shown in Figs. 2, 3 with their corresponding histograms.

3.1   Comparative Analysis of 2D Predictors for Computed Tomography (CT) Images

Analysis in Terms of Entropy: Comparative analysis is carried out for different samples of CT medical images taken from different database. These images are tested by all four predictors MED, GAP, DPCM and GED, which provides better assessment in contrast to entropy, PSNR, RMSE and SSIM. As GED predictor is based on threshold value and we got 44 as a optimal threshold when it is tested for different values of threshold from 8 to 256 at the difference of 16. Resolution Independent Gradient Edge Predictor (RIGED) is a GED predictor with threshold value 44 for efficient prediction. So for 8 bit depth images RIGED is efficient. It is estimated that performance of RIGED is better obtained than MED, DPCM and GAP as it takes the advantage of simplicity and efficiency from standard MED and GAP predictors.

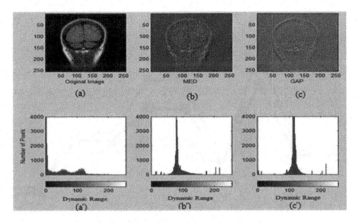

Fig. 2. (a) Original CT-scan image of brain, residual image obtained from (b) MED and (c) GAP predictors (a'), (b'), (c') corresponding histograms.

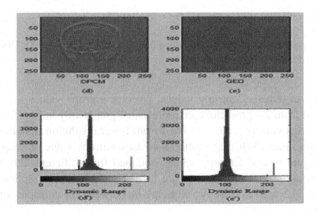

Fig. 3. Residual image of CT obtained from (d) DPCM and (e) RIGED predictors (d'), (e') respective histograms.

RIGED gave better results than MED and DPCM predictor and approximately same results as that of GAP even it is less complex than GAP. Entropy values of prediction error image obtained from MED, DPCM, GAP and RIGED for different CT images are represented in Fig. 4.

It is clear from above figure that for different CT image samples, entropy after prediction by 2D predictor is less as compare to entropy of original image. So it is depicted that lower number of bits are required to encode the image if prediction is done before encoding. Efficiency of predictor depends upon the entropy value, lower the entropy value, more efficient is the predictor. From the above figure, it is clear that RIGED achieved minimum value of entropy so it is efficient than other predictors.

Analysis of 2D Predictors for CT Images in Terms of Entropy Value for Varying Image Resolutions: Analysis of 2D predictors for CT images of varying resolutions is

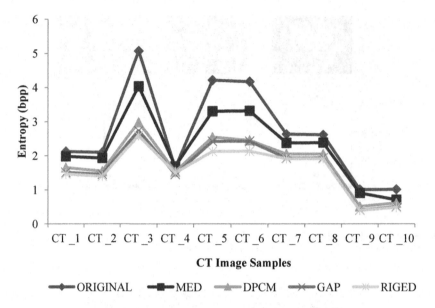

Fig. 4. Entropy values of original image residual image predicted from MED, DPCM, GAP and RIGED predictor for CT image samples.

also carried out in terms of entropy values. Average entropy values for different resolution obtained from 2D predictors are represented graphically in Fig. 5. It is depicted from the figure that entropy value obtained from lower resolution image is larger than higher resolution image. When resolution increases, entropy value of images decreases as shown in figure below. Entropy values obtained from different 2D predictors for 256×256 resolution is large as compare to 512×512. For resolution in between 256×256 and 512×512, entropy values are lie between the entropies of 256×256 and 512×512.

3.2   Analysis in Terms of Other Performance Metrics

In Terms of Root Mean Square Error: Analysis of 2D predictors is also done with reference to other performance metrics. Root mean error square of prediction error image or residual image is obtained that is shown in Table 2. Lower the value of RMS, better will the prediction and interpixel redundancy is also better removed. It is clear from the table below that RMSE of residual image calculated from GAP is lowest as compare to MED and DPCM. RIGED gave better results than MED, DPCM and approximately same values of error as that of GAP. GED is optimum combination of simplicity and efficiency. It is pointed that RMSE of prediction image is better obtained by RIGED as compare to other predictors.

In Terms of Peak Signal to Noise Ratio: Peak signal-to-noise ratio is also calculated for different image samples of CT-Scan as shown in Table 3 similar to the previous discussion. Optimal result of PSNR is achieved by RIGED. MED predictor gave lowest

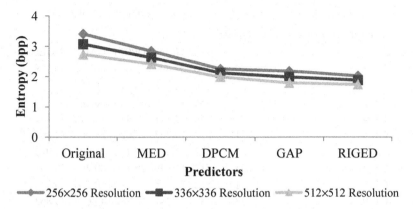

Fig. 5. Average entropy values of original image residual image predicted from MED, DPCM, GAP and RIGED predictor for CT image samples having different resolution.

Table 2. RMSE values for CT images having different resolutions

Medical images test samples	Image size	RMSE			
		MED	DPCM	GAP	RIGED
CT_1	256 × 256	18.707	4.231	3.888	3.695
CT_2	256 × 256	18.328	4.112	3.792	3.574
CT_3	256 × 256	33.618	5.1679	3.736	3.269
CT_4	256 × 256	11.245	5.405	4.377	4.836
CT_5	512 × 512	34.148	10.124	14.741	14.671
CT_6	512 × 512	33.724	9.998	14.497	14.434
CT_7	512 × 512	29.449	8.916	7.796	8.313
CT_8	512 × 512	30.219	9.075	8.190	8.680
CT_9	336 × 336	3.463	1.387	1.336	1.298
CT_10	336 × 336	5.221	1.235	1.145	0.996

value of PSNR as compare to other predictors but it has advantage of simplicity. GAP achieved good results in terms of PSNR but it is computationally complex predictor. RIGED achieved comparable values of PSNR and it is also simple to implement.

In Terms of Similarity Index: Another quality parameter Structural Similarity Index (SSIM) is also calculated for predicted image. It shows the similarity between predicted image and original image. Its value is in the range from 0 to 1 and if the SSIM of predicted image approaches value 1 then it is more similar to original image whereas approaching to 0 shows the dissimilarity between the images. Values of SSIM for various CT images from 2D predictors are given in Table 4.

It is seen from the above Table that RIGED achieved maximum values of SSIM for different CT test image. RIGED is highly efficient than other 2D predictors and it is also simple to implement.

Table 3. PSNR values for CT images having different resolutions

Medical images test samples	Image size	PSNR			
		MED	DPCM	GAP	RIGED
CT_1	256 × 256	22.690	35.600	36.337	36.778
CT_2	256 × 256	22.868	35.849	36.557	37.067
CT_3	256 × 256	17.599	33.864	36.702	37.840
CT_4	256 × 256	27.111	33.473	35.310	34.441
CT_5	512 × 512	17.463	28.023	24.760	24.801
CT_6	512 × 512	17.571	28.132	24.905	24.943
CT_7	512 × 512	18.749	29.126	30.293	29.735
CT_8	512 × 512	18.525	28.973	29.866	29.360
CT_9	336 × 336	37.341	45.286	45.619	45.863
CT_10	336 × 336	33.774	46.296	46.970	48.158

Table 4. SSIM values for CT images having different resolutions

Medical images test samples	Image size	SSIM			
		MED	DPCM	GAP	RIGED
CT_1	256 × 256	0.980	0.832	0.988	0.989
CT_2	256 × 256	0.981	0.836	0.989	0.990
CT_3	256 × 256	0.972	0.414	0.983	0.983
CT_4	256 × 256	0.944	0.859	0.960	0.957
CT_5	512 × 512	0.989	0.714	0.990	0.993
CT_6	512 × 512	0.989	0.724	0.990	0.993
CT_7	512 × 512	0.978	0.847	0.985	0.987
CT_8	512 × 512	0.979	0.846	0.986	0.987
CT_9	336 × 336	0.992	0.975	0.993	0.992
CT_10	336 × 336	0.995	0.965	0.996	0.997

4   Conclusion

For the lossless compression of medical images, predictive coding performs better as it is simple to implement and most essential it provides lossless compression with less storage space, low bandwidth and less transmission time. Different 2D predictors MED, DPCM, GAP and RIGED are used in this research work to removes interpixel redundancy of the image. Performance parameters such as entropy, RMSE, PSNR and SSIM are calculated after prediction for all these predictors. It is calculated from various experiments conducted that GED predictor at good threshold value (RIGED) can achieve comparable results as that of most efficient GAP predictor. RIGED is also simple to implement as that of MED and also provides efficient results.

References

1. Gupta, M.: Low complexity near lossless image compression technique for telemedicine. Int. J. Comput. Appl. **29**(7), 0975–8887 (2011)
2. Swathy, S., Jumana, N.: A study on medical image compression techniques. Int. J. Innovative Res. Comput. Commun. Eng. **5**(4), 8105–8110 (2017)
3. Ghadah, K.: Fast lossless compression of medical images based on polynomial. Int. J. Comput. Appl. **70**(15), 28–32 (2013)
4. Shridevi, S., Vijaykumar, V.R., Anuja, R.: A survey on various compression method for medical images. Int. J. Int. Syst. Appl. **3**, 13–19 (2012)
5. Verma, P., Sahu, A., Sahu, S., Sahu, N.: Comparison between different compression and decompression techniques on MRI scan images. Int. J. Adv. Res. Comput. Eng. Technol **1** (7), 109 (2012)
6. Gupta, M., Alam, S.: ROI based medical image compression for telemedicine using IWT and SPIHT. Int. J. Adv. Res. Comput. Sci. Manag. Stud. **2**(11), 340–348 (2014)
7. Chandrika, V., Parvathi, C.S., Bhaskar, P.: Medical image compression using EZW coding. IJEE. **5**(2), 87–91 (2013)
8. Urvashi, Sood, M., Bhardwaj, C.: Reconstruction methods in compressive sensing for biomedical images. J. Global Pharma Technol. **6**(9), 134–143 (2017)
9. Shrutika, S., Dharwadkar, N.V., Subodh, S.I.: A review on various medical image compression methods. Int. J. Innov. Res. Electr., Electron., Instrum. Control Eng. **4**(1), 27–29 (2016)
10. Avramovic, A., Banjac, G.: On predictive based lossless compression of images with higher bit depth. Telfor J **4**(2), 122–127 (2012)
11. Suma, Vidya, V.: A review of the effective techniques of compression in medical image processing. Int. J. Comput. Appl. **97**(6), 0975–8887 (2014)
12. Avramovic, A., Reljin, B.: Gradient edge detection predictor for image lossless compression. In: 52nd International Symposium ELMAR (2010)
13. Tomar, R., Jain, K.: Lossless image compression using differential pulse code modulation and its application. Int. J. Sig. Process., Image Process. Pattern Recogn. **9**(1), 197–202 (2016)
14. Al-Mahmood, H., Al-Rubaye, Z.: Lossless image compression based on predictive coding and bit plane slicing. Int. J. Comput. Appl. **93**(1) (2014)
15. Avramovicl, A., Savicl, S.: Lossless predictive compression of medical images. Serblan J. Electr. Eng. **8**, 27–36 (2011)
16. CIPR. http://www.cipr.rpi.edu/resource/sequences/sequence01.html
17. OsiriX Dataset. http://pubimage.hcuge.ch:8080/
18. Taubman, D., Marcellin, M.: JPEG2000: Image Compression Fundamentals, Standard and Practice. Kluwer Academic Publisher Group, Dordrecht (2004)
19. Wienberger M., Seroussi G.: LOCO-I; a low complexity, context based, lossless image compression algorithm. In: Conference on Data Compression. 140–149 (1996)
20. Puthooran, E., Anand, R.S., Mukherjee, S.: Lossless compression of medical images using a dual level DPCM with context adaptive switching neural network predictor. Int. J. Comput. Intell. Syst. **6**(6), 1082–1093 (2013)
21. Bhardwaj, C., Urvashi, Sood, M.: Implementation and performance assessment of compressed sensing for images and video signals. Int. J. Comput. Intell. Syst. **6**, 123–133 (2017)
22. Weinberger, M.J., Seroussi, G., Sapiro, G.: The LOCO-I lossless image compression algorithm: Principles and standardization into JPEG-LS. IEEE Trans. Image Proces. **9**(8), 1309–1324 (2000)
23. Gopi, K., Ramashri, T.: Medical image compression using wavelets. IOSR J. VLSI Sig. Process. **4**(2), 0106 (2013)

Mathematical Model for Dengue Virus Infected Populations with Fuzzy Differential Equations

A. Rajkumar[1(⊠)] and C. Jesuraj[1,2(⊠)]

[1] Hindustan Institute of Technology and Science, Chennai, India
arajkumar@hindustanuniv.ac.in, jesu2112@gmail.com
[2] IFET Colleges of Engineering, Villupuram, Tamilnadu, India

Abstract. The behaviors of Dengue Virus Infected Population model in Fuzzy and Interval Environment are discussed here. Modeling the environments in fuzzy differential equation and used to solve in different environments to get accurate solution by triangular fuzzy numbers. To identify these two different environments, how the behaviors of model can changes, finally we discussed briefly with two examples in each environment.

Keywords: Dengue virus · FDE (fuzzy differential equation) · Fuzzy number

1 Introduction

Modeling biological problems into mathematical problems is important for getting accurate solution of real life biological problems. In this paper, we introduce dengue virus affected population and then how virus transfers from persons to different persons is modeled, then the modeling problem is converted to the form of fuzzy differential equation. The model of fuzzy and interval environment are solved in triangular fuzzy number as an initial condition of fuzzy differential equations.

The Fuzzy derivative was first introduced by Zadeh and Chang in the year 1972 [1]. It's followed by Dubois and Prad in 1982 and Chen transformed the FDE into FIE and solved in 2008. In 2010 Allahviranloo and Ahmadi used Laplace Transform method in FDE. Later Mondal and Roy discussed and solved FDE of order one by Lagrange multiplier and RK methods in 2013; they used Fuzzy numbers like triangle, trapezoidal to solve FDE [4]. Barros et al. are taken dynamic model in Fuzzy environment and solved them. In 2012 Akin and Oruk used Prey predator model in Fuzzy [2, 11]. Zarei gives new formulation on HIV modeling in 2012. Mann used delay DE in predator prey analysis on stability model in 2013. Mondal et al. introduced glucose insulin regulatory system and diabetes in FDE in 2017 [5] and he discussed the behavior of aids in 2015.

Differential Equations play an important role for all real life problems. Mathematical modeling is to imitate real life problems so far as possible. In the field of bio-mathematical modeling is very important area for research in uncertainty and solution procedure is more valuable if the impreciseness comes the behavior of the Differential Equation can be changed and we can get a different way of solutions. In this paper, we

© Springer Nature Singapore Pte Ltd. 2019
A. K. Luhach et al. (Eds.): ICAICR 2018, CCIS 955, pp. 206–217, 2019.
https://doi.org/10.1007/978-981-13-3140-4_19

used Fuzzy and interval environments to find their changes of behaviors in the dengue virus model. Fuzzy and interval both are called imprecise.

In this paper the second sections are basic definitions and concept. In section 3rd we consider Dengue population dynamic model. The fourth section covered by the dengue virus model in fuzzy and interval environment. Fifth, we used examples for both environments separately. Sixth section covers conclusions of the paper and future research work.

2 Basic Definition and Concepts on Fuzzy Set Theory

2.1 Definition: Fuzzy Set

Let $\tilde{U}$ be a fuzzy set and we defined it

$$\tilde{U} = \left\{ (x, \mu_{\tilde{U}}(x) : \ x \text{ belongs to } U \right\}, \ \mu_{\tilde{U}}(x) \in [0, 1]$$

In this set of pair the first element $x \in U$ where U is classical set, second one is in [0, 1] is membership function.

2.2 Definition: α-Cut

α-cut contains $\forall$ elements of X that have membership function in $U \geq \alpha$. i.e.,

$$\tilde{U} = \left\{ (x, \ \mu_{\tilde{U}}(x) \geq \alpha, \ 0 < \alpha < 1, \ x \in X \right\}$$

2.3 Definition: Fuzzy Number

Let R be real number and R_F be fuzzy number is mapping such that $\tilde{u} : R \to [0, 1]$. If the following are satisfies

  i. $\tilde{u}$ - fuzzy convex
 ii. $\tilde{u}$ - normal
iii. $\tilde{u}$ - upper (semi) continuous
 iv. $\tilde{u}$ - compact.

2.4 Definition: Triangular Fuzzy Numbers

TFN's are given by $\tilde{u}$ and it is defined by (l, m, n) the membership functions are given below

$$\mu_{\tilde{U}}(x) = \begin{cases} 0; & x \le l \\ \frac{x-l}{m-l}; & l \le x \le m \\ \frac{n-x}{n-m}; & m \le x \le n \\ 0; & x \ge n \end{cases}$$

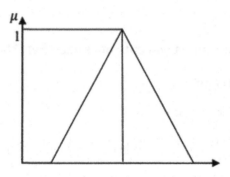

Triangular fuzzy number

2.5   Definition: Alpha-Cut

α-cut given by, Let $\tilde{u} = (l, m, n)$ be a fuzzy number then alpha cut is

$$U_\alpha = \begin{bmatrix} l + \alpha(m - l) \\ n - \alpha(n - m) \end{bmatrix}, \ \forall \alpha \in [0, 1]$$

2.6   Definition

Let $J : (l, m) \to E$ and $x_o \in (l, m)$. When f is strongly differential at x_o ∃ an element $f'(x_o) \in E$, ∋

(i)   For all $h > 0$ sufficiently small,
      there exists $J(x_o \oplus h) -^h J(x_o)$, $\exists J(x_o) -^h J(x_o - h)$ and
      $J'(x_o) = \underset{h \to 0}{lt} \frac{J(x_o \oplus h) -^h J(x_o)}{h} = \underset{h \to 0}{lt} \frac{J(x_o) -^h J(x_o - h)}{h}$ (or)

(ii) For all $\forall h > 0$ sufficiently small $\exists J(x_o) -^h J(x_o \oplus h)$, $\exists J(x_o - h) -^h J(x_o)$ and
      $J'(x_o) = \underset{h \to 0}{lt} \frac{J(x_o) -^h J(x_o + h)}{-h} = \underset{h \to 0}{lt} \frac{J(x_o - h) -^h J(x_o)}{-h}$.

2.7   Definition: Interval Number

Let I be denoted by closed interval $[I_m, I_n]$ and it is given by $I = [I_m, I_n]$

$$I = \{x, I_m \leq x \leq I_n, \ x \in R\}$$

3   Formulation of Dengue Virus Model

To derive the equation of mathematical classical model, we assume that dengue virus is virulent and no other microorganism that attacks the human body. Here we are developing the model into fuzzy environment it is given the following

$$\left.\begin{array}{l} \frac{ds(t)}{dt} = -\delta(\tilde{t})s(t) \\ \frac{dT(t)}{dt} = \delta(\tilde{t})s(t) = \delta(\tilde{t})(1 - T(t)) \end{array}\right\} \tag{1}$$

With initial condition s(0) = 1 and $T(t) = 0$.

In (1) $\delta(\tilde{t})$ is transference rate S(t) is proportion of infected population they are not having dengue in the beginning and T(t) is the proportion of the population that has developing dengue symptoms.

Let $\tilde{\delta}(t)$ = rt then the model becomes

$$\left.\begin{array}{l} \frac{ds(t)}{dt} = -r(t)(s(t)) \\ \frac{dT(t)}{dt} = r(t)(s(t)) = r(t)(1 - T(t)) \end{array}\right\} \tag{2}$$

Modeling of dengue virus infected population in fuzzy differential equation environment.

The following 3 - cases we consider

(i)   T(t) be the infected population here the initial condition is fuzzy numbers

(ii) $\tilde{\delta}(t)$ be the transference rate, in this the coefficients is fuzzy numbers

(iii) S(t)-both infected and transference rate are fuzzy numbers.

We discuss the above model by mathematical illustration. The problem is

$$\frac{ds_1(t,\alpha)}{dt} = -rts_2(t,\alpha)$$
$$\frac{ds_2(t,\alpha)}{dt} = -rts_1(t,\alpha)$$
$$\frac{dT_1(t,\alpha)}{dt} = rt(1 - T_2(t,\alpha))$$
$$\frac{dT_2(t,\alpha)}{dt} = rt(1 - T_1(t,\alpha))$$

With initial conditions

$$[s_1(t_0,\alpha), s_2(t_0,\alpha)] = [s_{01}(\alpha), s_{02}(t\alpha)], \ [T_1(t_0,\alpha), T_2(t_0,\alpha)] = [0,0]$$

From the given equation

$$\begin{bmatrix} \dfrac{ds_1(t,\alpha)}{dt} \\[2mm] \dfrac{ds_2(t,\alpha)}{dt} \\[2mm] \dfrac{dT_1(t,\alpha)}{dt} \\[2mm] \dfrac{dT_2(t,\alpha)}{dt} \end{bmatrix} = \begin{bmatrix} 0 & -rt & 0 & 0 \\ -rt & 0 & 0 & 0 \\ 0 & 0 & 0 & -rt \\ 0 & 0 & -rt & 0 \end{bmatrix} \begin{bmatrix} s_1(t,\alpha) \\ s_2(t,\alpha) \\ j_1(t,\alpha) \\ j_2(t,\alpha) \end{bmatrix} + \begin{bmatrix} 0 \\ 0 \\ rt \\ rt \end{bmatrix}$$

The solution of the above equation are given below

$$s_1(t,\alpha) = \left(\frac{s_{01}(\alpha) + s_{02}(\alpha)}{2} \right) e^{-\alpha \left(\frac{t^2 - t_0^2}{2} \right)} + \left(\frac{s_{01}(\alpha) - s_{02}(\alpha)}{2} \right) e^{\alpha \left(\frac{t^2 - t_0^2}{2} \right)} \tag{3}$$

$$s_2(t,\alpha) = \left(\frac{s_{01}(\alpha) + s_{02}(\alpha)}{2} \right) e^{-\alpha \left(\frac{t^2 - t_0^2}{2} \right)} - \left(\frac{s_{01}(\alpha) - s_{02}(\alpha)}{2} \right) e^{\alpha \left(\frac{t^2 - t_0^2}{2} \right)} \tag{4}$$

$$j_1(t,\alpha) = 1 - e^{-\alpha \left(\frac{t^2 - t_0^2}{2} \right)} \tag{5}$$

$$j_2(t,\alpha) = 1 - e^{\alpha \left(\frac{t^2 - t_0^2}{2} \right)} \tag{6}$$

4 Dengue Virus Infected Population in Interval Environment

The infected population are initial condition is interval numbers
    The problem is

$$\left. \begin{array}{l} \frac{ds(t)}{dt} = -r(t)(s(t;p)) \\[2mm] \frac{dT(t)}{dt} = r(t)(s(t;p)) = rt(1 - T(t;p)) \end{array} \right\} \tag{7}$$

$$\text{with } s(t_0;p) = (s_{0m})^{1-p}(s_{0n})^p \text{ and } j(t_0) = 0$$

The solution of the above problems is

$$s(t;p) = (s_{0m})^{1-p}(s_{0n})^p e^{-\alpha(t^2 - t_0^2)/2} \ \& \ j(t;p) = 1 - e^{-\alpha(t^2 - t_0^2)/2}$$

5 Numerical Examples

Example 5.1
Dengue virus model in fuzzy environment.

Consider s(0) = (0.6, 1.0, 1.3) and j(0) = 0, α = 0.15. When t = 2 find the solution. Value of $s_1(t, \alpha)$ and $s_2(t, \alpha)$; $j_1(t, \alpha)$ and $j_2(t, \alpha)$ *at* $t = 2$ for different α (Table 1, Figs. 1 and 2).

Table 1. Value of $s_1(t, \alpha)$; $s_2(t, \alpha)$; $j_1(t, \alpha)$ and $j_2(t, \alpha)$ *at* $t = 2$

α	$\{s_1(t, \alpha)\}$	$\{s_2(t, \alpha)\}$	$\{j_1(t, \alpha)\}$	$\{j_1(t, \alpha)\}$
0	0.2313	1.1762	0.9502	0.9502
0.1	0.2823	1.1327	0.9502	0.9502
0.2	0.3332	1.0891	0.9502	0.9502
0.3	0.3842	1.0456	0.9502	0.9502
0.4	0.4351	1.0021	0.9502	0.9502
0.5	0.4861	0.9585	0.9502	0.9502
0.6	0.5370	0.9150	0.9502	0.9502
0.7	0.5880	0.8714	0.9502	0.9502
0.8	0.6389	0.8279	0.9502	0.9502
0.9	0.6899	0.7844	0.9502	0.9502
1	0.7408	0.7408	0.9502	0.9502

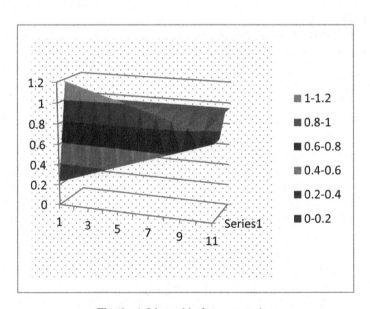

Fig. 1. 1-3d graphical representation

Remark 1

From above table $\{s_1(t, \alpha)\}$ and $\{s_2(t, \alpha)\}$ are increasing and decreasing function and we get strong solution. But $\{j_1(t, \alpha)\}$ and $\{j_1(t, \alpha)\}$ is crisp solution at t = 2.

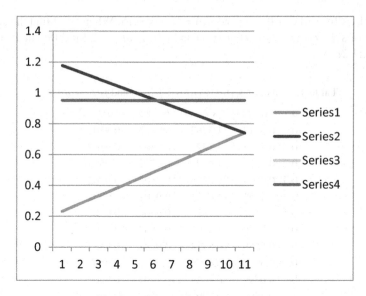

Fig. 2. 1-2d graphical representation

Example 5.2

Dengue virus model in fuzzy environment.

Consider s(0) = (0.9, 1.0, 1.5) and j(0) = 0, α = 025. When t = 3 find the solution.

Value of $s_1(t, \alpha)$ *and* $s_2(t, \alpha)$; $j_1(t, \alpha)$ *and* $j_2(t, \alpha)$ *at* $t = 3$ *for different* α (Table 2, Figs. 3 and 4).

Table 2. Value of $s_1(t, \alpha)$; $s_2(t, \alpha)$; $j_1(t, \alpha)$ and $j_2(t, \alpha)$ at $t = 3$

α	$\{s_1(t, \alpha)\}$	$\{s_2(t, \alpha)\}$	$\{j_1(t, \alpha)\}$	$\{j_1(t, \alpha)\}$
0	0.2947	1.2356	0.259	0.259
0.1	0.2824	1.2861	0.259	0.259
0.2	0.2702	1.3366	0.259	0.259
0.3	0.2579	1.3871	0.259	0.259
0.4	0.2457	1.4376	0.259	0.259
0.5	0.2335	1.4881	0.259	0.259
0.6	0.2212	1.5386	0.259	0.259
0.7	0.2090	1.5891	0.259	0.259
0.8	0.1968	1.6396	0.259	0.259
0.9	0.1845	1.6901	0.259	0.259
1	0.6376	0.6376	0.259	0.259

Remark 2

From above table $\{s_1(t, \alpha)\}$ and $\{s_2(t, \alpha)\}$ are increasing and decreasing function and we get strong solution. But $\{j_1(t, \alpha)\}$ and $\{j_1(t, \alpha)\}$ is crisp solution at t = 3.

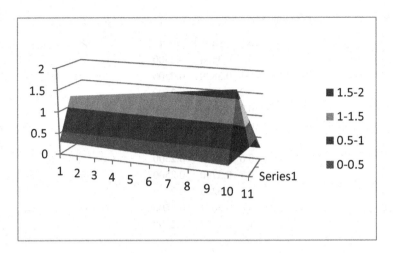

Fig. 3. 2-3d graphical representation

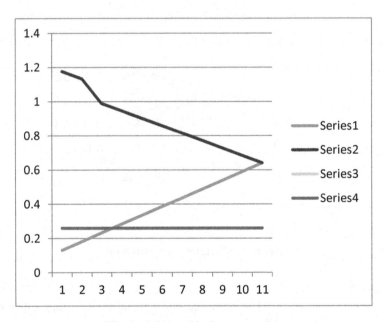

Fig. 4. 2-3d graphical representation

Example 5.3

Dengue virus model in interval environment.

Consider $s(0) = (0.8)^{1-p}(1.3)^p$, $j(0) = 0$, $\alpha = 0.15$ find solution after t = 3.
Values of $\{s(t, \alpha)\}$ and $\{j(t, \alpha)\}$.

The following tables give the values of different p in interval environment (Table 3, Figs. 5 and 6).

Table 3. Value of $s(t, \alpha); j(t, \alpha)$ *at* $t = 2$, $p = \alpha$

p	{s(t, p)}	{j(t, p)}
0	0.3564	0.2500
0.1	0.3820	0.2500
0.2	0.4094	0.2500
0.3	0.4388	0.2500
0.4	0.4703	0.2500
0.5	0.5040	0.2500
0.6	0.5402	0.2500
0.7	0.5790	0.2500
0.8	0.6205	0.2500
0.9	0.6651	0.2500
1	0.7128	0.2500

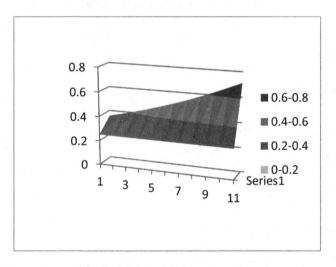

Fig. 5. 3-3d graphical representation

Remark 3

From above table $\{s_1(t, \alpha)\}$ is increasing function and we get strong solution. But $\{j_1(t, \alpha)\}$ is crisp solution at t = 2.

Example 5.4

Dengue virus model in interval environment.

Consider $s(0) = (0.8)^{1-p}(1.3)^p$, $j(0) = 0$, $\alpha = 0.15$ find solution after t = 3. Values of $\{s(t, \alpha)\}$ and $\{j(t, \alpha)\}$.

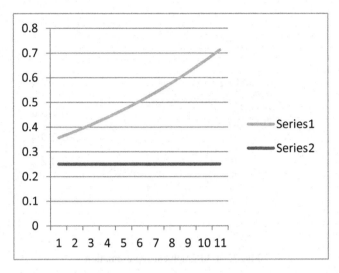

Fig. 6. 3-2d graphical representation

The following tables give the values of different p in interval environment (Table 4, Figs. 7 and 8).

Table 4. Value of $s(t, \alpha); j(t, \alpha)$ at $t = 3, p = \alpha$

p	{s(t, p)}	{j(t, p)}
0	0.5186	0.2592
0.1	0.5558	0.2592
0.2	0.5957	0.2592
0.3	0.6384	0.2592
0.4	0.6843	0.2592
0.5	0.7334	0.2592
0.6	0.786	0.2592
0.7	0.8424	0.2592
0.8	0.9029	0.2592
0.9	0.9677	0.2592
1	1.0371	0.2592

Remark 4

From above table $\{s_1(t, \alpha)\}$ is increasing function and we get strong solution. But $\{j_1(t, \alpha)\}$ is crisp solution at t = 3.

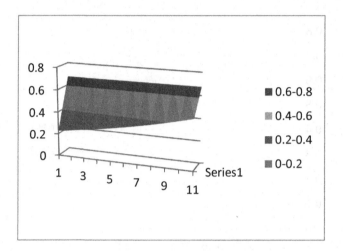

Fig. 7. 4-3d graphical representation

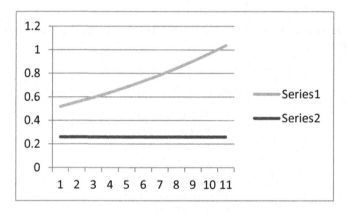

Fig. 8. 4-2d graphical representation

6 Conclusion

Any biological modeling is not sure that the solution, it is taken in an uncertain environment. Uncertainty plays a significant role in real life problems. This paper, we used fuzzy and interval model for the dengue virus infected environment, here we analyzed the behavior of the model is changed based on the environment. The crisp model is not suitable here. The stability of both models is related, but fuzzy environment model is more accurate than the interval. 'The solution method and procedure of fuzzy environment can help the researcher to solve some complex biological problems.

References

1. Chang, S.S., Zadeh, L.A.: On fuzzy mapping and control. IEEE Trans. Syst. Man Cybern. **2**, 330–340 (1972)
2. Bede, B., Ruda, I.J., Bencsik, A.L.: First order linear fuzzy differential equations under generalized differentiability. Inf. Sci. **177**, 1648–1662 (2007)
3. Akın, O., Oruc, O.: A Prey predator model with fuzzy initial values. Hacettepe J. Math. Stat. **41**(3), 387–395 (2012)
4. Mondal, S.P., Roy, T.K.: First order linear homogeneous fuzzy ordinary differential equation based on lagrange multiplier method. J. Soft Comput. Appl. **2013**, 1–17 (2013)
5. Mahata, A., Roy, B., Mondal, S.P., Alam, S.: Application of ordinary differential equation in glucose-insulin regulatory system modeling in fuzzy environment. Ecol. Genet. Genom. **3**, 60–66 (2017)
6. Sharma, S., Samanta, G.P.: Optimal harvesting of a two species competition model with imprecise biological parameters. Nonlinear Dyn. **77**, 1101–1119 (2014)
7. Pandit, P., Singh, P.: Prey predator model with fuzzy initial conditions. Int. J. Eng. Innov. Technol. (IJEIT) **3**(12) (2014)
8. Pal, D., Mahapatra, G.S.: A bioeconomic modeling of two-prey and one-predator fishery model with optimal harvesting policy through hybridization approach. Appl. Math. Comput. **242**, 748–763 (2014)
9. Mondal, S.P., Roy, T.K.: System of differential equation with initial value as triangular intuitionistic fuzzy number and its application. Int. J. Appl. Comput. Math. **3**, 449–474 (2015)
10. Paul, S., Mondal, S.P., Bhattacharya, P.: Discussion on fuzzy quota harvesting model in fuzzy environment: fuzzy differential equation approach. Model. Earth Syst. Environ. **2**, 70 (2016)
11. Mahata, A., Mondal, S.P., Alam, S., Roy, B.: Mathematical model of glucose-insulin regulatory system on diabetes mellitus in fuzzy and crisp environment. Ecol. Genet. Genom. **2**, 25–34 (2017)
12. Hussain, S.A.I., Mondal, S.P., Mandal, U.K.: A holistic-based multi-criterion decision-making approach for solving engineering sciences problem under imprecise environment. In: Handbook of Research on Modeling, Analysis, and Application of Nature (2018)
13. Kaleva, O.: Fuzzy differential equation. Fuzzy Sets Syst. **24**, 301–317 (1987)
14. Kaleva, O.: The Cauchy problems for fuzzy differential equations. Fuzzy Sets Syst. **35**, 389–396 (1990)
15. Buckley, J.J., Feuring, T., Hayashi, Y.: Linear systems of first order ordinary differential equations: fuzzy initial conditions. Soft Comput. **6**, 415–421 (2001)
16. Felix, A., Christopher, S., Devadoss, A.V.: A nonagonal fuzzy numbers and its arithmetic operation. IJMAA **2**, 185–195 (2015)
17. Atanassov, K.T.: Intuitionistic Fuzzy Sets. Physica-Verlag, Heidelberg (1999)
18. Kharal, A.: Homeopathic drug selection using intuitionistic fuzzy sets. Homeopathy **98**(1), 35–39 (2009)
19. Rajkumar, A., Jesuraj, C.: A new approach to solve fuzzy differential equation using intuitionistic nanaogonal fuzzy numbers. In: Proceedings of Second International Conference on FEAST 2018, pp. 187–194 (2018)
20. Buckley, J.J., Feuring, T.: Fuzzy differential equations. Fuzzy Sets Syst. **110**, 43–54 (2000)

Surface EMG Signal Classification Using Ensemble Algorithm, PCA and DWT for Robot Control

Yogendra Narayan[(✉)], Ram Murat Singh, Lini Mathew,
and S. Chatterji

Electrical Engineering Department,
National Institute of Technical Teachers Training and Research,
Chandigarh, India
narayan.yogendra1986@gmail.com,
linimathew1961@gmail.com, chatterjis@yahoo.com

Abstract. This paper presents a framework of surface electromyography signals based robotic arm prototype control using discrete wavelet transform, principle component analysis, ensemble algorithms and Arduino Uno controller. In this context, the sequential floating forward selection algorithm is used for sorting out the features based on their relevance. The performance of different ensemble algorithms is evaluated with various parameters like classification accuracy, sensitivity, specificity, false descriptive rate, positive predictive rate and speed. Among the all ensemble algorithm, the subspace discriminate ensemble was found the best method with the 100% accuracy, specificity, and sensitivity using 35 base classifiers. Subspace ensemble algorithm with principle component analysis and 4th scaling daubechies 4 wavelet filters produced the best performance. The main contribution of this work is that method has the potency of best classification of sEMG signal for elbow movement which can be beneficial for assistive robotic device development.

Keywords: sEMG signal · PCA · DWT · Ensemble classifier
SFFS algorithm

1 Introduction

The surface electromyographic (sEMG) signals are the non-invasive method in which EMG data is acquired with a surface electrode placed on suitable acupressure points [1]. The sEMG signals have been widely used in the field of rehabilitation robotics and neuromuscular disease classification [2]. So, the classifiers play a big role while controlling any robotic devices. One important application of sEMG signals lies in prosthetic limb development for rehabilitation of amputee as well as physically disables persons, due to the fact that sEMG signals contain information of muscle movement [3, 4]. But there is no universal model which can explains the relationship between gesture performed by human and recorded sEMG signals. Therefore, the identification of subject intention is a necessary step towards the development of such devices which could be solved by the associated features of sEMG signals [5]. The features of sEMG

© Springer Nature Singapore Pte Ltd. 2019
A. K. Luhach et al. (Eds.): ICAICR 2018, CCIS 955, pp. 218–230, 2019.
https://doi.org/10.1007/978-981-13-3140-4_20

signals can be three types: (i) time domain (TD), (ii) frequency domain (FD) and (iii) time-frequency domain (TFD). TFD feature is also called time scale feature or wavelet coefficient which can be extracted with the help of wavelet based techniques. The selection of suitable feature plays a vital role for achieving the good classification accuracy as well as smooth control of devices [6]. After sEMG signals acquisition, de-noising and other signal processing steps are performed followed by the feature extraction, classification and robotic device controlling.

The analysis of sEMG signals has started a new era of research by using advanced signal processing techniques in the field of biomedical signal processing [7]. The sEMG signal classification accuracy is important for developing reliable and robust methods of control. The comparative analysis of some classification techniques like pattern discovery/fuzzy inference system, Bayesian networks, naïve Bayesian net-works, tree augmented naïve Bayesian networks and evolutionary algorithms have been done for multi-sampled EMG signal [8, 9]. By using neuromodulation method (transcranial direct current stimulation), classification accuracy and quality of EMG signal of amputated limb has been enhanced for myoelectric control [10].

The objective of this study is to evaluate the performance of different ensemble algorithm to classify the sEMG signal using Discrete Wavelet Transform (DWT) for controlling the robotic arm prototype. The classification accuracy of sEMG signal improved by using DWT for de-noising and feature extraction purpose. The various features of sEMG signals like TD, FD and TFD are used to form a feature vector. The Sequential Floating Forward Selection (SFFS) algorithm is utilized for feature selection as well as searching the best feature set whereas Principle Component Analysis (PCA) is used for dimension reduction. Different performance measuring parameters are used to compare the classifier accuracy and speed. This paper is divided into four sections; the first section introduction of classification methods and related work, the second section describe data recording and a brief introduction of ensemble classifiers, the third section show the results and finally conclusions are given in the fourth section.

2 Materials and Methods

2.1 sEMG Data Recording and Pre-processing

The sEMG signals were gathered from total ten healthy volunteers including seven males and three females having age between 20 to 30 years with their signed consent. The placement of the surface electrode on arm acupressure point was done by Noraxon EMG and sensor system manual. Acquisition of sEMG signals was done with four-channel of myotrace 400 device, two channels were connected to brachioradialis and flexor carpi radialis muscle and remaining two were connected to triceps branchii (lateral and medial) muscles [11].

Total 466 observations were taken from ten right hand dominated volunteers. Full wave rectification, amplitude normalization, smoothing, and filtering operation was performed in the pre-processing stage. The system used for pre-processing had a base gain of 500, baseline noise less than 1 μV, input impedance greater than 100 MΩ and a common mode rejection ratio more than 100.

2.2   Feature Extraction

Feature extraction is carried out after the pre-processing of the sEMG signals to form a feature vector for classification purpose [12]. Classification accuracy of any classifier will depend on the suitable features chosen for feature vector [13]. SFFS algorithm is used for selecting the suitable features. Figure 1 shows the sEMG signal acquisition system to classify the elbow movement for controlling the robotic arm prototype. In this study, the features namely Standard Deviation (STD), Root Mean Square (RMS), Waveform Length (WL), Slope Sign Change (SSC), Integrated EMG (IEMG), Kurtosis (KUR), Mean Absolute Value (MAV), Variance (VAR), Fourth Order Auto-Regressive (AR) coefficient, Simple Square Integral (SSI), Wilson Amplitude (WAMP), Average Amplitude Change (AAC), Myopulse Percentage Rate (MYOP), Mean Power (MNP), Total Power (TTP), Skewness (SKEW) and DWT residual (four DWT features) are taken as suggested in a lot of literature [14, 15]. Table 1 shows the mathematical formulas used for sEMG feature calculation.

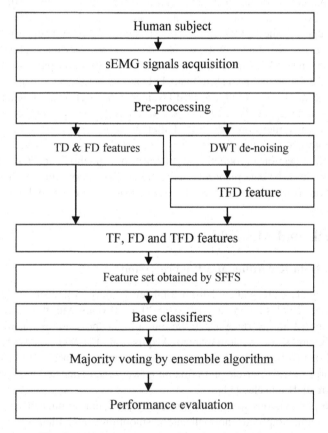

Fig. 1. Block diagram of sEMG signal classification

Table 1. Mathematical Equations of EMG feature

IEMG	$IEMG = \sum_{i=1}^{N}|X_i|$	(1)
SKEW	$SKEW = \frac{1}{N}\sum_{n=1}^{N}(x_n - \bar{x})^3 / (\frac{1}{N}\sum_{n=1}^{N}(x_n - \bar{x})^2)^{3/2}$	(2)
SSC	$SSC = \sum_{n=2}^{N-1}[f[(x_n - x_{n-1}) * (x_n - x_{n+1})]]$ $f(x) = \begin{cases} 1 \text{ if } x \geq threshold \\ 0 \text{ otherwise} \end{cases}$	(3)
STD	$STD = \sqrt{\frac{1}{N}\sum_{i=1}^{N}(x_i - \mu)^2}$	(4)
VAR	$VAR = \frac{1}{N-1}\sum_{n=1}^{N}x_n^2$	(5)
KUR	$KUR = \sum_{i=1}^{N}\frac{(x_i-\bar{x})^4/N}{STD}$	(6)
WL	$WL = \sum_{m=1}^{M-1}|x_{n-1} - x_n|$	(7)
AR Coefficient	$x_n = -\sum_{i=1}^{p}a_i x_{n-1} + w_n$	(8)
MAV	$MAV = \frac{1}{N}\sum_{i=1}^{N}|X_i|$	(9)
SSI	$SSI = \sum_{i=1}^{N}(X_i)^2$	(10)
RMS	$RMS = \sqrt{\frac{1}{N}\sum_{i=1}^{N}X_i^2}$	(11)
AAC	$AAC = \frac{1}{N}\sum_{i=1}^{N-1}|X_{i+1} - X_i|$	(12)
MYOP	$MYPO = \frac{1}{N}\sum_{i=1}^{N}[f(X_i)]$ $f(X) = \begin{cases} 1 \text{ if } X \geq threshold \\ 0 \quad\quad otherwise \end{cases}$	(13)
WAMP	$WAMP = \sum_{i=1}^{N-1}[f(|X_{n+1} - X_n|)]$ $f(X) = \begin{cases} 1 \text{ if } X \geq threshold \\ 0 \quad\quad otherwise \end{cases}$	(14)
MNP	$MNP = \frac{\sum_{j=1}^{M}P_j}{M}$	(15)
TTP	$TTP = \sum_{j=1}^{M}P_j$	(16)

2.2.1 Feature Selection: Order of Relevance

The SFFS algorithm is used for finding the set of best success rate features among the original feature set [16]. The SFFS is a heuristic algorithm used for searching the features having best success rate based on tracking the forward and backward step. The forward step involves the addition of new feature having the best success rate in combination with the already used feature. The least success rate feature is discarding as long as the resulting subset performs better than the previously evaluated one. The SFFS utilized a self-controlled backtracking approach in which trade-off between forward and backward steps take place dynamically and finally, it can find the better solution. The SFFS are used to sort the features in their order of relevance. In present study, 70% data used for training and 30% data for testing purpose. Total 20 subsets of best features are obtained by implementing algorithm 20 times randomly. A matrix bank of 20 (times) by 20 (features) is used for obtaining the best feature. Figure 2 shows the complete experimental setup for sEMG signals acquisition for controlling robotic arm prototype using Arduino Uno controller.

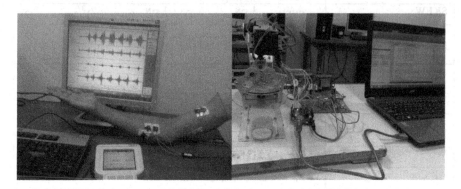

Fig. 2. sEMG electrodes on subject arm with complete setup

2.2.2 Feature Reduction: Principle Component Analysis

PCA generates a new set of a variable which is a linear combination of original variable and orthogonal to each other resulting no redundant information [17]. PCA is used for dimension reduction and feature extraction which transform d-dimensional data into lower dimensional space thereby reducing the space and time complexities. For any dataset, PCA can be found by calculating $d \times d$ covariance matrix and d-dimensional mean vector μ. It computes the value of eigenvectors as well as eigenvalues and orders them by eigenvalue, highest to lowest. Lesser significance component can be ignored because it does not lose some significant information [18]. For a d-dimensional data set, d eigenvectors and eigenvalues can be computed and if first most significant p eigenvectors are chosen then we obtain p dimensions data set. New feature vector are formed by arranging p eigenvectors as the column in matrix form. The final step is to transpose of the matrix obtained by eigenvectors and multiply it on the left side of mean-adjusted data transposed. In brief, all steps are as follow (i) Compute the means, (ii) Calculate the covariance matrix, (iii) Find the eigenvalue and corresponding eigenvector, (iv) Choose the most significant value eigenvector while ignoring lest significant value, and (v) Multiply the transposed matrix obtained by eigenvector to the mean-adjusted data transposed. In this way, PCA transformation of original inputs to new uncorrelated features is achieved [19].

2.3 Discrete Wavelet Transform

The wavelet transform is a powerful mathematical and signals processing tool that is used for multi-resolution analysis of a signal. In wavelet analysis, single function (mother wavelet) is shifted and dilated which consists of a linear combination of an individual set of functions. Dilated and translated wavelet can be defined in term of mother wavelet as

$$\emptyset_{a,b}(t) = \frac{1}{\sqrt{|a|}} \emptyset\left(\frac{t-b}{a}\right) \tag{17}$$

where a is scale and b is a translation parameter. $a < 1$, if compressing the wavelet and $a > 1$ if dilates the wavelet [20]. These parameters can be generated in time with midpoint localities and various frequencies which are called as wavelet atoms or baby wavelet. DWT was selected for this study due to its multi-resolution analysis capability and concentration in real-time engineering application [21]. Wavelet is used for the decomposition of signal the into details and approximations coefficient. These coefficients are the resultant of filtering process (high pass and low pass filter) and used for time scale feature extraction or wavelet coefficients. The approximations coefficient can be considered as low-frequency and high scale whereas the details coefficient as high-frequency with low scale respectively [22]. Details coefficient of the sEMG signals is obtained by using high pass filter followed by down sampler. Similarly, approximation coefficient can be found using low pass filtering followed by upsampler. Figure 3 shows the de-noised sEMG signal with approximations and details coefficient. In this ways, fourth level approximation and details coefficients (cA4, cD1, cD2, cD3, and cD4) are obtained [23]. In the present study, approximations coefficient of reconstructed signal by using 4th level Daubechies 4 (db$_4$) wavelet filter is utilized to form the feature vector.

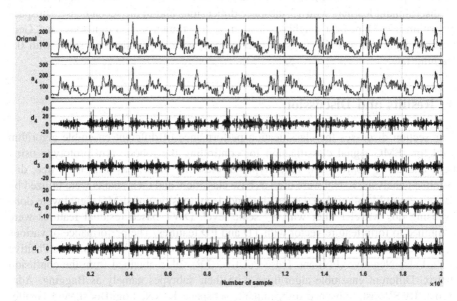

Fig. 3. Original sEMG signal with approximations and details coefficient obtained by DWT

2.4   Ensemble Classifiers

Generally, the base classifiers are used to construct the ensemble classifier. Three-fold cross validation is carried out using different ensemble algorithm. All bagging and boosting algorithm uses tree classifier as base classifiers whereas subspace algorithm can use either k-nearest neighbor (K-NN) learner or discriminant analysis classifier [24]. The Bagging algorithm forms a deep tree which is memory intensive and time-consuming resulting relatively slow predictions. It utilized the aggregated ensemble of complex decision trees. Boosted tree creates an ensemble of medium decision trees. As compared to bagging and boosting algorithm, AdaBoost algorithm require relatively little time or memory but might need more ensemble members. Bagged tree is also known as bootstrap aggregated which utilized the ensemble of complex decision trees. Subspace discriminant model creates an ensemble of discriminant classifiers using random subspace algorithm. It is good for many predictors, low on memory usage, relatively fast for fitting and prediction but the accuracy varies depending upon the data. RUSBoosted tree can be used for skewed data with many more observations of one class. RUS stand for the random undersampling. In the present study, bag, Ada-boost, RUSBoost, subspace, LogitBoost, GentleBoost ensemble methods are critically compared to each other to find the best methods for elbow movement classification. Bag ensemble algorithm uses 34 decision tree learners with 27 numbers of splits whereas AdaBoost and RUSBoost algorithms utilized the same number of the decision tree and split with 0.1 learning rate. In the first case, subspace ensemble algorithm uses 35 discriminant learners with 13 subspace dimensions and in the second case, subspace algorithm use 31 nearest neighbors learner with 9 dimensions. LogitBoost and Gen-tleBoost algorithm use 30 decision tree learners with 20 numbers of splits with 0.1 learning rate.

3   Results and Discussion

This section discusses the classification performance of different ensemble algorithm used for sEMG signal classification for controlling the robotic arm prototype using PCA and DWT approaches. Three types of classifier namely as a decision tree, discriminant analysis, K-NN were used as base classifiers and their results were utilized by various ensemble algorithm. De-noising and decomposition of sEMG signal were done by using db_4 wavelet filter with 4th scale level. DWT based residual features were combined to form feature vector with TD and FD features. The performance of various ensemble algorithms was done using the number of True Negative (TN), True Positive (TP), False Negative (FN) and False Positive (FP) value obtained from the confusion matrix. Different ensemble algorithms with their subtypes namely as Bagging, Ada-Boost, RUSBoost, subspace discriminant, subspace K-NN, LogitBoost, and Gentle-Boost were applied for classification of sEMG signals. Table 2 shows the comparative results of ensemble algorithms in term of various parameters and Table 3 shows the corresponding confusion matrix which is based on true class and predicted class relationship. The performance evaluation of classification algorithms is done on the basis of Accuracy (ACC) and Area Under Curve (AUC) but there are many different parameters like Specificity (SP) and Sensitivity (SE) which can also define the accuracy in other terms.

Table 2. Ensemble algorithms performance evaluation

Classification algorithm	ACC (%)	SP (%)	SE (%)	FDR (%)	PPV (%)	F-measure (%)	AUC (%)	Speed (obs/sec)
Bagging	98.7	98.3	99.1	0.7	98.3	98.7	100	380
AdaBoost	49.1	39.3	59	50.7	49.3	53.7	100	1100
RUSBoost	49.1	39.3	59	50.7	49.3	53.7	100	1200
Subspace discriminant	100	100	100	0	100	100	100	370
Subspace K-NN	97.3	97.3	97.3	0.6	97.3	97.3	99	240
LogitBoost	97.9	96.6	99.1	0.3	96.7	97.9	99	400
GentleBoost	97.9	96.6	99.1	0.3	96.7	97.9	99	400

Table 3. Confusion matrix of different classifiers

Serial no.	Classifier	Detector decision	Actual decision (%)	
			Flexion	Extension
1	Bagging	Flexion	99	1
		Extension	2	98
2	AdaBoost	Flexion	59	41
		Extension	61	39
3	RUSBoost	Flexion	59	41
		Extension	61	39
4	Subspace discriminant	Flexion	100	0
		Extension	0	100
5	Subspace KNN	Flexion	97	3
		Extension	3	97
6	LogitBoost	Flexion	99	1
		Extension	3	97
7	GentleBoost	Flexion	99	1
		Extension	3	97

3.1 Performance Metrics

The ensemble algorithms were compared by using False Discovery Rate (FDR), Positive Predictive Value (PPV), Specificity (true negative ratio), Sensitivity (true positive ratio), AUC, F-measure, and ACC. F-measure is also called F-score which is very familiar parameter playing a major role in classification accuracy estimation.

Receiver Operating Characteristic (ROC) curve yield relationship between specificity and sensitivity. The following parameters are calculated for performance comparison:

$$FDR = \frac{FP}{TP + FP} \times 100 \tag{18}$$

$$PPV = \frac{TP}{TP + FP} \times 100 \tag{19}$$

$$SP = \frac{TN}{TN + FP} \times 100 \tag{20}$$

$$SE = \frac{TP}{TP + FN} \times 100 \tag{21}$$

$$F-measure = \frac{2TP}{2TP + FP + FN} \tag{22}$$

$$ACC = \frac{TP + TN}{Total\ Population} * 100 \tag{23}$$

The experimental work showed that subspace discriminant algorithm performs the best as compared to any other ensemble classification algorithm. Subspace discriminant algorithm achieved the best ACC, SE, SP, F-measure as well as other parameters. Bagging algorithm exhibited the second best performance in term of ACC whereas Subspace K-NN has the highest speed and RUSBoost required less training time. AdaBoost and RUSBoost showed worst performance. Figure 4 is the graphical representation of result in term of ACC, SE and FDR.

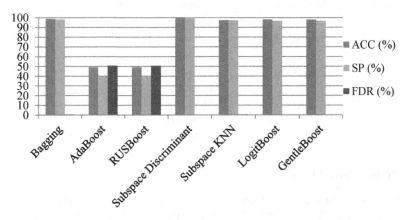

Fig. 4. Graphical representation of various classifiers performance

Subspace discriminant ensemble methods are more effective as compared to the any other ensemble classification algorithms which is also verified by ROC curve. ROC curve is drawn between true positive rate and false positive rate of classifier. Figure 5 shows the ROC curve of subspace discriminant ensemble algorithm which is ideal graph showing 100% true positive and 0% false positive rate. The overall performance and reliability of subspace discriminant algorithm is also shown by AUC value of curve. The AUC is one for subspace discriminant algorithm which is the best for the classification of sEMG signals.

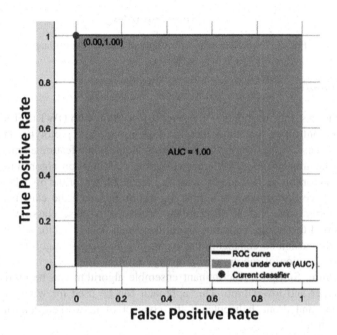

Fig. 5. ROC curve of subspace discriminant ensemble algorithm

3.2   Robotic Arm Controlling

After the classification of sEMG signals, the output of classifier *i.e.* ACC is utilized for generating the control signal using arduino microcontroller to control the elbow movement of the robotic arm prototype. The control signal generated from the microcontroller is in the form of pulse as shown in Fig. 6. This control pulse signal is used to interface the robotic arm through driver circuit. If the amplitude of control signal is 1 mV then it represents the elbow flexion class. If the amplitude of control signal is 0 mV, then it represents the elbow extension class. In this ways, the output of classifier is utilized for generating the control pulse to open and close the robotic arm prototype. This control signal can also be utilized for controlling the other motion of arm.

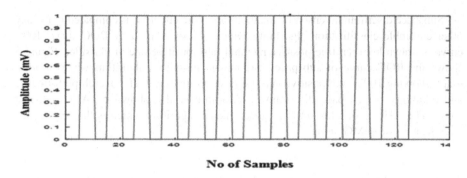

No of Samples

Fig. 6. Controller output for arm end effector controlling

4 Conclusion

This paper discusses the usefulness of ensemble algorithm with DWT, SFFS algorithm, and PCA for controlling the elbow motion of the robotic arm prototype. The 4th scale db_4 wavelet filter is utilized for better de-noising and residual feature extraction. Based on the classification results of different ensemble classification algorithms, subspace discriminant algorithm are found best with db_4 wavelet filter for the myoelectric control system. Subspace discriminant ensemble algorithm enhanced the classification accuracy by majority voting of 35 discriminant classifier as base classifier. The SFFS algorithm sorted the feature resulting low dimensional feature vector and PCA further reduces the dimension so enhancing the speed of classification algorithm for controlling the elbow motion of robotic arm prototype model.

In the future, Subspace discriminant ensemble algorithm can be used for developing the upper and lower limb. This approach can be used for wireless control of robotic device and drone helicopter if the concept of networked control system is combined with it.

References

1. Ryait, H.S., Arora, A.S., Agarwal, R.: SEMG signal analysis at acupressure points for elbow movement. J. Electromyogr. Kinesiol. **21**, 868–876 (2011)
2. Gams, A., Petric, T., Debevec, T., Babic, J.: Effects of robotic knee-exoskeleton on human energy expenditure. IEEE Trans. Biomed. Eng. **60**, 1–9 (2013)
3. Kloosterman, M.G.M., Buurke, J.H., de Vries, W., Van der Woude, L.H.V., Rietman, J.S.: Effect of power-assisted hand-rim wheelchair propulsion on shoulder load in experienced wheelchair users: a pilot study with an instrumented wheelchair. Med. Eng. Phys. **37**, 961–968 (2015)
4. Phinyomark, A., Phukpattaranont, P., Limsakul, C.: A review of control methods for electric power wheelchairs based on electromyography signals with special emphasis on pattern recognition. IETE Tech. Rev. (Institution Electron. Telecommun. Eng. India) **28**, 316–326 (2011)

5. Deep, A., Singh, J., Narayan, Y., Chatterji, S., Mathew, L.: Robotic arm controlling using automated balancing platform. In: International Conference Communication, Control and Intelligent Systems, CCIS 2015, pp. 282–285 (2016). https://doi.org/10.1109/ccintels.2015.7437924

6. Phinyomark, A., et al.: EMG feature evaluation for improving myoelectric pattern recognition robustness. Expert Syst. Appl. **40**, 4832–4840 (2013)

7. Khushaba, R.N., Takruri, M., Miro, J.V., Kodagoda, S.: Towards limb position invariant myoelectric pattern recognition using time-dependent spectral features. Neural Netw. **55**, 42–58 (2014)

8. Farid, D.M., Zhang, L., Rahman, C.M., Hossain, M.A., Strachan, R.: Hybrid decision tree and naïve Bayes classifiers for multi-class classification tasks. Expert Syst. Appl. **41**, 1937–1946 (2014)

9. Khushaba, R.N., Al-Timemy, A., Kodagoda, S., Nazarpour, K.: Combined influence of forearm orientation and muscular contraction on EMG pattern recognition. Expert Syst. Appl. **61**, 154–161 (2016)

10. Pan, L., Zhang, D., Sheng, X., Zhu, X.: Improved myoelectric control for amputees through transcranial direct current stimulation. IEEE Trans. Biomed. Eng. **9294**, 1–11 (2015)

11. Garg, C., Narayan, Y., Mathew, L.: Development of a software module for feature extraction and classification of EMG signals. In: 2015 Communication, Control and Intelligent Systems, CCIS, vol. 1, pp. 250–254 (2015)

12. Kumari, P., Narayan, Y., Ahlawat, V., Mathew, L.: Advance approach towards elbow movement classification using discrete wavelet transform and quadratic support vector machine. In: The International Conference on Communication and Computing Systems, ICCCS 2016, pp. 978–981 (2017)

13. Narayan, Y., Kumari, P., Mathew, L.: Elbow movement classification of a robotic arm using wavelet packet and cubic SVM. In: The International Conference on Communication and Computing Systems, ICCCS 2016, pp. 605–610 (2017). https://doi.org/10.1201/9781315364094-108

14. Phinyomark, A., Hu, H., Phukpattaranont, P., Limsakul, C.: Application of linear discriminant analysis in dimensionality reduction for hand motion classification. Meas. Sci. Rev. **12**, 82–89 (2012)

15. Narayan, Y., Mathew, L., Chatterji, S.: sEMG signal classification using Discrete Wavelet Transform and Decision Tree classifier. Int. J. Control Theory Appl. **10**, 511–517 (2017)

16. Pudil, P., Novovi, J.: Floating search methods in feature selection. Pattern Recognit. Lett. **15**, 1119–1125 (1994)

17. Alomari, F., Liu, G.: Novel hybrid soft computing pattern recognition system SVM-GAPSO for classification of eight different hand motions. Optik (Stuttg) **126**, 4757–4762 (2015)

18. Babita, Kumari, P., Narayan, Y., Mathew, L.: Binary movement classification of sEMG signal using linear SVM and Wavelet Packet Transform. In: 1st IEEE International Conference on Power Electronics, Intelligent Control and Energy Systems, ICPEICES 2016, pp. 2–5 (2016). https://doi.org/10.1109/icpeices.2016.7853640

19. Ryu, J., Kim, D.H.: Real-time gait subphase detection using an EMG signal graph matching (ESGM) algorithm based on EMG signals. Expert Syst. Appl. **85**, 357–365 (2017)

20. Yan, R., Gao, R.X., Chen, X.: Wavelets for fault diagnosis of rotary machines: a review with applications. Signal Process. **96**, 1–15 (2014)

21. Narayan, Y.: A comparative analysis for haar wavelet efficiency to remove Gaussian and speckle noise from image. In: 3rd 2016 International Conference on Computing for Sustainable Global Development (2016)

22. Virdi, P., Narayan, Y., Kumari, P., Mathew, L.: Discrete wavelet packet based elbow movement classification using fine Gaussian SVM. In: 1st IEEE International Conference on Power Electronics, Intelligent Control and Energy Systems, ICPEICES 2016, pp. 1–5 (2017). https://doi.org/10.1109/icpeices.2016.7853657
23. Garg, C., Mathew, L., Narayan, Y.: Fuzzy control of EMG based movement classification with six degree of freedom. Int. J. Eng. Technol. Manag. Appl. Sci. 3, 73–77 (2015)
24. Geethanjali, P., Ray, K.K.: A low-cost real-time research platform for EMG pattern recognition-based prosthetic hand. IEEE/ASME Trans. Mech. 20, 1948–1955 (2015)

Low Complexity Image Compression Algorithm Based on Uniform Quantization of RGB Colour Image for Capsule Endoscopy

Nithin Varma Malathkar[(✉)] and Surender Kumar Soni

Electronics and Communication Engineering Department, NIT Hamirpur,
Hamirpur 177005, HP, India
nithinvarma.a3@gmail.com

Abstract. Demand for wireless capsule endoscopy is increasing rapidly due to its simplicity and comfortable procedure. However, the wireless capsule endoscopy lack in complete diagnosing of gastrointestinal tract due to its limited power supply and size. Low complexity image compression algorithm plays vital role in saving power and size by reducing the data as transmitter consume 60% of capsule power. A high efficiency and lossless image compression algorithm is proposed, which is a combination of uniform quantization, simple predictive coding and Golomb Rice code. In the proposed algorithm, RGB colour image is quantized using uniform quantization. Then, differential pulse code modulation is applied, where current pixel value is subtracted with previous pixel value to provide a difference error value. The difference error value is encoded using Golomb Rice code. Several endoscopic images are considered for evaluating the performance and efficiency of proposed algorithm. The proposed algorithm provided the compression ratio of 72.5 with less computational complexity and memory usage.

Keywords: Wireless capsule endoscopy · RGB colour image
Uniform quantization · Golomb Rice code

1 Introduction

Wireless capsule endoscopy is a process of investigating the gastrointestinal (GI) tract of the human body using a tiny electronic device of capsule size. The capsule size device is swallowed by the patients, which travel thought the whole GI tract and capture the images using the inbuilt camera. The captured images are transmitted to data logger outside the body with the help of radio frequency (RF) antenna. The recorded data helps the doctor in diagnosing the GI tract [1]. WCE made diagnosing the complete small bowel possible for the doctors, where the conventional endoscopy failed. The WCE is preferred for its simple and comfortable procedure by the patients. However, the WCE still lack in complete diagnosing of GI tract due to its limited power supply (8 to 10 h) [2]. Total 60% of the capsule power is used by transmitter for transmitting image data. By reducing the data, power needed to transmit the data can be saved. The saved power helps in enhancing the life of capsule. The reduction of data within the limited bandwidth of capsule (2–3 Mbps) helps in increasing the frame rate.

© Springer Nature Singapore Pte Ltd. 2019
A. K. Luhach et al. (Eds.): ICAICR 2018, CCIS 955, pp. 231–240, 2019.
https://doi.org/10.1007/978-981-13-3140-4_21

The limited bandwidth of capsule is due to attenuation of human body towards the radio wave [2]. An image compression algorithm plays a vital role in WCE for reducing the data. To analyze the data accurately, quality image is preferred [3]. A lossless image compression algorithm provide good quality reconstructed image. Designing a lossless image compression algorithm with less computational complexity and no extra memory usage is a challenge.

The complementary metal–oxide–semiconductor (CMOS) sensor used in the capsule provide the output data in color filter array (CFA) pattern, where two green components, one red component and one blue component is obtained. The colour image consists of three components i.e. red, green and blue. The conversion of CFA data to colour data add some redundancy to the image [4]. To avoid the redundancy, conversion process has been skipped and image compression algorithm has been directly applied on CFA data in [5]. However, the reduction of data i.e. compression ratio obtained after data compression process is less due to non-homogeneity between neighboring pixels in CFA data. In [4], the filtration and transformation of CFA pixels has been done to acquire more compression ratio. The filtration and transformation process is not possible in WCE due to their high hardware cost. Recent capsules are equipped with RGB-YUV conversion transform [6], which help in achieving more compression ratio due to homogeneity between neighboring pixels. To utilize this advantage image compression algorithm has been applied on YUV colour space in [7, 8]. However, the RGB-YUV conversion lead to extra computational complexity and add some redundancy to image. Moreover, conversion process require some buffer memory. In [9–12], image compression algorithm has been applied on RGB colour image. However, the image compression algorithm used in it are mainly discrete cosine transform (DCT) based. The DCT based algorithm has been proposed for WCE in [10–13]. The DCT based algorithm are lossy and have high computational complexity. The DCT work with 8×8 pixels block, whereas CMOS send the data in raster scan fashion. For implementing DCT an image need to be stored, which consume extra buffer memory. The extra buffer memory consume extra power and hardware. The inherent nature of DCT lead to noise in image, which may affect the diagnosing rate of image. DPCM based image compression algorithm has been proposed in [14–17]. The DPCM is lossless algorithm, which is simple and need no extra buffer memory. To encode the value in binary form for transmitting, Huffman code has been proposed in [18]. The Huffman code need extra buffer memory to store Huffman table, extra memory consume extra power and size. LZW encoder based on dictionary code has been proposed in [11]. LZW don't need extra memory to store tables, but for storing dictionary code. In [1], simple and hardware efficient Golomb Rice code has been proposed for WCE. The G-R code don't required any extra buffer memory and has less computational complexity. In this article, high efficiency and lossless image compression algorithm is presented. In the proposed algorithm, first RGB colour image is quantized using uniform quantization, which is simple and near lossless quantization method. Then, quantized RGB colour image is compressed using DPCM, where current pixel value is subtracted with previous pixel value to provide difference error value. The difference error value is encoded using Golomb Rice code.

Later part of article is expressed as: in Sect. 2, step by step procedure of proposed algorithm is discussed. In Sect. 3 performance of the proposed algorithm is analyzed. Section 4 conclude the results of proposed algorithm.

2 Proposed Algorithm

The image compression algorithm reduces the data, which help in reducing the power consumption of transmitter in WCE and also reduces the data within the limited bandwidth of WCE. Figure 1 show the proposed algorithm block diagram, which consist of three stage process. First, the RGB colour image is uniform quantized. Then, DPCM applied on the quantized data to obtain the difference error value. Finally, the difference error value is transformed into binary form using G-R code.

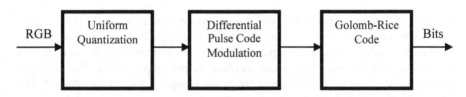

Fig. 1. Block diagram of proposed algorithm

2.1 Uniform Quantization of RGB Colour Image

The colour image is a combination of red, green and blue components. In Fig. 2a endoscopic colour image is shown. Figure 2b, represents the intensity distribution of colour image shown in Fig. 2a. From the Fig. 2b, it can be observed that red, green and blue colour in image shown in Fig. 2a, have wide range of intensity distribution. Since the intensity distribution of RGB colour is wide, less reduction of data is achieved due to homogeneity between consecutive pixels is less. Figure 2c represents the change in pixel for 128th row of image shown in Fig. 2a. From Fig. 2c, it can be observed that change in pixel value is more for all the components.

To reduce the change in pixel value, uniform quantization is used. The uniform quantization is a simple process with a combination of division and round off operation. In the uniform quantization, each value is divided with fixed value i.e. 4 and remainder obtained is round off to next nearest integer value. The uniform quantization is mathematically represented as

$$qRGB = round(\frac{RGB}{4}) \qquad (1)$$

The uniform quantization reduces the intensity distribution range of image by four times. Figure 3a represents the intensity distribution of quantized endoscopic colour image shown in Fig. 2a. From the Fig. 3a, it can be observed that intensity distribution of endoscopic image shown in Fig. 2a is narrow due to quantization of data. Figure 3b

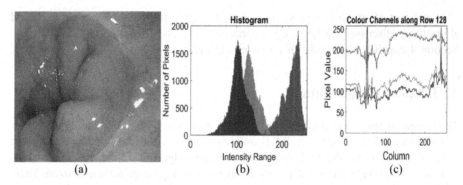

Fig. 2. (a) Endoscopic colour image of cardia, (b) Intensity distribution of endoscopic image, (c) Colour channels along row 128 of endoscopic image (Color figure online)

represents the change in pixels of 128th row of image shown in Fig. 2a after uniform quantization. From Fig. 3b, it can be observed that change in pixel value is reduced, which help in achieving more compression. However, uniform quantization produce quantization error. The error is the increment or decrement of pixel value. The maximum increment or decrement of reconstructed pixel value compared to original value is 2. This error is negligible as it doesn't affect much [19].

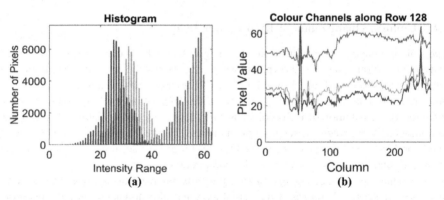

Fig. 3. (a) Intensity distribution of quantized RGB endoscopic image, (b) Colour channels along row 128 of image

In Table 1 comparison between quantized RGB and other standard colour space is done with regard to average standard deviation and entropy [20]. From Table 1, it can be observed that quantized RGB (qRGB) has overall less average standard deviation and entropy compared to other standards. It means that less number of bits is needed to transmit qRGB information compared to other color spaces. The qRGB is another representation of RGB colour space, which can be reversed to RGB colour space without any effect on information. qRGB is best choice for WCE application due to its less hardware cost.

Table 1. Average entropy and standard deviation of different colour space and proposed work

Colour space	Component	Std. dev	Entropy
RGB	R	45.0	7.2
	G	34.6	7.0
	B	32.2	6.8
YUV	Y	31.9	6.8
	U	3.9	3.8
	V	8.7	4.8
YEF	Y	36.2	7.0
	E	2.2	3.0
	F	3.2	3.5
qRGB	qR	11.5	5.2
	qG	8.7	5.0
	qB	8.1	4.9

2.2 Differential Pulse Code Modulation

The values between the consecutive pixels changes slowly in endoscopic images. Generally their difference value is small due to rare sharp edges in endoscopic images. The change in pixel values can be calculated using

$$dX = X_c - X_{c-1} \tag{2}$$

The X_c is the current pixel value and X_{c-1} is previous pixel value, where c represent the column in image. Figure 4 represent the change in pixels (difference value) for qRGB components at 128th row of image shown in Fig. 2a. From the Fig. 4, it can be observed that all the components has less change in pixel value. Here, differential pulse code modulation (DPCM) a lossless compression technique with low computational complexity is chosen to reduce the data. In DPCM, current pixel is subtracted with the previous pixel value to obtain difference error value. The difference error value can be represented in less bits compared to two consecutive pixels value.

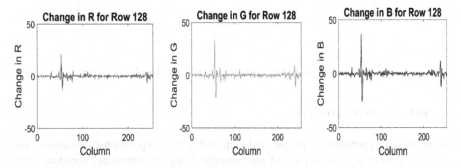

Fig. 4. DPCM at 128 row of endoscopic image for qRGB colour components

2.3 Golomb Rice Code

Golomb Rice (G-R) code is a simple and hardware supportive entropy coder based on
Golomb family codes. G-R code don't need any extra buffer memory to store tables or
dictionary code. It is a simple division operation. However, the G-R code don't work
with negative integers. So, all integer need to be mapped to positive. The mapping
process as follow: the positive integers are mapped to even numbers and negative
integers are mapped to odd numbers. The mapping is done using formula given below.

$$m\_dR = \begin{cases} 2|dR| - 1, & when \ dR < 0 \\ 2dR, & when \ dR \geq 0 \end{cases} \tag{3}$$

From the analyzing of m_dR it is observed that m_dR values ranges between 0–63,
which can be seen from Fig. 5. So, m_dR can be represented in 6 bits (I). The G-R
code encoding process as follows: the mapped integer is divided with 2 k (k = 1). The
quotient and remainder obtained after division operation are expressed in bits form. The
quotient value (Q) obtained is represented in the unary form of 1 s follow by 0 and
remainder value is expressed in binary form of k. The total bits needed to encode m_dR
value using G-R code is Q + 1 + k. For large value the G-R code produce large code
length, which effect the compression ratio. So code length need to be limited for large
value. klimit is proposed to limit the code length, where larger values are encoded to
fixed length code (klimit). The klimit is processed when the m_dR > 46, where klimit
is expressed as J number of unary 1 s followed by 0 and m_dR is represented in the
binary form of I bits. Total no of bits needed to represent the klimit is J + 1 + I. Here
klimit is considered as 30 and J as 23.

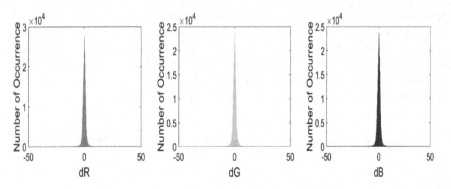

Fig. 5. Intensity distribution of dX for qR, qG and qB component

3 Performance Analysis

The proposed algorithm is simple and required less computational resources. The
proposed algorithm is implemented and verified using the personnel computer software. The proposed algorithm is applied on the 200 sample image of GI tract, from

larynx to anus. The performance of image compression algorithm is measured using two parameters compression ratio (CR) and peak signal noise ratio (PSNR). Since the algorithm is lossless, the PSNR is considered infinity. The compression ratio is measured using

$$CR = (1 - \frac{Total\ bits\ after\ compression}{Total\ bits\ before\ compression}) \times 100 \qquad (4)$$

In Table 2 comparison between proposed algorithm and YUV or YEN based compression algorithm in term of compression ratio is shown. From Table 2, it is observed that proposed compression algorithm which is combination of quantized RGB colour image, DPCM and G-R code provide better compression ratio than compression algorithms, which are combination of YUV [1] or YEF [14] colour space, DPCM and G-R code. Figure 6 show original endoscopic image and its reconstructed image. From Fig. 6, it can be observed that no change in reconstructed image compared to original image is observed as proposed algorithm is lossless and compression ratio obtained is 71.5.

Table 2. Compression methodologies classification

Colour space	Predictive code	Encoder	Compression ratio
YUV [1]	DPCM	G-R code	68.7
YEN [14]	DPCM	G-R code	69.0
qRGB (proposed)	DPCM	G-R code	72.5

In Table 3, the comparison between standard JPEG-LS [21] and proposed algorithm is done. From the Table 3, it can be observed that proposed algorithm provide better results in term of compression ratio than JPEG-LS. The computational complexity of JPEG-LS is more compared to proposed algorithm as it consist of 7 prediction modes, whereas proposed method consist of only one mode. In JPEG-LS, one row of image need to be stored as prediction modes are dependent on above row values. Storing one row of image consume extra buffer memory and also JPEG-LS need 1.9k register array for context parameters. The proposed algorithm don't required any extra buffer memory as prediction mode is dependent on previous pixel value only.

Table 4 represents the comparison between proposed algorithm and the other works. From the Table 4, it can be observed that proposed work provide good compression ratio compared to [1, 7, 9] at low computational complexity of O(n) and with no extra buffer memory usage. The algorithm presented in [2, 10–13] provide good compression ratio comparing to proposed one. However, they are lossy image compression algorithm based on discrete cosine transform (DCT). The DCT work with 8 × 8 pixels block, where the CMOS camera used in capsule send the data raster scan fashion. So image need to be stored, which need extra buffer memory. The extra buffer memory consume extra size and power, which are the bottleneck of WCE. The DCT has high computational complexity of O(nlogn). DPCM based compression algorithm is presented in [14–17], which provide good compression ratio at low computational

238   N. V. Malathkar and S. K. Soni

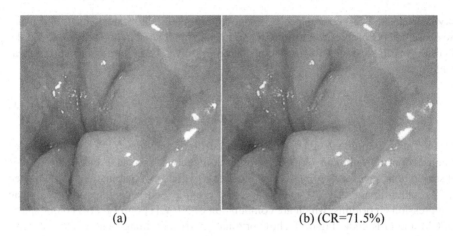

(a)   (b) (CR=71.5%)

Fig. 6. (a) Sample original endoscopic image, (b) Reconstructed endoscopic image

Table 3. Comparison between proposed algorithm and JPEG-LS

Parameters	JPEG-LS	Proposed
Colour plane	RGB	qRGB
Prediction modes	7	1
Extra memory	1.9 kb for context array + for storing one row of image	No
K-parameters	Dynamic(based on context array)	Fixed
Coding	Golomb-Rice	Golomb-Rice
Run mode	Yes	No
Avg. CR%	57.9	72.5

complexity of O(n) and no extra memory usage. Lossless compression algorithm based on DPCM is presented in [14, 17], from where it can be observed that they provide good compression ratio compared to proposed work. However, from Table 2, it can be observed that for common samples proposed work provide better compression ratio compared to work in [14], where DPCM is applied on YEN colour space. Work presented in [17] has more compression ratio compared to other DPCM based lossless compression algorithm. However in this algorithm DPCM techniques is directly applied on CFA image instead on colour image. The DPCM performance degrade on CFA images due to non-homogeneity between consecutive pixels in CFA images. To achieve good compression ratio, image is subdivided in to sub images using separable filters. This separable filters increases the hardware cost. Moreover G-R code used in this algorithm is based on the context array, where calculating context array for each components increases the computational resources. Whereas fixed context G-R code is used in proposed method, which do not require any extra resources.

Table 4. Comparison between proposed algorithm and other works

	Type	Colour plane	Buffer memory	Lossless	CR %	PSNR	Complexity
Chen et al. [9]	JPEG	RGB	Yes	No	56.7	46.6	O(n)
Dung et al. [10]	H.264 based DCT	RGB	Yes	No	82.0	36.2	O(nlogn)
Lin et al. [11]	DCT and LZW	RGB	Yes	No	79.6	32.5	O(nlogn)
Wu et al. [7]	Compressed Sensing	YUV	Yes	No	50.0	31.0	O(nlogn)
Wahid et al. [12]	DCT	RGB	Yes	No	87.1	32.9	O(nlogn)
Khan et al. [1]	DPCM and G-R	YUV	No	Yes	67.0	∞	O(n)
Turcza et al. [2]	DCT and G-R	YCgCo	Yes	No	91.2	34.7	O(nlogn)
Khan et al. [14]	DPCM and G-R	YEF	No	Yes	74.2	∞	O(n)
Fante et al. [15]	DPCM and G-R	YUV	No	No	82.1	46.6	O(n)
Turcza et al. [13]	DCT and G-R	YCbCr	Yes	No	91.6	36.1	O(nlogn)
Li et al. [16]	DPCM and G-R	YEF	No	No	80.0	40.0	O(n)
Mohammed et al. [17]	DPCM and G-R	YLMN	No	No	53.4	∞	O(n)
Proposed	DPCM and G-R	qRGB	No	Yes	72.5	∞	O(n)

4 Conclusion

A low complexity and lossless image compression algorithm based on qRGB, DPCM and Golomb Rice code is proposed. The performance of proposed algorithm is measured using compression ratio, where it is observed that proposed algorithm provide good compression ratio. The comparison between proposed algorithm and YUV and YEF based algorithm show that proposed algorithm perform better for endoscopic images. The proposed algorithm is also compared with standard JPEG-LS, which show that proposed algorithm work efficiently compared to JPEG-LS.

References

1. Khan, T.H., Wahid, K.A.: Lossless and low-power image compressor for wireless capsule endoscopy. VLSI Des. **2011**, 12 (2011)
2. Turcza, P., Duplaga, M.: Hardware-efficient low-power image processing system for wireless capsule endoscopy. IEEE J. Biomed. Health Inform. **17**, 1046–1056 (2013)

3. Ciuti, G., Menciassi, A., Dario, P.: Capsule endoscopy: from current achievements to open challenges. IEEE Trans. Bio-Med. Eng. **4**, 59–72 (2011)
4. Xie, X., Li, G., Wang, Z.: Low-complexity and high-efficiency image compression algorithm for wireless endoscopy system. J. Electron. Imag. **15**, 1–15 (2006)
5. Xie, X., Li, G.L., Wang, Z.H.: A near-lossless image compression algorithm suitable for hardware design in wireless endoscopy system. EURASIP J. Adv. Signal Process. **2007**, 82160 (2007)
6. Khan, T.H., Wahid, K.: Implantable narrow band image compressor for capsule endoscopy. In: International Symposium on Circuits and Systems, pp. 2203–2206. IEEE, Seoul (2012)
7. Wu, J., Li, Y.: Low-complexity video compression for capsule endoscope based on compressed sensing theory. In: International Conference on Engineering in Medicine and Biology Society, pp. 3727–3730. IEEE, Minneapolis (2009)
8. Khan, T.H., Wahid, K.A.: Subsample-based image compression for capsule endoscopy. J. Real-Time Image Process. **8**, 5–19 (2013)
9. Chen, X., Zhang, X., Zhang, L., et al.: A wireless capsule endoscopic system with a low-power controlling and processing ASIC. IEEE Trans. Biomed. Circ. Syst. **3**, 11–22 (2009)
10. Dung, L.R., Wu, Y.Y., Lai, H.C., Weng, P.K.: A modified H. 264 Intra-frame video encoder for capsule endoscope. In: International Conference on Biomedical Circuits and Systems, pp. 61–64. IEEE, MD (2008)
11. Lin, M.C., Dung, L.R., Weng, P.K.: An ultra-low-power image compressor for capsule endoscope. BioMed. Eng. Online **5**, 1–8 (2006)
12. Wahid, K., Ko, S., Teng, D.: Efficient hardware implementation of an image compressor for wireless capsule endoscopy applications. In: International Conference on Neural Networks, pp. 2761–2765. IEEE, Hong Kong (2008)
13. Turcza, P., Duplaga, M.: Energy-efficient image compression algorithm for high-frame rate multi-view wireless capsule endoscopy. J. Real-Time Image Process., 1–13 (2016)
14. Khan, T.H., Wahid, K.A.: Design of a lossless image compression system for video capsule endoscopy and its performance in in-vivo trials. Sensors **14**, 20779–20799 (2014)
15. Fante, K.A., Bhaumik, B., Chatterjee, S.: Design and implementation of computationally efficient image compressor for wireless capsule endoscopy. Circ. Syst. Signal Process. **35**, 1–27 (2015)
16. Siqing, L.I., Hua, L.: Development of a wireless capsule endoscope system based on field programmable gate array. J. Shanghai Jiaotong Univ. **22**, 156–160 (2017)
17. Mohammed, S.K., Rahman, K.M., Wahid, K.A.: Lossless compression in Bayer color filter array for capsule endoscopy. IEEE Access **5**, 13823–13834 (2017)
18. Turcza, P., Duplaga, M.: Low power FPGA-based image processing core for wireless capsule endoscopy. Sens. Actuators A: Phys. **172**, 552–560 (2011)
19. Pattanaik, S.K., Mahapatra, K.K., Panda, G.: A novel lossless image compression algorithm using arithmetic modulo operation. In: International Conference on Cybernetics and Intelligent Systems, pp. 1–4. IEEE, Bangkok (2006)
20. Shannon, C.E.: A mathematical theory of communication. Bell Syst. Tech. J. **27**, 379–423 (1948)
21. JPEG-LS public domain code. http://www.stat.columbia.edu/~jakulin/jpeg-ls/mirror.htm. Accessed 26 Apr 2018

KSUMM: A Compressed Domain Technique for Video Summarization Using Partial Decoding of Videos

Madhushree Basavarajaiah$^{(\boxtimes)}$ and Priyanka Sharma

Department of Computer Engineering, Institute of Technology,
Nirma University, Ahmedabad, India
{16ftvphde13, priyanka.sharma}@nirmauni.ac.in

Abstract. Generally, the videos are encoded before storing or transmitting. Traditional video processing techniques are compute intensive as they require decoding of the video before processing it. The compressed domain processing of video is an alternative approach where computational overhead is less because a partial decoding is sufficient for many applications. This paper proposes a video summarization technique, KSUMM, that works in the compressed domain. Based on the features extracted from just the I-frames of the video, frames are classified into a predefined number of classes using K-means clustering. Then, the frame which is located at the border of a class in the sequential order is selected to be included in the summary. The length of the summary video can be customized by varying the number of classes during clustering. The quality of the summary was evaluated using Mean Opinion Scores method and the result shows a good Quality of Experience.

Keywords: Video summarization · Machine learning · Video abstraction
Compressed video processing

1 Introduction

As per the Cisco Visual Networking Index, 75% of the mobile data traffic worldwide will be videos by 2020. Videos are an integral part of many applications. Mostly, a video is compressed after it is recorded for storing or transmission purpose. Even though modern video encoders are very efficient in compressing the video, they take longer time in decoding the video. Traditional video summarization techniques decode the video into a sequence of frames before processing it, which is an additional overhead in summarization process. On the other hand, we have compressed domain video summarization techniques which involve only a partial decoding of the videos in order to perform summarization task. This saves time and space in the overall process of summarization [1–4].

The process of summarization of videos can be defined as the generation of synopsis of a lengthy video so that it can be interpreted in less time. There are two types of video summarization [1]. They are: (i) Static Storyboard and (ii) Dynamic Video Skimming. Story board is a collection of keyframes selected from a static video.

© Springer Nature Singapore Pte Ltd. 2019
A. K. Luhach et al. (Eds.): ICAICR 2018, CCIS 955, pp. 241–252, 2019.
https://doi.org/10.1007/978-981-13-3140-4_22

Keyframes are the crucial frames of the original video which are included in the summary. Video skimming is the process of selecting important video clips from the original video.

Based on the working domain of the video, the process of video summarization is divided into two categories namely Pixel/uncompressed domain video summarization and Compressed domain video summarization. In uncompressed domain summarization, video is decoded before using it at the pixel level. In compressed domain, video is not decoded completely into frames. But, the information regarding the content of the video is extracted from partially decoded video [2]. Uncompressed domain video summarization involves three main issues as picturized in Fig. 1. The process of compressed domain summarization does not require complete decoding of the video before processing. A partial decoding of only I-frames is sufficient for extracting features from video based on which the key frames can be selected. This process is shown in Fig. 2.

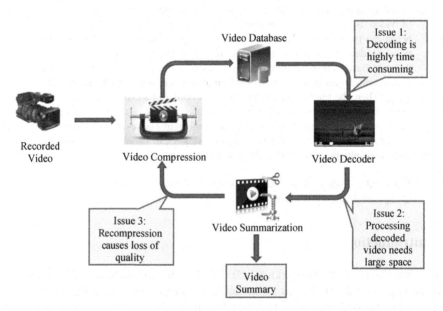

Fig. 1. The process of uncompressed domain video summarization and the issues involved in the process.

In this paper, the challenges faced in performing video summarization in the uncompressed video are addressed by implementing a new approach to obtain the summaries of lengthy videos in the compressed domain. The proposed approach, KSUMM, uses machine learning technique to find the frames in a video which are at the major changes in the content of the video. These frames are called keyframes and they are selected for including in the video summary. Video summaries are generated when a user requests for a summary and the quality of the summary is evaluated using a subjective measurement of Human Visual System [HSV]. In this evaluation method,

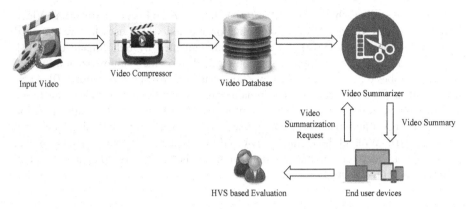

Fig. 2. The process of compressed domain video summarization

the video summary is shown to different users and the opinion score is recorded. A Mean Opinion Score (MOS) is calculated by taking average of all these scores.

The remaining part of the paper is structured as follows. Section 2 gives the literature review on compressed domain video summarization techniques. Section 3 explains the proposed work and the system overview. Implementation details are given in Sect. 4 and results are discussed in Sect. 5 with a trailing conclusion and future work in Sect. 6.

2 Literature Review

Video summarization is traditionally carried out on the uncompressed videos. But, there is a wide scope for research in processing a compressed video as it is less time consuming compared to pixel domain processing. Video summarization is one such problem in which compressed domain techniques are more in demand. In this section, we present a review of literature which use compressed domain techniques for videos summarization.

Video summarization can be performed on the basis of many characteristics of the video. Researchers have tried to implement summarization algorithms using such features of video. Also, summarization is performed in various application domains for example, sports, news, medical and online videos etc. Along with the visual features of the video content, audio and metadata accompanying with the video can also be used for summarization purpose. Similar amalgamation of video and audio features was used to summarize soccer videos by Kiani et al. [3]. A progressive generation mannered method was used to generate video summaries based on the visual content information extracted from the compressed domain video features by Almeida et al. [4, 5]. Yu et al. used semantic features along with metadata available in the compressed video to summarize MPEG [Moving Picture Experts Group] encoded videos [6]. User interaction can also be incorporated in the process of video summarization [7].

Some researchers have worked on specifically H.264/AVC [Advanced Video Coding] encoded videos. A video segmentation method which uses features attained from the entropy decoding of the video is implemented by Schöffmann et al. [8]. Herranz et al. united the content adaptation method into video summarization module [9]. Object tubes extraction was used by Zhong Rui et al. for summarization [10]. Apart from all these methods, compressed domain features like Discrete Cosine Transforms and Motion vectors are also used in summarization process. Video summarization through energy minimization in compressed domain was proposed using graph cut algorithm [10]. With all the literature reviewed in compressed domain, we can say that processing a video in compressed domain gives better results compared to pixel domain video processing [13].

3 Proposed Approach

The proposed work aims at solving the challenges faced in carrying out video summarization in uncompressed domain. This system can offer a video summary when a user requests for it based on the user requirements. Users can have the choice of deciding on the length of the summary. The major steps followed in the implementation are listed below.

Step 1: Extraction of compressed domain features from the video by decoding only the I-frames of the compressed video.
Step 2: Clustering of the frames depending on the features extracted using unsupervised machine learning technique.
Step 3: Selecting the frames which represents a scene change. These frames would later be included in the video summary.

3.1 Proposed Approach

In this proposed work, a summary of a video is created by selecting the important frames from a video sequence. A good video summary storyboard will provide the maximum information present in the input video in as less number of frames as possible. The outline of the proposed work is given away in Fig. 3.

The keyframes obtained from the video give the user a gist of the visual content of the video. In our approach, keyframes are selected when there are changes in the visual content or the scene change.

While compressing a video, MPEG encoder converts it into a sequence of I, B and P-frames. These frames are grouped together in the form of Group of Pictures (GoP). I-frames are the intra - coded frames which appear at the beginning of every GoP, followed by a specific number B and P-frames. This series of frames repeat till the end of the video. The number of these frames is decided by the encoding software [2]. I-frames hold most of the visual data of the video. Hence, only I-frames of the video are decoded for the summarization process here as shown in Fig. 4. The structure of a digital video compressed in MPEG format with I, B, and P-frames is shown in Fig. 5.

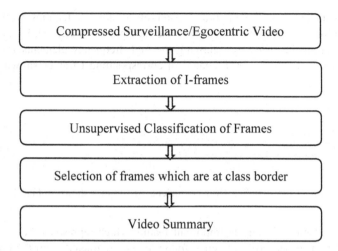

Fig. 3. Flow of the proposed approach

Fig. 4. Sample of decoded I-frames of Basketball 1920 × 1080_50.mp4 video

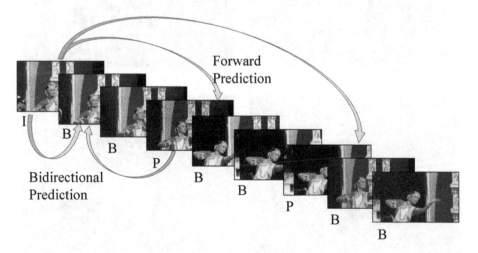

Fig. 5. Frames in a compressed video

DCT coefficients are the important compressed domain features which can be obtained without decoding the video. Because they are calculated while encoding the video to represent the video by removing the high frequency elements in the visual content. Figure 6 shows the DCT images of corresponding I-frames shown in Fig. 4.

Fig. 6. Corresponding DCT coefficients of I-frames shown in Fig. 4.

Similarly, Motion Vector, an important feature which represents the position of a macroblock with respect to a reference frame, can be extracted from the compressed video without decoding the video completely. Motion Vector can be used to find the movement of objects in the visual content of a video. Motion Vectors calculated from Basketball 1920 × 1080_50.mp4 video are shown in Fig. 7.

Fig. 7. Motion vectors represented in the frames of a sample video

4   Implementation

A simple and efficient technique is designed to produce a summary of a compressed surveillance/egocentric video. Consider a typical video V, as a set of frames, where f_i is the constituent frame of the video at position i and n represents the total number of frames of the video V.

$$V = \{f_1, f_2, f_3, \ldots, f_n\} \tag{1}$$

Similarly, a compressed video, CV, is a sequence of fi, fb and fp which represent the I, B, and P-frames respectively. A sample of I, B, and P-frames sequence is generalized in Eq. 2. An example sequence for the Eq. (2) looks like IBBPBBPI.

$$CV = \{fi_1, fb_1, \ldots, fb_{nb}, fp_1, fb_{nb+1}, \ldots, fb_{2nb}, fp_2, fb_{2nb+1}, \ldots, fb_{3nb}, fi_2, \ldots, fp_{np}, fi_{ni}\} \tag{2}$$

The number of I-frames is represented by ni, np represents the number of P-frames and nb is the number of B-frames which appear in sequence between an I and a P-frame. This number can be varied during the encoding of a video.

Only the I-frames of the compressed video are decoded since they contain the maximum information of the video. So, only a partial decoding of the encoded video is performed in the first step. The sequence of I-frames, represented as set I, acts as the input to the second step. The number of I-frames extracted from the video is n.

$$I = \{fi_1, fi_2, fi_3, \ldots, fi_n\} \tag{3}$$

Later, the feature extraction step is carried out to get the scene change or changes in the visual content of the video by extracting useful features from the frames of the video. The possible options for the features are DCT coefficients, Motion Vectors, Quantization Parameter, Color changes in the frames etc. In this implementation, each frame is divided into nine equal parts and the features are extracted based on the color histogram and the matrix having the positions of the greatest color histogram is constructed. This matrix with numerical values extracted from every frame forms the feature set using which the frame clustering is performed in the third step.

Unsupervised classification technique, the k-Means clustering method is used to classify the frames because the k-Means algorithm is well suited for general purpose clustering of numerical data with even cluster size and less number of clusters. The features extracted from the frames form matrix with 27 columns stand for the attributes of the data and the rows of the matrix represent the frames of the video. The feature set is given as an input to the unsupervised classification module that classifies the frames into a predefined set of classes of frames, C_k. k is the number of classes which can be defined by the user. fi_p is the first frame in the class and fi_q is the last frame.

$$C_k = \{fi_p, \ldots, fi_q\} \tag{4}$$

The last step is the selection of keyframes to form the video summary storyboard. The class labels assigned to each frame are sequentially scanned and a frame is selected if there is a change in the class label. For example, fi_1, fi_2 and fi_3 belong to C_1, then fi_1 and fi_4 are selected because fi_4 belongs to C_2. This process continues till all frames in the list are traversed. Finally, all the selected frames put together form the summary of a video, SV. fi_{C1} is the first frame from the class C_1, fi_{C2} is the first frame from class C_2 and so on. fi_{Ck} is the frame at the first frame from the last class C_k. fi_n is the last frame in the series of I-frames.

$$SV = \{fi_{C1}, fi_{C2}, fi_{C3}, \ldots, fi_{Ck}, fi_n\} \tag{5}$$

5 Result Analysis

The implementation of the proposed technique was carried out using Python. MPEG-4 videos were used for testing the summarization method. The number of frames included in the summary depends on the number of scene changes in the video as the technique selects frames based on the content change in the video. For example, a video from VSUMM dataset [12] containing 358 I-frames was summarized to 28 frames using KSUMM. That means a 7.8% of the frames were selected to be a part of the summary when a 5-class unsupervised classifier was used.

Increasing the number of classes increases the number of keyframes selected for the summary and vice-versa. Average complexity of the k-Means clustering algorithm is O (knT), where k is the number of classes, n represents the number of samples and T gives the number of iteration [11]. The summary frames of a sample surveillance video are shown in Fig. 8.

The evaluation of the summarization quality is a difficult process since there are no well-defined measures for the goodness of a summary and the usefulness of the summary majorly depends on the requirement of the user. Hence, the summary along with the original input video was shown to 20 volunteers who were asked to rate the summary quality based on the Quality of Experience (QoE) on a scale of 1 to 5 where 1 being the least and 5 being the best score. Mean Opinion Score (MOS) were calculated for every video summary based on the user rankings. An average score of 4.1 was given to the result shown in Fig. 8. The MOS for different test videos as obtained by the experiment are shown in Table 1. The summary frames of another sample surveillance video from VIRAT dataset [14] are shown in Fig. 9.

Fig. 8. Video summary result of a sample video from VSUMM dataset

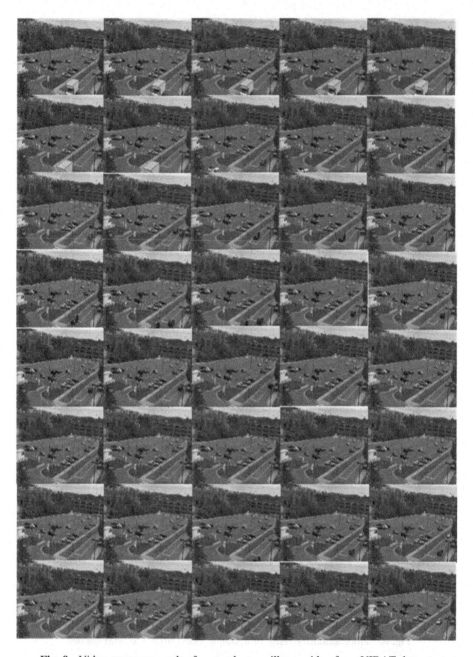

Fig. 9. Video summary result of a sample surveillance video from VIRAT dataset

Table 1. Result analysis using mean opinion score (MOS)

Sr. no.	Sample video	No. of classes	% of frames selected	MOS
1	video-1	5	7.8	4.1
2	video-2	5	6.9	3.8
3	video-3	5	5.5	3.5
4	video-4	5	6.4	4.2
5	video-5	3	4.6	3.6
6	video-6	3	3.2	3.7
7	video-7	3	3.8	3.9

6 Conclusion

This paper proposes a video summarization system called KSUMM that uses visual feature extraction from frames obtained from partial decoding of videos and unsupervised machine learning techniques to perform summarization tasks. The user can tweak the number of classes to be used in the clustering module to have the desired number of frames in the summary. With a 3-class classification, minimum of 3.8% of the frames are included in the summary and 6.4% with a 5-class classification. Number of frames included in the summary increase with the number of classes used in clustering the frames. In this research work, the surveillance video clips compressed using MPEG-4 technology have been used for summary generation. The algorithm for video summarization is designed in such a way that it can be parallelly computed by using graphic processors to speed up the overall process. The quality of the summary is evaluated using Mean Opinion Scores method. The outputs show that the video summary is generated with satisfying Quality of Experience. In future, the technique can be extended to work for other codecs like H.264 and HEVC and deep learning techniques can be employed to replace the manual features with machine learned features.

References

1. Truong, B.T., Venkatesh, S.: Video abstraction: a systematic review and classification. ACM Trans. Multimedia Comput. Commun. Appl. (TOMM) 3(1), 3 (2007)
2. Babu, R.V., Tom, M., Wadekar, P.: A survey on compressed domain video analysis techniques. Multimedia Tools Appl. 75(2), 1043–1078 (2014)
3. Kiani, V., Pourreza, H.R.: Flexible soccer video summarization in compressed domain. In: Proceedings of 3rd IEEE International Conference on Computer and Knowledge Engineering, pp. 213–218 (2013)
4. Almeida, J., Leite, N.J., Torres, R.D.S.: Online video summarization on compressed domain. J. Vis. Commun. Image Represent. 24(6), 729–738 (2013)
5. Almeida, J., Torres, R.D.S., Leite, N.J.: Rapid video summarization on compressed video. In: Proceedings of IEEE International Symposium on Multimedia, pp. 113–120 (2010)

6. Yu, J.C.S., Kankanhalli, M.S., Mulhen, P.: Semantic video summarization in compressed domain MPEG video. In: IEEE International Conference on Multimedia and Expo, Baltimore, MA, USA, 6–9 July, pp. 329–332 (2003)
7. Almeida, J., Leite, N.J., Torres, R.D.S.: VISON: VIdeo Summarization for ONline applications. Pattern Recogn. Lett. **33**(4), 397–409 (2012)
8. Schöffmann, K., Böszörmenyi, L.: Fast segmentation of H.264/AVC bitstreams for on-demand video summarization. In: Satoh, S., Nack, F., Etoh, M. (eds.) MMM 2008. LNCS, vol. 4903, pp. 265–276. Springer, Heidelberg (2008). https://doi.org/10.1007/978-3-540-77409-9_25
9. Herranz, L., Martínez, J.M.: An integrated approach to summarization and adaptation using H.264/MPEG-4 SVC. Sig. Process. Image Commun. **24**(6), 499–509 (2009)
10. Zhong, R., Hu, R., Wang, Z., Wang, S.: Fast synopsis for moving objects using compressed video. IEEE Sig. Process. Lett. **21**(7), 834–838 (2014)
11. Pedregosa, et al.: Scikit-learn: machine learning in Python. JMLR **12**, 2825–2830 (2011)
12. De Avila, S.E.F., Lopes, A.P.B., da Luz Jr., A., de Albuquerque Araújo, A.: VSUMM a mechanism designed to produce static video summaries and a novel evaluation method. Pattern Recogn. Lett. **32**(1), 56–68 (2011)
13. Babu, R.V., Tom, M., Wadekar, P.: A survey on compressed domain video analysis techniques. Multimedia Tools Appl. **75**(2), 1043–1078 (2016)
14. Oh, S., et al.: A large-scale benchmark dataset for event recognition in surveillance video. In: IEEE conference on Computer Vision and Pattern Recognition (CVPR), pp. 3153–3160 (2011)

A Machine Learning Approach to Employability Evaluation Using Handwriting Analysis

Prachi Joshi$^{(\boxtimes)}$, Pranav Ghaskadbi, and Sarvesh Tendulkar

MIT College of Engineering, Pune 411038, India
prachimjoshi@gmail.com, pranavghaskadbi@gmail.com,
sarvesh.tendulkar@gmail.com

Abstract. Writing is a process which is rooted deep within the creative processes of the mind. While writing, the mind and the hand synchronize to act as a smoothly functioning unit, thus enabling the pen to act as an extension of the person's innermost self. Emotional factors often dictate the writing strokes and mannerisms. The science of graphology can be applied to discern a person's behavior and inner psychological makeup from their handwriting. Certain features such as the page margins, handwriting size etc. are often reflective of mood changes and characterize the writer's state of mind at the moment of writing. An automated process for extracting these features and mapping them to the various personality traits can definitely prove to be a boon for many applications like - recruitment process or even psychological analysis. In this paper, we propose feature extraction methods implemented using image processing techniques to select features to be used further for this trait identification. Once the features have been selected, existing classifiers have been put to work to determine the employability evaluation of a candidate from an HR perspective.

Keywords: Graphology · Handwriting · Feature extraction
Template matching · Image processing · Machine learning

1 Introduction

People often construct an external persona that masks their mental and emotional state. While it is impossible to read minds, it is possible to discern the behavioral and psychological makeup of a person from their handwriting. Writing is a process which is rooted deep within the creative processes of the brain and requires the coordination of the brain, central nervous system and hand to manipulate the writing instrument. Each person's handwriting is unique and is a personal gesture representative of the person. It is rich in features which divulge information about the writer's personality.

Graphology is the technique used to analyze the physical characteristics and patterns handwriting, and can be used in the evaluation of the personality characteristics and behavior of a person [1]. It is primarily used as a recruiting tool to screen candidates during the assessment procedure. It is also used as a diagnostic tool by psychiatrists and psychologists in addition to the famous Rorschach inkblot test. In this paper, we propose a method to automate the personality profile prediction of a person

© Springer Nature Singapore Pte Ltd. 2019
A. K. Luhach et al. (Eds.): ICAICR 2018, CCIS 955, pp. 253–263, 2019.
https://doi.org/10.1007/978-981-13-3140-4_23

on the basis of specific features extracted from his handwriting. Features such as the page margin, pen pressure, letter size etc. can be extracted using novel algorithms and can then be analyzed and mapped to their corresponding personality traits. Then a personality profile of the individual can be created [2]. A number of classifiers such as Naïve Bayes, SVM and Random Forest classifier have been utilized for this purpose. In this paper, personality traits for determining the employability of a candidate have been identified and the classifiers have been trained accordingly to select the candidate with a suitable personality profile.

2 Literature Survey

Handwriting has been successfully used to understand a person's mind. Each person's handwriting depicts a different story about that person. A research work by Kedar et al. [3] elaborate on the different methodologies used to identify personality. The work comprises of three methods for Feature Extraction namely, Statistical, Structural and Global Transformation.

It has been observed that Machine Learning approach selection and the features employed during the trait determination have a large impact on the outcome. In a research work by Joshi et al. [4] on Handwriting Analysis for detection of personality traits, the authors propose Machine Learning algorithm KNN with incremental learning to improve efficiency of detection of personality traits. This paper also introduces various algorithms and techniques for handwriting analysis like Polygonalization, Template Matching and use of Artificial Neural Networks.

Another work by Dang et al. [5] exploit Back Propagation Neural Network for Human behavior analysis. Human behavior is predicted on the basis of signature by using neural network. The work highlights on the selection of features for categorization of the datasets. Heuristic selection process uses different features to categorize person in to one of the five categories viz. Good, Normal, Aggressive, Poor, Emotional.

Another paper discusses major approaches in the field of handwritten character recognition used in the last decade. Research work by Sharma et al. [6] presented various methods for Feature Extraction and Classification with supervised approaches along with their overall accuracy. It was observed that SVM classifier with Fourier descriptor with phase as feature extraction method had highest overall accuracy of 98.74%.

In yet another work by Champa et al. [7], the authors discuss about predicting the personality of a person from pen pressure, baseline and the characteristics of the letter t. They use Artificial Neural Network and above parameters were given as input to the ANN to predict the personality of the writer. More features like margin, size of letters and others for personality prediction can be used for further analysis as mentioned in the work.

From the literature survey it is observed that, there is a necessity to perform analysis on more significant parameters.

The proposed work explores the extraction of features from the scanned image using image processing along with application of existing machine learning approaches to determine the employability of a candidate from a HR perspective.

3 Proposed Methodology

The approach presented in this paper to implement handwriting analysis primarily focuses on characteristics such as the margin, baseline, letter size, t characteristics and the applied pen pressure. Here, a novel approach has been presented to extract features from each of the above mentioned characteristics.

The steps for the process shown in Fig. 1 are as follows:

SI := Scanned Input Image
Image := Image_Processing(SI)
where Image_Processing ∈ { BGR to Grayscale conversion, Binary thresholding, Erosion and Dilation, Obtaining contours }
{ margin, baseline, letter_size, t-characteristics, pen_pressure } ∋ Image
FV ∈ Image ∀ Image
Result := Classification_Method(FV)
Output := Personality_Trait ∃ Result

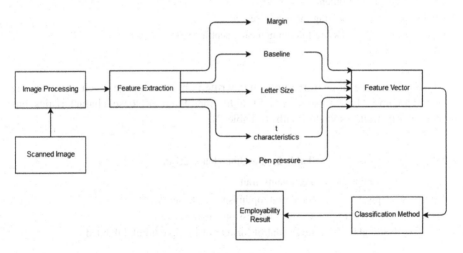

Fig. 1. Process flow diagram

3.1 Background

In this section we discuss a few characteristics of handwriting that are indicative of certain personality traits. Writing traits such as the margin, the baseline or letter style play a significant role in expressing the personality or emotional state of the writer at the moment of writing. Each mannerism has a unique personality trait that is typically associated with it [8].

1. Margin

The margin is the amount of space left by the writer on the left, right, top and bottom borders while writing on the blank page. The placement of writing on the page indicates the person's tastes such as social, cultural and artistic tendencies. The margin is associated with different characteristics for each of the case (Table 1).

Table 1. Margin characteristics

Margin	Personality trait
Wide left	Courage, communicative, vitality
Wide right	Fear of future, over-sensitive
Balanced	Awareness of social boundaries, order, control
Narrow upper	Lack of respect, indifference
Wide upper	Modesty, formality, respect
Wide all over	Withdrawn and aloof
Narrow on both sides	Lack of consideration and reserve, acquisitive
No margin all over	Causes strong reactions in others, eliminates barriers between self and others
Wide lower	Losing interest, reserved
Narrow lower	Desire to communicate, sentimental

2. Baseline

Baseline tells the slope of the line when written on a blank page. Each characteristic viz. Upwards, Downwards or a Straight line. Each of these characteristics has personality trait associated with it (Table 2).

Table 2. Baseline characteristics

Baseline slope	Personality trait
Upwards	Ambition, optimism, restlessness
Downwards	Fatigue, depressions, unhappiness
Straight	Over control for fear of losing control, inhibited

3. Letter Size

Letter Size is the average size of the letters on the page. It is measured in three values i.e. Small, Medium and Large (Table 3).

Table 3. Letter size characteristics

Letter size	Personality trait
Small	Modest, introvert, frugal, self-critical
Medium	Well adjusted, adaptable
Large	Expansive, extrovert, extravagant, like audience

4. T-Characteristics

Letter t plays a vital role handwriting analysis and is considered to be the most difficult part of computer aided graphology. The height and length of the t-bar on the stem reveals some personality traits for handwriting analysis (Table 4).

Table 4. Letter T characteristics

Template	Characteristics	Personality traits
1	Straight, medium height, average, bar on both sides	Healthy balance, calmness, self-control
2	Straight (curved stem), medium height, wide, bar on both sides	Easy to influence, kind, tolerant, kind
3	Straight, medium height, wide, bar on both sides	Energetic, bold, confident, persistent
4	Backward slant, medium height, average, bar on both sides	Shyness, inhibition, decisive
5	Forward slant, medium height, average, bar on right side	Impulsive, enthusiastic, passionate
6	Forward slant, medium height, narrow bar, bar on both sides	Passion, lack of objectivity in projects
7	Backward slant, medium height, average bar, bar on left	Cautiousness, indecisiveness, procrastination, shyness

5. Pen Pressure

Pen pressure is depicted by amount of force exerted by the writer on the paper while writing. It is also called as emotional intensity. Depending on the pressure three different categories have identified viz. Light pressure, Medium pressure and Heavy pressure (Table 5).

Table 5. Pen pressure characteristics

Pen pressure	Personality trait
Heavy pressure	Strong willed, firm, easily excited
Medium pressure	Healthy vitality and willpower
Light pressure	Sensitive, impressionable

3.2 Implementation

The proposed methodology follows the following algorithms:

Margin

To find the margin from the left and right sides as well as the top and the bottom of the page, the scanned page is logically divided into 4 quadrants. To determine the position of the text in each quadrant, the contours are obtained from each quadrant and are stored separately for each quadrant. Then the mean of closest 5 values from each border is considered as the margin value in each respective quadrant.

```
Algorithm
{
P = Scanned Page
UL, UR, BL, BR ∈ P ÷ 4
Where, UL is Upper Left
   UR is Upper Right
   BL is Bottom Left
   BR is Bottom Right quadrant of the scanned page
x[i], y[i], h[i], w[i] ∈ contour rectangle ∀ contours
∀ x[i] and y[i] ∈ { UL, UR, BL, BR }
   xvalues := xvalues + x[i]
   yvalues := yvalues + y[i]
x_sorted := f{sort(xvalues)}
y_sorted := f{sort(yvalues)}
margin_x := f{mean(f{min(x_sorted)})}
}
```

Baseline

To find the first line, it is necessary to find the closest contour from the top of the page by obtaining the contour with the minimum y value from the scanned image. Using this Y value, the first and the last contours on the same line are calculated. With the lowermost point of the first contour as the origin, an imaginary line parallel to the X-axis is drawn and the number of contours lying above, below or on or near this line are calculated. Depending upon the positional values (up, down and straight) of each contour, the slope of the handwriting is determined.

```
Algorithm
{
x[i], y[i], h[i], w[i] ∈ contour rectangle ∀ contours
Ymin := f{min(y)}
XFirst := f{min(x)}
YFirst := y[i] ∋ x[i] := XFirst
Ymax := Ymin + h[i] ∋ y[i] := YFirst
Loop  ∀ contours
  if y<YFirst
    up := up + 1
  if y>YFirst
    down := down + 1
  else
    straight := straight + 1
end Loop
if straight<=0.6*no_of_contours
  baseline := Straight
else if up>down
  baseline := Upwards
else
  baseline := Downwards
}
```

Letter Size
The average letter size is calculated by obtaining height of all the contours and computing their mean.

```
Algorithm
{
x[i], y[i], h[i], w[i] ∈contour rectangle ∀contours
hvalues := hvalues + h[i]
height := f{mean(hvalues)}
}
```

Template Matching
Template Matching is used to compare and extract single character [9], here the letter t. This algorithm performs template matching using matchTemplate method and Normalized Cross Correlation [10] method for 7 standard templates of letter t, each with distinct set of personality traits associated with it. Different scales of input image are considered to account for different sizes of handwriting.

```
Algorithm
{
curr_template ∈ template_set ∀ templates
curr_scale ∈ scale_set ∀scales
Repeat ∀templates:
  Repeat ∀scales:
    resized_image := f{resize(writing_img, writing_img *
curr_scale)}
    If f{size(resized_img)} < f{size(curr_template)}:
      break from loop
      result := f{matchTemplate(resized_image, template,
  Normalized Cross Correlation)}
      for curr_scale in (0.9, 1.0, 1.2):
        f{reduceBlocks(curr_template)}
        matches := f{check_matches()}
        temp_occurence
  ∀ matches ∈ result
  template_matches := f{crop(matches)}
  }
```

3.3   Dataset

The handwriting samples were obtained from students in the age group 20–24 years. A large proportion of these students were fresher candidates at the time of sampling. The dataset consists of 1890 samples records. Each record is a unique combination of different features where each feature is a personality trait which desirable or undesirable from an employer's perspective. The features extracted from a candidate's writing sample are fed to a classifier which outputs a Yes class when the candidate is employable or No class when a candidate ought to be rejected depending upon the values taken by those features. A feature vector includes input parameters like margin, baseline, letter size, t-template and pen pressure and corresponding output class.

3.4   Classification

Different classifiers such as Naïve Bayes, RandomForest and Support Vector Machine were compared on the basis of their performance. The extracted features were given as input to these classifiers to obtain the personality profile.

Figures 2, 3 and 4 are the line charts plotted for % Accuracy, Precision and Recall respectively on 10 fold Cross-validation of the dataset.

Since, the input dataset was skewed containing 380 samples with "Yes" class and 1510 samples with "No" class Synthetic Minority Oversampling Technique (SMOTE) is used to de-skew the dataset to obtain classes with 1520 samples for "Yes" class and 1510 samples for "No" class.

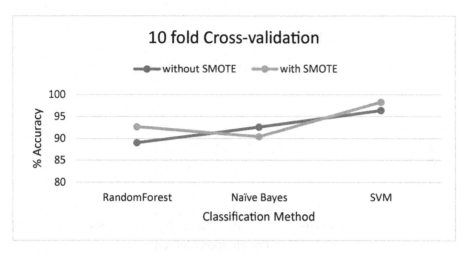

Fig. 2. Accuracy of classification methods

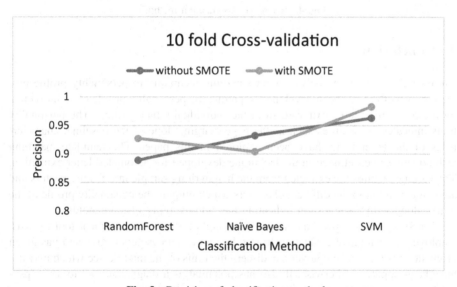

Fig. 3. Precision of classification methods

Figure 2 is a plot of % Accuracy vs Classification Method where RandomForest, Naïve Bayes and Support Vector Machine (SVM) Classifiers are used. 10 fold Cross-validation method is used to train the classifiers. It is compared with performance of classification methods after applying SMOTE algorithm.

Figure 3 is a plot of Precision vs Classification Method.

Figure 4 is a plot of Recall vs Classification Method.

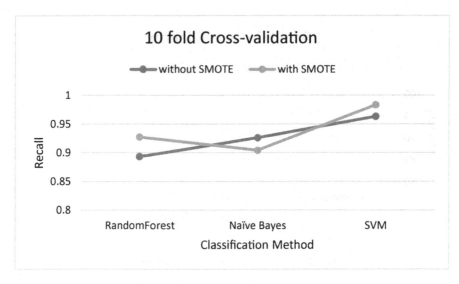

Fig. 4. Recall of classification methods

4   Conclusion

Automated handwriting analysis is an emerging technique in personality profile prediction. A method has been developed to predict the personality profile of an individual
on the basis of features extracted from the individual's handwriting. The personality
traits indicated by features such as the page margin, slope of the baseline, characteristics of the letter t etc. have been explored in this paper. The template matching
technique has been utilized in the technique developed for automated letter extraction.
The various features are extracted from the handwriting sample into feature vectors and
are given as input to the different classifiers which outputs the personality profile of the
writer along with a suggestion indicating the employability of the candidate.

The system developed has the potential application as a recruitment tool to assist
employers in candidate evaluation from a human resources perspective and has given
promising results. The employer can discern the traits of the interviewee which may not
have been apparent otherwise. It also has potential as a diagnostic tool to assist psychiatrists in patient therapy or investigators in forensic studies.

References

1. Champa, H.N., Anandakumar, K.R.: Automated human behavior prediction through
   handwriting analysis. Integr. Intell. Comput. (ICIIC) **1**, 160–165 (2010)
2. Antony, J.D., Cap, O.F.M.: Personality Profile Through Handwriting Analysis. Anugraha
   Publications, Dindigul (2008)
3. Kedar, S., Nair, V., Kulkarni, S.: Personality identification through handwriting analysis: a
   review. Int. J. Adv. Res. Comput. Sci. Softw. Eng. **5**, 548–556 (2015)

4. Joshi, P., Agarwal, A., Dhavale, A., Suryavanshi, R., Kodolikar, S.: Handwriting analysis for detection of personality traits using machine learning approach. Int. J. Comput. Appl. **130**, 40–45 (2015)

5. Dang, S., Kumar, M.: Handwriting analysis of human behaviour based on neural network. Int. J. Adv. Res. Comput. Sci. Softw. Eng. **4**, 227–232 (2014)

6. Sharma, N., Patnaik, T., Kumar, B.: Recognition for handwritten english letters: a review. Int. J. Eng. Innov. Technol. **2**, 318–321 (2013)

7. Champa, H.N., AnandaKumar, K.R.: Artificial neural network for human behavior prediction through handwriting analysis. Int. J. Comput. Appl. **2**, 36–41 (2010)

8. Amend, K., Ruiz, M.: Handwriting Analysis: The Complete Basic Book. New Page Books, New Jersey (1980)

9. Aravinda, C.V., Prakash, H.N.: Template matching method for Kannada Handwritten recognition based on correlation analysis. In: International Contemporary Computing and Informatics (IC3I), pp. 857–861 (2014)

10. Zhao, F., Huang, Q., Gao, W.: Image matching by normalized cross correlation. In: Acoustics, Speech and Signal Processing, ICASSP 2006 Proceedings, vol. 5, pp. 729–732 (2006)

Big Data Analytics Using Data Mining Techniques: A Survey

Shweta Mittal$^{(\boxtimes)}$ (ID) and Om Prakash Sangwan

Guru Jambeshwar University of Science and Technology, Hisar, Haryana, India
Shwetamittal019@gmail.com, Sangwan_op@yahoo.co.in

Abstract. Data collected now-a-days is quite huge in size. Also in the future, data will continue to grow at a much higher rate. The survey highlights the basic concepts of big data analytics and its application in the domain of weather prediction. More the data available to us, more accurate will be the results. Relatively small change in the accuracy of models benefits a lot to society. Huge number of statistical and predictive models for weather prediction exists in the literature but the methods are too time consuming and cannot handle unstructured as well as huge datasets. To overcome this problem, various authors have explored the Apache Hadoop Map Reduce framework for processing and storing Big Data. In this paper, we have discussed and analysed the work done by various researchers on weather prediction using big data analytics.

Keywords: Big data · Big data analytics · Weather prediction
Data mining · Hadoop

1 Introduction

Weather prediction is done by collecting data from various meteorological stations such as minimum temperature, maximum temperature, relative humidity, atmospheric pressure, wind speed, wind direction etc. on daily basis. The information is collected either manually with the help of certain instruments or via sensors which is then transferred to various numerical weather prediction models. The models then process the data and analyse it to make predictions for the future. It can be done on daily basis or for some days in advance. Data collected may have certain ambiguous or missing values, so it needs to be pre-processed. Also it may have several attributes, but only few are more relevant to us which helps in reducing the computation time. Thus, the use of appropriate feature selection techniques for dimensionality reduction is required.

Early and accurate weather predictions could help everyone in the society. Improving our ability to predict the weather is a difficult task. With the advent of science, there are certain technologies available with which we can efficiently handle the data storage as well as fast processing. Meteorological data is quite huge in size i.e. in Gigabytes or Terabytes due to which it is challenging for us to process it with the help of traditional methods. Also, more the data available for the prediction, more accurate will be the results.

© Springer Nature Singapore Pte Ltd. 2019
A. K. Luhach et al. (Eds.): ICAICR 2018, CCIS 955, pp. 264–273, 2019.
https://doi.org/10.1007/978-981-13-3140-4_24

1.1 Big Data

Now a days, data is growing at a very high rate, which comes from a number of sources such as social media, sensor data, historical data, online shopping, hospitality data etc. and will continue to grow further in future. Big Data is a term used for large and complex database which cannot be stored on a single machine or cannot be processed using traditional database systems. Some of the common challenges while designing the big data applications are: scalability, privacy and quickly able to respond to real time data [1]. With the size of the data alone, one cannot predict whether it is a big data. Five V's used to characterise the big data are as follows [2]:

- Volume: Data is generated in a very high volume.
- Variety: Data generated is of several types, which includes structured data such as data in form of tables, semi-structured such as XML files, E-mails as well as unstructured data such as social media data.
- Velocity: Speed of the data received/transmitted is very high.
- Veracity: Data generated have some missing/ambiguous values.
- Value: Information obtained from Big Data

Hadoop is an open source framework developed by Apache which is capable of storing and processing very large data sets with clusters of cheap hardware. It has two main components: (1) HDFS (Hadoop Distributed File System) which is particularly designed for storing the large data sets (2) Map Reduce for processing the data. In Hadoop, we can write the data only once but can read it any number of times. Once we have stored the data in HDFS, we cannot change the contents of file. When a file is stored in HDFS, it is divided into blocks and then these blocks are stored in nodes of the cluster. These blocks are then copied to some other nodes due to which it is fault tolerant. The default duplication factor in HDFS is 3 and the default block size is of 64 MB, or the multiple of it. No wastage of space is done while storing the files. Say, if we have a file of 35 MB, then remaining 29 MB space is not wasted yet allocated to some other file. HDFS offers three master services:

- Name Node: Manages HDFS storage, stores metadata information such as number of input splits, their location, replicas and other information.
- Secondary Name Node: Performs maintenance for the Name Node.
- Job Tracker: Accepts jobs, assigns task to various slave nodes, manage the entire process, handle failure if any.

There are two additional slave services as well:

- Data Node: Stores actual data in HDFS.
- Task Tracker: Responsible for executing actual Map and Reduce tasks.

Every slave service can communicate to each other. Also, master services can communicate to each other. Name Node can communicate with Data Node and Job tracker with the Task tracker. HDFS architecture [3] is described in Fig. 1. Say, if we have total 5 processors, then 1 node will act as a master node and remaining 4 will act as slave node. There will be 1 Name Node and 1 Job Tracker whereas 4 Data Node and 4 Task Tracker. Input file can be either one of the 4 formats:

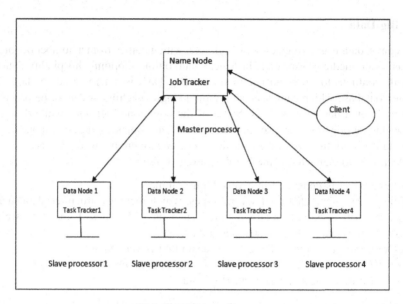

Fig. 1. HDFS architecture

- TextInputFormat
- KeyValueTextInputFormat
- SequenceFileInputFormat
- SequenceFileAsTextInputFormat

If file format is not specified, TextInputFormat is the default one. When client's request arrives, Input file is split into various blocks. RecordReader is an interface which reads one record at a time and converts it into (key, value) pair and then pass it to the Mapper. Number of Mapper used to process the given input file is equal to the number of Input splits. We have to write only one Mapper code that is shared by all the Task Trackers. Hadoop has an advantage of handling large size files as a lot of time is consumed during Map operation of reading and writing many small files.

We have various platform/tools which runs on top of HDFS framework:

1. Pig: Pig Latin is a dataflow scripting language initially given by Yahoo. It can process variety of datasets.
2. Hive: Apache Hive is built on top of Hadoop platform to provide data summarization, query and analysis. It provides HiveQL, an SQL like interface.
3. HBase: It is an open source, non-relational, column-oriented database that sits on top of HDFS.
4. Sqoop: Sqoop is an interface between RDBMS and HDFS for importing and exporting the data.
5. Oozie: It is a tool given by Apache used to coordinate different jobs.
6. Spark: Apache framework other than Hadoop. It provides the mechanism to handle real time data and is faster than Hadoop.

1.2 Big Data Analytics

Data Mining is a process used to unearth the useful information from the large data sets. Big Data analytics is the process of analysing huge datasets to acquire some useful information. It has its application in the various fields like agriculture, meteorology, healthcare, banking, telecom industry etc. which helps organizations in effective decision making process. In agriculture, it can be used for deciding what is an adequate time to plant the crop, how much fertilizers are required for good crop yield. If weather is predicted accurately, then it will be great advantage to farmers i.e. if the rainfall in a particular year is predicted to be low, choice of crops to be sown can be made accordingly. Also in banking, big data analytics is used for fraud detection. In telecom industry, effective marketing strategy can be planned by analysing the customer data. Customers who are more likely to churn can be targeted with good low price schemes. It has also been widely used in the field of healthcare [4].

Lot of researchers have made the use of various data mining techniques i.e. Decision Trees, Linear Regression, K-means clustering, Support Vector Machines (SVM) etc. on the data collected to reduce the computation time and to obtain better results. Challenges that may arise while processing these huge datasets using traditional data mining algorithms are as follows:

- How to schedule the jobs for parallel computing
- Modify the existing data mining algorithms to work on parallel systems and to process huge datasets
- To ensure the privacy of the user
- Security
- To reduce the complexity of data pre-processing operations.

2 Literature Review

Dang et al. [5] proposed efficient kNN classification algorithm for big data. First, k-means is applied on training dataset to partition the training data into smaller clusters. Then for test data, kNN is performed on the training cluster to find the nearest cluster. KNN is again applied on nearest cluster to obtain the solution, thereby reducing the time complexity of an algorithm. Number of clusters should be successfully chosen, as if number of clusters are very large, then overhead will increase and hence will impact the classification accuracy. The experimental results proved that proposed algorithm works well in terms of accuracy and efficiency. For larger number of clusters, accuracy is high while for smaller number of clusters, accuracy decreases.

Zhao et al. [6] introduced parallel k-means algorithm on Map Reduce platform. Input data was split and broadcasted to all the Mappers. Distance computations between different objects are independent and thus can be parallel executed. Mapper calculates the closest center point for each sample. Then, Combiner function calculates the new centroid. After that, the Reducer sums up all the samples and compute the total number of samples assigned to the cluster. The experimental results proved that proposed algorithm was efficiently able to deal with large datasets with respect to scaleup, speedup and sizeup.

Mailo et al. [7] implemented KNN algorithm i.e. MR-KNN on Map Reduce platform and compared the performance with sequential KNN. Input training set is split into several subsets and is assigned to the Mapper which performs the KNN algorithm on the data subset. There is a single Reducer which sorts the output received from all the Mappers. Afterwards, Cleanup performs the majority voting and determines the predictive class. The results proved that both MR-KNN and KNN have same accuracy but the runtime of KNN is very high as compared to MR-KNN. For both the algorithms, if value of k is increased, then there is an improvement in accuracy. Speedup was linear in almost all the cases i.e. speed of an algorithm increases with increase in the number of Mapper.

Tsai et al. [8] conducted a survey on how to design efficient data mining algorithm for big data analytics. The paper presented several challenges and modifications that need to be done in traditional data mining algorithm so that they can be used for mining of big data. As per survey, for measuring performance, several metrics like computation time, throughput, read-write latency, maximum size of data supported, concurrency, execution time of map-reduce jobs etc. can be used.

Majumdar et al. [9] implemented the various data mining techniques i.e. PAM, DBSCAN, CLARA and Multiple Liner Regression on the 6 years agricultural data of the Karnataka district to find out the best parameters to optimize the crop yield. Input parameters to the algorithm are year, district, soil type, crop, production, average temperature etc. As per the analysis based on quality metrics, it was found that DBSCAN performs better than PAM and CLARA with respect to clustering quality.

Fan et al. [10] proposed design for analysing big data in agricultural region. Data is taken from meteorological stations situated in 34 districts of China. Map Reduce framework was used to find the minimum, maximum and average temperature of all the months in the year. Nearest neighbour was used to find the similar years based on weather distances and then ARAMA model is used for prediction on the basis of nearest year. Proposed architecture was capable to forecast the weather long time in advance. Accuracy is beyond average, thus the above methodology can be used for making decisions in various fields.

Bendre et al. [11] analysed the meteorological data i.e. minimum temperature, maximum temperature, humidity and rainfall data of KVR (Krishi Vidyapeeth Rahuri (KVR), Ahmednagar India) weather station for past 10 years on daily basis. Historical data was then fed into Map-Reduce framework to evaluate mean and average values of temperature. It is able to forecast weather for the year 2013 using the regression model and also compared actual and predicted values to minimize the error.

Sneha and Majumdar [12] analysed the various parameters like crop, area, production, rainfall etc. of the 30 districts of Karnataka (10 years data) to find out the best soil required by the particular crop, expected yield, fertilizers and water required for the maximum crop yield. Kushwaha and Bhattachrya [13] introduced a new Agro algorithm to predict the suitability of a crop for a particular soil type using Hadoop. Nguyen et al. [14] proposed a design for collecting and analyzing agricultural big data. Input data can be from the various sources such as archival data from the various websites, real time data etc. For collecting the real time data and then transfer it to HDFS, Apache flume was used. Hadoop is used to collect the archival data such as huge data set from multiple websites. For importing and exporting the data between RDBMS and HDFS,

Sqoop interface is used. HBase is another storage platform which supports random access to data. Hive supports simple SQL style data queries and works on the top of Hadoop platform. Spark is a platform other than Hadoop which supports non-iterative jobs and hence has less execution time.

Reddy and Babu [15] reviewed the numerous weather prediction models. From the study, it was concluded that Map Reduce and Linear Regression gives better result for prediction. NN performs well for large scale weather forecast but for medium scale and daily forecast, NN gives less accurate results.

Shobha and Asha [16] studied agricultural data of Bangalore district of Feb, 2015 using R software. Input parameters include air temperature, humidity; rainfall and pan evaporation. Connectivity, Dunn index and Silhouette width were used for analysing performance. From the results, it was concluded that Hierarchical clustering outperforms K Means algorithm for each performance criteria.

Nikam and Meshram [17] proposed the model for rainfall prediction of Indian Meteorological Department (IMD), Pune data for rainy season using Bayesian model. The model has greater than 90% accuracy and can be used to predict both binary and multiclass attribute.

Tsagalidis and Evangelidis [18] studied how the performance of algorithm is impacted by the selection of the training set. For datasets greater than nine years, there is no impact on Bayesian and RIPPER algorithms. For training sets of size greater than six years, Multilayer Perceptron with BPNN (Back Propagation Neural Network) is preferable while for less than six years, Naive Bayesian is good alternative.

Navadia et al. [19] proposed a system that takes in the rainfall data i.e. humidity, precipitation etc. and forecasts the future rainfall using Apache PIG. Anchalia and Roy [20] implemented k-Nearest Neighbor method using Apache Hadoop on distributed systems. For large datasets, MapReduce kNN performs better than sequential kNN, Fang et al. [21] presented modified MK-means algorithm (MK-means) on MapReduce framework for NCDC data of 4 years using nine PCs and analysed that proposed algorithm is feasible and efficient.

Ismail et al. [22] collected NCDC (National Climatic Data Centre) data from weather stations and observations centres. The data provided by the weather stations is unstructured due to which it becomes difficult to analyze it. Experiment is carried out on 3 PCs, out of which one is a Name Node and the other two are Data Nodes. Using MapReduce with Hadoop, average, maximum and minimum temperature etc. are evaluated effectively.

Riyaz and Varghese [23] build data analytical engine for processing high velocity, huge volume temperature data from sensors using MapReduce on Hadoop of NCDC data, 2014. The results prove that if numbers of nodes are increased, then data processing speed also increases which is the major advantage of Hadoop.

Mazhar et al. [24] reviewed various data mining techniques applied in the field of weather prediction and it was found that Neural Network is the most widely used. Marjani et al. [25] proposed an architecture for big IoT data analytics. Alves and Cruvinel [26] proposed the framework to analyse computed tomography (CT) images using Hadoop for soil analysis.

Mohapatra et al. [27] build a model using Linear Regression for rainfall prediction based on 100 years of meteorological data. The results proved that model was accurate enough for rainfall prediction. Pandey et al. [28] build weather prediction model based on Hadoop platform. Fuzzy Logic (FL) and Artificial Neural Network Fuzzy Interface System (ANFIS) methods were implemented using Matlab and the results proved that ANFIS is better than FL. Also, time taken by FL is quite longer as compared to ANFIS. Kumar et al. [29] studied the impact of weather prediction on crop management and distribution channel.

Brief summary of weather prediction using big data analytics has been described in Table 1.

Table 1. Summary of weather prediction algorithms

Paper ref. no.	Dataset used	Technique	No. of I/P parameters	O/P parameters	Experimental results
[9]	Karnatka 28 districts, 6 years data	PAM,CLARA, DBSCAN and Multiple Linear Regression	16(district, crop, season, temp etc.)	Optimal best temp, worst temp. and rainfall for wheat production	Clustering quality: DBSCAN> CLARA> PAM
[10]	825 meteorological stations of China	MapReduce, Nearest neighbour, ARAMA model	3 (Precipitation, Intensity of sunshine, temp.)	Predict crop yield in advance	Nearest neighbour method using MapReduce achieves both accurate and timely predictions
[11]	KVR, Ahmednagar, 10 years data	MapReduce, Regression	3(Rainfall, Temp., Humidity)	Predict temp. and rainfall	Suggest decision for crop pattern and water management
[12]	30 districts of Karnatka, 9 years data	Chameleon clustering, Random forest, Regression	16(district, crop, season, temp etc.)	Best soil; For available water and fertilizers what yield is expected	Crop prediction
[16]	Meteorological data of 28 days, Feb. 2105	Hierarchical clustering,K Means algo, R software	8		Hierarchical clustering performs better than K Means
[17]	Indian Meteorological Department (IMD), Pune	Bayesian algo	7	Rainfall prediction	Good accuracy and good prediction performance
[19]	-	Apache PIG	Max humidity, Mean humidity, Precipitaion etc.	Rainfall prediction	Analysis and prediction of rain successfully done
[20]	-	MapReduce kNN, Sequential kNN	-	-	For datasets of larger size, MapReduce performs better than sequential kNN
[22]	NCDC data for more than 116 weather stations	MapReduce	2 (Temp, place)	Avg, Min and Max temp of a particular place	Proposed framework is highly scalable
[23]	NCDC data, 2014	MapReduce	2 (Temp, place	Avg, Min and Max temp of a particular place	If number of nodes are increased, then data processing speed also increases
[21]	China Meteorological Data, 4 years	Improved *MK*-means algorithm based on MapReduce	26		*MK*-means algorithm deployed in the large-scale meteorological data processing system is feasible and efficient

From the above table, it can concluded that analysis and prediction of rainfall, temperature etc. can be done effectively done with the help of various machine learning algorithms.

3 Proposed Methodology

Most of the data mining algorithms use the concept of centralized computing and are not designed to handle very large and complex data sets. Also, the algorithms have the assumptions that they have to process homogeneous datasets. Now, to use algorithms for processing big data, either we have to make the algorithm work on parallel systems, or we have to modify these algorithms. Input data to these algorithms are historical data as well as current data. Apache JFlume is used to process current archival data. If historical data is in unstructured form, we need to first convert it in semi-structured form before data pre-processing. In data pre-processing step, we will eliminate missing or ambiguous values. As the data available with us may have huge number of dimensions. So, we also need to reduce the complexity of these operations. ANOVA (Analysis of Variance), Chi-square, PCA (Principal Component Analysis), GA (Genetc Algorithm) are some frequently used algorithms for feature selection. To process the big data, various frameworks are available such as Apache Hadoop, Spark etc. Spark has an advantage over Hadoop that it can process non-iterative jobs. Next step is to apply data mining algorithms like Linear Regression; k means clustering, kNN so that it can be used for business purposes. Various visualization tools are also available in the market like Tableau, Infogram, Chartblocks etc. for representing the results in the form of graphs, charts etc. so that it can be easily understood by the user.

4 Conclusion and Future Work

From the survey done, it is concluded that there may occur several challenges while applying traditional data mining techniques for big data analytics. Few drawbacks of various MLT for Big data analytics are discussed below:

- Decision trees use splitting criteria on the nodes based on some quality criteria which makes it difficult to use for big data.
- SVM perform good only for moderate database size.
- For small data set, Conventional Neural Network algorithms have very longer learning time.

Thus, there is a need to explore various data mining approaches to deal with all the aspects of Big Data. Hybrid data mining algorithms also needs to be explored to obtain results. Processing time of traditional data mining algorithm is very high due to lack of parallel processing schemes. Hence, parallelisation needs to be incorporated in order to reduce the learning time of algorithms.

References

1. Evert, F., Fountas, S., Jakovetic, D., Cnnojevic, V., Travlos, I., Kempenaar, C.: Big data for weed control and crop protection. In: Big Data for Weed Control and Crop Protection. Weed Research (2017). https://doi.org/10.1111/wre.12255
2. Assuncao, M., Calheiros, R., Bianchi, S., Netto, M., Buyya, R.: Big data computing and clouds: trends and future directions. J. Parallel Distrib. Comput. **79–80**, 3–15 (2015). https://doi.org/10.1016/j.jpdc.2014.08.003
3. https://www.youtube.com/watch?v=DLutRT6K2rM
4. Giacalone, M., Cusatelli, C., Santarcangelo, V.: Big data compliance for innovative clinical models. Big Data Res. **12**, 35–40 (2018). https://doi.org/10.1016/j.bdr.2018.02.001
5. Dang, Z., Zhu, X., Cheng, D., Zong, M., Zhang, S.: Efficient KNN classification algorithm for big data. J. Neurocomput. **195**, 143–148 (2016). https://doi.org/10.1016/j.neucom.2015.08.112
6. Zhao, W., Ma, H., He, Q.: Parallel K-Means clustering based on MapReduce. In: Jaatun, M. G., Zhao, G., Rong, C. (eds.) CloudCom 2009. LNCS, vol. 5931, pp. 674–679. Springer, Heidelberg (2009). https://doi.org/10.1007/978-3-642-10665-1_71
7. Maillo, J., Triguero, I., Herrera, F.: A MapReduce-based k-Nearest neighbor approach for big data classification. In: IEEE Trustcom/BigDataSE/ISPA (2015). https://doi.org/10.1109/trustcom.2015.577
8. Tsai, C., Lai, C., Chao, H., Vasilakos, A.: Big data analytics: a survey. J. Big Data **2**, 21 (2015). https://doi.org/10.1186/s40537-015-0030-3
9. Majumdar, J., Naraseeyappa, S., Ankalaki, S.: Analysis of agriculture data using data mining techniques: application of big data. Open J. Big Data **4**, 20 (2017). https://doi.org/10.1186/s40537-017-0077-4
10. Fan, W., Chong, C., Xiaoling, G., Hua, Y.: Prediction of crop yield using big data. In: 8th International Symposium on Computational Intelligence and Design. IEEE (2015). https://doi.org/10.1109/iscid.2015.191
11. Bendre, M.R., Thool, R.C., Thool, V.R.: Big data in precision agriculture: weather forecasting for future farming. In: 1st International Conference on Next Generation Computing Technologies. IEEE (2015). https://doi.org/10.1109/ngct.2015.7375220
12. Sneha, N., Majumdar, J.: Big data application in agriculture to maximize the rice yield crop production using data mining techniques. Int. J. Innov. Res. Comput. Commun. Eng. (2017). https://doi.org/10.15680/ijircce.2017.0505045
13. Kushwaha, A., Bhattachrya, S.: Crop yield prediction using agro algorithm in hadoop. Int. J. Comput. Sci. Inf. Technol. Secur. (IJCSITS) **5**(2), 271–274 (2015)
14. Nguyen, V., Nguyen, S., Kim, K.: Design of a platform for collecting and analyzing agricultural big data. J. Digit. Contents Soc. **18**(1), 149–158 (2017). https://doi.org/10.9728/dcs.2017.18.1.149
15. Reddy, P., Babu, A.: Survey on weather prediction using big data analytics. In: Second International Conference on Electrical, Computer and Communication Technologies. IEEE (2017). https://doi.org/10.1109/icecct.2017.8117883
16. Shobha, N., Asha, T.: Monitoring weather based meteorological data: clustering approach for analysis. In: International Conference on Innovative Mechanisms for Industry Applications. IEEE (2017). https://doi.org/10.1109/icimia.2017.7975575
17. Nikam, V., Meshram, B.: Modeling rainfall prediction using data mining method. In: Fifth International Conference on Computational Intelligence, Modelling and Simulation. IEEE (2013). https://doi.org/10.1109/cimsim.2013.29

18. Tsagalidis, E., Evangelidis, G.: The effect of training set selection in meteorological data mining. In: Fourteenth Panhellenic Conference on Informatics. IEEE (2010). https://doi.org/ 10.1109/pci.2010.37
19. Navadia, S., Yadav, P., Thomas, J., Shaikh, S.: Weather prediction: a novel approach for measuring and analyzing weather data. In: International conference on I-SMAC (IoT in Social, Mobile, Analytics and Cloud). IEEE (2017). https://doi.org/10.1109/i-smac.2017. 8058382
20. Anchalia, P., Roy, K.: The k-Nearest neighbor algorithm using map reduce paradigm. In: Fifth International Conference on Intelligent Systems, Modelling and Simulation. IEEE (2014). https://doi.org/10.1109/isms.2014.94
21. Fang, W., Sheng, V.S., Wen, X., Pan, W.: Meteorological data analysis using MapReduce. Sci. World J. (2014). https://doi.org/10.1155/2014/646497
22. Ismail, K., Majid, M., Zain, J., Abu Bakar, N.: Big data prediction framework for weather temperature based on MapReduce algorithm. In: Conference on Open Systems. IEEE (2016). https://doi.org/10.1109/icos.2016.7881981
23. Riyaz, P.A., Varghese, S.: Leveraging map reduce with hadoop for weather data analytics. IOSR J. Comput. Eng. 17(3), 6–12 (2015). https://doi.org/10.9790/0661-17320612
24. Mazhar, A., Ikram, M.T., Butt, N.A., Butt, A.J.: Do we really have to consider data mining techniques for meteorological data. In: Fourth International Conference on Aerospace Science and Engineering. IEEE (2015). https://doi.org/10.1109/icase.2015.7489525
25. Marjani, M., et al.: Big IoT data analytics: architecture, opportunities, and open research challenges. IEEE Access 5, 5247–5261 (2017). https://doi.org/10.1109/ACCESS.2017. 2689040
26. Alves, G.M., Cruvinel, P.E.: Big data environment for agricultural soil analysis from CT digital images. In: Tenth International Conference on Semantic Computing. IEEE (2016). https://doi.org/10.1109/icsc.2016.80
27. Mohapatra, S., Upadhyay, A., Gola, C.: Rainfall prediction based on 100 years of meteorological data. In: International Conference on Computing and Communication Technologies for Smart Nation. IEEE (2017). https://doi.org/10.1109/ic3tsn.2017.8284469
28. Pandey, A., Agrawal, C., Agrawal, M.: A Hadoop based weather prediction model for classification of weather data. In: Second International Conference on Electrical, Computer and Communication Technologies (ICECCT). IEEE (2017). https://doi.org/10.1109/icecct. 2017.8117862
29. Kumar, M., Nagar, M.: Big data analytics in agriculture and distribution channel. In: Proceedings of the IEEE, International Conference on Computing Methodologies and Communication (2017). https://doi.org/10.1109/iccmc.2017.8282714

Comparative Analysis of Various Types of Classifier for Surface EMG Signal in Order to Improve Classification Accuracy

Ram Murat Singh[1(✉)], S. Chatterji[1], and Amod Kumar[2]

[1] National Institute of Technical Teachers Training and Research, Sector-26,
Chandigarh 160019, India
rammurat.singh@gmail.com
[2] CSIO, Sector-26, Chandigarh 160030, India

Abstract. Surface EMG is an important signal originating from human body while doing different movements. This can be utilized for various applications like movement classification, diagnosing neuromuscular disorders, prosthetic control and many more. Surface EMG signal analysis is complex in nature because of its random nature. Several researchers are trying to provide solutions for tackling this problem in the form of improving acquisition circuit for surface EMG signal, increasing the density of sensors during acquisition process, extracting novel features which could give more information and so on. One of the crucial stages while analyzing surface EMG signal is selection of feature sets and classification algorithm. In present work the authors tried different time domain feature sets and their combinations to improve classification accuracy. It was observed that a combination of feature sets improves classification accuracy (95.7%) but response time is increased. The present study explains the optimized solution for the aforesaid problem. It was also observed that Ensemble classifier in bagged tree variant gives maximum classification accuracy but takes too much time in training and classification.

Keywords: Acquisition of sEMG · Time domain features
Classification algorithms · Pattern recognition and sEMG control

1 Introduction

Electromyography (EMG) signals are the physical phenomena of electrical activity emanated by muscle acupressure points. Motor Unit Action Potential (MAUP) is a key element of any EMG signal. Electrical signals are generated by the muscle voluntary or involuntary contraction effect during the desired movement performed by the subject in the range of few μV due to the resulted sum of MAUP provided by pickup area electrode being used. Generally 20–50 motor units are conjoined together to form muscle fibers throughout the muscle area occupied by the surface electrode used for EMG signal for a particular muscle. sEMG signal originated the hidden concept of Human Robot Interaction (HRI) for rehabilitation process.

Surface electromyographic (sEMG) signals are the resultant of the motor unit action potential which is collected over the skin in the form of electrical activity during

© Springer Nature Singapore Pte Ltd. 2019
A. K. Luhach et al. (Eds.): ICAICR 2018, CCIS 955, pp. 274–283, 2019.
https://doi.org/10.1007/978-981-13-3140-4_25

contraction. The sEMG signals are acquired corresponding to some predefined movement performed by the subject with the help of multi-channel sEMG acquisition device to discriminate various motion [1]. The concept of sEMG based assistive robotic device has been applied for developing the myoelectric prostheses which utilized the result of classified sEMG signal for generating the desired control signal. The complete process consists of signal acquisition, feature extraction, and classification followed by the control of the robotic device [2]. In the modern era of patterns recognition, EMG signal based robotic device attracted the lots of research attention which utilized the various classifier namely Support Vector Machines (SVM), Self-Organizing Map (SOM), Linear Discriminant Analysis (LDA) and Self-Organizing Map (SOM) for developing the different EMG applications [3].

Better performance can be achieved in pattern recognition by considering the main key point i.e. feature extraction and feature selection which decide the reliability of the developed system. The sEMG signals feature can be categories in three type: first on is time domain (TD), second is frequency domain (FD) and Final is time-frequency domain (TFD) which is also known as time scale feature [4–6].

2 Data Acquisition of sEMG Signal

The **MYOTRACE 400** device is used for data acquisition with some signal processing facilities.

After acquiring the raw EMG signals from the subjects, Signal processing is done. Feature extraction and selection are then done in order to form the feature vector. For achieving the better and reliable output of the classifier, features set is divided into training as well as testing sets. In this study, three-fold cross-validation scheme is carried out for accurate computation. The data is acquired from 5 healthy subjects of the age group from 20 to 24 years. The hand movements are performed by the subjects under the predefined protocol. The EMG signal is sampled at 1000 Hz. Fifteen trails have been performed by each subject for each activity (flexion and extension) in a time period of 20 s. The surface electrodes are used for acquiring the data. The location of surface electrodes is fixed at the acupressure point of the right hand upper arm. The experimental set up is shown in Fig. 1.

In the present work, non-invasive type electrodes have been used. Generally used electrodes are pre-gelled in the form of Ag/Agcl electrode which has been recommended in the various literature. Ag/Agcl electrodes are easy for handling as well as fulfill all desired medical hygienic aspects as shown in Fig. 2. The diameter of electrode (conductive area) is 1 cm or even smaller than that, and the overall dimension is 50 mm × 35 mm × 1 mm.

The SEMG signal was acquired for two movements: elbow flexion and elbow extension.

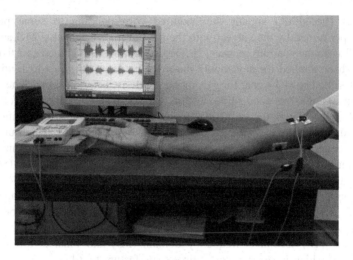

Fig. 1. Experimental setup

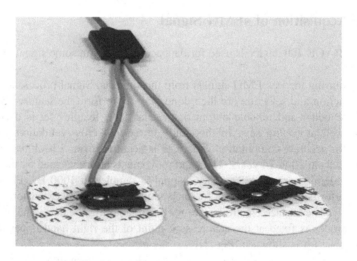

Fig. 2. Non invasive pre gelled electrodes

The muscles selected during elbow flexion are Flex Carp U., Flex Carp. R., Brachiorad and Biceps Br. as shown in Fig. 3.

The muscles selected during elbow extension are Lat. Triceps and Med. Triceps.

All processing steps such as feature extraction, selection and classification have been carried out using MATLAB.

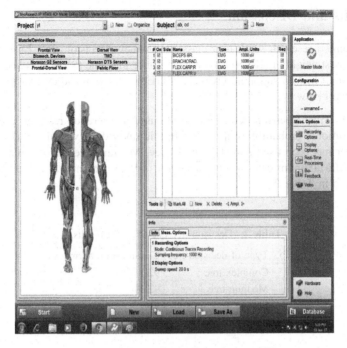

Fig. 3. Muscle selection in myotrace 400

3 Classification of sEMG Signal into Movements

Generally three main steps are followed for classifying the SEMG data for hand movements: (i) SEMG signal acquisition; (ii) Feature Extraction; (iii) Classification. The Time domain features are extracted as mentioned in Table 1 [7].

Table 1. Time domain features.

Features	Abbreviation
Root mean square	RMS
Waveform length	WL
Slope sign change	SSC
Skewness	SKEW
Kurtosis	KURT
Standard deviation	SD
Variance	VAR
Auto-regressive coefficients	AR

4   Results and Discussion

In the presented research work four classifiers namely Decision tree, Ensemble classifier, K nearest neighbor (KNN) and support vector machine (SVM) has been used for classification of SEMG signal into two classes (Elbow flexion and extension) [8]. They are explained below:

(i)   Decision Tree: Decision tree is commonly used in operation research and is based on conditional probabilities approach. In this study three variants of decision tree classifier has been used namely: simple tree, Medium tree and complex tree. We achieved Maximum classification accuracy of 92.3 percent was achieved. Results are given in Table 2.

Table 2. Decision tree classification results

S.No.	Type of decision tree	Classification accuracy
1	Complex tree	92.3
2	Medium tree	92.3
3	Simple Tree	91.1

Confusion matrices for various decision tree are shown in below given Fig. 4(a), (b) and (c) respectively. The confusion matrix represents the performance of classifier by demonstrating the true classified sample and false classified sample. The number of the correctly classified sample is shown by the diagonal element whereas misclassified sample by off-diagonal elements.

(ii)   Ensemble Classifier: This type of classification method utilize a set of the different weak classifier to discriminate between various classes. After the classification performed by the weak classifier, output of these classifiers are used to vote for the final decision of classification. Initially, the Bayesian averaging method was very famous but nowadays different others methods like bagging as well as boosting can also be considered.

In the present study the authors used 5 types of ensemble classifiers namely: Boosted trees, Bagged trees, Subspace discriminant trees, Subspace KNN Trees and RUS boosted trees. Highest classification accuracy of 95.7% was achieved in bagged trees type of ensemble classifier as shown in Table 3.

Confusion matrix for bagged trees ensemble classifier is shown below in Fig. 5.

(iii)   K- Nearest neighbor (KNN): The KNN classifier is a very popular method of biomedical signal classification which utilizes the density estimation technique to provide the suboptimal output. the algorithm is based on the strength of the nearest neighbor rule explained below. for the unknown feature vector x and a distance measure, then: Out of the N training vectors, identify the k nearest neighbors, irrespective of the class label. k is chosen to be odd for a two class problem, and in general not to be a multiple of the number of classes M.

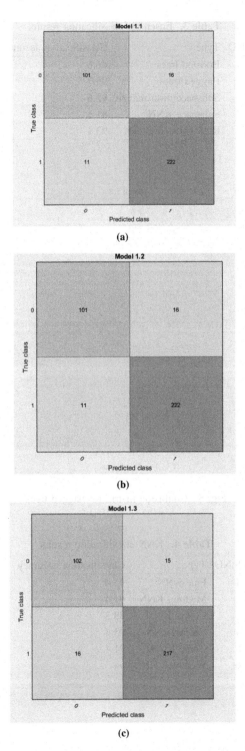

Fig. 4. (a) Confusion matrix for complex tree, (b) Confusion matrix for medium tree, (c) Confusion matrix for simple tree

Table 3. Ensemble classification results

S.NO	Type	Classification accuracy
1	Boosted trees	66.6
2	Bagged trees	95.7
3	Subspace discriminant	92.6
4	Subspace KNN	81.1
5	RUS boosted trees	93.1

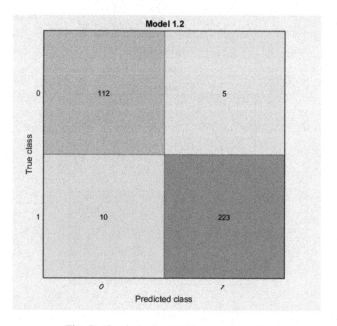

Fig. 5. Confusion matrix for bagged trees

Table 4. KNN classification results

S.NO	Type	Classification accuracy
1	Fine KNN	95.4
2	Medium KNN	91.4
3	Coarse KNN	88.3
4	Cosine KNN	93.4
5	Cubic KNN	91.4
6	Weighted KNN	94

- Out of these k samples, identify the number of vectors, Ki, that belong to class ωi, $i = 1, 2, ..., M$. Obviously, $\sum i\ ki = k$.
- Assign x to the class ωi with the maximum number ki of samples [9].

In the present study the authors used six variants of KNN namely Fine KNN, Medium KNN, Coarse KNN, Cosine KNN, Cubic KNN and weighted KNN. Highest classification accuracy of 95.4% was achieved in case of Fine KNN as shown in Table 4.

confusion matrix for fine KNN classifier are shown in Fig. 6.

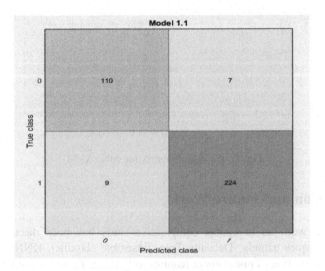

Fig. 6. Confusion matrix for fine KNN

(iv) Support Vector Machine (SVM) classifier: SVM algorithm attempts to identify the separating hyper plane, which is found to be the best in separating each class of signals from all the other classes [10]. In the present work 6 variants of SVM classifiers has been used namely: linear SVM, quadratic SVM, cubic SVM, fine Gaussian SVM, medium Gaussian SVM and coarse Gaussian SVM. The maximum classification accuracy of 95.1 percent has been achieved in the case of cubic SVM, as shown in Table 5.

Table 5. SVM classification results

S.NO	Type	Classification accuracy
1	Linear SVM	93.7
2	Quadratic SVM	94
3	Cubic SVM	95.1
4	Fine Gaussian SVM	94.6
5	Medium Gaussian SVM	92.6
6	Coarse Gaussian SVM	91.7

Confusion matrix for cubic SVM classifier are shown in Fig. 7.

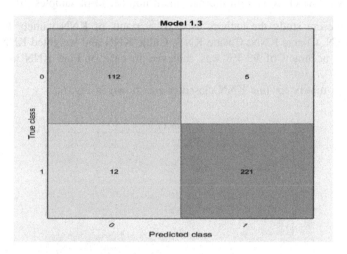

Fig. 7. Confusion matrix for cubic SVM

5 Conclusion and Future Work

In the present work an analytical comparative study has been discussed for four classifier techniques namely: Decision Tree, Ensemble classifier, KNN classifier and SVM classifier. Various Time domain features as listed in Table 1 have been extracted and feature vectors have been formed before applying the classification algorithms. The major outcome of the study is mentioned in the form of salient points provided below:

- Ensemble classifier technique provides highest classification accuracy of 95.7 in bagged trees type followed by 95.4 in case of KNN classifier in fine KNN technique.
- Ensemble classifier technique although provides the highest classification accuracy, consumes much more training time as well as response time.
- SVM classifier is best suited when compared classification accuracy, training time and also response time.
- The experimental result shows that increasing the feature vector increases the classification accuracy but the training and the response time are also increased.
- The experimental result also shows that increasing the length of feature vector also creates chances of error.

Application of time-domain, frequency domain and time-frequency domain features may be combined to frame the future scope of the present study in order to achieve even higher classification accuracy.

Also, a novel approach may be tried to generate the control signal by reducing the size of feature vector of EMG signals for robot having the more number of degree of freedom can be achieved depending on the requirements.

There is a great need of a reliable, safe and precise control scheme for the Myoelectric control of an Exoskeleton robots which establishes the majority of extensive research work for implementing the model in Real-time applications.

Acknowledgment. The authors wish to thank Department of Science and technology, Government of India for providing financial assistanceship.

References

1. Parker, P.A., Scott, R.N.: Myoelectric control of prostheses. Crit. Rev. Biomed. Eng. **13**, 283–310 (1986)
2. Parker, P.A., Englehart, K., Hudgins, B.: The control of upper limb prostheses. In: Merletti, R., Parker, P.A. (eds.) Electromyography: Physiology, Engineering, and Non-invasive Applications. Wiley/IEEE Press (2004)
3. Phinyomark, A., Phukpattaranont, P., Limsakul, C.: Feature reduction and selection for EMG signal classification. Expert Syst. Appl. **39**, 7420–7431 (2012)
4. Tsai, A.C., Hsieh, T.H., Luh, J.J., Lin, T.T.: A comparison of upper-limb motion pattern recognition using EMG signals during dynamic and isometric muscle contractions. Biomed. Signal Process. Control, 17–26 (2014)
5. Hogan, N., Mann, R.W.: Myoelectric signal processing: optimal estimation applied to electromyography-part I: derivation of the optimal myoprocessor, BME-27. IEEE Trans. Biomed. Eng., 382–395 (1980)
6. Englehart, K., Hudgins, B., Parker, P.A., Stevenson, M.: Classification of the myoelectric signal using time-frequency based representations. Med. Eng. Phys. **21**, 431–438 (1999)
7. Nurhazimah, N., Mohd, A.A.R., Shin-Ichiroh, Y., Siti, A.A., Hairi, Z., Saiful, A.M.: A review of classification techniques of EMG signals during Isotonic and Isometric contractions. Sensors **16**, 1304 (2016)
8. Chowdhury, R.H., et al.: Surface electromyography signal processing and classification techniques. Sensors, 12431–12466 (2013)
9. Theodorodis, S., Koutroumbas, K.: Pattern Recognition, 4th edn. Elsevier, Amsterdam (2009)
10. Lucas, M.-F., Gaufriaua, A., Pascuala, S., Doncarli, C., Farina, D.: Multi-channel surface EMG classification using support vector machines and signal-based wavelet optimization. Biomed. Sign. Process. and Control **3**(2), 169–174 (2008)

Modeling the Evolution of Coordinated Movement Strategies Using Digital Organisms

Zaki Ahmad Khan[1(✉)], Faraz Hasan[2], and Gabriel Yedid[1]

[1] Department of Zoology, College of Life Science,
Nanjing Agricultural University, Nanjing 210095, Jiangsu, China
Jmi.amul@gmail.com, gyedid04@njau.edu.cn
[2] Department of Computer Science,
Aligarh Muslim University, Aligarh 202002, U.P, India
faraz.hasan@live.in

Abstract. Intelligence is a fundamental characteristic of living beings. Even the simplest organisms exhibit intelligent behaviors in their routine actions. There are various levels of problems in computational science where evolutionary computation shows great potential for finding optimal or near-optimal solutions to problems that defy traditional analytical approaches. In line with this, an advanced problem associated with the evolution of movement in biological communities is examined here. We used the Avida digital life platform to explore the evolution of movements in model environments with a fixed landmark. Three prevailing movement strategies that emerged, Cockroach, Ziggurat, and Climber, show how both environmental constraints and movement coordination play a role in the emergence of intelligent behavior.

Keywords: Avida · Digital organism · Beacon · Habitat · Coordinated stasis

1 Introduction

In evolutionary computation, there are a variety of options available for examining the problems associated with movement of organisms. At the simplest scale, there are problems that focus on matching patterns of movement activation. At more complex scales, there are problems to identify specific patterns of optimal movement strategies and examine how exactly an individual agent coordinates its intrinsic states to obtain movement capability. In this contribution, our research focuses on a more abstract and generalized scale, where the focus is on how evolutionary processes make use of available movement capabilities in order to intelligently utilize given environmental conditions and the information they provide. Simply, instead of focusing towards assessment of optimal movement strategy in a particular environmental condition, this research focuses towards how the evaluation processes themselves utilize the existing movement capabilities to explore and generate intelligent behavior [1, 2]. Therefore, this work does not postulate any specific way of generating intelligent behavior, instead leaving that open for the evolving digital agents themselves to explore it via evolutionary processes. Providing a rich range of atomic building blocks to explore the use of movement capabilities by evolving agents in this way opens up a range of research

A. K. Luhach et al. (Eds.): ICAICR 2018, CCIS 955, pp. 284–295, 2019.
https://doi.org/10.1007/978-981-13-3140-4_26

questions directly comparable to work within biological systems, where examples abound ranging from route planning in delivery systems through chemical sensing in microorganisms.

1.1 Related Work

Computational studies related to movement of agents cover a variety of aspects. In one type, the actual details of movement are probably not modeled at all, but are basically allocated as a cost, as operates in artificial neural systems used on the Traveling Salesman Problem. In many cases, specifying a limited number of fixed movement strategies (which may be modified stochastically through parameter settings) may be enough, as has been applied in individual-based models (IBM) in ecology [5–7]. Considering evolutionary robotics, the interest in the movement of agents also spans several levels, ranging from tests monitoring environment recognition starting from a set of basic behaviours, evolving neural controllers for movement or kinematics for specific controller anatomies, and direct evolution of Turing-complete binary code for robots to accomplish obstacle-avoidance tasks [8–10].

1.2 Specific Problem

Our interest requires a more generalized and flexible approach than often-used approaches in computational intelligence. In general, to accomplish a task, the interest is on either solving or approximately solving it, instead of finding the means or processes by which the optimal solution is acquired. Following from exploring the evolution of intelligent behavior, our ultimate objective is to examine the impact of movement capabilities on "coordinated stasis" [3]. This a long-term evolutionary phenomenon in which multiple species living together in a biological community shows little to no morphological evolution (*evolutionary stasis*, [4]) over significant periods of time. Several hypotheses have been advanced to explain it; one of the most important is habitat tracking [3]. Put simply, if organisms are able to track and continually access patches of their preferred habitat, they will not evolve much over subsequent generations, as there is no real need for them to do so. The "coordinated" part of habitat tracking occurs when multiple co-existing species in a community migrate from one habitat patch to another. In fact, each species migrates individualistically seeking its own optimal living conditions, but it appears as though the whole community migrates as a unit.

1.3 Computational Approach

Our hypothesis is that given the capabilities of environment recognition, movement, and target sensing, evolutionary processes will result in organisms able to coordinately track their habitats. For testing of this hypothesis, the Avida artificial life platform is used [11–13]. Here, the digital organisms of Avida ("Avidians") have been granted the capabilities of sensing a habitat marker and movement, without providing any specific prescription on how to use these capacities in order to optimally exploit environmental conditions.

An important aspect of our approach towards the main problem is that we be able to explore patterns of emergence by which agents produced through evolutionary computation exhibit intelligent behaviors in order to track resource-based habitats. We should also be able to classify movement strategies based upon the parameter initialization and environmental conditions, which is one of the key properties of intelligence in applications of decision-making. Our goal is to investigate the pattern of emergence of intelligent strategies in the evolution of habitat tracking. In this work, as a preliminary approach, we examine the evolution of movement strategies in response to a "beacon" whose presence can be sensed by the organisms but whose precise location is never revealed directly to them. This beacon serves as the centre of the habitat, and its position on the grid is held static, although it can in principle be relocated.

The rest of the paper is organized as follows: Sect. 2 presents details of Avida digital evolution system and modifications to the Avida instruction set in order to permit evolution of strategic movement. In Sect. 3, the experimental evaluation of two evolutionary models for movement results is discussed. Future directions of stemming from the present work are included in Sect. 4. Finally, Sect. 4 concludes the paper.

2 Movement Evolution Approach

2.1 System and Methodology

The Avida digital evolution system creates populations of digital organisms held in a discrete two-dimensional grid of cells. A single organism (Avidian) may occur in a grid cell. An Avidian is composed of a genome (computer program) which it must successfully replicate in order to produce an offspring, and a virtual central processing unit CPU which executes the instructions in that genome. The Avida software creates a separate CPU in each grid cell for the Avidian's genome to be run on, and is also able to figure out how newborn organisms ought to be located into the population [11–13]. Further, every organism has a facing which orients it toward an adjoining grid cell.

In a standard Avida run, an Avidian tries to produce an identical copy of its own genome, and places that copy into the population, often by displacing another member of the population if the destination cell is already occupied [12]. During the copy procedure, mutations may alter the instructions that are copied into the child genome, resulting in offspring that differ in their genome, and may also differ in functionality, from their parent. Avida possesses certain additional features for implementing movement and specification of spatially distributed resources. Time in Avida is determined in updates, where each update corresponds to a specific number of instructions carried out, on average, by each Avidian in the population [15–19]. Avidians that can evolve the ability to perform particular rewarded computational functions can execute more instructions per update compared to individuals that lack these enhancements [11–19]. Hence, a key difference between Avida and more traditional genetic programming approaches is that evaluation of an Avidian's fitness does not rely only (or even at all) on an externally-supplied fitness function; Avidians must optimize both their ability to perform computational functions and also their ability and effectiveness of self-replication.

As the first step towards modeling an environment with a habitat of local resource that can be sensed and responded to, a beacon was placed at the centre of the population grid in a local region, with an implicit reward distribution based on distance established across the remainder of a bounded grid (see Fig. 1). No reward was gained by any organism without movement, but each step taken on move was rewarded by a movement bonus. Two different models of movement reward were used, called PERMISSIVE and STRINGENT.

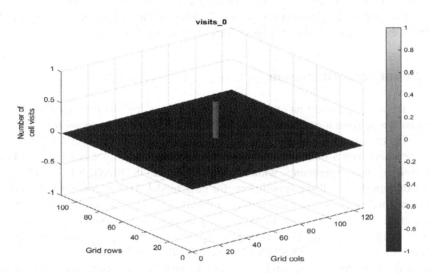

Fig. 1. Population distribution and beacon placement. The scale shows the cumulative number of times a particular cell has been visited.

In the PERMISSIVE model, the base level of reward for movement toward the beacon was set low and declined by a constant factor for each cell with increasing distance from the beacon. In the STRINGENT model, the reward declined as a function of the inverse of distance to the beacon, and required a higher base reward value. Following [2], placement of the Avidians' offspring was random within the population; local offspring placement in close proximity to the parent Avidian resulted in no ability to detect the beacon.

2.2 Problem-Specific New Implementation

In this work, we added four new instructions to the Avida instruction set, namely *pg-sense-beacon*, *pg-sense-dist*, *pg-sense-diff-faced-dist*, and *pg-beacon-move*. The *pg-sense-dist* instruction returns the squared distance to the beacon from an Avidian's current position as a value to be stored in one of the Avidian's registers. The *pg-sense-diff-faced-dist* instruction calculates the difference between the squared distance to the beacon from the Avidian's current position, and the squared distance to the beacon from the cell the Avidian currently faces, again storing the value in one of the Avidian's registers. The *pg-beacon-move* instruction moves the Avidian into the cell it faces and rewards it for movement towards the beacon. The amount of the reward declines with distance from the beacon. If an Avidian tries to move into a cell already occupied by another organism, the two simply swap places. The *pg-sense-beacon* instruction is an implementation of the vision model of Vickerstaff and DiPaolo [20], which produces two values of "activation energy" for the left and right "eyes" depending on an Avidian's orientation relative to the beacon and independent of distance from it; each "energy" value is stored in a different register. In addition, we also employed the previously-implemented *rotate-right, rotate-left,* and *tumble* instructions [2, 12], which permit facing changes. The former two instructions rotate the Avidian one grid cell facing to the right or left, while *tumble* changes the facing randomly (but never back to the current facing).

3   Results and Discussion

In this section, we present an experimental evaluation of the two movement evolution models. We perform a number of experiments to determine the capacity for evolution of intelligent movement strategies in this system. For the sake of general comparison, an experiment with a random model with no mutation capability was performed first, followed by the experiments with PERMISSIVE and STRINGENT models with mutation turned on. All the experiments for each model were performed with similar environmental settings and differed only in the random seeds for each replicate. With the random model, Avidians have the capacity to move in a random fashion by using *tumble* as their only way of changing facing, without the capability of sensing the beacon. Conversely, the PERMISSIVE and STRINGENT models both have the capability of beacon sensing and all aforementioned beacon- and movement-related instructions activated.

3.1   Movement Strategies as Revealed by Aggregate Cell Visits

Following the classification introduced in [2], three dominant movement strategies that emerged during our evolutionary runs were *Cockroach, Ziggurat,* and *Climber* (See Fig. 2). These movement strategies were classified based on Avidians' cell visit patterns. Following [2], the movement of Avidians primarily along the grid boundaries and across the diagonals of the grid was designated *Cockroach* movement. Populations in which *Ziggurat* movement was found prevalent indicate cell visits in the form of a stepped pyramid having a slight peak at the top. Finally, the *Climber* movement strategy shows a sharp peak near the beacon in terms of aggregate cell visits performed by Avidians, and represents the strongest ability to recognize and move around the beacon.

A Random model shows the same movement pattern throughout the time course of the experiment, with approximately equal total visits to all cells (Fig. 2, leftmost panel). By contrast, evolutionary runs produce multiple recognizable movement strategies throughout the time course of an experiment (See Fig. 2). A movement strategy found at the end of the experiment should demonstrate that evolved organisms can in most cases recognize and track the beacon, which is a fundamental characteristic of intelligence. Almost all runs produced successive evolution of two or more movement strategies (Fig. 3). The first panel in the figure reflects the state at 1000 updates having

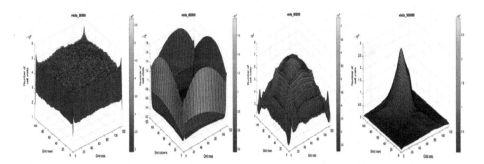

Fig. 2. Dominant Movement Strategies as shown in snapshots of space-time dynamics in experimental populations. Left: random mover; left-centre: *Cockroach*; right-centre: *Ziggurat*; right: *Climber*. The scale shows the cumulative number of times a particular cell has been visited.

most of the cell visits around two to three boundaries of a grid. The second panel shows the dominance in the population of *Cockroach* movement prior to update 2000 for this particular run. The third evolved movement strategy, *Ziggurat*, is dominant between 10000 and 115000 updates and fourth and final evolved movement strategy, *Climber*, appears in the fourteenth and subsequent plots, becoming dominant after 150000 updates. The series of plots clearly shows a mix of *Cockroach*, *Ziggurat*, and *Climber* movement strategies contributing to the grid cell visits, each successive strategy indicating increased ability to lock to the beacon.

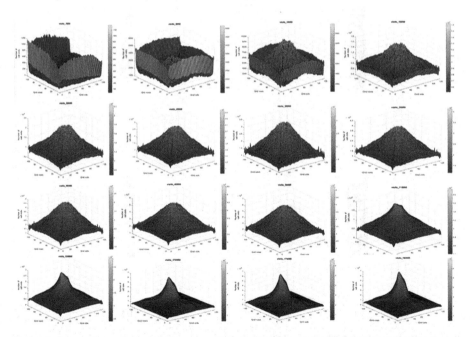

Fig. 3. Movement Transitions at various time intervals in a run by Avidians, resulting in evolution of a *Climber*-type population after progression through *Cockroach* and *Ziggurat* phases.

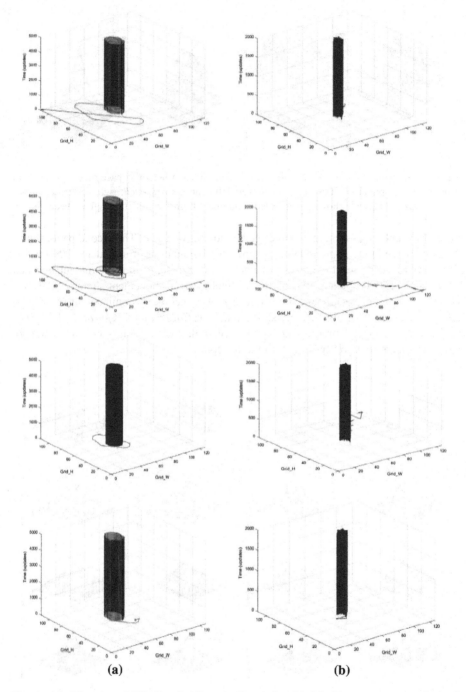

Fig. 4. (a). Diversity of Climber Avidians in Permissive Model. Movement traces obtained under this model feature rounded curves and orbital paths, (b). Diversity of Climber Avidians in Stringent Model. Movement traces obtained under this model are sharp, angular and with star-shaped or polygonal orbital paths.

3.2   Evolved Implementations and Movement Types

Different implementations of movement strategies were produced in different runs, under different settings. For example, in the PERMISSIVE model, evolved Avidians favoured using the *pg-sense-beacon* instruction. Under the STRINGENT model, Avidians instead favoured use of *pg-sense-distance-diff* instructions, producing distinctive movement-through-time traces (see Fig. 4(a) and (b)). We did not yet find any instances of an Avidian favouring use of these two instructions in combination, although there were some that very frequently used the *tumble* instruction in an exploratory manner when they were started far from the beacon. Hence, the coordinated evolved behavior shows evidence of both convergence and contingency of mutations in generating a diversity of movement capabilities upon which natural selection could act.

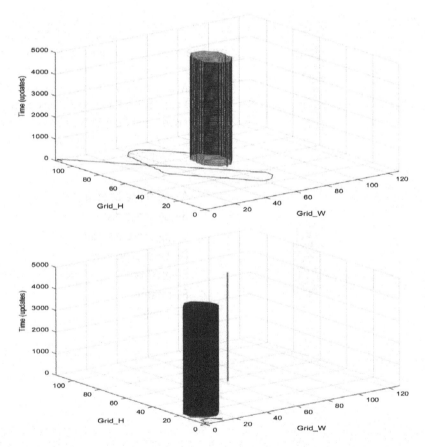

Fig. 5. Example of phenotypic plasticity in movement traces. The traces were produced by an Avidian from one of the permissive experiments. Top panel: when started at grid position (126, 112), the Avidian successfully moves to the vicinity of the beacon. Bottom panel: the same organism fails to move to the beacon when started at [0, 0].

3.3   Phenotypic Plasticity and Functional Genomics for Evaluating Informational Contribution of Instructions

Although we obtained Climber-type results under both settings, the Avidians did not evolve robust, generalized solutions under either set of conditions. The movement traces showed phenotypic plasticity [21], meaning that depending on starting position and/or value of random seed, the same Avidian could show different movement traces. (Figure 5). We therefore used functional genomics experiments [14] to determine how much each of the beacon-related instructions contributed to the observed movement behaviour. These experiments, in which each occurrence of a beacon-related instruction is replaced by a null instruction, showed that beacon-related instructions were not very

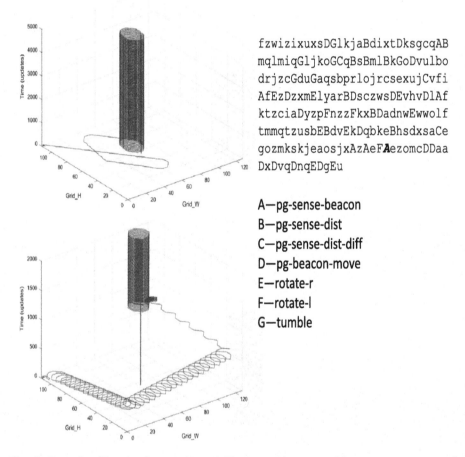

```
fzwizixuxsDGlkjaBdixtDksgcqAB
mqlmiqGljkoGCqBsBmlBkGoDvulbo
drjzcGduGaqsbprlojrcsexujCvfi
AfEzDzxmElyarBDsczwsDEvhvDlAf
ktzciaDyzpFnzzFkxBDadnwEwwolf
tmmqtzusbEBdvEkDqbkeBhsdxsaCe
gozmkskjeaosjxAzAeFAezomcDDaa
DxDvqDnqEDgEu
```

A—pg-sense-beacon
B—pg-sense-dist
C—pg-sense-dist-diff
D—pg-beacon-move
E—rotate-r
F—rotate-l
G—tumble

Fig. 6. Example of functional genomics test. Character string at top right represents genome of Avidian producing movement trace in top panel (beacon-related instructions identified below). Removal of the single red-highlighted *pg-sense-beacon* abolishes the Avidian's ability to lock to the beacon and produces the movement trace shown in the lower panel. (Color figure online)

well-used. Typically, only a single instance of a beacon-related instruction (out of all those present in the Avidian's genome) actually provided critical positional information (Fig. 6). In both the PERMISSIVE Avidians that used *pg-sense-beacon*, and the STRINGENT organisms that preferred *pg-sense-distance-diff*, null replacement of only a particular single instance of each of those instructions abolished the ability to react to the beacon (Fig. 6). No tested Avidians showed any use of the information provided by *pg-sense-distance*.

4 Conclusions and Future Work

There have been many computational approaches to dealing with the movement of individual agents, many of which require a particular way of specifying how movement-related behaviours are accomplished. Evolutionary computation does not require such specification, instead needing only a broad prescription to generate such behaviour and leaving them open to exploration via evolutionary processes. In this paper, we used digital evolution as implemented in the Avida platform to evolve intelligent strategies for detecting and moving to a fixed environmental landmark. One of the core characteristics of evolutionary processes is to produce and accumulate, and winnow variation in a population. Throughout the course of experiments, we examined two levels of variation i.e. intra-class and inter-class variation. The former level of variation was seen during examination of individual Avidian movement from within the most common movement classes, as movement paths of individual Avidians within particular movement classes could differ slightly from one another. As an example, within the *Climber* class of movement strategies, there were significant differences in the efficiency of individual Avidian runs (Fig. 5). The latter level of variation was observed between different classes of movement strategies, shown by our results of three distinct movement strategies with recognizably different patterns of movement based on aggregate population behavior, and the qualitatively different kinds of movement traces that were produced by each environmental model.

The evolved Avidian programs we obtained are instances of effective techniques, a limited number of steps that once performed lead to a specific result. Precisely what is rewarded within Avida is usually merely the accrual of greater worth in response to satisfying user-specified functions and environmental conditions, in the present case, the ability to move to the beacon and remain near it effectively according to the parameters that define the PERMISSIVE and STRINGENT environments. We were able to identify classes of behaviours evolved by Avidians and see them from different perspectives, such as the class of *Climber* movement strategies that approximate gradient ascent. In contrast to previous work [2], our implicit distance-based gradient is more flexible and more general than an environmentally-explicit resource-based gradient in which each cell's resource characteristics must be specified individually, effectively providing each cell with an environmental "signpost" that facilitates evolution of effective strategies [2].

The results presented here show the potential of evolutionary computation to produce effective movement strategies leading to intelligent locking to a fixed landmark feature using incomplete information. Our work shows that such strategies do indeed emerge and pass through multiple stages of varying effectiveness over the time course of a run. The variety of movement strategies obtained, seen both in aggregate and at the individual level, show the interplay between environmental configuration and evolutionary contingency, but the final solutions are suboptimal in that they remain sensitive to environmental variables. This may be a further example of "satisficing" [2], where a non-optimal but still "good enough" solution is retained over ones that are even less effective at addressing the problem; a *Climber* solution that shows plasticity but works well under at least some conditions is still better than one that is ineffective under all conditions i.e. *Cockroach* or random movement.

4.1 Future Work

Although this work yielded some promising initial results, it failed to produce evidence that the obtained movement strategies are robust, general results that could be applied to altered conditions. Further work will focus on: (1) ways to minimize or remove phenotypic plasticity, improve use of the information provided by the beacon-related instructions, and obtain improved solutions for static beacon-related movement; (2) following (1), introduction of a dynamic beacon that can be relocated during either an evolutionary run or during a movement assay, which will demonstrate the generality and "intelligence" of the evolved programs, i.e. ability for course correction in response to change of destination; (3) most importantly, introduction of a spatially and environmentally explicit resource-based ecological component in addition to the beacon, which can also be relocated dynamically, and which can be sensed by the Avidians through an analogue of smell. Use of this "resource field" will complete our habitat model, promote ecological diversification among Avidians, grant them the capacity for migration between spatially and temporally separate fields, and enable us to achieve our ultimate goal of using digital evolution to model the emergence of coordinated stasis through habitat tracking.

Acknowledgments. This work was supported by a grant from the National Natural Science Foundation of China (project # 31470435) to Gabriel Yedid. The authors wish to thank Dr. Laura Grabowski (University of Texas-Rio Grande Valley, Edinburg, TX, USA) for introduction to the vision model used in this work, and Dr. Matthew Rupp and Dr. Wesley Elsberry (Michigan State University, MI, USA) for useful discussion and assistance with experimental design and implementation.

References

1. Grabowski, L.M., Bryson, D.M., Dyer, F.C., Pennock, R.T., Ofria, C.: Clever creatures: case studies of evolved digital organism. In: 11th European Conference on the synthesis and simulation of Living Systems, pp. 276–283. Paris (2011)
2. Elsberry, W.R., Grabowski, L.M., Ofria, C., Pennock, R.T.: Cockroaches, drunkards and climber: modeling the evolution of simple movement strategies using digital organisms. In: 2009 IEEE Symposium on Artificial Life, pp. 92–99. Nashville (2009)

3. Brett, E.C.: Coordinated stasis reconsidered: a perspective at fifteen years. In: Talent, J.A. (ed.) Earth and Life. International Year of Planet Earth, pp. 23–36. Springer, Dordrecht (2012). https://doi.org/10.1007/978-90-481-3428-1_2

4. Gould, S.J.: The structure of evolutionary theory. Harvard University Press, Cambridge (2002)

5. Roese, J., Risenhoover, K., Folse, L.: Habitat heterogeneity and foraging efficiency: an individual-based model. Ecol. Model. **57**, 133–143 (1991)

6. Forrest, S., Jones, T.: Modeling complex adaptive systems with echo. Complex Syst.: Mech. Adapt. (1994)

7. Booth, G.: Gecko: a continuous 2D world for ecological modeling. Artif. Life **3**(3), 147–163 (1997)

8. Yamada, S.: Evolutionary behavior learning for action-based environment modeling by a mobile robot. Appl. Soft Comput. **5**(2), 245–257 (2005)

9. Mahdavi, S., Bentley, P.: Innately adaptive robotics through embodied evolution. Auton. Robots **20**(2), 149–163 (2006)

10. Matsushita, K., Yokoi, H., Arai, T.: Pseudo-passive dynamic walkers designed by coupled evolution of the controller and morphology. Robot. Auton. Syst. **54**, 674–685 (2006)

11. Cooper, T., Ofria, C.: Evolution of stable ecosystems in populations of digital organisms. In: 8th International Conference on Artificial Life, Sydney, pp. 227–232 (2002)

12. Ofria, C., Wilke, O.C.: Avida: a software platform for research in computational evolutionary biology. Artif. Life **10**, 191–229 (2004)

13. Adami, C., Ofria, C., Collier, T.C.: Evolution of biological complexity. Proc. Natl. Acad. Sci. U.S.A. **97**, 4463–4468 (2000)

14. Lenski, R.E., Ofria, C., Pennock, R.T., Adami, C.: The evolutionary origin of complex features. Nature **423**, 139–144 (2003)

15. Beckmann, B., Grabowski, L.M., McKinley, P., Ofria, C.: An autonomic software development methodology based on darwinian evolution. In: 5th IEEE International Conference on Autonomic Computing, pp. 202–203. Chicago (2008)

16. Abeywickrama, D.B., Ovaska, E.: A survey of autonomic computing methods in digital service ecosystems. Serv. Ori. Comp. Appl. **11**, 1–31 (2016)

17. Yedid, G., Heier, L.: Effects of random and selective mass extinction on community composition in communities of digital organisms. In: Pontarotti, P. (ed.) Evolutionary Biology: Mechanisms and Trends, pp. 43–64. Springer, Heidelberg (2012). https://doi.org/10.1007/978-3-642-30425-5_3

18. Yedid, G., Ofria, C.A., Lenski, R.E.: Historical and contingent factors affect re-evolution of a complex feature lost during mass extinction in communities of digital organisms. J. Evol. Biol. **21**, 1335–1357 (2008)

19. Wilke, C.O., Wang, J.L., Ofria, C., Lenski, R.E., Adami, C.: Evolution of digital organisms at high mutation rates leads to survival of the flattest. Nature **412**, 215–218 (2010)

20. Vickerstaff, R.J., DiPaolo, E.A.: Evolving neural models of path integration. J. Exp. Biol. **208**, 3349–3366 (2005)

21. Price, T.D., Qvarnström, A., Irwin, D.E.: The role of phenotypic plasticity in driving genetic evolution. Proc. Roy. Soc. B **270**(1523), 1433–1440 (2003)

Comparative Investigation of Different Feature Extraction Techniques for Lung Cancer Detection System

Pankaj Nanglia$^{(\boxtimes)}$, Sumit Kumar, Davinder Rathi, and Paramjit Singh

MAU, Baddi, India
nanglia.pankaj@gmail.com, kumarsumit@mau.edu.in,
jerryrathee@gmail.com, ppparamjitsingh@gmail.com

Abstract. The present work demonstrates the utilization of computer-aided diagnosis system for the detection of lung cancer diseases using computer tomography (CT) images, magnetic resonance images (MRI) and X-ray images. The feature extraction process in lung cancer images has been achieved by scale invariant feature transform (SIFT), speeded up robust features (SURF), and principal component analysis (PCA) techniques. In this work, a comparative investigation of different feature extraction technique such as SIFT, SURF, and PCA has been discussed in order to find the best descriptor for feature extraction of cancerous subjects to the normal subjects in terms of two parameters named as execution time and error rate. The main aspect of these learning approaches is to find the valid key points in minimum execution time with least error. The results reveal that the SURF technique has an average execution time of 0.448 s with an average error rate value of 25.704 which is least among three techniques. Hence, SURF extraction technique is best as compared to SIFT and PCA.

Keywords: Lung cancer · SIFT · SURF · PCA · Time and error rate

1 Introduction

Nowadays, the involvement of advanced technology in human life has shown as exponential rise almost in every field ranging from complex engineering to diversified medical sector. Subsequently, the addition of computer-aided diagnosis (CAD) system in medical industry opened up a new horizon for almost all the medical practitioners to diagnosis in an efficient manner with more reliability. The idea behind the whole concept is "Soft-Computing" that enable us to provide efficient computing technique to remove the hurdles of CAD system employed for diagnosis purpose. The improved and advanced CAD system provides the noninvasively mapping in the subject of Anatomy especially in clinical treatment and medical research [1–4]. Today cancer is considered one of the leading causes of death all over the world. It is estimated that 85% of male lung cancer patients and 75% of the female patient are caused by smoking [5–7]. The lung cancer patients increased in past few years and recently, in Africa due to the

© Springer Nature Singapore Pte Ltd. 2019
A. K. Luhach et al. (Eds.): ICAICR 2018, CCIS 955, pp. 296–307, 2019.
https://doi.org/10.1007/978-981-13-3140-4_27

tobacco epidemic that has resulted in the large dispersion of this disease [8]. Once diagnosed, lung cancer often reaches the terminal stage quickly, and thus patients lose the best treatment time. In this context, various techniques are employed to detect lung cancer that includes chest radiography, optical examination of trachea and the intra-pulmonary airways, cytological inspection of Saliva samples which are traditional and time consuming while modern methodologies are CAD be used such as Computerized tomography scans (CT) and magnetic resonance imaging (MRI) [9].Chest X-ray and CT scanning are often used to screen for early lung cancer patients, but the problems of low sensitivities and specificities exist. Hence coping with the cancer can be difficult and to confront this, a huge number of researchers are contributing in order to diagnosis with the help of captured images of affected regions [10–12]. This become possible by image processing for extracting the IP (Interest point) to obtain robust feature, using fully automated feature extraction techniques SIFT, SURF, and PCA [13]. Moreover, most of the researchers are using image processing techniques to diagnose the lung cancer using CT images. Leila et al. 2015 have presented a novel approach for the extraction of the invariant features from the interest region in which the novel descriptor was inspired by the unique SIFT descriptor [14]. The proposed system utilized SIFT, Local binary patterns (LBP) and Center-Symmetric Local Binary Pat-terns (CSLBP) descriptors for the improvisation of the matching results. In another work, by Jiaxi Wang and group has introduced SURF algorithm for the detection of feature points and Image mosaicking with the transformation matrix is used for the implementation of the work [15]. Image mosaicking can be used in different applica-tions like computer vision, photogrammetric, medical image analysis remote sensing image processing and computer graphics. Similarly B.L.Shivakumar et al. proposed a system which is based on SURF algorithm to identify the duplicated region [16]. The author obtained the key points in the forged region which will be quite similar to the original ones. The result indicates that detection along with copy-move forgery with a minimum false match for an image with high resolution can be achieved. While, M.M El-Gayar et al. describe the performance of F-SIFT(fast-SIFT) detection technique as compared to SIFT and SURF in terms of scale changes, rotation, blur and illumination changes [17]. In this paper, SIFT presents its stability and it is found its slow in most of the situations. The author found F-SIFT is the fastest one with excellent performance as the as SURF, SIFT and PCA-SIFT shows its advantage in the rotation and illumination changes. Finally, the author investigates the F-SIFT has the best overall performance above SIFT and SURF. Further, in another study by Anjali Kulkarni in proposed a novel algorithm for the detection of cancer at an initial stage that provides enhanced accuracy [18]. The execution time factor is considered for discovering the abnormality issues in the target images, and the accurate identification of the tumour region is achieved using watershed segmentation and Gabor filter. These method provides better results for the stage of pre-processing in terms of three parameters eccentricity, area, and perimeter were calculated from the extracted interest region. Based on these parameters, it has been identified that the tumors were of different dimensions.

Hence, a CAD system needs to perform the following actions training, classification and Optimization with maximum accuracy in each step which in turn depends on the precise extraction of features in an image. However, desired features would be obtained from the efficient feature extraction techniques. These techniques might have well-organized algorithms or a defined descriptor that can be utilized in order to detect the ROI in an image. Based on this theory it can be elucidated that feature extraction is a crucial phase, which represents the ultimate results to find out the normality or abnormality of an image or cell in case of cancer. Although the feature extraction process mainly falls into two sections called Named Feature Extraction and Feature Vector Extraction. Lung Cancer the most sophisticated disease, so features should be extracted precisely and very accurately (Table 1).

Table 1. Parameters required for obtaining ROI.

Sr No.	Features	Description	Formula
1	Area	Facilitates in obtaining the overall number of nodule pixel in the extracted ROI	$Area = Y\{y(n,m,xROI(area) = n,$ Y ROI(area) = m Here, n, m signifies the shape pixels, x ROI, and y ROI are the vectors contain ROI x location and y location respectively
2.	Perimeter	Facilitates the substantial nodule pixel in the ROI boundary	$Perimeter = Sm =$ where$\{S(n,m)\}$ X edge [S] = n Y edge[S] = m Here, X edge and Y edge represents the coordinate of nth and m^{th} pixels forming the curve respectively. It0
3.	Eccentricity	An irregular complex which generates roundness/circularity in ROI. Mean {= 1, for circular <1, for other forms	Eccentricity = Length of major axis of cell/Length of minor axis of cell

The second type of feature set is called a feature vector. In this we paper we investigate and elaborate the performance of the Feature extraction techniques SIFT, SURF and PCA [19].

2 Methodology

The proposed method finds out the computation time and error rate of feature extraction technique i.e., SIFT, SURF and PCA (Fig. 1).

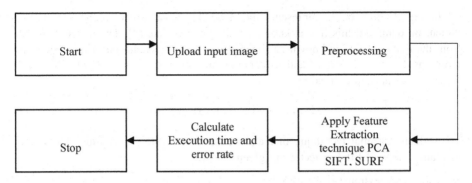

Fig. 1. Proposed implementation steps to determining the parameters

In this work we analyzed the feature extraction techniques SIFT, SURF and PCA. Here Feature extraction techniques transform the original features and generate new vital features those are more valid and more significant [17]. The main problem in the feature extraction techniques was facing to find out key point and give representation to multivariate data. In this context, PCA was implemented in the first phase. PCA was used to minimize the number of dimensions of a dataset consisting of many interrelated variables while preserving the changes that exist in the dataset. By transforming a variable into a new set of variables called the principal component and are orthogonal to each other. The differences that live in the original variable remain ascending when moving down in order [18]. In this way, the first PC retains the most extensive or massive change that exists in the original component. The principal components are the eigenvectors of the covariance matrix, so they are orthogonal [19].

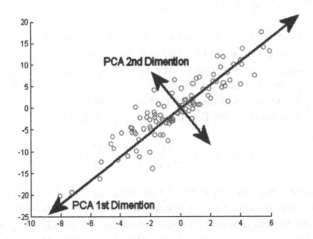

Fig. 2. Principal component analysis illustrations [20] (Color figure online)

In Fig. 2, blue circle represents the data, the broad arrow represents the 1st dimension data, and this line is known as the diagonal line [8]. The distance of data from the diagonal line is known as Eigen-value. Let us assume that Eigenvalues are represented as v1, v2, v3, v4 and let data is represented as x1, x2, x3, x4. Thus, their Eigenvectors are represented as

$$(x1, v1), (x2, v2), (x3, v3), (x4, v4) \tag{1}$$

Another essential technique of feature extraction is SIFT technique. The implementation steps of SIFT detector are given below:

a. Scale-space extreme detection
b. Key point localization
c. Orientation assignment
d. Key point descriptor
e. Key point Matching

The SIFT technique implemented on CT scan images. Start by identifying points of interest, which are called key points in the structure of the SIFT. The image is convolved with Gaussian filters on different scales, and then the difference of consecutive Gaussian-blurred images was performed. Then the key points are considered maxima/minima of the difference of Gaussian (DoG), which occur on several scales [21, 22]. The DoG image can be expressed as:

$$D(u, v, \sigma) = P(u, v, Li, \sigma) - P(u, v, Lj, \sigma) \tag{2}$$

Where $P(,,,)$ is the convolution of original image $R(u,v)$ with Gaussian blur

$$G(u, , L\sigma,) \text{ at scale } L\sigma, \text{i.e., } P(u, v, \sigma) = G(u, v, L\sigma,) \times R(u, v) \tag{3}$$

Hence, a DoG image between scales Li,σ and Li,σ is just the difference between the Gaussian blurred images at scales Li,σ and Li,σ. To match the data in an ideal location, we use the localization of key points. The DoG image can deflect the low contrast points that are represented along with the edge. This is done by interpolation, which further uses the Taylor series of the DoG spatial scale function to learn the original key points [23]. Mathematically, the Taylor series can be expressed as follows:

$$E(x) = E + \frac{\partial E^T}{\partial x} x + \frac{1}{2} x^T \frac{\partial 2_E}{\partial E^2} x \tag{4}$$

where E represents the derivative for determining the key points after finding the significant and prominent location of feature. It is called as **Orientation assignment** that is based on the local image gradient directions, in which every **key point** is assigned to more than one orientation [24]. While the orientation was calculated as:

$$P(x,y) = \sqrt{(M(x+1,y)-M(x-1,y)2 + (M(x,y+1) - M(x,y-1)2} \quad (5)$$

$$\theta(x,y) = atan2(M(x,y+1) - M(x,y-1), M(x+1,y - M(x-1,y)) \quad (6)$$

Where $P(x, y)$ is the gradient magnitude
$\theta(y, z)$ is the orientation

The magnitude and direction calculations for the gradient are performed for each pixel in the neighbouring region around the key point in a Gaussian blurred image P. An approximate 36-degree histogram is formed, with each box covering $10°$ [18]. Each sample in the adjacent window, added to the histogram, is weighted by its gradient value and a circular window with a Gaussian weight that is 1.5 times larger than the key point scale. The peaks in this histogram correspond to the dominant orientations. After filling the histogram, the priorities corresponding to the highest peak and local peaks within 80% of the maximum peaks are assigned to the key point. The work is intensively associated with statistical approaches that provide a visual representation of the extraction of key points those belong to the lung cancer images. In this case, we implement the algorithm SURF [12]. Here, three functional descriptors were used for various tasks, such as object identification, image registration, and classification. This algorithm is several times faster and more reliable than the SIFT algorithm. The description of each step are given below:

i. Key point detection: SURF uses square filters to determine DoG because this filter is much faster for integral images. The sum of the original image in the rectangle can be quickly estimated using an integral image. Bob detector based on the Hessine matrix is used to determine the point of interest. The Hessian matrix can be represented in the form as [24].

$$G(z,\sigma) = (Mxx(z,\sigma) \quad Mxx(z,\sigma)Mxy(z,\sigma) \quad Mxy(z,\sigma)) \quad (7)$$

$(z,)$ is the convolution of the 2nd order derivative of Gaussian with the image J(x, y) at point x [25].

ii. Scale-space illustration and positioning of interest points: The interest points could be found at various scales, thus, to calculate the point of interest requires an image for comparison. The scales are divided into octaves. Octave means a series of filter responses that are obtained by convolving a similar input image along with an increase in the size of the filter [26–28]. As far as localization of the point of interest is concerned, images are localized by suppression in the vicinity of 3 * 3 * 3. Currently, a fast variant is applied, and then the maximum of the Hessian matrix is determined.

iii. Interest point descriptor and matching: Surf uses Haar wavelet responses to extract the desired key points by the neighbour of the valid point of interest. Since the Haar wavelet was used to increase the dimension of the feature set in an attempt to improve the detection of objects in images. This was successful, as some of these functions are capable of better describing the object. Then, finally, a match is made. Any algorithm for extracting attributes extracts a set of vector functions, and it is not necessary that each row and each column from the resulting set be effective [29–31].

3 Experimental Results

Collectively, CT scan images from five different patients of Lung cancer have been considered with different image configurations. Table 2 represents the complete description of the dataset. In this paper evaluating key points by identifying the parameters like execution time and error Rate in each case of PCA, SIFT and SURF techniques. Initially, a pre-processing was performed in which the conversion of a colour image to a binary image was achieved by scaling the image, reducing the size of the image set and noise was removed. Later PCA technique was carried out in which orthogonal transformation has been performed on the corresponding images one by one illustrated in Table 2. PCA calculate, the principal components and corresponding Eigenvectors (256 * 1) for each image because it plots the ROI across the single column along with the dimension of an image. Similarly, the SIFT technique was executed for finding the key-points and extracted SIFT key points which are approximately similar for each image i.e., (252 * 252), because it scaling the images in the form of a matrix and plot the key points in the scaled dimension of the image. Concurrently the Surf technique was accomplished to extract the key points in order to plot these key points on the image. Moreover, a different configuration of the images got a different number of key points. The pictorial representation of entire process has been shown by Figs. 3 and 4.

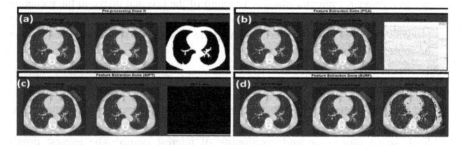

Fig. 3. Pictorial Representation and initial steps of different image techniques, (a) Preprocessing, (b) PCA, (c) SIFT, (d) SURF

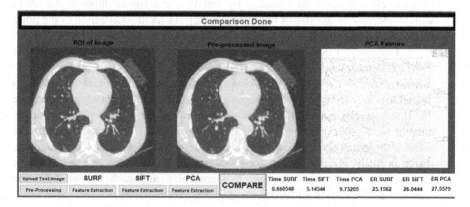

Fig. 4. Visual analysis SURF, SIFT, and PCA.

Table 2. Description of the dataset with image dimension corresponding to each feature set.

Image dimension	PCA (principle eigen vector)	SIFT (key points)	SURF (key points)
Image 1 (222 * 227)	256 *1	252*252	158*64
Image 2 (255 * 394)	256 *1	252*252	284*64
Image 3 (182 * 276)	256 *1	253*251	183*64
Image 4 (193 * 200)	256 *1	253*250	137*64
Image 5 (202 * 250)	256 *1	252*252	193*64

Table 3. Performance parameters of feature extraction algorithm for five samples

Image samples	Tic-Toc time			Mean square error		
	SURF	SIFT	PCA	SURF	SIFT	PCA
Image 1	0.42	6.36	9.51	25.20	26.60	27.79
Image 2	0.39	2.01	10.21	29.25	30.38	31.61
Image 3	0.35	2.10	9.97	22.45	23.50	24.72
Image 4	0.42	4.01	10.07	26.47	27.60	28.71
Image 5	0.66	5.14	9.72	25.15	26.04	27.55

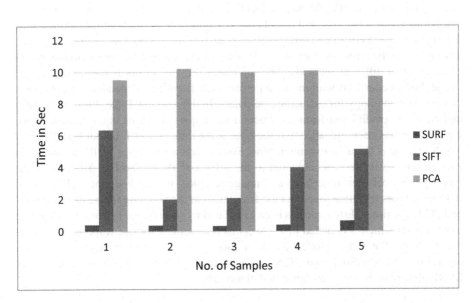

Fig. 5. Execution time chart for evaluation of feature extraction in SURF, SIFT and PCA techniques.

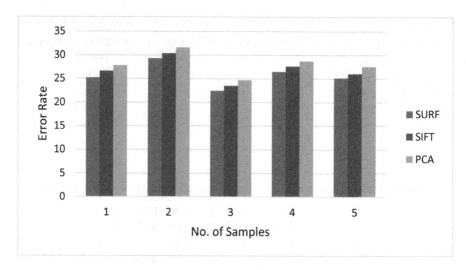

Fig. 6. Error rate of SURF, SIFT and PCA

The choice of the best feature or ROI function depends entirely on parameters such as the execution time and error rate in the different PCA, SIFT, and SURF methods. To detect lung cancer at an early stage, execution time plays a vital role. Finding the right key points is not a big task, but calculating key points in the minimum execution time with the minimum error rate corresponding to each point is a big task. The mean square error refers to the error between the positioning of the original key points to key points obtained from different methods. The minimum level of errors is the quality of the image. For a better ROI with minimal performance is entirely dependent on the choice of the best technology for extracting the points. In this context Table 3 shows the time and error rate of different feature extraction techniques. Tic time is the time at which input image has been uploaded and toc time is the time at which output image comes out. So tic-toc is the total execution time. Total execution time for SURF technique in each image is very less as compared to the SIFT and PCA. The Fig. 5 illustrates the graph plotted between time (sec) and image samples. It observed that SURF feature descriptor takes less time to extract the features from the test lung image than the SIFT and PCA descriptor. Error rate has been calculated by mean square error corresponding to each point which is depicted in Table 3 that represents error rate respectively. While Fig. 6 shows the graph plotted for error rate observed for three feature extraction algorithms (SURF, SIFT and PCA). It is observed that the error rate observed for SURF algorithm is less than other two algorithms.

4   Conclusion

The exploitation of non-invasive techniques for the detection of lung cancers has been investigated using soft computing methods. One of the possible ways is to utilize an advanced image processing approach which has the ability to differentiate the cancer image to the normal subject. The adopted technique must be simple, efficient and GUI based which requires less execution time with minimized error rate during the extraction process. This study reports an in-depth analysis of feature extraction algorithms and represents a comparative analysis of feature vector of SIFT, SURF and PCA in the terms of execution time and error rate. It has been found that the average value of execution time in five different samples by SURF, SIFT and PCA are 0.448, 3.924 and 9.896 s whereas the average value of error rate were 25.704, 26.824 and 28.076 respectively. Hence, it is clear from the obtained results that the SURF is best as compared to other two techniques in terms of execution time and calculated error rate ratios. Based on the measured parametric values, we proposed that *SURF* descriptor performs well for feature extraction process. Additionally, it is suggested that SURF as a feature extractor enhances the classification accuracy and helps in obtaining desired optimization which leads to an efficient lung cancer detection system.

Acknowledgement. The authors would like to thanks Honorable Vice-chancellor Dr. R.K Gupta of Maharaja Agrasen University Solan, Himachal Pradesh, India for continuous support during the execution of this work.

References

1. Sharma, S., Nanglia, P., Kumar, S., Shukla, P.: Detection and analysis of lung cancer using radiomic approach. In: International Conference on Computational Strategies for Next Generation Technologies (2017, in the press)
2. Radhakrishnan, M., Kuttiannan, T.: Comparative analysis of feature extraction methods for the classification of prostate cancer from the trus medical images. Int. J. Comput. Sci. **9**, 171–179 (2012)
3. An Information Resource on Lung Cancer Testing for Pathologists and Oncologists. https://Www.Verywell.Com/Non-Small-Cell-Lung-Cancer-2249281
4. Makaju, S., Prasad, P.W.C., Alsadoon, A., Singh, A.K.: Lung cancer detection using CT Scan images. In: 6th International Conference on Smart Computing and Communications Kurukshetra, pp. 107–114 (2017)
5. Chander, M.P., Rao, M.V., Rajinikanth, T.-V.: Detection of lung cancer using digital image processing techniques: a comparative study. Int. J. Med. Imaging. **5**, 58–62 (2017). https://doi.org/10.11648/j.ijmi.20170505.12
6. Ma, L., Wang, D.D., et al.: An eigen-binding site based method for the analysis of anti-EGFR drug resistance in lung cancer treatment. IEEE/ACM Trans. Comput. Biol. Bioinf. **14**, 1187–1194 (2017). https://doi.org/10.1109/tcbb.2016.2568184
7. El Hussein, A., Tynga, I.-M., Harith, M.-A.: Comparative study between the photodynamic ability of gold and silver nanoparticles in mediating cell death in breast and lung cancer cell lines. J. Photochem. Photobiol. Biol. **153**, 67–75 (2015). https://doi.org/10.1016/j.jphotobiol.2015.08.028
8. Song, Y., Cai, W., Zhou, Y., Feng, D.D.: Feature-based image patch approximation for lung tissue classification. IEEE Trans. Med. Imag. **30**, 797–808 (2013)
9. Firnimo, M., Morais, A.H., et al.: Computer-aided detection system for lung cancer in computed tomography scans: review and future prospects. In: Biomedical Engineering, pp. 1–16 (2014)

10. El Gayar, M.-M., Soliman, H., Meky, N.: A compative study of image low level featuteextection algorithm. Egypt. Inf. J. **14**, 175–181 (2013). https://doi.org/10.1016/j.eij.2013.06.003
11. Kabbai, L., Abdellaoui, M., Douik, A.: New robust descriptor for image matching. J. Theor. Appl. Inf. Technol. **87**, 451–460 (2016)
12. Wang, J., Watada, J.: Panoramic image mosaic based on SURF algorithm using Open CV. In: IEEE 9th International Symposium on Intelligent Signal Processing (WISP) Proceedings, pp. 1–6 (2015). https://doi.org/10.1109/wisp.2015.7139183
13. Saini, A.-K., Bhadauria, H.-S., Singh, A.: A Survey of noise removal methodologies for lung cancer diagnosis. In: Second International Conference on Computational Intelligence and Communication Technology (CICT) Ghaziabad, pp. 673–678 (2016). https://doi.org/10.1109/cict.2016.139
14. Teramoto, A., Fujita, H.: Fast lung nodule detection in chest ct images using cylindrical nodule-enhancement filter. Int. J. Comput. Assist. Radiol. Surg. **8**(2), 193–205 (2013)
15. Kulkarni, A., Panditrao, A.: Classification of lung cancer stages on CT scan images using image processing. In: IEEE International Conference on Advanced Communications Control and Computing Technologies, pp. 1384–1388 (2014). https://doi.org/10.1109/icaccct.2014.7019327
16. Han, G., Liu, X., Han, F., et al.: Lung diseases for computer-aided detection and diagnosis research and medical education. IEEE Trans. Biomed. Eng. **62**, 648–656 (2015). https://doi.org/10.1109/TBME.2014.2363131
17. Shivakumar, B.-L., Baboo, S.S.: Automated forensic method for copy-move forgery detection based on harris interest points and SIFT descriptors. Int. J. Comput. Appl. **27**, 9–17 (2011). https://doi.org/10.5120/3283-4472
18. Chumerin, N., Van, Hulle, M.-M.: Comparison of two feature extraction methods based on maximization of mutual information. In: Proceedings of the 16th IEEE Signal Processing Society Workshop on Machine Learning for Signal Processing, pp. 343–348 (2006). https://doi.org/10.1109/mlsp.2006.275572
19. Lambin, P., Velazquez, E.R., et al.: Radiomics: extracting more information from medical images using advanced feature analysis. Eur. J. Cancer **48**, 104–118 (2012). https://doi.org/10.1016/j.ejca.2011.11.036
20. https://stackoverflow.com/questions/30777569/significance-of-99-of-variance-covered-by-the-first-componentin-pca
21. Cateni, S., Vannucci, M., et al.: Variable selection and feature extraction through artificial intelligence techniques. In: Multivariate Analysis in Management, Engineering and Science vol. 6, pp. 103–118 (2013). https://doi.org/10.5772/53862
22. Peng, G., Tisch, U., Adams, O., et al.: Diagnosing lung cancer in exhaled breath using gold nanoparticles. Nat. Nanotechnol. **4**, 669–673 (2009)
23. Lowe, D.-G.: Distinctive image features from scale-invariant keypoints. Int. J. Comput. Vision **60**, 91–110 (2004)
24. Pang, Y., Li, W., Yuan, Y., Pan, J.: Fully affine invariant SURF for image matching. Neurocomputing **85**, 6–10 (2012). https://doi.org/10.1016/j.neucom.2011.12.006
25. Ha, S.W., Moon, Y.-H.: Multiple object tracking using SIFT features and location matching. Int. J. Smart Home **5**, 17–26 (2011)
26. Kang, H., Efros, A.A., Hebert, M., et al.: Image matching in large scale indoor environment. In: IEEE International Conference on Computer Vision and Pattern Recognition Workshop, pp. 33–40 (2009). https://doi.org/10.1109/cvprw.2009.5204357
27. Huijuan, Z., Qiong, H.: Fast image matching basedon improved SURF algorithm. In: IEEE International conference Electronics Communications and Control (ICECC), pp. 1460–1463 (2011). https://doi.org/10.1109/icecc.2011.6066546

28. Jin, X., Zhang, Y., Jin, Q.: Pulmonary nodule detection based on CT images using convolution neural network. In: 9th International Symposium On Computational Intelligence And Design (ISCID) (2016) https://doi.org/10.1109/iscid.2016.1053
29. Yin, Y., et al.: Tumor cell load and heterogeneity estimation from diffusion-weighted MRI calibrated with histological data: an example from lung cancer. IEEE Trans. Med. Imaging (2017)
30. Sangamithraa, P., Govindaraju, S.: Lung tumour detection and classification using EK-Mean cluster clustering. In: International Conference On Wireless Communications, Signal Processing and Networking (Wispnet) (2016). https://doi.org/10.1109/wispnet.2016.7566533
31. Sharma, S., Kumar. S., Aggarwal. E.: A study on adaptive wavelet technique for speckle noise removal. In: International conference on Communication and Computing Systems, pp. 131–136 (2016)

EEG Based Cognitive Brain Mapping in Time Domain to Analyze EM Radiation Effect on Human Brain

Rashima Mahajan$^{(\boxtimes)}$, Dipali Bansal, and Anshul Khatter

Faculty of Engineering and Technology, MRIIRS, Faridabad, India
{rashima.fet,dipali.fet}@mriu.edu.in,
anshul.khatter@gmail.com

Abstract. A progressive rise in the daily usage and dependency over electronic gadgets has been witnessed across the world since a decade. Most of the electronic gadgets involve the direct exposure to extremely harmful levels of highly dangerous electromagnetic radiations (EM). The chronic exposure of these EM radiations may adversely affect the human health. An attempt has been made to investigate the EM radiation effect on human brain using electroencephalography (EEG) analysis. A detailed event related potential and topographic map analysis of acquired EEG signals has been done using MATLAB and studied as an outcome during two states *viz.*, normal relaxed state and EM radiation exposure state. Significant rise in potential concentrations has been observed at frontal and frontal-temporal regions of scalp during radiation exposure state. This has also been inferred from three dimensional topographic scalp maps of human brain. This indicates that the time domain analysis of EEG responses possess the ability to be developed as a tool to assess the level of radiation exposure on cognitive functions of human brain. It could lead to explore and correlate a variety of health effects such as memory loss, cognitive impairment, brain tumors, headaches, frustration, anxiety, etc with the EM radiation exposure.

Keywords: Brain · Cognitive mapping · EEG analysis · EM radiations
Event related potential · Topographic map

1 Introduction

Exponential increase in usage of mobile phones, laptops and other gadgets which involve direct exposure of Electromagnetic (EM) radiations has become a potential threat to public health. Out of these EM sources, mobile phones are most crucial because of high number of users and longer usage time durations. In last two decades, mammoth increase in global mobile phone subscribers has been reported [1]. The figure is estimated to reach 6.8 billion marks which are approximately 94% of the global population. Though mobile phone phones proved to be better communication medium and highly convenient but the health hazards (mental and physical) due to their EM radiations are quite alarming [2].

A. K. Luhach et al. (Eds.): ICAICR 2018, CCIS 955, pp. 308–319, 2019.
https://doi.org/10.1007/978-981-13-3140-4_28

Mobile phones emit high concentration of microwave radiations (extremely strong near the antenna region of cell phone), the brain is eventually exposed to high frequency EM waves with significantly high specific absorption rate (SAR) [3] and that too increase exponentially with increase in frequency of signals. Also thermal effect due to mobile phone radio frequency (RF) emission is another issue but is not much of concern as studies does not showed any prominent adverse effect [4, 5]. Moreover its effect on reproduction of humans is quite prominent but for longer duration of usage [6]. Lot of research using highly precise imaging techniques such as positron emission tomography, has been done to investigate the variations in cerebral blood flow (CBF) due to mobile phone radiation. However their results are quite distinct with some reported 'no change' [7], 'increase' [8, 9] or decrease and increase in CBF [10, 11]. However these CBF variations are more related to vascular effects than neural signals. Increase in brain glucose metabolism due to long use of mobile phone has also been reported but the results only valid for the brain areas closest to the phone antennas [12].

Other than various imaging techniques, the analyzing EM effect on brain can be performed using a non-invasive technique of brain mapping known as electroencephalography (EEG). It is an established tool to determine a correlation between performed action, external stimulation and any cognitive activity with neural responses. A variety of feature extraction techniques in time and frequency domain can be utilized for required brain mapping. A very few research outcomes have been documented on EEG variations due to EM radiation exposure. Few major outcomes has been explored and quantified in tabular form below as Table 1.

Table 1. Literature summary

Sr. No.	Publication	Description
1.	Relova et al. [13] 2010	EEM radiations effects on epileptic subjects was characterized by EEG based spectral analysis and it shows significant increase in beta and gamma sub band power
2.	Murat et al. [14] 2011	Statistical study of the EEG patterns indicates decrease in alpha wave or right side of scalp during calling mode of cell phones but alpha wave of left side remains consistent
3.	Hareuveny et al. [15] 2011	Cognitive effects of cellular phone were studied by performing spatial working memory tasks by subjects. Response time and accuracy based results showed significant effect
4.	Isa et al. [16] 2012	Decrease in correlation of Power Asymmetric Ration (PAR) beta-alpha was recorded during transition from non-exposure to exposure state

Some of the research works involve signal processing techniques like wavelet energy, Higuichi's fractal dimension method and k-NN approach for determining EM exposure effect on brain [17–19]. Apart from all these positive results, few researchers showed negligible or no effect of mobile phone EM radiations on brain waves [20, 21].

Hence the current scenario of this problem is quite tentative and requires a concrete and multi modal study involving robust signal processing techniques. Also almost all prior works suffer from solid drawbacks like use of linear methods for EEG analysis, single or few channel analysis and study of limited skull area.

In this research paper, we address most of these problems to provide a substantial conclusion about effect of mobile phone generated EM radiation on human brain.

2   Materials and Methods

The methodology has been proposed to investigate the impact of cell phone exposure on human brain waves using EEG. The methodology is developed by analyzing and processing the EEG recordings performed before and during the phone calls using mobile phone. The functional block diagram of the proposed real time set up to investigate the EM radiations exposure via mobile phone on human neural state is shown in Fig. 1.

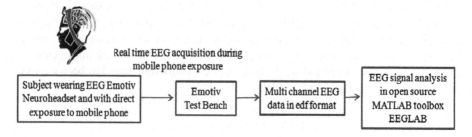

Fig. 1. Functional block diagram for the proposed set up to investigate EM radiation effect on human brain

2.1   Subjects

Five young and healthy male subjects (age 18–20 years) were involved in the proposed experiment to formulate the mobile phone exposure specific EEG signal database. Each participant equipped with EEG acquisition unit and a mobile phone was made to sit in a quiet and dark room. Extra precaution was taken to ensure that no other electromagnetic interference was present in the environment. It was ensured that all the subjects have given their written consent and are under no drug consumption before the experiment.

2.2   Experiment Protocol and EEG Signal Database Formulation

The human neural responses via EEG were acquired from designated subjects under three conditions. The protocol followed for the experimentation is depicted with the help of a flowchart as shown in Fig. 2. Each recording lasted for 20 s. A pair of 'start' and 'stop' markers was introduced manually at 5th second and 15th second respectively so as to enable extraction of EEG signal epochs at different channel locations. To minimize the eye movement related artifacts in the recorded signals, participants were asked to close their eyes while EEG signal acquisition. The first recording includes the baseline reading corresponding to the normal relaxed state of subject i.e. prior to mobile phone exposure. The second and third recordings include the readings corresponding to right exposure and left exposure respectively while the phone is in active session (voice is mute). The voice is switched in mute mode to reduce the effect of any external stimulation due to voice and emotional content modulation.

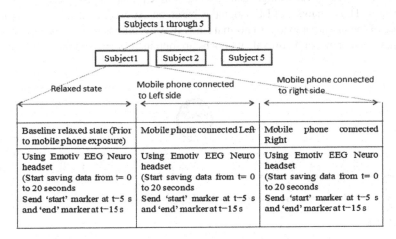

Fig. 2. Flow chart for followed protocol

The electroencephalograph (EEG) data was recorded using a Emotiv EEG Neuroheadset available with 14 channel sensors that are suitably placed on subject's scalp. The 14-assembly electrode sensors are AF3, F7, F3, FC5, T7, P7, O1, O2, P8, T8, FC6, F4, F8, AF4 with two reference electrodes P3 and P4. The acquired data, which is recorded at the sampling frequency of 128 Hz, is transmitted to receiver laptop and is saved as .edf (European data format) file.

2.3 EEG Data Analysis

EEG potential acquired in real time is processed using EEGLAB application software version 13.0.1 which is a standalone platform in MATLAB workspace. EEG signal is imported into EEGLAB in .edf format for further processing. Data is acquired by placing all the 14 electrodes/channels on the subject's head. Independent-Component-Analysis (ICA) is implemented to spontaneously recognize the temporal and spatial artifacts in the neural signals captured. Of all the ICA decomposition algorithms available in EEGLAB, the algorithm 'runica.m' which is based on Super Gaussian activity distribution, is used to work on 20 s EEG data acquired. To further understand the equivalent EEG dynamics in various conditions of EM wave exposure in the vicinity of mobile phones, channel specific statistics and ERPs were analyzed.

3 Result and Discussion

Results obtained from the EEG inspired BCI set up to study influence of mobile phone radiation on brain signals/cognitive abilities of a human being is presented in this section. The analysis here is based on data obtained from one subject but similar results are seen in case of other participants as well. The experimental procedure includes capturing brain signals in relaxed state when the participant is not subjected to any EM radiation followed by recordings made during mobile phone ringing kept on either side of the head. Thus, analysis of EEG signal is based on exposure of radiation on right and left side of the brain compared to normal state. ICA decomposition is done on real time acquired brain signal and equivalent epochs are obtained to analyze the radiation effect

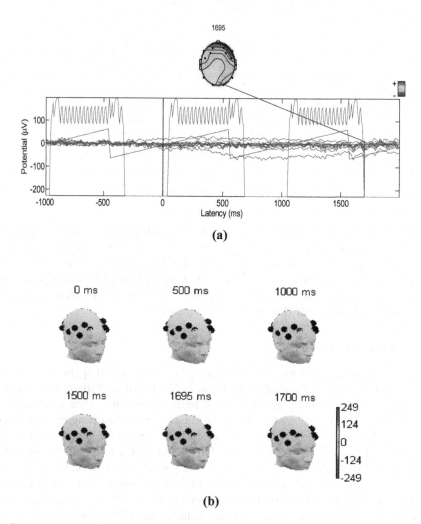

Fig. 3. (a) Average ERP (event related potential) during normal relaxed state (b) Three-D ERP scalp maps during normal relaxed state at different latencies (Color figure online)

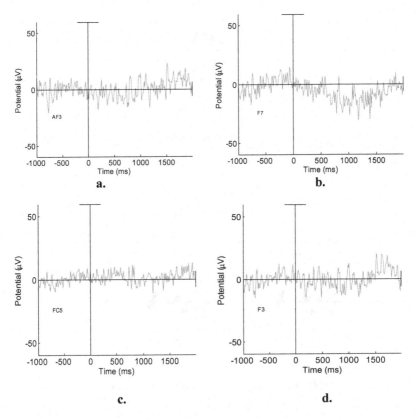

Fig. 4. EEG signal epoch on Frontal Channels (a) AF3, (b) F7, and Frontal Temporal Channels (c) FC5, (d) F3 of EMOTIV Neuro-headset during relaxed state

due to mobile phones. Analysis corresponds to 3 states viz. relaxed state with no exposure, mobile phone kept on right exposure and when kept on left side, respectively.

Average ERP and corresponding ERP scalp maps at particular latencies for entire dataset epoch during normal state of no exposure condition are plotted in Fig. 3a and b respectively. The individual plot in the figure characterizes the average of event related potential values captured across single scalp electrode. The topographic map plotted over the ERP graphs indicates the voltage concentration across distinct scalp regions. It is plotted at latency of around 1695 ms during normal condition. It shows the minimum potential distribution across scalp in blue and yellow color. The red color indicates the maximum potential distribution across scalp region.

EEG signal epochs obtained across Scalp Frontal Channels - AF3 & F7 and Frontal Temporal Channels - FC5 & F3 during relaxed state are plotted in Fig. 4a, b, c and d respectively. It is seen that the potential values are found to be lying in the very lower range of 0 to 20 µV.

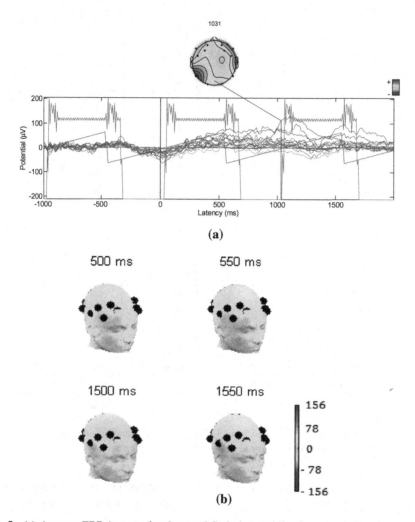

Fig. 5. (a) Average ERP (event related potential) during mobile phone in right exposure state (b) Three-D ERP scalp maps during mobile phone in right exposure state at different latencies (Color figure online)

Similarly, average ERP for entire dataset epoch during EM exposure due to ringing mobile phone kept on right side of the head and its corresponding topographic maps are plotted in Fig. 5a and equivalent 3-D ERP scalp maps are plotted in Fig. 5b, respectively. The scalp map overhead these ERP plots indicates the concentration of average potential values captured across distinct scalp regions at a latency of around 1031 ms which corresponds to the highest variations in event related potential values. It is seen that the average resultant potential rises across right frontal and temporal regions of

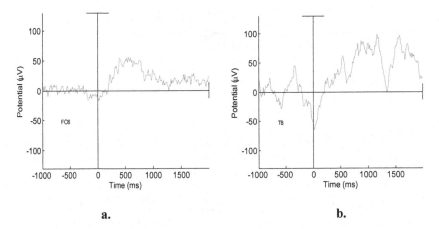

Fig. 6. EEG signal epochs acquired at right frontal-temporal channels (a) FC6 and (b) T8 of EMOTIV neuroheadset during mobile phone in right exposure state (active mode)

brain as indicated by bright red color. The 3D scalp map also indicates the maximum effect on right frontal and temporal regions and is reflected in the 3-D scalp maps depicted in Fig. 5b with red patches across right frontal regions.

The EEG signal epochs acquired across right Frontal Temporal scalp channels – FC6 and T8 during mobile phone in right exposure state are plotted in Fig. 6a and b respectively. It can be observed that the potential values are found to be above 50 µV which are much higher than potential values obtained during relaxed state.

Similar exercise is done to find the average ERP of entire dataset epoch during mobile phone kept on left side of the head. The resultant ERP scalp maps at particular latencies are plotted in Fig. 7a and corresponding ERP scalp maps in 3D are plotted in Fig. 7b respectively. The topographic map overhead these ERP plots indicates the concentration of average potential values captured across distinct scalp regions at a latency of around 1438 ms which corresponds to the highest variations in event related potential values during left exposure condition. It is seen that the average resulting potential rises across Left Frontal and Temporal regions of brain indicated by bright red color. The 3-D topographic map confirms the highest activation of Left Frontal and Temporal regions during radiation exposure and is clear from the 3-D scalp maps of Fig. 7b indicated by bright red shade. It is also clear from the 3-D scalp maps that effect of radiation on right side also persists during left exposure state which indicates the retention of after effects.

The EEG signal epochs acquired across scalp Frontal Channels - AF3, F7 and Frontal Temporal Channels - FC5, F3 during radiation exposure on the left side are plotted in Fig. 8a, b, c and d respectively. It can be seen that the potential values lay above 50 µV which are much higher than potential values obtained during no exposure state.

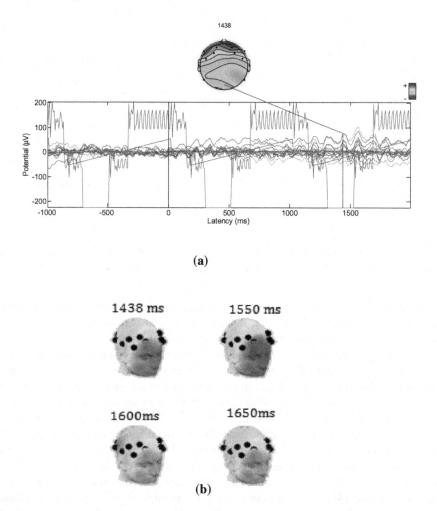

Fig. 7. (a) Average ERP (event related potential) during mobile phone in left exposure state (b) Three-D ERP scalp maps during mobile phone in left exposure state at different latencies (Color figure online)

Thus, it can be observed that the highest ERP activation due to radiation exposure due to vicinity of a mobile phone ringing can be observed at frontal and temporal regions of scalp. It can be easily confirmed from the obtained scalp maps plot. This is because of the intensity of stimulation/performed action corresponding to standard frequency EEG sub band power – delta, theta, alpha, beta or gamma of the EEG signal [22]. The analysis of equivalent band power activation shall be done using machine learning techniques in the future to investigate the effect of radiation due to mobile phone exposure on human brain.

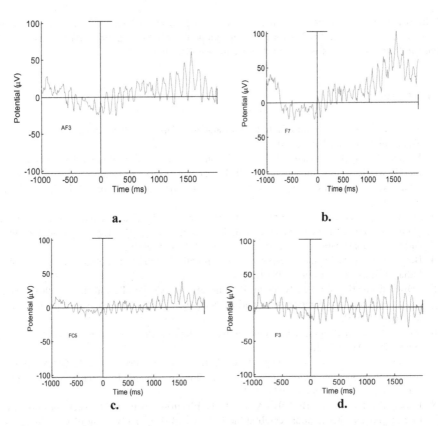

Fig. 8. EEG signal epoch obtained at Frontal Channels (a) AF3, (b) F7, and Frontal Temporal Channels (c) FC5, (d) F3 of EMOTIV neuro-headset during mobile phone in left exposure state

4 Conclusion

An attempt has been made to probe the effect of radiation exposure on human brain signals using EEG when in the vicinity of ringing mobile phone. Event Related Potential analysis and detailed topographic analysis is done to map the acquired EEG data under mobile phone exposure state. It is seen that the strength of potential activation in obtained EEG increases in the vicinity of ringing mobile phone. The Frontal and Temporal Scalp regions are found to be effected by mobile phone usage. It can also be used to analyze the cognitive abilities of human brain. The future work shall include the frequency domain analysis, channel spectral analysis of acquired dataset to map the radiation effect in EEG sub bands *viz.* Delta, Theta, Alpha, Beta and Gamma bands. These explorations may further lead to analysis of depression-related neurological syndromes such as stress, frustration, anxiety, etc.

Acknowledgement. Authors are thankful to management of Manav Rachna International Institute of Research and Studies for providing support to conduct required experiments and Mr. Dheeraj Rathee for his assistance in documenting initial phase of literature summary.

References

1. World Telecommunication/ICT Indicator database, 17th edn., December 2013. International Telecommunication Union (2013)
2. Kumar, A., Singh, T., Kaushal, V.: Radiation exposure during different data operations in mobile wireless communication. In: 2014 Recent Advances in Engineering and Computational Sciences (RAECS), pp. 1–4, 6–8th March 2014. https://doi.org/10.1109/raecs.2014.6799641
3. Stefanics, G., Thuroczy, G., Kellenyi, L., Hernadi, I.: Effects of twenty-minute 3G mobile phone irradiation on event related potential components and early gamma synchronization in auditory oddball paradigm. Neuroscience **157**, 453–462 (2008)
4. Behari, J.: Biological response of mobile phone radiofrequency exposure. Indian J. Exp. Biol. **48**, 959–981 (2010)
5. Tahvanainen, K., Nino, J., Halonen, P., Kuusela, T., Alanko, T.: Effects of cellular phone use on ear canal temperature measured by NTC thermistors. Clin. Physiol. Funct. Imaging **27**, 162–172 (2007)
6. Merhi, Z.O.: Challenging cell phone impact on reproduction: a review. J. Assist. Reprod. Genet. **29**, 293–297 (2012)
7. Mizuno, Y., Moriguchi, Y., Hikage, T., et al.: Effects of W-CDMA 1950 MHz EMF emitted by mobile phones on regional cerebral blood flow in humans. Bioelectromagnetics **30**(7), 536–544 (2009). (PubMed: 19475648)
8. Huber, R., Treyer, V., Borbély, A.A., et al.: Electromagnetic fields, such as those from mobile phones, alter regional cerebral blood flow and sleep and waking EEG. J. Sleep Res. **11**(4), 289–295 (2002). [PubMed: 12464096]
9. Huber, R., Treyer, V., Schuderer, J., et al.: Exposure to pulse-modulated radio frequency electromagnetic fields affects regional cerebral blood flow. Eur. J. Neurosci. **21**(4), 1000–1006 (2005). (PubMed: 15787706)
10. Haarala, C., Aalto, S., Hautzel, H., et al.: Effects of a 902 MHz mobile phone on cerebral blood flow in humans. NeuroReport **14**(16), 2019–2023 (2003). [PubMed: 14600490]
11. Aalto, S., Haarala, C., Bruck, A., et al.: Mobile phone affects cerebral blood flow in humans. J. Cereb. Blood Flow Metab. **26**(7), 885–890 (2006). [PubMed: 16495939]
12. Volkow, N.D., Tomasi, D., Wang, G., et al.: Effects of cell phone radiofrequency signal exposure on brain glucose metabolism. JAMA **305**(8), 808–813 (2011). https://doi.org/10.1001/jama.2011.186
13. Relova, J.L., Pértega, S., Vilar, J.A., López-Martin, E., Peleteiro, M., Ares-Pena, F.: Effects of cell-phone radiation on the electroencephalographic spectra of epileptic patients [telecommunications health & safety]. Antennas Propag. Mag. **52**(6), 173–179 (2010). https://doi.org/10.1109/map.2010.5723262
14. Murat, Z.H., AbdulKadir, R.S.S., Isa, R.M., Taib, M.N.: The effects of mobile phone usage on human brainwave using EEG. In: 2011 UkSim 13th International Conference on Computer Modelling and Simulation (UKSim), 30 March–1 April, pp. 36–41 (2011)
15. Hareuveny, R., Eliyahu, I., Luria, R., Meiran, N., Margaliot, M.: Cognitive effects of cellular phones: a possible role of non-radiofrequency radiation factors. Bioelectromagnetics **32**, 585–588 (2011)

16. Isa, R.M., Pasya, I., Taib, M.N., et al.: Assessment of brainwave asymmetry and hemisphere dominance due to RF radiation. In: 2012 Sixth UKSim/AMSS European Symposium on Computer Modeling and Simulation EMS, pp. 153–157. IEEE (2012)
17. Smitha, C.K., Narayanan, N.K.: Effect of mobile phone radiation on brain using wavelet energy. In: Goh, J. (ed.) The 15th International Conference on Biomedical Engineering. IP, vol. 43, pp. 192–195. Springer, Cham (2014). https://doi.org/10.1007/978-3-319-02913-9_49
18. Smitha, C.K., Narayanan, N.K.: Effect of mobile phone radiation on brain using EEG analysis by Higuichi's fractal dimension method. In: Proceedings SPIE, International Conference on Communication and Electronics System Design, vol. 8760, p. 87601C. https://doi.org/10.1117/12.2012177
19. Isa, R.M., Pasya, I., Taib, M.N., Jahidin, A.H., Omar, W.R.W., Fuad, N., Norhazman, H.: EEG brainwave behaviour due to RF exposure using kNN classification. In: 2013 IEEE 3rd International Conference on System Engineering and Technology (ICSET), 19–20 August 2013, pp. 385–388 (2013). https://doi.org/10.1109/icsengt.2013.6650205
20. Trunk, A., Stefanics, G., Zentai, N., Kovács-Bálint, Z., Thuróczy, G., Hernádi, I.: No effects of a single 3G UMTS mobile phone exposure on spontaneous EEG activity, ERP correlates, and automatic deviance detection. Bioelectromagnetics 34, 31–42 (2013). https://doi.org/10.1002/bem.21740
21. Loughran, S.P., Benz, D.C., Schmid, M.R., Murbach, M., Kuster, N., Achermann, P.: No increased sensitivity in brain activity of adolescents exposed to mobile phone-like emissions. Clin. Neurophysiol. 124(7), 1303–1308 (2013). https://doi.org/10.1016/j.clinph.2013.01.010
22. Bansal, D., Mahajan, R., Roy, S., Rathee, D., Singh, S.: Real-time man–machine interface and control using deliberate eye blink. Int. J. Biomed. Eng. Technol. 18(4), 370–384 (2015)
23. Mahajan, R., Bansal, D.: Depression diagnosis and management using EEG-based affective brain mapping in real time. Int. J. Biomed. Eng. Technol. 18(2), 115–138 (2015)

To Improve Code Structure by Identifying Move Method Opportunities Using Frequent Usage Patterns in Source-Code

Randeep Singh[(⊠)] and Ashok Kumar

Department of Computer Science and Engineering, Maharishi Markandeshwar
University, Mullana-Ambala 133-207, Haryana, India
randeeppoonia@gmail.com,
mailtodr.ashok@redikkmail.com

Abstract. A smelly code is generally an indication of the poor quality of the software and it increases the understandability and maintenance efforts at the software programmer's end. One technique to improve the quality is refactoring. Therefore, in this paper, we have identified the *Feature Envy* code smell and applied the corresponding *Move Method* refactoring. The code smell is tackled using the Frequent Usage Patterns (FUP's) present in the source-code of the software. The FUP's are identified at the method level and theyrepresent the set of member variables that are used by it either directly or indirectly. The identified FUP data is further used to cluster different methods using a newly proposed Clustering algorithm. Moreover, the proposed approach is successfully tested and evaluated on three standard open-source object-oriented software. The obtained results after evaluation confirm the ability of our proposed approach in enhancing the quality of the underlying software system.

Keywords: Code smell · Feature Envy · Move method refactoring
Quality · Cohesion · Frequent usage patterns · Hierarchical clustering

1 Introduction

Software development using object-oriented principle focus on creating classes that bind attributes and methods together. However, this activity is human-centric and it may result in the occurrence of traces of quality issues in the source-code. This ultimately results in a non-optimized system that requires more maintenance efforts. Software maintenance is a necessary phase of software development and it requires more efforts being devoted by the maintenance team side [1]. These involved efforts can be minimized if our software is well maintained. One method for this is to regularly examine the underlying system and move the state and behavior between classes [2]. This activity is known as refactoring and it helps us to remove various kinds of faults (aka code smells) in the source-code of the system. This action results in an increase in understandability of the underlying software system and hence reduced maintenance efforts and cost.

In order to perform refactoring, first of all, it is necessary to identify refactoring opportunities in source-code. Refactoring opportunities are termed as bad smells and

© Springer Nature Singapore Pte Ltd. 2019
A. K. Luhach et al. (Eds.): ICAICR 2018, CCIS 955, pp. 320–330, 2019.
https://doi.org/10.1007/978-981-13-3140-4_29

they identify design or structural flaws of the software system. Martin Fowler has identified various kinds of bad smells and refactoring activities [2]. In fact, there are many studies in the literature that rank different kind of code smells from the programmer's point of view [3, 4, 16, 18]. They have identified Feature Envy as the most commonly occurring smell that requires the most attention. Therefore, in this paper, we have targeted this code smell and proposed a new approach to efficiently identify it. Further, an efficient new clustering algorithm is proposed in this paper in order to perform the move method refactoring. The main contribution of this paper includes:

1. To propose a new, efficient approach (FUP based) to measure the relatedness among member variables and methods of a class.
2. To propose a new belongingness metric to measure the association of a method with the class in which it is present.
3. To propose a new clustering algorithm to ultimately perform the refactoring and to improve the underlying quality of the system.

This whole paper is further divided into following sections: Sect. 2 in this paper details about the survey of the related literature work; Sect. 3 in this paper details about the approach given by us along with a suitable example. Section 4 in this paper discussesabout the experimental setup done and the corresponding obtained results. In the last, Sect. 5 in this paper summarizes the whole research paper and also gives related future work in this direction.

2 Literature Survey

This section of the paper summarizes and discuss related research work already done in the area of the move method refactoring opportunities. The already proposed research work includes various techniques and tools by various researchers.

Steve et al. studied various kinds of code smells [5]. They have identified a total of 22 kinds of different code smells along with the related refactoring task. Foutse et al. studied about the chances of change proneness among classes in a software system [6]. They found that the set of classes that contain bad smells are more change prone as compared to classes without bad smells. Evolution of the bad smells over different versions of a software system was studied by [7, 17]. Based on the study, they found that the total number of code smells present in a software system goes on increasing as the software evolves over time. Rathee et al. also used the concept of usage pattern in improving the cohesion of the underlying software system [15]. Bansiya and Davis proposed a quality metric suite which is capable of determining the underlying software system's quality [8]. This suite is known as Quality Model for Object-Oriented Design i.e. QMOOD. This metric suite defines a total of 11 Object-Oriented design properties and binds them to different design metrics. Similarly, the authors in [9] gives a new approach called Method Book. This approach uses Relational Topic Model (RTM) [10] for detecting opportunities forthe Move Method refactoring.

Besidesthese, several semi/fully-automated tools are proposed to detect different kinds of code smells and to perform the refactoring. JDeodorant was proposed by [11] and this tool is capable of detecting four kinds of code smells in the Java program.

Another tool called iPlasma was developed by [12] for measuring the overall quality of the software system. This tool is capable of detecting various code smells such as duplicate code and various kinds of disharmonies in source-code. InFusion tool [13] is also proposed in the literature and this tool is capable of detecting 20 types of different code smells. This tool is an extension of iPlasma with extended functionalities.

Sincealready large number of approaches and tools were proposed in the literature to detect code smells and to perform the refactoring. They altogether aim at increasing the overall quality of the underlying software system. However, to the best of the author's knowledge, none of the above techniques and tools used the concept of FUP to detect Feature Envy code smell and none has utilized it to perform the move method refactoring.

3 Proposed Approach

This section of our paper gives details about our proposed methodology for identifying the Feature Envy code smell and mitigating the identified code smell by performing the well-known Move Method refactoring. Figure 1 depicts the overview of our proposed approach in this paper.

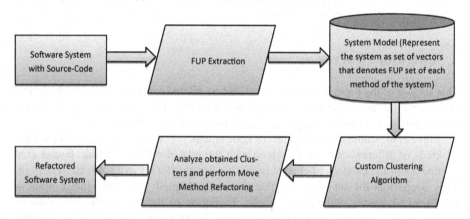

Fig. 1. The proposed approach for Feature Envy code smell identification and Move Method refactoring.

The proposed approach for increasing underlying code quality mainly consists of following four steps:

1. Frequent Usage Pattern (FUP) Extraction.
2. System Modeling.
3. Clustering.
4. Analysis and Refactoring.

These different steps of our proposed approach are explainedfurther in the upcoming subsections.

3.1 FUP Extraction

The first and most important step of our proposed approach is the FUP extraction for different methods and this step takes source-code of a software system as input. This step statically analyzes the source-code and returns all the member variables, which are directly or indirectly used by the underlying method belonging to a software element (mainly class in Object-Oriented software system) as output. The set of member variables constitutes the FUP of the underlying method. The FUP extraction is performed using a custom tool programmed by us and it considers the object-oriented software available with source-code as input and produces the list of member variables accessed by different methods belonging to different classes. Mathematically, this can be represented as follows: let us suppose that the software system consists of total n methods $M_1, M_2, M_3, \ldots\ldots\ldots, M_n$ belonging to different classes, then, this step produces total n sets $F_1, F_2, F_3, \ldots\ldots\ldots, F_n$ representing FUP sets for a corresponding method present in the system.

Any set F_i for method M_i contains the list of member variable names which are accessed by it directly or indirectly. In our custom tool designed for extracting FUP information for a different method, the member variable names in FUP list are maintained in the form *ClassName.MemberVariableName*. This is done based on manual inspection of the source-code and our finding that a software system may contain same variable name belonging to different classes also. The used representation scheme in our proposed approach helps us to uniquely identify different member variable names in FUP list.

In the above considered hypothetical example of Fig. 2, the FUP set for F1 = {C1. M1}, F2 = {C1.M1, C1.M2}, F3 = {C1.M3}, F4 = {C1.M4, C2.M5, C2.M5, C2. M6}, F5 = {C2.M5, C2.M5, C2.M6}, F6 = {C2.M5, C2.M6} and F7 = {C2.M6}. Here, since M7 member variable is not accessed by any of the methods, so, it is not part of any FUP set. The FUP set of F4 also contain member variables M5 and M6 because of indirect reference due to method call made to another method F5. Similarly, we can justify the formation of other FUP sets belonging to different methods in the considered system of Fig. 2.

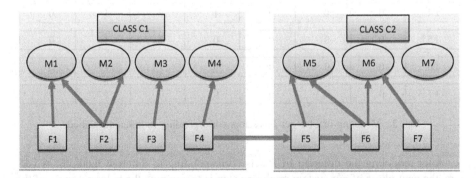

Fig. 2. Sample considered interaction between two classes in a hypothetical software system.

3.2   System Modeling

This is the second step in our proposed approach. After extracting the FUP set corresponding to different methods of the system, the next step is to represent that information in some meaningful format. This representation in our proposed approach is known as *System Modeling*. In our proposed approach, the system is modeled by representing each FUP set corresponding to different methods as a vector of size n where n is the total number of member variables present in the system. For example, for the considered hypothetical example in Fig. 2, the system is modeled by representing each FUP set as a vector of size 7 (total number of member variables). The member variable in the system is assigned a unique index in the vector and the corresponding value represents the frequency with which the corresponding method access the particular member variable (as identified in the FUP set). During system modeling, the FUP vector V_i for method M_i is initialized using the following equation:-

$$V_i[j] = \begin{cases} \geq 1; & \text{if } M_i \text{ uses the member variable at index } j; \\ 0; & \text{otherwise} \end{cases} \tag{1}$$

In the above Eq. (1), the value of $V_i[j]$ is ≥ 1, if the method M_i uses the member variable at index j and corresponding non-zero value represents the frequency with which it access the corresponding member variable. Figure 3 show the system modeling for the hypothetical example considered in the Fig. 2. Here, there are total seven vectors corresponding to different methods considered in the hypothetical example.

	C1.M1	C1.M2	C1.M3	C1.M4	C2.M5	C2.M6	C2.M7
F1	1	0	0	0	0	0	0
F2	1	1	0	0	0	0	0
F3	0	0	1	0	0	0	0
F4	0	0	0	1	2	1	0
F5	0	0	0	0	2	1	0
F6	0	0	0	0	1	1	0
F7	0	0	0	0	0	1	0

Fig. 3. Modeling of FUP set as vectors corresponding to different methods.

After modeling the different FUP sets corresponding to different methods as vectors, the next phase of our system modeling step is to compute the belongingness of the method to its original class. This is performed using the following proposed metric known as $Method_{Belong\_ness}$.

$$Method_{Belong_{ness}} = MB_i = \frac{InDeg_i}{InDeg_i + OutDeg_i} \tag{2}$$

Here, $InDeg_i$ is known as the In-Degree for Method M_i and it measures the total number of member variables that M_i accesses within the original class. Similarly, $OutDeg_i$ is known as Out-Degree for method M_i and it measures the total number of member variables that it accesses outside the original class. The value of the proposed belongingness metric MB_i lies between 0 and 1. More the value of $InDeg_i$ as compared to $OutDeg_i$, higher will be the belongingness metric value and vice-versa. A higher value for the MB_i metric indicates that the corresponding method is in the intended original class and any lower value for the same is an indication of feature envy code smell and it need to be refactored using the move method technique in its intended different class. For the example considered in the Fig. 3, the relatedness value for method $F4 = 1/1 + 3 = 0.25$ and the rest of the methods have relatedness value = 1. A lower value for F4 as compared to rest of the functions in the class shows that this method needs to be relocated to its intended place in another class.

3.3 Clustering

The third step in our proposed approach is to perform the complete linkage based hierarchical clustering in order to group different methods. The input to the hierarchical clustering algorithm is the belongingness score of different methods with different classes present in the software. This belongingness score with a particular class is computed using Eq. 1 as mentioned above. The belongingness score for the example considered in the Fig. 3 is shown in Table 1.

Table 1. Belongingness score of different methods with different classes.

	C1	C2
F1	1	0
F2	1	0
F3	1	0
F4	0.25	0.75
F5	0	1
F6	0	1
F7	0	1

The belongingness score as shown in Table 1 is used to perform clustering using the custom clustering algorithm specially designed for the problem. The algorithmic steps of the newly given clustering algorithm are mentioned in Fig. 4. The proposed clustering algorithm works iteratively and in each iteration it finds a (method, class) pair having the highest value for belongingness score. After identifying such pair, the corresponding method is added to the cluster group identified by the class number in the pair. In our proposed clustering algorithm, a total number of identified clusters is equal to the total number of classes in the system. These clusters are initially empty and after each iteration of the proposed algorithm, one of the methods is added to the intended cluster denoting unique class in the system.

Proposed Clustering Algorithm

1. $C = \{C_1=\phi, C_2=\phi, \dots , C_m=\phi\}$ /* Cluster Set. Total no. of clusters   are

    equal to the total number of classes i.e. m */

2. $|N_m| = n$ /* n is the total number of methods in system & */

3. $|N_c| = m$ /* m is the total number of classes in system */

4. While ($|N_m| < 0$) /* iteratively cluster different methods in cluster set C */

5. {

6. For j : 1 to $|N_c|$ /* read belongingness score for every class */

7. {

8.   Find the pair (i, j) from input data such that the corresponding entry is maximum.

9.   /* Here, i is the method number and j is the class number & the entry (i, j) de-

    notes

10.   that method i has highest belongingness with class j. */

11.   Add method i to the cluster number j. i.e. $C_j = \{F_i\}$ /* method belonging to class j

    */

12. $|N_m| = |N_m| - 1$

13. }

14. }

Fig. 4. Proposed clustering algorithm.

3.4   Analysis and Refactoring

This is the last phase of our proposed approach. In this phase, the obtained clusters are submitted to the software maintenance team. The team examines each of the identified move method refactoring opportunities in the system. Later, based on the analysis, the team can grant for move method refactoring or simply ignore suggested refactoring. The involvement of the maintenance team helps us to involve human knowledge in refactoring and thus improves the overall accuracy of the proposed approach.

4 Experimental Setup and Obtained Results

Experimental setup planned for evaluating the proposed approach is discussed in detail in this section of the paper. This section specifies the software systems considered for validating the proposed approach. Moreover, the experimental results are also presented and discussed.

4.1 Studied Dataset

For the evaluation of the approach of this paper, three standard open-source Object-Oriented software are considered. The considered systems are commonly used among the research community and are taken from the standard GitHub repository. The considered systems are of different sizes and belong to a different domain. Table 2 summarizes different system considered for experimentation.

Table 2. Studied software systems.

S. No.	System name	Version	# Classes	# Modules	# Connections
1	Apache commons email	1.5	20	3	98
2	JUnit	4.5	131	8	432
3	Apache commons logging	1.2	14	2	65

4.2 Experimentation and Analysis Steps

We analyze the software systems considered for experimentation using the built tool. The tool statically analyzes the source code and gives the FUP set corresponding to each of the methods in the system. Then, the system modeling is done and FUP set of every method is represented in the form of vectors. Further, clustering is performed using the proposed clustering algorithm. Finally, the clusters are analyzed and the underlying system is refactored using move method approach.

In order to evaluate the proposed approach, well-known modularization metric classed *TurboMQ* is used [14]. This metric measures the modularity of the system in terms of InDegree and OutDegree of the module/ cluster. This metric gives a perfect balance between cohesion and coupling computed at the module level. In our work, this metric is chosen since move method refactoring aims at placing a method into its intended class and thus minimizing the coupling (measured as OutDegree) and maximizing the cohesion (measured as InDegree). Any improvement in the value of this metric is an indication of the enhanced quality of the system.

Table 3 shows the value of TurboMQ metric in two different situations, namely original software system, and modified software system obtained after performing a refactoring operation.

Figure 5 displays the result of Table 3 in the form of bar-chart plot. It shows the comparison of an obtained TurboMQ metric score of different studied systems before refactoring and after refactoring. From the plots, it is clear that after performing

Table 3. Obtained results after experimentation and evaluation.

S. No.	Software name	TurboMQ score	
		Before	After
1	Apache commons email	1.57	1.95
2	Junit	0.45	0.58
3	Apache commons logging	0.96	1.21

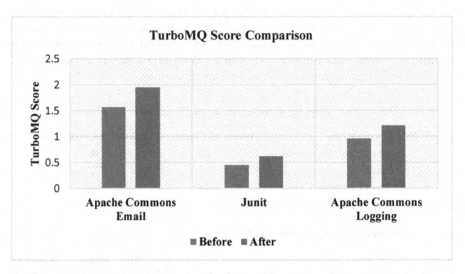

Fig. 5. TurboMQ score comparison of different software systems.

refactoring using the proposed approach, the underlying quality of the software system is increased (an increase of 20% to 35% in overall quality of the system).

5   Conclusion and Future Work

The aim of this research paper is to give a fresh approach to improving the overall quality of a software system. Hence, the proposed approach reduces the maintenance efforts. The quality of the software system is improved by identifying one probabilistic area in the source-code known as feature envy and removing it by performing move method refactoring. The paper proposes a FUP based approach to detect feature envy code smell. This paper also proposes a new clustering algorithm specially designed to detect feature envy and to suggest move method opportunities to the programmer. The new clustering algorithm utilizes the system modeled based on the FUP information extracted from the source-code at the method level. Finally, the suggested refactoring opportunities are examined by the maintenance team in order to finally approve or reject the suggested move method refactoring tasks. Later on, the approved refactoring is performed in order to improve the overall quality of the software system.

The future work related to our proposed approach can be many. One direction can in checking the feasibility of FUP based approach in detecting another type of code smells. Another direction can be in the evaluation of the proposed approach against other tools present in the literature. Finally, but not the last, efforts can be done by fully automating the proposed approach with human knowledge present in the form of some threshold values to the system.

References

1. Fuggetta, A.: Software process: a roadmap. In: Proceedings Conference on the Future of Software Engineering, Limerick, Ireland, pp. 25–34 (2000)
2. Fowler, M., Beck, K., Brant, J., Opdyke, W., Roberts, D.: Refactoring: Improving the Design of Existing Code. Addison Wesley, Boston (1999)
3. D'Ambros, M., Bacchelli, A., Lanza, M.: On the impact of design flaws on software defects. In: 10th International Conference on Quality Software (QSIC), pp. 23–31 (2010)
4. Sjoberg, D.I., Yamashita, A., Anda, B., Mockus, A., Dyba, T.: Quantifying the effect of code smells on maintenance effort. IEEE Trans. Softw. Eng. 39(8), 1144–1156 (2013)
5. Counsell, S., Hamza, H., Hierons, R.M.: An Empirical investigation of code smell 'deception' and research contextualization through Paul's criteria. J. Comput. Inf. Technol.-CIT 18 4, 333–340 (2010)
6. Khomh, F., Penta, M.D., Guéhéneuc, Y.: An exploratory study of the impact of code smells on software change proneness. In: Proceedings of the 16th Working Conference on Reverse Engineering (WCRE), 13–16 October. IEEE Computer Society Press, Lille (2009)
7. Chatzigeorgiou, A., Manakos, A.: Investigating the evolution of bad smells in object-oriented code. In: 7th International Conference on Quality of Information and Communications Technology (QUATIC), pp. 106–115 (2010)
8. Bansiya, J., Davis, C.G.: A hierarchical model for object-oriented design quality assessment. IEEE Trans. Softw. Eng. 28(1), 4–17 (2002)
9. Oliveto, R., Gethers, M., Bavota, G., Poshyvanyk, D., Lucia, A. De.: Identifying method friendships to remove the feature envy bad smell. In: 33rd International Conference on Software Engineering (ICSE), pp. 820–823 (2011)
10. Chang, J., Blei, D.: Hierarchical relational models for document networks. Ann. Appl. Stat. 4, 124–150 (2010)
11. Tsantalis, N., Chaikalis, T., Chatzigeorgiou, A.: JDeodorant: identification and removal of typechecking bad smells. In: Proceedings of CSMR, pp. 329–331 (2008)
12. Marinescu, C., Marinescu, R., Mihancea, P., Ratiu, D., Wettel, R.: iPlasma: an integrated platform for quality assessment of object-oriented design. In: Proceedings of 21st International Conference on Software Maintenance (ICSM) (2005)
13. InFusion. http://www.intooitus.com/inFusion.html
14. Mitchell, B.S., Traverso, M., Mancoridis, S.: An architecture for distributing the computation of software clustering algorithms. In: Proceedings of the IEEE/IFIP Conference on Software Architecture (2001)
15. Rathee, A., Chhabra, J.K.: Improving cohesion of a software system by performing usage pattern-based clustering. In: International Conference on Smart Computing and Communication (ICSCC), vol. 125, pp. 740–746. Elsevier (2018). Proc. Comput. Sci.

16. Palomba, F., Bavota, G., Penta, M.D., Fasano, F., Oliveto, R., Lucia, A.D.: A large-scale empirical study on the lifecycle of code smell co-occurrences. Inf. Softw. Technol. **99**, 1–10 (2018)
17. Taibi, D., Janes, A., Lenarduzzi, V.: How developers perceive smells in source code: a replicated study. Inf. Softw. Technol. **92**, 223–235 (2017)
18. Singh, S., Kaur, S.: A systematic literature review: refactoring for disclosing code smells in object oriented software. Ain Shams Eng. J. (2017, in press)

An Ontology Based Earthquake Recommendation System

Sarika Jain[1], Sonia Mehla[1], and Apoorv Gaurav Agarwal[2(✉)]

[1] National Institute of Technology, Kurukshetra, India
jasarika@nitkkr.ac.in, soniamehla9@gmail.com
[2] Birla Institute of Technology, Mesra, India
apoorv.agarwal.aga@gmail.com

Abstract. According to geographical statistics, 54% of the land in India is vulnerable to earthquakes, and several populous regions fall under Zone 4 or 5 in levels of seismicity. It is believed that a comprehensive earthquake recommendation system will significantly reduce the number of emergency services that are dispensed when disaster strikes and will also effectively minimize casualties. Various techniques have been employed to successively create such a recommendation system which provides efficiency in managing the dispensing of the emergency services. The paper focuses on determining the immediate course of action that should be taken during emergencies like earthquake to mitigate the damages to life and property using Ontology supported rule-based reasoning and case-based reasoning, i.e. the actions are determined using similar cases from the past, if any, and validated through existing rules and experience.

Keywords: Earthquake · Earthquake recommendation system
Ontology · Rule-based reasoning · Case-based reasoning

1 Introduction

An earthquake is a sudden movement of the Earth, caused by the abrupt release of the accumulated strain from the tectonic plates. For a long time, the accumulated strain forces of these tectonic plates have shaped the Earth causing the surface to slowly move over and brush against each other. This plate movement is generally gradual but sometimes when the plates are bound together, they have no outlet to release the accumulating energy. Strong enough accumulated energy causes the plate to break free of each other thereby producing the abrupt movement [1]. An earthquake occurring in a populated area can cause extensive damage to life and property. If a man-made structure (a building, road, bridge, etc.) is built across a fault or has a poor foundation with weak materials, the ground displacement during an earthquake could seriously damage or rip apart that structure. Dams or levees along a river can be ruptured by an earthquake which would then flood the area, damaging the buildings and sweeping away people. Tsunamis, created by seismic tremors, also cause a great deal of damage. Broken gas lines and power lines, or tipped over stoves can create local fires adding to the damage caused by the earthquake. Most of the hazards to the people come from the destruction of man-made structures—getting buried or crushed in a collapsing building,

© Springer Nature Singapore Pte Ltd. 2019
A. K. Luhach et al. (Eds.): ICAICR 2018, CCIS 955, pp. 331–340, 2019.
https://doi.org/10.1007/978-981-13-3140-4_30

drowning in a flood caused by a broken dam or levee, getting buried under a landslide, or damages caused by a fire. The damages caused by these hazards can be bridled by taking some timely countermeasures, and the project *'An Earthquake Recommendation system'* will play a cardinal role in tackling these hazards. India falls quite prominently on the global seismic belt (called the Alpine- Himalayan belt, which runs in an east-west direction), and hence, this undertaking is of much interest to India.

Parts of the Indian subcontinent are earthquake-prone with many of the populous regions lying in the Zone level 4 and 5. The reason for the intensity and high frequency of earthquakes is the Indian plate driving into Asia at a rate of approximately 47 mm/year. Timely warnings of an earthquake could spare time to take precautionary actions such as evacuating unsafe structures, taking cover in safe locations, stopping elevators, etc. to safeguard public. Several countries, including Japan and Mexico, have existing earthquake early-warning systems. As such, with the development in technology, there is much at stake, leading to the rising need of an emergency recommendation system which can both forewarn and suggest helpful measures to be taken by the personnel to ensure public safety.

Recommendations during an earthquake can greatly aid the organization in providing assistance for the damage mitigation process. Since no time will be available for the review of these recommendations, the actions provided must be accurately calculated with the efficient gathering and analysis of the data and decision-making for an earthquake scenario. These recommendations will also have to be fine-tuned considering a lot of factors like population density, building structures and the topography of the place. The aim of this system is to generate recommended actions for the operator in emergency situations like earthquakes. This system would be deployed all over the city, interconnected, and would provide an interface displaying the advised actions to be considered by the user. The targeted audience are chiefly the Government Organizations, viz. the PSUs and NGOs. The system can also serve as a basic model for other public/private institutions, which can enhance and customize it for better user experience. The recommendation system is expected to significantly alleviate major losses to people and infrastructure. It analyzes the resources that were provided or needed at the past instances. Thereafter, it attempts to search for the most similar case, if any, while also considering the imperative details and the geographic location. Various rules are applied on the data to analyze the actions if a similar case isn't found. Next, the system provides extensive lists of actions and resources, for example, the number of ambulances, helicopters, emergency contact numbers, required material aids and other likely desideratum. An Email is sent along with a SMS to the required authorities and personnel enlisting details of the Earthquake along with the recommended actions that can serve as prompt response to the immediate concerns.

The system makes use of the rule-based reasoning and the case-based reasoning supported by ontologies, which play a crucial role in reinforcing the machine readable logics that are needed to facilitate automation and can be effectively used for routing data and controlling the workflow of activities while assisting in query processing. The ontology can be divided into various branches which can contain the past records, the data of a place where module has been installed, the organizations which can be contacted, the emergency levels of an earthquake and the corresponding actions for a threat level. After referring the knowledge base, ontology can be used to refer the rules that have been defined for the adaption of the cases while new actions can also be recommended based on the generation rules.

2 Related Works

The Japan Meteorological Agency (JMA) has two Earthquake Early Warning schemes-one for the National Meteorological and Hydrological Services (NMHS) and the other for the general public. The agency is alerted upon detecting P-wave from the installed seismometers and a rough area of the earthquake's epicenter is predicted and analyzed. People residing in the affected prefectures are then warned using these rough predictions via TV and radio if a strong shaking is expected [2]. The Earthquake Early Warning helps minimizing the damages caused by an earthquake by making the people prepare for the upcoming calamity. People may take cover under table or steer clear of dangerous areas such as cliffs or lifts, trains may be stopped, and factory proceedings may be stopped before the shaking reaches them to minimize the damages.

The California Governor's Office of Emergency Services (CalOES) has been set up in California as a cabinet level agency which is responsible for providing recommendations for response actions taken by the local entities and measures that the general public can take for minimizing the damage in case of an emergency. In case of an Earthquake, the director of the agency requests California Earthquake Prediction Evaluation Council to provide a scientific evaluation regarding the short-term elevated likelihood of a damaging earthquake. A conference is held which then provides the recommended actions for the local government that helps in mitigating the damages.

Recent technological developments had led to an advancement in Mobile-based Emergency Response System (MERS) to automatically extract information from Short Message Service (SMS). The algorithm for Mobile-based Emergency Response System (MERS) is generally based on a maximum entropy statistical model which uses the ontology model to increase the efficiency of an information extraction system. The model makes use of various predefined functions which assists in estimating the probability of a certain expression appearing in a certain SMS texts. The algorithm comprises four main functions: collecting the unstructured information from an emergency SMS; extracting and aggregating the information; calculating the similarity of SMS texts; generating query and presenting the results [12].

In 2009, an ontology-based system was discussed for generating and managing the emergency alert notifications that are accessible to different kinds of people, paying special attention to impaired people and situational disabilities (e.g., smoke during a fire can cause low vision problems). By adapting alerts to different devices and users, blind or deaf people can be communicated using the Emergency Management Systems (EMSs) who otherwise are unreachable by usual channels [3]. Ontology was also used to address the information needs for sharing and integrating emergency notification messages over distinct emergency response information systems providing accessibility under different conditions and for different kind of users [4]. The research was further extended to include the concepts about evacuation, modelling the evacuation routes and procedures [5], which was later developed into a training system [6]. Efforts have been made to design and develop ontologies for an earthquake simulation grid such as

SERVOGrid project which introduces a web-based CBR retrieval system for performing the code selection for the earthquake simulation codes [7].

India currently lacks a proper, functioning Earthquake recommendation system or an early-warning system like other countries. Since the frequency of major earthquakes isn't very high in India, it is felt that early-warning system is not a primary need at the moment. However, there is an emerging necessity to create a citywide situational awareness and the required emergency management, helping the various experts in the earthquake management and city personnel in taking immediate decision in the state of earthquake emergencies [8], thereby reducing the number of casualties and efficiently dealing with the aftermath of an earthquake.

3 Materials and Methods

The damages due to earthquake are based on a lot of factors such as the magnitude of the earthquake, the population density of the area, building structures, density and their age, etc. As such, there is a need of a common understanding of the structure of information. The structure must be able to separate the domain and operational knowledge without affecting the reuse or the ability to analyze the domain knowledge. This is achieved through the use of Ontology. Ontology plays a crucial role in reinforcing the machine readable logics needed to facilitate automation and can be effectively used for routing data and controlling the workflow of activities while assisting in query processing. Ontology facilitates knowledge sharing and reuse, and have become a common denominator to structural real-life data [9] when it comes to address the semantic interoperability. In this paper, these recent advances were taken into consideration and a super ontology-based model [10] for our Knowledge base, designed in Protégé 5.2 and represented using OWL2, was used for organizing and storing the valuable earthquake data. The domain knowledge fed into the ontology consists of subclasses pertaining to the geography of the place, population density, the building topological structure and age of the building which will be fed by experts while installing the system in a city. The operational branch of the ontology will keep records of the emergency services which can be contacted in case of an emergency. The originated Knowledge base serves as the knowledge database which is integrated with all the sub-parts of the system. Various expert's knowledge are stored in the rule base of the knowledge base while consequences of the past earthquakes are stored in the case base. This enables all the past experiences and expert's knowledge to come under the same roof. Owing to the large dataset, the chronical cases were stored in a relational database developed using PostgreSQL improving the scalability and efficiency. The rule definitions used for generating the recommended actions from the procedural knowledge has been stored in the rule base [11].

Recommended actions were generated by applying Case based reasoning on the Ontology. Case based reasoning proves to be a convenient approach for decision support based on the knowledge and the previous actions taken by the authorities. These actions can be easily adapted to suit the situation. However, the demerits of this approach lies with the case with low similarity to the past situations making the adaptation somewhat less consistent with the situation on hand. Cases are the basis of any Case based reasoning system: a system without cases cannot be considered as a case-based system. However, using only cases makes it difficult to distinguish from a database retrieval system. This results in poor productivity due to inefficient retrieval based upon case-by-case search of the complete case base. This lack of heuristic knowledge is taken care of making the use of Rule based reasoning for the cases with low similarity to the past earthquakes, making the combined module an effective model for handling Knowledge-based structure [13]. Jena API has been used for accessing the ontology and applying the rules.

The input resources will feed the real time data to the system and would be processed and parsed for retrieving the earthquake properties. Knowledge Treasure, containing the ontologies and historical data in databases, is used for storing the details of the current earthquake. The input resources comprises the installed sensors in the city and the electronic-mail notification service provided by https://www.usgs.gov/. The installed sensor groups consists of Raspberry pi with an attached accelerometer to measure the intensity of shaking and determining the approximate earthquake magnitude. The generated report is then uploaded to the server in JSON format by these Raspberry pi units. This report, received by the server, is parsed to obtain the desired earthquake properties.

The Knowledge Base is analyzed using the parsed information so as to retrieve the case having similarity with the current earthquake scenario. Similarity value is calculated for retrieving the similar events from the Case Base with 0 being not similar and 1 being fully similar. The total similarity value is calculated by:

$$S = \frac{\sum_{i=1}^{n} \sum_{j=1}^{m} \left(1 - \left(\frac{C_{ij} - X_i}{\max(C_i) - \min(C_i)}\right) * W_i\right)}{N}. \tag{1}$$

where S_{ij} signifies the similarity value of the new case when compared to the old case. N is the number of parameters, C_{ij} is the value of the parameter i of the case j, X_i is the input value of the parameter i. W is the weight assigned to each parameter which will vary as per the city with the value stored in the ontology along with the associated unit information [13].

The system was implemented with the above formula and after some trial cases it was found that the actions can only be effectively adapted using the adaptation rules to meet the current situation if the Total Similarity Value is greater than 0.6953. However, if the Total Similarity Value is found out to be less than 0.6953, Rule Based Reasoner Module is applied to generate the new recommendations as per the rules defined in the ontology. The rules defined for the Rule Based Reasoner Module depends on the location of the Raspberry Pi sending the signals, its population density, the amount of services present in the location and the magnitude of the earthquake to calculate the estimated damage and deploy the Emergency Services likewise.

The occurrence of an earthquake causes a message prompt to be sent to the Operator for logging into the site for viewing the recommended actions. These actions are displayed on the site along with their clarifications and a framework which allows the operator to make changes to these recommendations and take actions accordingly. The framework is also associated with a server which can be used to send SMS and E-

Mail to the associated Authorities and City Personnel. The actions taken are passed to the server as feedback and recorded in the database for future usage. The pseudo code [13] used by the system is shown in Fig. 1.

Input: Parsed Information from the JSON file
Output: Most Similar Case with the degree of Similarity
Local Variables: Case A is retrieved from the knowledge base with its features- magnitude, location, date, etc. Weight W is the predefined weight factor of the feature. Similarity S is the calculated similarity between the properties if cases. Maximum similarity MS is the similarity of the most similar case.

Begin
    For each case A in the Knowledge Base
        Begin
            For *magnitude* feature, direct difference is calculated using above formula.
            For *location* feature, value 1 is added if the strings are equal. If not, difference in population density and topology is taken into consideration and total percentage change is added.
            For *date* feature, difference between the years is used while the maximum-minimum period is set be 10. The difference is subtracted from 1 and the final value is added.
            Calculate the average similarity of each retrieved case, multiplying each feature with its weight.
            If MS < S, then MS=S
        End
    If 0.70 ≤ S ≥ 1.0, Similarity is high do
        Begin
            Retrieve the case with similarity MS
            Calculate the difference between features and adjust the advices
        End
    If S ≤ 0.69, Similarity is low do
        Pass the features of the new case to the ontology to apply the pre-defined rules and generate the advices. Specific rules are designed for the different locations signifying the emergency level based on the magnitude of the earthquake.
    End

Fig. 1. Pseudo code for similarity measurement of the cases

4   Case Study

The severity of earthquakes in India might not be that high but there were three major earthquake in the past three decades. The damage caused by the earthquake could not be contained due to a lack of preparedness. The Knowledge Base has been fed with the data of the actions taken by the Government and the NGOs in the three major recent earthquake events [14]. Although most of the earthquake ranged from 3–5.5 on Richter scale, the lack of preparedness and the late response in the rescue only increases the destruction severity (Table 1).

Different units have been associated in the ontology for each field. Sample Run 1 and 2 aforementioned are among the various experimental runs conducted for the project.

Table 1. Table showing the dataset stored in the database.

Properties	Case 1	Case 2	Case 3
Date	26/01/2001	30/09/1993	08/10/2005
Magnitude	7.7	6.2	7.6
Location	Gujarat	Maharashtra	Kashmir
Deaths	20000	9745	13000
Injured	167000	16000	20000
Blankets	106000	8000	10000
Durries	8000	6000	7500
Tents	550	400	600
Sheets	1040	800	1200
Petrol	3104	2500	3500
Matchbox	5000	3000	5200
Pulses	200	210	250
Rice	400	350	420
Health center	991	800	1000
Hospitals	410	200	450
Doctors	550	180	600
Bandages	550	300	500
Kerosene	5719	4000	4500
Cranes	831	500	900
Bulldozers	395	200	450
Trucks	2679	2000	3000
Dumpers	1603	1200	1600
Ambulance	1603	1200	1600
Gas-Cutters	614	285	670
Helicopters	40	28	55
SRPF	10	8	12
CRPF	8	5	9
CISF	9	4	10
RAF	4	2	5
Police	3000	2800	3500

4.1 Sample Run 1

Input: Assuming an earthquake occurs on Ahemdabad, Gujarat of magnitude 7.4 on 19/8/2017, the Raspberry Pi passes the location: *Ahemdabad, Gujarat*, magnitude: *7.4* and date: *19/8/2017*. The information for Ahemdabad's population density and topology is already stored in the ontology.

Processing: Maximum Similarity MS = (1 − ((7.6 − 7.4)/10) * 1 + 1 * 1 + 1 − ((2017 − 2005)/10)*0.6))/3 = 0.90

Output: The Sample input shows 90% similarity with the Kashmir Earthquake, utilizes the rules defined in the ontology and displays the recommended actions as (Tables 2, 3 and 4):

Table 2. Table showing the output for humanitarian assistance.

Material aid		Medical aid	
Blankets	50000–80000	Health_centres	400–600
Match_boxes	2000–3500	Hospitals	300–400
Petrol	1000–2000		
Plastic_sheets	600–900		
Tents	500–800		

Table 3. Table showing the output for search and rescue.

Relief equipment		Rescue teams	
Cranes	400–650	Army	20–30
Gas Cutters	300–500	Police	1500–2500
Jeeps	800–1500	SRPF	2–4
Loaders	1000–2000	RAF	1–3
Bulldozers	150–300	CISF	5–8

Table 4. Table showing the output for rehabilitation and recovery

Food & rations	
Dal	200–220
Rice	400–450
Kerosene	4700–5500

4.2 Sample Run 2

Input: Assuming an earthquake occurs on Koynanagar of magnitude 6.0 on 19/8/2017, the Raspberry Pi passes the location: *Koynanagar*, magnitude: *5.0* and date: *19/8/2017*. The information for Koynanagar's population density and topology is already stored in the ontology.

Processing: Maximum Similarity $MS = (1 - ((6.2 - 6.0)/10)*1 + 0 + 1 - ((2017 - 2005)/10)*0.6))/ 3 = 0.567$

Output: The Sample input shows a maximum of 56.7% similarity with the Kashmir Earthquake. Thus the system uses predefined rules in the ontology to generate and display the recommended actions as (Tables 5, 6 and 7):

Table 5. Table showing the output for humanitarian assistance.

Material aid		Medical aid	
Blankets	30000–40000	Health_Centres	100–200
Match_Boxes	1000–1500	Hospitals	150–200
Petrol	700–900		
Plastic_Sheets	300–600		
Tents	300–600		

Table 6. Table showing the output for search and rescue.

Relief equipment		Rescue teams	
Cranes	200–450	Army	10–20
Gas Cutters	100–200	Police	500–1000
Jeeps	300–700	SRPF	1–2
Loaders	500–700	RAF	1
Bulldozers	50–100	CISF	2–4

Table 7. Table showing the output for rehabilitation and recovery

Food & rations	
Dal	80–120
Rice	100–150
Kerosene	1700–2500

5 Conclusion

The Paper focuses on determining the immediate course of action that should be taken during emergencies like earthquake to mitigate the damages to life and property using Ontology supported rule-based reasoning and case-based reasoning, i.e. the actions are determined using similar cases from the past, if any, and validated through existing rules and experience. As pointed out, the need for a recommendation situation arises due to the generation of immediate advices that reduces the damage to life and property by a huge margin. The suggestions are effectively provided on detection of the seismic activity based on the magnitude and population density of the place. The suggestions along with their reasoning can be reviewed by an Operator and thereby sent to the authorized personnel through SMS and E-Mails. This significantly reduces the response time and ensures the effective management of Emergency Services and also helps in mitigating the loss of lives. The collaboration of rule-based reasoning and case-based reasoning can counter the others' demerits and increase the efficiency of the system. The system can also serve as a basic model for other public/private institutions, which can enhance and customize it for better user experience. The advisory system is expected to significantly alleviate major losses to people and infrastructure.

Further work can be done by considering the post-earthquake calamities like floods, tsunamis, landslides or fires and expanding the research to mitigate the loss by these calamities. The advices generated can also be used for creating an efficient plan and devising an evacuation route. The recommendation system can also be expanded to include other natural disasters as well. With the collaboration of an early warning system, the recommendation system can keep the destruction caused during such a natural disaster to a bare minimum.

Acknowledgement. This research was partially supported by Defense Research and Development Organization. The author Dr. Sarika Jain is the principle investigator and the author Ms Sonia Mehla is Junior Research Fellow in this sponsored research project. Insight and expertise was also provided by other staff of the project that greatly assisted the research. We thank the members of the first project review committee meeting whose discussions initiated this part of the project.

References

1. Shedlock, K.M., Pakiser, L.C.: Earthquakes information. https://pubs.usgs.gov/gip/earthq1/earthqkgip.html
2. Japan Meteorological Agency. http://www.jma.go.jp/jma/indexe.html
3. Malizia, A., Acuña, P., Aedo, I., Díaz, P., Onorati, T.: An emergency notification system for all. Int. J. Emerg. Manag. **6**(3–4), 302–316 (2009)
4. Malizia, A., Onorati, T., Díaz, P., Aedo, I., Paliza, F.A.: An ontology for emergency notification systems accessibility. Expert Syst. Appl. **37**(4), 3380–3391 (2010)
5. Onorati, T., Malizia, A., Díaz, P., Aedo, I.: Modeling an ontology on accessible evacuation routes for emergencies. Expert Syst. Appl. **41**(16), 7124–7134 (2014)
6. Luo, H., Peng, X., Zhong, B.: Application of ontology in emergency plan management of metro operation. Procedia Eng. **164**, 158–165 (2016)
7. Aktas, M.S., Pierce, M., Fox, G.C.: A web based conversational case-based recommender system for ontology aided metadata discovery. In: Fifth IEEE/ACM International Workshop on Grid Computing, pp. 69–75(2004)
8. Jain, S.: Intelligent decision support for unconventional emergencies. In: Valencia-García, R., Paredes-Valverde, M.A., Salas-Zárate, M., Alor-Hernández, G. (eds.) Exploring Intelligent Decision Support Systems. SCI, vol. 764, pp. 199–219. Springer, Cham (2018). https://doi.org/10.1007/978-3-319-74002-7_10
9. Mishra, S., Malik, S., Jain, N.K., Jain, S.: A realist framework for ontologies and the semantic web. Procedia Comput. Sci. **70**, 483–495 (2015)
10. Malik, S., Mishra, S., Jain, N.K., Jain, S.: Devising a super ontology. Procedia Comput. Sci. **70**, 785–792 (2015)
11. Mishra, S., Jain, S.: A study of various approaches and tools on ontology. In: IEEE Conference CICT in ABES College of Engineering, pp. 57–61 (2015)
12. Zia, S.S., Akhtar, P., Mala, I., Memon, A.R.: Clinical Decision Support System: A Hybrid Reasoning Approach
13. Amailef, K., Lu, J.: Ontology-supported case-based approach for intelligent m-Government emergency response services. Decis. Support Syst. **55**(1), 79–97 (2013)
14. Details of the actions and aids provided by the organization has been taken from http://www.ndmindia.nic.in/recentdisaster/ and http://www.adrc.asia/counterpart_report/

An ANN Based Approach for Software Fault Prediction Using Object Oriented Metrics

Rajdeep Kaur[(⊠)] and Sumit Sharma

Department of Computer Science Engineering, Chandigarh University,
Gharuan, Mohali, Punjab, India
chahal.rajdeep03@gmail.com, cu.sumitsharma@gmail.com

Abstract. During recent years, the enormous increase in demand for software products has been experienced. High quality software is the major demand of users. Predicting the faults in early stages will improve the quality of software and apparently reduce the development efforts or cost. Fault prediction is majorly based on the selection of technique and the metrics to predict the fault. Thus metrics selection is a critical part of software fault prediction. Currently techniques been evaluated based on traditional set of metrics. There is a need to identify the different techniques and evaluate them on the bases of appropriate metrics. In this research, Artificial neural network is used. For classification task, ANN is one of the most effective technique. Artificial neural network based SFP model is designed for classification in this study. Prediction is performed on the basis of object-oriented metrics. 5 object oriented metrics from CK and Martin metric sets are selected as input parameters. The experiments are performed on 18 public datasets from PROMISE repository. Receiver operating characteristic curve, accuracy, and Mean squared error are taken as performance parameters for the prediction task. Results of the proposed systems signify that ANN provides significant results in terms of accuracy and error rate.

Keywords: Fault · Software fault prediction · Machine learning
Artificial intelligence · Neural network

1 Introduction

During recent years, the enormous increase in demand for software products has been experienced. This enormous rise in production henceforth of software products leads to the birth of various issues [1]. Reliability, security, and quality are the basic needs of users. Fulfillment of these requirements leads to the development of increased sized and complex software. Reliability and quality can be achieved through the testing process by detecting and removing defect but it requires time, efforts and extra cost, which makes it complex and time-consuming activity [2–4]. Software system undergoes errors, faults, and failures [4]. The error is a distinction among the output received and expected output. It is a human mistake that results in the incorrect output. It arises due to unspecified inputs or output, lack of understanding between user and development team. The software fault is a defect that causes software failure in an executable item. The software failure refers to the unsure results created because of numerous precise

© Springer Nature Singapore Pte Ltd. 2019
A. K. Luhach et al. (Eds.): ICAICR 2018, CCIS 955, pp. 341–354, 2019.
https://doi.org/10.1007/978-981-13-3140-4_31

conditions or surroundings that make defaults in a utility even as executing [5]. If these issues can be detected at the initial phases of the development, time and cost both can be minimized [6]. Error leads to faults. The existence of more than one fault in software leads to the failure of the software system.

Software fault prediction (SFP) can be referred as the activity in the development process which helps to predict the faulty data or modules at early phases of software development. Early prediction of faulty modules makes the testing process easy and less time-consuming. With the addition to this, it also improves the quality of software. By the prediction of faulty modules, extra efforts can be paid on these modules as compare to fault-free modules. The use of SFP makes the software product economic, efficient and reliable [7, 8]. SFP can only provide the advantages in terms of reduced budget, time complexity, and extra efforts if it can be applied at initial stages of software development life cycle. SFP is a popular technique for identifying faulty code during the development [9, 10]. SFP is a classification process which is used to make a prediction about the faulty or nonfaulty data [11].

In our research investigation, we have implemented ANN technique, which is most effective machine learning technique for prediction task. Datasets from PROMISE repository are used in our research. The organization of the paper is as follows: a brief summary of the previous studies is provided in Sect. 2. Section 3 includes details about data sets used in our work. Section 4 provides the proposed technique. Section 5 represents results of the proposed approach. The whole work is concluded in Sect. 6.

2 Related Work

In recent years, software fault prediction is the most emerging research areas. With the continuous growth in demand for software products, quality needs of users also increased day by day. SFP is known as one of the quality assurance tasks, improves the quality of the software by predicting the faulty data. Lots of research had been conducted on SFP by using various techniques. The commonly used techniques for predicting the faults are logistic regression [12–14], naïve Bayes [15–17], support vector machines, FIS [18, 19], KNN [20], decision tree [21, 22], random forest [23], linear or multiple regression [24–26], neural networks [27, 28], HySOM [29]. Researchers investigated that SFP using the software metrics is the most commonly used and best way to predict faults. Software metrics are important in order to measure the quality of the software product in terms of various factors such as coupling, cohesion, reliability, accuracy, completeness, complexity, inheritance etc. [30]. Commonly used metric set are CK metrics [31, 32], McCabe metrics [33], Halstead metrics [34]. Data sets from PROMISE repository [35–37] and NASA are mostly used in this research area.

Garvit et al. [38] discussed the impact of software metrics on the results. In this study, the author has developed new change metrics from the existing change metrics. He stated that existing change metrics cannot provide desired results. Classification or machine learning techniques are used in this research. Precision, F-measure, and recall parameters are used to evaluate the results. According to this study, KNN provides better results in terms of recall. Random forest algorithm is best suited for better results in precision parameter. Kumar et al. [39] investigated that machine learning techniques provide better results. He had conducted the research on public datasets from promise repository. In this paper, decision tree method is implemented on datasets to perform prediction. Five different machine learning algorithms are compared. Performance of all these models is evaluated on the basis of accuracy and F-mean. Owhadi-Kareshk et al. [40] implemented a shallow ANN technique to predict the faults. In this research, pre-training technique is used to train the Artificial neural network. Results of this approach are compared with ANN without pre-training and support vector machines. Results show that these three techniques are suitable for different data sets. ANN with pre-training is best suited for most of the datasets. Santosh et al. [41] performed prediction using ensemble method. The author states that ensemble methods are the best method for prediction tasks because these methods have the ability to combine the various methods for particular study. In this research, LRCR and GRCR are used. Linear and nonlinear ensemble methods are used in this study. Genetic programming and linear regression are used as base learning techniques. Output parameters of this study are average absolute or relative error and accuracy. 20 datasets are used for this study. Arshad et al. [42] implemented software fault prediction process by using DFCM clustering approach. Deep fuzzy c-mean approach is a clustering approach which works on semi supervised data. In this study, semi supervised data is divided into two parts i.e.; supervised or unsupervised with the help of max-min approach. Prediction is perfomed on both types of data (labeled data and unlabeled data). After that DFCM clustering approach is applied. It works by creating or updating the DFCM membership and finding the cluster center. Cluster centers are computed for both subsets of data set (labeled or unlabeled). Cluster centers are computed by DFCM clustering. Random under sampling approach is used to balance the features from both the subsets of dataset. The results of experiments are evaluated in terms of F-mean and AUC and results showed that DFCM approach provides acceptable results for labeled and unlabeled data. Diana-Lucia et al. [43] proposed a novel approach to predict faulty classes. In this research HyGRAR method is implemented. HyGRAR method is based on supervised classification. It combines ANN and rule mining technique to classify faulty or fault free modules. Data pre-processing is performed to sort the data. After that HyGRAR classifier is implemented. HyGRAR classifier classify the results into two classes i.e.; faulty classes or non faulty classes. According to the outcomes of this research, HyGRAR approach provides better results as compare to other techniques. Result are calculated using public data sets. Singh et al. [44] proposed a model for SFP which classify the software modules in to two categories. The prediction is performed on five defect datasets by using 9 different classifiers. In the first step data acquisition is performed. Boehm's model based classification is performed in this study. To classify the projects into various categories, COCOMO model is used. Projects are grouped into 3 categories i.e.; embedded, semidetached and organic datasets. KLOC metric is used in this research. Predictions are done in two ways i.e.; within dataset or cross dataset. To perform predictions, NNge, DTNB, PART, conjunctive rules, classification and regression tree, oneR, C4.5, ripper down rules and JRip classifiers are used. TPR, FPR, F-measure, accuracy, area under curve and precision are used as evaluation measures. Jin et al. [45] discussed about drawbacks of existing dimensionality reduction techniques which are used to select important features or to reduce unimportant features. Hybrid approach is proposed in this study which is the combination of QPSO and ANN approach. Features are selected using the QPSO which is based on the behaviour of natural swarms. According to the author QPSO provides significant results as compare to PCA or PLS. To perform this study, 21 metrics from Halstead, McCabe metrics etc. are used. QPSO reduces the dimensionality and select the metrics. It is the enhancement in the PSO. ANN is then applied to perform prediction. AUC, sensitivity and specificity parameters are used for evaluation of model. Erturk et al. [46] proposed a hybrid technique to predict faults. She has proposed an iterative approach. Two phases are designed for fault prediction. In the first phase, FIS is applied. FIS use rules created by expert knowledge and predict the results of initial versions of datasets. In the second phase, ANN or ANFIS system is used. OO metric set is used in this research. The result is measured by ROC curve. The result shows that ANFIS provides better results as compared to the ANN. Pardeep et al. [47] proposed a fuzzy inference system based approach for prediction task. The author states that prediction using the expert knowledge provides better outcomes as compared to supervised learning techniques. Data sets KC1, KC2, KC3 are used as input data. Then pre-processing of data is done. Useful metrics are selected by feature extraction technique. The author generates a large number of rules. Clusters are converted into fuzzy sets. Metric used in this study are McCabe metrics. According to the author performance of FIS is better than naïve Bayes or random forest algorithm. From this survey we concluded that there are various techniques which can provide better results for SFP. We concluded that machine learning techniques provide better results.

3 Dataset

To perform the prediction task, software metrics are taken as input parameters. Software metrics helps to measure characteristics of software in terms of various factors like performance, productivity, quality attributes and so on. Prediction based on software metrics can provide better results as compare with other models [48]. Set of 4 object-oriented metrics from CK metric set and 1 object-oriented metric from martin metric set are taken from PROMISE repository as a dataset. 18 dataset are taken from PROMISE repository. Table 1 shows the description of the dataset used.

Metrics used in this study are:

1. **Coupling between objects (CBO):** It describes the no. of classes to which particular class is coupled [49].
2. **Weighted methods per class (WMC):** WMC metric is calculated as the sum of complexities of all the methods invoked in clss [49].
3. **Response for class (RFC):** When an object of the class received a message, then the number of methods executed in response [50], that number of methods defines the value of RFC.
4. **The depth of inheritance tree (DIT):** It is the number of classes from which the particular class is inherited [50].
5. **Afferent coupling (Ca):** This metric contains the total number of classes that depend upon the particular class (measured class).

Table 1. Details of dataset

Name of dataset	wmc avg	wmc max	cbo avg	cbo max	rfc avg	rfc max	ca avg	ca max	dit avg	dit max
Lucene 2.0	9.26	57	9.76	80	23.15	129	5.48	5	1.74	66
Lucene 2.2	9.36	80	9.96	118	22.91	1711	5.65	5	1.77	93
Lucene 2.4	10.39	166	10.75	128	25.19	392	5.97	5	1.80	104
jEdít v3.2	12.53	399	12.04	162	37.74	487	7.15	6	2.83	137
jEdit v4.0	12.88	407	12.39	184	38.24	494	7.51	8	2.76	157
jEdít v4.1	13.13	413	12.98	197	39.87	505	8.46	8	2.74	169
jEdit v4.2	13.16	351	14.08	258	40.98	522	8.61	8	2.54	223
jEdít v4.3	12.35	351	14.32	346	39.85	540	8.74	8	2.37	291
Log4j 1.2	8.42	105	7.61	65	25.22	321	3.67	7	1.6	58
Camel 1.0	8.07	82	9.96	185	19.63	143	4.99	6	2.0	184
Camel 1.2	8.31	94	10.1	272	20.23	186	5.01	6	1.93	270
Camel 1.4	8.52	141	10.76	389	21.2	286	5.10	6	1.94	387
Camel 1.6	8.57	166	11.1	448	21.42	322	5.27	6	1.95	446
Ant v1.7	11.07	120	11.05	499	34.36	288	5.65	7	2.52	498
Xalan 2.4	11.45	123	14.5	171	30.16	355	6.74	8	2.56	155
Xalan 2.5	11.32	130	12.86	173	29.6	391	5.76	8	2.51	156
Xalan 2.6	11.03	133	12.07	168	29.29	409	5.81	8	2.51	152
Xalan 2.7	10.87	138	11.99	172	29.2	428	5.76	8	1.6	156

4 Proposed Methodology

Previous studies prove that the machine learning techniques are best suitable for prediction tasks in different areas like stock market, banking sector, disease prediction, net income prediction and so on. In our research work, Artificial neural network based SFP model is designed. ANN with 5 input parameters is used in this research. ANN use supervised machine learning algorithm for training purpose.

4.1 Artificial Neural Network (ANN)

An ANN is one of most commonly used machine learning technique which is inspired by the working of the human brain. It contains a number of artificial neurons which are interconnected with each other [51]. The various types of ANN are available. In this study, 3 layered feed forward (FF) ANN is used. ANN use supervised machine learning algorithms for the training purpose. Input values (software metrics) are assigned to the ANN at input layer. Weights are updated at every iteration in order to match the target value or to reduce the mean squared error. 5 metrics (Wmc, Cbo, Ca, Rfc, Dit.) from selected datasets are used as input for the ANN. Fault value of these datasets is taken as the target value. ANN is trained with Levenberg Marquardt (LM) algorithm. Dataset is separated into training part and testing part. 70% of total data is used as training data and rest is used for testing. ANN is defined as a:

$$X' = f(W, \dot{I})$$

Where X' refers to the output vector. W is the weight and $\dot{I}$ is the input vector.

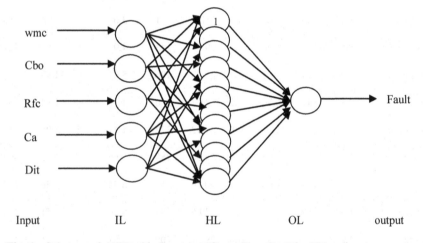

Fig. 1. Structure of ANN with 5 metrics (Wmc, Cbo, Ca, Rfc, Dit) as input parameter

Structure of ANN is defined in Fig. 1. Here, IL refers to input layer, HL refers to hidden layer, OL refers to output layer. Implementation details are described in Table 2 which shows a number of hidden neurons, training algorithms and a number of inputs.

Table 2. Implementation details of ANN

ANN type	Feedforward ANN
Layer count	3
No. of hidden neurons	20
No. of inputs	5
Training algorithm	Levenberg Marquardt (LM)
Output	Faultiness

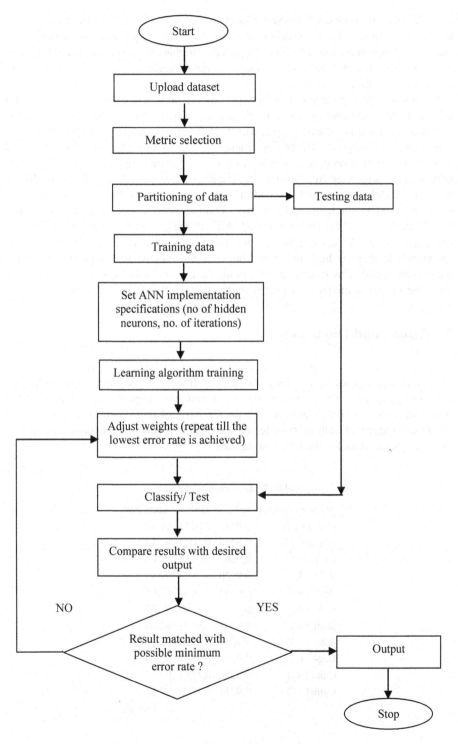

Fig. 2. Workflow of the proposed approach

The detailed process of the SFP model is shown in Fig. 2. Firstly upload metric dataset as a input. After uploading of dataset, extract dependent and independent metrics for the prediction task. The dependent variables act as output variables. Here fault data is used as a dependent variable. The output value is compared with values of dependent variables to find the performance of model. Software metrics acts as an independent variables. Selection of independent variable also affects the performance of SFP model. Here cbo, ca, wmc, dit, rfc acts as independent variable. After extraction of metrics, partition of dataset is performed. Data set is partitioned into two parts. i.e.; training set or testing set. Set the implementation requirements for building a proposed model. Implementation details include: layer count, hidden neurons, training algorithm, performance parameter etc. Perform the learning process by using LM algorithm to train the model. Weights are updated at every iteration in order to match the target value or to reduce the mean squared error. Training process stops automatically when maximum number of epochs are reached. After training, classification is performed on the test data set. Actual results and desired results are compared and error rate is calculated. If there is high difference between the outputs then adjustments in the weights are made. This process continues till the possible minimum MSE is achieved. Then the proposed model is evaluated on the base of performance parameters.

5 Results and Discussion

Results are analyzed in terms of ROC-AUC (receiver operating characteristics area under curve), accuracy and mean squared error (MSE). These three are used as performance parameters which measure the performance of the proposed technique. ANN with five input parameters is evaluated on the basis of these, output parameters and results are compared with existing techniques. Table 3 shows the approximate values of output parameters for the different dataset.

Table 3. Description of result

Name of dataset	ROC	MSE	Accuracy
Lucene 2.0	0.9215	0.0143	92.14
Lucene 2.2	0.9218	0.0003	92.18
Lucene 2.4	0.9207	0.0168	92.06
jEdit v3.2	0.9220	1.2529	92.19
jEdit v4.0	0.9205	1.7664	92.05
jEdit v4.1	0.9233	1.8806	92.32
jEdit v4.2	0.9208	1.8678	92.08
jEdit v4.3	0.9213	1.0223	92.12
Log4j-1.2	0.9204	0.2844	92.03
Camel 1.0	0.9236	0.1111	92.35
Camel 1.2	0.9214	0.1825	92.14

(*continued*)

Table 3. (*continued*)

Name of dataset	ROC	MSE	Accuracy
Camel 1.4	0.9209	0.1724	92.08
Camel 1.6	0.9217	0.1205	92.17
Ant v1.7	0.9207	0.4983	92.07
Xalan-2.4	0.9250	0.6209	92.50
Xalan-2.5	0.9215	0.7052	92.14
Xalan-2.6	0.9226	0.6919	92.26
Xalan-2.7	0.9202	0.7052	92.01

ROC is the receiver operating characteristic curve which defines the false positive rate and true positive rate of the prediction. ROC-AUC evaluate the performance by calculating the area under the curve (AUC). ROC-AUC is the widely used prediction parameter for SFP [52]. AUC = 1 signifies that there is no error in the prediction. AUC > 0.5 shows the usefulness of SFP model. Results less than 0.5 are not acceptable and shows the failure of the model [53]. In this study values of ROC-AUC varies for different datasets. Average ROC-AUC or this study is 0.92 approximately which shows the usefulness of the proposed ANN prediction model.

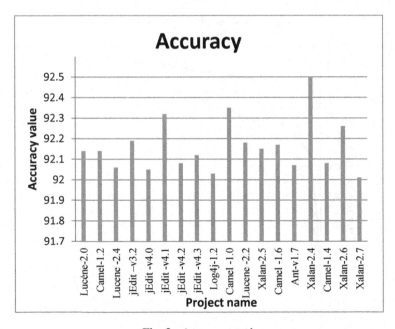

Fig. 3. Accuracy graph

Accuracy is defined as the number of correct prediction completed out of the overall prediction. Accuracy is recorded between 92–93% (Fig. 3).

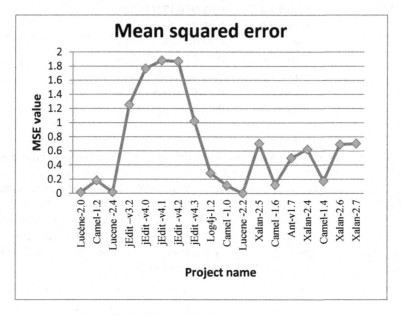

Fig. 4. MSE graph of various datasets

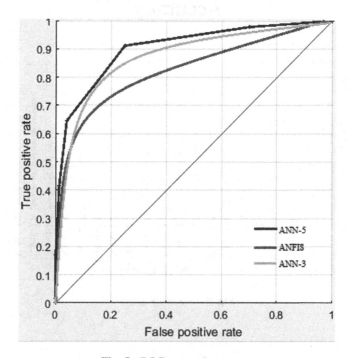

Fig. 5. ROC comparison curve

Figure 3 shows the accuracy graph of various datasets used in this study. MSE measures the average of the squares of the error. It is considered as the squared difference between the desired outcomes and actual outcomes. MSE parameters is used to measure the errors in prediction results. Mean squared error of this study varies between 0.0003–1.8806 (Fig. 4).

Our proposed technique is compared with existing techniques. These results show that proposed technique provides better results than ANN with 3 inputs and ANFIS technique. Table 3 shows the approximate values of output parameters for the different dataset. Figure 5 shows the ROC-AUC curve for the existing and proposed method. Average ROC value for ANFIS is 0.81 and the average value of ROC for ANN with 3 inputs is recorded as 0.90 approximately.

6 Conclusion

SFP is one of the most significant activities of the development process which helps to make the software product economic, efficient and reliable In this research, ANN-based SFP model is employed to classify the fault-prone modules. The proposed model used LM algorithm for the learning process and provides better prediction results as compared to existing techniques. This research is performed on 18 different datasets which are publically available. The Results are analyzed in terms of ROC(AUC), accuracy and mean squared error. Accuracy is recorded between 92–93% with mean squared error rate between 0.0003–1.8806. Results of the proposed systems signify that the ANN is the significant approach for prediction of faulty modules. It increases the accuracy of SFP model by minimizing the error rate. The results of proposed approach are compared with ANFIS and ANN with 3 inputs approach. The average ROC value for ANFIS is 0.81 and the average value of ROC for ANN with 3 inputs is recorded as 0.90 approximately and Average ROC-AUC for this study is 0.92 approximately. The comparison of proposed technique with existing techniques shows that proposed ANN model can predict the faulty modules with high accuracy. In future work, this SFP model will be converted into tool which can be applied to SDLC process.

References

1. Menzies, T., Greenwald, J., Frank, A.: Data mining static code attributes to learn defect predictors. IEEE Trans. Softw. Eng. 33(1), 2–13 (2007)
2. Cagatay, C.: Software fault prediction: a literature review and current trends. Expert Syst. Appl. 38(4), 4626–4636 (2011)
3. Pandey, A.K., Goyal, N.K.: Prediction and ranking of fault-prone software modules. In: Pandey, A.K., Goyal, N.K. (eds.) Early Software Reliability Prediction. Springer Series, vol. 303, pp. 81–104. Springer, Heidelberg (2013). https://doi.org/10.1007/978-81-322-1176-1_5
4. Fenton, E., Ohlsson, N.: Quantitative analysis of faults and failures in a complex software system. IEEE Trans. Softw. Eng. 26(8), 797–814 (2000)
5. Kaur, R., Sharma, E.S.: Various techniques to detect and predict faults in software system: survey. Int. J. Futur. Revolut. Comput. Sci. Commun. Eng. (IJFRSCE) 4(2), 330–336 (2018)

6. Porter, A., Selby, R.: Empirically guided software development using metric-based classification trees. IEEE Softw. **7**(2), 46–54 (1990)
7. Catal, C., Diri, B.: Investigating the effect of dataset size, metrics sets, and feature selection techniques on software fault prediction problem. Inf. Sci. **179**(8), 1040–1058 (2009)
8. Zheng, J., Williams, L., Nagappan, N., Snipes, W., Hudepohl, J.P., Vouk, M.A.: On the value of static analysis for fault detection in software. IEEE Trans. Softw. Eng. **32**(4), 1–14 (2006)
9. Jiang, Y., Cukic, B., Menzies, T.: Fault prediction using early lifecycle data. In: The 18th IEEE Symposium on Software Reliability Engineering ISSRE 2007, pp. 237–246. IEEE Computer Society, Sweden (2007)
10. Seliya, N., Khoshgoftaar, T.M., Zhong, S.: Analyzing software quality with limited fault-proneness defect data. In: Proceedings of the Ninth IEEE International Symposium on High Asssurance System Engineering, Germany, pp. 89–98 (2005)
11. Erturk, E., Sezer, E.A.: Software fault prediction using Mamdani type fuzzy inference system. Int. J. Data Anal. Tech. Strat. **8**(1), 14–28 (2016)
12. Olague, H.M., Etzkorn, L.H., Gholston, S., Quattlebaum, S.: Empirical validation of three software metrics suites to predict fault-proneness of object-oriented classes developed using highly iterative or agile software development processes. IEEE Trans. Softw. Eng. **33**(6), 402–419 (2007)
13. Cruz, E.C., Ochimizu, K.: Towards logistic regression models for predicting fault-prone code across software projects. In: 3rd International Symposium on Empirical Software Engineering and Measurement, ESEM 2009, pp. 460–463 (2009)
14. Burrows, R., Ferrari, F.C., Lemos, O.A., Garcia, A., Taiani, F.: The impact of coupling on the fault-proneness of aspect-oriented programs: an empirical study. In: 2010 IEEE 21st International Symposium on Software Reliability Engineering (ISSRE), pp. 329–338 (2010)
15. Kapila, H., Singh, S.: Analysis of CK metrics to predict software fault-proneness using bayesian inference. Int. J. Comput. Appl. **74**(2), 1–4 (2013)
16. Dejaeger, K., Verbraken, T., Baesens, B.: Towards comprehensible software fault prediction models using Bayesian network classifiers. Inst. Electr. Electron. Eng. IEEE Trans. Softw. Eng. **39**(2), 237–257 (2013)
17. Pai, G.J., Dugan, J.B.: Empirical analysis of software fault content and fault proneness using Bayesian methods. Inst. Electr. Electron. Eng. (IEEE) Trans. Softw. Eng. **33**(10), 675–686 (2007)
18. Mishra, B., Shukla, K.K.: Defect prediction for object oriented software using support vector based fuzzy classification model. Int. J. Comput. Appl. **60**(15), 8–16 (2012)
19. Singh, P., Pal, N.R., Verma, S., Vyas, O.P.: Fuzzy rule-based approach for software fault prediction. Inst. Electr. Electron. Eng. (IEEE) Trans. Syst. Man Cybern.: Syst. **47**(5), 826–837 (2017)
20. Goyal, R., Chandra, P., Singh, Y.: Suitability of KNN regression in the development of interaction based software fault prediction models. IERI Procedia **6**, 15–21 (2014)
21. Gyimothy, T., Ferenc, R., Siket, I.: Empirical validation of object-oriented metrics on open source software for fault prediction. IEEE Trans. Softw. Eng. **31**(10), 897–910 (2005)
22. Fokaefs, M., Mikhaiel, R., Tsantalis, N., Stroulia, E., Lau, A.: An empirical study on web service evolution. In: IEEE International Conference on Web Services (ICWS 2011), pp. 49–56 (2011)
23. Malhotra, R., Jain, A.: Fault prediction using statistical and machine learning methods for improving software quality. J. Inf. Process. Syst. **8**(2), 241–262 (2012)
24. Radjenović, D., Heričko, M., Torkar, R., Živkovič, A.: Software fault prediction metrics: a systematic literature review. Inf. Softw. Technol. **55**(8), 1397–1418 (2013)

25. Nagappan, N., Williams, L., Vouk, M., Osborne, J.: Early estimation of software quality using in-process testing metrics. In: Proceedings of the Third Workshop on Software Quality - 3-WoSQ (2005)
26. Pai, G.J., Bechta Dugan, J.: Empirical analysis of software fault content and fault proneness using bayesian methods. IEEE Trans. Softw. Eng. 33(10), 675–686 (2007)
27. Gondra, A.: Applying machine learning to software fault-proneness prediction. J. Syst. Softw. 81(2), 186–195 (2008)
28. Lu, H., Cukic, B.: An adaptive approach with active learning in software fault prediction. In: Proceedings of the 8th International Conference on Predictive Models in Software Engineering - PROMISE 2012 (2012)
29. Abaei, G., Selamat, A., Fujita, H.: An empirical study based on semi-supervised hybrid self-organizing map for software fault prediction. Knowl.-Based Syst. 74, 28–39 (2015)
30. Rathore, S., Gupta, A.: Investigating object-oriented design metrics to predict fault-proneness of software modules. In: 2012 CSI Sixth International Conference on Software Engineering (CONSEG) (2012)
31. Chidamber, S., Kemerer, C.: A metrics suite for object oriented design. IEEE Trans. Softw. Eng. 20(6), 476–493 (1994)
32. Basili, V., Briand, L., Melo, W.: A validation of object-oriented design metrics as quality indicators. IEEE Trans. Softw. Eng. 22(10), 751–761 (1996)
33. McCabe, T.: A complexity measure. IEEE Trans. Softw. Eng. 2(4), 308–320 (1976)
34. Chidamber, S., Kemerer, C.: Towards a metrics suite for object oriented design. In: Conference Proceedings on Object-Oriented Programming Systems, Languages, and Applications - OOPSLA 1991 (1991)
35. Chen, J., Liu, S., Chen, X., Gu, Q., Chen, D.: Empirical studies on feature selection for software fault prediction. In: Proceedings of the 5th Asia-Pacific Symposium on Internetware - Internetware 2013 (2013)
36. Chen, J., Liu, S., Liu, W., Chen, X., Gu, Q., Chen, D.: A two-stage data preprocessing approach for software fault prediction. In: 2014 Eighth International Conference on Software Security and Reliability (2014)
37. tera-PROMISE: Welcome to one of the largest repositories of SE research data. http://openscience.us/repo/
38. Choudhary, G., Kumar, S., Kumar, K., Mishra, A., Catal, C.: Empirical analysis of change metrics for software fault prediction. Comput. Electr. Eng. 67, 15–24 (2018)
39. Kumar, L., Sureka, A.: Analyzing fault prediction usefulness from cost perspective using source code metrics. In: 2017 Tenth International Conference on Contemporary Computing (IC3) (2017)
40. Owhadi-Kareshk, M., Sedaghat, Y., Akbarzadeh-T, M.: Pre-training of an artificial neural network for software fault prediction. In: 2017 7th International Conference on Computer and Knowledge Engineering (ICCKE) (2017)
41. Rathore, S., Kumar, S.: Towards an ensemble based system for predicting the number of software faults. Expert Syst. Appl. 82, 357–382 (2017)
42. Arshad, A., Riaz, S., Jiao, L., Murthy, A.: Semi-supervised deep fuzzy c-mean clustering for software fault prediction. IEEE Access 6, 25675–25685 (2018)
43. Miholca, D., Czibula, G., Czibula, I.: A novel approach for software defect prediction through hybridizing gradual relational association rules with artificial neural networks. Inf. Sci. 441, 152–170 (2018)
44. Singh, P.: Comprehensive model for software fault prediction. In: Proceedings of the International Conference on Inventive Computing and Informatics (ICICI 2017), pp. 1103–1108 (2017)

45. Jin, C., Jin, S.: Prediction approach of software fault-proneness based on hybrid artificial neural network and quantum particle swarm optimization. Appl. Soft Comput. **35**, 717–725 (2015)
46. Erturk, E., Akcapinar Sezer, E.: Iterative software fault prediction with a hybrid approach. Appl. Soft Comput. **49**, 1020–1033 (2016)
47. Singh, P., Pal, N., Verma, S., Vyas, O.: Fuzzy rule-based approach for software fault prediction. IEEE Trans. Syst. Man Cybern.: Syst. **47**(5), 826–837 (2017)
48. Pattnaik, S., Kumar Pattanayak, B.: Empirical analysis of software quality prediction using a TRAINBFG algorithm. Int. J. Eng. Technol. **7**(26), 259 (2018)
49. Meyer, B.: The role of object-oriented metrics. Computer **31**(11), 123–127 (1998)
50. Aggarwal, K., Singh, Y., Kaur, A., Malhotra, R.: Empirical study of object-oriented metrics. J. Object Technol. **5**(8), 149 (2006)
51. Erturk, E., Sezer, E.: A comparison of some soft computing methods for software fault prediction. Expert Syst. Appl. **42**(4), 1872–1879 (2015)
52. Castro, C., Braga, A.: Optimization of the area under the ROC curve. In: 2008 10th Brazilian Symposium on Neural Networks (2008)
53. An analysis of the area under the ROC curve and its use as a metric for comparing clinical scorecards. In: 2014 IEEE International Conference on Bioinformatics and Biomedicine (BIBM) (2014)

Sentiment Analysis of Tweets by Convolution Neural Network with L1 and L2 Regularization

Abhilasha Rangra$^{(\boxtimes)}$, Vivek Kumar Sehgal, and Shailendra Shukla

Department of Computer Science and Engineering,
Jaypee University of Information Technology, Wakhnaghat, India
abhilasharangra93@gmail.com, vivekseh@ieee.org,
shailendra.shukla@juit.ac.in

Abstract. Twitter data is one of the largest amounts of data where thousands of tweets are generated by the Twitter user. As this text is dynamic and huge so, we can consider it as a big data or a common example of Big data. The biggest challenge in the analysis of this big data is its improvement in the analysis. In this paper, there is an analysis by using semantic features like bigram, tri-gram and allow to learn by convolution neural network L1 and L2 regularization. Regularization is used to overcome the dropout and increase the training accuracy. In our experimental analysis, we demonstrated the effectiveness of a number of tweets in term of accuracy. In the result, we do not obtain any specific pattern but average improvement in the accuracy. For the analysis, we use 10 cross-validations and used to compare the outcome with max-entropy and SVM. Here we also analyze the effect of convolution layer on accuracy and time of execution.

Keywords: CNN · Tweets · Bigdata · Regularization · n-gram

1 Introduction

In the past few years, there was the enormous number of utilization of micro blogging platform like Facebook, Twitter, etc. For the purpose of growth and development, many organizations and companies used to extract the sentiments from the tweet data which also termed as big data. Big data is nothing but a large number of data like Twitter data which we use to analyze the sentiments. We can term tweet data as big data because big data are a set of large data that is used to analyze by using computation methods to demonstrate the trend, association, especially related to human behavior as we are used to exert in Twitter data. In the given paper, we also used to analyze the data from twitter data or we say big data [1, 2]. There are numbers of companies and organization which used to analyze the big data by using several means to identify the opinion of the masses about their product and services [1, 3]. The intention of this paper is to spot some light on the processes, issues, and methods used to analyze the sentiments of big data. This big data contains the number of Twitter messages termed as the tweet, Twitter post, etc. [1, 2]. There is numerous information

© Springer Nature Singapore Pte Ltd. 2019
A. K. Luhach et al. (Eds.): ICAICR 2018, CCIS 955, pp. 355–365, 2019.
https://doi.org/10.1007/978-981-13-3140-4_32

on the word floating in the big data whether it is related to any organization or any political and social issues. The content in the big data demonstrates real-time events in day to day life or daily routine, these contents are full of social information and temporal attributes. This information, data used to analyze sentiments of human beings, because every person uses to express their view on social sites. After analysis of these data valuable information can be extracted that helps to predict any situation or result easily. Twitter gives fine-grained information about each and every-events, instances, perspectives, etc. [5]. The main intention of sentiment analysis is to evaluate the state of mind of the speaker. In sentiment analysis, most of the work has been done to find sentiment regarding a general topic by taking an assumption that viewer talks about an individual topic. In such reviews, it is easy to analyze the sentiments of the subject [7]. This analysis is used to differentiate the opinion of users or speaker on the basis of its binary polarity. This analysis is done in documents, the single sentence or word for word. The classification of sentiments is done in two ways positive or negative. It is very difficult to make 100% accuracy while analyzing the sentiment, but the main goal of this paper is to provide such approach that assures to make the result as more as possible. We propose CNN for learning purpose which helps to give accuracy in the result. As there are various challenges during analysis of sentiments form big data like to evaluate the data parallel, if we have no previous result Real-time opinion mining becomes the very difficult task, classification of argument statement, the variation of sentiment from person to person or of a person with the passage of time. The sentiment of analysis is done by extracting (REST API), classifying (tokenization, stemming, stop word removal) and last learning (CNN). There is the number of methods, framework, models, etc. given by researchers to the analysis of sentiments of big data in an accurate manner some of the approaches are represented in Sect. 2. The rest of the paper is organized as follows: Sect. 2 gives the detail on the research given by a number of researchers in related work, in Sect. 3 there is a discussion about the proposed work and algorithm, in Sect. 4 there is a discussion about the experiments and result, and at last there is a summary of the conclusion of the whole paper, and the work which is to be done in the future given in Sect. 5.

2 Related Work

To analyze the sentiments of the tweets there is a utilization of lexicon approach and learning based method. Sentiment analysis is performed by collecting big data from the micro blogging site (Twitter) [9]. To execute the analysis, brilliant system with the help of machine learning like Naïve Bayes, Random Frost, or SVM are used [10, 18]. There is a complete description given by [11] about the working during analysis of twitter big data which start from extracting data from social sites and they allow for preprocessing and at last connected with the Alchemy API by Rest Call Method. There is also an evaluation of polarity and accuracy of twitter big data [12] by pre-processing. It is very difficult to analyze the complete paragraph taking adverb, adjective, and verb in a single framework. An AVA framework special for recognizing sentiments in a line, paragraph, etc., where the user has to select topic, line or paragraph, denoted as (t) and any document (d), AVA use to return a score that d used to express (t) [13]. This score expresses in the form of +1 or −1 where +1 means maximally positive and −1 maximally negative. As we discuss above CNN is used in this paper for learning process. Here to extract features from visual and textual modalities by using deep CNN. By using this method in multi-kernel learning classifier we can easily increase the performance to identify the multimodal emotion recognition and sentiment analysis on the different dataset [14]. To analyze the sentiments of the sentences CNN architecture is presented [15] here there is a utilization of 3 pairs of convolution layer and pooling layer in the given architecture. To enhance the given model [15] utilizes parametric rectified linear Unit (PReLU), normalization and Dropout technology.

3 Proposed Work

This section presents the explanation of the proposed methodology and proposed algorithm to analyze the sentiments on big data. Here we give a brief description about the working of CNN and preprocessing methods. Methodology is described in a number of steps with proper flow chart. In algorithm part there is a stepwise discussion about the working of whole methodology and sequence of their execution.

3.1 Preprocessing

In the given paper overall, proposed system is segregated into four steps. In the first step, we use to collect big data and it's pre-processing. In the third step, we use to extract the feature by its classification and at last applied CNN on the labeled feature and classify the outcomes by using soft-max classifier. In Fig. 1, initially, there is a collection of big data with the help of the REST API. Rest API is an application program interface which utilizes an HTTP request to GET, PUT, POST and DELETE data. It is an interface which helps to collect the Twitter data from its site. And in the second step, we use to pre-process the collected tweet for reducing noise. Then apply for tokenization, stop word removal and stemming. In tokenization, we use to make an alphanumeric sequence of collecting data having length character 3 or more. They use to segregate punctuation marks or special characters from the character length and to convert uppercase into lower case [16].

Fig. 1. Pre-processing of big data

In another method [16] given in Fig. 1, there is a removal of the stop word from the sentence and termed as stop word removal. Here it used to remove the word which seems to stop the word. For example, a) "I love Chandigarh but I also love Kinnaur" here, but is utilizing a stop word so this approach used to remove the word 'but'. It also uses to remove extra words or characters, for example "Blassssting day after many days, reeeallyyy enjooooyinggggg" here there are many extra words who only increasing the data size, this approach used to remove these extra words an left with " Blasting day after many days, really enjoying". It also helps to reduce the data size. This approach uses two methods for removing the words termed as TBRS methods which stand for Random sampling on the basis of a term expressed as:

$$S_z(r) = P_z(r).log_2 \frac{P_{z(r)}}{P_{(r)}} \tag{1}$$

And Mutual interference Method (MI)

$$P(B; M) = \sum_{b \in B} \sum_{m \in M} p(m, b) \log \left[\frac{p(m, b)}{p(m).p(b)} \right] \tag{2}$$

3.2   Semantic Features Extraction

In the third step of Fig. 1, stemming approach [17] is utilized to DE noise the tweets. In this approach, we use to recognize the root word or stem word from the given data. Here we use to remove the plural word like "foods → food and affix word from the data. These are the three methods which are used for the extraction, now we use to classify the given result in the form of n-grams (unigram, bigram and trigram). There are some formulas with help of which we used to classify the features; Fig. 4 represents the flow of feature classification after pre-processing.

In this process, we use to classify the outcome from preprocessed data in term of unigram, bi-gram, and tri-gram. Unigram is utilized to use every individual word as a feature. These features are used for utilization of term frequency, inverse document frequency as the feature value. In unigram n = 1 (Fig. 2).

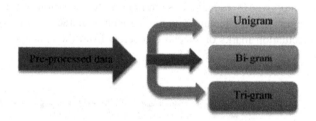

Fig. 2. Classification of feature

Where,

$$\text{Inverse document frequency} = \log\left[\frac{total\ number\ of\ documents}{number\ of\ documents\ containing\ -t}\right] \quad (3)$$

Bigrams are used, two consecutive words as features. It is a n-gram where n = 2. It helps to provide the previous token while allowing relation of conditional probability:

$$P\left[S_I|S_0\ldots\ldots\ldots S_{I-1}\right] \quad (4)$$

$$P\left(S_1^V\right) = \prod_{i=1}^{v} p(S_i|S_{i-1}) \quad (5)$$

and if we talk about the tri-gram having n = 3. It is a group of three consecutive written units like letter, syllables or words. There is one common example of all the three n-grams shown in Table 1.

$$P(S_i|S_0\ldots\ldots\ldots S_{i-1}) \approx P(S_i|S_{i-2}S_{i-1}) \quad (6)$$

$$P\left(S_1^v\right) = \prod_{i=1}^{v} p(S_i|S_{i-2}S_{i-1}) \quad (7)$$

Table 1. Accuracy variation in the given three parameters.

Number of tweets(K)	Statistical data for two classes			Statistical data for three classes		
	SVM (Accuracy)	Max-entropy (Accuracy)	CNN (Accuracy)	SVM (Accuracy)	Max-entropy (Accuracy)	CNN (Accuracy)
2	85.62	89.23	92.52	85.23	88.2	90.23
10	86.6	88.42	94.62	87.23	87.98	93.23
40	87.13	86.23	93.23	86.73	85.46	95.67
80	88.23	90.23	96.23	88	88.23	96.23
100	88.47	90.13	97.82	87.98	89.13	97

3.3 Learning Features with Label

After classification of features, we use to apply CNN tool which stands for convolution neural network for learning purpose. Before applying we use to give labeling to the feature by using the correlation method. We use labeled feature for learning like which feature having "positive" sentiments or "negative" sentiments or "neutral" sentiments. CNN is a tool which is very useful or enhanced tool in term of document recognition (LeCun et al. 1998) [18]. It contains any convolutional layers and many fully connected layers. There are two layers named as pooling layer and normalized layer in between the convolution layer. It is a supervised learning algorithm where parameters of various layers are used to learn from back propagation. In the previous year it is very hard to learn large feature set, but after the extension of the computational power of GPU, it is possible to train a deep convolution neural network on the large dataset (Krizhevskhy, Hinton 2012). In our work, there is a use of CNN to learn classified feature in terms of n-grams. There are three main processes in the CNN are pooling, convolution and soft-max model which perform their function on the features. The flow of CNN is represented in Fig. 3.

Fig. 3. Learning process

After labeling the data into a set of vectors which is instantly segregate into a training set and test set. The process of convolution is started from locating word indices into the lower dimensional vector where the distance of the word is directly proportional their sentiments in a layer termed as an embedded layer. In the next layer termed as convolution layer where convolution performs over the embedded words by using various filter sizes which are sliding over 6–7 words at a time. This is a method to understand the activity of words in terms of sentiments in n-grams. After every convolution, there is a utilization to segregate the most significant feature from the set of feature and used to convert them into the feature vector by using the max-pool layer or pooling layer [4]. The combination of convolution and pooling layer is used to make tensor with several shapes and has to create the layer for every individual layer and focus their result of a single big feature vector. Then at last there is a utilization of soft-max model to classify the features as an outcome of pooling layer. The main function of the soft-max model is to optimize the layer by the formula given below [6]. As it is a classifier, it is used to classify the features. [18] L_1 regularization express in Eq. 8.

$$\sum_{r=1}^{N} l(f(Z_r), I) + \lambda\left(\sum_{r.e=1}^{M+u} L\, f(Z_r) . f(Z_e), b(r, e)\right) \tag{8}$$

At last to examine the result from learning approach soft max classifier used to classify the outcome in term of accuracy and time execution. L_2 regularization is express in Eq. 9.

Algorithm 1

Step 1: Collection of tweets from Twitter by using REST API.

Step 2: *Pre-process the tweets*

Tokenization → Stop word removal → Stemming

Step 3: *Extraction of processed tweets in the form of n-grams where n = 1 or 2 or 3 respectively. The evaluation is done by using equation 4 and 5 for bigram and 6 and 7 for trigram from the above equation.*

Step 4: *String all the feature.*

Step 5: *Labeled the entire feature by using the correlation method.*

Step6: *These labeled features are applied for learning with the help of CNN.*

$$F_r(z) = \sum_{v=1}^{a} B_v^{0,r} \; y_v^M(z) + w^{0,r}, r = 1,2....K \tag{10}$$

Where,

M is the weight of random value

Optimization of feature by using soft-max layer equation (8).

Step 7: *Classification of features and the analysis of accuracy and time of execution of the model using equation (9)*

$$\xi_c : x \longrightarrow \sqrt{\frac{2}{\prod} \sum_{u \in \Omega_{c-1}} e^{\frac{-1}{w_c^2}\|u-x\|^2}} - \xi_{c-1}(u) \tag{9}$$

4 Experiment

4.1 Experiment Setting

Our experiment is executed on the analysis of sentiments of tweets where we use rest API for the collection of tweets and CNN as a learning approach for the collected data. We used to classify the data in two forms (a) two class which contains positive and negative sentiments (b) three class which contain positive, negative and neutral. We use to analyze the accuracy and execution time for different classes.

4.2 Datasets

To analyze the accuracy in terms of SVM, Max-entropy and CNN we use the dataset from 2 k which having various values for SVM stands for support vector machine, Max-entropy and CNN, similarly for 10 K, 40 K, 80 K and 100 K. These tweets are collected from twitter website with the help of rest API. Tables 1 and 2 shows the statistical data and also provides side-information about the accuracy in SVM, CNN, and max-entropy. Secondly, a number of convolution layers are used to analyze the execution time of CNN where time is considered in seconds. Execution time is represented in the different layer of CNN like 2, 4, 8 and 10 correspond to the accuracy of CNN. Tables 1 and 2 represents the time execution with the accuracy in CNN with the passage of convolution layers.

Table 2. Time taken by the classifier

Convolution layers	Statistical data for two classes		Statistical data for three classes	
	CNN (Accuracy)	Time of execution	CNN (Accuracy)	Time of execution
2	89.92	60	88.23	120
4	92.32	180	92.2	200
8	94.62	240	94.62	320
10	97.82	600	97	800

4.3 Baseline

To represent the analysis we use to compare the accuracy of two classifiers i.e. SVM and Max-entropy and also a deep learning method CNN. There is a comparison of these three approaches to demonstrate the accuracy of the analysis. Here we use to compare the accuracy rate of these three approaches. (Jaynes, 1957) states that max-entropy is the way by which one can explain the data in the best manner with its entropy value. (Berger, 1996) and (pang, 2002) demonstrate the efficiency of max-entropy as compare to NLP and naive Bayes. (Cortes, 1995) and (Renie, 2003) shows the efficiency in classification for selected documents or data. By taking these paper with [19] paper as a base paper, we use to analyze the sentiments of the tweet with statistical data. To generate the statistical data we use to study the behavior of approaches.

4.4 Evaluation Metrics

For recommendation we normally split our measures into three categories Accuracy used to evaluate the overall effectiveness of selected classifier. It is the ratio of Total corrected sentiment (positive + negative) to the complete data used for analysis or classification.

4.5   Results

For the purpose of comparison, we use the number of tweets collected by rest API. The number of tweets varied from 2 K to 100 K for both two class and three class (10-cross-validation). The comparison is done between SVM, CNN, and max-entropy. SVM stands for support vector machine is a state-of-the-art classifier for large data which is used to classify the sentiments of tweets whereas Max-entropy is also used for classification purpose. CNN is described in Sect. 3. Table 1 represents the accuracy variation in the given three parameters.

Table 2 represents the time taken by the classifier (CNN) for attaining the maximum accuracy in the different convolutional layer. There is the various layer of convolution where the value of time varies. Time execution is considered in seconds. Here we use the 100 K number of tweets in 2, 4, 8, 10 layers of convolutions. The given table shows the value of two classes and three classes of (100 K) for CNN execution time in seconds.

4.6   Results Analysis

Tables 1 and 2 demonstrate the values of CNN, SVM, and max-entropy in terms of accuracy and CNN and its execution time with respect to the convolution layers respectively. In Table 1 we use to compare the values of Entropy, SVM, and CNN in terms of accuracy and in Table 2 we use to compare the time with respect of accuracy given by CNN in different layers. The graphical representation of Tables 1 and 2 are shown in Figs. 4 and 5. Figure 4 represents the accuracy of two class and three class given by SVM, max-entropy and CNN for 2 K, 10 K, 40 K, 80 K and 100 K. The graphical result shows the superior performance of CNN in terms of accuracy as compared to the two classifiers in both the cases. Further Fig. 5 represents the execution time of CNN in seconds in term of accuracy. The graphical result demonstrates that with increase in the layer, time execution also increases and accuracy too. We can say that with the increase in this accuracy increase in the layer.

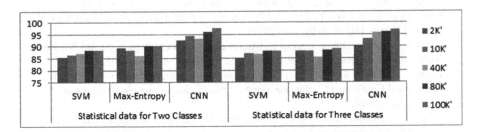

Fig. 4. Comparision of approaches in terms of accuracy

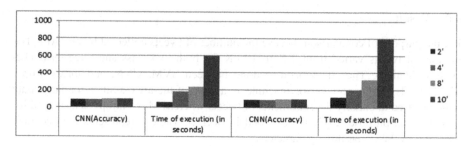

Fig. 5. Comparison of CNN accuary with time (seconds)

5 Conclusion

In the analysis of big data, the important factor is to understand the domain by number of instances. In this paper, experimental analysis is done by using various classifier with different number of instances which starts from 2 K to 100 K. In every case we use 10 cross-validations and generate accuracy. In the experimental result, CNN provides better or effective result as compare to max-entropy and SVM but it also requires more trade–off execution time for two class and three class. The accuracy is near about 97.82 with execution time 600 s and 97 with execution time 800 s for two class and three class respectively. So, if we ignore execution time then we can conclude that CNN shows effective enhancement in accuracy with L1 and L2 regularization from our experimental result in higher number of tweets.

References

1. Go, A., Bhayani, R., Huang, L.: Twitter sentiment classification using distant supervision. CS224 N Project Report, Stanford **1**, 12 (2009)
2. Agarwal, A., et al.: Sentiment analysis of twitter data. In: Proceedings of the Workshop on Languages in Social Media. Association for Computational Linguistics (2011)
3. Kouloumpis, E., Wilson, T., Moore, J.D.: Twitter sentiment analysis: the good the bad and the omg! Icwsm **11**(538-541), 164 (2011)
4. Bakliwal, A., et al.: Mining sentiments from tweets. In: Proceedings of the 3rd Workshop in Computational Approaches to Subjectivity and Sentiment Analysis (2012)
5. Singh, V., Dubey, S.K.: Opinion mining and analysis: a literature review. In: 2014 IEEE 5th International Conference Confluence The Next Generation Information Technology Summit (Confluence) (2014)
6. Bobicev, V., Sokolova, M., Jafer, Y., Schramm, D.: Learning sentiments from tweets with personal health information. In: Kosseim, L., Inkpen, D. (eds.) AI 2012. LNCS (LNAI), vol. 7310, pp. 37–48. Springer, Heidelberg (2012). https://doi.org/10.1007/978-3-642-30353-1_4
7. Rosenthal, S., Farra, N., Nakov, P.: SemEval-2017 task 4: sentiment analysis in Twitter. In: Proceedings of the 11th International Workshop on Semantic Evaluation (SemEval-2017) (2017)

8. Poursepanj, H., Weissbock, J., Inkpen, D.: uOttawa: system description for SemEval 2013 task 2 sentiment analysis in twitter. In: Second Joint Conference on Lexical and Computational Semantics (* SEM), Volume 2: Proceedings of the Seventh International Workshop on Semantic Evaluation (SemEval 2013), vol. 2 (2013)
9. Patil, H.P., and Mohammad A.: Applications, issues and challenges in sentiment analysis and opinion mining–a user's perspective. Int. J. Cont. Theory App. **10** (2017)
10. Meral, M., Diri, B.: Sentiment analysis on Twitter. In: 2014 22nd. IEEE Signal Processing and Communications Applications Conference (SIU) (2014)
11. Bhuta, S., et al.: A review of techniques for sentiment analysis Of Twitter data. In: IEEE 2014 International Conference on Issues and Challenges in Intelligent Computing Techniques (ICICT) (2014)
12. Das, T.K., Acharjya, D.P., Patra, M.R.: Opinion mining about a product by analyzing public tweets in Twitter. In: 2014 International Conference on IEEE Computer Communication and Informatics (ICCCI) (2014)
13. Gokulakrishnan, B., et al.: Opinion mining and sentiment analysis on a twitter data stream. In: 2012 International Conference on IEEE Advances in ICT for Emerging Regions (ICTer) (2012)
14. Poria, S., et al.: Convolutional MKL based multimodal emotion recognition and sentiment analysis. In: IEEE 16th International Conference on Data Mining (ICDM) 2016. IEEE (2016)
15. Ouyang, Xi, et al.: Sentiment analysis using convolutional neural network. In: 2015 IEEE International Conference on Computer and Information Technology; Ubiquitous Computing and Communications; Dependable, Autonomic and Secure Computing; Pervasive Intelligence and Computing (CIT/IUCC/DASC/PICOM). IEEE (2015)
16. Saif, H., He, Y., Alani, H.: Semantic sentiment analysis of Twitter. In: Cudré-Mauroux, P., et al. (eds.) ISWC 2012. LNCS, vol. 7649, pp. 508–524. Springer, Heidelberg (2012). https://doi.org/10.1007/978-3-642-35176-1_32
17. Martin, S., Liermann, J., Ney, H.: Algorithms for bigram and trigram word clustering1. Speech Commun. **24**(1), 19–37 (1998)
18. You, Q., et al.: Robust image sentiment analysis using progressively trained and domain transferred deep networks. In: AAAI (2015)
19. Singhal, P., Bhattacharyya, P.: Sentiment analysis and deep learning: a survey. (2016)

Failure Prediction and Health Status Assessment of Storage Systems with Decision Trees

Kamaljit Kaur[✉] and Kuljit Kaur

Computer Engineering and Technology, Guru Nanak Dev University,
Amritsar, India
kamal.auljla86@gmail.com, kuljitchahal@yahoo.com

Abstract. Prediction of imminent failures of large scale storage systems is critical to prevent loss of data. Various machine learning and statistical methods based on SMART attributes have been proposed by different researchers. Although they have achieved good prediction accuracy, but most of them focus on predicting the status of hard drives as "good" or "failed". Moreover, the performance of hard drives deteriorates slowly than abruptly as indicated by continuous change in their corresponding SMART attributes. So, these models cannot predict this kind of continuous change. This paper gives decision tree based failure prediction model for hard drives which gives a better prediction accuracy. Experiments show that decision tree based model anticipates through 99.99% of failures, along with a false alarm rate under 0.001%. Also, we introduce prediction of lead time that proactively quantifies health status of hard drives to generate warnings in advance for triggering backups. We test the proposed model on a real-world dataset.

Keywords: Fault tolerance · Decision trees · ID3

1 Introduction

Rapid development of information technology leads the storage systems to grow very quickly. Even hard drives are reliable but [1, 3] documented the hard drives as the most replaced hardware component. Theoretically Annual failure rate (AFR) of a distinct hard drive should be lesser than 1% but [3] observed that AFR in real data centers can exceed up to 10%. Hard drives may fail every day in petabyte-level storage systems.

In order to solve the issue of hard drive failure, both the proactive fault prediction and reactive fault tolerance have been investigated by different researchers. Analysis focus on erasure rules for storage devices reliability. It is a reactive fault-tolerant approach to reconstruct data after a drive failure. In contrast, prediction of drive failures before failure occurrence helps to take advance actions such as to trigger data backup. Now-a-days, SMART (Self-Monitoring, Analysis and Reporting Technology) is opted by hard drives. However, as concluded by [4], this cannot realize an expected performance of predictions. To raise failure prediction precision machine learning and statistical learning based ways possess based on SMART parameters [4–11]. Although

© Springer Nature Singapore Pte Ltd. 2019
A. K. Luhach et al. (Eds.): ICAICR 2018, CCIS 955, pp. 366–376, 2019.
https://doi.org/10.1007/978-981-13-3140-4_33

these methods performed well, there are few problems with their performance. Firstly, they do not consider the process of changing of hard drive's SMART parameters during its deterioration. Therefore, these models only profit binary classification of the hard drive status (i.e., good or failed), but could not differentiate among being close to and being far-off from failure. Secondly, they do not give stable functionality, and it is complicated to adjust their prediction. These restrictions inspire us to provide sequential information explicitly using SMART parameters to scale health of hard drives in our model.

Within this particular paper, we examine model for hard drive's failure prediction dependent on decision trees (also referred as classification and regression trees) that gives stable performance and high accuracy. On the dataset generated from real-world storage cloud, our decision tree based model anticipates through 99.99% of failures, along with false alarm rate under 0.001%. We also present prediction of failure probability to evaluate health status of hard drives and to predict lead-time to trigger alerts to initiate backups.

The rest part of paper is organized as follows: In Sect. 2 literature survey is discussed. Section 3 highlights the proposed approach which explored the capability of decision trees (classification and regression trees and ID3) for hard disk drives failure prediction using SMART parameters. Section 4 comprised of dataset description and preprocessing. Section 5 includes experimental results that justified the dependency between health status assessment of hard drives and the failure prediction. Section 6 describes the experimental setup. Section 7 evaluated the performance of health status assessment of decision trees. The paper is concluded in last Sect. 8.

2 Related Work

Since 1995, SMART is a technique for monitoring hard drive's conditions and failure warning [6]. However, the threshold-based algorithm implemented for drive's tracking can diagnose failure rate of about 3–10% through a low false alarm pace of 0.10% [3]. The reason of this lower FAR is that, to protect false alarm (FA) cost, they keep the thresholds conventionally to maintain the FAR to lessen which results in a low failure diagnose rate.

In 2001, Hamerly et al. [5] anticipated two Bayesian approaches for failure prediction of hard drives using dataset collected from Quantum Inc. having 1,927 drives in a small dataset, and among all drives only 9 drives get fail. They used two methods named as NBEM and a naive Bayes classifier. NBEM accomplished 35–40% accuracy for predicting failures under 1% FAR and the naive Bayes classifier predicted 55% accurate failures.

In 2002, Hughes and Murray [6] stated that the Wilcoxon rank-sum test suits the most to predict hard disk faults as the most significant SMART parameters are distributed. They suggested two methods: a multivariate test and an OR-ed single attribute test. Application of the above mentioned test was validated using dataset having 3,744 drives. Failure Detection Rate accomplished by these methods, as 60.0% at 0.50% FAR.

In 2003, Murray et al. [7] did performance comparison of various approaches, including support vector machine, statistical non-parametric tests (rank-sum and reverse arrangements test) and unsupervised clustering. They proved that the rank-sum test has given higher performance in comparison to SVM or others (33.23% FDR at 0.50% FAR). However, the best performance has been acknowledged by considering only one attribute and additional attributes lead to decrease in performance by increasing false alarms. In year 2005, they have extended their work by considering multiple attributes named Multiple-Instance Naïve Bayes also known as mi-NB [4]. In their work, all the methods were validated using dataset having 369 hard disk drives only with even distribution of good and failed drives. But such dataset does not contest the real-time data center's situation.

In 2011, Wang et al. [10] has given a new technique for disk's failure prediction using Mahalanobis distance. The experiment used attributes prioritization selected by failure modes, mechanisms and effects analysis (FMMEA) [5] did well than the others having all the attributes.

Later, in 2013, Wang et al. [11], used least redundancy utmost significance by filtering redundant parameters using FMMEA. Then constructed Mahalanobis space is using the right drive's data of significant attributes. This method detected 67% of drives' failure at 0% FAR. The majority of them could be detected in advance (about less than 20 h).

Recently, in 2011, Back-propagation Artificial Neural Network (BPNN) [9] and Classification and Regression Trees [12] have been achieved great improvement for hard drive failures prediction using SMART parameters. A dataset having 23,395 drives has been used for the validation of results. The BPANN method achieved outstanding FDR up to 95% with a quite little FAR.

The above-mentioned methods did not consider the sequential sequence of SMART parameters; rather all consider each SMART illustration as a participation instant. Zhao et al. [8] used Hidden Markov Models as well as Hidden Semi-Markov Models for the failure prediction of hard disk. They have also considered the time-sequence information of SMART parameters. The HMM and HSMM methods achieved an FDR of 46% and 30%, correspondingly by using the top single parameter. Also by considering the combination of two best parameters, the HMM method achieved a false detection rate of 52%.

In 2016, Xu et al. [13] presented a RNN-based approach to influence sequential sequence of SMART parameters for hard drive's failure prediction. They have adopted multi-level classification in the outer layer of the neural network to predict the health status of hard drives. Thus, this model predicted failures as well as gave drive health status using sequential sequence of SMART parameters.

Here, in this paper, we analyze hard disk drive failure prediction model dependent on decision trees (also termed as classification and regression trees) that gives stable performance and high accuracy.

3 The Proposed Approach

As mentioned in the last section, different ways given by many researchers do not make understanding of events that lead towards decisions given by them. Also, we disagree that hard disk failure detection issue fits into long-range reliance on SMART parameters. Within this paper, we have used the capability of decision trees (CART and ID3) and proposed decision tree with feature selection and voting-based failure detection mechanism for hard disk drive failure prediction by using featured SMART attributes. Along with high prediction accuracy, decision trees yield stable results.

3.1 Decision Tree

Decision trees use tree structure to build classification or regression models. It splits SMART attributes into smaller and smaller subsets using Information Gain and entropy as a splitting function. The result is a tree with decision nodes and leaf nodes. A conclusion node offers two or more branches. Leaf node presents the group or maybe conclusion or maybe conjecture in this case. A best conclusion node corresponds to the most beneficial predictor.

3.1.1 CART

Classification and regression trees are grown-up by recursive partitioning technique, till the node does not comply with split standards or includes simply one class. Parameters to control splitting of nodes are bucket size and a minimum number of splits. We have used entropy and information gain for splitting nodes in our model. The split function scans all values of the SMART features to determine the most effective splitting variable that raises the information gain. In support of a binary splitting, let us presume node K is splitting into child nodes K1 and K2 on the basis of some feature (SMART parameters) vi, Information Gain used for this split can be calculated as Eq. (1)

$$\text{gain}(K, vi) = \text{info}(K) - \text{info}(K, vi) \tag{1}$$

where info(K) is the information entropy on node K, and info(K, vi) is the summation of information entropy of child nodes subsequent to splitting. The information entropy is computed as Eq. (2)

$$\text{info}(K) = -p\log2(p) - q\log2(q) \tag{2}$$

where p, q are controlled by p + q = 1, indicate probability distributions of two classes samples at node K, respectively.

3.1.2 ID3

ID3 approach does not backtrack in searching. Therefore, algorithm can easily converge as local optima but not as global optimal answer. ID3 is a kind of greedy approach, dealing with large scale learning problems. ID3 is sensitive to noise, focus attention on selection of property. Therefore, ID3 when applied to SMART attributes after feature selection, give very good failure detection rate.

3.1.3 Decision Tree with Changed Attributes, Featured Selection and Voting

Basis on the general concept of decision tree, some of the smart attributes are seen with low like 0 importance. Therefore, after droping that attributes with the help of feature selection, data is again partitioned into leaves to get a target measure. We have used voting-based algorithm for the detection of failed drives [9] in our model. For drives health prediction, this model check the last N successive samples (voters) before time point, and predict the drive is about to fail if more than N/2 of samples will be classified as failed. In other cases the drive will be classified as a good drive. This justifies the dependency between health status assessment of hard drives and the failure prediction. We have taken the threshold value of voting-based detection algorithm as 80%, i.e. if 80% voters predict the health status of hard drive as failed, then only it will be considered as failed.

3.1.4 Health Status

As detected in real-world data centers and cloud storage, there is a regular drift towards the anomalous status of SMART parameters prior to a failure of hard drive. That is, health status of hard drive deteriorated gradually. We calculate the health status assessment of a hard disk drive as the time (in days) prior to a failure of hard drive, and defined a disk drive's health status according to its predicted remaining time before failure occurs. We termed this predicted remaining time as Lead Time. If the lead time is extremely small, this shows drive's health status as awfully meager. This helps to trigger failure alerts as well as backups. The health status assessment method can considerably improve the dependability as well as the availability of large scale distributed storage systems in comparison to the traditional binary failure prediction methods. With this recovery of different drives can be scheduled according to failure, importance and the residual lifetime of hard disk drives. We can also control the eminence of user services and data migration accordingly. Consequently, the likelihood of missing the most critical failures reduces and the related monetary loss can be avoided.

Figure 1 shows possible quantification of health status in our model. As shown in the diagram health status is divided into 9 different ranks according to the lead time (in days). Rank 9 designates that the disk drive works properly as predicted remaining time ranges from 6 months to 1 year. Rank 8 represents good health status. Ranks 6–7 shows the fair status of the hard disk drive. Ranks 2–5 shows that the hard disk drive is about to fail and rank 1 is the "critical alert" which indicates that the lasting time is about 2 days for the current hard drive. Therefore, immediate alert handling and backup initiation should be triggered.

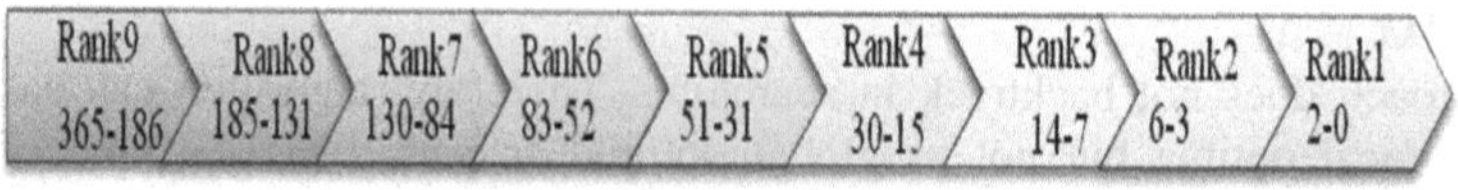

Rank9	Rank8	Rank7	Rank6	Rank5	Rank4	Rank3	Rank2	Rank1
365-186	185-131	130-84	83-52	51-31	30-15	14-7	6-3	2-0

Fig. 1. Health status of hard drives

4 Detail of Dataset

4.1 Dataset

Our dataset is collected from a real-world cloud storage 'blackbaze' [15]. The dataset provides SMART attributes of number of drives over a period of 4 years from 2013 to 2016. More than 45 attributes have been monitored for each hard drive in blackbaze cloud storage. We have taken one year data (2015 only) for failure prediction analysis of our model. There is 67,67,024 drives in the dataset, among them only 586 drives are labeled as failed. As this number is very small, so we sampled failure drive data to make count of failed drives as 97,205.

4.2 Feature Selection

For every hard drive, we can find 27 useful parameters from a SMART record. However, some SMART attributes are impractical for prediction of failures as their values remain same for good as well as for failed drives. So we filter out features according to feature importance and use only eighteen attributes for our prediction model. Table 1 lists the determined SMART features along with attribute importance. SMART is 48-bits raw value and 8-bits normalized value ranging from 1–253 which is modified through raw value [14]. The raw values of SMART parameters are not formatted by any standard specifications, but follow vendor-specifications. As several normalized values drop accuracy and their equivalent raw values are more critical towards hard drives health conditions, we have chosen ten raw values.

We have tested rate of change of SMART parameters with respect to different intervals of time and considered the most significant parameters. We have selected 8 features as important by considering 24-h change rates. The 8 parameters are: "Raw Read Error Rate", "Seek Error Rate", "Power on Hours", "Reported Uncorrected", "High Fly Writes", "Temperature Celsius", "Current Pending Sector", "Offline Uncorrectable".

5 Experimental Results

This section justifies the dependency between health status assessment of hard drives and the failure prediction.

5.1 Compared Model

KNN: This method is evaluated for hard drive failure prediction, by using desired training and testing variables. The distance concept used to find out how training set and target variable is to be examined. This procedure is repeated and maximum of k variable is to select. The value of k provides an effect on noise of the training set. As value of k increases the evaluated time also increases. Higher k reduces the effect of noise while training.

Table 1. Selected SMART attributes

Smart ID	Attribute name	Feature importance
1	Read error rate	4.09118531017
smart_1_diff		3.74839267095
3	Spin-up time	0.0
smart_3_diff		0.0
5	Reallocated sectors count	0.928684143926
smart_5_diff		0.0
7	Seek error rate	12.3707369654
smart_7_diff		0.0133497558702
9	Power-on hours count	50.6475628446
smart_9_diff		0.583214055371
187	Reported uncorrectable errors	3.40213863955
smart_187_diff		0.0075442541443
188	Command timeout	0.257551371663
smart_188_diff		0.0
189	High fly writes	10.3477533278
smart_189_diff		0.00444313837005
194	Temperature	9.12868939257
smart_194_diff		1.62027737629
197	Current pending sectors	0.451166076959
smart_197_diff		0.00216251221623
198	Off-line uncorrectable	2.39331743059
smart_198_diff		0.00183073353631

Logistic Regression: This method predicts the hard failure using binary values 0 or 1 and it is not normally distributed while predicting failure. Logistic curve gives the prediction results and concept of logarithm is applied rather than probability. As logarithm is calculated on both sides of linear line for this model prediction.

Decision tree with changed attributes, featured selection and voting: Basis on the general concept of decision tree, some of the smart attributes are seen with low like 0 importance. Therefore, after dropping that the attributes with the help of feature selection, data is again partitioned into leaves to get a target measure. These evaluated values are compared with, in addition to voting by voters to disk drives, and it gives the low value of false alarm rate.

6   Experimental Setup

In this experiment, SMART attributes (as mentioned) of different hard drives have been analyzed to predict the health of hard drives. This experiment is performed using jupyter tool using python 2.7. For the implementation of decision trees and other compared methods such as KNN, logistic regression, we split the dataset into training data and test data. Experiments are performed by changing that variation of training and test data as 60%–40%, 70%–30%, and 75%–25%, 10-fold cross validation. Results show only 75%–25% (train, test) as this ratio leads to good results. We carry out the experiments using a standard laptop as these methods does not oblige considerable computing capabilities. Training phase of each method considered in this paper is completed within 10 min approximately, and the rate of health status prediction is almost 10,000 disks per second. This time-cost tradeoff is suitable for real-time monitoring of distributed large scale data centers.

We have used voting-based algorithm for the detection of failed drives [9] in our model. For drives health prediction, this model check the last N successive samples (voters) before time point, and predict the drive is about to fail if more than N/2 of samples will be classified as failed. In other cases the drive will be classified as a good drive. This justifies the dependency between health status assessment of hard drives and the failure prediction. Figure 2 shows the results of prediction using Decision trees (with different variations), LR and KNN models using the voting-based failure detection algorithm. In our experiment, we have taken the threshold value of voting-based detection algorithm as 80%, i.e. if 80% voters predict the health status of hard drive as failed, then only it will be considered as failed.

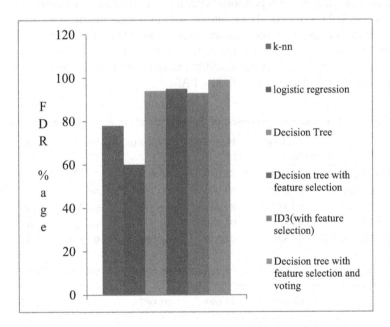

Fig. 2. Failure detection rate using different models

Figure 3 shows the correlation between false alarm rate and failure detection rate for decision tree using feature selection and voting-based failure detection for different simulation runs. It performs excellent to predict hard drive failures and correctly predicts 99.99% failed drives with 0.00% FAR.

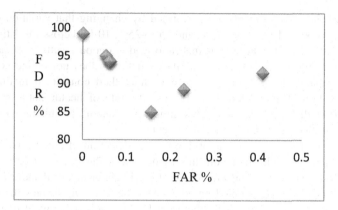

Fig. 3. Correlation b/w false alarm rate (FAR) and failure detection rate (FDR) for decision tree (with feature selection and voting)

Table 2 shows the parametric performance comparison of different models. From this table, it is clear that Logistic Regression (LR) performs worst in our case for hard drive failure prediction. KNN performs better than LR, but can only predict 78% failure correctly with 0.23% of FAR. If we further want to decrease FAR to increase FDR, it will not show any positive affect rather decrease the FDR value. Table 2 shows the different variations of decision trees and performs excellent to predict hard drive failures using voting-based detection algorithm along with feature selection. It correctly predicts 99.99% failed drives with 0.00% FAR.

Table 2. Performance comparison of different models in terms of FDR and FAR

Classifier	Accuracy (%)	Precision (%)	F-measure (%)	Recall (%)	FAR (%)	FDR (%)
k-nearest neighbors:	74.938	77.019	76.304	73.572	0.23	78
Logistic regression:	59.070	59.007	60.736	68.740	0.41	60
Random forest	90.493	84.405	88.813	93.706	0.156	85
Decision tree	94.777	93.740	94.134	94.532	0.063	94
Decision tree (Raw data)	95.549	94.637	95.003	95.371	0.054	95
Decision tree with feature selection	95.594	94.718	95.055	95.395	0.053	95
Decision tree (changed attribute and feature selection)	94.735	93.693	94.087	94.484	0.064	94
Decision tree with feature selection and voting	99.993	1.0	99.826	99.653	0.00	99
ID3	95.08	93.914	94.46	95.025	0.061	94

7   Health Status Assessment for Hard Drives

In this section, we evaluated the health status assessment of hard disk drives. We have predicted lead-time (predicted remaining time) of hard drives by extracting various parameters from our dataset such as

- First day: is the day when disk monitoring has been initiated using SMART parameters
- Last day: is the length of drive if drive doesn't fail or the day when drive failed
- Length: is last day - first day or the total time-period of disk operation
- Day of first occurrence: is the day when our model predicts that the drive is about to fail.

Prediction of health status assessment is performed by voting-based detection algorithm (threshold = 80%). Lead time (remaining predicted time) of hard drives has been predicted for each drive when our model says that the drive is going to fail. Figure 4 shows that according to above mentioned parameters, lead time can be predicted ranging from 2 days to 365 days. Due to lack of space very few results have been shown here. As shown, half of the drives may survive for a year or more after prediction. Very few hard drives are in very critical condition, i.e. just about to fail with 1–2 days, therefore for such drives alert should me managed critically or migrations can be initiated.

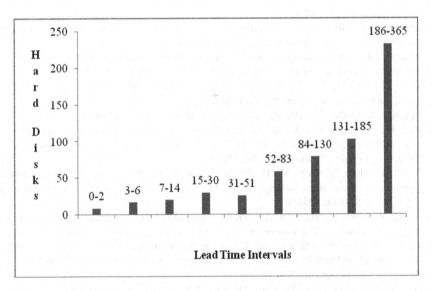

Fig. 4. Predicted remaining time (lead time) of different hard drives

8 Conclusion

Within this paper, we propose decision trees based model for hard disk drive failure prediction and for lead time prediction, that treats changed rate of SMART attributes for better prediction of the remaining lifetime of hard disk drives. Experiment results show that our model can achieve better performance in comparison to other binary prediction models.

References

1. Smith, T.F., Waterman, M.S.: Identification of common molecular subsequences. J. Mol. Biol. **147**, 195–197 (1981)
2. Schroeder, B., Gibson, G.A.: Disk failures in the real world: what does an MTTF of 1, 000, 000 hours mean to you? In: FAST, vol. 7, pp. 1–16 (2007)
3. Xin, Q., Miller, E.L., Schwarz, T., Long, D.D., Brandt, S.A., Litwin, W.: Reliability mechanisms for very large storage systems. In: Proceedings of 20th IEEE/11th NASA Goddard Conference on IEEE Mass Storage Systems and Technologies, 2003, pp. 146–156 (2003)
4. Murray, J.F., Hughes, G.F., Kreutz-Delgado, K.: Machine learning methods for predicting failures in hard drives: a multiple-instance application. J. Mach. Learn. Res. **6**, 783–816 (2005)
5. Hamerly, G., Elkan, C.: Bayesian approaches to failure prediction for disk drives. In: ICML, vol. 1, pp. 202–209 (2001)
6. Hughes, G.F., Murray, J.F., Kreutz-Delgado, K., Elkan, C.: Improved disk-drive failure warnings. IEEE Trans. Reliab. **51**, 350–357 (2002)
7. Murray, J.F., Hughes, G.F., Kreutz-Delgado, K.: Hard drive failure prediction using non-parametric statistical methods. In: Proceedings of ICANN/ICONIP (2003)
8. Zhao, Y., Liu, X., Gan, S., Zheng, W.: Predicting disk failures with HMM-and HSMM-based approaches. In: Perner, P. (ed.) ICDM 2010. LNCS (LNAI), vol. 6171, pp. 390–404. Springer, Heidelberg (2010). https://doi.org/10.1007/978-3-642-14400-4_30
9. Zhu, B., Wang, G., Liu, X., Hu, D., Lin, S., Ma, J.: Proactive drive failure prediction for large scale storage systems. In: 2013 IEEE 29th Symposium on Mass Storage Systems and Technologies (MSST), pp. 1–5. IEEE (2013)
10. Wang, Y., Miao, Q., Pecht, M.: Health monitoring of hard disk drive based on Mahalanobis distance. In: Prognostics and System Health Management Conference (PHM-Shenzhen), 2011, pp. 1–8. IEEE (2011)
11. Wang, Y., Miao, Q., Ma, E.W., Tsui, K.L., Pecht, M.G.: Online anomaly detection for hard disk drives based on Mahalanobis distance. IEEE Trans. Reliab. **62**, 136–145 (2013)
12. Li, J., et al.: Hard drive failure prediction using classification and regression trees. In: P2014 44th Annual IEEE/IFIP International Conference on IEEE Dependable Systems and Networks (DSN), pp. 383–394 (2014)
13. Xu, C., Wang, G., Liu, X., Guo, D., Liu, T.Y.: Health status assessment and failure prediction for hard drives with recurrent neural networks. IEEE Trans. Comput. **65**, 3502–3508 (2016)
14. Allen, B.: Monitoring hard disks with smart. Linux J. **117**, 74–77 (2004)
15. Hard Drive Data and Stat. https://www.backblaze.com/b2/hard-drive-test-data.html

A Study of Link Prediction Using Deep Learning

Anant Dadu[1], Ajay Kumar[1], Harish Kumar Shakya[1],
Siddhartha Kumar Arjaria[2(✉)], and Bhaskar Biswas[1]

[1] Indian Institute of Technology (BHU), Varanasi, India
[2] Information Technology, Rajkiya Engineering College, Banda, India
`ajayk.rs.cse16@itbhu.ac.in`

Abstract. Prediction of missing or future link is an arduous task in complex networks especially in the current scenario of big data where networks are growing at a high speed. We investigate into both the supervised and unsupervised learning approaches to solve this problem. Supervised approaches use the latent representation of nodes (representation learning) while unsupervised approaches work on the heuristic score given to each node pair having no edge in between them. In this work, Deep learning concept is explored to predict the missing links in the network as a part of the supervised classification. Our experiment on four real-world datasets represents that deep learning approach outperforms some existing supervised learning methods like the Random forest (RF) and the Logistic Regression (LR).

Keywords: Link prediction · Deep learning
Representation learning · Unsupervised learning · Supervised learning

1 Introduction

Network analysis has been identified as growing area of research due to exponential increase in data in the form of structural networks. Lots of networks are all around us, including web pages on the internet, telephone networks, transportation networks, social networks, etc. Graphs are compact representation of such networks. Enormous amount of knowledge can be extracted from real world networks by discovering typical patterns available in the network like predicting social relationships [1] in social networking sites, hyper-links among web pages [6] or in areas of biology like protein-protein interaction [7].

Social Networks are dynamic objects with the frequent addition or removal of edges and nodes. Link Prediction [19] is the effort to infer new interactions among the members that are likely to occur in near future. Tasks ranging from suggesting friends on social network, discovering relationship among genes or predicting citations of new articles can be solved by Link Prediction. It can also be seen as the problem of inferring missing links [2] in an observed network.

A. Dadu and A. Kumar—Authors equally contributed.

© Springer Nature Singapore Pte Ltd. 2019
A. K. Luhach et al. (Eds.): ICAICR 2018, CCIS 955, pp. 377–385, 2019.
https://doi.org/10.1007/978-981-13-3140-4_34

Good amount of work have been proposed in the past ten years in this area using learning techniques. A typical solution to the problem [2,19] is to provide score to each edge on the basis of degree of nodes to which the edge is connected. The different measures are analyzed to give scores to the edges like Jaccard coefficient, Adamic/Adar etc. The major drawback of these techniques is that they fail to exploit more structural information from the networks. The introduction of knowledge representation learning for networks boost the performance of analyzing graphs more clearly and easily. These features can be used to predict labels of nodes or for community detection using clustering techniques. Link Prediction can be converted to a binary classification problem which is described in further sections.

Recently, deep learning has been proved to be successful in many data mining application such as image classification, speech recognition and many others. To the best of our knowledge, deep learning has not been adequately investigated to solve link prediction. Therefore, we tried to exploit distributed representations generated by deep learning approaches to solve the problem. We also explored some existing unsupervised approaches and made comparison with our approach.

2   Background and Related Works

In this section, we discuss representation learning used in deep architectures to exploit the structural information and a brief review on deep learning.

2.1   Deep Learning

Recently, deep learning has gained lot of focus due to its ability to build much better models by exploiting the structural information from the features in complex networks. The power of deep learning can be seen through its applications in natural language processing, computer vision and speech recognition [5,8,16]. The technique involves multiple hidden layers with one input layer and one output layer. The feature vector is passed to the input layer of the neural network and the useful representation of the vector is learned by the model at each layer. The nonlinearity is provided by the activation functions at every level of neural network. Activation function can be relu ($max(0,x)$), logistic ($\frac{1}{(1+e^{-x})}$) or tanh ($\frac{1+e^x}{1+e^{-x}}$). At the end, the weights for each component of the input vector are calculated on the basis of cost function. For the binary classification problem, the cost function for the neural network is binary cross entropy given as

$$L = -t\log(p) - (1-t)\log(1-p) \tag{1}$$

where t is the target value and p is the predicted probability of getting t target value.

Very few deep learning approaches have been proposed in link prediction domain. Li et al. [26] proposed Conditional Temporal Restricted Boltzmann Machine (ctRBM), a deep learning framework for link prediction in dynamic networks. In the framework, local neighbor's influences and individual transition variance are used in prediction. A Neighbor Influence Clustering algorithm was proposed to improve efficiency by reducing the computational cost of prediction to linear. Experimental results on datasets (real and synthetic) show better performance over existing dynamic link prediction. Liu et al. [9] proposed a deep belief network (DBN)-based approach that predicts missing links in signed social network (SSN). A signed social network a directed network having both positive and negative relationships among nodes. In addition, they introduced DBN-based unsupervised link prediction model. Experiment results on three SSN datasets show promising results for both positive and negative links.

2.2 Representation Learning

The state-of-the-art methods for representation learning of graphs were introduced in past few years which include DeepWalk [24] and Node2Vec [10]. Both these techniques uses Skip-gram [23], which is a language model widely used in natural language processing for feature learning of words. Skip-gram models are basically the simpler version of the Neural Net Language Model (NNLM) [4] with the non-linear hidden layer removed. It is a three-layer neural network with one input layer, one hidden layer and one output layer. Major advantage of using skip-gram is that it is computationally inexpensive, hence, huge amount of words can be trained to generate high quality vectors.

In Deep Walk, the representation of nodes is learned on the basis of stream of random walks. The input layer is on-hot representation of nodes and output layer is the number of neighboring nodes according to random walks. Node2Vec introduces flexible biased random walk to explore the breadth first search (BFS) and depth first search (DFS). It allows to utilize both similarities in a graph namely, homophily and structural equivalence [11]. Structural equivalence is a similarity between two nodes that share similar neighbors and nodes that belong to similar kind of cluster or community in a network. It can be intuitively seen that BFS allows to exploit structural equivalence while DFS exploits the homophily. Deep-Walk can be thought as rigid strategy where node2vec can be controlled through its biased parameters. In [10], Node2vec showed better results than DeepWalk so we opt for Node2Vec in the experiments.

3 Methodology

Deep learning has been proved to be very successful in graph clustering [25]. Lots of works have implemented clustering for the link prediction [13], which makes us intuitively feel that this technique might work well for the link prediction problem. We apply deep learning to the vectorial representation of nodes to get the high quality low dimensional vectors of each edge.

3.1   Supervised Approach

Link prediction can be solved using binary classification algorithm. In a supervised setting, training set data is used to build a model and test set data is applied to assess the performance of the built model. To generate set of edges that can be treated as positive class samples, we took random 50% of the edges that are present in a network. While generating positive samples we have to take care that after removing the edges, the graph should remain connected. For the negative class samples, we chose the random edges that are not present in the actual graph. The sample size for each class is equal to half of the total number of edges in a graph. The node2vec is trained on the network after the removal of the edges present in positive examples. We proposed two deep learning architectures of feed forward neural network [3] as shown in Fig. 1. In the first architecture, the input vector for each edge is the combination of feature vector of both the nodes to which the edge is connected after applying binary operator. In second, the vectors of each node is separately passed to the input layer of neural network and combination is applied on the hidden layer. In Fig. 1, n is the number of dimensions of embedded vector, h is the hidden layer size, W and W' are the weight matrix from input and hidden layer respectively. We address the architecture shown in Figs. 1(a) and (b) as architecture 1 and architecture 2 respectively.

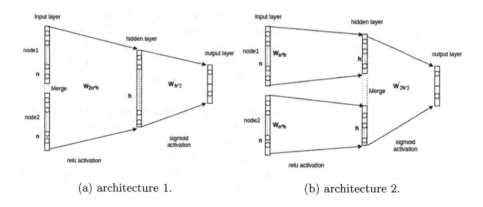

(a) architecture 1.   (b) architecture 2.

Fig. 1. Proposed deep architectures

There is a trade-off between time and model quality for these architectures. The first architecture is expected to be more accurate as the neural network will have more number of features to extract the desired information but expected to take more time than the second architecture. We compared the performance of neural network with Random Forest [18] and Logistic Regression [12]. For Random Forest (RF) and Logistic Regression (LR), only the first input layer is the feature vector of each sample in the dataset based on which the model is trained and tested.

3.2   Unsupervised Approach

Unsupervised approach evaluates how well the scores are given to the edges on the basis of node properties. Lots of different methods to assign heuristic score to every edge are available in the literature.

Common Neighbors [20]

This is a very simple heuristic to compute the similarity score between two nodes of a network. The common neighbor score of a node pair x and y is

$$S_{xy} = |\Gamma(x) \cap \Gamma(y)| \tag{2}$$

where S_{xy} is the score between x and y and $\Gamma(z)$ refers to the neighbors of z.

Jaccard Coefficient [21]

Jaccard heuristic is same as the common neighbors, additionally, it normalizes the common neighbor heuristic.

$$S_{xy} = \frac{|\Gamma(x) \cap \Gamma(y)|}{|\Gamma(x) \cup \Gamma(y)|} \tag{3}$$

Adamic/Adar [1]

Above two heuristics give more importance to the node pair having more number of common neighbors in score calculation. While this heuristic reduces the importance to such node pair.

$$S_{xy} = \sum_{z \in |\Gamma(x) \cap \Gamma(y)|} \frac{1}{\log |\Gamma(z)|} \tag{4}$$

Preferential Attachment [15]

This heuristic is the main crux of the evolution scale-free networks where the likelihood of incrementing new connection associating a node x is proportional to the degree of that node x. It is further extended for the node pair as follows.

$$S_{xy} = |\Gamma(x)| * |\Gamma(y) \tag{5}$$

3.3   Evaluation

The prediction accuracy is evaluated by a standard metric viz., area under the receiver operating characteristic curve (AUC) [14]. This is a single point summary statistics i.e., it is represented as a single value. This metric can be interpreted as the probability that randomly chosen missing link (link in positive examples) is given a higher score than a randomly chosen nonexistent link (link in negative examples). Among n independent comparisons, if there are n_1 missing links having higher score and n_2 occurrences of randomly positive example and negative examples having same score, AUC score can be formulated as:

$$AUC = \frac{(n_1 + 0.5 n_2)}{n} \tag{6}$$

The value of this evaluation metric ranges in the interval [0, 1] in which the value 1 represents perfect accuracy where as 0, worst accuracy. The value of area under the ROC curve (AUC) must be greater than 0.5 which is the accuracy of a random predictor. Higher AUC value of an approach represents the better approach.

4 Datasets and Experimental Settings

We choose four real world datasets to evaluate the performance of our model. Dolphin [22], Karate [27] and Facebook [17] are the social network datasets in which edges represents the interactions between living beings. BlogCatalog3 [28] is the social blog directory which manages the bloggers and their blogs. In this dataset, both the contact network and selected group membership information are included. The basic information of all these datasets are summarized in Table 1.

Table 1. Datasets description.

Dataset	#Nodes	#Edges
dolphin	62	159
karate	34	78
facebook	4,039	88,234
blogCatlog3	10,312	3,33,983

Table 2. Link prediction accuracy estimated by Area Under Receiver Operating Curve (AUC) scores using **unsupervised approaches.**

Dataset	Jaccard	AA	CN	PA
dolphin	0.6590	0.6630	0.6609	**0.6829**
karate	0.6220	0.6521	0.6382	**0.7226**
facebook	0.9641	**0.9706**	0.8311	0.9687
blogCatlog3	0.7785	0.9242	0.9193	**0.9495**

In supervised setting, we split the dataset into training and test set. We generated the five sets randomly for the better evaluation of the models. We set 128 as the dimension of node embedding vector. p and q are the parameters of node2vec which explains how fast the walk explores neighborhood. The values p and q are set to be 1. The number of hidden layer is 1 in both the architectures with size as 96 in architecture1 and 48 each in architecture2. The maximum number of epochs are 200, if the error does not converge. We select three binary operators to merge the layers;

(i) $Average(a, b) : \frac{(a_i + b_i)}{2}$,

(ii) $Hadamard(a, b) : (a_i * b_i)$, and

(iii) $Concatenation(a, b) : a_i + b_i$,

where a and b are two lists and a_i and b_i are i^{th} value of a and b respectively.

For unsupervised approach, the same set of positive and negative examples are chosen and 10000 independent trials are done to compute the AUC scores as described in Eq. 1. Some methods to calculate heuristic scores based on Jaccard coefficient [21], Adamic/Adar(AA) [1] Preferential Attachment(PA) [15], and Common neighbors(CN) are formulated in Table 2.

4.1 Results and Discussion

The results of unsupervised approach is given in Table 2, where preferential attachment method works better than others for all datasets except facebook. Highest scores are emphasized in bold.

Table 3. Link prediction accuracy estimated by Area Under Receiver Operating Curve (AUC) using **supervised approaches.**

Dataset	Merge-type	Architecture1	Architecture2	RF	LR
dolphin	Average	0.6544	0.6207	0.6863	0.5897
	Hadamard	0.7182	0.6863	0.7133	0.6287
	Concatenation	**0.7288**	0.6078	0.7173	0.6093
karate	Average	0.5992	0.6256	0.6238	0.4895
	Hadamard	0.5516	**0.7415**	0.6099	0.4565
	Concatenation	0.6464	0.6024	0.5659	0.5490
facebook	Average	0.9630	0.7582	0.9583	0.7124
	Hadamard	0.9645	**0.9663**	0.9595	0.9571
	Concatenation	0.9629	0.7620	0.9637	0.7157
blogCatlog3	Average	0.8847	0.8912	0.7428	0.8141
	Hadamard	0.7841	0.8827	0.7120	0.6947
	Concatenation	0.8877	**0.8913**	0.8545	0.8211

Our proposed deep architectures outperform random forest and logistic regression on all datasets shown in Table 3. As far as merge-type is concerned, hadamard operator proves to be better than others for facebook and karate dataset while concatenation is better in dolphin and blogCatalog3. Moreover, the architecture 2 performs best on the three large datasets. The experimental results suggest that the we should use architecture1 for smaller datasets (like dolphin) and architecture 2 for the larger datasets. The possible reason of this misclassification is that one layer neural network cannot emulate average or hadamard operation at the input layer on larger datasets, so it is important to perform that operation on hidden layer (representation generated by neural net).

Comparing the proposed method with unsupervised approach we observe that architecture 1 beat all methods on karate network where as architecture 2 outperform on dolphin network. Our method shows comparable results on other two datasets viz., facebook and blogCatlog3.

5   Conclusion

In this paper, we proposed a novel approach to predict missing links in networks using deep learning. The two different architectures (i.e., deep architectures) of feed forward neural network are exploited to extract useful information from the node pair of an edge. We applied three binary operators to merge the node properties to generate accurate representation of an edge. Models are evaluated using area under the ROC curve (AUC). The experimental result shows that the proposed approach outperforms other supervised algorithms on four datasets; with hadamard operator as the best one. In unsupervised approach, preferential attachment works better as compared to others except facebook dataset.

In future, we can exploit time series deep learning methods like LSTM and Recurrent neural network in link prediction. We wish to explore the Hidden Markov Models for the representation learning of node vectors. Overall, we have taken a step towards the use of deep learning in graph mining and we would like to extend its domain to other related problems as well.

References

1. Adamic, L.A., Adar, E.: Friends and neighbors on the web. Soc. Netw. **25**(3), 211–230 (2003)
2. Backstrom, L., Leskovec, J.: Supervised random walks: predicting and recommending links in social networks. In: Proceedings of the Fourth ACM International Conference on Web Search and Data Mining, pp. 635–644 (2011)
3. Bebis, G., Georgiopoulos, M.: Feed-forward neural networks. IEEE Potentials **13**(4), 27–31 (1994)
4. Bengio, Y., Ducharme, R., Vincent, P., Jauvin, C.: A neural probabilistic language model. J. Mach. Learn. Res. **3**(Feb), 1137–1155 (2003)
5. Collobert, R., Weston, J., Bottou, L., Karlen, M., Kavukcuoglu, K., Kuksa, P.: Natural language processing (almost) from scratch. J. Mach. Learn. Res. **12**(Aug), 2493–2537 (2011)
6. Zhu, J., Hong, J., Hughes, J.G.: Using Markov models for web site link prediction. In: Proceedings of the Thirteenth ACM Conference on Hypertext and Hypermedia, HYPERTEXT 2002, pp. 169–170 (2002)
7. Airodi, E., Blei, D., Xing, E., Fienberg, S.: Mixed membership stochastic block models for relational data, with applications to protein-protein interactions. In: Proceedings of International Biometric Society-ENAR Annual Meetings (2006)

8. Dahl, G.E., Yu, D., Deng, L., Acero, A.: Context-dependent pre-trained deep neural networks for large vocabulary speech recognition. IEEE Trans. Audio Speech Lang. Process. **20**(1), 30–42 (2012)
9. Liu, F., Liu, B., Sun, C., Liu, M., Wang, X.: Deep belief network-based approaches for link prediction in signed social networks. Entropy **17**(4), 2140–2169 (2015)
10. Grover, A., Leskovec, J.: node2vec: scalable feature learning for networks. In: Proceedings of the 22nd ACM SIGKDD International Conference on Knowledge Discovery and Data Mining, pp. 855–864 (2016)
11. Ho, P.D., Raftery, A.E., Handcock, M.S.: Latent space approaches to social network analysis. J. Am. Stat. Assoc. **97**(460), 1090–1098 (2002)
12. Hosmer Jr., D.W., Lemeshow, S., Sturdivant, R.X.: Applied Logistic Regression, vol. 398. Wiley, Hoboken (2013)
13. Huang, Z.: Link prediction based on graph topology: the predictive value of generalized clustering coefficient. In: LinkKDD (2006)
14. Hanley, J.A., McNeil, B.J.: The meaning and use of the area under a receiver operating characteristic (ROC) curve. Radiology **143**(1), 2936 (1982). https://doi.org/10.1148/radiology.143.1.7063747
15. Jeong, H., Neda, Z., Barabasi, A.L.: Measuring preferential attachment in evolving networks. EPL (Eur. Lett.) **61**(4), 567 (2003)
16. Krizhevsky, A., Sutskever, I., Hinton, G.E.: Imagenet classification with deep convolutional neural networks. In: Advances in Neural Information Processing Systems, pp. 1097–1105 (2012)
17. Leskovec, J., Mcauley, J.J.: Learning to discover social circles in ego networks. In: Advances in Neural Information Processing Systems, pp. 539–547 (2012)
18. Liaw, A., Wiener, M.: Classification and regression by random forest. R News **2**(3), 18–22 (2002)
19. Liben-Nowell, D., Kleinberg, J.: The link-prediction problem for social networks. J. Assoc. Inf. Sci. Technol. **58**(7), 1019–1031 (2007)
20. Newman, M.E.J.: Clustering and preferential attachment in growing networks. Phys. Rev. E **64**, 025102 (2001). https://doi.org/10.1103/PhysRevE.64.025102
21. Jaccard, P.: Distribution de la flore alpine dans le bassin des dranses et dans quelques regions voisines. Bull. Soc. Vaud. Sci. Nat. **37**, 241–272 (1901)
22. Lusseau, D., Schneider, K., Boisseau, O.J., Haase, P., Slooten, E., Dawson, S.M.: The bottlenose dolphin community of doubtful sound features a large proportion of long lasting associations. Behav. Ecol. Sociobiol. **54**(4), 396–405 (2003)
23. Mikolov, T., Chen, K., Corrado, G., Dean, J.: Efficient estimation of word representations in vector space. arXiv preprint arXiv:1301.3781 (2013)
24. Perozzi, B., Al-Rfou, R., Skiena, S.: Deepwalk: online learning of social representations. In: Proceedings of the 20th ACM SIGKDD International Conference on Knowledge Discovery and Data Mining, pp. 701–710 (2014)
25. Tian, F., Gao, B., Cui, Q., Chen, E., Liu, T.Y.: Learning deep representations for graph clustering. In: AAAI, pp. 1293–1299 (2014)
26. Li, X., Du, N., Li, H., Li, K., Gao, J., Zhang, A.: A deep learning approach to link prediction in dynamic networks. In: Proceedings of the 2014 SIAM International Conference on Data Mining, pp. 289–297 (2014)
27. Zachary, W.W.: An information flow model for conflict and fission in small groups. J. Anthropol. Res. **33**(4), 452–473 (1977)
28. Zafarani, R., Liu, H.: Social computing data repository at ASU (2009). http://socialcomputing.asu.edu

Hindi Story Heading Generation Using Proverb Identification

Leena Jain[1] and Prateek Agrawal[1,2(✉)]

[1] IKG-Punjab Technical University, Kapurthala, Punjab, India
leenajain.79@gmail.com, prateek061186@gmail.com
[2] Lovely Professional University, Phagwara, Punjab, India

Abstract. This paper explains 02 methods to generate the headings or titles of Hindi stories. We have developed a title generation tool that takes a story (without any length limit) as input and suggests some titles based on (i) keyword matching and (ii) proverb sensing. In keyword matching approach, it deals with database which includes keywords associated with each proverb. The corpora contain 35135 Hindi words which are classified separately among Nouns, Adjectives, Verbs, Adverbs, and Quantifiers etc. Both algorithms for generating the titles are described in this paper. RD Parts Of Speech Tagger (an open source POS tagger) has been referred and some tagged word enhancements have been done in the POS tagger corpora to improve the efficiency. Our proposed tool was tested on randomly selected 40 common Hindi short stories and the system produces more than 90% relevant (The results were verified and validated by 02 School Hindi Teachers having more than 10 years experience (St. Soldiers Public School, Jalandhar, Punjab, India)) titles using proverb sensing method. This application can be recommended as an informative tool for school going students as well as for school Hindi teachers as an effective pedagogy tool for teaching and learning. It can also be helpful to Hindi newspaper editors, blog writers and technical writers in finding the tentative titles for their articles.

Keywords: Transliteration · Heading generation · Language teaching tool
Natural language processing

1 Introduction

Title creation is one of the most challenging tasks that bloggers or article-writers usually face [1]. As per Indian Censes 2001 report, there were approximately 42 million Indians having Hindi as their first language [2]. Recent research has shown a lot of automatic work done text written in English language [3–5], title generation for articles [6–8, 10] but the scenario for Hindi language is not appreciable. According to English language there is a categorization of alphabets into two parts: 21 Consonants and 05 Vowels. On the other hand, Hindi language alphabets have larger categorization of consonants and vowels in comparison to English. There are 40 consonants known as "'व्यंजन'" and 12 vowels known as "'स्वर'" in Hindi language [9] (Fig. 1).

A. K. Luhach et al. (Eds.): ICAICR 2018, CCIS 955, pp. 386–396, 2019.
https://doi.org/10.1007/978-981-13-3140-4_35

क ख ग घ ङ   च छ ज झ ञ
ट ठ ड ढ ण   त थ द ध न
प फ ब भ म   य र ल व
श ष स ह

Fig. 1. Consonants of Hindi [14]

There are 12 vowels in hindi language as shown in Fig. 2. These vowels include sign, *maatra*, half letters and *halants* etc.

अ	आ	इ
ई	उ	ऊ
ए	ऐ	ओ
औ	अं	अः

Fig. 2. Vowels in Hindi [13]

So, due to this major difference between English and Hindi language the methods which are applicable for English language are not directly suitable to use for the systems of Hindi language. A very large area of India is covered by Hindi language. Various novels, documents, newspaper, government notice, books, magazines, etc. are written in Hindi language so there is need for development of title generation tools for Hindi.

NLP is an approach for learning of computers for various natural languages. Interaction between computers and humans introduces number of challenges [10]. Computers operates using binary digits only but it is not feasible for a human being to deal everything by the use of binary digits. So a huge database is required which can be stored in a system for processing of human understandable words by machine. NLP provides an approach through which human can interact with computer using any desired natural language. NLP technique is one of the famous approaches to generate the title of the given story in Hindi. Title of story can be used to understand that what the story is about? The most common and suitable language used for NLP is Java.

2 Related Work

According to the already existing systems, their main aim is to provide an English headline for the English as well as Non-English document. Two approaches suggested by them for generating an English headline is : a statistical system (HMM Hedge) and Hedge trimmer. *Informative abstract is a* headline that summarizes a story whereas an indicative abstract is a headline which identifies the topic or topics of a story. From here we get an idea of title generation which is the central theme of the story, not the headline, as they focus on informative abstract and our focus area is indicative abstract i.e. central theme of the story. The major drawback is their system is they need to do translation because they are generating English headline but we will focus on generating Hindi title for Hindi story [1].

In other system, they designed and implemented an automatic tagger which extract a free text and then tag it. The main aim of the research is to implement an automatic and perfect tagging system that can be used as a main core component or reusable component for NLP applications. The words disambiguation is solved in Arabic POS taggers but not for Hindi language. This problem of tagging is solved in our system [2].

3 Proposed Approach

This proposed system is implemented using number of steps as parts of speech tagging, tokenization, text segmentation, database generation, classification of sentences, paraphrasing etc shown in the Fig. 3.

3.1 Input Text

Firstly, the text will be given as an input by user. Considering those users who are not comfortable to operate the system with an English text so here is a provision of Hindi text. Interface of this system is provided with a Hindi keyboard through which user can input the text in Hindi. User needs to select Hindi keyboard to type text in Hindi language. User can use virtual keyboard for Hindi typing by clicking on virtual keyboard button mentioned on interface. In virtual keyboard interface, there is a provision to exit from it by clicking on exit button. By clicking on reset button, entire Hindi text can be reset and new text can be typed using virtual keyboard. The order of Hindi alphabets in virtual keyboard is same as their actual order so it makes convenient and user friendly to novice users to search any alphabet easily in virtual keyboard.

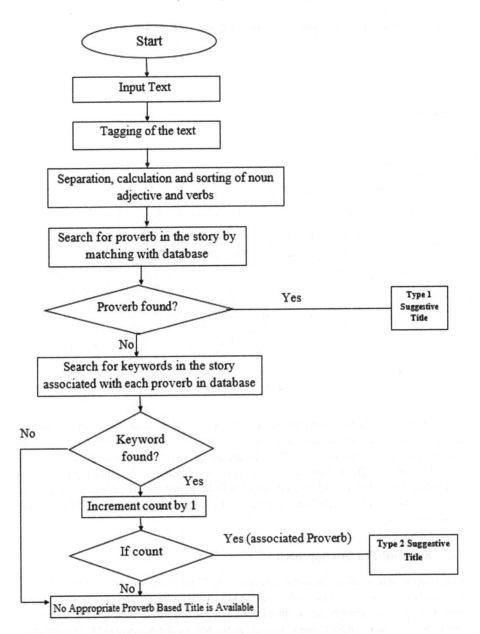

Fig. 3. Processing steps of proposed approach

The interface having keyboard is shown below in Fig. 4.

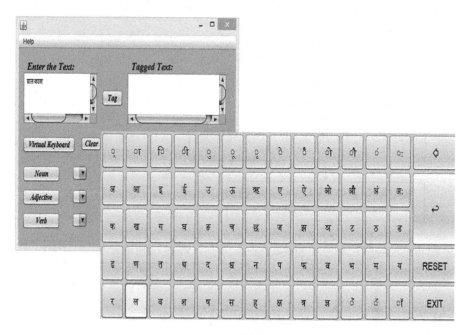

Fig. 4. Hindi keyboard

Exit button is there to leave the keyboard section. There is another way to enter the text by the process of transliteration. User can type in English language and then with the transliteration process text will automatically convert the text to Hindi language [11]. Unicode of Hindi language is mapped to transliterate English alphabets into equivalent Hindi letters and desired output will be generated by calling the algorithm [18, 19]. Third way to write Hindi text can be by doing copy and paste of Hindi text in input text area.

3.2   Keyword-Proverb approach

In this approach we again make a database which includes proverbs with their some keywords [17]. System will search for these keywords in the given passage and if it will found all the keywords or some threshold value of keywords then it will suggest the corresponding proverb for those keywords as the title of the passage [15]. This database of keywords is generated after surveying large numbers of articles and stories of Hindi language. Firstly we collected 3–4 stories for each proverb and afterwards in collaboration of all the stories 8 keywords are searched which will match to a particular proverb [14]. The following Fig. 5 shows the structure of Keyword-Proverb database table made in wamp_server:

Algorithm

```
Input = Hindi paragraph or story
P = List of Hindi Proverbs and Idioms with their relevant keywords
for each Pᵢ in P
        If "Pᵢ" is found in Hindi Story,
        Return Title = Pi
        else
                Keyword_Proverb (Input)
                        Database Connectivity;
                        Keywords_list = add all keywords given in database
                        corresponding to particular proverb to array list;
                count = 0;
                        for (i=1 to length of keywords) // for columns one by one in each
                        record(row)
                                String keyword = rst.getString(i);
                                if(k.contains(keyword))
                                        count++;

                If (count>=4)
                        title_list.addItem (rst.getString(10));  // add idiom as title
                        suggestion
```

id	k1	k2	k3	k4	k5	k6	k7	k8	idiom
1	ताकतवर	ताकत वाले	बड़ा आदमी	अमीर इन्सान	बलवान	गरीब आदमी	कमजोर इन्सान	कमजोर	जिसकी लाठी उसकी भैंस
2	मेहनत	बड़ा पाने के लिए	बड़े काम का बड़ा नतीजा	कठिन मेहनत	बड़ी उपलब्धी	बड़ी सफलता	बड़ा प्रयत्न	बड़ा काम	ओस चाटने से प्यास नहीं बुझती
3	गरीब	लालची	खराब	बुरा	खड़ा	दुखी	खुश	बेईमान	जैसे को तैसा

Fig. 5. Keyword-proverb database table

4 Results

This system will generate the title of the entered text on the basis of two approaches; one is the keyword-proverb approach and another is the highest priority nouns. The following Fig. 6 shows the interface of the system resulting in the generation of title by the above discussed two approaches.

Table 1 shows the result analysis of the system. This table includes the actual title of the story and the title generated by the tool. The title generated by the tool are based on two approaches i.e. keyword-proverb approach and highest priority noun approach. The testing of the system is performed in two ways: firstly by checking for those stories

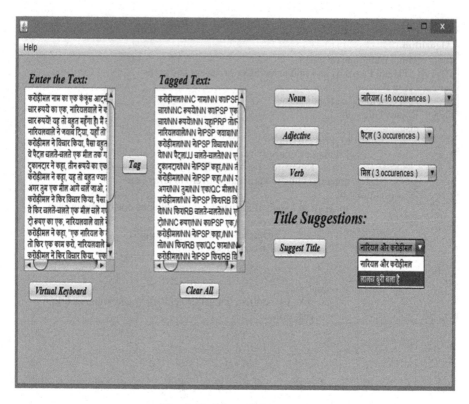

Fig. 6. Interface of the system

Table 1. Result analysis

Sr. No.	Story No.	Actual Title	Generated by Tool	Relevance Analysis
1	1	कंजूस करोड़ीमल	लालच बुरी बला है	Most relevant
2	2	जैसा बोओगे वैसा काटोगे	जैसे को तैसा	Most relevant
3	3	मछुआ और मंत्री	जैसे को तैसा	Most relevant
4	4	लकड़हारा और देवदूत	ईमानदारी का फल मीठा होता है	Most relevant
5	5	एकता का बल	एकता में बल है	Most relevant

which already had titles. Secondly by the Hindi professional tutors who test our system generated titles with the associated story. From the table, it is clear that our tool was able to identify the suitable proverb and extracted the same as relevant story title. For given 5 story samples [16], accuracy is found 100%.

5   Conclusion

In this proposed system we have discussed the generation of the title of Hindi text or story based on a unique approach of keyword and proverbs. Our system also generates the title on the basis of highest priority nouns. This system is intended to design for the use of technical writers, students, scholars and researchers. Proposed system can prove itself as an optimized and robust tool for editors of the magazines or newspapers to find the appropriate heading or title. Moreover this can also be used to get appropriate phrase as well. This tool can also be used as an effective learning tool for school going students and it can also assist Hindi teachers to teach the students. Moreover, anybody can easily perform the sentence analysis.

Story 1

करोड़ीमल नाम का एक कंजूस आदमी था। एक दिन वह नारियल खरीदने के लिए बाजार गया। उसने नारियलवाले से नारियल की कीमत पूछी। चार रूपये का एक, नारियलवाले ने कहा। चार रूपये! यह तो बहुत महँगा है। मैं तो तीन रूपये दूँगा।करोड़ीमल ने कहा। नारियलवाले ने जवाब दिया, यहाँ तो नही, यहाँ से एक मील की दूरीपर आपको जरूर तीन रूपये में एक नारियल मिल जाएगा। करोड़ीमल ने विचार किया, पैसा बहुत मेहनत से कमाया जाता है। मीलभर पैदल चल लेने पर कम-से-कम एक रूपये की तो बचत हो जाएगी। वे पैदल चलते-चलते एक मील तक गए, तो वहाँ उन्हें एक नारियलवाले की दुकान दिखाई दी। उन्होंने दुकानदार से नारियल की कीमत पूछी। दुकानदार ने कहा, तीन रूपये का एक। करोड़ीमल ने कहा, यह तो बहुत ज़्यादा है। मैं तो अधिक से अधिक दो रूपये दूँगा। अगर तुम एक मील आगे चले जाओ, तो वहाँ तुम्हें दो रूपए में मिल जाएगा। दुकानदार ने कहा। करोड़ीमल ने फिर विचार किया, पैसा बहुत मूल्यवान होता है। एक रूपया बचाने के लिए मीलश्र पैदल चलने में क्या हर्ज है? वे फिर चलते-चलते एक मील चले गए। वहाँ उन्हें नारियल की एक दुकान दिखाई दी। उन्होंने नारियलवाले से नारियल की कीमत पूछी। दो रूपए का एक, नारियलवाले वाले ने जवाब दिया। करोड़ीमल ने कहा, "एक नारियल के दो रूपये? यह तो बहुत अधिक है। मैं तो केवल एक रूपए दूँगा।" तो फिर एक काम करो, नारियलवाले ने कहा, "तुम समुद्र के किनारे-किनारे एक मील तक चलते जाओ। वहाँ नारियल की कई दुकानें है। तुम्हें एक रूपए में ही नारियल मिल जाएगा वहाँ।" करोड़ीमल ने फिर विचार किया, "एक रूपया बचाने के लिए एक मील चल लेने में क्या हर्ज है? पैसा बहुत मूल्यवान होता है!" करोड़ीमल वहाँ से चलते-चलते एक मील दूर समुद्र-तट पर पहुँच गए। वहाँ नारियलवालों की कई दुकाने थीं। करोड़ीमल ने एक दुकानदार से नारियल की कीमत पूछी। दुकानदार ने कहा, "एक रूपया का एक नारियल।" करोड़ीमल ने कहा, "एक रूपया! मैं तो इसके पचास पैसे दूँगा।" नारियलवाले ने कहा, "तो फिर सामनेवाले नारियल के पेड़ पर चढ़ जाओ और तोड़ लो जितने चाहिए उतने। तुम्हारा एक पैसा भी खर्च नहीं होगा।" हाँ यही ठीक रहेगा। करोड़ीमल ने कहा और देखते-ही-देखते वे एक नारियल के पेड़ पर चढ़ गए। उन्होंने अपने दोनों हाथों से एक नारियल पकड़ा और उसे जोर का झटका दिया। नारियल तो टूट गया, पर साथ-ही-साथ पेड़ से उनके पैर की पकड़ भी छूट गयी। फिर क्या था, करोड़ीमल नारियल सहित समुद्र की रेत पर आ गिरे। उनके पैर की हड्डी टूट गई और शरीर पर भी कई जगह खरोंचें आ गईं। तभी दुकानदार ने बोला "लालच बुरी बला है"। एक नारियल के लिए कंजूस करोड़ीमल को सिर्फ इतनी ही कीमत अदा करनी पड़ी!

Story 2

तीन चोर थे। एक रात उन्होंने एक मालदार आदमी के यहाँ चोरी की। चोरों के हाथ खूब माल लगा। उन्होंने सारा धन एक थैले में भरा और उसे लेकर जंगल की ओर भाग निकले। जंगल में पहुँचने पर उन्हें जोर की भूख लगी। वहाँ खाने को तो कुछ था नहीं, इसलिए उनमें से एक चोर पास के एक गाँव से खाने का कुछ सामान लाने गया। बाकी के दोनों चोर चोरी के माल की रखवाली के लिए जंगल में   ही   रहे।

जो चोर खाने का सामान लाने गया था, उसकी नीयत खराब थी। पहले उसने होटल में खुद छककर भोजन किया। फिर उसने अपने साथियों के लिए खाने का समान खरीदा और उसमें तेज जहर मिला दिया। उसने सोचा कि जहरीला खाना खाकर उसके दोनों साथी मर   जाएंगे   तो   सारा   धन   उसी   का   हो   जाएगा।

इधर जंगल में दोनो चोरों ने खाने का समान लाने गए अपने साथी चोर की हत्या कर डालने की योजना बना ली थी। वे उसे अपने रास्ते से   हटाकर   सारा   धन   आपस   में   बाँट   लेना   चाहते   थे।

तीनों चोरों ने अपनी-अपनी- योजनाओं के अनुसार कार्य किया। पहला लालची चोर ज्योंही जहरीला भोजन लेकर जंगल में पहुँचा कि उसके साथी दोनों चोर उसपर टूट पड़े। उन्होंने उसका काम तमाम कर दिया। फिर वे निश्चिंत होकर भोजन करने बैठे। मगर जहरीला भोजन   खाते   ही   वे   दोनों   भी   तड़प-तड़प   कर   मर   गए।

इस प्रकार इन बुरे लोगों का अंत भी बुरा ही हुआ जैसे कहते हैं कर बुरा तो होय बुरा । तभी कहते है कि जैसा बोओगे वैसा काटोगे।

Story 3

एक राजा था। उसे रोज तुरंत पकड़ी गई मछलियाँ खाने का शौक था । एक दिन समुद्र में भयंकर तूफान आया। कोई भी मछुआ समुद्र में मछली मारने नही गया। इसलिए राजा को तुरंत पकड़ी हुई मछली नही मिल सकी। राजा ने घोषणा करा दी । कि उस दिन जो भी तुरंत पकड़ी हुई मछली राजा के पास लाएगा। उसे भरपूर इनाम दिया जाएगा। एक गरीब मछुए ने यह घोषणा सुनी जान जोखिम में डालकर समुद्र से मछलियाँ पकड़ी और राजमहल पहुँचा राजमहल के पहरेदारो ने उसे फाटक पर रोक दिया वे उसे राजा के   मंत्री   के   पास   ले   गए   ।

मंत्री ने मछुए से कहा, "मैं तुम्हे राजा के पास जरूर जाने दूँगा पर तुम्हे राजा से जो इनाम मिलेगा । उस में आधा हिस्सा होगा ।" मछुए को मंत्री का यह प्रस्ताव पसंद नही आया और उसे बहुत बुरा लगा। फिर भी उसने न खुश होते हुए भी उसे स्वीकार किया। इसके बाद पहरेदार उसे लेकर राजा के पास गए। मछुए ने राजा को मछलियाँ दी। राजा मछुए पर बहुत प्रसन्न हुआ। बताओ क्या इनाम चाहिए। तुम जो माँगोगे वह मैं तुम्हे अवश्य दूँगा। मछुए ने कहा, "महाराज मैं चाहता हूँ मेरी पीठ पर पचास कोड़े लगाए जाएँ। बस मुझे यही इनाम चाहिए ।" मछुए की यह बात सुनकर सभी दरबारी चकित रह गए। राजा ने मछुए की पीठ पर पचास हल्के कोड़े लगाने का आदेश दिया जब नौकर मछुए की पीठ पर पच्चीस कोड़े लगा चुका। तो मछुए ने कहा, "रूको! अब बाकी के पच्चीस कोड़े मेरे साझेदार की पीठ पर लगाओ ।" राजा ने मछुए से कहा, "तुम्हारा हिस्सेदार कौन है?" मछुए ने कहा,"महाराज आपके मंत्री महोदय ही मेरे हिस्सेदार है ।" मछुए का जवाब सुनकर राजा गुस्से से तमतमा उठा। उसने मंत्री को अपने सामने हाजिर करने का आदेश दिया। मंत्री के सामने आते ही राजा ने नौकर को आदेश दिया इन्हे गिनकर पच्चीस कोड़े लगाओ ध्यान रखो। इनकी पीठ पर कोड़े जोर जोर से लगने चाहिए। इसके बाद राजा ने बेईमान मंत्री को जेल मे डाल दिया और मंत्री को बोला जैसी करनी वैसी भरनी। फिर राजा ने मछुए को मुँहमाँगा इनाम दिया।

Story 4

एक लकड़हारा था । एक बार वह नदी के किनारे एक पेड़ से लकड़ी काट रहा था । एकाएक उसके हाथ से कुल्हाड़ी छूटकर नदी में गिर पड़ी । नदी गहरी थी । उसका प्रवाह भी तेज था । लकड़हारे ने नदी से कुल्हाड़ी निकालने की बहुत कोशिश की पर वह उसे नही मिली इससे लकड़हारा बहुत दुखी हो गया । इतने देवदूत मेवहाँ से गुजरा लकड़हारे के मुँह लटकाए खड़ा देख कर उसे दया आ गई । वह लकड़हारे के पास आया और बोला चिंता मत करो । मैं नदी से तुम्हारी कुल्हाड़ी अभी निकाल देता हूँ । यह कहकर देवदूत नदी में कूद पड़ा देवदूत पानी से निकला तो उसके हाथ में सोने की कुल्हाड़ी थी । वह लकड़हारे को सोने की कुल्हाड़ी देने लगा । तो लकड़हारे ने कहा , "नही नही यह कुल्हाड़ी मेरी नही है । मैं इसे नही ले सकता ।"

देवदूत ने फिर नदी में डुबकी लगाई इसबार वह चाँदी की कुल्हाड़ी लेकर बाहर आया ईमानदार लकड़हारा ने कहा, "यह कुल्हाड़ी   मेरी   नही   है   ।

देवदूत ने तीसरी बार पानी में डुबकी लगाई इस बार वह एक साधारण सी लोहे की कुल्हाड़ी लेकर बाहर आया । हाँ   यह   मेरी   कुल्हाड़ी   है   ।   लकड़हारे   ने   खुश   होकर   कहा   ।

उस गरीब लकड़हारे की ईमानदारी देखकर देवदूत बहुत प्रसन्न हुआ । उसने लकड़हारे को उसकी लोहे की कुल्हाड़ी दे दी । देवदूत ने बोला ईमानदारी का फल मीठा होता है इस लिए यह सोने और चाँदी की कुल्हाड़ियाँ भी तुम्हे पुरस्कार के रूप में दे रहा हु ।

Story 5

एक बूढ़ा किसान था । उसके तीन बेटे थे । तीनों ही जवान और हट्टे-कट्टे थे । पर वे बहुत ही आलसी थे । पिता की कमाई उड़ाने में उन्हें बड़ा मजा आता था । मेहनत करके पैसे कमाना उन्हें अच्छा नहीं लगता था । एक दिन किसान ने अपने बेटों को बुलाकर कहा, "देखो, तुम लोगों के लिए मैंने अपने खेत में एक छोटा-मोटा खजाना गाड़ रखा है । तुम लोग खेत को खोद डालो और वहा जो गड़ा खजाना मिलेगा उस खजाने को निकालकर आपस में बाँट लो",दूसरे दिन बड़े सबेरे उस किसान के तीनों लड़के कुदालियाँ लेकर खेत पर पहुँच गए और खुदाई शुरू कर दी । पर, उन्होंने खेत की एक-एक इंच जमीन खोद डाली । पर, उन्हें कहीं भी खजाना नही मिला । अंत में निराश होकर वे पिता के पास पहुँचे । उन्होंने कहा, "पिताजी, हमने पूरा खेत खोद डाला, पर हमें कहीं भी खजाना नही मिला ।" किसान ने जवाब दिया, "कोई बात नही! तुम लोगों ने खेत की बहुत अच्छी खुदाई कर दी है । अब मेरे साथ आओ,   हम   इसकी   बोआई   करें   ।"

बाप-बेटों ने मिलकर खूब लगन से खेत की बुआई की । संयोग से उस वर्ष बरसात भी समय पर और बहुत अच्छी हुई । खेत में खूब पैदावार हुई । फसल पक जाने पर खेत की शोभा देखते ही बनती थी । तीनों बेटे ने बड़े गर्व से अपने पिता को लहलहाती   फसल   दिखाई   ।

किसान ने कहा, "वाह, क्या खूब फसल हुई है! यही है वह खजाना, जिसे मैं तुम लोग को सौंपना चाहता था । मेहनत का फल हमेशा मीठा होता है अगर तुम लोग इसी तरह कड़ी मेहनत करते रहोगे, तो ऐसा ही खजाना तुम्हें हर वर्ष मिलता रहेगा ।"

References

1. http://thetimefinder.com/title-generator-saves-time/. Accessed 31 July 2016
2. http://www.censusindia.gov.in/Census_Data_2001/Census_Data_Online/Language/Statement1.aspx. Accessed 10 Oct 2016
3. Dorr, B., Zajic, D., Schwartz, R.: Cross-language headline generation for Hindi. ACM Trans. Asian Lang. Inf. Process. 2(3), 270–289 (2003)
4. Sethi, N., Agrawal, P., Madaan, V., Singh, S.K.: A novel approach to paraphrase hindi sentences using natural language processing. Indian J. Sci. Technol. 9(28), 1–6 (2016)
5. Jain, L., Agrawal, P.: Text independent root word identification in Hindi language using natural language processing. Int. J. Adv. Intell. Paradigm 7(3/4), 240–249 (2015)
6. Jain, L., Agrawal, P.: English to sanskrit transliteration: an effective approach to design natural language translation tool. Int. J. Adv. Res. Comput. Sci. 8(1), 1–4 (2017)
7. Sethi, N., Agrawal, P., Madaan, V., Singh, S.K., Kakran, A.: Automated title generation in english language using NLP. Int. J. Control Theory Appl. 9(11), 5159–5168 (2016)
8. Madaan, V., Agrawal, P., Sethi, N., Kumar, V., Singh, S.K.: A novel approach to paraphrase english sentences using natural language processing. Int. J. Control Theory Appl. 9(11), 5119–5128 (2016)
9. Yousif, J.H.: Natural language processing based soft computing techniques. Int. J. Comput. Appl. 77(8), 43–50 (2013)
10. Haque, R., Dandapat, S., Srivastava, A.K., Naskar, S.K., Way, A.: English-Hindi transliteration using context-informed PB-SMT: the DCU system for NEWS 2009. In: Proceedings of the 2009 Named Entities Workshop Shared Task on Transliteration (NEWS 2009), pp. 104–107 (2009)
11. http://www.baraha.com/help/Keyboards/dev_phonetic.html. Accessed 19 Feb 2016
12. Patterson, D.W.: Introduction to AI and Expert Systems, 2nd edn. Prentice Hall, Upper Saddle River (2012)
13. Rich, E., Knight, K., Nair, S.V.: Artificial Intelligence, 3rd edn. Tata McGraw Hill, New York (2009)
14. http://www.learning-hindi.com/consonants/. Accessed 21 Mar 2016
15. https://www.pinterest.com/saee_subhedar/marathi-blog/. Accessed on 2 Mar 2016
16. http://www.guide2india.org/hindi-moral-story-for-kids/. Accessed 26 Feb 2016
17. http://www.achhikhabar.com/proverbs-sayings-idioms-with-meaning-in-hindi-and-english. Accessed 27 Mar 2016
18. http://unicode.org/charts/PDF/U0900.pdf. Accessed 3 Jan 2016
19. http://jrgraphix.net/r/Unicode/0900-097F. Accessed 4 Jan 2016

Investigating Developers' Sentiments Associated with Software Cloning Practices

Sarveshwar Bharti[✉] and Hardeep Singh

Department of Computer Science, Guru Nanak Dev University, Amritsar, India
{sarveshwar.dcsrsh,hardeep.dcse}@gndu.ac.in

Abstract. Researchers through empirical observations have established that efficiency of software development tasks and their output relies upon software developer's associated persuasions. Thus, empathizing software developer's sentiments has now become one of the goals of an effective Software Engineering. This paper presents the developers' sentiments associated with software cloning practices. SentiStrength, a frequently used Sentiment Analysis tool in software engineering is used to explore the sentiment polarity of the developers during programming tasks. 39 responses collected via online industrial survey were analyzed with SentiStrength tool. Sentiment Analysis performed on the developer responses mainly indicate the neutral polarity i.e. developers under study don't think clones and cloning practices as good or bad practice, instead 71.79% expressed neutral sentiments. The collected opinions indicate neither the acceptance nor rejection of harmfulness or benefits of clones, rather depicted the neutral opinion of software developers towards clones.

Keywords: Developers' behavior · Sentiment analysis · Software cloning

1 Introduction

Exact or nearly identical copy of the original code fragment is referred to as a clone. Software clone literature discusses clones mainly into two different categories viz. syntactic and semantic clones. Syntactic clones have further three categories viz. type 1, type 2 and type 3 whereas semantic clones are also referred to as type 4 clones. To manage clones i.e. to identify, analyze and remove clones, there are various approaches discussed in the literature [1]. It has been empirically evidenced that software clones have a direct impact on the software quality with increased maintenance effort [2, 3]. Thus despite some benefits software clones are mainly referred to as bad smells.

There have been various studies conducted in past few years to identify developers' intentions behind cloning practices [2, 4, 5] etc., but no study performed sentiment analysis of programmers associated with software cloning practices. Thus, it motivates us to perform a sentimental analysis on the responses collected from an online industrial survey involving 20 software developers.

Sentiment analysis has now found its way into software engineering also. It is an opinion mining technique used to identify the sentiments from the text. There are various sentiment analysis tools available to identify the polarity of the developers' sentiments. SentiStrength is a tool best suited for use in software engineering studies.

© Springer Nature Singapore Pte Ltd. 2019
A. K. Luhach et al. (Eds.): ICAICR 2018, CCIS 955, pp. 397–406, 2019.
https://doi.org/10.1007/978-981-13-3140-4_36

It detects strengths as well as the polarity of the sentiments. The main contributions of this paper are the mined opinions reflected by the developers gained after applying sentimental analysis tool, SentiStrength.

Next section presents the motivations behind this study along with research questions. Section 3 will discuss the study design and the methodology adopted by this study. Source and type of data for analysis are discussed in Sect. 4. How sentiment analysis is performed is presented in Sect. 5. Section 6 presents the results and discussions. Section 7 identifies various threats to the validity of this study. Work related to our study is then discussed in Sect. 8. Then, finally, conclusion and future work is presented in Sect. 9 along with acknowledgments and then references in support of this paper.

2 Motivation and Research Questions

Reuse approach via copy and pasting is the most prevalent activity among software developers. Adding to this activity, there are other reasons also that lead to duplicated code into the software system. This duplicate code is found to cause code bloat and other quality and maintenance issues leading to degradation of software quality and increase in maintenance cost. To study the developer behavior various studies have been performed, but to the best of our knowledge, no study dealt with the analysis of developers' sentiments concerning software cloning. This instigated us to perform sentiment analysis of developers applied to developer responses collected from an online industrial survey. Based on the motivations we identified four research questions that we attempted to seek answers as listed below:

RQ1: What are the general sentiments expressed by the software developers towards software cloning?

RQ2: What are the sentiments reflected by the developers when asked about reasons for multiple occurrences of code fragments?

RQ3: Do developers think copy and paste programming is a bad programming practice or good?

RQ4: What are the developers' general opinions towards code clones?

3 Study Design and Methodology

The experimental design involved two major elements viz. online industrial study and sentimental analysis. Figure 1 represents the detailed methodology adopted in this paper to perform sentiment analysis. At the initial stage, authors' responses were collected by conducting the online industrial survey. Then these responses were manually analyzed and then finally fed to the sentiment analysis tool SentiStrength. The output from the tool was then analyzed for different trends and then finally findings are presented.

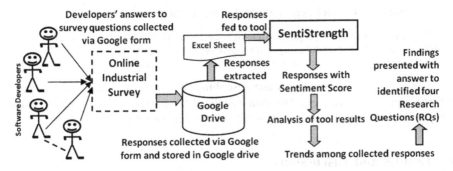

Fig. 1. Overview of the methodology adopted

4 Dataset Used

Authors conducted an online industrial survey in which an email containing a link to the questionnaire created using Google Form was sent to the professional software developers. This survey involved 20 software developers who contributed about 39 responses. All the responses were acquired in Google Drive. The data used in this paper is the part of the industrial survey. The communicated questionnaire contained three open-ended questions as listed below:

Q1: In your opinion, what is the reason of multiple occurrences of code fragment i.e. code cloning?
Q2: In your view, what is the reason of copy and pasting i.e. code cloning?
Q3: In your view, what is a code clone?

The answers in response to these above-mentioned questions served as a dataset for conducting software developers' sentiment analysis associated with software cloning.

5 Sentiment Analysis Approach

To analyze software developers' emotions, sentiment analysis techniques have now been applied to a number of different software engineering tasks/artifacts viz. commit messages, reviews, etc. These developers' messages or reviews express their emotion or we can say sentiments. There are various sentiment analysis tools available for use in software engineering viz. SentiStrength, NLTK, EmoText, Stanford CoreNLP etc. Out of the list, SentiStrength is the most used tool for Software Engineering. It helps in analyzing the polarity of reviews/comments. It assigns a sentiment score to each word and adding up the individual score, sentence sentiment is derived. The negative score ranges from −1 to −5 and positive score from 1 to 5.

Let's take a real example form the analysis done. For example, the sentence under analysis that was fed to SentiStrength is as:

"One reason might be due to insufficient skills of developer who is using duplicate code for developing same type of functionality"

The output of the tool SentiStrength for this input sentence is:

"One[0] reason[0] might[0] be[0] due[0] to[0] insufficient[−1] skills[0] of[0] developer[0] who [0] is[0] using[0] duplicate[0] code[0] for[0] developing[0] same[0] type[0] of[0] functionality [0] [[Sentence = −2,1 = word max, 1–5]][[[1,−2 max of sentences]]]"

The senti score i.e. positive value describing sentence sentiments is derived as 1 whereas negative score is −2. We then calculated the final sentiment score by adding the positive and negative sentiment score, and in this case it is −1.

6 Results and Discussions

In this section, results of various research questions identified in Sect. 2 are presented along with the analysis and discussions. After applying sentiment analysis, the gathered results are discussed as under:

6.1 Answer to Research Question 1

To answer the research question RQ1, the results across all the responses were accumulated as shown in Table 1. Overall sentiments across all the developer responses indicate 71.79% neutral sentiments with just 10.25% positive and rest as negative sentiments. We noticed that most of the responses neither fall in positive nor in negative senti score range but had a sentiment score 0.

Table 1. Overall sentiments across all responses

Sentiment	Final sentiment score	Number of responses	Sentiment percentage
Positive	1	4	10.25%
Negative	−2	1	17.95%
	−1	6	
Neutral	0	28	71.79%
	Total	39	

6.2 Answer to Research Question 2

The motivation behind RQ2 was to explore the sentiments of software developers related to multiple occurrences of code fragments. In a way to find the answer to this research question, Q1 identified in Sect. 4 was utilized. Total of gathered 16 responses from developers were fed to the SentiStrength. The positive, negative and neutral responses with the corresponding positive, negative and final sentiment core are listed in Table 2.

The overall sentiments across all the responses for the Q1 are presented in Table 3. Results clearly indicate 68.75% of neutral sentiments shown by the software developers with 18.75% negative and just 12.5% positive sentiments.

Table 2. Positive, negative and neutral responses for Q1

Sentiment	Developer's response	Positive score	Negative score	Final sentiment score
Positive	Mostly to deviate from doing the same work again and again. Instead I like to devote my time in something new	3	−2	1
	We try to save time and energy involved and make some changes in existing code and use it	2	−1	1
Negative	One reason might be due to insufficient skills of developer who is using duplicate code for developing same type of functionality	1	−2	−1
	Sometimes requirement is there as we need to do the same if we are in block or in else block	1	−2	−1
	Lack of knowledge of core basics of the technology. Strict timelines and rush to deliver the solution	1	−2	−1
Neutral	We don't do code cloning. What we do is we create functions and then use that function anywhere	1	−1	0
	Also in country like India, most of software engineer are indulge in copy paste funda	2	−2	0
	When we make different modules for different clients and after some time or years, we try to integrate both modules, Then we face code cloning	1	−1	0
	When multiple people are working on same piece	1	−1	0
	Or when one piece might get updated in future and you don't want same to be updated in future	1	−1	0
	Multiple modules of applications may be using similar functionality	1	−1	0
	Repeat code for using same command on different web pages or on different locations in software	1	−1	0
	Not aware of it due to big code	1	−1	0
	Having same type of functionality that is requested by the client for their business logic and getting used in one or another part of the application	1	−1	0
	Easy availability of code over internet easy availability of code over internet	1	−1	0
	Code cloning mainly arises when we are not following the Oops concepts. We can prevent code cloning by sharing the common code that will be residing in some server and then we can use that as web services	1	−1	0

Table 3. Sentiment across all responses for Q1

Sentiment	Final sentiment score	Number of responses	Sentiment percentage
Positive	1	2	12.5%
Negative	−1	3	18.75%
Neutral	0	11	68.75%
	Total	16	

6.3   Answer to Research Question 3

The motive of RQ3 was to find the opinion of software developers regarding copy and paste programming practice. To explore this, Q2 listed in Sect. 4 was utilized. Total of 15 responses for Q2 from software developers was collected in Google Drive. The sentiment score (positive, negative, final) for positive, negative and neutral sentiments after applying sentiment analysis tool SentiStrength on the acquired responses are listed in Table 4.

Table 4. Positive, negative and neutral responses for Q2

Sentiment	Developer's response	Positive score	Negative score	Final sentiment score
Positive	It saves time in implementation and moreover it maintains same code standards	2	−1	1
	For our comfort we do copy and pasting	2	−1	1
Negative	Lack of knowledge of core basics of the technology. Strict timelines and rush to deliver the solution	1	−2	−1
	Less chances of error if same code is required	1	−2	−1
Neutral	Because we do not want write that code again and again for same command	1	−1	0
	I prefer creating a function	1	−1	0
	But sometimes to make the code easier to develop and to minimise jumps, copy pasting is better option	1	−1	0
	Time saving and of course don't want to mess my brain when something is already implemented and can be reused	1	−1	0
	Most of the developers hesitate to code same thing again and again	1	−1	0
	Its already working and tested	1	−1	0
	Reduce time, you get already tried and tested code	1	−1	0
	If requirement is same, no need to write it same. Although we can call that code if we want but it increases processing time for code. So, it depends on requirement to requirement	1	−1	0
	Code cloning mainly arises when we are not following the Oops concepts. We can prevent code cloning by sharing the common code that will be residing in some server and then we can use that as web services	1	−1	0
	Reduce time, you get already tried and tested code	1	−1	0
	Time saving	1	−1	0

Table 5 indicates that 73.33% responses possess neutral sentiments along with 13.33% positive and negative sentiments each.

Table 5. Sentiment across all responses for Q2

Sentiment	Final sentiment score	Number of responses	Sentiment percentage
Positive	1	2	13.33%
Negative	−1	2	13.33%
Neutral	0	11	73.33%
	Total	15	

6.4 Answer to Research Question 4

To explore the general opinion of developers towards code clones and thus to answer RQ4, Q3 identified in Sect. 4 was utilized. Just 8 responses were collected from the software developers with sentiment score extracted after applying SentiStrength tool listed in Table 6.

Table 6. Positive, negative and neutral responses for Q3

Sentiment	Developer's response	Positive score	Negative score	Final sentiment score
Negative	Or to make the useless checks	1	−3	−2
	It if you have knowledge of other running functionality, then your requirement is quite similar to that, then you can copy the required module/line/function from that code to save time, efforts/brain. it might called code cloning but it don't feel any harm in that	2	−3	−1
Neutral	It's a duplication of the code	1	−1	0
	Doing the same code again and again	1	−1	0
	Code clone is the exact copy of the business logic	1	−1	0
	Replica of code has already been used in the program	1	−1	0
	Some code with same functionality	1	−1	0
	A piece of code occurring multiple times	1	−1	0

Overall sentiment score for Q3 indicates neutral sentiments with the percentage of 75% and 25% negative sentiments as shown in Table 7.

Table 7. Sentiment across all responses for Q3

Sentiment	Final sentiment score	Number of responses	Sentiment percentage
Negative	−2	1	25%
	−1	1	
Neutral	0	6	75%
	Total	8	

7 Threats to Validity

SentiStrength, a sentimental analysis tool was applied that may possess the precision issues for the utilized dataset containing technical terms. The other major issue that may arise is the small dataset including just 39 comments, but still, this study may serve as a benchmark for further research as we gathered the data from online industrial survey and sentiment analysis of software developers' in association with software cloning practices was done that itself is a novel approach.

8 Related Work

To the best of our knowledge, till now no study has performed software developers' sentiment analysis related with software cloning. But still few studies that may somehow relate are discussed in this section. Lesiuk [6] in 2005 presented the study on the emotional impact of music on the performance of software developers. Khan et al. [7] in the year 2010 came up with analysis of software developers' emotions and its impact on debugging performance. In the year 2014, Murgia et al. [8] conducted an observation on issue reports. Guzman et al. [9] in 2014, analyzed the relationship of emotions possessed by a software developer with a programming language, day and time of the week, team distribution and project approval. Sinha et al. [10] in 2016 presented investigation of developer sentiments in commit logs. Singh and Singh [11] in the year 2017 analyzed impact of refactoring activities on developers' sentiments. Complimenting all the above-mentioned literature, this paper presented a study on an unexplored data that was collected from the industrial survey and thus may serve as a benchmark for further research in this direction.

9 Conclusion and Future Work

Developers' sentiment analysis associated with the software cloning practices was the main aim of this paper. For conducting sentiment analysis, SentiStrength, a most adopted sentiment analysis tool for software engineering was utilized for this purpose.

The dataset was collected from the online industrial survey involving 20 professional software developers.

In this study, we observed that most of the developers expressed neutral sentiments towards cloning practices. As out of total 39 responses, 71.79% represented neutral sentiments. While studying the developers' sentiment association with the multiple occurrences of code fragments, it has been observed that 68.75% expressed neutral sentiments. Regarding the copy and paste activity, results indicate that 73.33% possessed neutral sentiments. In case of developer opinion regarding code clones, 75% expressed neutral sentiments.

Results presented in this paper clearly indicate that developers don't consider cloning practices as a bad or good programming practice, rather are neutral about the practice of cloning and the existence of clones in the software systems.

In future, we are planning to extend our study to cover more software developers and thus utilization of large dataset that may present better inference applicable to the industry practitioners.

Acknowledgments. We present our sincere gratitude to UGC, Government of India for Senior Research Fellowship to the first author and also would like to thank Department of Computer Science, Guru Nanak Dev University, Amritsar for the infrastructural and scholastic support towards the ongoing research.

References

1. Roy, C.K., Cordy, J.R., Koschke, R.: Comparison and evaluation of code clone detection techniques and tools: a quantitative approach. Sci. Comput. Programm. **74**(7), 470–495 (2009)
2. Roy, C.K., Cordy, J.R.: A survey on software clone detection research. Technical report 2007-541, Queen's University, Kingston (2007)
3. Rattan, D., Bhatia, R., Singh, M.: Software clone detection: a systematic review. Inf. Softw. Technol. **55**(7), 1165–1199 (2013)
4. Zhang, G., Peng, X., Xing, Z., Zhao, W.: Cloning practices: why developers clone and what can be changed. In: 28th IEEE International Conference on Software Maintenance (ICSM), Trento, Italy, pp. 285–294 (2012)
5. Kim, M., Bergman, L., Lau, T., Notkin, D.: An ethnographic study of copy and paste programming practices in OOPL. In: Proceedings of the 2004 International Symposium on Empirical Software Engineering (ISESE 2004), Redondo Beach, CA, USA (2004)
6. Lesiuk, T.: The effect of music listening on work performance. Psychol. Music **33**(2), 173–191 (2005)
7. Khan, I.A., Brinkman, W.-P., Hierons, R.M.: Do moods affect programmers' debug performance? Cogn. Technol. Work. **13**(4), 245–258 (2011)
8. Murgia, A., Tourani, P., Adams, B., Ortu, M.: Do developers feel emotions? An exploratory analysis of emotions in software artifacts. In: Proceedings of the 11th Working Conference on Mining Software Repositories, Hyderabad, India, pp. 262–271 (2014)
9. Guzman, E., Azócar, D., Li, Y.: Sentiment analysis of commit comments in GitHub: an empirical study. In: Proceedings of the 11th Working Conference on Mining Software Repositories, Hyderabad, India, pp. 352–355 (2014)

10. Sinha, V., Lazar, A., Sharif, B.: Analyzing developer sentiment in commit logs. In: Proceedings of the 13th International Conference on Mining Software Repositories, Austin, Texas, pp. 520–523 (2016)
11. Singh, N., Singh, P.: How do code refactoring activities impact software developers' sentiments? - An empirical investigation into GitHub commits. In: 24th Asia-Pacific Software Engineering Conference (APSEC), Nanjing, China, pp. 648–653 (2017)

A Brief Review of Image Quality Enhancement Techniques Based Multi-modal Biometric Fusion Systems

Tajinder Kumar[1(✉)], Shashi Bhushan[2], and Surender Jangra[3]

[1] IKGPTU, Jalandhar, India
tajinder_114@jmit.ac.in
[2] CGC, Landran, Mohali, India
shashibhushan6@gmail.com
[3] GTBC, Bhawanigarh, Punjab, India
jangra.surender@gmail.com

Abstract. An extensive amount of system needs reliable schemes for personal recognition to confirm the individual identity demanding the services. The aim of these schemes is the authentication of services that can be executed from the genuine user only. Tremendous growth has been seen from last few years in biometric recognition because of the increased requirement of consistent personal identification with the varied government and commercial applications. The biometric recognition is termed as automatic individual recognition on the basis of physiological or behavioural characteristics. This paper provides a brief outline of biometric field and sums up the biometric modalities, biometric framework, and biometric system classification with Image Quality Improvement Techniques. Work done by number of authors in the similar field has been analyzed and defined. The review has also shown the observation of different modalities for recognition accuracy with FAR and FRR.

Keywords: Biometric recognition · Biometric modalities
Unimodal and multimodal biometric system
Image Quality Improvement Techniques

1 Introduction

Extensive variety of system needs schemes of dependable individual recognition to verify the individuality of an entity demanding the services. The cause of these methods is the confirmation of render services can be executed by the correct user [1]. The example of these applications contains safe utilization of computer systems, mobile phones, buildings, ATMs and the laptops. When strong personal recognition methods are not available then the mentioned methods are prone to the fraud tricks. The term "Biometric recognition" is the human being recognition on the basis of behavioral and physiological individuality. With the usage of biometrics, it is possible to develop individual identity defining "who he is" than "what he possesses" (like ID [identity

© Springer Nature Singapore Pte Ltd. 2019
A. K. Luhach et al. (Eds.): ICAICR 2018, CCIS 955, pp. 407–423, 2019.
https://doi.org/10.1007/978-981-13-3140-4_37

card]) or "what he remembers" [like password] [2]. Computer science has defined Biometric as an area of automatic recognition of human beings with the unique attributes such as Physiological (face, fingerprint, iris and so on) or behavioral (signature, voice and so on). Further, attributes of biometric cannot be transferred, lost or stolen and guarantee more re security as it is difficult to forge them. Eve, the attributes needs the genuine user presence when granting the access to exact resources [3].

This document deals with the brief description of biometric field with the description of each biometric trait or modalities. Later, the biometric framework has been defined following the biometric system functionalities. The level of fusion and the biometric system classification has been defined subsequent to Image Quality Improvement Techniques. Work done by different authors in the area of biometric recognition is analyzed and described in the end (Fig. 1).

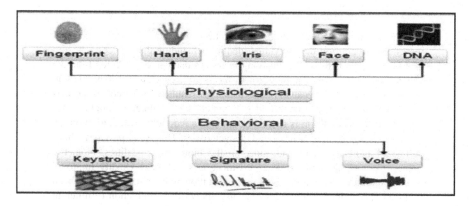

Fig. 1. Biometric traits

Following criteria should be met by physiological and behavioral traits [4]:

i. Distinctiveness: similar characteristics possessed by two persons that doesn't exist.
ii. Universality: every individual should have this characteristic.
iii. Collectability: defines the truth that biometric might be quantitatively calculated.
iv. Permanence: it should be invariant for more time span.
v. Acceptability: shows the degree in which the provided biometric characteristic is established by the user.

2 Biometric Frameworks

General biometric framework is consisted of four principles, particularly, extractor, sensor, choice modules and matcher. The sensor is used for securing the biometric information from human being [5]. The calculation of quality estimation is utilized for learning whether the attained biometric information is enough to be arranged by the resulting parts. When the information is not sufficient for top notch, it is normally re-procured form the users. The work of element extractor is to integrate the best data from the obtained biometric example to frame other representation of biometric characteristic, known as list of capabilities. In this perfect world, the list of capabilities should be one of the types for each individual, in addition, invariance for the variation in varied examples of same biometric quality taken as of the similar individual. In between of the confirmation, the capabilities are eliminated from the biometric speci-men compared with the layout by the matcher that decides the likeliness level among the capabilities. The modules are settled on client character of similitude level among inquiry and format [6] (Fig. 2).

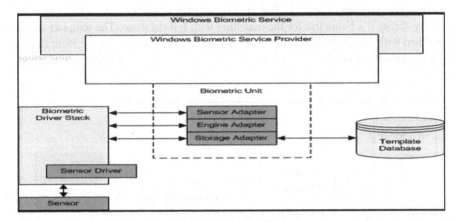

Fig. 2. Biometric framework

2.1 Biometric System Functionality

According to the context of the applications, biometric system can execute modes like identification or verification [7].

i. Verification mode

It is termed as 1:1 matching. It is also referred as Authentication in which the user maintains individuality and the scheme confirms regarding the maintenance of the system (Fig. 3).

ii. Identification mode

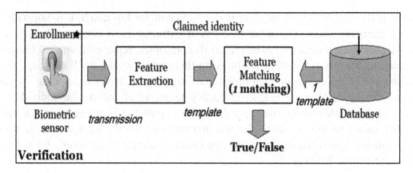

Fig. 3. Process of verification

It is taken as 1: m matching. The identity of user is not known in this mode and uniquely shows it's biometric for the matching with full database. The template of user is matched with each template being stored in the similar database for the identification of high similarity (Fig. 4).

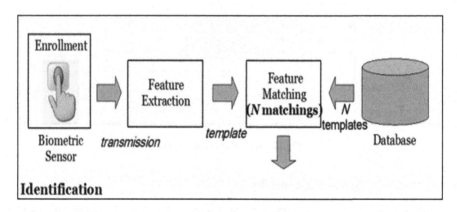

Fig. 4. Process of identification

3   Biometric Modalities

The comparison of varied biometric modalities has been described in this section. The various modalities are: fingerprint, face, and voice and Iris recognition. The pros and cons of each biometric trait are also defined in tabular form [8] (Table 1).

Table 1. Biometric modalities comparison

Biometric modalities	Pros	Cons
Face	Doesn't need some co-operation of test subject	Not that efficient for less resolution images
	The system being set up can find the user from the crowd	Not perfect and takes the challenges for the instance integrated with varied face positions
	Executes enormous identification that other biometric cannot execute	Doesn't perform in bad sunglasses, lightning or some another object that defines subject's face
Iris	Can be executed in the range of 10 cms to some metres	Difficult to adjust the scanning devices and can annoy varied people of varied heights
	Enhanced accuracy and high process speed	The scanning devices accuracy can be affected by wrong lightning effects and the illumination from surface reflective types
	The process of data capturing can be executed even when the user has glasses or contact lenses	The Iris scanner is more costly as compare to other modalities
Fingerprint	May be utilized with easiness with enhanced verification procedure for accuracy and speed	The scanning system in fingerprint can be cheated by applying artificial fingers and depicts other person's finger
	The pattern contains unique distinctive composition and the characteristic would remain the same with time	Number of times, it can take number of swipes of fingerprint to register
	A person should not need to remember long passwords, a person need to swipe only the fingers on the scanner	
Voice/ Speech	Speech may be considered as a natural I/P as it doesn't consider some training and it is quicker than other I/P	This system might develop mistake when the some noise or disturbance is taken place in the surroundings
	The method assists the people having difficulty in using the hands	The system of voice recognition can be hacked with few pre-recorded with some voice messages
	The major benefit of voice recognition is that is can cut back the wrongly spelled words/texts by which the typist can suffer a issue while typing	Different words sound more similar

4 Fusions in Biometrics

Because the feature set has extended the knowledge for input biometric data with contrast to the equivalence of score/ output matcher decision, so, at features level be taken for providing the required recognition outcome. Though, the fusion at the defined level is compound for achieving in practice as the feature sets of different modalities cannot be appropriate and number of popular systems cannot guarantee the failure access that they consider. Three levels are there for the fusion as described in below Table 2:

Table 2. Fusion levels

Levels of fusion	Description
At feature extraction level [9]	Processing of signals is done initially
	Extraction of feature vector is from the biometric attribute. For the classification, the merging of features is considered that develops a complex feature vector
	As the features suffer from huge information as contrasted to the matching score, so, fusion at the feature level is shown for the best outcome for the recognition
At matching score level [10]	It is also known as confidence level fusion
	The processing of feature vectors is done completely and the determination of individual matching score is taken place and according the matching score are fused for developing classification
	Different mathematical learning methods could be implemented for merging the match scores
At decision level [11]	Every modality is processed individually means ebery biometric attribute has been apprehended and then the features can be extracted from exact attribute
	The resulted classification is dependent on fusion of the output of varied modalities
	It is the prior level of fusion by means of human interface
	It can also be said that the choice from every biometric can be integrated for delivering the last decision

5 Biometric System Classifications

The classification of biometric system is into two types, namely, unimodal biometric system and multimodal biometric system.

5.1 Unimodal Biometric System

It is a system that utilizes single biometric trait or one information source for identification or verification. This system has steadily improved in reliability as well as accuracy [12]. Though, the unimodal system suffers from issues in the enrolment procedure as of non-universal biometric modalities, lack of accuracy and spoofing because of the noisy data. Thus, a technique for solving the issues is developing a usage of multimodal biometric authentication system. The problems linked with unimodal biometric systems are discussed below [13]:

- Noisy data: The noise is generally resides in biometric data when the sensors are not maintained properly. For instance, the dirt that lies in the fingerprint scanner sensor that resulted in noisy fingerprint.
- Lack of individuality: The biometric system is known to be universal when the users may define the biometric modalities for identification. Though, not each biometric modality is universal.
- Non-universality: The modalities produced from the biometric system like face recognition system deal with the face image can be moderately same. The example can be taken as father or son and identical twins. This results an enhancement in false match rate which is because of its uniqueness.
- Susceptibility to circumvention: It is probable to imitate anyone's modality from an imposter with the spoofed traits like the designing bogus fingers with the utilization of fingerprints and utilizing them for gaining access wrongly for a biometric system.

5.2   Multimodal Biometric System

It can be describes as the one that integrates the result taken from varied features of biometrics for identification. Variety of multimodal biometric traits can be used that resulted in more secure and accurate biometric identification system. Because there are other biometric technology system are implanted so it can be consider that some failure or error cannot affect anyone [14]. As shown in Fig. 5 below, the initial module known as the sensor module, the data may get stored before some raw biometric data and it is mandatory to integrate the biometric sensor with the appropriate user interface. Then, the raw biometric data can be taken and can be send again for feature extraction. When the procedure takes place, the obtained biometric data can be executed on the basis of processing quality. Therefore, the digital illustration of the modalities can be produced as an input to the matching module for thereafter comparison [15].

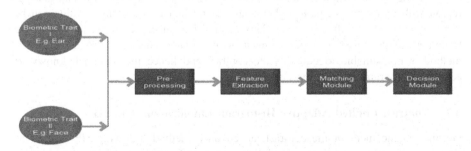

Fig. 5. Multimodal biometric system

The comparison of extracted features with the template has been taken place at the matching level for achieving a matching score which is calculated by means of data quality and in the end, the decision making module has been informed that whether the user is unique or not [16].

6   Image Quality Improvement Techniques

This section defines the various image quality improvement or image enhancement techniques used in biometric recognition.

6.1   Histogram Equalization (HE)

HE method is used to adjust the contrast of an image by using image's histogram in image processing. Before applying histogram on any image user must know about the probability mass function (PMF) and Cumulative distributive function (CDF). A probability mass function which provides the value that is approximately equal to some value. Its values must be positive and sum is equal to 1. Cumulative distributive function (CDF) is providing the region under the probability density function. An example of histogram equalization is shown below [19] (Fig. 6):

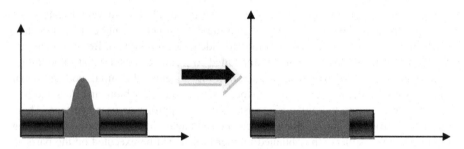

Fig. 6.   Before and after HE image

By using HE method the intensities can be distributed in a better way and thus the region with less contrast, gain higher contrast and hence the intensity value can be distributed in a more effective way. This method has an disadvantage that when the brightness of the image changes in most of the area parents in the image then this method is not suitable to equalize the contrast and hence the approach known as adaptive histogram equalization is used.

6.2   Contrast Limited Adaptive Histogram Equalization (CLAHE)

For the enhancement of the contrast, an advance method following HE is used as adaptive histogram equalization technique. It is different from HE approach as it measures a number of histograms at a time from the different image area and thus utilizes them for equalizing the contrast and hence increases the edges of the every image. AHE method has a disadvantage that it over-amplifies noise in the homogeneous area of the image. This problem is resolved by using a method known as contrast limited adaptive histogram equalization [20] (Figs. 7).

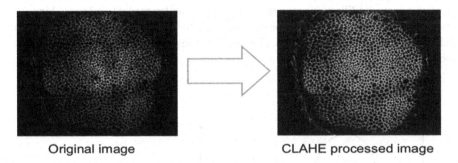

Original image   CLAHE processed image

Fig. 7. Before and after CLAHE processed image

CLHE method works on the small parts of the image rather than on the whole image. These small parts are known as tiles. The contrast of every tiles is enhanced and then integrated by using bilinear interpolation so that the artificial boundaries can be eliminated.

6.3 De-correlation Stretching

This method is used to increase the color separation of a test image using essential band to band relationship. By using this technique the visual quality of the image can be enhanced in MATLAB this function can be applied by using the command "decorrstretch". Mainly there are three colours but this scheme can be applied in several color bands [21].

The above Fig. 8 represents the river image before and after applying the Decorrelation stretching function on the image. From the above figure it is clear that when Decorrelation function is applied on the image the color range is expanded in a wide rage. The colour intensities of the image are modified into the color correlation matrix.

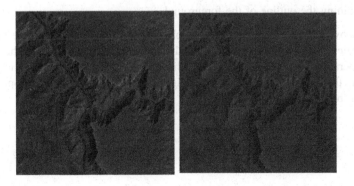

Fig. 8. Before and after De-correlation stretching image (Color figure online)

6.4   Linear Contrast Adjustment

This type involves contrast stretching, linear expansion of the original digital image in which the data is sensed remotely. The entire sensitivity range of the display device can be covered by expanding the true value of the image. Linear contrast improvement also creates exact modifications to the data more understandable. These kinds of improvements are suitably implemented for distantly sensed pictures having Gaussian indicating, the illumination values in a restricted histogram range and merely single mode is manifest [22] (Fig. 9).

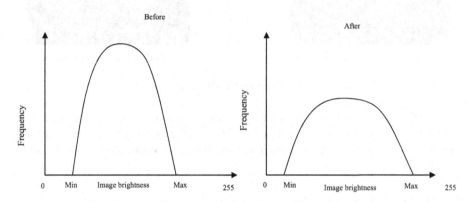

Fig. 9. Linear contrast adjustment

6.5   Morphological Operators

The main function performed by the morphological operator is:

a. Contracting the foreground
b. Extending the foreground
c. Excluding holes in the foreground
d. excluding stray foreground pixels in the framework
e. Detecting the boundary of the foreground
f. Determining the outline of the foreground

The above Fig. 10 represents the morphological operation. It must be noted that morphological operation is always applied on the binary image. Here the morphological operation is applied to separate the circles in the image. This is done by contracting the circle or by removing the edges of the circles so that the property of the circles can be determined [22].

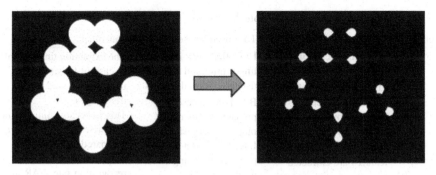

Fig. 10. Before and after morphological image

7 Related Work

In this section, the work performed by a number of authors in the field of biometric authentication system as discussed in tabular form. The below Table 3 different authors in the field of uni-modal and multi-model system.

Table 3. A glance of existing techniques in uni-model and multi-model biometric system

Reference	Proposed technique	Tool used/dataset	Outcomes
[14]	Face recognition and fingerprint recognition system is integrated for increasing the security of the system	NFIQ simulator is used that is designed by NIST The dataset has been taken from FVC2004-DB1 dataset	The results are measured on the basis of ROC (receiving operating curve)
	For the face image rotation of face, illumination and face expressions are used	This dataset is comprises of 1000 fingerprint of 100 various users that consist 10 fingerprint of each user	The parameters such as Genuine acceptance rate, FRR and FAR have been measured The comparison of these parameters has been shown for both face and fingerprint recognition
	The multimodal system has been trained for randomly selected 40 users	For face recognition dataset has been taken from FERET-b series dataset that comprises of 2200 face images of 200 persons. 11 face pictures of each person	It is concluded that the security is less when weighted sum method is used as compared to the multimodal biometrics
			Also when fuzzy logic is used the system performs well

(*continued*)

Table 3. (*continued*)

Reference	Proposed technique	Tool used/dataset	Outcomes
[15]	Iris and fingerprint biometric traits are used The RoI (region of interest) has been extracted by using the pre-processing technique In figure print Minutia features are extracted whereas in iris image the segmentation is done by excluding the eyelids and eyelashes For eyelashes position gablor filter has been used	FVC2002 DB2 is used for finger print and BATH database is used for Iris BATH-S1 dataset is prepared by using 10 random users whereas Bath S2 dataset is prepared by using 50 users BATH-S3 is used 50 databases	The extraction time of RoI in case of finger print is less as compared to the iris images This is because fingerprint comprises of less points as compared to iris image The parameters such as recognition rate, FAR and FRR have been measured The accuracy rate up to 95.62% has been obtained The value of FAR and FRR measured for the fusion system are 036% and 8.38% respectively
[16]	Iris and 3D cornea biometric traits are used to increase the efficiency of the system Authors shows that how one can use cornea as a biometric traits for the security purpose Zernike polynomial equation has been used to extract the features from the cornea Gabor filter along with phase encoding scheme have been used for extracting the features from the Iris image Minimum, maximum and weighted sum rule are used to determine the matching score of the fused image	A manual database has been created by using 22 women and 17 men The images of their iris are captured by using 2.0 microsope webcam The resolution of the image generated is 2000*1600 pixels For capturing the corena image a cornea topographer has been used	The parameters such as FAR and FRR have been measured When iris is used alone then the value of FAR plus FRR observed are 0.1% and 1.37% correspondingly For multimodal, FAR plus FRR values measured are 0% and 0.1% correspondingly
[17]	Proposed a signature biometric system based on Markov model	The dataset has been taken from Samsung Galaxy and WACOM intuos The Samsun database comprises of 500 numbers of signatures.	It is concluded that WACOm perform well than that of mobile dataset. This because of the forgery images The FAR of mobile database obtained is 0.2302. The FAR value

(*continued*)

Table 3. (*continued*)

Reference	Proposed technique	Tool used/dataset	Outcomes
		Total 25 persons are used and 10 signatures have been taken from each user The WACVOM dataset comprises of total 100 signatures in which there are 20 true genuine signature and 20 skilled forgeries signature from the users	obtained for forgery images is 0.01818
[18]	Voice authentication system has been designed for the identification and authentication of the system	MYSQL database has been used that is managed by the JAVA JDBC	There is no need to memorize the password It enhances the usability of the user authentication The average recognition rate up to 80.6% has been obtained The FAR and FRR rate obtained for the proposed voice authentication system are 0.01% and 15% which is not as per requirement
	The model comprises of three main components named as client Agent, Relying Party, and Identity Provider	The model is designed in window 7 by using JAVA programming	
		The database is comprises of 7 Men and 8 Women	
	Mel Frequency Cepstral coCoefficients (MFCC) has been used to extract the features		
[23]	Comparison of uni-modal and multi modal systems like iris multimodal, finger print face, finger vein multimodal and iris, finger vein, face	PCA (Principal component analysis) with Euclidean distance matcher	The advantage of utilizing uniform data with the multi modals of training and testing mostly by SDUMLA-HMT as homogeneous database having the advantage of fusion at feature level particularly as suitable feature extractor

8 Comparative Analyses of Fusion Modalities

This section describes the comparison of various modalities to examine the performance parameters by considering FAR (False Acceptance Rate), FRR (False Rejection Rate) and accuracy. The observation has been shown below in tabular and graphical form as shown below:

i. FAR (False Acceptance Rate)

It is the inaccuracy in the pattern-recognition-system that can be calculated as:

$$FAR = \frac{\text{Total Number of Features} - \text{Total Number of Falsely Accepted Features}}{\text{Total Number of Features}}.$$

ii. FRR (False rejection rate)

It is the rate by which the falsely rejected features can be calculated with the total number of features. It can be defined as:

$$FRR = \frac{\text{Total Number of Features} - \text{Total Number of Falsely Rejected Features}}{\text{Total Number of Features}}$$

iii. Accuracy

It is the common term utilized for achieving the system performance. It can be described as:

Table 4. Analysis of recognition accuracy in multimodal biometric system

Modalities	Recognition accuracy
Face, fingerprint and iris	94
Face, fingerprint and finger vein	95
Face and iris	93
Face and finger vein	91
Face and fingerprint	90

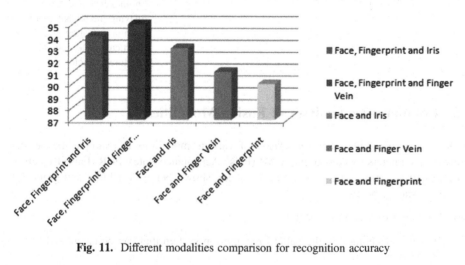

Fig. 11. Different modalities comparison for recognition accuracy

$$\text{Accuracy} = 100 - (\text{FAR} + \text{FRR})$$

Above Table 4 and Fig. 11 shows the comparison of Recognition accuracy for different modalities. It has been analyzed from [23]. The aim of depicting the comparison is that if the fusion of Face, fingerprint and Iris can be consider, than the recognition accuracy is 94, if the fusion of Face, Fingerprint and Finger Vein, than the recognition accuracy is 95, if the fusion of Face and Iris is 93, if the fusion of Face and Finger Vein is consider than the recognition accuracy is 91 and if the fusion of Face and Fingerprint is consider than the recognition accuracy is 90. It can be concluded from the observation that the best accuracy is for Face, Fingerprint and Finger Vein. It has been analyzed that this fusion has achieved its maximum accuracy; therefore, there this fusion cannot have more enhancement in terms of recognition accuracy. So, the fusion of Face, Fingerprint and Iris has more chances in the improvement that can be improved with the use of optimization techniques with classifier.

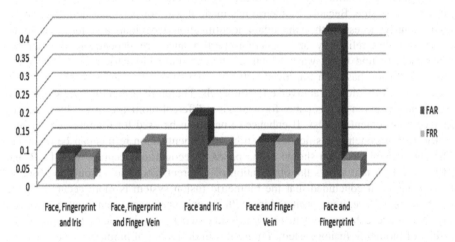

Fig. 12. Comparison of different modalities for FAR and FRR (Color figure online)

Table 5. Analysis of FAN and FRR in Multimodal biometric system

Modalities	FAR	FRR
Face, fingerprint and iris	0.07	0.06
Face, fingerprint and finger vein	0.07	0.1
Face and iris	0.17	0.09
Face and finger vein	0.1	0.1
Face and fingerprint	0.4	0.05

The above Fig. 12 and Table 5 depicts the comparison of FAR and FRR as observed from [23]. FAR is shown in red bar and FRR is shown in blue bar. The observation has shown that when the fusion of Face, Fingerprint and Iris is taken, FAR is 0.07 and FRR is 0.06, when Face, Fingerprint and Finger Vein is considered, FAR is 0.07 and FRR is 01, when face and Iris is considered, FAR is 0.17 and FRR is 0.09, when the fusion of Face and Finger-vein is considered, FAR is 0.1 and FRR is 0.1 and when the fusion of Face and Fingerprint is considered, FAR obtained is 0.4 and FRR is 0.05. It has been observed that in the fusion of face, fingerprint and iris, the probability of error rate is less because FAR and FRR is less and is in equilibrium state for the same fusion.

9   Conclusions

Identity authentication may provide access to high security services, executes trans-action and permit the people cross the border, therefore, exact user authentication is considered as critical in linked and fast moving world. As biometric fusion can be utilized for digital and physical identity authentication, it is significant to enhance current biometric reliability of existing biometric fusion systems. The biometric system has initiated the journey by uni-biometric system that has utilized single biometric information source. Because biometric has made it way for personal identification for high security access with mainstream identification technique and turn out to be imperative that reliability and matching performance are dependable that let the researchers to find novel ways which resulted in multi biometric fusion. The multi biometric fusion has been improved with the integration of varied systems and com-bination of biometric data at diverse fusion levels. Therefore, a concise review of varied researchers is given in this paper for analyzing different biometric fusion by means of image enhancement process. If enhanced image can be used for training and for bio-metric fusion system classification, then better authentication results can be obtained. The comparison has been shown in the paper of recognition accuracy with FAR and FRR from [23] that shows the observation of different modalities. From the observa-tion, it has been concluded that the biometric fusion system is more accurate in the combination of face, fingerprint and iris with the enhance image as an input. So, we can say that image enhancement in pre-processing step is a major factor to improve the results of biometric fusion system. Future lies in designing of biometric fusion system with the combination of different feature extraction techniques with feature optimiza-tion algorithms for the improvement of recognition accuracy in fusion model with face, finger and iris. Future lies in designing of biometric fusion system with the combination of different feature extraction techniques with feature optimization algorithms for the improvement of recognition accuracy in fusion model with face, finger and Iris.

References

1. Leyvand, T., et al.: Biometric recognition. US Patent No. 9,539,500. US Patent and Trademark Office, Washington (2017)
2. Prabhakar, S., Ivanisov, A., Jain, A.: Biometric recognition: sensor characteristics and image quality.IEEE Instrum. Meas. Mag. 14(3), 10–16 (2011). https://doi.org/10.1109/mim.2011.5773529

3. Jain, A.K., Ross, A., Prabhakar, S.: An introduction to biometric recognition. IEEE Trans. Circ. Syst. Video Technol. **14**, 4–20 (2004)
4. Delac, K., Grgic, M.: A survey of biometric recognition methods. In: 46th International Symposium on Electronics in Marine, 2004 Proceedings Elmar, pp. 184–193 (2004)
5. Prabhakar, S., Pankanti, S., Jain, A.K.: Biometric recognition: security and privacy concerns. IEEE Secur. Priv. **2**, 33–42 (2003)
6. Ratha, N.K., Govindaraju, V. (eds.): Advances in Biometrics: Sensors Algorithms and Systems. Springer, Heidelberg (2007)
7. Chauhan, S., Arora, A.S., Kaul, A.: A survey of emerging biometric modalities. Procedia Comput. Sci **2**, 213–218 (2010)
8. Goudelis, G., Tefas, A., Pitas, I.: Emerging biometric modalities: a survey. J. Multimod. User Interfaces **2**, 217 (2008)
9. Kisku, D.R., Gupta, P., Sing, J.K.: Feature level fusion of biometrics cues: human identification with Doddington's caricature. In: Ślęzak, D., Kim, T., Fang, W.C., Arnett, K. P. (eds.) SecTech 2009. CCIS, vol. 58, pp. 157–164. Springer, Heidelberg (2009). https://doi.org/10.1007/978-3-642-10847-1_20
10. Zhang, D., Song, F., Xu, Y., Liang, Z.: Matching score level fusion. In: Advanced Pattern Recognition Technologies with Applications to Biometrics, pp. 305–327. IGI Global (2009)
11. Zhang, D., Song, F., Xu, Y., Liang, Z.: Decision level fusion. In: Advanced Pattern Recognition Technologies with Applications to Biometrics, pp. 328–348. IGI Global (2009)
12. Jain, A.K., Dass, S.C., Nandakumar, K.: Soft biometric traits for personal recognition systems. In: Zhang, D., Jain, A.K. (eds.) ICBA 2004. LNCS, vol. 3072, pp. 731–738. Springer, Heidelberg (2004). https://doi.org/10.1007/978-3-540-25948-0_99
13. Solayappan, N., Latifi, S.: A survey of unimodal biometric methods. In: Proceedings of the 2006 International Conference on Security and Management, pp. 1609–1618 (2006)
14. Rodrigues, R.N., Ling, L.L., Govindaraju, V.: Robustness of multimodal biometric fusion methods against spoof attacks. J. Vis. Lang. Comput. **20**, 169–179 (2009)
15. Conti, V., Militello, C., Sorbello, F., Vitabile, S.: A frequency-based approach for features fusion in fingerprint and iris multimodal biometric identification systems. IEEE Trans. Syst. Man Cybern. Part C (Appl. Rev.) **40**, 384–395 (2010)
16. Kihal, N., Chitroub, S., Polette, A., Brunette, I., Meunier, J.: Efficient multimodal ocular biometric system for person authentication based on iris texture and corneal shape. IET Biomet. **6**, 379–386 (2017)
17. Zareen, F.J., Jabin, S.: Authentic mobile-biometric signature verification system. IET Biomet. **5**, 13–19 (2016)
18. Yan, Z., Zhao, S.: A usable authentication system based on personal voice challenge. In: Advanced Cloud and Big Data (CBD), pp. 194–199 (2016)
19. Abdullah-Al-Wadud, M., Kabir, M., Akber Dewan, M., Chae, O.: A dynamic histogram equalization for image contrast enhancement. IEEE Trans. Consum. Electron. **53**(2), 593–600 (2007). https://doi.org/10.1109/tce.2007.381734
20. Yadav, G., Maheshwari, S., Agarwal, A.: Contrast limited adaptive histogram equalization based enhancement for real time video system. In: 2014 International Conference on Advances in Computing, Communications and Informatics ICACCI, pp. 2392–2397 (2014)
21. Gillespie, A.R.: Enhancement of multispectral thermal infrared images: decorrelation contrast stretching. Rem. Sens. Environ. **42**, 147–155 (1992)
22. Mustapha, A., Hussain, A., Samad, S.A.: A new approach for noise reduction in spine radiograph images using a non-linear contrast adjustment scheme based adaptive factor. Sci. Res. Essays **6**, 4246–4258 (2011)
23. Sarhan, S., Alhassan, S., Elmougy, S.: Multimodal biometric systems: a comparative study. Arab. J. Sci. Eng. **42**, 443–457 (2017)

Heart Disease Prediction Using Fuzzy System

Sumit Sharma[1], Vishu Madaan[1(✉)], Prateek Agrawal[1],
and Narendra Kumar Garg[2]

[1] Lovely Professional University, Phagwara, Punjab, India
sumitsharma1754046@gmail.com,
vishumadaan123@gmail.com, prateek061186@gmail.com
[2] Amity University, Gwalior, Madhya Pradesh, India
narendra.gwl.mits@gmail.com

Abstract. There are numerous Artificial Intelligence (AI) techniques that are being applied within certain applications in such a manner that the requirements are satisfied. Providing solutions to the issues which simulate human behavior of experts used within the specific areas is done with the help of Expert Systems (ES's). The Shells are used in order to generate the ES which are further utilized by the users. The expert system can be designed using the technique of artificial intelligence. The fuzzy logic is the technique of artificial intelligence in which output is generated on the basis of given inputs. In this research, the heart disease prediction expert system is designed on the basis of certain parameters. To increase efficiency of the system, ECG parameter will be added in future which increase accuracy of heart disease prediction.

Keywords: Disease diagnosis · Medical expert system · Fuzzy logic
Fuzzy rule based system

1 Introduction

An extensive variety of diseases are familiar a number of the people across the globe. Some diseases might be cured even as others might be triumphing at some point of the complete lifespan. The hassle could be similarly compounded with non-detection or while detection takes location within the superior degrees. A range of illnesses will be cured with suitable precautions taken during the early degree of prevalence of the disease [1]. One such disease is Heart Disease. An early detection of the identical should gain wealthy dividends. Computer generation gear assist docs to organize keep and retrieve relevant clinical information needed to recognize the elaborate instances and deliver them ideas approximately a proper prognosis, analysis and treatment selections. There is huge information management gear available inside health care systems, but evaluation gear is not enough to discover hidden relationships amongst the records. Expert Systems (ES) of an smart laptop is based totally on interactive selection tool that uses information and guidelines to clear up actual existence issues, based on expertise acquired from one or greater of a human expert in a selected location [2]. In domain of heart sickness risk, smoke, cholesterol, blood strain, diabetes, sex and age are predominant chance factors that affect on heart disease threat. Because of the

© Springer Nature Singapore Pte Ltd. 2019
A. K. Luhach et al. (Eds.): ICAICR 2018, CCIS 955, pp. 424–434, 2019.
https://doi.org/10.1007/978-981-13-3140-4_38

numerous and unsure threat factors within the heart ailment risks, now and again coronary heart disorder analysis is hard for experts. In the alternative word, there exists no strict boundary among what is Healthy and what is diseased, as a result distinguishes is uncertain and indistinct [3]. Having so many factors to research to diagnose the heart ailment of an affected person makes the physician's activity difficult. So, experts require an accurate tool that considering these danger elements and display positive brings about unsure term.

A diagnosis decision relies upon the knowledge and perception of a physician. Good judgment capability of Fuzzy offers effective reasoning techniques which can deal with uncertainties and vagueness. Fuzzy logic is a technique to render particular what is obscure in the world of drugs. FES plays a very important role in medicinal drug for symptomatic diagnostic remedies. The researchers diagnosed potential and the capability of FES to prove its diagnosing accuracy in a special field. The computer based totally diagnostic technology and knowledge base truly facilitates for early analysis of any disease [4]. As per current trends, the usage of computer technology within the discipline of drugs has tremendously accelerated. The use of neural network approach, fuzzy common sense, genetic set of rules and neuro-fuzzy systems has especially helped in complicated and uncertain symptoms of patients. Research work of last few years has proved that neural networks and fuzzy systems are the effective and accurate approaches to deal with uncertain and vague data collected from patients for analysis of disease [5].

2 Literature Review

In a medical field analysis is a system for ID or acknowledgment of an ailment in view of few signs and side effects that shows up. With ceaseless upgrades in social insurance information framework, assurance of the valuable learning from the accessible learning is testing undertaking. Agrawal et al. composed a framework in light of fuzzy rationale to upgrade the control techniques in the medicinal field with the advancement of therapeutic master framework fit for identifying human ailments [6]. Proposed technique makes weighted fuzzy set lead to manage the medicinal diagnosing issues from the preparation information. This exploration is an endeavor to support the PC innovation ahead of time to create programming that will help the specialists, doctors or a typical individual at essential level in settling on redress choices before taking any interview from the pro of eyes, ear-nose-throat (ENT) and liver.

In developing nations growth of cervix harrows the vast majority of the ladies. Sharma et al. arrange the clinical dataset of cervical disease to recognize the phase of growth which helps in appropriate treatment of patient experiencing tumor [7]. This examination work essentially advances toward the recognition of cervical disease utilizing Pap spread pictures. Investigation of Pap spread of cervical district is an effective method to think about any variation from the norm in cervical cells. The proposed framework right off the bat portion the pap picture utilizing Edge Detection to isolate the cell cores from cytoplasm and foundation and after that concentrate different highlights of cervical pap pictures like zone, border, lengthening and afterward these highlights are standardized utilizing min-max strategy. After standardization KNN strategy is utilized to order malignancy as per its anomaly. The classification precision with 84.3% of greatest execution with no approval and order exactness with 82.9% of most extreme execution with 5 Fold cross approval is accomplished.

A savvy framework is a machine with an installed PC that has the ability to assemble and investigate information and speak with different frameworks. Agrawal et al. recognize the conduct of human in light of his/her body signal [8]. Body motion acknowledgment is imperative and prime element to recognize the conduct of the individual so conduct and outlook of any individual can be judged from one's body motion. The proposed framework catches a picture of a man and perceives distinctive signals identified with head, hands and legs positions. The distinctive kinds of standards are characterized in fuzzy framework that will create the conduct and state of mind subsèquent to breaking down the caught picture with information base.

There are various Artificial Intelligence (AI) methods that are being connected inside specific applications in such a way, to the point that the necessities are fulfilled. Giving answers for the issues which reenact human conduct of specialists utilized inside the particular zones is finished with the assistance of Expert Systems (ES's). The Shells are utilized as a part of request to produce the ES which are additionally used by the clients. The master framework can be planned utilizing the method of computerized reasoning. The fuzzy rationale is the procedure of counterfeit consciousness in which yield is produced based on given information sources. Other experiment is done to diagnose the diseases related to gynecology [9]. To build effectiveness of the framework, ECG parameter will be included future which increment precision of coronary illness expectation.

Soft Computing systems have been utilized as a part of a wide assortment of utilizations and medicinal field is no exemption. In spite of the fact that its utilization is dominating in territories like heart and diabetes, adequate measure of research has not been led in investigating its use in the working of lungs. Keeping in see this perspective, the work did places a lot of significance in the way the lung capacities and furthermore in distinguishing issues related with lungs fundamentally Asthma and Chronic Obstructive Pulmonary Disease (COPD). Anand et al. planned a fuzzy master framework that considers subtle elements of different patients and recognizes the issue the patient is probably going to experience [10].

The intelligent reasoning of medicinal experts assumes critical part in basic leadership about conclusion. It displays variety in choices as results of their ways to deal with manage vulnerabilities and unclearness in the learning and data. Fuzzy rationale has turned out to be the momentous apparatus for building insightful basic leadership frameworks for surmised thinking that can fittingly deal with both the vulnerability and imprecision. Sikchi et al. build up a bland fuzzy master framework structure that can be utilized to outline particular fuzzy master frameworks for specific therapeutic area [11]. Chaudhari et al. outlined a fuzzy master framework for the expectation of coronary illness [14]. Despite the fact that innovation has made its essence felt generously in the field of prescription, the levels of pressure displayed in people over the globe has been on the expansion in unselfish extents. A critical need is felt in enhancing the wellbeing remainder of human race. With this view in context, a specific space in particular expectation of Coronary Heart Disease (CHD) has been concentrated upon. Studies have demonstrated that early forecasts prompt better conclusion and thus better medications and even conceivable cures.

These days the utilization of PC innovation in the fields of pharmaceutical region conclusion, treatment of sicknesses and patient interest has very expanded. Kumar et al. composed fuzzy master framework for Heart Disease Diagnosis with take after enrollment capacities, input factors, yield factors and lead base [12]. Coronary illness is a turmoil that influences the heart, the main enemy of human group. Kumar et al. led an investigation to analyze heart patients [13]. The parts of this investigation are Fuzzification, Advanced Fuzzy Resolution Mechanism and defuzzification. Fresh qualities are moved into fuzzy qualities through the fuzzification (Table 1).

Table 1. Comparative study of various techniques

Sr. No.	Reference No.	Author	Technique proposed	Findings
1	[15]	Biyouki et al.	Presented a fuzzy rule-based expert system in order to diagnose the thyroid disease	This helped the experts as well as the non-experts to provide diagnosis to people suffering
2	[21]	Duisenbayeva et al.	Presented various problems that are arising during the design of Fuzzy Expert System in order to diagnose the cardiovascular diseases	This will help in preventing the faults to occur
3	[24]	Hanafiah et al.	Presented the study which is related to Discus Fish.by	Higher accuracy achieved with the application of this proposed algorithm
4	[25]	Kalach et al.	Presented various algorithms that are utilized for implementing the loosely coupled navigation system	This paper identifies the boundaries of any transit able object from a state of rotation
5	[26]	Maylawati et al.	Stated a study based on the pregnancy which is an important part of human lives	Higher accuracy of results achieved with the application of ANN based technique
6	[22]	Sanjani et al.	Presented that prediction of electric load is very important within the power systems	The analysis of receiver operating characteristic curves was utilized for testing the correctness of the system function
7	[23]	Iman et al.	Presented that there is an increase in demand	The users can easily identify their problems

(*continued*)

Table 1. (*continued*)

Sr. No.	Reference No.	Author	Technique proposed	Findings
			of the non-functional requirements by the users with the growth in software technologies	and remove them which can help them develop a better interface
8	[16]	Khayamnia et al.	Presented a study related to the patients suffering from migraine headache	Provide early diagnosis and accurate results
9	[17]	Zheng et al.	Presented product design process using the fuzzy TOPSIS	The optimal combination of design form elements can be attained with the help of an expert system
10	[18]	Suzdaltsev et al.	Presented utilization of fuzzy rules in order to conduct the predictive diagnostics with the help of expert system	The validity of the fuzzy rules achieved is confirmed
11	[19]	Kostrov et al.	Presented technique for smart management of the computing resources	Level of accuracy was improved along with the enhancement is various other parameters
12	[20]	Thapar et al.	A fuzzy expert system that helps in diagnosing malnutrition in infants	Level of nourishment can be detected here in accurate level and can help in providing benefits to the users which can help prevent it

3   Research Methodology

This research work is based on the expert system which is designed to predict the heart disease. In the existing work, the 19 parameters are taken as input to predict the heart disease. In the 19 parameters most important features are Blood Pressure, Heart Rate Cough and Total Cholesterol. On the basis of these parameters the chances of heart disease that whether chances are low, medium or high is predicted. The tables are described below which are used for the heart disease prediction:

Inputs

- **Age:** As the age of the person increases the possibility of having heart disease also increases. According to mayo-clinic the men at the age of 45 and women at the age of 55 or older having possibility of getting heart disease.
- **Smoking:** Smoking the major factor which is responsible for coughing which leads to heart disease. Second hand smoker is high heart disease risk rate.
- **High BP (Blood Pressure):** High B.P can make a bad impact on the arteries that may cause atherosclerosis later. Blood pressure increases due unhygienic food, Smoking, any operations, diabetes.
- **Cholesterol:**
  See (Table 2).

Table 2. Types of cholesterol test

Sr. No.	Name
1	HDL cholesterol
2	LDL cholesterol
3	VLDL cholesterol
4	TRIGLYCERIDE
5	Total cholesterol

- **TRIGLYCERIDE:** TRIGLYCERIDE is related type of blood fat (Density of blood increases).
- **High Density Lipoprotein (HDL) Cholesterol:** It is the good type of the cholesterol that protects the heart from getting the heart disease.
- **Low Density Lipoprotein (LDL) Cholesterol:** It is the Bad cholesterol which is responsible for heart disease.
- **Total Cholesterol:** It is the ratio of the HDL and LDL cholesterol i.e. good cholesterol and bad cholesterol.
- **Family History:** If the patient have heart disease in their family member like parents or sibling that also increases the heart disease risk rate.
- **Lack of physical Activity:** To maintain the cholesterol level physical activity like jogging or exercise is more important. The people who exercise regularly have less risk of getting heart disease.
- **Diabetes:**
  See (Table 3).

Table 3. Types of diabetes test

Sr. No.	Name
1	Fasting blood sugar
2	Random blood sugar
3	AC1 test
4	Oral glucose test

- **Random Blood Sugar:** Random blood sugar is the test done by taking the sample of blood at random time to check the random sugar level.
- **Fasting Blood Sugar:** Fasting blood sugar is the test done by taking the blood sample by doing overnight fast.
- **AC1 Test:** It is used to measure the percentage of blood sugar level attached to hemoglobin. It indicates the average sugar of the patient.

Flow Chart of Proposed Methodology

See (Fig. 1).

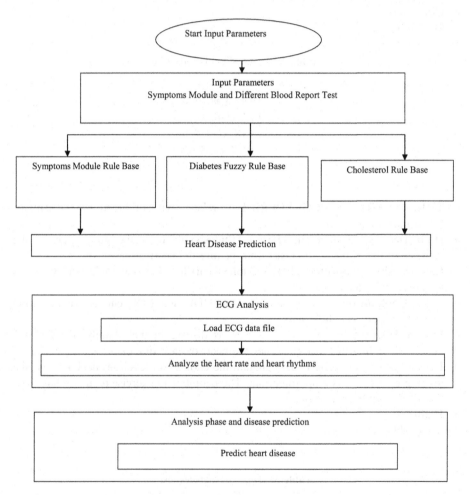

Fig. 1. Flow chart of proposed process

4   Experimental Results

The proposed approach is implemented in MATLAB and the results are evaluated as shown below.

As shown in Fig. 2, the interface is designed for the heart disease prediction. In the interface the Symptoms are input, sugar level and Lipid test is given as input and output is generated of the heart disease prediction.

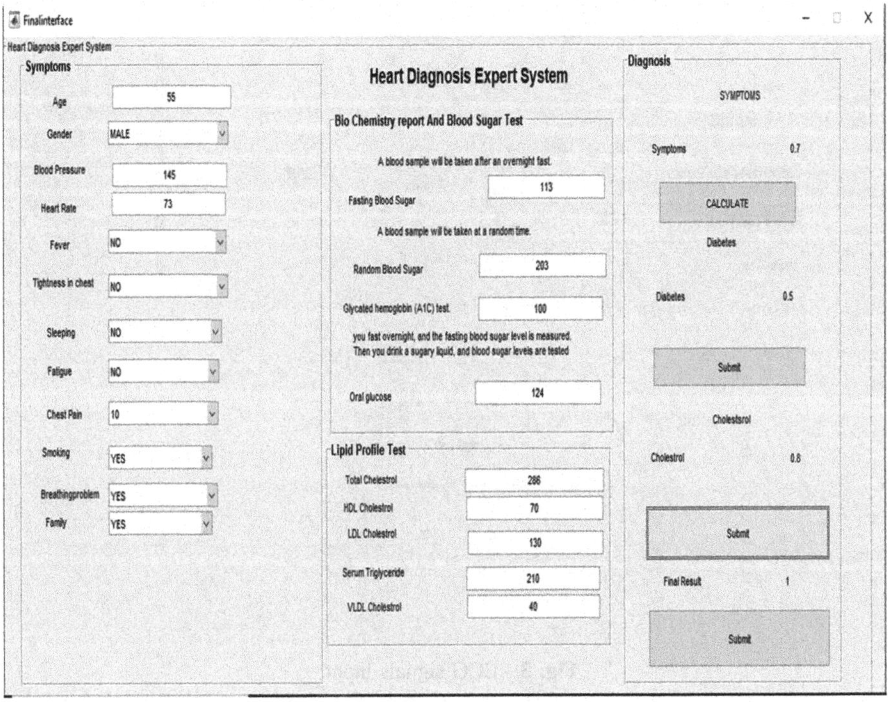

Fig. 2. Interface design

As shown in Fig. 3, the ECG signals are generated which are used for the heart disease prediction. The ECG signals can predict the chances of heart disease.

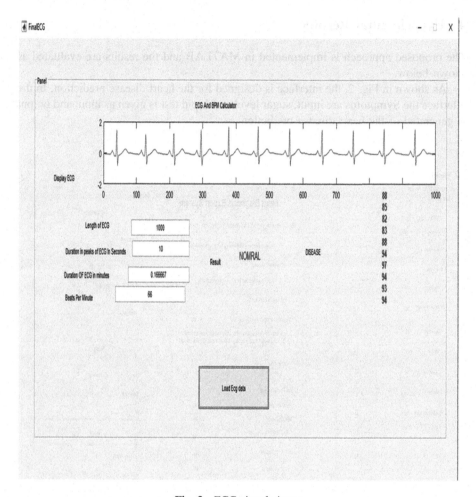

Fig. 3. ECG signals input

5 Conclusion

The expert system is designed to take output according to the given input. The fuzzy logic is applied to design efficient expert system. In the fuzzy logic technique certain numbers of inputs are given on the basis of which output is generated. In this research work, the expert system is designed to predict heart disease. The 19 input parameters are used to derive output system in which chances of heart disease can be low, medium or high is predicted. To increase efficiency of the expert system parameter of ECG will be given as input with the other parameters which predict chances of heart disease.

References

1. Anand, S.K., Sreelalitha, A.V., Sushmitha, B.S.: Designing an efficient fuzzy controller for coronary heart disease. ARPN J. Eng. Appl. Sci. **11**(17), 10319–10326 (2016)
2. Angbera, A., Esiefarienrhe, M., Agaji, I.: Efficient fuzzy-based system for the diagnosis and treatment of tuberculosis (EFBSDTTB). Int. J. Comput. Appl. Technol. Res. **5**(2), 34–48 (2016)
3. Adeli, A., Neshat, M.: A fuzzy expert system for heart disease diagnosis. In: International Multi Conference of Engineers and Computer Scientists, pp. 134–139 (2010)
4. Sikchi, S.S., Sikchi, S., Ali, M.S.: Generic medical fuzzy expert system for diagnosis of cardiac diseases. Int. J. Comput. Appl. **66**(13), 35–44 (2013)
5. Opeyemi, O., Justice, E.O.: Development of neuro-fuzzy system for early prediction of heart attack. Int. J. Inf. Technol. Comput. Sci. **9**, 22–28 (2012)
6. Agrawal, P., Madaan, V., Kumar, V.: Fuzzy rule-based medical expert system to identify the disorders of eyes, ENT and liver. Int. J. Adv. Intell. Parad. **7**(¾), 352–367 (2015)
7. Kaur, R., Madaan, V., Agrawal, P.: Fuzzy expert system to calculate the strength/immunity of a human body. Indian J. Sci. Technol. **9**(44), 1–8 (2016)
8. Agrawal, P., Madaan, V., Kundu, N., Sethi, D., Singh, S.K.: X-HuBIS: a fuzzy rule based human behaviour identification system based on body gestures. Indian J. Sci. Technol. **9**(1), 2–6 (2016)
9. Sethi, D., Agrawal, P., Madaan, V.: X-Tumour: fuzzy rule based medical expert system to detect tumours in gynecology. Int. J. Control. Theory Appl. **9**(11), 5073–5084 (2016)
10. Anand, S.K., Kalpana, R., Vijayalakshmi, S.: Design and implementation of a fuzzy expert system for detecting and estimating the level of asthma and chronic obstructive pulmonary disease. World Appl. Sci. J. **23**(2), 213–223 (2013)
11. Sikchi, S.S., Sikchi, S., Ali, M.S.: Design of fuzzy expert system for diagnosis of cardiac diseases. Int. J. Med. Sci. Public Health **2**(1), 56–61 (2013)
12. Kumar, S., Kaur, G.: Detection of heart diseases using fuzzy logic. Int. J. Eng. Trends Technol. **4**(6), 2694–2699 (2013)
13. Senthil Kumar, A.V.: Diagnosis of heart disease using advanced fuzzy resolution mechanism. Int. J. Sci. Appl. Inf. Technol. **2**(2), 22–30 (2013)
14. Chaudhari, A.A., Akarte, S.P.: Fuzzy and data mining based disease prediction using KNN algorithm. Int. J. Innov. Eng. Technol. **3**(4), 22–66 (2014)
15. Biyouki, S.A., Zarandi, M.H.F., Turksen, I.B.: Fuzzy rule-based expert system for diagnosis of thyroid disease. In: IEEE, vol. 8, no. 3, pp. 47–62 (2015)
16. Khayamnia, M., Yazdchi, M., Vahidiankamyad, A., Foroughipour, M.: The recognition of migraine headache by designation of fuzzy expert system and usage of LFE learning algorithm. In: 2017 5th Iranian Joint Congress on Fuzzy and Intelligent Systems (CFIS), vol. 4, no. 6, pp. 16–35 (2017)
17. Zheng, F., Lin, Y.-C.: A fuzzy TOPSIS expert system based on neural networks for new product design. In: Proceedings of the 2017 IEEE International Conference on Applied System Innovation, vol. 3, no. 6, pp. 17–22 (2017)
18. Suzdaltsev, V.A., Suzdaltsev, I.V., Bogula, N.Y.: Fuzzy rules formation for the construction of the predictive diagnostics expert system. In: 2017 IEEE, vol. 4, no. 6, pp. 17–22 (2017)
19. Kostrov, B.V., Ruchkin, V.N., Makhmudov, M.N., Romanchuk, V.A., Fulin, V.A.: Expert system of multi-criterion fuzzy management in selection of computing resources. In: 2017 International Conference on Mechanical, System and Control Engineering, vol. 8, no. 6, pp. 17–44 (2017)

20. Thapar, A., Goyal, M.: A fuzzy expert system for diagnosis of malnutrition in children. In: IEEE Region 10 Humanitarian Technology Conference (R10-HTC), vol. 4, no. 3, pp. 17–22. IEEE (2016)
21. Duisenbayeva, A., Atymtayeva, L., Beisembetov, I.: Using fuzzy logic concepts in creating the decision making expert system for cardio - vascular diseases (CVD). In: 10th International Conference on Application of Information and Communication Technologies (AICT), pp. 1–5. IEEE (2016)
22. Sanjani, M.A.: The prediction of increase or decrease of electricity cost using fuzzy expert systems. In: 4th Iranian Joint Congress on Fuzzy and Intelligent Systems (CFIS), pp. 1–5. IEEE (2015)
23. Iman, M.R.H., Rasoolzadegan, A.: Quantitative evaluation of software usability with a fuzzy expert system. In: 5th International Conference on Computer and Knowledge Engineering (ICCKE 2015), pp. 325–330. IEEE (2015)
24. Hanafiah, N., Sugiarto, K., Ardy, Y., Prathama, R., Suhartono, D.: Expert system for diagnosis of discus fish disease using fuzzy logic approach. In: IEEE, pp. 56–61 (2015)
25. Kalach, G.G., Romanov, A.M., Tripolskiy, P.E.: Loosely coupled navigation system based on expert system using fuzzy logic. In: IEEE, pp. 167–169 (2016)
26. Maylawati, D.S., Ramdhani, M.A., Zulfikar, W.B.: Expert system for predicting the early pregnancy with disorders using artificial neural network. In: IEEE, pp. 1–6 (2017)

An Adaptive Web Based Educational System Using HMM Approach for C Programming

Aditya Khamparia$^{(\boxtimes)}$, Babita Pandey, Aman Singh, Shrasti Tiwari, and Parampreet Kaur

Lovely Professional University, Phagwara 144411, Punjab, India
aditya.khamparia88@gmail.com,
shukla_babita@yahoo.co.in, amansingh.x@gmail.com,
shrastitiwari@gmail.com, Paramnagpal16@gmail.com

Abstract. The usage of web enabled e-learning systems has been increased for education in recent years. In present study, a Hidden Markov Model (HMM) driven approach is used to predict the future lecture topics or paths of C programming those has been accessed by students in an adaptive web enabled educational system. Data has been preprocessed and collected from e-learning system then HMM parameters were adjusted and used modified algorithm to train the data. This system help faculty to identified the student's problems and provide assistance to them as per their need. The experiment result shows the accuracy of prediction in proposed system is 80.23% which is better than neural network multilayer perceptron model whose accuracy rate is 78.15%.

Keywords: Prediction · E-learning · HMM · Perceptron · Questionnaire

1 Introduction

With the invention and growth of WWW technologies, latest gadgets in past decades have resulted in new e-learning opportunities. Web based learning has shifted the education from the teacher centered into learner centered. Traditional web-based system put the static learning material on the web and does not delivered the learning material to individual learner based on his attributes, background experiences and demand [1]. There is a need to build adaptive intelligent system which represents goals, interests, skills, preferences, knowledge of individual student and update it according to their skills acquiring ability and adapt the content to student needs. These systems are able to predict student future learning actions, next path sequences to visit based on their current and previous knowledge base or information to improve their accuracy and performance. In our C programming-based e-learning system we have three modules: Course module, Instructor module and student module. In course module, all the lectures and course content of programming has been organized which are divided into several concepts depend on topic coverage.

Instructor module has three functions: (1) Uploading the course content; (2) Providing learning path sequence; (3) Providing assignments and evaluating students. In this system, HMM works as an instructor for providing learning path sequence and evaluating students. Student module allows students to interact with different course

© Springer Nature Singapore Pte Ltd. 2019
A. K. Luhach et al. (Eds.): ICAICR 2018, CCIS 955, pp. 435–447, 2019.
https://doi.org/10.1007/978-981-13-3140-4_39

content i.e. lectures as well as instructor to resolve their problems. The status of student knowledge related to lecture component is computed with help of prediction model known as Hidden Markov Model (HMM).

HMM are used to predict the future student actions and improves the delivery of lecture content based on individual student requirements. The use of HMM in learning task is to find the best set of transmission and emission probabilities on basis of given set of sequences. The purpose is to derive the maximum likelihood estimate (using Baum-Welch) of parameters of HMM given the sequences. With the effective usage of sequence profiles, the probabilistic sequential datasets have been analyzed. HMM mostly used in speech and gesture identification, health informatics and educational-hypermedia systems etc. HMM preferable used in web based English modules where students are classified in experimental and control groups and adaptive course sequencing provided to them according to their needs and preferences [1].

Multimedia driven networked system had been used to capture the future behaviour of specific users and deliver lecture according to personalized behavior from dedicated courseware [2]. HMM able to detect gene encoding in different strands of DNA through sequencing of eukaryotes [3]. Hasan and Nath presented HMM approach for stock market forecasting [4].

In this study, we proposed an adaptive web driven educational system based on HMM approach which predicts the future actions and next lecture content of C programming to be visited by student based on history of lecture contents and delivers the learning material according to their ability and preferences. The paper is organized as follows. Section 2 represents the proposed approach. Section 3 deals with implementation and Sect. 4 discussed system evaluation in comparison to perceptron model and finally Sect. 5 concludes this paper.

2 Proposed Approach

We have divided our approach into three phases: Starting, Intermediate and Final. Data has been collected from events recorded in web-based e-learning system. Our proposed system able to facilitates student of university with help of faculty module in which student able to interact with faculty at other site [6–9]. The complete procedure for prediction of student actions using HMM is shown in Fig. 1.

In starting phase, for every students HMM (λ) is developed on the basis of their earlier lecture content access sequence as shown in Fig. 2. If the student is studying first time the course then we provide the learning path as prescribed by expertise [10–12].

HMM model characterized by:

Total number of Hidden states i.e. N

$L = \{L_0, L_1, L_2 \ldots L_{N-1}\}$ which denotes the count of lectures in the system, q_t specified unobservable state at instantaneous time t.

M represents the number of observable states with $V = \{V_0, V_1 \ldots V_{M-1}\}$ the set of observable symbols and O_t the observation state at time t.

$A = \{a_{ij}\}$ represents the probability mapping from L_i and L_j i.e. hidden states transition matrix.

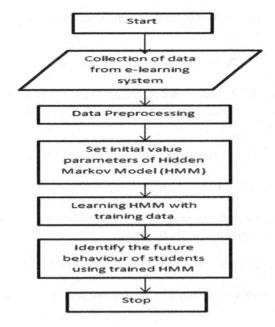

Fig. 1. Proposed approach

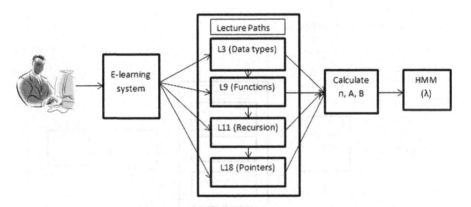

Fig. 2. Starting phase of HMM

$B = \{b_j(k)\}$ determines the identified states V_k probability in unobservable state L_j.
$\prod = \{\Pi_i\}$, the initial state probabilities.

In the intermediate phase, we have used Baum Welch concepts to identify the starting HMM (λ) and to enhance the path sequence of new observed lecture path which is also known as observed sequences as shown in Fig. 3.

This algorithm comprised of two stated variables i.e. forward (α) and backward (β). The probability of non-fully observable lecture content sequence at time t is denoted by forward variable, and unobservable (hidden) state S_i at time t using parameters $\lambda = (A, B, \Pi)$.

$$\alpha_t(i) = \text{Probability of } (O_1, O_2, O_3 \ldots O_t, q_t = L_i, \lambda) \tag{1}$$

The probability of observable lecture content sequence from time $t + 1$ to T is denoted by backward variable, given unobservable state L_i at instantaneous time t using $\lambda = (A, B, \Pi)$.

$$\beta_t(i) = P(O_{t+1}, O_{t+2}, O_{t+3} \ldots O_T, q_t = L_i, \lambda) \tag{2}$$

$$\xi_t(i,j) = P(q_t = L_i, q_{t+1} = L_j | O_1, O_2, \ldots, O_T, \lambda) \tag{3}$$

The probability of being in state L_i at time t given the observation sequence $O = O_1, O_2, \ldots O_T$ and model $\lambda = (A, B, \Pi)$.

$$\gamma_t(i) = P(q_t = L_i | O_1, O_2, O_3 \ldots O_T, \lambda) \tag{4}$$

As per Baum Welch algorithm [5], the starting and intermediate phase can be generalized in 4 steps.

1. For each student HMM $\lambda = (A, B, \Pi)$ is initialized.
2. Calculate $\alpha_t(i)$, $\beta_t(i)$, $\xi_t(i,j)$, $\gamma_t(i)$, $t = 1 \ldots T$, $i = 0, 1, 2 \ldots N-1$, $j = 0, 1, \ldots N-1$.
3. Adjust $\lambda = (A, B, \Pi)$.
4. If $P(O|\lambda)$ increased proceed to 2.

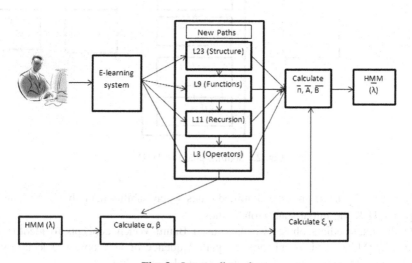

Fig. 3. Intermediate phase

In final phase, probability $\alpha_t(i)$ of each lecture content can be denoted as states for programming course is determined by forward algorithm as shown in Fig. 4. After computation [13–16], maximum value will determine the next future action or lecture content to be visited by students.

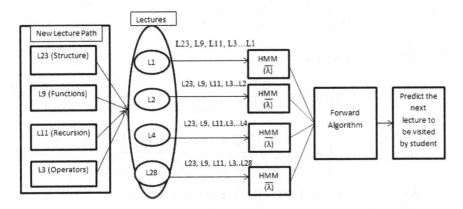

Fig. 4. Final phase

Forward Algorithm:

1. Set $\lambda = (A, B, \Pi)$ with random initial condition.
2. Set LTH = 1 where LTH is the length of the observations or lecture path.
3. Increment LTH by 1. C = 0 is the current iteration.
4. If (LTH < H) where H is previous history of count of lectures used for course then
   Set H = LTH
   Else
   Set LTH = H
5. The HMM model based on Baum Welch algorithm $\lambda = (A, B, \Pi)$ is settled on the basis of last H sequence observations or lecture paths $O_{LTH-H+1}$, $O_{LTH-H+2}$, $O_{LTH-H+3}$ ... O_{LTH}.
   5.1 Calculate α recursively.

$$\alpha_{LTH-H+1}(i) = \frac{\Pi_k \cdot b_k(O_{LTH-H+1})}{\sum_{i=0}^{N-1} \Pi \cdot b_i(O_{LTH-H+1})} \tag{5}$$

Where i = 0, 1, 2...N − 1 and $\alpha_{LTH-H+1}(i)$ denoted the probability of ($O_{LTH-H+1}$) and hidden state L_k.

$$\alpha_t(j) = \frac{\sum_{i=0}^{N-1} \alpha_{t-1} \cdot a_{ij} b_j(O_t)}{\sum_{j=0}^{N-1} \sum_{i=0}^{N-1} \alpha_{t-1}(i) \cdot a_{ij} \cdot b_j(O_t)} \tag{6}$$

LTH = LTH − H + 2, LTH − H + 1, ..., LTH, J = 0, 1, 2...N − 1, where $\alpha_t(j)$ is the probability of partial lecture paths until time t ($O_{LTH-H+1}.....O_{LTH}$) and hidden state L_j at time t.

$$\alpha_T(j) = P\left(O_{LTH-H+1}, O_{LTH-H+2}, ..., O_{LTH}, q_{LTH} = L_j | \lambda\right) \tag{7}$$

$$P(O_{LTH-H+1}, O_{LTH-H+2}, ..., O_{LTH} | \lambda) = \sum_{j=0}^{N-1} \alpha_{LTH}(j) \tag{8}$$

5.2 Calculate β recursively.

$$\beta_{LTH}(i) = \frac{1}{\sum_{j=0}^{N-1} \sum_{i=0}^{N-1} \alpha_{LTH-1}(i) \cdot a_{ij} \cdot b_j(O_{LTH})} \tag{9}$$

$$\beta_{LTH}(i) = \frac{\sum_{j=0}^{N-1} a_{ij} \cdot b_j(O_{t+1}) \cdot \beta_{t+1}(j)}{\sum_{j=0}^{N-1} \sum_{i=0}^{N-1} a_{ij} \cdot b_j(O_{t+1}) \cdot \beta_{t+1}(j)} \tag{10}$$

Where, t = LTH − 1, LTH − H + 1, and i = 0, 1, 2...N − 1
5.3 Calculate ξ

$$\xi_t(i, j) = \frac{\alpha_t(i) \cdot a_{ij} \cdot b(O_{t+1}) \beta_{t+1}(j)}{\sum_{i=0}^{N-1} \sum_{j=0}^{N-1} \alpha_t(i) \cdot a_{ij} \cdot b_j(O_{t+1}) \beta_{t+1}(j)} \tag{11}$$

t = LTH − H + 1, ..., LTH − 1, i = 0, 1, 2...N − 1.

Here $\xi_t(i, j)$ denoted the unobservable state probability L_i at time t and perform transition to state L_j at timestamp t and performing a transition to L_j at t + 1, having various sequence as $O_{LTH-H+1}, O_{LTH-H+2}, ...O_T$.

5.4 Calculate γ

$$\gamma_{LTH}(i) = \sum_{j=0}^{N-1} \xi_t(i, j) \tag{12}$$

t = LTH − H + 1, ..., LTH − 1, i = 0...N − 1.

$\gamma_{LTH}(i)$ is state L_i probability at time stamp t and sequence $O_{LTH-H+1}, O_{LTH-H+2}, ..., O_{LTH}$.

5.5 Adjust Π

$$\Pi_i = \gamma_{LTH-H+1}(i)$$

Π_i denoted the maximum frequency count where hidden state is L_i at t = LTH − H + 1

5.6 Adjustment on A

$$a_{ijnew} = \frac{\sum_{t=LTH-H+1}^{LTH-1} \xi_t(i,j)}{\sum_{t=LTH-H+1}^{LTH-1} \gamma_t(i)} \tag{13}$$

5.7 Adjust B

$$b_j(k)_{new} = \frac{\sum_{t=LTH-H+1}^{LTH-1} 1_{yt=vk}\gamma_t(j)}{\sum_{LTH-H+1}^{LTH-1} \gamma_t(j)} \tag{14}$$

Here $1_{yt=vk}$ is an indicator function.

5.8 Increment c.

5.9 If $P(O_{LTH-H+1}...O_{LTH} |\lambda_{new}) > P(O_{LTH-H+1}.....O_{LTH}| \lambda)$ then go to 5.

6. The next observation symbol or lecture path O_{LTH+1} can be predicted at time LTH with the help of adjusted model $\lambda_{new} = (A_{new}, B_{new}, \Pi_{new})$.

6.1 Take out unobservable state L_i at LTH, i = 0, 1, 2...N − 1, maximize $\alpha_{LTH}(i)$.

6.2 Take out next unobservable state L_j at LTH + 1 j = 0, 1, 2...N − 1, maximize a_{ijnew}.

6.3 Identify V_k next lecture at LTH + 1, k = 0, ..., M − 1, maximize $b_j(k)_{new}$.

7. If procedure goes in continuation then LTH = LTH + 1 and proceed to step 4.

8. End.

3 Implementation

The web-based e-learning system identified the next lecture path or sequence to be visited by certain students based on their preference and skills [17, 18]. We have developed our e-learning system in Java language. The main entities used in our system are: students and faculty which are implemented as JSP class. They communicate each other by means of JSP MySQL database using the Apache web server.

Every lecture topics present in course curriculum of C programming is represented through letter L along with a number, i.e. the lecture topic "Structure" is coded by L23. Lecture coding is not sequential, it is random. It can be interchangeable i.e. L15 can represent string also. The entire lecture topics covered in course module is shown in Table 1.

To obtain which next lecture path or topic sequence is visited by students there is a need to provide proper sequence with help of browsing option or can directly paste it in text field as shown in Fig. 5 In this sequence two options are provided for prediction: predicting a single lecture topic or predicting a multiple lecture topic in succession. In the system the user has choice to select the sequence related to single or multiple concepts. Single concept refers when the topic is individual and not associated with any other major topics like array is related to function or structures. Multiple concepts refer when the topic is associated with multiple major topics like array with function or structure.

Table 1. Lecture topics of C programming

Lecture number	Lecture topics/paths/concept	Lecture number	Lecture topics/paths/concept
L1	Identifiers and keywords	L15	Array application
L2	Data types	L16	String
L3	Operators	L17	Manipulation of string
L4	Control transfer statements	L18	Pointers
L5	For, while, do-while	L19	Operation on pointers
L6	Formatted and unformatted functions	L20	Passing pointer to functions
L7	Type conversion	L21	Array of pointers
L8	Type modifiers	L22	DMA
L9	Functions	L23	Structures
L10	Parameters passing techniques	L24	Nested structures
L11	Recursion	L25	Union
L12	Storage class	L26	File handling modes
L13	Arrays and types	L27	File handling operations
L14	Passing array to function	L28	Macros

Fig. 5. Adaptive HMM system

In this system, we have provided faculty module as shown in Fig. 6 through which they can monitor student progress and instruct them to take suitable decisions based on their requirement. On the demand of students, faculty has right to deliver and instruct the exact learning material i.e. they can alter the learning material content and also changes the sequence of lecture prediction list produced by web-based system [19–21].

In order to provide suggestion to students based on lecture path they followed, a sequence with suggestions as shown in Fig. 7 is presented to them where they want to know where to go next or which topic to be followed. Sequence has been provided to

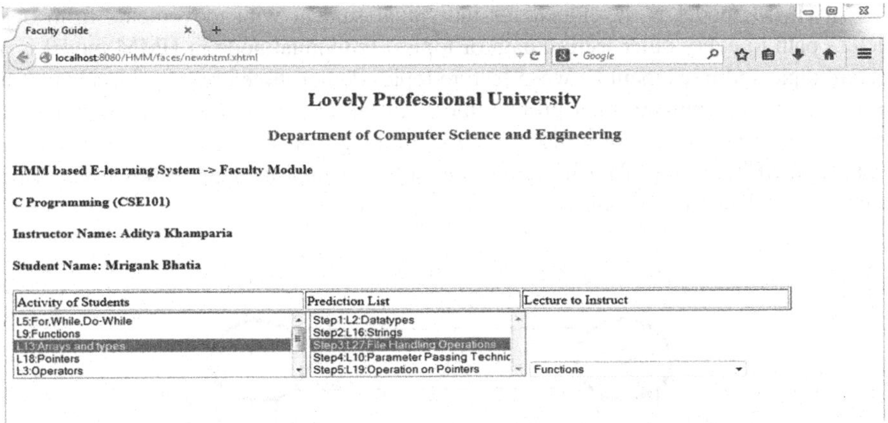

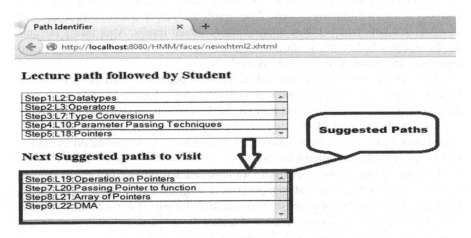

Fig. 6. Faculty module

student based on their previous knowledge, skills and ability. The path finding navigation and prediction is performed through sequences i.e. short and long sequence of students. These single sequence or lecture paths are demonstrated as training data of HMM prediction and testing data could be sequences with multiple paths. For example, student1 has lecture topic to be followed in sequence like L1 (Identifiers and Keywords), L2 (Data types), L3 (Operators), L18 (Pointers), L19 (Operation on pointers), L20 (Passing pointer to functions), L21 (Array of pointers), whereas for student2 it can be L18 (Pointers), L19 (Operation on pointers), L1 (Identifiers and keywords), L3 (Operators), L2 (Data types), L21 (Array of pointers), L20 (Passing pointer to functions). Student3 has navigation sequence for lecture topic it can be L1 (Identifiers and keywords), L19 (Operation on pointers), L20 (Passing pointer to functions) L21 (Array of pointers), L2 (Data types), L3 (Operators), L18 (Pointers).

Fig. 7. Sequence path suggestions

An HMM model is developed for individual student with movements from one lecture path to every other lecture path or topics. Individual node in HMM model is a lecture topic and movement between lecture topics demonstrated by transition between several nodes to compute final probabilities. All the lecture topics are represented as states to represent all lecture series of C programming course. As shown in Fig. 8 only partial HMM has been taken into consideration in which navigation has been made between different lecture topics.

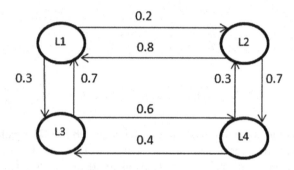

Fig. 8. Partial HMM

4   System Evaluation

To obtain some feedback about our adaptive web-based e-learning system, we demonstrate effectiveness of our HMM model through several experiments using C programming course taught in university. In this section Exercise/quizzes module selected for students as shown in Fig. 9 and present feedback to them. A questionnaire has been prepared and distributed to students registered for C programming course in adaptive system. Two groups of 25 students each have been randomly selected to test the system. First group of 25 students use offline paper exercise/quiz and second group used our adaptive e-learning system. After result analysis or comparison, it has been observed that both groups obtain approximately similar results. After taking the quiz, all the students had to fill in questionnaire with general questions regarding C programming and based on assessment methods.

After getting response it has been observed that student who used the web-based e-learning system obtained their marks immediately after submitting response to server. Student who had given offline quiz they received the results the day after exam. Based on result analysis, most of the students are interested to know their grade details immediately after exam which shows they trust more a computer-based evaluation system rather than conventional methods.

To compare our proposed approach, we designed a Multilayer perceptron network to predict the student actions and their progress in programming in coming months. The input of network is student actions. There are total 4 inputs that can be enrollment of student to programming course, decision of lecture topics, participation in exercise/quiz assessments, and interaction with faculty while asking questions, suggestions and

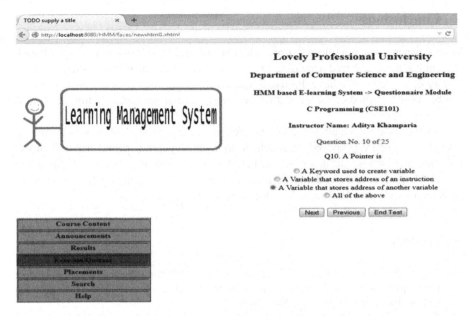

Fig. 9. Exercise/quiz module

discussion in class. The network has one output i.e. rate of improvement in student actions in coming time. The proposed model has 3 layers as 5-20-1 (input-hidden-output). It has been tested with record of 50 student's data and evaluated with 25 data and performance rate achieved was 78.15 compared to HMM i.e. 80.23 which show that our HMM based approach is more effective in terms of performance.

As shown in Fig. 10 the percentage of positive predictions reaches up to 80% using 100% of training set which shows the number of correctly predicted concepts based on student actions.

Fig. 10. Test results

5 Conclusions

In this paper, data is collected from adaptive e-learning system and action of each student has been gathered according to every lecture topic which they visited based on history of concepts. We have discussed how HMM along with Baum-Welch algorithm has been used to predict the student future behaviour and navigation actions within an e-learning system.

On the basis of result achieved, prediction percent of student actions equals to 80.23. To compare proposed approach, Multilayer perceptron neural network model was designed whose accuracy rate equals to 78.15. It shows that our method has acceptable performance and can be used as good tool for predicting future action of students to visit next lecture path or topics in C programming.

References

1. Fok, A., Wong, H.S., Chen, Y.S.: Hidden Markov model based characterization of content access patterns in an E-learning environment. In: IEEE International conference on Multimedia and Expo, pp. 201–204 (2005)
2. Ping, J., Jim, K., Beverly, W.: Student behavioral model based prefetching in online tutoring. University of Massachusetts, Technical report, pp. 01–27 (2001)
3. Birney, E.: Hidden Markov model in biological sequence analysis. IBM J. Res. Dev. **45**, 834–846 (2001)
4. Hassan, M.R., Nath, B.: Stock market forecasting using hidden Markov model: a new approach. In: Proceedings of 5th International Conference on Intelligent Systems Design and Applications, pp. 192–196 (2005)
5. Homsi, M., Lutfi, R., Carro, R., Ghias, B.: A hidden Markov model approach to predict student actions in an adaptive and intelligent web based educational system. In: IEEE Xplore, pp. 236–245 (2007)
6. Huang, X., Yong, J., Li, J., Gao, J.: Prediction of student actions using weighted hidden Markov model. In: IT in Medicine and Education, IEEE International Symposium on Digital Object Identifier (2008)
7. Anari, M.S., Anari, S.: Intelligent e-learning systems using student behavior prediction. J. Basic Appl. Sci. **8**(3), 12017–12023 (2012)
8. Deeb, B., Hassan, Z., Beseiso, M.: An adaptive HMM based approach for improving e-learning methods. IEEE Proceedings, pp. 456–468 (2014)
9. Wang, Y., Tseng, M.H., Lia, H.C.: Data mining for adaptive learning in a TESL based e-learning system. Expert Syst. Appl. **38**, 6480–6485 (2011)
10. Wang, T.H.: Developing web-based assessment strategies for facilitating junior high school students to perform self-regulated learning in an e-learning environment. Comput. Educ. **57** (2), 1801–1812 (2011)
11. Seters, J.R., Ossevoort, M.A., Tramper, J., Goedhart, M.J.: The influence of student characteristics on the use of adaptive e-learning material. Comput. Educ. **58**, 942–952 (2012)
12. Pandey, B., Mishra, R.B., Khamparia, A.: CBR based approach for adaptive learning in e-learning system. In: IEEE conference on Computer Science and Engineering (Asia Pacific World Conference, Fiji), pp. 1–6 (2014). https://doi.org/10.1109/apwccse.2014.7053877
13. Tseng, S.S., Su, J.M., Hwang, G.J., Tsai, C.J.: An object oriented course framework for developing adaptive learning systems. Educ. Technol. Soc. **11**(2), 171–191 (2008)

14. Chookaew, S., Panjaburee, P., Wanichsan, D., Laosinchai, P.: A personalized e-learning environment to promote students conceptual learning on basic computer programming. Procedia – Soc. Behav. Sci. **116**, 815–819 (2013)
15. Hsieh, T.-C., Wang, T.-I.: A mining based approach on discovering courses pattern for constructing suitable learning path. Expert Syst. Appl. **37**(6), 4156–4157 (2010)
16. Chang, T.Y., Chen, Y.T.: Cooperative learning in e-learning: a peer assessment of student-centered using consistent fuzzy preference. Expert Syst. Appl. **36**(4), 8342–8349 (2009)
17. Yarandi, M., Tawil, H., Rehman, A.: A personalized adaptive e-learning approach based on semantic web technology. Webology **2**, 243–256 (2013)
18. Dayhoff, J.E.: Neural Network Architecture. Van Nostrand, New York (1990)
19. Kristofic, A., Bielikova, M.: Improving adaptation in web based educational hypermedia by means of knowledge discovery. In: Proceedings of Sixteenth ACM Conference on Hypertext and Media (2005)
20. Khamparia, A., Pandey, B.: Knowledge and intelligent computing methods in e-learning. Int. J. Technol. Enhanc. Learn. **7**(3), 221–242 (2015)
21. Khamparia, A., Pandey, B.: A novel method of case representation and retrieval in CBR for e-learning. Educ. Inf. Technol. **22**, 337–354 (2015). https://doi.org/10.1007/s10639-015-9447-8

Performance Evaluation of Robot Path Planning Using Hybrid TSP Based ACO

Ankita Khurana[✉], Sunil Kumar Khatri, and Ajay Vikram Singh

Amity Institute of Information Technology (AIIT),
Amity University Uttar Pradesh (AUUP), Noida, India
ankitakhurana43@gmail.com, sunilkkhatri@gmail.com,
skkhatri@amity.edu, ajayavs.iitr@gmail.co

Abstract. Path problem is a motivating theme in robotics framework/system these days. The relevant quantity of inspection had always been committed to this specific complex issue lately. This ant colony optimization calculation is an elective strategy only to tackle such a problematic situation. Every ant drops an amount of simulated pheromone at each node that the ant has just finished covering up. This specific pheromone fundamentally deviates the likelihood that the following ant winds up included to a specific network node. The proposed directs the ants to make a path line inclusive of all factors to reach the goal point. This paper purposes ant colony based approach which is useful in taking care of way arranging problem for self-sufficient automated (robotic) application.

Keywords: Robot path planning · Ant colony optimization (ACO)
Traveling salesman problem (TSP)
Dubin travelling salesman problem with neighborhood
Asymmetric traveling salesman problem (ATSP) · Path map (PM)

1 Introduction

Under Ant Colony Optimization (ACO) method, the ants look through the food by succeeding some illustrative ways. The ant acknowledges it and the food source by noticing the ways that how they can grasp the food source via door. Ant tries to form their pheromone on the affecting path to follow a routine. They likewise utilize the system to keep away from obstructions or defeat the obstructions coming in the way. The hybrid style of the complete ant framework is introduced in the proposal of this paper to unravel the Robot Path Planning (RPP) problems. The planning of path of robots are presented to such extent that they can discover and select their path towards the focused area with no human intervention yet utilizing the Path Map (PM), which is really the predefined chart that incorporates every meaning of the path of the region wherever the robot group is found. The PM is fundamentally introduced in the robot's remembrance and robots take after that PM while reaching toward the goal. The changed cross breed Traveling Sales Person algorithm and Ant Colony Optimization algorithm (TSP-ACO), with use of Robot path planning is equipped for finding the most limited path proficiently with the execution of Path Map (PM). The principle comparability between the ants' framework and the robot framework is that the ant can

© Springer Nature Singapore Pte Ltd. 2019
A. K. Luhach et al. (Eds.): ICAICR 2018, CCIS 955, pp. 448–457, 2019.
https://doi.org/10.1007/978-981-13-3140-4_40

possess a scent reminiscent of the food and the robot can detect for the way to grasp from the protected area.

2 Literature Review

The Traveling Salesman Problem (TSP) involves limiting a path, or visit, given an arrangement of hubs, that visits every hub once. It is a prevalent problem in the optimization group and broadly inquired about [1]. Albeit relevant to a wide range of fields, the model is constrained by the way that every hub is a settled point. The problem of planning the path seeks to control the ideal arrangement of waypoint to visit in a direction to perceive positive task objective though curtailing cost, by way of the full distance of the mission [2, 3]. Path planning problem naturally trust on resembling the charge of the job length of the key to a traveling salesman problem (TSP), where the cost to travel the distance from one node to another is calculated by Euclidean Distance formula. By this calculation, the overall result for the route selection gets simplified but it may lead to the absurd routes that may deviate from the goal of getting the optimal route to the reach point. All the rigid limitations related to mechanics are out of scope. The other scope of kinetic research is the path the robot is following to achieve the final node while getting the optimal control over the path in the shortest possible time. In the year 1957, Dubin explained that for the shortest model of the airship progression, the appropriate movement between the two nodes can be selected amongst the available six possible ways [4]. Same results were proved later in [5] also by using tools from optimal theory in [6], the important agenda for all the authors is chose the best possible dubine path without actual calculating those best six possible paths. The substantial quantity of researches had gone through joining the problems of motion planning and path planning in robots [7–11]. In all these work, the elements of the rigidity are heated over by using the dubine path show while determining the ideal procedure of nodes. This issue is classically stated as the Dubin Traveling Salesman Problem (DTSP). The third area of the UAV problem related research is the part of the path planning that effects the statement of the sensors of the plane. This problem the best described as a Traveling Salesman Problem with Neighborhoods (TSPN). Now what exactly matters is the control of the arrangement of the area at the entry as well as the exit reachability point. A lot of the Researchers had already talked about this issue with various viewpoints, but maximum had used the distance as cost function as described by Euclidean [12, 13]. Obermeyer was amongst the first author to handle with the TSPN with the Dubin's automobile display in [14] with the help of optimization genetic approach, at that point later in [15] by an investigative roadmap scheme, which they called RCM that proved to be the determination in this paper. The author presented a new technique, which is Distance Travelling Salesman Problem with Neighborhoods (DTSPN) that is changed into a general salesman Travelling problem (GTSP) with non-covering hub sets, and after that to an Asymmetric Traveling Salesmen Problem (ATSP) through a version of the noon and bean transformation [19].

3 Modified Ant Colony Algorithm

The Robot Path Planning (RPP) is dependent on Modified Ant Colony Algorithm and Travelling Sales Person Algorithm. This proposed algorithm guides the robot to the correct method of crusade.

There are mainly two types of moves:

a. The forward path: The robot begins to collect the information or other things necessary in its journey to reach to the goal point.
b. The reverse path: After collecting the desired information, the robot returns to the its original point from where it had started.

If entire ants have completed their routes on the basis of minimum cost level of travelling sales, for a *shortest path* is found among the Xsnew routes. When all ants finish and move to the next route Xprev routes for the sale and position defined on the basis of $\cos(\Theta)$ for horizontal and $\sin(\Theta)$ is completed when are route get executed the destination vertex.

Suppose, Robot start walking from a fixed source point (X_s, Y_s).

(A) Robot first move
Now Moving of Robot as at first travelling sales first step.
In the moving of Robot (X_s, Y_s) is changed to (X_{snew}, Y_{snew}) while the robot travels 1st step fast with the help of given down calculation:

$$X_{snew} = X_{prev} + Step*\cos(\Theta) \tag{1}$$

$$Y_{snew} = Y_{prev} + Step*\sin(\Theta) \tag{2}$$

Where X_{prev}, Y_{prev} signifies exactly at which point the robot is situated currently. The succeeding position of the robot is dictated by including the result of step estimate and the function $\cos(\Theta)$ and $\sin(\Theta)$ where Θ is dynamic point and it can be used Eqs. (1) and (2) to find out steam ahead for next goal

$$\Theta = \tan^{-1} X_{prev}/Y_{prev} \tag{3}$$

(B) Encounter with obstacle
Above Eq. (3) find out next goal obstacle to out quiet moving in our planned work with X_{snew} obstacles are made casually, which is zig-zac form obstacle, is settled which an imperative in our work is.

(C) Take previous step that having low Θ angle
At any point the involvement of robot with problem, robot quit moving and makes three strides back by utilizing the accompanying condition:

$$X_{snew} = X_{prev} - (Nmin)Step*\cos(\Theta) \tag{4}$$

$$Y_{snew} = Y_{prev} - (Nmin)Step*\sin(\Theta) \tag{5}$$

$$\Theta = \tan^{-1} X_{prev}/Y_{prev} \qquad (6)$$

Where Nmin is shorten distance for previous obstacle.

(D) Path Mapping to reach Goal Point
Goal finally robot needs to reach at the point (Xs, Ys), which is settled. Robot needs Eq. (4) for finding next obstacle and the following perfect route needs to reach to target point using Eq. (6).

(E) Node to node mapping
Check all coordinate using Eqs. (3), (4) and rotational angle is Θ where sidestep the obstacle ACO is utilized to discover the ideal one likelihood insect k is situated at node i, utilizes the pheromone save di the edge (i, j) to process the likelihood of picking directly below Eq. (7)

$$P_{ij} = \begin{cases} \dfrac{\tau_{ij}\alpha}{\sum_{j\epsilon N_{i(k)}} \tau_{ij}\alpha} & if\ j\epsilon N_{i(k)} \\ 0 & otherwise \end{cases} \qquad (7)$$

Wherever α signifies significance of pheromone level track and Ni(k) demonstrates the arrangement of closest of subterranean insect k once situated at hub I except for the last hub went for P_{ij} applying next pheromone value would be consider

$$\dot{\eta}_j = \{X_{snew} * P_{ij} + Y_{snew} * P_{ij} + Nmin\} \qquad (8)$$

using Eq. (8) find out closest value of next obstacle and put value in Eq. (9) for evaluation of pheromone refreshing.
Where, $\dot{\eta}_j \in (0,1)$ is the evaporation rate and $\Delta\tau ij$ (k) and is the amount of pheromone deposit on the node i and node j selected the best ant and k. the point of pheromone refreshing is to build the pheromone esteem related with ideal way. The pheromone deposited on arc (i, j) by the best ant k $\Delta\tau ij$ (k). Where,

$$\Delta\tau_{ij}(k) = P_{ij}/L_k \qquad (9)$$

Now Pij is a consistent & L_k is the measurement of the way crossed through the greatest

$$\Delta\tau_{ij}(k) = \frac{\{X_{snew} * P_{ij} + Y_{snew} * P_{ij} + Nmin\}\ for\ local\ best\ tour}{\sum_{i=1} \{X_{snew} * P_{ij} + Y_{snew} * P_{ij} + Nmin\}\ for\ global\ best\ tour} \qquad (10)$$

Using above Eq. (10) with the help of Eq. (9) which finding with (x, y) pheromone deposited on arc facilitate and put in a proper cell in matrix there is no path exists the cell will be indicated by zero. The separation between two urban areas is figured by

$$d = \sqrt{(Xsnew + Ysnew\,)^2 + (Xsnew - Ysnew)^2} \qquad (11)$$

For TSP Dist. (X_s, Y_s) = d (if path exists between the urban areas). 0 (if no path between the urban areas).

For (Xs, Ys) = 1 (if no obstacles in the cell). 0 (if obstacle in the cell).

(F) Enumeration of Candidate Paths

Fill all possible path using Eq. (11) and find the possible paths are recognized double diverse for these two components for distributed area using urban areas which find out components of all the hopeful paths are to be same component.

(G) Travelling sales based RPP Candidate Paths

The RPP applicant path would be the objective cell of the matrix type of design space is improved solution found. The recent derived solution becomes the new best solution using Eq. (8) also the pheromone path strength of the nodes forms the unswerving routes using Eq. (11) at same time, pheromone strength on all ends reduces (evaporates) to evade boundless buildup of pheromone (Fig. 1).

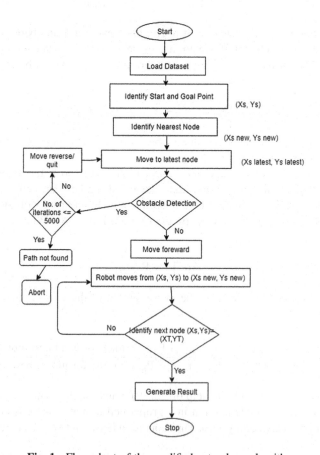

Fig. 1. Flow chart of the modified ant colony algorithm

4   Result Analysis

In this section we agreed on view MATLAB simulation experimentation for the instance demonstrated in Fig. 2 with the help of TSP & ACO. The model factors existed established equally: iteration = 5000, No of ants = 200. Now the result of experimental simulation is displayed in Fig. 4, those opinions involved the facts planned through workstation through proposed method and the precise ideas desirable to be approved in Fig. 4, and this remained a whole path. Figure 3 showed the Tour length cost for path planning procedure of the optimum explanation produced through the technique, after that we can get process had produced actual established optimum explanation in around five 1000 cycles.

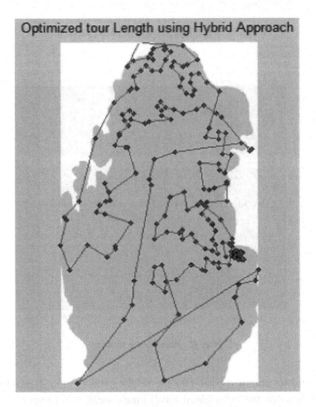

Fig. 2. Optimized tour length using hybrid approach

Before building our models, we investigate visit length and issue measure information to increase some knowledge concerning how the optimal visit length changes as the administration locale step by step ends up extended.

The base collision-free separation from source to goal would now be able to be discovered utilizing a basic briefest path calculation on the broadened path arranging, where each edge is given a cost that compares to its path length. Once more, this

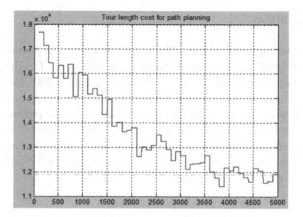

Fig. 3. Tour length cost for path planning

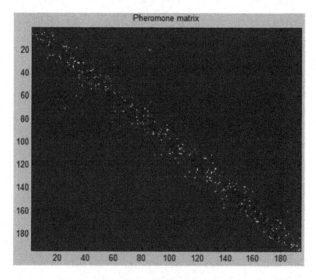

Fig. 4. Pheromone matrix

separation should be changed over into the relating travel time. Keeping in mind the end goal to ensure that the determined travel times speak to a lower bound on the real direction lengths, we again need to accept that the returned paths are constantly crossed with most extreme speeding up maximum acceleration.

Above figure insect speaks with elective one by changing their neighborhood area. The ants achieve this undertaking by setting down pheromone along their trails. ACO-TSP takes care of basically combinatorial advancement issues clear finished discrete inquiry spaces (Fig. 5).

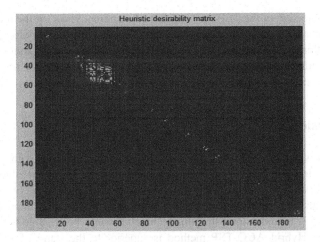

Fig. 5. Heuristic desirability matrix

The probability function used in the Improved TSP-ACO algorithm, which is a variation on the function presented by Hsiao et al. [19], is given by:

$$P_{ij} = \frac{[\tau_{ij}]^{\alpha}[\eta_{ij}]^{\beta}}{\sum_{j\epsilon s}[\tau_{ij}]^{\alpha}[\eta_{ij}]^{\beta}} \tag{12}$$

Here P_{ij} is the possibility of traveling from node I to node j. η_{ij} defines the desirability of travelling after node i to node j based on the direction amongst the present node and the probable node interrelated to the direction among the current node and the area node, τ_{ij} defines the no. of pheromone amid nodes i and j, β is heuristic weighting value, α is the pheromone weighting value, and S is the population of allowable nodes (Fig. 6).

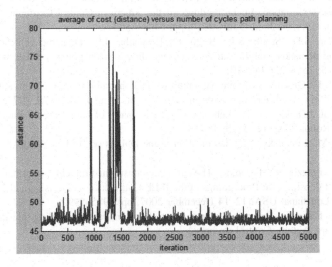

Fig. 6. Average of cost (distance) versus number of cycles path planning

It is the objective of the TSP-ACO to discover optimal visits for the robots with the end goal that all the given separation on the segment can be handled in the given process duration. The robot arms are outfitted with various welding tongs and can just process particular weld focuses. Amid every one of these activities the robot arms must not crash into each other and security clearances must be kept.

5   Conclusion

This research shows a Hybrid TSP-ACO algorithm for dynamic path planning. By adding the desirability matrix and Pheromone matrix to the ACO-TSP algorithm, faster convergence speeds with better solutions were found. Leaving the old pheromone trails when re-initializing the system when the path was blocked also improved the processing speed. It is understood that this technique would be feasible for overall path planning. The Hybrid ACO-TSP method is superior to the standard ACO and TSP algorithms, as it results in shorter average path lengths and vastly reduced processing times.

Future work on this algorithm would include testing the algorithm with an actual robot in a known environment with moving obstacles.

Acknowledgement. Authors express their deep sense of gratitude to The Founder President of Amity University, Dr. Ashok K. Chauhan for his keen interest in promoting research at Amity University and have always been an inspiration for achieving great heights.

References

1. Sariff, N.B., Buniyamin, O.: Ant colony system for robot path planning in global static environment. In: Selected Topics in System Science and Simulation in Engineering, pp. 192–197. ISSN: 1792-507X, ISBN: 978-960-474-230-1
2. Klein, D.J., Schweikl, J., Isaacs, J.T., Hespanha, J.P.: On UAV routing protocols for sparse sensor data exfiltration. In: Proceedings of the American Control Conference, Baltimore, Maryland, USA, 30 June–2 July 2010, pp. 6494–6500
3. Bopardikar, S.D., Smith, S.L., Bullo, F., Hespanha, J.P.: Dynamic vehicle routing for translating demands: stability analysis and receding-horizon policies. IEEE Trans. Autom. Control **55**, 2554–2569 (2010)
4. Dubins, L.E.: On curves of minimal length with a constraint on average curvature, and with prescribed initial and terminal positions and tangents. Am. J. Math. **79**, 497–516 (1957)
5. Boissonnat, J.D., Cerezo, A., Leblond, J.: Shortest paths of bounded curvature in the plane. J. Intell. Robot. Syst. **11**, 5–20 (1994)
6. Shkel, A.M., Lumelsky, V.: Classification of the Dubins set. Robot. Auton. Syst. **34**, 179–202 (2001)
7. Le Ny, J., Frazzoli, E., Feron, E.: The curvature-constrained traveling salesman problem for high point densities. In: Proceedings of the IEEE Conference on Decision and Control, New Orleans, Louisiana, USA, 12–14 December 2007, pp. 5985–5990
8. Le Ny, J., Feron, E., Frazzoli, E.: On the curvature-constrained traveling salesman problem. IEEE Trans. Autom. Control (in press)

9. Savla, K., Frazzoli, E., Bullo, F.: Traveling salesperson problems for the Dubins vehicle. IEEE Trans. Autom. Control 53, 1378–1391 (2008)
10. Ma, X., Castanon, D.: Receding horizon planning for Dubins traveling salesman problems. In: Proceedings of the IEEE Conference on Decision and Control, San Diego, California, USA, 13–15 December 2006, pp. 5453–5458
11. Rathinam, S., Sengupta, R., Darbha, S.: A resource allocation algorithm for multiple vehicle systems with non-holnomic constraints. IEEE Trans. Autom. Sci. Eng. 4, 98–104 (2007)
12. Dumitrescu, A., Mitchell, J.S.B.: Approximation algorithms for TSP with neighborhoods in the plane. J. Algorithm 48, 135–159 (2003)
13. Elbassioni, K., Fishkin, A.V., Mustafa, N.H., Sitters, R.: Approximation algorithms for euclidean group TSP. In: Proceedings of the International Colloquim on Automata, Languages and Programming, Lisbon, Portugal, 11–15 July 2005, pp. 1115–1126
14. Yuan, B., Orlowska, M., Sadiq, S.: On the optimal robot routing problem in wireless sensor networks. IEEE Trans. Knowl. Data Eng. 19, 1252–1261 (2007)
15. Obermeyer, K.J.: Path planning for a UAV performing reconnaissance of static ground targets in terrain. In: Proceedings of the AIAA Conference on Guidance, Navigation, and Control, Chicago, Illinois, USA, 10–13 August 2009
16. Obermeyer, K.J., Oberlin, P., Darbha, S.: Sampling-based roadmap methods for a visual reconnaissance UAV. In: Proceedings of the AIAA Conference on Guidance, Navigation, and Control, Toronto, Ontario, Canada, 2–5 August 2010
17. Noon, C.E., Bean, J.C.: An efficient transformation of the generalized traveling salesman problem. Technical report 91–26. Department of Industrial and Operations Engineering, University of Michigan: Ann Arbor, MI, USA (1991)
18. Osipov, V., Sanders, P., Singler, J.: The Filter-Kruskal Minimum Spanning Tree Algorithm, pp. 52–61. Copyright © by SIAM
19. Hsiao Y.-T., Chuang C.-L., Chien C.-C.: Ant colony optimization for best path planning. In: Proceedings of the 1st International Symposium on Information and Communication Technologies, vol. 1, Sapporo, Japan, 26–29 October 2004, pp. 109–113 (2004)
20. Buniyamin, N., Sariff, N., Wan Ngah, W.A.J., Mohamad, Z.: Robot global path planning overview and a variation of ant colony system algorithm. Int. J. Math. Comput. Simul. 5(1), 9–16 (2011)
21. Mei, H., Tian, Y., Zu, L.: A hybrid ant colony optimization algorithm for path planning of robot in dynamic environment. Int. J. Inf. Technol. 12(3), 78–88 (2006)

Sentiment Analysis and Prediction Using Neural Networks

Sneh Paliwal$^{(\boxtimes)}$, Sunil Kumar Khatri, and Mayank Sharma

Amity Institute of Information Technology, Amity University,
Noida, Uttar Pradesh, India
sneh.paliwal@student.amity.edu, sunilkhatri@gmail.com
{skkhatri,msharma22}@amity.edu

Abstract. Sentiment Analysis or opinion mining have taken many leaps and turns from its starting in early 2000s till now. Advancement in technology, mobile & internet services and ease of access to these services have resulted in more and more engagement of people on the social media platforms for expressing their views and collaborate with people who share similar thoughts. This has led to generation of a large amount of data on the internet and subsequently the need of analysing this data. The sentiment analysis helps different organisations to know how people look to their products and services and what changes are required to improve them. The paper performs sentiment analysis i.e. classification of tweets into positive, negative and neutral on views of a particular product using an inbuilt python library called TextBlob for three platforms i.e. twitter, Facebook and news websites and further it talks about how Artificial Neural Networks (ANN) offer a platform to perform sentiment analysis in a much easier and less time-consuming manner. In this paper Feed-Forward Back propagation neural networks are used to split the data into train and test data and a min-max approach was applied to the data to scale the data and analyse the prediction accuracy of a sentiment using ANN. Precision, recall and accuracy have been calculated to provide a quantitative approach to the results and measure the performance of ANN. We found that such type of neural network is very efficient in predicting the result with a high accuracy.

Keywords: Sentiment analysis · Artificial Neural Networks (ANN)
Machine learning · Feed-forward networks · Activation function

1 Introduction

Sentiment Analysis or more commonly called opinion mining has been helping different organisations and industries to analyse and predict trends for nearly two decades. With increase in access to internet and its services more and more people are joining and participating in social media activities. This has led to generation of a huge amount of data on the social media platforms like twitter, Facebook, YouTube etc. Today most of the organisations analyse user sentiments through this social media content. It helps them to improve their business decisions and hence maximise profits. Many scientists have been working on different methods to classify and analyse the data generated through these platforms. Some of the methods include Naïve Bayes theorem, Support

© Springer Nature Singapore Pte Ltd. 2019
A. K. Luhach et al. (Eds.): ICAICR 2018, CCIS 955, pp. 458–470, 2019.
https://doi.org/10.1007/978-981-13-3140-4_41

vector Machine (SVM), Maximum entropy etc. These algorithms have been proved to be very efficient with data which is smaller in size. But the increase in the amount of data in terms of velocity, veracity and volume have generated a need for much efficient algorithms which could analyse a large amount of data and provide a greater precision. In this paper we are performing sentiment analysis for 'iPhoneX' using twitter API, Facebook API and data collected from news websites using python as a platform and around 36,500 tweets, comments and votes from each platform have been collected and cleaned. The polarity and sentiment of the tweets was recorded using the inbuilt TextBlob library. Further ANN are applied to the collected data using R. The data collected is partitioned into train and test dataset in the ratio 80:20 respectively. The train data is used to train the neural network and test dataset is used to determine the accuracy of the results predicted by ANN. This paper is categorized as follows: Sect. 2 gives an overview of the literature survey. Section 3 states the proposed approach. Section 4 gives the methodology adopted. Section 5 tabulates the results. Conclusion is stated in Sect. 6 of the paper.

2 Related Work

Much research work is done on classifying data and performing sentiment analysis using the traditional methods of sentiment analysis like Naïve Bayes, Lexicon based approach, Support Vector Machine (SVM), Maximum entropy etc. The authors have used twitter data to find and analyze the sentiment of the tweets. After collecting the tweets, score of the tweets were calculated and finally a performance analysis was done. The authors have used Random Sampling technique to select a sample dataset from the whole dataset. On the same grounds, Sampling Analysis and comparative analysis was performed for sample dataset and between sample and whole dataset respectively [1]. In this paper a module is trained with the help of Hadoop and MapReduce, Classification was based on Naïve Bayes, Time Variant Analytics and the Continuous learning System. Real time analysis done in this paper was a major highlight of this paper [2]. In this paper, the authors have tried to implement dictionary based methodology of sentiment analysis and in order to estimate the sentiment of the public an algorithm was developed that is employed to large amount of data. An acronym dictionary was used by the authors to identify the acronyms and moreover emoticons were also detected from the tweet. They have done both document level and aspect level analysis [3]. In this paper the authors have tried to ease information extraction from financial documents available online. For the above job the authors have classified the text on the basis of genre and sentiment. To classify text on the basis of genre, Support vector Machine has been used and to classify the text on the basis of sentiment, an attribute extraction algorithm has been designed on the basis of Apriori Algorithm to extract attributes from the text and design a lexicon. The results were satisfactory when authors have used sentiment intensity calculation [4]. In this paper, the author has implemented two algorithms i.e. Naïve Bayes (NB) and Maximum Entropy. Through the observations it was very clear that maximum Entropy classifier is better than any other classifier for predicting the sentiment with 74% accuracy [5]. Through this paper the authors have performed sentiment analysis on the comments of the users on YouTube videos by using Natural Language Processing (NLG) and SentiStrength to improve the relevancy and quality of YouTube videos. Around one million user comments have been used to perform the analysis and the authors have shown the efficiency of up to 75.4% [6]. The experiment performed in this paper indicated that SVM shows better results as compared to Naive Bayes and Maximum Entropy classifiers. The observation showed accuracy of SVM is 91%, the accuracy of Naive base is 83% and the accuracy of Maximum Entropy is 80% [8]. In this paper the author is trying to compare various classification algorithms such as Random Forest, Gradient Boosting, Decision Tree, Adaptive Boost, Logistic Regression and Gaussian Naïve Bayes to recognize sarcasm in tweets from the Twitter Streaming API [9]. In this paper the authors have performed sentiment analysis on the reviews of the customers given for different mobile phones. The authors have included the sentiments like anger, disgust, fear, joy, trust etc. to classify the text as positive or negative. The authors have performed a sentence level classification of the reviews by using an inbuilt package named 'Syuzhet'. The results after being cross validated using Support Vector Machine (SVM) give an accuracy of 84.87% [10]. In this paper the authors have performed sentiment analysis on Delhi Corporation Election results by using different supervised machine learning classifiers. Through this paper authors are trying to figure out the most effective and accurate algorithm for prediction. The results show that Multinomial Naïve Bayes classifier is the most effective predictor for sentiments with an accuracy of 78% [11]. Authors have used Rapid Miner to implement machine learning algorithms and perform opinion mining. The Support Vector Machine algorithm classified the text into positive, negative and neutral depending on their polarity [12]. In this paper authors have made a comparative analysis of various algorithms and suggested that among traditional algorithms used so far SVM has given better results but also points towards the limitations of using SVM and suggests that the use of artificial neural networks (ANN) in sentiment classification and analysis can overcome these problems. The authors have concluded that machine learning approaches and ANN implementations would result in better classification and analysis. A methodology has also been proposed which suggests how ANN can be applied to large datasets and better results can be obtained [14]. In the proposed work, ANN has been applied to different datasets obtained from social media platforms like twitter, Facebook and reviews of a product on news websites, to check the performance of ANN and supervised learning approach (which is used to train the dataset obtained) by calculating precision, recall and accuracy.

3 Proposed Approach

A. *Artificial Neural Networks and Their Need*

An artificial neural network (ANN) is a computational model in light of the structure and elements of natural or biological neural systems. Structure of an ANN is based in the data that traverses through the network as based on the fact that a neural network, whether it is artificial or biological, learns according to the data that is fed into it and the output it gives.

ANNs are considered nonlinear statistical data modelling tools in which the intricate relationship between inputs and outputs are used to recognise or identify some patterns. Instead of using the whole dataset, ANN's use a sample of the data to find and reach the solution so this saves both time and money in finding and arriving at the result. ANNs are regarded as fairly simple mathematical models to upgrade the present data analysis technologies. Just like there are neurons in the brain for passing information, there are nodes in a neural network for doing a similar task. Nodes are nothing but mathematical functions. ANNs have three interconnected layers just like a neuron in our body. The first layer is similar to dendrites where the input value is received. The second layer is analogous to soma where the summation of the information is done and the output is given at the last i.e. the output layer which is like the axon of a neuron (Fig. 1).

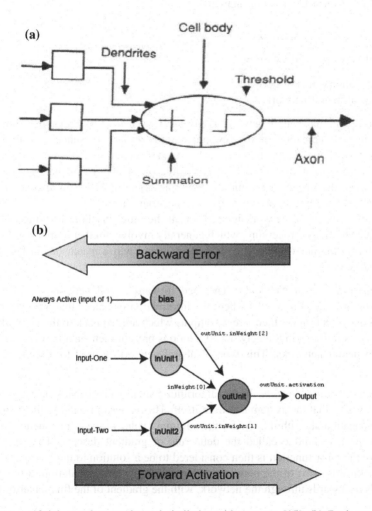

Fig. 1. (a) Artificial neural networks and similarity with neurons [15]. (b) Back propagation model [16]

Components of Artificial Neural Networks:

Neurons: Each neural network comprises of several neurons which constitutes an input neuron, inner neurons and an output neuron. The value in each neuron is stored depending on the predecessor neuron (except the input neuron) and is forwarded to the successor neuron after the applying the activation function.

Connections and weights: Two neurons form a connection between them and each connection is assigned a weight.

Propagation function: This function computes the input to the next neuron by processing the weight from the connection.

Learning Rule: This learning rule implies an algorithm that modifies the weights and threshold variables for a neural network.

B. *Types of Neural Networks*

A neural network is of two types:

1. Convolutional neural network.
2. Artificial neural network.

A convolutional neural network is primarily used for tasks related to image processing like classification of images into various groups, presence of a tumour etc. Convolutional networks perform optical character recognition (OCR) to digitize text and make natural-language processing possible on analogue and hand-written documents, where the images are symbols to be transcribed. CNNs can also be applied to sound when it is represented visually as a spectrogram.

An artificial neural network is used for all the other machine learning tasks other than related to image processing, which generally involve number crunching (like stock prediction, to predict whether a certain team would win a match or not based on its performance etc.)

Feed-Forward Neural Networks: The feed forward neural network or a multilayer perceptron are neural networks where the information or values that are fed into them flows in one direction i.e. there are no outputs which are fed back to the network. There are no cycles or loops in the network. If a loop is present then such networks are called recurrent neural networks. This type of neural network is used to test the data after training.

Back Propagation Algorithm: In this algorithm a small value is back propagated to the hidden layer so that the system can train itself. This is used in training the dataset. The Backpropagation algorithm looks for the minimum value of the error function in weight space using a technique called the delta rule or gradient descent. The weights that minimize the error function is then considered to be a solution to the learning problem. The "backwards" part of the name comes from the fact that calculation of the gradient proceeds backwards through the network, with the gradient of the final layer of weights being calculated first and the gradient of the first layer of weights being calculated last. Partial computations of the gradient from one layer are reused in the computation of the gradient for the previous layer. This backwards flow of the error information allows for efficient computation of the gradient at each layer versus the naive approach of calculating the gradient of each layer separately.

C. *Types of Learning*

Supervised Learning: This is a machine learning task where a function is learnt by the machine by mapping input and output pairs. It requires a training dataset which provide the machine with required input and output pairs. In this type of learning the system is provided the output in order to train it and then it performs the prediction operation. It is similar to training a child. In the same way, the system first learns about the input-output pairs and then predicts the output whenever it encounters the same input.

Unsupervised Learning: This type of learning is also a machine learning algorithm which is used to draw inference from a dataset. It takes data without responses as input so there is no measure of accuracy. His learning technique do not provide the system with output and the system marks them on the basis of some characteristics like shape, colour, size etc. and the output is predicted on this basis.

4 Methodology

Using the twitter API and python as a tool, 36,500 tweets were collected and filtered by removing unwanted words, special characters and spaces. A dataset was created which include date, number of positive tweets, number of negative tweets, number of neutral tweets, polarity. The polarity of the tweets was determined by an inbuilt library in python i.e. TextBlob.

TextBlob is a Python library for processing textual data. An API is provided to perform sentiment analysis. When a text is fed as input, it uses Naïve Bayes classifier to classify the text. This analyser is apparently based on Stanford Natural Language Tool Kit (NLTK). The training data for Stanford NLTK are the movie reviews.

The same procedure is applied for collecting data from Facebook and news websites. Using R programming, the data was partitioned as train and test dataset in the ratio of 80:20 respectively. The train dataset was given to a feed forward neural network which uses supervised learning approach to train the neural network. A neural network graph was then created with three inputs to the input layer which include number of positive tweets, number of negative tweets and number of neutral tweets. The second layer is the hidden layer and the third layer is the output layer which determines the overall polarity of the data that is fed into the neural network. A confusion matrix was then created to calculate the accuracy of the results obtained (Fig. 2).

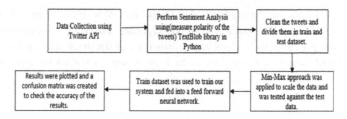

Fig. 2. Flowchart of the approach

Also, to validate the results precision and recall values are computed for all the three datasets used in the study.

A. *Implementation*

Using the twitter application interface, Facebook graph API's and web scraping using python as the programming language, last one year tweets, comments and votes related to 'iphoneX' were collected limiting the number of tweets per day to be 100 which resulted in a total of 36,500 tweets, 36,500 comments and 36,500 votes for performing data analytics. The data collected from twitter includes the date, text of the tweet and its sentiment by using twitter API. Similarly, data from Facebook is collected using Facebook's graph API and data from news websites is collected using web scraping. After that the data was cleaned by removing unwanted symbols and spaces. The collected data was analyzed using TextBlob library and sentiment of the data was noted. Now the number of positive, negative and neutral tweets, comments and votes were recorded per day with the overall polarity of the day. The polarity of the tweets, comments and votes was calculated by subtracting number of positive and the negative data. The data collected contains date of the tweet, No. of positive tweets, No. of negative tweets, No. of neutral tweets, polarity of the data and scaled polarity whose value lies between 0 and 1.

To apply the neural networks, R programming language has been used to predict and analyze the results. The dataset was divided into train and test dataset in the ratio of 80:20 respectively. The train dataset is now scaled using min-max approach to scale the values between 0 and 1. The Fig. 3 shows a sample of scaled data.

	No_of_positive_tweets	No_of_negative_tweets	No_of_neutral_tweets
1	0.1126760563	0.00000000000	0.3510638298
6	0.5211267606	0.16666666667	0.7553191489
13	0.4647887324	0.66666666667	0.1382978723
27	0.4084507042	0.83333333333	0.8510638298
31	0.2957746479	1.00000000000	0.5212765957
36	0.4084507042	0.08333333333	0.3829787234

Fig. 3. Scaled data

From the train dataset number of positive, negative and neutral tweets were fed into the input layer. Similar work is done for data from Facebook and news websites. The neural network applied here is a feed forward neural network and uses back propagation to train itself. The train dataset is required to train our neural networks and the predicted results will be tested against the test dataset. After training the neural network a neural net graph was plotted which is shown in Fig. 4.

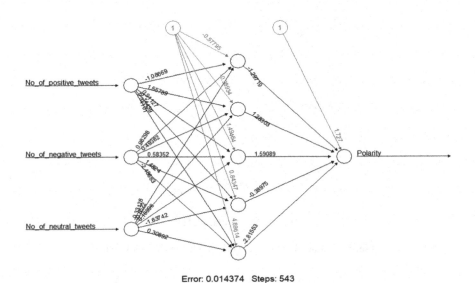

Error: 0.014374   Steps: 543

Fig. 4. Artificial neural network graph for twitter data

The Fig. 4 has an input layer which provides three inputs to the neural network i.e. the number of positive, negative and neutral tweets per day to the neural network and gives polarity of the tweet as a result in the output layer. Similar neural nets were plotted for Facebook and new websites data. Similar figures shows neural nets for Facebook and news websites data. Input for Facebook data were the number of positive, negative and neutral comments and for news website data the input consist of number of up votes, down votes and neutral votes and the output of all the neural nets was polarity of the input data (Fig. 5).

The test dataset was now fed to the trained neural network and a matrix was taken as output which showed actual and predicted values of the polarity (Fig. 6).

Program Code: The code used for plotting the neural network graph is given below:

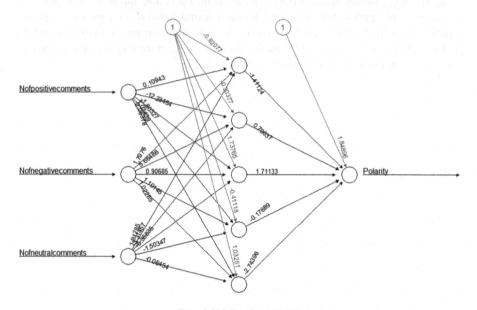

Error: 0.035171   Steps: 2151

Fig. 5. Artificial neural network graph for Facebook data

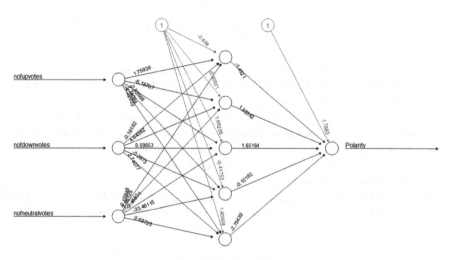

Error: 0.038528   Steps: 7416

Fig. 6. Artificial neural network graph for news website data

```
getwd()
setwd('C:/Users/Sneh')
getwd()
data = read.csv("perDate_Sentiment.csv", header=T)
samplesize = 0.80 * nrow(data)
#set.seed(80)
index = sample( seq_len ( nrow ( data ) ), size = samplesize )
datatrain = data[ index, ]
datatest = data[ -index, ]
data <- data[, sapply(data, is.numeric)]
maxs <- as.numeric(apply(data, 2, max) )
mins <- as.numeric(apply(data, 2, min))
scaled <- as.data.frame(scale(data, center = mins, scale = maxs - mins))
library(neuralnet)
trainNN = scaled[index , ]
testNN = scaled[-index , ]
set.seed(2)
NN = neuralnet(Level ~ No_of_positive_tweets+ No_of_negative_tweets+
No_of_neutral_tweets, trainNN, hidden = 5 , linear.output = T )
plot(NN)
```

Now the actual and predicted values are rounded to one place of decimal and a confusion matrix was plotted. With the help of confusion matrix we calculate the precision, recall and accuracy of the result. Figures 7(a), (b) and (c) shows the confusion matrices.

The following formulae depicted in Eqs. 1, 2 and 3 are used to calculate Precision, Recall and Accuracy. Precision measures how often a sentiment is rated correctly. Recall measures how many tweets, comments or votes with sentiment are rated as sentimental. This also determines how well ANN's can identify neutrality. The third parameter i.e. accuracy checks how many sentiments that were rated as positive or negative were rated correctly.

$$\text{Precision} \ = \ \text{TP} \ / \ (\text{TP} + \text{FP}) \tag{1}$$

$$\text{Recall} \ = \ \text{TP} \ / \ (\text{TP} + \text{FN}) \tag{2}$$

$$\text{Accuracy} \ = \ (\text{TP} + \text{TN}) \ / \ (\text{TP} + \text{FP} + \text{TN} + \text{FN}) \tag{3}$$

where

TP = True Positive
FP = False Positive
TN = True Negative
FN = False Negative

A similar confusion matrix was constructed for Facebook and news website data as shown in Figs. 7(b) and (c) respectively.

Precision, recall and accuracy were computed for both the matrices and the results are shown in Table 1.

(a)

Actual/Prediction	0	0.1	0.2	0.3	0.4	0.5	0.6
0	2	2	0	0	0	0	0
0.1	1	7	1	0	1	0	0
0.2	0	1	5	2	0	0	0
0.3	0	1	1	4	1	2	1
0.4	0	2	2	1	4	1	1
0.5	0	0	0	2	2	3	2
0.6	0	1	1	1	1	1	6
0.7	0	0	0	0	0	1	1
0.8	0	0	0	0	0	0	0

(b)

Actual/Prediction	0	0.1	0.2	0.3	0.4
0	0	2	0	0	0
0.1	0	8	1	0	0
0.2	0	1	4	2	2
0.3	0	2	2	3	2
0.4	0	2	1	1	5
0.5	0	0	0	2	1
0.6	0	0	0	1	1
0.7	0	1	0	0	0
0.8	0	0	0	0	0

(c)

Actual/Prediction	0	0.1	0.2	0.3	0.4	0.5	0.6
0	0	2	0	0	0	0	0
0.1	0	3	1	1	0	0	0
0.2	0	3	6	0	2	1	0
0.3	0	2	1	5	1	1	1
0.4	0	1	2	1	4	1	1
0.5	0	0	0	1	1	4	0
0.6	0	0	0	0	0	2	2
0.7	0	0	0	0	1	1	1
0.8	0	0	0	0	0	0	1

Fig. 7. (a) Confusion matrix for twitter data. (b) Confusion matrix for Facebook data. (c) Confusion matrix for news website data

Table 1. .

Datasets used	Variables computed		
	Precision	Recall	Accuracy
Twitter dataset	0.56	0.79	0.86
Facebook dataset	0.65	0.73	0.87
News sites dataset	0.40	0.62	0.79

5 Result

In the present study, 36,500 tweets from twitter, 36,500 comments from Facebook and 36,500 votes of people from news sites were collected with an average of 100 per day for one year i.e. April 2017 to March 2018 which were related to 'iphoneX' using Python. The data was then scaled using min-max approach and neural networks were applied using R. The data was segmented into train and test dataset in the ratio 80:20 respectively. The actual and predicted values were used to define a confusion matrix. Precision, recall and accuracy of the result was calculated using this matrix. The Table 1 shows the values for all three datasets used in the present study.

6 Conclusion

From the above study we infer that Artificial Neural Networks can prove to be a better medium to perform sentiment analysis to a large amount of dataset as the accuracy obtained is between the range 79–87% and we do not need any extra amount of space to store the intermediate datasets as is the case with traditional methods used so far. Also the time consumed in training and testing of the data is also very less.

Acknowledgments. We thank open data platforms like twitter, Facebook and different news sites, which provide data to students like us to perform several types of studies and infer results from them. Also, we would like to thank free software providers like Anaconda platform, which is used in this study, to help people across the data science community to code, develop and analyse different problems.

References

1. Yazhini Priyanka, D., Senthilkumar, R.: Sampling techniques for streaming dataset using sentiment analysis. In: Fifth International Conference on Recent Trends in Information Technology(ICRTIT), pp: 1–6 (2016)
2. Trupthi, M., Pabboju, S., Narasimha, G.: Sentiment analysis on twitter using streaming API. In: 2017 IEEE 7th International Advance Computing Conference, pp. 915–919 (2017)
3. Ray, P., Chakrabarti, A.: Twitter sentiment analysis for product review using lexicon method. In: 2017 International Conference on Data Management, Analytics and Innovation (ICDMAI), pp. 211–216 (2017)
4. Fang, B., Liang, S., Zou, Q., Huang, W.: Research on sentiment analysis of financial texts based on web. In: 7th IEEE International Conference on Electronics Information and Emergency Communication (ICEIEC), pp. 248–252 (2017)
5. Soni, A.K.: Multi-lingual sentiment analysis of twitter data by using classification algorithms. In: Second International Conference on Electrical, Computer and Communication Technologies (ICECCT), pp. 1–5 (2017)
6. Bhuiyan, H., Ara, J., Bardhan, R., Rashedul Islam, Md.: Retrieving youtube video by sentiment analysis on user comment. In: IEEE International Conference on Signal and Image Processing Applications (IEEE ICSIPA 2017), pp. 474–478. Malaysia (2017)

7. Likhar, M., Kasar, S.L.: Sentiment analysis using sentence minimization with natural language generation (NLG). In: 1st International Conference on Intelligent Systems and Information Management (ICISIM), pp. 134–140 (2017)
8. Ul Hassan, A., Hussain, J., Hussain, M., Sadiq, M., Lee, S.: Sentiment analysis of social networking sites (SNS) data using machine learning approach for the measurement of depression. In: International Conference on Information and Communication Technology Convergence (ICTC), pp. 138–140 (2017)
9. Prasad, A.G., Sanjana, S., Bhat, S.M., Harish, B.S.: Sentiment analysis for sarcasm detection on streaming short text data. In: 2nd International Conference on Knowledge Engineering and Applications, pp. 1–5 (2017)
10. Singla, Z., Randhawa, S., Jain, S.: Statistical and sentiment analysis of consumer product reviews. In: 8th ICCCNT, pp. 1–6 (2017)
11. Juneja, P., Ojha, U.: Casting online votes: to predict offline results using sentiment analysis by machine learning classifiers. In: 8th ICCCNT, pp. 1–6 (2017)
12. Sindhu, C., Vyas, D.V., Pradyoth, K.: Sentiment analysis based product rating using textual reviews. In: International Conference on Electronics, Communication and Aerospace Technology ICECA, vol. 2, pp. 727–731 (2017)
13. Wang, H., Wang, N., Yeung, D.-Y.: Collaborative deep learning for recommender systems, KDD '15, pp. 1235–1244 (2015)
14. Borele, P., Borikar, D.A.: An approach to sentiment analysis using artificial neural network with comparative analysis of different techniques. IOSR J. Comput. Eng. (IOSR-JCE) 18(2). e-ISSN: 2278-0661, p-ISSN: 2278-8727
15. Image 1[a] source: https://www.doc.ic.ac.uk/~nd/surprise_96/journal/vol4/cs11/report.html
16. Image 1[b] source: https://inst.eecs.berkeley.edu/~cs182/sp07/assignments/a3-bp.html

Diabetes Detection and Prediction Using Machine Learning/IoT: A Survey

Neha Sharma[(✉)] and Ashima Singh

Department of CSE, Thapar University, Patiala, India
nehasharma.pw@gmail.com, ashima@thapar.edu

Abstract. A healthcare system using modern computing techniques is the highest explored area in healthcare research. Researchers in the field of computing and healthcare are persistently working together to make such systems more technology ready. Recent studies by World Health Organization have shown an increment in the number of diabetic patients and their deaths. Diabetes is one of the basic sicknesses which has long-haul complexities related to it. A high volume of medical information is produced. It is important to gather, store, learn and predict the health of such patients using continuous monitoring and technological innovations. An alarming increase in the number of diabetic patients in India has become an important area of concern. With the assistance of innovation, it is important to construct a framework that store and examine the diabetic information and further see conceivable dangers. Its early detection and analysis remain a challenge among researchers. This review gives present status of research in determining diabetes and proposed frameworks.

Keywords: Diabetes · Machine learning · IoT

1 Introduction

Diabetes is a disease which is detected on a blood test when the blood sugar is higher than normal value i.e. between (72 to 99 mg/dL) when fasting and up to (140 mg/dL) 2 h subsequent to eating. Naturally, the pancreas emancipates insulin to assist the body to stock and use the sugar fat from the food eaten. Periodically body doesn't make sufficient insulin or doesn't take insulin well. Glucose then remains in blood and doesn't stretch out at cells. There are 3 categories of diabetes Type 1, Type 2 and Gestational diabetes. About 10% of all diabetes cases are type 1 the body don't generate insulin in this compose and about 90% of every of cases of diabetes global are of Type 2 the body don't provide sufficient measure of insulin for absolute purpose. Diabetes effect females during pregnancy are known as Gestational. Diabetes will be the seventh driving reason for death in 2030 as predicted by WHO.

1.1 Internet of Things

Internet of Things (IoT) is considered as biological group of affiliated corporal items which are obtainable on internet. The 'thing' in IoT can be a man with heart screen or vehicle including worked in-sensors i.e. things that have been doled out an IP address.

© Springer Nature Singapore Pte Ltd. 2019
A. K. Luhach et al. (Eds.): ICAICR 2018, CCIS 955, pp. 471–479, 2019.
https://doi.org/10.1007/978-981-13-3140-4_42

It can assemble and share data on network with no physical aid. The implanted technology in the devices causes to associate with inner situation or with outside situation, which then affect the conclusion. There is an expanding awareness and commitment of individuals with respect to their health. Medical examination depletes a huge part of hospital bills. Technology can change by sending medical checks to the patient's home from a hospital (home-driven) so; the Healthcare business is between the fastest to take on the Internet of Things. With utilizing of technology-based healthcare procedure, there is an unequalled likelihood to do better the standard and effectiveness of treatments. There are different benefits of using IoT like Simultaneous reporting and monitoring, End-to-end connectivity and affordability, Data assortment and analysis. Figure 1 exemplifies how this dramatic change in practice of medicine will examine in IoT hospital. A patient suffering from diabetes will have an ID card that when examined will be linked to secure cloud that hold their electronic health documents and medical treatment chronicles. Doctors and attendants will easily utilize the record on tablet or computer.

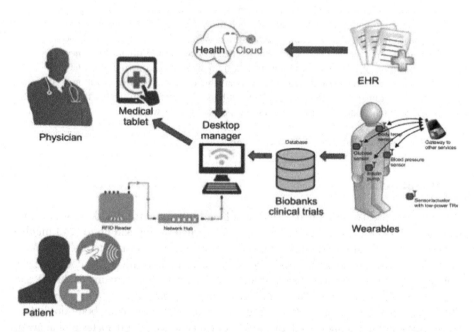

Fig. 1. Exemplifies the dramatic change in practice of medicine will be examined in IoT hospital.

1.2 Machine Learning

Electronic health records are becoming progressively usual in ambulatory care practices and in inpatient care. The transformation to digital records also describes an important transformation in how patient data are in order and made approachable for utilizing never visualize with paper documentation. Early detection and screening play main role ineffectual prevention of diabetes. The procedure of learning starts with survey or data, such as examples, exact occurrences, or commands, in order to gaze for patterns in data and make satisfactory decisions in the future based on the examples. Machine learning is an information investigation procedure that instructs PCs to do what falls into place without any issues for people and creatures: gain for a fact. It is tract of computerized reasoning. The goal of machine learning for the every part is to grasp the structure of data and so capable that data into models which can be understood and utilized by people. Machine learning categories are supervised learning, reinforcement learning, semi-supervised learning and unsupervised learning.

Supervised Learning: In supervised learning, the PC is given an illustration input which is decided with their coveted yields. The reason for this technique is for the calculation to have the capability to "discover" by distinction between its genuine yield and the "instructed" yields.

Unsupervised Learning: In unsupervised learning, data is unlabeled, so the learning calculation is left to find out mutual features. The purpose of unsupervised learning might be as straight as discovering concealed examples inside a dataset.

Semi-supervised Learning: In the above two specified types, either for all the observation in the dataset there is no labels or just labels are available for total the observing. In many empirical conditions, the amount of label is completely high, since it needs an experienced human specialist to do that. In this way, in the lack of description in the larger number of the inspections but available in hardly, semi-supervised algorithms are the most appropriate applicant for the model building.

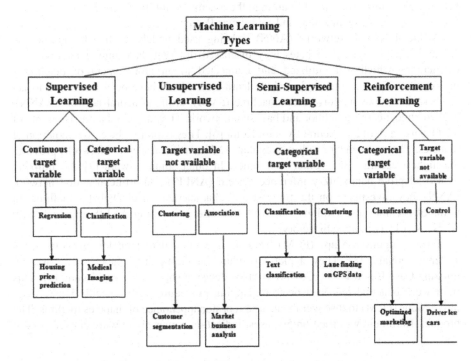

Fig. 2. Applications of different types of machine learning

Reinforcement learning: Reinforcement learning, with regards to computerized reasoning, is a kind of powerful programming that trains calculations utilizing an arrangement of reward and discipline. A reinforcement learning calculation, or specialist, learns by associating with its condition. The operator gets remunerates by performing effectively and punishments for performing mistakenly.

In Fig. 2 different machine learning applications are showcased depending upon the type of learning.

2 Related Work

2.1 Diabetes Prediction Using Machine Learning

Existing models: Xu et al. [1]: They initiate random forest prediction algorithm which focus for inspecting some accessible measures like age, weight, waist, and hip that impacts on diabetes. Random forest utilizes decision trees to prepare the examples and combine significance of every tree to acquire last outcomes. Gandhi and Prajapati [2]: They apply information digging innovation for anticipating diabetes and performed a pre-handling venture to manage dataset like feature determination strategy, standardization and evaluated the machine-learning method for example SVM. Panwar [3]: They proposed the methodology, in view of novel pre-processing systems and K-closest neighbor classifier. Sowjanya [4]: They utilize portable/android application for responses to overcome the absence of care about disease diabetes. Four machine learning algorithms were used to arrange the assembled information such as J48, naïve Bayes, support vector machine and multilayer Perceptron.

Artificial Neural Networks (ANN) is being used widely in diabetes prediction. Heydari [5]: For type 2 diabetes they discussed different data mining methods and calculations which were utilized and connected to an arrangement of displaying information. The execution of machine learning methods have been contrasted to get the best result like support vector machine (SVM), artificial neural network, (ANN), decision tree, nearest neighbor and bayesian network. They achieved a precision rate of 97.44% using Artificial Neural System. Komi [6]: They explored the early prediction of diabetes. The experiment result proves that ANN (Artificial Neural Network) provides the highest accuracy than other techniques. In other studies Swain [7]: By utilizing hybrid adaptive neuro-fuzzy inference system (ANFIS) and artificial neural network (ANN) they investigate on the forecast and characterization of Diabetes mellitus. In terms of accuracy this explorer uncovers that after comparing ANFIS approach with ANN, ANFIS is more satisfactory.

Fuzzy Cognitive Maps (FCM) have been employed to model knowledge-based systems: Doualia [8]: They depict procedure on Gestational diabetes forecast and utilizing Case Based Fuzzy Cognitive Maps decision support system. Bhatia [9]: This framework is actualized on delicate registering procedure, to be specific Fuzzy Cognitive Maps (FCM) to discover the nearness or nonappearance of diabetes mellitus. The product instrument was tried on 50 cases, indicating comes about with an exactness of 96%.

Owing to the use of detection through iris image is a remarkable progress in medical imaging technology in the recent decade: Samant [10]: The capability of the determination utility of the iridology alongside machine learning modes. The proposed model was connected to a systemic disease with ocular effects. 200 subject information of 100 every diabetic and non-diabetic was assessed, 89.66% accuracy was achieved by the using random forest classifier.

2.2 Different Techniques Applied to Predict Diabetes

IoT starts to become the main method of information procurement and transmission and would turn an important technology across several kinds of sensors to gather, investigate and deal with the whole data: Chang [11]: The intuitive to m-well being system (ImHS) gives continuous, two-route communication between diabetes patients and guardians by using Internet of Things innovation. Gomez [12]: The system created quiet monitoring in light of Internet of things which can be utilized to assist persons having constant infections.

Smart devices associated to a system or different gadgets and they have the capability to interact. Over the recent couple of years, there has been gained remarkable advancement in the innovation of sensors. They are more inexpensive, simple to install and affordable. Gupta [13]: The engineering proposed depends on the installed sensors of the hardware as opposed to utilizing wearable sensors and smart phone sensors to utilize the estimation for essential well being interconnected variables. The design presented here was assessed for appropriation, forecast investigation of physical activities, proficiency and safety. Antonovici [14]: They developed an application on the Android platform which trains for recording data which estimates the Diastolic blood pressure (DBP), Systolic blood pressure (SBP) and Heart Rate by electronic sphygmomanometer which conveys utilizing Bluetooth TM procedure. The application provides the probability of sending medical data by means of mobile internet or remote. Information will be compared with standard esteems and if these qualities are not in the normal range, the patient is cautioned, including family specialist, or in the most pessimistic scenario the emergency benefit. Al-Taee [15]: The mobile well being (mHealth) approach takes into consideration multiple care dimensions of diabetes by means of remote gathering and monitoring of patient information and arrangement of information on a smart phone platform. Such help to self-management of diabetes empowers ongoing clinical communication and input customized to the individual needs of the patient. Nataraja [16]: The normal outcome is Raspberry Pi gathers and stores the medical information through the sensors joined. The gathered information is exchanged to the client through applications. Rathore [17]: They propose a Real-time response system of medical emergency which includes light of the human body by IoT-construct medical sensors sent in it. Additionally, the system proposed comprises of the information investigation building called BIntelligent Building which is depicted by the layered proposed engineering. The information gathered from millions of body-joined sensors is sent to Intelligent Building for handling and for performing essential activities utilizing different units. Jara [18]: The proposed arrangement depends on Internet of things all together to; on the one hand, bolster a patient's profile management engineering in view of individual Radio-frequency identification (RFID) cards.

These Frameworks aim to improve care for people with diabetes: Rahman et al. [19]: This examination introduces a technique for checking ketone level by utilizing breath estimation. The method comprises to encourage the procedure of patient's diagnosis by advancement of equipment association with the Internet of Things (IoT) framework. In this framework, to sense the breath arduino board was utilized. Bhat and Bhat [20]: The embraced methodology uses IR spectroscopy to choose the blood glucose level in a person. A section based quickly adaptable care framework with a Wi-Fi module, gives prepared administration in unending thought condition (Android Application). The areas in their framework consolidate patients, specialists, relatives and medicinal administrations providers. The framework was created for the home use of patients that ought to be ceaselessly or intermittently watched. Winterlich et al. [21]: They have demonstrated how the proving ground will give the framework to mobile well-being self management devices including quiet instruction, wearable sensors and supporting applications and administrations so individuals with type 1 or sort 2 diabetes make the best decision at the perfect time to self-manage their condition.

A robot is intelligent in the sense that it has embedded observing, detecting capabilities and at the same time can get sensor information from other sources which are fused for the 'acting' reason of the device. Mall et al. [22]: They introduced the eHealth mind stage by utilizing Robots which was associated through IoT for giving customized various care approaches especially to a diabetic patient. The robot contains sensors for medical and dietary observing of the diabetic person which subsequently gives them complete multidimensional-care (Table 1).

Table 1. Significant studies in the prediction of diabetes using Machine Learning/IoT

Author	Year	Technique	Accuracy	Datasets
Gandhi [2]	2014	Support vector machine	98%	PIMA India
Panwar [3]	2016	K-nearest neighbor		
Sowjanya [4]	2015	Mobile application and J48, naive bayes, support vector machine and multilayer perceptron	J48 algorithm demonstrated to give preferred outcomes over different algorithms	
Heydari [5]	2013	Artificial neural network	97.44%	Tabriz, Iran
Swain [7]	2016	Hybrid adaptive neuro-fuzzy inference system (ANFIS) and artificial neural network (ANN)	Best accuracy was obtained with adaptive neuro-fuzzy inference	
Doualia [8]	2015	Fuzzy cognitive maps decision support system	90.2%	
Bhatia [9]	2015	Fuzzy cognitive maps	96%	
Samant [10]	2017	Random forest	89.66%	Iris image

(continued)

Table 1. (*continued*)

Author	Year	Technique	Accuracy	Datasets
Chang [11]	2016	IoT by using GPRS BGM and a smart phone		
Gomez [12]	2016	IoT		
Gupta [13]	2016	Internet-of-Things on cloud centric architecture		
Antonovici [14]	2014	Electronic sphygmomanometer, bluetooth TM technique		
Al-Taee [15]	2015	Mobile health (mHealth) approach		
Natarajan [16]	2016	IoT		
Rathore [17]	2016	IoT medical sensors		
Jara [18]	2011	RFID cards		
Bhat [20]	2017	Spectrophotometry		
Winterlich [21]	2016	IoT		
Mall [22]		By internet of things assisting robot		
Istepanian [23]	2011	Non-invasive glucose level sensing by m-IoT		
Ephizbah [24]	2011	Fuzzy logic	78%	UCI

3 Conclusion

Every time for glucose level prediction we need to pierce the finger with a sharp needle and after that place a fall of blood on a test strip and afterward put the strip into a meter that displays glucose levels. We need to have devices like glucotrack, sugarbeat, dia-vit which will not need the blood sample for it. As diabetes is the most occurring medical problem during pregnancy representing 3.3% of all live births. Most of the doctor's states that Diabetes occurs because of avoided or delayed with consume less calories, physical activity, medication and consistent screening. Projects initiated by the government like mDiabetes which will contribute to improving familiarity with diabetes and assisting healthy diets and active lifestyle which are vital to the anticipation of diabetes.

References

1. Xu, W., Zhang, J., Zhang, Q., Wei, X.: Risk prediction of type II diabetes based on random forest model. In: Advances in Electrical, Electronics, Information, Communication and Bio-Informatics (AEEICB). (2017). https://doi.org/10.1109/aeeicb.2017.7972337
2. Gandhi, K.K., Prajapati, N.B.: Diabetes prediction using feature selection and classification. Int. J. Adv. Eng. Res. Develop. (2014). https://doi.org/10.21090/ijaerd.0105110
3. Panwar, M., Acharyya, A., Shafik, R.A., Biswas, D.: K-nearest neighbor based methodology for accurate diagnosis of diabetes mellitus. In: Embedded Computing and System Design (ISED), pp. 132–136. IEEE (2016). https://doi.org/10.15417/1881
4. Sowjanya, K., Singhal, A., Choudhary, C.: MobDBTest: a machine learning based system for predicting diabetes risk using mobile devices. In: Advance Computing Conference (IACC), pp. 397–402. IEEE (2015). https://doi.org/10.1109/iadcc.2015.7154738
5. Heydari, M., Teimouri, M., Heshmati, Z., Alavinia, S.M.: Comparison of various classification algorithms in the diagnosis of type 2 diabetes in Iran. Int. J. Diabetes Develop. Countries, 167–173. (2016). https://doi.org/10.15417/1881
6. Komi, M., Li, J., Zhai, Y., Zhang, X.: Application of data mining methods in diabetes prediction. Image Vision Comput. (ICIVC) (2017). https://doi.org/10.1109/icivc.2017.7984706
7. Swain, A., Mohanty, S.N., Das A.C.: Comparative risk analysis on prediction of diabetes mellitus using machine learning approach. In: Electrical, Electronics, and Optimization Techniques (ICEEOT), pp. 3312–3317 (2016). https://doi.org/10.1109/iceeot.2016.7755319
8. Douali, N., Dollon, J., Jaulent, M.-C.: Personalized prediction of gestational diabetes using a clinical decision support system. In: Fuzzy Systems (FUZZ-IEEE), pp. 1–5 (2015). https://doi.org/10.1109/fuzz-ieee.2015.7337813
9. Bhatia, N., Kumar, S.: Prediction of severity of diabetes mellitus using fuzzy cognitive maps. Adv. Life Sci. Technol. **29**, 71–78 (2015)
10. Samant, P., Agarwal, R.: Diagnosis of Diabetes using computer methods: soft computing methods for diabetes detection using iris (2017). https://doi.org/10.1016/j.cmpb.2018.01.004
11. Chang, S.H., Chiang, R.D., Wu, S.J., Chang, W.T.: A context-aware, interactive M-health system for diabetics. IT Prof. **18**(3), 14–22 (2016)
12. Gomez, J., Oviedo, B., Zhuma, E.: Patient monitoring system based on internet of things. Proc. Comput. Sci. **83**, 90–97 (2016). https://doi.org/10.1016/j.procs.2016.04.103
13. Gupta, P.K., Maharaj, B.T., Malekian, R.: A novel and secure IoT based cloud centric architecture to perform predictive analysis of users activities in sustainable health centres. Multimed. Tools Appl. **76**(18), 18489–18512 (2017). https://doi.org/10.1007/s11042-016-4050
14. Antonovici, D.-A., et al.: Acquisition and management of biomedical data using Internet of Things concepts. In: International Symposium on Fundamentals of Electrical Engineering (ISFEE). IEEE (2014). https://doi.org/10.1109/isfee.2014.7050625
15. Al-Taee, M.A., Al-Nuaimy, W., Al-Ataby, A., Muhsin, Z.J., Abood, S.N.: Mobile health platform for diabetes management based on the Internet-of-Things. In: Applied Electrical Engineering and Computing Technologies (AEECT) (2015). https://doi.org/10.1109/aeect.2013.6716427
16. Natarajan, K., Prasad, B., Kokila, P.: Smart health care system using internet of things. J. Netw. Commun. Emerg. Technol. (JNCET) **6**(3) (2016)

17. Rathore, M.M., Ahmad, A., Paul, A., Wan, J., Zhang, D.: Real-time medical emergency response system: exploiting IoT and big data for public health. J. Med. Syst. **40**(12), 283 (2016)
18. Jara, A.J., Zamora, M.A., Skarmeta, A.F.: An internet of things—based personal device for diabetes therapy management in ambient assisted living (AAL). In: Personal and Ubiquitous Computing (2011). https://doi.org/10.1007/s00779-010-0353-1
19. Rahman, R.A., et al.: IoT-based personal health care monitoring device for diabetic patients. Comput. Appl. Industr. Electron. (ISCAIE) (2017). https://doi.org/10.1109/iscaie.2017.8074971
20. Bhat, G.M., Bhat, N.G.: A novel IoT based framework for blood glucose examination. In: Electrical, Electronics, Communication, Computer, and Optimization Techniques (ICEEC-COT), pp. 205–207 (2017). https://doi.org/10.1109/iceeccot.2017.8284666
21. Winterlich, A., et al.: Diabetes digital coach: developing an infrastructure for e-health self-management tools. In: Developments in Systems Engineering (DeSE), 9th International Conference (2016). https://doi.org/10.1109/dese.2016.56
22. Mall, S., Gupta, M., Chauhan, R.: Diet monitoring and management of diabetic patient using robot assistant based on Internet of Things. In: Emerging Trends in Computing and Communication Technologies (ICETCCT) (2017). https://doi.org/10.1109/icetcct.2017.8280339
23. Istepanian, R.S., Hu, S., Philip, N.Y., Sungoor, A.: The potential of Internet of m-health Things "m-IoT" for non-invasive glucose level sensing. In: Engineering in Medicine and Biology Society, EMBC, pp. 5264–5266, Aug 2011
24. Ephzibah, E.P.: Cost effective approach on feature selection using genetic algorithms and fuzzy logic for diabetes diagnosis. Int. J. Soft Comput. (IJSC) **2**, 1–10 (2011). https://doi.org/10.5121/ijsc.2011.2101

Prediction Technique for Time Series Data Sets Using Regression Models

Pinki Sagar[1]([⊠]), Prinima Gupta[1], and Indu Kashyap[2]

[1] Manav Rachna University, Faridabad, Haryana, India
[2] Manav Rachna International Institute of Research and Studies, Faridabad, Haryana, India

Abstract. Data mining techniques are the set of algorithms intended to find the hidden knowledge from the data sets, some of the popular techniques of data mining are prediction, sequential patterns, association, classification, clustering, and decision tree. Classification and regression are used for forecasting. Regression algorithms are based on various regression model i.e. linear regressions, non-linear regression, multiple regressions, logistic regression, and probabilistic regression. Forecasting of time series data sets with improved parameters has been discussed in the proposed methodology. For preprocessing the data set, sliding window or classification algorithms are used. Then coefficients values for the regression model are identified to fit the regression model.

Keywords: Data mining · Prediction · Linear regression · Non linear
Stream data · Time series data

1 Introduction

All data mining methodologies are divided in to two major categories Predictive and Descriptive mining. Descriptive Mining: How data aggregation and data mining to provide insight into the past and answer: "What has happened?" Predictive Mining: statistical methods and prediction techniques are used to understand the future and answer: "What could happen?" In data mining many techniques are used and each has its own application in various areas. Regression and Classification are the predictive methods which are used for analysis, forecasting and extraction of data sets of data ware houses.

2 Prediction Techniques for Stream Data

Stream data is continuous data; it is collected with fixed time interval in time. It can be one dimensional and two dimensional stream data. Below are the techniques for predicting stream data (Fig. 1):
FIPM: Frequent item Prediction Method [3]
FTP_DS: Frequent Temporal Pattern Data Stream [10]
SFA-PR: Sequence Forecast Algorithm for plane Regression [2].

© Springer Nature Singapore Pte Ltd. 2019
A. K. Luhach et al. (Eds.): ICAICR 2018, CCIS 955, pp. 480–488, 2019.
https://doi.org/10.1007/978-981-13-3140-4_43

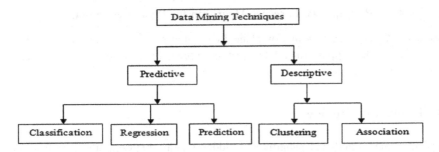

Fig. 1. Data mining techniques.

2.1 Frequent Item Prediction Method (FIPM)

The method used for analysis of stream data using regression (one dimensional). Prediction of stream data is to be done by linear regression model. Firstly, the data would be preprocessed and converted in to the form of sample value for using in further techniques of regression.

The key characteristics of Frequent Item Prediction Method are the following:

(i)   Formulate the data according to the accruing of time, when similar types of data are occurred.
(ii) Find out the difference of time intervals when particular variables are occurred and Form the pairs using intervals in the form of (X, Y). Make the pairs in the form of two type variables: dependent variables and independent variables.
(iii) Fit the data in to linear regression model (preprocessed).

2.2 Frequent Temporal Pattern Data Stream (FTPDS)

FTPDS algorithm was introduced by Teng [10]. There was two important attributes for Frequent Temporal Pattern Data Stream (FTPDS) algorithm, first is the frequent occurrences of data sets sequence and its support values and second is the pattern representation. The key characteristics of Frequent Temporal Pattern Data Stream are the following:

(i)   This algorithm checks the flow of transaction (online) and generates frequent patterns for real time data.
(ii) Second significant characteristics of Frequent Temporal Pattern Data Stream (FTP-DS) compact pattern representation based on regression techniques. Particularly, to meet up the space restriction, partition for pattern representation a compressed Accumulated Frequency and time form to aggregately include all complete the information which is necessary for further regression study.
(iii) In comparison of other linear regression model. FTP-DS perform the identification of errors during prediction is very effectively.
(iv) Frequent Temporal Pattern Data Stream algorithm is used for prediction for two dimensional stream data.

2.3 (SFA-PR) Sequence Forecast Algorithm for Plane Regression

Sequence Forecast Algorithm for plane Regression calculates support for particular sequence and then applies the plane equation to predict the sequences or assurances of data sets in the future.

3 Literature Review

In data mining significant patterns and hidden relation between attributes from large amounts of data are automatically determined. Prediction techniques of Data mining identify correlations between variables. Linear regression is used in any system for forecasting one dimensional and two dimensional data. Frequent item sets are generated from the Association Matrix and then association rules are generated from the frequent item set which are already generated.

Zhou, Liu, Wong [1], explains that logistic regression is a specific method for designing of prediction model for categorical data or binary data like 0 or 1. The result of logistic regression has been improved for classification of disease and data sets for disease in the form of microarray.

Zhao and Li [2] proposed a method which is based on plane regression. Plane regression based forecasting algorithm SFA-PR (sequence forecast algorithm). It predicts the sequences of two dimensional frequent stream data. SFA-PR mining algorithm gives better result in comparing with other prediction algorithms which are used in forecasting of sequence data sets. SFA-PR can cover many fields and never neglect the exceptions.

Chai, Kim, Jin [3] introduced a method (FIPM) for the prediction of one dimensional frequent stream data sets. Frequent Stream data has characteristics of continuous and infinite. Tiwari [4] introduced a method for improving prediction of two dimensional stream data (FTP_DS) Frequent Temporal Pattern data stream algorithm with non linear regression, so the more exceptions can cover by sequence trends.

Nishara Banu [5] introduced a method to predict the heart disease through classification algorithms. Gupta [6] discussed about the framing of linear regression technique, with the designing of linear regression method, training data sets or test data sets are used to fit a equation of linear regression. It is the very simplest method for regression analysis, and find out the suitable values for coefficients a and b to predict the value of y based upon a assigning value of X.

Greven and Scheipl [8] the framework enclose various existing as well as novel models. It comprises regression for 'generalized' functional data and quintile regression as well as generalized preservative models for location, shape and scale (GAMLSS) for functional data. It admit various flexible linear, smooth or interact terms of scalar and functional covariates as well as arbitrary effects and provide flexible options of bases—mainly splines and functional principal components—and communicate penalty for each term. It includes functional data observed on common grids or dense or specific on curve or sparse grids.

Sagar [9] Data Mining (sometimes called data or knowledge discovery) is the process of analyzing data from different perspectives and summarizing it into useful information–making it more accurate, reliable, efficient and beneficial. In data mining various techniques are used-classification, clustering, regression, association mining.

Bae and Kim [7], suggests a methodology called a smart ubiquitous data mining (UDM) that consolidates uniform models in a smart ubiquitous computing background. It induces rules from the dataset using diverse rule extraction algorithms and combines the rules to build a meta-model.

3.1 Literature Conclusion

In literature survey it has been studied various prediction techniques by using regression and classification for different types of data. Data could be stream data, time series data frequent data. Three algorithms used for forecasting are, FIPM, FTPDS, SFAPR In earlier FIPM (based on linear regression). In non linear regression based FIPM and FTPDS we get the improved results but in FIPM based on non linear regression. The error detection rate find out by algorithm SFA-PR is much higher than method Frequent Temporal Pattern Data Stream. The SFA-PR helps to clarify or explain prediction more intruding than FPT-DS algorithm so that it covers each and every data set. Logistic regression is based on binary values such as 0 or 1 and it is used to forecast the chances of a gene related with ailment by considering the prior information as the dependent variables in various category and label which are related to feature vectors termed as estimator variables. The forecasting approach could be applied to dataset of medical field which helps in predicting of the factors that affect risk with level of risk and the patients based on selective factors item sets.

4 Objective of Proposed Work

Conceptual understanding of different type of regression: linear, nonlinear, logistic etc. Regression analysis uses the independent variable to check the predicted value of dependent variable. Understand the association or relation between dependent and independent variables, plotting of values in the regression model and the difference value (errors) of dependent variable and independent values on graph line.

5 Methodology

Methodology of Regression is a quantitative research method which involves modeling and analyzing many variables, where the relationship includes a dependent variable and independent variables (one or more).

STEP 1:   Collection of data is done from online repository (UCI Repository).
　　　　　Characteristics of data sets are:
　　　　　　(i)   Data type: time series data set
　　　　　　(ii) Attribute characteristics: Real
　　　　　　(iii) Associated task: Regression
　　　　　Source: UCI repository

STEP 2:   An outlier or an error is an observation that lies an irregular distance from other values in a sample data (randomly selected) from a population data It means that, the analyst decide what should be considered and should not be considered. Before unusual observations could be selected out, it is mandatory to find the feature of normal observations.

STEP 3:   Data preprocessing is a step of data mining technique that involves conversion of raw data into a model so that regression could be applied or an understandable form. Real-time or dynamic data is often not complete, not consistent, deficient in certain behaviors or sequence trends, and it may have contain many errors. Huge data sets are usually incomplete due to several reasons, absence of attribute values, incorrect data, non relevant data and corrupted data.

(a) Data cleaning: It is the method of removing of corrupt or inaccurate data from a data sets, and refers to identifying imperfect, wrong, erroneous or irrelevant parts of the data sets and then updating, or removing the dirty data. Steps for data cleaning:
   (i)   Fill It is the procedure of fill up the missing values or ignores the row, usually done when class label is missing.
   (ii) Fill the attribute mean value in the place of missing value for all samples belonging to the same class.
   (iii) Learning algorithms are used to predict the missing values. Consider the missing value attribute as a dependent variable and run a learning algorithm to predict the missing values.
(b) Binning is the method which is used to Sort the attribute values and partitions them into bins. Then smooth by bin means, bin median, or bin boundaries.
(c) Data transformation: It is the practice of normalizing the data. It is the procedure of Scaling attribute values to fall within a particular range.
(d) Data reduction: It is the method of dropping the count of attributes by Data cube aggregation operations, slice or dice, roll-up, operations., filtering and wrapper method are attribute selection method for removing of non relevant attributes. Principle component analysis is a method for searching the lower dimensional space that can represent the data in best way.

STEP 4:   Calculation of coefficients (depend on regression model).

Linear Regression, co efficient are a0 and b1

$$Y = a_0 + b_1 X_1 \tag{1}$$

Nonlinear regression uses following equation:

$$\mathbf{Y} = \mathbf{f}(\mathbf{X}, \beta) + \varepsilon \tag{2}$$

Where:

X = a vector of p predictors,

β = a vector of k parameters,

ε = an error term.

Multi Linear regression

$$Y = a_0 + b_1 X_1 + b_2 X_2 + b_3 X_3 + \varepsilon \tag{3}$$

STEP 5:   Apply the Regression model, depend on type of data for example if they are using two dimensional data in number format they will use linear and nonlinear regression model. If processed data is in binary forms then they will apply logistic regression. And so on.

STEP 6:   After applying regression model the accuracy of prediction can be analyzed. It is based on independent and dependent variable. Percentage of accuracy is found out using standard error. The standard error of the estimate is a measure of the accuracy of predictions

$$\sigma_{est} = \frac{\sqrt{\sum (Y - Y')^2}}{N}$$

Error = Actual value-Predicted value.

STEP 7:   During Prediction of data they can find the standard error data analysis which is identified by difference of actual data and predicted data. Data Analysis is a method that help describe facts, test hypotheses and detect patterns. This includes data quality assurance, statistical data analysis, modeling, and interpretation of results.

Correlation Analysis: Some Databases may have data sets that contain some irrelevant attributes. Finding two attributes of the data base are interrelated or not can be only analyzed using correlation analysis. In correlation analysis, we measure the relationship between more than one continuous variable (for example: between an independent and a dependent variable or between two independent variables).

Regression Analysis: In regression analysis More than one variable are included, one is independent variable and second is dependent variable. In multi linear regression multiple independent (more than one variable) are used. Regression analysis is the procedure of checking error rate during the prediction or it is a way of predictive modeling. It is used in the analysis of relationship between a target and predicator. It is also used in forecasting or predicting of the datasets based on previous data sets or historical data. Regression techniques are used in finding out the relationship between the dependent and independent variables in data sets. For example, relationship between road accidents and rough driving by a driver is best studied through regression (prediction model). Regression is a statistical process for estimating the relationships or correlation among different attributes of data sets. Analysis could be done through using many regression techniques for model and analyze different attributes, whether the main focus is on the correlation between dependent variable and more than one independent variables (Fig. 2).

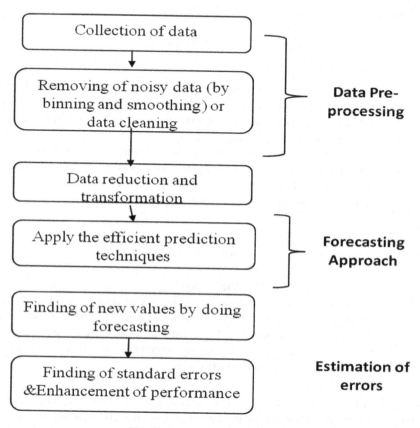

Fig. 2. Process for the prediction

6   Analysis

In the earlier study it has been analysed that frequent item prediction method [3] forecasting is applied using linear regression model in frequent temporal pattern data stream [2], sequence forecast algorithm [2] are used for forecasting of two dimensional stream data through linear fregression and plane regression.ftpds and sfapr coverup the limitations of fipm algorithm.ftpds and sfapr are more efficient algorithms in comparison of fipm in concern of following parameters: mean square error, percentage of accuracy, execution time, covering of each time stamp, prediction rate (Fig. 3).

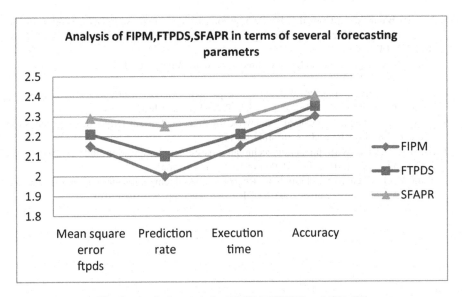

Fig. 3. Analysis graph for FRIPM, FTPDS and SFA-PR

7   Conclusion

In this paper we have discussed prediction techniques for stream data. These techniques are: FIPM, FTPDS, and SFAPR. In these prediction algorithms linear and nonlinear regression are applied. A novel method is introduced for the prediction of time series data which is multidimensional which has been collected on daily basis at the same time. Our novel approach will overcome the limitations of fipm [3] (for one dimensional data sets..ftpds [3] and sfa pr [2] (for two dimensional data set: stream data) For the better result best regression model will be applied and it will give the better result in the prediction and reduce the residuals.

References

1. Zhou, X., Liu, K.-Y., Wong, S.T.: Cancer classification and prediction using logistic regression with Bayesian gene selection. J. Biomed. Inf. **37**(4), 249–265 (2004)
2. Zhao, F., Li, Q.H.: A plane regression-based sequence forecast algorithm for stream data. In: Proceedings International Conference on Machine Learning and Cybernetics. pp. 18–21 Aug. IEEE (2005)
3. Chai, D.J., Kim, E.H., Jin, L., Wang, B., Ryu, K.H.: Prediction of frequent items to one dimensional stream data. In: Fifth International Conference on Computational Science and Applications 0-7695-2945-3/07. IEEE (2007)
4. Tiwari, S.: Sequence forecast algorithm based on nonlinear regression technique for stream data, Vol. 1, No. 2, pp. 285–288 (2010)

5. Nishara Banu, M.A., Gomathy, B.: Disease forecasting system using data mining methods. In: International Conference on Intelligent Computing Applications 978-1-4799-3966-4/14. IEEE (2014)
6. Gupta, S.: A regression modeling technique on data mining. Int. J. Comput. Appl. (0975 – 8887) **116**(9) (2015)
7. Bae, J.K., Kim J.: A personal credit rating prediction model using data mining in smart ubiquitous environments. Research Article Published in February (2015)
8. Greven, S., Scheipl, F.: General framework for functional regression modelling. Published February 28. Sage Journals, California (2017)
9. Sagar, P.: Analysis of prediction techniques based on classification and regression. Int. J. Comput. Appl. (2017). Foundation of Computer Science
10. Teng, W.G., Chen, M.S., Philip, S.Y.: Regression based temporal pattern mining scheme for pattern data. In: Proceedings 2003 VLDB Conference pp. 93–104 (2013)

Enhancement Methods for Low Visibility and Fog Degraded Images

Gurveer Singh$^{(\boxtimes)}$ and Ashima Singh

Department of CSE, Thapar University, Patiala, India
gurveer7393@gmail.com, ashima@thapar.edu

Abstract. Image processing methods are widely used to improvise the quality of an image to extract the hidden information in it. Phenomena of scattering and atmosphere absorption results inhaze smoke and fog. Weather conditions majorly influence the visual system as well as detection and identification of the targets and degrade the picture quality. In the previous year, researchers have been focused on the high-quality images or videos for enhancement as well as to detect objects. In this paper, we have reviewed previous papers and compare based on used techniques and performance parameters.

Keywords: Image processing · Visual system · Image enhancement and low visibility techniques

1 Introduction

Image Processing is a technique to execute few operations on a particular image, to get an improved image or to withdraw a coded message hidden in an image. This is a kind of signal processing, here, an image is inserted as input and extracted results can be an image or any other characteristics linked with an image as shown in Fig. 1. Recently, Image processing is widely used technology and it is an active research area in several fields like biomedical images, computer vision, and object detection. Initially, image processing comprised of three steps: Importing an image with the help of acquisition equipment; Analysing alteration made in an image; Results can be achieved as a modified image or analysis-based report of an image [1]. Digital and analogue processing are two techniques generally used for image processing. Analog technique is used for hard copies such as photos or document printout while digital methods are used to manipulate advanced images with the help of computers. Pre-processing, display, enhancement and extraction are common stages of digital processing of data [16]. The main goal of image processing is Visualization, Restoring and Sharpening Images, Retrieving Images, Pattern Measurement, and Image Recognition [17].

Several major disciplines where image processing helps researchers for its wide usage:

1. *Restoration and Image Sharpening:* It is the important and challenging task to recover the corrupted, noisy or poor-quality images. Hu and Xu [23] proposes this to remove noise from the sequences of images i.e. video with digital lock-in

A. K. Luhach et al. (Eds.): ICAICR 2018, CCIS 955, pp. 489–498, 2019.
https://doi.org/10.1007/978-981-13-3140-4_44

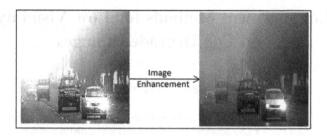

Fig. 1. Image processing

method. Maru and Parikh [22] discussed direct inverse filter, Wiener filter, and order statistic filter for the restoration of corrupted images.

2. *Medical Field:* PET scan, CT scan, UV imaging, X-ray are common medical implementations. Alsayem and Kadah [2] tried to obtain a high-resolution image using the methodology of super-resolution reconstruction.

3. *Transmission/Encoding:* The first picture was transmitted from London to New York in 3 h. Presently footage can be seen within seconds from one continent to other. Various methods are developed for low to high frequency for encoding and streaming over the internet.

4. *Pattern Recognition:* it comprised of the study of image processing, machine learning, etc. where image processing helps in object recognition and machine learning helps in system training for pattern changes.

This paper is divided into five parts: section two gives a literature review along with comparison table to discuss different techniques and performance. Further, third section discusses enhancement technique for the image and section fourth gives knowledge of deep learning algorithms. Last Sect. 5 is the conclusion part to the paper.

1.1 Motivation

In recent years, maximum work has been done over image processing. It covers a wide area in the fields of medical, science, nature, technology, and professional. High-resolution images and videos are preferred to detected objects or for other processing like encoding, transmission, and processing. Poor quality images like blur or corrupted images are the idea generator to work with hazy or foggy images so that objects identify easily as well as the occurrence of accidents can be mitigated.

2 Literature Review

Foggy Images are characterized as indefinite quality on the surface of an image caused by a mixture of water droplets. Hazy pictures have some positive adjustment in nature of an image. The essential picture parameters like standard deviation and mean of picture changes in the extent to the amount of cloudiness fused. Contingent upon these two essential parameters, [4] hazy images are categorised as a Non-Hazy colour image; Slight Hazy colour image; Medium Hazy colour image; Extreme Hazy colour image.

Deformation of pictures has various utilizations from liveliness, to transforming and therapeutic imaging. To execute such deforming, the client chooses some arrangement of operations to control the level of the distortion. These operations may appear as focuses, lines or even polygon networks [3]. As the client adjusts the position and introduction of these handles, the picture ought to disfigure in an instinctive manner. The twisting as a capacity f that maps indicates in the un-deformed picture the disfigured picture. Capacity f is applied to every point v to the un-deformed picture makes the twisted picture. Then consider a picture with an arrangement of operations p that client achieves different position q. There are some important properties for the deformation of capacity f: first is *Interpolation* in which operation p must map to q directly under twisting; Second property is *Smoothness* where f must provide firm deformations. Whereas, third property is *Identity* defined as in case, deformed operates q and it is similar with p, then f has also similar functions. (i.e.; $q_i = p_i => f(v) = v$) [5].

These three properties are fundamentally the same as those utilized as a part of scattered information insertion. The initial two properties essentially express that the capacity f inserts the scattered information esteems and is plain. The last property expresses that if the information is inspected from a direct capacity, at that point the interpolant replicates that straight capacity. Given these likenesses, it shocks no one that numerous deformation techniques get methods from scattered information interjection [5].

Sangeetha and Anusudha [6] centred to improve the visibility and contrast of hazy images with the help of various enhancement methods and analyse on the basis of standard parameters explained in the table. Best algorithm is carried out i.e. Discrete Wavelet Transform (DWT) based on a number of changing pixel rate (NPCR).

Choo and Franconeri [7] examined if the size averaging process depends on moderately early question portrayals or on later protest portrayals that have experienced iterative preparing. Individuals can quickly judge the normal size of a gathering of items with extensive exactness. They requested members to judge the normal size of an arrangement of circles and, in a few conditions, introduced two extra circles that were either littler or bigger than the normal. The extra circles were encompassed by four-speck covers that either waited longer than the circle exhibit, averting further handling with question substitution concealing (OSM) or vanished all the while with circle cluster, enabling the hover portrayal to achieve later visual preparing stages.

Hurtos et al. [8] proposed the utilization of a Fourier-based enrolment system fit for taking care of the low determination, clamour, and ancient rarities related with sonar picture development. Vehicle tasks in submerged situations are regularly traded off by poor permeability conditions. E.g. the discernment scope of optical gadgets is intensely obliged in turbid waters, in this way entangling route and mapping undertakings in situations like harbours, inlets or waterways. In case, the qualities of the sonar information present troubles in picture enrolment, a key advance in mosaicking and movement estimation applications.

Lin and Murray [9] gauged the awareness level in two sessions and found that the session-subordinate impact was because of a mindfulness distinction. A current report recommended that oblivious reaction restraint is kept up when subliminal jolts are blended with supraliminal boosts that are related with reaction hindrance (blended session), however, it is nullified when they have exhibited alone (single session). Be that as it may, the consciousness of the subliminal boosts is probably going to contrast in the 2 sessions due to the preparing of for subliminal jolts is lifted (e.g., no longer subliminal) when blended with supraliminal jolts.

Van Damme [10] reviewed Computer Vision Photogrammetry thinks positively about manual chronicle techniques both in recording effectiveness and in the nature of the last outcomes. The software used for under-water sites by archaeologists in the field of underwater archaeology is PhotoScan. Computer Vision Photogrammetry enables archaeologists to precisely record submerged locales in three measurements utilizing straightforward 2D picture or videos, consequently handled in committed programming. The results of the case study are compared with manual results obtained both in the terms of quality and efficiency of the final results (Table 1).

Table 1. Literature survey in techniques and performance parameters.

Author name	Thrust area	Technique used	Parameters
Sangeetha and Anusudha [6]	Various enhancement methods for image defogging	Boost filter, power law filter, homomorphic filtering, wiener filtering, DCT and DWT	Counting of pixel rate change and peak signal to noise ratio
Choo and Franconeri [7]	Objects with reduced visibility still contribute to size averaging	Object substitution masking	Point of subjective equality and accuracy rate
Hurtos et al. [8]	Low visibility in ocean water	Region-based technique	Phase difference matrix, mean and max error
Lin and Murray [9]	Automaticity in responses of unconscious	Priming awareness	Reaction time and accuracy

3   Image Enhancement Techniques

Basically, image enhancement is enhancing the interpretability or impression of data in image, so that these results can be used for another analysis purpose. The vital target of an image improvement is to upgrade an image attributes so that specific results can be achieved for particular task [11]. The enhancement techniques are broadly classified as Spatial and Frequency Domain Methods.

In Spatial methods deals straightforwardly with pixels of an image. Pixels are altered to get desired results whereas, in frequency-based methods, Fourier transforms are calculated and all operations and calculations are executed on Fourier's to get resulting image. Several methods used for image enhancement are:

1. *Histogram Equalization:* It's a common method to improvise the image's appearance. Assuming a picture is transcendently dull. At that point, its histogram is skewed to the lower end of the dark scale and all picture detail is packed into the dull end of the histogram. HE extends out the histogram over the whole range of pixels (0–255). It expands the differentiation of pictures for conclusiveness of human assessment and can be connected to standardize brightening varieties in picture understanding issues. Histogram equalization is the activities used to get new pictures on the basis of histogram characteristics or alteration.

2. *Local Enhancements:* Earlier techniques for histogram adjustments and histogram coordinating are used worldwide. Thus, the local improvement was utilized. Characterize square or rectangular surroundings (cover) and move the inside from pixel to pixel. For every area, ascertain histogram of the focuses in the area. Acquire histogram evening out/detail work. Guide dim level of pixel focused in the neighbourhood. It can utilize fresh pixel values and existing histogram to ascertain further histogram.

3. *Log Transforms:* The log changes map a restricted scope of low information dim level esteems into a more extensive scope of yield esteems. The reverse log change plays out the inverse change. Log capacities are especially helpful when the info dark level esteems may have an amazingly expansive scope of qualities. Once in a while, the dynamic scope of a

4. Handled picture far surpasses the ability of the show gadget. This change maps a restricted scope of low-level dim scale powers into a more extensive scope of yield esteems. Log Transformations is utilized to grow estimations of dull pixels and pack estimations of splendid pixels.

5. *Threshold Transformation:* Threshold changes are especially helpful for division required to isolate a question of enthusiasm from a foundation. Picture edge is the way toward isolating the data (objects) of a picture from its experience, henceforth, threshold is normally connected to dark level or shading record checked pictures. Threshold can be classified into two fundamental classifications: Local and Global. Global threshold strategies pick one limit an incentive for the whole report picture, which is frequently in light of the estimation of the foundation level from the force histogram of the picture. Local versatile threshold utilizes distinctive esteems for every pixel as per the neighbourhood.

6. *Contrast Stretching:* To grow the scope of brilliance esteems in a picture the differentiation upgrade procedures are utilized, with the goal that the picture can be productively shown in a way wanted by the expert. The level of differentiation in a picture may fluctuate because of poor light or ill-advised setting in the securing sensor gadget. Hence, there is need to control the difference of a picture with a specific end goal to adjust for troubles in picture procurement. The thought of complexity extending is to build the dynamic scope of the dark levels in the picture being handled [12].

7. *High Boost Filtering:* The high-help sifting technique upgrades high recurrence part while as yet holding the low recurrence segment. This strategy is made out of an all-pass channel and an edge identification channel. Along these lines, it accentuates edges as well as results in sharper of an image. This technique melds the cover

picture and unique picture to enhance the high recurrence segment, which can upgrade the permeability and edge data of the picture.

8. *Homomorphic Filtering:* Homomorphic separating is used to remedy non-uniform light in pictures. Moreover, it constricts low frequencies, however, save fine subtle elements. The enlightenment reflectance model of picture arrangement expresses that the power at any pixel, which is the measure of brightness in an image thought about by a point the protest is defined by the result of the brightening of the site as well as the reflectance in the scene of the objects.

Above-mentioned image enhancement methods are popular and required improve the quality of the image. There are so many other methods like deblurring, Contrast and filtrations.

4 Deep Learning

Deep Learning grants computational models, which are mostly designed by different level layers to learn portrayals of information with variety of reflection to levels. These approaches have dramatically improved best discourse acknowledgement in the class, Visual protest acknowledgement, question recognition and other various different areas, genomics as well as tranquillize revelation are good examples. Profound learning identifies multifaceted design in huge informational collections with the use of the back-spread estimations, which shows machine changing its inner parameters, which trained to register in every layer of the portrayal from the portrayal last layer. Deep convolution nets contain realized leaps which are forward in handling picture, videos, sound and discourse; and intermittent nets described light on successive information. For instance-speech and text [13]. Several Deep Learning techniques that are stated as follows:

A. *Linear Regression:* It is used for gauge genuine esteems into the light of nonstop variables. The connection amongst autonomous and subordinate factors is set up through best line fitting and called as relapse line. Direct condition is "Y = a * X + b". Direct Regression is of mainly two writes first one is (MLR) Multiple Linear Regression and other is (SLR) Simple Linear Regression. Basic Linear Regression illustrates through one free factor. More than that, Multiple Linear Regression as name implies is portrayed through multiple free factors. At the same time as, discovers best fit line, you can easily fit a relapse that is curvilinear and polynomial. Therefore, relapse called as the polynomial and curvilinear relapse known as polynomial or curvilinear relapse.

B. *Decision Tree:* Depicts a type of managed learning calculations, generally obtained for order problems. Horrifically, it performs for clear-cut as well as for persistent ward factors. From calculation, we divide the populace into two homogeneous sets. This at whole worked in the light of majority of autonomous factors, which makes as mainly gathering could be expected must be under the circumstances. To part the populace into various heterogeneous gatherings, it utilizes different strategies like Gini, Information Gain, Chi-square, entropy [18].

C. *SVM*: It is a grouping technique. In this calculation, every datum thing is plotted in n-dimensional space which is a point (n is a number of highlights) with the calculations of every element become the estimation of a particular facility. Like, a condition if only two highlights, for instance Hair and Height of a person is available, at that point these two factors, the first plot must be in space that is two dimensional and every point has the two coordinates (otherwise called Support Vectors) [19].

D. *Naives Bayes:* An arrangement scheme in light of Bayes hypothesis with the supposition of an autonomy. Basically, a Naive Bayes classifier assumed that closest of particular component is disconnected in a class which is the nearest other element. Innocent Bayesian model's manufacture is complex and difficult mainly, the vast informational index. Next to it, it is straightforward, Naive Bayes called to out flank even making the refined settlement scheme [20].

E. *KNN:* It is applicable to grouping as well as for relapse problems. In case, it is most usually obtained part of grouping problems in any the business. K nearest neighbour is a straight forward estimation, which collects each attainable case and distinguishes new case through share vote of its k neighbours. The case, which is assigned to class, is the primary among its K nearest neighbours intended with the use of distance function. Distance functions should be Euclidean, Manhattan, Minkowski and Hamming separation.

F. *K-means:* this is the unsupervised estimations that cares about the problems, which generated in the bunching. The methodology is the main and simple technique to arrange an informational collection by the use of particular number of bunch that accept k groups. The information is homogeneous and heterogeneous mainly focus inside the bunch.

G. *Random Forest:* it is a trademark term, which is used for a group of choice trees. In this forest, the gathering of choice trees exists called as Woods. To combine another question in terms of qualities, each tree provides a characterization and votes for the class. Wood collected order, which have the majority of votes that are seen from every one vote from the woods at backside.

Deep learning shows the powerful advantages in the field of extraction. It is commonly used in the computer vision and also it has replaced the existing machine learning techniques. Above mentioned are not only the techniques, there are so many other available algorithms for the deep learning that can be used.

5 Existing Performance Parameters and Comparison

Several existing parameters used to calculate performance states as:

5.1 DCT

The discrete cosine change (DCT) is utilized broadly for flag pressure because of it inhibits properties of energy compaction instead of the discrete Fourier change. For a flag of length, N the DCT work restores a vector of coefficients of length N, every coefficient speaking to how nearly the flag maps to that cosine work. The primary coefficient speaks to a level capacity. Accordingly, if the information is all a similar esteem the primary coefficient will be a non-zero esteem while every other coefficient ought to be near zero. Various DCT variants exist, every one having extraordinary properties [6].

5.2   DWT

Discrete Wavelets Transforms (DWT) is a scientific instrument for progressively disintegrating a picture by dissolving a flag into set of essential capacity called wavelets. DWT is a multi-determination investigation which at various frequencies split down the flag and thereby produces exceptional outcomes. Wavelets are clarified as capacities gained over a settled interim and get zero as normal esteem. The adjustment is amazingly mandatory path utilized for flag examination and picture handling administration, for the most part for multi-determination affirmation [14]. Wavelet is a little flag that vary and disintegrated in time area. DWT is present and computationally solid method. Wavelet examination have advantages of Fourier Transformation as it executes nearby and multi-determination investigation and uncover perspectives like discontinuities, split down and so on. Therefore, exhibits more proficient behaviour than Fourier Transformation. Multi Resolution Analysis (MRA) is examining signal with one of a kind frequencies and distinctive resolutions [15].

Table 2. The table describes the comparative analysis with quality of de-fogging enhancement methods. The results states that discrete wavelet transformation method has attained better results in terms of NPCR, Peak Signal to Noise Ratio for both input database images.

Table 2. Comparative study with various methods in image enhancement [6]

Techniques	PSNR	NPCR	Contrast gain
DWT (Discrete Wavelet Transformation)	32.10	1	0.9598
Power law transformation	30.68	1	0.6848
High Boost filtering	30.80	0.0414	0.6233
Holomorphic filtering	30.31	1	0.6848
Wiener filtering	30.25	1	0.7353
DCT	30.68	1	1

6   Conclusion and Future Scope

Image preparing strategies are applied vitally to filter the degraded image to remove the unfavourable data in it. Foggy or cloudy climate significantly affect the visual framework and in addition, location and distinguishing proof of the objectives and corrupts the photo quality. In this paper, we have assessed finish picture handling including the pictures, preparing and its applications. We have done survey on a few existing papers and look at based on utilized strategies and execution parameters. In addition, we have talked about a few methods for the improvement of an image and examined a view of execution parameters. A few issues happened because of low permeability of items because of a few reasons. Furthermore, existing issues are look upon and discussed.

For the future work, there can be enhancement of obtained results by combining DWT with guide filter, which leads to accessibility of large data set by applying the above-mentioned deep learning algorithms and thereby identification of invisible objects in fog and hazy environment can be done with ease, which in future can be proficient for the betterment of society.

References

1. Russ, J.C.: The Image Processing Handbook. CRC Press (2016)
2. Alsayem, H.A., Kadah, Y.M.: Image Restoration Techniques in Super-Resolution Reconstruction of MRI Images (2016). IEEE. 978-1-4673-9652-3/16
3. Ručka, L., Peterlík, I.: Fast reconstruction of image deformation field using radial basis function. In: IEEE 14th International Symposium on (2017). https://doi.org/10.1109/isbi.2017.7950719
4. Thakur, R.K., Saravanan, C.: Classification of colour hazy images. In: International Conference on Electrical, Electronics, and Optimization Techniques (ICEEOT), pp. 2159–2163. IEEE, Mar 2016
5. Schaefer, S., McPhail, T., Warren, J.: Image deformation using moving least squares. ACM Trans. Graph. (TOG) 25(3), 533–540 (2006)
6. Sangeetha, N., Anusudha, K.: Image defogging using enhancement techniques. In: 2017 International Conference on Computer, Communication and Signal Processing (ICCCSP), pp. 1–5. IEEE, Jan 2017
7. Choo, H., Franconeri, S.L.: Objects with reduced visibility still contribute to size averaging. Atten. Percept. Psychophys. 72(1), 86–99 (2010)
8. Hurtós, N., Ribas, D., Cufí, X., Petillot, Y., Salvi, J.: Fourier-based registration for robust forward-looking sonar mosaicing in low-visibility underwater environments. J. Field Robot. 32(1), 123–151 (2015)
9. Lin, Z., Murray, S.O.: Automaticity of unconscious response inhibition: Comment on Chiu and Aron (2014) (2015)
10. Van Damme, T.: Computer vision photogrammetry for underwater archaeological site recording in a low-visibility environment. Int. Arch. Photogram. Remote Sens. Spat. Inf. Sci. 40(5), 231 (2015)
11. Maini, R., Aggarwal, H.: A comprehensive review of image enhancement techniques (2010). arXiv preprint arXiv:1003.4053
12. Sawant, H.K., Deore, M.: A comprehensive review of image enhancement techniques. Int. J. Comput. Technol. Electron. Eng. (IJCTEE) 1(2), 39–44 (2010)
13. LeCun, Y., Bengio, Y., Hinton, G.: Deep Learning. Nature 521(7553), 436 (2015)
14. Kaur, A., Kaur, R., Kumar, N.: A review on image steganography techniques. Int. J. Comput. Appl. 123(4) (2015)
15. Tiwari, A., Yadav, S.R., Mittal, N.K.: A review on different image steganography techniques. Int. J. Eng. Innov. Technol. (IJEIT) 3, 19–23 (2014)

16. Chitradevi, B., Srimathi, P.: An overview on image processing techniques. Int. J. Innov. Res. Comput. Commun. Eng. (IJIRCCE) **2**(11) (2014)
17. https://www.engineersgarage.com/articles/image-processing-tutorial-applications
18. Gupta, V., Lehal, G.S.: A survey of text mining techniques and applications. J. Emerg. Technol. web Intell. **1**(1), 60–76 (2009)
19. Tang, X., Liu, K., Cui, J., Wen, F., Wang, X.: Intentsearch: capturing user intention for one-click internet image search. IEEE Trans. Pattern Anal. Mach. Intell. **34**(7), 1342–1353 (2012)
20. Nehru, E.I., Mala, T.: Automatic e-content generation. In: Conference Papers Conference Papers, p. 109, Sept 2009
21. Introduction to the Image Processing. https://www.engineersgarage.com/articles/image-processing-tutorial-applications
22. Maru, M., Parikh, M.C.: Image restoration techniques: a survey. Int. J. Comput. Appl. **160** (6) (2017) (0975–8887)
23. Hu, Y., Xu, Y.: An image restoration method based on cross-correlation. In: 2017 6th International Conference on Computer Science and Network Technology (ICCSNT). IEEE (2017)

Image Processing by Using Different Types of Discrete Wavelet Transform

Shaveta Thakral$^{(\boxtimes)}$ and Pratima Manhas$^{(\boxtimes)}$

ECE Department, FET, Manav Rachna International Institute of Research and
Studies, Faridabad, India
{shaveta.fet,pratima.fet}@mriu.edu.in

Abstract. Image processing is emerging research area which seeks attention in biomedical field. There are lots of image processing techniques which are not only useful in extracting useful information for analysis purpose but also saves computation time and memory space. Transformation is one such type of image processing technique. Examples of transform techniques are Hilbert transform, Fourier transform, Radon Transform, wavelet transform etc. Transform technique may be chosen based on its advantages, disadvantages and applications. The wavelet transform is a technique which assimilates the time and frequency domains and precisely popular as time-frequency representation of a non stationary signal. In this paper different types of Discrete wavelet transform is applied on an image. Comparative analysis of different wavelets such as Haar, Daubechies and symlet 2 is applied on image and different filters respond are plotted using MATLAB 15.

Keywords: Pixel · Discrete wavelet transform · Image · Filters
Stationary · Reference

1 Introduction

Transformations of signals not only extract useful information from any real signal but also process it as per demanding application. Natural signal in raw form is taken and processed in one form or other depending upon application. The transformed signal after processing can be used further to retrieve useful information. e.g. time domain (raw signal) can be transformed to frequency domain (processed signal) using Fourier transform. Examples of transform techniques are Hilbert transform, Fourier transform, Radon Transform, wavelet transform etc. Transform technique may be chosen based on its advantages, disadvantages and applications.

A time domain signal provides time information and frequency domain signal provides frequency information. If both type of information are required simultaneously, then wavelet transform is a nice choice. A practical signal may be stationary or non stationary. A stationary signal preserve all frequency components for full time slot means frequency components won't change with time whereas in non stationary signal frequency may changes at all points of time. e.g. chirp signal. Fourier transform seems good for stationary signals whereas non stationary signals are better analyzed by

© Springer Nature Singapore Pte Ltd. 2019
A. K. Luhach et al. (Eds.): ICAICR 2018, CCIS 955, pp. 499–507, 2019.
https://doi.org/10.1007/978-981-13-3140-4_45

wavelet transformation. Wavelet transformation finds its application in biomedical fields for ECG, EEG and EMG signals.

The wavelet transform is a technique which assimilates the time and frequency domains and precisely popular as time-frequency representation of a non stationary signal. Although time frequency information can be extracted using short time Fourier transform yet wavelet transform is a better approach as it overcomes fixed resolution problems suffered by using short time Fourier transform. Short term Fourier transform method broke the signal into small chunks, where chunks can be assumed to be stationary.

In wavelet transform the signal in time domain is decomposed by passing it through high pass filter and low pass filter to produce two different versions i.e. low pass (L) version and high pass (H) version. Low pass version can be further decomposed by passing it to again a group of low pass (LL) and high pass (LH) filters. Similarly High pass version can be further decomposed by passing it to again a group of low pass (HL) and high pass (HH) filters. This process can be further continued till a given signal gets decomposed to a pre-defined reference level. Then in depth decomposition generates a group of signals specifying different frequency bands but in total represent a single signal. Then signals corresponding to different bands can be put together and plotted on a three dimensional graph.

Time, frequency and amplitude represents three axis on a three dimensional graph. The scale in three dimensional graphs will be inverse of frequency. The low frequencies components represent high scales and large peak and high frequency components represent low scales and little peak. The term wavelet means a small wave. Wavelet can be continuous or discrete and hence can be classified as continuous wavelets transform or discrete wavelet transform. The discrete wavelet transform (DWT) is a computerized technique to compute fast wavelet transform of a signal. The discrete wavelet transform (DWT) is an optimum solution for computational time overhead. It is easier in operation and implementation.

Croiser, Esteban, and Galand proposed a technique to decompose discrete time signals in 1976. Various techniques were proposed like Subband coding, pyramidal coding. Discrete wavelet transforms can be used for image processing. As resolution of image increases, it requires a lot of disk space. DWT is used to reduce the size of an image without compromising on quality and hence resolution increases.

1.1 Types of Wavelet Transform

Wavelet transform is used to suppress the noise which is out of frequency band of the signal [7]. There are various types of wavelet among which Haar wavelet is the simplest technique [11]. Haar transform is mathematical operation applied on Haar wavelets. Due to its simplicity Haar transform can be taken as reference for all other wavelet transforms. The Haar transform is based on decomposition principle where a discrete signal is broken into two sub signals of each half of original length. Average running subsignal is known as trend and the difference running subsignal is known as fluctuation. Haar transform is simple and low cost and easy to apply. Limitation of Haar wavelet transform technique is its inability in providing compression and noise removal for audio signal processing applications. The Daubechies wavelet is an alternative to Haar wavelet but faces with limitations of its complexity and cost. The other type of wavelet is Symlets which are a modified version of Daubechies wavelets. It increases the symmetry.

2 Discrete Wavelet Transform

In Discrete wavelet transform the signal is decomposed into two levels such as coarse approximation and detail information. DWT have two sets of functions. Scaling functions are performed by low pass filter and wavelet functions are performed by high pass filter. A signal in time domain is decomposed into different frequency bands by passing it into successive high pass and low pass filters. The original signal is passed through a half band high pass filter which is followed by low pass filter [12]. The signal is then down sampled by 2, simply by ignoring every other sample. This constitutes one level of decomposition and this process can be further repeated for both high pass and low pass filter in order to get in depth transformation (Fig. 1).

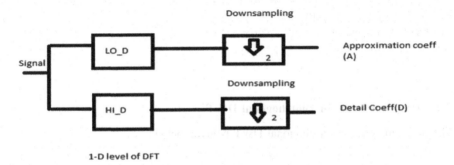

Fig. 1. 1-D level of Discrete wavelet transform

2.1 Algorithm for Different Discrete Wavelet Transform

The following steps are used to provide to apply wavelet transform:

(1) Get the gray scale image of 256 * 256 pixel value.
(2) Apply the MATLAB code for the Discrete wavelet transform (e.g. haar, db1).
(3) Plot stem function for both original and DWT image.
(4) Apply different wavelet transforms (such as orthogonal and bi orthogonal) for the original image such as haar, db1, db2, db10, bi orthogonal and symlets.
(5) Plot the original image for different wavelet transforms.

3 Program Code

3.1 Program Code for DWT

The program code for DWT is given below:

```
x= imread('flower.jpg');
subplot(6,1,1);title('original');
imshow(x);title('original');
sx=size(x);
[LL,LH,HL,HH]=dwt2(x,'haar');
subplot(6,1,2);title('Low filter');
imshow(LL); title('Low filter');
subplot(6,1,3);title('low high');
imshow(LH); title('Low high');
subplot(6,1,4);title('high low');
imshow(HL); title('high low');
subplot(6,1,5);title('high high');
imshow(HH); title('high high');
X=idwt2(LL,LH,HL,HH,'haar',sx);
subplot(6,1,6);title('inverse');
imshow(X);title('inverse');
```

3.2 Program Code for Biorthogonal DWT

The program code for biorthogonal DWT is given below:

```
x= imread('flower.jpg');
subplot(6,1,1);title('original');
stem(x);title('original');
sx=size(x);
[LL,LH,HL,HH]=dwt2(x,'bior1.3');
subplot(6,1,2);title('Low Low filter');
stem(LL); title('Low filter');
subplot(6,1,3);title('low high');
stem(LH); title('Low high');
subplot(6,1,4);title('high low');
stem(HL); title('high low');
subplot(6,1,5);title('high high');
stem(HH); title('high high');
X=idwt2(LL,LH,HL,HH,'bior1.3',sx);
subplot(6,1,6);title('inverse');
stem(X);title('inverse');
xlabel('DWT using Biorthogonal DWT bior1.3')
```

4 Results

The results of original image and DWT image is shown in Fig. 2 using Haar transform. It has shown in the Fig. 2, all the types of filters (Low Low, High Low, High Low and High High filters). The another name of db1 is haar filters. The Haar wavelet is response is discontinuous and looks like a step function. Daubechies (db1) is an alternative name of Haar wavelet [8] (Fig. 3).

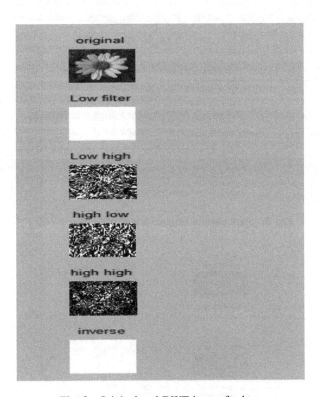

Fig. 2. Original and DWT image for haar

4.1 Results for Biorthogonal (Bior 1.3) Wavelet Transform for Original Image

The different decomposition filters for bior 1.3 wavelet transform has been shown in Fig. 4.

The stem plot for original and DWT image for different decomposition levels for bior 1.3 is shown in Fig. 5.

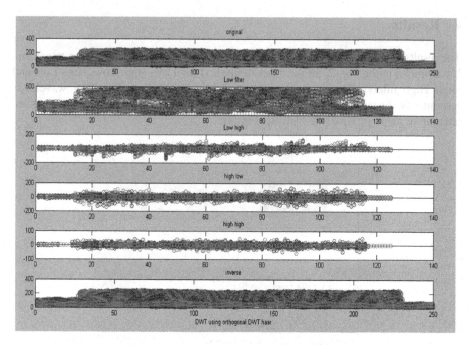

Fig. 3. Stem plot for original and DWT image for haar

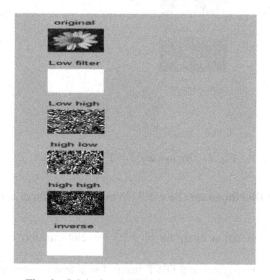

Fig. 4. Original and DWT image for bior 1.3

4.2   Results for Sym2 Wavelet Transform for Original Image

Daubechies wavelets can be further modified to form Symlets wavelet increased and it enhances the symmetry (Fig. 6).

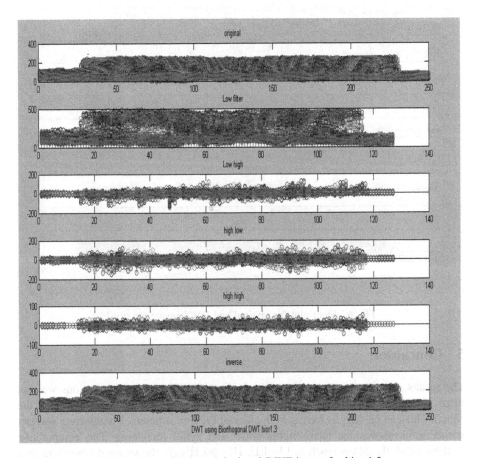

Fig. 5. Stem plot for original and DWT image for bior 1.3

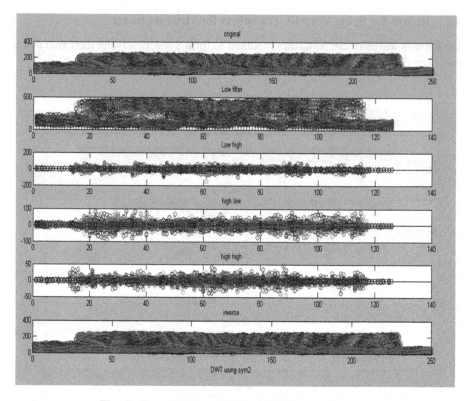

Fig. 6. Stem plot for original and DWT image for sym2

5   Conclusion

The results show the performance of original and DWT image using various wavelet filters. In DWT the zooming is present into both low and high frequency bands of the signal. This can be seen as having both sides of the tree structure. The discrete wavelet transform is shown for haar, biorthogonal and sym2 transform. The comparative analysis of all the filters (such as LL, LH, HL and HH) is shown for different wavelet transforms such as haar, biorthogonal and sysm2. The biorthogonal wavelet is best for decomposing the signal.

References

1. Debnath, L.: Wavelets and Signal Processing. Birkhauser Boston, Boston, U.S.A (2003)
2. Onur, G.: Guleryuz.: iterated denoising for image recovery. In: Data Compression Conference (DCC'02), SnaoBird, Utah. IEEE (2002)
3. Strang, G., Nguyen, T.: Wavelets and Filter Banks. Wellesley-Cambridge Press (1996)
4. Zhang, Q., Zhang, J., Wang, X.: A wavelet-based image edge enhancement algorithm. Comput. Appl. **26**(z1), 49–50 (2006)

5. Wiaux, Y., McEwen, J.D., Vandergheynst, P., Blanc, O.: Exact reconstruction with directional wavelets on the sphere. Mon. Not. R. Astron. Soc. **388**, 770–788 (2008)
6. Tang, J., Peli, E., Acton, S.: Image enhancement using a contrast measure in the compressed domain. IEEE Signal Proc. Lett. **10**(10), 289–292 (2003)
7. Rosca, D.: Haar wavelets on spherical triangulations. In: Dogson, N.A., Floater, M.S., Sabin, M.A. (eds.) Advances in Multiresolution for Geometric Modelling. Springer, Berlin, pp. 407–419(2005)
8. Manhas, P., Soni, M.K.: Performance analysis of DWT-OFDM and FFT-OFDM using various digital modulation techniques and channel coding. Int. J. Comput. Appl. **128**(11), 34–39 (2015) (0975–8887)
9. Lidong, H., Wei, Z., Jun, W., Sun, Z.: Combination of contrast limited adaptive histogram equalisation and discrete wavelet transform for image enhancement. IET Image Proc. **9**(10), 908–915 (2015)
10. Singh, R.P., Dixit M.: Histogram equalization: a strong technique for image enhancement. Int. J. Signal Proc. Image Proc. Pattern Recogn **8**(8), 345–352 (2015)
11. Thakral, S., Manhas, P., Kumar, C.: Virtual reality and m-learning. Int. J. Electron. Eng. (2010)
12. Gu, K., Zhai, G., Lin, W., Liu, M.: The analysis of image contrast: from quality assessment to automatic enhancement. IEEE Trans. Cybern. **46**(1), 284–297 (2016)
13. Antoine, J.-P., Murenzi, R., Vandergheynst, P., Ali, S.T.: Two-Dimensional Wavelets and Their Relatives. Cambridge University Press, Cambridge, UK (2004)
14. Thiruvengadam, S.J., Chinnadurai, P., Kumar, M.T., Abhaikumar, V.: Signal detection algorithm using discrete wavelet transform and radon transform. IETE J. Res. (2004)
15. Heil, C., Walnut, D.F. (eds.): Fundamental Papers in Wavelet Theory. Princeton University Press, Princeton, NJ (2006)
16. Tan, Y.: A wavelet thresholding image enhancement method based on edge detection. Inf. Dev. Econ. **17**(18), 206–208 (2007)

Hybrid Min-Median-Max Filter for Removal of Impulse Noise from Color Images

Prity Kumari$^{(\boxtimes)}$, Deepti Kakkar, and Neetu Sood

Dr. B R Ambedkar National Institute of Technology, Jalandhar, Punjab, India
prity030991@gmail.com, {kakkard, soodn}@nitj.ac.in

Abstract. In this paper, an improved median based hybrid Min-Median-Max filter (M3F) has been proposed, to restore original image that is corrupted by impulse noise. The identification of the contaminated pixels is performed by local extrema intensity, i.e. using Min-Max noise detector. If any pixel is found corrupted, it will be changed by the resultant value of M3F algorithm, and uncorrupted pixels remain unchanged. Different color images have been considered to test the proposed method and better results have been found in terms of quantitative measures and visual perception. The presented algorithm can effectively reconstruct noise-free image from image which is corrupted with 70% noise level and also maintains the edges. Even up to 90% noisy image can be identified using proposed method. Experimental observations indicates that the proposed method removes high density impulse noise efficiently at high noise level and also keeps the originality of pixel's value.

Keywords: Impulse noise · Median filter · Noise removal · PSNR

1 Introduction

Different kinds of noises often deteriorate the quality of images, and also cause loss of some important information [1]. Noises can be caused in an image when it is sent from one place to other via electronics devices. Noise is also caused by sensor heat while capturing an image. Nowadays, impulse noise is of high interest of research. Any abrupt change in the image pixel value can cause impulse noise. The existence of impulse noise may corrupt important details of the images. Therefore, to suppress the impulse noise in images is a challenging issue. Salt-and-Pepper Noise is another name for impulse noise. It appears with equal probability in any image and are distributed over the complete image. The key objective of noise removal techniques is to eliminate noises from the image by keeping its other important details preserved.

Several linear as well as nonlinear filtering approach have been developed which deal with the impulse noise [2]. Primarily, linear filters were used to suppress impulse noise. The linear filters operate well in case of removing impulse noise of low noise density. For high noise density, linear filtering approach tend to obscure the images and fail to restore the edges accurately. The nonlinear filtering techniques provide better performance and have better preservation capability than linear filtering techniques in case of impulse noise. In this paper, nonlinear filtering methods have been studied and proposed for impulse noise removal. The aim of these non-linear techniques is

© Springer Nature Singapore Pte Ltd. 2019
A. K. Luhach et al. (Eds.): ICAICR 2018, CCIS 955, pp. 508–518, 2019.
https://doi.org/10.1007/978-981-13-3140-4_46

suppression of noise while keeping the image information preserved and maintaining the edges simultaneously.

Standard median filter (MF) [3] is the most commonly known technique for removal of impulse noise. The MF is a nonlinear order-statistic filter in which every pixel's value in reconstructed image is equal to the median of its nearest neighbors existing in the input image. A square, sliding window is utilized to determine the size of neighborhood. MF has good denoising capability & computational efficiency, but fails to preserve image fine details at high noise level. The Weighted Median Filter (WMF) [4] involves similar operation as that for MF except that WMF has weight corresponding to each of its element. These weights correspond to a more accurate calculation of median value. However, preservation of image details highly depends on the weight coefficients and unfortunately; it is difficult to find suitable weight coefficients for this filter in practical cases.

Conventional median filters do not check for the processing pixel whether it is noisy or noise free and apply the filtering operation to each and every pixel. Thus, the image information imparted from the noise free pixels is also filtered resulting in obscuring the whole image and deteriorating the picture quality. To solve this situation, the median filters approach are being accomplished in two stage way. Firstly, in order to take decision about pixels whether it is corrupted or uncorrupted pixel, an impulse noise detector is used. Secondly, corrupted pixel is modified and uncorrupted pixels remain unaltered. Some two-stage filtering approach include: Adaptive Center Weighted Median Filters [5], Adaptive Median Filters (AMF) [6] and Switching Median Filters (SMF) [7, 8]. These two-stage approaches have achieved better results than single-stage approach at low noise levels. Many fuzzy MFs [9–12] have been presented for removal of random valued impulse noise. In case of fuzzy based filters, fuzzy logics are used to identify and estimate the corrupted pixels. The fuzzy filters can keep the details preserved very well while removing low-noise-level impulse noises. However, fuzzy filters don't provide satisfying output when images are highly corrupted. A combination of mean and median filtering techniques can also be used to eliminate impulse noise [13]. Another method to remove high noise level impulse noise is to use morphological operations [14].

The above discussed techniques have efficient noise reduction. However, most of the techniques have difficulties in overcoming impulse noise especially at high noise level. This paper aims to restore original image that is highly contaminated with impulse noise. In this paper, firstly the corrupted pixel has been identified based on local maximum & minimum intensity in the grayscale range and then a median based hybrid M3F algorithm has been utilized for removal of impulse noise. Proposed algorithm has been applied to the noisy R, G, and B channels of contaminated RGB color image and has been recovered efficiently.

The proposed method has been discussed in Sect. 2. In Sect. 3 the Simulation results of proposed method with different RGB color images have been presented, and the conclusions are finally discussed in Sect. 4.

2 Proposed Method

Several MF-based filters exist for removal of impulse noise from contaminated images. Some of them utilize an individual impulse noise detector and a noise removal process. Some uses detection and removal in single stage. The proposed method uses a single algorithm for noise detection and removal process. It can also be referred as automatic noise detection and removal technique. In this paper, a variable size square window has been used to scan each pixel in the image. The smallest size taken is 3 × 3 and it is increased as per requirement. In this paper, the processing pixel is first identified whether it is corrupted pixel or uncorrupted pixel. The pixels having the either minimum value, i.e. '0' or the maximum value, i.e. '255' in the range have been identified as noisy pixels. Once, the pixel is found as corrupted pixel, its value is modified by the median value calculated within selected window, if this calculated median value ranges between the minimum and the maximum values. If the calculated median value is also a noisy pixel value, then the median value is re-calculated by incrementing the window size by one and modify that noisy pixel by the re-calculated median value, and so on. If any pixel is found as uncorrupted pixel, its value remains unchanged.

An overview of proposed methodology is shown below in Fig. 1 and the description of proposed algorithm is given in Sect. 2.1.

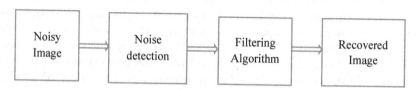

Fig. 1. Proposed methodology

2.1   Algorithm Description

Step 1: Take Noisy Image (I_noise)
Step 2: Calculate the Weight map
Step 3: Create 3×3 Mask (window) using meshgrid
Step 4: Calculate the P_{min}, P_{median} & P_{max} within selected window as:
$\qquad P_{min} = \min (I\_noise\,(POS))$
$\qquad P_{median} = \mathrm{median}\,(I\_noise\,(POS))$
$\qquad P_{max} = \max (I\_noise\,(POS))$
Step 5: for each pixel $P(i, j)$
$\qquad$ if $(P_{min} < P_{median}$ && $P_{median} < P_{max})$
$\qquad\qquad$ if $(I\_noise(i, j) > P_{min}$ && $I\_noise(i, j) < P_{max})$
$\qquad\qquad\qquad R\_Image(i, j) = I\_noise(i, j)$
$\qquad\qquad$ else
$\qquad\qquad\qquad R\_Image(i, j) = P_{median}$
$\qquad\qquad$ end
else
$\qquad$ % Increase the size of window by one and go back to *Step 4.*
$\qquad R\_Image(i, j) = P_{median}$
$\qquad$ end
end

Where,

POS is used to determine the position of selected window in the noisy image
P_{min}, P_{max} & P_{median} are the minimum, maximum and the calculated median values within selected window
R_Image is the output recovered image

The flow diagram of proposed methodology is demonstrated in Fig. 2 and the detailed explanation of its different cases is illustrated through examples in Sect. 2.2.

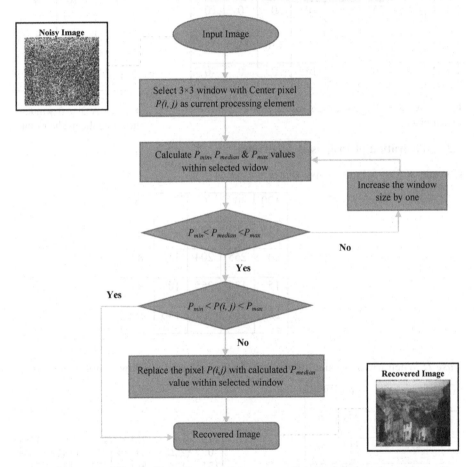

Fig. 2. Flow diagram of the proposed methodology

An 8 × 8 noisy image matrix indicating the corrupted and un-corrupted pixels is shown in Fig. 3. The shaded portion represents the noisy pixels and remaining all are uncorrupted pixels. A 3 × 3 window has been selected. For this 3 × 3 selected window the median value is '136', considering all elements present within this window. For median filtering the central processing pixel i.e. '0' is replaced by this median value, shown in Fig. 4.

0	139	0	0	255	139	0	255
141	0	255	142	0	139	136	255
255	0	0	139	0	126	138	0
0	139	255	0	136	0	255	0
137	137	138	141	0	255	136	0
138	255	255	255	0	0	0	0
137	0	136	0	137	136	137	139
142	141	0	255	142	0	0	0

Fig. 3. An 8 × 8 noisy image matrix denoting the corrupted pixel

0	139	0
255	136	136
138	141	0

Fig. 4. A 3 × 3 window denoting the median value

2.2   Illustration of Proposed Algorithm

Consider a 5 × 5 Input Noisy Image matrix as

$$I\_{Noise} =$$

120	0	0	0	255
115	0	178	255	0
0	255	204	110	87
151	134	255	109	96
255	164	201	146	255

Case I: When Median value of elements within selected window is noise-free pixel

120	0	0	0	255
115	0	178	255	0
0	255	204	110	87
151	134	255	109	96
255	164	201	146	255

$$\Rightarrow \quad \begin{bmatrix} 115 & 0 & 178 \\ 0 & (255) & 204 \\ 151 & 134 & 255 \end{bmatrix} \Leftrightarrow \begin{bmatrix} 115 & 0 & 178 \\ 0 & (151) & 204 \\ 151 & 134 & 255 \end{bmatrix}$$

1-D Array after sorting all elements in increasing order = [0 0 115 134 151 178 204 255 255]

$P_{min} = 0$

$P_{median} = 151$

$P_{max} = 255$

Since Median value lies between the Minimum & the Maximum value and '255' is a noisy pixel, replace it by P_{median}, i.e. '151'.

Case II: When Median value of elements within selected window is again a noisy pixel.

120	0	0	0	255
115	0	178	255	0
0	255	204	110	87
151	134	255	109	96
255	164	201	146	255

$$\Longrightarrow \quad \begin{bmatrix} 0 & (0) & 0 \\ 0 & 178 & 255 \end{bmatrix}$$

1-D Array after sorting all elements in increasing order = [0 0 0 0 178 255]

$P_{min} = 0$

$P_{median} = 0$

$P_{max} = 255$

Since P_{median} is equal to P_{min}, and it is a noisy pixel, increase the window size by one.

120	0	0	0	255
115	0	178	255	0
0	255	204	110	87
151	134	255	109	96
255	164	201	146	255

$$\Longrightarrow \begin{bmatrix} 120 & 0 & (0) & 0 & 255 \\ 115 & 0 & 178 & 255 & 0 \\ 0 & 255 & 204 & 110 & 87 \end{bmatrix} \Leftrightarrow \begin{bmatrix} 120 & 0 & (110) & 0 & 255 \\ 115 & 0 & 178 & 255 & 0 \\ 0 & 255 & 204 & 110 & 87 \end{bmatrix}$$

1-D Array after sorting all elements in increasing order = [0 0 0 0 0 0 87 110 115 120 178 204 255 255 255]

Min = 0;

Median = 110;

Max = 255

Since Median value lies between the Minimum & the Maximum value and '0' is a noisy pixel, replace it by P_{median}, i.e. '110'.

After checking every pixels of the input corrupted image and modifying the value of corrupted pixels, a noise free recovered image matrix has been obtained as:

$R\_Image =$

120	58	110	89	128
115	115	178	110	99
125	151	204	110	87
151	134	164	109	96
158	164	201	146	128

3   Simulation Results

In this paper, different RGB color images (Barbra, Pills, Goldhil, Girl, Sailboat and Baboon [15]) of size 256×256 have been taken and each image has been considered as corrupted image with noise level ranging from 10% to 90%. The presented algorithm has been performed using *MATLAB R2015a* and on a desktop machine with operating system Window 8. The presented method has been tested with many standard color test images corrupted by impulse noise for different noise level. The visual quality results obtained for restored images has been presented in Fig. 5 and the quantitative evaluation is computed by Peak Signal to Noise Ratio (PSNR) and is given in Table 1.

The PSNR computation can be calculated by formula as follow:

$$PSNR(indB) = 10 * \log_{10} 10 \left(\frac{255 * 255}{MSE} \right)$$

Where, MSE for color image is defined as:

$$MSE = \frac{1}{3 * mn} \sum_{i=0}^{m-1} \sum_{j=0}^{n-1} \sum_{k=1}^{3} \left[Y(i,j) - \hat{Y}(i,j) \right]^2$$

Where, $Y(i, j)$ = Original Noise-free Image

$\hat{Y}(i, j)$ = Recovered Image, and

$m \times n$ = Dimension of Image

PSNR generally defines the measurement of peak error between original input image and recovered output image and is most commonly used for measuring the quality of restoration. The higher PSNR values represent the higher quality of reconstruction.

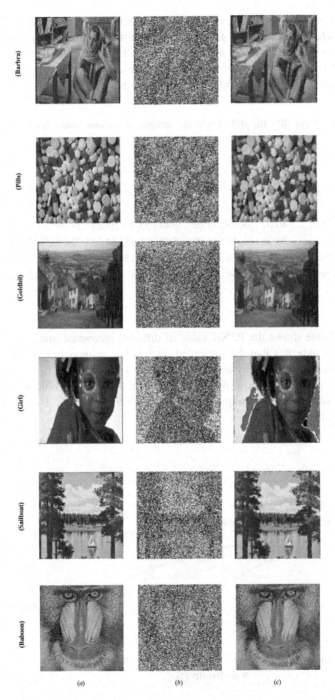

Fig. 5. Simulation results for different images using proposed method. (a) Original 256 × 256 color image. (b) Image with 70% noise level. (c) Restored image

Above figure shows the visual simulation results for different color images using proposed technique. From this figure it can be observed that the original image has been restored very well without any loss in image details and quality of restored image is well improved. For the restored images using proposed method higher value of PSNR has been obtained, providing better image quality.

Table 1. PSNR (in dB) for different color images at various noise levels using proposed technique

Noise level (%)	10	20	30	40	50	60	70	80	90
Barbra	39.76	38.36	37.09	35.81	34.65	33.75	32.80	31.79	30.52
Pills	42.07	39.57	37.74	36.32	34.99	33.92	32.88	31.74	30.28
Goldhill	40.07	38.83	37.66	36.44	35.30	34.31	33.29	32.20	31.00
Girl	36.78	36.44	35.99	35.45	34.88	34.35	33.59	32.93	31.78
Sailboat	40.07	38.74	37.35	36.23	35.13	34.20	33.28	32.32	31.04
Baboon	36.62	35.84	34.81	33.84	32.87	32.00	31.19	30.38	29.53

Above Table shows the PSNR value of different recovered images with proposed method. This indicates that the presented method has achieved high values of PSNR providing better image quality as increased PSNR value provides better image quality.

Figure 6 and Fig. 7 show the comparison of proposed technique with previous existing noise removal techniques in terms of PSNR for color Barbra and Baboon image respectively.

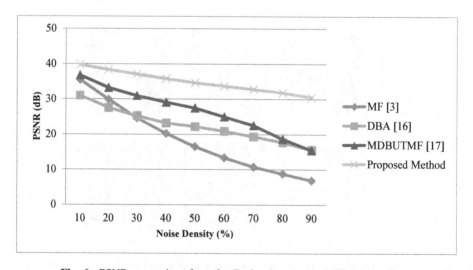

Fig. 6. PSNR comparison for color Barbra image using different methods

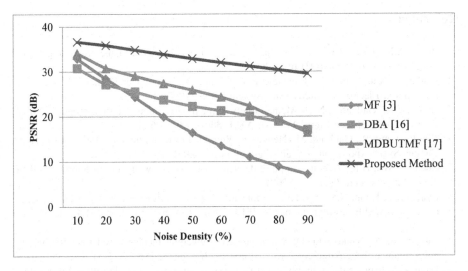

Fig. 7. PSNR comparison for color Baboon image using different methods

Above figures show the PSNR values of Barbra & Baboon images with proposed method and also with some existing methods. From this figure it is clear that the proposed method has achieved greater PSNR value than existing methods at low noise level as well as at high noise level, thus provides better image quality.

4 Conclusion

In this paper a hybrid M3F algorithm has been presented to removes high density impulse noise from corrupted image and restores the original image better than MF, SMF, AMF, and other slandered median filters. The presented algorithm utilizes a variable window size. If any pixel is found uncorrupted, it is kept unchanged. If any pixel is found corrupted, it is changed by the median value calculated for the selected window. Six different images have been tested using proposed method by varying the noise level from 10% to 90%. From Fig. 5, it can be seen that, the above images which are corrupted with 70% noise level have been recovered well using proposed algorithm and visual quality of restored image is much better at high noise level. The quantitative performance of the presented method has been evaluated and compared with other existing impulse noise removal techniques in terms of PSNR. The comparison concludes that the presented method has obtained better PSNR values for recovered images than other existing methods. The presented method can identify the image corrupted with noise level up to 90% and can be applied to grayscale images as well.

References

1. Boyat, A.K., Joshi, B.K.: A review paper: noise models in digital image processing. Signal Image Process. Int. J. (SIPIJ) **6**(2) (2015)
2. Astola, J., Kuosmanen, P.: Fundamentals of Linear and Nonlinear Digital Filtering. CRC Press Book, Electronics Engineering System Series (1997)
3. Nodes, T.A., Gallagher, N.C.: Median filters: some modifications and their properties. IEEE Trans. Acoust. Speech Signal Process. **ASSP-30**(5), 739–746 (1982)
4. Yin, L., Yang, R., Gabbouj, M., Neuvo, Y.: Weighted median filters: a tutorial. IEEE Trans. Circuits Syst. Expo. Analog Digit. Signal Process. **43**(3), 157–192 (1996)
5. Chen, T., Wu, H.R.: Adaptive impulse detection using center-weighted median filters. IEEE Signal Process. Lett. **8**(1), 1–3 (2001)
6. Ibrahim, H., Kong, N.S., Ng, T.F.: Simple adaptive median filter for the removal of impulse noise from highly corrupted images. IEEE Trans. Consum. Electron. **54**(4), 1920–1927 (2008)
7. Fabijańska, A., Sankowski, D.: Noise adaptive switching median-based filter for impulse noise removal from extremely corrupted images. IET Image Process. **5**(5), 472–480 (2011)
8. Duan, F., Zhang, Y.J.: A highly effective impulse noise detection algorithm for switching median filters. IEEE Signal Process. Lett. **17**(7), 647–650 (2010)
9. Yuksel, M.E., Besdok, E.A.: simple neuro-fuzzy impulse detector for efficient blur reduction of impulse noise removal operators for digital images. IEEE Trans. Fuzzy Syst. **12**(6), 854–865 (2004)
10. Wu, C.B., Liu, B.D., Yang, J.F.: A fuzzy-based impulse noise detection and cancellation for real-time processing in video receivers. IEEE Trans. Instrum. Meas. **52**(3), 780–784 (2003)
11. Rahman, T., Uddin, M.S.: Removal of high density impulse noise from color images using an adaptive fuzzy filter. In: IEEE International Conference on Electrical Engineering and Information & Communication Technology (ICEEICT), pp. 1–5 (2014)
12. Chang, J.Y., Liu, P.C.: A fuzzy weighted mean aggregation algorithm for color image impulse noise removal. In: IEEE International Conference on Automation Science and Engineering (CASE), pp. 1268–1273 (2015)
13. Roy, A., Singha, J., Manam, L., Laskar, R.H.: Combination of adaptive vector median filter and weighted mean filter for removal of high-density impulse noise from color images. IET Image Process. **11**(6), 352–361 (2017)
14. Ze-Feng, D., Zhou-Ping, Y., You-Lun, X.: High probability impulse noise-removing algorithm based on mathematical morphology. IEEE Signal Process. Lett. **14**(1), 31–34 (2007)
15. Database are available at: http://homepages.cae.wisc.edu/∼ece533/images/
16. Srinivasan, K.S., Ebenezer, D.: A new fast and efficient decision based algorithm for removal of high-density impulse noises. IEEE Signal Process. Lett. **14**(3), 189–192 (2007)
17. Esakkirajan, S., Veerakumar, T., Subramanyam, A.N., PremChand, C.H.: Removal of high density salt and pepper noise through modified decision based unsymmetrical trimmed median filter. IEEE Signal Process. Lett. **18**(5), 287–290 (2011)

Double Image Encryption Based on 2D Discrete Fractional Fourier Transform and Piecewise Nonlinear Chaotic Map

Gurpreet kaur[1]([⊠]), Rekha Agarwal[2], and Vinod Patidar[3]

[1] USICT, Guru Gobind Singh Indraprastha University,
Dwarka, New Delhi 110078, India
gurpreet.preeti.82@gmail.com
[2] Department of ECE, Amity School of Engineering and Technology,
New Delhi 110061, India
[3] Department of Physics, Sir Padampat Singhania University,
Bhatewar, Udaipur 313 601, Rajasthan, India

Abstract. Secure transmission of sensitive data over open networks is a challenge in the present scenario of digital signal transmissions. Especially in 2D image signals, the adjacent pixel correlation is high which makes it a challenge to encrypt or hide the information from being fraudulently interpreted. Optical signal processing is preferred for image encryption owing to its high speed parallel processing. Fractional transforms are used for the digital implementation of the optical processing due to the fact that fractional orders enable to analyze a time variant signal where each fractional order correspond to an arbitrary angle of rotation. In this work, we apply a fractional Fourier transform for double image encryption, as fractional orders provide randomness and serve as secret key. The complex outcome of transform becomes a limitation due to requirement of double memory for storage and transmission besides computational complexity. To overcome this issue, a reality preserving scheme is applied to obtain real output from transform. A piecewise nonlinear chaotic map is used to introduce chaotic blending in the double image data. The larger key space of PWNCA based blending offers yet another security layer to the optical transform based encryption. The simulation results give testimony to the acquired randomness in the encrypted data. The proposed scheme is quite sensitive to keys and is robust against potential attacks.

Keywords: Discrete fractional fourier transform · Reality preserving
Piecewise nonlinear chaotic map

1 Introduction

Dissemination of information across the internet and storage of sensitive data on open networks creates an environment where it becomes easier for intruders to disclose the confidential information. The robustness and reliability of information transmission can be achieved by suitable encryption method. Particularly for multimedia messages that includes 2D images have highly correlated adjacent pixel values and therefore securing

© Springer Nature Singapore Pte Ltd. 2019
A. K. Luhach et al. (Eds.): ICAICR 2018, CCIS 955, pp. 519–530, 2019.
https://doi.org/10.1007/978-981-13-3140-4_47

these images with hiding or encryption technique is a challenge. LCT is a family of transforms that generalizes many classical transforms like Fourier, Laplace, Fresnel with four parameters and one constraint. In *optical transforms*, a paraxial optical system that is implemented entirely with thin lenses and propagation through free space are Quadratic Phase systems (QPS). Thus the effect of any QPS on an input wave field can be described using LCT. Optical information technologies offer high speed parallel processing and find applications in signal and image analysis for them to be converted to different domains by mathematical transforms. On the other hand Chaos theory owing to its inherent properties like randomness, sensitivity and ergodicity serve as an excellent technique for cryptographical applications. We propose to use this class of integral transforms along with the Chaos theory to implement a robust and efficient double image encryption scheme.

The fractional transforms are the generalization of full transforms. The beauty of these fractional transforms lies in the fact that they can be used to analyze the time variant signals which otherwise is not possible with full transform orders as they can only analyze the time invariant signals. Fractional order corresponds to the value with range [0, 1]. The fractional order can be used as a secret key for security purpose. Also it is likely to mention that different fractional orders correspond to the different angle of rotation in transform domain. This provides a degree of freedom to the encrypted data.

Namias in [1] first introduced the concept of fractional Fourier transform. The applicability of fractional Fourier for optical implementation is described by Ozakatas in [2]. His work describe various mathematical analyses for realization of fractional transform besides which it described the digital implementation methods for the same where signals with time-bandwidth product 'N' has their fractional transforms in O (NlogN) time. Almeida [3] explained main properties of the FRFT, its interpretation as rotation in time-frequency planes and also its relation with several time-frequency representations that support the interpretation as rotation like Wigner distribution, short term FT and spectrogram. Later Pei and Hsue [4, 5] in their series of work on FRFT generalized the continuous FRFT to discrete FRFT and derived Eigen values and Eigen vector decomposition for generating a fractional transform matrix coefficients. Fractional transforms although give randomness to the image signals for encryption purpose but lack on the desired key space thus requires some means to increase the key space by combining with other confusion/diffusion strategies. Hennely and Sheridan in [6] proposed a method to eliminate the random phase keys to be known at receiver and to align the keys while decrypting by jigsaw algorithm where image is encrypted by juxtaposition of sections of image in FrFT domain. During the past decade there is enormous development in the combined approach towards attaining image encryption with optical transform based confusion and chaos based diffusion methods. An optical transform is implemented for creating confusion in the pixel values (substitution) and a chaos based diffusion for spreading the pixel values (permutation). The DRPE scheme of encryption was first introduced Refreiger and Javidi [7] where a random phase multiplied in input and in Fourier plane serves as key for encryption. Unnikrishnan in [8] proposed to use DRPE based scheme used with fractional Fourier transform to encrypt image into a white noise. Using a complete random phase as secret key and transmitting it over the insecure channel can be a risk. Using a chaos based random phase generation is much beneficial as it requires only parameters of the chaotic map to be used as private key. Singh in [9] proposed multiple canonical transforms and multiple chaotic maps for multiple image encryption. Zhou in [10] used HSI (Hue, saturation and Intensity)components for image encrypting such that S component is fractional Fourier transformed by random phase, I-component is transformed by DRPE based on FrFT using H-component, making it a single channel image along with a chaos based scrambling. Shan in [11] proposed double image encryption by encoding two images into amplitude and phase by initially scrambling one image by a chaotic map and using it as a phase image to form a single image for transmission. Zhang in [12] proposed double image encryption with Chirikov standard map and chaos based fractional random transform (CBFrRT) which is said to exhibit the advantage of both chaos system and optical transform. Bhatnagar in [13] proposed to encrypt a biometric image by using dual parameter FrFT along with NLCM (non linear chaotic map) based random phase generator. Ran in [14] proposed a novel transform which is neither periodic, nor can be expressed as expansion of two 1D transforms in spatial domain or in Wigner space-frequency domain.

All fractional integral transforms including the proposed DFrFT (discrete fractional Fourier transform) generate complex coefficients in transform domain. Although a chaos based random phase generation eliminates the transmission of whole random phase matrix over insecure channel but still complex outcome is a limitation in terms of memory requirement and complex computation. Venturini and Duhamel in [15] proposed a reality preserving alternative to the complex fractional sine and cosine transforms. This scheme can be applied to other fractional transforms as well. Lang in [16] proposed a multiple parameter discrete fractional Fourier transform (MPDFrFT) and logistic function along with reality preserving scheme. The algorithm thus takes advantage of both decentralization of the chaos based pixel scrambling technique and multiple parameter feature of the MPDFrft spectrum. Recently Mishra in [17] proposed a reality preserving FrFT based image encryption with Arnold cat map based scrambling, cyclic shift in horizontal and vertical direction and reality preserving FrFT for image encryption.

This paper is divided into 5 sections. Section 1 is the introduction part and includes literature part. Next section describes the principle of DFrFT, reality preserving algorithm and chaotic mapping used in proposed scheme. Section 3 describes proposed encryption/decryption procedure. Section 4 presents the results and analysis. Finally paper is concluded in Sect. 5.

2 Preliminaries

2.1 Fractional Fourier Transform

Fractional integral transforms are a class of Linear Canonical Transforms and find applications in the field of quantum mechanics, optics and signal processing. During the discovery of Calculus, Gottfried Willhelm Leibniz introduced the symbolic method for nth derivative, where 'n' is a non negative number as $\frac{d^n y}{dx^n} = D^n y$ and L'Hospital then asked about the possibility of 'n' being fractional. In true sense that was when the fractional order integral transforms were initially discovered. Any integral transform is useful if it enables to convert a complicated problem to a simpler one. For instance a Fourier transform is used to convert a signal in time domain to its frequency domain to make its spectral analysis easier. Similarly in optical systems, a set up comprising of lens, SLMs (Spatial light modulators), CCD (Charged couple devices) are used to analyze the mathematical transforms. FrFT kernel for a 1D function in continuous domain is defined as:

$$\mathcal{F}_\alpha(u,v) = \left(\frac{1-jcot\alpha}{2\pi}\right)^{1/2} \exp(j\frac{v^2+u^2}{2}cot\alpha - ju\ vcsc\alpha) \tag{1}$$

Therefore in discrete domain, for N x N DFT matrix of F is given by:

$$|F|_{a,b} = \frac{1}{N}e^{-j\left(\frac{2\pi}{N}\right)a.b}; \quad 0 \leq a,b \leq N-1 \tag{2}$$

By eigen decomposition, this can be further expressed as:

$$F = \sum_{l=0}^{N-1} \lambda_l e_l e_l^T \tag{3}$$

where T: Transpose operation, $e_k : e_0, e_1, e_2, \ldots \ldots e_{N-1}$ are orthonormal eigen vector basis, $\lambda_k = \lambda_0, \lambda_1, \lambda_2, \ldots \ldots \lambda_{N-1}$ are eigen values of DFT. Here F has four distinct values $\{1, -j, -1, j\}$. Thus DFT of a signal is combination of 4 parts: original signal, its DFT, a circular flipped version of signal and a circular flipped version of its DFT. Therefore DFrFT of a signal is considered as:

In discrete domain for 1D signal

$$F^\alpha = e_l . \lambda_l^\alpha . e_l^T$$
$$\alpha : \text{fractional order} \tag{4}$$

In a 2D image signal this can be represented as

$$F^{(\alpha_1,\alpha_2)} = e_l . \lambda_l^{(\alpha_1,\alpha_2)} . e_l^T$$
$$\alpha_1, \alpha_2 : \text{are the fractional orders in each dimension} \tag{5}$$

2.2   Reality Preserving Fractional Transform

The fractional transforms when applied to a signal gives the transform coefficients in complex domain. This is a limitation in terms of storage and transmission of these transformed images. The memory requirement is increased twice and also the computation complexity increases. In order to overcome this issue Venturini and Duhamel in [15] proposed a reality preserving algorithm. We have applied it to DFrFT obtained from Eq. (5) to get the transform outcome in real domain.

The procedure is as follows:

(1) For a 1-dimensional DFrFT of length, M. Let $F_{a,\frac{M}{2}}$ be a complex valued fractional Fourier transform matrix with size $\frac{M}{2}, M :$ even The real input signal, $y = \{y_0, y_1, y_2, \ldots \ldots \ldots y_{M-2}, y_{M-1}\}^t$ from which a permutation matrix is constructed as, $y' = \{y'_0, y'_1, y'_2, \ldots \ldots \ldots y_{M-2}' y_{M-1}'\}^t : y' = Py$

(2) The complex vector built from y as

$$\hat{y} = \left\{ y'_0 + jy_{\frac{M}{2}}' \middle| y_1' + y_{\frac{M}{2}+1}' \middle| \ldots \ldots y_{\frac{M}{2}-1}' + jy_2' \middle| y_{\frac{M}{2}-1}' + jy_{M-1}' \right\}^t$$

Further a transform output is obtained from this complex vector such that, $\hat{z} = FrF^a(\hat{y})$

(3) The Reality preserving transform is obtained as $z' = \{(Re\ \hat{z}), (Im\ \hat{z})\}; z = P^{-1}z'^t;$ Thus $z = P^{-1}RPFrFT_aPy$ and is obtained from $F_{a,M/2} + jF_{a,M/2}$ as:

$$RPFrFT_a = \begin{bmatrix} Re(F_a) & -Im(F_a) \\ Im(F_a) & Re(F_a) \end{bmatrix} \tag{6}$$

The basic properties like orthogonality,Inversability, Commutativity and periodicity of a transform are however maintained in the Reality preserving fractional Fourier transform thus obtained.

2.3 Chaotic Mapping with PWNCA

Chaos theory plays a major role in the field of electrical engineering for communication, PRNG generator and for information security. There are three significant characteristics of the chaotic maps that make them highly suitable for data encryption specially in images where classical methods of encryption does not work due to highly correlated adjacent pixel values in the image. These inherent characteristics are sensitivity to initial parameters, randomness and ergodicity. A chaotic map can be 1D or multi dimensional. The complexity and randomness increases with the dimensions but at the cost of difficulty in hardware implementation and complexity in designing. On the other hand 1D chaotic map are simple and relatively easier in hardware implementation but then these 1D maps are weak and are vulnerable to certain attacks. PWLCM is a piecewise linear chaotic map with uniform invariant density function and is considered to be much better than other 1D chaotic maps in terms of its LE(Lyapunov Exponent) which is positive for the entire range of the control parameter [18]. However the small key space and dynamical degradation due to discretization of PWLCM is still an issue [19] which can be further resolved by using a PWNCA (Piecewise non linear chaotic map) [20].

A PWNCA can be mathematically defined as:

$$\psi(\zeta, \vartheta) = \frac{\vartheta^2 \Gamma(\zeta)}{1 + (\vartheta^2 - 1)\Gamma(\zeta)} \tag{7}$$

$\Gamma(\zeta)$: is a piece wise linear chaotic map defined as:

$$\Gamma(\zeta) = \begin{cases} \frac{\zeta}{p}, & 0 \le \zeta \ge p \\ \frac{\zeta - p}{1 - p}, & p \le \zeta \ge 1 \end{cases}; p \in [0, 1] \tag{8}$$

The measure of a chaotic behavior of the map is generally done by calculating its LLE(Largest Lyapunov Exponent) which should be positive for the chaotic region. LE is the average of log of the differential of the function and is given by: $\lambda = 1/Nlog(\sum_{i=1}^{N} \Gamma'(\zeta))$. However sometimes its calculation is a trivial task so another measure known as its invariant measure can be used. The invariant measure associated with PWNCA is given by

$$\mu(\zeta, \vartheta, p) = \frac{1 - \vartheta}{\ln\left(\frac{1-p}{\vartheta-p}\right)} \frac{1}{\vartheta - p + (1 - \vartheta)\zeta}, \zeta > p \tag{9}$$

The Kolmogorov Sinai entropy (KS-entropy) which is equivalent to LE measure is based on the invariant measure given by Eq. (9) and is defined as:

$$H_{ks} = \frac{1 - \vartheta}{\ln\left(\frac{1-p}{\vartheta-p\vartheta}\right)} \left[\ln(\vartheta p) \ln\left(\frac{\vartheta(1 - p)}{\vartheta - p}\right) - 2\ln(\vartheta p) \ln(1 - p) + \right.$$

$$2ln.p.\ln\left(\frac{\vartheta - p}{\vartheta}\right) - 2lg_2 + 2lg_2\left(\frac{p}{\vartheta}\right) + \ln \vartheta(1 - p) \ln\left(\frac{\vartheta - p}{\vartheta(1 - p)}\right) - \tag{10}$$

$$\left. \left(\ln(1 - p)\right)^2 + (\ln \vartheta(1 - p))^2\right]$$

Thus a PWNCA can be expressed using Eqs. (8) and (7) as:

$$\psi(\zeta_2, \vartheta, p) = \begin{cases} \frac{\vartheta^2 \left(\frac{\zeta_2}{p}\right)}{1 + (\vartheta^2 - 1)\frac{(\zeta_2)}{(p)}}, & 0 \le \zeta_2 \le p \\ \frac{\vartheta^2 \left(\frac{\zeta_2-p}{1-p}\right)}{1 + (\vartheta^2 - 1)\frac{(\zeta_2-p)}{(1-p)}}, & p \le \zeta_2 \le 1 \end{cases} \tag{11}$$

$$\text{with} \quad p = \begin{cases} \zeta_1, & 0 < \zeta_1 \le 1 \\ \frac{1}{\zeta_1}, & \zeta_1 > 1 \end{cases}$$

Here ζ_1 is a positive real number which is used to determine the probability parameter $p \in [0, 1]$ of Eq. (11).

3 Proposed Scheme for Coverting Images

The entire process of encryption and decryption requires a set of 5 keys that comprises of the two initial conditions for PWLCM and PWNCA, two control parameters and number of iterations to be discarded for further enhancing the security of the first level which is basically a scrambling process. After scrambling the two images in spatial domain, next step is to obtain the optical transform with yet another set of keys. This set of keys are the fractional transform orders of RPFrFT. The transform coefficients obtained are in collective time–frequency domain. Thus the entire scheme has a total of 7 keys for gray scale images. However if the images are in RGB format then the total keys will be 21 as a separate set of 7 keys will be used for each color channel. The encryption process is shown in Fig. 1. Initially two plain images are concatenated into a single image and then blended with a piecewise non linear chaotic map (PWNCA) which is iterated through another chaotic map, that is piecewise linear(PWLCM) in spatial domain. This is to increase the key space which otherwise is small for a 1D chaotic map. After the combined image is scrambled/permuted with PWNCA. The scrambled image in spatial (real) domain is then subjected to an optical transform with RPFrFT that requires another set of keys (α, β) for obtaining a 2D transform with 1D in x-direction using fractional order $'\alpha'$ and another 1D transform in y-direction with parameter $'\beta'$ to get the final encrypted image that can be optically transmitted over insecure channel.

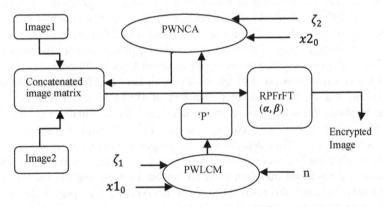

Fig. 1. Schematic diagram for proposed encryption procedure

The decryption process, delineated in Fig. 2, is exactly reverse of that of encryption with exactly same set of secret keys as are used during encryption. The encrypted image is first inversely optically transformed with fractional orders (α, β) and then PWNCA is iterated by set of 5 keys and an inverse blending/permutation/scrambling is performed.

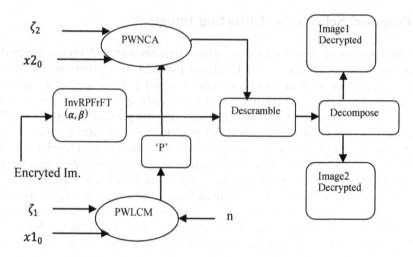

Fig. 2. Schematic diagram for the decryption procedure

4 Results and Analysis

4.1 Sensitivity Analysis

The major concern for coverting an information is its security against different types of statistical and differential attacks. In this section we have made an attempt to check for the sensitivity of keys. As shown in Fig. 3(b) is the scrambled image, Fig. 3(c) is the optically transformed image with rotation in time–frequency domain by angle (α, β). Figure 3(d–f) shows decrypted images with incorrect keys at different stages keeping all other keys correct. This proves high sensitivity of keys to different types of attacks. Again in Fig. 4(a–c), the incorrect parameters of PWLCM and PWNCA give no information about the actual image in the decrypted result. Finally Fig. 4(d) is the decrypted image with all correct keys. This decrypted image has a $(psnr = \infty; MSE = 0)$. This depicts that the proposed scheme is a lossless image encryption with complete recovery of data. There are various schemes mentioned in Sect. 1 that use fractional transforms but are unable to overcome the issue of degradation of data, although the resultant value of decrypted image psnr > 28 (required value for recognition of image visual contents).

4.2 Histogram Analysis

An image histogram is the plot of probability of occurrence of a particular image intensity value in the entire pixel range of image details. Thus it can disclose some of the crucial information regarding the statistical data. Image histogram can reveal statistical information for an intruder to plan for the potential attacks. Therefore histogram should be completely different from that of plain image histogram. The image scrambling scheme only changes the positions of the pixel values and therefore histogram plot for scrambled image in Fig. 3(b) will be similar to that of Fig. 3(a). The

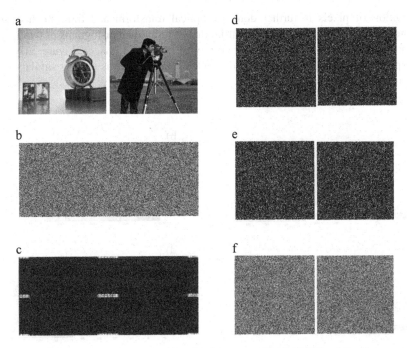

Fig. 3. (a) original plain images (b) scrambled images with PWNCA with all correct keys $(x1_0, \zeta_1, x2_0, \zeta_2)$; (c) optically transformed image with RPFrFT (α, β); (d) decrypted double image with incorrect order (β); (e) decrypted images with incorrect order (α); (f) decrypted images with incorrect key $(x1_0)$

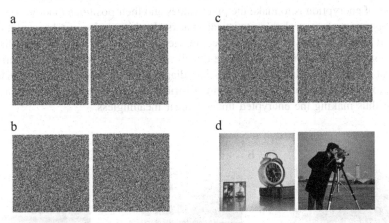

Fig. 4. (a) decrypted images with incorrect control parameter for PWLCM (ζ_1); (b) decrypted images with incorrect key of PWNCA $(x2_0)$; (c) decrypted images with incorrect key (ζ_2); (d) correctly decrypted images with all correct keys $(psnr = \infty; MSE = 0)$

substitution of pixels is further done by optical transform and thus the histogram obtained in Fig. 5(c) is quite different from that of individual histograms of two images in Fig. 5(a). Figure 5(b) is the histogram plot of combined images. Figure 5(d) is the corresponding histogram of correctly decrypted image which is exactly similar to that of plain images.

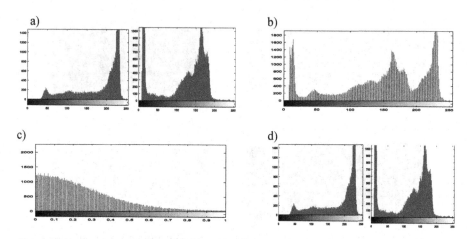

Fig. 5. Histogram plots: (a) two plain images; (b) for concatenated image; (c) for encrypted image; (d) decrypted images

4.3   Correlation Analysis

2D images with a meaningful visual content are highly correlated to each other. The purpose of encryption is to make the pixel values and their positions random so that the image is immune to probable statistical attacks. In this section we have plotted the adjacent image pixels of the encrypted image in horizontal, vertical and diagonal positions of the double image. Figure 6(a, b and c) shows the plots for horizontal adjacent pixels, vertical adjacent pixels and diagonal adjacent pixels respectively. All these plots shows that pixels are randomly distributed over the entire range of intensity values, thus making the encrypted image appear meaningless.

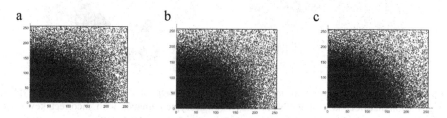

Fig. 6. Correlation plot for encrypted image (a) Horizontal shifted pixels; (b) Vertical shifted pixels; (c) Diagonally shifted pixels

5 Conclusion

In this work, we have proposed a double image encryption scheme using fractional Fourier transform and yet maintaining the real outcome to a real input domain along with a non linear preprocessing with chaos based permutation of the input double image with piecewise non linear chaotic map. The distinct features of the proposed scheme can be summarized as:

1. The optical transforms based on DRPE scheme gives a complex outcome which not only makes the computation extensive but also requires double memory for storage and making transmission tedious In contrast, the proposed encryption scheme gives real domain transform coefficients, making storage and transmission much easier and also economical in hardware implementation.
2. For the chaos part, 1D maps like Logistic, Sine or Tent map, although are simple and easy to implement, but have some weak characteristics like shorter chaotic range, non- chaotic windows in their bifurcation making them vulnerable to different analytic attacks. PWNCA based on PWLCM is used as a solution to shorter key space and gives good randomness characteristics.
3. The proposed method offers lossless encryption/decryption as the recovered data has $psnr = \infty, MSE = 0$ which is not possible with DRPE based schemes, although those methods claim to have high $psnr(\gg 28)$ but still are far from the ideal measure.

References

1. McBride, A.C., Kerr, F.H.: On Namias's fractional Fourier transforms. IMA J. Appl. Math. **39**(2), 159–175 (1987)
2. Ozaktas, H.M., Arikan, O., Kutay, M.A., Bozdagt, G.: Digital computation of the fractional Fourier transform. IEEE Trans. Signal Process. **44**(9), 2141–2150 (1996)
3. Almeida, L.B.: The fractional Fourier transform and time-frequency representations. IEEE Trans. Signal Process. **42**(11), 3084–3091 (1994)
4. Pei, S.C., Tseng, C.C., Yeh, M.H., Shyu, J.J.: Discrete fractional Hartley and Fourier transforms. IEEE Trans. Circuits Syst. II: Analog. Digit. Signal Process. **45**(6), 665–675 (1998)
5. Pei, S.C., Yeh, M.H., Tseng, C.C.: Discrete fractional Fourier transform based on orthogonal projections. IEEE Trans. Signal Process. **47**(5), 1335–1348 (1999)
6. Hennelly, B., Sheridan, J.T.: Optical image encryption by random shifting in fractional Fourier domains. Opt. Lett. **28**(4), 269–271 (2003)
7. Refregier, P., Javidi, B.: Optical image encryption based on input plane and Fourier plane random encoding. Opt. Lett. **20**(7), 767–769 (1995)
8. Unnikrishnan, G., Singh, K.: Double random fractional Fourier domain encoding for optical security. Opt. Eng. **39**(11), 2853–2860 (2000)
9. Singh, N., Sinha, A.: Chaos based multiple image encryption using multiple canonical transforms. Opt. Laser Technol. **42**(5), 724–731 (2010)

10. Zhou, N., Wang, Y., Gong, L., He, H., Wu, J.: Novel single-channel color image encryption algorithm based on chaos and fractional Fourier transform. Opt. Commun. **284**(12), 2789–2796 (2011)

11. Shan, M., Chang, J., Zhong, Z., Hao, B.: Double image encryption based on discrete multiple-parameter fractional Fourier transform and chaotic maps. Opt. Commun. **285**(21–22), 4227–4234 (2012)

12. Zhang, Y., Xiao, D.: Double optical image encryption using discrete Chirikov standard map and chaos-based fractional random transform. Opt. Lasers Eng. **51**(4), 472–480 (2013)

13. Bhatnagar,G., Wu, Q. J.:Biometric inspired multimedia encryption based on dual parameter fractional fourier transform. IEEE transactions on systems, man, and cybernetics: systems 44 (9) 1234–1247(2014)

14. Ran, Q., Yuan, L., Zhao, T.: Image encryption based on nonseparable fractional Fourier transform and chaotic map. Opt. Commun. **348**, 43–49 (2015)

15. Venturini, I., Duhamel, P.: Reality preserving fractional transforms[signal processing applications]. In: Acoustics, Speech, and Signal Processing, France, pp. 205–207 (2004)

16. Lang, J.: Image encryption based on the reality-preserving multiple-parameter fractional Fourier transform and chaos permutation. Opt. Lasers Eng. **50**(7), 929–937 (2012)

17. Mishra, D.C., Sharma, R.K., Suman, S., Prasad, A.: Multi-layer security of color image based on chaotic system combined with RP2DFRFT and Arnold Transform. J. Inf. Secur. Appl. **37**, 65–90 (2017)

18. Li, S.J.: Analyses and new designs of digital chaotic ciphers (Doctoral dissertation, Xi'an Jiaotong University) (2003)

19. Li, S., Chen, G., Mou, X.: On the dynamical degradation of digital piecewise linear chaotic maps. Int. J. Bifurc. Chaos **15**(10), 3119–3151 (2005)

20. Behnia, S., Akhshani, A., Ahadpour, S., Mahmodi, H., Akhavan, A.: A fast chaotic encryption scheme based on piecewise nonlinear chaotic maps. Phys. Lett. A **366**(4–5), 391–396 (2007)

A Framework for Testing Object Oriented Programs Using Hybrid Nature Inspired Algorithms

Madhumita Panda[(✉)] and Sujata Dash

NOU, Baripada, Odisha, India
madhumita.panda3@gmail.com

Abstract. Software testing is a very vital and inevitable phase of software development for ensuring the quality and trustworthiness of software. In this work a framework has been proposed for effective testing of object oriented programs by generating test cases using UML behavioral models. The proposed technique ensures the transition coverage as well as path coverage. In this framework we have employed a hybrid simulated annealing based cuckoo search algorithm to generate optimized test cases for bench mark triangle classification problem.

Keywords: Object oriented testing · Nature inspired algorithm
Transition path coverage · Hybrid simulated annealing

1 Introduction

Software testing is an indispensable part of software quality assurance, ensuring the correct functioning of the individual modules along with the complete software. The main purpose of testing is to identify an appropriate set of test cases that are able to reveal hidden faults of the software, avoiding bugs and system failure in the feature. This is the main reason that software development organizations spent more than 40 percent of the project development cost on software testing [9].

As object oriented programs show dynamic behavior, the traditional static code based testing approaches cannot be applied on object oriented testing [6]. The behavioral models of UML are widely used in past decade by the test researchers to design and generate test cases intended for grey box testing of object oriented programs. The UML has thirteen models and out of these the behavioral models represent the dynamic system behavior in a very abstract way, therefore the models are specifically used in testing in comparison to other models. The most common behavioral specification models include Use case, Sequence, State chart, and State activity diagrams. The widespread research approaches used for test data generation from those behavioral models first and foremost include formal approach, graph based testing, heuristic testing and direct approach using UML design [6]. The adoption of UML specifications models made a paradigm shift in the process of software development as well as testing.

© Springer Nature Singapore Pte Ltd. 2019
A. K. Luhach et al. (Eds.): ICAICR 2018, CCIS 955, pp. 531–539, 2019.
https://doi.org/10.1007/978-981-13-3140-4_48

Although many research work has been performed and proposed in the last few years for test case generation using UML models but still very few concrete and clear methodologies are available in this paradigm of model based testing [6]. Similarly the search based testing approaches have been used in the area of software testing, but they have mainly used the Genetic algorithms and Particle swarm optimization algorithms [12], a few papers have used some recent swarm based algorithms but the area is still budding especially for model based testing of object oriented programs.

Nature inspired algorithms are inspired from nature or natural species. These algorithms are developed either simulating the food searching behavior or mate selection processes adopted by natural species for improving their adaptability with the environment as well as the survival of their own race. Those computing techniques developed by observing the adaptableness of natural beings led to the development of algorithms named as Nature Inspired Algorithms (NIA) [2–4]. Those algorithms are included in the area of computational intelligence and are proving themselves to be highly effective in solving complex optimization problems. The engineering problems are getting more and more complicated due to their high dimensions, large number of variables, time complexity, more space complexity etc. For handling the above described complex engineering problems nature-inspired algorithms are becoming popular in recent years, specifically to resolve complex optimization problems whose definite solutions are very hard to calculate (NP hard).

Nature inspired algorithms include both evolutionary algorithms as well as swarm intellect based algorithms. The Evolutionary algorithms are developed observing the evolution and adaptability features of natural systems. These algorithms are based on the natural selection theory proposed by Darwin. The well-liked evolutionary algorithms include Genetic Algorithms (GAs), Differential Evolution algorithm (DE), Gravitational Search algorithms (GSAs) etc.

Swarm intellect based algorithms are derived from the collective behavior and intelligence used by natural species, particle swarm optimization (PSO) is developed observing the food searching behavior of birds, ant colony algorithm (ACO) is developed observing the collective behaviour of ants, artificial bee colony algorithm (ABC) from the food and nest establishment behaviour of honey Bees, Cuckoo search algorithm (CO) from the egg laying habit of cuckoo birds [5] etc.

The foremost intent of nature enthused algorithms is to locate the global optimal solution from a probable set of best solutions for a specific problem. The main factors common and controlling all nature inspired algorithms are exploration and exploitation. Exploration is performed for the random selection of a new solution space to get the global optimum solution and exploitation is done to find out the local best solution in a randomly selected solution space. A proper balance between the two factors i.e. exploration and exploitation is very crucial for any nature inspired algorithm [2–4].

It is a very challenging task to analyse UML models, specifically the behavioral models as they capture the dynamic system behavior. Therefore in this paper first the UML Sequence model and State chart models are converted to flatten system level

Sequence diagram and state chart diagram and then Cuckoo Search, Simulated Annealing and Hybrid Cuckoo Search algorithms are applied to generate suitably best test cases. The capabilities of those algorithms are verified using bench mark triangle classification problem [15].

This paper is ordered as follows, the Sect. 2 highlights some important earlier works in this field of model based software testing using nature inspired search algorithms, Sect. 3 describes some important aspects of Cuckoo Search, Simulated Annealing and the hybrid technique used in this work, Sect. 4 presents proposed approach, Sect. 5 includes the experimental research carried out, Sect. 6 ends with the conclusion.

2 Related Works

The Nature-inspired algorithms are search based algorithms that are premeditated following nature and when these are used to solve software testing problem, first the test goal is converted into an optimization problem [12].

Starting from 1990s, a lot of research articles are available in search based testing (SBST) area [12]. The most popular algorithms in this domain are Genetic Algorithms (GAs), Ant Colony Optimization (ACO), Particle Swarm Optimization (PSO) etc. Genetic Algorithms, are developed from the evolution theory, Ant Colony Optimization, copies the behaviour of ants during their search of food, Bacterial Foraging Algorithm (BFO) is derived from the behaviour of E.coil bacteria, Particle Swarm Optimization (PSO) adopts the food searching behaviour of birds, gravitational Search algorithm(GSA) is derived from Newton's laws of gravitational forces, artificial bee colony optimization algorithm(ABC) is developed following the searching pattern of honey bees [13–15] (Fig. 1).

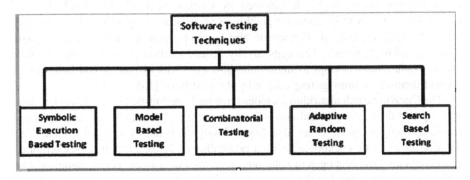

Fig. 1. Software testing techniques

3   Simulated Annealing

Simulated Annealing (SA) is a metaheuristic, probabilistic algorithm used in a large solution space to reach at a global optimum. Simulated Annealing is inspired from the annealing process adopted in metallurgy; it is a process involving first the heating of a metal and then the molten metal is cooled in a controlled manner. It was formulated [11] to be used as a function minimization approach. The SA has efficiently solved many problems like travelling salesman problem, Boolean satisfiability problem (SAT) etc.

Basically, SA works as follows:

Algorithm1: SA

Fix an initial temperature T_i
Randomly generate an initial set of solutions S.
Step: 1   Begin with an initial solution (S) generated randomly to solve a given problem.

Step: 2 Select randomly another new solution (S_i) from the solution space.

Step: 3 Evaluate the new solution, if the new solution is superior than the current solution, then replace the current best solution with the new solution, Otherwise, keep the current best solution based on the decreasing probability of acceptance.

Step: 4 Adjust the temperature by implementing either kinetic equations for density functions or using the stochastic sampling method

Step: 5 Terminate searching when the stopping condition is satisfied; otherwise, go back to Step 2.

3.1   Cuckoo Search

Cuckoo search (CS) is a metaheuristic optimization algorithm motivated from the intelligent egg laying approach followed by Cuckoo birds [9, 10]. Cuckoo is an extraordinary bird with its attention-grabbing sweet voice along with a very opposing parasitic egg laying pattern. The female bird lays her egg in the nest of different host birds of different species. The eggs lay by female cuckoo as well as the recently hatched little chicks attempt to imitate the host eggs, chicks pattern and behavior to prevent themselves from getting caught by the host birds [15].

The Cuckoo Search algorithm includes three basic optimistic rules; one cuckoo lays one egg and drops it on a randomly selected host nest. The number of nests is determined and only a few nests are abandoned if only the host bird is capable enough to identify the parasitic cuckoo egg with a probability of P_a (0, 1). A tiny proportion of nests containing the best eggs or solutions are carried over to the next generation. The cuckoo search algorithm has the similar characteristic of preserving the best nests to the next generation just like the elitism property of genetic algorithms. It includes both the features of nature inspired algorithms i.e. the process of exploitation using random walks and exploration using levy flights.

```
Algorithm2:CS

Randomly generate a population of n hosts
Nests hᵢ,where i = 1, 2,..., n
For all hᵢ do
Calculate the fitness value Fᵢ = f (hᵢ)
End for
While the number of objective Evaluation < MaxNumber of Evaluations do
Generate a cuckoo bird egg(hⱼ) by a levy flight
Fⱼ=f (hⱼ)
Randomly choose a  nest i
If (Fⱼ<Fᵢ) then
hᵢ ◄—hⱼ  Fᵢ ◄—Fⱼ
Endif
Discard a fraction of worst nests φ̇ₐ
Construct new nests at new locations
Evaluate the fitness of newly constructed  nests
Rank all solutions
End While
```

3.2   Hybrid Simulated Annealing and Cuckoo Search (HSA-CS)

The Simulated Annealing [7] and Cuckoo Search algorithm are hybridized [1] to improve the speed of convergence as well as quality of solutions. We already know that the capability of Cuckoo Search algorithm in finding the global optimal solution is superior in comparison to its local searching capability that is relatively poor. Therefore the Simulated Annealing procedure is integrated into Cuckoo Search algorithm to improvise its exploration as well as exploitation capability (Fig. 2).

```
Algorithm3:HSA-CS
Start
Objective function f(x), x=(x₁,... , xₘ)
Randomly Generate an initial population of n number of host nests xᵢ (where i=1,2,...,n)
While (t<MaxIterations) do
xᵢ ◄— Simulated Annealing
A small fraction Pa of worse nests are discarded and some new ones are built
Preserve the best solutions
Rank the obtained solutions to figure out the current best
End While
Stop
```

According to literature there are four variations of CS and SA used for hybridization [1]. Here the number of iterations of SA and CS are kept same i.e. 10. First the hybrid algorithm is tested using bench mark triangle classification problem, and the experimental results illustrated in Figs. 4, 5, 6, 7 and 8 indicate that the hybrid algorithm is showing better results generating test suites covering the feasible paths of bench mark example triangle classification problem.

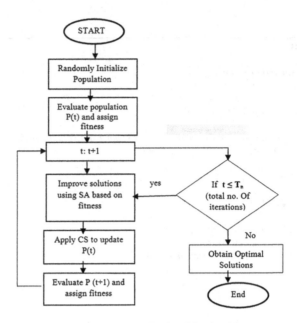

Fig. 2. Flow chart of HSA-CS Algorithm

4 Proposed Methodology

This paper suggests a framework to generate test suits using UML sequence diagram, state chart diagram and a amalgamation of sequence as well as state chart diagram. First the diagrams are converted to sequence graph using sequence diagram, state chart graph using state chart diagram and system graph using a combination of both sequence and state chart graph. Then the nodes of the graphs are assigned weights, here the parent node number is the weight for the child node and if a child node has many parent nodes then the sum the parent's weights is provided as the weight of the child node [8]. Then Depth first search is applied to trace the paths and the total path cost is the sum of node weights assigned to each path. Here the total path weight is the fitness function for each feasible path [13–15]. Then cuckoo search, Simulated Annealing and hybrid cuckoo search is applied to generate test cases covering all paths (Fig. 3).

4.1 Transformation of Sequence Diagram to Sequence Graph

The sequence diagrams capture the entire message passing events between a set of objects along with control flow for successful completion of any functionality of one particular use case. A message is a service request from one object to another which are method calls. When any message is send to an object it invokes an operation in that object.

It is normally difficult to construct direct test cases using UML sequence diagram; therefore it is first transformed to a sequence graph. The sequence graph S_G is

$$S_G = \{S_i, E_i, S_F, S_L\}$$

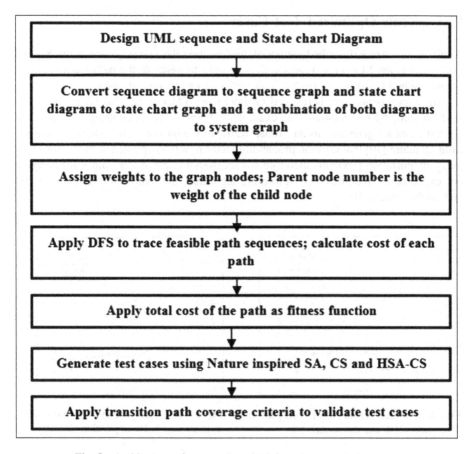

Fig. 3. Architecture of proposed methodology to generate test cases

Where S$_i$, holds the set of nodes presenting every message and return statement, E$_i$ is the total set of edges representing flow of the massage between nodes, S$_F$ is the first node, and S$_L$ is the last node.

4.2 Construction of State Chart Graph from State Chart Diagram

The state chart diagram captures the behavior of an object in response to a set of events. It mainly includes a collection of events along with a collection of guard conditions.

A state chart graph is represented as,

$$SC_G = \{S_n, T_i, G_c, S_{init}, S_{final}\}$$

Where S$_n$ the states that the object enters through in response to some events, T$_i$ the set of transitions that the object makes, Gc includes a set of guard condition, S$_{init}$, the initial state of the object and S$_{final}$ is the final state of the object.

5 Generate Optimized Test Cases

Applying the above described methodologies we first derived sequence graph S_G and state chart graph SC_G then traversed those graphs to generate the path sequences and finally applied CS, SA and HSA-CS algorithms to generate test cases.

The experiments were performed on Intel Core TM i3 CPU, 2.0 GHz with 4 GB RAM running 64-bit windows. The example problem is developed using Java and then the test cases are generated using Matlab R2016b. We have used the parameter setting, from literature [10] that says the probability factor $p_a = 0.3$ is proved to be the finest for many optimization problems therefore we set the same parameter values for carrying our experiments, for Simulated Annealing algorithm, the temperature is fixed at 100 and cooling rate at 0.01.

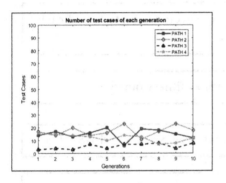

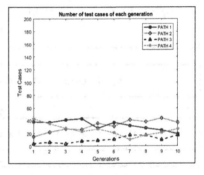

Fig. 4. Test case generated for each path at generation = 10, population size 100

Fig. 5. Test case generated for each path at generation = 10, population size 200

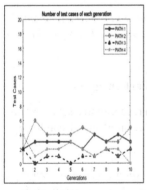

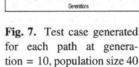

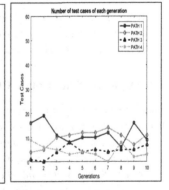

Fig. 6. Test case generated for each path at generation = 10, population size 20

Fig. 7. Test case generated for each path at generation = 10, population size 40

Fig. 8. Test case generated for each path at generation = 10, population size 60

6 Conclusion

In this paper, a framework for test suite generation using hybrid Cuckoo Search (CS) and Simulated Annealing algorithms has been proposed. The finest part of cuckoo search algorithm is its exploration and exploitation ability to get optimal result in a selected search space that has been exploited in the proposed framework to generate appropriate test suite for every feasible path. Here, the bench mark triangle classification problem has been used to evaluate the performance of the hybrid Cuckoo Search (CS) and Simulated Annealing algorithms in comparison with the performance of Simulated Annealing and Cuckoo Search algorithms individually. The simulation results illustrate that the proposed approach offers better results in terms of generating test suits for transition path coverage of every feasible paths and converges faster in comparisons to Cuckoo Search and SA algorithms. This framework can be extended by using other hybrid approaches in future.

References

1. Alkhateeb, F., Abed-alguni, B.H.: A hybrid cuckoo search and simulated annealing algorithm. J. Intell. Syst. (2017)
2. Khari, M., Kumar, P.: An effective meta-heuristic cuckoo search algorithm for test suite optimization. Informatica **41**, 363–377 (2017)
3. Agarwal, P., Mehta, S.: Nature-inspired algorithms: state-of-art problems and prospects. IJCA **14**, 0975–8887 (2014)
4. Yang, X.S.: Mathematical analysis of nature-inspired algorithms. J. Comput. Intell. (2018)
5. Saeed, A., Ab Hamid, S.H., Mustafa, M.B.: The experimental applications of search-based techniques for model-based testing: taxonomy and systematic literature review. J. Appl. Soft Comput. **49**, 1094–1117 (2016)
6. Shirole, M., Kumar, R.: UML behavioral model based test case generation. ACM SIGSOFT Softw. Eng. Notes **38**, 1–13 (2013)
7. Waeselynck, H., Thévenod-Fosse, P., Abdellatif-Kaddour, O.: Simulated annealing applied to test generation: landscape characterization and stopping criteria. Empir. Softw. Eng. **12**, 35–63 (2007)
8. Sumalatha, V.M.: Object oriented test case generation technique using genetic algorithms. IJCA **61** (2013)
9. Srivastava, P.R., Singh, A.K., Kumhar, H., Jain, M.: Optimal test sequence generation in state based testing using cuckoo search. IJAEC **3**, 17–32 (2012)
10. Yang, X.S., Deb, S.: Cuckoo search via Lévy flights. In: Nature & Biologically Inspired Computing, NaBIC, World Congress, pp. 210–214. IEEE (2009)
11. Kirkpatrick, S., Gelatt, C.D., Vecchi, M.P.: Optimization by simulated annealing. Science **220**, 671–680 (1983)
12. Harman, M., Jones, B.F.: The SEMINAL workshop: reformulating software engineering as a metaheuristic search problem. ACM SIGSOFT Softw. Eng. Notes **26**, 62–66 (2001)
13. Madhumita, P., Partha, P.S.: Performance analysis of test data generation for path coverage based testing using three meta-heuristic algorithms. IJCSI **3**, 2231–5292 (2013)
14. Madhumita, P., Mohapatra D.P.: Generating test data for path coverage based testing using genetic algorithms. In: ICICIC Global Conference. Springer (2014)
15. Madhumita, P., Partha, P.S., Sujata, D.: Automatic test data generation using metaheuristic cuckoo search algorithm. IJKDB **5**, 16–29 (2015)

Firefly Algorithm Based Multilingual Named Entity Recognition for Indian Languages

Sitanath Biswas[1(✉)], Sujata Dash[1], and Sweta Acharya[2]

[1] North Orissa University, Baripada, Odisha, India
sitanathbiswas2006@gmail.com, sujata238dash@gmail.com
[2] Centurian University, Balangir, Odisha, India
sweta_acharya20@yahoo.co.in

Abstract. Named Entity Recognition (NER) is considered as a very influential undertaking in natural language processing appropriate to Question Answering system, Machine Translation (MT), Information extraction (IE), Information Retrieval (IR) etc. Basically NER is to identify and classify different types of proper nouns present inside given filelike location name, person name, number, organization name, time etc. Multilingual NER is a task where NE can be recognized for variety of Languages by implementing one or more methods. In this paper, we have implemented Conditional Random Field (CRF) as a base and firefly Algorithm (FA) to effectively combine different feature representation. For better performance of this system, we have combined both the methods. We have taken three Indian languages Hindi, Bengali, and Odiya for the purpose of evaluation. A promising result is observed for all three languages while implementing FA with CRF.

Keywords: Firefly Algorithm · Conditional Random Field
Named Entity Recognition · Recognition · Information extraction
Machine Translation · Information Retrieval · Multilingual NER
NER

1 Introduction

The increasing diversity of languages for example, English, Urdu, Portuguese, Japanese and many more, used on the web has created a new level of complexity to for the system like Information Retrieval (IR) and Machine Translation (MT) systems. Named Entity Recognition (NER) [1] is considered as a very influential undertaking in the field of natural language processing [11] appropriate to Question Answering system, Machine Translation (MT), Information extraction (IE), Information Retrieval (IR) etc. Basically NER is to identify and classify every genuine nouns present inside a text as location name, human name, institution name, digit, time etc. [1]. For last twenty five years, NER is considered a tremendously dynamic region of research in the field of NLP. But NER still remains a big problem for Multilingual Named Entity Recognition even after a lot of progress has been made in detecting named entities.

A multilingual NER system is basically responsible for recognizing named entities in a variety of languages. The very advantage of multilingual named entity recognition

A. K. Luhach et al. (Eds.): ICAICR 2018, CCIS 955, pp. 540–552, 2019.
https://doi.org/10.1007/978-981-13-3140-4_49

(NER) is utilizing the identical method for numerous languages [3] and implementing fresh languages is very effortless and quick. The greatest challenge to develop Multilingual NER system for Indian Languages is:

Indian languages have many different language families, the Dravidian lang0uages, Indo-European languages, and Indo-Aryan are the major ones [4].

Morphologically rich –As Indian languages are morphologically very rich, it is very difficult to identify the root word, therefore it requires morphological analysers.

Capitalization feature - In English, capitalization plays a big role to identify NEs but it is not found in Indian languages [4].

Ambiguity – thousands of ambiguities are present in common and proper nouns.

Spell variations – When it comes to web, then a same thing can be spelled differently in different domain.

From last two decades, NER is the prime attention of NLP researchers [19, 20]. The initiative in the field of NER taken during Message Understanding Conferences (MUCs) [19, 20]. During the development of GATE system. Precise finding of NEs was reported and later standardised by the inventers [3]. NER was also got tremendous importance during the development of Information Extraction System [21], question-answering systems [22], machine translation [23]. In the early times, researchers were using finite state automata to match against a series of words general regular expression matcher. LaSIE-II by University Of Sheffield's [24], NetOwl by ISOQuest [25] and LTG by University Of Edinburgh [26] are the English NER. These systems were actually based on rule and therefore these systems are not robust and have issue like portability. Developing rule based system is quite expensive because every time we use new text as input, we need to manipulate the existing rule to manage the optimal performance. In recent days, machine-learning (ML) [14] approaches are extensively implemented in NER. The basic advantage of using ML is that one can train it easily, ML is very adapting in nature to various domains and languages and to maintain is very less expensive [13]. Different machine learning techniques [13] used in NER so far is Hidden Markov Model (HMM) [27], Maximum Entropy (ME) [13] systems, New York University's MENE [28], in the New York University's system, Decision Tree was implemented [29], CRF [30]. Shallow parsing approach by Pattern-directed for NER in Bengali was reported by Bandyopadhyay and Ekbal [10]. The paper describes two different model of NER, where one model uses lexical contextual designs and additional uses language based characteristics with lexical contextual patterns of same set. A NER system using HMM was reported by Ekbal [10], to handle unknown entities, the author uses maximum number of contextual information and named entity suffixes during probability (emission). More recent contributions in Bengali NER can effortlessly be get in [4, 7] with a CRF, and a SVM technique, commonly. These NER tools were developed by using various contextual features and orthographical word based characteristics in association with a variety of characteristic took out, out of the gazetteers. The NER work on the language Hindi was reported by Li and McCallum [5] with CRF technique that implements a technique known as characteristic ordination to build the characteristics automatically to grow the conditional likelihood. Cucerzon and Yarowsky had introduced a novel Hindi NER method which was language independent.

In this paper we have implemented FA to search for the correct feature selection. The features we have considered here are morphological information, suffix and prefix, Orthographic features, part-of-speech (POS) tagging data along with the neighbouring word information of the Oriya language. For more accuracy in identification of NEs, We have implemented gazetteers to identify title, person designation etc. We have also used gazetteers in our system for person and location name entities. It is well proved that the linguistic rule acts as very significant character to better detect NEs therefore we had implemented a number of handcrafted linguistic rules for this system, for example, the rule for recognizing time, number etc. We have used a language independent classifier CRF as base classifier which requires less computing overhead.

We have taken three Indian languages, Hindi, Bengali and Odiya for the purpose of evaluating the proposed approach. Hindi is known as the Indian national language and popular as third speaking language in this universe. Bengali is the Governmental language in Bangladesh and it is second most used language of India. We have taken Odiya language as significant work is not done for this language.

The remaining part of our paper is arranged like this. Section 2 presents Conditional Random Field (CRF) [6]. Section 3 describes Firefly Algorithm (FA). Section 4 gives Architecture of our hybrid system, Sect. 5 describes the results of experiment and Sect. 6 gives conclusion.

2 Conditional Random Field (CRF)

Conditional Random Fields (CRFs) [4] is the unique cases of graphical representation which is undirected in nature. It represent to finite state automata which is conditionally trained and probabilistic by nature. Due to its conditional training, the CRF can very easily combine a huge number of non-independent and arbitrary features even if having well ordered methods for training and finite-state inference which is non-greedy in nature [4]. CRF is very much popular and successful in various sequence modelling tasks like for example, table extraction, noun phrase segmentation and many more. CRF is basically implemented to find out the conditional probability of appointed nodes for output for specified rates on other appointed input nodes. To calculate the conditional probability of a given state series $s = (s_1, s_2 \ldots s_T)$ and observation series $o = (o_1, o_2, \ldots, o_T)$ the following equation is used:

$$P \wedge (so) = exp \left(\sum_{t=1}^{T} \sum_{k=1}^{K} \imath k \, X f_k (S_t - 1, S_t, o, t) \right)_{,,}$$

Where $f_k (s_t - 1, s_t, o, t)$ is the feature function and the weight λk should to be gained through training. The feature functions worth may fall in a range between $-\infty \ldots + \infty$, but it should be mandatorily binary. We should find out the normalization factor in order to create all conditional probabilities added to 1

$$Z_0 = \sum_s exp\left(\sum_{t=1}^{T}\sum_{k=1}^{K} \lambda k \times f_k(S_t - 1, S_t, o, t)\right),$$

In order to teach a CRF, the objective function has to be increase, this objective function is the punished log-likelihood series of the state, for the given series of observation:

$$L_\wedge = \sum_{i=1}^{N} \log\left(P\wedge\left(s^{(i)} | o^{(i)}\right)\right) - \sum_{k=1}^{K} \frac{\lambda_k^2}{2\sigma^2},$$

The labelled training data is $\{o^{(i)}, s^{(i)}\}$. The 2nd sum represents to the zero-mean, σ^2 is the variance of Gaussian prior over parameters, that actually gives the optimization if we make the probability surface as firmly convex. To increase the punished log-likelihood implementing restricted memory BFGS, we set parameters λ, a quasi Newton technique which is actually very effective thus outcomes in solely slight differences in correctness owing to minor differences in λ. When we apply CRFs for the Named entity recognition case, we consider, for a given text, a series of observation is nothing but a token of a line or file. Here the state series is its analogous label series. Here, f_k ($s_t - 1$, s_t, o, t) is a feature function and for most of the cases, has a value of 0. And when $s_t - 1$, s_t can only be set to 1, here $s_t - 1$, s_t are assertive position and the scrutiny has few assertive characteristics. For segmenting or labelling sequential data, In this paper, we had implemented the C++ based CRF++ package version IV, an open source implementation of CRF which is a very simple and customizable. http://crfpp.sourceforge.net (Figs. 1 and 2).

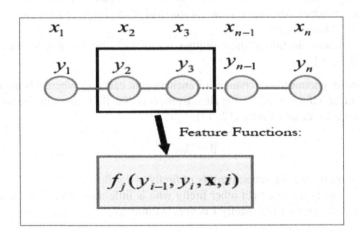

Fig. 1. Conditional random fields: feature functions

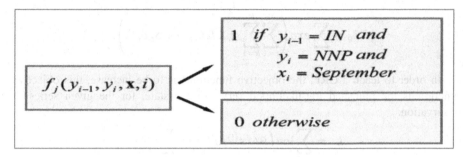

Fig. 2. Feature functions

3 Firefly Algorithm (FA)

In recent days, the most popular meta-heuristic algorithm which is inspired by nature and frequently used to solve optimization issues is firefly algorithm. Fireflies are capable to generate light by a process called bio-luminescence; most of the fireflies generate rhythmic flashes and shot. In order to communicate among them, fireflies use these flashes. This process basically attracts closest predators or potential prey and possibly partner for mating. Fireflies react depending on the perceived intensity of light [2].

The FA performs searching operations on the population of individuals known as fireflies employing the below mentioned assumptions:

- As attraction between fireflies happens irrespective of their sex, therefore they are considered as unisex [11].
- The criteria for attraction is relatively proportional to the intensity of the light or brightness, which changes with the distance. This regulates the movement of fireflies i.e., brighter one attracts less bright and if no brighter fireflies found then movement becomes random [3].
- The evaluation function of these fireflies is directly corresponding to brightness of these fireflies [3].

In order to amount to the changes of enchantment called β, where r is the distance among them, and if we consider, the attractiveness is directly varies with the strength of light observed by nearby firefly [12, 13].

$$\beta = \beta_0 e^{-\gamma r2}, \tag{1}$$

Here β_0 represents the attractiveness of firefly at r = 0.

When a Firefly try to attract other firefly who is little more attractive (in this case "brighter"), the motion j of a firefly i is decided through:

$$x_i^{t+1} = x_i^t + \beta_{0e} - \gamma r_{ij}^2 (x_i^t - x_i^t) + \alpha_t \in_i^t, \tag{2}$$

Here the 2nd term appeared because of the allure. The 3rd phrase is appeared due to the property of randomness with α_t. Where α_t is the framework for randomization and

$\in_i^t$ represent the vector of haphazard digits which is derived from a uniform scattering or Gaussian distribution in interval t. If simple random walk is required, it is represented by $\beta_0 = 0$. Subsequently, if $\gamma = 0$, then this decreases to the special case called particle swarm optimisation. Taking further $\in_i^t$ is such a randomization, which may be considered of extension of other kinds of distributions like Levy flights [14–16].

Settings up the Parameters: As αt usually command the randomness (or, may be up to certain extent, the variety of solutions) [17]. During iterations, it is possible to adjust the parameter in order to adapt with the iteration counter called t. Then the better option for expressing αt will be the use of $\alpha t = \alpha 0 \delta t, 0 < \delta < 1$).

Where we have taken $\alpha 0$ as the basic arbitrariness factor for scaling. Here δ considered as a factor for cooling, we can use $\delta = 0.95$ to 0.97 for almost all optimisation problem.

As per the result of simulation, it was observed that FA is better than other optimisation techniques if $\alpha 0$ is accompanied along the scaling to design variables. If L is considered as the median range of a given task, we may initially set $\alpha 0 = 0.01L$. In order to reach a target in absence of jumping very long in less step then random walk is needed for few step so the factor 0.01 comes in. As the attractiveness is controlled by the parameter "β", it is well studied that $\beta 0 = 1$ is useful for most of the application. Here γ is too associated with the scaling of L. Normally we can fix $\gamma = 1/\sqrt{L}$. We can also fix $\gamma = O(1)$, if the variation in scaling is not significant. We have used the following Matlab code for the simulation.

https://in.mathworks.com/matlabcentral/fileexchange/29693-firefly-algorithm.

Pseudo code for Firefly Algorithm:

Start

Calculation of Objective function f(y), $y = (y_1, ..., y_d)^T$

Create basic inhabitancy for fireflies $y_i = (i=1,2,....,n)$

Light strength of I_i at Y_i is obtained by $f(Y_i)$

Derive coefficient of light efficiency "γ"

while (*t < MaximumGeneration*)

for *i=1*:n *all n number of fireflies*

    for *j=1*:n *all n number of fireflies (inside loop)*

    if *($I_i < I_j$)* shift the firefly *i* close to *j*; **end if**

        Alter attraction along length r through [-γr]

        Calculate updated result and renew the light strength

    end for *j*

end for *i*

Rank assignment of fireflies and discover present global best g *

end while

After procedure outcome analysis and visualization

This pseudo code was adapted from [18] (Fig. 3).

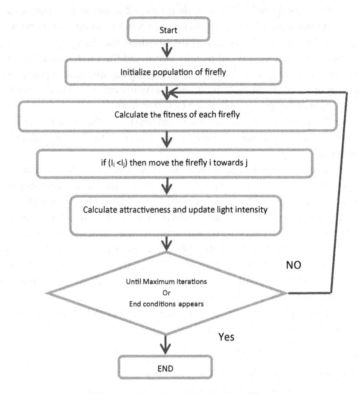

Fig. 3. Flowchart of firefly algorithm.

Algorithm Complexity:

Nature Inspired Metaheuristic algorithms are generally simple when it comes to complexity, and implementation of these algorithms are very easy. For iteration "t", FA uses two internal loops and one external loop. Therefore complexity of this algorithm in worst situation is $O(n^2 t)$, when n is little (say n = 38) and t is big (may be t = 4500), The very basic computational value is the evaluations of objective functions, therefore the algorithm is inexpensive in terms of computational cost. The greatest computationally large scale part of this algorithm is the evaluation of objective. The complexity of FA can be $O(nt \log(n))$ if n is comparatively large. In that case, we can use single internal loop based on the allure or brilliance of whole fireflies. The ranking will be done for choosing the attractiveness by using standard sorting algorithm.

4 Architecture

See Fig. 4.

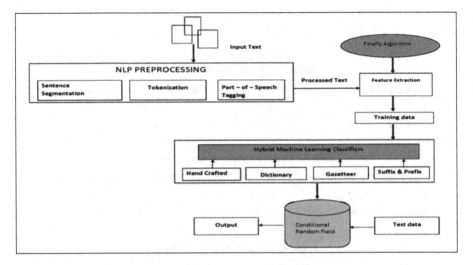

Fig. 4. Architecture of firefly algorithm based multilingual named entity recognition system.

5 Experimental Results

The accomplishment of our methods was studied with regard to recall, precision and *F*-measure:

Precision = (valid positives) / (valid positives + invalid positives)
Recall = (valid positives) / (valid positives + invalid negatives)
F measure = (2* Precision * Recall) / (Precision + Recall) [8]

Where:

- *Valid* positives indicates the number of Named Entities classified correctly

- *Invalid* positives indicates the number of Named Entities classified for non NEs

- *Invalid* negatives indicates the number of Named Entities not categorized for correct Name Entities.

In this work, we have used IJCNLP-08 Shared Task [12] data on South and South East Asian Languages (NERSSEAL) [12] and also manual annotated data for Odiya. We have got a very promising result while implementing FA with CFR (Tables 1, 2, 3 and 4).

Table 1. Data set

Name of language	Total words for training	Total name entities in training	Total words for test	Total name entities in test
Hindi	318,010	42067	41110	5091
Bengali	451,003	33102	13905	2019
Odiya	89,831	6977	11150	2173

Table 2. Overall result for Hindi

Prototype	Recall (percentage)	Precision (percentage)	F-measure (percentage)
FA	76.27	84.95	77.99
Baseline	73.31	82.13	76.79

Table 3. Comprehensive result for Bengali

Prototype	Recall (percentage)	Precision (percentage)	F-measure (percentage)
FA	78.12	88.25	83.19
Baseline	67.39	80.63	73.15

Table 4. Overall result for Odiya

Model	Recall (in %)	Precision (in %)	F-measure (in %)
FA based approach	66.11	95.25	74.91
Baseline	60.29	92.95	67.92

Comparison with Earlier Work: Genetic Algorithm with CRF

Earlier we have used IJCNLP-08 [12] Shared Task data on South and South East Asian Languages (NERSSEAL) [12] and also manual annotated data for Odiya [1] where we have implemented GA with CRF and got the result mentioned in the table below (Tables 5, 6, 7 and 8):

Table 5. Data set

Name of language	Total words for training	Total name entities in training	Total words for test	Total name entities in test
Hindi	314,760	38031	34810	4421
Bengali	432,113	28122	8965	1089
Odiya	87,238	4970	8460	1178

Table 6. Overall result for Hindi

Prototype	Recall (percentage)	Precision (percentage)	F-measure (percentage)
GA	71.27	83.95	77.09
Baseline	71.15	81.53	75.99

Table 7. Comprehensive result for Bengali

Prototype	Recall (percentage)	Precision (percentage)	F-measure (percentage)
GA	74.72	87.15	80.46
Baseline	62.39	80.63	70.35

Table 8. Overall result for Odiya

Prototype	Recall (percentage)	Precision (percentage)	F-measure (percentage)
GA	60.91	94.15	73.97
Baseline	50.89	91.55	65.42

If we compare both the result from table number one and table number two, it is clearly ascertained that combination of FA with CRF is giving better result in comparison with GA and CRF.

A Named Entity tagset is described in Table 9 which was used to train CRF model. Different gazetteers implemented in our analysis are described in table number four. The Gazetteers was prepared mostly manually and sometimes semi automatically from different sources like newspaper, news corpus etc. (Table 10).

Table 9. Tagset for named entity adapted from [3, 9]

Tag for NE	Interpretation	Instance
PER [10]	One-word person name	Tapan/PER
B-PER [10] I-PER [10] E-PER [10]	Starting, Inside or End of a multiple word person name	Tapan/B-PER Kumar/I-PER Mohapatra/E-PER
LOC [10]	One-word	Bhubaneswar/LOC
B-LOC [10] I-LOC [10] E-LOC [10]	Starting, Inside or Ending of a multiple word place name	Naveen/B-LOC Pattnayak/I-LOC lane/E-LOC
ORG [10]	One-word organization name	NALCO/ORG
B-ORG [10] I-ORG [10] E-ORG [10]	Starting, Inside or End of a multiple word institution name	Indian/B-ORG Institute/I-ORG For/I-ORG Technology/E-ORG
MISC [10]	One-word miscellaneous name	20%/MISC
B-MISC [10] I-MISC [10] E-MISC [10]	Starting, Inside or End of a multiple word miscellaneous name	10e/B-MISC Sravan/I-MISC 1502/E-MISC
NNE [10]	Word which is not NEs	Neta /NNE

Table 10. Gazetteers for three different language

Language	Gazetteer	Number of entries
Hindi	NE suffix	105
	Institution suffix	74
	Person prefix	215
	Middle name	1221
	Surname	3214
	Common Place	621
	Action verb	134
	Designation words	831
	Beginning names	59761
	Location name	4312
	Organization name	1871
	Month name	12
	Weekdays	07
	Measurement expressions	43
Bengali	NE suffix	115
	Organization suffix	64
	Person prefix	195
	Middle name	921
	Surname	4214
	Common Location	781
	Action verb	94
	Designation words	631
	Beginning names	51009
	Location name	3976
	Organization name	1171
	Month name	12
	Weekdays	07
	Measurement expressions	43
Odiya	NE suffix	89
	Organization suffix	59
	Person prefix	205
	Middle name	721
	Surname	3987
	Trivial Location	885
	Action verb	74
	Designation words	587
	First names	45009
	Location name	3452
	Organization name	1097
	Month name	12
	Weekdays	07
	Measurement expressions	43

6 Conclusions

In this paper, for the first time, we have introduced a FA based technique for NER. We have taken CRF as base classifier here. The value of the median F-measure of CRF classifier was obtained and training was done using the set of characteristics obtained from the objective function of FA. The very strong attribute of this paper is that we have used many features which are not at all any language dependent. One can easily derive these features for many different languages. For the purpose of evaluation, we have taken Hindi, Bengali and Odiya language. The comprehensive recall, precision and F-measure values we have obtained are 76.27%, 84.95% and 77.99%, for Hindi, 78.12%, 88.25% and 83.15%, are for Bengali and 66.11%, 95.25% and 74.91%, are for Odiya. Therefore we can conclude that FA is giving better performance than GA.

References

1. Biswas, S.: Hybrid multilingual named entity recognition for Indian languages. Int. J. Control Theory Appl. **10**(18), 57–62 (2017)
2. Dash, S.: An enhanced chaos-based firefly model for Parkinson's disease diagnosis and classification. In: 2017 International Conference on Information Technology. IEEE Computer Society (2017)
3. Dash, S.: A parallel firefly meta-heuristics algorithm for financial option pricing. IEEE Computer Society (2017)
4. Ekbal, A.: Classifier ensemble selection using genetic algorithm for named entity recognition. In: Research on Language and Computation. Springer
5. Wei, L., McCallum, A.: Rapid development of Hindi named entity recognition using conditional random fields and feature induction (short paper). In: ACM Transactions on Computational Logic (2004)
6. Dimililer, N., Varoğlu, E., Altınçay, H.: Vote-based classifier selection for biomedical NER using genetic algorithms. In: Proceedings of 3rd Iberian Conference on Pattern Recognition and Image Analysis (IbPRAI 2007), vol. 4478, pp. 202–209 (2007)
7. Gabrys, B., Ruta, D.: Genetic algorithms in classifier fusion. Appl. Soft Comput. **6**(4), 337–347 (2006)
8. Ekbal, A., Bandyopadhyay, S.: Bengali named entity recognition using support vector machine. In: Proceedings of Workshop on NER for South and South East Asian Languages, 3rd International Joint Conference on Natural Language Processing (IJCNLP), pp. 51–58, India (2008)
9. Ekbal, A., Bandyopadhyay, S.: A conditional random field approach for named entity recognition in Bengali and Hindi. Linguist. Issues Lang. Technol. (LiLT) **2**(1), 1–44 (2009)
10. Ekbal, A., Naskar, S., Bandyopadhyay, S.: Named entity recognition and transliteration in Bengali. Named Entities: Recogn. Classif. Use, Spec. Issue Lingvisticae Investigationes J. **30**(1), 95–114 (2007)
11. Abdullah, A., Deris, S., Mohamad, M., Hashim, S.: A new hybrid firefly algorithm for complex and nonlinear problem, pp. 673–680. Distributed Computing and Artificial Intelligence, Springer, Berlin, Heidelberg (2012)
12. Apostolopoulos, T., Vlachos, A.: Application of the firefly algorithm for solving the economic emissions load dispatch problem. Int. J. Comb. **2011** (2010)

13. El-Sawy, A., Zaki, E., Rizk-Allah, R.: A novel hybrid ant colony optimization and firefly algorithm for solving constrained engineering design problems. J. Nat. Sci. Math. **6**(1), 1–22 (2012)

14. Farahani, S., Abshouri, A., Nasiri, B., Meybodi, M.: A Gaussian firefly algorithm. Int. J. Mach. Learn. Comput. **1**(5), 448–453 (2011)

15. Gandomi, A., Yang, X., Alavi, A.: Mixed variable structural optimization using firefly algorithm. Comput. Struct. **89**(23), 2325–2336 (2011)

16. Hassanzadeh, T., Meybodi, M.: A new hybrid algorithm based on Firefly Algorithm and cellular learning automata. In: 20th Iranian Conference on Electrical Engineering, (ICEE), pp. 628–633. IEEE (2012)

17. Tilahun, S., Ong, H.: Modified firefly algorithm. J. Appl. Math. 1–12 (2012)

18. Yang, X.: Nature-Inspired Metaheuristic Algorithms, 2nd edn. Luniver Press, Frome (2010)

19. Chinchor, N.: MUC-6 Named Entity Task Definition (Version 2.1). In: MUC-6. Maryland (1995)

20. Chinchor, N.: MUC-7 Named Entity Task Definition (Version 3.5). In: MUC-7. Fairfax (1998)

21. Moldovan, D., et al.: LCC tools for question answering. In: Text REtrieval Conference (TREC) (2002)

22. Babych, B., Hartley, A.: Improving machine translation quality with automatic named entity recognition. In: Proceedings of EAMT/EACL 2003 Workshop on MT and Other Language Technology Tools, pp. 1–8 (2003)

23. Humphreys, K., et al.: University of Sheffield: description of the LaSIE-II system as used for MUC-7. In: MUC-7, Fairfax, Virginia

24. Aone, C., Halverson, L., Hampton, T., Ramos-Santacruz, M.: SRA: Description of the IE2 system used for MUC-7. In: MUC-7, Fairfax, Virginia (1998)

25. Mikheev, A., Grover, C., Moens, M.: Description of the LTG system used for MUC-7. In: MUC-7, Fairfax, Virginia (1998)

26. Mikheev, A., Grover, C., Moens, M.: Named entity recognition without gazeteers. In: Proceedings of EACL, pp. 1–8, Bergen, Norway (1999)

27. Miller, S., et al.: BBN: description of the SIFT system as used for MUC-7. In: MUC-7, Fairfax, Virginia (1998)

28. Borthwick, A.: Maximum Entropy Approach to Named Entity Recognition. Ph.D. thesis, New York University (1999)

29. Borthwick, A., Sterling, J., Agichtein, E., Grishman, R.: NYU: description of the MENE named entity system as used in MUC-7. In: MUC-7, Fairfax (1998)

30. Bennet, S.W., Aone, C., Lovell, C.: Learning to tag multilingual texts through observation. In: Proceedings of Empirical Methods of Natural Language Processing, pp. 109–116, Providence, Rhode Island (1997)

Color Based Segmentation Towards Structural Distribution of Image Data

Rashima Mahajan[1](✉) and Pragya Gupta[2]

[1] Faculty of Engineering and Technology, MRIIRS, Faridabad, India
rashima.fet@mriu.edu.in
[2] SRM Institute of Science and Technology, Chennai, India
pragyagupta291999@gmail.com

Abstract. This paper analyses the digital image acquired in real time using color based segmentation to estimate the structural distributions of image data. Structural distribution using computer systems has become a major field of interest. Furthermore, distribution of data in a digital image with different colors has gained much importance in the last decade due to its wide applications. An image is acquired in real time through image acquisition toolbox and is exported to MATLAB workspace. Color based image segmentation has been explored and implemented to locate different colored structures in an acquired image. This is followed by the plotting of corresponding histograms of individual red, green and blue planes, respectively to indicate brightness at each point that in turn, represents the pixel count. Finally, the segmented pixels are classified using the Nearest Neighbor rule. It is observed that the designed algorithm possesses the capability to determine the structural distribution of input image data. The results suggest that the methodology adopted can further be used for brake light detection system, to locate different colored objects in satellite images, for authentication of paper currency, in fashion industry etc.

Keywords: Color image · Segmentation · Histogram · Pixels
Nearest neighbor · Image acquisition

1 Introduction

Structural distribution and subsequent localization of an image data has gained much importance in the last decade due to its wide applications. It is done to isolate and identify distinct structures from their background and exactly locate their position and orientation in an acquired image [1]. Identification of different structures is performed using digital image processing techniques [2, 3] by retrieving non-redundant information from a test image. A plethora of image processing algorithms has been evolved from time to time to recognize homogeneous image segments, region of interests in image data, supervised segmentation of images, edge identification of acquired objects in images, and distinct sized/shaped/colored/textured objects in an image [4–6].

Image segmentation is a basic mechanism that is aimed to identify specific Regions-of-Interest (ROI) in an input acquired image data and thus to identify and locate distinct structures. Image segmentation subdivides the input pixel elements of an

© Springer Nature Singapore Pte Ltd. 2019
A. K. Luhach et al. (Eds.): ICAICR 2018, CCIS 955, pp. 553–561, 2019.
https://doi.org/10.1007/978-981-13-3140-4_50

input image-data into different clusters possessing homogeneous kind of features on the basis of four properties of an image *viz.*, color, intensity, edges and texture of that image [7–9]. Analyzing input images on the basis of these properties via image segmentation leads to development of several applications including video-surveillance, satellite imaging, recognition of faces (biometrics), and image retrieval, removing noise from an image, medical imaging analysis, and recognizing and classifying distinct structures in a given image [10]. A very less literature has been published to efficiently determine the structural based distribution of acquired image-data. Some used the Gaussian-Mixture models [11], the Dirichlet-Mixture models [12], while some tried to implement a segmentation model using a single starting Kernel by estimating the possible maximum-likelihood factor [13]. However, the non-Gaussian and Asymmetric image-data-distributions are difficult to be estimated by the Gaussian-Mixture models and thus, results obtained are not up to the mark [14]. In such instances, the modeling of input image-data is preferred by implementing the Dririchlet-Mixture based distribution models. These are implemented by applying a generalization in multivariate domain to the Beta-distribution. This paper implements a color based segmentation technique to automatically identify and localize different structures in an image. Color based image-data segmentation has become a major field of interest to estimate the structural distributions of image data. It further aids the identification of specific Regions-of-Interest and associated properties from an acquired image for subsequent image analysis.

Color based image segmentation is then followed by suitable pattern recognition task for structure classification. Several classification algorithms has been implemented in the literature including neural networks, clustering techniques, edge based and fuzzy based techniques [15, 16]. However, the nearest neighbor algorithm is easy to implement and possesses less execution time [17]. Thus, is selected for classification task in this research paper.

2   Materials and Methods

In this work, an algorithm for real time image acquisition and structural distribution system has been developed and implemented using color-based image segmentation. The functional block diagram of designed system is sketched in Fig. 1. It involves a series of modules for image acquisition, image processing and image segmentation, respectively.

An image is acquired in real time through image acquisition toolbox and is exported to MATLAB workspace in .jpg image format. The color based image segmentation has been explored and implemented to locate different colored structures in an acquired image. This is followed by the plotting of corresponding histograms of individual red, green and blue planes, respectively to indicate brightness at each point that in turn, represents the pixel count. Finally, the segmented pixels are classified using the Nearest Neighbor rule. The detailed methodology implemented is given in flow chart as in Fig. 2.

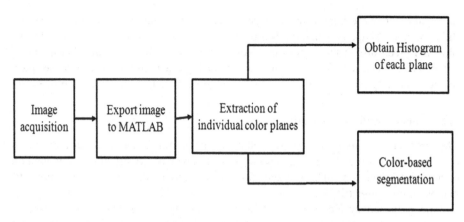

Fig. 1. Block diagram for real time image acquisition and structural distribution system using color-based segmentation

2.1   Image Acquisition

At first an image is acquired in real time using image acquisition toolbox by creating a video input object. The resolution of 288 × 352 is selected for acquisition of an image. A single frame of data has been captured and is exported to MATLAB workspace in. jpg image format.

2.2   Histogram Based Classification

The histogram based classification involves the determination of number of pixel elements of an image at each and every individual intensity point [18]. At first the range of intensity values present in an image are estimated and a graph of number of pixel elements versus respective intensity points is plotted. The construction of histogram of an image involves the single-pass scanning of an input image. It is done for the whole image using a single color filter. The aim is to determine and store a running pixel element count captured at individual intensity point. As color is the most important parameter to further extract image features/identifying structures of input image-data. Thus, color-specific histograms can also be constructed; either different histogram constructed for individual color planes *viz.*, Red, Green and Blue or a three-dimensional histogram where all the three Red, Green and Blue color planes are represented by respective three axes. Here, the pixel-element count is indicated by the respective brightness-level at individual intensity point [19]. The color histogram based classification techniques are widely applied to Content based Retrieval systems [20, 21] and are proven to be successful. However, the details the logic behind the spatial distribution of respective colors is missing.

The major limitation of histogram based classification lies in the fact that the comparison is performed on the basis of identified color of the input image structure while completely ignoring it's spatial or shape information. The plotted color based histograms can be misleading as there is always a possibility to have same color histograms for two different input image datasets possessing similar color content but different object/shape information. It is hard to differentiate a blue and green ball from a blue and green disc if the respective color content of ball/disc is same. Furthermore, color histogram based classification shows very high sensitivity towards noise inter-ference including intensity variations due to lightning. It causes quantization errors also.

2.3   Color Based Segmentation

The proposed solution to above inefficient histogram based classification is to classify/identify structures in a given image using color based structural segmentation of an input image data. The segmentation of an input image data involves the esti-mation of constituent image regions.

The proposed system uses the L*a*b (luminosity-chromaticity) color space to identify structures of an acquired input image. It has been identified as the most appropriate color-space as per specifications provided by the International Commission on Illumination. Each and every individual color visible to Human-Eye is described in

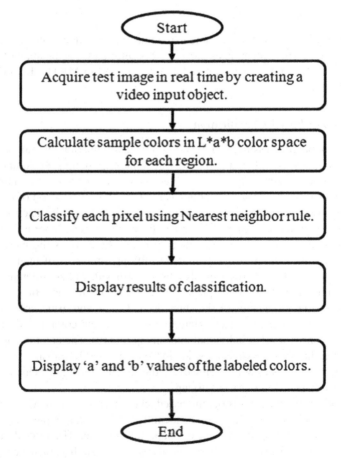

Fig. 2. Flow chart for object identification using color based segmentation

this space [22]. Further, these color spaces has been found to be the best suited to perform segmentation by calculating the Euclidean-Distance to determine differences in respective colors [22].

The ranges of sample colors 'L', 'a' and 'b' are calculated for region classification. The L*a*b color space includes luminosity (L) known as brightness layer, chromaticity layer (a) representing the instance of specific color fall along the Red-Green axis, and chromaticity layer (b) representing the instance of specific color fall along the Blue-Yellow axis. Once 'a' and 'b' value for each color marker is obtained, individual pixel-element in the acquired image-data has been classified using Nearest Neighbor Rule [17]. It includes calculation of Euclidean distance of a selected pixel from individual color-marker. The smallest the distance, more closely the selected pixel-element matches the specific color-marker. This leads to the labeling of selected pixel-element to that particular color-marker. This process in continuation would assign respective color labels to individual pixel-elements of an acquired image-data. It constitutes a label matrix that in turn is used to segment structures in an input acquired image by color-based segmentation.

3 Result and Discussion

The various results obtained using histogram based classification and color-based segmentation are presented and discussed in this section. Figure 3 shows the test image acquired in real time using image acquisition toolbox. The original test image

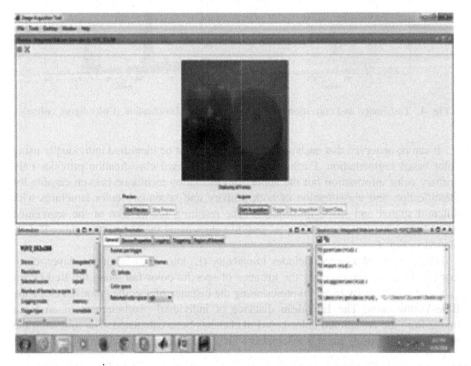

Fig. 3. Test image acquired in real time using image acquisition toolbox

constitutes of four color structures including blue background (four balls and one disk). The different colored objects have been included for better understanding of the algorithm used for color based image segmentation.

At first the individual histogram of red, green and blue color planes are constructed and are shown in Fig. 4. But color-based histograms can be misleading as there is always a possibility to have same color histograms for two different input image datasets possessing similar color content but different object/shape information. Thus an efficient color based segmentation technique has been implemented in order to identify different color structures and the corresponding results are shown in Fig. 5.

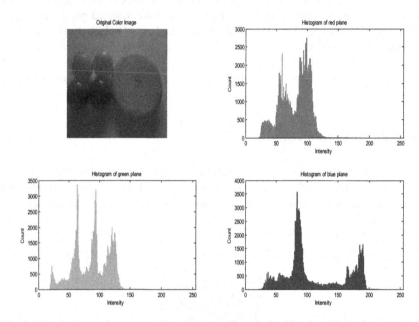

Fig. 4. Test image and corresponding histogram based classification (Color figure online)

It can be observed that each and every structure can be identified individually using color based segmentation. Furthermore, histogram based classification provides only primary color information but the applied segmentation technique is even capable for identification and classification of both primary and secondary color structures with different spatial and shape information. The resulting scatter plot of the segmented labeled pixels with corresponding 'a' and 'b' values using the Nearest Neighbor Rule is plotted in Fig. 6.

The L*a*b color space includes luminosity (L) known as brightness layer, chromaticity layer (a) representing the instance of specific color fall along the Red-Green axis, and chromaticity layer (b) representing the instance of specific color fall along the Blue-Yellow axis. The Euclidean distance of individual pixel-element of an input image from the considered color-based marker has been calculated. The minimum the distance, more closely pixel is associated with selected color. The scatter plot shows the

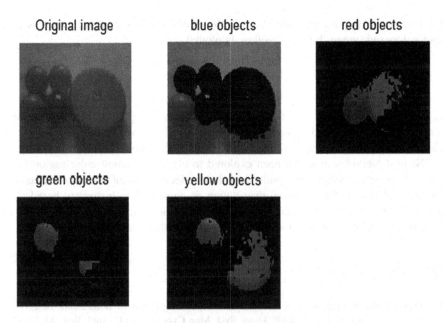

Original image   blue objects   red objects

green objects   yellow objects

Fig. 5. Test image and corresponding color based segmentation

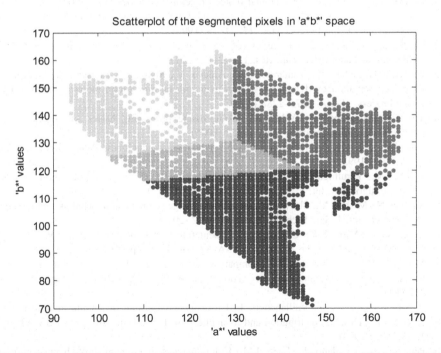

Scatterplot of the segmented pixels in 'a*b*' space

Fig. 6. Scatter plot of the segmented labeled pixels with corresponding 'a' and 'b' values (Color figure online)

individual color population using 'a' and 'b' values. Here, the segmentation of four input colors red, green, blue and yellow is plotted.

4 Conclusion

An algorithm for structural distribution of image data using color based image segmentation is implemented in real time. The system is developed to locate different colored structures in an acquired image along with their spatial and shape information. The Nearest Neighbor rule has been explored to classify different color region in an acquired image. Experimental results reveal the effectiveness of the color based segmentation algorithm for structural distribution as compared to histogram based classification. The future work shall include development of a medical image analysis system for tumor classification and paper currency authentication system.

References

1. Foresti, G.L., Pellegrino, F.A.: Automatic visual recognition of deformable objects for grasping and manipulation. IEEE Trans. Syst. Man Cybern. Part C Appl. Rev. **34**(3), 325–333 (2004)
2. Gonzalez, R.C., Woods, R.E.: Digital Image Processing. Prentice Hall (2002)
3. Chen, T. (Guest Ed.).: The past, present and future of image and multimedia signal processing. IEEE Sig Process Mag. **15**, 21–58 (1998)
4. Bhattacharyya, S.: A brief survey of color image preprocessing and segmentation techniques. J. Pattern Recognit. Res. 1, 120–129(2011)
5. Ugarriza, L., Saber, E., Vantaram, S.R., Amuso, V., Shaw, M., Bhaskar, R.: Automatic image segmentation by dynamic region growth and multiresolution merging. IEEE Trans. Image Process. **18**(10), 2275–2288 (2009)
6. Trussell, H.J., Saber, E., Vrhel, M.: Color image processing basics and special issue overview. IEEE Sig. Process. Mag. 14–22 (2005)
7. Pal, N.R., Pal, S.K.: A review on image segmentation techniques. Pattern Recognit. **26**, 1277–1294 (1993)
8. Lalitha, M., Kiruthiga, M., Loganathan, C.: A survey on image segmentation through clustering algorithm. Int. J. Sci. Res. **2**(2), 348–358 (2013)
9. Sharma, N., Mishra, M., Shrivastava, M.: Colour image segmentation techniques and issues: an approach. Int. J. Sci. Technol. Res. **1**(4), 9–12 (2012)
10. Lucchese, L., Mitra, S.K.: Color image segmentation: a state-of art survey. In: Proceedings of Indian National Science Academy (INSA-A), vol. 67-A, pp. 207–221 (2001)
11. Medasani, S., Krishnapuram, R.: A comparison of Gaussian and Pearson mixture modelling for pattern recognition and computer vision applications. Pattern Recognit. Lett. **20**, 305–313 (1999)
12. Bouguila, N., Ziou, D., Vaillancourt, J.: Unsupervised learning of a finite mixture model based on the Dirichlet distribution and its application. IEEE Trans. Image Process. **13**(11), 1533–1543 (2004)
13. Penalver, A., Escolano, F., Saez, J.M.: Color image segmentation through unsupervised Gaussian mixture models. LNAI **4140**, 149–158 (2006)

14. Raftery, A.E., Banfield, J.D.: Model-based Gaussian and non-Gaussian clustering. Biometrics **49**, 803–821 (1993)
15. Dongand, G., Xie, M.: Color clustering and learning for image segmentation based on neural networks. IEEE Trans. Neural Netw. **16**(4), 925–936 (2005)
16. Khan, W.: Image segmentation techniques: a survey. J Image Gr. **1**(4), 166–170 (2013)
17. Cover, T., Hart, P.: Nearest neighbor pattern classification. IEEE Trans. Inf. Theory **13**(1), 21–27 (1967)
18. Chakravarti, R., Meng, X.: A study of color histogram based image retrieval. In: 2009 Sixth International Conference on Information Technology: New Generations 2009, pp. 1323–1328
19. Kunttu, I., Lepistö, L., Rauhamaa, J., Visa, A.: Binary histogram in image classification for retrieval purposes. J. WSCG **11**(1), 1213–1217 (2003)
20. Niblack, W. et al.: The QBIC project: querying images by content using colour, texture and shape. In: SPIE Proceedings of Storage and Retrieval for Image and Video Databases, vol. 1908, pp. 173–187 (1993)
21. Ogle, V., Stonebraker, M.: Chabot: Retrieval from a relational database of images. IEEE Comput. **8**(9), 40–48 (1995)
22. http://en.wikipedia.org/wiki/Lab_color_space. Accessed on 27 April 2014

An Analysis of Interactions Among Barriers on the Implementation of Green Computing: Using Multi-objective Decision Modelling ISM

Harshit Khandelwal, Saru Dhir$^{(\boxtimes)}$, and Madhurima

Amity University, Noida, Uttar Pradesh, India
h.khandelwal096@gmail.com, sarudhir@gmail.com,
mhooda@amity.edu

Abstract. Green computing is the process of utilizing computer systems and their related resources in an ecological and environment friendly manner. It incorporates designing, building, utilizing and assembling of computing devices in a way that decreases their harmful ecological effect. In the past few years, green-computing concepts had been adopted by the industries due to increase in harmful effects of computing systems. This paper emphasizes on the important computing practices which are influencing on the environment. Significant practices and the essential barriers are recognized and analysed for the adoption of green systems. In this research, significant green barriers have been identified from the literature study and by the judgement of the specialists. The paper focuses on identifying and ranking the barriers for application, developing and studying the interrelationship between the identified barriers using the Interpretive Structural Modelling (ISM) and preparing a structure for the implementation of green computing.

Keywords: Green practices · Barriers · Interpretive system modelling (ISM)

1 Introduction

In the past few years, computer systems had been harming the environment rapidly in different ways like the increased power consumption, energy wastage, increased carbon footprint, lack of proper disposal, etc. The concept of green computing was introduced to deal with these effects [3]. The notion of green computing was brought up to reduce the effects of computers on the environment and enhancing the throughput of the computing systems. The main areas of focus of green computing are:

- To decrease the power consumed by systems.
- To increase the use of green energy.
- To make the systems more economical without sacrificing the productivity.
- To decrease the amount of electronic waste.

Although, green computing is an efficient way to provide services to the world as well as it also faces some barriers, such as: lack of resources, lack of techniques and eco-literacy etc. which hinder its performance [16, 18]. To further motivate the

© Springer Nature Singapore Pte Ltd. 2019
A. K. Luhach et al. (Eds.): ICAICR 2018, CCIS 955, pp. 562–570, 2019.
https://doi.org/10.1007/978-981-13-3140-4_51

companies to embrace green computing, these barriers should be eliminated. These barriers impact each other and the knowledge of the common relationship they share is very important. These barriers can be independent, dependant or interrelated.

Different decision-making techniques are used to evaluate the relationship between different attributes [9]. In this paper, the "Interpretive Structural Modelling (ISM)" is used for establishing the relationship between the barriers. It is known to be a firmly established methodology to recognize and encapsulate relationships amongst explicit variables, which are used for defining an issue or a problem [15].

This paper tries to increase the amount of knowledge by following the given points:

- Identifying the relationship between the barriers.
- Developing a model for feasible implementation of green computing.

This paper is further categorized into the following subsections. Second section comprises of the barriers affecting green computing are defined. A brief description of ISM is given in the third section. Section four discusses the ISM model for the barriers. Finally, the fifth section comprises of the conclusion.

2   Literature Review

The whole concept behind green computing is to reduce carbon footprint and cost cutting. Various number of research work has been done focusing entirely on the availability of resources, overall cost, performance of the computing systems and the data centres in the long run.

Larumbe et al. [1] had given a way for improving the design of networks for providing improved performance while reducing the overall consumption of energy and cost of the system. It is a new energy awareness system which supports the new computer architecture while providing a low power consumption environment.

The Eco Value 21 model gave a 7-step environment credit rating (AAA-CCC), while the GCI (Green Competitive Index) model developed by Samsung and rates the competitiveness between countries based on low carbon index and green industry index [5, 6].

Gartner and Molla catches the whole concept of green in ICT but is only limited to the direct influences of ICT on the environment [2, 17].

Principles of virtualising server can help large industries to conserve the over usage of power by 80% and can help to increase the use of hardware resource to maximum. According to a research, in 1990's IBM company saved 4 billion of kilowatts in power [4]. The data centres are more responsible in power consumption and uses more than 50% of the office space.

ISM technique was used by Sharma et al. for developing a ranking of actions essential for achieving the upcoming motive of managing waste [14].

Diabat et al. utilized this methodology for developing a framework of the drivers which affected the application of green computing [10]. The enablers for supply chain agility were examined using the ISM technique by Faisal et al. [7].

Madaan et al. used ISM to provide a multi-objective decision model for enriching and initiating the green computing activities in an industry [8]. Mudgal et al. used this approach for modelling and analysing key barriers of Green Computing [11]. The relationships among the main barriers preventing the practise of energy saving were examined by Wan et al. in China [12].

3 Barriers Affecting Green Computing

- Privacy issues (security issues) (B1)
- Budget issues (B2)
- Adoption issues(B3)
- Reluctance to change (B4)
- Lack of management(B5)
- Lack of motivation (B6)
- Frequent changes in the technology (B7)
- Lack of technology (B8)
- Lack of resources (B9)
- Low eco-literacy (B10).

4 Interpretive Structural Modeling (ISM)

The ISM, created by J.W. Warfield, is a well-known technique to study the synergic impact of different variables over the whole system. The process of ISM comprises of finding the factors, defining their contextual relationships, and imposing a hierarchical rank order to eliminate complex problems from a system's point of view.

The ISM process helps in transforming uncertain, poorly segmented mental frameworks of systems into observable, distinct frameworks beneficial for various motives.

Many researchers have used ISM for understanding the interrelationships between different attributes in several organisations since it is a well-established methodology that can be used in different fields. Methodology for developing the model using ISM:

A step-to-step procedure is followed for developing the ISM framework. Ravi and Shankar defined some steps or stages which are listed below [13]:

- Stage 1: Variables affecting the system are taken into consideration.
- Stage 2: An interdependent relationship among the variables is defined.
- Stage 3: SSIM is created for the variables which defines the relationship of a variable with another.
- Stage 4: From the SSIM, reachability matrix is derived and examined for transitivity.
- Stage 5: Reachability matrix is divided into various levels.
- Stage 6: A directed graph is drawn and remove the transitive links.
- Stage 7: Subsequent digraph is then transformed into ISM.
- Stage 8: The developed ISM model is revised, and essential alterations are made.

5   ISM Model

5.1   Structural Self Interaction Matrix (SSIM)

Ten barriers are chosen from the literature and judgement of experts. The next point of focus is identifying and analysing the contextual relationship between the barriers. ISM encourages the usage of opinions of experts and minimum group discussion techniques for identifying the relationship. Four symbols are defined to understand the connection among the barriers.

V: B_I influences the barrier B_j
A: B_i is influenced by the barrier B_j
X: B_i and B_j influence each other
O: B_i and B_j are not inter-related

Based on the interrelationships between the variables, the final SSIM is created which is shown in Table 1.

Table 1. SSIM

	B1	B2	B3	B4	B5	B6	B7	B8	B9	B10
B1	1	A	A	A	V	V	V	A	A	A
B2	V	1	V	V	V	V	V	O	V	V
B3	V	A	1	A	V	V	V	O	V	V
B4	V	A	V	1	O	V	V	O	V	V
B5	A"	A	A	O	1	X	V	O	V	V
B6	A	A	A	A	X	1	A	o	O	A
B7	A	A	A	A	A	V	1	o	O	V
B8	V	O	O	O	O	O	O	1	O	V
B9	V	A	A	A	A	O	O	O	1	V
B10	V	A	A	A	A	V	A	A	A	1

5.2   Initial Reachability Matrix

This matrix is derived from the SSIM by substituting the values of A, V, O, X by binary digits (0, 1) according to the rules of transformation. The rules are listed below (Table 2):

Table 2. Rules of transformation

If the (i, j) entry in the SSIM is	Entry in the initial reachability matrix	
	(i, j)	(j, i)
V	1	0
A	0	1
X	1	1
O	0	0

The initial reachability matrix is organized following the above rule as shown in Table 3.

Table 3. Initial reachability matrix

	B1	B2	B3	B4	B5	B6	B7	B8	B9	B10
B1	1	0	1	0	1	1	1	0	0	0
B2	1	1	0	1	1	1	1	0	1	1
B3	1	0	1	0	1	1	1	0	1	1
B4	1	0	1	1	0	1	1	0	1	1
B5	0	0	0	0	1	1	1	0	1	1
B6	0	0	0	0	1	1	0	0	0	0
B7	0	0	0	0	0	1	1	0	0	1
B8	1	0	0	0	0	0	0	1	0	1
B9	1	0	0	0	0	0	0	0	1	1
B10	1	0	0	0	0	1	0	0	0	1

5.3   Final Reachability Matrix

For creating the final reachability matrix, modify the initial reachability using the concept of transitivity. If an element 'i' affects an element 'j' and 'j' affects an element 'k' then transitivity states that 'i' should affect 'k'. The final reachability matrix is represented in Table 4. In Table 4, transitivity is shown in cells marked by '*'.

Table 4. Final reachability matrix

	B1	B2	B3	B4	B5	B6	B7	B8	B9	B10	Driving power
B1	1	0	1	0	1	1	1	0	1*	1*	7
B2	1	1	1*	1	1	1	1	0	1	1	9
B3	1	0	1	0	1	1	1	0	1	1	7
B4	1	0	1	1	1*	1	1	0	1	1	8
B5	1*	0	0	0	1	1	1	0	1	1	6
B6	0	0	0	0	1	1	1*	0	1*	1*	5
B7	1*	0	0	0	1*	1	1	0	0	1	5
B8	1	0	1*	0	1*	1*	1	1	0	1	7
B9	1	0	1*	0	1*	1*	1*	0	1	1	7
B10	1	0	1*	0	1*	1	1*	0	0	1	6
Dependencies	9	1	7	2	10	10	10	1	7	10	67

5.4 Level Partitioning

Firstly, the reachability and antecedent sets are derived from final reachability matrix. The reachability matrix is formed by the barrier itself and the different barriers which are influenced by it. The antecedent set is made up of the barrier and other barriers which might affect it. The intersection set comprises of the intersection of the reachability sets and antecedent sets for every barrier. Finally, the levels of various barriers are deduced. If the reachability sets and the antecedent sets of a barrier are identical, the highest level is allotted to that barrier in the ISM hierarchy. In the hierarchy, the highest-level barriers do not allow any other barriers above their own level (Table 5, 6, 7 and 8).

Table 5. Barriers of Level I

Barrier	Reachability set	Antecedent set	Intersection set	Level
B1	B1, B3, B5, B6, B7, B9, B10	B1, B2, B3, B4, B5, B7, B9, B10	B1, B3, B5, B7, B9, B10	
B2	B1, B2, B3, B4, B5, B6, B7, B9, B10	B2	B2	
B3	B1, B3, B5, B6, B7, B9, B10	B1, B2, B3, B4,	B1, B3	
B4	B1, B3, B4, B5, B6, B7, B9, B10	B1, B4	B1, B4	
B5	B1, B5, B6, B7, B9, B10	B1, B2, B3, B4, B5, B6, B7, B8, B9, B10	B1, B5, B6, B7, B9, B10	I
B6	B5, B6, B7, B9, B10	B1, B2, B3, B4, B5, B6, B7, B8, B9, B10	B5, B6, B7, B9, B10	I
B7	B1, B5, B6, B7, B9, B10	B1, B2, B3, B4, B5, B6, B7, B8, B9, B10	B1, B5, B6, B7, B9, B10	I
B8	B1, B3, B5, B6, B7, B8, B10	B8	B8	
B9	B1, B3, B5, B6, B7, B9, B10	B1, B2, B3, B4, B5, B6, B9	B1, B3, B5, B6, B9	
B10	B1, B3, B5, B6, B7, B10	B1, B2, B3, B4, B5, B6, B7, B8, B9, B10	B1, B3, B5, B6, B7, B10	I

Table 6. Barriers of Level II

Barrier	Reachability set	Antecedent set	Intersection set	Level
B1	B1, B3, B9	B1, B2, B3, B4, B8, B9	B1, B3, B9	II
B2	B1, B2, B3, B4, B9	B2	B2	
B3	B1, B3, B9	B1, B2, B3, B4	B1, B3	
B4	B1, B3, B4, B9	B1, B2, B3, B4	B1, B3, B4	
B8	B1, B3, B8	B8	B8	
B9	B1, B3, B9	B1, B2, B3, B4, B9	B1, B3, B9	II

Table 7. Barriers of Level III

Barrier	Reachability set	antecedent set	Intersection set	Level
B2	B2, B3, B4	B2	B2	
B3	B3	B2, B3, B4	B3	III
B4	B3, B4	B2, B3, B4	B3, B4	III
B8	B3, B8	B8	B8	

Table 8. Barriers of Level IV

Barrier	Reachability set	Antecedent set	Intersection set	Level
B2	B2	B2	B2	IV
B8	B8	B8	B8	IV

5.5   Building the ISM Model

The model created with the known barriers in green computing is depicted in Figs. 1 and 2. It clearly shows that the successful elimination of barriers B2 and B8 (Budget issues and lack of technology respectively) would lead to better implementation of green computing as they form base level of ISM hierarchy whereas B5, B6, B7 and B10 (lack of management, lack of motivation, frequent changes in technology and low eco-literacy) leans on other barriers and appear highest in the hierarchy.

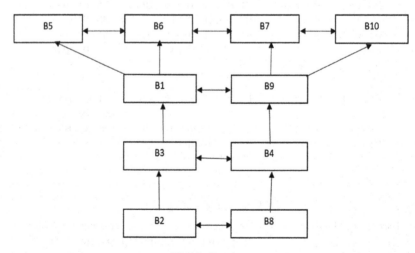

Fig. 1. Barriers

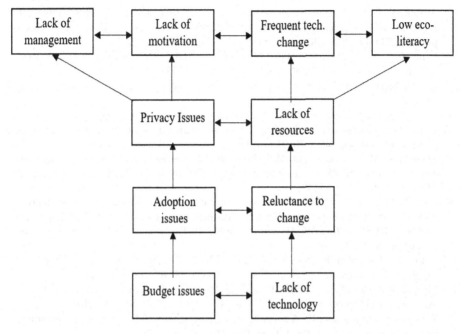

Fig. 2. ISM Model

6 Conclusion

This paper guides the practitioners in the successful implementation of green computing by eliminating the barriers in systematic way. This model provides a relationship between the barriers and it will help the practitioners and industries for understanding the connection. This research shows that barriers are modelled based on their driving power and dependencies. Barriers with weak dependence (or strong driving power) should be dealt firstly as they lead the other barriers.

Using the ISM model, successful management and utilization of resources will lead to the removal of barriers and a successful and profitable implementation of green computing. Proper study and research of this area may help in acting like a road map for the future in Green ICT. It would be a light house to researchers and industries.

References

1. Larumbe, F., Sanso, B.: A tabu search algorithm for the location of data centers and software components in green cloud computing networks. IEEE Trans. Cloud Comput. 1(1), 22–35 (2013)
2. Gartner: Introducing the gartner green and sustainable it infrastructure and operations maturity model (2013)

3. Mishra, A., Garg, A., Dhir, S.: A cybernetic approach for controlling employee attitude for implementation of green organization. In: 2012 World Congress on Sustainable Technologies (WCST), London, UK, 19–22 November 2012. IEEE (2012)
4. Lamb, J.: The Greening of IT: How Companies Can Make a Difference for the Environment. IBM Press, Indianapolis (2009). ISBN-13: 978-0137150830
5. BSDGlobalHome: Innovestcasestudy. http://www.iisd.org/business/viewcasestudy.aspx?id=75
6. SERI: The advent of green growth era, CEO Information, October 2008
7. Faisal, M.N., Banwet, D.K., Shankar, R.: Supply chain agility: analysing the enablers. Int. J. Agile Syst. Manag. 2(1), 76–91 (2007)
8. Madaan, J., Mangla, S., Gupta, M.P.: Multi-objective decision modeling using Interpretive Structural Modeling (ISM) for Green Supply Chains. In: POMS 23rd Annual Conference, Chicago, Illinois, U.S.A. (2012)
9. Dhir, S., Kumar, D., Singh, V.B.: Requirement paradigms to implement the software projects in agile development using analytical hierarchy process. Int. J. Dec. Supp. Syst. Technol. (IJDSST) 9(3), 28–41 (2017). Article 2 (Thomson Reuters (Web of Science), Scopus Indexed)
10. Diabat, A., Govindan, K.: An analysis of the drivers affecting the implementation of green supply chain management. Resour. Conserv. Recycl. 55, 659–667 (2011)
11. Mudgal, R.K., Shankar, R., Talib, P., Raj, T.: Modelling the barriers of green supply chain practices: an Indian perspective. Int. J. Log. Syst. Manag. 7(1), 81–107 (2010)
12. Wan, H.-D., Frank Chen, F.: A leanness measure of manufacturing systems for quantifying impacts of lean initiatives. Int. J. Prod. Res. 46(23), 6567–6584 (2008)
13. Ravi, V., Shankar, R.: Analysis of interactions among the barriers of reverse logistics. Technol. Forecast. Soc. Chang. 72, 1011–1029 (2005)
14. Sharma, H.D., Gupta, A.D., Sushil: The objectives of waste management in India: a future inquiry. Technol. Forecast. Soc. Chang. 48, 285–309 (1995)
15. Rai, P., Dhir, S.: Impact of different methodologies in software development process. Int. J. Comput. Sci. Inf. Technol. (IJCSIT) 5(2), 1112–1116 (2014)
16. Dhir, S., Kumar, D., Singh, V.B.: Success and failure factors that impact on project implementation using agile software development methodology. In: Hoda, M.N., Chauhan, N., Quadri, S.M.K., Srivastava, P.R. (eds.) Software Engineering. AISC, vol. 731, pp. 647–654. Springer, Singapore (2019). https://doi.org/10.1007/978-981-10-8848-3_62
17. Molla, A., Cooper, V.: Green it readiness a framework and preliminary proof of concept. Australas. J. Inf. Syst. 16(2) (2010)
18. Shradha, M., Dhir, S.: IoT for healthcare: challenges and future prospects. Presented in 5th International Conference on Computing for Sustainable Global Development (INDIACom 2018), 14–16 March 2018. IEEE Xplore (2018, to be published)

Automated Testcase Generation and Prioritization Using GA and FRBS

Muhammad Azam[1], Atta-ur-Rahman[2], Kiran Sultan[3],
Sujata Dash[4(✉)], Sundas Naqeeb Khan[5],
and Muhammad Aftab Alam Khan[2]

[1] Barani Institute of Information Technology (BIIT), PMAS-AA University,
Rawalpindi, Pakistan
Mazam770@yahoo.com
[2] College of Computer Science and Information Technology,
Department of Computer Science, Imam Abdulrahman Bin Faisal University,
P.O. Box 1982, Dammam, Kingdom of Saudi Arabia
{aaurrahamn,mkhan}@iau.edu.sa
[3] Department of CIT, JCC, AbdulAziz University, King Jeddah,
Kingdom of Saudi Arabia
Kkhan2@kau.edu.sa
[4] Department of Computer Science, North Orissa University, Baripada, India
Sujata238dash@gmail.com
[5] Faculty of Computer Science and Information Technology,
Universiti Tun Hussein Onn Malaysia, 86400 Parit Raja, Johor, Malaysia
Sndskhan87@gmail.com

Abstract. Software Quality Assurance (SQA) is a process in which the quality of software is assured by adequate software testing techniques that mainly comprise of verification and validation of the software. Software testing is the process of assessing the features of a software item and evaluating it to detect differences between given input and expected output. This process is done during the development process just prior to deployment. The SQA process is usually a manual process due to the diverse and versatile nature of the software products. That means a technique devised to test one type of software may not work that efficiently while testing another kind of software etc. Moreover, it is a time consuming process; according to a survey it consumes almost half of the total development cost and around two third of the total development time. To address the above-mentioned issues, in this research an intelligent toolkit for automated SQA is proposed and compared them with the existing famous tools like Selenium. This research focuses on automated test case/test data generation and prioritization of test cases. For this purpose, Genetic Algorithm is investigated for automatic test case generation and a fuzzy based system is proposed for test case prioritization.

Keywords: SQA · Testcase generation · Testcase prioritization
Automated testing · GA · FRBS

© Springer Nature Singapore Pte Ltd. 2019
A. K. Luhach et al. (Eds.): ICAICR 2018, CCIS 955, pp. 571–584, 2019.
https://doi.org/10.1007/978-981-13-3140-4_52

1 Introduction

Testing is a vital phase of Software life Cycle (SDLC). It is principally done on all type of applications like Desktop; Web based applications and smart phone apps etc. Moreover, it is one of the major techniques that deal with the customer requirements means it ensures that the product is built as per customer requirements. In other words, software testing means delivering a bug-free quality product as per the requirements of end user. It is done to detect the differences between the expected and actual output of the software also the presence of faults which cases failure. In short testing is a verification and validation process carried out prior to software deployment.

Testing can be done manually or automatically by using different testing tools like Selenium, QTP and MTM etc. It is found that manual testing is time consuming as compared to automated testing. However, different testing tools are available in the market now a day with their own pros and cons. These tools basically deal with the automatic test case generation. In this regard, various techniques have been introduced for effective test case generation and prioritization of test cases automatically using population based stochastic algorithms like Genetic Algorithms, fuzzy logic, neural networks and genetic programming [1–3].

The SQA process is usually a manual process due to the diverse and versatile nature of the software products. That means a technique devised to test one type of software may not work that efficiently while testing another kind of software etc. Moreover, it is a time-consuming process; according to a survey it consumes most of the total development cost and total development time. To overcome above cited problem of laborious manual work involved in testing phase of software development life cycle, following approaches are made.

Automatic Test case/test data generation

This phase concerns with generation of test cases automatically for a given application being tested. In this regard, the field IDs and their corresponding values are once assessed and then these values are fed to Genetic Algorithm as a initial population to come up with all the possible test cases related to that application of concern. All the test cases generated by the Genetic Algorithm are eventually stored in an Excel file.

Test case prioritization

This approach involves in the prioritization of test cases. This is done for two reasons. Firstly, that important test cases must be conducted first. Secondly to avoid the duplication of test cases, which eventually reduces the time complexity of testing. Its role is more significant with the large applications having several test cases. In this regard, a fuzzy rule based system (FRBS) is projected, that considers, various factors, to prioritize a test case.

Rest part of the paper is organized as follows: section two throws light on the related works, section three holds the proposed work. Section four includes results and discussion while section five provides the conclusions.

2 Related Work

The past literature shows the growing research interests towards the software testing area from last few decades. However, Software Quality Assurance is the emerging field in Information Technology.

As described by Singh et al. [1] proposes a hybrid Genetic Particle Swarm technique algorithm. This is used for Software Test Case Generation. It also describes the research done in software testing using soft computing techniques, such as Genetic Algorithms (GA) Particle Swarm Optimization techniques (PSO) and their hybridizations. These are used to compare and find the minimum software test case for testing the software. The new proposed solution produces 100% results as compared to GA and PSO and their hybrid.

According to Arora and Baghel [2] a method is describe for optimizing software testing by discovering the most defective paths in the software. This can be achieved by meta-heuristic technique that is by using genetic algorithm and particle swarm optimization. Our goal is the generation of test cases using both algorithms and their comparative study. Comparative study shows that GA can be more useful and how PSO overcomes the drawbacks of GA.

As described by Sharma et al. [3] present a survey of GA approach for addressing the various issues like effective generation of test cases and prioritization of test cases etc. encountered during the software testing also the applications of GA algorithm.

According to Brar and Garg [4] presents a survey on automatic test case generation methodologies adopted to generate optimum set of test data without human intervention based on test adequacy criteria. The main objective of the paper is to go through the current researchs performed in the automated test data generation field, the various sub optimal startigies (ACO, PSO GA, SA etc.) and the hybridization of those meta-heuristics techniques (ACSGA, GAPSO etc.). Results show that the PSO is competitive with GA and even outperforms them for complex cases. According to Ahmed et al. [5] software testing has a few fundamental concerns, that are too important and proper attention should be given on those properties. These characteristics are effective in the generation as well as prioritization of test cases. Applications of softcomputing are not just limited to software testing but wide in variety [6–9].

Evolutionary algorithms have a momentous role in the process of automatic test case generation and researchers are focusing on it. In this study software testing related concepts are addressed using the genetic algorithms based approach. In addition to this it is found that after applying some analysis, better solutions are produced, that are feasible and reliable. This paper provides an expert system for the optimization of test case generation using genetic algorithms [10, 16, 17]. Similar approaches arecarried out in [11–15].

3 Proposed Approach

This section is further comprised of following sections.

- Automated test data generation for data driven testing using GAs
- Optimization as well as prioritization of test cases using FRBS

In both manual and automated Software testing there is no mechanism to create test data automatically. Tester make this data through its assumptions created from the requirements and use these test data for multiple test cases. So, in this research, a solution for automatically test data generation through Genetic algorithm is proposed. This algorithm works based on Test case inscription techniques (Equivalence Class Partitioning along with Boundary Value Analysis) and creates test data automatically which is populated into an excel file. Later this excel file is read through the application and the result of the test cases is written against that test data input. In this way we can limit the test cases and prioritize them according to the severity of the test data applying the proposed fuzzy based system.

3.1   Automatic Test Data Generation by Applying Genetic Algorithms

In software testing we have various techniques which divide the software input test data to trim down the number of test cases. Which are as follows;

1. Equivalence class partitioning
2. Boundary value analysis

Equivalence class partitioning: In this method, the entire input domain data set is divided into diverse equivalence data classes. Like we need to test the values between 1 and 100 then we can break this into four classes like 1–25, 26–50, 51–75 and 76–100.

In a nut shell we can say, it is the process of selecting the entire set of possible test cases and placing them in a number of classes. single test value is chosen from every class while testing. This is a complex process which is carried out manually. Inserting so many values is humanly not possible. That is why Genetic Algorithm is used to reduce the search space. To show how Genetic Algorithm works, here an example is shown.

Example 1: Test cases for input box accommodating numbers in the range of 1 and 1000.

1. One can make class from 1 to 99 and pick one or two values as input data.
2. One can make another class from 100 to 9999 and pick one or two values as input data.
3. One can make another class from 10000 to above to test the negative values as input data.
4. Similarly, can also make another class below 1 to test the negative values as input data.

This process is shown in the Table 1.

Table 1. Example 1

Classes	Boundary value 1	Boundary value 2
Class 1	0	−99
Class 2	1	99
Class 3	100	333
Class 4	1000	Above

After creating the classes, we can apply Boundary value analysis for picking the test data input. So,

1. First data input for input box is 0.
2. Second data input for input box is −99.
3. And so on

Example 2: There is another example of Username text field accepting the Alpha Numeric values using the black box strategies Equivalence class Partitioning along with Boundary Value Analysis.

1. One can make the classes like for 0a to −99yz.
2. Second class is from 1a to 99yz.
3. Third class should be 100abc to 999xyz.
4. Fourth class should be 1000abcd to above.

Also, one can make the classes separately for alphabetically and numeric values and depending upon the algorithm you have used to create classes. Here this is carried out by the Genetic Algorithm to find and return best random cases (Table 2).

Table 2. Example 2

Classes	Test cases	Username	Result
Class 1	Test case 1	0a	Pass
	Test case 2	99xy	Pass
Class 2	Test case 3	100abe	Pass
	Test case 4	999xyz	Pass

So, in Username text field 0a is the test data input and after applying this test data it is Test case1 and 99xy is the second test data input and after applying it is Test case 2 and so on.

After creating the excel file we also prioritize the test cases according to the severity of test data. Which was a manual process but now it is done by proposed fuzzy based system described in subsequent section. Eventually, after creating the excel file of test data we can use the Data Driven frame work using Selenium web driver to execute the test cases.

3.2 Data Driven Testing

In data driven automated testing, initially a test data set is created in the excel sheet, and is the data set is imported into an automation testing tool that feeds it to the software under test.

Why data drive tests? Often there might several test data sets that can be used to test the different features of an application. Repeating the same test manually with different data sets is a quite time-consuming and error prone task. Let us explain the scenario with an example.

Suppose we need to test the login or Register feature of a form with multiple input fields out of 100 different data sets. To test it, three different approaches are available

1. Create 100 scripts, one for each dataset and then execute them one by one.
2. Alter the dataset in the script and execute it multiple times.
3. Import the test data from created excel sheet and execute the script multiple times with different set of data.

As the above described initial two scenarios are laborious, time-consuming. Hence, we have followed the third technique in this research. That is first importing the test data from the excel sheet and then executing the script multiple time with different sets of test data selected randomly.

The Question is where the Test data comes from in the excel file. So, the answer is, either tester makes it manually which is basically a time-consuming task or automatically? Which we have proposed in this research by using the Genetic Algorithm. In the next section, we will show the results of both manual test data creation through the algorithm shown in Fig. 1 and compare them.

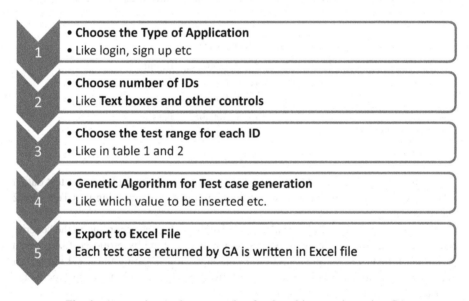

Fig. 1. Automatic test data generation for data driven testing using GA

3.3   Optimization and Prioritization of Test Cases Using FRBS

This section contains the construction of fuzzy rule based system (FRBS) for optimization and precogitation of the test cases generated by the Genetic Algorithm, explained in the previous section. Here prioritization means sequencing or sorting the test cases based on their importance. That means which test case will be applied first, second and so on based on some priority number. While optimization means that there could be more than one test cases (in excel file) related to same testing, then which one to choose and which one to drop. This process will further reduce the complexity of testing the software quality. Prioritization is mainly based on some key factors usually set by the tester based on his experience. Following is the set of most common and factors in this regard.

This process deals with, the calculation of prioritization factors such as:

- The priority (CP) allotted by Customer

This factor is suggested by the customer based on his intention that which component he wants to assign more or less importance. Value of this factor lies between 1 and 20. Where one is the lowest and 20 is the highest priority.

- Developer observed code execution complexity (EC)

This measure usually comes from the development team based on their assigned complexity value. The complexity value ranges between 1 and 20. Complex codes are more vulnerable to errors. That is why a higher value is given to more complex codes and vice versa.

- Changes in requirements (CHG)

It is a grade assigned by the developer in the range of 1 to 20 that indicates the number of times the requirement is changed during the development cycle with respect to its origin. The volatility values for all those needs are expressed on a 20-point scale where the need is changed more than 20 times. The number of changes for any requirement 'i' is divided to the maximum number of changes that yields the change in requirement Ri where the requirement is 'i'.

If the i_{th} requirement is changed M times and N is the maximum number of requirements, then the requirement change R_i can be calculated as follows:

$$R_i = (M/N) * 20 \qquad (1)$$

- Fault impact (FI)

This impact is measured as the frequency of change requirements during software development. The impact value may vary between 1 and 20 where 1 leads to lowest and 20 leads to highest impact.

- Completeness (COM)

This part indicates the requirement based function that are to be executed, the success rate, the limitations and specifically those limitation that manipulate the expected solution. (boundary constraints). The purchaser assigned values range between 1 and 20. Where 1 reveals least and 20 reveals most completeness value.

- Traceability (TR)

The relationship between the requirements and assessments can be adjusted by means of Traceability. Impact value may vary between 1 and 20 where 1 leads to lowest and 20 leads to highest value of traceability.

Those factors are vital for prioritizing the test cases as they are used in the prioritization algorithm. We have assigned weights to each test case in the software testing according to those factors. Then, the test cases are prioritized based on those assigned weights.

3.4 Design of Fuzzy Rule Based System

The proposed fuzzy rule based system is designed in such a way that it takes values of all factors and provide a joint priority to the test case. This can be written as.

$$Final\text{-}priority = FRBS(F1, F2, F3, F4, F5, F6)$$

where F1 to F6 are the factors discussed above, final-prirority is the outcome by the proposed fuzzy rule based system. FRBS takes these factors as inputs and generates the said output by inferring it.

3.4.1 Input/Output Variables

Here the input to the proposed fuzzy rule based system are the above-mentioned factors that contributes to obtain the final priority of the given test case, given in Fig. 2.

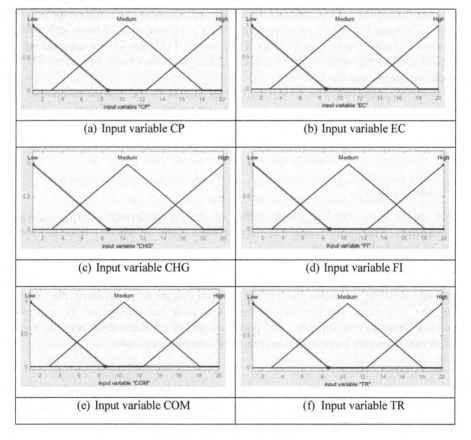

(a) Input variable CP	(b) Input variable EC
(c) Input variable CHG	(d) Input variable FI
(e) Input variable COM	(f) Input variable TR

Fig. 2. Fuzzy input variables

The range of all the variables is between 1 and 20 where 1 corresponds to lowest and 20 corresponds to the highest value of priority. The sets in all the input variables are kept three that are low, medium and high while the number of fuzzy sets in output variable are five. Namely, very_low, Low, Medium, High and Very_high. Triangular fuzzifiers have been used in all those input output variables.

Figure 4 shows the overall picture of fuzzy rule based system that is comprised on all input and output variables. This shows that there are six input variables and one output variable. Moreover, the inference engine used is Mamdani Inference Engine (MIE) that infers to the output based on the given set of inputs at any given time.

Output variable final-priority is given in Fig. 3.

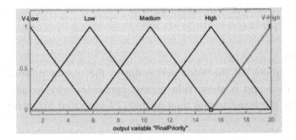

Fig. 3. Fuzzy output variable

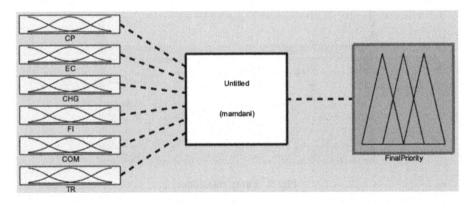

Fig. 4. Fuzzy rule based system

3.4.2   Implication System
The parameters of the proposed Fuzzy Rule Based System are given in Table 3.

Table 3. FRBS parameters

Sr.	Parameter	Value
1	Number of inputs	6
2	Number of output	1
3	Type of fuzzifiers	Triangular
4	Inference engine	Mamdani inference engine
5	AND Method	Min
6	OR Method	Max
7	Implication	Min
8	Aggregation	Max
9	Defuzzifier	Centroid
10	Cardinality of Input output	6 × 1

3.4.3   Rulebase

The rule base contains all the rules pertaining to the output priority by given input priorities. Figures 5 and 6 show rule editors (provides way to add rules) and rule surface (visualize the input output relationship) of proposed fuzzy rule based system.

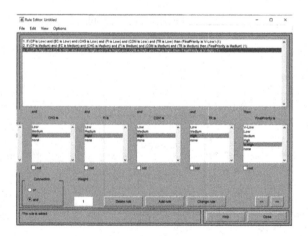

Fig. 5. Fuzzy rule editor

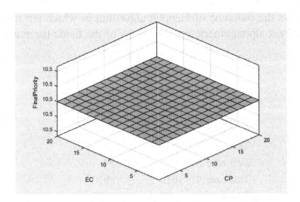

Fig. 6. Fuzzy rule surface

4 Results and Discussion

This section contains the results of the proposed automated software quality assurance process and related discussion. Here a case study has been provided that reflects the effectiveness of the projected methodology.

4.1 Example

Suppose there is a login page having two text fields Username and Password accepting alpha numeric values. So According to Class Partitioning we can make the classes to shorten the input data and with minimum input data we can test the validity of text field. Providing the following guidelines (Table 4), we can obtain the test cases by Genetic Algorithm.

Table 4. Class partitioning

Classes	Values
Negative class	Empty value
Positive class 1	a, b, c, …, z and 0 to 9
Positive class 2	a, b, c, …, z and 10 to 99
Positive class 3	a, b, c, …, z and 100 to 999
Positive class 4	a, b, c, …, z and 1000 to 9999
Positive class 5	a, b, c, …, z and 10000+

Now the above information is fed to the Genetic Algorithm as a seed or initial population. Although the permutations of the possible values are huge in number and it is of no use in assessing each of them. However, the number of samples must be enough to test the whole scenario of possible combinations of username and passwords.

Table 5 shows the outcome of Genetic algorithm in which ten test cases are generated with different alphanumeric combinations of the fields username and password respectively.

Table 5. Generated test cases

Test Cases	Username	Password
Test case 1	Empty	Empty
Test case 2	a0	a0
Test case 3	z9	z9
Test case 4	ab10	ab10
Test case 5	yz99	yz99
Test case 6	abc100	abc100
Test case 7	xyz999	xyz999
Test case 8	abcd1000	abcd1000
Test case 9	wxyz9999	wxyz9999
Test case 10	vwxyz10000	vwxyz10000

The sample test cases for the example are enlisted in the Table 5 are the outcome of Genetic Algorithm. Although the generated test cases are more than the listed but these are mentioned for sake of example purpose here.

Now when the fuzzy rule based system is employed on a given set of test cases duly generated by the Genetic Algorithm, it resulted in assigning the priorities to the test cases based on the knowledge provided in the inference engine through rules. That can be seen in the Table 6, where each test case has been assigned a priority values.

Table 6. Test cases prioritized

Test Cases	Username	Password	P
Test case 1	Empty	Empty	10
Test case 2	a0	a0	20
Test case 3	z9	z9	20
Test case 4	ab10	ab10	20
Test case 5	yz99	yz99	20
Test case 6	abc100	abc100	20
Test case 7	xyz999	xyz999	20
Test case 8	abcd1000	abcd1000	20
Test case 9	wxyz9999	wxyz9999	20
Test case 10	vwxyz10000	vwxyz10000	20

From the values of Table 6 it is observed that in the first test case empty values corresponds to the medium the priority. This is because the test case is less obvious. Rest all the test cases contain highest priority that means all the test cases must be executed during the testing phase.

5 Conclusion and Future Work

This research focuses on generation of an intelligent toolkit for automated software quality assurance process. In the automation, two aspects are the most important. First is test case/test data generation and second it prioritization of the generated test cases. To address these issues, in this research Genetic Algorithm (GA) and a Fuzzy Rule Based System (FRBS) are modeled as well as investigated that are intended for automatic case/test data generation and case/test data prioritization, respectively. From the experiments it was observed that the projected schemes are promising for automated test case generation along with prioritization. In our research the major focus was on boundary values testing in the light of class partitioning.

In future, other testing methodologies may also be investigated in terms of automation using same schemes or some other set of techniques.

References

1. Singh, A., Garg, N., Saini, T.: A hybrid approach of genetic algorithm and particle swarm technique to software test. Int. J. Innov. Eng. Technol. (IJIET), **3**(4), 208–214 (2014)
2. Arora, D., Baghel, A.S.: Application of genetic algorithm and particle swarm optimization in software testing. IOSR J. Comput. Eng. (IOSR-JCE) **17**(1), 75–78, Ver. II (2015), e-ISSN: 2278-0661, p-ISSN: 2278-8727
3. Sharma, C., Sabharwal, S., Sibal, R.: Applying genetic algorithm for prioritization of test case scenarios. IJCSI Int. J. Comput. Sci. Issues **8**(3), 2, 433–444 (2011), Derived from UML Diagrams
4. Brar, K.M., Garg, S.: Survey on automated test data generation. Int. J. Comput. Appl. (0975–8887) **108**(15), 1–4 (2014)
5. Mateen, A., Nazir, M., Awan, S.A.: Optimization of test case generation using genetic algorithm (GA). Int. J. Comput. Appl. (0975–8887) **151**(7), 6–14 (2016)
6. Atta-ur-Rahman, Qureshi, I.M., Malik, A.N., Naseem, M.T.: QoS and rate enhancement in DVB-S2 using fuzzy rule base system. J. Intell. Fuzzy Syst. (JIFS) **30**(1), 801–810 (2016)
7. Atta-ur-Rahman, Qureshi, I.M., Malik, A.N., Naseem, M.T.: Dynamic resource allocation for OFDM systems using differential evolution and fuzzy rule base system. J. Intell. Fuzzy Syst. (JIFS) **26**(4), 2035–2046 (2014). https://doi.org/10.3233/ifs-130880
8. Atta-ur-Rahman, Qureshi, I.M., Malik, A.N.: Adaptive resource allocation in OFDM systems using GA and fuzzy rule base system. World Appl. Sci. J. (WASJ) **18**(6), 836–844 (2012)
9. Atta-ur-Rahman, Qureshi, I.M., Malik, A.N.: A fuzzy rule base assisted adaptive coding and modulation scheme for OFDM systems. J. Basic Appl. Sci. Res. **2**(5), 4843–4853 (2012)
10. Abhishek, S., Chandna, S., Bansal, A.: Optimization of test cases using genetic algorithm 1 (2012)
11. Deepa, C., Sehgal, A.: Automated test data generation using soft computing techniques. Int. J. Adv. Res. Comput. Eng. Technol. (IJARCET) **4**(4), 1165–1169 (2015)
12. Sathi, N., Rani, S., Singh, P.: Ants optimization for minimal test case selection and prioritization as to reduce the cost of regression testing. Int. J. Comput. Appl. (0975–8887) **100**(17), 48–54 (2014)
13. Kire, K., Malhotra, N.: Software testing using intelligent technique. Int. J. Comput. Appl. (0975–8887) **90**(19), 22–25 (2014)

14. Singla, S., Kumar, R., Kummar, D.: Natural computing for automatic test data generation approach using spanning tree concepts. Procedia Comput. Sci. **85**, 929–939 (2016)
15. Badanahatti, S., Murthy, Y.S.S.R.: Optimal test case prioritization in cloud based regression testing with aid of KFCM. Int. J. Intell. Eng. Syst. **10**(2), 96–106 (2017)
16. Panda, M., Dah, S.: Automatic test suite generation for object oriented programs using metaheuristic Cuckoo search algorithm. Int. J. Control Theory Appl. **10**(18), 71–79 (2017)
17. Panda, M., Dash, S.: Automatic test data generation using bio-inspired algorithms: a travelogue. In: Dash, S., Tripathy, B.K., Rehman, A. (eds.) Handbook of Research on the Modeling. Analysis and Application on Nature-Inspired Metaheuristic Algorithms, pp. 140–159. IGI-Global, USA (2017)

A Survey on Metaheuristic Approaches and Its Evaluation for Load Balancing in Cloud Computing

Deepak Garg[(✉)] and Pardeep Kumar

Department of Computer Science and Application, Kurukshetra University,
Kurukshetra, Haryana, India
erdeepakgarg21@gmail.com, pmittal@kuk.ac.in

Abstract. In daily life there exist many problems whose objective are to either maximize or minimize some value with following some constraints (like load balancing in cloud with aim to maximizing QoS, Travelling salesman problem with aim to minimize total length of trip). These types of problems are optimization problems. Out of these problems there exist many problems which comes under NP-Hard category. To get nearby optimal solution of these problems in polynomial time the metaheuristics approaches are used. Metaheuristics are nature inspired algorithms which provides optimal solution by utilizing combination of exploration and exploitation. This paper provides a survey of Metaheuristic approaches (consisting of need, applications, characteristics, general classification and fourteen approaches under it). Compared all approaches corresponding to key parameters, mechanism. On the basis of literature survey and comparison, cuckoo search has been considered better due to global search via levy flight and generality (because of single parameter setting in cuckoo search). Implemented Randomized algorithm, Genetic Algorithm and Cuckoo Search to solve Load Balancing problem in Cloud Computing with aim to minimize makespan time and proved through results that cuckoo search is better. These experimental results were obtained using CloudSim 3.0.3 toolkit by extending few base classes.

Keywords: Cloud computing · Cuckoo search · Genetic algorithms
Load balancing · Metaheuristic algorithms

1 Introduction

Meta- It means beyond or higher level.

Heuristics- It means to search solution by trial and error.
The word "metaheuristic" was coined by Fred Glover et al. in his seminal paper in 1986 [1], and a metaheuristic can be assumed as a "master strategy that guides and modifies other heuristics to produce solutions beyond those that are normally generated in a quest for local optimality".

Furthermore, Glover call all the modern nature inspired algorithms as metaheuristics [2].

© Springer Nature Singapore Pte Ltd. 2019
A. K. Luhach et al. (Eds.): ICAICR 2018, CCIS 955, pp. 585–599, 2019.
https://doi.org/10.1007/978-981-13-3140-4_53

1.1 Need of Meta-Heuristic

Heuristics: It is a procedure that provides a possible solution for a problem, which is approx. optimal or can proved that no solution exists. But it is not generally applicable.

- It's design is usually problem centred.
- Easily gets stuck at local optima.

Metaheuristics: These are more general as compared to heuristic alone, these combine general structure & strategy guidelines to develop a specific heuristic approach to fit a particular problem. Below are reasons as need of methaheuristic:

- Meta-heuristic fits to many problems.
- Applicable on Multimodal Optimization.
- Applicable on Discontinuous, non-linear functions etc.

1.2 Components of Meta-Heuristic

Intensification or Exploitation: It is identifying the best fitted solution within current local region knowing that a better solution was found in the region. It helps in convergence.

Diversification or Exploration: It is identifying the better solution globally via randomization. It prevents to get stuck at local optima and at same time, it increases the diversity within population of solutions.

In a good metaheuristic algorithm a good mixture of these 2 components is required to get global solution.

1.3 Characteristics of Metaheuristic

Following are the important characteristics that almost all meta-heuristics approaches shares.

- Inspired from nature. (Based on physics, biology or ethology etc. principles).
- Use stochastic components. (use of random variables).
- No restricted use of Hessian matrix or gradient.
- Generally have several parameters that need to be configured corresponding to problem.

1.4 Applications of Metaheuristic Optimization

1. NP hard Optimization Problems solutions in polynomial time.

- Flow Shop Scheduling Problem
- Load Balancing/Task Scheduling in Cloud Computing
- Travelling Salesman Problem
- P-Median Problem.

2. Complicated Search Problems in Many Applications.

- Automatic Test Data Generation
- Feature Selection in Pattern Recognition
- Automatic Clustering.

2 General Classifications

2.1 Gradient/Derivative Based and Non-gradient Based

Gradient Based: The key trait in this class is focusing on derivative or gradient of a function under consideration. For example to optimize function f(x), Evaluation of first derivative (f′(x) = 0) is done to find the possible potential locations for that function & using the second derivative at these potential locations \(f″(x)\) to ensure that if the solution maximizes or minimizes.

Derivative-Free Algorithms: These class of algorithm do not use derivative function but these directly uses values of function itself like f(x).
Generally, function in this category have discontinuities. That's why derivatives cannot be used. Eg: Nelder-Mead downhill simplex become very useful.

2.2 Single Agent/Trajectory Based and Population Based

Trajectory-based algorithm: These type of algorithms uses a single trajectory or agent or individual to find solution at a time. Or we can say in these algorithms the population size of individuals is one only.
    Eg: Hill climbing comes under this category, it starts from a single seed position & links that with the final maximum or minimum point via searching.

Population - Based Algorithm: On the other hand, It uses more than one agents at a same time which will interact and trace out multiple paths as the iterations goes on.
    Eg: Particle Swarm Optimization Can be Parallelized.

2.3 Deterministic and Stochastic

Deterministic: In this category of algorithm, solution is found by only using fixed deterministic way without taking help of any randomness. The main feature of algorithm under this is that these will reach the same final solution position if started with the same initial point.
    Eg: Hill-climbing is good example of deterministic algorithms.

Stochastic: These category algorithm takes the help of randomness in addition with fixed approach.
    Thus on starting with same initial point the final solution may be different always.

2.4   Local and Global Search

Local search algorithms: Algorithm which mostly get premature converged to local optima falls under this category.

Furthermore, these can't escapes from local optima generally.

Eg: Hill-climbing an example of this.

Global Search: These tend to be suitable for global exploration of search space & optimization, though not always successful or efficient.

– The key feature in this is role of randomness.

Eg: Hill Climbing suffers from local optima but random starting point, random jumps can turn this into global search.

3   Literature Survey

In 1975, Holland proposed a nature inspired algorithm named as Genetic algorithm [3] It is motivated from the "evolution in nature" which is the theory of Darwin. It replicates the method of natural selection for survival. The Performance of Genetic Algorithm depends upon four factors which are population size, mutation probability, crossover probability & number of generations or iterations. In each iteration a sequential process of selection, crossover, mutation, replacement of individuals is done. To determine survival chances of each individual within population a fitness function is determined corresponding to phenotype structure of individual. After selecting good individuals corresponding to fitness function they are crossover to form new offspring. Crossover is performed on genotype structure. It is kind of exploitation of good features within parents to form better offspring. Mutation is like exploration by random changes. It is also like global search. In replacement out of old population and generated population new offspring population has been selected. This sequence of steps are iterated till fulfillment of maximum iterations or till some convergence condition.

In 1983, Kirpatrick et al. proposed Simulated Annealing. It is type of random search & mimics the method of slowly cooling of molten metal to get the minimum energy function value in this minimization problem [4]. Initially temperature starts from high, which shows that the selection pressure is low. Then the temperature is gradually decreased, which means that raise in selection pressure. In the minimization problem, any better moves or changes in individual solution that lowered the value of objective function is permitted; however, the main feature is that it also accept not better steps with some probability.

In 1986, Glover et al. proposed Tabu search. It is inspired from the mechanisms of human memory [2]. In this a list or memory has been created named as tabu list, which starts to store searched better distinct moves and does not permit to coming back at already searched move. Thus it prevents endless repeated cycling of same solution search and within this process it also allow to accept not better move as compared to repeated move. The key feature of this search is length of tabu list. Short length allows local search while long length allows global search.

In 1992, Dorigo [5] proposed algorithm based on the ants food searching behavior and named it as Ant colony optimization. In the search of food Ants intelligently discover the shortest path between ant nest and the food source. Initially ants moves randomly in search of food leaving pheromone in their path and when they find food they came back leaving pheromones again. Other ants follows the path with strongest pheromones scent. While some ants continuously search for other good food source or search for other better path nearby current good path. Each ant is considered as a potential solution to the objective function. Pheromones concentration in each path is considered as quality of solution. Within this whole process rate of pheromone evaporation and pheromone deposition plays role. In computer science problems, ACO is considered as iteration cycle of construction of ant solutions, updation of pheromones, daemons actions and this cycle is repeated till satisfaction of convergence criteria.

In 1992, Moscato et al. suggested a memetic method for the TSP (traveling salesman problem) [6]. Memetic means study of memes and their social and cultural effects. It is also motivated by Dawkin's theory which is evolution in nature. As compared to genetic algorithm in memetic algorithm, a set memes are assumed to form the chromosomes rather than genes. In the GA, after the selection of the individuals the crossover and mutation methods starts immediately but in Memetic Algorithm, an individual solution takes time to acquire experience memes & then these crossover or mutation like operations are performed. In Memetic algorithm local search may include after every step (like after crossover, mutation). For example after crossover two offspring are produced then they are allowed to search locally by using hill climbing for better solutions.

In 1995, Kennedy et al. suggested Particle Swarm Optimization [7]. Particle Swarm Optimization is centered on the flocking behavior (together flying of large no. of birds for migration) of birds. The birds fly in a possible solution space and the flocking behavior finds the optimum position or velocity as solution. Birds follow some path randomly or depending upon personal best and global best to reach to their food destination. Particular or personal best position or solution is the shortest path followed by that bird. Global best solution is best shortest path originate so far by any bird or particle. Then Bird tends to flew or move towards its personal or local best position solution. Birds also keep track of the gbest (global best) solution. Every particle or bird is linked with a velocity parameter, by which bird moved towards the its local best path & the global best path, keeping track of the position in 'n' dimension & position with respect to global best and localbest. Every Birds interact with each other to follow this strategy and regularly updates important parameters after a certain time. This whole process is iterated till satisfaction of convergence criteria.

In 2002, Passino et al. developed Bacterial foraging optimization Algorithm [8]. It involves 3 key steps: chemotactic, reproduction and elimination-dispersal step. In first step i.e. chemotactic, bacteria moves or swims towards the direction of rich nutrient area while it get tumbled when a harmful or noxious area has been contacted. The main objective of this algorithm is to minimize the cost movement of bacteria towards rich nutrient area. After this first step, all the bacteria are sorted in decreasing order of movement cost or fitness value. In second step i.e. reproduction step, the first half of bacteria having high cost get died because they did not got necessary nutrient to survive and the every remaining (half population) bacteria got split into two bacteria thus keeping population size fixed. In last step i.e. elimination- dispersal step, bacteria scattered or dispersed in complete surface for searching good nutrient surface. Newly reproduced bacteria takes position of died or eliminated bacteria. Bacteria with least minimum cost or best fitness value, represents the solution. This sequence of steps is repeated till fulfillment of coverage criteria.

In 2003, Eusuff et al. proposed Shuffled Frog Leaping Algorithm (SFLA) [9]. It mixes the best features of 2 algorithms: MA & PSO. It is motivated from leaping & shuffling nature of frogs to share information related to food search. Every frog is considered as a possible solution of the problem. Fitness value of each frog is evaluated and then they are sorted into decreasing order of their fitness. After this all frogs are divided in number of groups named as memeplexes. In every memeplex local best solution is evaluated and local evolution is done within every memeplex. After a fixed no. of memetic evolutions, for global evolution all the frogs are shuffled together. This whole process is iterated unless stopping criteria is satisfied.

In 2005, Karaboga et al. developed Artificial Bee Colony Algorithm (ABC) [10, 11]. The algorithm mimics the honey bees for food searching behavior. Authors termed bee as artificial bee because of difference in behavior with actual bee as compared to assumed one. There are three types of bees, Scout bee, employed bees and onlooker bees. Scouts randomly searches for food source. Employed bees exploits searched food positions by scouts and communicate to onlooker bees the nectar quantity of food found at particular position. Onlooker bees keeps and updates the best food position source (having maximum nectar quantity) and sends the employee bees to neighborhood of best food source to find much better food position. Thus output is food source with highest nectar quantity.

In 2007, Xin-She Yang et al. developed Firefly Algorithm (FFA) [12]. The algorithm is motivated by mimicking the flashing pattern or behavior of the fireflies for attracting other fireflies for mating purpose and to attract prey for food [13]. Fireflies are unisex thus every firefly gets attracted towards other firefly depended upon brightness of each other. Brightness increases or decreases corresponding to distance between the flies. Fireflies having lower light intensity flies or move to the high light intensity firefly, thus with decrease in distance updating is done towards its own brightness. When there is no brighter firefly then that firefly will move randomly. Desired output is the firefly with high brightness & least distance.

In 2008, Dan Simon et al. proposed BBO (Biogeography Based Optimization) [14]. It is inspired from the migrating behavior of the species in the habitat. Here, every habitat assumed as a possible solution of the problem. In this the key attribute is HSI (Habitat suitability index) corresponding to every habitat. It represents the desirability of living in habitat. There are two other parameters which depends upon this one is habitat immigration (no. of species arriving in that habitat) & other is emigration (no. of species leaving from that habitat). High HSI habitat is considered as good solution and supposed to have suitable environment for reproduction and feeding, thus high HSI habitat contains large no. of species than the low HSI habitat. Emigration rate is also higher as compared to low HIS habitat. On Migration, the migrating species passes the characteristics of the high Habitat suitability index habitat to the low Habitat suitability index habitat. Every habitat suitability is indicated as suitability index variable (SIV).

During reproduction within a habitat mutation causes unexpected species in the habitat which reasons disturbance in the equilibrium state. Equilibrium state of habitat is when emigration rate & immigration rate are same or equal. This change reasons the change in the value of SIV. This iterative process lasts up to required no. of iterations or unless certain convergence criteria occurred.

In 2009, Xin-She Yang et al. developed Cuckoo Search Algorithm (CSA) [15, 16] after inspiring from the breeding behavior of the cuckoo bird. Rather than creating their own nest cuckoo bird lay its egg in some others bird nest for reproduction and drop down the host bird's egg. When host bird arrives, then the host bird either drop the cuckoo egg or leave the whole nest. Few female cuckoo mimics their eggs in terms of shape, size, weight, color corresponding to host bird egg, sometimes even before laying of host bird egg. This causes increase in probability of cuckoo chick survival. In real life problems, every egg in nests assumed as one possible solution & cuckoo bird's egg assumed as a new solution prepared using levy flight. Levy flight is like combination of global random walk and local random walk. In this there is only one key parameter that is discovering probability of alien egg by host bird "Pa". If host bird identifies cuckoo egg as not his own egg then host bird abandon nest and builds new nest using levy flight [17] The whole process is continued upto specified iterations or unless convergence criteria is satisfied.

In 2010, Xin-She Yang et al. proposed Bat Algorithm [18]. It is inspired from the echolocation behavior of the microbats as the microbats can produce very high echolocation to find its prey or which echoes back with a frequency. Method of detecting the position of object by originating sound and getting back reflected sound is termed as echolocation. By identifying the reflected or bounced sound frequency, bats are also able to differentiate between the obstacle & prey and also can make idea about distance between them and to their nearby surroundings. Initially bats fly randomly with any velocity, sound (loudness or frequency) in search for food. Overall aim of bat is to find prey at the minimum distance. The zooming around the particular possible position and frequency parameters keeps the balance between exploitation and exploration. This whole process is continued till satisfaction of some convergence criteria.

In 2012, Xin-She Yang proposed FPA (Flower Pollination Algorithm) [19]. It is motivated from the fertilization (pollination) method of flowers. In this method, there are two types of pollination one is abiotic or self-pollination and other is biotic or cross pollination. First one is assumed as local while other one is considered as global pollination. Corresponding to optimization problem Yang [20] supposed that every plant has only one flower & every flower has only one pollen grain. Pollinators such as flies, insects or wind plays the role of pollination. There exist flower constancy which is assumed as the reproduction probability and which is proportional to similarity of the two flowers involved. That's why every flower (or pollen) is assumed as a potential solution. Objective function searches the best flower, who is capable of maximum pollination.

In 2016, Yang included [21] all the existing algorithms optimization algorithms, application areas, previous work that has been done. This paper has provided many models for computational problem solutions, consisting of optimizations centered on swarm intelligence displayed by fireflies, ants, bats and many more. Theoretically compared all important algorithm, their needs, challenges and applications in real life problems.

4   General Comparison of Cuckoo Search with Others

After deeply studying all above papers, it has been clear that metaheuristic optimization algorithm are good approaches to solve NP hard problems and for complicated searching problems. Xin-She Yang et al. has proposed many algorithms like Flower Pollination Algorithm, Cuckoo Search Algorithm, Firefly Algorithm, and Compared theoretically the traditional metaheuristic optimization algorithms with proposed algorithms. Furthermore, many studies & applications have showed that CS is better in terms of generality and global solution [17, 21, 23–25]. Overall in support of Cuckoo search some points has been given in Table 1.

Table 1. CS general difference with other algorithms

#	Parameter	Description in support of CS
1	Use of Levy flight/global search	Levy flights is considered to have infinite mean & variance. Thus, Cuckoo search can explore problem search space efficiently than the other approaches
2	No. of parameters	Only one that is Pa which is too less as compared to other algorithms
3	MetaPopulation Algo.	Every nest can have more than one host eggs represented as solutions
4	Multimodal & multiobjective	Can show all optima at once so good for multimodal & multi objective
5	Generally applicability	As no. of parameter is one, so can be applied on large no. of problems
6	Showing all optima	If No. of nest > no. of local optima can show All optima Simultaneously
7	Efficient-randomization	In CS step length is fully tailed thus effective randomization

A main advantage of cuckoo search is that the use of levy flight as global search as compared to simple random walks [17, 22]. In Levy Flight the mean and variance is supposed to be infinite. So, CS explore the search space more effectively than any other optimization algorithms.

Theoretical studies has also proved that cuckoo search fulfills the global search needs & that's why it shows and ensures global convergence features [22]. Cuckoo search has two search capabilities: one is local search and other is global search, which are balanced or controlled by a single parameter named as alien egg discovery probability Ps.

5   Cuckoo Search

It is motivated from the mimicking behavior of cuckoo bird species. Cuckoo bird does not builds its own nest but it lays egg in nest of host bird like warbler. Host bird accept those mimicked cuckoo eggs corresponding to some discovering probability. Host bird raises the cuckoo eggs till they hatched. Cuckoo do this by mimicking the color, texture & size of the host bird nest [15, 16].

To simply describe standard Cuckoo Search, following 3 rules has been used:

- Cuckoo lays a single egg at a time and drop it in a host nest (which is chosen randomly).
- Evolutionary aim is that the best nests having high-quality eggs will be forwarded to the next generations.
- The no. of host nests are fixed. When host bird arrives then it can identify cuckoo egg with a probability pa $\in$ (0, 1). After identification host bird left the egg or abandon the nest & built a new nest at random location.

In addition to the algorithm steps, CS involves three important equations, two for the renewal (Eqs. 1 and 2) and last for reestablishment (Eq. 3) of the nests. Equations 1 & 2 can be considered as local random walk while Eq. 3 is considered as global random walk. These equations are given as follows:

$$x_i^{t+1} = x_i^t + \alpha \oplus \text{Levy}(\beta) \tag{1}$$

$$\alpha = \alpha 0 \left(x_i^t - x_{\text{best}}^t \right) \tag{2}$$

$$x_i^{t+1} = x_i^t + \varepsilon \cdot \left(x_j^t - x_k^t \right) \tag{3}$$

For i = 1, 2,···, N. in this N represents number of the nests; xi, xj and xk are the location of host nests within possible solution domain (i $\neq$ j $\neq$ k) and xbest is best solution in current generation; α represents step size (greater than zero) and $\alpha 0$ is constant (value = 0.01); Levy (β) is random vector step length. It is generated by using Eq. 4 & $\varepsilon \sim$ U(0,1) is zoom factor.

$\alpha 0$ is taken as 0.01 by xin she yang considering that if it taken as too large in local random walk then it may happen that the new solutions jumps out of the specified domain which further result in wastage of evaluations.

5.1 Lévy Random or Levy(β)

Yang and Deb [15, 16] have used Mantegna's algorithm as levy random generation method shown in below 4–6 equations.

$$s = u/|v|^{1/\beta} \tag{4}$$

$$u \sim N(0, \sigma_u), v \sim N(0, \sigma_v) \tag{5}$$

$$\sigma_u(\beta) = \left[(\Gamma(1+\beta). \text{Sin}(\pi \beta/2))/\beta\Gamma((1+\beta)/2).2^{((\beta-1)/3)} \right]^{(1/\beta)}, \sigma_v = 1 \tag{6}$$

In above equations, u and v represents random vector obeying normal distributions. β (beta) $\in[0.3, 1.99]$ is a distribution's parameter & usually taken value as $\beta = 3/2$ in CS. Value of v is from 0 to 1 while value of u is from 0 to $\sigma(3/2)$. In Eq. 6, "Γ" is gamma function is extended version of factorial function, with argument shifted below by 1. Suppose, if n is positive integer, $\Gamma(n) = (n-1)!$. Steps of Cuckoo search is given below.

5.2   Cuckoo Search Algorithm (Pa)

begin
Input: N, pa
   Objective function Minimize f(x), x= (x1, x2,....xp)^T
   Initial population of N host nests xi (i=1, 2,....N)
   And evaluate its fitness fi
   Gbest=min(f1,f2....fN)
   While (t <MaxIterations of stop criterion)
        Get a host nest randomly say i with fitness fi
        Generate a cuckoo egg corresponding to choosen host nest using eq. 1.1, 1.2 (local random walk)
        Evaluate fitness of cuckoo egg say Fi
        If (Fi<fi)
           Replace xi by generated cuckoo egg.
        Endif
        If (rand<pa=0.25)// discovering probabitliy is //greater
           That nest is abandoned
           Built new nest using eq. 2 (global random walk) accept it & Evaluate its fitness Fk.
        Endif
     G*=min(f1,f2....fN)
     If (G* < Gbest)
        Update Gbest, Xbest
     Endif
   Endwhile
Output:Gbest, Xbest
end

Pros: Xin she yang et al. (creator of CS, FA, FPA) & many other researchers conclude that cuckoo search is better among all existed algorithms in terms of following:

- Levy Flights is considered to have infinite mean and variance.
- Only one parameter that is Pa in CS so, it is generally applicable.
- Good for multimodal problem.

If No. of nest > no. of Local Optima then it can show All optima simultaneously.

6   Experimental Settings

Evaluation and comparisons of CS, GA and Randomized algorithms has been done for Load Balancing in Cloudsim 3.0.3 with the help of a suitable example. Due to space constraints 6 Cloudlets and 2 VMs has been considered in these experiments. At infrastructure level there are 2 processing elements. For every VMs and Cloudlets the required processing element for them is considered one. Out of 2 PEs, one is with 1000 MIPS and other is with 2000 MIPS processing capability. In case of Multipopulation algorithms no. of schedules or size of population has been taken as 4.

Table 2 represents six cloudlets with their size in terms of Millions of instructions and CL-ids.

Table 2. Cloudlets properties

CL-id	Length in MI (millions of instruction)
0	2227
1	1693
2	2725
3	1581
4	2014
5	2386

Table 3 represents two VMs with their processing capabilities MIPS and VM-ids.

Table 3. Processing capabilities of VMs

VM-id	MIPS (millions of instruction per second)
0	1000
1	2000

Table 4 represents a sample Load schedule by using randomized scheduling as example. Below is the sample code for randomized scheduling as example in java.

Table 4. Load schedules by using randomized scheduling

Pop [schedule, CL]	CL0	CL1	CL2	CL3	CL4	CL5
0	0	1	1	1	1	0
1	1	0	0	1	1	0
2	0	0	0	0	1	0
3	1	1	0	0	0	0

Sample Code for Randomized Scheduling:

```
c-No. of Cloudlets=6
v-No. of VMs=2
s-No. of Schedules=4
int pop[ ][ ]=new int[s][c];
Random robj1=new Random();
for (int i=0;i<s;i++)
    {
        for (int j=0;j<c;j++)
            {
                pop[i][j]=robj1.nextInt(v+1);
            }
    }
```

Where, robj1.nextInt(v + 1) returns a pseudo random, which is uniformly distributed int value between 0 (inclusive) and v + 1 (exclusive).

7   Experimental Results

In this sections experimental results have been performed corresponding to Average Makespan of schedule of Cloudlets criteria. These have been observed on 3 algorithms (Randomized algorithm, Genetic Algorithm, Cuckoo Search with Levy Flight) in Figs. 1 and 2. To conclude results average of time parameters has been taken corresponding to regularly increase in iterations of load balancing with CloudletSchedulerSpaceShared mode and CloudletSchedulerTimeShared mode.

Mode 1: CloudletSchedulerSpaceShared-

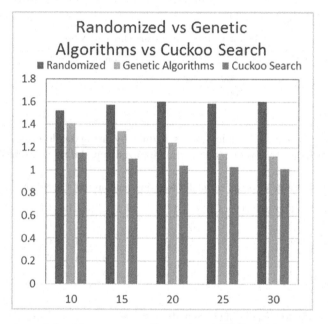

Fig. 1. Comparison of algorithms corresponding to Avg. MSSCL (Makespan time of schedule of Cloudlets) in CloudletSchedulerSpaceShared mode

Mode 2: CloudletSchedulerTimeShared-

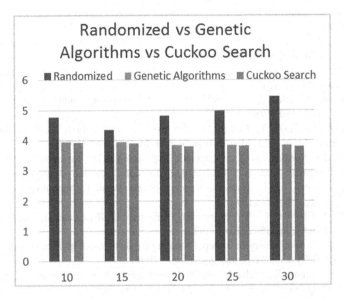

Fig. 2. Comparison of algorithms corresponding to Avg. MSSCL (Makespan time of schedule of Cloudlets) in CloudletSchedulerTimeShared mode.

In all cases X and Y axis are treated as below:

X axis: No. of Iterations the Load Balancing is done.

Y axis: Avg. of Maksespan or Response Time of schedules (one in case of single population like randomized schedule or four in case of multi population like genetic algorithm) of Cloudlets after n iterations.

MSSCL-Makespan time of schedule of Cloudlets.

8 Conclusion

In this paper, the need of metaheuristic algorithms, its components, characteristics, classifications, literature survey have been done deeply on fourteen approaches. On the basis of literature survey, comparison has been done among fourteen approaches corresponding to key parameters, main mechanism and used applications areas. Theoretically found Cuckoo search as optimal algorithm out of all due to global levy flight and generality (because of one parameter only). Furthermore, load balancing in cloud computing problem has been solved by randomized algorithm, genetic algorithm and cuckoo search with aim to minimize makespan time to improve quality of services. Results have been compared and concluded that cuckoo search with levy flight is more general and optimal. Furthermore, a lot of work can be done in future to improve its performance by adjusting to optimal value of pa (discovering probability).

References

1. Boussaid, I., Lepagnot, J., Patrick S.: A survey on optimization metaheuristics. In: Web of Science, Elsevier Information Science, vol. 237(5), pp. 82–117 (2013)
2. Glover, F.: Future paths for integer programming and links to artificial intelligence. Comput. Op. Res. **13**(5), 533–549 (1986)
3. Holland, J.H.: Adaption in Natural and Artificial Systems. The University of Michigan Press, Ann Harbor, MI (1975)
4. Kirkpatrick, S., Gelatt, C.D., Vecchi, M.P.: Optimization by simulated annealing. Science **220**(4598), 671–680 (1983)
5. Dorigo, M., Maniezzo, V., Colorni, A.: Ant system- optimization by a colony of cooperating agents. IEEE Trans. Syst. Man Cybern. Part B **26**(1), 29–41 (1996)
6. Moscato, P., Norman, M.G.: A memetic approach for the traveling salesman problem implementation of a computational ecology for combinatorial optimization on message-passing systems. In: International Conference on Parallel Computing and Transputer Application, pp. 86–177 (1992)
7. Kennedy, J., Eberhart R.: Particle swarm optimization. In: IEEE International Conference on Neural Networks, pp. 1942–1948 (1995)
8. Passino, K.M.: Biomimicry of bacterial foraging for distributed optimization and control. In: IEEE Control Systems Magazine, pp. 52–67 (2006)
9. Eusuff, M., Lansey, K., Pasha, F.: Shuffled frog-leaping algorithm: a memetic meta-heuristic for discrete optimization. Eng. Optim. **38**(2), 129–154 (2006)
10. Karaboga, D., Basturk, B.: On the performance of artificial bee colony (ABC) algorithm. Appl. Soft Comput. **8**, 687–697 (2007)
11. Karaboga, D., Basturk, B.: A powerful and efficient algorithm for numerical function optimization- artificial bee colony (ABC) algorithm. J. Glob. Optim. **39**, 459–471 (2007)
12. Yang, X.S., He, X.: Firefly algorithm- recent advances and applications. Int. J. Swarm Intell. **1**(1), 36–50 (2013)
13. Yang, X.S.: Firefly algorithm, stochastic test functions and design optimization. Int. J. Bio-Inspir. Comput. **2**(2), 78–84 (2010)
14. Simon, D.: Biogeography-based optimization. IEEE Trans. Evol. Comput. **12**(6), 702–713 (2008)
15. Yang, X.S., Deb, S.: Cuckoo search via Lévy flights. In: IEEE Conference Publication World Congress on Nature & Biologically Inspired Computing (NaBIC), pp. 210–214 (2009)
16. Yang, X.S., Deb, S.: Engineering optimisation by cuckoo search. Int. J. Math. Modell. Numer. Optim. **1**(4), 330–343 (2010)
17. Yang, X.S., Deb, S.: Cuckoo search- recent advances and applications. Neural Comput. Appl. **24**(1), 169–174 (2014)
18. Yang, X.S.: Bat algorithm- literature review and applications. Int. J. Bio-Inspir. Comput. **5** (3), 141–149 (2013)
19. Yang, X.S., Karamanoglu M.: Multi-objective flower algorithm for optimization. In: International Conference on Computational Science, Elsevier Science, pp. 861–868 (2013)
20. Yang, X.S.: Flower pollination algorithm for global optimization, unconventional computation and natural computation. Lect. Notes Comput. Sci. **44**(5), 240–249 (2012)
21. Yang, X.S., Deb, S., Fong, S., Xingshi, H., Zhao, Y.: From swarm intelligence to metaheuristics- nature-inspired optimization algorithms. IEEE Comput. Soc. **49**(9), 52–59 (2016)

22. Wang, F., Yang, X.S., Yang, S.M.: Markov model and convergence analysis based on cuckoo search algorithm. Comput. Eng. **38**(11), 180–185 (2012)
23. Gandomi, A.H., Yang, X.S., Alavi, A.H.: Cuckoo search algorithm- a metaheuristic approach to solve structural optimization problems. Eng. Comput. **29**(1), 17–35 (2013)
24. Gandomi, A.H., Yang, X.S., Talatahari, S., Deb, S.: Coupled eagle strategy and differential evolution for unconstrained and constrained global optimization. Comput. Math Appl. **63**(1), 191–200 (2012)
25. Srivastava, P.R., Chis, M., Deb, S., Yang, X.S.: An efficient optimization algorithm for structural software testing. Int. J. Artif. Intell. **9**(12), 68–77 (2012)

Hybrid Live VM Migration: An Efficient Live VM Migration Approach in Cloud Computing

Abhishek ku. Shakya$^{(\boxtimes)}$, Deepak Garg, and Prakash Ch. Nayak

Department of Computer Application, National Institute of Technology
Kurukshetra, Kurukshetra, Haryana 136119, India
abhishakya44@gmail.com, erdeepakgarg21@gmail.com,
12prak@gmail.com

Abstract. The whole world is moving towards digitalization via internet. And the internet world is ruled by cloud computing because of its simplicity and user satisfactory quality of service. Handling such a huge number of users and providing uninterrupted services is only can be done by live virtual machine migration (pre copy and post copy) in cloud data center. We know that pre copy migration degrades the application performance when memory transfer rate is higher than network bandwidth. And post copy migration also not able to give optimum performance because of high page fault. To achieve optimum performances during VM migration we propose a hybrid VM migration approach which is a combination of pre copy and post copy method through this paper. The approach basically uses push and pulls method for migration of VM. During migration process both the highly loaded and less loaded server participate to push and pull the VM. The main concept of the approach is highly overloaded server actively pushes the VM to less loaded server and the less loaded server also help the process by pulling the VM. The proposed migration process is simulated and the outcome is compared with existing live migration considering CPU uses, network, and memory as parameter. And by the comparison it is proved that the proposed approach really works better than the existing migration process in many scenarios.

Keywords: Broadcasting · Multicasting · Hybrid-copy · Pre-copy
Post-copy · Push · Pull

1 Introduction

Cloud computing is one of the prominent technique in modern internet world. For providing infrastructure, platform and software as service it uses live virtual machine (VM) migration technique [1]. Cloud computing basically provides the computing facility and charges the user as per the use. But for managing large number of users too much energy is used by cloud data center [2, 3]. To reduce the energy use and maintaining the work load, prominent live VM migration technique such as pre copy and post VM migration are used. In live migration technique, services provide is not interrupted, the VM is migrated in background without user attention [4].

© Springer Nature Singapore Pte Ltd. 2019
A. K. Luhach et al. (Eds.): ICAICR 2018, CCIS 955, pp. 600–611, 2019.
https://doi.org/10.1007/978-981-13-3140-4_54

1.1 Cloud Data Center

These are online service provider. They provide services and charges as per use. Datacenter contains many physical machines for storing and processing the data and providing service to users. A cloud data center actually provides Services via web link. But due to internal fragmentation, cost increases and performance reduces to provide the service [5].

1.2 Virtual Machine Migration

Before virtual machine (VM) migration the cloud computing is known as grid computing. In grid computing there is no virtualizations layer. So all the physical machine (PM) only can do its own work. It can't help other PM for reducing work load. For this cause the work performance of grid computing is reduced. To overcome this and to maintain high number of users virtualization technique is introduced [5]. Virtualization uses VM migration for isolating the data center and maintaining the workload of server. It migrate the processor state (I/O, CPU, memory) between physical machines [1]. To reach underutilized server by resource rich server, and to provide better service when number of user increases cloud data center uses VM migration technique [3]. Basically two migration patterns are implemented for migration of VM such as live migration and non-live migration. In non-live migration, service providing is stop during migration. In live migration, service providing is not stopped during migration [6–9] (Fig. 1).

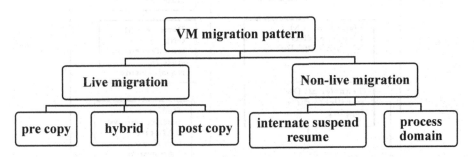

Fig. 1. Virtual machine migration patterns.

1.2.1 Live VM Migration

Uninterrupted service is provided live VM migration. Without user knowledge VM migrated in background. The aim of live VM migration consists: (1) Application performance optimization during VM migration, (2) Efficient bandwidth utilization and (3) Minimize high migration time and down time during migration [10].

Pre-copy VM Migration
Memory pages copied iteratively in this VM migration. For this migration time increases rapidly. And to transfer dirty memory pages, system resources and network both occupied. This migration process consists of many rounds, such as memory

migration and VM migration. During memory migration phase CPU actively pushes the dirty pages and then VM migration is done from source server to destination. Works well, when there is less memory transfer. Migration mode is more optimal if less page fault occurs during VM migration. But performance level is not optimal [7].

Post-copy VM Migration
In this migration the VM transfer to destination first and then memory pages are transferred. It is just reverse of pre-copy migration. To do this, a part of VM pauses for some time at the source host, and a small part of running state of virtual machine (CPU Registers) is sent to the destination. After this virtual machine starts it's working at the destination [8].

1.2.2   Flow Chart for Pre Copy and Post Copy VM Migration
See Figs. 2 and 3.

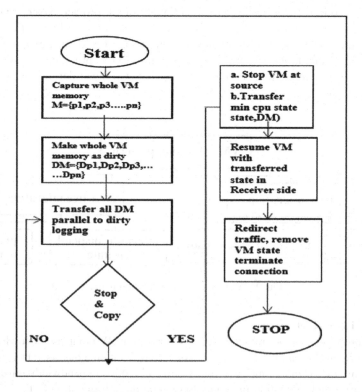

Fig. 2. Pre-copy migration flowchart.

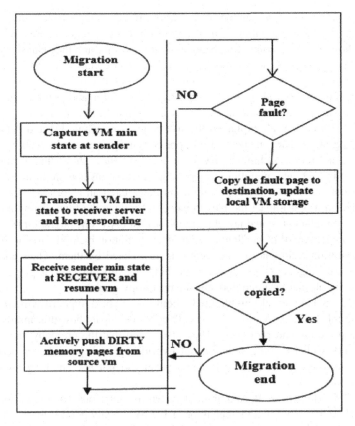

Fig. 3. Post-copy migration flowchart.

2 Literature Review

- In 2002, Kozuch et al. were discussed about ISR (internet suspend and resume) Technique used for VM migration [12]. They stated its usefulness for VM migration. And discussed that in this non live migration technique service provide is interrupted because of internet suspend. They also discussed how to avoid hardware transfer physically during VM migration.
- In 2010, Hirofuchi proposed an advanced live migration and also stated how to allocate VM on machine within a few milliseconds [11]. They also stated that if memory transfer is done after the VM migration it will take less time for switching the server and service providing.
- In 2010, Ranjan proposed about the simulation toolkit for Cloud computing [4]. This Simulation toolkit is written in java and it provides many scenarios of cloud

computing working as example. User can use these example to test and predict the working of cloud computing. This is a platform for future generation. Who want to know how the cloud computing behave in various condition they can simulate on it.

- In 2011, Svärd et al. demonstrated that using delta compression in live migration [10] Can reduce time for migration, and interruption of service providing to the user is also reduced. They also shown some practical situation and user their algorithm in it and by their compression method they easily handle the migration.

- In 2011, Ibrahim et al. explained the live migration technic [7] and details of pre copy Migration. They also stated that pre copy migration works well by using the iterative migration technique. By their analysis they show that if more cores included in VM then migrating it by pre copy method takes more time. So to reduce the migration time for pre copy migration they stated an algorithm and prove that this algorithm not impact the performance but reduce the time of migration.

- In 2013, Singh et al. stated novel method for post copy VM migration [8] technique with Comparison of its challenges with other migration method. How to implement this migration technique in data center is also stated by them. They said that pre paging, pushing pages on demand, pushing actively all chosen pages and self-ballooning are the basic component for post copy migration.

- In 2012, Sahani et al. highlighted about the hybrid type of virtual machine migration [9] And it's various aspects. They also compare how this approach is best among pre copy and post copy. They also stated that the pre copy and post copy may work well for some situation but hybrid approach gives better performance where the both of them fails. But this paper did not say anything about implementation [13, 14].

- In 2012, Deshpande et al. said about a system for inter-rack live migration (IRLM) [15]. They discussed that the behavior of IRLM is really good if there is more than one VM associated with the one host. They show that if there are 6 host each rack and each host contains 4 VM then IRLM reduces 44% page transfer as compare to KVM and 17% as compare to gang migration.

- In 2015, Ahmad et al. explained categorization of live migration [6]. They inspected all The current migration method as per their performance, advantages and disadvantages.

3 Proposed Hybrid Virtual Machine Migration

As the cloud users are increasing rapidly similarly the need of service providing data centers are also increasing accordingly. But the main question is to implement such a datacenter which consume less energy by optimally utilizing the capacity to maintain more servers and to provide best QOS (quality of services) to the cloud users. For this the load is evenly distributed among the servers and service level agreements (SLA) are fulfilled. This is run time problem. For this purpose live virtual machine migration is more important. To optimize resource management two questions arises which are as follows:

When to migrate virtual machine?

Where to migrate virtual machine so as to reduce migration time?

The main aim and objective is based on the question proposed above. To overcome these situations we proposed hybrid virtual machine migration. This algorithm basically works for identifying the particular servers which need to migrate their work load to less loaded server to reduce the traffic. So first objective is to find the high loaded server from which the VM should migrate and also find a suitable target server which is less loaded and can have the capacity to take the load. The second objective is to instantiate migration process by both the loaded and less loaded server. The loaded server which known as hotspot has the ability to push the workload to less loaded server. And the less loaded server known as cold spot can have the capability to pull work load from the overloaded server automatically. Synchronizations of the above expressed problem and solve them can lead the datacenter for efficient resource management. Smooth service provide to the user is also included into the objectives.

3.1   Push Algorithm for Proposed Virtual Machine Migration

1. If load >= Threshold then push
2. if HOTSPOT = 0 then
   Set HOTSPOT to recent time
   Multicast HOTSPOT MESSAGE with VM property
3. while not timeout do
   Listen for HOTSPOT REPLY
   Grab value from HOTSPOT REPLY and save
   them into VM status
   end **while**
4. for all VM do
   Calculate migration costs
   end **for**
5. if TIMEOUT then
   Multicast RESOURCE RELEASE
   Set HOTSPOT to 0
6. else
   Send MIGRATION to top bidder
7. if migration successfully finished then
   Set COUNT to 0

3.2 Pull Algorithm for Proposed Hybrid Virtual Machine Migration

1. **If** load <= Threshold PULL then
2. **if** COLDSPOT = 0 then
   Set COLDSPOT to recent time
   Multicast STEAL **BROADCAST**
3. **while** not TIMEOUT do
   Listen for **BROADCAST** REPLY
   Grab the VM contain and
   end while
4. **for** all VMs do
   if VM fits the available resources
   PULL then Append VM to VM_candidates for PM
   Calculate migration cost(pair cost)
   end if
   end for
5. **if** receive STEAL BROADCAST then
   Generate local PM information and information of all
   running unlocked(not in VMs_locked) VMs
   Send back STEAL BROADCAST REPLY
   elif receive STEAL ATTEMPT then
6. **if** Migration_id of STEAL ATTEMPT is in VMs_locked then
   Set ack to 'NOT OK'
   Else Set ack to 'OK'
7. Append Migration_id of STEAL ATTEMPT to VMs_locked
   end if Send back STEAL ATTEMPT REPLY with ack
8. **if** ack = 'OK' then
   Send MIGRATION to MP
   Run migration: migrate Migration_id to the Source node of
   STEAL ATTEMPT
9. **if** migration succefully finished then
   Send MIGRATION ACKNOWLEDGMENT to both MP and the
   Source node of STEAL ATTEMPT
   End if End if

4 Working of Proposed Algorithm

This algorithm basically implements push and pull technique with hotspot and cold spot as working variable. The overloaded sever sets its HOTSPOT variable ON and the less overloaded server sets their COLDSPOT variable ON. If the workload is more than threshold capacity, server multicast its hotspot variable to all other servers in the network where less overloaded server multicast cold spot variable to all other. After receiving the response from the target server the sender pushes its memory as well as VM state to target server if it is in hotspot and if it is in cold spot it will pulls the memory as well as VM state from target server.

4.1   Designing

The prototype of proposed Hybrid migration is implemented by using multicasting and broadcasting technique. When servers need to migrate service state it multicast to all other server in the network. And when it tries to migrate the VM (by push and pull method) it uses broadcasting (for target and migrate) (Figs. 4, 5).

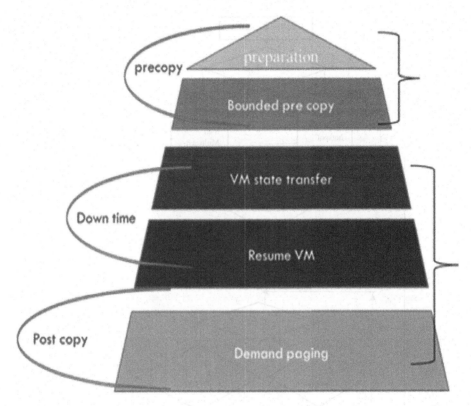

Fig. 4. Proposed Hybrid copy migration working.

4.2   Experimental Parameters

V_M	Size of VM's memory
V_{mig}	Amount of network traffic required to perform migration
T_{mig}	Time required for the total Migration of time
V_{thr}	Threshold value for load
B	Available Bandwidth
D	Dirty page cost
V_c	CPU use
V_m	Memory use
V_n	Network use

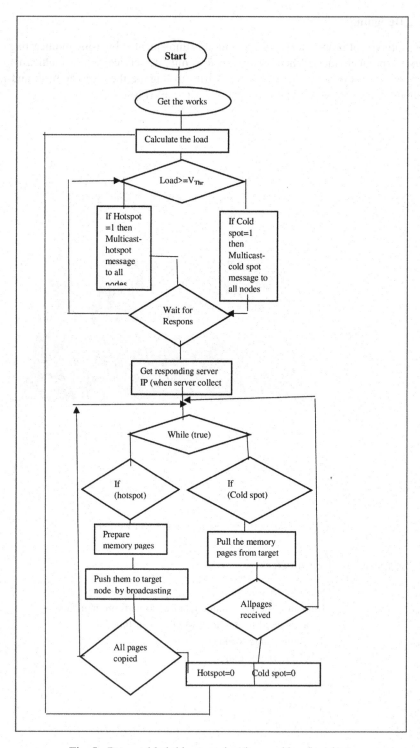

Fig. 5. Proposed hybrid copy migration working flowchart.

4.3   Result of Simulation

By simulation we conclude that in some scenario pre copy and post copy may work well but by our experiment it has been seen that in most of the case hybrid migration is best among these two. And it also tested that in pre copy and post copy migration more time is wasted by searching the target server among all other server. But by our

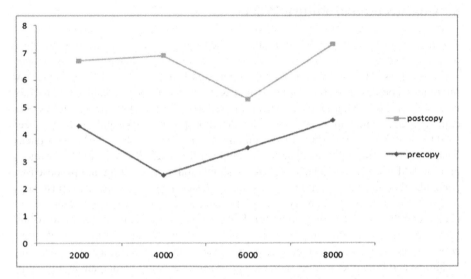

Fig. 6. Comparison among pre copy and post copy migration with time (sec) in y-axis and system load in x-axis.

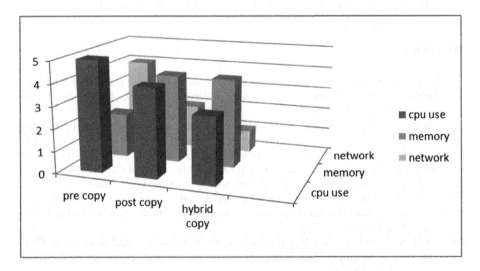

Fig. 7. Comparisons among pre copy, post copy, hybrid copy live VM migration.

algorithm we completely remove these issues. As per our implementation the high loaded and the less loaded server instantiate the migration process by themselves and multicast it to all other servers. By this the time wasted for searching the server is completely reduces. And the second advantage of our method is that the entire server has the ability to communicate all other server as well as individual server by multicasting and broadcasting which reduces the traffic and overhead (Figs. 6, 7).

5 Conclusion and Future Work

The most widely used live VM migration scheme like pre-copy, post-copy has been deeply studied. And these methods have been reviewed as per their strength, weakness, and challenges. The highly critical aspects and significant features of the existing VM migration schemes have been investigated & reviewed through qualitative analysis. A new Hybrid VM Migration has been proposed and all these three approach has been compared under simulation. All three variables (hot spot, cold spot and stable) has been used to identify the server (high loaded and the less loaded). Implemented push strategy push the VM from high loaded server to targeted less loaded server and pull strategy pull the VM from high loaded server. After simulation of all existing and proposed we conclude that hybrid algorithm works really faster than pre copy and post copy migration as no iterative memory migration (required memory pages are combine to a packet and this packet is only migrate). Furthermore, tests has been done and results proved that migration time in proposed hybrid VM migration algorithm is less than pre copy and post copy migration, because hybrid copy migration don't need any searching technique and both over loaded and less loaded server actively participate in migration.

As per the implementation there are some sections where the algorithm needs to improve to work efficiently. Like wise to migrate the memory with less page fault and in less time is the real challenge. In many cases to synchronize the server and reduce the workload in less network bandwidth is also need to be optimized.

References

1. Beloglazov, A., Buyya, R.: Managing overloaded hosts for dynamic consolidation of virtual machines in cloud data centers under quality of service constraints. IEEE Trans. Parallel Distrib. Syst. **24**, 1366–1379 (2013)
2. Uddin, M., Shah, A., Alsaqour, A., Memon, J.: Measuring efficiency of tier level data centers to implement green energy efficient data centers. Middle East J. Sci. **15**, 200–207 (2013)
3. Beloglazov, A., Buyya, R.: Energy efficient resource management in virtualized cloud data centers. In: Proceedings of the 2010 10th IEEE/ACM International Conference on Cluster, cloud and Grid Computing. IEEE Computer Society, New York, pp. 826–831, (2010)
4. Ranjan, R.: CloudSim: a toolkit for modeling and simulation of cloud computing environments and evaluation of resource provisioning algorithms. In: Wiley Online Library (wileyonlinelibrary.com) (2010)
5. Sahani, S., Verma, V.: A hybrid approach to live migration of virtual machine. In: Cloud Computing in Emerging Markets (CCEM), IEEE International Conference on Bangalore, India, pp. 257–265 (2012)

6. Abash, M.: Secure live virtual machines migration: issues and solutions. In: 28th International Conference on Advanced Information Networking and Applications Workshops, pp. 654–662 (2014)
7. Ibrahim, K., Hofmeyr, S.: Optimized pre-copy live migration for memory intensive applications. Seattle, Washington, USA Copyright 2011 ACM 978-1-4503-0771, pp. 12–18 (2011)
8. Singh, R., Chalon, K.: Comparative study of virtual machine migration techniques and challenges in post copy live virtual machine migration. In: International Journal of Science and Research (IJSR) ISSN (Online), pp. 2319–7064 Index Copernicus Value (2013)
9. Svärd, P., Hoodia, B., Tordsson, J., Elm Roth, E.: Evaluation of delta compression techniques for efficient live migration of large virtual machines. ACM Sigplan Not. **46**, 111–120 (2011)
10. Hirofuchi, T., Nakada, H., Itoh, S., Sekiguchi, S.: Enabling instantaneous relocation of virtual machines with a lightweight vmm extension. In: 10th IEEE/ACM International Conference on Cluster, Cloud and Grid Computing (CCGrid), pp. 73–83 (2010)
11. Kozuch, M., Satyanarayanan, M.: Internet suspend/resume. In: Proceedings Fourth IEEE Workshop on Mobile Computing Systems and Applications. IEEE, New York, pp. 40–46 (2002)
12. Ahmad, R.: Virtual machine migration in cloud data centers: a review, taxonomy, and open research issues. Springer Science+Business Media, New York, pp. 2474–2515 (2015)
13. Deshpande, U., Kulkarni, U., Gopala K.: Inter-rack live migration of multiple virtual machines. In: Proceedings of the 6th International Workshop on Virtualization Technologies in Distributed Computing Date. ACM, New York, pp. 19–26 (2012)
14. Jihun, K., Dongju, C.: Guide-copy: fast and silent migration of virtual machine for datacenters. Department of Computer Science and Engineering, POSTECH (2000)
15. Shribman, A., Benoit, H.: Precopy and postcopy VM live migration for memory intensive applications. In: Euro-Par 2012: Parallel Processing Workshops, pp. 539–547 (2013)
16. Sammy, K., Shengbing, R., Wilson, C.: Energy Efficient security preserving VM live migration. Data Int. J. Comput. Sci. **9**(2), 33–39 (2012)
17. Leelipushpam, P., Sharmila, J.: Live VM migration techniques in cloud environment—a survey. In: Proceedings of IEEE Conference on Information and Communication Technologies (ICT), pp. 408–413 (2013)
18. Ge, C., Sun, Z., Wang, N., Xu, K., Wu, J.: Energy management in cross-domain content delivery networks: a theoretical perspective. IEEE Trans. Netw. Serv. Manag. **11**(3), 264–277 (2014)
19. Bari, M., Zhani, Q., Ahmed, R., Boutaba, R.: CQNCR: optimal VM migration planning in cloud data centers. In: Proceedings of Networking Conference IFIP, pp. 1–9 (2014)
20. Deshpande, E.: Agile live migration of virtual machines. In: Proceedings of IEEE International Parallel Distributed Processing Symposium, pp. 1061–1070 (2016)
21. Zhang, F., Fu, X., Yahyapour, R.: CBase: a new paradigm for fast virtual machine migration across data centers. In: Proceedings of 17th IEEE/ACM International Symposium on Cluster, Cloud and Grid Computing, pp. 284–293 (2017)
22. Tsakalozos, K., Verroios, V., Roussopoulos, M., Delis, A.: Time-constrained live VM migration in share-nothing IaaS-clouds. In: Proceedings of IEEE 7th International Conference on Cloud Computing (CLOUD), pp. 56–63 (2014)
23. Arif, M., Kiani, A., Qadir, J.: Machine learning based optimized live virtual machine migration over WAN links. Telecommun. Syst. **64**(2), 245–257 (2017)
24. Haikun, L., Hai, J., Cheng, X., Xiaofei, L.: Performance and energy modeling for live migration of virtual machines. Clust. Comput. **16**(2), 249–264 (2013)

Comparison, Classification and Survey of Aspect Based Sentiment Analysis

Ahmed Sabeeh[✉] and Rupesh Kumar Dewang

Motilal Nehru National Institute of Technology, Allahabad, Uttar Pradesh, India
ahmedmnnit@gmail.com, rupeshdewang@mnnit.ac.in

Abstract. Sentiment Analysis is the study of sentiments expressed by people. Aspect based Sentiment Analysis is the study of sentiments expressed by people regarding the aspect of an entity. Aspect based Sentiment Analysis is becoming an important task in realising the finer sentiments of objects as described by people in their opinions. In the present paper we describe several techniques which have come up in recent years involving aspect term extraction and/or aspect sentiment prediction.Present paper describes the taxonomy of aspect based sentiment analysis with detailed explainaton of recent methods used. This paper also gives the pros and cons of research papers discussed. In the present paper we have compared all the papers with table enteries.

Keywords: Aspect Based Sentiment Analysis · Sentiment Mining Supervised · Unsupervised Learning · etc

1 Introduction

Aspect Based Sentiment Analysis (ABSA) [25] deals with extracting and predicting the users sentiment regarding an aspect of the object in the opinionated corpus. ABSA is the extraction of user's opinion about an aspect expressed over the internet in different sources. With the evolution of the internet and the dependence on the services provided by the internet sentiment analysis has become one of the most sought-after research areas in computer science. After the boom of social media it has become obvious to analyse the opinion of people. Aspect/feature based sentiment analysis model extracts opinions on aspects/features of the given entity. After extraction the aspect is categorised into one of the aspect classes pertaining to the given entity. The class may or may not be predefined. The classified aspect is then opinionated based on the users review. This collective result of aspects and their polarities can then be used to know the finer details of what features exist and how good they are which is more beneficial than just knowing the overall opinion of the product. This data can also be used by companies to improve their product quality. For example Google Play Store uses the reviews to rate the individual features of applications.

© Springer Nature Singapore Pte Ltd. 2019
A. K. Luhach et al. (Eds.): ICAICR 2018, CCIS 955, pp. 612–629, 2019.
https://doi.org/10.1007/978-981-13-3140-4_55

Much work has been done on aspect based sentiment analysis. The latest being Aspect Based Sentiment Analysis Survey [54] it gives a review on supervised, semi supervised and unsupervised algorithms which focus on aspect and opinion extraction. Present paper goes ahead of the latest survey on ABSA and gives a summary on papers focusing on ABSA which were not included in that paper. With SemEval (International Workshop on Semantic Evaluation) completing its task of ABSA there are now lot of techniques/algorithms to summarize now and with Google Play Store having started using aspect in review of its products it is now time to finalise the current progress of this technology in the industry.

2 Methodology

In this survey paper we have included most recent research papers. Feldman [20] reported more than seven thousand articles on different areas of sentiment analysis. Nowadays supervised learning is giving very good results in this field of research and it has been observed that most of recent research papers [63,64,66] are using supervised learning or deep learning for aspect based sentiment analysis. We have summarized 40 research papers some of which are [31,63,64,66] and classified these papers on the basis of sub-tasks of aspect based sentiment analysis. The three main subtasks of aspect based sentiment analysis are- aspect extraction, aspect category detection and sentiment analysis. In aspect extraction, all the target words are extracted which are important to determine the polarity of sentiment. After that those words are categorised into similar clusters. Aspect can be implicit or explicit. Most of the papers summarized here are for implicit and explicit aspect extraction. And in sentiment analysis, polarity of aspect is detected. It is useful in order to determine whether the users attitude towards a particular topic or product is positive, negative, or neutral. Due to variation of papers, we have classified it into five categories- aspect extraction, aspect category detection, sentiment analysis, joint aspect extraction and sentiment analysis, joint aspect extraction, aspect category extraction and sentiment analysis. Then further classify into various techniques.

3 Aspect Extraction

In aspect based sentiment analysis, extraction of aspects is the main subtask. We have classified the techniques of aspect extraction into supervised and unsupervised learning. Supervised learning is then classified into dictionary based, frequency based, neural network, conditional random fields (CRF) [7], support vector machine (SVM), latent dirichlet allocation LDA [9]. Unsupervised learning is further classified into syntax based. The summary is classified into tabular form.

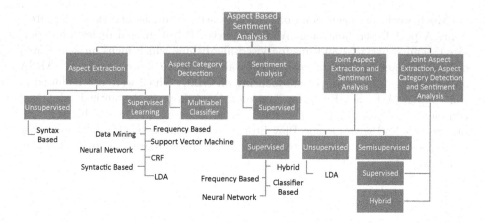

Fig. 1. Taxonomy of survey

3.1 Supervised Learning

Supervised learning infers a function from training data with given outputs of the respective inputs consisting of a set of training examples. As compared to others techniques, supervised techniques have been applied to other domains. Most research papers have used supervised learning for aspect extraction in English language.

Support Vector Machine (SVM). SVM algorithm outputs an optimal hyperplane which classifies the data into two. This hyperplane can be used to classify new data. Falk et al. [46] describes the participation in SemEval-2016 for *Opinion Target Expression*. The author describes the challenges to find domain specific aspect in sentence. Focus was done on determining domain specific aspect using the grammatical dependency relationships of word vectors to classify each word in a sentence into non-target or target. They have used L2-regularized L2-loss support vector dual classification provided by the LIBLINEAR [15] library for classification of each word of sentence into target and non-target tag. After that they use heuristics, based on observations and statistical information. The key observation here is that the aspect expression is usually composed of noun or proper nouns. The system achieved an F1 score of 56.81%. Here the drawback with this system is that it uses heuristics function for target phrase labelling which in some cases is unable to select the full target phrase and can be improved by using more sophisticated techniques.

Frequency Based (FB). FB assumes that words with higher frequency are more important and hence they are aspect. Islam et al. [37] extracted features by proposing a criterion for the intrinsic and extrinsic domain relevance technique. The author proposed a method with a modification to Intrinsic and Extrinsic Domain Relevance (IEDR) [21]. It has been observed that most of the aspects are domain specific and rare to be found in other domains. So syntactic rules can be applied for extraction of aspects. In spite of using weight equation of term frequency inverse document frequency, a modified weight equation is used. Domain relevance calculation is used excluding the inverse document frequency. The experimental dataset is opinRank dataset which has reviews of cars and hotels. The F1 score of this system is 45.42%.

Convolutional Neural Network (CNN). A network similar to the interconnected group of neurons in the brain, a convolutional neural network is a class of deep and feed-forward neural networks that apply a convolution operation to the input. Poria et al. [38] used a convolutional neural network (CNN) and a non-linear supervised classifier to extract aspects. They used a seven layer deep CNN to tag each word in sentences as non-aspect or aspect word. Additionally, they use linguistic patterns in addition to the CNN to improve the performance of the method. The dataset domain are Canon, Nikon, DVD, Mp3, Cell phone, laptop, and restaurant. The F1 score of the system in domain canon (92.59%), Nikon (82.6%), DVD (90.29%), Mp3 (90.75%), Cell phone (92.75%).

Conditional Random Field (CRF). CRF is a statistical modelling method used for structured prediction it can take context into account. Gunes [39] proposed a technique to extract aspect terms from opinionated documents by using sequential learning approach. The author used semi-markov [12] conditional random fields. While incorporating into the learning process the word embedding as features . In all domain for aspect phrase extraction, semi-markov CRFs performs slightly better than the conditional random fields. The author showed that the detection accuracy for opinion targets and aspect terms can be improved by using word embeddings. The dataset contained data from the domains hotels, laptops and restaurants.

Syntactic Based. Maharani et al. [30] proposed a technique to extract aspects from unstructured review using syntactic pattern based on features observation, along with a comprehensive analysis of varied pattern. A new pattern is observed by features using bag-of-words feature and POS tagging. This research used review datasets from Hu and Liu research [10, 14] and [13] and the dataset collected from Amazon.com and cnet.com websites. Since this is a syntactic based approach it cannot extract implicit aspects.

Data Mining. Mars and Gouider [63] used text analysis techniques to extract product features opinions from customer reviews in social networks. The author didn't use any data mining discussed so far and hence we categorise it simply as a data mining technique. The author constructed a tree of negative and positive words and then design the ontology representing the product. For feature extraction text mining and natural language processing was used. This system gives an F1-score of 56%.

Latent Dirichlet Allocation (LDA). LDA allows a set of data to be explained by the unobserved set of data which in turn helps to explain the reason of data similarity. Asnani and Pawar [57] focussed on finding aspect in code mixed content by enhancing LDA. Here code-mixed content refers reviews consisting of sentences which is written as a mixture of two languages such as Hindi and

English. The authors enhanced LDA by improving the relevance of aspect clusters by not including in the clusters unimportant words and including coherent words to process code-mixed data to generate topic clusters which are semantically related to each other. They performed experiment in both the domain monolingual and code-mixed content. This technique is important in solving real world problem as most of the interaction on the web through social networks and text forums is a random mix of languages.

3.2 Unsupervised Learning

Unsupervised learning constructs a function from the training dataset wherein the output for any of the inputs is not given or simply stating unsupervised learning works on unlabelled training data.

Syntax method. Zhu et al. [16] addressed the challenge of identifying multiple single-aspect and single-polarity terms in one sentence, called as aspect-based sentence segmentation. The authors proposed two baseline methods comma-based method and full-stop based method. Comma-based methodology is to phase a sentence in terms of comma, and therefore the full-stop primarily based methodology is to think about the entire sentence as a single-aspect phase. And it was observed that these baseline method gives best results over 3 state-of-art text summarization methods [5] such as Dotplotting [2,3] , C99 [5] and Fragkou [11] method.

4   Aspect Category Detection

4.1   Multi-label Classifier

Multi-label classifier can classify each entity with multiple labels. Machacek [40] described a technique for Aspect Category Detection. The author modelled the task as multi-label classification with binary relevance transformation, where label is the pair of entity and aspect. The author preformed logistic regression using gradient descent function with suared cost function. For each entity-aspect to train the resulting binary classifier. The disadvantage of this model is that review constext is not taken into consideration.

5   Sentiment Analysis

5.1   Supervised

Pateria and Choubey [31] hypothesised that aspect polarity is only affected by terms related to aspect. The authors used a supervised model which used Support Vector Machine with Radial Basis Function as classifier.They however hypothesised that only the terms related to aspect affect the aspect polarity. The only problem with the system is that it determines the polarity about some specific aspects only and other aspects are ignored. And there is one more research done in improving sentiment analysis with the help of neural network they divided the task into two, first they find the category of aspect and secondly, determine the sentiment of that aspect according to category hence increase the accuracy of system. The authors used single layer feedforward network for aspect category classification and sequential labelling classifier for polarity or sentiment detection. The system is unconstrained and uses a lot of external resources for feature generation.

Backpropagation artificial neural network also improves sentiment analysis which is described by Sharma and Dey [19]. A model using back-propagation artificial neural network (BPANN) was proposed by the authors for sentiment classification. Three sentiment lexicons and Information Gain (HM dataset [4], GI dataset [1] and opinion lexicon [10]) were used to retrieve sentiment terms that are used to train and test the back-propagation artificial neural network. Movie review corpus has been used. This gives far better results than the most recently previous research papers.

HEAT with artificial neural network gives results into next level which is described by Chernyshevich [43]. The author has made a simple neural network that predicts polarity of word sequence based on the heat map of sentence that regions with higher or lower sentiment intensity.This system fails ar identifying neutral opinions.

The last research paper in this category is in different language domain which is authored by Mayorov and Andrianov [47]. The author describes aspect-based polarity detection system for Russian language. The system is a combination of two classifiers for opinion target expressions and for implicit opinion target mentions. Both the classifiers used linear SVM with L2 regularization as their base for sentiment classification into three classes. Russian restaurant reviews dataset was used.

Apart from these there is also one technique that is supervised leaning with distributed approach that is described by Zahedi et al. [58]. The author shows a distributed approach based on topic modelling for sentiment analysis. The Kitchen, Book, Electronics, Sport, Movie and Music reviews data sets obtained from Amazon site were used for evaluation. The author describes the problems related to low speedup and low efficiency and garbage collection.

6   Joint Aspect Extraction and Sentiment Analysis

6.1   Supervised

Frequency Based. Frequency based supervised approach for aspect extraction and sentiment analysis gives good result in closed domain which is deeply described by Ströat et al. [66] the author focuses on extraction of aspect and their sentient from game reviews. Word frequency is used to identify a word as aspect i.e. the word who appears more will be having higher chances of becoming aspect. And after that sentiment analysis is performed online, through an online crowd sourcing service. Another method that is using features and linguistic rules are described by Kansal and Toshniwal [23] linguistic rules were used for polarity detection, and an online dictionary was used to find and eliminate the context independent words and find the aspect term. For classification of left out opinion words, opinion words and features were used together because same opinion can have different polarity in same domain. They termed this methodology as Interaction Information. Assumes features as nouns or noun phrases.

Classifier Based. Using multiple an ensemble of multiple classifiers to obtain better results. Xenos et al. [32] for Aspect Category (Aspect Extraction) the author used multiple ensembles, basing it on Support Vector Machine classifiers. To achieve the task of Opinion Target Expression Extraction a sequence labelling approach using CRF (Conditional Random Fields) was employed. For Aspect Polarity, an ensemble of two supervised classifiers, one based on word embeddings and another based on hand crafted features was employed. The authors assigned a tag to every word to indicate if it was an aspect term or not. Not only it supports vector machine but naive Bayes classifier gives good results. Naive Bayes classifier is used for aspect extraction.The author gives scores to aspects based on the driving factor for aspect based sentiment classification and aspects with more driving factors decide the polarity of the review the most. Linear classifier is also used to detect sentiment of aspects which is described by Peleja and Magalhaes [28]. For aspect extraction the authors used short text and extracts target words and then used linear classifier (VW3) to determine polarity detection.

Hybrid. A hybrid model is used to address the problem of finding the aspect based sentiment analysis. Similar approach is described by Cheng et al. [61] who present the HiErarchical ATtention (HEAT) network for aspect based sentiment classification. The HEAT network is made up of a hierarchical attention module the constituents of which are sentiment and aspect attention modules. The aspect attention module extracts the aspect based information and the sentiment attention module extracts the aspect determining sentiment words. With the help of Bernoulli attention mechanics the HEAT network can retrieve aspect terms while also classifying them. Their system cannot handle certain special cases like the comparative sentiment. Another hierarchical approach is described by Panchendrarajan et al. [65] hierarchical relationships between different aspects was represented by the taxonomy developed. A total of 400 random sample reviews from pre-processed reviews were used to develop this taxonomy. The model is trained by using a standard maximum entropy classifier which helps in explicit aspect extraction with bigrams as the feature of this classifier. Eventually sentiment scores related the extracted aspects are calculated using Analytic Hierarchy Process (AHP) [18].

Neural Network. Nowadays Neural network model is giving good results in domain of sentiment analysis which is proved by Jebbara and Cimiano [36]. The architecture given by the authors breaks down the task in two subtasks: aspect based sentiment extraction and aspect term extraction. The problem is framed as a sequence labelling task and aspects are extracted by using a recurrent neural network. Further, a sentiment is predicted by a recurrent network. Sentiment and wordnet is used for features extraction. Pham and Le proposed a new multilayer approach of neural network to solve this problem [56] to generate the aspect sentiment from the review the authors proposed a multiple layer representation. It contains six layers:

1. Word representation
2. Sentence representation
3. Aspect representation
4. Higher aspect representation
5. Aspect rating
6. Overall rating.

LRNN-ASR (Latent Rating Neural Network-Aspect Semantic Representation) is the name of this model.

6.2 Unsupervised

Unsupervised learning for sentiment analysis has always been a challenge in field of research yet some researchers achieved notable success in this field. Zhi et al. [62] proposed an aspect opinion mining algorithm by combining word embedding and dependency parsing. They have chosen the best performance of the lexicons -aspect lexicon based on word embeddings and sentiment lexicon based on words embedding too. The authors extracted language patterns of aspects by combining two lexicons and dependency parsers. The authors discovered all of the sentiment words by combination of aspect lexicon for each aspect and the the language patterns of aspects from the test dataset. Next, the sentiment was computed by clustering aspects and computing the sentimental orientation of each cluster. Another success in unsupervised learning is using self-organizing results that gives good results in sentiment analysis. Chifu et al. [29] performed aspect level sentiment analysis using an unsupervised method which used the Growing Hierarchical Self-organizing Maps [8]. The authors made a domain specific ontological taxonomy associated with aspects having a tree-like structure. Then the authors classified the sentences against this data structure. The authors perform hierarchical classification by using unsupervised neural network based on Kohonen Self-organizing Maps [6] the Enrich-GHSOM [17], which is a hierarchical self-organizing map.

Latent Dirichlet Allocation (LDA). Akhtar et al. [60] focussed on the summarization and analysis of the hotel reviews mentioned on the TripAdvisor website. The reviews and metadata from the website were crawled and classified. The classes were predefined into common aspects. Implicit and hidden aspects and information was uncovered by using Topic modelling technique -LDA. The classified sentences were then followed with sentiment analysis.

6.3 Semi-supervised

Anand and Naorem [53] proposed a scheme without using labelled data. They classified the data into two classes and proposed a scheme to detect aspects and the corresponding opinions. They used aspect clue words and a collection of hand crafted rules. 3 techniques for choosing of aspect clue words are explored

- Manual labelling
- Review guided clustering
- Clustering.

The effectiveness of this method was only tested on individual statements.

The aspect-based extraction on the review should be effected by filtering plot sentences out but it needs to be joined with efficient techniques for incorporating opinions across various review sentences. Applying user interests derived through these methods the lack of large datasets for testing this technique can be lightened.

7 Joint Aspect Extraction, Aspect Category Detection and Sentiment Analysis

7.1 Supervised

Supervised learning gave best results in SemEval task and Araque et al. [48] proposed an alternative pipeline for aspect based sentiment analysis task that is- aspect extraction, aspect level classification, aspect context detection and sentiment detection. The author developed an aspect classifier module by proposing a hybrid model made up of word embeddings used along with semantic similarity measures. And extend the context detection algorithm to increase its efficiency. For aspect extraction authors used POS (Parts Of Speech) tagger and Name entity recognition (NER) for aspect categorization they have used SVM linear classifier on the basis of word2vec as a feature. For context detection they used dependency graph and parameter based filtering. Then sentiment analysis is done using linear regression classifier, which takes skip-gram model as an embedding. Dataset is used is: Yelp-extracted, SemEval16 train and SemEval16 test. The accuracy of sentiment analysis was increased by using distributed supervised learning methodology. This paper uses word embedding and similarity measures to find aspect which works positively for it. But accuracy of system can be increased by extracting domain specific aspects. Kumar et al. [44] described the system incorporating with distributional thesaurus, domain dependency graph features and unsupervised lexical induction with the help of an unlabelled external dataset for aspect level sentiment analysis. The author used Support Vector Machine (SVM) as the baseline classifier for aspect level category detection and sentiment polarity classification, and Conditional Random Fields (CRF) [7] for opinion target expression identification. This system purely works on domain specific aspect extraction which gives good result but for aspect category extraction the system has some inconsistency which leads to decrease in accuracy achieved. Next, neural network and deep learning is used in researches to increase accuracy here we describe two papers who solved all three tasks of sentiment analysis. Toh and Su [49] proposed a system consisting of two components: binary classifiers and sequential labelling classifiers. Binary classifiers were trained using single layer feedforward neural network and were used for aspect category classification and sequential label classifier was used for opinion target extraction. For aspect category classification, they have used CNN architecture which consists of one input layer, one max pooling layer, one hidden dense layer, one SoftMax layer. Stochastic gradient descent algorithm was used to train the model. For opinion target extraction the sequential labelling classifiers are trained using Conditional Random Fields (CRF). Another one is using recurrent neural network which is described by Toshihiko et al. [55]. They proposed an approach based on Neural attention [26] which learns relations between tokens and entity-attribute pairs through backpropagation in RNN this was used for aspect category detection. Opinion target extraction was done based on a rule-based system that examines several verb-centric relations related to entity-attribute pair. Sentiment polarity was done using two techniques one by using a deep learning approach proposed by Wang and Liu [27] and other was a rule based approach.

7.2   Hybrid

One hybrid approach for sentiment analysis uses both supervised and unsupervised learning is described by Alvarez-López et al. [42]. For aspect category detection the author have used SVM classifier combined with the words lists. For Opinion target expression CRF are used and used an unsupervised system for polarity detection, based on context-based polarity lexicons and syntactic dependencies. The dataset domain is restaurant and laptop data.The problem with the system is that it gives poor result in sentiment analysis due to unsupervised approach although the main benefit is that there is no need of labelled dataset manual tagging of which is both time and resource consuming.

8   Comparison of Works

We have given tabular description of all studied papers in two tables. Table 1 is performance analysis table which describes performance of various papers in terms of recall, precision and F1 score. Some papers only give accuracy of their system so we have included that in F1 score column. The scores included are of those tests which gave the highest result of all the data the author tested it in. This Table 1 gives the year the paper was published in, the accuracy of the technique in the paper in terms of precision, recall and F1-score if available or only accuracy and the dataset on which this accuracy was achieved in. Table 2 is for evaluation techniques for various papers. It includes information about techniques and dataset used. we have found most of dataset used are annotated

Table 1. Comparison of performance of various papers on aspect based sentiment analysis.

References	Year	Performance			Dataset
		Precision (%)	Recall or accuracy (%)	F1-score (%)	
[16]	2009	69	56	62	Chinese restaurant reviews
[19]	2012	-	86	-	Movie review corpus
[22]	2014	81.12	76.56	78.78	Movie reviews of Stanford AI
[23]	2014	-	82.3	-	Amazon product review
[28]	2015	71	-		SemEval-2015: restaurant
[29]	2015	-	44.38	-	Camera review dataset
[30]	2015	52.4	68.6	60	Amazon and CNET reviews
[31]	2016	50	50.6	71.7	SemEval-2016: restaurant
[34]	2016	-	86.7	-	Movie and restaurant reviews
[32]	2016	67.75	75.77	71.54	SemEval-2016: restaurant
[36]	2016	65.9	71	68.4	SenticNet and WordNet
[37]	2016	40.45	45.42	42.57	opinRank dataset
[38]	2016	88.27	86.1	88.27	SemEval-2016: restaurant
[39]	2016	84.76	81.38	83.07	SemEval 2014: restaurant
[40]	2016	-	71.49	72.396	Semeval 2015: restaurant
[41]	2016	-	81.09	-	SemEval-2016: restaurant
[42]	2016	-	69.96	-	SemEval-2015: restaurant
[43]	2016	-	83	-	SemEval-2016: restaurants
[44]	2016	-	86.7	-	SemEval-2016: restaurants
[45]	2016	-	68.1	-	SemEval-2016: restaurant
[46]	2016	-	56.81	-	SemEval-2016: restaurant
[47]	2016	-	77.92	-	Russian restaurant reviews
[48]	2016	80	82	79	Yelp and SemEval-2016
[49]	2016	-	73.03	-	SemEval-2016: restaurant
[50]	2016	-	81.12	-	News dataset
[51]	2016	72.69	73.08	72.88	SemEval 2016
[52]	2016	-	88.12	-	SemEval 2016
[53]	2016	-	52	-	Amazon movie reviews
[55]	2014	62.61	67.32	64.88	SemEval-2016: restaurant
[59]	2017	62.5	58.08	60.21	Reviews from Play store
[61]	2017	-	85.5	-	SemEval 2015: laptop
[62]	2017	73.17	76.6	74.8	Reviews of a video software
[63]	2017	-	56	-	Product tweets
[64]	2017	94	85	89	Reviews of Canon SD500
[65]	2017	94.7	97.5	75.8	Restaurant reviews (Yelp)

dataset by SemEval and they mainly focus on restaurant, laptop, camera domain. We also observed that mostly used approach by papers is supervised in nature. The highest F1-score is achieved so far is 89% for reviews of Canon SD500. This Table 2 gives the technique used in the paper, whether the algorithm was supervised, unsupervised or semi-supervised, the task achieved and the dataset used.

Table 2. Comparison of techniques of various papers on aspect based sentiment analysis.

S. No.	Reference	Year	Evaluation task	Technique used	Type	Dataset used
1	[16]	2009	Aspect extraction	Syntax method	Unsupervised	Chinese restaurant reviews
2	[19]	2012	Both	Neural Network (RNN)	Semi-supervised	Movie review corpus
3	[22]	2014	Both	Probablistic	Supervised	Movie reviews from Stanford AI Lab
4	[23]	2014	Both	Probablistic (Naive Bayes + Decision Tree)	Semi-supervised	Amazon product review
5	[28]	2015	Sentiment detection	Linear classifier	Supervised	SemEval-2015
6	[29]	2015	Sentiment detection	Neural network	Unsupervised	Camera review dataset
7	[30]	2015	Aspect extraction	Rule based (using patterns)	Unsupervised	Review dataset from amazon and cnet
8	[31]	2016	Both	SVM with RBF	Supervised	SemEval-2016
9	[34]	2016	Both	Rule-based	Supervised	Movie and restaurant reviews
10	[32]	2016	Both	CRF + SVM + IDF	Supervised	SemEval-2016
11	[36]	2016	Both	Neural network (RNN)	Supervised	SenticNet and WordNet
12	[37]	2016	Aspect extraction	Frequency based	Supervised	OpinRank Dataset
13	[38]	2016	Aspect extraction	Neural network (CNN)	Supervised	word2vec and Glove and amazon
14	[39]	2016	Aspect extraction	CRF	Supervised	SemEval-2014
15	[40]	2016	Aspect extraction	Multi-label classifier	Supervised	Semeval 2015
16	[41]	2016	Both	Topic modelling	Supervised	SemEval-2016
17	[42]	2016	Both	Hybrid	Supervised	SemEval-2015
18	[43]	2016	Sentiment detection	Neural network	Supervised	SemEval-2016
19	[44]	2016	Both	SVM + CRF	Supervised	SemEval-2016
20	[45]	2016	Both	CNN	Supervised	SemEval-2016
21	[46]	2016	Aspect extraction	SVM+linear classifier	Supervised	SemEval-2016

(continued)

Table 2. (*continued*)

S. No.	Reference	Year	Evaluation task	Technique used	Type	Dataset used
22	[47]	2016	Sentiment detection	SVM with L2 regularization	Supervised	Russian restaurant reviews dataset
23	[48]	2016	Both	SVM+linear classifier	Supervised	Yelp and SemEval-2016
24	[49]	2016	Both	Neural network	Supervised	SemEval-2016
25	[50]	2016	Both	LSTM	Supervised	Text and news dataset
26	[51]	2016	Both	CNN with SVM	Supervised	SemEval 2016
27	[52]	2016	Aspect extraction	CRF	Supervised	SemEval 2016
28	[53]	2016	Both	Rule based and clustering	Semi-supervised	Amazon movie reviews
29	[55]	2016	Both	NN	Supervised	SemEval-2016
30	[56]	2017	Both	CNN	Supervised	Hotel reviews from tripadvisor.com
31	[57]	2017	Aspect extraction	Code-mixed-semantic LDA	Supervised	FIRE 2014 dataset
32	[58]	2017	Sentiment detection	Distributed	Supervised	Movie reviews from amazon
33	[59]	2017	Both	LDA	Unsupervised	Reviews from Play store
34	[60]	2017	Both	LDA	Supervised	Hotel reviews from tripadvisor.com
35	[61]	2017	Both	HiErarchical ATtention	Supervised	SemEval: 2014, 2015, 2016
36	[62]	2017	Sentiment detection	Dependency parsing and language pattern	Unsupervised	Reviews of a video software
37	[63]	2017	Aspect extraction	Data mining	Supervised	Product tweets
38	[64]	2017	Both	Ontology based	Supervised	Canon SD500 digital camera
39	[65]	2017	Both	Hybrid	Supervised	Restaurant reviews (Yelp)
40	[66]	2017	Sentiment detection	Frequency based	Supervised	Reviews on game Dragon Age

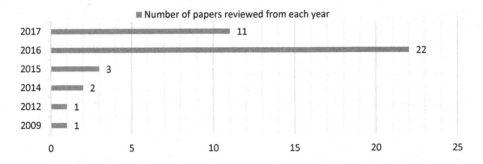

Fig. 2. Number of papers reviewed.

9   Conclusion

Aspect based sentiment analysis is growing subtask of Natural Language Processing (NLP). The presented paper surveys on aspect based sentiment analysis and its various techniques which have been discussed above in brief. To understand all subtask of aspect based sentiment analysis clearly, we have studied 40 papers some of which are [63,64,66] for trend analysis. Aspect based sentiment analysis deals with every word of sentence to know the attitude of customer towards features of product and services. We have categorized all the papers based on subtasks of aspect based sentiment analysis such as the extraction, category detection, polarity detection, joint extraction and polarity detection and joint extraction, category detection and sentiment analysis of aspect and we further classified based on algorithms and techniques. Nowadays most of research is going in field of applying neural networks in aspect based sentiment analysis. Some papers used Convolution Neural Networks (CNN) approach and showed great increase in accuracy of finding aspect from reviews. One more key observation we made in this survey paper is that most of the papers follow supervised approach and very few follow semi-supervised or unsupervised approach. This paper has clear bifurcation of subtasks and techniques along with active research area. We have analyzed that multi-word aspect is still a problem to most of the systems available. All the systems available extract multiword aspect with low accuracy hence it has greater scope of improvement. Although we are still limited to extract domain specific aspects. We have limitation of finding polarity of aspects according to domain.

10   Future Scope

The future scope of this work would be to find and survey unsupervised techniques which needs huge improvement in accuracy. There is a lack of domain independent techniques in this field which means that for every domain we need a test dataset if we want to use any of the techniques. The lack of accurate unsupervised techniques also demand the presence of datasets which is difficult to obtain.

References

1. Stone, P.J., Dunphy, D.C., Smith, M.S.: The general inquirer: a computer approach to content analysis (1966)
2. Church K.W.: Chart align: a program for aligning parallel texts at the character level. In: Proceedings of the 31st Annual Meeting of the Association for Computational Linguistics, pp. 1–8 (1993)
3. Reynar J.C.: An automatic method of finding topic boundaries. In: Proceedings of the 32nd Annual Meeting of the Association for Computational Linguistics, pp. 331–333 (1994)
4. Hatzivassiloglou, V., McKeown, K.R.: Predicting the semantic orientation of adjectives. In: Proceedings of the 35th Annual Meeting of the Association for Computational Linguistics and Eighth Conference of the European Chapter of the Association for Computational Linguistics pp. 174–181. Association for Computational Linguistics (1997)
5. Choi, F.Y.Y.: Advances in domain independent linear text segmentation. In: Proceedings of the 1st Meeting of the North American Chapter of the Association for Computational Linguistics, pp. 26–33 (2000)
6. Kohonen, T.: Self-organizing Maps, 3rd edn. In: Springer Series in Information Sciences, vol. 30. Springer, Berlin (2001)
7. Lafferty, J., McCallum, A., Pereira, F.C.: Conditional Random Fields: Probabilistic Models for Segmenting and Labeling Sequence Data (2001)
8. Dittenbach, M., Merkl, D., Rauber, A.: Organizing and exploring high-dimensional data with the growing hierarchical self-organizing map. In: FSKD, pp. 626–630 (2002)
9. Blei, D.M., Ng, A.Y., Jordan, M.I.: Latent dirichlet allocation. J. Mach. Learn. Res. 3(Jan), 993–1022 (2003)
10. Hu, M., Liu, B.: Mining and summarizing customer reviews. In: Proceedings of the Tenth ACM SIGKDD International Conference on Knowledge Discovery and Data Mining. ACM, 2004. pp. 168177 (2004)
11. Fragkou P., Petridis V., Kehagias A.: A dynamic programming algorithm for liner text segmentation. J. Intell. Inf. Syst. 23(2), 179–197 (2004)
12. Sarawagi, S., Cohen, W.W.: Semi-markov conditional random fields for information extraction. In: NIPS (2004)
13. Hu, M., Liu, B.: Opinion extraction and summarization on the web. AAAI. 2006. pp. 1621–1624 (2006)
14. Ding, X., Liu, B., Yu, P.S.: A holistic lexicon-based approach to opinion mining. In: Proceedings of the 2008 International Conference on Web Search and Data Mining. ACM, pp. 231–240 (2008)
15. Fan, R.E., Chang, K.W., Hsieh, C.J., Wang, X.R., Lin, C.J.: LIBLINEAR: a library for large linear classification. J. Mach. Learn. Res. 9, 1871–1874 (2008)
16. Zhu, J., Zhu, M., Wang, H., Tsou, B.K.: Aspect-based sentence segmentation for sentiment summarization. In: Proceedings of the 1st International CIKM Workshop on Topic-Sentiment Analysis for Mass Opinion. ACM, pp. 65–72 (2009)
17. Chifu, E.S., Letia, I.A. : Self-organizing maps in Web mining and semantic Web. In: Matsopoulos, G.K. (ed.) Self-Organizing Maps, INTECH, pp. 357–380 (2010)
18. Qiu, G., Liu, B., Bu, J., Chen, C.: Opinion word expansion and target extraction through double propagation. Comput. linguist. 37(1), 9–27 (2011)
19. Sharma, A., Dey, S.: An artificial neural network based approach for sentiment analysis of opinionated text. In: Proceedings of the 2012 ACM Research in Applied Computation Symposium pp. 37–42. ACM (2012)

20. Feldman, R.: Techniques and applications for sentiment analysis. Commun. ACM **56**(4), 82–89 (2013)
21. Hai, Z., Chang, K., Kim, J.J., Yang, C.C.: Identifying features in opinion mining via intrinsic and extrinsic domain relevance. IEEE Trans. Knowl. Data Eng. **26**(3) (2014)
22. Parkhe, V., Biswas, B.: Aspect based sentiment analysis of movie reviews: finding the polarity directing aspects. In: 2014 International Conference on InSoft Computing and Machine Intelligence (ISCMI), pp. 28–32. IEEE (2014)
23. Kansal, H., Toshniwal, D.: Aspect based summarization of context dependent opinion words. Procedia Comput. Sci. **35**, 166–175 (2014)
24. Patra, B.G., Mukherjee, N., Das, A., Mandal, S., Das, D., Bandyopadhyay, S.: Identifying aspects and analyzing their sentiments from reviews. In: 2014 13th Mexican International Conference on Artificial Intelligence (MICAI), pp. 9–15. IEEE (2014)
25. Liu, B.: Sentiment Analysis: Mining Opinions, Sentiments, and Emotions. Cambridge University Press (2015)
26. Luong, M.T., Pham, H., Manning, C.D.: Effective approaches to attention-based neural machine translation. In: Proceedings of the 2015 Conference on Empirical Methods in Natural Language Processing, pp. 1412–1421 (2015)
27. Wang, B., Liu, M.: Deep learning for aspect based sentiment analysis. Reports for CS224d, Stanford University (2015)
28. Peleja, F., Magalhaes, J.: Learning text patterns to detect opinion targets. In: 2015 7th International Joint Conference on Knowledge Discovery, Knowledge Engineering and Knowledge Management (IC3K), Vol. 1, pp. 337–343. IEEE (2015)
29. Chifu, E.S., Letia, T.S., Chifu, V.R.: Unsupervised aspect level sentiment analysis using self-organizing maps. In: 2015 17th International Symposium on Symbolic and Numeric Algorithms for Scientific Computing (SYNASC), pp. 468–475. IEEE (2015)
30. Maharani, W., Widyantoro, D.H., Khodra, M.L.: Aspect extraction in customer reviews using syntactic pattern. Procedia Comput. Sci. **59**, 244–253 (2015)
31. Pateria, S., Choubey, P.: AKTSKI at SemEval-2016 Task 5: Aspect Based Sentiment Analysis for Consumer Reviews. InSemEval@ NAACL-HLT, pp. 318–324 (2016)
32. Xenos, D., Theodorakakos, P., Pavlopoulos, J., Malakasiotis, P., Androutsopoulos, I.: AUEB-ABSA at SemEval-2016 Task 5: Ensembles of Classifiers and Embeddings for Aspect Based Sentiment Analysis. InSemEval@ NAACL-HLT, pp. 312–317 (2016)
33. Yanase, T., Yanai, K., Sato, M., Miyoshi, T., Niwa, Y.: bunji at SemEval-2016 Task 5: Neural and Syntactic Models of Entity-Attribute Relationship for Aspect-based Sentiment Analysis. InSemEval@ NAACL-HLT, pp. 289–295 (2016)
34. Ismail, S., Alsammak, A., Elshishtawy, T.: A generic approach for extracting aspects and opinions of arabic reviews. In: Proceedings of the 10th International Conference on Informatics and Systems, pp. 173–179. ACM (2016)
35. Wang, H., Zhang, C., Yin, H., Wang, W., Zhang, J., Xu, F.: A unified framework for fine-grained opinion mining from online reviews. In: 2016 49th Hawaii International Conference on System Sciences (HICSS), pp. 1134–1143. IEEE (2016)
36. Jebbara, S., Cimiano, P.: Aspect-based sentiment analysis using a two-step neural network architecture. In: Semantic Web Evaluation Challenge, pp. 153–167. Springer, Cham (2016)

37. Islam, J., Badhon, Z.A., Shill, P.C.: An effective approach of intrinsic and extrinsic domain relevance technique for feature extraction in opinion mining. In: 2016 5th International Conference on Informatics, Electronics and Vision (ICIEV), pp. 428–433. IEEE (2016)

38. Poria, S., Cambria, E., Gelbukh, A.: Aspect extraction for opinion mining with a deep convolutional neural network. Knowl. Based Syst. **108**, 42–49 (2016)

39. Gunes, O.: Aspect term and opinion target extraction from web product reviews using semi-markov conditional random fields with word embeddings as features. In: Proceedings of the 6th International Conference on Web Intelligence, Mining and Semantics, p. 6. ACM (2016)

40. Machacek, J.: BUTknot at SemEval-2016 Task 5: supervised machine learning with term substitution approach in aspect category detection. In: Proceedings of the 10th International Workshop on Semantic Evaluation (SemEval-2016) pp. 301–305 (2016)

41. Jiang, M., Zhang, Z., Lan, M.: Ecnu at semeval-2016 task 5: extracting effective features from relevant fragments in sentence for aspect-based sentiment analysis in reviews. In: Proceedings of the 10th International Workshop on Semantic Evaluation (SemEval-2016), pp. 361–366 (2016)

42. Alvarez-López, T., Juncal-Martinez, J., Fernndez-Gavilanes, M., Costa-Montenegro, E., Gonzlez-Castano, F.J.: Gti at semeval-2016 task 5: Svm and crf for aspect detection and unsupervised aspect-based sentiment analysis. In: Proceedings of the 10th International Workshop on Semantic Evaluation (SemEval-2016), pp. 306–311 (2016)

43. Chernyshevich, M.: Ihs-rd-belarus at semeval-2016 task 5: detecting sentiment polarity using the heatmap of sentence. In: Proceedings of the 10th International Workshop on Semantic Evaluation (SemEval-2016), pp. 296–300 (2016)

44. Kumar, A., Kohail, S., Kumar, A., Ekbal, A., Biemann, C.: IIT-TUDA at SemEval-2016 task 5: beyond sentiment lexicon: combining domain dependency and distributional semantics features for aspect based sentiment analysis. In: Proceedings of the 10th International Workshop on Semantic Evaluation (SemEval-2016), pp. 1129–1135 (2016)

45. Ruder, S., Ghaffari, P., Breslin, J.G.: Insight-1 at semeval-2016 task 5: deep learning for multilingual aspect-based sentiment analysis (2016). arXiv preprint arXiv:1609.02748

46. Falk, S., Rexha, A., Kern, R.: Know-center at SemEval-2016 task 5: using word vectors with typed dependencies for opinion target expression extraction. In: Proceedings of the 10th International Workshop on Semantic Evaluation (SemEval-2016), pp. 266–270 (2016)

47. Mayorov, V., Andrianov, I.: MayAnd at SemEval-2016 task 5: syntactic and word2vec-based approach to aspect-based polarity detection in Russian. In: Proceedings of the 10th International Workshop on Semantic Evaluation (SemEval-2016), pp. 325–329 (2016)

48. Araque, O., Zhu, G., Garca-Amado, M., Iglesias, C.A.: Mining the opinionated web: classification and detection of aspect contexts for aspect based sentiment analysis. In: 2016 IEEE 16th International Conference on Data Mining Workshops (ICDMW), pp. 900–907. IEEE (2016)

49. Toh, Z., Su, J.: NLANGP at SemEval-2016 task 5: improving aspect based sentiment analysis using neural network features. In: Proceedings of the 10th International Workshop on Semantic Evaluation (SemEval-2016), pp. 282–288 (2016)

50. Jin, L., Duan, M., Schuler, W.: OCLSP at SemEval-2016 task 9: multilayered LSTM as a neural semantic dependency parser. In: Proceedings of the 10th International Workshop on Semantic Evaluation (SemEval-2016), pp. 1212–1217 (2016)
51. Khalil, T., El-Beltagy, S.R.: NileTMRG at SemEval-2016 task 5: deep convolutional neural networks for aspect category and sentiment extraction. In: Proceedings of the 10th International Workshop on Semantic Evaluation (SemEval-2016), pp. 271–276 (2016)
52. Brun, C., Perez, J., Roux, C.: Xrce at semeval-2016 task 5: feedbacked ensemble modeling on syntactico-semantic knowledge for aspect based sentiment analysis. In: Proceedings of the 10th International Workshop on Semantic Evaluation (SemEval-2016), pp. 277–281 (2016)
53. Anand, D., Naorem, D.: Semi-supervised aspect based sentiment analysis for movies using review filtering. Procedia Comput. Sci. **84**, 86–93 (2016)
54. Laskari, N.K., Sanampudi, S.K.: Aspect based sentiment analysis survey. OSR J. Comput. Eng. (IOSR-JCE) (2016). e-ISSN 2278–0661
55. Yanase, T., Yanai, K., Sato, M., Miyoshi, T., Niwa, Y.: bunji at semeval-2016 task 5: neural and syntactic models of entity-attribute relationship for aspect-based sentiment analysis. In: Proceedings of the 10th International Workshop on Semantic Evaluation (SemEval-2016), pp. 289–295 (2016)
56. Pham, D.H., Le, A.C.: Learning multiple layers of knowledge representation for aspect based sentiment analysis. Data Knowl. Eng. (2017)
57. Asnani, K., Pawar, J.D.: Automatic aspect extraction using lexical semantic knowledge in code-mixed context. Procedia Comput. Sci. **112**, 693–702 (2017)
58. Zahedi, E., Baniasadi, Z., Saraee, M.: A distributed joint sentiment and topic modeling using Spark for big opinion mining. In: 2017 Iranian Conference on Electrical Engineering (ICEE), pp. 1475–1480. IEEE (2017)
59. Deewattananon, B., Sammapun, U.: Analyzing user reviews in Thai language toward aspects in mobile applications. In: 2017 14th International Joint Conference on Computer Science and Software Engineering (JCSSE), pp. 1–6. IEEE (2017)
60. Akhtar, N., Zubair, N., Kumar, A., Ahmad, T.: Aspect based Sentiment oriented summarization of hotel reviews. Procedia Comput. Sci. **115**, 563–571 (2017)
61. Cheng, J., Zhao, S., Zhang, J., King, I., Zhang, X., Wang, H.: Aspect-level sentiment classification with HEAT (HiErarchical ATtention) network. In: Proceedings of the 2017 ACM on Conference on Information and Knowledge Management, pp. 97–106. ACM (2017)
62. Zhi, S., Li, X., Zhang, J., Fan, X., Du, L., Li, Z.: Aspects opinion mining based on word embedding and dependency parsing. In: Proceedings of the International Conference on Advances in Image Processing, pp. 210–215. ACM (2017)
63. Mars, A., Gouider, M.S.: Big data analysis to features opinions extraction of customer. Procedia Comput. Sci. **112**, 906–916 (2017)
64. Marstawi, A., Sharef, N.M., Aris, T.N.M., Mustapha, A.: Ontology-based aspect extraction for an improved sentiment analysis in summarization of product reviews. In: Proceedings of the 8th International Conference on Computer Modeling and Simulation pp. 100–104. ACM (2017)
65. Panchendrarajan, R., Ahamed, N., Sivakumar, P., Murugaiah, B., Ranathunga, S., Pemasiri, A.: Eatery: a multi-aspect restaurant rating system. In: Proceedings of the 28th ACM Conference on Hypertext and Social Media, pp. 225–234. ACM (2017)
66. Stråât, B., Verhagen, H., Warpefelt, H.: Probing user opinions in an indirect way: an aspect based sentiment analysis of game reviews. In: Proceedings of the 21st International Academic Mindtrek Conference, pp. 1–7. ACM (2017)

Use of Similarity Measure in Recommender System Based on Type of Item Preferences

Ashishkumar B. Patel[1,2]([⊠]) and Kiran Amin[3]

[1] LDRP Institute of Technology and Research, Gandhinagar, Gujarat, India
abp5@live.com
[2] C U Shah University, Wadhwan, Gujarat, India
[3] U V Patel College of Engineering, Kherva, Mehsana, Gujarat, India
kiran.amin@ganpatuniversity.ac.in

Abstract. During last twenty years recommender system have emerged as a research field. Recommender System is rooted in the field of Information Retrieval, Machine Learning and Decision Support System. Most of the users do not have enough knowledge to make automatic decisions. So they need recommendation of different items for better choice. Because of this many researchers tried to understand the algorithmic techniques for recommendation to the given user. It is very important factor to identify similar items related to the target user's test. To find similar items RS uses item preference of an item. In different RSs, the item preferences are available in different forms, i.e. preferences are either available, Boolean preference (yes/no) or not available. We test various User Similarity Measures for dataset with preferences, without preferences and Boolean preferences. We tested various similarity measures for User Based Collaborative Filtering techniques in Apache Mahout.

Keywords: Recommendation system · Item preference · User similarity
Collaborative filtering · Item similarity

1 Introduction

In our daily life we face different opinions and options i.e. thing we would like, don't like and even we don't care. We buy items online or from different stores. We watch movies online today. We listen songs on radio because it is of our choice or we don't notice it all. Same thing happens with hotel choice, tourism destinations, different websites, friend's updates, news etc. Although people's choice may vary, but there are some hidden patterns in their choices or in liking areas. People like the things which are liked by similar kind of other people or they like the things which they have knowledge or experienced in past. Recommender System (RS) is the area which predict about this hidden pattern, and by using these patterns to discover new things which user do not able to find it even if it is useful for them [4]. In real world the user has very large options available for choice, which are not even known to him/her. In such case recommender systems may help them to find relative items based on their choice. Such recommender systems uses preferences of items for recommendations.

© Springer Nature Singapore Pte Ltd. 2019
A. K. Luhach et al. (Eds.): ICAICR 2018, CCIS 955, pp. 630–638, 2019.
https://doi.org/10.1007/978-981-13-3140-4_56

Figure 1 shows the concepts of recommendation [8]. A user who is seeking for recommendation may ask for a recommendation to the system, or a recommender system (recommender engine) may produce the list of recommended items to the user. After visiting the items recommended by recommender, the user rate the item based on his/her experience. Sometimes recommender system ask to provide the preference or rating of the item. The preferences provided by the user are stored in universe of alternatives or preference database, which will further help the recommender engine for accuracy of next recommendation in future.

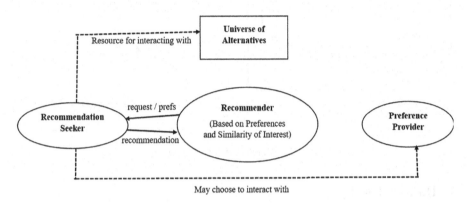

Fig. 1. Model of the recommendation process

2   Mahout – Collaborative Filtering Library

Apache Mahout [1] is a collaborative filtering library from Apache Software Foundation. It is also an open source library which includes machine learning and collaborative filtering algorithms in a single package. Mahout can be used for recommender engine with classification and clustering algorithms. Mahout is used to process scalable data. It can be used to process very large collection of data in a single machine. It has also support of Hadoop for distributed computing and Big Data. We implement and test various methods which uses inbuilt similarity algorithms in Mahout. Our methods takes preference of items from users and based on that it estimates preferences for other items.

Mahout generally uses collaborative filtering for recommendation. It takes users' preferences of rich set of items and find recommended items based on estimated preferences for target item. The Fig. 2 shows different components used for user based recommendation.

Top-level packages define the Mahout interfaces to these key abstractions:

- DataModel
- UserSimilarity
- ItemSimilarity
- UserNeighborhood
- Recommender

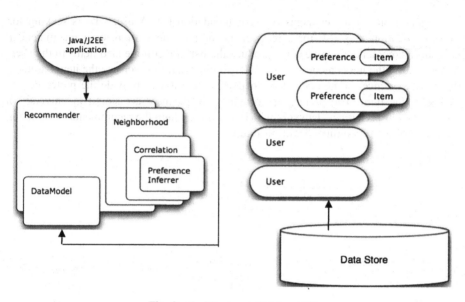

Fig. 2. Architecture of Mahout [4]

3   Dataset Used

MovieLense [10] data sets was by the GroupLens Research Project at the University of Minnesota. This dataset 943 users had rated 1682 movies. The rating of each movie in range 1 to 5. This dataset contains total 100000 ratings. In this dataset every user rated about 20 movies. This project was carried out in Computer Science Department of the University of Minnesota. In the dataset, the data is randomly ordered and tab separated.

user id | item id | rating | timestamp.

We used this data set for comparing similarity measures. By using this dataset several algorithms are tested. In this implementation the output will display the top-n items with their item id.

4   Evaluation Parameters for Recommender System

To understand or measure the accuracy of recommender systems several accuracy measures are used. The popular accuracy measures are Precision, Recall and F-Measures [2]. To derive the accuracy parameters the confusion matrix is often used [12]. The confusion matrix is as shown in Table 1.

Table 1. Confusion matrix

Actual/Predicted	Negative	Positive
Negative	A	C
Positive	C	D

Precision, Recall and F-Measure

Precision and Recall are the well-known metrics for measuring the accuracy of recommends in classical information retrieval (Table 2).

Table 2. Categorization of all possible recommendations

	Recommended	Not Recommended	Total
Used	True – Positive (TP)	False – Negative (FN)	Total Used
Not Used	False – Positive (FP)	True – Negative (TN)	Total not Used
Total	Total Recommended	Total Not Recommended	Total (T)

$$\text{Precision} = \text{count } (N) / N \qquad \text{Precision} = TP / (TP + FP) \qquad (1)$$

$$\text{Recall} = \text{count } (N) / R \qquad \text{Recall} = TP / (TP + FN) \qquad (2)$$

Recall is the ratio of number of items system correctly recall (TP) to the total number of all correct items (R). However precision is the ratio of no. of relevant records (TP) retrieved to the total no. of irrelevant (FP) and relevant (TP) records retired which is expressed in percentages [11]. It is the ration of number of items correctly recall to the number of all items called.

"Precision is defined as the proportion of relevant items in the predicted items and recall is defined as the proportion of predicted items in the relevant items" [11]. If R is the no. of relevant items in the list, then precision and recall are defined as in Eq. 1 and 2 where N is the total no. of items. In some RSs if trying to improve precision often worsen recall. F-measure is introduced as a measure of the harmonic mean of precision and recall.

$$\text{F-Measure} = 2 * (\text{Precision} * \text{Recall}) / (\text{Precision} + \text{Recall}) \qquad (3)$$

5 User Based Recommender System

Sometime people like the same items which are liked by similar kind of people [15]. The user based recommender finds the items which are preferred by similar kind of users based on different parameters like age, location, choice, qualification etc (Fig. 3).

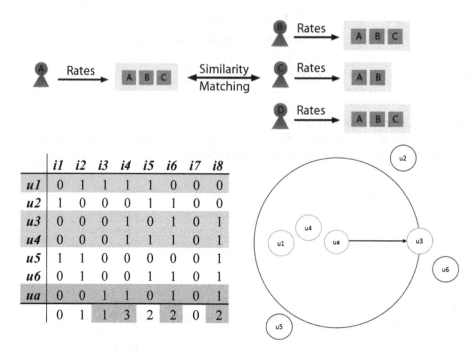

Fig. 3. User based collaborative filtering [3, 9].

As shown in figure the left hand side array is known as preference array. Each cell of preference array represents the preference of an item assigned by the user. If any cell has value 0 means he/she has not visited that item. Value 1 means user has visited and assigned the preference 1. Here we consider only Boolean preference of the items, means user has visited it or not. Sometimes the preference values may vary from 1 to 5 or 1 to 10. In user based Collaborative Filtering, system finds the neighbour users based on difference similarity modes as we experimented in this paper. In the figure the no. of neighbour n = 3 then the similar users related to ua are u1, u3 and u4. Based on the items preferred by similar users system finds items i5 and i2 are recommended items in descending order of some accuracy measures.

The UserSimilarity is one of the required components of the user based recommender method in Apache Mahout, which encapsulates some notion of similarity among users. The UserNeighborhood finds similar users.

6   Item Based Recommender System

In some cases user likes items which they know or for which they have knowledge or which they have purchased in past. The item based RS works on the information of users own preferences of items which he/she referred in past [4] (Fig 4).

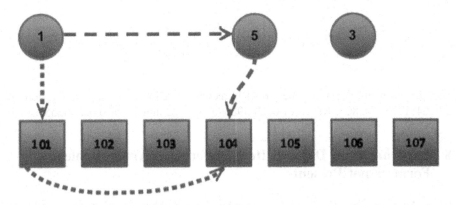

Fig. 4. Item based collaborative filtering [4].

As shown in figure if we want to find recommended items for user 1, then item based RS finds the items which user 1 have referenced in past (here item 101). Then it will find the items which are similar to item 101 (here item 104). Item based RS recommends item 104 to user 1.

7 Experiment on Dataset: Item Preferences Are Considered

For User Similarity, we have implemented and tested two similarity measures, Uncentered Cosine Similarity and Pearson Correlation Similarity.

A. Cosine Similarity

In this similarity [14] the result is the cosine of the angle formed between the two preference vectors. In this similarity metric, the item ratings or preferences are used as a vector to find the normalized dot product of the two users. Cosine similarity is the angular difference between two preference vectors. The expression of Cosine Similarity is:

$$Similarity = \cos(\theta) = \frac{\Sigma Ai * Bi}{\sqrt{\Sigma (Ai)^2} * \sqrt{\Sigma (Bi)^2}} \tag{4}$$

This similarity will always between 0 and 1. Value 0 means no similarity between users or items and 1 means total similar. Based on this construct our experiment finds top-10 recommended items with Precision of 0.00522979397781299, Recall of 0.00584735743214348 and F1 of 0.010459588.

B. Pearson Correlation Similarity

The correlation is the association between two users or items. Correlation values are range from −1 to +1 [5]. Positive correlation states positive association and negative correlation states negative association. If we have two users X and Y, then Pearson correlation is term as:

$$Person(x,y) = \frac{\Sigma xy - \frac{\Sigma x\,\Sigma y}{N}}{\sqrt{(\Sigma x^2 - \frac{(\Sigma x)^2}{N})(\Sigma y^2 - \frac{(\Sigma y)^2}{N})}} \qquad (5)$$

Our experiment generate the top-10 recommended items with Precision of 0.0164817749603803, Recall of 0.0185985963323522 and F1 of 0.03296355.

8 Experiment on Dataset: Item Preferences Are in Boolean Form or not Present

It not always possible for some recommender systems to have explicit items ratings are available [9]. As example, for news website which recommends news to user based on his/her previous news watched or read. In such recommender systems the mapping of user with news articles available but not with explicit rate or preference of the news. In such RSs it is not common to all users to rate the news.

A. Loglike Similarity

Sometimes there are such situation possible in which there are some common items preferences are possible between dissimilar users [7]. For example if you and I have rated 100 items each, and 50 overlap, we're probably similar. But if we've each rated 1000 and overlap in only 50, maybe we're not. This similarity measure is useful where two users are not similar but their overlap is due to chance (the numerator part of the expression). The denominator is the likelihood that it is not at all due to chance, i.e. that the overlap is because of our tastes are similar and the overlap is exactly what we would expect given that. When the numerator is relatively small, in such cases we are similar.

Based on this construct, our experiment gives the top-10 recommended items with Precision of 0.1256735340729, Recall 0.159425703720473 of and F1 of 0.251347068.

B. Tanimoto Coefficient Similarity

Tanimoto coefficient/ Jaccard Distance [13] is such a similarity which is used to measure surprise factor between two items [11]. This similarity focus on weather users have expressed items or not instead of the actual preference value. It is the total number of items expressed (intersection) by two users versus either user expressed (union). As illustrated in Fig. 5.

Based on this construct our experiment gives the top-10 recommended papers with Precision of 0.15949427480916, Recall of 0.156943501119412 and F1 of 0.31898855.

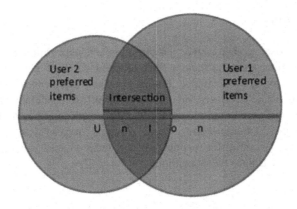

Fig. 5. The Tanimoto coefficient

9   Comparison Between Similarity Measures

According to above experiments, it is clear that the recommendations are more accurate when preferences are not considered. Both Loglike and Tanimoto Similarities are superior than similarities with item preferences are considered. Such algorithms may lead towards the serendipity of the recommender system [11] (Table 3 and Fig. 6).

Table 3. Comparison between all similarity measures on precision, recall and F1

Similarity	Precision	Recall	F1
Cosine	0.00523	0.005847	0.01046
Pearson	0.016482	0.018599	0.032964
Loglike	0.125674	0.159426	0.251347
Tanimoto	0.159494	0.156944	0.318989

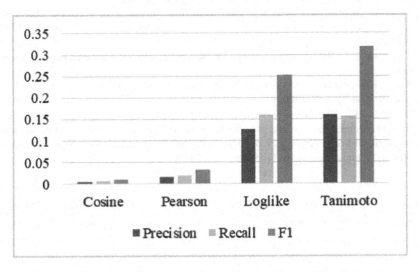

Fig. 6. Comparison between similarity measures for movielense dataset

10   Conclusion

We tested user based collaborative filtering approach with different similarity algorithms. Our methods tests the dataset with different cases of items preferences, i.e. items preferences explicitly available, Boolean (yes/no) preferences and in the case of preferences not available. Based on our experiments we conclude that when item preferences not considered then recommender system's accuracy in terms of precision and recall is higher. Tanimoto and Loglike similarity measures are promising algorithms which may be useful for recommender systems which focus on uncertainty or surprise which may trigger the Serendipity .

References

1. Apache Mahout, https://mahout.apache.org/
2. Ziegler, C.-N., McNee, S.M., Konstan, J.A., Lausen G.: Proceedings of the 14th International World Wide Web Conference (WWW '05), May 10–14, 2005, Chiba, Japan. To appear
3. Asanov, D.: Algorithms and methods in recommender systems. Technology (2011)
4. E. Friedman et.al.: Mahout in action. In: Manning Shelter Island (2012)
5. Ricci, F., Rokach, L., Shapira, B., Kantor, P.B.: Recommender systems handbook. In: Media (2011)
6. Bobadilla, J., et al.: Knowledge based systems. Knowl. Based Syst. **46**, 109–132 (2013)
7. Keshav, R., et al.: Int. J. Comput. Sci. Inf. Technol. (IJCSIT) **5**(3), 4782–4787 (2014)
8. Terveen, L., Hill, W.: Beyond recommender systems: helping people help each other recommendation: examples and concepts (1), 1–21 (2001)
9. Hahsler, M.: Developing and testing top- N recommendation algorithms for 0–1 data using recommenderlab, 1–21 (2011)
10. MovieLense, http://www.movielens.org/
11. Patel, A., Amin, K.: Serendipity in recommender systems. Int. J. Eng. Technol. (IJET) **10**(1), pp (2018). https://doi.org/10.21817/ijet/2018/v10i1/181001067
12. Stehman, Stephen V.: Selecting and interpreting measures of thematic classification accuracy. Remote Sens. Environ. **62**(1), 77–89 (1997). https://doi.org/10.1016/S0034-4257(97)00083-7
13. Tanimoto, T.T.: IBM Internal Report 17th Nov 1957. http://en.wikipedia.org/wiki/Jaccard_index
14. Su, X., Khoshgoftaar, T.M.: A survey of collaborative filtering techniques. Adv. Artif. Intell. **2009**(Section 3), 1–20 (2009)
15. Stephen, S.C., Xie, H., Rai, S.: Measures of similarity in memory-based collaborative filtering recommender system: a comparison. In: Proceedings of the 4th Multidisciplinary International Social Networks Conference (MISNC 2017). ACM, New York, Article 32, 8 pp (2017). https://doi.org/10.1145/3092090.3092105

Effect of Package Cohesion on Evaluation of Reusability of Aspect Oriented Systems: A Fuzzy Approach

Puneet Jai Kaur[1(✉)] and Sakshi Kaushal[2]

[1] Department of Information Technology, U.I.E.T, Panjab University,
Chandigarh, Punjab, India
puneet@pu.ac.in
[2] Department of Computer Science and Engineering, U.I.E.T, Panjab University,
Chandigarh, Punjab, India
sakshi@pu.ac.in

Abstract. Reusability is the ability to reuse without significant changes. Software reusability reduces development time, effort and cost. Software reuse is the process of developing new software from legacy software and not starting from scratch. However the predicting software reusability is a difficult process. Aspect oriented software development is a new approach that introduces the concept of aspects for implementing concerns. By applying an aspect oriented approach, issues related to crosscutting concerns can be isolated to increase reusability of the system. However, many research works aimed at accessing the software reusability of object oriented system but it remained unexplored for aspect oriented system. In this paper, reusability of aspect oriented systems is evaluated using package cohesion by following fuzzy logic technique.

Keywords: Aspect oriented systems · Reusability
Package cohesion (PCohA) · Fuzzy logic

1 Introduction

Software engineering aims at improving the quality of software products in terms of their internal and external characteristics. Quality of software products and processes can be measured with the help of software metrics. But with the increase in the complexity of software, there was the need of better techniques. Object Oriented Approach (OOA) has evolved as a programming language where problem solutions are framed by decomposing them into objects that integrate functions and data in a single unit [1, 2]. Although OOA has many advantages in modelling constructs for modularity, polymorphism etc., it has some limitations also. In OOP, the implementation of concern is scattered in multiple classes. Such scattered concerns are called crosscutting concerns. Examples of such concerns are *logging, synchronization, exception handling etc*. [4]. Aspect Oriented technology provides the solution to this problem of crosscutting concerns which remained unsolved in Object oriented and other traditional

© Springer Nature Singapore Pte Ltd. 2019
A. K. Luhach et al. (Eds.): ICAICR 2018, CCIS 955, pp. 639–650, 2019.
https://doi.org/10.1007/978-981-13-3140-4_57

languages.. Aspect Oriented software development (AOSD) emerged as technology that modularize crosscutting concerns with the introduction of new concept termed as aspect [3].

According to Salamon and Wallace [5], National Institute of Standard and Technology (NIST) provides measurement information for determining the reusability of software. The report prepared by NIST researchers identified ten indirect Quality characteristics for software products based on extensive research in the available literature, which also includes OO technology. The listed characteristics include parameters like- understandability, modularity, portability, reliability, completeness, maintainability, adaptability, flexibility, expandability, efficiency, completeness and generality. As Aspect Oriented Technology is an extension of OO technology and has some new features, some quality parameters needs to be redefined for aspect oriented technology. The important characteristics which contribute in assessment of reusability of AOS cannot be measured directly.

In order to provide solution to the problem Brichau and Hondt [6] proposed a reusability quality model. According to this proposed model, for measuring external quality characteristics internal characteristics such as complexity, cohesion, coupling and size are very helpful. The reusability model established the relationship among external Quality characteristics and internal characteristics by using the metrics for internal characteristics. According to this model reusability is mainly affected by Cohesion, Coupling, Size and SoC.

A high maintainable and quality software system has an advantage of reusing the existing packages, if the cohesion of these packages is maximized. As stated by Vinay and Vandana [7], Package level cohesion measure plays a crucial role in analyzing the reusability, maintainability and understandability of software. Martin et al. [8] in his work had proposed the package cohesion principles to address the goal of package structuring. According to Martin packages must contain classes that can be reused together and that are being affected by the same changes.

In this paper, effort is made to evaluate reusability of AOS using package cohesion measure PCohA, along with other package level metrics effecting reusability. Evaluation is carried out by using Fuzzy logic approach for predicting reusability using package level metrics.

The rest of the paper is organised as: Next section gives the related work done in this field which is followed by the factors affecting reusability. Then the fuzzy logic model for evaluating reusability using internal quality attributes is discussed which is followed by the case study of AspectJ project AJHotdraw for validating proposed model. In the last conclusion and future work is given.

2 Related Work

Nowadays, real world systems are evolving so fast that they are capable to meet challenges among the users and developers. A well modularized designing of software is required to meet the functional and non-functional requirement. AOSD has emerged as the development technology that modularizes the crosscutting concerns to handle the problem of scattering and tangling of concerns. Although AOSD has emerged as a solution for OO problems, but it has its own limitations. The related work will discuss the work done so far by many researchers in the area of OO and AO approach for assessing software reusability.

According to Salamon and Wallace [5], the National Institute of Standards and Technology (NIST) has defined the structural quality of software systems by specifying ten quality characteristics for software products. These quality characteristics are listed as- understandability, modularity, portability, reliability, completeness, maintainability, adaptability, flexibility, expandability, efficiency, correctness, and generality. To measure these indirect quality measures, inter quality attributes are required. According to the report, internal characteristics for assessing reusability and maintainability include - size, complexity, cohesion, coupling etc.

First quality model for AOS was proposed by Kumar et al. [9], known as AOS-QUAMO. This model was an improvement of ISO Quality Model [10]. AOSQUAMO includes various external quality attributes like Complexity, Reusability, Modularity and Code-Reducibility. New attribute, evolvability is added to AOSQUAMO by Kumar [11], and the new model was named as AOSQ model. The author added some parameters as sub-characteristics of evolvability like Design Stability, Configurability etc.

Sant' Anna et al. [12] proposed a framework to assess reusability and maintainability for AOS using internal attributes. Authors had proposed a metrics suite and a quality model for AOS. The authors have concluded that the quality of AOS can be assessed using structural design properties such as coupling, cohesion, and SOC. Leite et al. [13], has worked on enhancing the quality of software in terms of its reusability using goal driven process to. Authors have proposed a method for using quality parameters for calculating software reuse. Cunha et al. [14] had explored the use of quality characteristics like reusability, modularity and understandability for AspectJ along with java programming to enhance the AO development. Zhang et al. [15] had worked on using AOS for designing reusable connectors. Aljassere et al. [16] has proposed a new language ParaAJ, to enhance reusability in AOS by modularizing aspects.

Singh et al. [17], has proposed a model to predict maintainability for AOS using fuzzy logic. They had considered the four main internal quality attributes for assessment: coupling, cohesion, size and SOC. All these metrics are class level metrics. Nerurkar et al. [18] in their work has demonstrated the process of automating the prediction of reusability using external parameters - Understandability, maintainability, adaptability and AOS using fuzzy logic approach by considering internal parameters - cohesion, coupling, Size and SOC. Singh et al. [19], in their another research work had used fuzzy logic for assessing reusability for AOS. They concluded that using fuzzy logic for assessing reusability can help in selecting best quality software. Singh, Sangwan and Srivastava [20]) had also proposed reusability assessment model for AOS using Multi Criteria Decision Making (MCDM) approach. They have validated the proposed model by using Analytic Hierarchy Process (AHP) and cross validated it by applying Fuzzy AHP. Singh and Singhal [21] worked on assessing reusability for component based software system using fuzzy logic approach. They have used various factors like modularity, maintainability etc. for predicting the reusability.

All the frameworks for assessing OOS and AOS quality are defined on the basis of class level metrics. In this paper efforts have been made to assess Reusability, using the fuzzy model approach for AOS using package level metrics. Here, Package level metrics like Package cohesion (PCohA) [22], coupling *etc.*, are used to assess reusability.

3 Factors Affecting Reusability

Package level metrics for reusability is proposed [23] as:

1. *ECA (Efferent Coupling in Aspects)*: This is defined as the number of packages (aspects) on which a package (aspect) depends upon.
2. *PCohA (Package level Cohesion in AOS)*: It is defined as the percentage of number of relations of each class present in the aspect to the number of classes in the aspect, averaged over the total number of classes in the aspect.
3. *Aspect Design Size (ADS)*: This is the total number of classes and interfaces in aspect (Package).
4. *Messaging (IP)*: Messaging can be calculated by counting the interface size of the package. Interface size of the package is the count of public classes in the package.

These metrics are defined on the basis of formula given in Eq. (1):

$$Reusability = -0.25 * coupling + 0.25 * Cohesion + 0.5 * Messaging + 0.5 * Design\ size \tag{1}$$

4 Proposed Fuzzy Framework

This section gives the description of fuzzy logic approach for assessing of reusability for AOS.

Fuzzy logic approach for prediction was introduced with the idea of fuzzy set theory by Lotfi Zadeh [25]. It is defined to present the theory of incomplete facts, where the fact value may vary from totally true to totally false [26]. According to Sivanandam *et al.* [26], the fuzzy model can be implemented with the help of Fuzzy inference system (FIS). FIS works by mapping input variables with output variable using fuzzy set. It consists of four modules - Fuzzification, Inference, Composition and Defuzzification. FIS works through five steps:

1. Fuzzification of the inputs using the membership functions,
2. Constructing Fuzzy Rules for fuzzified inputs,
3. Mapping the input rules with the output membership function, to find the weightage of the rule.
4. Analyzing the results to get predicted value of output.

Input variables are the internal characteristics that are used to assess the output attribute. The output variable is the dependent attribute which is to be predicted after fuzzification of input attributes. For the proposed fuzzy approach, input variables are the internal attributes of software such as cohesion, coupling etc. and the output variable is the external attribute such as Reusability etc. Membership functions are defined for input and output attributes to link their values. Measurement values of all attributes (inputs and outputs) are taken in scale of 0 to 1. To evaluate output variable using input variables in MATLAB, Mamdani fuzzy system is used.

Membership functions links input attributes with output attributes with the help of rules defined on inputs. Rules are constructed in Rule editor, the graphical interface for constructing rules in fuzzy model. The rules are of the form *"If'abc' and/or'xyz' then' XYZ' "*. The rules constructed with the help of rule editor can be viewed through rule viewer. It consists of columns representing input and output variables. If there are n columns in the rule viewer, then last column represents the 'then' part of each rule and rest n-1 columns are referring to input variables.

5 Assessing Reusability for AOS Using Fuzzy Approach

5.1 Input and Output Variables for Fuzzy Model

For implementing proposed fuzzy model, input and output variables are required. Here, output variable is quality parameter Reusability for Aspect Oriented system and input variables for assessing Reusability are as follows:

1. Coupling: **ECA** (Efferent Coupling in Aspects)
2. Cohesion: **PCohA** (Package level Cohesion in AOSD)
3. Design size: **ADS** (Aspect Design Size)
4. Messaging: **IP** (Interface size of Package)

These input variables are mapped with output variables for predicting their effects using MATLAB Mamdani fuzzy system.

5.2 Membership Functions

FIS links the input values with output using membership functions. In this work, membership functions for input and output variables scaled in the range of 0 to 1 using the triangular (trimf) membership functions of MATLAB. Table 1 shows the scaled membership functions.

Table 1. Scaling of Input and output variables

Input variables	Scale	Output variables	Scale
Low	0–0.35	Very low	0–0.2
Medium	0.37–0.7	Low	0.17–0.4
High	0.67–1.0	Medium	0.37–0.6
–	–	High	0.57–0.8
–	–	Very high	0.77–1.0

5.3   Rule Base for Proposed Model

In this work, three input variables are used for predicting output parameter reusability for all three cases and scaled them to three values (Table 1). So, total number of rules for each output variable is 3^3 which are 27 rules i.e. there are 27 if-then rules constructed using Rule Editor for each output. Figure 1 shows the rule editor for AOSReusability.

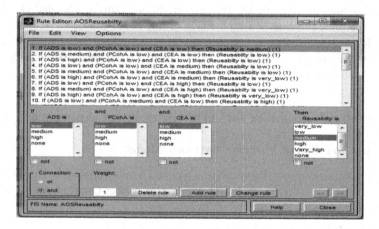

Fig. 1. Rule editor for AOSReusability

Rules are constructed on the basis of knowledge for software Reusability. For example, reusability of any software is positively correlated with cohesion and is adversely affected by coupling value [24]. Then rule can be constructed as - If Size and Coupling is low and Cohesion is high, then Reusability is high. In the similar ways, all the 27 rules are constructed for AOSReusability. Some sample rules for are given in Table 2.

Table 2. Rules for AOSReusability

Inputs			Output
ADS	PCohA	CEA	AOSReusability
Low	Low	Low	Medium
Medium	Low	Medium	Low
Low	Medium	Low	High
Low	High	Low	Very high
High	Low	High	Very low

Different set of input values are given as input into the fuzzy model to find the corresponding effect on output variable Reusability. Suppose the value of input variables is: PCohA = 0.5, CEA = 0.5 and ADS = 0.5. These inputs value are provided to the fuzzy model to obtain the output as 0.48 i.e. Medium. Table 3 shows the results of giving some rules as input to the proposed fuzzy based system for AOSReusability.Table 3 shows the results of giving some rules as input to the proposed fuzzy based system for AOSReusability.

Table 3. Values obtained from rule viewer for AOSReusability

Inputs			Output	
ADS	PCohA	CEA	AOSReusability	
0.53	0.843	0.182	0.885	Very high
0.216	0.923	0.614	0.685	High
0.873	0.122	0.878	0.1	Very low
0.893	0.286	0.241	0.285	Low
0.455	0.575	0.445	0.485	Medium

It is concluded from the predicted results that the proposed fuzzy model is best suitable for determining the estimations for external quality attributes for AOS. It is clear from the predicted values that cohesion has positive effect on Reusability.

The next section presents a case study AspectJ project AJhotdraw, for validating predictions made for Reusability using proposed fuzzy model approach.

6   Case Study: AJhotdraw

In this section, AJhotdraw an aspectJ project has been studied for validating the predictions made in the proposed fuzzy model for measuring Reusability.

AJhotdraw is the aspect refactoring of Jhotdraw, drawing application developed as display good design patterns in java. AJhotdraw is written in AspectJ, an aspect language that extends java with crosscutting functionality. Many researchers have used AJhotdraw for their research oriented studies on AOS. There are 4 versions of AJhotdraw. Here, AJhotdraw 0.4 release is analysed for measuring Reusability. It is composed of 24 packages, 330 classes and total lines of code are 21542. For this research 20 packages have been analysed. Composition of those 20 packages of AJhotdraw is shown in Table 4.

Since we are assessing reusability using package level metrics, Table 5 gives the value of Reusability for each package of AJhotdraw.

Figures 2, 3 and 4 shows the relationship of package cohesion (PCohA), design size and package level coupling with Reusability respectively for each package. It is clear from the above figures that Reusability is positively affected by package cohesion whereas coupling and size has negative effects on Reusability of the packages. Karl Pearson Product Moment correlation is used to calculate the correlation between three input parameters and reusability using the values from Table 5. Correlation values are given in Table 6.

Table 4. Composition of AJhotdraw

Package No.	Package name	LOC	No. of Classes/Aspects	# Interfaces
P1	Applet	372	1	0
P2	Applications	732	1	0
P3	Ccconcerns	3	1	1
P4	Ccconcerns.commands	246	7	1
P5	Ccconcerns.undo	576	18	1
P6	Ccconcerns.Figs.Figselectionobserver	98	4	1
P7	Ccconcerns.Figs.persistence	167	7	0
P8	Ccconcerns.handles.undo	11	1	0
P9	Ccconcerns.tools.undo	74	5	0
P10	Contrib.dnd	730	9	1
P11	Contrib.html	1347	34	9
P12	Contrib..zoom	832	10	0
P13	Framework	518	26	21
P14	Samples.javadraw	647	10	0
P15	Samples.minimap	38	2	0
P16	Samples.net	131	2	0
P17	Samples.nothing	63	2	0
P18	Samples.pert	346	5	0
P19	Util.collections.jdk11	229	5	0
P20	Util.collections.jdk12	28	1	0

Table 5. Package level metric values for AJhotdraw.

Package	CE	IP	ADS	PCohA	Reusability	Rating
P1	1	1	1	1	1	9
P2	1	1	1	1	1	9
P3	0	1	2	0.5	1.62	8
P4	5	7	8	0.16	6.29	4
P5	10	18	18	0.11	16.02	2
P6	3	4	4	0.15	3.79	7
P7	7	7	7	0	5.25	5
P8	1	1	1	1	1	9
P9	5	5	5	0	3.75	7
P10	5	9	9	0.19	8.29	5
P11	18	34	34	0.04	34	1
P12	7	10	10	0.12	8.28	4
P13	9	26	26	0.02	34.25	1
P14	10	10	10	0.1	7.52	3
P15	2	2	2	0.5	1.62	8
P16	2	2	2	0.5	1.62	8
P17	2	2	2	0	1.5	8
P18	5	5	5	0.35	3.83	7
P19	1	5	5	0.25	4.81	6
P20	1	1	1	1	1	9

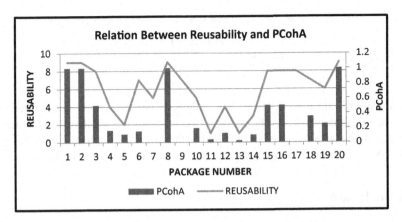

Fig. 2. Relation between reusability and PCohA

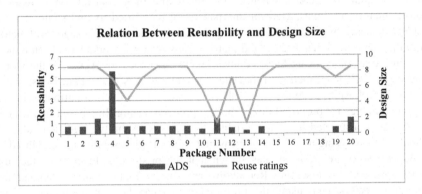

Fig. 3. Relation between reusability and Design Size

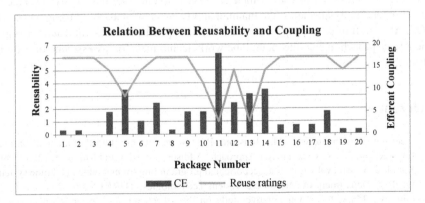

Fig. 4. Relation between reusability and coupling

Table 6. Correlation between Reusability and Internal attributes

	PCohA	CEA	ADS
Reusability	0.71	−0.88	−0.84

Correlation values in Table 6, has validated the predictions made through the proposed fuzzy model. It is validated that, the reusability is positively correlated with PCohA, whereas it is negatively correlated with Size and Coupling. Hence for system to be more reusable, its coupling must be low and cohesion must be high.

7 Conclusion

In this paper, a framework is proposed to assess Reusability of AOS using rule based fuzzy model. Since measuring internal quality attributes is not an easy task, it is very difficult to quantify them and hence difficult to find their contribution in assessing external quality attributes. Here in this paper, we have tried to find solution to this problem by using fuzzy logic for assessing Reusability using the package level metrics. From the literature, it has been found that very few research works have been done on assessing Reusability using Package level quality attributes for AOS. All the work is done using class level metrics. From literature review it is found that, Reusability is affected by cohesion, coupling, size, inheritance etc. These internal attributes are used as input variables for proposed Fuzzy model approach. Using Rule based fuzzy model, 27 rules are constructed for input variables to assess Reusability. Predicted values are validated by analyzing the results of measured values for Reusability using AJhotdraw, an AspectJ software. Analysis has shown that the predictions made from the fuzzy model approach for assessing Reusability are similar to the values obtained from AJhotdraw. Assessment using the proposed model can help in predicting software reusability automatically, for a module as well for the whole AOS.

The assessment framework proposed in this paper, will help in encouraging software organizations to software which are less maintainable and highly reusable. In future, other quality attributes like maintainability etc. can be assessed using metrics for AOS. Also, in future the proposed model can be applied and cross validated for Aspect oriented approach using the neural network techniques for assessment of external attributes.

References

1. Jacobson, I., Christerson, M., Jonsson, P., Overgaard, G.: Object Oriented Software Engineering: A Use Case Driven Approach. Addison - Wesley Publishing, Boston (1992)
2. Kartal, Y.B.: An evaluation of aspect oriented programming for embedded real time systems. In: IEEE Department of Microwave System Technologies. TURKEY (2007)
3. Filho, C., Mary, C.: A Quantitative study on the aspectization of exception handling. In: Proceedings of ECOOP, Workshop on Exception Handling in Object Oriented System (2005)

4. Salamon, W.J., Wallace, D.R.: Quality characteristics and metrics for reusable software (Preliminary Report). US DoC for US DoD Ballistic Missile Defence Organization. NISTIR 5459 (1994)
5. Brichau, J., D'Hondt.: An Introduction to Aspect Oriented Software Development AOSD. Europe (2005)
6. Vinay, V.: Assessing package reusability in object oriented design. Int. J. Softw.Eng. Appl. **8** (4), 75–84 (2014)
7. Filman, R., Elrad, T., Clarke, S., Aksit, M.: Aspect oriented Software Development. Book by Pearson Education (2014)
8. Kumar, A., Grover, P.S., Kumar, R.: A quantitative evaluation of aspect oriented software quality model. ACM SIGSOFT Softw. Eng. Notes **34**(5), 1–9 (2009)
9. ISO/IEC 9126–1, 2001, ISO/IEC 9126-2, 2003, ISO/IEC 9126-3, 2003 and ISO/IEC 9126-4, 2004, "Information Technology - Product Quality, Quality Model, External Metrics, Internal Metrics, Quality in use Metrics", International Standard ISO/IEC 9126, International Standard Organization
10. Kumar, P.: Aspect oriented software quality model- the aosq model. Adv. Comput. Int. J. **3** (2), 105–118 (2012)
11. Sant' Anna, C., Garcia, A., Chavez, C., Lucena, C., Staa, A.: On the reuse and maintenance of aspect-oriented software: an assessment framework. XXIII Brazilian Symposium on Software Engineering, Manaus, Brazil (2003)
12. Leite, J.C., Yu, Y., Lui, L., Yu, E.S.K., Mylopoulos, J.: Quality based software reuse, advanced information system engineering.In: Proceedings of 17th International Conference, pp. 535–550. Portugal (2005)
13. Cunha, C.A., Sobral, J. L., Monteiro, M.P.: Reusable aspect-oriented implementations of concurrency patterns and mechanisms. In: Proceedings of 5th International Conference on Aspect-Oriented Software Development, pp. 134–145. ACM, New York (2006)
14. Zhang, J., Li, H., Cai, X.: Research on reusability of software connector based on AOP. In: IEEE Proceedings of International Conference on Computer Science and Information Technology (ICCSIT 2008), pp. 113–117 (2008)
15. Aljasser K., Schachte P.: ParaAJ -toward reusable and maintainable aspect oriented programs. In: Proceedings of 32nd Australasian Computer Science Conference, pp 53–62. Wellington, New Zealand (2009)
16. Singh, P.K., Sangwan, O.P., Srivastava, A.: An essence of software maintenance prediction using the fuzzy model for aspect oriented software. ARPN J. Eng. Appl. Sci. **9**(9), 1598–1605. (2014)
17. Nerurkar, N.W., Kumar, A., Shrivastava, P.: Assessment of reusability in aspect oriented systems using fuzzy logic. ACM SIGSOFT Softw. Eng. Note **35**(5), 1–5 (2010)
18. Singh, P.K., Sangwan, O.P., Singh, A.P., Pratap, A.: A framework for assessing the software reusability using fuzzy logic approach for aspect oriented software. Int. J. Inf. Technol. Comput. Sci. (2), 12–20 (2015)
19. Singh, P.K., Sangwan, O.P., Srivastava, P.: A quantitative evaluation for reusability for aspect oriented software using multi-criteria decision making approach. World Appl. Sci. J. **30**(12), 1966–1976 (2014)
20. Singh, C., Pratap, A., Singhal, A.: An estimation of software reusability using fuzzy logic techniques.In: IEEE proceedings of International Conference on Signal propagation and Computer Technology (ICSPCT), pp: 250–256 (2014)
21. Kaur, P.J., Kaushal, S., Sangaiah, A.K., Picialli, F.: A framework for assessing reusability using package cohesion measure in aspect oriented system. Int. J. Parallel Progr. Spec. Issue Progr. Models Algorithms Data Anal HPC Syst. 1–22 (2017)

22. Kaur, P.J., Kaushal, S.: Package level metrics for reusability in aspect oriented systems. In: Proceedings of IEEE International Conference on Futuristic Trend in Computational Analysis and Knowledge Management (ABLAZE), pp: 364–368 (2015)
23. Bansiya, J., Davis, C.G.: A hierarchical model for object oriented design quality assessment. IEEE Trans. Softw. Eng. **28**(1) (2002)
24. Zadeh, L.A.: Fuzzy logic, neural networks and soft computing. Commun. ACM **37**(3), 77–84 (1994)
25. Novak, V., Perfilieva, I., Mockor, J.: Mathematical principles of fuzzy logic. Dodrecht Kluwer Academic. ISBN 0-7923-8595-0 (1999)
26. Sivanandam, S.N., Sumathi, S., Deepa, S.N.: Introduction to Fuzzy Logic using MATLAB. Springer-Verlag, Berlin Heidelberg (2007)

Improved Zoning and Cropping Techniques Facilitating Segmentation

Monika Kohli[1(✉)] and Satish Kumar[2]

[1] Department of Computer Science and Applications, Panjab University,
Chandigarh, India
monikakrajotia@gmail.com
[2] Department of Computer Applications, Panjab University,
SSG Regional Centre, Hoshiarpur, Punjab, India

Abstract. In the advent of digital computers and era where work force is shifted to be inclined on robotic process, Optical Character Recognition (OCR) has immense potentials to ease some these processes. Segmentation is one of the pre-processing phases- the pivotal essence of the process where lingual scripts and their characteristics vary to a much larger extent. This paper focuses on techniques which facilitates segmentation in Devanagari script (Hindi) for offline handwritten words i.e. Headline detection in handwritten word images of Hindi for extracting upper and middle zone characters and cropping. Experiments are performed on the handwritten legal amount words ICDAR database [1] on 106 words by 80 writers and on Self created touching character database on 106 words by 15 writers. The proposed zoning technique i.e. CPT (Continuous pixel technique) and cropping techniques is implemented on 10070 and 530 legal amount words with 98.89% accuracy and 80.94% respectively.

Keywords: Handwritten data · Optical character recognition (OCR) Segmentation · Zoning

1 Introduction

The prominence of utility of mother tongue has been increasing in past half decade, has opened opportunities for tools inclined in providing functionality of OCR. Thus the process involved in recognizing native linguistic characters is a major challenge that has been prevailing for more than a decade. The research involves exploring phases for optical character recognition is pre-processing & segmentation, feature extraction and recognition. The recognition accuracy of character can be enhanced by applying improved pre-processing & segmentation technique to extract appropriate features.

Moreover, recognition of handwritten words is complex activity where achieving accuracy for multilingual script is more challenging. Offline handwritten data adds more complication and reduced recognition accuracy as compare to online data due to varying stroke width, writing style, pen/pencil used, mood of the writer, paper used, skew.

© Springer Nature Singapore Pte Ltd. 2019
A. K. Luhach et al. (Eds.): ICAICR 2018, CCIS 955, pp. 651–657, 2019.
https://doi.org/10.1007/978-981-13-3140-4_58

According to the literature survey, improper segmentation in handwritten data is a major topic of research. S. Kumar [2] discussed various irregularities in Devanagari script. Number of papers are available dealing with segmentation problem in Roman characters/numerals [3–7] and in other Indian languages[8–10] but very few are available in Devanagari script (Hindi) [11, 12].

Zoning is required to divide words into upper zone, middle zone and lower zone. Literature survey has shown that Horizontal Profile, Vertical profile, Hough transform are used for zoning.

Due to the presence of large character set in Devanagari script (Hindi), segmentation becomes more complicated. Character set in Hindi not only consists of characters but includes vowels, consonants, conjuncts, compound characters, modifiers. The paper is an attempt to propose techniques for zoning (CPT), to detect Headline and perform zoning. The paper is organized as follows. Section 2 gives the basic technique used in the literature for pre-processing, formulation of Headline detection for zoning to extract middle and upper zone characters, cropping. Section 3 introduces the database used and experimental results. Conclusion and future scope is given in Sect. 4.

2 Pre-processing

Character segmentation is an approach which decomposes an image consisting sequence of characters into sub-images or sub-units for recognition. Pre-processing consists of scanning the handwritten document and processes it to Binarization, remove noise, skew, smoothing the image, Headline detection/removal, zoning which aid segmentation. Variations in the handwritten data necessitate addressing various intricacies of handwritten text.

Detection of Headline is a challenging task in handwritten text. Soumen et al. [11] used thinning and global max density of a row for removal of Headline with accuracy of 95.45% on 11550 words. Detection of header line is performed after straightening is proposed in [13]. Garg et al. [14] used two-stripe projection for Headline detection. Contour-tracing used in [15] used structural approach for the detection of Headline by finding the maximum number of pixels in a row. The detection of Headline by finding the row with maximum pixel density is widely used by authors but fails for skew variable text.

In literature, Hough Transform is used for skew detection and line segmentation. Continuous Pixel Technique (CPT) - based on Hough Transform function is used for Headline line detection is proposed in this paper which facilitates zoning. The proposed algorithm eliminate the problem due to unusual size of upper modifier.

Formal definition of Line detection is given as:

The function uses the polar representation of lines to represent lines in binary image.

$$x * \cos \theta = y * \sin \theta$$

The function returns an accumulator array based on the threshold value which determines minimum number of pixels that belong to line in an image space. θ defines the angle of detected lines in the polar coordinates system. It gives set of all straight line at a single point in plane corresponds to a sinusoidal curve which is unique to that point. Line detection and zoning using CPT (Continuous Pixel technique) is given in Sect. 2.1.

2.1 Zoning - CPT (Continuous Pixels Technique)

Devanagari script consists of core character in the middle strip and optional modifiers above and below the core characters. Characters form a word when they are joined by a Headline ('shirorekha'). The purpose of zoning is to extract middle, upper and lower components. The proposed technique for zoning is applied on Binarized, smoothened image.

Step1. Contiguous pixel with maximum length is calculated using Houghline detection algorithm.

Step2. Threshold of value 20 is used for finding Houghlines.

Step3. The result of the step I and step II, results a row connecting common row between the upper and the middle zone of the word.

Step4. The upper zone is considered for further manipulation as it contains matra/matras/Chandra bindu/bindu else it will be discarded on the basis of number of rows of white pixels in the upper zone. The Figs. 1a, b, c shows the result of the applied algorithm.

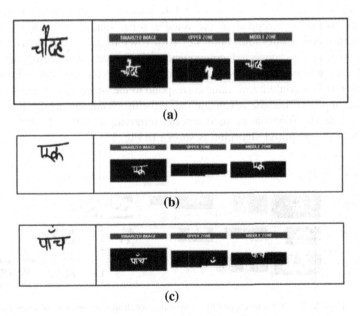

(a)

(b)

(c)

Fig. 1. (a) Images containing word matra in the upper zone, (b) Images containing word without matra in the upper zone, (c) Images containing Chandra Bindu in the upper zone

2.2 Cropping

The presence of Headline in languages like Hindi, Gurumukhi, and Marathi etc. makes the task of segmentation more difficult as compare to scripts without Headline line Roman script. To segment each of the constituent character of a word, various techniques of segmentation are reported in the literature using Headline removal approach and other without removing the Headline [16, 17].

In literature various Headline removal techniques in printed [18, 19] or handwritten (online) [20] is discussed based on the number of pixels present per stroke. But the same task becomes difficult if the text is handwritten (offline). Variability in handwritten text by the user can be due to varying width of stroke, writing style, pen/pencil used, mood of the writer, paper used, skew etc. Varying Headline add more complexity.

The approach for character cropping without removing the Headline is used in the paper. The reason behind using this approach is that even an individual Hindi character is written with a Headline present on it and other reason is the availability of handwritten word database used consists of characters with Headline. Segmentation approaches which consider the removal of Headline need to create database consisting of characters without Headline or adding the Headline to each character after segmentation. Such approach will increase the computation for removal and then adding of Headline and hence reduce the overall efficiency of the proposed algorithm.

In this paper, new idea is proposed to extract individual components of Devanagari word image. Headline is not considered while finding the component but considered when components are cropped in the middle zone. Initially the proposed idea is implemented using a threshold value i.e. 10% rows from the top of the image are excluded to find the connected component and included while cropping. Due to variability in width of the strokes in handwritten data, results are further improved by calculating rzone(maximum row value correspond to the header line + threshold value) value. This approach has the advantage that existing characters databases consists of characters with Headline can be used without removing Headline from the database. The result of the proposed algorithm is shown in Fig. 2.

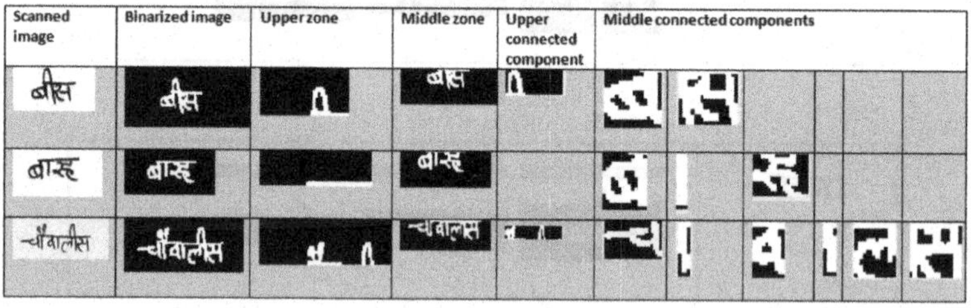

Fig. 2. Zoning and cropping on words containing touched characters

2.2.1 Cropping Algorithm

In handwritten data, width of the stroke is not fixed. The pixels contributing to Headline also vary in length as well as in width. In the proposed algorithm for cropping individual components, lower sub-part of the middle zone is considered. The upper sub-part of the middle zone image is not to be considered while finding connected components in the image .

The lower sub-part is calculated by adding maximum row value correspond to the header line to threshold value.

Algorithm:

im_i= Input image(middle zone image after applying CPT)
im_o= Output image
im_{iu}= Part of the image which is not to be considered while finding connected components in the image.
im_{ol}= Part of the image which is to be considered while finding connected components in the image.
Size(im)= returns maximum row number and maximum column no of image(im).
rzone= maximum row value correspond to the header line + threshold value.
rc=connected component row.
cc=connected component column.
Total Connected Components=N
im_o=N

Step 1:   Connected components are extracted from image im_{ol}
            [r c] = size (im_i)
            im_{ol} = im_i (rzone: r, 1: c)
Step 2:   For connected component for i = 1 to N
            [rc cc] = size(i)
            im_o = crop_img(1: rc; cc)
            end
Step 3:   Save im_o[i] where i $\geq$ 0 and i $\leq$ N

3   Experimental Results

The performance of CPT is evaluated and verified manually. The experiment is performed in MATLAB R2009b under Microsoft Windows environment with X86 based PC, 2.40 GHz CPU and 4 GB RAM.

3.1 Database Used for Experiment

The database consists of 8480 handwritten legal amount words containing non-touching characters by 80 writers provided by ICDAR [1]. The benchmark database for touching characters word in Hindi is not available. We have prepared dataset consisting of 1590 legal amount words for touching characters by 15 writers. The database consists of Binary images. The efficiency of the CPT (Continuous Pixels technique) algorithm is verified manually on 10070 words and for cropping 530 randomly selected images out of 10070 are used.

3.2 Results

Table 1 shows the accuracies obtained with the dataset. It is observed that 98.89% accuracy is obtained using CPT (Continuous Pixels technique) and 80.94% cropping.

Table 1. Accuracy of the proposed algorithms.

Algorithm	Words	Correctly detected	Accuracy (%)
CPT	10070	9958	98.89
Cropping	530	429	80.94

4 Conclusion and Future Scope

In this paper, technique for zoning-CPT (Continuous Pixels technique) and cropping are proposed. CPT facilitates division of upper and middle zone of handwritten Hindi words by finding the contiguous pixels in the Headline. Cropping facilitates extraction of individual components of a Devanagari word image taking into consideration its one of the major characteristic i.e. Headline. Accuracy of cropping can be further enhanced by finding addressing the solution to shadowed characters. Future work will focus on extracting individual components of the word image considering constraint like shadowed characters.

Acknowledgment. I am thankful to Jayadevan R., ICDAR for support and providing word database of offline handwritten words database in Hindi.

References

1. Jayadevan, R., Kolhe, S.R., Patil, P.M., Pal, U.: Database development and recognition of handwritten Devanagari legal amount words. In: Proceedings of the International Conference on Document Analysis and Recognition, ICDAR, pp. 304–308 (2011)
2. Kumar, S.: An analysis of irregularities in Devanagari script writing—a machine recognition perspective. Int. J. Comput. Sci. Eng. **2**, 274–279 (2010)
3. Choudhary, A., Rishi, R., Ahlawat, S.: New character segmentation approach for off-line cursive handwritten words. Procedia Comput. Sci. **17**, 88–95 (2013)

4. Elnagar, A., Alhajj, R.: Segmentation of connected handwritten numeral strings. Pattern Recognit. **36**, 625–634 (2003)
5. Jayarathna, U.K.S., Bandara, G.E.M.D.C.: A junction based segmentation algorithm for offline handwritten connected character segmentation. In: International Conference on Computational Intelligence for Modelling, Control and Automation, 2006 and International Conference on Intelligent Agents, Web Technologies and Internet Commerce, p. 147 (2006)
6. Kim, K.K., Kim, J.H., Suen, C.Y.: Segmentation-based recognition of handwritten touching pairs of digits using structural features. Pattern Recognit. Lett. **23**, 13–24 (2002)
7. Saba, T., Sulong, G., Rehman, A.: Non-linear segmentation of touched roman characters based on genetic algorithm. Int. J. Comput. Sci. Eng. **2**, 2167–2172 (2010)
8. Reddy, L.P., Babu, T.R., Rao, N.V., Babu, B.R.: Touching syllable segmentation using split profile algorithm. Int. J. Comput. Sci. Issues (IJCSI) **7**(3), 1–10 (2010)
9. Bag, S., Bhowmick, P., Harit, G., Biswas, A.: Character segmentation of handwritten Bangla text by vertex characterization of isothetic covers. In: 2011 Third National Conference on Computer Vision, Pattern Recognition, Image Processing and Graphics (NCVPRIPG), pp. 21–24 (2011)
10. Venkatesh, M., Majjagi, V., Vijayasenan, D.: Implicit segmentation of Kannada characters in offline handwriting recognition using hidden Markov models. Implicit arXiv1410.4341, pp. 1–6 (2014)
11. Bag, A.S., Krishna: Character segmentation of Hindi unconstrained handwritten words. In: International Workshop on Combinatorial Image Analysis, vol. 9448, pp. 247–260. Springer, Cham (2015)
12. Garg, N.K., Kaur, L., Jindal, M.K.: The hazards in segmentation of handwritten Hindi Text. Int. J. Comput. Appl. **29**, 30–34 (2011)
13. Palakollu, S., Rani, R.: Handwritten Hindi text segmentation techniques for lines and characters. In: Proceedings of the World Congress on Engineering and Computer Science (2012)
14. Garg, N.K.: A new method for line segmentation of handwritten Hindi text key words. In: Seventh International Conference on Information Technology, pp. 392–397 (2010)
15. Hanmandlu, M.B.L., Agrawal, P.: Segmentation of handwritten Hindi text: a structural approach. Int. J. Comput. Proc. Languages **22**(01), 1–20 (2001)
16. Bhujade, M.V.G., Meshram, M.C.M.: A technique for segmentation of handwritten Hindi text. Int. J. Eng. Res. Technol. **3**, 1491–1495 (2014)
17. Ramteke, A.S., Rane, M.E.: Offline handwritten devanagari script segmentation. Int. J. Sci. Res. **1**, 142–145 (2012)
18. Garain, U., Chaudhuri, B.B.: Segmentation of touching and fused Devanagari characters. Pattern Recognit **32**, 449–459 (2002)
19. Bansal, V., Sinha, R.M.K.: Segmentation of touching and fused Devanagari characters. Pattern Recognit. **35**, 875–893 (2002)
20. Kumar, M.: Segmentation of isolated and touching characters in offline handwritten Gurmukhi script recognition. Int. J. Inf. Technol. Comput. Sci. **2**, 58–63 (2014)

Enhancement in Brain Tumor Diagnosis Using MRI Image Processing Techniques

Vikul J. Pawar$^{(\boxtimes)}$, Kailash D. Kharat$^{(\boxtimes)}$, and Suraj R. Pardeshi

Computer Science and Engineering Department, Government Engineering
College, Aurangabad, Maharashtra, India
{vikul.pawar,kailashdkharat,surajrp}@geca.ac.in

Abstract. The analysis of Brain tumor is always ended by the doctors but its consultation about grading of tumor May gives dissimilar conclusion and those conclusions may differ from one doctor to another. This Paper describes the different image processing techniques for automatic brain tumor detection. As we know that the proper diagnosis of brain disorder is a complex task. The tumor in human brain causes the different impairments such as in loss of memory, speech learning, listening impairments, difficulties in talking and understanding. Tumor is a disease which may hamper the human life very badly, as far as medical and engineering field is concern it is challenging fact for technologists. This paper presents the various techniques for processing MRI images for the identification of brain tumor automatically. These techniques are include the image enhancement Acquisition and pre-processing, image segmentation and classification steps.

Keywords: Brain tumor · Image processing · MRI image · Enhancement
Acquisition · Classification

1 Introduction

When we think about the tumor one question arises in a mind that what is tumor and what are the causes of the tumor in human brain? Then the answer is as per medical term the human brain tumor is anomalous development of cell around human_brain or in the skull. [4, 11] A brain tumor is an intracranial_neoplasm. It will find when the cells growth find abnormally. Generally the tumor will grow in the brain cells and blood vessel.

There are three different types of the tumor First Benign Second Premalignant and Third Malignant. In Benign type tumor is not in a cancerous stage it can easily recover by taking medicines but in premalignant type tumor may be in cancerous or in non cancerous stage so it will require the radiologists examine process by using the MRI Magnetic Resonance Imaging and CT scan [13]. Two different common test used to detect presence of tumor in human brain [3] (Fig. 1).

Slow growing tumors will damage pressure but it will not extend into the neighbouring tissues of the brain. But if tumor is growing rapidly then it will damage the normal brain cells by using the pressure and by producing inflammation on the different parts of the brain and the pressure will be increase on the skull.

© Springer Nature Singapore Pte Ltd. 2019
A. K. Luhach et al. (Eds.): ICAICR 2018, CCIS 955, pp. 658–666, 2019.
https://doi.org/10.1007/978-981-13-3140-4_59

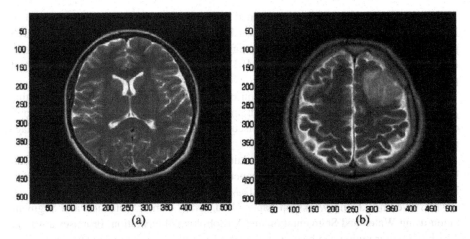

Fig. 1. (a) MRI image with Non-infected Brain. (b) MRI Image with infected Brain

MRI images are used to show the structure of the brain, infected area (tumor location) and tumor size. Tumor diagnosis become easy by using MRI images which gives the information about tumor location so it will become easy to plan the surgical approach for its removal [4].

In the field of medical, doctors do not have any specific or standard method for the brain tumor detection and that is why which leads to varying conclusions on tumor detection. Due to which the medical field requires the computerised system for the diagnose of the grading of brain tumor which will be easier and unique way for the conclusions in brain tumor detection.

2   Literature Review

Several researchers' studies are presented in literature review of the automatic detection of the brain tumor. These studies are listed below in short.

Mr. Badran and Mahmoud performed on "brain tumor detection algorithm in MRI". In his paper Images computer based methods has been applied on MRI images for automatic recognition of tumor in human brain, that method include different steps of image_processing like Image Pre-processing on images, Segmentation of Image, Extracting features and categorisation using neural network. In pre processing images are converted in to accessible form to use for the further processing and to apply the detection methods.

Mr. Kailash Kharat and Pradyumna Kulkarni performed on "Brain tumor detection by using Neural network methods". This research paper contains how MRI images are pre-processed and used for the next steps to detect the brain tumor. Two methods are used for the detection of tumor Feedforward and backpropogation methods are used to detect the tumor. Both methods are used to generate the accurate results of the tumor detection and also used to diagnose the tumor.

Mr. Karnan and Logeshwari performed work on "An enhanced implementation of Brain tumor detection using segmentation based on soft computing". In this research paper contains descriptions about image segmentation methods. There are two phase in the process of segmentation first one is MRI images are collected and after that different pre processing techniques are used to convert into standard form.

Dr. Samir Kumar work on "Detection of brain tumor a proposed method". In this paper the author describes the types of brain tumor, its anatomy with its symptoms and different classification techniques are discussed. Also different computer aided diagnosis techniques are described.

Mr. Viji and Jayakumari proposed, Automatic detection of brain tumor based on MRI image using CAD system. In this paper water shade segmentation on 3D image of MRI data software is used to convert 2D MRI image to 3D Image.

Mr. swe and khaing works on paper titled, Brain Tumor Detection and Segmentation using Watershed Segmentation and Morphological Operation. Proposes a way in which the tumor region can be extract the ROI from the slice of single MRI image. The region of interest can be detected by using operations of morphological. And to obtain these precise outcome of tumor ROI the size of the tumor is calculated.

3 Proposed System

In MRI image processing and tumor detection various steps are like MRI image collection, Pre-processing, Symmetry Methods and feature based Methods for transferring image from original to accessible form, tumor classification neural network approach these are shown in below figure (Fig. 2).

4 Image Enhancement

Proposed Approaches for the Image Enhancement

(1) LSBM Methods (Local_Symmetry_Based_Methods)
(2) GSBM (Global_Symmetry_Based_Methods)
(3) FBM Methods (Feature_Based_Methods)

The different FBM Methods features of midsagittal plane are used, like low intensity and linear shape values of CSF in IF. FBM method works on a lower intensity and also works on the difference between value of the intensity differences.

In lower intensity the value of that image with respect to plane is minimum and when we consider the differences of intensity then values are maximum with respect to plane. But in SBM methods find plane for optimization of symmetry measures by assuming the bilateral symmetry to midsagittal in hemispheres [14].

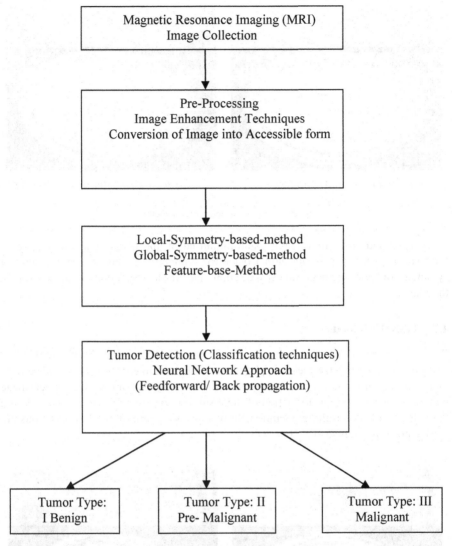

Fig. 2. Proposed computer aided system for the MRI image processing to enhancing the brain tumor diagnosis

4.1   LSBM Methods

In Local symmetry SBM method initially it attempts to trace the mid part of the brain nearly and then locally perform the optimization of the symmetry measure [16].

As the local symmetry methods only consider the part of brain that is why they are time consuming than the GSBM methods. The main Moto of local symmetry is that GS (global_symmetry) of heads will not represent the hemispheres symmetry [1] (Fig. 3).

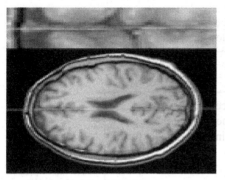 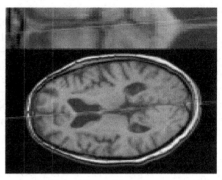

a)   Original MRI Image   b)Resulting MRI Image (LSBM)

Fig. 3. Local symmetry based methods

In local symmetry midsagittal plane initialised in mid of the image and segment lines are perpendicular to midsagittal plane for symmetry [1]. For the optimization of symmetry of Line_segment intensity rotation and translations are apply to position of the plane.

4.2   GSBM Methods

Brain always has a bilateral symmetry as per the hemispheres of cerebrum and that fact is used by the symmetry methods [15]. The Global symmetry based method reflects input images on sagittal axis to achieve firm registrations to support the reflect image with original image. Transformation of the result use to gain mid plane by considering the half part of the resulting alteration. In this generic approach several variations are exist with some changes [5] (Fig. 4).

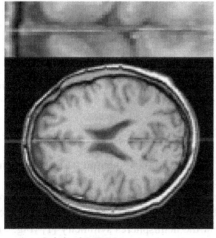 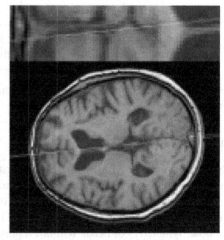

a)   Original MRI Image   b) Resulting MRI Image (GSBM)

Fig. 4. Global symmetry based methods

Several changes to generic approaches include use of similarity metrics, in this approach registration is speed up by using some part of image, derivative images and approach of multi resolution. Some symmetry methods use the firm registration on 2D traversals slice to fit plane by using the resulting mid lines [10].

4.3   FBM Methods

The FBM methods are well known and popular method by brummer, used the convert to identify linear shapes of IF. largely the feature methods are based on the low intensity of CSF. The methods which are based on intensity of the image are initialising the plane in mid of MRi image for optimization in the plane position by using number of rotations and the translations [6] (Fig. 5).

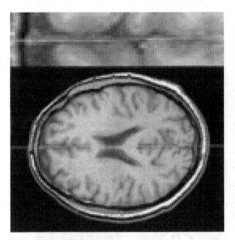 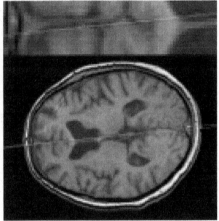

a)   Original MRI Image   b) Resulting MRI Image (FBM)

Fig. 5. Feature based methods

In this optimization intensity value with plane have be minimized when we use lower intensity and when we use the difference between intensity values then this will have maximum. In this method it varies in approach with: Meany lines inspect from exact left_right direction, CSF with lower intensity is detected [9].

5   Tumor Classification & Detection

Tumor Classification and Detection Approaches

• Neural Network Approach.

In this Method neuron model is used with number of neurons as an input to the network with weighted connections [8]. To obtain values of the weights at each connection two different approaches are used:

(a) Feedforward Neural Network Approach
(b) Back Propagation Neural Network Approach

In Feedforward approach that neuron network work in forward direction only weights are calculated at each connection in this approach there is no chance for the correction of the weight at each node that's why the accuracy of that approach is less as compare to the back propagation neural network approach [2] (Fig. 6).

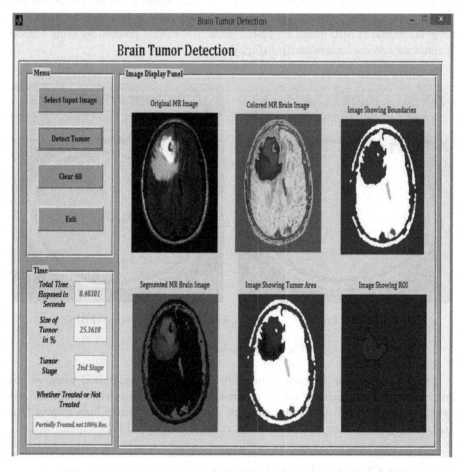

Fig. 6. Brain tumor classification and detection using neural network

In back propagation approach that neuron network work in forward and backward direction both directions are used to the calculation and correction of weights at each node and the accuracy of the result in this approach is more as compare to other [2].

• MRI images of brain represent the Non Infected (Healthy) Brain and Infected (Tumor) Brain [7].

- MRI images after applying Image Enhancement techniques are used.
- Weight calculation is used in this method for classification of tumor.
- This Method gives good accuracy in classification of tumor.

6 Result

Image enhancement techniques enhance the MRI images for the next level and in image enhancement techniques lower intensity and intensity difference values are used. In these methods angular errors and volume error of each approach are tabulated as below (Table 1),

Table 1 Result of evaluation showing angular error and volume error

Measure, mean (sd)	AE (o)	VE (ml)	Time (s)
FBM methods	1.28(0.52)	1.57(0.59)	0.51
GSBM methods	1.53(0.61)	1.66(0.54)	33.60
LSBM methods	1.47(0.60)	1.67(0.62)	1.80

7 Conclusion

This research paper includes the details of image enhancement techniques to transfer the image from original form to accessible form and that techniques are useful to improve the accuracy of the result of the computerised system for the diagnose of the brain tumor identification and classification. This paper also contains the neural network method with Feedforward and back propagation approach in last stage of the computerised system for the classification of human brain tumor. This approach gives more accuracy in the results of human brain tumor discovery and classification.

Acknowledgement. We, Vikul J Pawar, Kailash D Kharat and Prof. S. R. Pardeshi author of this paper are express our gratitude towards Dr. P. B. Murnal, Principal and Professor of Government Engineering College, Aurangabad (Maharashtra)India, Dr. V. P. Kshirsagar, HEAD CSE Government College of Engineering, Aurangabad, Dr. Avinash K. Gulve, Asso. Prof., Dept of MCA, Government College of Engineering, Aurangabad for their support and motivation. Our special thanks to Prof. S. G. Shikalpure for huge motivation from him.

References

1. Shah, D.B., Modi, N.: A review-Various segmentation techniques for brain tumor Detection. IJESRT 3(12). ISSN: 2277-9655 (2014)
2. Kharat, K.D., Kulkarni, P.: Brain Tumor classification using neural network based methods. IJCSI Nagpur 1(4) (2012). ISSN: 2231-5292
3. Bhateja, V., Raj, A., Shrivastav, A.: Computer Aided detection of Brain tumor in magnetic resinance Images. Int. J. Eng. Technol. 3(5) (2011)

4. Zwanenburg, J.J., Biessels, G.J., Bouvy, W.H., Kuijif, H.J., Kappelle, L.J.: Visualization of perivascular spaces and perforating arteries with 7T magenetic resonance imaging. Invest Radiol. **49**(5) (2014). ISSN No: 0020-9996
5. Iliff, J.J.: Cerebral arterial pulsation drives paravascular CSF-interstitial fluid exchange in the murine brain. Neuro Sci. 33–46, ISSN No: 18190-18299 (2013)
6. Zhu, Y.C.: Severity of dilated Virchow robin spaces is associated with age blood pressure and MRI markers of small vessel disease: a population based study. STROKE 41–11 (2010). ISSN No: 2483-2490
7. Ghafaryasl B.: A Computer Aided Detection System for Cerebral Microbleeds in Brain MRI, pp. 138–141 (2012)
8. Badran, E.F., Mohmoud, E.G., Hamdy, N.: An algorithm for detecting brain tumors in MRI images. In: IEEE Conference (2010)
9. Jensesn, T., Schmainda, K.: computer aided detection of brain tumor invasion using multiparametric MRI. J. Magn. Reson. Imaging **33**(3), 481–489 (2009)
10. Logeswari, T., Karnan, M.: An enhanced Implementation of brain tumor detection using segmentation based on soft computing. In: International Conference on Signal Acquieition and Processing (2010)
11. Bandopadhyay, S.K.: Detection of brain tumor a proposed method. J. Glob. Res. Comput. Sci. **2**(1) (2011)
12. Viji, K.S.A., Jayakumari, J.: Automatica detection of brain tumor based on magnetic resonance image Using CAD system with watershed segmentation. In: Proceeding in ICSCCN (2011)
13. Zhang, Y., Wang, S., Ji, G., Dong, Z.: Genetic pattern search and Its application to brain Image classification. Math. Probl. Eng. Article No 580876 (2013)
14. Bhavani, R., Rajini, N.H.: Classification of MRI Brain images using k-nearest neighbor and artificial neural network. ICRTIT 563–568 (2011)
15. Gad, A., Hassan, N.M.H., Abul, R., Nassef, T.M.: Automatic machine learning classification of alzheimers disease based on selectyed slices from 3D magnetic resonance imaging. Int. J. Biomed. Sci. Eng. **4**(6) (2016)
16. Stegmann, M.B., Skoglund, K., Ryberg, C.: Mid-sagittal plane and midsagittal surface optimization in brain MRI using a local symmetry measure. In: International Symposium on Medical Imaging, vol. 5747, pp. 568–579 (2005)

Smart Trash Monitoring and Segregation System Using Emerging Technology—A Survey

Kruti Dhyani[1](✉) and Nehal Patel[2]

[1] U and P U. Patel Department of Computer Engineering, CSPIT, Charusat,
Changa, Gujarat, India
krutidhyani.ce@charusat.ac.in
[2] Department of Information Technology, CSPIT, Charusat,
Changa, Gujarat, India
nehalpatel.it@charusat.ac.in

Abstract. Global warming and pollution is the most growing problem world-wide. One of the causes is trash generation and it's not recycle properly. Most of the developing and developed countries are now focus on proper management of garbage through its different stages from generation to destroy of garbage. To develop such effective system, modern technologies are used like IoT (Internet of Things), Embedded System, Cloud Computing, Big Data, Data Transfer technology. Using these technologies different approaches is proposed around the world by researchers which cover mainly three aspects, smart waste detection, smart garbage segregation and smart trash collection. This paper covers literature survey on waste monitoring, segregation and collection system with the use of innovative techniques. Merits are, environment become clean, most of the disease are cured which are generated through pollution and recycle of waste.

Keywords: IoT · Cloud computing · Smart trash · Sensors

1 Introduction

Nowadays, IoT is a platform where each device turns into smarter and through intelligent processing, communication turns into revealing. It is a crucial driver for innovation in customer facing, automation, optimization of data driven and business models through all regions. Internet of Things structures a block which helps to achieve an enhanced perception towards real meaning. There are six chief fundamentals of the IoT to deliver its functionalities. 1. Identification 2. Sensing 3. Communication 4. Computation 5. Services 6. Semantics. Furthermore, IoT have some common standards to exemplify, Service Discovery Protocols, Infrastructure Protocols, Influential Protocols and Application Protocols [1]. IoT may be categorized as the container of significant utility factors to demonstrate Self-configuring, Interoperable communication protocols, Dynamic and self-adapting, Context-awareness, Integrated into information network, Intelligent decision making capability and Unique identity [2].

The Swachh Bharat Abhiyan is the utmost important project to make the India a clean country by the Government of India. For instance, the city of Indore entitled

© Springer Nature Singapore Pte Ltd. 2019
A. K. Luhach et al. (Eds.): ICAICR 2018, CCIS 955, pp. 667–674, 2019.
https://doi.org/10.1007/978-981-13-3140-4_60

India's cleanest city as Narendra Modi's Swachh Bharat mission creates actual evolution. It climbed from 149th placed in 2014 to the 25th position in 2016 and top of the heap in 2017. Where there is a life and humans are alive wastes are produced. Hence, garbage levels are also increasing significantly with the growing population. There are three foremost types of objects of garbage management such as user who generate garbage, garbage collectors and stake holders [3]. Therefore, garbage management is a still challenging task which is faced for developing advanced countries.

2 Literature Survey

In this paper, various research, review and survey papers are inspected on the smart garbage system and based on that a literature survey is done on different technologies and sensors used to develop different techniques. Major of the researchers have used Cloud Computing to store the Data, RFID sensor to gather the information tag on that objects, microcontroller and Arduino Uno board to generate small computer to test and mange the system and GPS Technology to transfer data. Some of them also used Big Data analytics to analyze the trend and make decision out of its result. In the following Table 1 the technologies and sensors used in different researches are shown.

Table 1. Technologies + Sensors used in different existing garbage monitoring system

Sr. no.	Paper title	Publications	Year	Technology/sensor used
1	Smart garbage monitoring system using Internet of Things [4]	IJIREEICE	2017	Microcontroller, Wi-Fi modem, IoT, GSM, Ultrasonic sensor
2	Smart garbage monitoring system for waste management [5]	EDP Sciences	2017	Microcontroller, HC-SR04 ultrasonic sensor, GPS module, SIM900A GSM module, Arduino Uno board
3	Smart garbage monitoring and clearance system using internet of things [6]	IEEE	2017	Embedded, IoT, GSM, Microcontroller, Web server, Ultrasonic Sensor, Force sensor
4	Smart waste management using Internet-of-Thing [7]	IEEE	2017	Wi-Fi, Embedded, IoT, MySql, AI, Ultrasonic Ranging module HC-SR04
5	Smart garbage monitoring system using sensors with RFID over Internet of Things [27]	Journal of Advanced Research in Dynamical and Control Systems	2017	IR sensor, Radio sensor, Photoelectric sensor, Weight sensor, RFID
6	Multipurpose street smart garbage bin based on IOT [28]	International Journal of Advanced Research in Computer Science	2017	Ultrasonic sensors, GSM, Arduino

(continued)

Table 1. (*continued*)

Sr. no.	Paper title	Publications	Year	Technology/sensor used
7	Garbage monitoring system using IoT [29]	IOP Conference Series: Materials Science and Engineering	2017	Ultrasonic sensors, GSM, Arduino, Blynk app
8	Challenges & Opportunities of waste management in IoT-enabled smart cities: a survey [30]	IEEE Transactions on Sustainable Computing	2017	RFIDs, sensors, and Actuators, WSN, GPs
9	Smart city technology based architecture for refuse disposal management [8]	IEEE	2016	Arduino UNO microcontroller board, proximity sensor, light, odor, force sensitive refuse bin and PC, K-NN classifier, GSM/GPRS, Wi-Fi module
10	IoT based smart garbage alert system using Arduino UNO [9]	IEEE	2016	Arduino UNO, Microcontroller, Ultrasonic sensor, Wi-Fi module, RFID, Android application
11	A cloud-based dynamic waste management system for smart cities [10]	ACM	2016	Load sensor SEN-10245, Ultrasonic sensor, Cloud server, Microcontroller and GPRS
12	Efficient waste collection system [11]	IEEE	2016	Microcontroller, Ultrasonic sensor, Gas equality, Wi-Fi module
13	Automatic waste segregator and monitoring system [12]	STM	2016	Ultrasonic sensor, proximity sensor, Arduino Uno board, Microcontroller, GSM module
14	Cloud-based smart waste management for smart cities [3]	IEEE	2016	RFID, load cell sensor, Cloud, Big Data Analytics
15	Smart dustbin-an efficient garbage monitoring system [13]	IJESC	2016	GSM, Arduino Uno, Ultrasonic sensor HC-SR04
16	An integrated node for smart-city applications based on active RFID tags; Use case on waste-bins [17]	IEEE	2016	RFID, Ultrasonic sensor
17	Cloud computing based smart garbage monitoring system [18]	IEEE	2016	Microcontroller, ultrasonic sensor, wireless sensor network, cloud computing, decision forest regression

(*continued*)

Table 1. (*continued*)

Sr. no.	Paper title	Publications	Year	Technology/sensor used
18	Smart garbage monitoring system [31]	ACM	2016	WSN, GPS, Ultrasonic sensor
19	Smartbin: smart waste management system [22]	IEEE	2015	Wireless mesh network, Cloud, GPS module and Web technology
20	Waste management as an IoT-enabled service in smart cities [20]	Springer	2015	Load Cell, RFID, GPS module, Web technology
21	Smart and wireless waste management [24]	IEEE	2015	Microcontroller, load cell, ultrasonic sensor, GPS module, GSM/GPRS module
22	Real time solid waste bin monitoring system framework using wireless sensor network [14]	IEEE	2014	Accelerometer, hall effect, ultrasound, temperature, humidity, load cell sensor, ZigBee-PRO, GPRS, central server database
23	Smart recycle bin: a conceptual approach of smart waste management with integrated web based system [16]	IEEE	2014	Microcontroller, RFID, web technology
24	A novel approach for waste segregation at source level for effective generation of electricity—GREENBIN [23]	IEEE	2014	Moisture sensor, Metal sensor, Methane sensor, Odour sensor
25	An approach for monitoring and smart planning of urban solid waste management using smart M3 platform [25]	IEEE	2014	Load cell, Proximity sensor, Radio or ZigBee
26	SVASTHA: an effective solid waste management system for Thiruvalla Municipality in Android OS [15]	IEEE	2013	Microcontroller, RFID, GPS module, Android, Bluetooth
27	Solid waste management architecture using wireless sensor network technology [21]	IEEE	2012	Microcontroller, GPS, GPRS, GSM module
28	RFID-based real-time smart waste management system [19]	IEEE	2007	RFID, Load cell

3   Existing System Flow

In Fig. 1 [26], demonstrates the general design of Smart Garbage Management System using Cloud. It is demonstrated that omnipresent accessibility of information uploads on the cloud which can be helpful for various elements and partners in various methods. Investigation and arranging can begin from when squander begins assembling then up to once reprocessing and import and/or export connected matters are directed.

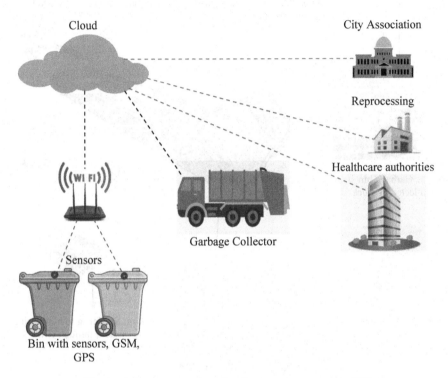

Fig. 1. Smart system using cloud garbage management [26]

In Fig. 2, depicts the segregation scenario of trash using embedded and GSM technology. In simple words, First garbage is collected and sent it to trash segregator house. Then after, garbage is put it in to conveyor belt and simultaneously blower in blowing air at some frequency of time so that light weight trash is separated. Starting and Ending of the Conveyor belt ultrasonic sensor is connected and microcontroller identify that metal is present or not through NPN sensor. If metal is present, ultrasonic sensor generate waves and metal particles is separated by robotic arms and put it in to separate bin. This method uses electromagnets mechanism to attract metals. At the end, if bins are full then message is sent to monitoring system through GSM technology.

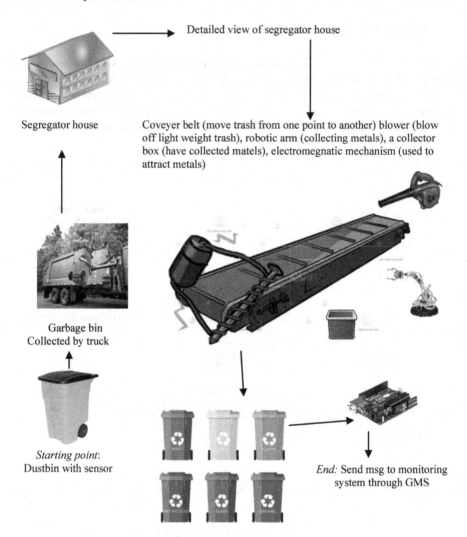

Detailed view of segregator house

Segregator house

Coveyer belt (move trash from one point to another) blower (blow off light weight trash), robotic arm (collecting metals), a collector box (have collected matels), electromegnatic mechanism (used to attract metals)

Garbage bin
Collected by truck

Starting point:
Dustbin with sensor

End: Send msg to monitoring
system through GMS

Segregated trash and If bins are full

Fig. 2. Smart trash segregator and monitoring system using GSM and embedded technology

4   Conclusion and Future Work

The word Internet of Things has been famous for last few decades. Garbage management is one of the difficult tasks that urban communities need to manage. Garbage management comprises of various procedures for instance, gathering, transport, preparing, overseeing, and checking of unwanted materials. These procedures cost huge amount of time, labour, and money. To enhance various garbage management forms which help societies to spare money that can be utilized to address different difficulties that smart urban societies need to manage. In this paper, we have reviewed on smart trash monitoring and segregation system using emerging technology which ensures that strong way of managing the waste. Hence, which is not only the entire procedure turn into effective, nonetheless too, the disposal of garbage is done in a dynamic way.

In the future, this idea can be implemented for a nation precise garbage generation drifts. Moreover, Big Data analysis would apply on the collected information from diverse metropolises.

References

1. Al-Fuqaha, A., et al.: Internet of things: A survey on enabling technologies, protocols, and applications. IEEE Commun. Surv. Tutor. **17**(4), 2347–2376 (2015)
2. Ray, P.P.: A survey on Internet of Things architectures. Ournal King Saud Univ.-Comput. Inf. Sci. (2016)
3. Aazam, M., et al.: Cloud-based smart waste management for smart cities. In: 2016 IEEE 21st International Workshop on Computer Aided Modelling and Design of Communication Links and Networks (CAMAD). IEEE (2016)
4. Chaware, S.M., Dighe, S., Joshi, A., Bajare, N., Korke, R.: Smart garbage monitoring system using Internet of Things (IoT). Int. J. Innov. Res. Electr. Electron. Instrum. Control. Eng. **5**(1) (2017)
5. Yusof, N.M., Jidin, A.Z., Rahim, M.I.: Smart garbage monitoring system for waste management. In: MATEC Web of Conferences, vol. 97. EDP Sciences (2017)
6. Kumar, S.V., Kumaran, T.S., Kumar, A.K., Mathapati, M.: Smart garbage monitoring and clearance system using internet of things. In: 2017 IEEE International Conference on Smart Technologies and Management for Computing, Communication, Controls, Energy and Materials (ICSTM), pp. 184 − 189. IEEE (2017)
7. Shyam, G.K., Manvi, S.S. Bharti, P.: Smart waste management using Internet-of-Things (IoT). In: 2017 2nd International Conference on Computing and Communications Technologies (ICCCT), pp. 199 − 203. IEEE (2017)
8. Adeyemo, J.O., Olugbara, O.O., Adetiba, E.: Smart city technology based architecture for refuse disposal management. In: IST-Africa Week Conference. IEEE (2016)
9. Kumar, N.S., et al.: IOT based smart garbage alert system using Arduino UNO. In: 2016 IEEE Region 10 Conference (TENCON). IEEE (2016)
10. Sharmin, S., Al-Amin, S.T.: A cloud-based dynamic waste management system for smart cities. In: 2016 Proceedings of the 7th Annual Symposium on Computing for Development. ACM (2016)
11. Dugdhe, S., et al.: Efficient waste collection system. In: International Conference on Internet of Things and Applications (IOTA). IEEE (2016)
12. VJ, A., Balakrishnan, K., Rosmi, T.B., Swathy Krishna, K.J., Sreejith, S., Subha, T.D.: Automatic Waste Segregator and Monitoring System
13. Monika, K.A., Rao, N., Prapulla, S.B., Shobha, G.: Smart dustbin-an efficient garbage monitoring system. Int. J. Eng. Sci. Comput. **6**(6), 7113 − 7116 (2016)
14. Al Mamun, M.A., Hannan, M.A., Hussain, A.: Real time solid waste bin monitoring system framework using wireless sensor network. In: 2014 International Conference on Electronics, Information and Communications (ICEIC). IEEE (2014)
15. Issac, R., Akshai, M.: SVASTHA: an effective solid waste management system for Thiruvalla Municipality in Android OS. In: 2013 IEEE Global Humanitarian Technology Conference: South Asia Satellite (GHTC-SAS). IEEE (2013)

16. Wahab, M.H.A., Kadir, A.A., Tomari, M.R., Jabbar, M.H.: Smart recycle bin: a conceptual approach of smart waste management with integrated web based system. In: 2014 International Conference on IT Convergence and Security (ICITCS). IEEE (2014)
17. Karadimas, D., et al.: An integrated node for smart-city applications based on active RFID tags; Use case on waste-bins. In: Emerging Technologies and Factory Automation (ETFA). IEEE (2016)
18. Joshi, J., et al.: Cloud computing based smart garbage monitoring system. In: 2016 3rd International Conference on Electronic Design (ICED). IEEE (2016)
19. Chowdhury, B., Chowdhury, M.U.: RFID-based real-time smart waste management system. In: 2007 Telecommunication Networks and Applications Conference, ATNAC 2007, Australasian. IEEE (2007)
20. Medvedev, A., et al.: Waste management as an IoT-enabled service in smart cities. In: Conference on Smart Spaces. Springer, Cham (2015)
21. Longhi, S., et al.: Solid waste management architecture using wireless sensor network technology. In: 2012 5th International Conference on New Technologies, Mobility and Security (NTMS). IEEE (2012)
22. Folianto, F., Low, Y.S., Yeow, W.L.: Smartbin: smart waste management system. In: 2015 IEEE Tenth International Conference on Intelligent Sensors, Sensor Networks and Information Processing (ISSNIP). IEEE (2015)
23. Rajkamal, R., et al.: A novel approach for waste segregation at source level for effective generation of electricity—GREENBIN. In: 2014 International Conference on Science Engineering and Management Research (ICSEMR). IEEE (2014)
24. Thakker, S., Narayanamoorthi, R.: Smart and wireless waste management. In: 2015 International Conference on Innovations in Information, Embedded and Communication Systems (ICIIECS). IEEE (2015)
25. Catania, V., Ventura, D.: An approach for monitoring and smart planning of urban solid waste management using smart-M3 platform. In: Proceedings of 15th Conference of Open Innovations Association FRUCT. IEEE (2014)
26. Perera, C., et al.: Sensing as a service model for smart cities supported by internet of things. Trans. Emerg. Telecommun. Technol. 25(1), 81 – 93 (2014)
27. Satyamanikanta, S.D., Narayanan, M.: Smart Garbage Monitoring System Using Sensors with RFID Over Internet of Things
28. Kaushik, D., Yadav, S.: Multipurpose street smart garbage bin based on Iot. Int. J. Adv. Res. Comput. Sci. 8(3) (2017)
29. Bajaj, A., Reddy, S.: Garbage monitoring system using IoT. Int. J. Pure Appl. Math. 114 (12), 155–161 (2017)
30. Anagnostopoulos, T., et al.: Challenges and opportunities of waste management in IoT-enabled smart cities: a survey. IEEE Trans. Sustain. Comput. 2(3), 275 – 289 (2017)
31. Joshi, J., et al.: Smart Garbage monitoring system. In: Proceedings of the 7th International Conference on Computing Communication and Networking Technologies. ACM (2016)

Raw Materials Management for Time Dependent Supply Chain Network

Ayan Chatterjee[1($\boxtimes$)] and Mahendra Rong[2]

[1] Operation Management Group, Indian Institute of Management Calcutta,
Kolkata, India
ayanchatterje2012@gmail.com
[2] Department of Mathematics, Bangabasi Evening College, Kolkata, India
mahendrarong@gmail.com

Abstract. Purchasing raw materials from proper locations play an important role in supply chain network design. In this paper, a mathematical model is developed to optimize the cost of purchasing raw materials and transportation cost of these raw materials from market locations to production unit(s) to meet the demand of the products timely. This model is developed considering multiple products, single production unit and time dependent demands of the products. Capacity of the paths from market locations to production unit(s), demand of raw materials in each time interval and for each product are taken as constraints in this mathematical formulation. Key decisions of the formulation are suitable locations and purchasing amount of each raw material in each time interval. The proposed approach is examined with a standard data set in LINGO platform and efficacy is shown with optimality.

Keywords: Supply chain management · Multi products
Raw materials management · Market location

1 Introduction

Supply chain management is defined as the optimal balance between demand and supply of products/services [9]. Major three phases of supply chain network are- (i) raw materials management, (ii) manufacturing of products and (iii) selling the products to the customers [9, 10, 12]. The interconnection among these three phases is shown in Fig. 1. A small description of each step is given in the following.

1.1 Raw Materials Management

Raw materials management is the initial phase of supply chain. Moreover, it is a crucial stage of supply chain management. This is divided into three major subparts- (i) Purchasing raw materials, (ii) storing raw materials in production units and (iii) transportation of raw materials from market location to production unit(s). Each subpart consists of a separate cost. At the time of purchasing raw materials, two important facts should be noted. These two facts are quality and cost of raw materials. In general way, it is observed that multiple raw materials are bought from different market locations.

© Springer Nature Singapore Pte Ltd. 2019
A. K. Luhach et al. (Eds.): ICAICR 2018, CCIS 955, pp. 675–686, 2019.
https://doi.org/10.1007/978-981-13-3140-4_61

So, selection of proper location corresponding to a particular raw material is a vital decision in raw materials management. Beside this, if a particular raw material is available in more than one market, then purchasing amount of each raw material from market locations should be decided properly. To maintain this, various factors are involved with this platform. Actually, at the time of optimizing the raw materials cost with quality, transportation cost and inventory cost also should be optimized. Inventory is dependent on time and transportation is dependent on distance from market location (s) to production unit(s) and condition of road. Therefore, the objective of raw materials management is to optimize all of purchasing cost, inventory and transportation costs with fulfilling the demands of all raw materials maintaining the quality as per as required.

1.2 Manufacturing of Products

Production of goods is the second most important phase of supply chain management. This phase is the task of manufacturer. The function of this phase is to prepare the goods maintaining quality of product and demand from customers. The major decision in this phase is to estimate the amount of products, required to prepare at a specific time interval considering the demand and safety stock. This particular decision plays a very important role in the case of assembling of semi finished goods in different production units. These semi finished goods are generally stored in each production unit for a specific time period. So, there is an inventory cost in each production unit. In fact, in the case of single product and single production unit, inventory acts an important role also. Therefore, the objective of the manufacturing phase is to optimize the costs of products, inventory cost of semi-finished and finished goods and cost of transportation from one manufacturing unit to another unit (only in the case of assembling of goods) with maintaining time specification of demand and quality of products.

1.3 Selling of Products

The last stage of supply chain is selling of products to the intended customers in the market. After preparing the products in the production units, these are transported to the retailing markets according to requirement. But in most of the cases, distribution centers are established in between the production units and local retailing shops. So, one of the most crucial decision in this phase is to select the proper locations of distribution centers and to estimate the strength of distribution centers. Another important decision in this phase is to estimate the amount of products to be transported from production unit(s) to distribution center(s) and distribution center(s) to retailing market(s). Also, safety stock estimation in both of distribution centers and retailing shops are important decisions to optimize the inventory cost. So, overall objective of this particular stage is optimization of transportation cost(s), inventory cost(s) and ordering cost(s) with maintaining the supply of products timely.

In the Fig. 1, flow of three phases for supply of products is shown. Also, the particular workers, who are involved in the corresponding phases, are shown in the diagram. Here, it is observed that purchasing raw materials from proper locations is an important decision in supply chain. More specifically, quality of product(s) is

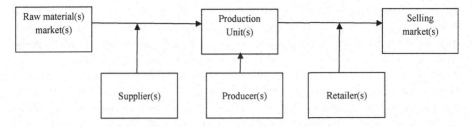

Fig. 1. Architecture of supply chain network

dependent on quality and quantity of corresponding raw materials [11]. Another important factor regarding this is availability of raw materials in market locations. In most of the reality, an uncertainty occurs at the time of obtaining raw materials in production units. Therefore, at the time of designing supply chain network, availability of the raw materials should be analyzed properly with optimum purchasing cost. The capacity of the paths from raw material(s) purchasing location(s) to production unit(s) is an important factor regarding this also. But most of the papers in supply chain consider the production and distribution phases. Very few models are developed considering the fact raw materials handling. In this paper, an optimization model is proposed to handle raw materials in proper way with minimization of purchasing and carrying costs of the raw materials.

The remaining of the paper is designed in the specified structure. In Sect. 2, a literature survey of previously developed raw materials handling model is carried out with their basic properties, uniqueness and bottlenecks. The enhancement over previous models is described and structured as mathematical formulation in Sect. 3. Feasibility of the proposed model is shown with a small standard set in Sect. 4. At the end of the paper, a conclusion of the proposed model is drawn followed by the future scope in Sect. 5.

2 Literature Survey

In this part, a small description of previously developed works is listed shortly. In the scheme of Arntzen et al. [1], an integrated deterministic supply chain model is developed for multiple products. The objective of this model is minimization of number of production days, raw materials cost, storage cost, overhead cost, and cost of transportation. Here, amount of purchasing raw materials is considered as decision variable. But location selection for purchasing raw materials and availability of raw materials in each location are not considered in this model. Another technique [2] on supply chain, developed by Cohen and Moon, keeps the fact of raw materials flow handling in a deterministic way. In this model, a constraint is set up considering requirement of raw materials. But the drawback of previous development [1] still exists in this model. In the model of Voudouris [3], a supply chain model is developed with the factor resource handling. Consideration of time dependency is a special inclusion of this model. But location of market(s) for purchasing raw materials is not considered in this mathematical approach. A stochastic supply chain model [4] considering material flow is developed by Cohen and Lee. Material requirements are considered in each stage of the system. As a result, cost of raw materials can be optimized properly. Another stochastic model [5] considers raw materials flow in each site individually. Actually, the decision of purchasing raw materials is dependent on stock level analysis of each manufacturing unit. This fact is taken into account in this model. After that, huge developments occur in supply chain. Most of the papers consider production and selling phases. Very few models take the management of raw materials providing high propriety. In the paper of Agarwal [6], flow of raw materials is considered in a high density. This model is developed for multiple production units with different type raw materials. Amount of availabilities of raw materials are considered also in the market locations. But here it is assumed that all materials are available in each location with differentiation of quantities. In the scheme of Liu and Yang [7], a model of procure control with pricing consideration is developed. The novelty of this stochastic approach is fluctuation of raw materials purchasing cost is taken into account in this model. Nilsen [8] developed a model of production delay with uncertain storage of raw materials. In the scheme of Andrea et al. [13], a raw materials handling decision support system is developed with a particular case study. Actually, assembling of raw materials is considered in this model before manufacturing a specific product. The importance of this approach is consideration of environmental issue during assembling phase. In the case study of Suryaningrat [14], raw materials management is analyzed for fruit processing industries. In this particular case, all the fruit manufacturing industries of Indonesia are taken into account for analytical purpose. This particular business is combined agriculture and industrial development. Normally fruits are purchased from whole sellers to prepare different fruit products at the production units. Whole sellers buy the fruits from the farmers. This is the structure of large scale fruit processing industries. In the case of small scale fruit processing industries, farmers are directly connected with manufacturer. The uniqueness of this particular contribution is properly analysis of financial flow and fruit processed products flow. But in normal cases, fruit is perishable in nature. In similar way, fruit processing products are also perishable. The drawback of this analysis is not consideration of the perishable condition. In the model of Mancheri et al. [15], the supply chain procedure of tantalum is analyzed. A sustainable supply chain model is developed in this contribution. More specifically, in the phase of raw materials management, three important facts resistance, rapidity and flexibility are considered. As a result, uniqueness of this model is easily handling of four crucial situations. These are supply diversity, substitution of materials, stockpiling and altering of properties of materials. It is observed from experimentation part of this model that a large gap of data occurs between manufacturing and consumption of the product tantalum. An important contribution regarding raw materials management is developed by Schimf et al. [16]. This particular paper shows the future directions of raw materials handling improvement considering various scenarios. The objective of this analysis is properly investigation of different application areas of raw materials handling, like economic framing and research, environmental policy improvement etc. In general way, all the facts of technological, economic and political issues are taken into account for the scenario analysis. The categorization of the considered papers with specific novelties is listed in Table 1.

Table 1. A categorization of raw materials handling models with specifications

Models	Categorization type		Novelty of the works
	Deterministic	Stochastic	
[1]	×		Minimization of number of production days, raw materials cost, storage cost, overhead cost, and cost of transportation
[2]	×		Development of a constraint considering requirement of raw materials
[3]	×		Consideration of time dependency
[4]		×	Consideration of multi stages raw materials requirement
[5]		×	Consideration of multiple production units
[6]	×		Consideration of multiple production units with multiple raw materials
[7]		×	Procurement control with pricing consideration
[8]	×		Consideration of production delay with uncertain storage of raw materials
[13]	×		Consideration of environmental issue during assembling phase of the raw materials
[14]	NA		Development of properly analysis of financial flow and fruit processed products flow with a case study of the fruit manufacturing industries of Indonesia
[15]	×		Easily handling of four crucial situations- supply diversity, substitution of materials, stockpiling and altering of properties of materials with resistance, rapidity and flexibility
[16]	NA		Properly investigation of different application areas of raw materials handling, like economic framing and research, environmental policy improvement etc.

But any model doesn't consider the continuation of a particular raw material in consecutive time intervals. In the proposed approach, raw materials handling mathematical model is developed with an uncertainty of existence of raw materials at a particular location in a specific time interval.

3   Proposed Model

In this section, proposed development on raw materials handling in deterministic nature is described with a brief discussion. This description is divided into three consecutive subsections. In Subsect. 3.1, the considered problem is described with particular assumptions. The symbols and notations used to formulate the mathematical model are described shortly in Subsect. 3.2. In the last Subsect. 3.3, proposed mathematical model is given with real meanings of objective function and constraints.

3.1   Problem Description

In the initial phase of supply chain, purchasing raw materials from proper locations is an important decision. Here, it is considered that multiple products can be manufactured in a single production unit with differentiation of quantities. But demand of product(s) in each interval is different. Actually, the demand of a particular product at a specific moment is known to the producer. Also, the raw material types required to make each particular product that is also known to the user. The specification of this proposed work is that all materials may not available in all market locations and each product reserves different set of raw material types. At the time of transportation, load capacities of the paths are taken into account. Ultimately it is decided from the model is that the amount of raw material should be transported in such a way that the requirement of these in each time interval can be met properly according to the demand of the products. To develop this decision making model, the considered assumptions are listed as follows:

- This is a multi products and single manufacturing unit based raw materials handling decision making model.
- Purchasing costs of raw materials are uniform in different time intervals.
- A particular raw material may be available in more than one market location; but it is not necessary that all raw materials are available in all market locations.
- Transportation cost is dependent on type of raw materials and feasible paths between market locations between market locations to production units.
- All raw materials are required at each instant of the production unit. No inventory (previous storage) is considered in this model.
- Set of raw materials is different for various products.
- At a particular time t, purchasing amount of raw materials = transported amount of that raw material
- Amount of demand of the products are not considered in this model. Only product type is taken here. For simplicity, one unit demand of product is considered everywhere.

3.2 Symbols and Notations Description

Suppose, there are 'P' no. of products are manufactured in the production unit of an organization. So, the set of products is denoted by 1, 2,…, P. The raw materials 1, 2,…, R are required to manufacture the products. The data element 'RP' represents a particular raw material is required or not to produce a particular product. There are 'T' time intervals, namely 1, 2,…, T; considered in this model and a unit amount of demand of each product from the customers at each time interval. The data element 'PT' represents a particular product is manufactured or not in a specific time interval. In similar manner, it should be known that a particular raw material is required or not to make a particular product. The data element 'D' represents the requirement of a particular raw material to manufacture one unit of a product. There are 'N' market locations, namely 1, 2,…, N to purchase raw materials 1, 2,…, R. The data elements 'c' and 'TC' represent per unit purchasing cost of a raw material from a specific market location and transportation cost of a raw material from a particular location to manufacturing unit respectively. But previously it is mentioned that all raw materials are not necessarily available in all the market locations. The data element 'Rm' denoted a particular raw material is available or not in a location at instant time. Loading capacities of the routes from locations to production unit is considered through the data element 'CAP'. The outputs of the model are amount of purchased raw materials from proper locations and requirement of each raw material in t-th time interval. All the symbols, to develop this mathematical model are listed in the following:

Index:

$$i : Index\ of\ raw\ material\ type$$

$$j : Index\ of\ market\ location$$

$$k : Index\ of\ product\ type$$

$$t : Index\ of\ time\ period$$

Notations for data elements:

$$R : No.\ of\ different\ type\ raw\ materials$$

$$N : No.\ of\ raw\ materials\ purchasing\ market\ locations$$

$$P : No.\ of\ products$$

$$T : No.\ of\ time\ intervals$$

$$c_{ij} : Per\ unit\ purchasing\ cost\ of\ i-th\ raw\ material\ from\ j-th\ market\ location$$

$$TC_{ij} : Per\ unit\ transportation\ cost\ of\ i-th\ raw\ material\ from\ j\\-th\ market\ location\ to\ production\ unit$$

$$Rm_{ij}^t = \begin{cases} 1, & if\ i-th\ raw\ material\ is\ available\ in\ j-th\ location\ in\ t-th\ time\ period \\ 0, & otherwise \end{cases}$$

$$PT_k^t = \begin{cases} 1, & if\ k-th\ product\ is\ manufactured\ in\ t-th\ time\ period \\ 0, & otherwise \end{cases}$$

$$RP_{ik} = \begin{cases} 1, & if\ i-th\ raw\ material\ is\ required\ to\ manufacture\ k-th\ product \\ 0, & otherwise \end{cases}$$

$$CAP_j : Capacity\ of\ the\ route\ from\ j-th\ market\ location\ to\ production\ unit$$

$$D_{ik} : Requirement\ of\ i-th\ raw\ material\ to\ produce\ k-th\ product$$

Decision variables:

$$x_{ij}^t : Amount\ of\ purchased\ i-th\ raw\ material\ from\ j-th\ market\ location\ in\ t\\-th\ time\ period$$

$$RM_{ij}^t = \begin{cases} 1, & if\ i-th\ raw\ material\ is\ purchased\ from\ j-th\ location\ in\ t-th\ time\ period \\ 0, & otherwise \end{cases}$$

$$d_i^t : Requirement\ of\ i-th\ raw\ material\ in\ t-th\ time\ period$$

3.3   Mathematical Model

The proposed mathematical model is designed as follows:

$$Minimize\ Z = \sum_{i=1}^{R} \sum_{j=1}^{N} c_{ij} \sum_{t=1}^{T} x_{ij}^t Rm_{ij}^t RM_{ij}^t + \sum_{i=1}^{R} \sum_{j=1}^{N} TC_{ij} \sum_{t=1}^{T} x_{ij}^t Rm_{ij}^t RM_{ij}^t \tag{1}$$

Subject to

$$\sum_{j=1}^{N} x_{ij}^t Rm_{ij}^t RM_{ij}^t = d_i^t \ \forall t = 1, 2, \ldots, T; i = 1, 2, \ldots, R \tag{2}$$

$$\sum_{t=1}^{T} \sum_{i=1}^{R} x_{ij}^t Rm_{ij}^t RM_{ij}^t \leq CAP_j \ \forall j = 1, 2, \ldots, N \tag{3}$$

$$PT_k^t \sum_{i=1}^{R} RP_{ik} \sum_{j=1}^{N} x_{ij}^t Rm_{ij}^t RM_{ij}^t \geq \sum_{i=1}^{R} D_{ik} RP_{ik} \ \forall k = 1, 2, ..P; t = 1, 2, \ldots, T \tag{4}$$

$$\sum_{i=1}^{R} d_i^t \geq PT_k^t \sum_{i=1}^{R} D_{ik} RP_{ik} \ \forall k = 1, 2, ..P; t = 1, 2, \ldots, T \tag{5}$$

$$x_{ij}^t \geq 0 \ \forall i = 1, 2, \ldots, R; j = 1, 2, \ldots, N; t = 1, 2, \ldots, T \tag{6}$$

$$RM_{ij}^t \in \{0, 1\} \ \forall i = 1, 2, \ldots, R; j = 1, 2, \ldots, N; t = 1, 2, \ldots, T \tag{7}$$

$$d_i^t \geq 0 \ \forall i = 1, 2, \ldots, R; t = 1, 2, \ldots, T \tag{8}$$

Here, objective function (1) is minimization of raw materials purchasing cost and transportation cost of raw materials from market locations to production unit. Constraint (2) is demand fulfilling constraint in all the time intervals. The loads of the paths are considered in constraint (3) Constraints (4) and (5) define the product based and time based demands of raw materials respectively. Feasibility conditions are defined in the constraints (6–8).

4   Experiments and Results

Two small standard data sets are considered to realize the effectiveness of the proposed scheme. The proposed model is examined in LINGO platform. The data sets and corresponding outputs are given in the following.

At the time of coding, two symbols are distinguished from the original notations. Here, the data element 'DD' represents the requirement of a particular raw material to manufacture one unit of a product in place of the notation 'D'. Other one is the decision variable 'RM' is renamed with 'R' in the LINGO code. All other symbols are kept same with the actual mathematical model.

4.1   Data Set 1 and Corresponding Output

```
SETS:
MARKET;
RAWMATERIALS;
PRODUCTS;
TIME;

S1(RAWMATERIALS,MARKET):c,TC;
S3(RAWMATERIALS,MARKET,TIME): Rm;
S4(PRODUCTS,TIME): PT;
S5(RAWMATERIALS,PRODUCTS): RP,DD;
S6(MARKET): CAP;

V1(RAWMATERIALS,MARKET,TIME): x;
V2(RAWMATERIALS,MARKET,TIME): R;
V3(RAWMATERIALS,TIME): d;
ENDSETS

DATA:
MARKET=M1 M2;

RAWMATERIALS= RA1 RA2;
PRODUCTS= 1 2;
TIME= T1 T2;

c= 2 3
   2 4;
TC= 3 4
    8 3;

Rm= 1 0
    0 1
    0 1
    1 1;
PT= 0 1
    1 0;

RP= 1 0
    0 1;
CAP= 5 7;
DD= 2 5
    4 6;
ENDDATA
```

The output of this model is listed given in the following:

```
Variable              Value              Reduced Cost
X( RA1, M1, T1)       1.234568           0.000000
X( RA1, M1, T2)       1.234568           0.000000
X( RA1, M2, T1)       0.000000           0.000000
X( RA1, M2, T2)       1.234568           0.000000
X( RA2, M1, T1)       0.000000           0.000000
X( RA2, M1, T2)       1.234568           0.000000
X( RA2, M2, T1)       1.234568           0.000000
X( RA2, M2, T2)       1.234568           0.000000
D( RA1, T1)           4.000000           0.000000
D( RA1, T2)           4.000000           0.000000
D( RA2, T1)           7.000000           0.000000
D( RA2, T2)           8.000000           0.000000
```

4.2   Data Set 2 and Corresponding Output

```
SETS:
MARKET;
RAWMATERIALS;
PRODUCTS;
TIME;

S1(RAWMATERIALS,MARKET):c,TC;
S3(RAWMATERIALS,MARKET,TIME): Rm;
S4(PRODUCTS,TIME): PT;
S5(RAWMATERIALS,PRODUCTS): RP,DD;
S6(MARKET): CAP;

V1(RAWMATERIALS,MARKET,TIME): x;
V2(RAWMATERIALS,MARKET,TIME): R;
V3(RAWMATERIALS,TIME): d;
ENDSETS
DATA:
MARKET=M1 M2 ;
RAWMATERIALS= RA1 RA2 ;
PRODUCTS= 1 2 ;
TIME= T1 T2 ;
```

```
c= 200 300
    400 500 ;
TC= 300 400
    800 300;

Rm= 0 1
    1 1
    0 1
    1 0 ;
PT= 1 0
    0 1;

RP= 1 1
    0 1 ;
CAP= 500 700 ;
DD= 200 500
    400 600 ;
ENDDATA
```

The output of this model is listed given in the following:

Variable	Value	Reduced Cost
X(RA1, M1, T1)	0.000000	0.000000
X(RA1, M1, T2)	8.297247	0.000000
X(RA1, M2, T1)	9.317333	0.000000
X(RA1, M2, T2)	10.33896	0.000000
X(RA2, M1, T1)	0.000000	0.000000
X(RA2, M1, T2)	22.36068	0.000000
X(RA2, M2, T1)	17.32051	0.000000
X(RA2, M2, T2)	0.000000	0.000000
D(RA1, T1)	400.0000	0.000000
D(RA1, T2)	700.0000	0.000000
D(RA2, T1)	300.0000	0.000000
D(RA2, T2)	500.0000	0.000000

From the output of the proposed model with the standard data set, the feasibility is observed with optimality of costs of raw materials.

5 Conclusions

In this paper, a mathematical model is developed for handling raw materials properly of a multi products manufacturing organization. A different set of raw materials is required for each product. So, raw materials purchasing amount from markets and transportation of them are managed properly to meet the demand of the products timely. Consideration of uncertainty of availability of raw materials in deterministic way is the novelty of the proposed approach. But the main bottleneck of the model is the amount of product(s) demand is not considered here. In other words, the demand of each product is assumed as one unit. Beside this, the amount of each raw material is taken as one unit also. Another drawback of this development is no consideration of any storage or inventory of raw materials and finished goods in the production unit. These assumptions can be relaxed as future improvement corresponding to the proposed model.

References

1. Arntzen, B.C., et al.: Global supply chain management at digital corporation. Interfaces **25**, 69–93 (1995)
2. Cohen, M.A., Moon, S.: Impact of production scale economies, manufacturing complexity, and transportation costs on supply chain facility networks. J. Manuf. Oper. Manag. **3**, 269–292 (1990)
3. Voudouris, V.T.: Mathematical programming techniques to debottleneck the supply chain of fine chemical industries. Comput. Chem. Eng. **20**, S1269–S1274 (1996)
4. Cohen, M.A., Lee, H.L.: Strategic analysis of integrated production-distribution systems: models and methods. Oper. Res. **36**(2), 216–228 (1988)
5. Lee, H.L., Billington, C.: Material management in decentralized supply chains. Oper. Res. **41**(5), 835–847 (1993)
6. Agarwal, A.: Managing raw materials in supply chains. Eur. J. Oper. Res. **239**(3), 685–698 (2014)
7. Liu, Y., Yang, J.: Joint pricing-procurement control under fluctuating raw materials costs. Int. J. Prod. Econ. **168**, 91–104 (2015)
8. Nilsen, J.: Delayed production and raw materials inventory under uncertainty. Int. J. Prod. Econ. **146**, 337–345 (2013)
9. Benita, M.: Beamon, supply chain design and analysis: models and methods. Int. J. Prod. Econ. **55**, 281–294 (1998)
10. Mula, J., et al.: Mathematical programming models for supply chain production and transport planning. Eur. J. Oper. Res. **204**, 377–390 (2010)
11. Saldanha-da-Gama, F., et al.: Facility location and supply chain management – A review. Eur. J. Oper. Res. **196**, 401–412 (2009)
12. Achzet, B., Helbig, C.: How to evaluate raw material supply risks- an overview. Resour. Policy **38**, 435–447 (2013)
13. Kolotzek, C.: A company-oriented model for the assessment of raw material supply risks, environmental impact and social implications. J. Clean. Prod. **176**, 566 – 580 (2018)
14. Suryaningrat, I.B.: Raw material procurement on agroindustrial supply chain management: a case survey of fruit processing industries in Indonesia. Agric. Agric. Sci. Proc. **9**, 253–257 (2016)
15. Mancheri, N.A., et al.: Resilience in the tantalum supply chain. Resour. Conserv. Recycl. **129**, 56–69 (2018)
16. Schimf, S., et al.: The world of raw materials 2050: scoping future dynamics in raw materials through scenarios. Energy Proc. **125**, 6–13 (2017)

Design and Development of Leukemia Identification System Through Neural Network and SVM Approach for Microscopic Smear Image Database

M. V. Rege[1(✉)], B. W. Gawali[1], and S. Gaikwad[2]

[1] Department of CS and IT, Dr. B.A.M. University, Aurangabad, MS, India
regemangesh2007@gmail.com, bharti_rokde@yahoo.co.in
[2] Department of Computer Science,
Model College, Ghansawangi, Jalna, MS, India
santosh.gaikwadscsit@gmail.com

Abstract. The recognition of blood disorder through the visual observation is the most challenging job. In the current technological era computer become the most important part of medical science. The haematological disorders of white blood cells (WBC) are really frequent in medical practices. The objective of this research is to design and development of automated identification of Leukemia using microscopic blood smear image database. This proposed scheme uses the most significant steps of image processing like, pre-processing, image segmentation, extraction of features and classification. The Leukemia smear image database is segmented using Otsu image segmentation. The feature extraction extracts the area, perimeter, solidity, orientation, eccentricity, centroid, entropy and energy features. The classification method applied using neural network, Support vector machine and QDA approach. In the neural network the 60% dataset has been passed for the training, 35% towards the testing and remaining 05% is used for the validation. The SVM and QDA classify the dataset for the two groups such as normal and leukaemia. The classification is done on the extracted 08 features of each image. The performance of the neural network is achieving 98.97% with 1.0246 error rate. The support vector machine is shows the 99.35% accuracy with 0.6500 error rate. The QDA classification reported the 99.70% accuracy with 0.300% error rate. From the reported accuracy the QDA and support vector machine proved as dominant as the neural network.

Keywords: Leukemia · Microscopic · Smear · Otsu · SVM · QDA
Neural network

1 Introduction

In the day to day life the medical diagnosis for any diseases is the major task. The treatment of concern diseases using medical pathology is essential work [1]. The statistics of blood based dieses is increasing day by day. In the era of medical science the most of the dieses is edification is done using the computer based automated system [2]. The leukemia is the most dangerous cancer through blood. The adaptability of

© Springer Nature Singapore Pte Ltd. 2019
A. K. Luhach et al. (Eds.): ICAICR 2018, CCIS 955, pp. 687–700, 2019.
https://doi.org/10.1007/978-981-13-3140-4_62

leukemia dieses varies as per age group. Compared the all types of cancer, the leukemia is the common type. Leukemia is most frequently diagnosed among people aged 65–74 [3]. Generally, leukemia is classified into two main types such as Acute and Chronic. Acute then classified into two types Acute Lymphocytic Leukemia (ALL) & Acute Myeloid Leukemia (AML).Chronic has two types Chronic Lymphocytic Leukemia (CLL) and Chronic Myeloid Leukemia (CML) [4]. The types of Leukemia and occurrences in an age group are shown in Fig. 1.

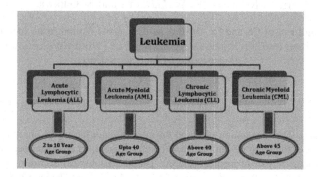

Fig. 1. Types of Leukemia and its occurrences in age group

There is a large scope to develop the automated leukemia identification system using the image processing approach.

The other of this paper is arranged as follows: Sect. 2 the development of the microscopic Leukemia Image database. Section 3 describes the Methodology: Otsu Image segmentation feature extraction and classification in details. The experimental work is explained in Sect. 4. Section 5 is highlighting conclusion followed by references.

2 Database Collection

This research work contributes the accumulation of microscopic smear image database. The images were taken by microscope under (100X) oil immersed setting and with effective magnification of 1000 the volunteer of the database is selected are from leukemia patients of Government Medical College & Hospital, Aurangabad. Each image is represented by RGB color scale. The graphical representation of normal microscopic blood smear image is shown in Fig. 2. The Fig. 3 shows the leukemia microscopic blood sample image.

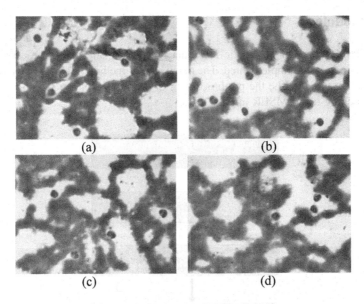

Fig. 2. Normal microscopic blood smear image

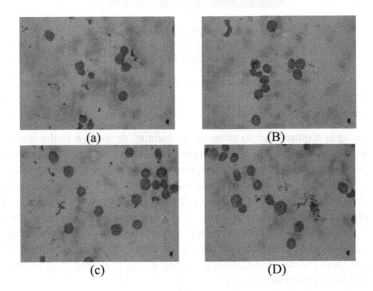

Fig. 3. Leukemia microscopic blood smear image

3   Methodology

For the development of automatic leukemia detection using image processing techniques, basic steps are implemented. The detail step of methodology is shown in Fig. 4. In this section we describe the pre-processing of image, Otsu image segmentation and image matching using MSER approach.

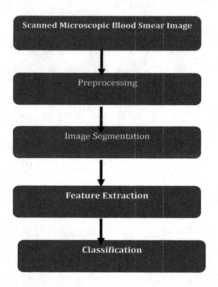

Fig. 4. Flow diagram for proposed system

3.1   Pre-processing

Pre-processing is required due to unnecessary staining or shadow in the image. This is the second step shown in the above image. The image has three different parts for observation such as RBC WBC and background. In the image, an area of interest is the WBC. The WBCs are examined to check whether they are infected or not. There are two different methods for input images, color images & gray scale images. Selective median filtering with un-sharp masking and contrast Enhancement techniques are employed. Color images used partial contrast, dark, stretching and bright stretching for image enhancement [5]. Established on the outcome, the partial contrast stretching method is regarded as the best technique among all contrast stretching techniques that helps to improve quality of image [6].

3.2   Image Segmentation

An image is a manner of transferring information and it contains lots of useful information. Understanding the image and extracting information from the image to carry out application works is a most important step of image processing technology. This important step of extracting information is known as image segmentation [7, 8]. Otsu image segmentation method gives the better results as compare to the other segmentation method [9].

3.2.1 Otsu Segmentation

Segmentation divides an image into two regions [10]. The Otsu algorithm of image segmentation has been worked on noisy as well as without noisy image database.

3.3 Feature Extraction

For the extraction of features the prominent features of the scale image are area, solidity and perimeter. The features are plays a vital role in the procedure of classification. The detail features of the each image such as area, perimeter, solidity, orientation, eccentricity, centroid, entropy and energy are caring the prominent information.

Shape, color and texture are important fundamental primitives in human visual perceptions. In this section for extracting important features with distinctive texture, color and shape are discussed. The possibility of extracting prominent visual features like color, shape and texture from images without user assistance is focused. Shape features are very useful in many image databases and pattern matching applications.

3.4 Classification

For the classification the artificial neural network, support vector machine and quadratic discrimitive analysis have been a best choice for the researcher. The working structure of artificial neural network is describes in Fig. 5.

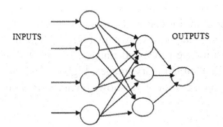

Fig. 5. Structure of artificial neural network

QDA is not really that much different from LDA except that you assume that the covariance matrix can be different for each class. This quadratic discriminate function is very much like the linear discriminate function except that because Σk, the covariance matrix, is not identical, you cannot throw away the quadratic terms [12].

3.5 Maximally Stable Extremely Regions (MSER)

The analysis of the proposed system includes an assessment of all possible errors and mean square error (MSE) good idea of the efficiency for verification [11]. The accuracy is calculated on the basis of given formula.

Accuracy = 100 − Error Rate

4 Experimental Analysis

For this experiment we acquired the more than 200 microscopic images from Government Medical College, Aurangabad. The graphical representation of sample Leukaemia Image is shown in Fig. 6. All the images are cropped and converted into the binary images. The features are collected from the Leukaemia and normal image, both for training and testing based on the border clearing.

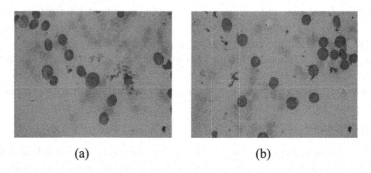

(a)   (b)

Fig. 6. Sample Leukaemia images collected from blood smear database

The pre-processing of the image has done using histogram method. The pre-processing stage is important for clarify the image sample. The graphical representation of normal pre-processed images is shown in Fig. 7. The Fig. 8 shows the graphical representation of leukemia pre-processed images. Figure 9 shows normal binary images. Figure 10 shows Leukaemia binary images. Figure 11 shows binary complemented normal images without noise. Figure 12 shows binary complemented leukemia images without noise.

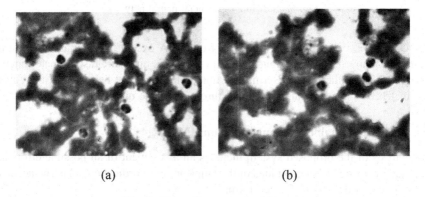

(a)   (b)

Fig. 7. Normal pre-processed images

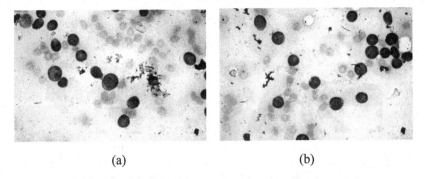

(a)   (b)

Fig. 8. Leukemic pre-processed images

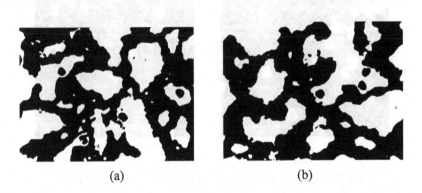

(a)   (b)

Fig. 9. Binary normal images

(a)   (b)

Fig. 10. Binary Leukemia images

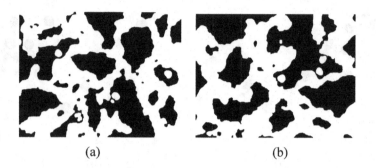

(a)   (b)

Fig. 11. Binary complemented normal images without noise

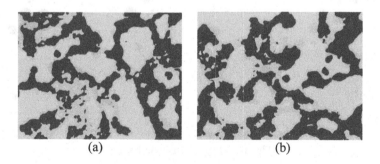

(a)   (b)

Fig. 12. Binary complemented Leukemia images without noise

For the segmentation of the pre-processed images, we are targeted the Otsu segmentation image. The graphical representation of normal images showed in Fig. 13 and leukemia images shown in Fig. 14.

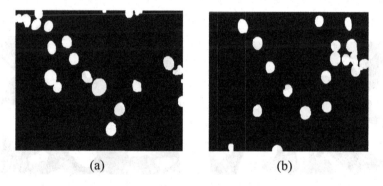

(a)   (b)

Fig. 13. Otsu image segmentation for normal images

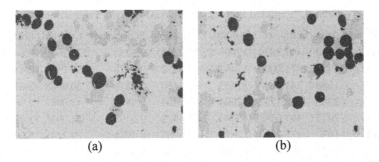

(a)   (b)

Fig. 14. Otsu image segmentation for Leukemia images

For the feature extraction we have extracted the 07 features namely Area, Perimeter, Solidity, Orientation, Eccentricity, Centroid and Entropy. The extracted features of normal images are shown in Table 1. The leukaemia image features are described in Table 2.

Table 1. Extracted features of normal blood smear image sample

Slide no.	Area	Perimeter	Solidity	Orientation	Eccentricity	Centroid	Entropy
1.JPG	535	87.4975	0.9727	−72.7998	0.6311	20.2467	0.9123
2.JPG	602	88.6690	0.9869	35.7242	0.5446	16.6827	0.9844
3.JPG	598	90.3259	0.9868	89.9617	0.3198	19.5635	0.9465
4.JPG	467	78.4264	0.9811	55.1041	0.3572	17.0086	0.9516
5.JPG	631	91.4975	0.9829	−53.5102	0.5494	20.1569	0.9735
6.JPG	603	90.1838	0.9742	1.3448	0.5456	20.4527	0.9803
7.JPG	487	81.0122	0.9722	47.5111	0.5252	20.6012	0.9153
8.JPG	593	90.0833	0.9690	−34.2071	0.5514	18.0742	0.9878
9.JPG	551	88.0833	0.9650	−79.4979	0.5137	19.9546	0.9660
10.JPG	622	91.4975	0.9765	87.7943	0.4087	21.4678	0.9437
11.JPG	487	81.0122	0.9663	44.7891	0.3432	18.5133	0.9308
12.JPG	608	88.7696	0.9886	4.9046	0.5799	18.7878	0.9975
13.JPG	646	92.3259	0.9833	9.9120	0.2311	21.6269	0.9812
14.JPG	569	94.5685	0.9595	−30.9659	0.8292	17.6538	0.9611
15.JPG	553	87.2548	0.9634	26.0117	0.6096	20.7830	0.9473
16.JPG	538	91.4975	0.9624	45.2362	0.7931	19.3011	0.9158
17.JPG	622	93.4975	0.9584	68.4120	0.5233	18.0113	0.9759
18.JPG	468	79.4975	0.9730	−46.3289	0.5552	21.9658	0.8813
19.JPG	434	79.0122	0.9414	−77.8204	0.6851	15.9654	0.9571
20.JPG	526	111.6396	0.8738	−57.7581	0.6328	22.1597	0.9681

Table 2. Extracted features of Leukemia effected image dataset

Slide no.	Area	Perimeter	Solidity	Orientation	Eccentricity	Centroid	Entropy
1.JPG	3130	491.5879	0.7995	−33.2393	0.3254	37.1042	2.6430
2.JPG	1471	1471.0000	0.7444	−57.3612	0.3776	32.2549	2.4702
3.JPG	1688	341.4630	0.7355	61.3460	0.5473	30.9988	3.6745
4.JPG	2383	452.1737	0.7604	−35.3203	0.8542	42.0982	2.9098
5.JPG	2073	407.6468	0.7446	−77.4322	0.6498	31.0926	3.4745
6.JPG	1630	276.2082	0.7814	−0.5982	0.4986	29.2245	2.9242
7.JPG	2024	354.0904	0.7764	19.6594	0.5523	38.3207	3.0914
8.JPG	1528	320.5929	0.7450	27.5361	0.7296	29.8154	2.9750
9.JPG	1301	236.8356	0.7781	−15.7476	0.6194	29.7832	2.3236
10.JPG	1800	334.6346	0.7755	41.1787	0.5892	25.8817	3.8853
11.JPG	808	177.4386	0.8064	35.6037	0.2205	21.7884	2.6628
12.JPG	1201	227.0366	0.8066	35.7461	0.6851	28.2540	2.7478
13.JPG	1961	357.5046	0.7745	50.6080	0.2953	24.6859	3.4123
14.JPG	965	254.3503	0.7510	−0.1308	0.4712	20.2819	3.2137
15.JPG	1460	386.9605	0.7419	−59.5357	0.5361	26.9788	3.3402
16.JPG	1050	253.8234	0.8159	73.5678	0.6842	24.1124	2.7250
17.JPG	2039	332.3919	0.7583	−25.9293	0.7465	36.6999	3.0419
18.JPG	1718	337.8478	0.8085	−74.6390	0.3315	23.9144	3.7343
19.JPG	1621	273.8061	0.7865	4.2427	0.6386	27.2702	3.1294
20.JPG	1199	290.1493	0.7333	−8.3777	0.4147	22.6697	4.0511

The classification of the proposed system is done using the Artificial Neural Network (ANN), Support Vector Machine (SVM) and Quadratic Discrimitive Analysis (QDA). The graphical representation of extracted performance results is shown in Fig. 15. The training state, ROC curve, confusion matrix of the neural network graphically showed in Figs. 16, 17 and 18.

The validation and testing are varies as per the variation in the hidden layer. The performance of the neural network with respective to different hidden layer is described in Table 3.

Table 3. Performance of neural network with respective to hidden layer

Sr.no	Hidden layer	Error	Accuracy
1	03	2.08	97.92
2	05	1.91	98.09
3	10	1.086	98.91
4	15	0.0364	99.96
5	20	0.0106	99.98
Average performance		1.0246	98.97

The support vector machine based classifier works for the two supportive groups such as normal and leukaemia image dataset. The graphical representation of support vector machine based classifier is shown in Fig. 19. Figure 20 represent the graphical representation of QDA based outcome results (Figs. 16, 17, 18, 19 and 20).

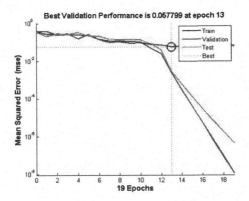

Fig. 15. Performance of the proposed system using neural network.

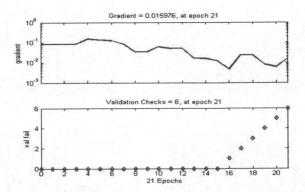

Fig. 16. Training state of the neural network for the proposed system

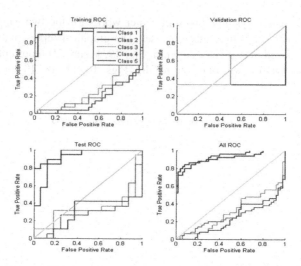

Fig. 17. ROC curve of extracted outcome from proposed system using neural network

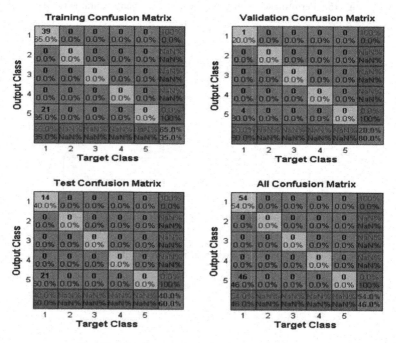

Fig. 18. Confusion matrix for training and testing

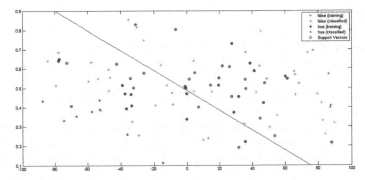

Fig. 19. Performance of proposed system using Support Vector Machine (SVM)

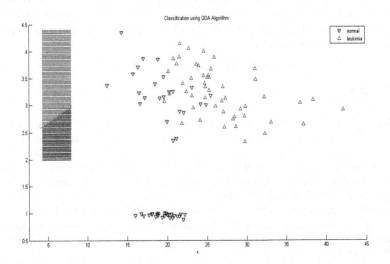

Fig. 20. Performance of proposed system using QDA technique.

The comparative performance of the proposed system based on Artificial Neural Network, Support Vector Machine and QDA is shown in Table 4.

Table 4. The comparative performance of the proposed system

Sr.no	Classifier	Error rate (%)	Accuracy (%)
1	Neural network	1.0246	98.97
2	Support vector machine	0.6500	99.35
3	QDA	0.300	99.70

5 Conclusion

For the design and development of Automatic Leukemia identification system, we are tested experiment on 200 samples of Leukemia and normal microscopic smear images. In this research paper, we highlighted the results of 10 test images. For the pre-processing of the database binarization, histogram and edge detection techniques are used. The pre-processed images are segmented using the Otsu image segmentation. The classification has been done using Artificial Neural Network (ANN), Support Vector Machine (SVM) and Quadratic Discrimitive Analysis (QDA). In the neural network the 60% dataset has been passed for the training, 35% towards the testing and remaining 05% is used for the validation. The SVM and QDA classify the dataset for the two groups such as normal and leukaemia. The classification is done on the extracted 08 features of each image. The performance of the neural network is achieving 98.97% with 1.0246 error rate. The support vector machine is shows the 99.35% accuracy with 0.6500 error rate. The QDA classification reported the 99.70% accuracy with 0.300% error rate. From the reported accuracy the QDA and support vector machine proved as dominant as the neural network.

References

1. Virmani, J., Kumar, V., Kalra, N., Khandelwal, N.: A rapid approach for prediction of liver cirrhosis based on first order statistics. In: Proceedings of the IEEE International Conference on Multimedia, Signal Processing and Communication Technologies, IMPACT-2011 (2011)
2. Mohapatra, S., Patra, D., Satpathi, S.: Image analysis of blood microscopic images for Leukemia detection. In: International Conference on Industrial Electronics, Control and Robotics, pp. 215–219. IEEE (2010)
3. National Cancer Institute. https://seer.cancer.gov/statfacts/html/leuks.html
4. Virmani, J., Kumar, V., Kalra, N., Khandelwal, N.: Characterization of primary and secondary malignant liver lesions from B-mode ultrasound. J. Digit. Imaging 26(6), 1058 –1070 (2013)
5. Salihah, A.A., Mashor, M.Y., Harun, N.H., Rosline, H.: Colour image enhancement techniques for acute Leukemia blood cell morphological Features, pp. 3677–3682. IEEE (2010)
6. Rajeswari, R., Ramesh, N.: Contrast stretching enhancement techniques for acute leukemia images. Int. J. Publ. Probl. Appl. Eng. Res. Pap. 4(1), 190–194 (2013)
7. Haralick, R.M., Shapiro, L.G.: Image segmentation techniques [J]. Comput. Vis. Graph. Image Process. 29(1), 100–132 (1985)
8. Fan, W.: Color image segmentation algorithm based on region growth [J]. JisuanjiGongcheng/Comput. Eng. 36(13) (2010)
9. Kang, W.X., Yang, Q.Q., Liang, R.P.: The comparative research on image segmentation algorithms. In: IEEE Conference on ETCS, pp. 703–707 (2009)
10. Gonzalez, R.C., Woods, R.E.: Digital Image Processing, 2nd edn. Publishing House of Electronics Industry, Beijing (2007)
11. Niknejad, M., Mirzaei, V., Heydari, M.: Comparing different classifications of satellite imagery in forest mapping. Int. Res. J. Appl. Basic Sci. 8(7), 1407–1415 (2014)
12. QDA. https://newonlinecourses.science.psu.edu/stat857/node/80/

Multiple Faults Diagnosis of Induction Motor Using Artificial Neural Network

Rajvardhan Jigyasu[✉], Lini Mathew, and Amandeep Sharma

Electrical Engineering Department, National Institute of Technical Teachers
Training and Research, Sector 26, Chandigarh 160019, India
rajvardhan1991@gmail.com,
engineer.amandeep@gmail.com, lenimathew@yahoo.com

Abstract. This paper presents multiple fault diagnosis and detection using artificial neural feed forward network. In this work analysis is done on induction motor, as these motor are widely used in industries because of their robustness, easy maintenance etc. The current and vibration responses of healthy motor, motor with bearing, rotor and stator defects are analysed. The feature extraction process is done in time domain only. From the results it is cleared that among various transfer functions in ANN the trainlm performs best and traingdm performs worst for fault detection.

Keywords: Induction motor · Fault detection · Fault diagnosis
Artificial intelligence · ANN · Transfer functions · Time domain analysis

1 Introduction

Early prediction of faults in induction motor is very important because it reduces the maintenance cost which is very important during the production in order to maintain the process economical. Induction motor used in industries due to simple construction, high efficiency, robustness, low cost and constant speed operation. Although induction motors are highly reliable, their failure probability cannot be ruled out. Induction motors (IMs) are subject to thermal and mechanical stresses, due to which they may develop defects such as broken rotor bar, bearing, stator winding short circuit etc. [1, 2]. Thus, these motors require continuous monitoring and timely maintenance. An incipient stage fault, if left unattended may build up into a major fault causing abrupt breakdown of motor and interruption in manufacture process. To avoid such failures continuous monitoring of three phase induction motors is necessary. Various major motor related faults such as bearing faults, broken rotor bars, eccentricity, stator faults, etc., have been investigated by various investigators in the past [3, 4]. A typical condition monitoring process involves monitoring of motor parameters to estimate the condition of operating motor. These motor parameters could be vibration, current, voltage, acoustic noise and temperature etc. [3, 5–7].

Among the widely used methods of fault diagnosis the motor current signature analysis (MCSA) [8] and vibration based analysis [9] are best, because of their non invasiveness, low cost and ability to detect most of the motor related faults. MCSA can be applied for online diagnosis of motor faults, i.e. the motor parameters are acquired

© Springer Nature Singapore Pte Ltd. 2019
A. K. Luhach et al. (Eds.): ICAICR 2018, CCIS 955, pp. 701–710, 2019.
https://doi.org/10.1007/978-981-13-3140-4_63

from the operating motor. Monitoring is usually done by checking the absolute limits of motor parameters or by computing features of the signal either in time, frequency or time-frequency domain. These computed features are than fed to some pretrained classifiers such as artificial neural networks (ANN) [10], K-nearest neighbor (KNN) [11], support vector machine (SVM) [12], decision trees [13], random forest [14] and linear discriminant analysis classifiers [15] etc. to estimate the type and severity of faults.

Most frequently used time-domain features include the analysis of RMS value, kurtosis, crest factor, mean and variance etc. Most commonly used time-domain method is Empirical mode decomposition (EMD) which is used for feature extraction. In [16], the authors proposed a two-step method for detection of defect in plastic bearings, firstly it extracts frequency and time domain features by envelope analysis and EMD; secondly the frequency and time domain features are utilized to identify bearing defect and build K-NN classifier to identify different types of bearing faults. Palacios et al. in [17] proposed a method for evaluation of pattern classification methods for motors fault identification using the amplitudes of current signals in the time domain with the help of naive Bayes, k-NN, SVM and ANN as classification techniques.

In this paper, the classification of induction motor faults, viz. bearing faults, eccentricity, stator and broken rotor bar faults with different severity levels is carried out using ANN. The classification is made based on power of current signal acquire from a single phase of a 0.5 hp, 3-phase induction motor and vibration signal using single axis accelerometer. Features are extracted and given to ANN classifier for finding the classification accuracy using different ANN transfer functions.

2   Fault Diagnosis Using ANN

Human brain works as a parallel computer which actually computes with more speed than the most powerful computers in existence today. It performs much complex computations due to its capability to organize its structural constituents called neurons. Human beings take decisions or develop their behaviour based on their past incidents. ANN is analogues to simple biological neural units called neurons. ANN comprises of neurons which are organised as input, hidden and output layers, where all neurons in the three layers have a weighted interconnection to neurons in succeeding layer. Nodes present in the hidden and output layer contains processing units generally called as artificial neurons. ANN consists of multilayer or three dimensional designs, where the signal passes through from input layer towards the output layer neurons. ANNs have ability to learn and model non-linear and complex relationships; it can generalize the model and predict on unseen data, many studies have shown that ANNs can better model heteroskedasticity.

Training is provided to the neural network so that it can identify various states of the system under test. The neurons present in the input layer are the same as number of input features. It is believed that neural networks having only two layers of weights and having sigmoid activation function for hidden layer nodes can approximate any design boundary to arbitrary accuracy [18]. The suggested methodology in [19] will reduce the risk of misalignment fault and can be very useful for on-line monitoring the technique used was Multi-scale Entropy and Artificial Neural Network. The success of the proposed misalignment detection methodology is evident in two ways; first, it requires only one sensor, and second, it does not require extensive computation in frequency domain. In [20], diagnosis of the three-phase induction motor using thermal imaging has been done using the Nearest Neighbour, K-means and Back propagation Neural Network. In [21], blade faults diagnosis has been done using ANN technique where the performance of the ANN trained with statistical features extracted from the operating frequency achieved the highest classification accuracy of 88.43%.

For classification purpose in this paper Feed-forward network is trained with different back propagation training algorithms. Single layer network is utilized, in which number of hidden layer is find out using trial and error method. The numbers of hidden layer neurons are bit by bit expanded in ventures in order to achieve the required classification accuracy and quick convergence. The network is trained and tested using various training algorithm and it is practical that LM algorithm converges more quickly. Tansigmoid transfer function (TANSIG) and linear (PURELIN) activation function are used for hidden layer and output layer neurons correspondingly. Initially the network weights and biases are selected haphazardly. Stopping criteria for training procedure is taken as attainment of any one criteria, i.e. Mean Square Error (MSE) =10-10, gradient =10-10 or 1000 epochs.

3 Experimental Setup

The experimental setup consisted of a 0.5 hp induction motor, 3-phase, and 4 poles, connected to mechanical load using belt pulley arrangement. A single axis accelerometer of sensitivity 100 mV/g was mounted on motor body close to the drive end bearing is used for acquiring vibration signals. Measurements from motor were obtained using data acquisition system comprising of NI-cDAQ-9178 and NI-9234, 9227, 9244 modules.

The data was acquired from motor for different condition with motor running at 80% of rated load. Sampling of data is taken at the rate of 12,800 samples per second for 96,000 samples which is repeated for 5 times nor overlapped. 11 time domain features were computed for each reiteration for different fault conditions: (i) Healthy, (ii) Inner race defect, (iii) Outer race defect, (iv) BRB, (v) eccentricity, (vi) stator. The obtained features were normalized to improve the classification accuracy and discriminate any bias. Thus, 40 sets of eleven normalized features were gotten for each fault condition, out of which 28 sets are chosen arbitrarily to train the system, 8 sets were utilized for testing and 4 for validation.

Training and Testing were performed for different number of hidden layers using different transfer functions such as traingdm, trainlm, trainbfg, trainrp, trainscg, traincgb, traincgf, traincgp, trainoss, traingdx and traingda to find out optimal solution. Output accuracy was considered as optimization criteria because goal is the fault detection.

4 Features Extraction

Feature selection is an important aspect, which has a significant importance in pattern recognition problems. To diagnose faults time domain features were extracted from current and vibration data. The time domain current and vibration signal were split into subsections before feature extraction. The extracted time domain features include root-mean-square (RMS), variance (VAR), kurtosis (KUR), peak value (PV), skewness (SKW), median (MED), crest factor (CF), margin factor (MF), impulse factor (IF), shape (SH) and median range (MR). The mathematical expression for the same is given as under (where, N = total number of observations):

$$\text{RMS} = \sqrt{\frac{1}{N} \sum_{i=1}^{N} (x_i)^2} \tag{1}$$

$$\text{Mean} = \frac{1}{N} \sum_{i=1}^{N} x_i \tag{2}$$

$$\text{Variance} = \frac{1}{N} \sum_{i=1}^{N} (x_i - \bar{x})^2 \tag{3}$$

$$\text{Skewness} = \frac{E(x - \mu)^3}{\sigma^3} \tag{4}$$

$$\text{Kurtosis} = \frac{\sum_{i=1}^{N} (x_i - \bar{x})^4}{(\text{RMS value})^4} \tag{5}$$

$$\text{Crest\_factor} = \frac{\text{Peak magnitude}}{\text{RMS}} \tag{6}$$

$$\text{Impulse factor} = \frac{\max(x)_{\text{absolute}}}{\text{mean}(x)_{\text{absolute}}} \tag{7}$$

$$\text{Shape factor} = \frac{\text{RMS}}{\text{mean}(x)_{\text{absolute}}} \tag{8}$$

$$\text{Median} = \frac{(n+1)}{2} \tag{9}$$

$$\text{Range} = \max(x) - \min(x) \tag{10}$$

$$\text{Margin factor} = \frac{\max(x)_{\text{absolute}}}{\text{mean}\left(\sqrt{x_{\text{absolute}}}\right)^2} \tag{11}$$

where μ is the mean of x, σ is the standard deviation of x, and $E(t)$ represents the expected value of the quantity t, x_{rms}, x_{abs} are root mean square value and absolute value respectively.

5   Results and Discussions

Induction motor is run at around 80% loading. From acquired data parameters are fetched and after normalization applied to the ANN for finding accuracy. The following results were obtained after analysis of current and vibration signatures. For accessing the performance of neural network, the training was performed using and without using validation. The training of neural network is performed with different number of hidden layer neurons, with and without validation data. For with validation cases, 10% data is selected for validation, 20% for testing, while 70% data is used for training. For training with no validation, training data is taken as 75% and testing data is 25% of the total training samples. The average accuracies are obtained for classification using 'patternnet' neural network having different number (2, 4, 6..16) of hidden layer neurons.

5.1   Using Current Signatures

Current signal is acquired using DAQ acquisition system and extracted features are undergone for analysis and following results were found.

5.1.1   No Validation
The following results are obtained for no validation case (Tables 1, 2, 3 and 4).

Table 1. Accuracy obtained for different transfer function used in analysis using different number of processing elements without validation.

Processing elements	Trainscg	Trainbfg	Traincgb	Traincgf	Traincgp	Traingda	Traingdx	Trainlm	Trainoss	Trainrp
2	99.2	99.2	90.8	98.8	98.8	84.2	80.8	99.2	94.6	99.2
4	99.2	96.7	98.8	99.6	98.3	97.1	97.1	97.9	99.6	98.3
6	97.5	95.4	97.9	97.1	99.2	97.1	99.2	99.6	98.3	97.1
8	98.8	95.4	99.6	96.3	99.6	96.3	97.5	98.8	98.8	97.9
10	97.9	95.8	99.6	99.2	97.9	98.3	98.3	99.6	97.5	97.9
12	99.2	92.5	99.8	97.9	97.5	98.3	97.1	98.8	97.5	97.1
14	98.8	94.2	98.8	98.8	99.6	97.5	98.8	99.6	98.3	98.8
16	99.6	96.3	97.1	100	97.6	98.3	99.2	97.9	99.2	95.8
Average	98.7	95.6	97.8	98.4	98.5	95.8	96	98.9	97.9	97.7

Among all the training functions trainscg, traincgf, traincgp and trainlm performed the best for no validation case. Traingdm however performed poorly with an average accuracy of about 22%, and thus not included in the table. Number of processing elements in hidden layer has very little effect on network performance. An accuracy of 100% is achieved using traincgf with 16 processing elements.

Table 2. Accuracy obtained for different transfer function used in analysis using different number of processing elements with validation.

Processing elements	Trainscg	Trainbfg	Traincgb	Traincgf	Traincgp	Traingda	Traingdx	Trainlm	Trainoss	Trainrp
2	40.8	17.5	68.8	22.1	70	50	75	100	34.2	59.6
4	93.3	81.7	82.5	70.4	89.6	89.2	89.2	98.8	81.7	94.2
6	92.1	42.1	92.1	72.5	97.1	96	97.5	99.2	93.3	96.3
8	95	38.8	92.1	89.6	98.3	91.7	97.5	99.6	92.1	94.6
10	97.5	95.4	91.3	93.3	96.3	96.7	98.3	99.2	86.3	95.4
12	99.2	90	96.7	95	94.6	97.5	97.5	99.2	91.3	88.8
14	96.3	93.3	95	97.5	94	97.1	98.8	98.3	89.6	95.8
16	97.9	75	98.8	97.5	94.2	95.4	100	99.2	90.8	97.5
Average	89.0	66.7	89.6	79.7	91.7	89.2	94.22	99.1	82.4	90.2

Table 3. Accuracy obtained for different transfer function used in analysis using different number of processing elements without validation.

Processing elements	Trainscg	Trainbfg	Traincgb	Traincgf	Traincgp	Traingda	Traingdx	Trainlm	Trainoss	Trainrp
2	73.3	64.2	75.8	80.8	82.1	43.3	47.9	84.6	55.8	57.1
4	87.1	80	86.7	83.8	93.8	70.8	73.8	95	85	67.9
6	94.6	83.8	96.7	87.5	95.8	83.4	83.8	95.4	94.2	88.8
8	95.8	88.9	93.3	93.8	95	87.9	91.7	92.5	91.7	94.6
10	93.8	89.6	92.9	95	93.8	92.1	94.6	93.8	92.5	92.9
12	94.6	92.9	93.4	95	92.9	93.3	95	94.4	94.6	94.2
14	94.2	92.5	94.2	94.2	94.6	94.6	95.4	93.3	92.1	91.7
16	94.6	92.1	96.6	95	94.2	95.8	95	94.6	93.8	94.6
Average	91	85.5	91.2	90.6	92.7	82.6	84.65	92.9	87.4	85.2

Table 4. Accuracy obtained for different transfer function used in analysis using different number of processing elements with validation.

Processing elements	Trainscg	Trainbfg	Traincgb	Traincgf	Traincgp	Traingda	Traingdx	Trainlm	Trainoss	Trainrp
2	49.2	25.8	27.8	30	45.4	39.6	29.2	87.1	30	39.2
4	60	48	67.5	58.3	61.3	55.8	60	80.8	45	65
6	65.4	52.4	65	61.7	70.4	56.3	61	86.3	46.3	68.8
8	80.8	58.8	71.7	64	76.7	70.4	54.2	87.5	60	75
10	65	73.8	66.6	72.3	78	72.1	79	92.5	70	81.3
12	75.4	40	80.8	70.4	77.6	69	88.3	86.7	81.3	83.4
14	69.2	62.1	80	68.8	75	85	83.8	92.5	84.4	84.2
16	82.1	75.8	81.7	68.3	76.7	76	84.6	90	76.6	78
Average	68.3	54.5	67.6	61.7	70.1	65.5	67.5	87.9	61.7	71.8

5.1.2 With Validation

The following results are obtained for with validation case.

Validation protects against over fitting. Trainlm performs the best with an average accuracy of 99.1875% for different number of processing elements. For trainlm, it is also seen that the classification accuracy is independent of number of hidden layer neurons, i.e. the accuracy is almost constant for varying processing elements number. However for other training functions the accuracy improves with increasing number network size.

5.1.3 Average Accuracy

After combining both the results i.e with and without validation the following average accuracy plot we obtained which is shown below.

Figure 1 shows the average accuracies obtained using different training functions for the time domain features. The training of neural network was performed with different number of hidden layer neurons, with and without validation data. For with validation case, 10% data was selected for validation, while 70% data was used for training and 20% for testing. For training with no validation, training data is taken as 75% and testing data is 25% of the total training samples.

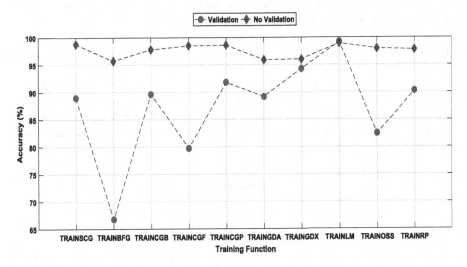

Fig. 1. Average accuracies obtained for training functions for different number of processing elements.

The average accuracies are obtained for classification using 'patternnet' neural network having different number (2, 4, 6..16) of hidden layer neurons. It is seen that the 'trainlm' performs best for both cases, i.e. training process without any validation data and with 10% validation.

5.2 Using Vibration Signatures

Vibration signal is acquired using DAQ acquisition system and extracted features are undergone for analysis and following results are found.

5.2.1 No Validation

The following results are obtained for no validation case.

In no validation case for vibration based diagnosis trainlm again showed highest percentage average accuracy of 92.95% followed by traincgp with 92.775% average accuracy. Trainbfg, traingda, traingdx, trainoss and trainrp showed average accuracy percentage below 90%, thus they are not able to classify the fault patterns properly in training data. In this case again the traingdm performed worst with average percentage accuracy of 19.2%..

5.2.2 With Validation

The following results are obtained for with validation case.

For with validation case 70% samples of total data were used for training, 10% for validation and 20% were used for testing the neural network. For training with validation the trainlm performed best with average percentage accuracy of 87.925%. Further all other training methods gave unsatisfactory results.

5.2.3 Average Accuracy

After combining both the results i.e with and without validation the following average accuracy plot we obtained which is shown below.

Figure 2 shows the average accuracies obtained using vibration signatures with different training functions for the time domain features. The training of neural network was performed with different number of hidden layer neurons, with and without validation data. For validation case 10% data was selected for validation. The average accuracies were obtained for classification using 'patternnet' neural network having different number (2, 4, 6..16) of hidden layer neurons. Again it was seen that the 'trainlm' performs best for both cases, i.e. training process without any validation data and with 10% validation.

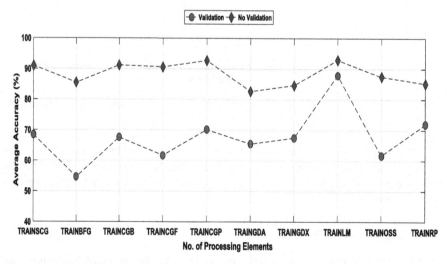

Fig. 2. Average accuracies obtained for training functions for different number of processing elements.

6 Conclusion

Condition monitoring and diagnosis based on stator current and vibration are the most widely used and established methods. Various signal processing and fault diagnosis techniques have been developed over the past few decades utilizing vibration and current signatures. In this paper a comparison of current and vibration based diagnosis using artificial neural networks for various types of motor faults such as bearing, stator, rotor and eccentricity is performed. Different transfer functions are used to evaluate the performance of neural network with different number of hidden layer neurons. It is found that the Trainlm performed best in all the cases i.e. current features, vibration features with validation and without validation and traingdm performed worst because of that no included in table. Also the current time domain analysis found better than the vibration time domain analysis. From the analysis it is found that as the number of iterations are increased the percentage accuracy increases, also the average accuracy of no validation case is much higher than the validation case in this analysis.

References

1. Motor Reliability Working Group: Report of large motor reliability survey of industrial and commercial installations, Part I. IEEE Trans. Ind. Appl. **1**(4), 865–872 (1985)
2. Lu, B., Gungor, V.C.: Online and remote motor energy monitoring and fault diagnostics using wireless sensor networks. IEEE Trans. Ind. Electron. **56**(11), 4651–4659 (2009)
3. Benbouzid, M.E.H.: A review of induction motors signature analysis as a medium for faults detection. IEEE Trans. Ind. Electron. **47**(5), 984–993 (2000)
4. Zhongming, Y., Bin, W.: A review on induction motor online fault diagnosis. In: 2000 Proceedings of the Third International Power Electronics and Motion Control Conference, IPEMC 2000, vol. 3, pp. 1353–1358. IEEE (2000)
5. Nandi, S., Toliyat, H.A., Li, X.: Condition monitoring and fault diagnosis of electrical motors—A review. IEEE Trans. Energy Convers. **20**(4), 719–729 (2005)
6. Vas, P.: Artificial-Intelligence-Based Electrical Machines and Drives: Application of Fuzzy, Neural, Fuzzy-Neural, and Genetic-Algorithm-Based Techniques, vol. 45. Oxford University Press (1999)
7. Kliman, G.B., Stein, J.: Induction motor fault detection via passive current monitoring-A brief survey. In: Proceedings of 44th Meeting of the Mechanical Failures Prevention Group, pp. 49–65 (1990)
8. Jung, J.H., Lee, J.J., Kwon, B.H.: Online diagnosis of induction motors using MCSA. IEEE Trans. Ind. Electron. **53**(6), 1842–1852 (2006)
9. Li, B., Chow, M.Y., Tipsuwan, Y., Hung, J.C.: Neural-network-based motor rolling bearing fault diagnosis. IEEE Trans. Ind. Electron. **47**(5), 1060–1069 (2000)
10. Huang, X., Habetler, T.G., Harley, R.G.: Detection of rotor eccentricity faults in a closed-loop drive-connected induction motor using an artificial neural network. IEEE Trans. Power Electron. **22**(4), 1552–1559 (2007)
11. Casimir, R., Boutleux, E., Clerc, G., Yahoui, A.: The use of features selection and nearest neighbors rule for faults diagnostic in induction motors. Eng. Appl. Artif. Intell. **19**(2), 169–177 (2006)
12. Konar, P., Chattopadhyay, P.: Bearing fault detection of induction motor using wavelet and Support Vector Machines (SVMs). Appl. Soft Comput. **11**(6), 4203–4211 (2011)

13. Yang, B.S., Oh, M.S., Tan, A.C.C.: Fault diagnosis of induction motor based on decision trees and adaptive neuro-fuzzy inference. Expert Syst. Appl. **36**(2), 1840–1849 (2009)
14. Patel, R.K., Giri, V.K.: Feature selection and classification of mechanical fault of an induction motor using random forest classifier. Perspect. Sci. **8**, 334–337 (2016)
15. Widodo, A., Yang, B.S., Han, T.: Combination of independent component analysis and support vector machines for intelligent faults diagnosis of induction motors. Expert Syst. Appl. **32**(2), 299–312 (2007)
16. He, D., Li, R., Zhu, J.: Plastic bearing fault diagnosis based on a two-step data mining approach. IEEE Trans. Ind. Electron. **60**(8), 3429–3440 (2013)
17. Palácios, R.H.C., da Silva, I.N., Goedtel, A., Godoy, W.F.: A comprehensive evaluation of intelligent classifiers for fault identification in three-phase induction motors. Electr. Power Syst. Res. **127**, 249–258 (2015)
18. Bishop, C., Bishop, C.M.: Neural Networks for Pattern Recognition. Oxford University Press, Cambridge (1995)
19. Verma, A.K., Sarangi, S., Kolekar, M.: Misalignment faults detection in an induction motor based on multi-scale entropy and artificial neural network. Electr. Power Compon. Syst. **44**(8), 916–927 (2016)
20. Moghadasian, M., Shakouhi, S.M., Moosavi, S.S.: Induction motor fault diagnosis using ANFIS based on vibration signal spectrum analysis. In: 2017 3rd International Conference on Frontiers of Signal Processing (ICFSP), pp. 105–108. IEEE (2017)
21. Ngui, W.K., Leong, M.S., Shapiai, M.I., Lim, M.H.: Blade fault diagnosis using artificial neural network. Int. J. Appl. Eng. Res. **12**(4), 519–526 (2017)

Duplication Based Performance Effective Scheduling

Monika Sharma[✉] and Raj Kumari

UIET, Panjab University, Chandigarh, India
kashyap.monika.09@gmail.com, rajkumari@pu.ac.in

Abstract. In cloud computing (CC), mainly list scheduling algorithms are widely used in task scheduling. The existing list scheduling algorithms are generally not efficient in reducing overall execution time (makespan). So in this paper, we have presented a list scheduling algorithm namely, Performance Effective Task Scheduling (PETS) which is merged with the task duplication method named as Duplication based Performance Effective Scheduling (DPES). Most of the duplication algorithms mainly focus on obtaining high performance by minimizing the makespan without reviewing the energy consumed by an application. But DPES algorithm not only reduces the makespan but also examines the energy consumption. Duplication strategy is used in which the parent tasks have been replicated in order to minimize the makespan while to lower the energy consumption, Dynamic Voltage and Frequency Scaling (DVFS) technique has been applied. In this paper, the DPES algorithm is compared with the PETS algorithm on various performance metrics and DPES algorithm proves to be better in each metrics comparison.

Keywords: Task scheduling · List scheduling · Task duplication DVFS

1 Introduction

Cloud Computing is an emerging computing technology that preserves data and applications with the use of the internet and central remote servers. It helps in configuring and customizing the applications efficiently. CC has many advantages such as high processing speed, better performance, scalability, flexibility, low service cost, fast accessibility of resources and many more [1, 2, 3]. Apart from many advantages, it also faces many challenges like security [4, 5], reliability [2], resource allocation [6], scheduling [7] etc. Task scheduling is one of the major challenges. Task scheduling is the technique to schedule the tasks among different processors to provide the optimal results without violating the time deadline. In the task scheduling phase, an application is considered as a series of tasks. Multiple tasks are being processed in certain sequence and scheduling can be termed as a technique to identify the best mapping of the tasks to the available set of resources in order to obtain the efficient and optimal results. Task scheduling helps to utilize the available resources in better way as well as it provides quality of service. Task scheduling is an issue in acquiring high performance in heterogeneous frameworks. Task scheduling in heterogeneous frameworks is a NP-

© Springer Nature Singapore Pte Ltd. 2019
A. K. Luhach et al. (Eds.): ICAICR 2018, CCIS 955, pp. 711–724, 2019.
https://doi.org/10.1007/978-981-13-3140-4_64

problem; consequently a few heuristic methodologies were proposed to explain it. These heuristics are sorted into a few classes namely list based, clustering and task duplication scheduling as shown in Fig. 1.

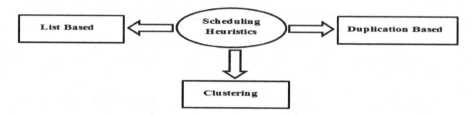

Fig. 1. Different types of static heuristic based scheduling

In the list scheduling technique, the task sequence should satisfy the precedence constraints and mostly the ranking is assigned to the tasks to process the task at each level. While in clustering based technique, the heavily communicating tasks are scheduled on the same processor regardless of the other processors available. During this there is balance maintained between parallelism and interprocess communication. In task duplication, one task may be processed on more than one processor so as to reduce the waiting time of its dependent tasks. If task scheduling algorithm is performed in a heterogeneous system where multiple processors are present and each processor take different time span to complete the same task, then complexity of the problem rises. Now a day, parallel computing systems proved to be more beneficial systems in order to gain the high processing speed and to execute the task in less time. The effectiveness of executing parallel applications on heterogeneous frameworks fundamentally relies upon the techniques used to schedule the tasks of a parallel application.

In our work, we combine the list scheduling algorithm with the task duplication scheduling in order to perform better with less energy consumption and reduced makespan. Initially, the duplication strategy is applied in which the parent tasks are being duplicated on the processors so as to get the better makespan. This proves to be useful technique as it minimizes the communication cost between the tasks. But, with the increase in duplications, it can results in high energy consumption by the processors during the dynamic time spans. To overcome this problem we applied the Dynamic Voltage and Frequency Scaling (DVFS) technique. This technique checks the dynamic and idle power consumption by each processor and ensures that the total energy consumed after duplication do not exceeds the threshold energy.

The rest of the paper is structured as follows: In Sect. 2, we discussed the related work, while Sect. 3 describes the application model and energy model. In Sect. 4, proposed algorithm has been explained and Sect. 5 presents a numeric example. In Sect. 6, the results are presented. Finally, Sect. 7 concludes the paper.

2 Related Work

The scheduling algorithms (the HEFT Algorithm and the CPOP Algorithm) for heterogeneous processors are discussed in [8, 9]. For the produced arbitrary task graphs, the HEFT algorithm beats alternate algorithms in all performance metrics, i.e., average schedule length ratio (SLR), speedup, and time-complexity. So also, the CPOP Algorithm is superior to or if nothing else is equivalent to according to the existing algorithms. The Communication Leveled DAG with Duplication (CLDD) algorithm for heterogeneous distributed computing systems (HeDCS) are proposed in [10]. In this algorithm, the tasks are prioritized by assigning rank to each of them. The CLDD algorithm additionally utilizes task duplication with low time complexity in order to limit the communication overhead. As indicated by the simulation results, it is noticed that the CLDD calculation is superior to ECTS, HEFT, CPOP algorithms in terms of time complexity, schedule length, speedup and efficiency. SHEFT scheduling algorithm was proposed in [11] so as to obtain high Scalability, minimised execution time. This algorithm scheduled the workflow elastically on a cloud environment. This SHEFT not only performs better than HEFT [9], but in addition to this it empowers resources to scale elastically during execution. A new scheduling algorithm has been proposed in [12] for heterogeneous distributed computing systems (HDCS) to improve scheduling execution. This algorithm is based on Critical Path Merge (CPM) method and task duplication strategy. The NDCP algorithm duplicates MP for VIT only. The simulation results demonstrated that the proposed NDCP algorithm outperforms over HCPT, PHTS, HEFT and CPOP algorithms. In [13], authors presented Heterogeneous Critical Task (HCT) scheduling algorithm that describe the critical task and idle time slot. This algorithm then duplicates the critical task to processors in idle time slot in order to minimize overall execution time. The Earliest Starting and Finishing time Duplication based (ESFD) algorithm in [14], has three-stages with a dynamic stage where priority is assigned to each task. Authors in [15], proposed an algorithm named Selective Duplication (SD) which is based on duplication technique that produces result without duplicating the redundant task that don't helps in increasing the overall performance. An algorithm named Heterogeneous Critical Parents with Fast Duplicator (HCPFD) is proposed [16]. The algorithm consists of two mechanisms: first is to select the task through a simple listing mechanism rather than classical prioritization phase of list-scheduling, and second is to assign a processor to each task based on task-duplication. In [17], authors proposed a new energy-aware scheduling algorithm called Energy Aware Scheduling by Minimizing Duplication (EAMD). This algorithm considers the energy consumption as well as the makespan of applications.

3 Models

3.1 Application Model

An application is supposed to be decomposed into multiple tasks and directed acyclic graph (DAG) is used to represent these tasks set. The DAG, $G = (N, E, P)$, where N is the set of n tasks to be processed and t_i is the time units required for computation to compute the n_i task. E is the set of edges indicating the precedence constraints between the tasks and Communication Cost ($C_{i,j}$) is the cost of transferring the data from task n_i to n_j, if both the tasks are scheduled on different processors. P is the set of p processors and $W_{i,j}$ is the processing time of task i on processor j. It is assumed that n_i is the parent task of n_j, and n_j cannot be executed until its parent task (n_i) is not executed completely. A task with no predecessors is called an entry task (n_{entry}), while the task with no successors is known to be exit task (n_{exit}). If there are multiple entry and exit task then these multiple tasks are connected to a dummy entry and exit task respectively. These dummy tasks will have the zero computation cost and zero communication cost. For simplicity, it is assumed that there is only one entry task and one exit task for each task graph.

$LST\_d(n_i, p_j)$ and $LCT\_d(n_i, p_j)$ denote the latest start time and latest completion time of a given task respectively. It can be calculated using Eqs. 1 and 2. Also, the LST for entry task should be zero.

$$LST\_d(n_i, p_j) = \max\{(Avail[j], (AFT(n_t + C_{t,i}))\} \tag{1}$$

t is immediate predecessor of the task i

$$LCT\_d(n_i, p_j) = W_{i,j} + LST\_d(n_i, p_j) \tag{2}$$

Where $Avail[j]$ is the earliest time at which processor p_j is ready for task execution and $AFT(n_t)$ is the actual finish time of task n_t while $AST(n_t)$ is the actual start of the task n_t.

In a task graph, makespan tells the performance of workflow and it is calculated as finish time minus start time of a workflow as mentioned in Eq. 3

$$makespan = Finish\_Time - Start\_Time. \tag{3}$$

3.2 Energy Model

3.2.1 Computation Energy Model

The DVFS technique helps to scale the voltage and frequency of the processors. The task execution can have two types of energy consumption. One is dynamic energy dissipation ($Energy_{dynamic}$) while the other one is static energy dissipation ($Energy_{static}$). The dynamic power dissipation ($Power_{dynamic}$) is considered to be one of the main factors of energy consumption. The $P_{dynamic}$ is related to the voltage (v) and frequency (f) as shown in Eq. 4

$$Power_{dynamic} = k * v^2 * f \tag{4}$$

Where k is the application related constant. The dynamic energy dissipation can be determined using Eq. 5

$$Energy_{dynamic} = Power_{dynamic} * t \tag{5}$$

Where t is the time period.

The voltage and frequency of the processor at the idle stage cannot be considered to be null, so the energy dissipation by the processor at the idle state ($Energy_{static}$) is calculated by taking the voltage and frequency of the processor when it is lowest (i.e. v_{lowest} and f_{lowest}) and t_{idle} is the time when processor is ideal.

$$Energy_{idle} = \left(k * \left(v_{lowest} \right)^2 * f_{lowest} \right) * t_{idle} \tag{6}$$

So the total energy consumption by processors can be illustrated using Eq. 7

$$Energy_{comp} = Energy_{dynamic} + Energy_{idle}. \tag{7}$$

3.2.2 Communication Energy Model

The bandwidth is assumed to be same among the different pair of tasks as the network is considered to be homogeneous. Thus, every pair consumes the similar link power. Assume $Elink_{t,i}$ is the energy consumed in transmitting the data from task n_t to task n_i, these tasks (n_t, n_i) are processed on different processors (say, p_j and p_s respectively) having energy consumption rate as PL. So, the energy consumed in transmitting the data from task n_t to task n_i can be defined using Eq. 8

$$Elink_{t,i} = PL * C_{t,i}. \tag{8}$$

Subsequently, the energy consumed because of network interconnection is expressed as

$$EL = \sum_{t=1}^{u} \sum_{\substack{i=1 \\ i \neq t}}^{u} \sum_{j=1}^{p} \sum_{\substack{s=1 \\ s \neq j}}^{p} \left(x_{t,j} \cdot x_{i,s} \cdot PL \cdot C_{t,i} \right) \tag{9}$$

Where, $x_{t,j}$ and $x_{i,s}$ is 1 if n_t is scheduled on p_j and n_i is scheduled on p_s respectively, else 0.

So, total energy consumed (both computation and communication) of an application can be calculated using Eq. 10

$$Energy_{total} = Energy_{comp} + EL. \tag{10}$$

In Table 1, important notations used in the DPES algorithm are listed and its definitions are briefed with notations.

Table 1. Notations used in the DPES algorithm

N, E, P	Number of tasks, edges and processors used in DAG respectively
$C_{i,j}$	Communication cost to transfer message from n_i to n_t scheduled on different processors
$W_{i,j}$	processing time of task i on processor j
$LST(n_i, p_j), LCT(n_i, p_j)$	Start and completion time of ith task on jth processor without duplication
$LST\_d(n_i, p_j), LCT\_d(n_i, p_j)$	Start and completion time of ith task on jth processor with duplication of its immediate predecessors
$AST(n_i, p_j), AFT(n_i, p_j)$	Actual start and finish time of ith task on jth processor
PL	Power consumption of interconnect
$Energy_{comp}$	Total energy consumption of processor
EL	Total energy consumption of interconnect

4 Proposed Algorithm: Duplication Based Performance Effective Scheduling (DPES)

The proposed DPES algorithm has three phases namely, Level sorting, task prioritization, processor selection with task duplication and energy consumption estimation.

In DPES algorithm some important parameters are calculated and these parameters [18] are listed in Table 2.

Table 2. Important notation and parameters

Notation	Definition
ACC	Average computation cost
DTC	Data transfer cost
DRC	Data receiving cost
$Rank(n_i)$	Rank of task n_i

The average computation cost of each task on N available processors can be calculated using the given Eq. 11.

$$ACC(n_i) = \sum\nolimits_{i=1}^{x} \frac{W_{i,j}}{N}, \qquad x \text{ is the number of immediate successors of } n_i \quad (11)$$

The communication cost is defined in two ways: Data Transfer Cost (DTC) and Data Receiving Cost (DRC). The DTC of a given task is the measure of cost required to transfer data to all its immediate successor tasks and it can be calculated as given in Eq. 12. While DRC of a given task is the measure of cost required to receive the data from its predecessor tasks. DRC can be computed using the Eq. 13

$$DTC(n_i) = \sum_{i=1}^{x} C_{i,j}, \; x \text{ is the number of immediate successors of } n_i \qquad (12)$$

$$DRC(n_i) = \{rank(n_j)\}, \; n_i \text{ is the predecessor of } n_j \qquad (13)$$

Rank of the task n_i can be computed by adding its ACC, DTC and DRC values. $Rank(n_i)$ at each level i, can be calculated by using Eq. 14. After computing the rank, the priority is assigned to each task at each level (L_i). The task with maximum rank value will be assigned highest priority and minimum rank value will be assigned lowest priority.

$$Rank(n_i) = ACC + DTC + DRC \qquad (14)$$

4.1 Pseudo Code for DPES

1. BEGIN
2. Read DAG.
3. Interpret the number of processors used.
4. For each task (n_i) at respective level (L_i) of DAG, calculate the task's ACC, DRC, DTC values using Eq. 11, 12 and 13.
5. Compute $Rank(n_i)$ using Eq. 14.
6. Construct a priority queue.
7. For scheduling the tasks from priority queue to the processors using duplication strategy and ensuring energy consumption not to exceed the threshold energy.
   Initialize $threshold\_energy$
   n_i = first unscheduled task from the priority queue.
   for all $p_j \in P$
       find $LST(n_i, p_j)$ and $LCT(n_i, p_j)$ and $LST\_d(n_i, p_j)$ and $LCT\_d(n_i, p_j)$
   end
   if $(LCT(n_t) - LST(n_i) < C_{t,i})$ //Allow duplication where n_t is immediate predecessor of n_i
       {
       $Energy_{usage}(n_i, p_j) = (Energy_{comp}(n_i, p_j) - Elink_{i,t})$
       if $(Energy_{usage}(n_i, p_j) < threshold\_energy)$
           { $AST(n_i, p_j) = LST\_d(n_i, p_j)$
             $AFT(n_i, p_j) = LCT\_d(n_i, p_j)$
           }
       else
           { $AST(n_i, p_j) = LST(n_i, p_j)$
             $AFT(n_i, p_j) = LCT(n_i, p_j)$
           }
       end
   else
       { $AST(n_i, p_j) = LST(n_i, p_j)$
         $AFT(n_i, p_j) = LCT(n_i, p_j)$
       }
   end

8. Return the makespan and total $Energy_{usage}(n_i, p_j)$. This should be always less than or equal to the $threshold_{energy}$.
9. END

5 A Numeric Example

A random generated DAG has been shown in Fig. 2. The DAG has eight tasks, 0 is the entry task present at level zero. Tasks 1, 2, 3, 4 are present at level one while tasks 5 and 6 are present at level two of DAG. At last level, exit task 7 is present. Table 3 shows the computation cost matrix for each task shown in Fig. 2.

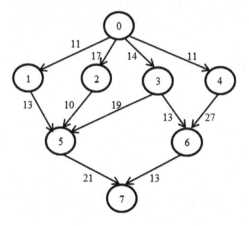

Table 3. Computation cost of task n_i at processor p_j

Tasks	P_1	P_2	P_3
0	11	13	9
1	10	15	11
2	9	12	14
3	11	16	10
4	15	11	19
5	12	9	5
6	10	14	13
7	14	15	10

Fig. 2. Directed Acyclic Graph (DAG)

The ACC, DTC, DRC, rank and priority value for each of the task is calculated using Eqs. 8–11 and is shown in Table 4. The task in each level is given highest priority if its rank value is maximum and the task with minimum rank value is given the lowest priority.

Table 4. Computed ACC, DTC, DRC values and priority assigned to tasks

Level	Tasks	ACC	DTC	DRC	Rank	Priority
1	0	11	53	0	64	1
2	1	12	13	64	89	3
2	2	11.66	10	64	85.66	4
2	3	12.33	32	64	108.33	1
2	4	15	27	64	106	2
3	5	8.66	21	108.33	138	1
3	6	12.33	13	108.33	134	2
4	7	13	0	138	151	1

In Table 5, the latest start time **(LST)** and latest completion time **(LCT)** of PETS algorithm are calculated using Eqs. 1 and 2 respectively. The task on one of three processors which has minimum latest completion time, is being selected to schedule the task and that processor become the favourable processor for that particular task.

Table 5. Calculating the LST and LCT in PETS algorithm

Ordered tasks	P_1		P_2		P_3		Favourable processor
	LST	LCT	LST	LCT	LST	LCT	
0	0	11	0	13	0	**9**	P3
3	23	34	23	39	9	**19**	P3
4	20	35	20	**31**	19	38	P2
1	20	30	31	46	19	**30**	P3
2	26	**35**	31	43	30	44	P1
5	43	55	43	52	45	**50**	P3
6	58	68	32	**46**	58	71	P2
7	71	82	71	86	59	**69**	P3

In Table 6, the latest start time with duplication (**LST_d**) and latest completion time with duplication (**LCT_d**) of DPES algorithm are calculated.

Table 6. Calculating the LST_d and LCT_d in DPES algorithm

Ordered tasks	Immediate predecessor	P_1		P_2		P_3		Duplicate predecessor	Favourable processor
		LST_d	LCT_d	LST_d	LCT_d	LST_d	LCT_d		
0	–	0	11	0	13	0	**9**	–	P3
3	0	11	22	13	29	9	**19**	No	P3
4	0	11	26	13	**24**	19	30	Yes at P_2	P2
1	0	11	**21**	24	39	19	30	Yes at P_1	P1
2	0	21	**30**	24	36	19	33	No	P1
5	2	30	42	36	45	33	**38**	Yes at P_3	P3
6	4	45	55	24	**38**	38	51	No	P2
7	6	55	69	38	**53**	51	61	No	P2

The Schedules obtained by the PETS algorithm are shown in Fig. 3(a). The overall makespan of this algorithm is equal to 69 units. While in Fig. 3(b), the schedules obtained by DPES algorithm are shown. Task 0 is duplicated on the processors P1 and P2, while task 2 is duplicated on processor P3, so as to minimize the overall execution time. The makespan of this algorithm is 53 units. The difference between the makespan of both the algorithms is 16 units.

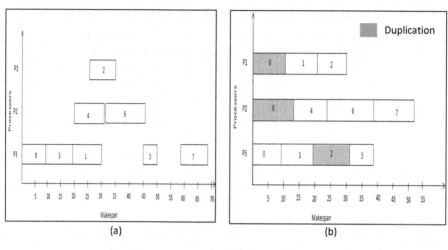

Fig. 3. Illustrating the schedules of (a) PETS algorithm and (b) DPES algorithm

6 Performance Evaluation and Results

6.1 Experimental Setup

For simulation experiments, we adopt the MATLAB (The Math Works Company, United States). By utilizing the randomly generated directed acyclic graphs, PETS algorithm and DPES algorithm has been used in standard experiments in order to get a comparatively objective evaluation. This simulator has been built on the machine with configuration: RAM of 4.00 GB, Operating System is Windows 8 (64-bit), Processor is Intel(R) Core(TM) i5-4200U CPU @ 1.60 GHz.

The three real heterogeneous processors are selected namely, AMD Turion MT-34, Pentium M processor and AMD Athlon-64. Their voltage-frequency pairs [19] are listed in Table 7. The numbers of nodes are 4,8,12,16,20,24 and three processors used for each type.

Table 7. Voltage-relative speed pairs

Levels	Processor pair 1		Processor pair 2		Processor pair 3	
	Voltage (V)	Frequency (MHz)	Voltage (V)	Frequency (MHz)	Voltage (V)	Frequency (MHz)
0	1.20	1800	1.484	1400	1.50	2000
1	1.15	1600	1.436	1200	1.40	1800
2	1.10	1400	1.308	1000	1.30	1600
3	1.05	1200	1.180	800	1.20	1400
4	1.00	1000	0.956	600	1.10	1200

6.2   Comparison Metrics

The performance of an algorithm can be determined using the following three comparison metrics.

Schedule Length Ratio (SLR): It is the ratio of the makespan to the summation of minimum computation costs of the critical path tasks on the processor. Its value should not be less than 1. It can be determined using Eq. 15.

$$SLR = \frac{makespan}{\sum_{n_i \in CP} min_{p_j \in P}\{w_{i,j}\}}, CP \text{ is the critical path.} \qquad (15)$$

SpeedUp: It is the ratio of sequential execution time (cumulative computation cost of tasks) to the parallel execution time (makespan). It can be defined using Eq. 16.

$$SpeedUp = \frac{min_{p_j \in P}\{\sum_{n_i \in V} w_{i,j}\}}{makespan} \qquad (16)$$

Efficiency: It is the ratio of the speed up value to the number of processors used. It can be expressed using Eq. 17.

$$Efficiency = \frac{Speed\ Up}{No.of\ Processors} \qquad (17)$$

6.3   Experimental Results

The makespan of a DAG can be calculated using Eq. 3. The makespan of a DAG is inversely proportional to its performance. In Fig. 4(a), the makespan of two algorithms (i.e. PETS and DPES algorithm) are shown while Fig. 4(b) demonstrates the energy consumed by the two (PETS and DPES) algorithms. In each kind the makespan of our proposed algorithm DPES algorithm consumes lesser energy than PETS algorithm and generates the schedule with reduced makespan. Therefore, the DPES algorithm proves to have better performance.

The SLR values for the DPES algorithm are minimum as compared to PETS algorithm as shown in Fig. 5(a). As the SLR value of any algorithm decreases, the performance increases i.e. $SLR \propto \frac{1}{Performance}$. So, we computed that DPES algorithm performs better than the PETS algorithm when SLR comparison metric is considered.

When SpeedUp metrics is calculated, then it is indicated that the speedup value for DPES algorithm is greater than PETS algorithm in each case as illustrated in Fig. 5(b). Greater the SpeedUp value, better the performance of an algorithm i.e. $SpeedUp \propto \frac{1}{makespan} \propto Performance$.

In terms of Efficiency, the DPES algorithm is more efficient than the PETS algorithm as depicted in Fig. 5(c). More the efficiency value better will be the performance. Efficiency depends upon SpeedUp i.e. $Efficiency \propto SpeedUp$.

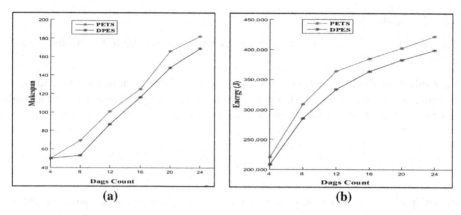

Fig. 4. (a) Comparison on basis of makespan (b) Comparison on basis of energy consumed

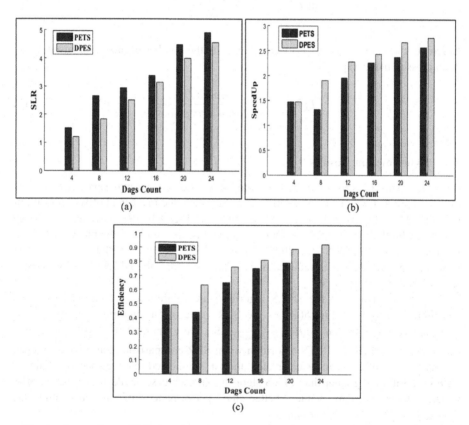

Fig. 5. Comparison of DPES and PETS algorithm based on different comparison metrics

7 Conclusion

In this paper, the task duplication-based scheduling algorithm is proposed i.e. Duplication based Performance Effective Scheduling (DPES), which is implemented on the randomly generated directed acyclic graphs in heterogeneous environment. DPES algorithm makes the use of DVFS technique in order to choose the appropriate voltage and frequency pair for the DAG in order to minimize the energy consumption by the processors without increasing the makespan of the DAG. We concluded that DPES algorithm reduces the makespan as well as it is energy efficient algorithm. The DPES algorithm proves to be a better alternative for the PETS algorithm in terms of obtaining better makespan without violating the energy consumption rate. The proposed (DPES) algorithm is compared with the existing (PETS) algorithm in terms of various comparison metrics (SpeedUp, SLR, Efficiency) and it outstands in all the aspects. According to our best knowledge, till now the task duplication technique is not applied to the PETS algorithm.

References

1. Kim, W.: Cloud computing: today and tomorrow. J. Object Technol. **8**(1), 65–72 (2009)
2. Avram, M.G.: Advantages and challenges of adopting cloud computing from an enterprise perspective. Procedia Technol. **12**, 529–534 (2014)
3. Marston, S., Li, Z., Bandyopadhyay, S., Zhang, J., Ghalsasi, A.: Cloud computing-The business perspective. Decis. Support Syst. **51**(1), 176–189 (2011)
4. Chen, D., Zhao, H.: Data security and privacy protection issues in cloud computing. In: 2012 International Conference on Computer Science and Electronics Engineering, vol. 973, pp. 647–651 (2012)
5. Jensen, M., Schwenk, J., Gruschka, N., Lo Iacono, L.: On technical security issues in cloud computing. In: 2009 IEEE International Conference of Cloud Computing, pp. 109–116 (2009)
6. Selvi, S.T., Valliyammai, C., Dhatchayani, V.N.: Resource Allocation Issues and Challenges in Cloud Computing (2014)
7. Foster, I., Kesselman, C.: Globus: a metacomputing infrastructure toolkit. Int. J. High. Perform. Comput. Appl. **11**(2), 115–128 (1997)
8. Topcuoglu, H., Hariri, S., Wu, M.: Performance-effective and low-complexity task scheduling for heterogeneous computing. IEEE Trans. Parallel Distrib. Syst. **13**(3), 260–274 (2002)
9. Topcuoglu, H., Hariri, S.: Task scheduling algorithms for heterogeneous processors. In: Proceedings of Eighth Heterogeneous Computing Workshop, pp. 3–14 (1999)
10. Nasr, A.A.: Task scheduling algorithm for high performance heterogeneous distributed computing systems. Int. J. Comput. Appl. **110**(16), 23–29 (2015)
11. Lin, C., Lu, S.: Scheduling scientific workflows elastically for cloud computing. In: Proceeding-2011 IEEE 4th International Conference of Cloud Computing, pp. 746–747 (2011)
12. Nasr, A.A., El-Bahnasawy, N.A., El-Sayed, A.: Performance enhancement of scheduling algorithm in heterogeneous distributed computing systems. Int. J. Adv. Comput. Sci. Appl. **6**(5), 88–96 (2015)

13. Zhenxia, Y., Fang, M., Sheng, S.: Scheduling algorithm based on task priority in heterogeneous computing environment. In: 2008 International Conference on Computer Science and Information Technology, vol. 19, no. 2, pp. 12–16 (2008)
14. Hosseinzadeh, M., Shahhoseini, H.S.: An effective duplication-based task-scheduling algorithm for heterogeneous systems. Simulation **87**(12), 1067–1080 (2011)
15. Bansal, S., Kumar, P., Singh, K.: An improved duplication strategy for scheduling precedence constrained graphs in multiprocessor systems. IEEE Trans. Parallel Distrib. Syst. **14**(6), 533–544 (2003)
16. Hagras, T., Janeček, J.: A high performance, low complexity algorithm for compile-time task scheduling in heterogeneous systems. Parallel Comput. **31**(7), 653–670 (2005)
17. Mei, J., Li, K.: Energy-aware scheduling algorithm with duplication on heterogenous computing systems. In: Proceedings of the IEEE/ACM International Conference on Grid Computing, pp. 122–129 (2012)
18. Thambidurai, E.I.P., Mahilmannan, R.: Performance effective task scheduling algorithm for heterogeneous computing system. In: Proceedings of 4th International Symposium on Parallel Distributed Computing, pp. 0–7 (2005)
19. Huang, Q., Su, S., Li, J., Xu, P., Shuang, K., Huang, X.: Enhanced energy-efficient scheduling for parallel applications in cloud. In: 2012 12th IEEE/ACM International Symposium Cluster, Cloud and Grid Computing (CCGRID 2012), pp. 781–786 (2012)

Reducing Forgery in Land Registry System Using Blockchain Technology

U. M. Ramya[✉], P. Sindhuja, RA Atsaya, B. Bavya Dharani,
and SS Manikanta Varshith Golla

Department of Computer Science and Engineering, Amrita School of
Engineering, Amrita Vishwa Vidyapeetham, Coimbatore, India
um_ramya@cb.amrita.edu, sindhujaparnam@gmail.com,
atsyatchul7@gmail.com,
bavyabalasubramaniam@gmail.com,
satyavrshth6@gmail.com

Abstract. Forgery of land documents is one of the major problems faced by any state government in land registration system. Even though the documents are now secured in the database, but these records can be tampered because there is no proper security and time-stamping present in the database system. To overcome this problem, the use case can be deployed using Blockchain. Blockchain being a distributed system, data is available to everyone in the network. Every block added into the blockchain is time stamped and proof-of-work is required to add the block, making the data very hard to be tampered. In this paper, we have used a private-permissioned Blockchain - Multichain, where the authority lies with the registrar making the process faster because proof-of-work [13] is not required. The implementation of land registration use-case involves recording the documents into blockchain and verifying it with the one stored in digital locker thereby reducing forgery of documents.

Keywords: Multichain · Distributed ledger · Streams · Hash value
Consensus protocol · Digilocker

1 Introduction

Blockchain can be understood easily by taking the Bitcoin [1] use case. Smart contracts [3, 5] can be deployed. They are used in various use cases [4] like health care, legal, education, supply chain [2, 7]. Blockchain is a universal digital ledger for recording all transactions or digital events executed by participating parties. Block chain's core technology uses cryptography as well as distributed database architecture that is open ledger and a peer-to-peer protocol to create shared ledgers among different parties. Each transaction before getting added into blockchain is verified using any one of the consensus protocols [9] by the nodes present within the network. Once a block is written into the blockchain, the information in the blockchain is immutable –meaning it cannot be manipulated or erased. The distributed ledger chronologically stores information in "blocks" containing a verifiable record of every single transaction, as well as the sequence in which the transactions were executed. A third party is not required to

© Springer Nature Singapore Pte Ltd. 2019
A. K. Luhach et al. (Eds.): ICAICR 2018, CCIS 955, pp. 725–734, 2019.
https://doi.org/10.1007/978-981-13-3140-4_65

monitor, manage and validate transactions. Transactions such as money transfers or stock purchases require a third party to monitor and record these activities. In a blockchain, in order to perform any transaction accepted by the rest of the network before adding block into the blockchain, a participant(miner) must show "proof of work" – a mechanism for protecting the integrity of information and preventing fraud. Once captured, information in the blockchain is immutable – meaning it cannot be manipulated or erased.

2 Literature Survey

Presently the records are stored in database. Database is authorised wholly by a single entity, this may lead to single point failure. There is no time stamping in database. ChromaWay [8] a Bitcoin blockchain company is working on land registration using the blockchain technology.

Blockchain Characteristics

- Decentralized data(an open ledger to every node in the network).
- Mutual consensus by participants.
- Use of cryptography.
- Digital signature for identity verification.
- Strict controls and time-stamped data.
- Direct, secure and immediate access to data (which is immutable).

Types of Blockchain

- Public blockchain/Permissionless blockchain [12]
  As the name suggests it is a blockchain of public where there is no in charge to write into the blockchain. But while deploying the land registration use case the government should have the authority so here we use private/permissioned blockchain.
- Private blockchain/Permissioned blockchain [12]
  Permissioned Blockchain type [6] requires permission to connect, read the data on the blockchain, limits the number of participants who can connect, transact on the blockchain and serve the network by creating new blocks into the chain. Eg Ripple [10], Multichain, HyperLedger, Ethereum [11], Hydrachain [14].

Similarities Between Public and Private Blockchain

Both of these are peer-to-peer and decentralised networks avoiding single point failure, where every node in the network has a copy of a shared append-only ledger of digitally signed transactions.

- Both maintain the copies which are consistent through a consensus protocol.
- Both the Blockchains make sure that the data which is present in the blockchain cannot be manipulated even in the presence of completely faulty or malicious node in the network.

Difference Between Public and Private Blockchain

- Nodes participating in the network.
- Nodes executing the consensus protocol.

  A public blockchain network is open and anyone can join the network, can access and read or write data from the ledger. Presently Bitcoin [1] is one of the largest public blockchain networks. The major drawback of a public blockchain is very high consumption of computational power required by the miners to solve complex problems and produce proof-of-work. When a new node wants to join the private blockchain network, it requires permission to connect to the network which is given by the blockchain creator. Organisations that deploy a private blockchain will generally use a permissioned network. So there are restrictions on who can be part of the network, and only in particular transactions. The privileges given to the nodes in the network differ. In order to join the network, nodes need to get permission from the network creator. Nodes existing in the network depending on their privilege get to decide new joiners into the network. A regulatory authority or consortium could issue licenses for participation. Once a node enters the network, it maintains the blockchain in a decentralized manner. The creator of the blockchain has the authority to make the records available for every node present in the network to read, but the privilege to write/add the blocks is not given to every one in the network keeping in mind the security of the network and mining. With permissioned Blockchains, it's not mandatory to use POW (Proof-of-Work) for achieving consensus from the nodes which actually requires high computational power or some other system requirement.

3 System Architecture

Figure 1 given below shows the overall view of our proposed system. The proposed system is explained in the following steps

1. If the seller wants to sell the land he should have the hard copy of the land document and soft copy of the same i.e. present in the digilocker [15] (which gets uploaded by the government).
2. The sender will send the copy to the registrar.
3. The registrar converts the received soft copy of the document into hash value and verifies the hash value of the corresponding document i.e. already present in the blockchain.
4. At the same time the buyer witnesses the whole process. If he is convinced with the process he will registrar to transfer the ownership from the seller to buyer.
5. The registrar prepares the hard copy of the new document.
6. The registrar scans the document and puts it into the database of the government.
7. When the buyer requests the government for the document he should be able to get the soft copy of the document into his digilocker account.
8. The registrar should convert the scanned document into a hash value and upload it into the blockchain.

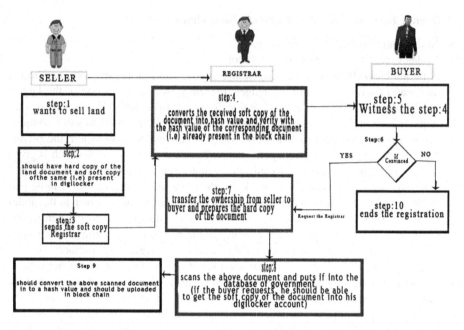

Fig. 1. System architecture

4 Implementation

In this proposed system, we have used Multichain platform to deploy the land registration use case. It is a readily available platform for the creation and deployment of private Blockchains, either within or between the organizations. It provides the privacy and control required in a easy-to-use package. Multichain supports Windows, Linux and Mac servers and provides a simple API and command-line interface. Multichain solves the problems of mining, privacy and openness through coordinated management of user permissions. The main functionality 'Streams' implemented in Multichain platform enable blockchain to be used as an all-purpose append-only database, with the blockchain providing time stamping, notarization and immutability of documents present in it. There is no constraint on the number of streams that could be created. The restriction is, items can only be added to it. Each item that gets added to the stream represents a blockchain transaction. Without knowing the underlying mechanism, developer scan read and write streams. The vital part of streams is in indexing and retrieval. Each participant in the network can subscribe to any stream of their choice with the blockchain making sure of consistency of the open ledger. As Blockchain is a peer-to peer decentralized network, items in a stream gets added from various nodes across the network irrespective of the order of arrival.

Multichain-Console Commands
The Following are the steps to be followed in a console for creating and dealing with Multichain private blockchain:

1. Creating a Blockchain

server1:

multichain-util create chain1

2. To Initialize

server1:

multichain-util create chain1

On doing so, IP address and port number is obtained.

3. Connecting the Blockchain

Server2:

multichaind chain1@[ip-address]:[port]

Server2 is added to the list of peers.

4. To Get Permission

Server1: multichain-cli chain1 grant 1.

connect, receive

5. To Switch to Interactive Mode

On both servers:

multichaind chain1 –daemon

6. Creating a Stream

Server1:

create stream stream1 false

7. To Publish into Stream

Server1:

publish stream1 key1 73747265616d2064617461

8. To Subscribe to this Stream and View its Contents

Server2:

1. liststreams
2. subscribe stream1
3. liststreamitems stream1

5 Limitations

Since blockchain technology is a new technology, it is still in an emerging state across industries. The real implementation of the system is very costly, and hence system is developed in a testing environment. Computational power is a major limitation for a public blockchain which can be overcome by private one. Since even a small change to the original hard copy of the document (e.g.: ink mark, letters getting faded, etc.) will affect the hash value drastically, a digital copy of the document should be present with the owner. digilocker app can be used to have the permanent soft copy of the document since it can't be deleted.

6 Sample Screen Shots of Implementation of Land Registration Use-Case

See Figs. 2, 3, 4, 5, 6, 7 and 8.

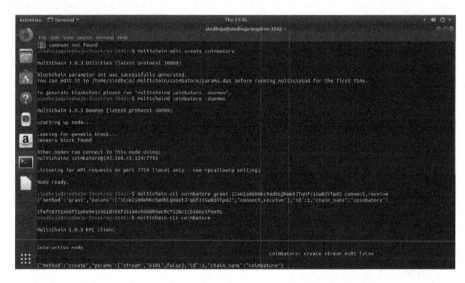

Fig. 2. Creation of the Blockchain "Coimbatore" from the Host server (registrar)

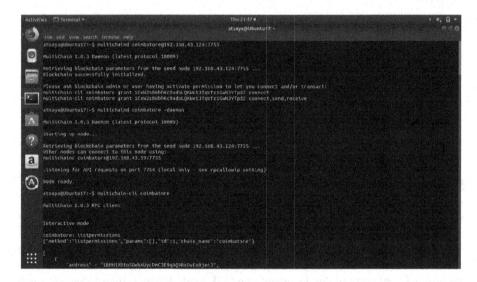

Fig. 3. Connecting to the created Blockchain by the buyer from his server.

7   Future Work

The proposed work can be extended and implemented in practical use. Since there are chances for the document to get spoilt atleast a little after several years, digital copy of the document must be present and carried with the original document to proceed with transaction. Because even a very small change such as an ink mark on the paper will generate a drastically different hash and hence the authentication will be difficult to be

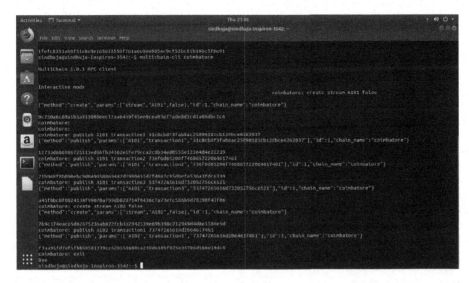

Fig. 4. Creating stream "A101" and putting the hashed documents into the Blockchain

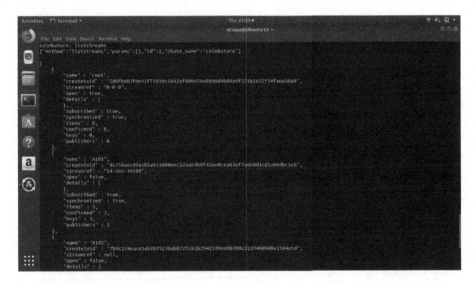

Fig. 5. To find the available land streams in the Blockchain by the buyer

verified. Thus to make it simple, the soft copy of the document must be updated in the government database so that any time when the owner asks for the copy it can be given. And also the government can take initiative to make the land documents available to the owner through the digilocker app. As mentioned earlier, once data is put in the digital locker it cannot be deleted by the user. This prevents us from losing the softcopy of the document.

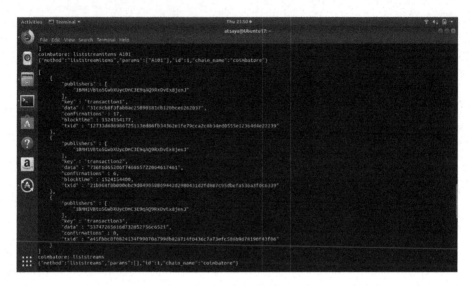

Fig. 6. To see the transactions for the land "A101" by the buyer

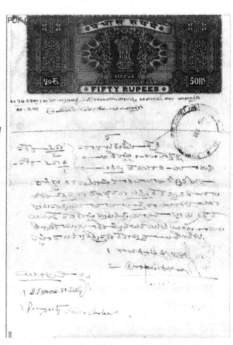

hex: 31c38cb8f3fabf8ac25090181c6120bce6262037

HEX: 31C38CB8F3FABF8AC25090181C6120BCE6262037

h:e:x: 31:c3:8c:b8:f3:fa:bf:8a:c2:50:90:18:1c:61:20:bc:e6:26:20:37

base64: McOMuPP6v4rCUJAYHGEgvOYmIDc=

Fig. 7. Hash value of original document

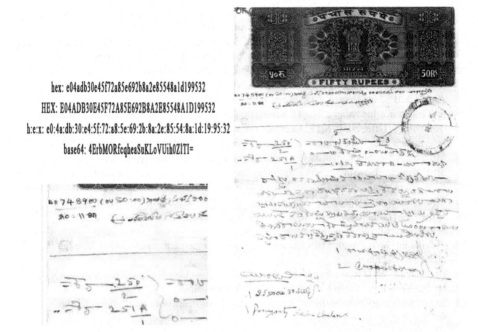

hex: e04adb30e45f72a85e692b8a2e85548a1d199532

HEX: E04ADB30E45F72A85E692B8A2E85548A1D199532

h:e:x: e0:4a:db:30:e4:5f:72:a8:5e:69:2b:8a:2e:85:54:8a:1d:19:95:32

base64: 4ErbMORfcqheaSuKLoVUih0ZlTI=

Fig. 8. Hash value after a change in doucment

8 Conclusion

Thus, the use-case land forgery prevention is achieved with the blockchain technology. Unlike current existing system, the document as such cannot be viewed by the buyer since the hashed value of the document only is available (because a hashed value cannot be de-hashed) thus providing user's privacy. The documents cannot be claimed by someone later by tampering because it changes the hash value and hence the transaction will become invalid and will not be proceeded further. Another advantage is that the time-stamp of the original document created in the blockchain will be used to cross-verify and thus the document and the land becoming totally safe. This system thus helps in a complete forgery less land transaction.

References

1. Nakamoto, S.: Bitcoin: a peer-to-peer electronic cash system. White Paper (2008)
2. The Blockchain Imperative: The Next Challenge for P&C Carriers. Cognizant
3. Kosba, A., Miller, A., Shi, E., Wen, Z., Papamanthou, C.: Hawk: the Blockchain model of cryptography and privacy- preserving smart contracts. In: 2016 IEEE Symposium on Security and Privacy (SP), San Jose, CA, USA, pp. 839–858 (2016). https://doi.org/10.1109/sp.2016.55

4. Implementing Blockchain for cognitive IOT applications: integrate device data with smart contracts in IBM Blockchain. IBM Developer Works
5. Christidis, K., Devetsikiotis, M.: Blockchains and smart contracts for the internet of things. IEEE Access **4**, 2292–2303 (2016). https://doi.org/10.1109/ACCESS.2016.2566339
6. Nugent, T., Upton, D., Cimpoesu, M.: Improving data transparency in clinical trials using blockchain. Firstpublished: 20 Oct 2016, 2541 Latest published 20 Oct 2016, 2541
7. Archa, A.B., Achuthan, K.: Trace and track: enhanced pharma supply chain infrastructure to prevent fraud. In: Kumar, N., Thakre, A. (eds.) Ubiquitous Communications and Network Computing. UBICNET 2017. Lecture Notesof the Institute for Computer Sciences, Social Informatics and Telecommunications Engineering, vol. 218. Springer, Cham (2018)
8. Mizrahi, A.: A blockchain-based property ownership recording system
9. Siva Sankar, L., Sindhu, M., Sethumadhavan, M.: Survey of consensus protocols on Blockchain applications. In: 2017 International Conference on Advanced Computing and Communication Systems (ICACCS 2017), Jan. 06–07 (2017). Coimbatore, INDIA
10. Schwartz, D., Youngs, N., Britto, A.: The ripple protocol consensus algorithm (2014)
11. Multichain. https://www.multichain.com/
12. On Public and Private Blockchain. https://blog.ethereum.org/2015/08/07/on-public-and-private-blockchains
13. Blockchain: What is in a block? https://dev.to/damcosset/blockchain-what-is-in-a-block-48jo
14. Hydrachain. https://github.com/HydraChain/hydrachain
15. https://www.ndtv.com/business/list-of-documents-you-can-store-on-digilocker-from-aadhaar-card-to-your-pan-card

Mobile Application for Dissemination of Advisories on Pest and Diseases of Rice & Mustard

Rakhee[1(✉)], Amrender Kumar[1], Anshu Thakur[1], Ajanta Birah[2], and Rahul Nigam[3]

[1] AKMU, ICAR-IARI, New Delhi 110012, India
rakheesharma234@gmail.com
[2] ICAR-NCIPM, New Delhi 110012, India
[3] SAC-ISRO, Ahemdabad 380015, India

Abstract. In agricultural field, dissemination of information regarding pest population and their occurrence is very important for taking remedial measures in advance to save the crops to a great extent. The information dissemination through mobile application is adapted due to effective and efficient way to communicate to end users at proper time. In this study mobile application development and its implementation is discussed. The application is developed with push notification feature in order to disseminate the advisories about the infestation of pest and remedial measures based on the objective forewarning of pests through statistical modeling.

Keywords: Mobile application · Google could messaging · Android studio Weather based predictive modeling · Push notification

1 Introduction

At present more than 70% of the Indian population uses android mobile phones for its new trends and applications installed in it. The application installed on the users mobile phones is for the information, news, games, lifestyle, shopping etc. The growing popularity of mobile application is due to its fast processing and ease in usages. Many of the applications utilize notification features to engage its user's more often. The push notification is a message that pops up on the device on a specified time interval or on any trigger factor such as new upload on websites, new results, any updated information etc. The push notification provides convenience and added value to application users. There are mainly two types of notifications local notifications and remote notification, the local notifications are build by the developer within the applications in both cases of android and ios respectively. In the remote notifications, the notifications were send at certain specific time from the specific demographic locations. The push notification engage the application users with the personalized messages. Another important advantage of push notification is that it gets the insight behaviour of the users by tracking various matrices associated with it. Without push notification, applications take space in the mobile phones doing nothing but when the apps have instant

A. K. Luhach et al. (Eds.): ICAICR 2018, CCIS 955, pp. 735–743, 2019.
https://doi.org/10.1007/978-981-13-3140-4_66

notifications about the activities it instantly inform the users to what's new and thus driving them into action. Originally the android applications are designed to make information available on platform such as Gmail, news, weather information etc. Now various applications related to medicine, education, technologies, games, farming, agriculture etc. were also found. There are many android based applications which are implemented for the farmers *viz.* Kisan suvidha, Pusa Krishi, Crop insurance mobile app, agro app [1] etc. to promote communications between farmers, researchers, scientist to disseminate the information. Technology advancement in agriculture practice is a great tool to support farming. Introduction of ICT in agriculture in past few years has upgraded the farmers knowledge, usages of the pesticides for the crops, perception of e-Agriculture [2].

Researchers have also attempted to explain the challenges faced by developer team in making an android application [3]. Mobile applications are broadly classified into three types *viz.* native applications, web-based applications and hybrid applications respectively. The native applications resides on the device only and utilizes full features of that device e.g. of native applications are calendar, calculator and in some latest android phones news applications and gaming applications are also native. The web-based application presents the web-view of the developed system. These applications require a browser to open the links associated with the web view and requires an internet connection as well, the third type of android application i.e. hybrid application is the mix of two application type features. Some of the feature of this application can work offline and some may require the internet connections. The application utilizes the features of the device on which it is installed. In this study web based application is developed with the feature of push notification about the infestation of major pests/disease for a target crop. The notification is an important information which provides details to end users about the pest infestation and its control.

2 Data

For model development historical data on pest/disease [Rice- Yellow Stem Borer (YSB) & Blast and Mustard-Aphid & Alternaria Blight] were obtained from the experimental stations along with agro-metrological data on mustard (Bharatpur, Hisar and Berhampur) and Rice (Chinsura and Raipur). Forecasts models were developed and validated for a target locations using agromet and satellite based agromet data. Satmet data is provided by Space Application Center (SAC)-ISRO, Ahmedabad. The weather data on maximum & minimum temperature, relative humidity morning & evening, rainfall, bright sunshine hours were considered for model development.

3 Methodology

3.1 Model Development

Weather indices based regression model were developed for a target pest and crop on various character such as (i) crop age at first appearance of pest/disease (ii) crop age at peak population of pest/disease (iii) Maximum severity/population of pest/disease. Besides this, models were also developed on weekly basis after peak population/severity of the pest/disease [3–7].

3.2 Web-Based Forewarning System

The web-based forewarning system is developed using three tier architecture as shown in Fig. 1 namely presentation layer, application layer and data layer respectively. The presentation layer deals with the user interface and to make system as user friendly as possible. The user selects the options for crop, pest, location, year and characteristics of the pests based on the requirement they needed. The presentation layer is formed in such a way that user feels free to use the system, links are provided to easily navigate from one system to another. The application layer is the bridge between the presentation layer and the data layer The application tier is composed of scripts running on web server which forms the way of communication between the user interface and the database. Java programming is used to generate the codes. Through ASP, database connection is also established so that when user requests information, the application tier immediately fetch the data from database and provide the resulting information to the end user in the form of webpage itself. Application tier was implemented through NetBeans 8.0.2 IDE (Integrated Development Environment) which is a data editor. Glass fish server was used to test the system on local host. The application tier is composed of scripts running on web server which forms the way of communication between the user interface and the database. The script consists of Active Server Pages (ASP) and to make the web pages more interactive and dynamic, Hypertext Markup Language (HTML) along with Cascading Style Sheet (CSS) is used. Database is the collection of the organized data which can be used to access, modify and update the information. Three tier architecture for developing the model is used because it manages complexity. This approach brings numerous benefits including increased understandability and maintainability. The other benefits of the architecture are maintainability, scalability, reusability, reliability and most importantly flexibility. Maintainability ensures that the component in one tier should have no effect on other tiers. All the tiers can be managed independently and can be integrated as and when required. This three-tier architecture provides developer a good flexibility and ease to work with. PostgreSQL is used to create the database for the web-enabled system. The developed forecast model discussed in previous section is implemented at the backend of this forewarning system. The system can be browsed from any client machine using browsers such as chrome, Mozilla, Internet Explorer.

3.3 Mobile Application Development

Web-based forewarning system for major pest in Mustard & Rice crop was developed on responsive template which means that the design of the system adapts on any layout of the devices used i.e. on different laptops, tablets and mobile phones. Making system responsive means to enhance the user experience of using application while pruning the amount of information displayed. The web-enabled system developed is converted into android mobile application by generating web view of it through java programming.

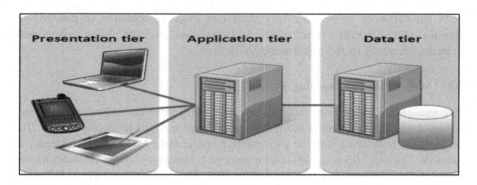

Fig. 1. Three tier architecture

The codes are written on Integrated Development Environment Android studio version 1.5. The mobile application is based on famous Google Cloud Messaging (GCM) services which are adapted for getting notifications on installed mobile applications. These notifications were about the advisories for the farmers and researchers so that they can take appropriate action before the pest infestation reaches to high level to save their crops and at the right time. The application is developed to push advisories in the form of notifications to android mobiles. GCM is used to notify application running on a device about the new information available on it. The process of push notification is as follows:

1. First of all android device sends sender ID and application ID to the GCM server for registration.
2. When the devices are successfully registered with GCM, it will provide registration ID to android device.
3. After receiving registration ID, device will send this registration ID to the application server.
4. The application server will then store the registration ID into the database for later usage as and when required.
   a. Whenever new document is uploaded on the Krishikosh website, a push notification is needed, the application server is then sends a message to GCM server along with the device registration ID (stored in the database).
   b. GCM server will delivers the message to respected device using device registration ID.

The pictorial representation of the process is shown in Fig. 2.

Google Cloud messaging (GCM) developed by Google works on notification services. It allows the developer to send notification on the registered mobile devices. Required packages for mobile application were installed using Android SDK (Software Development Kit) manager. It has package Google APIs (x86 System Image) which is necessary to form the emulator device having Google APIs functionality.

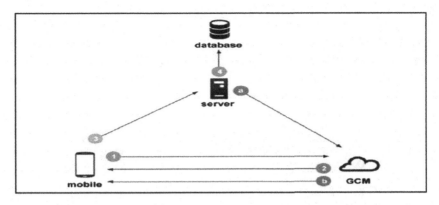

Fig. 2. Architecture of push notification through GCM

3.3.1   Android Studio

Android Studio an Integrated Development Environment (IDE), is used for the development of mobile application. It has powerful tools to create user interface and emulator a virtual device for the testing purpose without having an actual android device. It offers tools for integrating applications, running server side code locally for the testing purpose. Android studio offers a virtual Android device for testing the codes time to time as shown in Fig. 3. The device *viz.* emulator utilizes multi-core CPUs, making the entire process very fast. Any modifications in the code can be tested using this device which is the perfect replica of any other android mobile devices. Android studio makes code writing and executing faster as well, it's in built methods and classes is much easier and accurate, it has a feature of intelligent code editor which is equipped with IntelliJ IDEA interface. After installing the android studio tool, required packages were installed using Android SDK (software development kit) manager as shown in Fig. 4.

Fig. 3. Emulator- a virtual device

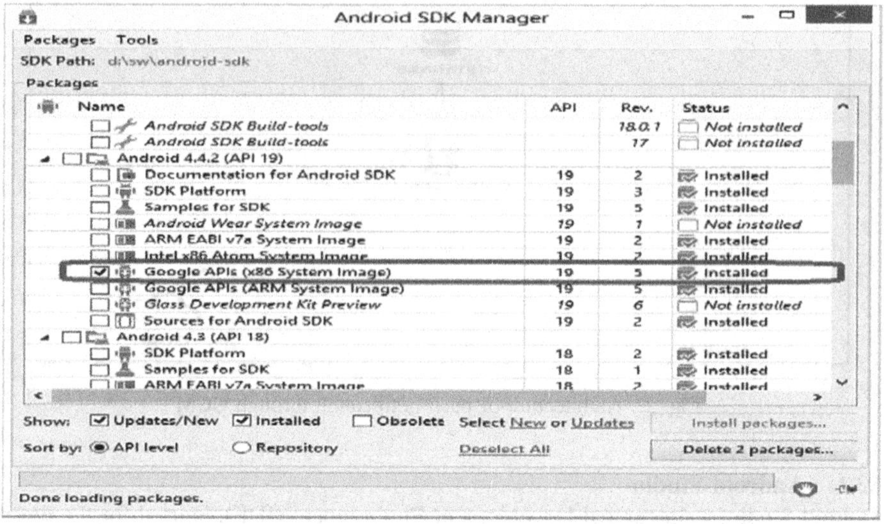

Fig. 4. Package installation in android SDK manager

The android mobile application icon is shown in Fig. 5. The icon is designed keeping in mind the crops and pests majorly involved in the project *viz.* Paddy & Mustard crops and Yellow Stem Borer (YSB), Blast, Alternaria Blight (ALB), and Aphids as pests respectively. Figure 6 represents different WebPages designed for Web-based forewarning system. The first page is the splash screen which immediately comes when user click the icon to open the android application, the second page is the home page of the developed system, the third page is the selection of the crops, in the proceeding pages users can select the pest, year, characteristics to forecast and get the results. These results are stored back into the database, results are then compared with the economic threshold values and then advisories related to the comparison made is pushed on to the device. The push notification is flashed on the device which has installed the application as shown in Fig. 7. Android operating system is a software components consisting of stacks of five layers namely Linux Kernel, Libraries, Android Runtime, Application Framework and Applications respectively. The Linux Kernel consists of all the drivers for the hardware such as cameras, keypads, display settings etc. On the top of the kernel there is set of libraries having browser engines and database used for storing the content and also used for sharing the content of the applications, playing and recording the videos and audios. The third stack is the Android Runtime which provides Java Virtual Machine. This stack also provides a set of core libraries which enable Android application developers to write Android applications using standard Java programming language. The Application Framework has Activity Manager, Content Providers, notification manager etc. The Android application is found at the top of all the layers, this layer is to write the application for the android systems.

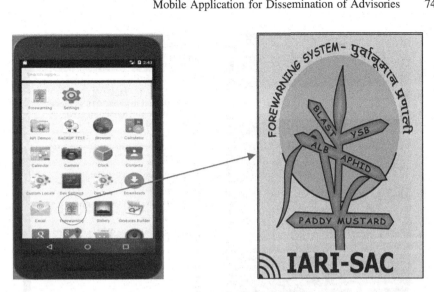

Fig. 5. Android mobile application icon

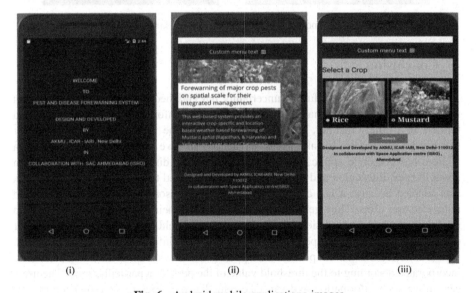

Fig. 6. Android mobile applications images

The above virtual device represents the actual android device, developer use an android emulator as a target platform to run and test the applications on the system. The emulator provides all the capabilities of a real android device, testing the developing applications on emulator is faster and easier than dosing so on physical device. It comes with predefined configuration which developer has to select while creating the emulator on the android studio.

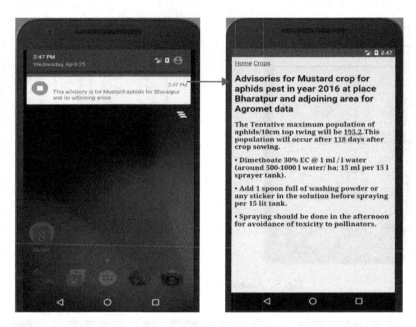

Fig. 7. Push message and the advisory issue (after clicking on the push message)

4   Conclusion

Agricultural field which is full of uncertainty but enriched with sensitive information needs to have a proper channel to disseminate its information to researchers and farmers in a timely manner. Prior information about the forthcoming pests and their severity let researchers to take necessary actions to save the crops. In this study an android based mobile application is developed to help disseminating the information about the pest infestation and necessary advisories related to it. The mobile application was adapted because it has ability to send instant advisories via push notification to registered app users. They get the pop up message on their device to monitor the crop age when maximum population of pest appears on the field and also what is the number of maximum population of pest. When user click such information in the notification, then advisories related to pest count appears on the screen. The advisories were incorporated according to the threshold value of the pest for a particular crop. The users can utilize such information and can take remedial measures to save their crop from future harm. These advisories will become an important source of pest management dissemination for the farmers. This application will help in the horizontal spreading of these information to their fellow farmers. This will disseminate the information in neighboring villages through farmers as well. Moreover, such an application also implicitly addressing the climate change impacts on the pest and disease situation in rice and mustard. Farmers can apply appropriate pest management measures as per advisories at right time, and thereby, heavy loss caused by the above mentioned pests can be checked or minimized.

Acknowledgments. We are thankful to SAC (ISRO), Ahmedabad for providing financial support to carry out the research work.

References

1. Aggarwal, M., Kaushik, A., Sengar, A.: Agro App: an application for healthy living, ISCON (2014). https://doi.org/10.1109/iciscon.2014.6965213
2. Thankachan, S., Kirubakaran, S.: A survey conducted on E-Agriculture with Indian Farmers. Int. J. Comput. Sci. Mob. Comput. 3(2), 8–14 (2014)
3. Kathuria, A., Gupta, A.: IJCSMC, challenges in android application 14(5), 294–299 (2015)
4. Kumar, A. et al.,: Web enabled and weather based forewarning of yellow stem borer [*Scirpophaga incertulas* (Walker)] and leaf folder [*Cnaphalocrcis medinalis* (Guenee)] for different rice growing locations of India, Mausam 67(4), 861–868 (2016)
5. Agrawal, R., Mehta, S.C.: Weather based forecasting of crop yields, pests and diseases - IASRI models. J. Ind. Soc. Agril. Statist 61(2), 255–263 (2007)
6. Chattopadhyay, C. et al.,: Forecasting of *Lipaphis erysimi* on oilseed Brassicas in India - a case study. Crop Protect. 24, 1042–1053 (2005)
7. Chattopadhyay, C., et al.: Epidemiology and forecasting of Alternaria blight of oilseed Brassica in India - a case study. Zeitschrift für Pflanzenkrankheiten und Pflanzenschutz 112, 351–365 (2005)

Impact of Neighboring Agent's Characteristics with Q-Learning in Network Multi-agent System

Harjot Kaur[(⊠)] and Ginni Devi

Department of Computer Science and Engineering,
Guru Nanak Dev University Regional Campus, Gurdaspur 143521, Punjab, India
harjotkaursohal@rediffmail.com, ginnithapa@yahoo.com

Abstract. In a Network Multiagent System (NMAS), agent learning is one of the most investigated attribute and vital issues in terms of enhancing the global productivity of the system. The work in this paper implements a new approach that uses neighboring agent characteristics to improve the learning performance of an agent in NMAS considering social networks. The main contributions of this work are: First, it presents the basic principles of multi-agent learning while considering various learning issues. Second, it reviews the main research developments in the field of multi-agent learning. Third, it introduces a network multi-agent learning framework by considering the neighboring agent characteristics, i.e., the relative degree of neighboring nodes and past interaction histories of neighboring agents in a social network. Furthermore, the proposed framework is experimentally assessed by implementing various social networks (scale-free and small-world) in the form of a NMAS.

Keywords: Q-learning · Relative degree of neighboring nodes
Multi-agent systems · Social networks · Multi-agent learning

1 Introduction

In a Network Multiagent System (NMAS) [8, 15, 21], agent learning is one of the most investigated attribute and vital issues in terms of enhancing the global productivity of the system. The environment of NMAS can be considered as a shared environment, where numbers of independent agents [22] interact with one another in the form of network in order to meet their desired objectives. With the purpose of successful interaction and hence goal achievement, agents [19] in a NMAS will cooperate, coordinate, and arbitrate with other agents. These agents exercise the process of multi-agent learning (MAL) [21] for improving their learning performance via experience. Multiple agents in NMAS interact in a common environment [18] where each agent learns how to select its own action, how rest of the member agents select actions, and what are the goal, plans, and perspectives of other member agents. For learning, agents in NMAS can use the technique of multi-agent reinforcement learning, which is one of the proven and established techniques used for MAL.

© Springer Nature Singapore Pte Ltd. 2019
A. K. Luhach et al. (Eds.): ICAICR 2018, CCIS 955, pp. 744–756, 2019.
https://doi.org/10.1007/978-981-13-3140-4_67

Multi-agent reinforcement learning (MARL) [5] can be represented as an environment where agents interact to maximize the begotten rewards over time. The environment comprises a set of agents Ag, a set of states S and a set of actions A per state. When an agent interacts in the environment, it receives state (s) from the environment and produces an action (a). With this state and action pair, the environment provides an agent a new state (s') and a reward (r). A huge successive addition of rewards can be influenced by recognizing a mapping from states to actions. In order to manage learning issues and their consequences in NMASs, several multi-agent reinforcement learning algorithms [4, 6, 12, 13] have been introduced. In most of the learning frameworks that have been considered in the literature, two or more fixed players interact with each other and learn their optimal policies [1, 15] by interacting with the same opponent time and again.

More work needs to be performed in the direction of MAL in addition to foregoing learning frameworks in order to enhance the learning efficiency for various scenarios in NMAS. This paper considers characteristics of neighboring agents of an agent in a NMAS when it is performing an action in a multi-agent reinforcement learning environment. This in turn will result in improved learning of the same and help achieve optimal outcomes.

The remainder of the paper proceeds as follows. Section 2 summarizes background work based on several previously proposed MAL approaches, Sect. 3 presents the proposed multi-agent learning framework, various algorithms and Q-Learning concepts. Section 4 demonstrates the experimental analysis performed in this work. Various experimental results are discussed in Sect. 5 and conclusions and future work are covered in Sect. 6.

2 Background Work and Motivation

This section presents a comprehensive description of existing work in the area of multi-agent learning in social networks

Claus and Boutilier [1] exhibited the simplest form of reinforcement learning, i.e., Q-learning and have considered two types of learners i.e., IALs(Individual Action Learners) and JALs(Joint Action Learners) in their work. The authors investigated the performance of agents by simulating them in the form of two-player repeated cooperative games. After simulation, the outcomes of the work demonstrated that there was negligible performance difference between both types of learners. Franchi [2] introduced a multi-agent system, which implemented a fully distributed Social Network System (SNS). The goal of the proposed system was to help individuals to keep their profiles as FOAF (Friend of a Friend) profiles and to assist them to preserve their private information in their profiles.

Franchi and Poggi [3] discussed various multi-agent system models and techniques that can be implemented for social network analysis. The authors considered various previous research works, which have been done in the domain of social network analysis for multi-agent simulation and have also highlighted some approaches of agent-based modeling and their simulation methods (ABMS) which can be used for social network systems and theories.

Tuyls and Weiss [21] discussed some basics of MAL and have also presented a survey of various milestones in MAL by focusing on the main research achievements accomplished in it. The authors have identified the main challenges in MAL and also investigated several optimal learning mechanisms, i.e., transfer learning and swarm intelligence. An observation mechanism was introduced by Hao and Leung [5] in their proposed social learning framework in order to reduce the amount of communication among agents. The framework was comprehensively analyzed in step-by-step manner by implementing the test-bed of general-sum games and by comparing the results with previous research [9, 16]. Hao and Leung [7], also investigated the multi-agent learning problem considering their previously proposed and above-mentioned learning framework, for evaluating the performance of both IALs and JALs, and by considering various types of cooperative gaming environments.

Jiang et al. [10] presented a well-organized research based on task allocation in a multi-agent system using social network (MAS-SN) and have proposed a task allocation mechanism based upon the negotiation reputation. Jiang and Jiang [11] have classified various related surveys on social networks in their work. After surveying a good amount of works, they were able to correlate a strong relationship between multi-agent systems and social networks which could be expressed in a multi-agent learning perspective as well.

Hao et al. [6] pursued research towards improving learning performance in CMAS and investigated various coordination issues in multi-agent cooperative games by implementing them on the networked social learning framework rather than simple social learning framework. Hao et al. [8] further considered two more network topologies i.e., random and ring networks in addition to small and scale-free networks to represent agents' interaction. They investigated how various network structures and different factors considered in these networks influence the learning performance of agents in various environments.

Silva et al. [20] proposed a multi-agent advising framework in which each agent can learn through environment exploration and can speed up its learning process by taking advise from its neighborhood. The proposed framework was experimentally evaluated using Robot-Soccer environment. A set of Actor-Critics methods were explored by Lowe et al. [14] in which an actor agent considered action policies of neighboring agents and learn policies based on local information at the time of execution. The work was one of the primary attempts to improve the multi-agent learning policies in mixed cooperative-competitive environments.

In the last few years, there has been a growing interest in the field of learning in multi-agent systems. All the above-surveyed works have considered multi-agent learning issues and implemented various approaches to deal with them and hence serve as motivation for the proposed research idea. This work widens the scope of MAL by considering neighboring agent characteristics for a particular node (agent) in NMAS. It primarily investigates the impact of relative degree of a node (agent) w.r.t. Q-learning in a NMAS.

3 Multi-agent Learning Framework Based on Q-Learning

This work primarily proposes a Multi-agent learning (MAL) Framework, assuming that a network multi-agent system consists of agents with a cooperative environment, in which each agent interacts with a randomly selected agent from set of its neighboring agents (Fig. 1). This work uses Q-learning (multi-agent reinforcement learning) to improve the learning performance in NMAS. The learner agents use observation mechanism during interaction that allows them to observe the characteristics of other agents. Two neighboring agent characteristics are considered in this work, i.e., both past interaction extracted by using Q-learning and relative degree for various neighboring agents of an interacting agent in a network. For agent interaction, two social network topologies, i.e. scale-free and small-world are considered in this work.

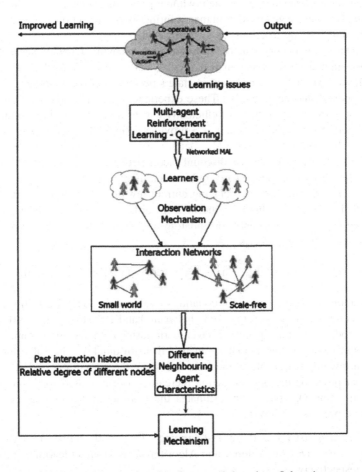

Fig. 1. Multi-agent learning framework based on Q-learning

3.1   Q-Learning Algorithm

Introduction. Q-learning [1] is a reinforcement learning technique in machine learning, in which "Q" is identical to a value that serves as a returned reward, used to assign reinforcement and can be expressed as the "quality" of action performed in a given state. In Q-learning and other relevant algorithms, an agent attempts to learn the best optimal policy by taking into consideration its history of interaction with various neighboring agents or the environment.

The history of an agent's interaction in Q-learning can be presented as a sequence of state-action-rewards such as:

$$((s_0, a_0, r_1), (s_1, a_1, r_2), (s_2, a_2, r_3), (s_3, a_3, r_4), \ldots \ldots (s_n, a_n, r_m))$$

where s_0 is the current state of the agent while it performs action a_0, resulting in reward r_1 and moves to next state i.e., s_1; and then it further performs action a_1, which results in reward r_2, and ends up in next state s_2; and so on.

The interaction history can be considered as a chain of experiences, where an experience gained by an agent in a particular state can be defined as a experience quadruple <s, a, r, s'> ; i.e., an agent in state s performed some action a, got reward r and then moved into next state s'. These experiences are preserved as an interaction history that helps an agent to learn efficiently and to find what to do in future.

An experience quadruple <s, a, r, s'> provides a single data-set to estimate $Q_{new}(s, a)$ matrix. This data-set is expressed in such a way that an agent receives the future value of $r + \gamma V(s')$, where γ is a discount factor between 0 and 1. If $\gamma = 0$, an agent will consider only immediate rewards rather than future rewards. And if $\gamma = 1$, an agent will consider future rewards by delaying current rewards. And, $V(s') = \max_a Q(s', a)$; i.e., discounted estimated future value of a reward. This new data-set is called as a return. The Eq. (1) is considered for updating the estimate for $Q_{new}(s, a)$ by an agent having an old estimate as $Q_{old}(s, a)$:

$$Q_{new}(s, a) \leftarrow Q_{old}(s, a) + \alpha[r + \gamma \max_a Q(s', a) - Q_{old}(s, a)] \qquad (1)$$

The parameters that are used for updating Q-value are α and γ, i.e. learning rate and discount factor respectively, set possibly between 0 and 1 randomly. If $\alpha = 0$, Q-values are never updated, and an agent will never learn during the interaction. And, if $\alpha = 0.9$ (a very high value), it means that an agent will learn quickly. The value $\max_a$ is the maximum reward, achievable in the state following the current one, i.e. it is the best reward that proceeds the optimal action thereafter. The proposed work progresses to define a function $Q_{new}(s, a)$ that estimates the best action (a) in state (s) so as to maximize a progressive reward.

Algorithms proposed based on Q-Learning. This work defines two Q-Learning based algorithms, i.e., Algorithm 1 and Algorithm 2 as Train_Q-learning and Test_Q-learning respectively.

Algorithm 1 is used to demonstrate the learning experience of an agent where each episode is treated as a single training session. In each training session, an agent usually traverses in an environment, receives reward (if any available) continuously till it reaches the goal state. The aim of this training is to improvise the "learning" of an agent represented by matrix Q. The number of episodes together contributes to optimised Q and when Q is optimised, an agent will find the best and fastest path to the state with goal node.

Algorithm 1. Train_Q-learning

```
1. Set learning rate, α = "x" where    0<x<1.
2. Set discount factor, γ = "y" where 0<y<1.
3. Set Environment reward matrix, R(s, a).
4. Initialize matrix Q(s, a) = 0.
5. Repeat (for each episode):
6.      Initialize state's' randomly
7.      Repeat (for each step of an episode: Update Q-
value)
8.         Select 'a' for s
9.         if T(s, a) ≠ null
10.           s' ← T(s, a), where s' is next state, T
stores state transitions
11.           r ← R(s, a), where r is reward, R stores re-
wards obtained
12.        else
13.           Choose 'a', observe 'r'and s'
14.           T(s, a) ← s'
15.           R(s, a) ← r
16.           Compute Q(s, a)_new ← Q(s, a)_old + α[r + γmax_aQ(s',
a) − Q(s,a)_old]
17.        Set next state as current state,
             Set s ← s'
18.        Until 's' is reached on termination condition.
19.     End of loop
20. End of loop
```

Algorithm 2 is used to find the trace of actions that have the maximum reward values recorded in Q for each state of interaction and moves to the next state until it reaches the termination condition.

Algorithm 2. Test_Q-learning

```
1. Set current state, s = 0
2. Let goal = "x"
3. From s, find max_aQ(s, a)
4. Set s ← s'
5. Repeat step 2 to 4 while s! = x.
```

3.2   Learner Agents

Learners [1, 6, 18] are agents who have capability to learn from the environment. Learners can perceive their individual actions and Q-values along with payoffs for all the neighboring agents. The experience for an agent 'i' can be recorded as $<a_i, r(a_i)>$, where a_i is the action performed by an agent 'i' and $r(a_i)$ is the reward for an action 'a_i'. Learning of an agent is based upon Eq. (2)

$$Q_{new}(a) = (1 - \lambda)Q_{old}(a) + \lambda.r(a) \tag{2}$$

Learners perform their tasks, obtain a reward corresponding to the action performed by them and update their Q-values without considering the tasks performed by other interacting agents in the environment. At the end of each state transition t, each agent is able to perceive the information about its neighbors. Information that each agent 'i' perceives at the end of state transition t, can be represented as the set S_i^t:

$$S_i^t = \{ < S_i^t, \ a_i^t, \ r_i^t, \ S_i^{t+1} > , \ <S_{x,1}^t, \ x_1^t, \ r_1^t, \ S_{x,1}^{t+1} > , \ ......, \ <S_{x,N(i)}^t, \ x_{N(i)}^t,$$
$$r_{N(i)}^t, \ S_{b,N(i)}^{t+1} > \}$$

where quadruple $<s_i^t, a_i^t, r^t, s_i^{t+1}>$ denotes current state s_i^t of an agent 'i', action a_i^t performed in its current state, reward r^t returned after performing action 'a' and the next state s_i^{t+1} to which agent moves after receiving its reward and the rest of quadruples comprise the corresponding current states, actions, rewards and next state information for all the neighbors of an agent i in the set S_i^t.

3.3   Interaction Networks

When agents in NMAS interact with each other in order to achieve their individual or societal goals, they form an interaction network. The proposed framework is validated using two types of interaction networks, i.e., small-world and scale-free networks.

Small-World Networks. Small-world networks [17] have two independent structural properties i.e. high clustering coefficients and short average path lengths. Most of the nodes in this type of networks have the same number of connections. The proposed MAL framework uses Watts and Strogatz model which is one of very basic graph models used to construct small-world networks for simulation.

Scale-Free Networks. Scale-free networks [17] exhibit the property of degree distribution, based on power law. One of the main properties of this network is all nodes are not equal, i.e., most of the nodes in the scale-free network have very few connected nodes and only a few nodes have large number of connections. The Barabasi-Albert model is used in the proposed MAL framework to generate a scale-free network for simulation and experimental analysis.

It is assumed that an interaction stops when the agent reaches the final, i.e., goal state and is able to discover the most efficient route using Q-Learning in multi-agent learning environment. During each episode, an agent interacts with another agent by selecting it from its neighborhood set by comparing their relative degrees. The basic interaction protocol which is followed during each round of interaction when an agent plays cooperative games is demonstrated as Algorithm 3.

Algorithm 3. Interaction protocol for the network-multi-agent learning framework in cooperative games.

```
1 for a number of episodes do
2   for each agent in the MAS do
3     if a single agent has multiple interacting partners
4       Choose a neighboring agent from its neighborhood
by comparing the relative degrees i.e.  deg(v) |v∈V(G)
5     else
6       The interacting partner is selected from the
neighborhood in random manner
7     end if
8   Play a two-player cooperative decision game.
9   Update policy that depends on its experience gained
in the current episode
10  end for
11 end for
```

4 Simulation

The experimental analysis is performed by modeling a social network (SN) [2] using the proposed MAL framework in the form of NMAS (Fig. 2). The SN comprises various types of nodes modeled as agents which can be positively or negatively rewarded. The normal, start and goal nodes are presented by green, black, blue and red colors respectively. An agent aims to reach its goal state by discovering the most efficient route. During its traversal, an agent will interact with other neighboring agents and will choose the best neighboring agent based on their relative degrees. In this Q-Learning based NMAS, the simulation is based upon constant trial and error approach, in which an agent gathers data about its environment and other agents in order to achieve its goal.

During the simulation, first of all, an agent's past interaction histories during the training session will be stored in order to enhance the learning set of an agent. During each session, an agent will continuously interact with other neighboring agents, receives its rewards and reaches the goal state. A number of training sessions will be executed to enhance the learning set of an interacting agent. Secondly, after each training session, an agent gets ready to further move to the testing phase where it will use the stored interaction history to finally reach its destination with maximum reward.

This will happen because now an agent can easily analyze which node(s) has the highest reward value(s) that could result in best and optimal route. Finally, in the testing session, agent will find an efficient sequence of states with the highest reward from the initial to goal state. This sequence will decide the optimal route followed by

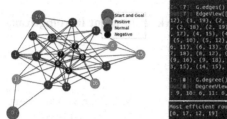 

Fig. 2. Simulation of network multi-agent system (Color figure online)

Table 1. Simulation Parameters used for Experimental Analysis of MAL framework

Simulation parameters	Value
Environment	Social network
Typologies used	Scale-free and small-world
Modeling structure	Graph
No. of nodes/Population	20
Learning rate (α)	0.5
Discount factor (γ)	0.8

an agent to reach its goal state. The parameters used for the simulation of proposed MAL framework in NMAS (shown in Fig. 2) are described in Table 1.

An agent will consider a number of interactions with other agents (nodes) in a network to reach its goal node. In this setting, the goal of the experiment is to improve the learning between the interacting nodes which depends upon the optimal learning policies and the best action selection. Here, decline in number of interactions by an agent results in the improved learning efficiency in the multi-agent learning environment (NMAS).

5 Results and Interpretations

To validate the proposed MAL framework, the experiments were performed with a static agent population n; n = 20. For the scale-free network G_n^m, the default degree distribution exponent is m; m = 2; for the small-world network $G_n^{k, \, p}$, the default 'k' nearest neighbor connected to each node is set to be 2 and the rewiring probability is ρ; $\rho = 0.5$. The initial Q-matrix is initialized to 0, then its value is changed from 0, if it is a viable path and 100 if it is a goal path. Finally, the training function and testing functions are executed (around 8000 times) using the Q-Learning technique to discover the most efficient route in a network.

5.1 Scale-Free-Graph

In the first setting, Q-learning is only implemented in a scale-free graph without considering relative degrees of different neighboring nodes in the environment. An agent has to just reach its goal by choosing the best node on each step based on Q-learning algorithm. As shown in the results (Fig. 3), when the value of 'm' is increased from 2 to 5, 7, and 10, the number of interactions required to reach its goal also increased, and this happened due to lack of learning efficiency of an interacting agent in a complex social network.

To improve the learning performance, Q-learning algorithm is implemented along with the relative degree of a neighboring node of the interacting agent. In the next setting, some environmental information such as number of nodes differentiated based upon the relative degree of every neighboring node is added to the network, where an interacting agent will prefer to choose node having the lesser relative degree i.e., deg (v) < 6 and avoids the node that has higher relative degree, i.e. deg(v) > 9 in order to choose most efficient route.

As shown in the results, (Fig. 4) this improves the learning performance of an interacting agent. And after analyzing the results it is observed that as the value of m increases, the number of interactions required by an agent decrease in order to reach its goal point.

5.2 Small-World-Graph

The same experiment is again performed for small-world network where value of k is increased simultaneously. The results were analyzed without adding the information of relative degrees of the neighboring nodes in the environment which resulted in increase in the number of interactions when 'k' was increased from 2 to 5, 7 and 10, to reach its goal (Fig. 5). But, it was observed that the difference in the results was very less as compared to the scale-free graph. But after applying relative degree and differentiating nodes on the basis of degree, where agent tries to interact with the node having lesser relative degree, i.e., deg(v) <=7 and avoids a neighboring agent with a higher relative degree, i.e. deg(v) > 10. It was analyzed that as k increased, the number of interactions gradually decreased but after few numbers of attempts, started increasing (Fig. 6).

After comparison of the results for both types of networks, it can be interpreted that in a scale-free network, learning is performed quickly as compared to a small-world network (Table 2). The proposed technique (Q-Learning + neighboring agent characteristics) has improved the learning performance of agents in case of both the networks.

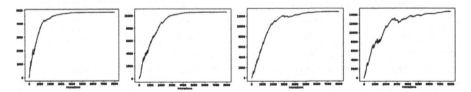

Fig. 3. Experimental results before considering relative degree of neighboring nodes with m = 2, 5, 7, 10 respectively.

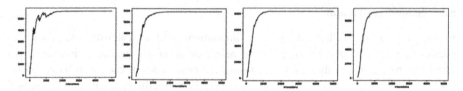

Fig. 4. Improved performance after considering relative degree of neighboring nodes with m = 5, 7, 10, 12 respectively

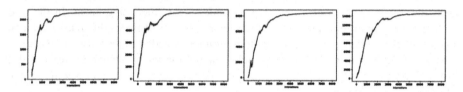

Fig. 5. Experimental results before considering relative degree of neighboring nodes with k = 2, 5, 7, 10 respectively.

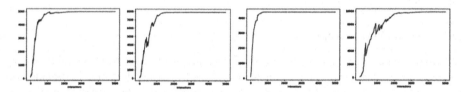

Fig. 6. Improved performance after considering relative degree of neighboring nodes with k = 5, 7, 10, 12 respectively

Table 2. Results for the proposed MAL framework for scale-free and small-world networks respectively.

Scale-free graph			Small-world graph		
m	Number of interactions (appx.) (before considering relative degrees)	Number of interactions (appx.) (after considering relative degrees)	k	Number of interactions (appx.) (before considering relative degrees)	Number of interactions (appx.) (after considering relative degrees)
5	4200	1800	5	3100	1800
7	5500	1700	7	4000	1500
10	8000	1300	10	4200	800
12	>8000	800	12	8000	2300

6 Conclusions and Future Work

In this paper, we have investigated and analyzed the impact of relative degree of nodes in NMAS while implementing Q-learning algorithm for the proposed MAL framework. This is accomplished by first modeling a NMAS in the form of a social network (both small-world and scale-free topologies) along with various neighboring agent characteristics for a particular node in the network. Then, these social networks are experimentally analyzed and simulated by varying the relative degrees of neighboring nodes to investigate learning performance in each session by selecting most efficient state.

Experimental results show that there is increase in learning performance of an interacting agent when it considers relative degrees of neighboring nodes in NMAS. Also, the underlying topology of a network indeed matter in the learning performance, since scale-free networks learnt quickly as compared to small-world networks as shown in experimental analysis.

As a future research direction, the proposed work can be performed in a better environment with a broader domain and higher agent dependence on one another, i.e. more number of agents can start their traversal and compete (if competitive agents) or cooperate (if cooperative agents) with other neighboring agents to reach their goal state. Furthermore, the proposed methods can also be investigated to improve the learning performance by considering the relative degrees of different neighboring nodes along with other characteristics of neighboring agents in a network, which an agent can learn from the system requirements automatically.

References

1. Claus, C., Boutilier, C.: The Dynamics of reinforcement learning in cooperative multiagent systems. In: Proceedings of the Fifteenth National Conference on Artificial Intelligence, pp. 746–752 (1998)
2. Franchi, E.: A multi-agent implementation of social networks. In: Proceedings of the 11th {WOA} 2010 Workshop, Dagli Oggetti Agli Agenti, Rimini, Italy (2010)
3. Franchi, E., Poggi, A.: Multi-Agent systems and social networks. Handbook of Research on Business Social Networking: Organizational, Managerial, and Technological Dimensions. IGI Global, Hershey, Pennsylvania, pp. 84–97 (2011)
4. Hao, J., Leung, H.: The dynamics of reinforcement social learning in cooperative multiagent systems. In: Proceedings of IJCAI 2013, Beijing, pp. 184–190 (2013)
5. Hao, J., Leung, H.: Achieving socially optimal outcomes in multiagent systems with reinforcement social learning. ACM Trans. Auton. Adapt. Syst. 8(3), 1–23 (2013)
6. Hao, J., Huang, D., Cai, Y., Leung, H.: Networked reinforcement social learning towards coordination in cooperative multiagent systems. In: 26th IEEE International Conference on Tools with Artificial Intelligence (2014)
7. Hao, J., Leung, H.: Reinforcement social learning of coordination in cooperative multiagent systems (extended abstract). In: Proceedings of AAMAS 2013, Saint Paul, pp. 1321–1322 (2013)
8. Hao, J., Huang, D., Cai, Y., Leung, H.: The dynamics of reinforcement social learning in networked cooperative multiagent systems. In: Proceedings of AAAI 1958, pp. 111–122 (2017)

9. Hao, J.Y., Leung, H. F.: Learning to achieve social rationality using tag mechanism in repeated interactions. In: Proceedings of ICTAI 2011, pp. 148–155 (2011)
10. Jiang, Y., Zhou, Y., Wang, W.: Task allocation for undependable multiagent systems in social networks. IEEE Trans. Parallel Distrib. Syst. **24**(8), 1671–1681 (2013)
11. Jiang, Y., Jiang, J.C.: Understanding social networks from a multiagent perspective. IEEE Trans. Parallel Distrib. Syst. **25**(10), 2743–2759 (2013)
12. Kapetanakis, S., Kudenko, D.: Reinforcement learning of coordination in cooperative multiagent systems. In: Proceedings of the AAAI 2002, pp. 326–331 (2002)
13. Lauer, M., Riedmiller, M.: An algorithm for distributed reinforcement learning in cooperative multi-agent systems. In: Proceedings of ICML 2000, pp. 535–542 (2012)
14. Lowe, R., Wu, Y., Tamar, A., Harb, J., Abbeel, P., Mordatch, I.: Multi-Agent actor-critic for mixed cooperative-competitive environments. In: Proceedings of 2017 Conference on Neural Information Processing Systems (2017)
15. Matignon, L., Laurent, G.J., Le For-Piat, N.: Independent reinforcement learners in cooperative Markov games: a survey regarding coordination problems. Knowl. Eng. Rev. **27**, 1–31 (2012)
16. Matlock, M., Sen, S.: Effective tag mechanisms for evolving coordination. In: Proceedings of AAMAS 2007, pp. 1340–1347 (2007)
17. Matthew, E.G., Marie des, J.: Social network structures and their impact on multi-agent system dynamics. In: Proceedings of FLAIRS 2005, pp. 32–37 (2005)
18. Multi-Agent system. Wikipedia, Wikipedia Foundation. https://en.wikipedia.org/wiki/Multi-agent_system. Accessed 5 Jan 2018
19. Glavic, M.: Agents and Multi-Agent Systems: A Short Introduction for Power Engineers. http://www.montefiore.ulg.ac.be/ ~ glavic/MAS-Intro_Tech_report.pdf
20. Silva, F., Glatt, R., Costa, A.H.R.: Simultaneously learning and advising in multi-agent reinforcement learning. In: Proceedings of the 16th Conference on Autonomous Agents and MultiAgent Systems (AAMAS 2017). International Foundation for Autonomous Agents and Multiagent Systems, Richland, pp. 1100–1108 (2017)
21. Tuyls, K., Weiss, G.: Multiagent learning: basics, challenges, and prospects. AI Mag. **33**(3), 41–50 (2012)
22. Wooldridge, M.: An Introduction to Multiagent Systems. John Wiley, Hoboken (2002)

A Diagnostic System Based on Fuzzy Logic for Clinical Examination of Patients in Ayurveda

Ranjit Kaur[⊠] and Kamaldeep Kaur

School of Computer Science Engineering, Lovely Professional University,
Phagwara, Punjab, India
reetbansal09@gmail.com, kaurdeep230@gmail.com

Abstract. Ayurveda accentuate on 'Personalized Treatment' as it considers very individual different in terms of physical and mental traits. Hence Ayurvedic Physicians carry out Dashvidh Prakisha (Ten Fold Examination) of patients to assess various aspects of personality, temperament, health status of the patient. This examination will help the physicians to provide the personalized treatment and appropriate dose of medicine to the patients. The prime objective of this research is to develop a tool based on fuzzy logic to automate the clinical examination of patients. A fuzzy controller is designed which has all the input and output parameters acquired by rigorous consultation with Ayurvedic Physicians. A knowledge base constructed by mapping input parameters to an appropriate output parameter based on the expertise of Ayurvedic Physicians is fed into the fuzzy controller. Comparative study is applied for assessing the performance of the proposed system. Diagnosis carried out by the Ayurvedic Physicians and results generated by the system and are compared for 150 patients.

Keywords: Fuzzy logic · Human Constituents · Immunity · Ayurveda
Inference engine · Defuzzification

1 Introduction

Ancient Indian culture has many precious gems in its basket. One of these indispensable gem is Ayurveda, which has been succoring the mankind to maintain a healthy and prosperous life. Ayurveda is a science of ancient times which deals with curing the diseases of patients. Ayurveda accentuate on 'Personalized Treatment' as it considers very individual different in terms of physical and mental traits. Following the principle of personalized treatment, Ayurvedic physicians emphasizes that the examination of patients is as important as the examination of diseases [1].

- Examination of disease (Roga Pariksha).
- Examination of patient (Rogi Prakisha).

For the examination of patient Dashvidh Pariksha(Ten Fold Examination) in Ayurveda is considered through which a thorough examination of patient is done to accumulate maximum information about the patient before prescribing any medicine,

© Springer Nature Singapore Pte Ltd. 2019
A. K. Luhach et al. (Eds.): ICAICR 2018, CCIS 955, pp. 757–771, 2019.
https://doi.org/10.1007/978-981-13-3140-4_68

drug or treatment. The Ten Fold Examination (Dashvidh Pariksha) was introduced by Acharya Charaka thousands of years ago. This examination is carried out to assess and evaluate various aspects of personality, temperament, health status of the patient. Figure 1 shows the ten factors considered during the examination of patient [1].

1.1   Examination of Human Constitution (Prakriti Pariksha)

Prakriti literary means 'Nature'. In reference to the human beings, Prakriti means the distinctive psychological and physical nature [7]. In Ayurveda, individuals are classified according to their physical structure and their mental attributes. Analysis of prakriti guides the physicians to help their patients live a healthy life. Prakriti is genetic in nature which means it is decided at the time of conception and it depends upon many parental, antenatal and postnatal factors. Human constitution or Prakriti can be of seven types: Vatt, Pitt, Kapha, Vatt-Pitt, Vatt-Kapha, Pitt-Kapha and Vitt-Pitt-Kapha.

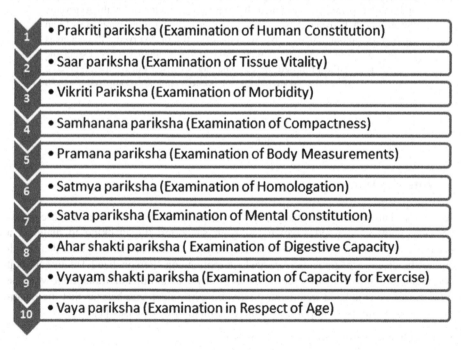

Fig. 1. Tenfold examination of the patients

1.2   Examination of Tissue Vitality (Saar Pariksha)

There are seven vital tissues of which the whole human body is made up of. They are namely, Rasa (Lymph or plasma), Mamsa (Muscle), Rakta (Blood), Asthi (Bone), Majja (Bone Marrow), Meda (Fat tissues), Sukra (Reproductive Tissues). These tissues play a vital role in maintaining and nourishing the whole body. Saar Pariksha is one of the most reliable and practical examination for determining the strength or immunity of the individual's body. This examination helps the physicians to prescribe the treatment and dose of the medicines.

This research works mainly focuses on modeling a system for first two factors of 'Dashvidh Pariksha' i.e. Examination of Human Constituents and Tissue Vitality.

2   Literature Review

Computer base methods enhance the quality in field of medical science. In artificial intelligence, development of expert system is emerging field which uses human knowledge to diagnose the disease accurately. In 1970s, the first expert system which is developed for infectious blood diseases is MYCIN. It is rule base system, implemented with 500 rules in LISP and deals with certain degree of belief using combining functions [2]. With the advancement, many expert systems in various field is designed like DENDRAL, PROSPECTOR, ENT, cancer, dengue, gynecology, tumor, asthma and diabetes.

Başçiftçi and Avuçlu developed a medical expert system to diagnose the cancer type as Breast, Lung, Renal and Cervical opening cancer using Boolean function minimization. There were 13 input symptoms as risk factor and 4 outputs used to diagnose the type of cancer [3]. An android application was used as interface. Kurniawan, Sihwi and Gunarhadi (2017), designed an expert system using java program to diagnose the student with severity level of dysgraphia. Knowledge acquisition were done from experts based on interviews and observations. Decision tree was implemented to represent the knowledge using forward chaining approach. The system was tested on 19 students from grade 3 to 6 with 97.41% accuracy [4]. Amiri and Khadivar designed the fuzzy system to diagnose the seven types of disorders in wrist and defined treatment for the diseases in MATLAB software. Mamdani inference system was used for the diagnosis of musculoskeletal disorders in wrist. The method used for the collection of data was Fuzzy Delphi. Based on the input parameters fuzzy system generated the output in form of score. From the score, the disease was diagnosed. The accuracy of that system was 86.7% which was compared by SPSS software [5]. Zirra designed an expert system that diagnosis the severity level of osteomyelitis (bone infection disease), usually affect the long bones in children and adults. To diagnose this disease fuzzy system took four parameters (pain, age, swelling, fever) as input and severity level of disease as output. Range for all input parameter was taken from 0 to 1. The parameter pain was categorized as case 1 ignore pain, case 2, case 3 and case 4 severe pain whereas swelling and fever were categorized as very mild, mild, moderate, severe and very severe. Total 500 rules were made for diagnosis of severity level of osteomyelitis [6].

3   Knowledge Engineering

Parameters for determining the Human Constituent type and vitality of the seven tissues (blood tissue, lymph, fat tissue, bone marrow, bone tissue, reproductive tissues, muscle tissue) as well as the vitality of mind are acquired through rigorous consultation with the Ayurvedic physicians. The acquired and identified parameters for every tissue and constituent type are displayed in Tables 1 and 2 respectively. A questionnaire is developed to gather information of patients considering these factors.

Table 1. Acquired parameters for determining Human Constituents.

Class	Sub-Class	Acquired Parameters	PITT	VATT	KAPH	Assigned Priority
Physical Traits	Anatomical Traits	Complexion	Whitish	Dark	Fair	Non-Prime
		Eyes	Moderate size	Small	Big	Non-Prime
		Hair	Normal	Dry	Soft	**Prime**
		Physique	Medium	Thin	Heavy	Non-Prime
		Skin	Medium	Dry & Rough	Oily	**Prime**
		Tendons & veins	Fairly Visible	Visible	Covered	Non-Prime
	Physiological traits	Voice/Speech	High Pitch	Stammering & weak	Strong & deep rooted	Non-Prime
		Sexual Activeness	Medium	Less	High	Non-Prime
		Eating habits	Medium	Fast	Slow	Non-Prime
		Walk	Medium	Swift	Slow	Non-Prime
		Appetite	Heavy	Changeable	Less and regular	**Prime**
		Stool	Loose stool and regular	Dry and constipated	Thick and sluggish constipation	**Prime**
	Homeostatic traits	Immunity	Medium	Low	High	Non-Prime
		Cold tolerance	Medium	Very Less	High	Non-Prime
		Energy	Medium	Low	High	Non-Prime
		Sweating	More	Less	Medium	**Prime**
		Sleep	Moderate	Irregular	Sound & deep	**Prime**
		Thirst	Excessive	Changeable	Less	**Prime**
Mental Traits	Behavioral Traits	Activities	Moderate	Hyperactive	Slow, Measured	**Prime**
		Jealous	Moderate	More	Less	Non-Prime
		Friendship	Medium	Short lived	Strong & long lived	Non-Prime
		Patience	Medium	Less	High	Non-Prime
		Talk	Medium	Talkative & garrulous	talk to the point	Non-Prime
		Temper	Short tempered	Sometimes	Calm & Quiet	**Prime**
	Intellectual Traits	Concentration	Medium	Low	Good	Non-Prime
		Intelligence	Moderate	Low	High	Non-Prime
		Memory & retention	Moderate	Short	Long	**Prime**
		Grasping power	High	Medium	Low	Non-Prime

Table 2. Sign and symptoms for the tissue vitality

Tissues	Signs tissue vitality
Plasma	Smooth, shiny and soft skin delicate, small and deep rooted body hairs
Blood tissue	Reddish and shiny lips, eyes, forehead, tongue, palms, face, sexual organs and foot sole
Bone tissue	Firm and big ankle, heel, collar bones, knee joint, jaw/chin, teeth, nails and head
Bone marrow tissue	Round, long, stable and stout joints, smooth voice
Fat tissue	Soft and smooth nails, hairs, teeth, smooth voice, Oily skin
Muscle tissue	Healthy, bulky and stable mass on eyes, forehead, shoulder, jaws, armpit, abdomen, chest, nape of neck and cheeks
Reproductive tissues	Soft spoken, Cheerful, equal sized teeth, heavy buttocks, smooth complexion

4 Research Methodology for Implemented System

The implemented system works in two phases. In the first phase the system determines the Human Constituents (Prakriti) of an individual which will assist the ayurvedic physicians to distinguish each individual and provide personalised treatment according to the constituent's type. In second phase the system determines the vitality of tissues which will assist the physicians to identify the immunity level of the patient. Based on the immunity level, dosage of the medicines will be decided accordingly for each patient. The system is designed using MATLAB software. All the fuzzified input parameters are fed into the Mamdani Inference system and crisp output is obtained by defuzzifying output parameters using centroid method as shown in Fig. 2.

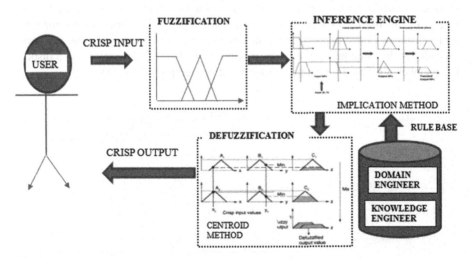

Fig. 2. Research methodology for proposed system

4.1 Choosing Membership Functions

Membership functions are used to tackle with the vague input and output parameters. Matlab provides various membership functions like Guassian, Triangular, Trapezoidal. For the proposed system, Triangular and Trapezoidal meberiship functions are used as shown in Fig. 3. A trapezoidal membership function can be defined as (1) [7].

$$\mu(x; q, r, s, t) = \max\left(\min\left(\frac{x-q}{r-q}, 1\frac{t-x}{t-s}\right), 0\right) \tag{1}$$

The triangular membership function can be defined as (2) [8].

$$\mu(x; q, r, s) = \max\left(\min\left(\frac{x-q}{r-q}, \frac{s-x}{s-r}\right), 0\right) \tag{2}$$

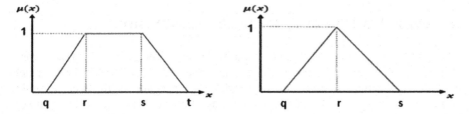

Fig. 3. Trapezoidal and Triangular membership functions

4.2 Fuzzification of Linguistic Variables

After choosing the appropriate membership function, all the input and output parameters are fuzzified. Fuzzification is the process of transforming real numbers into fuzzy value ranging from 0 to 1 [9, 10]. The fuzzified input and output variable for determining Human Constituents is shown in Tables 3 and 4. The fuzzified input and output variable for determining Immunity level is shown in Table 5. Figures 4 and 5 displays the membership functions employed for input and output parameters.

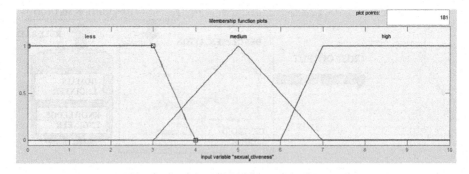

Fig. 4. Fuzzification of input linguistic variables

$$\mu_{LESS}(z) = \begin{cases} \frac{4-z}{1}, & 3 \le z \le 4 \\ 1, & z \le 3 \end{cases} \tag{3}$$

$$\mu_{MEDIUM}(z) = \begin{cases} \frac{z-3}{4-3}, & 3 \le z \le 4 \\ 1, & z = 5 \\ \frac{7-z}{7-6}, & 6 \le z \le 7 \end{cases} \tag{4}$$

$$\mu_{HIGH}(z) = \begin{cases} \frac{z-6}{1}, & 6 \le z \le 7 \\ 1, & z \ge 7 \end{cases} \tag{5}$$

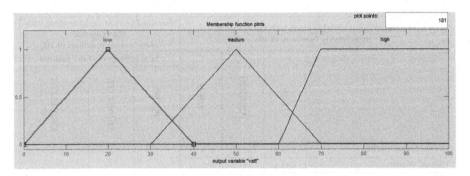

Fig. 5. Fuzzification of output linguistic variables

$$\mu_{LOW}(z) = \begin{cases} \frac{40-z}{1}, & 30 \le z \le 40 \\ 1, & z \le 30 \end{cases} \tag{6}$$

$$\mu_{MEDIUM}(z) = \begin{cases} \frac{z-30}{40-30}, & 30 \le z \le 40 \\ 1, & z = 50 \\ \frac{70-z}{70-60}, & 60 \le z \le 70 \end{cases} \tag{7}$$

$$\mu_{HIGH}(z) = \begin{cases} \frac{z-60}{1}, & 60 \le z \le 70 \\ 1, & z \ge 70 \end{cases} \tag{8}$$

Table 3. Fuzzified input variables and the ranges of membership functions for determining Human Constituents

Fuzzified input variable	Ranges of membership functions (0–10)		
	Low	Medium	High
	−1 to 4	3 to 7	6 to 11

Table 4. Fuzzified output variables and the ranges of membership functions for determining Human Constituents

Fuzzified output variable	Ranges of membership functions (0–100)		
	Low	Medium	High
PITT	0 to 40	30 to 70	60 to 110
VATT	0 to 40	30 to 70	60 to 110
KAPHA	0 to 40	30 to 70	60 to 110

Table 5. Input and output variable along with their membership ranges for determining Immunity level

Fuzzified Input variable along with the ranges of membership functions (0-10)				Fuzzified Output variable along with the ranges of membership functions (0-10)		
				Immunity level of the patients		
	LOW	*MEDIUM*	*HIGH*	*POOR*	*MODERATE*	*EXCELLENT*
Bone Tissue vitality	0 to 4	3 to 7	6 to 11			
Blood vitality	0 to 4	3 to 7	6 to 11			
Lymph Tissue vitality	0 to 4	3 to 7	6 to 11			
Bone Marrow vitality	0 to 4	3 to 7	6 to 11	0 to 4	3 to 7	6 to 11
Muscle Tissue vitality	0 to 4	3 to 7	6 to 11			
Fat Tissue vitality	0 to 4	3 to 7	6 to 11			
Mind vitality	0 to 4	3 to 7	6 to 11			
Reproductive Tissues vitality	0 to 4	3 to 7	6 to 11			

4.3   Design of Knowledge Base

After Fuzzification the next step is to design the knowledge base. The rules are formed in IF-THEN form. IF x is the input parameter, z is the output parameter, M is the fuzzified input linguistic variable and N is the fuzzified output linguistic variable then the fuzzy rules are represented as IF (x is M) THEN (y is N) [11, 12].

Tables 6 and 7 displays some sample rules designed with the help of Ayurvedic experts for determining Human Constituents and Immunity Level of patients respectively.

Table 6. Sample rules for Human Constituents where input parameters are Hair, Skin, Physique, Tendons & viens, Complexion, Eyes and output parameters are VATT, PITT, KAPH

#Rule	Hair	Skin	Physique	Tendons & viens	Complexion	Eyes	VATT	PITT	KAPH
1.	Dry	Dry	Thin	Visible	Dark	Small	**High**	**Low**	**Low**
2.	Dry	Dry	Thin	Fairly Visible	Wheatish	Medium	**Medium**	**Medium**	**Low**
3.	Normal	Medium	Medium	Visible	wheatish	Medium	**Low**	**High**	**Low**
4.	Normal	Medium	Thin	Covered	Fair	Large	**Low**	**Medium**	**Medium**

Table 7. Sample rules for Immunity Level where input parameters are Vitality of Blood, Bone, Lymph Bone Marrow, Fat, Reproductive Tissue, Muscle, Mind and output parameter is Immunity Level

#Rule	Lymph	Blood	Bone	Bone marrow	Fat	Muscle	Reproductive tissue	Mind	Immunity level
1.	Low	Low	Low	Low	Low	Low	High	High	Moderate
2.	High	High	High	High	High	High	High	High	Excellent
3.	Low	Moderate	Moderate	Moderate	Moderate	Moderate	Moderate	Moderate	Low

4.4   Inference Mechanism

Mamdani Inference Engine is used to implement the proposed system. Five fuzzy inference systems are constructed for determining the Human Constituents in first phase. In second phase nine fuzzy systems are constructed for calculating the immunity level of the patients. Figure 6 shows one of the fuzzy inference system designed for the proposed system. Figure 7 shows the rule viewer and Fig. 8 shows the surface view for the fuzzy inference system.

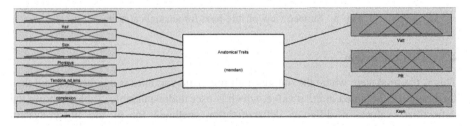

Fig. 6. Mamdani inference process for anatomical traits

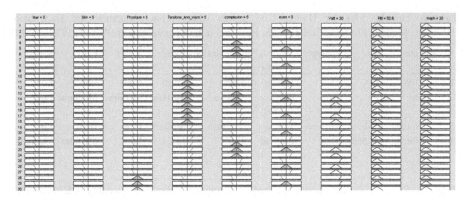

Fig. 7. Fuzzy rule base view for anatomical traits

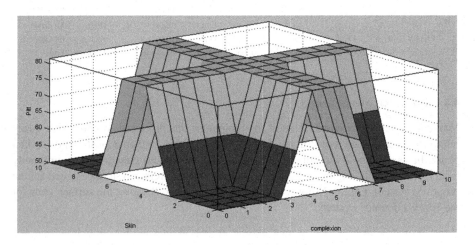

Fig. 8. Surface view of rule base for anatomical traits

4.5   Defuzzification

This is the final step, where the output of all linguistic variables is aggregated, and then final output is obtained in crisp value, which is user understandable. Table 8 shows the defuzzified values of different defuzzification methods for of the fuzzy system designed. Different methods of defuzzification are mentioned below [13, 14]:

- Center of area (COA): The defuzzification method named center of area, calculates the centroid under the aggregation function for that area. It is calculated with the below mentioned formula:

$$Z_{COA} = \frac{\int \mu_A(z)zdz}{\int \mu_A(z)zdz} \tag{9}$$

Table 8. Defuzzified values of different defuzzification methods for anatomical traits

INPUTS (Anatomical Traits)	Hair		1	2.2	3	5	5.6	6.5	7.5	8	9.4
	Skin		1.5	2.7	3.5	4.5	5.1	6	6.5	7	8.4
	Physique		2	3.2	4	4	4.6	5.5	7	7.5	8.9
	Tendons & veins		1.8	3	3.8	4.5	5.1	6	6.8	7.3	8.7
	Complexion		1	2.2	3	4.2	4.8	5.7	6.5	7	8.4
	Size of eyes		2	3.2	4	5.5	6.1	7	7.5	8	9.4
Defuzzified values according to different defuzzification methods	MOM	VATT	85	84	50	20	20	20	20	20	20
		PITT	20	20	50	82.5	82.5	50	20	20	20
		KAPH	20	20	20	20	20	50	82.5	85	85
	SOM	VATT	70	68	38	10	10	10	10	20	20
		PITT	20	16	38	65	65	40	10	20	20
		KAPH	20	16	8	10	10	40	65	70	70
	LOM	VATT	100	100	62	30	30	30	30	20	20
		PITT	20	24	62	100	100	60	30	20	20
		KAPH	20	24	32	30	30	60	100	100	100
	CENTROID	VATT	82.6	82.2	61.5	20	20	20	20	20	20
		PITT	20	20	39.5	81.5	81.4	62.5	30.8	20	0
		KAPH	20	20	20	20	20	39.2	72	82.6	82.6
	BISECTOR	VATT	83	82	58	20	20	20	20	20	20
		PITT	20	20	42	81	81	58	27	20	20
		KAPH	20	20	20	20	20	42	74	83	83

- Bisector of area (BOA): BOA divides the region vertically, where whole area is divided into two equal parts. Sometime, the center of area and bisector of area lies on same line but not always.

$$\int_{a}^{BOA} \mu_A dz = \int_{BOA}^{\beta} \mu_A(z) dz \qquad (10)$$

- Largest of Maximum (LOM): Largest value will be return of the aggregation function.
- Smallest of Maximum (SOM): It returns smallest value of aggregation output membership function.
- Mean of Maximum(MOM): This function calculates arithmetic mean of the aggregated membership functions and return the maximum value with the below mentioned formula.:

$$Z_{mom} = \frac{\int z dz}{\int dz} \qquad (11)$$

5 Graphical User Interface of the System

A perfect GUI should be user friendly so that non- expert can also easily understand how to give input and where to fill values etc. For the proposed expert system Fig. 9 shows graphical user interface (Main window) for Examination of patients. GUI has two tabs namely Physical Constitution and Strength of Body. User will be navigated to the next pages on click of these tabs for calculating the Human Constituents and Immunity of an individual. An excel sheet is prepared which contains the inputs for calculating the vitality of all the seven tissues and Human Constituents. The user enters the value between 1 to 10 in the excel sheet for all the parameters mentioned in the sheet. For instance, user can enter value between 1 to 3 if the physique is thin, 4 to 6 can be entered if the physique is medium or 7 to 10 can be entered if physique is heavy. This excel sheet is imported and displayed when the user clicks on Browse button. Vitality of all the seven tissues and mind are calculated and displayed on the GUI. According to the values calculated for tissue vitality of all the seven tissue, the immunity level of the individual is determined and shown on the GUI. Similarly the value of Human Constituents in terms of Vatt, Pitt and Kaph is displayed.

Fig. 9. Graphical user interface for the proposed system

6   Results

For the testing of the proposed system comparative study is applied in which the system generated results are compared with the outputs provided by the ayurvedic physicians as shown in Tables 9 and 10. The study has shown that the system has produced satisfactory results. This study is approved by the Ayurvedic Specialists of "Government Ayurvedic Dispensary (GAD), Bombeli, Hoshiarpur, Punjab, India".

Table 9. Some sample test results of FIS for determining Human Constitutients

PATIENT ID	OUTPUTS GENERATED				RESULTS
	Human Constituents (Stated by the Ayurvedic Expert)	Human Constituents (Result generated by the System)			
		PITT	VATT	KAPH	
PID-01	PITT- KAPH	41.71	16.58	41.71	True
PID-02	VATT- PITT	33.93	47.27	18.09	True
PID-03	PITT	55.09	24.96	19.96	True
PID-04	KAPH	22.66	27.78	49.57	True
PID-05	PITT- KAPH	40.54	23.89	35.54	True
PID-06	VATT- PITT	38.97	42.19	18.85	True
PID-07	VATT-KAPH	22.68	44.49	32.82	True
PID-08	PITT	52.31	28.85	18.83	True
PID-09	PITT-VATT	40.56	30.54	28.87	True
PID-10	KAPH- PITT	33.87	23.87	42.23	True
PID-11	PITT-VATT	44.43	37.76	17.76	True
PID-12	VATT	23.83	52.31	23.83	True

Table 10. Some sample test results of FIS for determining Immunity Level

Patient ID	INPUTS GIVEN TO THE SYSTEM								OUTPUTS GENERATED		RESULTS
	Blood Tissue Vitality	Fat Tissue Vitality	Muscle Tissue Vitality	Lymph Tissue Vitality	Bone Marrow Tissue Vitality	Reproductive tissue Vitality	Bone Tissue Vitality Tissue Vitality	Mind Vitality	Immunity Level (Stated by the Ayurvedic Expert)	Immunity Level (Result generated by the Fuzzy System)	
PID-01	5	8.15	5	4	8.15	8.26	5	8.15	Medium	50	True
PID-02	5	8.15	5	4	5	5	5	5	Poor	20	True
PID-03	5	5	2	4	5	5	5	5	Poor	20	True
PID-04	5	5	5	4	5	5	5	5	Poor	20	True
PID-05	5	5	5	5	5	8.26	5	5	Poor	20	True
PID-06	8.15	8.15	8.26	7	8.15	8.15	8.15	8.15	Excellent	82.63	True
PID-07	5	5	5	6.5	5	5	5	8.15	Medium	39.17	False
PID-08	8.15	5	8.26	4	5	8.26	5	5	Medium	50	True
PID-09	8.26	3.08	5	6..5	5	5	7.19	8.26	Medium	50	True
PID-10	7.19	8.15	8.26	6.5	8.26	8.26	7.19	8.15	Excellent	71.97	True
PID-11	8.26	5	5	6.5	5	5	5	8.26	Medium	50	True
PID-12	2	5	5	4	5	5	5	8.15	Poor	20	True

7 Discussion and Conclusion

The proposed system is designed to assist the ayurvedic practitioners and physicians for clinical examination of patients. Ayurveda follows Dashvidh Pariksha (Ten-fold Examination) for clinical examination of patients out of which two factors Prakriti Prakisha (Examination of Human Constituents) and Saar Pariksha (Examination of tissue vitality) are implemented in this proposed system. Examination of Human Constituents will help the vedic practitioners to provide personalized treatment for the patients whereas Examination of tissue vitality will help them to decide the dose of the medicine to be prescribed to the patients.

This proposed research work can further be extended for implementing rest of the factors in Dashvidh Pariksha. The system could also be designed using Adaptive Neuro-Fuzzy technique and genetic algorithm.

Acknowledgement. The authors wish to express special thanks of gratitude to the expert Dr. Rabjyot Kaur working as Ayurvedic Medical Officer at Government Ayurvedic Dispensary (GAD), Bombeli, Hoshiarpur, Punjab, India for her persistent assistance during the development and testing phase of the proposed system.

References

1. Sharma, R., Dash, B.: Charaka Samhita. Chowkhamba Sanskrit Series (2009)
2. Daniel, M., Hájek, P., Nguyen, P.H.: CADIAG-2 and MYCIN-like systems. Artif. Intell. Med. **9**(3), 241–259 (1997)
3. Başçiftçi, F., Avuçlu, E.: An expert system design to diagnose cancer by using a new method reduced rule base. Comput. Methods Programs Biomed. **157**, 113–120 (2018)
4. Bahrami, A., Bahrami, A.: An expert system for diagnosing dilated cardiomyopathy. Int. J. Eng. Sci. Invent. **3**(3), 38–42 (2014)
5. Amiri, F.M., Khadivar, A.: A fuzzy expert system for diagnosis and treatment of musculoskeletal disorders in wrist. Teh Vjesn - Tech. Gaz **24**(Suppl. 1), 147–155 (2017)
6. Zirra, P.B.: A fuzzy based system for determining the severity level of osteomyelitis. Int. J. Adv. Res. Comput. Sci. Softw. Eng. **6**(6), 174–183 (2016)
7. Ranjit, K., Vishu, M., Prateek, A., Sanjay Kumar, S., Amandeep, K.: Fuzzy expert system for identifying the physical constituents of a human body. Indian J. Sci. Technol. **9**(28) (2016)
8. Mashood, A.H., Adewole, K.S.: Rule-based expert system for disease conference paper. In: International Conference on Science, Technology, Education, Arts, Management and Social Sciences (2015)
9. Putra, I.K.G.D., Prihatini, P.M.: Fuzzy expert system for tropical infectious disease by certainty factor. Telkomnika **10**(4), 825–836 (2012)
10. Sethi, D., Agrawal, P., Madaan, V.: X-Tumour: fuzzy rule based medical expert system to detect tumours. Indian J. Sci. Technol. **9**(11), 5073–5084 (2016)
11. Ranjit, K., Madaan, V., Agrawal, P.: Fuzzy expert system to calculate the strength/immunity of a human body. Indian J. Sci. Technol. **9**(44) (2016)
12. Amandeep, K., Madaan, V., Agrawal, P., Ranjit, K., Singh, S.K.: Fuzzy rule based expert system for evaluating defaulter risk in banking sector. Indian J. Sci. Technol. **9**(28) (2016)

13. Sethi, D., Agrawal, P., Madaan, V., Kumar Singh, S.: X-Gyno: fuzzy method based medical expert system for gynaecology. Indian J. Sci. Technol. **9**(28) (2016)
14. Hartley, S., Boucho-meunier, B.: Design and implementation of a fuzzy expert system for detecting and estimating the level of asthma and chronic obstructive pulmonary disease. Middle-East J. Sci. Res. **14**(11), 1435–1444 (2013)

Automatic Magnification Independent Classification of Breast Cancer Tissue in Histological Images Using Deep Convolutional Neural Network

Shallu$^{(\boxtimes)}$ and Rajesh Mehra

National Institute of Technical Teachers Training and Research,
Chandigarh, India
{shallu.ece,rajeshmehra}@nitttrchd.ac.in

Abstract. This paper proposes a new model for automatic classification of breast cancer tissues images using convolution neural network on BreakHis dataset. The main characteristic of the proposed model is its independency on the magnification factors of the images. The presence of pooling layer only in the last convolutional layer is the beauty of this model, which assists in the prevention of information loss. Data augmentation technique was used to increase the size of the dataset as convolution neural network relies on the size of the dataset for its better performance. For model evaluation, the classification performance of the proposed model was compared with the recent work and found that the proposed model outperforms the existing one with an average accuracy of 85.3% as well as robust to the images with different magnification factor. Employment of additional data, deeper architecture and consideration of factors like filter size, pooling strategy, optimiser, loss function can be the future possibilities for this work.

Keywords: Breast cancer · Histopathology · Convolutional neural networks
Magnification factor · Computer-aided diagnosis

1 Introduction

The term cancer is associated to a group of diseases that cause uncontrollable growth and alteration in the cells of the body which named by a body part from where it originates like lung cancer, cervical cancer, prostate cancer, endometrial cancer, breast cancer. According to the statistics provided by World Health Organization (WHO), in every year nearly 1.5 million women are affected by breast cancer [1]. In 2015, breast cancer accounted for 570,000 deaths among women which were 15% of all cancer deaths [1]. According to American Cancer Society (ACS) [2, 3], breast cancer was the leading cause of deaths in females up to the year 1987, but later lung and bronchus cancer became the leading factor for causing deaths as depicted in Fig. 1. ACS also provided an estimation of new cases and deaths in 2018 due to cancer for both male and female combined where breast cancer hold first position and fourth position in the context of new cases and deaths respectively. Most of time breast cancer originates

© Springer Nature Singapore Pte Ltd. 2019
A. K. Luhach et al. (Eds.): ICAICR 2018, CCIS 955, pp. 772–781, 2019.
https://doi.org/10.1007/978-981-13-3140-4_69

either in lobules or the ducts, and finally forms a lump which termed as a tumour. Common symptoms of cancer in breasts include stiffness, heaviness and breast pain, swelling or redness and abnormalities like bloody discharge, shrinking or erosion of nipples [2].

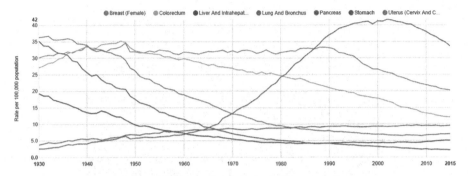

Fig. 1. Trends in death rates (Female), 1930–2015 [2]

Broadly, there are two types of breast cancer: in-situ (benign) and invasive (malignant) in which invasive breast cancer is life-threatening and about 80% breast cancers are invasive [2]. The diagnosis of breast cancer includes screening examination such as mammography, magnetic resonance imaging, ultrasound, positron emission mammography, thermography, breast-specific gamma imaging and tissue sampling etc. Surgical incision or biopsy is another method of screening which based on size and location of lump, patient, resources available and preferences [4]. All the imaging screening techniques are evident that images are playing an amazing role in the detection of breast cancer. Dispersion of various breast cancer patterns is being assessed to interpret this imaging data. In the diagnosis of breast cancer, analysis of breast tissue is a necessary step in order to provide a differential diagnosis. However, the differential diagnosis becomes difficult in some cases due to almost similar clinical expression or textures of benign and malignant cancer. Therefore, to avoid such kind of difficulties, the research community is performing outstanding work in this direction by designing computer-aided diagnosis systems (CAD). Such systems would help the radiologists to make a differential diagnosis by raising the diagnostic accuracy and reducing the observer variability.

In this paper, histopathology images of the breast are considered, attained by tissue sampling to classify the breast tissue in the two classes: benign and malignant. Examples of typical breast cancer pattern obtained from BreakHis database are depicted in Fig. 2 [5]. The variations in tissue image appearance are the major challenges in the analysis of histopathology images, which arises due to improper fixation, staining, mounting, and variability among human skills for tissue sample preparation [5]. Therefore, a large annotated datasets are always required that should available publically to provide a common platform for validation and comparison of algorithms as well as develop the more robust algorithm. In this context, this work is performed on the BreakHis [6] dataset that consists of breast cancer histopathology images collected from 82 patients with different magnification factors of 40X, 100X, 200X and 400X. Further details of the BreakHis dataset are discussed in Sect. 2.

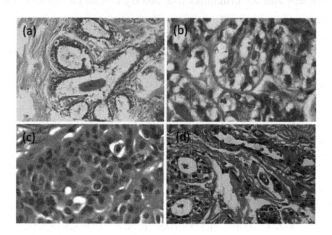

Fig. 2. Examples of typical breast cancer pattern obtained from BreakHis Database (Hematoxylin and eosin stained tissue sample) (a) & (b) Benign, and (c) & (d) Malignant

2 Materials and Method

In this section, first, the dataset used in this work is described which is essential for better understanding of the problem. Further, a full description of the proposed Convolutional Neural Network (CNN) architecture is provided.

2.1 Database

The BreakHis dataset is a very popular database for breast cancer histopathology images; built in collaboration with the Prognostics and Diagnostics (P&D) Laboratory, Parana, Brazil [6]. In order to prepare the dataset, Images were collected via a clinical study after taking the consent of all the patients referred to the lab. The dataset consists of 7,909 images where 2480 images for benign and 5429 images for malignant cancer; collected from 82 patients with the four different magnification factors, i.e. 40X, 100X, 200X, 400X. Samples present in the dataset were collected through excisions or surgical open biopsy (SOB), and then embedded in paraffin after formalin fixation for the tissue preparation. A section of thickness about 3–5 μm is cut with a microtome from paraffin and then mount on glass slides. Further, the section dyed with hematoxylin and eosin (H&E) to highlight the structure of interest in the tissue: nuclei and cytoplasm. The hematoxyline dyes the nuclei in blue-purple color as it binds to DNA; and eosin dyes the cytoplasm in pink color as it binds to proteins. After staining, a glass coverslipping is performed over the sections, and sent to the anatomopathologists to detect the tumoral area in each sample slide by a microscopical analysis. Eventually, an experienced pathologist produced a final diagnosis for each case which further confirmed by complementary screening examination like immunohistochemistry

(IHC) analysis or tissue micro-arrays (TMAs) [5]. To acquire the digital image of tissue slides, a digital camera was coupled with the microscope. The acquired images have true color space with size 700 × 460 pixel, and stored in PNG format. Each file in dataset stored in same format, consist of information about biopsy procedure, tumor class, tumor type, year, slide id, magnification factor, and sequence number for example: SOB_M_DC-14-2523-40-010.png where SOB for surgical open biopsy, M stands for malignant tumor, and DC represents ductal carcinoma, a subtype of malignant tumor [7] (Table 1).

Table 1. Distribution of images regarding magnification and tumor class in BreakHis

Magnification Factor	Benign	Malignant	Total
40X	625	1,370	1,995
100X	644	1,437	2.081
200X	623	1,390	2,013
400X	588	1,232	1,820
Total	2,480	5,429	7,909
Pateints	24	58	82

2.2 Proposed CNN

Data understanding is very important step to solving a classification problem via machine learning techniques. Only by nature of the problem, the optimal architecture of classification model and its configuration can be decided. Similar to interstitial lung diseases (ILD) patterns in computed tomography (CT) images; breast cancer tissue is also characterized by local textural features [8]. The texture may be defined as an array of primitive texels or textural elements in some regular or repeated fashion. In a study by Spanhol et al. [7], the authors performed several experiments and evaluated six textural descriptors and different classifiers. The authors also reported a good range of accuracy rate, i.e. 80% to 85%. However, the conventional texture descriptors require domain expertise and significant efforts for its feature extraction step. Also, the conventional machine learning techniques depend on the feature extraction step for their better performance. However, the dependency on feature extraction step is the major drawback of the conventional machine learning techniques [9]. Hence, there is a need for a machine learning approach that would able to learn discriminative information directly from the data. CNN is a special type of deep learning which can learn representation directly from the data [10]. In convolution, a bank of filters is repeatedly applied throughout an image to highlight the structures that match the convolution kernel over the image. This property of CNN's encourages us to use it in the analysis of breast cancer tissue images.

Architecture: In the proposed **CNN** architecture, three convolutional layers are used where each layer is followed by an activation layer. However, the pooling layer follows only the last one to prevent information loss that occurs due to subsampling. In the first two convolutional layers, 32 filters with size 3 × 3 are applied to the input. In third convolutional layer, 64 filters with same filter size are used. The value of hyper-parameters, zero padding and stride are set to 1 for all the three layers. The zeros are padded around the image patch to maintain the size of the input, and the output equal to each other. The input for this network is an image patch of size 128 × 128. Max-pooling operation [11] is chosen for sub-sampling the input dimension for the third convolutional layer only. The size of the receptive field to perform pooling is set to 2 × 2 to obtain invariance to spatial transformation for all of the convolutional layers with stride value of 2. Later, ReLU activation function; i.e. $f(x) = \max(0, x)$ is applied to enhance the nonlinear properties of the decision function as well as to speed up the process of training [12]. Eventually, two fully-connected layers are concatenated after the convolutional layers where each fully connected layer composed of 128 neurons and followed by an activation layer (i.e., ReLU) as well as dropout [13]. Simultaneously, a softmax layer is placed after the last fully connected layer to compress the output into a discrete probability distribution (Table 2).

Table 2. Summary of proposed CNN architecture

Components	Layers				
	1	2	3	4	5
Layer type	Conv. + ReLU	Conv. + ReLU	Conv. + Max Pool + ReLU	Fully Connected + ReLU + Dropout	Fully Connected + ReLU + Dropout
No. of filters	32	32	64	128	128
Filer size	3 × 3	3 × 3	3 × 3	–	–
Convolution stride	1 × 1	1 × 1	1 × 1	–	–
Pooling size	–	–	3 × 3	–	–
Pooling stride	–	–	2 × 2	–	–
Zero-padding size	2 × 2	2 × 2	2 × 2	–	–

Training Procedure: In the training of a neural network, a measure of error is required to compute error between the targeted output and the computed output of training data known as loss function [14]. An optimisation algorithm is needed to minimise this function. Here, Adam optimiser [15] is chosen to minimize the cross-entropy with its default settings. To update the weights, the number of epochs is set to 1,000, and a batch of size 20 is considered.

3   Experimental Setup and Results

In this section, results are presented with a detailed discussion but before that the description of the experimental setup is provided.

3.1   Experimental Framework

Performance Evaluation Measures: In this study, a magnification independent classification is performed for breast cancer tissue as images of all magnification considered collectively. The dataset has been divided into 80%-20% ratio where 80% used for training and 20% for testing purpose. The data used for testing is kept isolated from the training set and never seen by the model during training. To evaluate the breast cancer tissue classification, we computed the recognition rate at the image level [16] over the two different classes, which defined as follows:

$$Image\ Recognition\ Rate = \frac{correctly\ classified\ images\ of\ cancer}{total\ number\ of\ images\ in\ test\ set} \quad (1)$$

Implementation: The proposed CNN model is implemented using the Tensorflow [17] framework, and coded in python. The experiment was performed on a machine with configuration Intel(R) Core(TM) i7-7500U @ 2.90 GHz, 8 GB RAM and, GPU NVIDIA GeForce 940MX.

4   Results

The section is demonstrating the results gained after the implementation of the proposed model to classify the breast cancer histopathology images. This section is divided into two parts where the first part presents a comparative analysis of the proposed model with the existing state-of-the-art technique. In the second part, the additional performance of the system is analyzed.

Comparison with Previous Work: In the current experiment, the performance of the proposed model for the magnification independent classification is presented. Also, data augmentation is performed to increase the size of the dataset, in which images are rotated about their centre with the three angles: 90°, 180°, and 270° [18, 19]. The obtained accuracy at image level for the binary classification of breast cancer tissue images are shown in Table 3:

Table 3. Image recognition rate at image level (Magnification Independent)

Recognition rate at	Layers				
	40x	100x	200x	400x	Average
Image Level	90.4 ± 1.5	86.3 ± 3.3	83.1 ± 2.2	81.3 ± 3.5	85.3

Table 4 depicts the existing state-of-the-art technique used in [20] where four strategies were used by the author to generate image patches and then utilized for training:

Table 4. Image recognition rate at image level [20]

Recognition rate at	Strategy	Layers				
		40x	100x	200x	400x	Average
Image level [18]	1	79.9 ± 1.5	80.8 ± 1.5	**84.0** ± 1.5	80.7 ± 1.5	81.4
	2	80.6 ± 1.5	81.0 ± 1.5	82.7 ± 1.5	**80.8** ± 1.5	81.3
	3	81.8 ± 1.5	82.3 ± 1.5	82.4 ± 1.5	80.3 ± 1.5	81.7
	4	**89.6** ± 1.5	**85.0** ± 1.5	82.8 ± 1.5	80.2 ± 1.5	**84.4**

From the Table 5, it can be seen that the mixing of all the images from the BreakHis database without due consideration of their magnification factors incremented the classification performance of the model. The reason behind this enhanced performance of the model is the increased size of the dataset for training. The application of pooling strategy only at the last convolutional layer is another reason for its better performance as this step prevents the loss of information at a low level. Low level features combined to form the high-level features in the convolutional neural network. Thus, low-level features play a very crucial role in the characterization of textures.

Table 5. Comparison of model performance between [20] and the proposed approach based on average image recognition rate

Recognition rate at	[20]	Proposed approach
Image level	84.4	85.3

System's Performance Analysis: For a better understanding of the proposed framework, the performance curves obtained during the training of the model are provided. In Fig. 3, the blue curve is representing the training accuracy and red curve to validation accuracy; gained at the time of model's training. In Fig. 4, the 32 filters' kernel of the first convolution layer of this model is displayed. These filters' kernels are responsible for the extraction of features like edge and corner at lower representation level and then learn complex features when combined at higher representation level. A normalised confusion matrix for the classification of test set consists of breast cancer tissue images with magnification factor 40x is illustrated in Fig. 5. The main reason for confusion between benign and malignant breast tissue is their similar textures or expression. Here, Fig. 6 is showing some images that were misclassified. Therefore, careful description of texture is required to remove the confusion between the two classes.

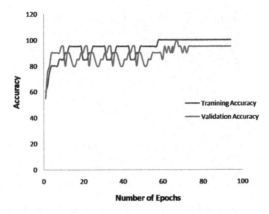

Fig. 3. Training and validation accuracy curves at the time of training (Color Figure online)

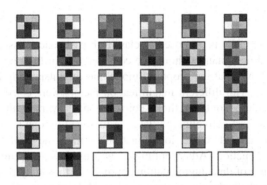

Fig. 4. 32 Filters from the first convolution layer of the proposed model with kernel size (3 × 3)

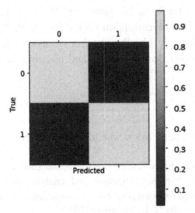

Fig. 5. Confusion matrix for the test set with magnification factor (40x) 0: Benign and 1: malignant

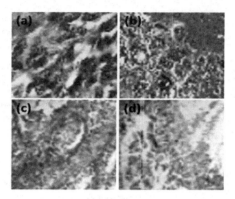

Fig. 6. Misclassified images of breast cancer tissue, (a) & (b) are Benign but classified as malignant, and (c) & (d) are Malignant but classified as benign

5   Conclusion

In this work, a deep CNN is proposed to classify breast cancer tissue images into two classes, benign and malignant without due consideration of their magnification factor. This experiment shows that the proposed model has an outstanding performance even when all the images with different magnification factors were considered collectively. This deep architecture contains three convolutional layers with ReLU activation function where only last convolutional layer is followed by one layer of max pooling. Cross-entropy was considered as loss function to train the model correctly and to minimise this loss function 'Adam optimiser' was used as an optimisation technique. Additionally, the use of data augmentation approach in this study positively affects the performance of the model because of expansion in the size of training data which is the foremost requirement of a deep network for its proper working. From the results, it is concluded that the current approach outperforms the state-of-the-art technique previously reported on BreakHis database. Random initialization of weights and slow training are the major drawbacks of this approach. In future, further improvement could be possible with the detailed investigation on the factors that affect the performance of the model directly or indirectly like the number of layers, filter size, pooling strategy, size of the dataset, optimizer, loss function, and learning rate.

References

1. World Health Organization. www.who.int/cancer/prevention/diagnosis-screening/breast-cancer/en/
2. American Cancer Society. https://cancerstatisticscenter.cancer.org/
3. Shallu, Nanglia, P., Kumar, S.: Detection and analysis of lung cancer using radiomic approach. In: International Conference on Computational Strategies for Next Generation Technologies (NextCom 2017). in the press (2017)
4. National Cancer Institute. https://www.cancer.gov/types/breast/patient/breast-screening-pdq#section/_13

5. Veta, M., Pluim, J.P.W., Diest, P.J.V., Viergever, M.A.: Breast cancer histopathology image analysis: a review. IEEE T Bio-Med. Eng. **61**(5), 1400–1411 (2014)
6. Spanhol, F., Oliveira, L.S., Prtitjean, C., Heutte, L.: A dataset for breast cancer histopathological image classification. IEEE T Bio-Med. Eng. **63**(4), 1455–1462 (2016)
7. Laboratório Visão Robótica e Imagens. https://web.inf.ufpr.br/vri/databases/breast-cancer-histopathological-database-breakhis/
8. Delorme, S., Keller-Reichenbecher, M.A., Zuna, I., Schlegel, W., Kaick, G.V.: Usual interstitial pneumonia: quantitative assessment of high resolution computed tomography findings by computer assisted texture based image analysis. Invest. Radiol. **32**(9), 566–574 (1997)
9. LeCun, Y., Bengio, Y., Hinton, G.: Deep learning. Nature **521**, 436–444 (2015)
10. Shallu, Mehra, R., Kumar, S.: An insight into the convolutional neural network for the analysis of medical images. In: IEEE International Conference on 'Nanofim 2017'. In the Press (2017)
11. Lee, C.Y., Gallagher, P.W., Tu, Z.: Generalizing pooling functions in convolutional neural networks: mixed, gated, and tree. IEEE T. Pattern. Anal. **40**, 863–875 (2018)
12. Xu, B., Wang, N., Chen, T., Li, M.: Empirical evaluation of rectified activations in convolutional network. ICML Deep Learn, pp. 1–5 (2015)
13. Srivastava, N., Hinton, G., Krizhevsky, A.: Dropout: a simple way to prevent neural networks from overfitting. J. Mach. Learn. Res. **15**, 1929–1958 (2014)
14. Li, F., Yang, Y.: A loss function analysis for classification methods in text categorization. In: Proceedings of the Twentieth International Conference on Machine Learning, pp. 472–479 (2003)
15. Kingma, D.P., Ba, J.L.: Adam: a method for stochastic optimization. In: International Conference on Learning Representation, pp. 1–13 (2015)
16. Spanhol, F.A., Cavalin, P.R., Oliveira, L.S., Petitjean, C., Heutte, L.: Deep features for breast cancer histopathological image classification. In: IEEE International Conference on Systems, Man, and Cybernetics, pp. 1868–1873 (2017)
17. Tensorflow. https://www.tensorflow.org/
18. Setio, A.A.A., et al.: Pulmonary nodule detection in CT images: false positive reduction using multi-view convolutional networks. IEEE T Med Imaging **35**(5), 1160–1169 (2016)
19. Dosovitskiy, A., Springenberg, J.T., Brox, T.: Unsupervised feature learning by augmenting single images. CoRR, pp. 1–7 (2013)
20. Spanhol, F.A., Cavalin, P.R., Oliveira, L.S., Petitjean, C., Heutte, L.: Breast cancer histopathological image classification using convolutional neural networks. In: International Joint Conference on Neural Networks, pp. 2560–2567 (2016)

Queueing Analysis of Migration of Virtual Machines

Surabhi Sachdeva$^{(\boxtimes)}$ and Neeraj Gupta

K. R. Mangalam University, Gurugram, Haryana, India
surabhisachdeva@gmail.com, neerajgupta3729@gmail.com

Abstract. Live migration is a prerequisite feature of virtualization that allows transfer of a working virtual machine from one data center to another. It is a useful tool for optimization of resources and is one of the issues of research. The work [22] proposes an analytical model based approach for quality evaluation of cloud by considering the rejection probability, expected request completion time, system overhead as key metrics. In this paper, we are exploring only rejection probability of jobs. The work in [22] has been done in two phases and M/M/1/K queueing model has been applied to the first phase of the work in order to find the rejection probability of jobs. We are considering the variable buffer sizes and different distribution models. To study the impact of changing buffer sizes on the rejection probability of the jobs is the main point of concern here. We have proposed application of M/G/1/∞, M/G/1/K models to it. And, in order to validate the correctness of the proposed model, we simulate the data and the graphs are drawn in Matlab showing the comparison of the proposed model with work presented in [22]. It is observed that in case of M/M/1/K, with an increase in the request arrival rate, the rejection probability of jobs increases, but if we change the model to M/G/1/∞, the rejection probability of jobs decreases. With an increase in execution rate, the rejection rate of jobs decreases, but if we change [22] to M/G/1/∞, then the rejection probability decreases more as compared to it. Hence, changing buffer size proves to be gainful. And the changing of queueing model is advantageous as it leads to decrease in the rejection probability of the jobs. So, we can say that general distribution queueing model is more effective in migration as compared to exponential distribution model as it leads to a decrease in rejection rate of jobs.

Keywords: Load balancing · Rejection probability · Queueing models
Virtual machine migration · Buffer size · Matlab

List of abbreviations used

PM	Physical machine
VM	Virtual machine
RJ	Overall rejection probability(rejection rate)
VMM	Virtual machine migration
QoS	Quality of service

© Springer Nature Singapore Pte Ltd. 2019
A. K. Luhach et al. (Eds.): ICAICR 2018, CCIS 955, pp. 782–793, 2019.
https://doi.org/10.1007/978-981-13-3140-4_70

1 Introduction

Cloud computing is a promising paradigm which delivers the services over the internet efficiently by using the feature of pay-as-you-go and provides an on demand access to the resources. Cloud promises to provide a shared set of services to its users through the use of virtualization. The mechanism of virtualization enables one to create multiple versions of anything. It allows concurrent running of multiple VMs on the same PM. In order to manage the load efficiently, it provides a feature of virtual machine migration. It is a very effective tool to enable data center management in a non-disruptive manner. Performance of VM migration is affected by different parameters namely migration time, migration downtime, bandwidth and many more. In our study, the performance of migration is calculated on the basis of rejection rate of waiting jobs (RJ). To offer a satisfactory service to these waiting jobs, modeling of jobs can be done by applying queueing theory to it. Jobs arrive at the rate of λ jobs/minute and executed at the rate of μ jobs/minute. K is the finite capacity buffer of the system. This paper provides a comprehensive study of three different distribution queueing models relating to migration of VMs. The queueing models that we have considered are M/G/1/∞, M/G/1/K and M/M/1/K. The fundamental point of this paper is to relate the rejection rate of jobs to the different distribution queueing models. The simulations are carried out in Matlab in order to note the variations taking place in the graphs of the rejection rate (RJ) formula by taking the same assumed parameter values as that of [22]. This is a mathematical paper featuring the points of interest of the RJ formula and utilization of the two more models on the same. The main objective of this study is to evaluate the details of general and exponential distribution queueing models for virtual machine migration and to draw a comparison between them so as to arrive at a conclusion about the best out of general and exponential distribution queueing model for migration.

The remaining sections of the paper are systematically organized as follows: the next section reviews studies of migration and queueing theory in literature survey. The comparison of general and exponential queueing models in virtual machine migration is there in Sect. 3. Section 4 provides observations of the Matlab implementations & results. And, Sect. 5, the last section concludes the paper.

2 Literature Survey

A lot of work has been done in the field of virtual machine migration. M/G/1/K*PS queueing model for a web server has been introduced and expressions for average response time, throughput and blocking probability were made in [1]. A measure of time devoured by the application while preparing the demand of the user is named as response time [2]. By the utilization of queueing hypothesis, a model for the outlining of distributed computing structures are also displayed. Runtime test data used by the authors to evaluate the performance and cost of executing the montage workflow on clouds in [3]. Keeping in mind the end goal to anticipate the execution of the administration uncovered by the cloud in [4] proposed a queueing hypothesis based model and analyzed expected request completion time. Also, a percentile of response time used as a QoS metric, introduced M/M/1 model taking arrival and service rates as inputs but failed to include failure/repair rates. Keeping in mind the main aim to spare vitality, [6] proposed a packing algorithm-based strategy along with the proposal and validation of a web application execution. The issue of demonstrating of PC benefit execution as for reaction time, throughput, usage of system has been examined in [2, 4, 6, 7]. In [6], a similar study using sequential queueing network carried out ignoring failure/repair rates. An experiment based performance evaluation of live migration of virtual machines is presented in [8]. In [9] a theory based probability distribution of service time considering failure/repair rates were derived. A multivariate probabilistic model was given in [16] to study the effect of VM relocation plans. A comprehensive QoS model taking into consideration all the aspects was given in [11]. Proposal of a queue-construct a display for execution administration in light of the cloud in which the web applications are modeled as queues and virtual machines are modeled as service centers [17, 24] utilized M/M/1 model to ascertain the limit with a specific end goal to control the relocation. Quantitative examination of live relocation inside a data center has been given in [27]. Virtualization may induce significant performance penalties as given in [34]. Work done by the author [22] is in two phases CMU handling phase & Job execution phase. Queueing theory has been applied by the author in phase 1 in order to find the rejection rate of the jobs. A model system in which job arrival rate represented by λ jobs/minute and execution rate represented by μ jobs/minute. ρ represents the utilization factor We further analyze and compare the rejection rates of the exponential distribution queue of [22] with other two general distribution queues.

3 Comparison of Exponential and General Distribution Queueing Models in VMM

The abbreviations used in the text are there in the list at the beginning. The symbols of various parameters used have already been introduced in the Table 1. According to the model [22], the work has been done by the author in two phases CMU handling phase & Job execution phase. Exponential finite capacity distribution M/M/1/K has been utilized by the author in phase 1 of [22]. We are using general distribution queueing models having variable buffer sizes with an interest of finding the rejection rate of the model. Also, in order to find the best out of exponential and general distribution, a comparison of the rejection rates of [22] with M/G/1/∞ and M/G/1/K is to be drawn. The main objective of this paper is to study the effect of changing buffer size and changing distribution of the queueing model on the rejection rate of the jobs. In our study, the nature of the output depends on the buffer size and the type of distribution applied. By taking into consideration both the types of distribution models one by one, so as to discover the rejection rate of that model.

We know that utilization factor,

$$\rho = \lambda/\mu_c \tag{1}$$

$$P_i = \rho^i P_0 \tag{2}$$

Table 1. Meaning of symbols used

λ = 10 jobs/min	Request arrival rate
μ = 20 jobs/min	Execution rate
λ_{eff}	Number of jobs getting served
ρ = 10/20 = 1/2	Utilization factor
P_i	Steady state probability of ith request
RJQ	Job rejection due to insufficient queue capacity
RJC	Request rejection probability
RJP	Job rejection probability
RJH	Job rejection due to non existing hot PM
Po	Probability of no arrivals
Pn	Probability of n arrivals
i	Number of hot PMs

$$RJC = P_{Nc} \tag{3}$$

After performing calculations and analyzing the formulas of [22] a general formula for rejection rate of jobs in both the cases of exponential and general distribution models can be framed as:

$$RJ = 1 - (1 - \rho^i P_0)) \tag{4}$$

$$P_0 = 1 - \rho \tag{5}$$

$$P_n = \rho^n P_o \tag{6}$$

So,

$$P_n = \rho^n (1 - \rho) \tag{7}$$

So, the rejection rate for:

$$M/G/1/\infty = 1 - \left(1 - \rho^i * (1 - \rho)\right) \tag{8}$$

Also, on comparing and analyzing, the rejection rate of:

$$M/M/1/K \text{ model} = 1 - (1 - \rho^i \times (\frac{1 - \rho}{1 - \rho^{K+1}})) \tag{9}$$

$$M/G/1/K \text{ model} = 1 - \left(1 - \rho^i/(1 + \rho)\right) \tag{10}$$

The mathematical expressions of RJ of different models are obtained as:

$$M/G/1/\infty \qquad 1 - (1 - \rho^{i}{}^{*}(1 - \rho)) * (63/64).^{\wedge}2) \qquad (11)$$

$$M/G/1/K \qquad 1 - (1 - \rho^{i}{}^{*}(1 - \rho/1 - \rho^{K+1})) * (62/63).^{\wedge}2) \qquad (12)$$

$$M/G/1/K \text{ model} \qquad 1 - (1 - \rho^{i}/(1 + \rho)) * (47/48).^{\wedge}2 \qquad (13)$$

Table 2 shows a brief comparison of the different distribution queueing models taken into consideration.

Table 2. Comparison of assumed queueing models with [22].

Queueing model	Type of distribution	No. of servers	Buffer size	Jobs served	Jobs rejected
M/G/1/∞	General	1	infinite	No limit	Never
M/M/1/K [17]	Exponential	1	K	Only K jobs	(K+1)th job
M/G/1/K	General	1	K	Only K jobs	(K+1)th job

The net effect of changing the type of distribution used in the queueing model affected the values of request rejection probability and job rejection probability as given in [22]. Further, on solving each of them one by one, first of all we get the values of the different parameters which are required for drawing the graphs and then the graphs are drawn to check the variations of the RJ lines. Table 3 below summarizes the calculated values of parameters.

Table 3. Parameter values for drawing graphs

Parameters	M/M/1/K	M/G/1/∞	M/G/1/k
RJC	1/63	1/64	1/48
RJQ	0000000	0000000	0000000
RJH	1000101	1000101	1000101
RJP	1/63	1/64	1/48
RJ	$1 - (1 - \rho^{i} * (\frac{1-\rho}{1-\rho^{K+1}})))$	$1 - (1 - \rho^{i} * (1 - \rho))$	$1 - (1 - \rho^{i}/(1 + \rho))$

4   Results

In this section, we implement the work with Matlab 9.3 platform. The implemented program is capable of calculating RJ (rejection rate/rejection probability), given input request arrival rate, queue capacity, the execution rate of jobs, number of initial hot PMs. We considered $\lambda = 10$, $\mu = 20$. Figure 1 Representing RJ versus the arrival rate of exponential distribution [22]. Figure 2(a) and (b) are representing RJ versus the arrival rate of general distribution M/G/1/∞ and M/G/1/K models respectively. For a specific number of hot PMs, an increase in the request arrival rate results in an increase in rejection probability. With an increase in the number of hot PMs, all the considered queueing models shown a decrease in RJ. We are taking into consideration M/G/1/K & M/G/1/∞ models for studying the changing behavior of the system of RJ. Though the RJ of M/G/1/K model is continually increasing, but on comparing the RJ of M/M/1/K [22] and M/G/1/∞ model, we can judge out that the RJ of M/M/1/K is increasing higher as compared to M/G/1/∞ model. Hence, for finding the rejection rate of the jobs, general distribution queueing models are better than the exponential distribution model used in [22] as on using the general distribution models, the rejection rate of job is showing a decrease in the values.

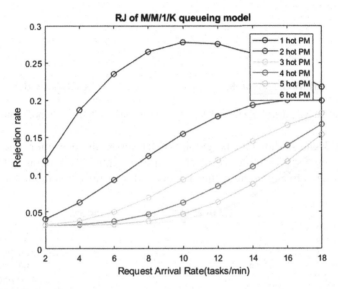

Fig. 1. RJ of exponential distribution M/M/1/k model [22] versus arrival rate with different no. of initial hot PMs.

In the Figs. 1 and 2 drawn above, it shows that with an increase in the number of hot PMs the RJ is also increasing. However, taking into consideration an individual instance of 1 hot PM, it is plainly visible that with an increase in the request arrival rate, the rejection rate of jobs (RJ) is also increasing. Initially, in case of general distribution M/G/1/∞ model the rejection rate of jobs continued increasing and finally, it started decreasing showing that the values of RJ decreases with an increase in the request arrival rate and the number of hot PMs. With an increase in the number of hot PMs, the values of RJ of M/G/1/K continued decreasing. Also, the system under consideration having 1 hot PM is indicating the highest initial value of 0.23. This is on the grounds that the estimation of RJ is increasing with an increase in the request arrival rate in case of M/G/1/K.

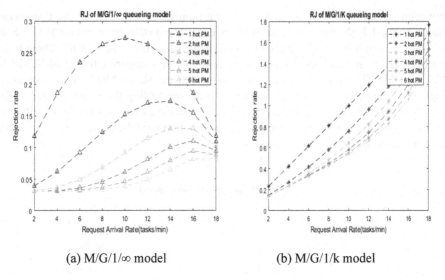

(a) M/G/1/∞ model   (b) M/G/1/k model

Fig. 2. RJ of general distribution models versus arrival rate with different no. of initial hot PMs

Figures 3 and 4 showing the graphs of RJ versus the execution rate of various models. Figure 3 representing the RJ lines of exponential distribution M/M/1/K [22]. Figure 4(a) and (b) representing the RJ lines of general distribution M/G/1/∞ and

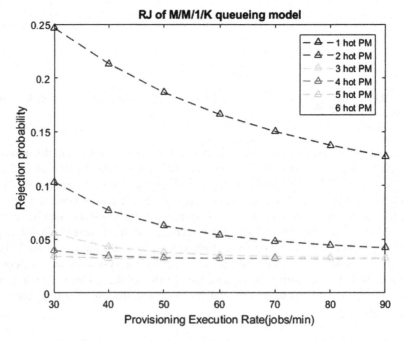

Fig. 3. RJ of the exponential distribution M/M/1/K model [22] versus execution rate with different no. of initial hot PMs

M/G/1/K models respectively. As can be seen in these figures, an increase in execution rate results in a decrease in RJ. Also, for a specific number of hot PMs, with an increase in the execution rate, again RJ decreases. The only difference is in the initial value of RJ lines of all the models. The initial value of RJ lines is least in case of M/M/1/K and M/G/1/∞ models So, on changing the model to M/G/1/∞, there can be a comparable decrease in rejection probability as that of M/M/1/K [22]. We have taken two different parameters. One is request arrival rate and the other is execution rate. Individual graphs of different distribution queueing models are already drawn with both the above mentioned parameters. Further, drawing graphs of RJ of different queueing models together in order to show the comparisons of different distribution queueing models so as to prove the better of the two distributions considered.

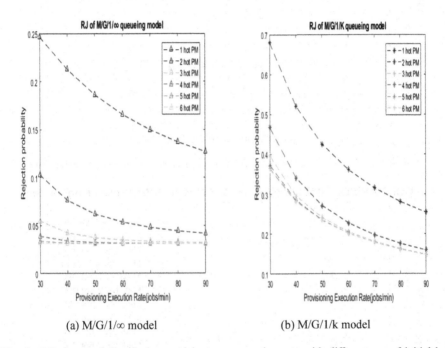

(a) M/G/1/∞ model   (b) M/G/1/k model

Fig. 4. RJ of general distribution model versus execution rate with different no. of initial hot PMs

In Fig. 5. Showing a comparison of RJ versus request arrival rate of all the models. It can be seen that with an increase in the request arrival rate, the RJ of M/G/1/K is also increasing which shows that choosing M/G/1/K model can lead to decrease in the performance of the system. Though, on comparing M/M/1/K [22] to M/G/1/∞ we see that with an increase in the number of hot PM, RJ of M/M/1/K is increasing. Hence, we can say that changing to general distribution infinite buffer queueing model can lead to a decrease in RJ. Out of all the three models, M/G/1/∞ is showing the best results.

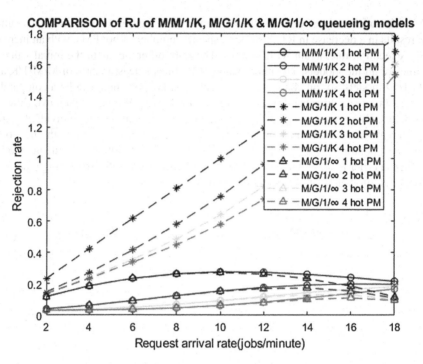

Fig. 5. Comparison of RJ of different queueing models versus request arrival rate.

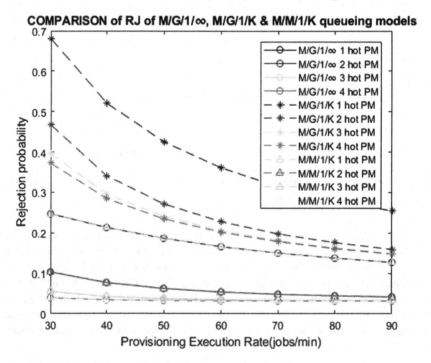

Fig. 6. Comparison of RJ of different queueing models versus execution rate.

And, lastly, Fig. 6 showing comparison of RJ versus execution rate of all the models. An increase in the number of hot PMs showing a decrease in the values of RJ lines of M/M/1/K [22] & M/G/1/∞ in almost similar fashion, whereas, the values of RJ of M/G/1/K are also decreasing but the initial value of RJ is more as compared to the other two models considered. Hence, on comparison, general distribution queueing model shown better results.

5 Conclusion

The topic of rejection probability of jobs has been discussed and mathematically analyzed. It is giving details about exponential and general distribution queueing models of variable buffer sizes. Exponential distribution finite capacity M/M/1/K model applied in the CMU handling phase to compute the RJ (rejection rate of jobs) [22]. We applied general distribution M/G/1/∞ and M/G/1/K models to compute the rejection rate. On changing the queueing model the formulas got changed which graphically outcomes in a decrease in RJ. Graphs drawn using MATLAB show that with an increase in the request arrival rate, the RJ of M/G/1/K is also increasing which shows that M/G/1/K model can lead to decrease the performance of the system, but if we shift from M/M/1/K to M/G/1/∞ there is a decrease in the values of RJ lines as compared to the exponential distribution model of finite capacity used. Lastly, with an increase in execution rate, the values of RJ of not only M/G/1/∞ but also M/M/1/K are decreasing, and the initial value of RJ in M/G/1/∞ is less as compared to the other two models considered. Hence, we can get better results by switching to the general distribution queueing model. M/G/1/∞ is the best possible choice for handling the requests at the CMU handling phase (the first phase) of the process of migration.

References

1. Cao, J., Andersson, M., Nyberg, C., Kihl, M.: Web server performance modeling using an M/G/1/K* PS queue. In: Telecommunications 10th International Conference, vol. 2, pp. 1501–1506. IEEE (2003)
2. Karlapudi, H.: Web application performance prediction. In: Proceedings of International Conference on Communication and Computer Networks, IASTED, pp. 281–286 (2004)
3. Deelman, E., Singh, G., Livny, M., Berriman, J.B., Good, J.: The cost of doing science on the cloud: The Montage example. In: Procedia. International Conference High Performance Computing Network. Storage Analysis, pp. 1–12 (2008)
4. Xiong, K., Perros, H.: Service performance and analysis in cloud computing. In: 2009 World Conference on Services-I, pp. 693–700. IEEE (2009)
5. Li, B., Li, J., Huai, J., Wo, T., Li, Q., Zhong, L.: Ena Cloud: An Energy Saving Application Live Placement Approach for Cloud Computing Environments. IEEE (2009)
6. Yang, B., Tan, F., Dai, Y.-S., Guo, S.: Performance evaluation of cloud service considering fault recovery. In: Jaatun, M.G., Zhao, G., Rong, C. (eds.) CloudCom 2009. LNCS, vol. 5931, pp. 571–576. Springer, Heidelberg (2009). https://doi.org/10.1007/978-3-642-10665-1_54

7. Dai, Y.S., Yang, B., Dongarra, J., Zhang, G.: Cloud service reliability: Modeling and analysis. In: 15th IEEE Pacific Rim International Symposium on Dependable Computing, pp. 1–17. IEEE (2009)
8. Hines, M.R., Deshpande, U., Gopalan, K.: Post-copy live migration of virtual machines. In: ACM SIGOPS Operating Systems Review, vol. 43, no. 3, pp. 14–26. ACM (2009)
9. Voorsluys, W., Broberg, J., Venugopal, S., Buyya, R.: Cost of virtual machine live migration in clouds: A performance evaluation. In Procedia International Conference Cloud Computing, pp. 254–265 (2009)
10. Ghosh, R., Trivedi, K.S., Naik, V.K., Kim, D.S.: End-to-end performability analysis for infrastructure-as-a-service cloud: An interacting stochastic models approach. In: 2010 IEEE 16th Pacific Rim International Symposium on Dependable Computing (PRDC), pp. 125–132. IEEE (2010)
11. Loganayagi, B., Sujatha, S.: Creating virtual platform for cloud computing. In: International Conference on Computational Intelligence & Computing Research (ICCIC 2010), 1–4, pp. 28–29. IEEE (2010)
12. Sahoo, J., Mohapatra, S., Lath, R.: Virtualization: A survey on concepts, taxonomy and associated security issues. In: 2010 2nd International Conference on Computer and Network Technology (ICCNT), pp. 222–226. IEEE (2010)
13. Chen, H.P., Li, S.C.: A queueing based model for performance management on cloud. In: International Conference, pp. 83–88. IEEE (2011)
14. Strunk, A.: Costs of virtual machine live migration: A survey. In: 2012 IEEE 8th World Congress on Services (SERVICES), pp. 323–329. IEEE (2012)
15. He, S., Guo, L., Ghanem, M., Guo, Y.: Improving resource utilisation in the cloud environment using multivariate probabilistic models. In: 5th International Conference Cloud Computing (CLOUD), pp. 574–581. IEEE (2012)
16. Loganayagi, B., Sujatha, S.: Enhanced cloud security by combining virtualization and policy monitoring techniques. Procedia Eng. 30, 654–661 (2012)
17. Mastelic, T., Brandic, I.: Recent trends in energy efficient cloud computing. J. Latex 11(4) (2012)
18. Zheng, J., Ng, T.E., Sripanidkulchai, K., Liu, Z.: Pacer: A progress management system for live virtual machine migration. In: IEEE Transactions on Cloud Computing, pp. 369–382. IEEE (2013)
19. Chanchio, K., Thaenkaew, P.: Time-bound, thread-based live migration of virtual machines. In: 14th IEEE/ACM International Symposium on Cluster, Cloud and Grid Computing (CCGrid), pp. 364–373. IEEE (2014)
20. Anala, M.R., Shetty, J., Shobha, G.: A framework for secure live migration of virtual machines. In: 2013 International Conference of Advances in Computing, Communications and Informatics (ICACCI), pp. 243–248. IEEE (2013)
21. Sarker, T.K., Tang, M.: Performance-driven live migration of multiple virtual machines in datacenters. In: International Conference of Granular Computing (GrC), pp. 253–258. IEEE (2013)
22. Xia, Y., Zhou, M., Luo, X., Zhu, Q., Li, J., Huang, Y.: Stochastic modeling and quality evaluation of infrastructure-as-a-service clouds. IEEE Trans. Autom. Sci. Eng. 12(1), 162–170 (2015)
23. Sandhya, S., Revathi, S., NK, C.: Performance analysis and comparative analysis of process migration using genetic algorithm. Int. J. Sci. Eng. Technol. Res. 5(11) (2016)
24. Pham, C., Hong, C.S.: Using Queueing Model to Analyse the Live Migration Process in Data Centers, pp. 1136–1138. IEEE (2014)
25. Durairaj, M., Kannan, P.: A study on virtualization techniques and challenges in cloud computing. Int. J. Sci. Technol. Res. 3(11), 147–151 (2014)

26. Yu, L., Chen, L., Cai, Z., Shen, H., Liang, Y., Pan, Y.: Stochastic load balancing for virtual resource management in datacenters. In: IEEE Transactions on Cloud Computing. IEEE (2014)
27. Baghshahi, S.S., Jabbehdari, S., Adabi, S.: Virtual machine migration based on Greedy algorithm in cloud computing. In: Int. J. Comput. Appl. **96**(12) (2014)
28. Kumar, N., Saxena, S.: Migration performance of cloud applications-a quantitative analysis. Procedia Comput. Sci. **45**, 823–831 (2015)
29. https://youtu.be/2aPlzhsEsIw
30. https://www.youtube.com/watch?v=PavZX3hAL6I&t=7s
31. https://www.youtube.com/watch?v=WWHCfTlLTOs
32. http://nptel.ac.in/courses/117103017/22
33. Vilaplana, J., Solsona, F., Teixidó, I., Mateo, J., Abella, F., Rius, J.: A queueing theory model for cloud computing. J. Supercomput. 492–507 (2014)
34. Baliga, J., Ayre, R.W., Hinton, K., Tucker, R.S.: Green cloud computing: balancing energy in processing, storage, and transport. Proc. IEEE **99**(1), 149–167 (2011)

Wavelet Based Sleep EEG Detection Using Fuzzy Logic

Chetna Nagpal[1](✉) and Prabhat Kumar Upadhyay[2]

[1] Department of EEE, Birla Institute of Technology Offshore Campus,
Ras Al Khaimah, UAE
chetnakochhar0@gmail.com
[2] Department of EEE, Birla Institute of Technology, Mesra, Ranchi, India
uprabhatbit@gmail.com

Abstract. The Sleep stage classification has been accomplished using fuzzy inference system, where the prerecorded data of sleep EEG has been processed with the help of wavelet transform. The investigation on sleep stage detection reveals the quantitative presence of three different stages of sleep i.e. Awake, SWS (slow wave sleep) and REM (rapid eye movement). The proposed work approaches to correctly identify the three classes of sleep EEG using fuzzy classification method based on fuzzy rule base. The 3- channel data is preprocessed by wavelet transform via signal processing tools and further processed to identify the stages of sleep EEG. The extracted features from the processed data are EEG sub-band frequencies, standard deviation measures for EMG and EOG and variance measures for EMG and EOG. These features are required to make the fuzzy rules for FIS (Fuzzy inference system) and further used to identify the sleep stages correctly. Performance analysis of the proposed fuzzy model was accurately evaluated in terms of fuzzy variables and the result shows that the proposed approach is able to classify the EEG signals with the average accuracy of 93% in which SWS stage was best detected among other stages of sleep EEG.

Keywords: EEG · EOG · EMG · Fuzzy logic · Wavelet transform
Awake · SWS · REM

1 Introduction

Sleep can change the performance of day- to- day activities in a normal life like productivity, learning, memorization and concentration, which is related to a healthy sleep. Deprived from sleep can lead to the risk of hypertension, diabetes cardiovascular disease, metabolic irregularities, obesity which lowers the immune system [1].

Sleep evaluation is important to diagnose the sleep disorder. The method used to evaluate the sleep is polysomnography (PSG) [2], which is the recording of different physiological signals like EEG (Electrocencephalogram), EMG (Electromyogram), EOG (Electrooculogram), pulse oximetry and respiration. Analysis of sleep can be done when system changes in awake homeostasis. In visual observation of PSG, medical examiner can examine the individual sleep by evaluating the sleep stages [3]. According to Rechtschaffen and Kales, the main stages of vigilance are wakefulness,

© Springer Nature Singapore Pte Ltd. 2019
A. K. Luhach et al. (Eds.): ICAICR 2018, CCIS 955, pp. 794–805, 2019.
https://doi.org/10.1007/978-981-13-3140-4_71

REM (Rapid Eye Movement) and Non REM, where non REM is further divided in to four more stages. In the present work, the sleep stages are divided in to three stages namely: Awake, REM and SWS. EEG, EMG and EOG are the three polysomnographs which have been recorded to determine the vigilance stages of sleep EEG, where EEG signals are used for brain activities and EOG, EMG are used to detect the presence of rapid movement of eye and muscular tone. EEG signals are also used to detect spindles which have frequency of 12–14 Hz. The polygraph method also keeps the record of other signals which are used by the experts to investigate the important information; e.g. ECG used for detection of body movements, abdominal ventilatory movement, body temperatures, and oxymetry [4]. Study of brain activities and with addition to the widespread application in diagnosis of sleep EEG, various developments have been undertaken in the field of signal processing and analysis of bioelectric signals.

The electrical activity of the brain and cerebral cortex is very complicated and produced by different types of neurons, nerves and nerve fibers. This occurs due to large number of neurons, synapses and various properties of synapses, such as inhibition, summation, facilitation etc. which are integrated together to give rise to rhythmic electrical potential changes [5]. EEGs are recording of these minute rhythmic electrical potentials produced by cortical cell discharging of the brain. Cortical dendrites are the sites of forest of dense units placed in the superficial layers of the cerebral cortex and non-propagated hypopolarising local potential changes in the excitatory and inhibitory axo-dendritic synapses [6]. When the excitatory axo-dendritic synapses are activated, current flow in and out in between the cell body and axo-dendritic endings, causing a wave-like potential fluctuation [7].

Intelligent automated sleep scoring systems are needed to support the tedious visual examination of polygraphic recordings. Almost all biomedical systems are required to be analysed for the different electroencephalogram (EEG) waveforms. Many researchers have proposed the different algorithms for classifying the sleep EEG. In the computerized detection of alpha waveforms, amplitude and duration of the signal varies individually [4]. Intelligence of the method can be attributed to the features extracted and the way they are selected. The ranges of the fuzzy rules are determined based on feature statistics in most of the applications.

Three various stages of sleep EEG can be classified without human interpolation automatically with the proposed approched, where the preprocessing has been done through the wavelet transform and the detection is done through fuzzy inference system. As wavelet transform provides better time - frequency resolution, many researchers have exploited this inherent property to analyse such complex and non linear signals. In order to extract the main features, authors have used various approaches based on amplitude, frequency, and entropy [8]. These features which are extracted from multichannel EEG signals are combined using fuzzy algorithms both in feature domain and in spatial domain. One major application of fuzzy logic in the field of biomedical engineering is the analysis of EEG where multistage fuzzy rule-based algorithm were mainly used for epileptic seizure onset detection [9].

Previous classifiers such as back propagation neural network, LDA etc. includes the high mathematical complex calculations for the categorization of the EEG signals, but fuzzy qualitative approach adapts the parameters to achieve the best classification of the signals [10]. This method helps to minimize the effort which is used to refrain the associated parameters of classifier to classify the various stages of sleep.

The three channel data which has been acquired from the recordings are EEG, EMG and EOG, where the sub-band frequencies were extracted with the help of DWT (Discrete wavelet transform) techniques. EEG contains waveforms in a series which are classified into four frequency sub-band that are delta, theta, alpha and beta. Distribution of different frequency sub-bands of the EEG is as shown in Table 1.

Table 1. Different frequency sub-bands of EEG

Different frequency bands of EEG	
0.5–4 Hz	delta or ∂
4–8 Hz	theta or θ
8–12 Hz	alpha or α
12–40 Hz	beta or β

EEG recordings give the information in the form of voltage with respect to time. So, for any time 'T' seconds, the voltage in mV can be measured to read the EEG graphs. For the automated analysis of the EEG, the recording must be converted into the frequency domain by using the discrete values of voltage. Digital signal processing tools are used to acquire the EEG data in the discrete form [6]. EOG keeps the record of eye movements and the technique used for measuring the retinal potential is called Electrooculography. Electric dipoles generate the potential difference due to the positive and negative cornea. Electrodes are placed on the eyes to get the potential difference due to the motion of the eyes balls. This signal has an amplitude ranging from 0.001–0.3 mV and frequency 0.1–100 Hz [11]. EMG keeps the record of electrical activity generated from active muscles. It describes the physiological properties of muscular tissue during rest or activity. These signals are produced due to the activation of muscles of the eye, eye blinks, and head movement. The signal has frequency range of 50–150 Hz [12]. As frequency analysis is not commonly evaluated in EMG, it is used to avoid the unnecessary features like frequency or noise.

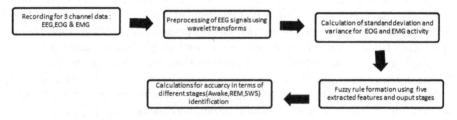

Fig. 1. Block diagram of EEG system

2 Materials and Methods

For the identification of sleep stage, the proposed algorithm is shown in Fig. 1 in which the process starts from the recording of 3 channel data and then preprocessing is done by extracting the wavelet coefficients from raw EEG. DWT has been used to extract the time - frequency signal from the time domain EEG signal. Standard deviation and variance of EMG and EOG have also been calculated to find the sleep awake stages.

2.1 Data Acquisition

In the experiment, 3- channel data was recorded continuously for four hours from normal healthy subjects. The acquired EEG data is preprocessed with DSP (Digital signal processing) techniques i.e. wavelet transforms. The data was recorded at the 256 Hz sampling frequency and features were extracted from the selected data. The recordings represent the three sleep states: Awake, REM and SWS and they were further subdivided into 2 s epoch. Each epoch contains 512 data points as the sampling frequency was selected as 256 Hz.

Some examples of two seconds epochs of unprocessed EEG recordings for Awake, SWS sleep and REM conditions have been presented in Figs. 2. It depicts the recordings of unprocessed sleep-EEG with its corresponding EMG and EOG signals with baseline drift unadjusted.

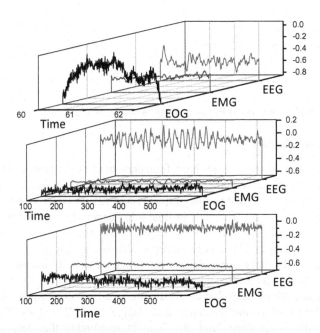

Fig. 2. Two seconds long epoch of recorded unprocessed sleep-EEG (Awake, SWS, REM) with its corresponding EMG and EOG signals

2.2   Data Processing Using Wavelet Transform

Use of wavelet decomposition enables segmentation of EEG into standard clinical bands [13]. The entropy of the wavelet coefficients in each level of decomposition reflects the underlying statistics and the degree of bursting activity associated with the recovery phenomena. With the help of wavelet analysis, changes in frequency for each signal (MAT files) were visually examined and analyzed. In the orthogonal wavelet decomposition procedure, the signal is decomposed into a vector of approximation coefficients and detail coefficients and new approximation coefficient vector is further split without considering the succeeding particulars. The analysis of the signal starts from a scale-oriented decomposition and examines the different frequency bands for EEG signal. With these four frequency bands of EEG and the other features (EMG, EOG), different stages i.e. Awake, REM, and SWS signals were clearly indentified.

Calculation of wavelet co-efficients has been done in MATLAB. Continuous wavelet transform using Daubechies order-4 wavelet was applied to Awake, REM, and SWS sleep EEG data of size [512, 1] over scales 1:128, which gives coefficients as a function of time and scale (translation vector and scale). With the ease of wavelet processing, recorded signals for all three states were split into an epoch of two seconds length. Two seconds long processed EEG signals for the three sleep states - Awake, SWS and REM have been shown in Fig. 3.

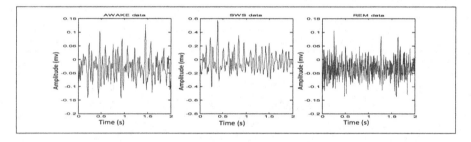

Fig. 3. Processed EEG signals of Awake, SWS and REM states

2.3   Features Selection

In this study, feature vectors of sub-band frequency have been calculated to implement the sleep stage classification. Other features namely standard deviation and variance of EMG and EOG were calculated from Eqs. (1) and (2). Wavelet transform has been applied to represent the EEG signals in time - frequency domain. Total five features were selected to frame the rules for fuzzy rule base engine in the proposed work, whereas various features like energy entropy, Shannon's entropy, amplitude, R.M.S value and mean value have been taken to determine the activity feature vectors of the EOG in [14]. Since, frequency domain analysis is not required, these features can suitably represent the changes that can distinguish various sleep stages. Various deep sleep stages lead to muscular relaxation and change the EMG values. These changes can help classify sleep stages and also help in reinforcing the sleep stages result achieved using EEG [14].

Following are the standard deviation and variance calculations of the EOG and EMG activities.

2.3.1 Standard Deviation

It is the measure of dispersion of a set of data points from its mean value. It is calculated as the radical of variance by determining the variation between each data point relative to the mean [15].

$$S.D\,(\sigma) = \sqrt{\frac{\sum(x - \mu)^2}{N}} \tag{1}$$

where,

σ = standard deviation
μ = mean of all data values in the data set
N = total number of values
x = each value in the data set.

2.3.2 Variance

It is defined as the square of standard deviation [16] which is a measure of the amount of alteration in probable values and its probability of the variable.

$$\text{variance}\,(\sigma^2) = SD^2 = \frac{\sum(x - \mu)^2}{N} \tag{2}$$

3 Fuzzy Logic Implementation

Fuzzy logic approach is mainly used in computing words or linguistics which depends on granularity and imprecision. In human brain, the perceptive organs interpret the complex and incomplete sensor informations. Similarly, the fuzzy theory also provides the same approach to deal these linguistic information with words. It uses the membership functions to perform computations.

Fuzzy rule system, fuzzy models, fuzzy associative memories and fuzzy controllers are different terms known for Fuzzy inference systems. Fuzzy logic implementation involves the following steps.

- Preprocessing
- Fuzzification
- Rule base engine/Knowledge base engine
- Defuzzification
- Post processing

Fuzzy logic is widely used in different fields e.g. robotics, data classification, expert system, automation, time series analysis decision making,, pattern and signal classification, system identification etc. [17]. FIS depends on three components i.e. a rule base which consists of fuzzy rules, a database having membership functions and a mechanism which is used in fuzzy inference to generate output.

Fuzzification: In this module, the crisp inputs are transformed in to fuzzy sets. Fuzzy operator is used to find the if-then rule of the antecedent and consequent. Fuzzy membership values can be described by antecedent and consequent. The linguistic variables are used to define the degree of association with given membership functions [18]. The method used for evaluation of degree of association to the crisp input in given fuzzy set is called the fuzzification. Membership functions which are used in fuzzy sets can be trapezoidal, triangular, gaussian or bell shape etc. In fuzzification, there is a loss of information due to degree of the membership which is just because of nonlinear transformation of the inputs [18, 19].

When membership functions of trapezoidal or triangular are used, there is loss of information where the slope is zero and resultant membership also becomes zero. Thus, the problems in these functions occur due to learning from data. There are some smoother membership functions such as Gaussian or Gaussian bell functions which are used to overcome the above problem.

Fuzzy Inference System (FIS): Implementation of fuzzy if-then rules are used to define input–output relationships and model the qualitative inputs and reasoning process for creating the output. The fuzzy inference systems incorporate a set of antecedent and consequent fuzzy membership functions as well as a set of fuzzy IF–THEN rules which are considered to form a firm basis for developing the core of any system which might be used for making decisions in vague and inaccurate situations.

Aggregation: In this module, aggregation of all outputs for each rule is done in fuzzy set. Three methods of aggregations can be applied: maximum, probabilistic OR, or simply the sum of each rule's output set.

Logical operators OR and AND are used in the method of aggregation [19]. The conjunction of linguistic statements can be applied by using logical t-conorm and the t-norm operator. Classification of task uses the Min and Max operators. In Identification and approximation process, the product operators are used for the smoothness and differentiability. It has many advantages in Neuro-fuzzy schemes.

Defuzzification: In order to get the crisp output of the given system, defuzzification is needed at the final fuzzy output. For the conversion of fuzzy sets to crisp sets, different defuzzification methods such as bisector of area, smallest (absolute) of maximum (som), mean of maximum (mom), largest (absolute) of maximum (lom) and center of gravity are used.

This method is used to generate a single number from above step of aggregation. In this, centroid calculation method is popularly used which gives the center of area under the aggregated output curve. Other methods like bisector and average of certain range of aggregated output curve are also used for defuzzification.

3.1   Fuzzy Rule Based Model

FIS (Fuzzy Inference System) model is based on various concepts such as fuzzy sets, fuzzy rule base engine and fuzzy logic reasoning. Formation of fuzzy rules is an essential component of Fuzzy model. The basic structure of a FIS (shown in Fig. 4) includes three main components viz. a rule base engine which consists of the stipulated fuzzy rules, knowledge based engine i.e. database which defines the membership functions for the entire fuzzy rule formation, and the reasoning mechanism, required to execute a inference model with the framed rules to achieve a reasonable output or conclusion.

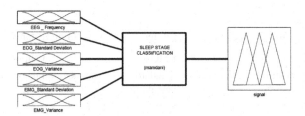

Fig. 4. Fuzzy inference system

Following rules are framed for the classification of sleep stages as shown in Table 2.

Table 2. Rules for the classification of sleep stages

EEG frequency	EMG		EOG		EEG stage
	Standard deviation	Variance	Standard deviation	Variance	
Low	Low	Low	High	High	REM
High	Medium	Medium	Low	Low	SWS
Medium	High	High	Medium	Medium	Awake

The extracted parameters such as frequencies, standard deviation and variance are taken as input variables to the Fuzzy inference system subjected to selection process block. The fuzzy rules have been framed after extracting the features to classify the EEG in to three classes: Awake, REM and SWS stages. Mapping was done between input feature vectors and output classes by an inference system using FL [20]. The processed EEG signals for Awake, REM and SWS are shown in Fig. 3.

4 Result

4.1 Membership Function for Input and Output Variables

A Membership function is a curve that defines how each point in the input space is mapped to a membership value or degree of membership between 0 and 1. The membership function associated with each input is described in Fig. 5. Triangular membership function has been taken for each linguistic variable (low, medium and high). The range of the input has been decided on the basis of EEG frequency sub-bands and mean of EOG and EMG. The study of the frequency sub-bands of the EEG reflects changes which are further reinforced by the sleep stages rules as discussed in Table 3.

Table 3. Identification of different stages based on features

EEG	EOG		EMG		Output	
Frequency	Standard deviation	Variance	Standard deviation	Variance	Fuzzy score	Sleep stage
9.26	4.92	7.2	5.49	6.38	4.47	Probably Awake
9.26	9.21	10	1.98	1.9	2.57	Marginally Awake
31.6	9.21	8.54	10	8.84	5.35	Definitely REM
7.1	0.263	6.16	10	8.69	6.62	Probably REM
3.01	9.72	8.99	0	0	8.25	SWS

The output will be in the form of fuzzy score. Fuzzy score is the value that is calculated by FIS considering all input values, constraints and membership functions. Table 3 shows the fuzzy score of all inputs and outputs which is decided by the fuzzy rules. As shown in Table 3, the system is able to find the different sleep stages accurately which may be further used for the purpose of clinical diagnosis. Five

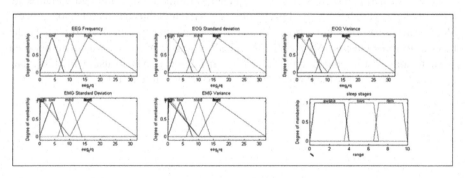

Fig. 5. Membership function for input and output

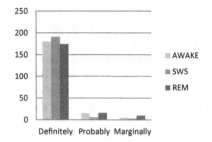

Table 4. Accuracy breakdown of different stages of sleep

Different stages of sleep	Definitely	Probably	Marginally	Accuracy
Awake	180	15	5	91%
SWS	191	6	3	95%
REM	174	16	10	89%

Fig. 6. Identification of correct sleep stages

features namely frequency, standard deviation and variance of EOG and EMG have been fed to the FIS. Once the corresponding input is presented, the corresponding rule gets fired and estimates the stage of sleep EEG.

Each membership function of all five features has been described with three linguistic variables (Low, Medium and High) which represent the particular range of each input. For the output stages three trapezoidal memberships have been chosen for the entire range as specified in Fig. 4, where each membership function defines the stage of sleep EEG as Awake, REM or SWS. For the precise identification of all stages, they are further classified as probable, marginal and definite. Fuzzy score is evaluated on the basis of five features and further the stage is identified on the basis of the rule base engine which is fed in to the fuzzy inference system. The fuzzy rule base engine generates the fuzzy score after evaluation of all fuzzy rules and its constraints. The output obtained from the fuzzy score lies between 0 and 10. The range of fuzzy score is classified in to nine categories i.e. definitely awake (0–2.5), marginally awake (2.5–3.5), probably awake (3.5–4.5), definitely SWS (4.5–5.5), marginally SWS (5.5–6.5) probably SWS (6.5–7), definitely REM (7–8.5), marginally SWS (8.5–9.5) and probably REM (9.5–10). Table 3 shows the detailed overview of fuzzy score for the sample identification of sleep EEG.

Performance of the fuzzy system for sleep stage classification has been assessed and experimental results have been plotted as shown in Fig. 5. Table 3 confirmed that the proposed model has potential in classifying the EEG signals with the average accuracy of 93%. The accuracy of each stage is 91% for Awake, 95% for SWS and 89% for REM stage (Fig. 6 and Table 4).

5 Discussion

As the applications of soft-computing and digital signal processing tools in solving brain electrophysiological problems and systems modeling of various brain functions have great clinical and pathophysiological importance, the design of such types of systems with development of a clinical software package, after some training to the clinical and research persons definitely will reduce the labor involved in clinical diagnosis [21]. Review of literature reveals that neural network along with the various

804   C. Nagpal and P. K. Upadhyay

transforms (such as Fourier transform, wavelet transform) has been applied for finding the solution of complex problems associated with human brain [22]. Many researchers have reported on the automated sleep scoring techniques using wavelet transform as a pre-processor. Applications like event related potentials, sleep spindles detection, spike detection, epileptic seizures have also been discussed in past years with different supervised and unsupervised classifier techniques [23, 24], but very less works have been reported till now which investigate the frequency and powers changes for different stages of EEG with the help of fuzzy logic.

6 Conclusion

The soft-computing tools are very effective tools for automatic identification of small changes occuring in EEG signals associated with various stress stimuli [16]. Therefore, the proposed research work will help the neurologists and doctors to find the sleep-awake correlation. By means of Fuzzy logic approach, sleep stage classification on the subject's polygraphs under consideration have been studied. EEG, EOG and EMG have been used in this study where the range of EEG sub-band frequencies are cata-gorised into 4 frequency bands: delta (0.5–4 Hz), theta (4–8 Hz), alpha (8–12 Hz), beta (12–40 Hz). The proposed work approaches the classification of the sleep stages through the use and attributes of fuzzy logic and fuzzy inference system accompanied by wavelet transform. The sleep stage identification has been done with an accuracy of 91% (Awake), 95% (REM) and 88% (REM) with the help of proposed algorithm with an accuracy. The goal of this study is to improve an available computerized diagnostic system to investigate the abnormalities in sleep EEG signals for normal and abnormal conditions.

References

1. Regan, D.: Human Brain Electrophysiology-Evoked Potentials and Evoked Magnetic Fields in Science and Medicine. Elsevier, New York (1989)
2. Zhang, J., Wu, Y.: Automatic sleep stage classification of single-channel EEG by using complex convolved neural network. Biomed. Eng. Biomed. Tech. 63(2), 177–190 (2018)
3. Koley, B., Dey, D.: Automatic detection of sleep apnea and hypopnea events from single channel measurement of respiration signal employing ensemble binary SVM classifiers. Measurement 46(7), 2082–2092 (2013)
4. Heiss, J.E., Held, C.M., Estevez, P.A., Perez, C.A., Holzmann, C.A., Perez, J.P.: Classification of sleep stages in infants: a neuro fuzzy approach. IEEE Eng. Med. Biol. Mag. 21(5), 147–151 (2002)
5. Sinha, R.K.: Artificial neural network detects changes in electro-encephalogram power spectrum of different sleep-wakes in an animal model of heat stress. Med. Biol. Eng. Comput. 41, 595–600 (2003)
6. Sandya, H.B., Hemanth Kumar, P., Bhudiraja, H., Rao, S.K.: Fuzzy rule based feature extraction and classification of time series signal. Int. J. Soft Comput. Eng. (IJSCE) 3(2) (2013) ISSN: 2231–2307

7. Sarbadhikari, S.N.: Neural network aided analysis of electrophysiological signals from the brain of an animal model of depression subjected to chronic physical exercise. Ph.D. thesis, School of Biomedical Engineering, Banaras Hindu University, 1995
8. James, C.J., Jones, R.D., Bones, P.J., Carrol, G.J.: Spatial analysis of multi-channel EEG recordings through a fuzzy-rule based system in the detection of epileptiform events. In: Proceeding of 20th International Conference of the IEEE Engineering in Medicine and Biology Society (CD-ROM), Hong Kong, p. 4 (1998)
9. James, C.J., et al.: Detection of epileptiform discharges in the EEG by a hybrid system comprising mimetic, self-organized artificial neural network, and fuzzy logic stages. Clin. Neurophy. 110, 2049–2063 (1999)
10. Jansen, B.: Feature extraction methods for EEG analysis. Electroencephalogr. Clin. Neurophysiol. 61(3), S222 (1985)
11. Sarbadhikari, S.N.: Neural network aided analysis of electrophysiological signals from the brain of an animal model of depression subjected to chronic physical exercise. Ph.D. thesis, School of Biomedical Engineering, Banaras Hindu University (1995)
12. Cesarelli, M., Clemente, F., Bracale, M.: The flexible FFT algorithm for processing biomedical signals using a PC. J. Biomed. Eng. 12, 527–530 (1990)
13. Tagluk, M., Sezgin, N., Akin, M.: Estimation of sleep stages by an artificial neural network employing EEG, EMG and EOG. J. Med. Syst. 34(4), 717–725 (2009)
14. Estévez, P., Held, C., Holzmann, C., Perez, C., Pérez, J., Heiss, J., Garrido, M., Peirano, P.: Polysomnographic pattern recognition for automated classification of sleep-waking states in infants. Med. Biol. Eng. Comput. 40(1), 105–113 (2002)
15. Jacques, G., et al.: Multiresolution analysis for early diagnosis of Alzheirmer's disease. In: Proceedings of the 26th Annual International Conference of the IEEE EMBS San Francisco, CA, USA. Sept. 1–5 (2004)
16. Robert, C., Guilpin, C., Limoge, A.: Review of neural network application in sleep research. J. Neurosci. Methods 79, 187–193 (1998)
17. Kaur, M., Tiwari, P.: Developing brain computer interface using fuzzy logic. Int. J. Inf. Technol. Knowl. Manag. 2, 429–434 (2010)
18. Sarbadhikari, S.N., Dey, S., Ray, A.K.: Chronic exercise alters EEG power spectra in an animal model of depression. Indian J. Physiol. Pharmacol. 40(1), 47–57 (1996)
19. Hasan, J.: Automatic analysis of sleep recording: a critical review. Ann. Clin. Res. 17, 280–287 (1985)
20. Sukanesh, R., Harikumar, R.: Analysis of Fuzzy Techniques and Neural Networks (RBF&MLP) in Classification of Epilepsy Risk Levels from EEG Signals. IETE J. Res. 53(5), 465–474 (2007)
21. Kumar, R.H., Sukanesh, R.: Fuzzy techniques with aggregation operators for classification and optimization of epilepsy risk level from EEG signals. IETE J. Res. 51(5), 379–388 (2005)
22. Bankman, I.N., Sigillito, V.G., Wise, R.A., Smith, P.L.: Feature-based detection of the K-complex wave in the human electroencephalogram using neural networks. IEEE Trans. Biomed. Eng. 39(12), 1305–1310 (1992)
23. Gupta, L., Molfese, D.L., Tammana, R.: An artificial neural network approach to ERP classification. Brain Cogn. 27(3), 311–330 (1995)
24. Oropesa, E., Cycon, H.L., Jobert, M.: Sleep Stage Classification Using Wavelet Transform and Neural Network. International Computer Science Institute (1999)

Efficient Digital Filter Banking Algorithm for Wireless VoIP

Ravindra Luhach[1], Chandra Kr. Jha[1], and Ashish Kr. Luhach[2($\boxtimes$)]

[1] Banasthali University, Banasthali, Rajasthan, India
ravindraluhach@gmail.com, ckjhal@gmail.com
[2] Maharshi Dayanand University, Haryana, India
ashishluhach@acm.org

Abstract. Due to advancement in Today's information and communication technology, Voice over IP (VoIP), emerged as one of the most reliable and cost efficient technology over the traditional ones, the same used to transmit the voice data over available computer networks using standardized protocols such as Internet Protocol (IP). Along with the advantages such as scalability and security, VoIP has some threats to deal with such as voice quality and interference. In this research article, an efficient digital filter banking scheme is proposed and the same is implemented after decoding the signal into the system as post-processor. To analysis the performance of the proposed, it is evaluated under various network conditions. Later, the proposed scheme is compared with the traditional one. The proposed scheme shows better results in terms of speech quality with the rational ones.

1 Introduction

Voice over Internet Protocol (VoIP) has emerged as one of the most significant technology in the field of communication and evolved as a substitute to the conventional communication method as the Public Switched Telephone Network (PSTN). Voice over Internet Protocol (VoIP) is the technology used to transmit the voice through internet or local area networks and based on packet switching. The packets in the same are transmitted through the most efficient path from the available ones. The conventional communication system such as public switched telephone network (PSTN) was using circuit-switching for communication which requires a dedicated line [1]. The conventional communication systems was using analog infrastructure. The analog infrastructure lacks in robustness and is not able to deal with the noise occurring from various sources but in digital communication such as VOIP, noise can be handled for example by using repeaters the original signal can be recovered [2]. Singh et al. [3] discussed the evolution of voice communication over the period of the time beginning from packet switched networks to modern VoIP. The authors describe that, for providing voice communication to the users VoIP can be the best alternative of the PSTN telecommunication services. Later, the authors summarized the advantages & disadvantages, compression & measurement schemes for the VoIP system. Han et al. [4], this research work focused on the noise removal and reduction in VoIP transmission. To achieve their research objective of noise reduction in VoIP transmission, authors used the modified Weiner filter. The Weiner filter lowered the signal to noise ratio at each frequency. In this research work, authors proposed a system to reduce the noise by using pre-processing of the voice signal. By using the proposed scheme, authors observed better results in terms of MOS score.

Bolot et al. [5] in this research work, authors observed very interesting facts about VoIP transmission. The authors choose the times scales of the interest scales very efficiently from a small amount of milliseconds to couple of minutes. During their experiment, authors recorded rapid fluctuations of queuing delay over small interval of time. Such as, loss of packets are mainly random until and unless they consume a large portion of the existing bandwidth. Later the authors discussed the effects of the said results on the design and implementation of control mechanisms for the internet. For speech applications Noor et al. [6] proposed noise canceller using multirate filter bank by splitting the input signal spectrum and applied the Least Mean Square (LMS) algorithm to control the finite impulse response filter. In the proposed systems, authors concluded that computational power is significantly decreased by implementing the polyphase and the noble identities. Samad et al. [7] focused on the noisy environments and proposed a new feature extracting method for the same. In the proposed method, the speech signals are decomposed into subbands to find out noisiest subband. After decomposing of the speech signal, adaptive filtering methods are applied to the same. In the research work, decomposition of the speech signal is performed with the help low complexity octave filter bank. The adaptive filtering is calculated by applying normalized least mean square algorithm. Ninkovic et al. [8] discussed that there is a need of implementing a loss recovery method to address the VOIP quality challenges where the packet loss is very high. The authors also discussed the disturbing effect of the heavy packet loss in VOIP. The authors emphasized that, the traditional loss recovery methods are dependent on various other factors.

2 VOIP Success Over PSTN

In the section, various factors are discussed which attract the user to migrate towards VOIP from PSTN:

- **Low Cost:** Low cost is one of the most attracting features of the VOIP in comparison with PSTN. VOIP system does not require new infrastructure as it can use the existing one such as computers, laptops etc. to make communication cheaper. The low cost feature also attracts the small and medium sized organization to adopt VOIP.
- **Scalable:** Number of the connecting ports can be added in the PSTN to make it expandable but for the same extra cost is also involved but VOIP is a software based solution where updates can be very easily integrated at no extra cost.
- **Disaster Recovery:** In VOIP system, it chooses the most efficient path from the available ones; if one path is disturbed due to some reason other paths can be chosen. Due to interconnection of various routers and switches, there is more than one path to research the destination as compared to PSTN where there is only dedicated path available.

- **Advance Features:** In VOIP various advance features are very easily integrated without heavy cost such as call forwarding, caller-id and broadcasting of message in comparison to PSTN.
- **Security:** High level of security can be achieved in VOIP than PSTN by using Virtual Private Network (VPN).

3 Demerits of VOIP System

VOIP system is very well implemented due to its advantages; this section is focused on the demerits of the VOIP System, which are as follows:

- **Voice Quality:** The quality of voice signals received by the receiver is not up to the mark, sometimes due to the distortion in the signal over wireless VoIP system. The factors affecting the same are network speed, connectivity and the hardware used for implementation of the wired/wireless VoIP system.
- **No Power No Service:** In the case of power failure, VOIP phone system becomes unreachable as it is needs continuous power supply for working. Although the same is not applicable for the regular telephone system as the power supplied through the telephone line. To make maximum use of VOIP telephone system it requires continuous power supply.
- **Security:** Wireless VOIP uses the computer network for communication and the same is also used by many other users. Wireless VOIP are going to face the same security issues as in computer networks. The major security issues over VoIP are network identity theft of service; phishing attacks, virus's attacks, service denial, tampering of calls.
- **Interference:** Interference can be caused during the transmission of signal into a channel from source to destination. Interference is one of the major limiting factors in the performance of wireless system and the same is also responsible for dropped calls. It also results in crosstalk on voice channels while communicating.

4 Methodology

To enhance the signal quality of the narrowband and wideband wireless VoIP system, which could be degraded due to the loss of voice packets during the communication, the computationally efficient scheme has been proposed. The step by steps plan is as under (Fig. 1):

Step 1:   The original speech signal has been fed into the system

Step 2:   The speech signal has been encoded with various narrowband wireless VoIP speech encoders at different data rates

Step 3:   The compressed version of the speech signal has been packetized into the VoIP packets to transmit over the IP network. To check for network efficiency, the packet size can be varied

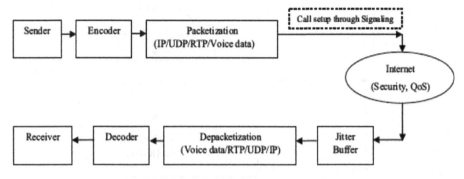

Fig. 1. General architecture of VOIP system

Step 4:   The IP network impairments into the speech signals has been introduced through 2-state Gilbert-Elliot model. The signal has been degraded with different packet loss rates

Step 5:   The degraded VoIP signal has been depacketized and then decoded with the corresponding decoders

Step 6:   The digital filtering schemes has been incorporated into the system as post processor, after the decoder

Step 7:   The signal measurement and evaluation had been performed with PESQ

The methodology of the proposed work is presented in Fig. 2.

5   VoIP Simulations

In this section, the VoIP simulation results are discussed. The proposed scheme is implemented on the various modulation schemes such as DBPSK, DQPSK and QAM64. For the experiment simulator is designed according to the available network conditions. The speech signal encoded into the VoIP frames using G.711, G.729 and AMR-NB encoder. The VoIP frames were designed by Gilbert-Elliot mode and then resulting stream decoded into degraded voice. The measurements were carried out through PESQ. The set of speech recordings were taken from [11] for VoIP simulations. The speech signal is degraded with various packet loss rates as described in Table 1. The performance of the proposed filter is analyzed for various loss rates for G.711, G.729A& AMR-NB based wireless VoIP system (Fig. 4).

6   Results and Discussion

Simulations of synthesis and dyadic filtering based VoIP system had been performed for narrowband G.711, G.729A & AMR-NB (7.95 kbps) coders. The variation of the packet loss rates and PESQ-MOS scores for G.711, G.729A and AMR-NB coders in VoIP system are shown in Figs. 3, 5 and Tables 2, 4. The significant increase in

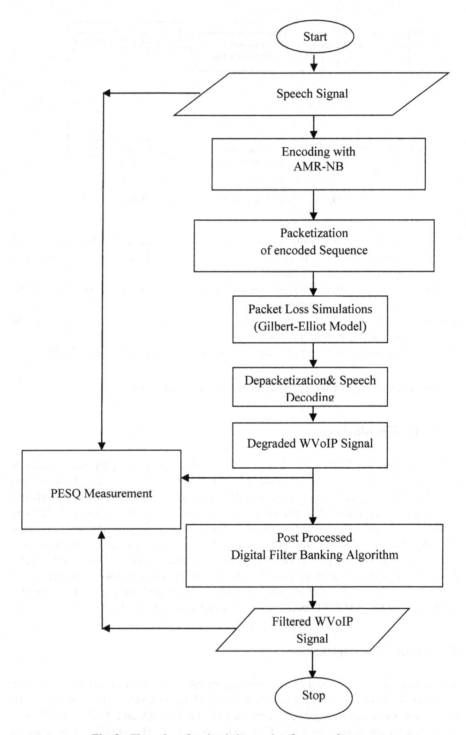

Fig. 2. Flow chart for simulation study of proposed system

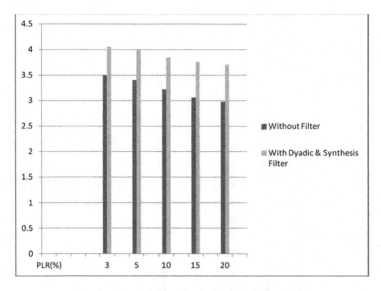

Fig. 3. Dyadic & synthesis filter bank for G.711

Table 1. Simulated loss rates

Packet loss rate (%)	p	q	e
3	0.98	0.032	0.005
5	0.95	0.053	0.005
10	0.91	0.101	0.005
15	0.84	0.151	0.005
20	0.81	0.201	0.005

PESQ-MOS scores is achieved at various packet loss rates with the Dyadic filters. The evaluation results presented in indicated that the DBPSK modulation scheme work well in wireless VoIP system. The proposed scheme is much effective at high packet loss rates as presented in results. The proposed scheme effectively conceals the lost packet during VoIP speech transmission to improve the signal quality (Table 3).

7 Discussion

It is observed form the comparison results that the signal quality of the wireless VoIP signal is significantly increased with Synthesis & Dyadic filtering scheme as compared to the without filters as presented in Figs. 3, 5 and Tables 2, 4. The much improvement in PESQ-MOS scores is observed with Dyadic filter for wireless VoIP speech signal. The results of the G.729A can be compared with recovery by reinitialization (RbR) [12] method where the increase in the signal quality was 0.0065–0.17 (with packet loss rates 10% to 50%), which is very low as compared to the proposed work.

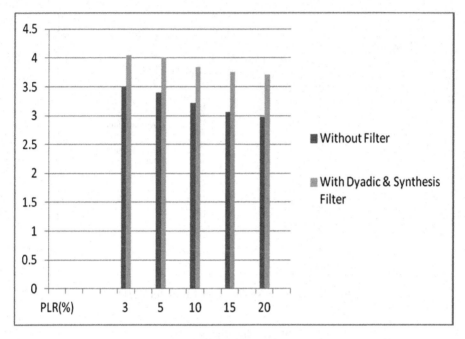

Fig. 4. Dyadic & synthesis filter bank for G.7.29A

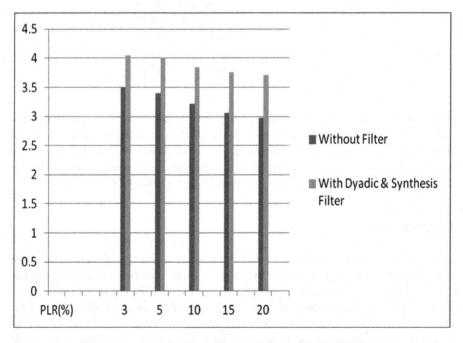

Fig. 5. Dyadic & synthesis filter bank for AMR-NB 7.95 kbps

Table 2. MOS scores for G.711

PLR (%)	MOS scores	
	DBPSK	
	Without filter	With dyadic & synthesis filter
3	2.28	3.01
5	2.20	2.89
10	2.02	2.68
15	2.01	2.48
20	1.89	2.42

Table 3. MOS Scores for G.729A8kbps

PLR (%)	MOS scores	
	DBPSK	
	Without filter	With dyadic & synthesis filter
3	2.39	3.27
5	2.28	3.14
10	2.02	2.92
15	1.96	2.79
20	1.87	2.52

Table 4. MOS scores for AMR-NB 7.95 kbps

PLR (%)	MOS scores	
	DBPSK	
	Without filter	With QMF
3	2.48	3.35
5	2.39	3.23
10	2.25	3.01
15	2.09	2.89
20	2.02	2.68

8   Conclusion

The synthesis and dyadic filtering based VoIP system had been performed for narrowband G.711, G.729A & AMR-NB (7.95 kbps) coders in this work. It had been observed that the proposed scheme works well for both narrowband wireless VoIP systems, since the proposed scheme enhances the signal quality. The enhancement in signal quality was measured through PESQ measurement schemes and it had been found that results of the filtering based wireless VoIP system were better than that of without filtering based system with DBPSK modulation scheme. In future the work can be extended for noisy environment and implemented on TMS320C6713 DSP processor.

References

1. Meisel, J.B., Needles, M.: Voice over Internet protocol (VoIP) development and public policy implications. Info **7** (2005)
2. Davidson, J., Peters, J., Bhatia, M., Kalidindi, S., Mukherjee, S.: Voice Over IP Fundamentals. Cisco Press, Indianpolis (2006)
3. Singh, H.P., Singh, S., Singh, J., Khan, S.A.: VoIP: state of art for global connectivity—A critical review. J. Netw. Comput. Appl. **37**, 365–379 (2014)
4. Han, S.H., Jeong, S., Yang, H., Kim, J.: Noise reduction for VoIP speech codecs using modified wiener filter. In: Elleithy, K., (ed.) Innovations in Systems, Computing Sciences and Software Engineering, pp. 393–397. Springer, Dordrecht (2007)
5. Bolot, J.C.: End-to-end packet delay and loss behavior in the internet. In: Proceedings of ACM Symposium on Communications Architectures, Protocols and Applications, pp. 289–298 (1993)
6. Noor, A.O.A., Samad, S.A., Hussain, A.: Improved low complexity noise cancellation technique for speech signals. World Appl. Sci. J. **6**(2), 272–278 (2009)
7. Samad, S.A.: Feature extracting in the presence of environmental noise, using subb and adaptive filtering. In: Industrial Electronic Seminar (2009)
8. Ninkovic, N., Gajin, S., Reljin, I.: Packet dispersion strategy evaluation from the perspective of packet loss pattern and VoIP quality. Comput. Sci. Inf. Syst. **13**(1), 71–92 (2016)
9. Mitra, S.K.: Digital Signal Processing: A Computer-Based Approach, with DSP Laboratory Using MATLAB, 2nd edn. McGraw-Hill, New York (2001)
10. Proakis, J.D., Manolakis, D.G.: Digital Signal Processing: Principles, Algorithm and Applications, 4th edn, p. 701p. Prentice Hall, Upper Saddle River (2007)
11. Open Speech Repository. http://www.voiptroubleshooter.com/open_speech/
12. Montininy, C., Aboulnasr, T.: Improving the Performance of ITU-T G.729A for VoIP. In: Proceedings of the IEEE International Conference on Multimedia and Expo, vol. 1, pp. 433–436 (2000)

Speed and Torque Control of Induction Motor Using Adaptive Neuro-Fuzzy Interference System with DTC

Ranjit Kumar Bindal$^{(\boxtimes)}$ and Inderpreet Kaur

Electrical Engineering Department, Chandigarh University, Gharuan, Mohali,
Punjab, India
ranjit19782002@gmail.com, inder_preet74@yahoo.com

Abstract. Every industry needs speed and torque ripple control of induction motor in large number of applications. The number of induction motor takes more time during starting, settling and transient period. As more time is taken by the motor so there are more losses, more heat, less efficiency and more ripples are produced. To overcome these drawback, direct torque control technique known as conventional technique, is used with induction motors, but with up to certain limits the drawbacks are reduced. In this paper a new technique an Adaptive Neuro-Fuzzy Interference System (ANFIS) with DTC is proposed to overcome the drawbacks of conventional DTC technique. Now by implementing and comparing the proposed technique ANFIS with conventional one it is seen that the system becomes less complicated, the performance of the speed and torque control of the induction motor is also improved. It is also seen that as we compared the proposed technique with conventional one the rise time is reduced by 256 ms settling time is reduced by 687 ms and transient time is reduced by 202 ms and torque ripples are also reduced and the overall performance of the induction motor is improved.

Keywords: Three-phase induction motor
Adaptive Neuro-Fuzzy Interference System (ANFIS) direct torque control

1 Introduction

The electrical power generated in the world about 60% of it is consumed by three phase Induction motors [1]. Induction motors are extensively utilized in industries, as it is easy in construction, minimum operating cost, require less repair cost, more efficient and economical as compared to the other machines of the same rating [2]. Three phase induction motor has highly efficient at low loads. The induction motor has a drawback of wide speed control. The speed control of an induction machine is becoming easy with power electronics devices [3, 4]. Now a day vector control, scalar control and direct torque control (DTC) techniques are utilized to control the torque of an ac motors. Unlike vector control, In direct torque control, there is no need for coordination transformation, no encoder, and no current regulator [5, 6]. A DTC limit the torque and flux of induction motor directly depends upon instantaneous errors. DTC technique is one of the main control technique presented by German Scientist Blaschke and

© Springer Nature Singapore Pte Ltd. 2019
A. K. Luhach et al. (Eds.): ICAICR 2018, CCIS 955, pp. 815–825, 2019.
https://doi.org/10.1007/978-981-13-3140-4_73

Depenbrock in 1971 and 1985. Later on, ABB Company replaces the previous conventional techniques with latest AC drive techniques [7–9].

The main aim of this paper is to limit the torque and flux of an ac machine with direct torque control and ANFIS technique. The proposed controller not only has a simple structure but also has all of the functions for a high accurate speed control for working with all the speed range. In this paper, a presented method ANFIS is also compared with a conventional method.

The remaining paper is prepared as follows: Sect. 2 presents the Mathematic modelling of a three-phase induction motor, while Sect. 3 describes the principal model of DTC for the induction motor. Section 4; discuss the proposed ANFIS method is discussed in detail in Sect. 5 shows the simulation results and discussion. At last, Sect. 6 gives the conclusions discussion.

2   Mathematical Model of Three-Phase Induction Motor

The three-phase induction motor consists of stationary stator frame and rotating wound rotor, which are the main parts of motor. A stator consists of the stationary part and rotating part is known as the rotor. The parameters of three-phase induction motors are stator resistance, rotor resistance, self-inductance, stator reactance, mutual inductance and rotor reactance of the motor [10–13]. The equivalent circuit of an ac machine is drawn in Fig. 1 [14–16]. A voltage source inverter model is shown in Fig. 2.

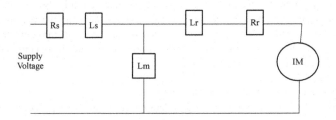

Fig. 1. The equivalent circuit diagram of three phase AC machine

$$V(t) = \frac{2}{3}[V_a(t) + ZV_b(t) + Z^2V_c(t)] \tag{1}$$

where

$$Z = e^{i2/3\pi} \tag{2}$$

V_a, V_b, and V_c are the per phase instantaneous voltages. The Eqs. (1) and (2) shows that Eqs. (1) has 6 non-zero states and Eq. (2) has 2 null states. The phasor diagram of Eqs. (1) and (2) shown in Fig. 3 and the voltage vector/switching table is shown in Table 1. Normally V_d and V_q are the torque and flux parameters of voltage vector,

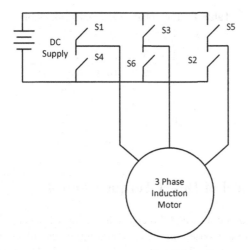

Fig. 2. Voltage source inverter circuit

where V_d controls the flux of the system and V_q controls the torque of the motor. A voltage source inverter is utilized to limit the supply voltage easily. The voltage space phasor using Eq. (1) along D-axis is V_t [17–20]. The voltage vector/switching table is shown in Table 1.

$$V(t) = \frac{2}{3}V_d[S_a(t) + ZS_b(t) + Z^2S_d(t)] \tag{3}$$

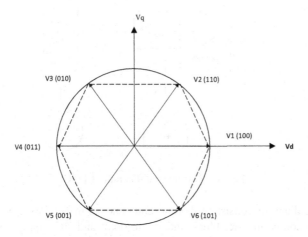

Fig. 3. DTC with space vector

Table 1. The voltage vector/switching table

V_Ψ	V_{Te}	1	2	3	4	5	6
↑	↑	ε_2	ε_3	ε_4	ε_5	ε_6	ε_1
	0	ε_0	ε_0	ε_0	ε_0	ε_0	ε_0
	↓	ε_6	ε_1	ε_3	ε_2	ε_4	ε_5
↓	↑	ε_3	ε_4	ε_5	ε_6	ε_1	ε_2
	0	ε_0	–	–	–	–	–
	↓	ε_6	ε_5	ε_1	ε_2	ε_3	ε_4

3   Principle Model of Direct Torque Control

The torque and speed is controlled directly using different voltage vector in DTC. The voltage vector selection is based on the error among the calculated torque and flux and their respective base values. These values should be remaining within the limits of hysteresis comparators. The stator flux and stator torque be able to restrict directly as choosing a particular inverter switching states of the DTC [21, 22].

The voltage and current can be calculated by the use of electromagnetic flux and torque of induction motor. The stator flux linkage was obtained by the integrating the stator voltages and the torque are obtained by the multiplication of stator flux linkage vector and measured induction machine current. Now the calculated values are then compared with base values. As per the error values obtained voltage vector selection takes place. The DTC block diagram is drawn in Fig. 4 [23, 24].

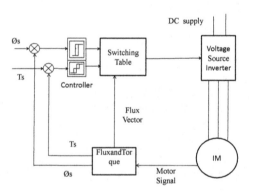

Fig. 4. Fundamental diagram of DTC

The block diagram consist of Torque and flux controller block, switching table block, voltage source inverter block, induction motor and DC supply voltage. The dc supply is connected to voltage source inverter; here the dc supply is converted into three phase supply by using the parks transformation ratio. This three phase supply is connected to the three phase induction motor. The take off point is taken from the supply and fed back to the torque and flux controller block. This block control the torque and flux and fed to the torque and flux comparator. Here the toque and flux are compared with reference torque and flux and fed to the switching table. The switching table control the input with different switching position, and fed to the voltage source inverter.

$$V_s = R_s i_s + \frac{1}{\omega_0} \frac{d}{dt}(\psi_s) + \omega K_m \left(\frac{\pi}{2}\right)(\psi_s) \tag{4}$$

$$V_r = R_r i_r + \frac{1}{\omega_0} \frac{d}{dt}(\psi_r) + (\omega_k - \omega_m) M \left(\frac{\pi}{2}\right)(\psi_r) \tag{5}$$

$$i_s = \left[i_{ds} i_{qs}\right] \tag{6}$$

$$T_e = \psi_s * i_s = M\left(\frac{\pi}{2}\right)\psi_s \cdot i_s = \psi_{ds} * i_{qs} - \psi_{qs} * i_{ds} \tag{7}$$

$$i_r \psi_r = L_m i_r \cdot i_s = \frac{L_m}{L_r}\psi_r * i_s \tag{8}$$

$$\psi_s = \int (V_s - i_s R_s) dt \tag{9}$$

$$\psi_s = \frac{Z^{-1}}{1 - Z^{-1}}(T_s)(V_s - i_s R_s) \tag{10}$$

Here V_s and V_r are the three-phase stator voltages and, V_d is stator voltage direct axis and V_q is stator voltage of quadrature axis. i_s and i_r are three-phase stator and rotor currents respectively, while i_{sd}, i_{sq}, stator current of direct axis and quardature axis and i_{rd}, i_{rq} rotor current of direct axis and quardature axis.

4 Principle of ANFIS

An adaptive Neuro-Fuzzy controller is the mixture of the Fuzzy logic controller and artificial neural network controller. Neural network controller provides combined construction and learning outcomes of a Fuzzy logic system and the fuzzy logic controller provides the neural system with a standard structure with high-level fuzzy rules of thoughts and analysis. The ANFIS is proposed technique using a combination of fuzzy logic and artificial neural network [25–27].

Here the electro-magnetic torque of an ac machine is controlled by changing the values of torque. The produced value is forwarded to fuzzy interference system for the generation of fuzzy rules. The ANFIS is created by different stages, first stage is known as training stage and the second stage is known as testing stage [28, 29]. A basic working of the Training phase and Testing phase is discussed as under.

Training Phase: In this phase training data set is generated for ANFIS. In this control technique, the torque and variable torque is produced in the form of phasor/vectors for induction motor that is connected to neural system. After the preparation of values by back Propagation, then algorithm is prepared to calculate the actual torque control of induction motor. Now, the prepared information is utilized to produce the fuzzy rules. There for the fuzzy based control rules are produced consequently in ANFIS [30].

Testing Phase/Stage: In this phase tested speed control is created that is used in ANFIS. In this testing stage, the real torque and the difference in the torque of the induction motor are connected to the input, there for the suitable control electromagnetic torque is produced for the ANFIS.

ANFIS Structure: The basic ANFIS structure consists of different layers that are known as input layer, membership function input layer, rule layer, and members function output layer and last layer output layer. The basic structure is shown in Fig. 5 and the working of ANFIS network layers is as under [31–34].

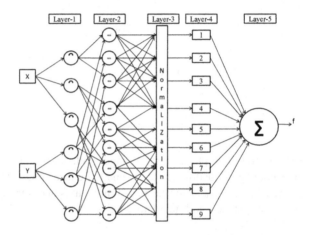

Fig. 5. Structure of ANFIS

1: Every node of this layer generates the membership function of the input variable with node function.
2: The outgoing of layer second is a multiplication of the entire inward coming signals.
3: In this layer the calculated weight is normalized.
4: All the nodes of this layer include the linear function.
5: This Layer includes the addition of all output of layer-4.

5   Results and Discussion

The simulation structure of a presented ANFIS controller is drawn in Fig. 6, Supply voltage of ANFIS with DTC is drawn in Fig. 7, Stator current of direct axis and quadrature axis is drawn in Fig. 8, Rotor speed is shown in Fig. 9, Electro-magnetic Torque and stator current is shown in Fig. 10 and Output vector of ANFIS with DTC (Fig. 11).

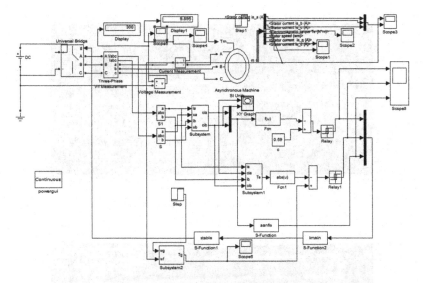

Fig. 6. Simulation diagram of ANFIS with DTC

Fig. 7. Supply voltage of ANFIS with DTC

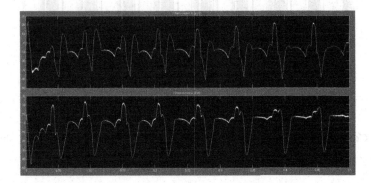

Fig. 8. D-axis and Q-axis of stator current of ANFIS

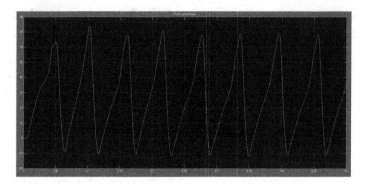

Fig. 9. Rotor speed of ANFIS with DTC

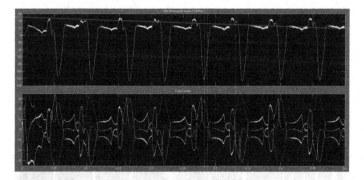

Fig. 10. Electromagnetic Torque and stator current ANFIS with DTC

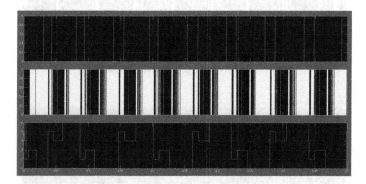

Fig. 11. Output vector of ANFIS with DTC

The Comparative analysis of presented and conventional technique is shown in Table 2.

Table 2. Comparative analysis of presented and conventional technique

S. No.	Technique	Rise Time (ms)	Settling Time (ms)	Transient time (ms)	Electro- magnetic Torque (Nm)	Current in (Amp)	Speed in (Wm)	Supply voltage (Volts)
1.	Conventional DTC	260	725	520	54	37	178	300
2.	ANFIS with DTC	3.2	38	318.3	52	35	74	300

From the comparative analysis it is seen that the proposed ANFIS technique improves the performance of induction machine for rise time, settling time, transient times and torque ripples are reduced than the conventional technique.

6   Conclusions and Discussion

In this paper, ANFIS control technique is used for speed and torque control of the induction motor is proposed. The proposed control technique is easy to construct and easy to use in a large number of practical applications. The proposed technique is compared with conventional technique on the basis of rise time, settling time transient response and torque ripples for an induction motor. From the comparative analysis, it is seen that the rise time is reduced by 256 ms, the settling time is reduced by 687 ms, transient time is reduced by 202 ms and torque ripples are also reduced. The proposed technique also control speed and reduce the torque ripples with a good extent of three phase Induction motor. As a point of discussion we can say that, there is an overall improvement in the performance of induction motor when the proposed technique ANFIS is implemented as compared to conventional technique. For further enhancement of the DTC model in induction motor, a μ–controller can be design based on artificial intelligence.

Appendix

The presented control methods have been tested on a 5.4 HP (4 KW) three phase induction motor.

Voltage = 400 V
Frequency = 50 Hz
Inductance of Stator = 5.839 mH
Speed = 1430 rpm
Resistance of rotor = 1.394 Ω
Stator resistance = 0.8 Ω
Inductance of rotor = 2.6 mH
Mutually inductance Lm = 172.2 mH

Pole = 4

Rotor inertia (J) = 0.0129 kg/m^2

References

1. Sekhar, D.C., Marutheswar, G.V.: Direct torque control of three phase induction motor with ANFIS and CUCKOO search algorithms. Int. J. Pure Appl. Math. **114**, 501–514 (2017)
2. Mishra, R.N., Mohanty, K.B.: Implementation of feedback-linearization-modelled induction motor Drive through an adaptive simplified neuro-fuzzy approach. Sadhana **42**, 2113–2135 (2017)
3. Swain, S.D., Ray, P.K., Mohanty, K.B.: Improvement of power quality using a robust hybrid series active power filter. IEEE Trans. Power Electron. **32**, 3490–3498 (2016)
4. Mishra, R.N., Mohanty, K.B.: Real time implementation of an ANFIS-based induction motor drive via feedback linearization for performance enhancement. Eng. Sci. Technol. Int. J. **19**, 1714–1730 (2016)
5. Li, J.Q., Li, W.L., Deng, G., Ming, Z.: Continuous-behaviour and discrete-time combined control for linear induction motor-based urban rail transit. IEEE Trans. Magn. **52**(7), 1–4 (2016)
6. Alexandridis, A., Chondrodima, E., Sarimveis, H.: Cooperative learning for radial basis function networks using particle swarm optimization. Appl. Soft Comput. **49**, 485–497 (2016)
7. Krishna, V., Mamanduru, R., Subramanian, N., Tiwari, M.K.: Composite particle algorithm for sustainable integrated dynamic ship routing and scheduling optimization. Comput. Ind. Eng. **96**, 201–215 (2016)
8. Venkataramana, N.N., Thankachan, J., Singh, S.P.: A neuro-fuzzy direct torque control using bus-clamped space vector modulation. IET Tech. Rev. **33**, 205–217 (2016)
9. Venkataramana, N.N., Singh, S.P.: A comparative analytical performance of F2DTC and PIDTC of induction motor using the space ds-1104. IEEE Trans. Ind. Electron. **62**, 7350–7359 (2015)
10. Ramesh, T., Panda, K.: Type-2 fuzzy logic control based MRAS speed estimator for speed sensor less direct torque and flux control of an induction motor drive. ISA Trans. **57**, 262–275 (2015)
11. Mishra, R.N., Mohanty, B.K.: Performance enhancement of a linearized induction motor drive using ANFIS based torque controller. In: Proceedings of the 12th India International Conference (INDICON), vol. 5, pp. 1–6 (2015)
12. Igoulalenei, I., Benyoucef, I., Tiwari, M.K.: Novel fuzzy hybrid multi-criteria group decision making approaches for the strategic supplier selection problem. Expert Syst. Appl. **42**, 3342–3356 (2015)
13. Uddin, M.N., Huang, Z.R.: Development and implementation of a simplified self-tuned neuro-fuzzy-based IM drive. IEEE Trans. Ind. Appl. **50**, 51–59 (2014)
14. Sekhar, D.C., Marutheshwar, G.V.: Modelling and field oriented control of induction motor by using an adaptive neuro fuzzy interference system control technique. Int. J. Ind. Electron. Electr. Eng. **2**, 75–81 (2014)
15. Wang, S.Y., Tseng, C.L., Chiu, C.J.: Design of a novel adaptive TSK-fuzzy speed controller for use in direct torque control induction motor drives. Appl. Soft Comput. **31**, 396–404 (2015)
16. Lia, Y., Weib, H.: Research on controlling strategy of dual bridge matrix converter-direct torque control of induction motor. Energy Proc. **16**, 1650–1658 (2012)

17. Duanx, X., Deng, H., Li, H.: A saturation-based tuning method for fuzzy PID controller. IEEE Trans. Ind. Electron. **60**, 577–585 (2013)
18. Kumar, G.D., Pathak, M.K.: Comparison of adaptive neuro-fuzzy based space vector modulation for two level inverter. Int. J. Electr. Power Energy Syst. **38**, 9–19 (2012)
19. Pimkumwonga, N., Onkronga, A., Sapaklomb, T.: Modelling and simulation of direct torque control induction motor drives via constant volt/hertz technique. Proc. Eng. **31**, 1211–1216 (2012)
20. Mohammed, T.L., Muthanna, J.M., Ahmed, I.S.: Space vector modulation direct torque speed control of induction motor. Proc. Comput. Sci. **5**, 505–512 (2011)
21. Geyer, T.: Computationally efficient model predictive direct torque control. IEEE Trans. Power Electron. **26**, 2804–2816 (2011)
22. Rubaai, A., Jerry, J., Smith, S.T.: Performance evaluation of fuzzy switching position system controller for automation and process industry control. IEEE Trans. Ind. Appl. **47**, 2274–2282 (2011)
23. Tang, Z.R., Bai, B., Xie, D.: Novel direct torque control based on space vector modulation with adaptive stator flux observer for induction motors. IEEE Trans. Magn. **46**, 3133–3136 (2010)
24. Areed, F.G., Haikal, A.Y., Mohammed, R.H.: Anadaptive neuro-fuzzy control of an induction motor. Ain Shams Eng. J. **1**, 71–78 (2010)
25. Uddin, M.N., Chy, M.I.: A novel fuzzy logic controller based torque and flux controls of a synchronous motor. IEEE Trans. Ind. Appl. **46**, 1220–1229 (2010)
26. Geyer, T., Papafotiou, G., Morari, M.: Model predictive direct torque control—part I, part-II: concept, algorithm, and analysis. IEEE Trans. Power Electron. **56**(6), 1894–1905 (2009)
27. Karakas, E., Vardarbasi, S.: Speed control of motor by self-tuning fuzzy PI controller with artificial neural network. Sadhana **32**, 587–596 (2007)
28. Kouro, S., Rodriguez, J.: High-performance torque and flux control for multilevel inverter fed induction motors. IEEE Trans. Power Electron. **22**(6), 2116–2123 (2007)
29. Toufouti, R., Meziane, S., Benalla, H.: Direct torque control for induction motor using intelligent techniques. J. Theor. Appl. Inf. Technol. **3**(3), 35–44 (2007)
30. Changyu, S., Lixia, W., Qian, I.: Optimization of Injection modeling process parameters using combination of artificial neural network and genetic algorithm method. J. Mater. Process. Technol. **183**, 412–418 (2007)
31. Lin, F.J., Huang, P.K., Chou, W.D.: Recurrent-fuzzy neural- network-controlled linear Induction motor servo drives using Genetic algorithms. IEEE Trans. Ind. Electron. **54**, 449–1461 (2007)
32. Grabowski, P.Z., Bose, B.K., Blaabjerg, F.: A simple direct-torque neuro-fuzzy control of PWM-Inverter-fed induction motor drive. IEEE Trans. Ind. Electron. **47**, 863–870 (2000)
33. Bindal, R.K., Kaur, I.: Performance of three phase induction motor of direct torque control using fuzzy logic controller. Int. J. Pure Appl. Math. **118**, 159–175 (2018)
34. Bindal, R.K., Kaur, I.: Comparative analysis of different controlling techniques using direct torque control on induction motor. In: 2016 2nd International Conference on Next Generation Computing Technologies (NGCT), pp. 191–196. IEEE (2016)

Author Index

Printed in the United States
By Bookmasters